THE CHILDREN'S
ANIMAL
WORLD
ENCYCLOPEDIA
IN COLOUR

HAMLYN
LONDON · NEW YORK · SYDNEY · TORONTO

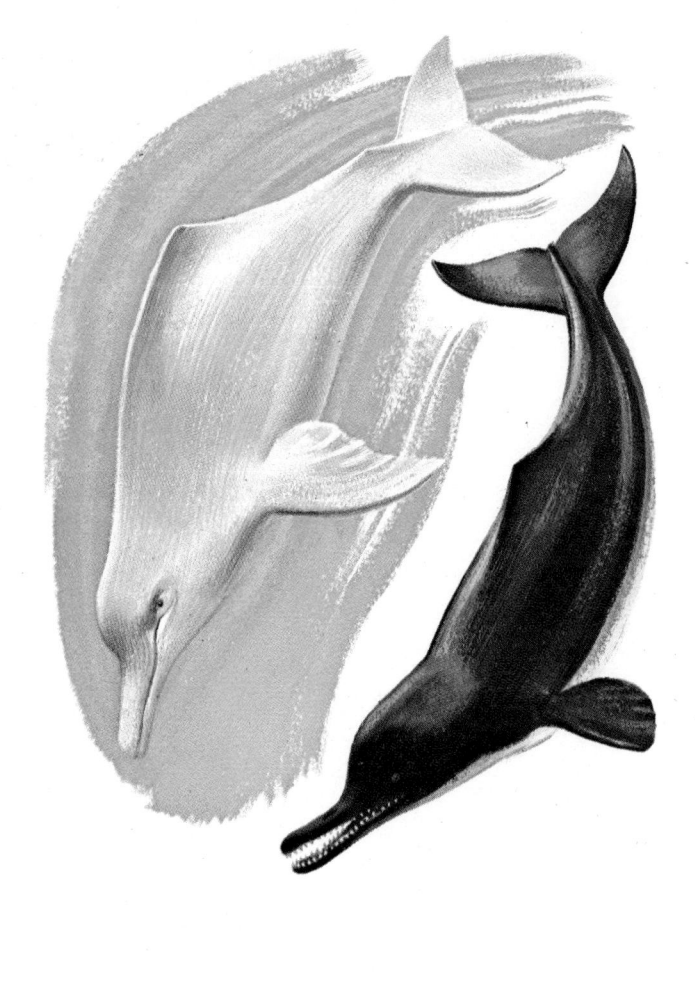

This revised edition first published in 1967
Eighth impression 1977
Published by THE HAMLYN PUBLISHING GROUP LIMITED
LONDON • NEW YORK • SYDNEY • TORONTO
ASTRONAUT HOUSE • FELTHAM • MIDDLESEX • ENGLAND
by arrangement with WESTERN PUBLISHING COMPANY INC.

ISBN 0 601 08084 X

Printed in Italy

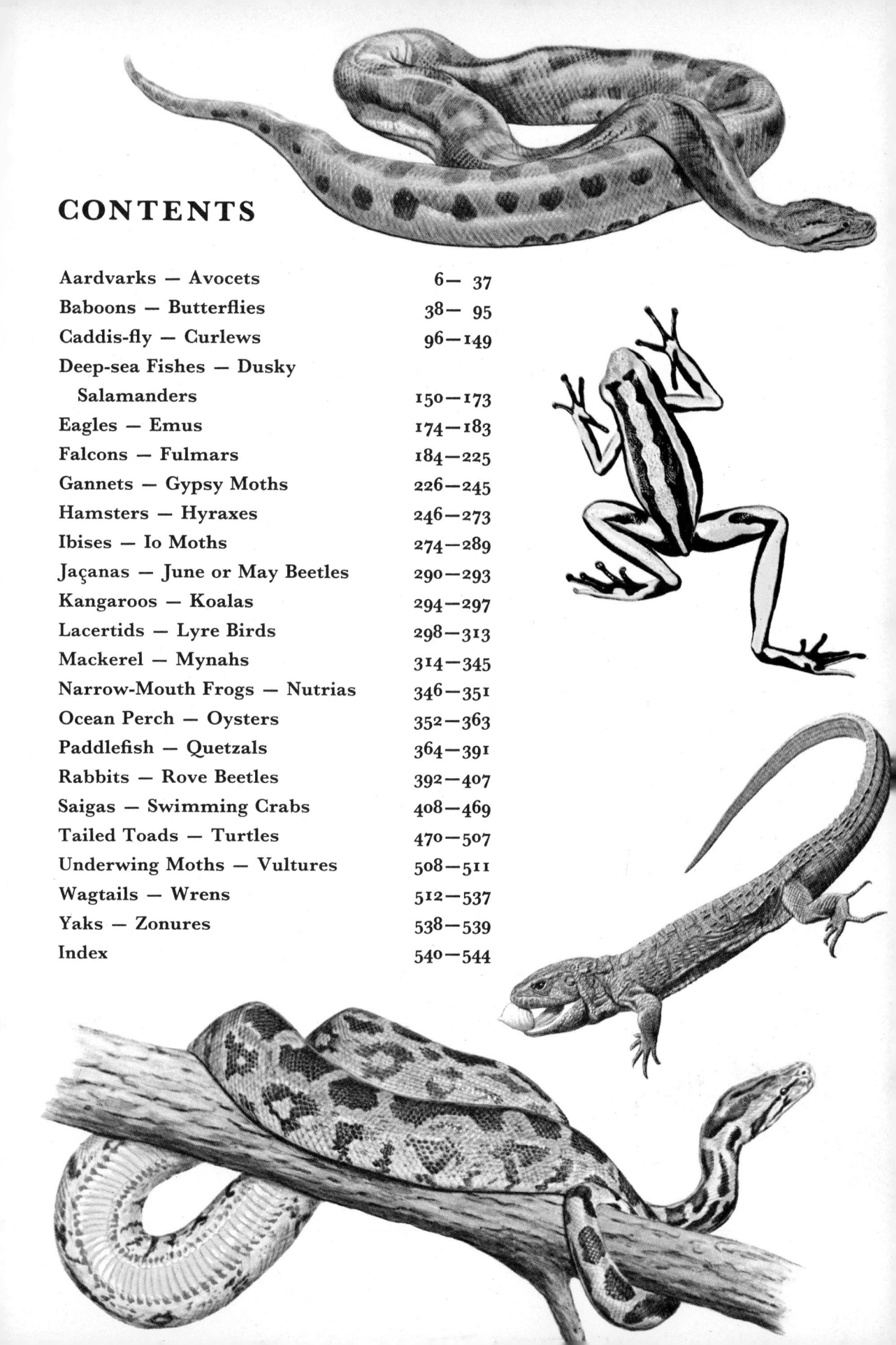

CONTENTS

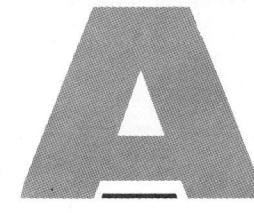

A

AARDVARKS *(Orycteropus)*, also called African Antbears, are mammals found only in the grass regions of Africa. Their name means "earth pig" in Dutch. About the size of large pigs (up to six feet long including tail, and 140 pounds in weight), they live in large burrows. They have long snouts, tiny heads, and long, slender ears. Their bodies are thinly covered with bristly, yellowish brown hairs. Aardvarks use the powerful claws on their front feet for digging into termite or ant hills. As the Aardvark digs — which it does with great speed — it folds its ears against its body to protect them from the flying dirt. As soon as the nest is torn apart, the Aardvark uses its tongue, which is up to eighteen inches long and is covered with a sticky saliva, to pick up termites. The Aardvark is able to close its nostrils to keep out the insects. They are nocturnal animals and are not often seen. Natives dig Aardvarks from their burrows and eat them.

AARDWOLVES *(Proteles cristata)* look like hyenas and are closely related to them; they are not wolves. Their weak teeth and jaws are not suited for crushing bones or tearing flesh, and they feed almost entirely on insects.

Aardwolves live in the dry areas of eastern and southern Africa. They are active at night and sleep by day, mostly in holes dug by the Aardvark, and they may also feed on the termites left by the Aardvark. Aardwolves are usually found separately, but sometimes in pairs and rarely in packs. They can emit an unpleasant scent as a defence against an enemy.

ABALONES *(Haliotis* spp.*)* are sea snails with flattened, open, oval shells, usually with a series of four to eight holes along the upper edge through which water passes for breathing. They are greatly prized for their shells, which are made into jewellery and table ornaments, and also for their large muscular foot which is a delicacy. Abalones are most common along the Pacific coasts of North America, Japan and Asia. Some of the species caught commercially are protected by law. Largest is the valuable Red Abalone (10 to 12 in.). Smallest of American abalones and one of the only two Atlantic species is Pourtales' Abalone ($\frac{1}{2}$ to 1 in.), which lives in deep

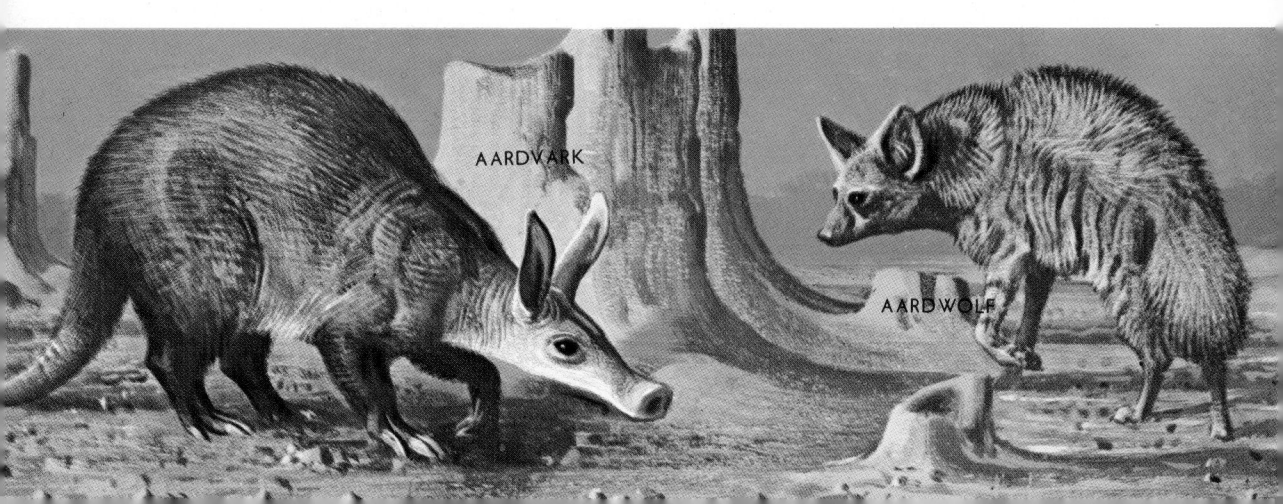

AARDVARK

AARDWOLF

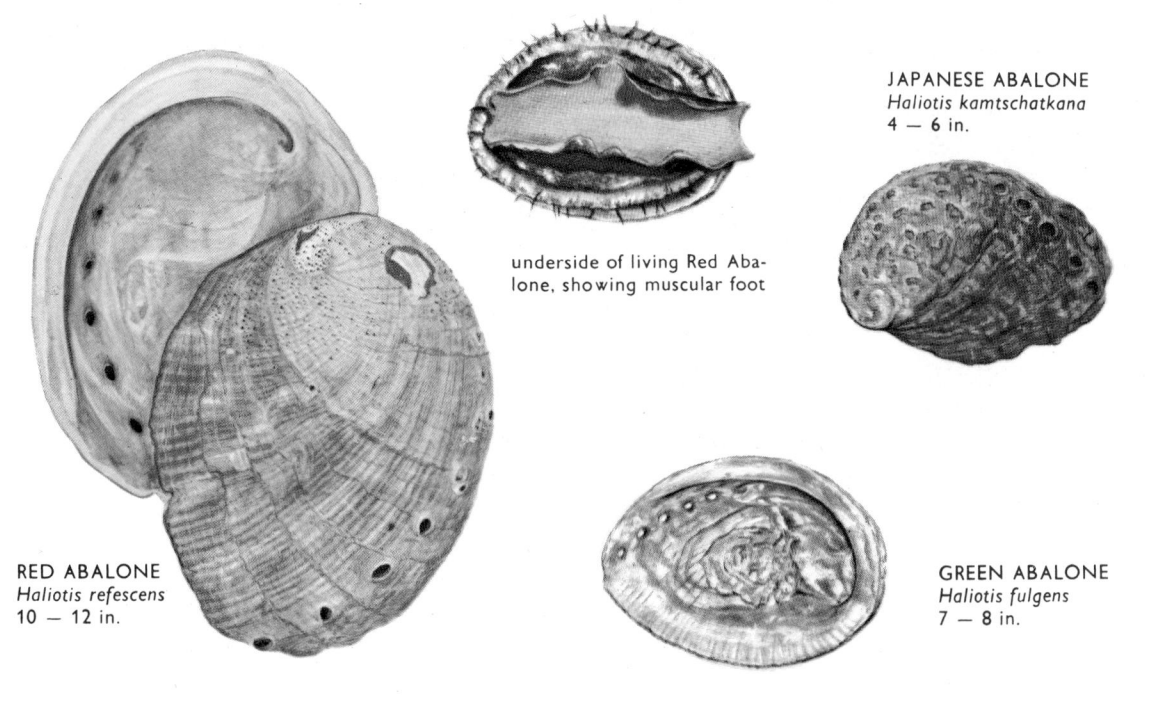

JAPANESE ABALONE
Haliotis kamtschatkana
4 — 6 in.

underside of living Red Abalone, showing muscular foot

RED ABALONE
Haliotis refescens
10 — 12 in.

GREEN ABALONE
Haliotis fulgens
7 — 8 in.

water off Florida and the West Indies. Abalones are prized by the Chinese and Japanese. Large quantities are canned and shipped to the United States. They are often included on the menus of Chinese-American restaurants.

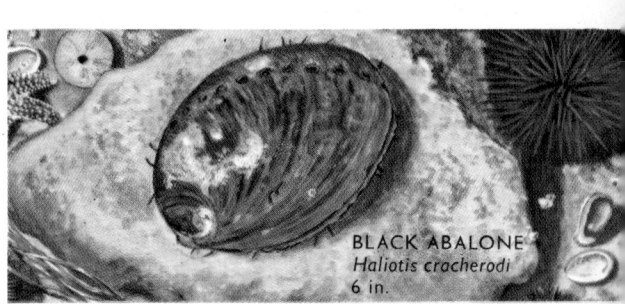

BLACK ABALONE
Haliotis cracherodi
6 in.

ADDERS *(Vipera berus)* are the only poisonous snakes in Britain. The species has a wide distribution in Europe and Asia, reaching well within the Arctic Circle and extending across Northern Asia to China. It is absent from Southern Europe. The zigzag line down the middle of the back, coupled with the thick-set body and short tail, distinguish it from the other two snakes found in Britain.

The Adder is one of the few snakes that show colour differences between sexes and it is possible to tell the sex of an adder from its colour alone, males being silvery white or grey-olive while females are often brick-red or golden.

It shows a habitat preference for dry hillsides, open moors and sandy heaths, and feeds chiefly on lizards and small mammals. Its chief predator is man, who kills it deliberately, and also unconsciously by

destroying its habitat when clearing ground; but among the animal population the hedgehog takes pride of place, this mammal having a certain immunity to the adder's venom. The adder produces live young. (See VIPERS.)

AGAMIDS are a group, containing many species, of rough-scaled, gangling lizards that occur only in the Eastern Hemisphere. Most abundant in the tropics and subtropics, they live both in jungles and on sandy deserts. They are Old World counterparts of the New World iguanids (see IGUANAS). In each family there are species occupying the same sort of habitats and often astonishingly similar in appearance. Iguanids, however, have teeth loosely anchored on the inside of the jaw; these

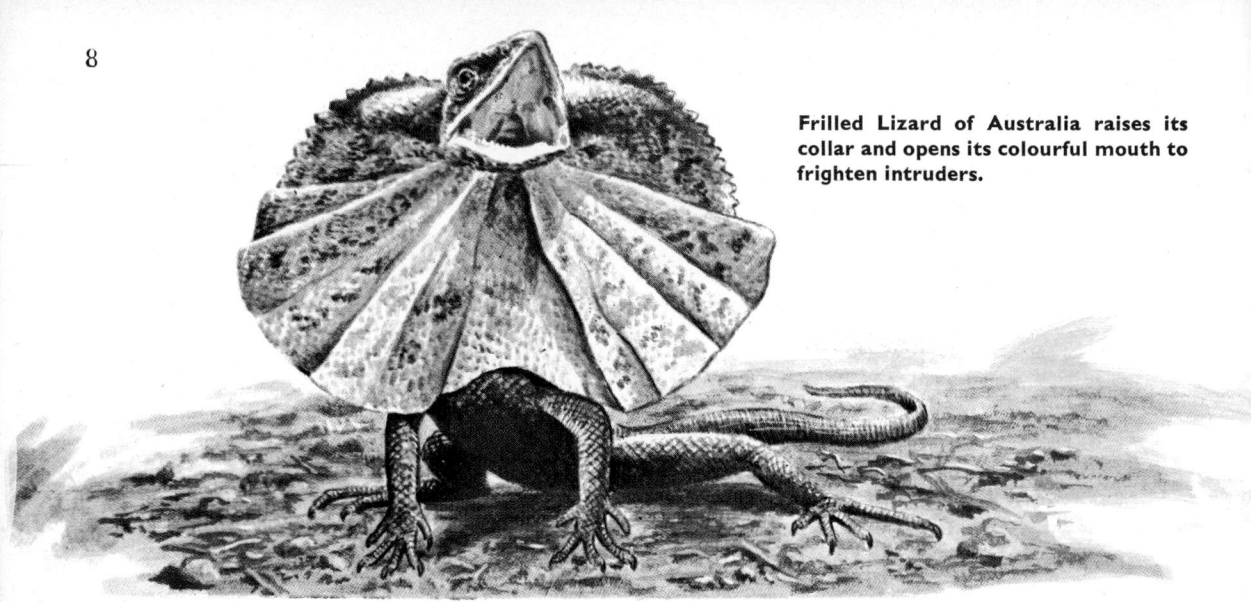

Frilled Lizard of Australia raises its collar and opens its colourful mouth to frighten intruders.

teeth are often replaced. Agamids have stronger teeth permanently anchored on the crest of the jaw, and their teeth are not replaced if lost. The short, fleshy tongues of agamids are smooth. Tongues of iguanids are covered with tiny, soft projections. Both have small granular scales on the sides of the body, and often on back and belly, and both are able to change colour.

Most grotesque of the agamids is the Australian Thorny Devil *(Moloch horridus)*. It has larger spines than its American counterpart, the Horned Lizard, but they are alike in refusing to bite, eating only ants, and living in sandy, semi-arid regions.

Water-lizards *(Physignathus* and *Hydrosaurus)*, often seen in zoos, have a low crest on the body. One species reaches a length of three feet and has a high tail-crest.

The Frilled Lizard *(Chlamydosaurus)* of Australia has a large, umbrella-like membrane attached around its head. Normally this frill is collapsed and draped along its neck and shoulders, but it can be spread

suddenly. With the frill spread and its mouth wide open, this big lizard ($1\frac{1}{2}$ ft.) attempts to intimidate enemies. The Australian Bearded Lizard *(Amphibolurus)* has a similar, smaller throat fan.

True agamids *(Agama),* of some 50 species, live in the deserts of Africa, south-western Asia, and south-eastern Europe. Moderately large ($1\frac{1}{2}$ to 2 ft.), the tails of some kinds are ringed with short spines. Most agamids are insect-eaters, but the spiny-tailed agamas eat vegetation. They have broad-crowned rear teeth for chewing, and sharp rat-like front teeth for nipping the tips of growing plants.

Toad-headed agamas *(Phrynocephalus)* are burrowers in desert sands. These dwarfs (4 to 8 in.) have long, spineless tails, and fringes of scales around their eyes to protect them from sand. Bloodsuckers *(Calotes)* are tropical tree lizards. Mostly tail and long limbs, these lizards do not suck blood, but can change in colour from greyish brown to red. When two males fight, for

Thorny Devil, or Moloch, is a sluggish agamid lizard that lives in desert regions of Australia.

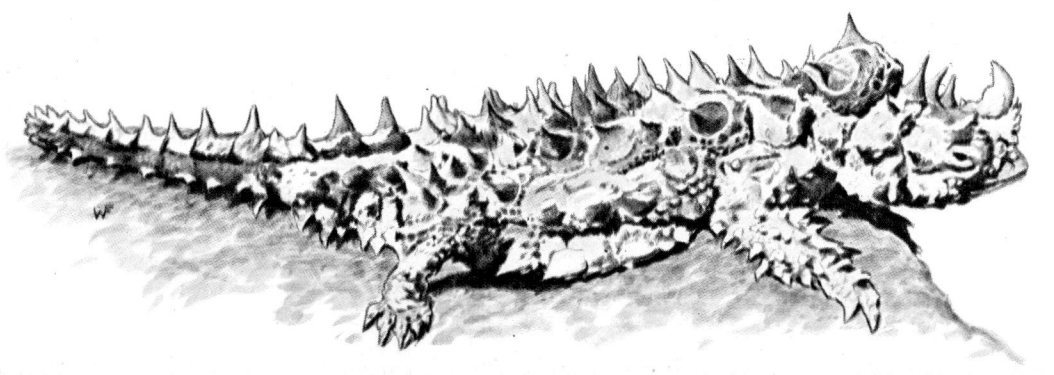

example, the winner turns red, while the loser slinks off in its dullest colours. The similar, tree-dwelling, angle-headed agamas (*Gonyocephalus*) live in jungles from S.E.-Asia to Australia. (See FLYING LIZARDS.)

AGOUTIS (*Dasyprocta* spp.) are rabbit-sized South American rodents related to the Guinea Pig. They have long legs, a short tail, and large eyes. Agoutis hide in dense thickets and, when pursued, combine graceful running with long leaps. Bright patches on their rumps show conspicuously. Agoutis feed on leaves, fruit and nuts, holding them in their front paws like squirrels. South American pacas (*Cuniculus* spp.) are closely related to agoutis.

ALBACORES (*Thunnus alalunga*) are swift, streamlined members of the tuna family. They are truly mystery fish of the sea. Large schools of Albacores live in warm and temperate seas throughout the world. They are uncommon near the equator and in cold arctic waters. Little is known about where Albacores lay their eggs or how their young develop, however. Also, the migration routes used by Albacores through the open sea are still not understood.

Every year commercial fishermen off the western coast of the United States catch millions of pounds of Albacores in the deep waters. Tremendous schools appear in offshore waters in early summer and may still be present in the autumn. Later the schools appear off the coast of Japan and also in the waters off the Hawaiian Islands. Schools of smaller fish show up first, then the heavyweights.

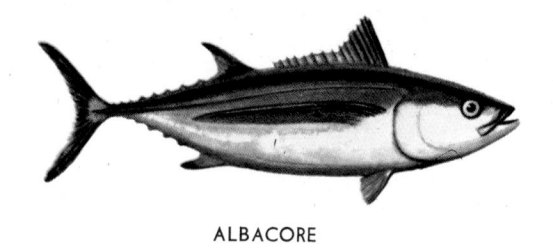

ALBACORE

Albacores are fast swimmers. Their dorsal fins fit into slots on their backs so that they create no friction when the fish are travelling at top speed. An Albacore tagged by biologists off the coast of California was caught two weeks later by fishermen near Japan. It had travelled about 400 miles per day.

Albacores are caught on hook and line by trolling lures or live baits through their schools. They fight hard, taking the lure or bait deep into the water. As soon as they stop, the fishermen begin "pumping" them up. The record catch weighed 69 pounds, but Albacores are reported to weigh over 80 pounds. (See TUNAS.)

South American agoutis eat plants and can be pests in fields and gardens. Young agoutis tame quickly.

W. Suschitzky

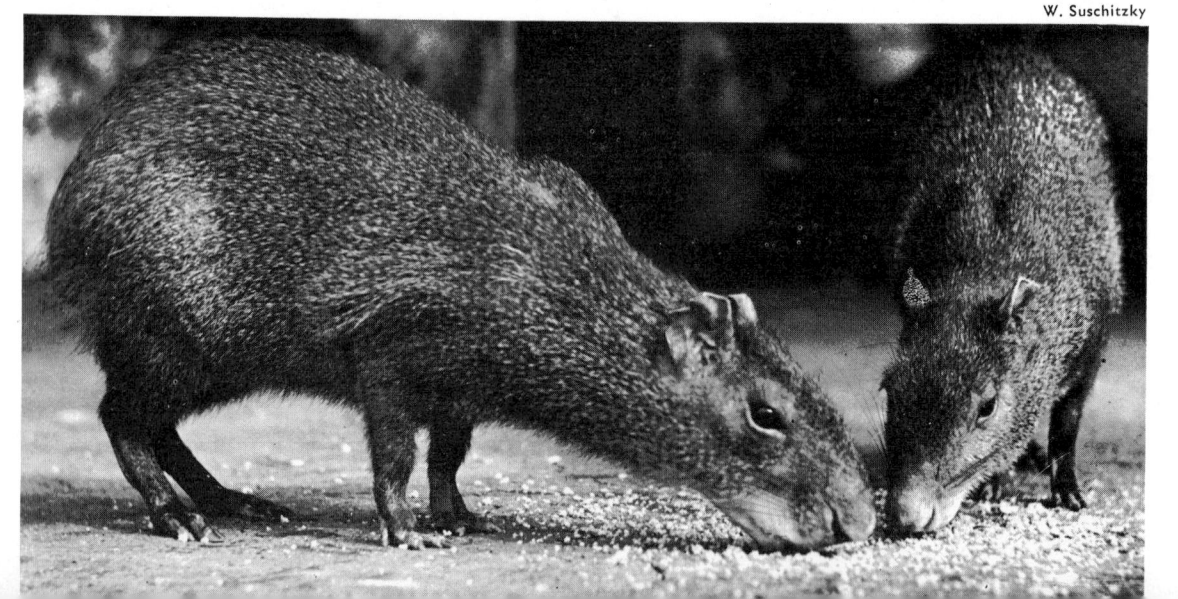

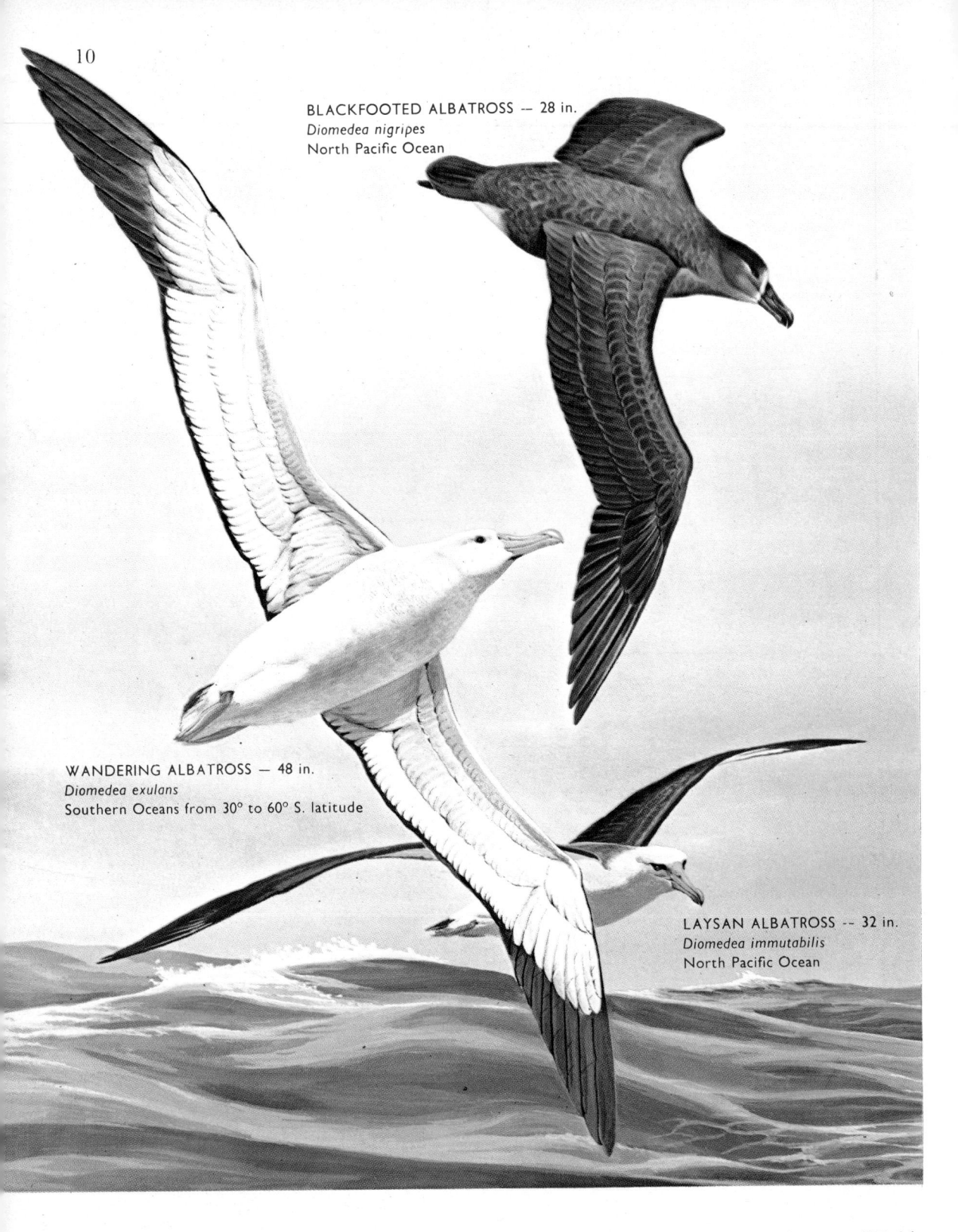

BLACKFOOTED ALBATROSS — 28 in.
Diomedea nigripes
North Pacific Ocean

WANDERING ALBATROSS — 48 in.
Diomedea exulans
Southern Oceans from 30° to 60° S. latitude

LAYSAN ALBATROSS — 32 in.
Diomedea immutabilis
North Pacific Ocean

ALBATROSSES are graceful sea birds known in all oceans of the world except the North Atlantic. The short, horny tubes formed by their nostrils on top of their long, hooked bills identify them as "Tubinares", members of the *Procillariformes*, the Shearwater and Petrel family.

Albatrosses excel as flyers. Their exceed-

ingly long, very narrow wings make them notable gliders. They ride the winds and, when gales blow, can go faster than ships. On land they are slow and awkward.

Albatrosses feed on small marine animals, and also on galley refuse when following ships at sea. They breed in colonies on oceanic islands. The breeding of some species has never been investigated. The females lay one large egg (white or white spotted with brown) on the bare ground, or on carelessly heaped grass or seaweeds.

The Wandering Albatross has longer wings than any other bird in the world. They measure 11 feet from tip to tip. This big bird has been known to travel 6,000 miles over open seas. Often it follows ships. Whaling captains and shipwrecked sailors have scratched messages on tin or wood or put them in small bottles, then attached them to Wandering Albatrosses. Several such messages have brought rescue to marooned sailors.

The Wandering Albatross nests in colonies on small islands a little north of the Antarctic continent. It ranges over all southern seas. English seamen named it the "gooney", which comes from an old English word meaning "a simpleton". They do not seem stupid when flying, but only on land or in the water.

The Black-footed Albatross, a sooty grey bird with black feet and legs, is the smallest of the 13 different albatrosses. Its wing-spread is only seven feet. It lives in the North Pacific and often comes within five miles of the shore. It is well known along the west coast of North America.

The Laysan Albatross is a slightly larger North Pacific bird with a white body and a black back and wings. It seldom comes within 20 miles of land except when nesting.

Both the Laysan and Black-footed Albatrosses breed on small islands west of Hawaii. All have solemn, comical dances when courting. Nesting birds are tame.

ALLIGATOR LIZARDS *(Gerrhonotus* spp.*)*, of the western United States south to Panama, belong to the family *Anguidae*, as do Glass Lizards and the Slow-worm. A species that lives in the California Mountains bears its young alive. One that lives at a lower altitude lays eggs. A bright-green Mexican species with patches of yellow-orange skin around its eyes lives in evergreen trees growing at 7,000 feet elevation. At night and in winter it takes refuge in air plants that grow in trees.

In the same family are the tropical American Galliwasp Lizards *(Diploglossus* spp.)*. All Galliwasps have smooth, flat, rounded scales (similar to fish scales). Galliwasp Lizards resemble the skinks (see SKINKS). They have weak legs, the hind legs being small, or almost lacking in many. Some species bear their young alive.

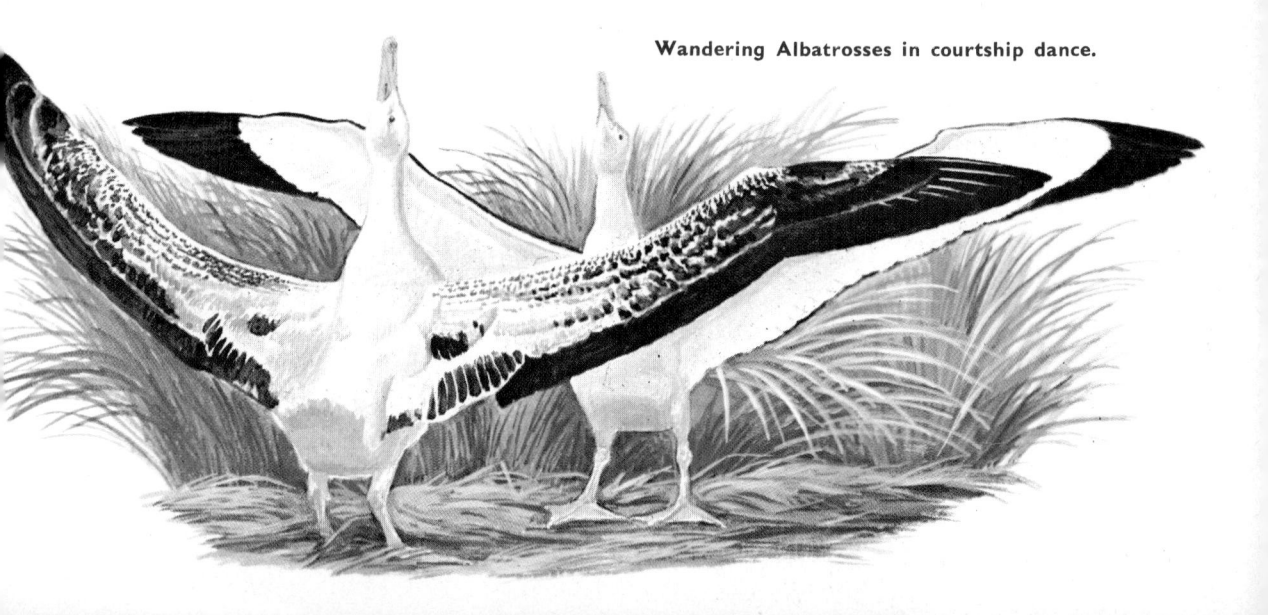

Wandering Albatrosses in courtship dance.

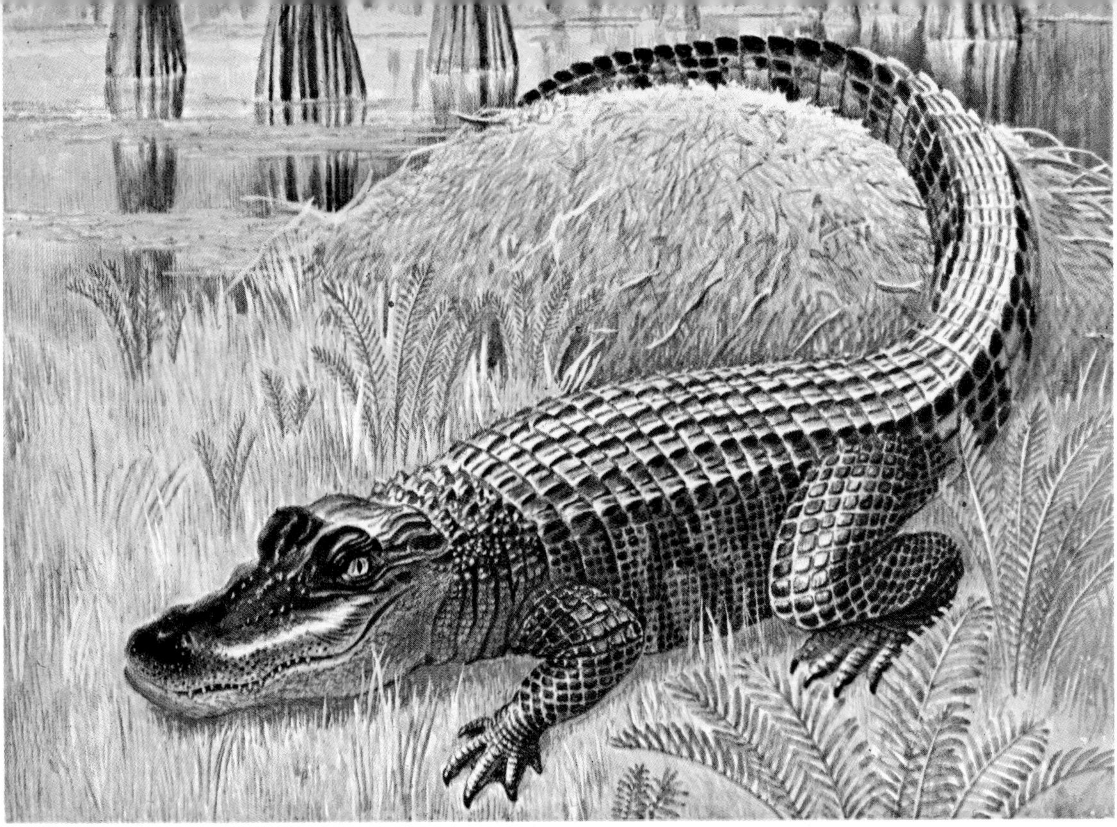

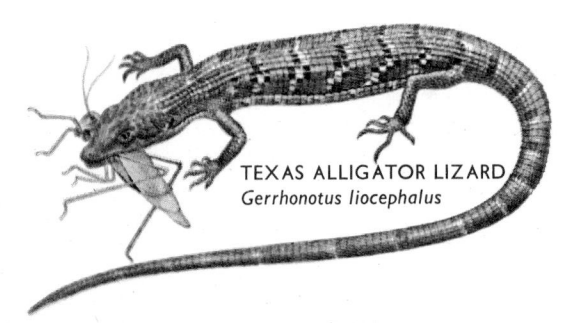

An American Alligator guards her nest. The heat of the sun and decaying vegetation incubates the eggs.

Fossil species of this family are found in rock deposits of Cretaceous age — 75 million years old. All living species have long tails, which they shed as a defence mechanism when attacked. Most kinds have long bodies. Many are burrowers, and almost all are insect-eaters; but one, which lives on a South American island, feeds on marine crustaceans (q.v.). Those that lay eggs stay close to their nests, brooding the eggs and protecting their newly-hatched young for several days. (See GLASS LIZARDS; SLOW-WORMS.)

ALLIGATORS. Only two species of true alligators are known. One species (*Alligator mississipiensis*) occurs in the south-eastern United States, the other (*Alligator sinensis*)

in eastern China. Six species of Caimans, members of the same family, are found in Central and South America, one ranging to southern Mexico.

All members of this family have a broad snout, in which there is a pocket on each side receiving the big canine (fourth tooth) when the mouth is closed. Some crocodiles have broad snouts, but the fourth tooth of the lower jaw fits in a groove outside the upper jaw when the mouth is closed. No broad-snouted crocodiles live in the same region with alligators and caimans. (See CROCODILIANS.)

In spring the female American Alligator builds a mound of mud and swamp vegetation which she carries to the site in her jaws. In the top of the mound she lays 20 to 70 eggs — each three inches or so

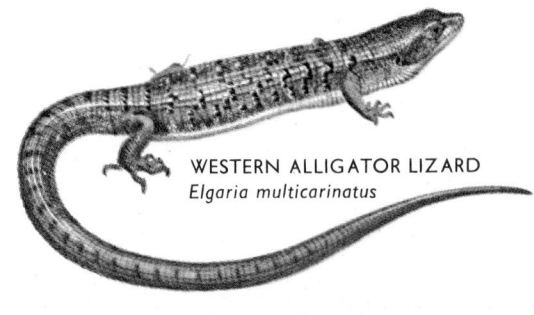

WESTERN ALLIGATOR LIZARD
Elgaria multicarinatus

TEXAS ALLIGATOR LIZARD
Gerrhonotus liocephalus

in diameter — and covers them with more mud and vegetation. For the nine or ten weeks the eggs require to hatch, the female guards her nest fiercely, occasionally wetting and damping it. The squeaking calls of the 8-inch young as they scramble from the eggs acts as a signal to the female, who tears the nest open to help release them. If the female is not there to help, the young die without getting out of the nest. The female herds her newly-hatched young into the water, and guards them much as a duck does her ducklings. The young use high-pitched grunts to locate or to signal the mother.

Young alligators eat minnows, crayfish, or other small animals. Bigger alligators eat snakes, turtles and larger fishes, and very large ones sometimes attack calves, deer or pigs, dragging them into deep water to drown. Like other crocodilians, alligators tear off chunks of food by rotating their body rapidly and powerfully to twist off whatever is held in their jaws. Turtles are crushed to pulp in the alligators' jaws.

In the spring the roars of adult males, or bulls, carry a mile or more across the swamp country. As they roar, the bulls vibrate their bodies. They rise on their legs and then sink back slowly. At the same time a strong scent is sprayed from glands under the lower jaw. Both the loud bellows and the odour are used to attract females for mating.

Alligators have been hunted heavily for their hides and their numbers greatly reduced. Fifty years ago as many as 250,000 hides, were marketed every season. In Florida's swamp country, a hunter could take as many as 10,000 a year. In most areas alligators are now protected by law. In some places killing them is not allowed at all; in others they can be killed only when they reach large size (usually 6 feet) or when they have become a nuisance. Sometimes alligators wander into residential areas or centres of cities at night and are unable to find their way out. Occasionally an alligator stalks a dog and kills it or,

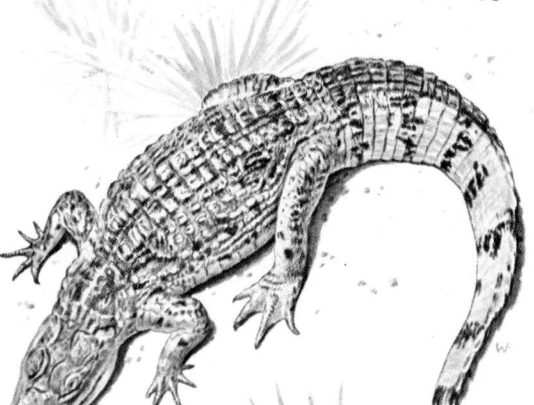

Black Caimans of the Amazon Basin and the Guianas grow to a length of more than nine feet. They are ill-tempered and are known to attack humans.

less commonly, attacks a person. The most dangerous are those near-pets that are fed by people and tormented or molested by them. Those that live in the wild are wary.

Alligators keep waterways open in the swamps. This helps to prevent pools in which mosquitoes breed from becoming stagnant. Small fish that eat the mosquito larvae also travel along alligator channels. In the dry season, pools in front of alligator dens are sources of water for wild life and for livestock in open-range country.

The Black Caiman (*Melanosuchus niger*) approaches the American Alligator in size but has a more vicious, crocodile-like temperament. The two species of smooth-fronted Caimans (*Paleosuchus*) are among the smallest of all crocodilians. One reaches a length of five feet, the other only four feet. These small South American caimans are the most heavily armoured of living crocodilians. Interlocking bony plates under the belly scales are adaptations to their life in rocky streams. Alligators, which have bony plates only under the scales on their back, would have survived civilisation much better with more armour, for the bony plates make the hides of caimans useless for leather. There are four species and sub-species of the common and widely distributed Spectacled Caimans (*Caiman*).

They reach a maximum length of about nine feet, but in many parts of their range seldom exceed six feet. A ridge of bone between their eyes looks somewhat like the nose-piece on a pair of spectacles.

Because laws prevent sale of American Alligators as pets, Spectacled Caimans are imported from the American tropics. Caimans are even less hardy and more difficult to feed than baby alligators, however. Most of those sold either die from neglect or improper care, or they are turned over to zoos. No crocodilian makes a satisfactory house pet.

ALPACAS AND LLAMAS are domesticated animals native to South America, where their wild relatives, the Guanaco (*Lama huanacos*) of the plains and the Vicuña (*Lama vicugna*) of the Andes, are still hunted for their hide and wool. Vicuña fleece is especially long, fine and lustrous. Despite a number of attempts, neither has been introduced successfully in countries outside their homeland.

The Alpaca (*Lama pacos*) resembles a sheep but has a long neck and a camel-like head. It is raised for its long, silky wool, and each animal yields a fleece about

Llamas, such as this mother and young, live in the Andes Mountains at high altitudes.

W. Suschitzky

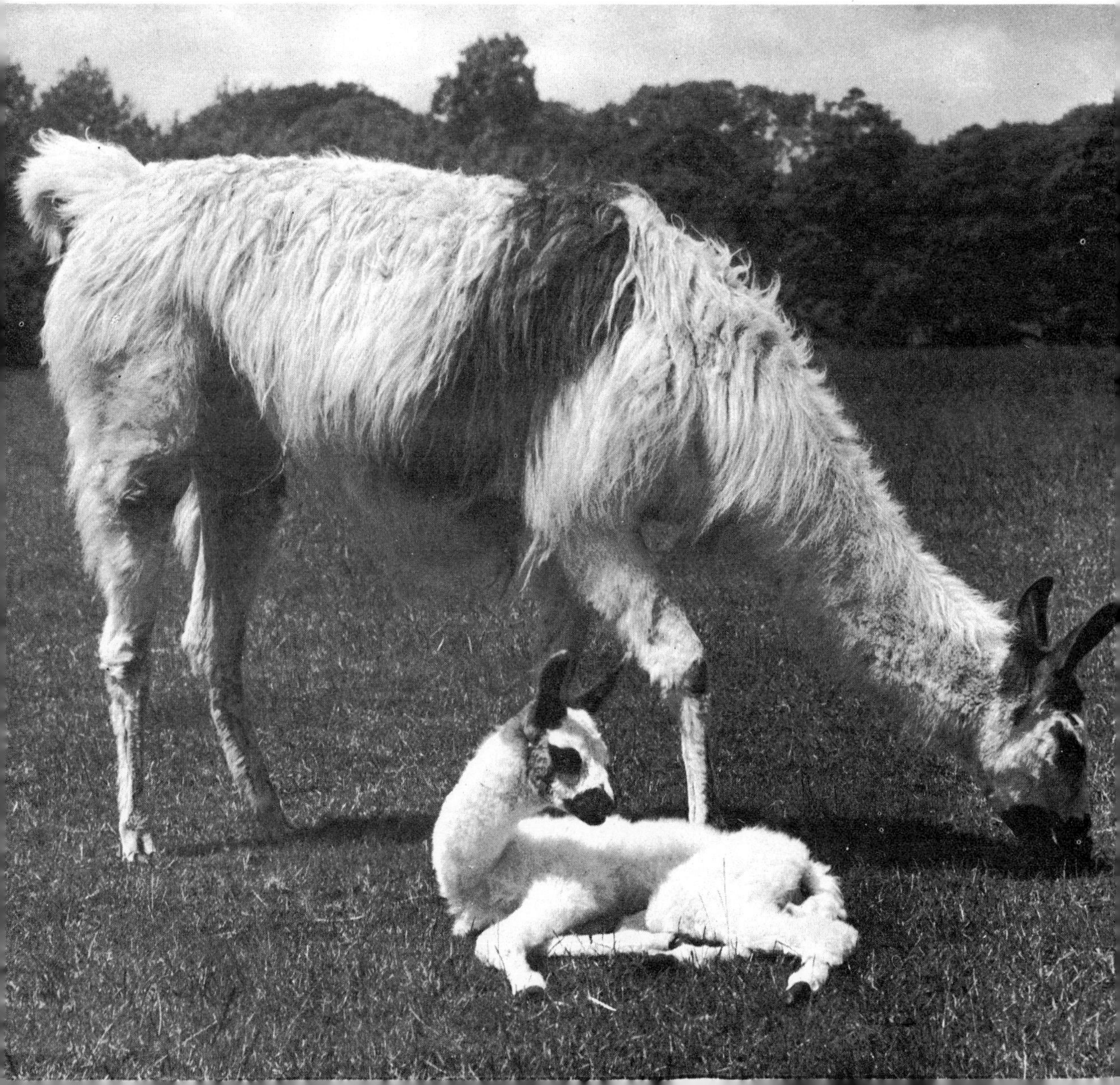

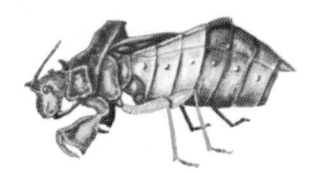

AMBUSH BUG
Phymata

AMBUSH BUGS *(Phymatidae)* are heavy-bodied bugs that sit and wait — in ambush — for food to come to them. Usually greenish-yellow in colour, they blend well with the flowers, such as goldenrods, in which they hide. They feed mostly on small bees and flies that visit the flowers for nectar. When a bee or fly comes close enough, they grab the victim with their powerful front legs, pierce its body with their sharp beak, and draw out its body fluids. About 15 species are found in temperate North America, and over 150 in the tropics of the Americas and Asia.

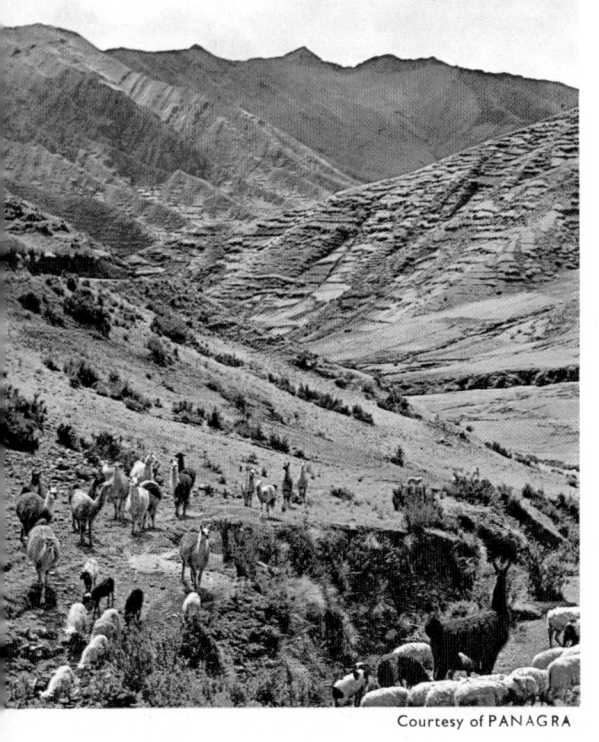

Courtesy of PANAGRA

Llamas pictured in their natural surroundings.

eight or nine inches long every year.

The Llama *(Lama glama)* is slightly larger than the Alpaca, and males stand about four feet high at the shoulder. Although its short wool is woven into fabrics by the Indians and it is sometimes a source of meat and milk, the Llama was developed primarily as a pack animal. Males can carry loads weighing up to 100 or 120 pounds as far as 12 miles in a day. Llamas are highly independent, and if an animal thinks that it has been burdened with too heavy a load, it will lie down and refuse to move. If angered, it will kick and spit.

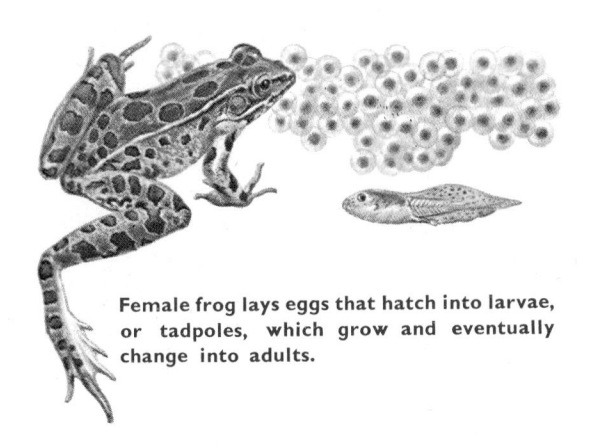

Female frog lays eggs that hatch into larvae, or tadpoles, which grow and eventually change into adults.

AMPHIBIANS appeared about 335 million years ago. They were the first animals with backbones at least partly adapted to life on land. Until then fishes were the only backboned (vertebrate) animals.

Amphibians spread quickly throughout the world. Only severe winter cold or dryness limited their distribution, but in those ancient times tropical climates extended to Alaska, Greenland and Siberia.

A few living fishes, such as the lung-fishes of Africa, Australia and South America, and the recently discovered coelacanths in the ocean off southern Africa, resemble the ancient ancestors of amphibians. These primitive fishes have fleshy, leg-like fins;

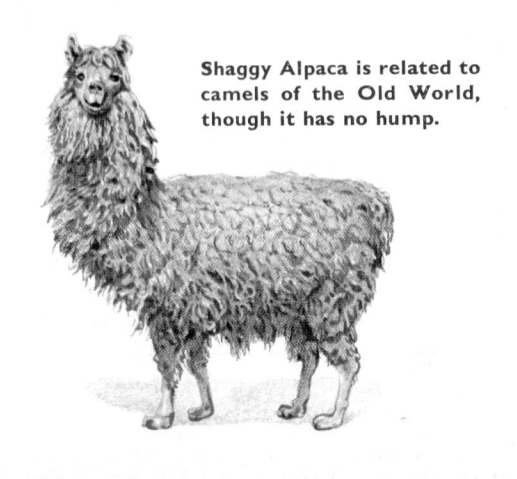

Shaggy Alpaca is related to camels of the Old World, though it has no hump.

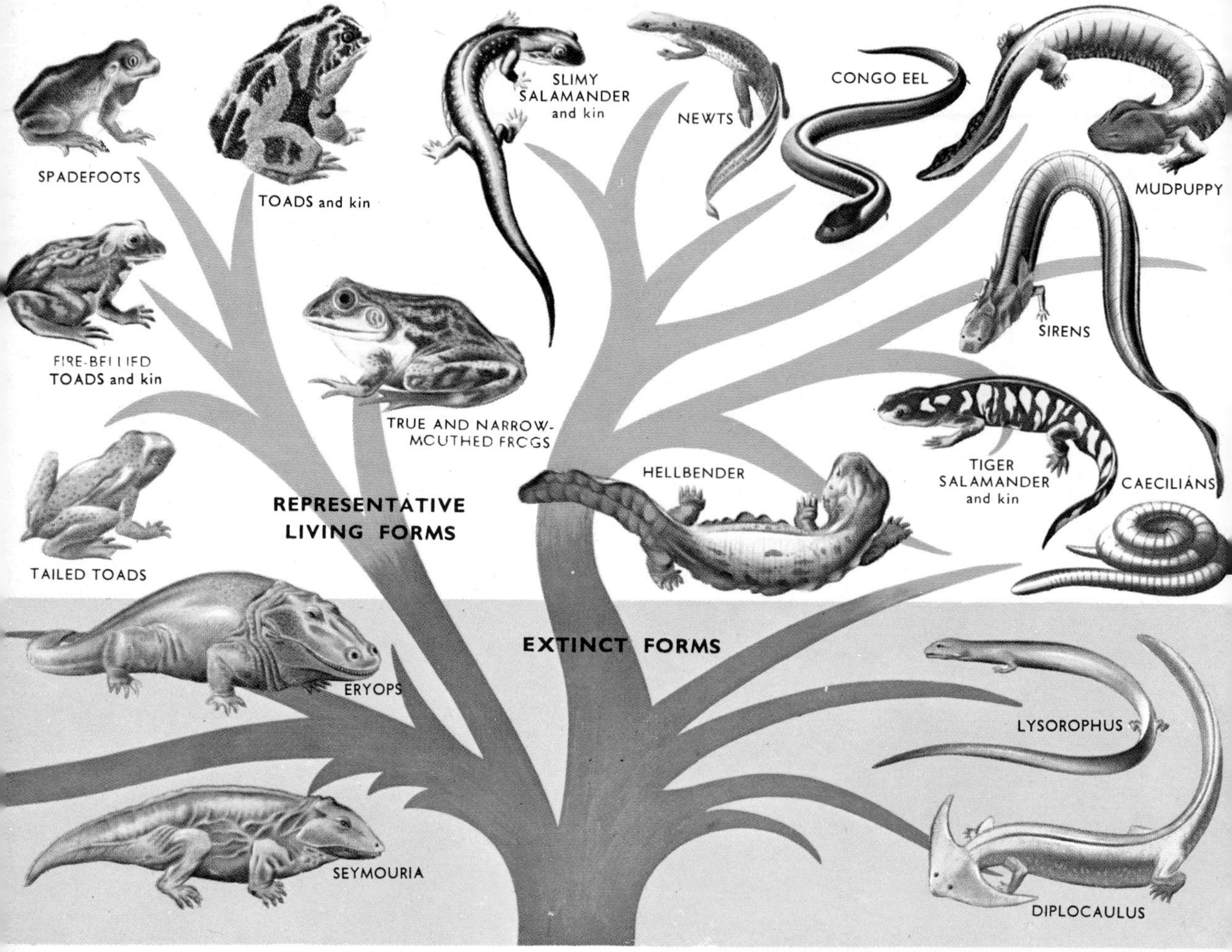

SPADEFOOTS

TOADS and kin

SLIMY SALAMANDER and kin

NEWTS

CONGO EEL

MUDPUPPY

FIRE-BELLIED TOADS and kin

SIRENS

TRUE AND NARROW-MOUTHED FROGS

REPRESENTATIVE LIVING FORMS

HELLBENDER

TIGER SALAMANDER and kin

CAECILIANS

TAILED TOADS

EXTINCT FORMS

ERYOPS

LYSOROPHUS

SEYMOURIA

DIPLOCAULUS

nostrils that open into their mouth, rather than into blind pockets as in most fishes; and an air-bladder that serves as a lung. (See COELACANTHS; LUNG-FISHES.)

Most adult amphibians have true lungs and breathe air directly — they also breathe through their skin or through the lining of the mouth — but, because of their moist skin, they must always remain in or near water, and part of the development of their young also takes place around water. Only three groups of amphibians exist today: salamanders and newts, caecilians, and anurans, or frogs and toads. Some nine major groups are now extinct.

Living amphibians — about 2,500 species — vary greatly in body form. Caecilians are limbless and worm-like. Salamanders are slender, long-tailed, and have either two or four legs. Frogs and toads have four legs and no tail. In the fossil groups

there were still other types, most notably those with broad bodies and oddly-shaped, flattened heads.

Some tiny salamanders of Mexico are only three-quarters of an inch long when fully grown. Frogs found in the southeastern United States and Cuba are only about three-eighths of an inch long when mature. These are the smallest amphibians known. The largest living amphibian is the Giant Salamander of Japan. It may measure five feet in length and weigh 100 pounds. The Goliath Frog of Africa reaches a length of 12 inches and a weight of 15 pounds. All living amphibians are small, however, compared to some of the bulky fossil kinds which were as much as eight feet long and weighed 150 pounds.

Numerous microscopic glands in the skins of all amphibians secrete a moistening fluid. Many kinds "breathe" through this

fluid, particularly during hibernation. In some this fluid is also a poison powerful enough to kill predators — even human beings. As amphibians grow they shed their skin from time to time, often eating it.

Amphibians lack direct control of their body temperature. The anurans particularly cannot withstand temperatures more than a degree or two below freezing. In winter they enter a state of deep sleep or inactivity, called hibernation. During dry periods in summer, they also become inactive, a dormancy known as estivation. In both conditions their life processes are almost at a standstill. They use almost no oxygen and consume no food, getting their energy from the fat stored in their bodies. Most amphibians hibernate in holes in the ground, or beneath rocks or logs. Some survive severe winters in northern Canada or Eurasia at the bottom of lakes.

Amphibians, and also reptiles and fishes, are sometimes known as "cold-blooded" animals. In the sun, however, they may become as "warm-blooded" as a mammal or a bird. An amphibian's body temperature is controlled by its environment. A frog in warm sun may keep cool for some time by the evaporation of moisture from its

Frog skin, moist

Lizard skin, dry

skin. A lizard, in contrast, has a scaly skin through which it does not lose moisture. Its body temperature may be 10 or 20 degrees higher than its surroundings.

Most amphibians hatch from eggs into larvae with gills. The larvae grow in the water and later change (metamorphose) into air-breathing imagos, which are small "images" of mature adults. They grow considerably in size before becoming mature.

Amphibians of northern temperate and sub-arctic regions generally lay their eggs in water. Depending partly on the temperature of the water, the eggs hatch into larvae in as short a time as a day, or as long as three weeks. The larvae grow rapidly. Some are big enough to leave the water within a week; others stay for as long as five years. In the water they breathe through gills. When the larvae reach the right size and age, they change rapidly into air-breathing imagos. They develop lungs, legs, and a thick skin which

Lobe-finned fishes that lived in the Devonian era, some 300 million years ago, may have been the ancestors of present-day amphibians. They were among the first vertebrates to show an adaptation to life on land.

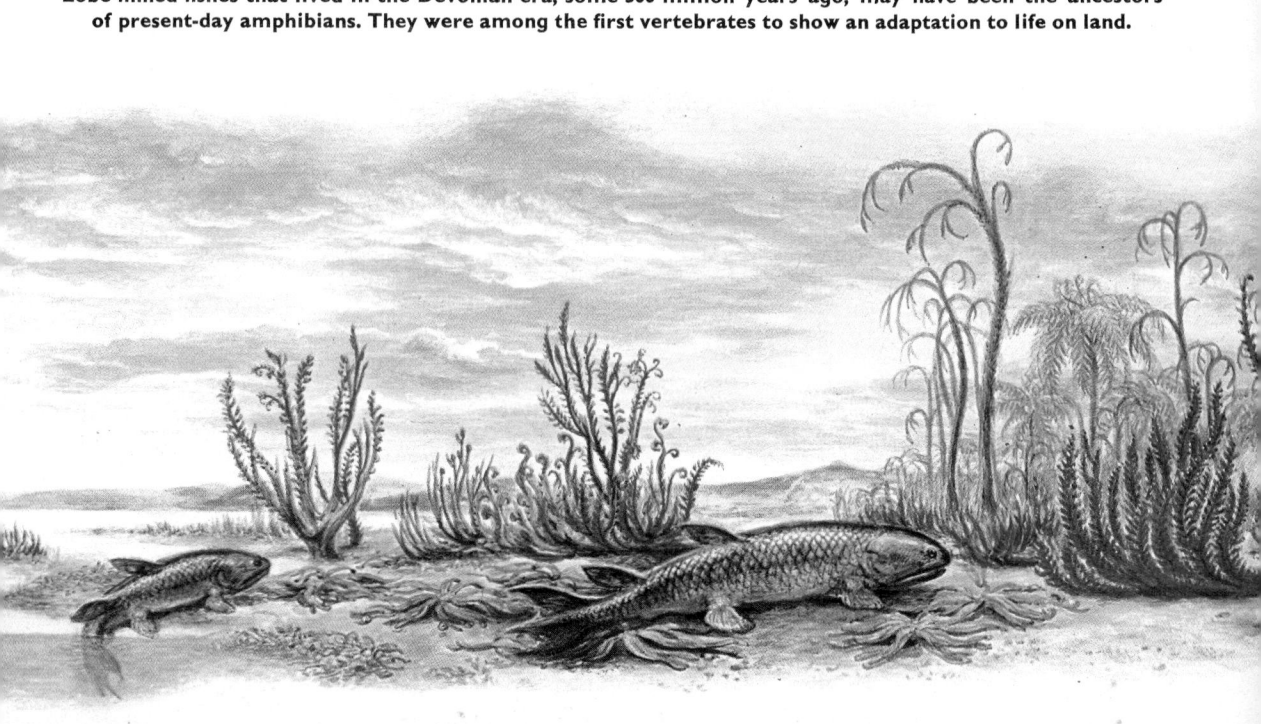

Fossils of *Eryops*, a giant amphibian that lived about 225 million years ago, are evidence that the beasts crawled about clumsily on land.

helps to prevent loss of body fluids by evaporation. They also acquire jaws and begin eating animal foods. Their digestive tract becomes greatly reduced in length. Some imagos mature in a few months; others require several years.

Some amphibians lay their eggs on land rather than in water. Others give birth to their young, and yet another group goes through the larval stage while still in the egg or in the female's body, emerging as air-breathing imagos not larvae. Some salamanders never have an imago stage.

In most amphibians the eggs are fertilised outside the female's body. A male frog or toad generally clasps the female and rides on her back until she lays her eggs; then he fertilises them. Males of primitive salamanders fertilise the eggs after they are laid, but in most salamanders the eggs are fertilised before they are laid. Males of some kinds deposit sperm packets

in shallow water where they are picked up by the females; in other salamanders there is direct mating.

Amphibian eggs are round and opaque. When fresh, most are dark coloured above and light below. Each egg is usually surrounded by several layers of gelatine, at first scarcely visible. This gelatine soon absorbs water, swelling to as much as five times the diameter of the egg. In some

TIGER SALAMANDER

egg mass   larva

Female salamanders lay jelly-like egg mass from which larvae hatch and subsequently develop into adults, retaining the tail.

species, a kind of algae grows in the gelatine and supplies extra oxygen for the developing egg. The egg, in turn, gives off carbon dioxide which is used by the algae in its manufacture of food.

In many kinds of amphibians the gelatine around the egg simply dissolves when the egg is ready to hatch, and the larvae float free. In others, the larvae struggle through the jelly to gain their freedom. Some

Bones in amphibian's leg and fin of a lobe-finned fish are alike in structure but differ in function.

lobe-finned fish   amphibian

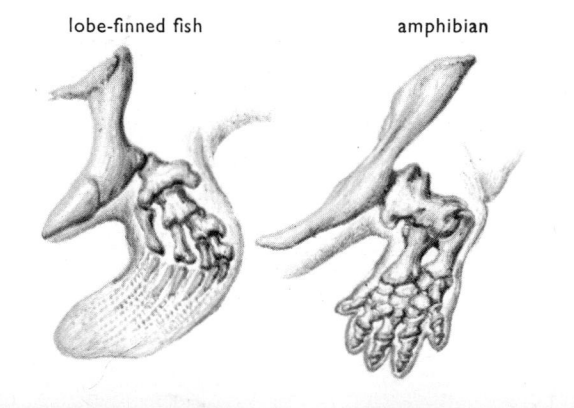

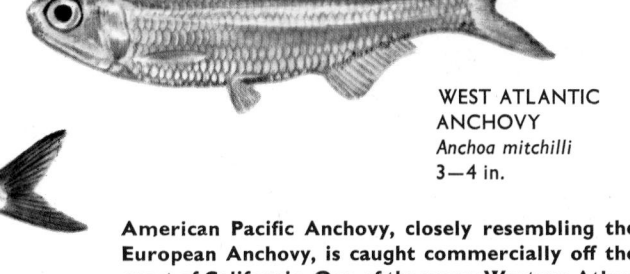

**AMERICAN PACIFIC
ANCHOVY**
Engraulis mordax
to 9 in.

**WEST ATLANTIC
ANCHOVY**
Anchoa mitchilli
3—4 in.

American Pacific Anchovy, closely resembling the European Anchovy, is caught commercially off the coast of California. One of the many Western Atlantic Anchovies is also shown.

larvae have in their snouts special glands which secrete a substance that dissolves a hole in the gelatine. Then the larvae either wriggle out through this hole, or are shot out like bullets as the water pressure inside is released.

ANCHOVIES resemble herrings, but have a pointed snout and an "under-slung" lower jaw. The European Anchovy *(Engraulis encrasicolus)* grows to about 6 inches, but there is an Australian anchovy that reaches a foot in length.

Great numbers of anchovies are caught by commercial fishermen in the Atlantic Ocean off the coasts of Spain and Portugal. Anchovies are not so common off British coasts. One well-tried method of catching them is to use lights as a means of attraction, surrounding the seething mass of little fish which assembles with nets. The anchovies are cleaned and placed in barrels, each layer of fish separated by a layer of salt. Many are canned in olive oil; others are made into anchovy paste. They are used in salads or for appetisers. Sport fishermen use anchovies for bait; but anchovies are most important as food for larger fish.

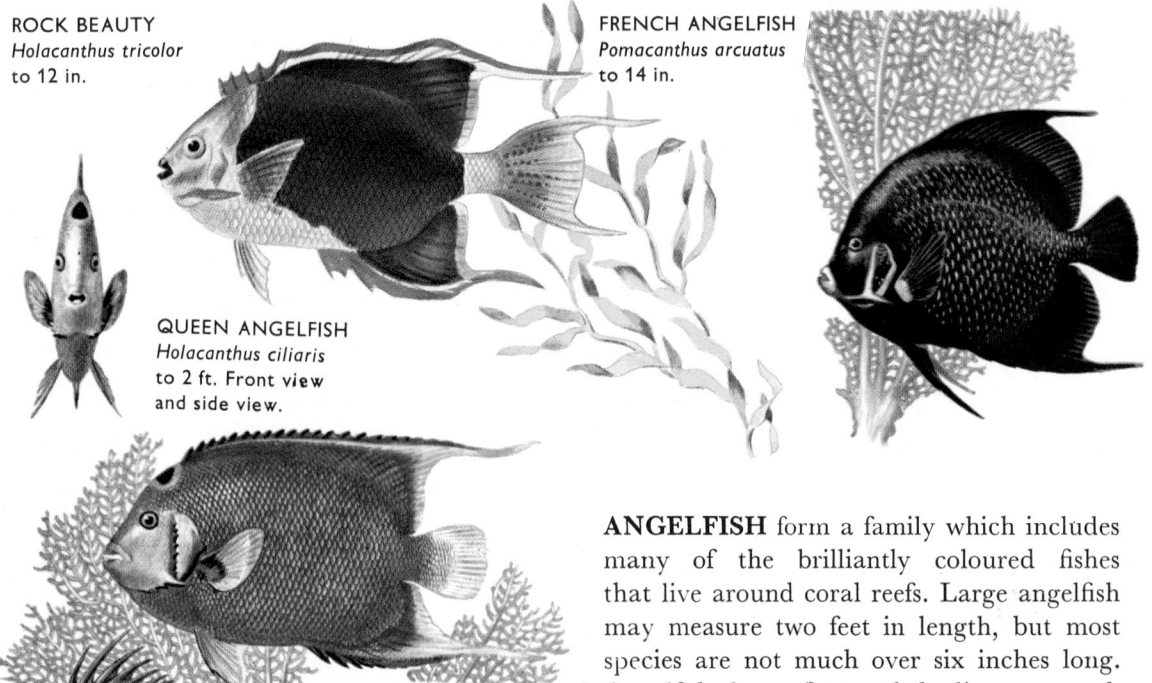

ROCK BEAUTY
Holacanthus tricolor
to 12 in.

FRENCH ANGELFISH
Pomacanthus arcuatus
to 14 in.

QUEEN ANGELFISH
Holacanthus ciliaris
to 2 ft. Front view
and side view.

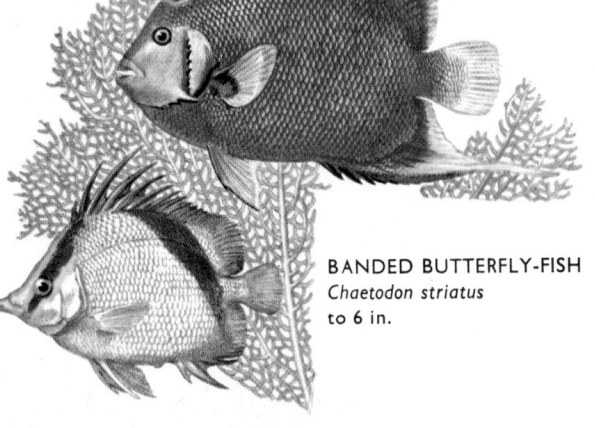

BANDED BUTTERFLY-FISH
Chaetodon striatus
to 6 in.

ANGELFISH form a family which includes many of the brilliantly coloured fishes that live around coral reefs. Large angelfish may measure two feet in length, but most species are not much over six inches long. Angelfish have flattened bodies — much taller than wide. They are decorated with stripes and splotches of colour. Typically their mouths are a different colour from

their bodies, so that their lips look as though they have been painted. Their dorsal and ventral fins extend into long, slim filaments that often trail as far behind the fish as their tails do.

Butterfly-fishes *(Chaetodontidae)*, smaller but similar in appearance, are also found in the coral reefs. They seem to "flutter" as they swim — hence their name. Many butterfly-fishes have large "eye-spots" near their tails. These spots make them appear to be swimming backwards, particularly since their real eyes may be hidden behind a dark stripe. A butterfly-fish's fins are rounded and do not have long filaments. Their lips are generally extended into sharp snouts, with which they probe into coral crannies for food. Like angelfish, they have many small, sharp teeth which they use to scrape plant and animal food from the coral.

ANGLER FISH are strange fishes that use "fishing rods and lures" to catch their food. Their rods are long filaments developed from the first spines of their dorsal fins. Those that live in the lighted areas of the sea have fleshy bulbs at the tip of the rods, and sometimes they can wiggle or vibrate these lures. Those that live in the dark waters of the deep sea have a luminous lure. These baits attract smaller fishes, which swim close and are promptly gobbled up by the angler fish. Angler fish are poor swimmers. Many kinds use their fins like stubby legs to crawl about slowly over the bottom. Most of them are dull in colour and have fringed fins so that their body outlines are not easily distinguished.

Largest of the anglers is the Goosefish *(Lophius americanus)*, which may grow to four feet in length and weigh as much as 70 pounds. It has a cavernous mouth — so huge, in fact, that it can swallow a fish almost as large as itself. The Goosefish has been known to catch ducks and geese, hence its name. Its many teeth are sharp and curved back, like a snake's, so that it is difficult for prey to escape once the Goosefish has a grip on it. In Europe, especially in the Mediterranean countries, the Goosefish is often eaten. Those caught in deep water — found at depths of up to half a mile — have firm flesh. Those taken from shallow bays are less flavoursome.

Many different kinds of anglers are found in all types of seas — warm and shallow, cool or deep. Some prefer clear water; others like muddy or weedy waters. (See BATFISH; DEEP-SEA FISHES.)

GOOSEFISH
Lophius americanus
max. of 4 ft. and 70 lbs.

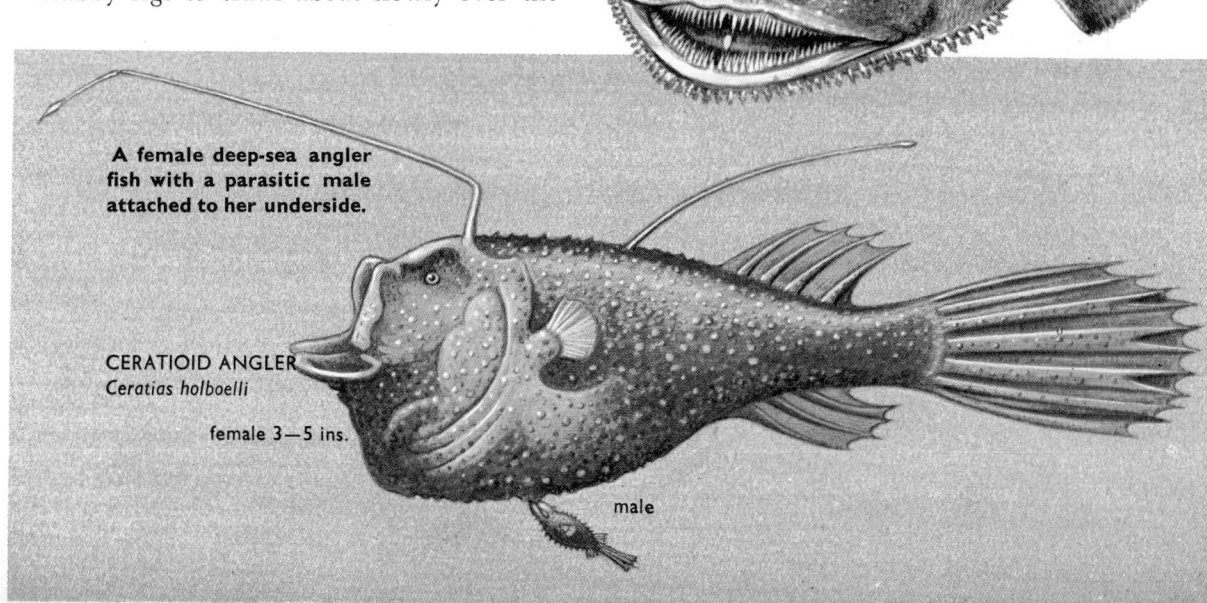

A female deep-sea angler fish with a parasitic male attached to her underside.

CERATIOID ANGLER
Ceratias holboelli

female 3—5 ins.

male

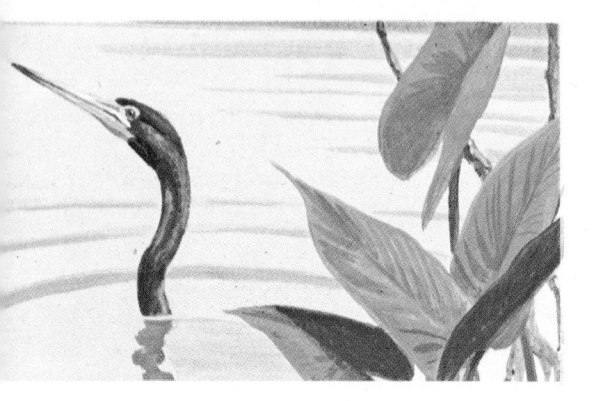

Anhingas swim in ponds, streams and canals with only their head and neck above the water.

ANHINGAS are a family of four slender cormorant-like birds, one species to each of the following regions: the Americas; southern Asia; parts of Africa; and Australia. They have long slender necks, with the head little thicker than the neck, and a thin, sharp dagger bill. They are known as darters or snakebirds, and the American species goes by the name of water turkey.

Anhingas spear their prey. They hunt with their necks folded, and then dart their heads out at their prey like a snake striking. A special joint in the neck makes it possible to dart the head forward with extreme speed. When a bird spears a fish or a frog, it waits for the victim to stop struggling, then throws it into the air and catches it, always swallowing it head first.

Anhingas are fine swimmers. Their more solid bones and fewer air-sacs (see BIRDS) make it possible for them to sink without a ripple, until only their snaky heads and necks can be seen above the water.

In spite of webbed feet which make perching difficult, Anhingas spend much of their time on tree limbs. They sit in groups in the sun, spreading their wings to dry. Unlike ducks, their feathers are not waterproof. Anhingas are awkward birds on the ground or perched in a tree, but they are very graceful in flight. With their long necks held straight out before them, they soar with ease. Often on sunny days they ride air currents above their roosts, soaring for long periods of time. With their wings motionless, head and neck held out stiffly in front and the long tail sticking out at the rear, they form a perfect cross.

Anhingas build nests of sticks and leaves in trees 5 to 15 feet above ponds or marshes. The 3 to 6 young that hatch from the bluish-white eggs are blind, naked and helpless. Both parents participate in feeding them regurgitated food. Within two weeks the young can swim, and, when frightened, they tumble out of the nest into the water to hide. When the danger has passed, they clamber back into the nest again, using their bills, feet and wings for climbing. The young are fully feathered and leave the nest in 6 to 8 weeks.

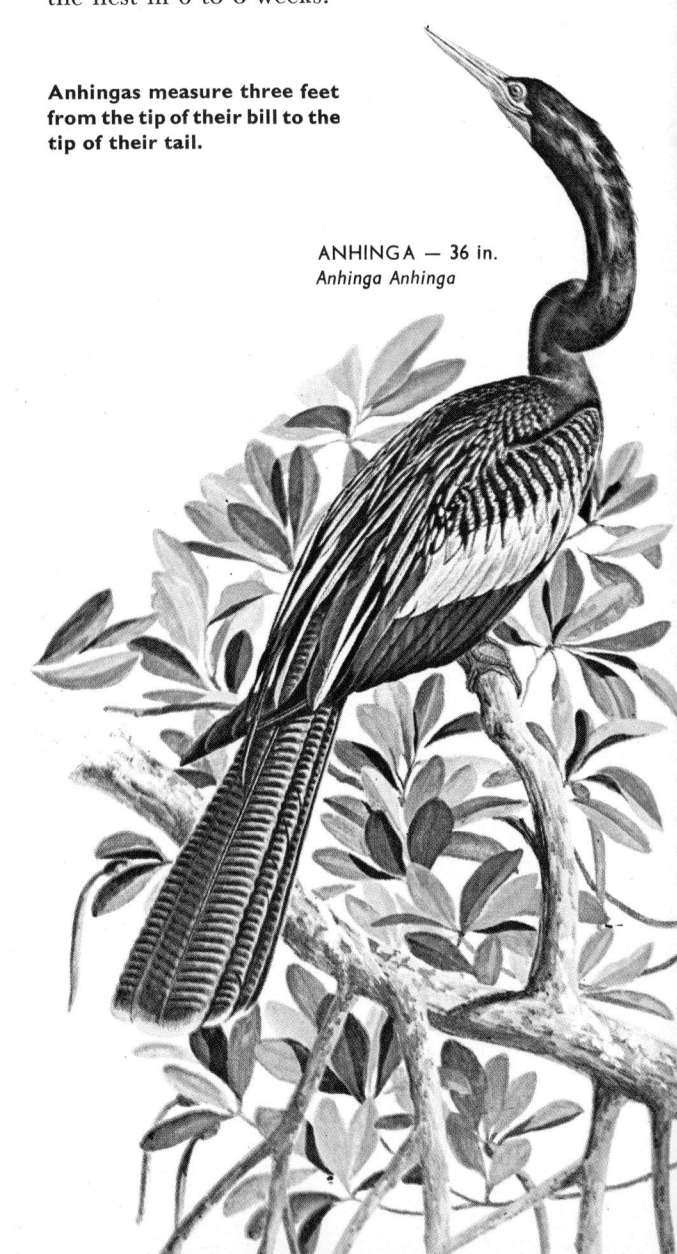

Anhingas measure three feet from the tip of their bill to the tip of their tail.

ANHINGA — 36 in.
Anhinga Anhinga

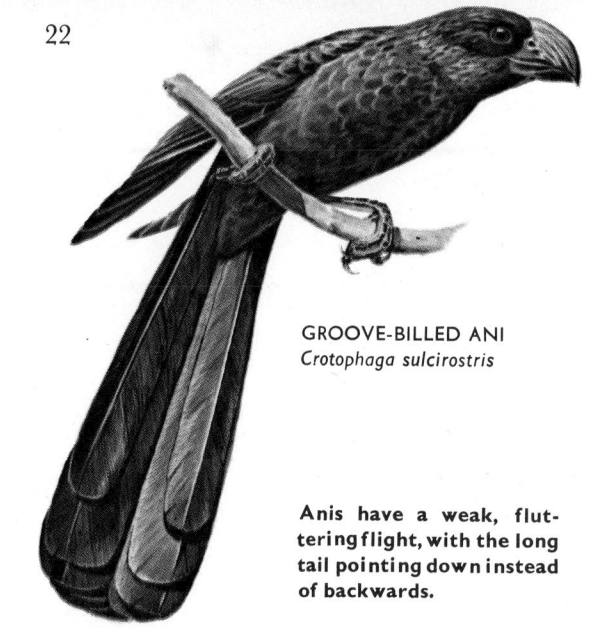

GROOVE-BILLED ANI
Crotophaga sulcirostris

Anis have a weak, fluttering flight, with the long tail pointing down instead of backwards.

ANIS, which live in eastern South America and the West Indies, are dull black birds with high, curved bills. They fly weakly on short, rounded wings, their long tails dangling. They belong to the cuckoo family (see CUCKOO).

The Anis are interesting because of their intensely sociable behaviour. Not only do they nest communally, but at other times resting birds huddle close together and may preen one another. The Ani is called the "black witch" in the West Indies.

Anis roost and nest in colonies and may go through their breeding cycle at any time of the year. The nest is usually a foot in diameter and six inches deep. Often while one bird is laying or incubating another is still adding to the nest. Sometimes as many as 15 birds use one nest. There are always more males than females in a group. The group often builds several nests each season, but only one is selected for the community project of raising one or several broods of young. Both sexes work at nest building and incubating, and often as many as three birds incubate the same eggs at the same time.

ANOLES, or American Chameleons (*Anolis* spp.), are the largest group of iguanid lizards (see IGUANAS) and are quite different from the true chameleons (see

CHAMELEONS), which belong to the Old World. Anoles, of which there are numerous species, range from the southeastern United States through Mexico, the West Indies and most of South America.

Anoles have two distinctive features: widened toes and a "dewlap", which is a loose fold of skin on their throats. The dewlap can be spread by swinging downwards a long, flexible rod of cartilage attached near the chin. In some species only males have dewlaps, and those of males are always larger. Brightly coloured in most species, the dewlap is a threatening or warning flag when enemies or males of the same species approach.

In most anoles the scales on the under surface of the fingers and toes are wide and form pads that aid in climbing, as in geckos (see GECKOS). Their innumerable tiny hooks catch in irregularities of a surface. An anole can climb a dirty pane of glass, but slips on a freshly-cleaned glass.

The Carolina Anole is very abundant in the Gulf States. Thousands are sold to carnivals and other retailers, who in turn sell them to boys and girls as "pets". They are alert, interesting and harmless animals for a few weeks, but seldom live in captivity even as long as a year. In nature, too, the

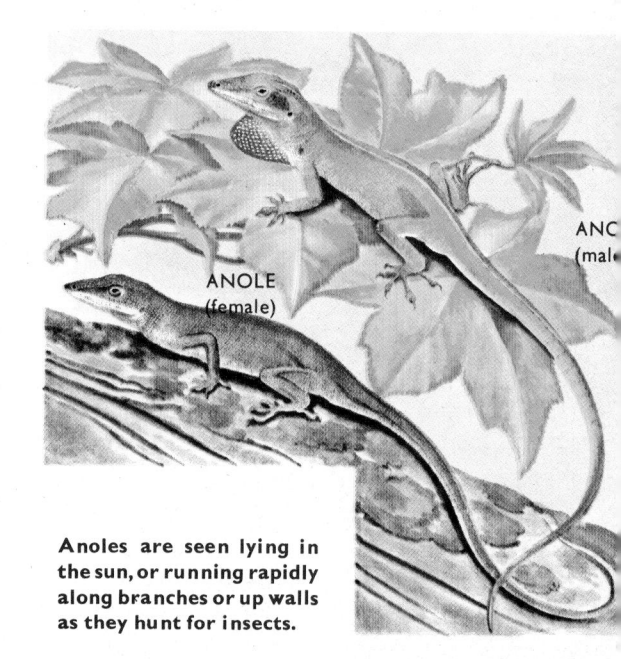

ANOLE
(female)

ANC
(mal

Anoles are seen lying in the sun, or running rapidly along branches or up walls as they hunt for insects.

average life expectancy is an astonishingly low 10 months, the least of any reptile; only under ideal conditions would an age of two years be reached. Other kinds of anoles live longer. The giant Cuban Anole has lived at least six years in captivity.

ANT-EATERS are clumsy-looking, toothless mammals with long, sticky tongues used to capture termites and ants. Most ant-eaters are found in the tropics of Central and South America. Scaly Ant-eaters, or Pangolins, live in Africa and Asia.

Giant Ant-eaters *(Myrmecophaga jubata)* are nearly eight feet long, and about half this length is bushy tail. They use the powerful, curved claws on their front feet to rip open the hard nests built by tropical termites. They also use them to dig in rotting logs on the jungle floor. These claws are so large that, when walking, they are forced to turn them inwards. The single offspring frequently rides on the mother's back. The mouth, less than a half-inch wide, is at the tip of a nozzle-shaped snout. Through this they stick their narrow tongues, nearly 12 inches long, to lick up termites or ants. They feed at night and, during the day, Giant Ant-eaters roll up in a ball to sleep, covering their heads and bodies with their bushy tails.

Tamanduas *(Tamandua tetradactyla)* usually live in trees, where they feed on the termites or other insects. Their long, flexible tail, half the length of the body, is used for climbing. These ant-eaters appear to be

The Giant Ant-eater feeds on ants and termites in forests and swampy grasslands of tropical South America.

W. Suschitzky

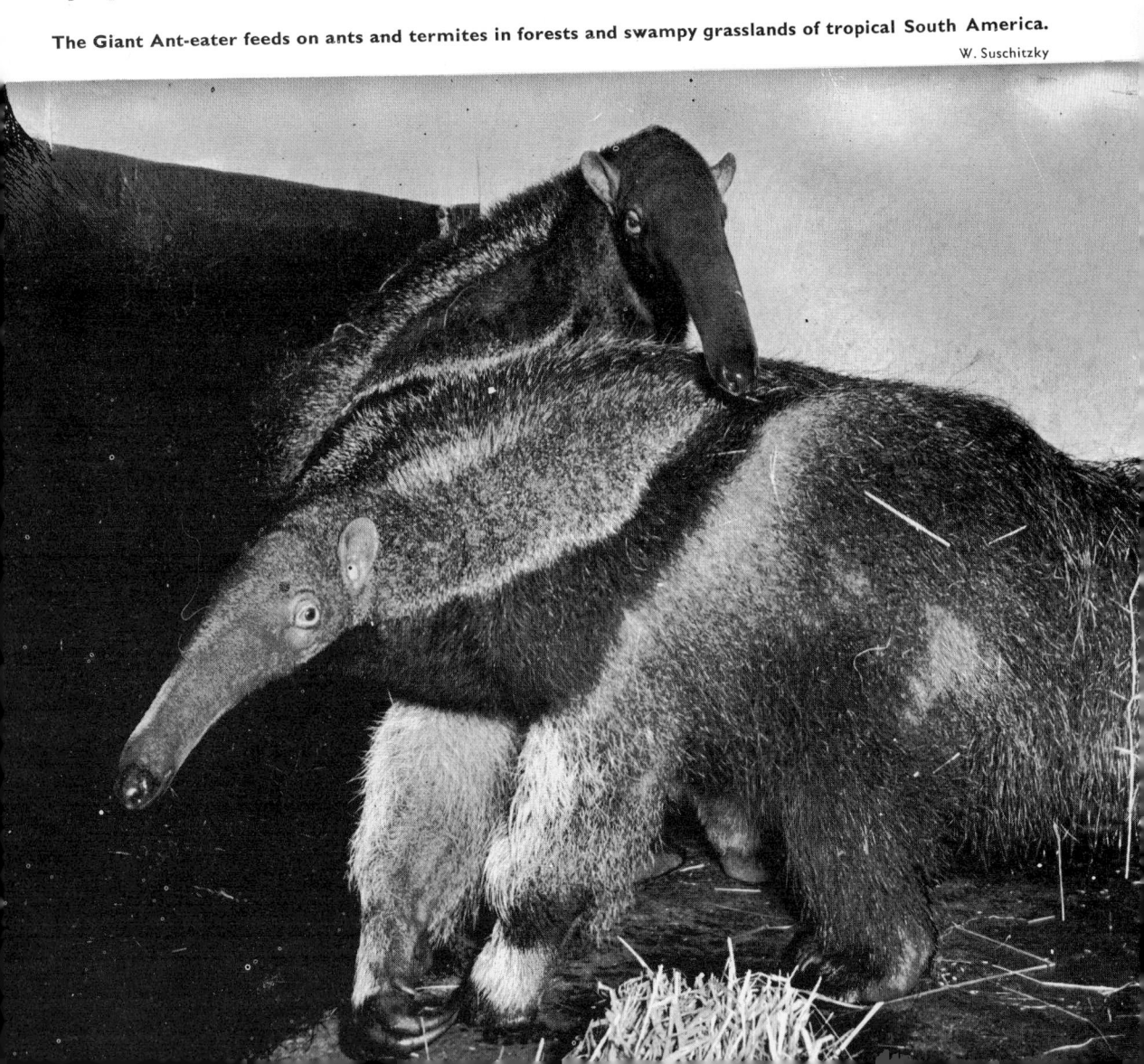

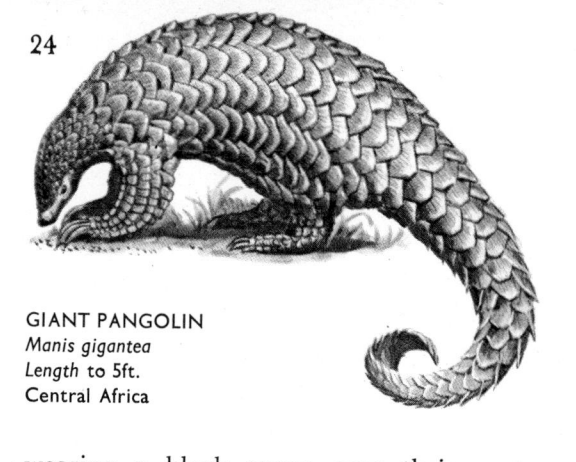

GIANT PANGOLIN
Manis gigantea
Length to 5ft.
Central Africa

southern and eastern Africa. The slightly larger Roan Antelope *(Hippotragus equinus)* lives in the same area and western Africa.

The male Greater Kudu *(Strepsiceros strepsiceros)* is slightly larger than the Sable Antelope, with horns 5 feet or a little more in length. It lives in the bushy country of South and East Africa.

Blackbucks *(Antilope cervicapra),* the most

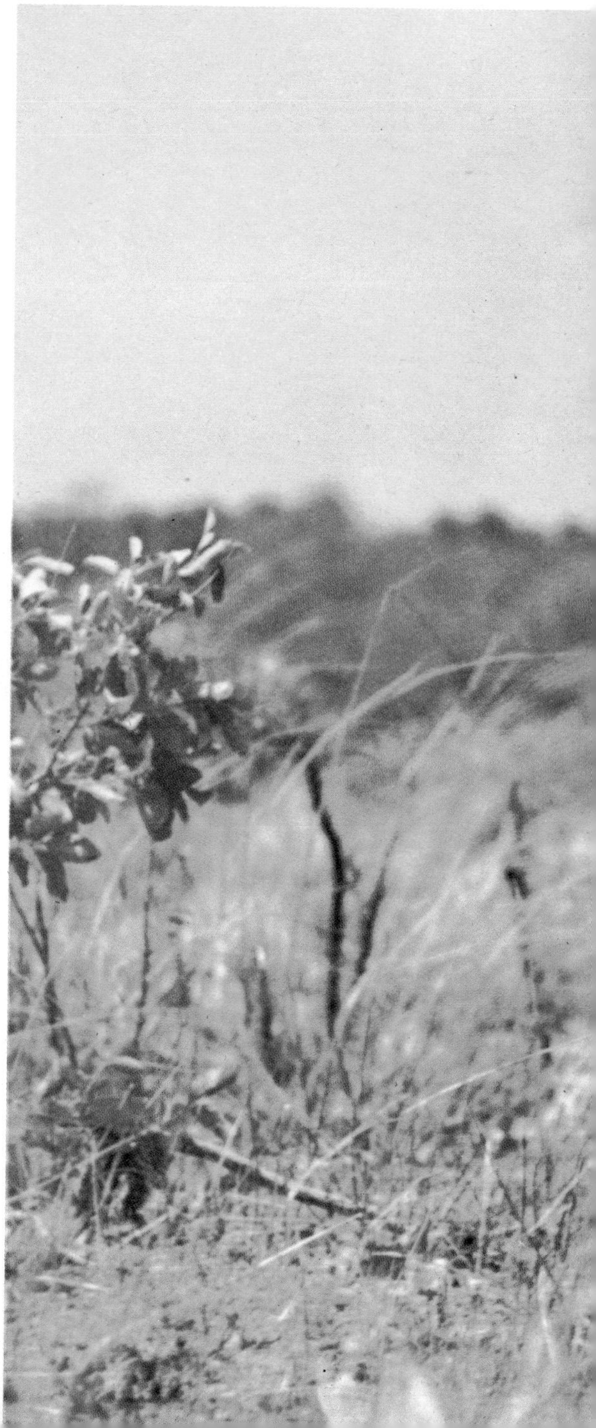

wearing a black apron over their coats.

Two-toed Ant-eaters *(Cyclopes didactylus)* are only about $1\frac{1}{2}$ feet in length and have long tails which make up nearly half their length. Their fur is the silkiest of all the ant-eaters. Tree-dwellers, they feed on termites and other insects at night and sleep by day on the branches, holding on to branches with their legs and tails.

Scaly Ant-eaters, or Pangolins *(Manis* spp.), are Old World ant-eaters found in Africa and Asia. Their strong claws are used to open the nests of ants and termites on which they feed. Some kinds live on the ground; others in trees. Scaly Ant-eaters are covered with horny scales. They have hair only sparsely on their heads, bellies, and the insides of their legs. Their hard scales are modified hairs and are good protection, especially when the animals roll up in tight balls and wrap their tails around themselves. Tree-climbing Pangolins use their long tails to help in climbing.

ANTELOPE is a name given to a number of swift, graceful mammals that live in the brush or grasslands of Africa and southern Asia. They are often grouped by the shape of their horns: sickle-shaped, as in Roan and Sable antelopes; straight-horned, in Oryxes; and screw-horned, in the Kudu.

Sable Antelopes *(Hippotragus niger),* which weigh as much as 500 pounds, have beautifully curved horns that may exceed five feet in length. Small herds forage in the savannas and lightly forested regions of

A graceful antelope stands in the bush of southern Africa, homeland of so many related species.

common antelopes in India, travel the open plains in small herds. Only the males have horns, which are corkscrew shaped. Older bucks, which stand about three feet high at the shoulder, command herds of about 50. Blackbuck are capable of running at 50 miles per hour. Nevertheless, some are caught by large cats (see CHEETAHS) and are frequently hunted by sportsmen. Old males are blackish-brown; females are brown. All are creamy-white below.

The straight-horned antelopes include the Gemsbok *(Oryx gazella)* of the desert regions of southern and south-western Africa. Both males and females have rapier-like horns as much as four feet long. They use these horns to protect themselves from lions or other predators. In open country, small herds of

Afrique-Photo

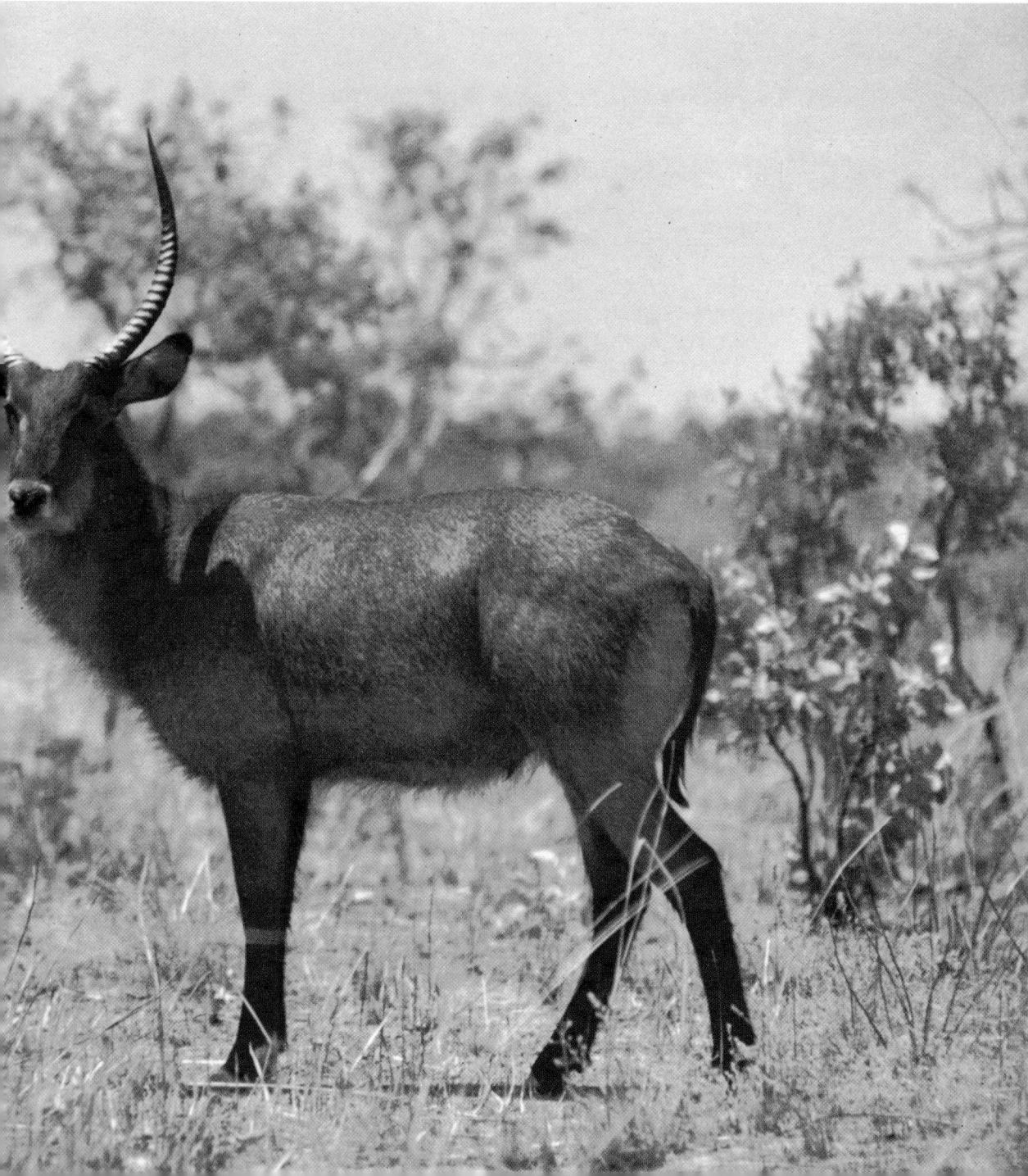

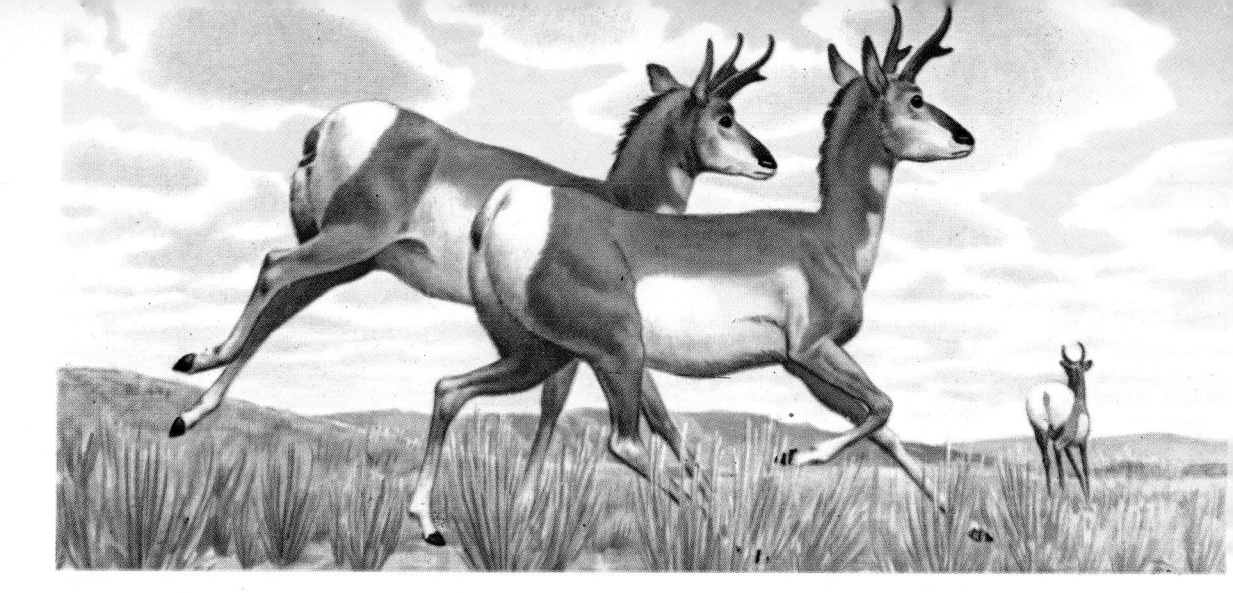

The horns, which occur on both male and female American Pronghorns, are formed of tightly-fused hairs.

Gemsboks are usually seen trotting along in single file. The East African Oryx, or Beisa (*Oryx beisa*), is similar to the Gemsbok. The White or Scimitar Oryx (*Oryx algazel*) is a near relative of the straight-horned antelopes. It is very light-coloured, with slightly curved horns, and lives in the desert lands

Gemsbok and Kudu are African antelopes; the Blackbuck is from India.

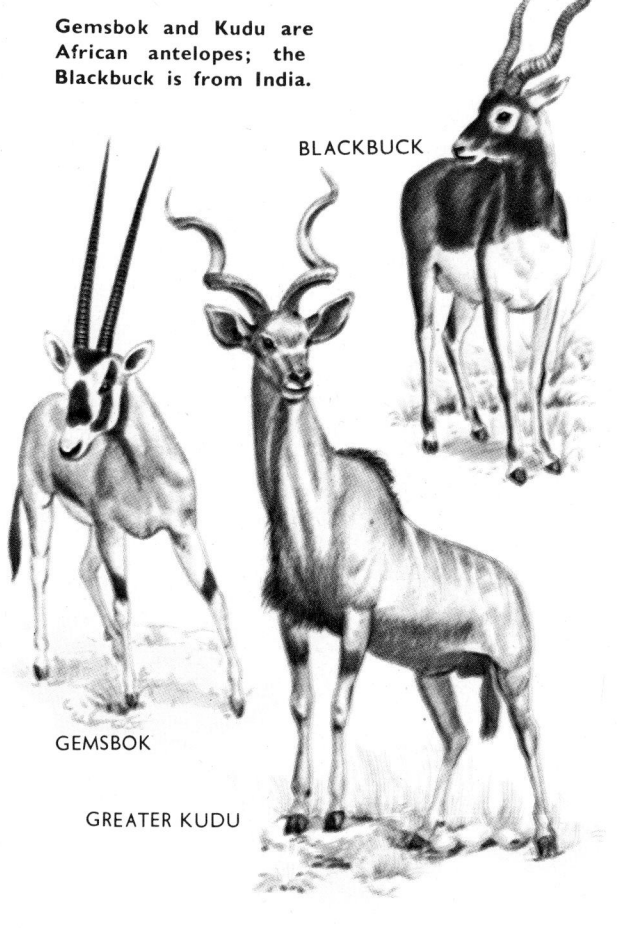

BLACKBUCK

GEMSBOK

GREATER KUDU

of the western Sudan in central Africa.

American Pronghorns (*Antilocapra americana*), frequently called Pronghorned Antelopes, are not closely related to the antelopes of the Old World, although they are somewhat similar in size and appearance. Klipspringers (*Oreotragus oreotragus*), small antelopes of the mountainous parts of eastern and southern Africa, measure only about 20 inches in height at the shoulder. Like the Mountain Goats of North America and the Chamois of the Alps, these antelopes are adept at springing up and down steep, rocky slopes. (See DIK-DIKS; DUIKERS, GAZELLES; GNUS.)

ANT-LIONS, or Doodlebugs (*Myrmeleontidae*), are fascinating insects that pass their early existence in dry, sandy places. Most ant-lions dig funnel-shaped pits in which they trap other insects that stumble over the edge, slide down and fall to the bottom. The ant-lion, hidden in the sand at the pit's base, grabs the victim with its long, sickle-shaped mandibles. When the desperate prey attempts to climb up the side of the pit, the loose, sandy side crumbles beneath it, while the ant-lion throws sand at the victim by snapping its head. This generally knocks the prey down into the pit again. Its prey secure, the ant-lion sucks the juices from its catch, and then it flips the shell of

the body out of their funnel-like pit.

These voracious creatures are actually the larvae of graceful insects that resemble dragon-flies. Females lay their eggs in the sand, and as soon as they hatch, the young larvae begin digging pits. As they grow in size, the larvae increase the size of their pits. Ant-lions are found in such dry, protected places as beneath buildings or under overhanging ledges, because rain destroys their pits and moist soil packs too tightly for their purpose.

Most of the more than 600 species live in the tropics or sub-tropics. Some kinds do not build pits, but lie in wait for ants or other prey beneath bark, rocks or wood. All belong to the order Neuroptera.

ANTS *(Formicidae)*, social insects of the order Hymenoptera, are probably the best known of all insects, and also more numerous than any other land animal. Their colonies may contain only a few dozen individuals, or several thousand. Ants inhabit nearly every kind of land area, from desert to rain forest and from the arctic to the tropics. Although the many species (more than 6,000) vary greatly in size and shape, almost all are easily recognised as ants. All ants have elbowed antennae and a bump, or spine, on the slender stalk, or pedicel,

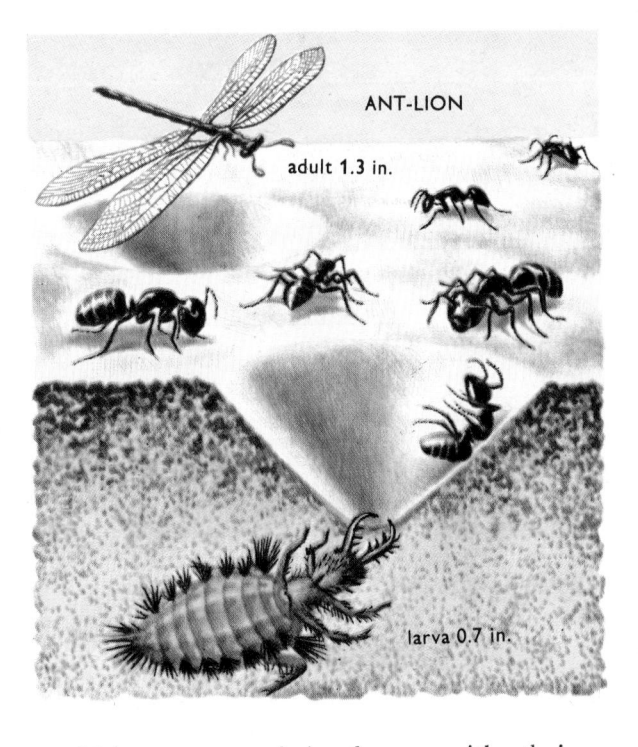

ANT-LION

adult 1.3 in.

larva 0.7 in.

which connects their thorax with their abdomen.

Each colony contains three basic castes, or kinds of individuals: queens, males and workers. Queens have wings and are much larger than other members of the colony. Males have wings, too, but are smaller than the queens. Workers, still smaller, do not have wings and are the most abundant members of a colony. In some species, also,

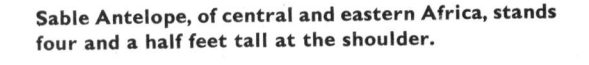

Sable Antelope, of central and eastern Africa, stands four and a half feet tall at the shoulder.

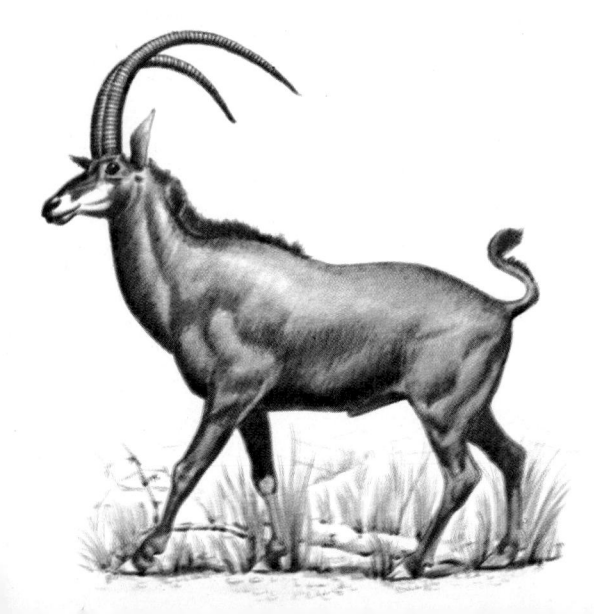

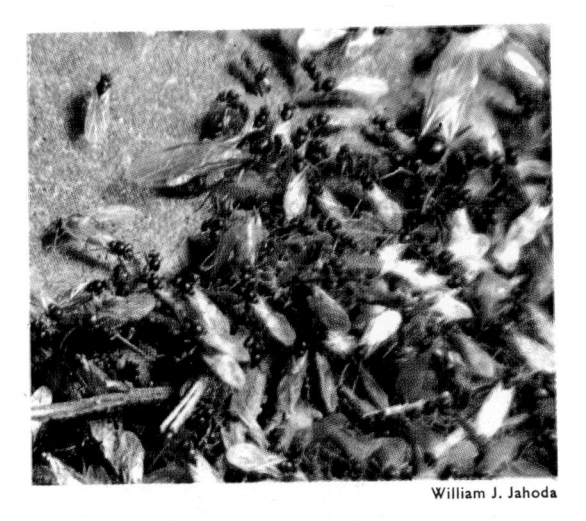

William J. Jahoda

Winged males and females swarm from colony and mate. Then the females establish new colonies.

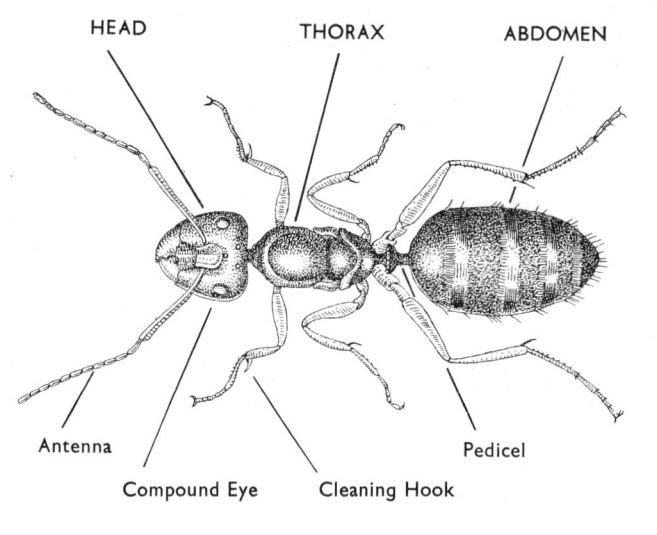

HEAD   THORAX   ABDOMEN

Antenna

Compound Eye   Cleaning Hook

Pedicel

there are several forms within each caste.

New ant colonies are formed when males and females fly away from an old colony. After mating, the males die. The females soon shed their wings and find a suitable spot to make a nest. Some species nest in the ground, under logs, or beneath stones; many build mounds. Others construct nests in hollow stems, fruit or nuts; a few kinds even build paper-like nests as wasps do. The queen tends the first batch of eggs herself, and also cares for the larvae until they become adults. These become the new colony's

first workers. The queen is then free to do nothing but lay eggs and, once mated, can lay fertilised eggs for the rest of her life. After the colony is well established, winged males and females are produced; they soon fly away to establish new colonies.

Army or legionary ants, found mostly in the tropics, do not build permanent nests, nor do the queens have wings. Shortly before the queen becomes swollen with eggs, army ants settle in an area, and within about a week the queen lays several thousand eggs. The eggs hatch in a few days, and at about the same time young adults from the previous batch of eggs emerge from pupa which the ants have carried with them. At this time the migratory stage begins and continues until the new larvae spin cocoons. The ants are probably triggered to migrate by physical contact between the larvae and the new workers. When the larvae spin cocoons, the exchange of food between workers and larvae ceases, and the ants settle. Army ants on the march eat nesting birds, small mammals, snakes, turtles, other insects — and nothing seems to stop them.

Harvester ants are seed-eaters that collect and store seeds in special chambers in their underground nests. Seeds that get wet and

Leafcutter ants cut fragments from leaves and have been known to strip a tree of its foliage in one night.

E. S. Ross

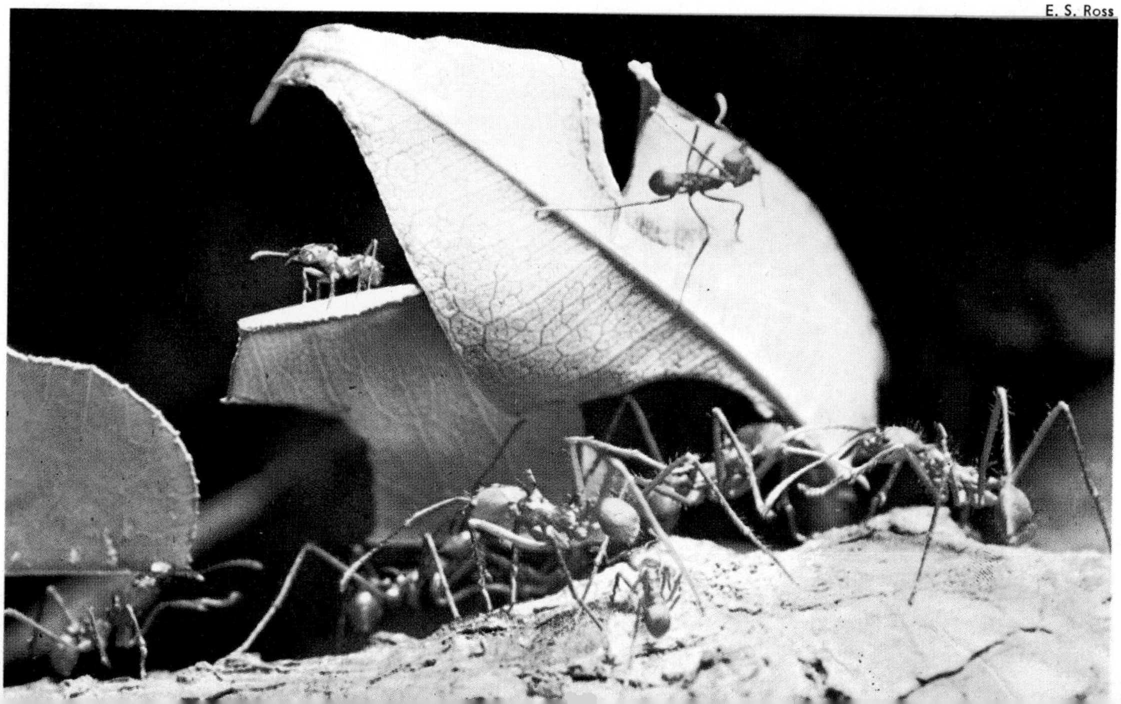

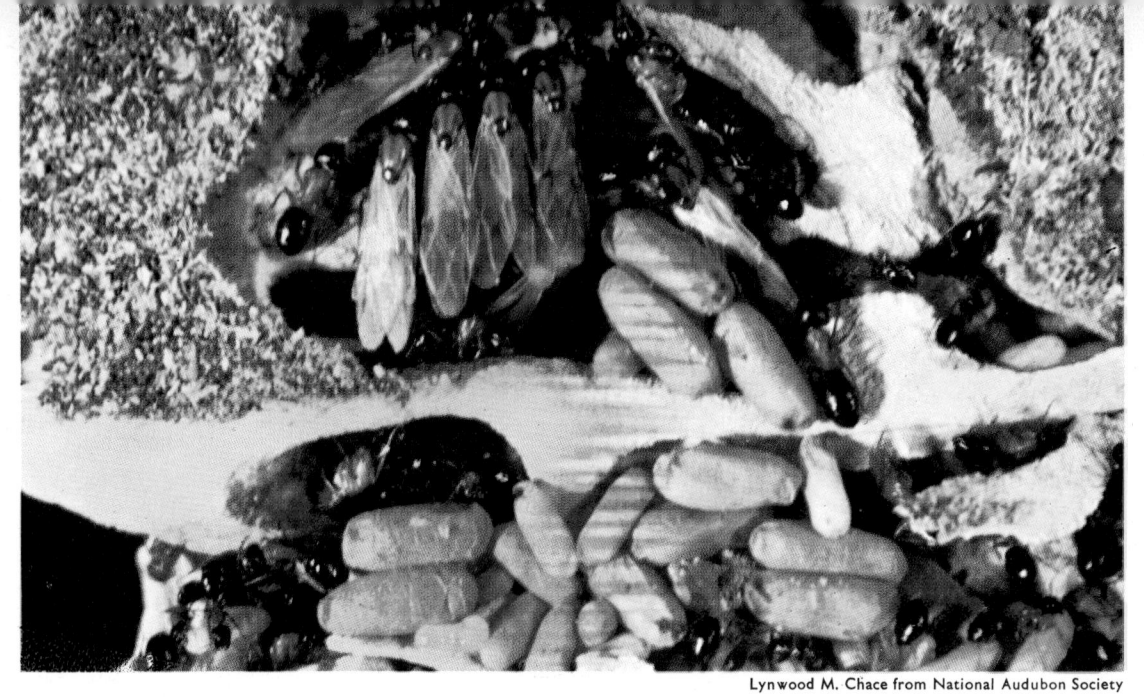

Lynwood M. Chace from National Audubon Society

In the top chamber of this ant nest is a group of young winged queens. Beneath them, workers are tending cocoons, or pupae, often mistakenly called "ant eggs". Adult ants will hatch from the pupae.

germinate are placed outside the nest but are not actually planted there, as was once believed. Closely-related ants do maintain gardens of fungi, however; each species of ant grows a particular species of fungus. Some grow the fungus on pieces of leaves; others use excrement or grain.

Other ants keep herds of "cows" —— aphids that secrete honeydew on which the ants feed. These ants protect their aphids when danger threatens, and some build shelters over the stem on which the aphids are feeding. Often they move the aphids to better food plants.

Perhaps the most unusual are the honey ants. Honeydew, their principal food, is stored in a special caste of workers, called repletes. These ants hang from the roof of

A leafcutter ant worker carries a leaf to the colony's underground garden to be compost for the fungus crop.

E. S. Ross

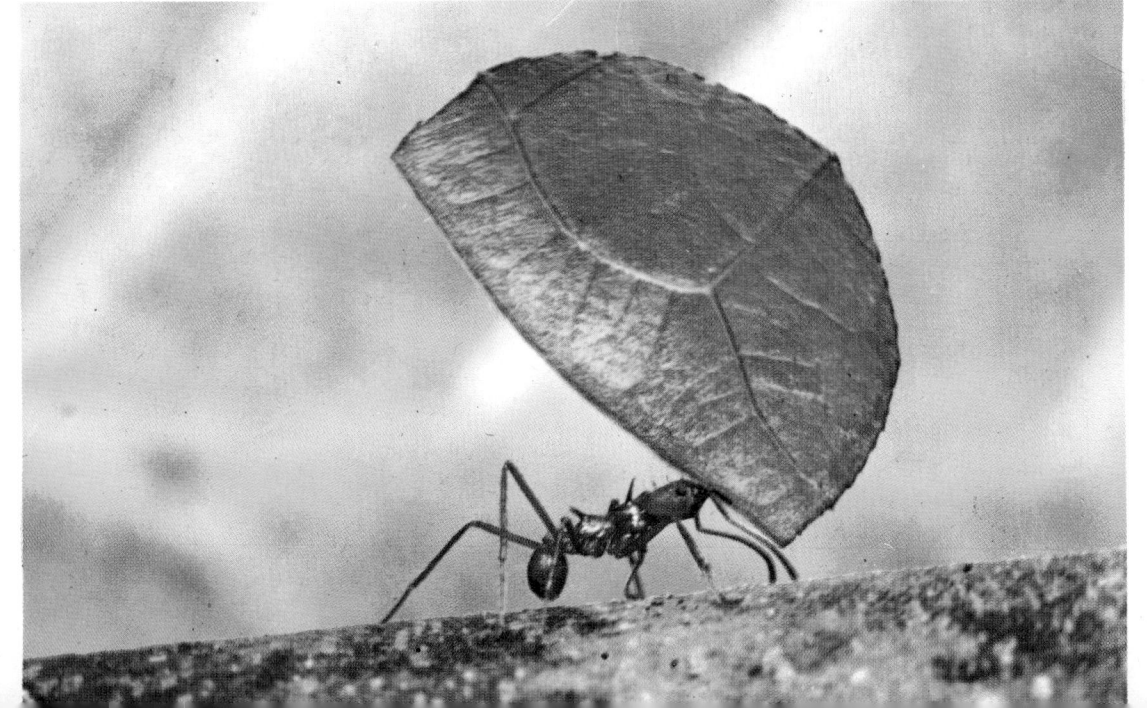

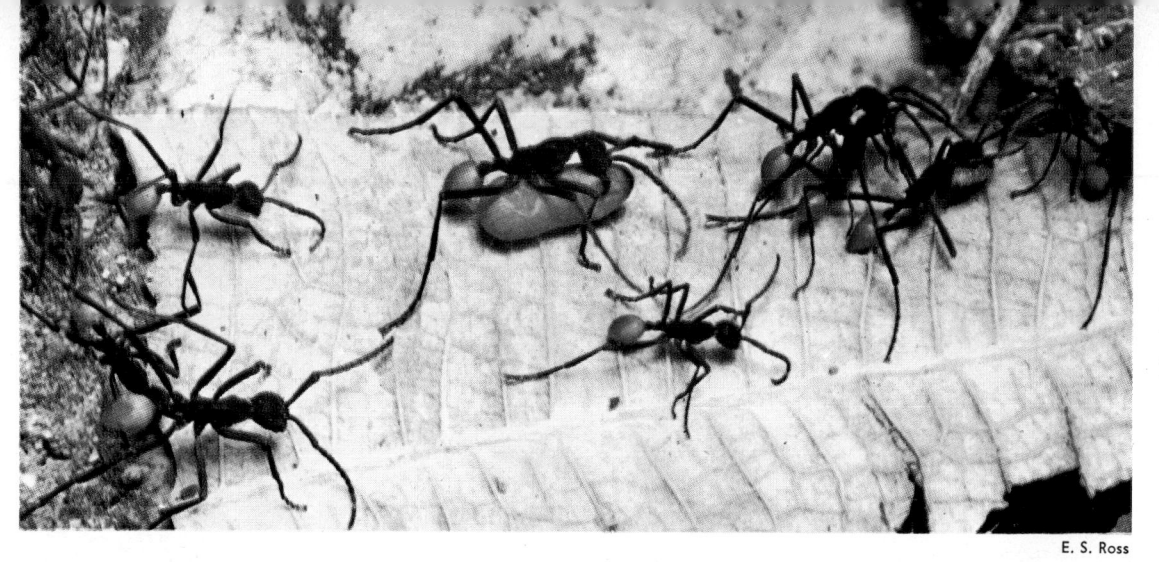

E. S. Ross

Army, or legionary, ant workers carry the cocoons (pupae) with them when the colony is on the move.

a special chamber in the nest. Their abdomens become swollen to many times normal size. Workers feed them honeydew collected from aphids, and the repletes feed it back to the workers to use as needed.

Fire ants got their name from the burning pain caused by their sting. They have been reported to cause the death of newly-hatched birds and other small animals, as well as causing considerable damage to crops. Their hard, mound-like nests make it impossible to use farm machinery in infested fields. Fire ants from South America have spread through the south-western United States in recent years, in spite of major efforts to control them.

Carpenter ants, among the larger species of common ants, build their nests in the woods of logs or timbers, or in the dead areas of living trees.

Slave-making ants raid other ant colonies and carry off their pupae. Some of the pupae

These army ant workers are busily attending the colony's queen, who spends most of her life laying eggs.

T. C. Schneirla

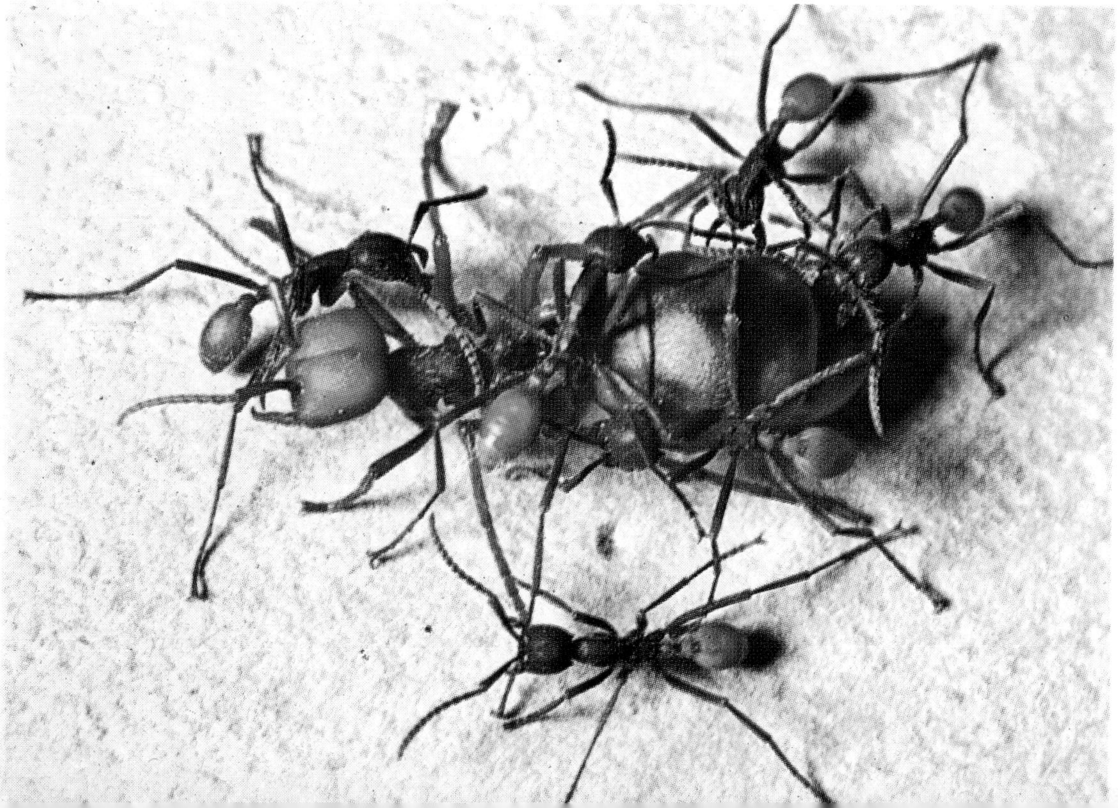

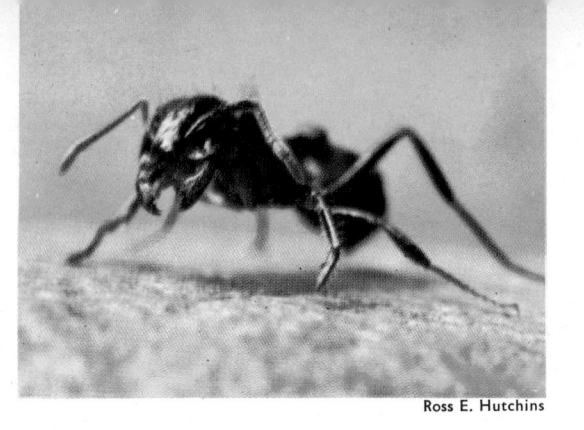

Ross E. Hutchins

Fire ants feed on insects, which they sting to death.

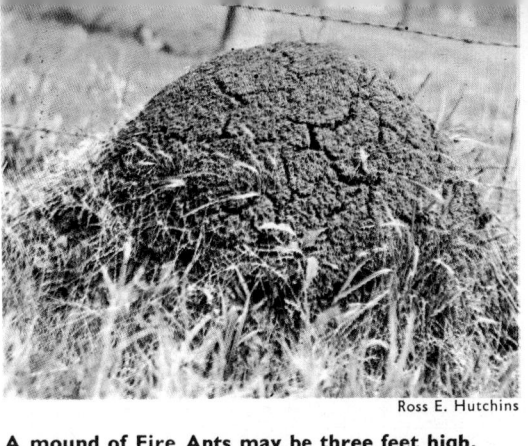

Ross E. Hutchins

A mound of Fire Ants may be three feet high.

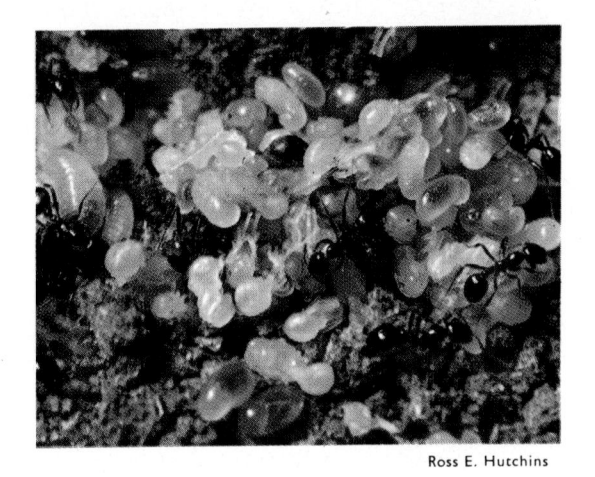

Ross E. Hutchins

Fire Ant workers tend larvae and pupae.

are eaten, but others are allowed to develop, becoming worker "slaves". Queens start new colonies by robbing another ant nest of its pupae, and then guarding them until they emerge as adult workers to serve her.

Leafcutter, or parasol, ants occur in the south-western United States, but are most abundant in Mexico and in Central and South America. In chambers a dozen feet or more beneath the surface they grow fungi, enriching their gardens with a compost of leaves. Each species of leafcutter cultivates a particular kind of fungus and weeds out any other that starts to grow in the garden. Workers move in a steady procession from the colony to trees or other leafy plants, where each ant uses its scissor-like mandibles to cut a fragment of leaf. In the nest the worker chews the leaf into tiny bits and packs them into the garden. The ant larvae feed on the fungus. Each young queen carries in her mouth a bit of fungus from her parent colony, to be used in starting the new colony. Large colonies may contain several hundred gardens.

APES, which include the Gibbons, Orang-utans, Chimpanzees and Gorillas, are members of one of the two major groups of primates. The most primitive group includes the Lemurs, Tarsiers and Lorises. In the second group are monkeys, apes and man. Apes are more human in habits and appearance than are any other living animals. They have extremely long arms, but rather short legs, so they lean forward on their hands as they walk, and they lack tails. In the distant past, apes and man had a common

ancestor which was very different from either modern apes or modern man. (See CHIMPANZEES; GORILLAS; ORANG-UTANS; PRIMATES.)

APHIDS, also called Plant Lice *(Aphididae)*, are very small ($\frac{1}{10}$ to $\frac{1}{50}$ of an inch) soft-bodied insects of the order Homoptera. They are usually found clustered in large numbers on leaves and stems of plants. Both winged and wingless forms occur, depending on the species or the stage of development. Most aphids are pear-shaped, their bodies broader at the rear than in front, and most kinds have a pair of tube-like organs at the rear of their abdomen. Some aphids are covered with a powdery or cottony wax-like substance, the product of dermal glands.

Aphids often have a complex life cycle. Typically, eggs that overwinter hatch into wingless females called "stem mothers". Without mating, these females give birth

to living young that are also usually wingless and that reproduce again in the same manner. Several generations may be produced in this way. Later, winged individuals may appear and fly to a different host plant, where they continue to produce new individuals. In the autumn they return to the original host plant and produce both males and females. After mating, females lay eggs on stems of plants, and the eggs do not hatch until spring. Adults normally die in winter.

Aphids feed only on plant juices that they suck out through their beaks inserted in the plants. Heavy infestations may injure a plant's growth or deform it, or the aphids may transmit various plant diseases. They secrete from the end of their abdomen a sweet, sticky fluid called honeydew, which collects on the plant stem. Honeydew is eaten by flies, bees and ants.

About 2,000 species of aphids occur in temperate regions around the world. They are rare in the tropics. Some have smooth bodies, others hairy. Green is a common colour, but others are black, brown, white, red or orange. Some are duo-toned.

ARK SHELLS (*Arca* spp., *Anadara* spp., and others) are common molluscs of shallow waters and are most abundant in the Atlantic. They are unusual among invertebrates in having red blood. One member of the group along the Pacific Coast of Central America is caught commercially for food. Turkey Wing Arks and Ponderous Arks are washed up on Florida's sand beaches, both ranging from the Carolinas to the Gulf of Mexico. Ponderous Arks often have stalks of sea feathers attached to their shells. Many Ribbed and Baily's Miniature Arks are found along the California coast. All arks have a series of teeth along the hinge. Some are sand-dwellers; most live attached to rocks by a strong holdfast (byssus) that grows out of a gap between the valves.

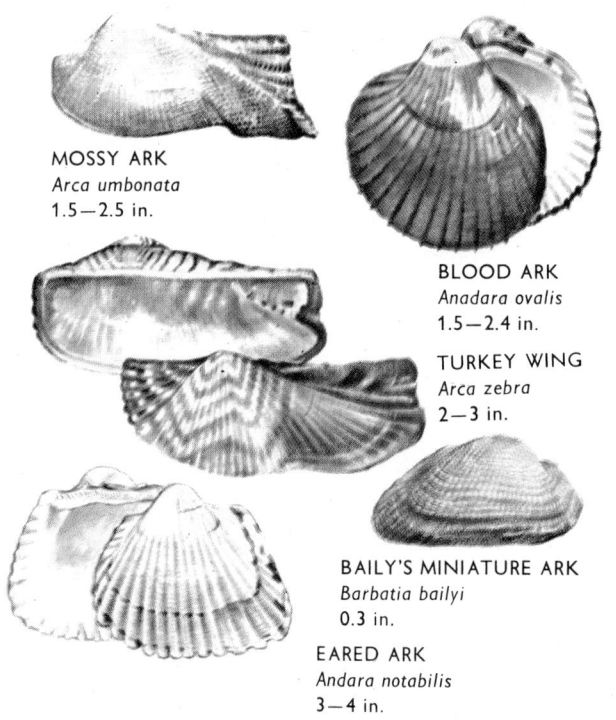

MOSSY ARK
Arca umbonata
1.5—2.5 in.

BLOOD ARK
Anadara ovalis
1.5—2.4 in.

TURKEY WING
Arca zebra
2—3 in.

BAILY'S MINIATURE ARK
Barbatia bailyi
0.3 in.

EARED ARK
Andara notabilis
3—4 in.

Ants that tend aphides move the "herds" to favourable locations, guard them, and extract their honeydew.

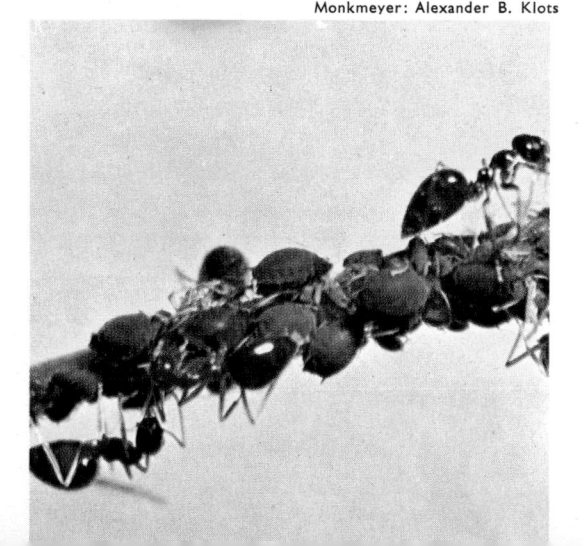

Monkmeyer: Alexander B. Klots

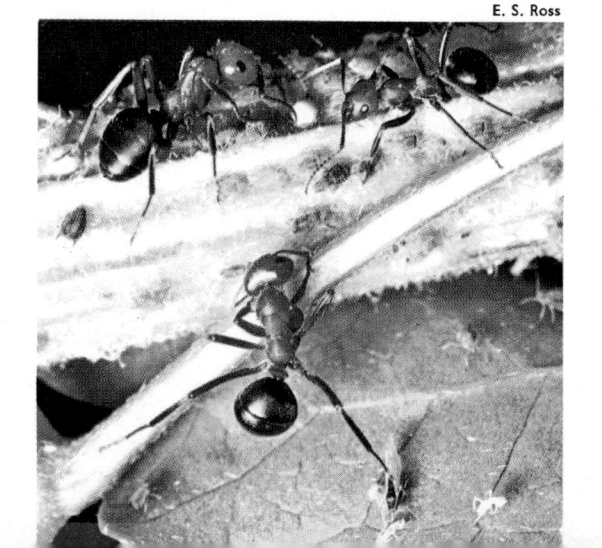

E. S. Ross

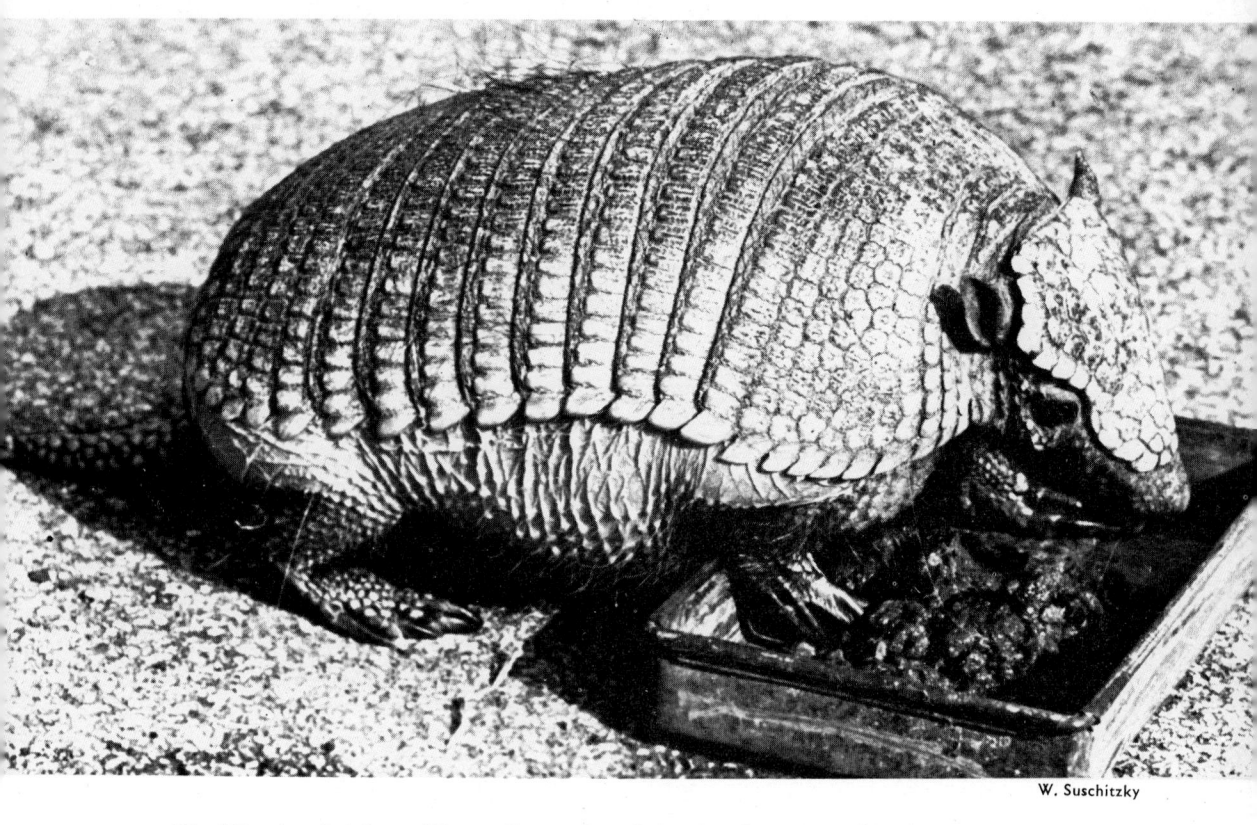

W. Suschitzky

The Nine-banded Armadillo swallows a lot of air when it wants to float in water.

ARMADILLOS, found only in North and South America, are strange mammals with horny plates forming a coat of armour. The plates are separated by soft skin on which a few hairs grow. At birth, an armadillo's skin is like soft leather; as the animal gets older, its skin hardens.

Armadillos have simple but numerous teeth. They feed mostly on ants and other insects, but sometimes eat plants. Most armadillos are not good runners. Some kinds can avoid enemies by rolling up in their "shells". The number of young at birth is often four in some armadillos, which are all of the same sex, since they develop from a single egg that divides twice to form four embryos.

Nine-banded Armadillos *(Dasypus novemcinctus)* are the only armadillos found as far north as the southern United States. They are swift enough runners to escape most enemies. More than 90 per cent of their food consists of insects (mostly beetles), earth-worms, crayfish, and other invertebrate creatures. These heavy animals gulp down large quantities of air to make themselves float in water.

Giant Armadillos *(Priodontes gigas)*, found in the tropical forests of South America, measure five feet in length, including tail. They have a greatly enlarged middle claw on each front foot, for the purpose of tearing apart termite nests.

Hairy Armadillos *(Euphractus villosus)*, found from Argentina to Uruguay, have a coat of hair that arises from between the body plates and is commonly heavy on the underside of the body. The hair may be so dense that it conceals the hard armour.

Three-banded Armadillos *(Tolypeutes tricinctus)*, of Bolivia, Paraguay and Brazil, completely enclose themselves in their hard shells. Their armoured heads and tails form part of the ball.

Pygmy Armadillos *(Chlamyphorus truncatus)*, sometimes called Fairy Armadillos

FAMILY TREE OF ARTHROPODS

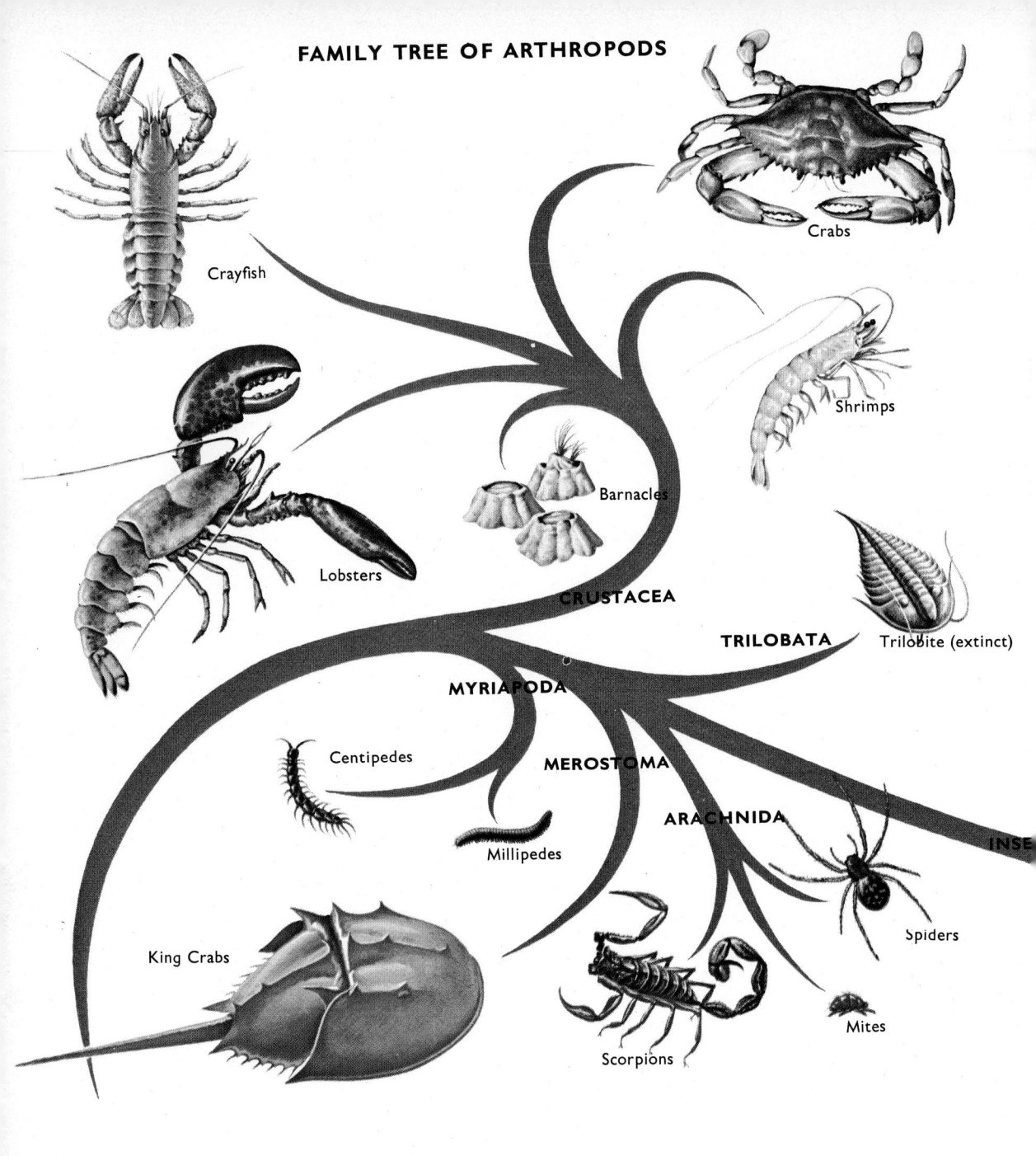

Crayfish

Crabs

Shrimps

Lobsters

Barnacles

CRUSTACEA

Trilobite (extinct)

TRILOBATA

MYRIAPODA

Centipedes

MEROSTOMA

Millipedes

ARACHNIDA

INSE

Spiders

King Crabs

Mites

Scorpions

or Pichiciagos, are the strangest of all the armadillos. Found only in the pampas of South America, many are only five inches long. They live in burrows, and have whitish fur and pink "shells" which do not cover them completely. A separate plate of armour at their tail-end serves as a shield to plug their burrow.

Extinct glyptodonts of late Cenozoic time were closely related to armadillos. Their bodies were covered by a massive, bony dome (up to 5 feet long). Both head and tail were heavily armoured. In some, the heavy tail ended in a spiked, bony knob. (See SLOTHS.)

ARMY-WORMS are the larvae of greyish-brown moths that belong to the family *Noctuidae*. They are called army-worms because they frequently move in large numbers

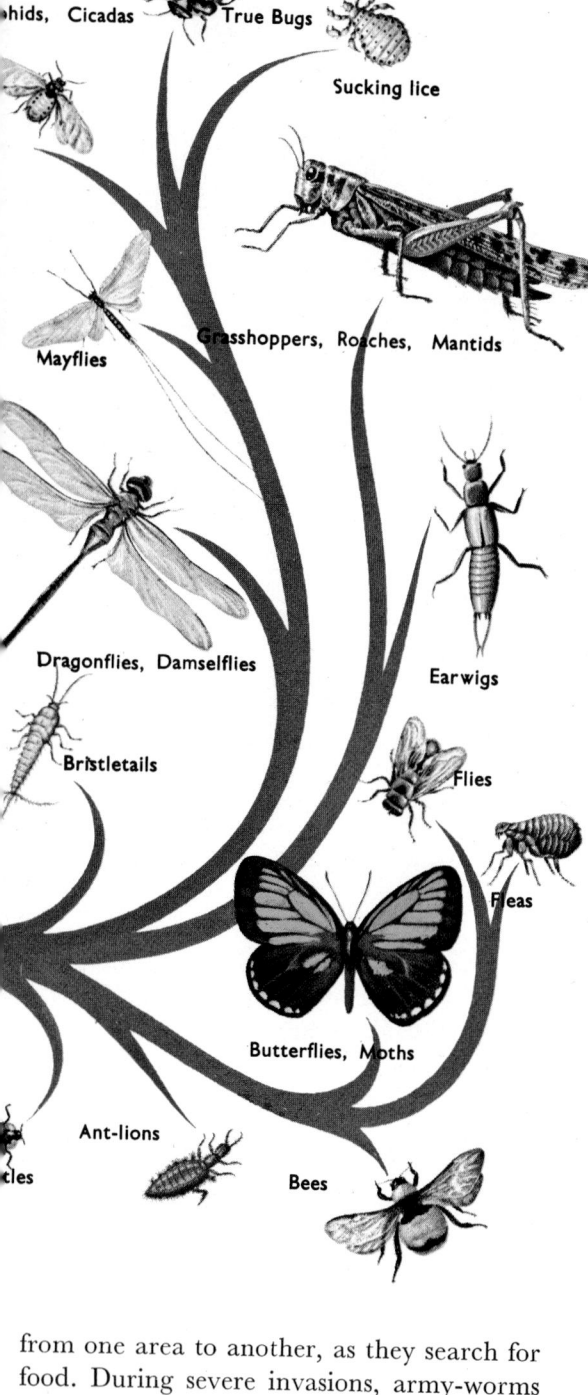

hids, Cicadas   True Bugs

Sucking lice

Grasshoppers, Roaches, Mantids

Mayflies

Dragonflies, Damselflies

Earwigs

Bristletails

Flies

Fleas

Butterflies, Moths

Ant-lions

cles   Bees

used, farmers dug ditches around their fields when an army-worm invasion was expected. The army-worms would either fall or crawl into the ditches, and were then unable to get out; there they were easily killed by the farmers.

ARTHROPODS include crabs, shrimps, insects, barnacles, spiders, centipedes, and the extinct eurypterids (sea scorpions) and trilobites. All have paired, jointed legs, and a jointed external covering. Their bodies consist of a number of segments, and they have well-developed digestive, nervous, circulatory and reproductive systems.

This largest group (phylum) in the animal kingdom contains about a million named species, and 90 per cent of these are insects. Arthropods live in almost every environment, from ocean deeps to mountain peaks. They are one of the most successful of all animal groups and also one of the oldest — from Cambrian to Recent.

The outer skeleton of adult arthropods consists of a tough, complex material called chitin. In many arthropods additional chemical compounds, such as lime, are deposited over the chitin, causing the skeleton to be hard. Between the body segments and the joints of the appendages there are no deposits, and the chitin remains flexible.

As an arthropod increases in size, it must

ARMY-WORM
Pseudaletia unipuncta
1—2 in.

from one area to another, as they search for food. During severe invasions, army-worms have been known to destroy vegetation over many square miles, and have been observed crossing roads in bands several yards wide to reach fresh fields.

Female moths lay their eggs, often as many as 500 in a cluster, on the lower leaves of grasses. The worms begin eating as soon as they hatch. Before insecticides were widely

shed this outer covering, and a new covering is formed beneath to take its place. While the new shell is still soft and is expanding to accommodate the larger size, the animal is especially vulnerable to predators.

No species of arthropods has ever become giant size, partly because of their heavy outer skeleton. The largest are those that live in the sea, where their body is buoyed by the water. Some species are microscopic (see index for those treated separately).

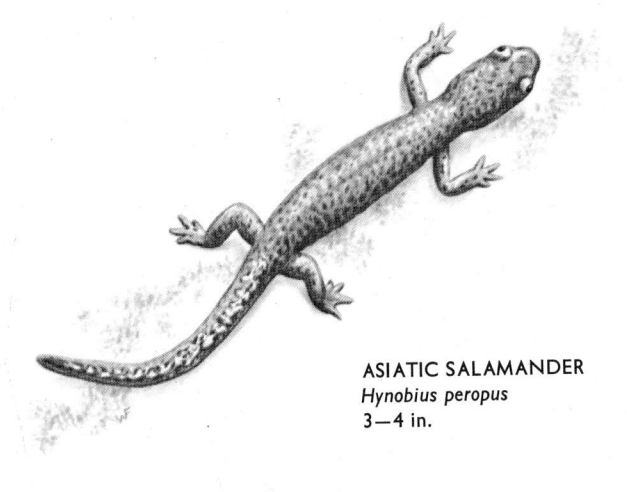

ASIATIC SALAMANDER
Hynobius peropus
3—4 in.

ASIATIC SALAMANDERS are small (3 to 4 in.) salamanders in a family *(Hynobiidae)* of 25 species found from Siberia and Turkestan to Japan. Adults lack gills, but all have water-dwelling larvae with gills. As many as 75 eggs are laid in long strings in the water. Those species that live in fast-moving mountain streams lay their eggs under rocks.

Most species are land-dwellers as adults and breed in still waters. Those few kinds that live in mountain streams have lost their lungs; this reduces their buoyancy, so that they can crawl about in the flowing water without being carried away. Since these aquatic types also lack gills, they breathe through their skin.

ASSASSIN BUGS *(Reduviidae)* live on the blood or juices of other insects. Occasionally they attack man and other mammals. More than 3,000 species are known, most of them tropical. Their long, slim heads are pointed

in front, then become narrow again just behind the eyes. Their beaks, usually short and curved, rest in a groove beneath their heads, and their abdomens are sometimes slightly wider than their wings. Most are dull, but a few are brightly coloured. Many kinds live on flowers, where they catch bees or other insects that come for nectar; others hide under rocks, logs, or other objects on the ground.

The Wheel Bug is unusual because of the cogwheel-like crest on its thorax. Another well-known assassin bug is the Kissing Bug, or Bloodsucking Conenose, which occasionally invades houses and can inflict painful bites. Some are carriers of disease.

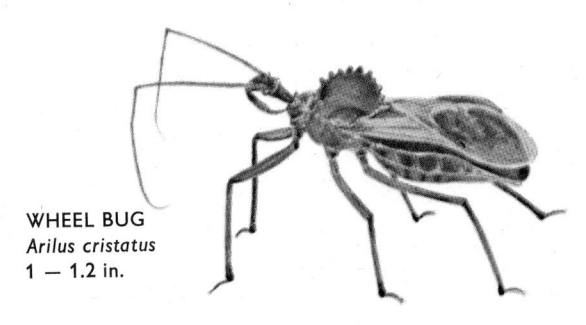

WHEEL BUG
Arilus cristatus
1 — 1.2 in.

AUKS, a circumpolar family of birds, breed in the far north and migrate south to the north temperate zones in winter. Puffins, razorbills, guillemots and little auks belong to this family of powerful swimmers and expert divers.

On the surface of the sea they all swim with closed wings, using their feet with their wings, as though flying underwater, and steer with their feet.

Members of the auk family are clumsy on

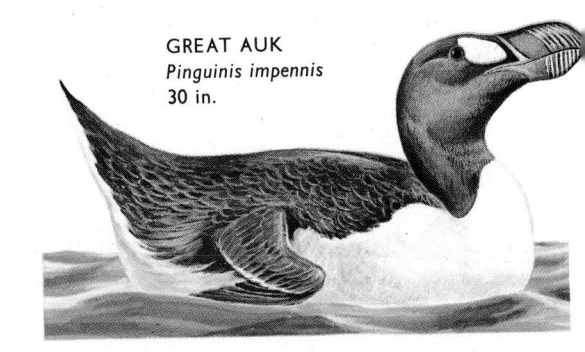

GREAT AUK
Pinguinis impennis
30 in.

land. They stand erect and waddle much like penguins. Although they have difficulty taking off, except from a height, once in the air they fly well. They never soar.

The Great Auk, an extinct flightless bird, was as big as a goose. It lived in the North Atlantic and nested on small islands off the coasts of Newfoundland, Iceland, Scotland and Norway, and in winter swam south as far as Florida. Men caught these auks on their nesting grounds, drove them into pens, and killed them for their meat and oil. The last Great Auk was killed in Iceland in 1844.

The Razorbill, about the size of a duck, breeds as far north as the Arctic Sea and winters off the coasts of the North Atlantic Ocean. In the spring the inside of the Razorbill's mouth turns bright yellow. It courts with its mouth open to show the brilliant colour. Like the slender-billed Guillemot, it comes to land only to nest; both species use cliff-ledges, the Razorbill preferring dark corners, the Guillemot in close-packed ranks on ledges or flat-topped stacks. The growling murmur of their calls, heard at a distance, has given them their name of "murres". The large, pear-shaped egg is laid on bare rcok. Parent birds coax the chick into the water before it can fly.

Auklets are very small auks, some no bigger than the Robin. Most of them live in the North Pacific and the Bering Sea; the Little Auk is the only one that reaches the Atlantic. It breeds within the Arctic Circle and migrates south in winter into the North Atlantic, often appearing near the coasts when driven onshore by heavy winter storms.

AVOCETS are long-legged wading birds. They live all over the world in temperate zones, near shallow salt water in marshes, sandy flats and salt meadows. Avocets swim and fly well, and are extremely graceful.

Avocets feed by sweeping their bills from side to side in shallow salt water, catching tiny fish and aquatic insects. Their upcurved bills move parallel to the surface and bed, even though their heads are bent down.

Courting Avocets are sometimes seen

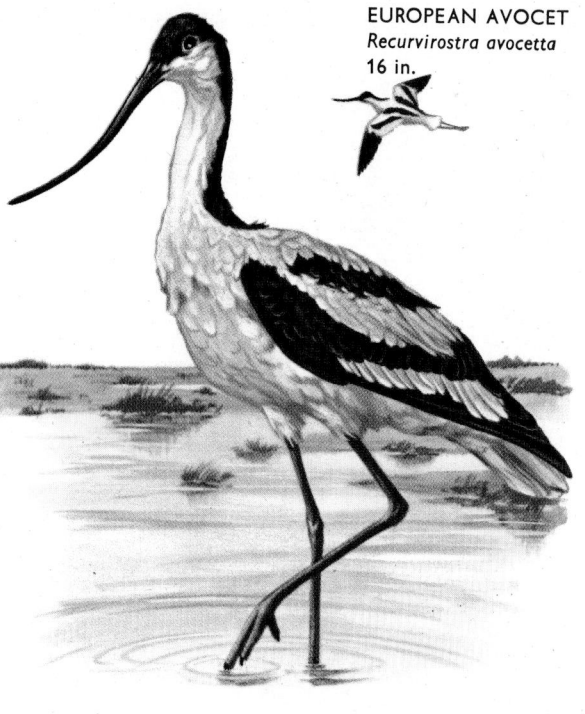

EUROPEAN AVOCET
Recurvirostra avocetta
16 in.

running side by side, with the male's half-open wing stretched over the female's back, as though the bird were protecting its mate. Both birds incubate the eggs, which are laid in a depression in the sand or dry mud. They take turns, and always greet each other with bowing ceremonies as they change places.

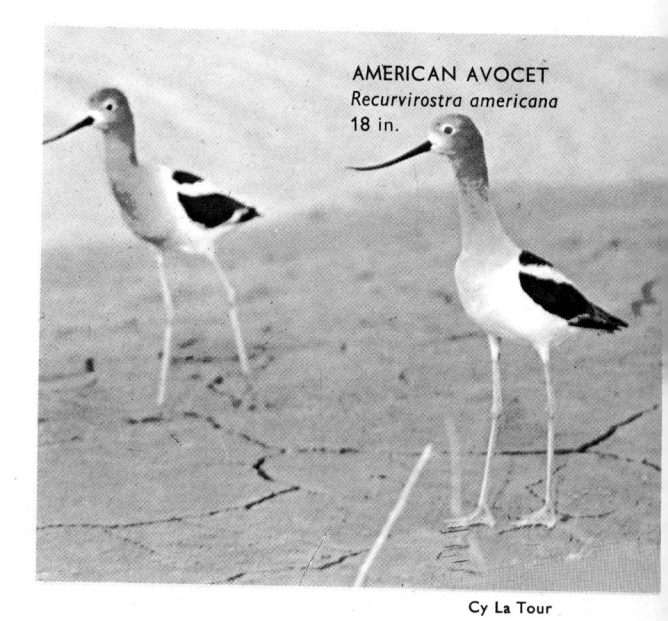

AMERICAN AVOCET
Recurvirostra americana
18 in.

Cy La Tour

American Avocets nest in the western United States and winter south to Guatemala. When they migrate, they travel in small flocks.

B

BABOONS (*Papio* spp.), found mostly in Africa, are among the largest of the monkeys. They may measure $2\frac{1}{2}$ feet in length, exclusive of the 2-foot tail. Because of the shape of their heads, baboons are sometimes called "dog-faced monkeys". Ground dwellers, they rarely climb trees. Their fore and hind legs are about the same length, so they can walk or run comfortably on all fours. Baboons travel in well-organised herds or troops, and defend themselves fiercely against much larger enemies. Baboons are easily trained and make intelligent pets.

Chacma Baboons *(Papio ursinus)* of South Africa sleep in caves or natural rock shelters and forage for food during the day. Closely-related Yellow Baboons *(Papio eynocephalus)* are found from Angola and Rhodesia north to East Africa and the Congo.

The Hamadryas Baboon, found in East Africa north to Arabia, was the Sacred Baboon of the Ancient Egyptians, often pictured on their temples and monuments. Mummies of these baboons are found in Ancient Egyptian tombs. Much has been written about the social behaviour of Hamadryas Baboons. They travel in packs of several hundred, and where they are abundant they become pests, raiding crops or even ransacking houses.

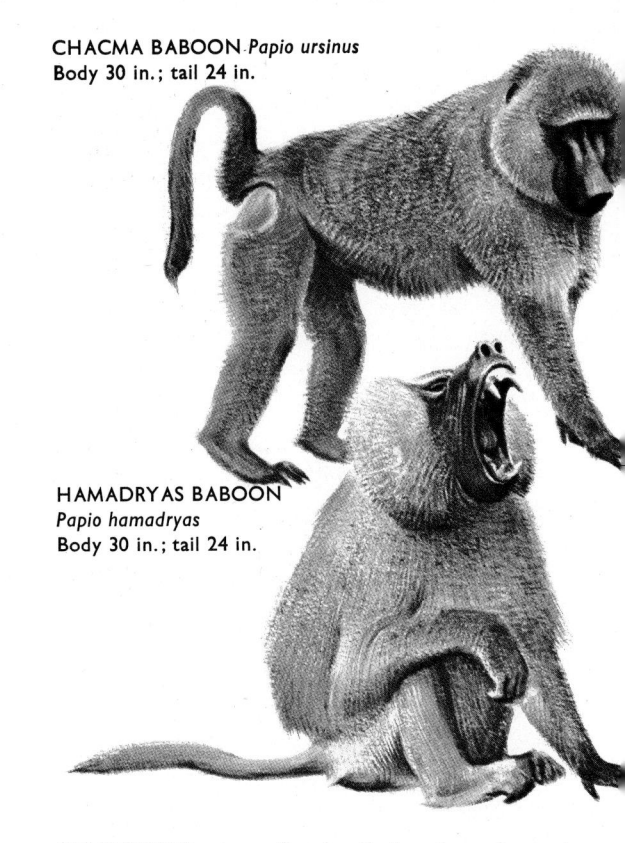

CHACMA BABOON *Papio ursinus*
Body 30 in.; tail 24 in.

HAMADRYAS BABOON
Papio hamadryas
Body 30 in.; tail 24 in.

BADGERS are flat-bodied, short-legged, digging mammals. They are closely related to skunks and weasels, but do not have such well-developed scent glands. Badgers eat a wide variety of foods, from burrowing mammals to crawling insects and snails; but they also vary their diets by eating fruit or by robbing bees' nests to get honey.

Badgers are found in Europe, the northern part of Asia and in North America. The badgers of Europe and Asia are 3 feet or a little more in length and are nocturnal, feeding at night on insects, snails, slugs and small mammals, with some vegetable food. They inhabit extensive burrows, known as sets, and are usually to be found in woodland, especially on hillsides.

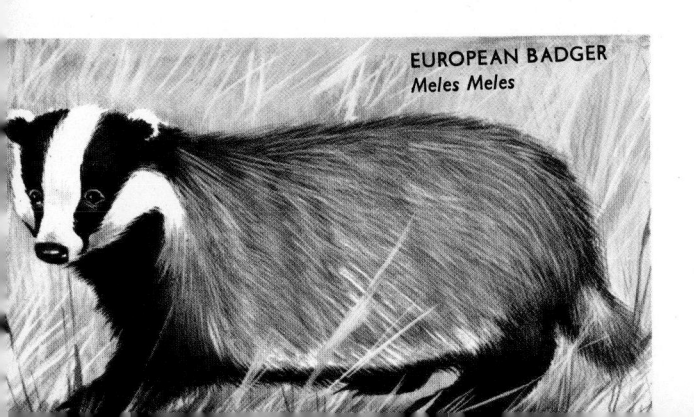

EUROPEAN BADGER
Meles Meles

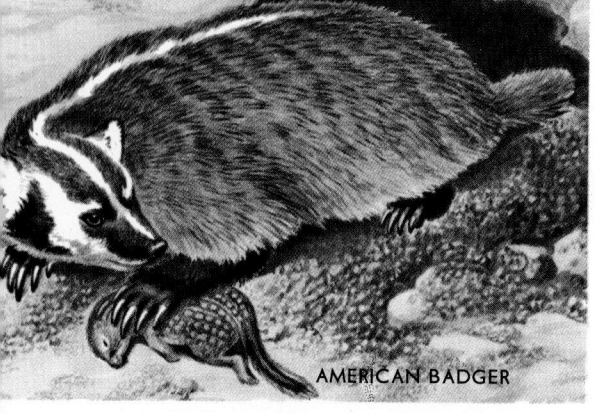

Badgers have sharp claws and powerful front legs. They dig rapidly to catch prey or to escape enemies.

American badgers are very similar to those of Europe and Asia, but are slightly smaller. They live on ground squirrels, marmots, prairie dogs and other small rodents, and burrow rapidly after prey.

Honey Badgers, or Ratels *(Mellivora ratel)*, found in Africa and southern Asia, are especially fond of honey and often raid the nests of ground-dwelling bees to satisfy this taste. Their thick hair and tough hides protect them from stings. Honey Badgers often follow birds called Honey-guides to find nests of bees (see HONEY-GUIDES). They also eat rodents, insects, termites, and other small animals.

BAGWORMS *(Psychidae),* the larval stage of a moth, spin silken bags, often covered on the outside with twigs, pine-needles, leaves, or other debris. They feed on leaves, flowers and stems or bark of many kinds of plants, and eventually pupate in the bags. The dull-coloured male moths that eventually emerge from these bags have wings and look like other moths. Females, however, have neither wings nor legs. They never emerge from the bag. Males search for a bag containing a female. They mate, and the female lays her eggs inside the bag.

The Evergreen Bagworm, a common species, attacks cedars or arbor vitae, but may also feed on other kinds of plants.

BALLYHOO, an American member of the halfbeak family *(Hemirhamphidae),* is a popular bait for sailfishes. The halfbeaks, close relatives of the flying fishes and needle fishes, have a normal upper jaw, but a long lower jaw that sticks out like a beak — hence their name. They are abundant in all warm seas, swimming close to the surface, generally in large shoals. Most species are less than a foot in length, but one South American species reaches 6 feet; it is greatly feared by the fisherman. (See FLYING FISHES; NEEDLE FISHES.)

BARNACLES are marine crustaceans that live attached to such hard surfaces as pilings, rocks, ship bottoms and hard-shelled animals. There are two common kinds: conical species, common on intertidal rocks; and goose barnacles, which have flattened shells at the end of long leathery necks, or stalks.

All barnacles begin life as free-swimming larvae. They soon cement themselves firmly to some surface and transform into typical barnacles. Based on their final position, barnacles are said to lie on their backs and kick their food into their mouths with their feet. Actually they feed on plankton, which they catch with their feathery appendages. Some are parasites. *Sacculina,* for example,

BAGWORM
Thyridopteryx ephemeraeformis
1.3 in.

larva carrying bag
0.8 in.

tail of Ballyhoo

HALFBEAK
Hyporhamphus unifascatum

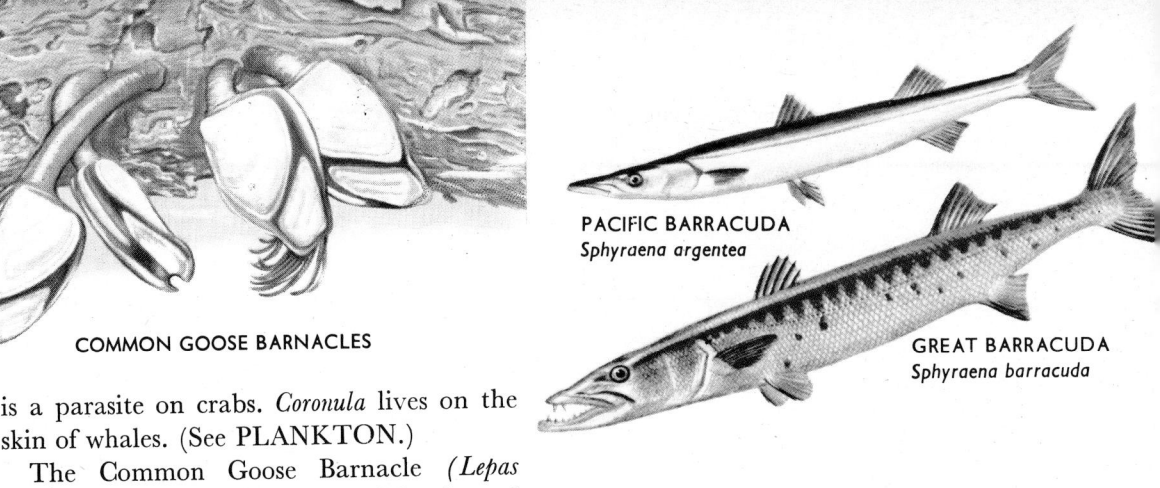

PACIFIC BARRACUDA
Sphyraena argentea

GREAT BARRACUDA
Sphyraena barracuda

COMMON GOOSE BARNACLES

is a parasite on crabs. *Coronula* lives on the skin of whales. (See PLANKTON.)

The Common Goose Barnacle *(Lepas fascicularis)* occurs in both the Atlantic and Pacific. It is often found on driftwood cast on shore. It got its name from an Irish myth that these barnacles transformed into geese, if they dropped into the water from tree roots along the shore. Another reason for their name is their long, goose-like necks.

Barnacles often foul ship bottoms, causing the vessel to lose speed and consume more fuel. Many barnacles can live for several days out of water.

BARRACUDA *(Sphyraena* spp.), known as the fierce "tigers of the sea", are found in warm oceans everywhere in the world. There are about 20 different kinds. All have numerous sharp teeth and enormous appetites for other fish. Many of these slim, cigar-shaped fish can change colour to blend with their surroundings. Small barracudas travel in schools; large ones more often hunt alone.

The Great Barracuda *(Sphyraena barracuda)* occurs on both sides of the Atlantic and in the western Pacific. It may grow to a length

Rock Barnacles feed in water but often grow where they are exposed at low tides.

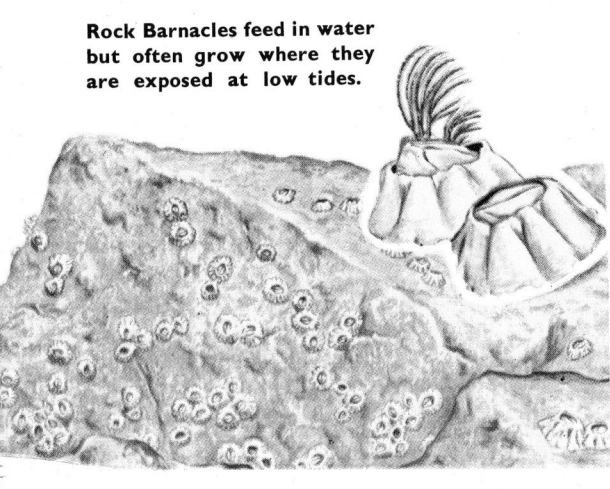

of eight feet and a weight of more than 60 pounds. The European Barracuda *(S. sphyraena)* is the common eastern Atlantic and Mediterranean species, where the name Spet is often used for it.

Barracudas are fearless and have great curiosity. They will follow a man walking along the shore, and will approach to within a few feet of a swimmer or diver. As a rule, they dart away as soon as they know that they are being watched.

There are many reports of people being bitten by barracudas. Apparently, these fish may attack in murky water, mistaking the splashes of a swimmer for a school of fish; or they may be attracted to shiny objects worn by swimmers or divers. Some of the stories about barracuda attacks may not be true, but it is probable that many of them are. These fish are too large and capable of being dangerous not to be respected.

Sport fishing for barracudas is popular, and fishermen soon discover that barracudas are just as suspicious as they are inquisitive. Small barracudas are generally less wary than large ones.

In many places barracudas are eaten regularly, but the flesh of some large barracudas is poisonous. Fishermen sometimes cut barracudas into strips and dry them. When strips are suncured, they are eaten like smoked fish or dried beef.

BASILISKS *(Basiliscus* spp.) are swift lizards that live along streams in the American tropics. A frightened basilisk dashes away frantically, running so fast that it scampers on its hind legs across the surface of water.

Males have high crests that extend from head to tail; females lack crests. Basilisks are members of the iguanid family (see IGUANAS), as are the beautifully coloured, long-legged Helmeted Lizards (*Corythophanes* spp.). Helmeted Lizards, however, are slow-moving climbers that live in vines and bushes. In Casque-headed Lizards (*Laemanctus* spp.), the top of the head is extended in a broad shelf over the back of the lizard's neck.

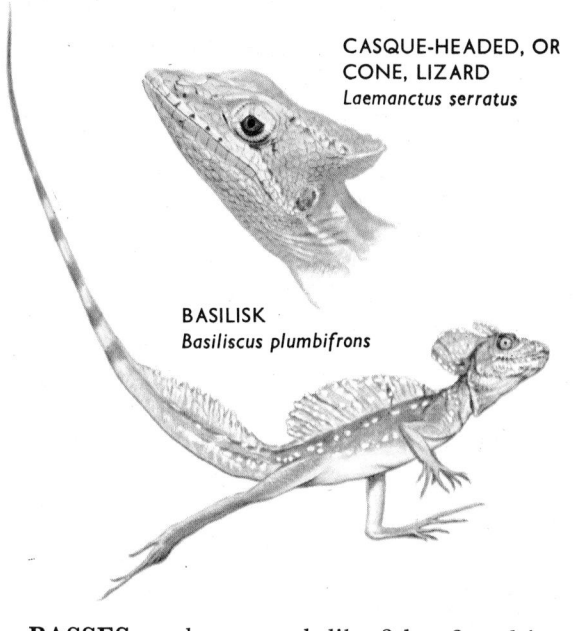

CASQUE-HEADED, OR CONE, LIZARD
Laemanctus serratus

BASILISK
Basiliscus plumbifrons

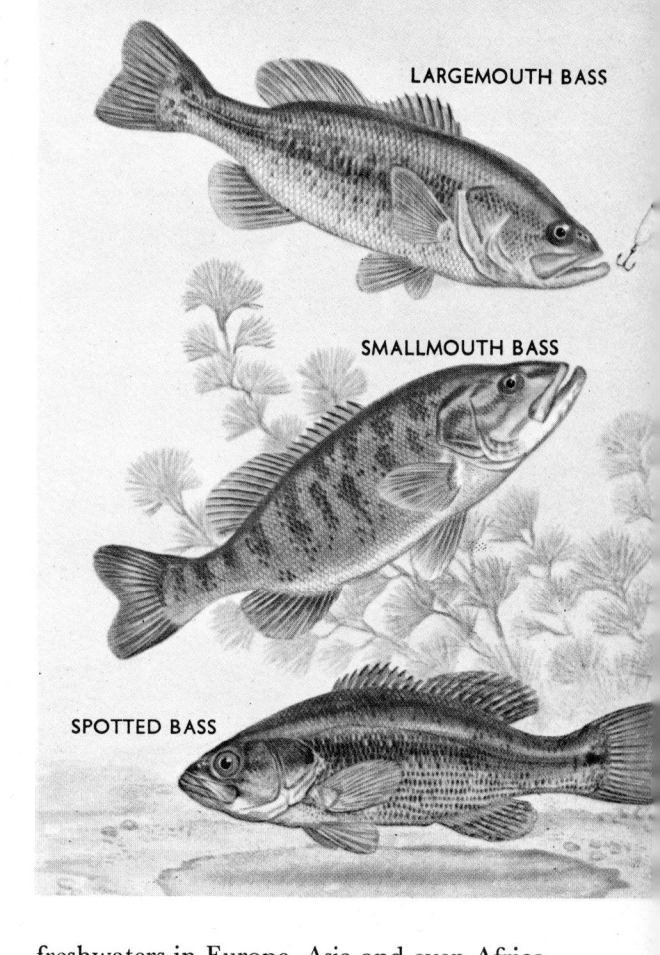

LARGEMOUTH BASS

SMALLMOUTH BASS

SPOTTED BASS

BASSES are large perch-like fishes found in salt waters throughout the world, mainly in warm seas. However, in the United States the term bass is applied to certain large and important members of the sunfish family. These are entirely freshwater fishes.

Freshwater Basses, belonging to the family *Centrarchidae,* are also known as black basses in the United States. Although originally occurring only in North America, black basses have now been stocked into freshwaters in Europe, Asia and even Africa.

The largest and most widely distributed is the Largemouth Bass (*Micropterus salmonoides*), which may grow to 10 pounds in the southern States of America; the record weight is over 22 pounds. The Smallmouth and the Spotted Bass are smaller species, but all three are popular sport fishes.

The black basses are voracious predators, feeding greedily on small fish, frogs and crayfish, striking at almost anything that moves near them. They are often used in fish ponds as a means of controlling the numbers of smaller fishes to prevent overcrowding.

Sea Basses and Grouper belonging to the family *Serranidae,* are chiefly marine and most species are found in tropical waters. However, in British waters, the Bass (*Morone labrax*) may travel some distance up rivers in southern England during the summer.

The serranids may grow to a considerable size, and include some of the world's most important food fishes. The Giant Sea Basses, sometimes called Jewfishes, can reach 800

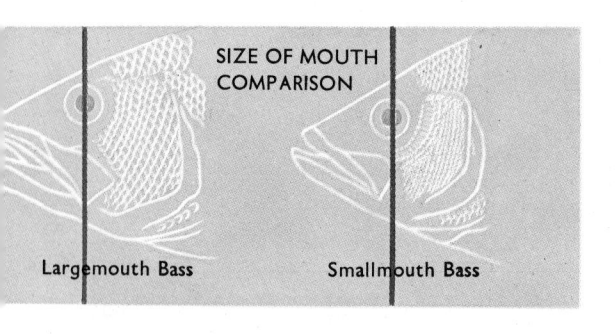

SIZE OF MOUTH COMPARISON

Largemouth Bass   Smallmouth Bass

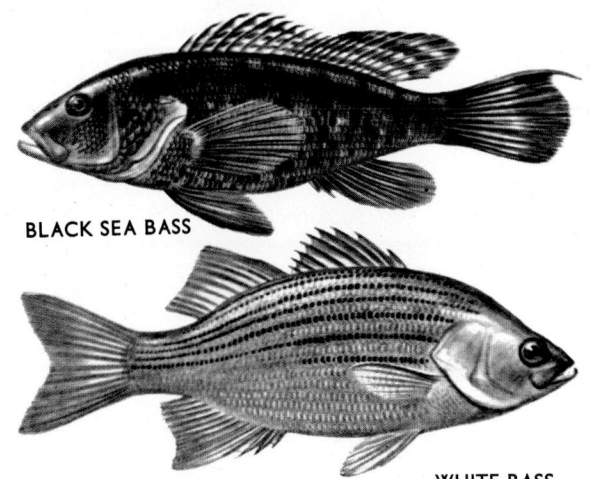

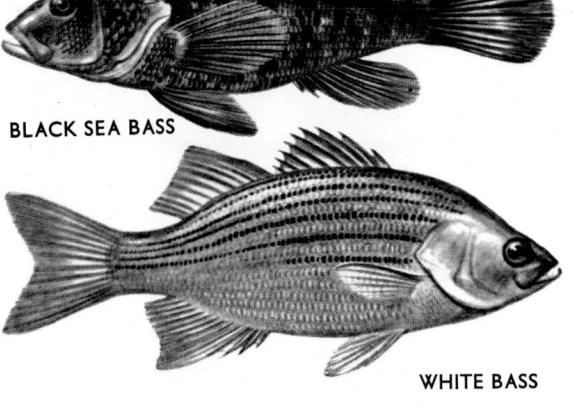

BLACK SEA BASS

WHITE BASS

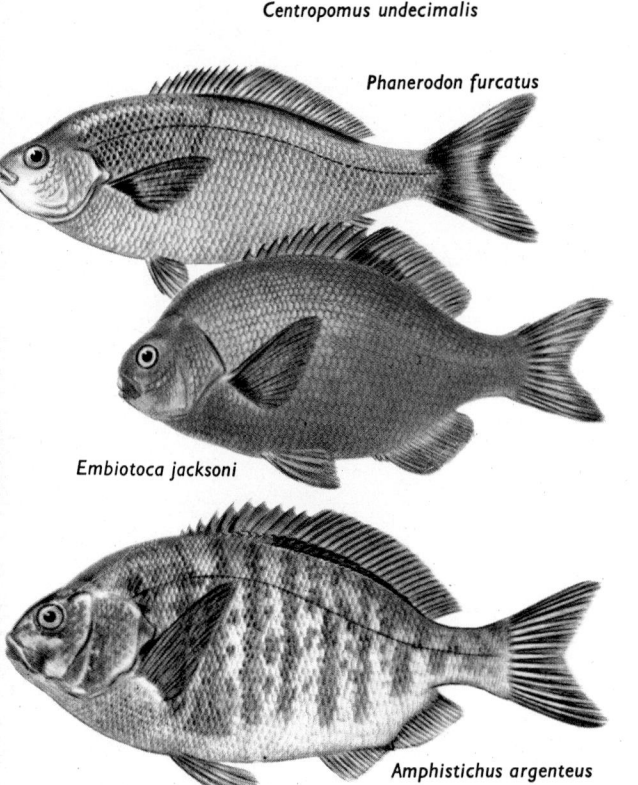

Centropomus undecimalis

Phanerodon furcatus

Embiotoca jacksoni

Amphistichus argenteus

pounds in weight, and the Queensland Grouper, an Australian species, is said to grow to 12 feet and 1,000 pounds in weight.

Some serranids show a remarkable ability to change colour. A Western Atlantic grouper, *Epinephalus striatus*, has eight colour phases, ranging from dark brown to cream, and can show several of these within the space of one minute.

Another peculiarity of the serranids is that some species are able to function as both males and females, either at the same time (as in *Serranellus subligarius*), or at different periods in their lives (e.g., the American *Centropristis striatus* begins life as a female, but after five years can function as a male).

A rare visitor to British coasts is the Wreckfish, or Stone Bass (*Polyprion americanus*), so-called because of its reputation

GIANT SEA BASS

KELP BASS

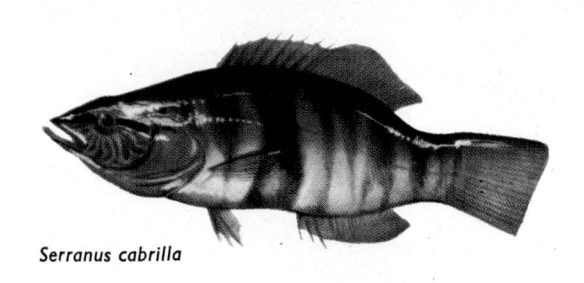

Serranus cabrilla

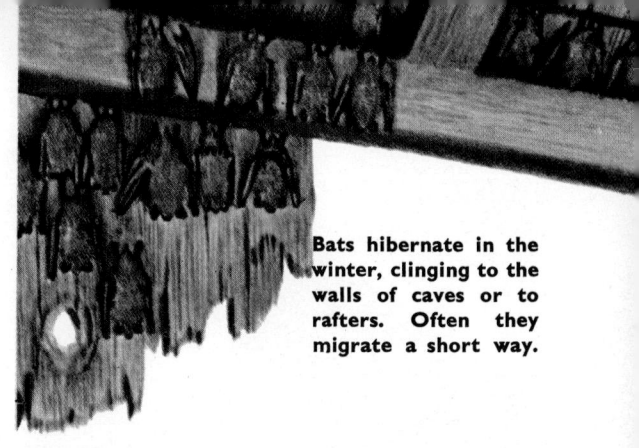

for occurring in numbers near the site of wrecks. It may reach a length of up to 6 feet.

Most of the serranids, and especially the larger species, spend much of their time sitting on the bottom or lurking in rocky holes. The majority are carnivorous, having large mouths and sharp teeth. They have given rise to stories of skin-divers being swallowed alive by giant groupers. Normally, they feed on small fishes, and their man-eating reputation is probably undeserved.

BATFISH *(Ogcocephalus nasutus)* are strange-looking fishes that live in tropical seas throughout the world. In summer they may stray into temperate zones; often they are seen close to shore.

Batfish, like the Angler Fish *(q. v.)*, catch fish by means of a lure. Their rod is a small filament that hangs in front of the mouth. A fleshy, wiggly lure at its tip entices fish to swim too close.

Most unusual is the Batfish's method of locomotion, for it walks about on the bottom on its stubby, leg-like fins. When it is frightened or in a hurry, it "hops" along like a toad.

BATS are the only mammals capable of true flight. Their wings consist of thin membranes joining their greatly elongated fingers, and extending to their legs and tails. There are many different species of bats and they are found throughout the world, except in the cold polar regions. Some can fly considerable distances, and many avoid objects, or seek their food of insects, while in flight by means of a sonar (or echo-location)

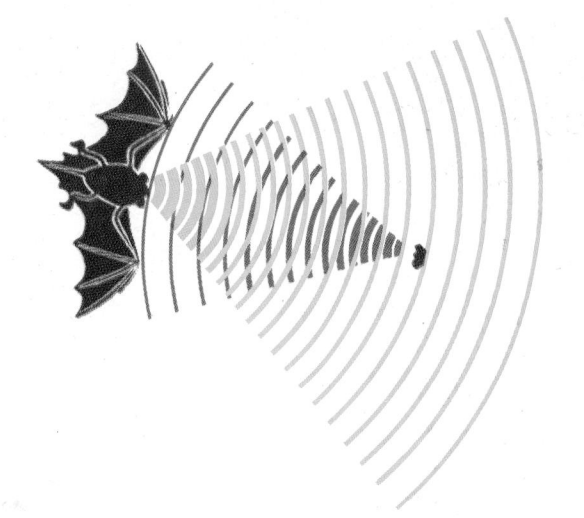

Bats locate insects or objects in their path by emitting squeaks, then listening for the echoes to return.

system. Active only at night, bats sleep during the day, hanging head downwards, often in caves, mine-shafts or dark attics. Others live in hollow trees or crevices in bark, and some hide among leaves. Some cave-dwellers, such as the Mexican Free-tailed Bat, form very large colonies, and a number of species hibernate during the colder months in the temperate regions.

Most bats feed either on fruit or insects.

Batfish, 8 to 10 inches long, are slender, flattened fish with stubby fins when seen from the side, but they appear quite broad when viewed from above.

top view

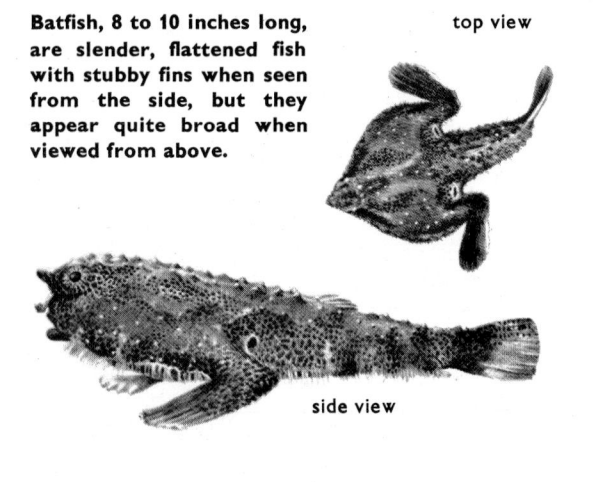

side view

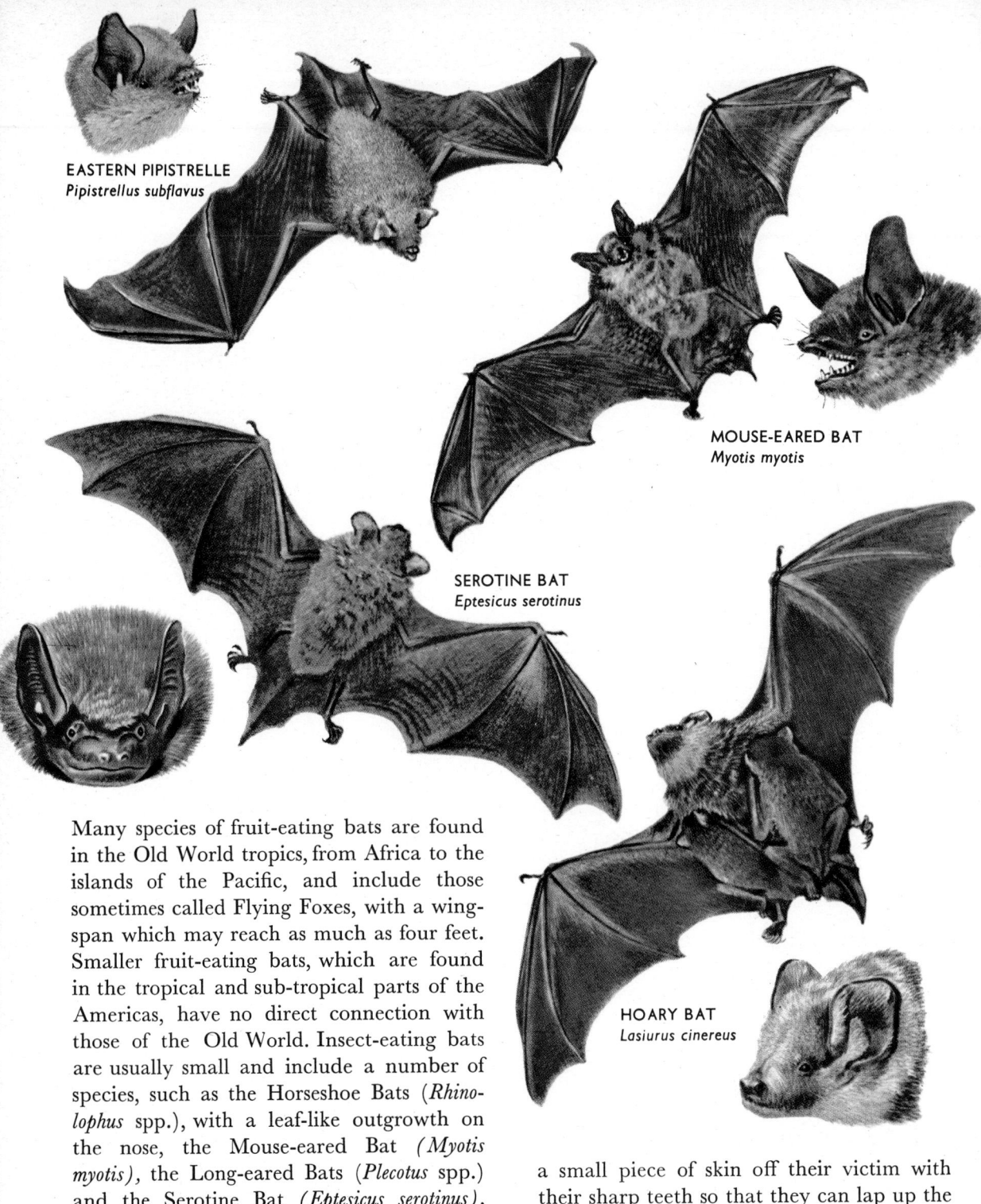

EASTERN PIPISTRELLE
Pipistrellus subflavus

MOUSE-EARED BAT
Myotis myotis

SEROTINE BAT
Eptesicus serotinus

HOARY BAT
Lasiurus cinereus

Many species of fruit-eating bats are found in the Old World tropics, from Africa to the islands of the Pacific, and include those sometimes called Flying Foxes, with a wing-span which may reach as much as four feet. Smaller fruit-eating bats, which are found in the tropical and sub-tropical parts of the Americas, have no direct connection with those of the Old World. Insect-eating bats are usually small and include a number of species, such as the Horseshoe Bats (*Rhino-lophus* spp.), with a leaf-like outgrowth on the nose, the Mouse-eared Bat *(Myotis myotis)*, the Long-eared Bats (*Plecotus* spp.) and the Serotine Bat *(Eptesicus serotinus)*, which are found in Europe. Mastiff Bats *(Eumops perotis)*, of Central America and the southern part of North America, have ears of a peculiar shape. Vampire Bats *(Desmodus rotundus, Diphylla ecaudata)* are found in Central and South America and live on blood, which they obtain by scraping

a small piece of skin off their victim with their sharp teeth so that they can lap up the oozing blood. False Vampire Bats *(Mega-derma* spp.) come from south-eastern Asia and are not really vampires; they live on small animals such as birds, lizards and frogs. Fish-eating Bats *(Noctilio leporinus)*, of Central and South America, have elonga-ted toes and claws with which to grasp small

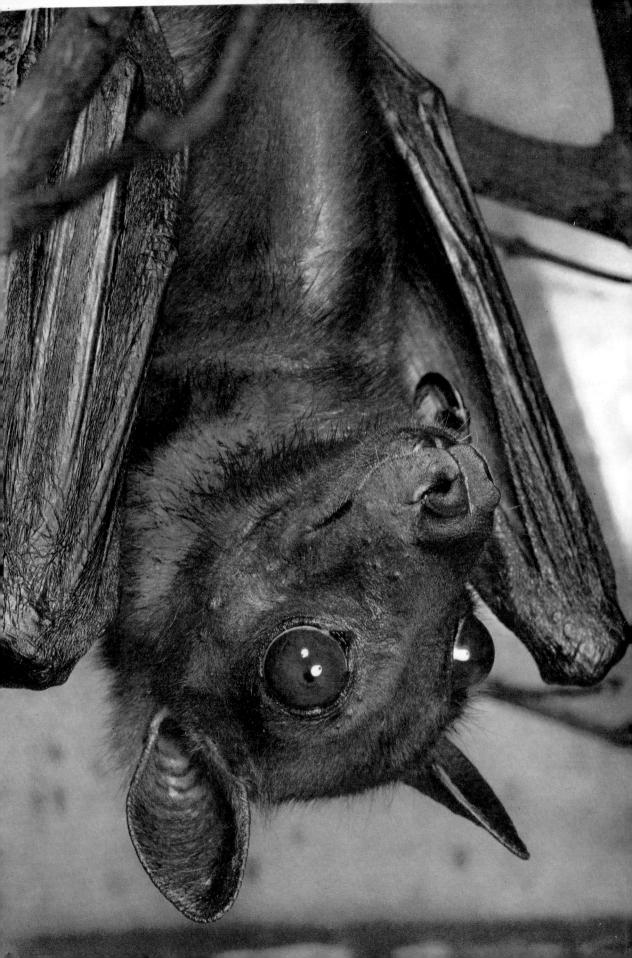

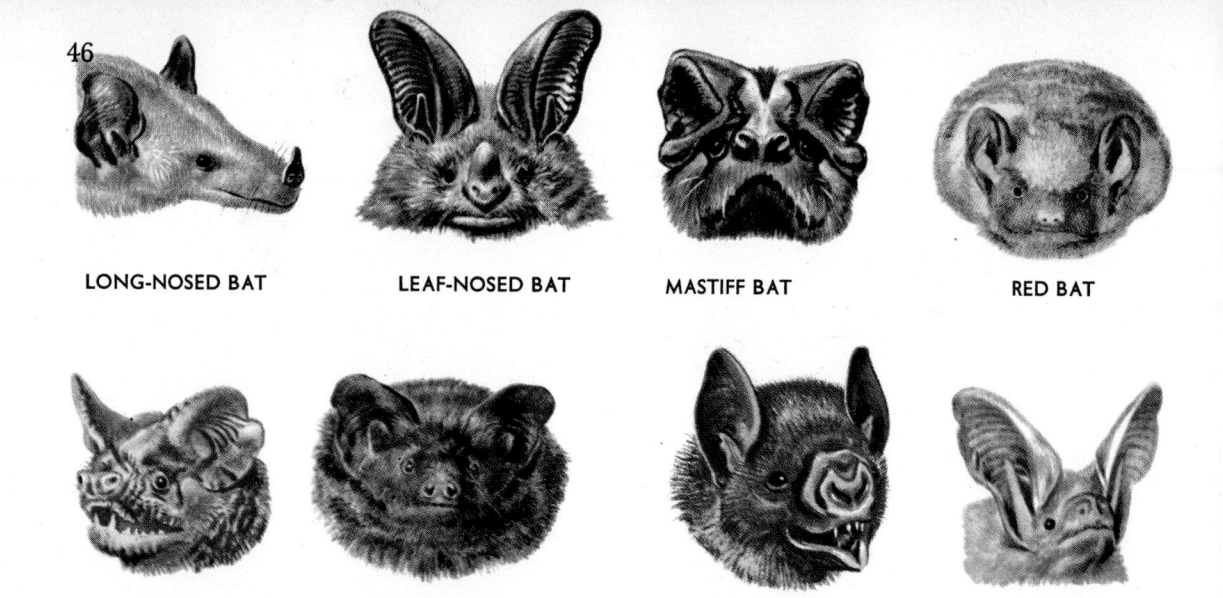

LONG-NOSED BAT   LEAF-NOSED BAT   MASTIFF BAT   RED BAT

MEXICAN FREE-TAILED BAT   SILVER-HAIRED BAT   VAMPIRE BAT   PALLID BAT

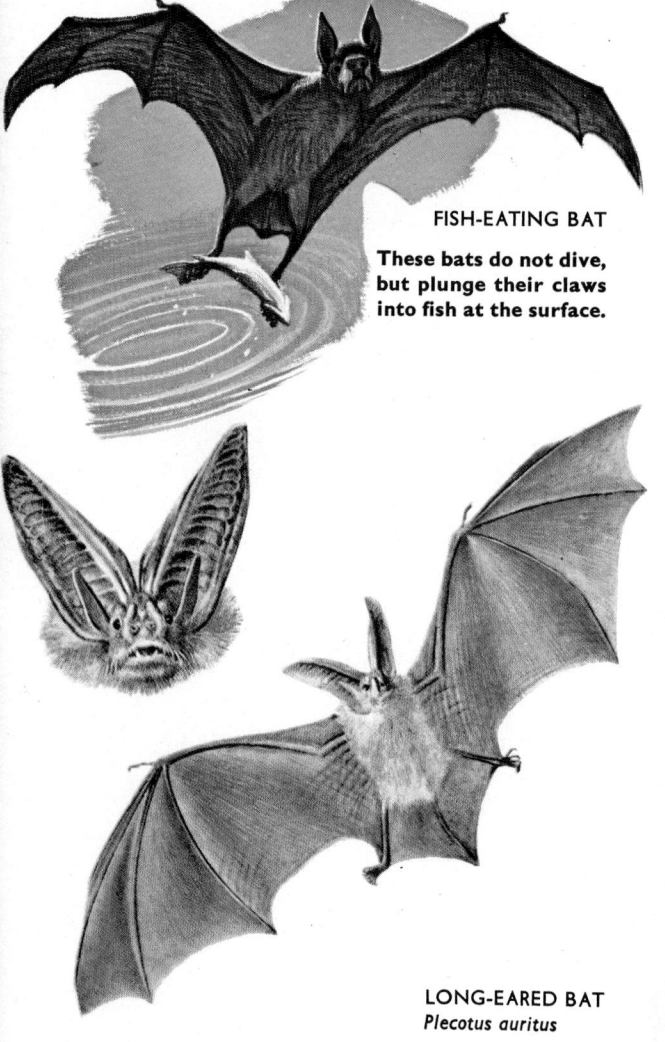

FISH-EATING BAT

These bats do not dive, but plunge their claws into fish at the surface.

LONG-EARED BAT
Plecotus auritus

fish from the surface of the water. Other bats, such as the Long-nosed Bat *(Leptonycteris nivalis)*, live on nectar and pollen. The tip of the tongue is covered with fine hairs, to which the pollen clings.

BEARS are a family *(Ursidae)* of large mammals that walk with a flat-footed, shuffling gait. They feed on fruits, roots, grasses, insects and meat. Most bears give birth to two young at a time, and the cubs require several years to mature. Bears do not truly hibernate (see MAMMALS). All bears live in the Northern Hemisphere, except the Spectacled Bear *(Tremarctos ornatos)* of northern South America.

Black bears *(Ursus americanus)* of North America feed on everything from honey and wild berries to insects and small mammals. Although typically black, they may be brown, cinnamon, or nearly white. Black Bears have short claws on their front feet and do not have humps between their shoulders as do Brown Bears *(Ursus arctos),* of North America, Europe and northern Asia, and Grizzly Bears *(Ursus horribilis)* of North America. Once common throughout Canada and the continental United States, Black Bears are now found only in wild, forested tracts and mountainous areas. Alaskan Brown Bears, the largest carniv-

orous land mammals, have long claws on their front feet, humps between their shoulders, and hollow rather than full faces. Grizzly Bears are much the same as Brown Bears, only slightly smaller. Their brownish-coloured hair is usually tipped with white, giving them their grizzled appearance. Alaskan Brown Bears, found on offshore islands and along the coast of Alaska, reach a length of nearly eight feet and are more than four feet tall at shoulder height when they stand on all four feet; males may weigh nearly three-quarters of a ton. Kodiak Bears *(Ursus middendorffi)*, the largest of these brown bears, prey on salmon, mice and ground squirrels, but also eat such plant foods as bark, roots, fruits and berries.

Polar Bears *(Thalarctos maritimus)*, which may weigh nearly 1,000 pounds, live on the snow and ice fields of the northern polar regions. They feed mostly on seals and

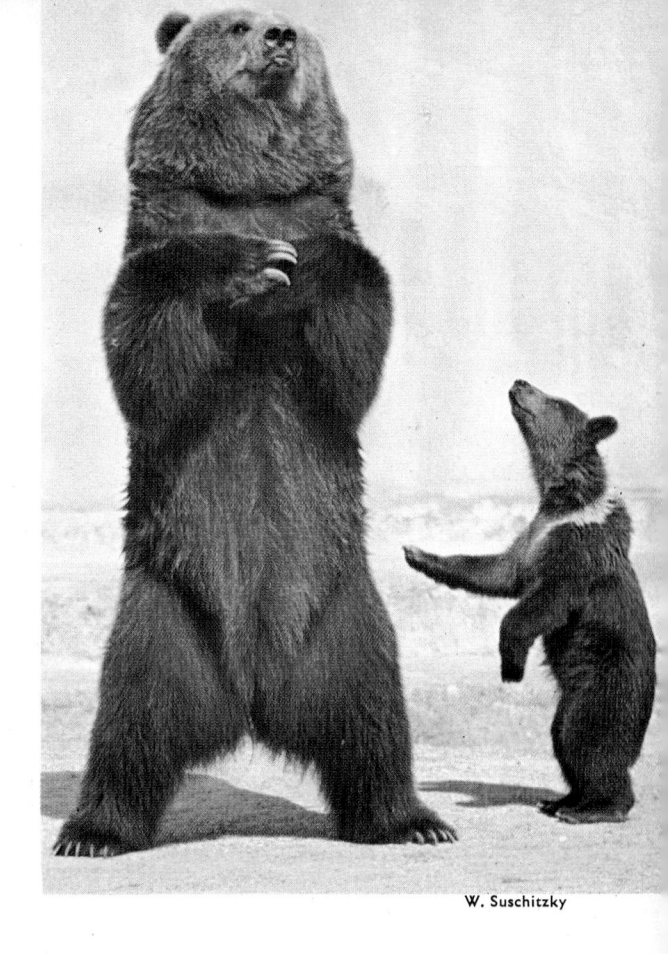

The largest of the bears, the Kodiak, was photographed in a zoo with the small Himalayan Bear.

W. Suschitzky

Polar Bears have hair on the soles of their paws, giving them a sure-footed grip on ice.

W. Suschitzky

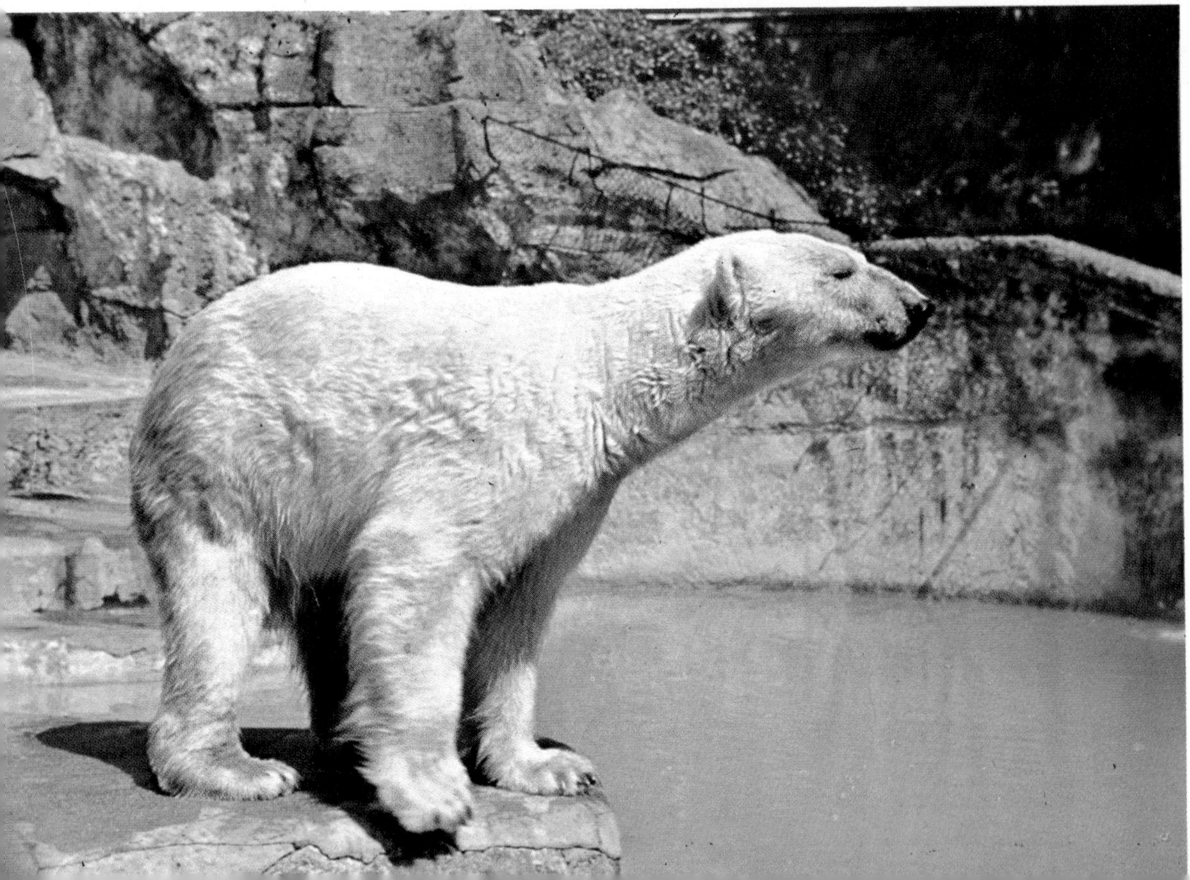

fish, and rear their young in dens dug in snow banks. Excellent swimmers, they cross wide expanses of open water. Polar Bears have always been important to the Eskimos, who eat their flesh, make clothes from their hides, and shape a variety of useful implements from their bones. Polar Bears are active all the year around.

Sun Bears *(Helarctos malayanus),* found in the dense jungles of south-eastern Asia, are the smallest of the bears, usually weighing less than a hundred pounds. They have glossy black hair with orange or yellow crescents on their chests. This has been interpreted to represent the rising sun and gave rise to their name. Sun Bears feed on honey, insects, other small animals, and tropical fruits. They are agile climbers.

BEAVERS *(Castor canadensis),* the largest water-dwelling rodents of North America, have thick coats of reddish-brown fur and long, flattened tails. They keep busy from sunset until sunrise, cutting down trees to get the tender branches, building dams, or constructing the houses, or lodges, in which they live. Tree bark is their most important food. Trees are cut down with their powerful chisel-like incisor teeth. Contrary to popular belief, beavers cannot control which way a tree will fall. Beavers also feed on cat's-tails or other aquatic plants. They store food in piles underwater to eat in winter. Beavers' flat tails serve as rudders when swimming, as props when they sit up to cut trees, or as alarm signals when slapped on the surface of the water.

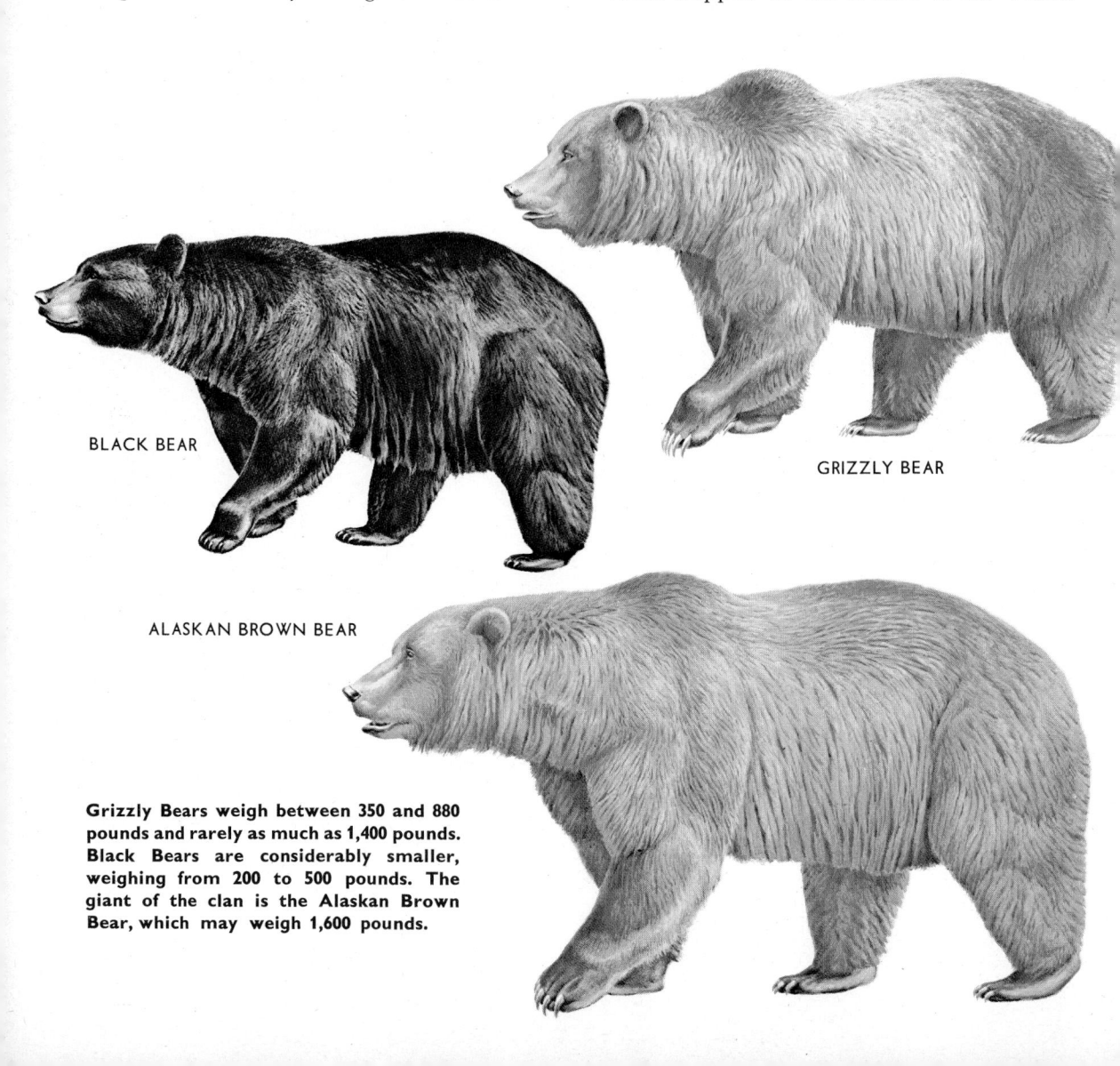

BLACK BEAR

GRIZZLY BEAR

ALASKAN BROWN BEAR

Grizzly Bears weigh between 350 and 880 pounds and rarely as much as 1,400 pounds. Black Bears are considerably smaller, weighing from 200 to 500 pounds. The giant of the clan is the Alaskan Brown Bear, which may weigh 1,600 pounds.

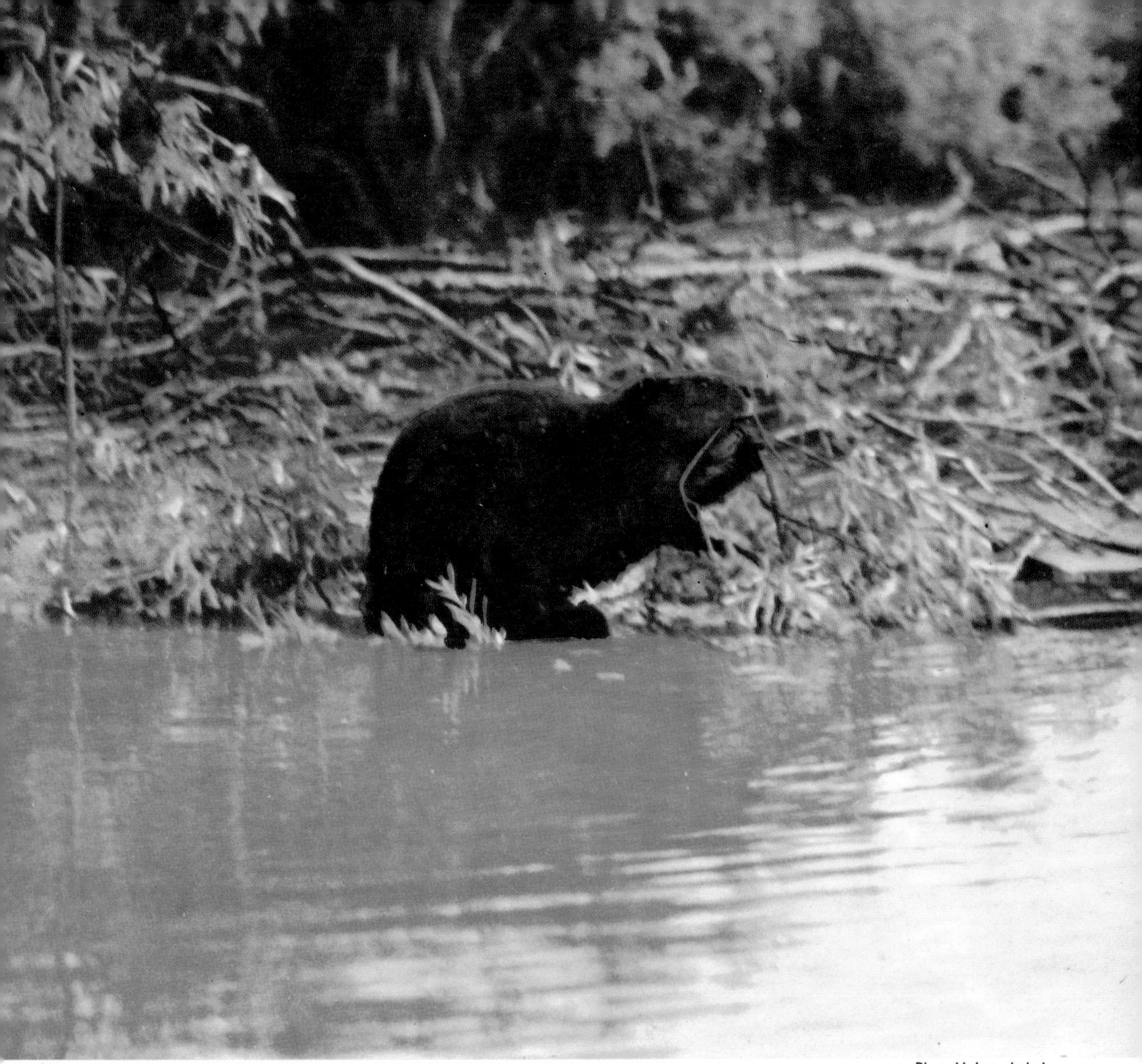

Beavers use their hind legs for driving power when swimming.

Beaver dams are built of logs and stones, plastered together with mud. The ponds or small lakes formed by these dams are used by beavers as sites for their dome-shaped lodges. The entrance is beneath the water, but the nest itself, which consists of only one room, is above the high-water level. If the pond becomes filled with silt

Ponds formed by beaver dams become homes for fish and aquatic invertebrates. Waterfowl and large mammals, such as minks, muskrats and otters, are also attracted to the ponds, which hold a reserve supply of water over the dry season. Eventually, the pond silts up to become a marsh and meadow.

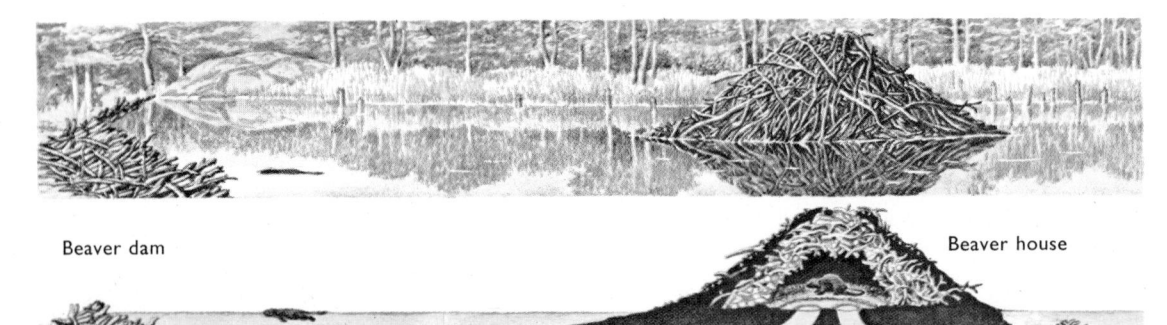

Beaver dam

Beaver house

after several years, a new dam is built or the old one is made higher. Beavers sometimes build their dens along the banks of lakes or streams. When they do this, they usually do not construct a dam to regulate the water level.

Beavers are found in North America, and in Europe and Asia. Trappers have sought their fur for many centuries, and in many parts of their range they have been exterminated by over-trapping.

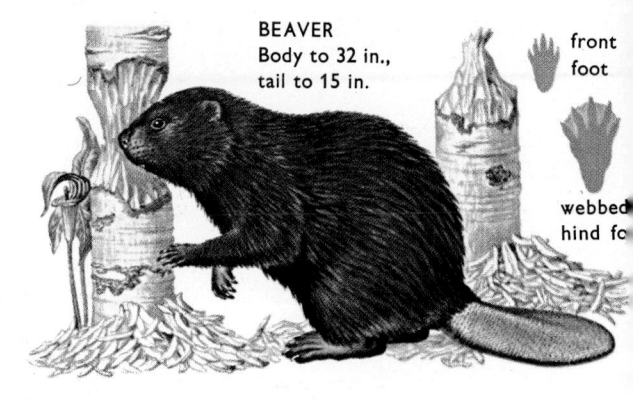

BEAVER
Body to 32 in.,
tail to 15 in.

front foot

webbed hind fo

BEDBUGS *(Cimicidae)* are small, flat, wingless true bugs that suck the blood of warm-blooded animals. They usually feed at night and hide during the day in cracks or crevices. During their lifetime, female bedbugs lay from 50 to 200 eggs, depositing them in cracks of walls, floors, or similar locations. The eggs generally hatch within eight days and the nymphs become adults in about two months. They moult five times and require a blood meal between each moult. Adults live for six months or longer and can also go without food for long periods. They feed at night, gorging themselves quickly and then getting off their host to hide nearby until hungry again.

A bedbug's bite produces irritation and swelling in some people, but bedbugs probably are not important carriers of any human disease. Some species live only on certain host animals, such as bats, birds or poultry.

BEES. Members of several families of insects in the order *Hymenoptera* are called bees. Most familiar are bumblebees and honeybees. Bees supply their young with pollen and honey for food, rather than with insects or spiders as do wasps. Even

those wasps that do collect pollen have not got pollen baskets on their legs as bees have, and bees that lack pollen baskets on their legs can be distinguished from wasps by the hairs on their bodies; the hairs on a bee's body are branched or plumed, while those on a wasp are not. The pollen from various flowers that the bees visit adheres to these branched, or plumose, body-hairs, and by their means it is transferred from one blossom to another. Adult bees are thus among the most important agents for pollinating flowers. Some kinds of bees restrict their pollen-gathering to certain plants; e.g., some *Andrenidae*

When a honeybee hive becomes crowded, the queen bee and some of her workers swarm. While scouts seek a new place for a colony, the swarm rests.

Hugh Spencer

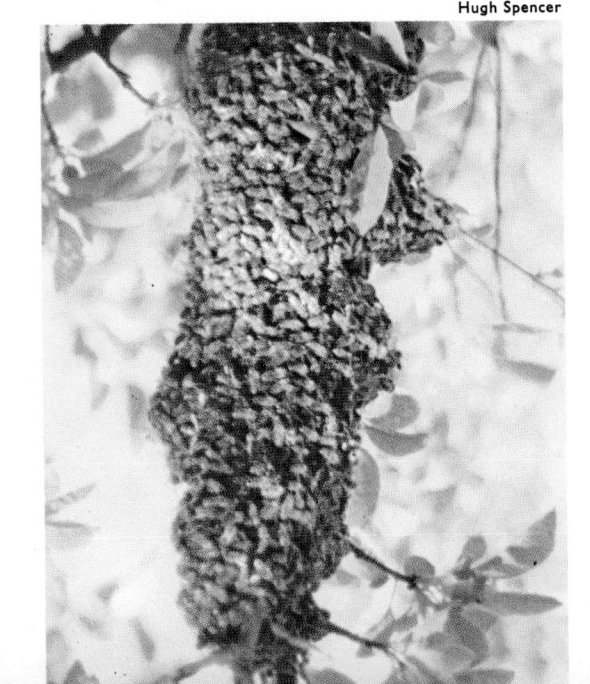

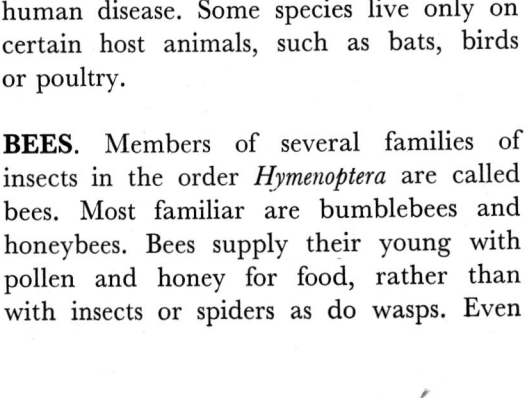

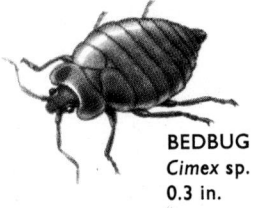

Bedbugs are bloodsucking true bugs. They are more annoying than dangerous.

BEDBUG
Cimex sp.
0.3 in.

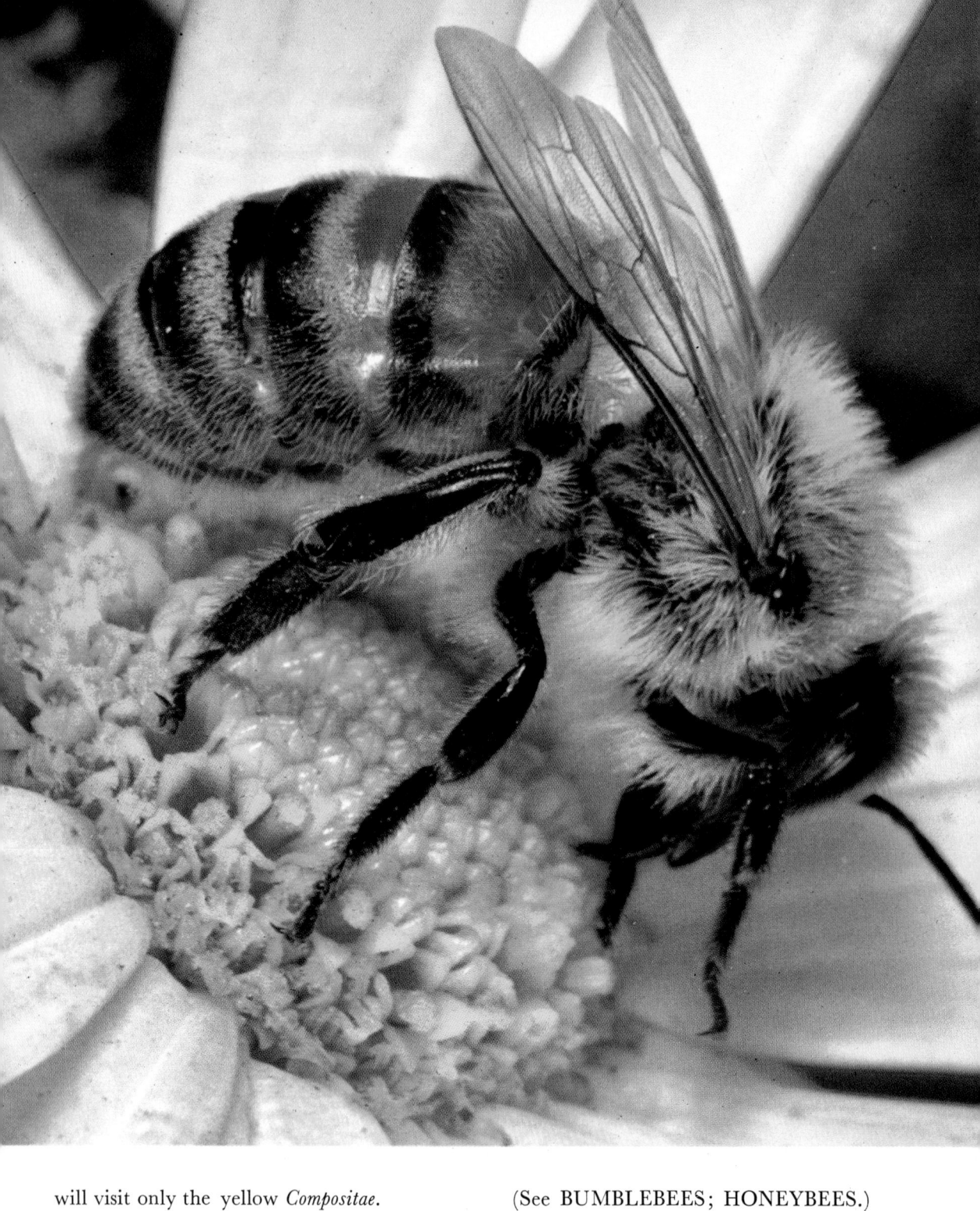

will visit only the yellow *Compositae*.

Most bees are solitary. They nest in cavities in plants or in tunnels in the ground. Honeybees and bumblebees are social. Their colonies are composed of one queen (a female), a few drones (males), and many workers (sexually undeveloped females).

(See BUMBLEBEES; HONEYBEES.)

Leafcutter bees *(Megachilidae)* line their cells with neatly-cut circular pieces of leaves. The holes these bees cut in leaves are easier to find than are their nests. Sometimes their nests are in holes in the ground, but most are built in rotten wood.

MORPHOLOGY OF THE BEE

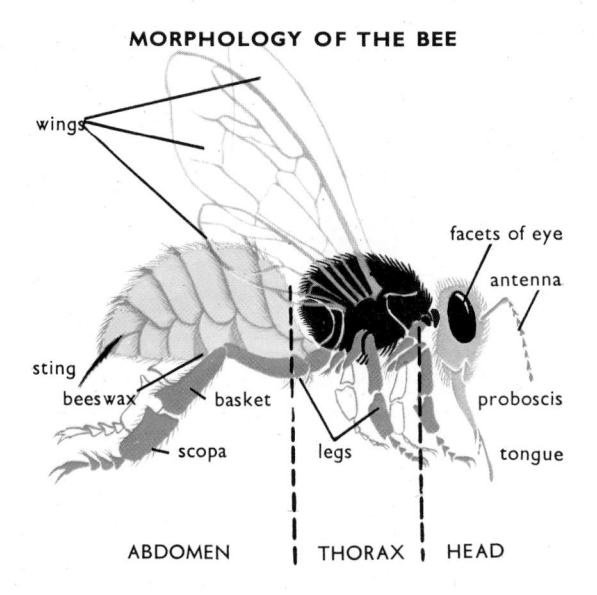

wings

facets of eye

antenna

sting

beeswax

basket

proboscis

scopa

legs

tongue

ABDOMEN   THORAX   HEAD

A mixture of pollen and honey is placed in the partially completed, leaf-lined cell, and on top of this food the female deposits an egg. Then she plugs the cell with more pieces of leaves. Often several cells are made in a single tunnel.

Carpenter bees *(Andrenidae)* build their nests in wood. Small, metallic-blue carpenter bees make their nests in plant stems that have a soft pith. The Large Carpenter

Bee, nearly an inch long, resembles a bumblebee. It builds its nest in solid wood. Mining bees, members of the same family, build their nests in tunnels in the ground. Often metallic in colour they are solitary bees, although they commonly nest together in large numbers and use the same entrance. Some kinds of mining bees are called "sweat bees", because they are attracted to the odour of perspiration.

BEETLES form the largest order of insects *(Coleoptera)*. More than 220,000 species — about one-third of all insects known — are beetles, and they are found in nearly every type of habitat throughout the world. Many beetles feed on plants. Some eat only leaves; others, roots. Still others bore into the stems or woody trunks of trees. Some beetles feed on decaying plants or animals, or on over-ripe fruit, and many kinds eat insects or other animals. Some are household pests, feeding on various food or stored products. The size of beetles is about as varied as their habitats. Some fungus beetles are almost microscopic; but others, such as the gigantic tropical Atlas

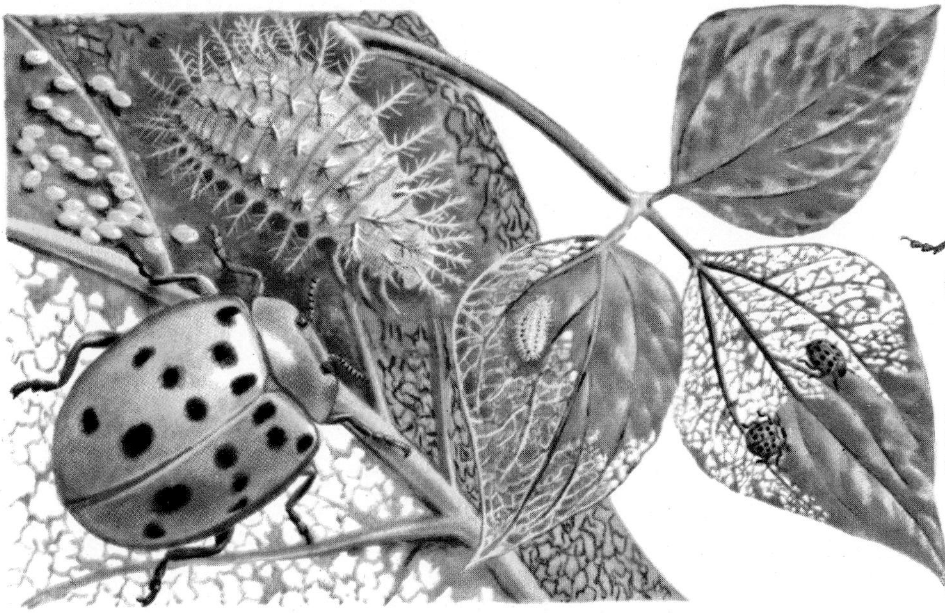

SPOTTED ASPARAGUS BEETLE
Crioceris duodecimpunctata
0.3 in.

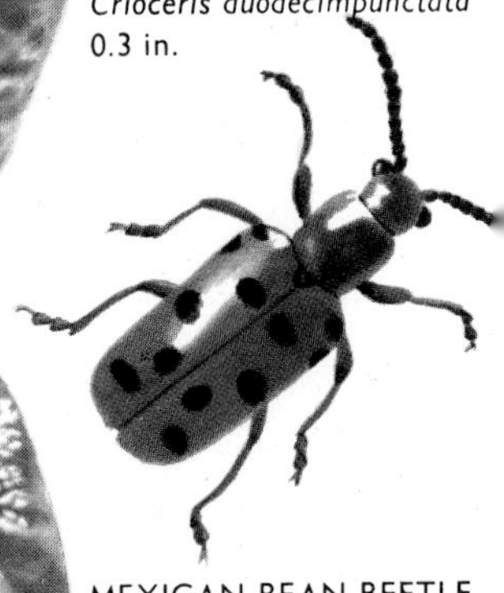

MEXICAN BEAN BEETLE
Epilachna varivestis
0.3 in.

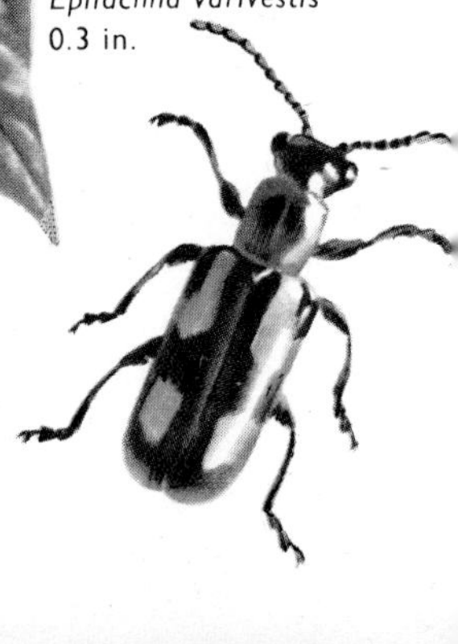

Both the adults and the larvae of the Mexican Bean Beetle feed on the foliage of plants of the large bean family. They are not pests of other vegetables.

ASPARAGUS BEETLE
Crioceris asparagi
0.3 in.

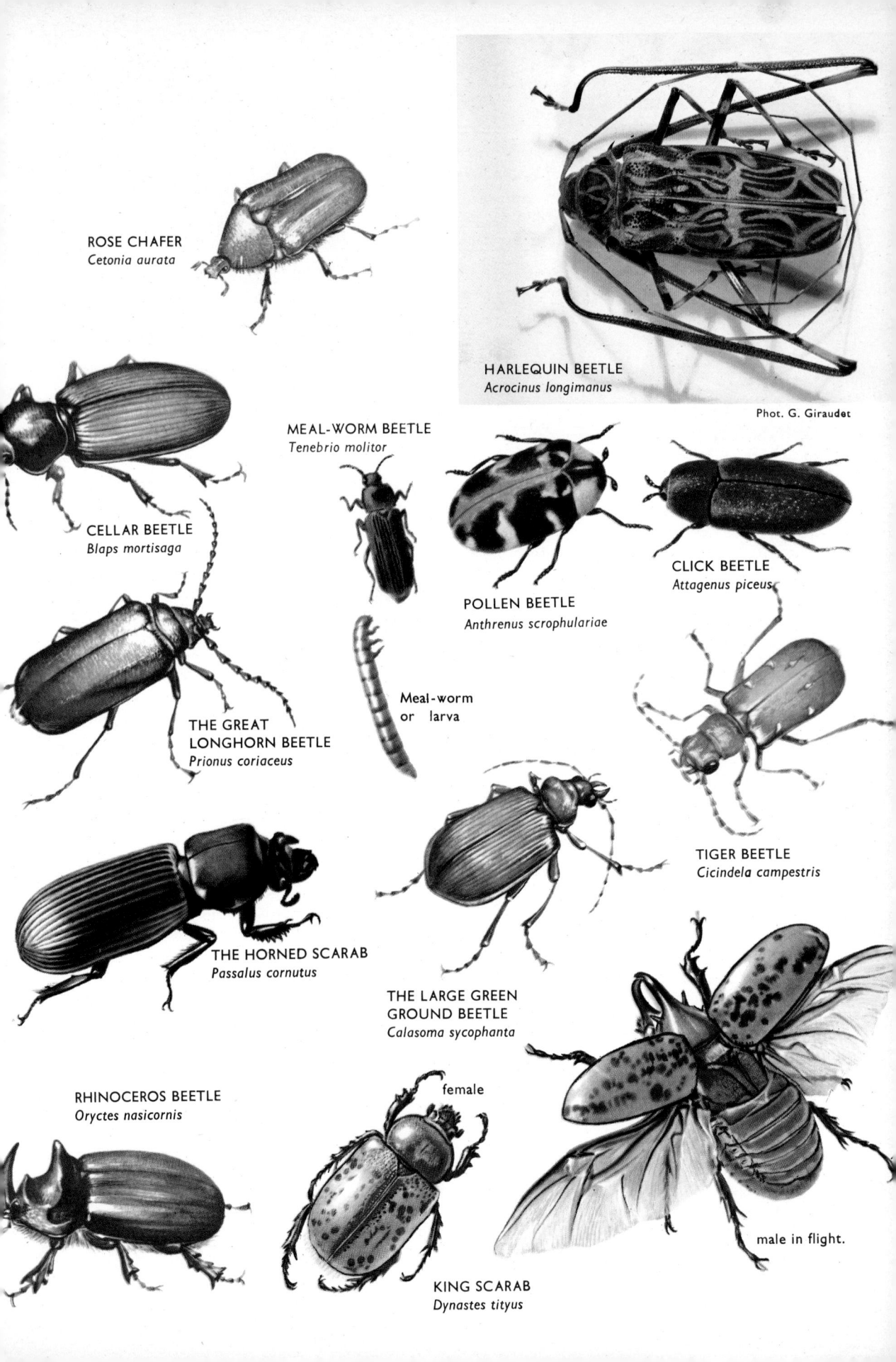

ROSE CHAFER
Cetonia aurata

HARLEQUIN BEETLE
Acrocinus longimanus

Phot. G. Giraudet

CELLAR BEETLE
Blaps mortisaga

MEAL-WORM BEETLE
Tenebrio molitor

POLLEN BEETLE
Anthrenus scrophulariae

CLICK BEETLE
Attagenus piceus

THE GREAT
LONGHORN BEETLE
Prionus coriaceus

Meal-worm
or larva

TIGER BEETLE
Cicindela campestris

THE HORNED SCARAB
Passalus cornutus

THE LARGE GREEN
GROUND BEETLE
Calasoma sycophanta

RHINOCEROS BEETLE
Oryctes nasicornis

female

male in flight.

KING SCARAB
Dynastes tityus

Beetle, are the most massive of all insects.

Nearly all beetles can be recognised by their hard, thick front wings that meet in a straight line down the middle of their back. These outer wings cover thin hind wings with which the beetles fly. In a few species, such as fireflies, only the males have wings, and the females are flightless.

Beetles undergo a complete metamorphosis (egg, larva, pupa and adult) that may require only a few weeks or as long as several years. In most species there is only one generation each year.

Among the many kinds are carpet beetles and larder beetles *(Dermestidae)*, many of which are very destructive. The larvae do most of the damage, eating carpets, upholstered furniture and stored clothing. Adults are commonly found on flowers. Larder beetles are pests of stored food products and also feed on leather goods.

Striped Cucumber Beetles and Spotted Cucumber Beetles *(Chrysomelidae)* are pests of vegetable crops, and both adults and larvae cause damage. They belong to a large family of plant-feeders.

Male Unicorn (or Rhinoceros) Beetles have a prominent horn on their head. There may be a second horn just behind the first. These are among the largest beetles in the world. Hercules Beetles of the West Indies are six inches long. Children often play with these beetles for, though large, they are harmless. (See index for list of beetles described separately in this volume.)

BIG-HEADED TURTLE

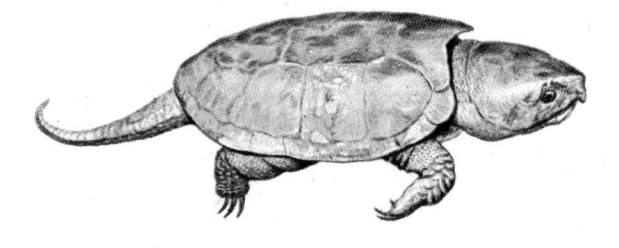

BIG-HEADED TURTLES *(Platysternum megacephalum)* live in south-eastern Asia. The tails of these seven-inch turtles are equal to or exceed the length of their shells,

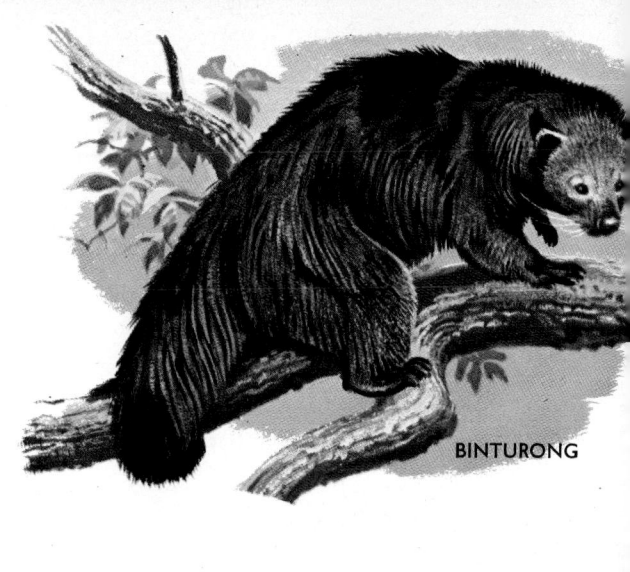

BINTURONG

and their heads are so large they cannot be drawn into the shell. Big-headed Turtles live in mountain streams in forested areas and are agile climbers of trees. They sun themselves frequently, lay only two eggs in a nest, and are reputedly pugnacious.

BINTURONGS *(Arctictis binturong)* are large civet-like mammals, almost the size of Wolverines. They live in trees of the dense tropical forests of Burma, Malaya, Indo-China, Sumatra, Java and Borneo. They have heavy black coats and long, bushy, grasping tails, which they use in climbing trees. Their ears have long, hairy tufts. Fruit is their main food. Like other civets, Binturongs are equipped with strong scent glands. (See CIVETS.)

BIRDS form one of the five groups of "higher" animals. They are so important, so useful, and so interesting, that a great many people watch and study birds as a fascinating hobby.

All birds possess a spinal column, or backbone, made up of small bones called vertebrae, linked together. Other vertebrate animals are mammals (cows, dogs, squirrels), reptiles (snakes, lizards, alligators, turtles), amphibians (frogs, toads, salamanders), and fishes (bass, perch, mackerel).

One thing sets birds apart from all other animals. Birds are the only living creatures that have feathers. The feathers grow from the bird's skin as hair and fingernails do

on humans; but, unlike these, the feathers grow to a definite size and then stop.

Feathers are firmly fixed in the skin, but may become looser and more easily lost when the bird is seized by a predator. They suffer from wear and become worn and frayed. They are renewed by a process called moulting, old feathers being shed and new ones growing in their place. Most birds moult only once a year, usually soon after raising their young, but some moult on two or more occasions annually.

As birds must be in balance at all times to be able to fly, they moult the same number of feathers from the same place on each wing at the same time. They shed and replace tail feathers the same way: a pair at a time, one from each side of the tail.

Many species of ducks and geese moult their flight feathers all at once. This occurs at a time when the young are not old enough to fly, and the adults, for a period of several weeks, are therefore also flightless. The family stays near water, and takes to it if alarmed. Penguins also moult all over at once. During this "eclipse" period, they never go near the water, but stand about on the nesting grounds, looking ragged and unhappy.

Feathers grow in definite patterns from special parts of the skin called feather tracts. In a few primitive birds, like ostriches and penguins, the entire skin is feather tract, so feathers grow all over the bird. In all other birds, feather tracts are so placed that feathers cover the patches of bare skin between them. Each type of bird has its own pattern of feather tracts.

PARTS OF A BIRD

Primary Coverts
Greater Coverts
Lesser Coverts
Scapulars
Back
Crown
Auricular Patch
Eye Ring
Iris
Nape
Forehead
Nostril
Upper Mandible ⎫ Bill
Lower Mandible ⎰
Primaries
Secondaries
Belly
Chin
Side
Flank
Front Toes
Hind Toe
Tertiaries
Tarsus
Tail Feather
Under Tail
Coverts   Tibia   Heel
Rump
Upper Tail Coverts
Tail Feathers or Retrices

Birds are the only animals that have feathers. Light in weight and filled with air spaces, feathers insulate the body from heat and cold. They give the body its shape and make flight possible.

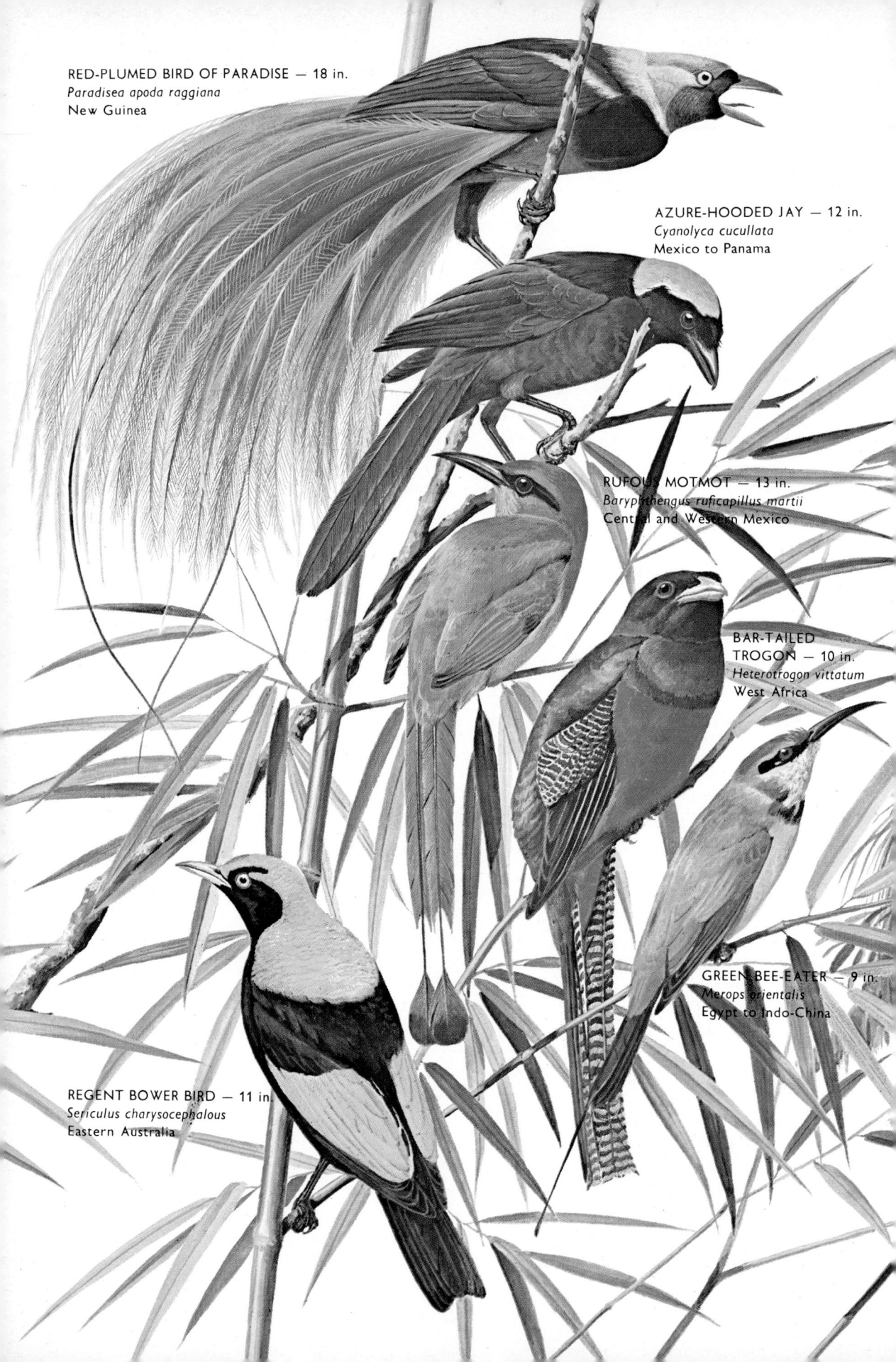

RED-PLUMED BIRD OF PARADISE — 18 in.
Paradisea apoda raggiana
New Guinea

AZURE-HOODED JAY — 12 in.
Cyanolyca cucullata
Mexico to Panama

RUFOUS MOTMOT — 13 in.
Baryphthengus ruficapillus martii
Central and Western Mexico

BAR-TAILED
TROGON — 10 in.
Heterotrogon vittatum
West Africa

GREEN BEE-EATER — 9 in.
Merops orientalis
Egypt to Indo-China

REGENT BOWER BIRD — 11 in.
Sericulus charysocephalous
Eastern Australia

Feathers give a bird its balance and shape, and protect it from heat and cold. They help swimming birds to float and give all birds beauty; most important, they make flying possible.

FLIGHT. All birds take off with a great flapping of wings, but once airborne they can fly in three different ways. They "power fly" when they propel themselves through the air by flapping their wings continuously; they also "soar", which is wind-riding, or gliding; and they employ "mixed flying", a combination of power flying and soaring.

Birds' wings are designed for the type of flying they do. Birds that soar and glide, and stay in the air for the longest periods of time, have the longest wings. Those that fly the least have the shortest wings.

Soaring is sailing through the air on wind currents as a glider does. This requires hardly any wing-flapping. To soar, a bird must know where the wind currents are and how to use them. From the ground, soaring looks like easy, lazy flying, as though the bird is resting on air; and that is exactly what it does. With wings rigid, a soaring bird coasts along, floating on updraughts of air, steering with its tail, and tipping its wings and body to bank in sharp turns, the way an aircraft does.

Birds soaring over land can go higher than birds soaring over the sea, because updraughts over land go higher. Mountains and valleys, cliffs, high buildings, cleared land and tall trees create these updraughts, and also cause sudden wind changes.

Land soaring birds have broader wings than sea soaring birds. Their wing-tips are usually rounded instead of pointed, and the feathers can be spread so that there are slots between them. This helps the bird change direction quickly, which the sea soarers seldom have to do.

Some wonderfully efficient land soarers are eagles, kites, hawks and vultures. Condors are especially skilled at soaring. The finest sea soarers are albatrosses, frigatebirds, shearwaters and gulls. Some water birds, like the White Pelican, soar mostly over land and they have rounded, slotted wings.

Most of the world's birds use power flying to get about. They take advantage of wind currents when they can, but they do not depend on them. Their flapping wings are their propellers; the breast muscles are the motors.

Wings of most power flyers are short and broad. Birds that fly low and for short distances through bush and woodland generally have the shortest and most rounded wings. Wings of birds that fly fast and fairly high for a long time are more pointed.

Birds can twist the "wrist" part of their wings to change the angle the wing-tip makes with the air. As the pressure of the air varies during the wing stroke, the slant of the feathers at the end of the wing changes automatically to give the bird the same kind of lift that wing-flaps give aeroplanes. Strong power flyers, such as geese, ducks, cormorants, thrushes and most finches, have this arrangement. Some soarers have this ability also.

A bird's wing-area compared to its weight relates to the kind of flying it does. Pilots call this relationship "wing-load". Soarers have low wing-loads; power flyers have higher ones. Each square foot of a vulture's wing lifts only one pound or less. A square foot of a duck's wing has to lift $2\frac{1}{2}$ times as much.

Some birds flap their wings faster than others during steady flight. Swallows flap their wings four times per second; redstarts three times; thrushes twice. When a bird is frightened or is chasing prey, it flaps its wings faster for a short time to put on an extra spurt of speed.

The third way of flying, a combination of flapping and soaring, is done in different ways by different birds. Ibises flap their wings several times, then glide. Woodpeckers and nuthatches use a similar method, but their faster wing-beats, and their downward swoop when gliding, give them an undulating flight.

ANATOMY OF A BIRD

Feathers with air spaces, streamlined shape — these are among the external features that reveal a bird's specialisation for flight.

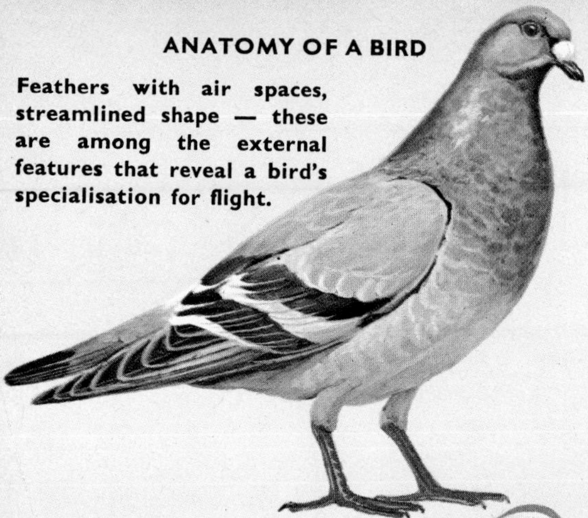

A bird's skeleton is compact, with many bones fused. Note the broad keel on the breastbone where powerful flight muscles attach.

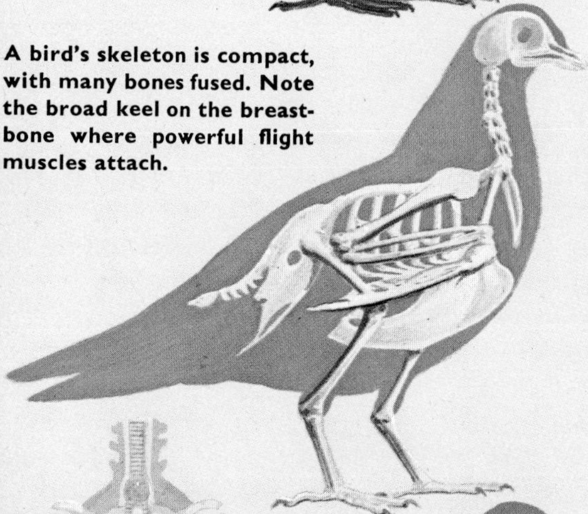

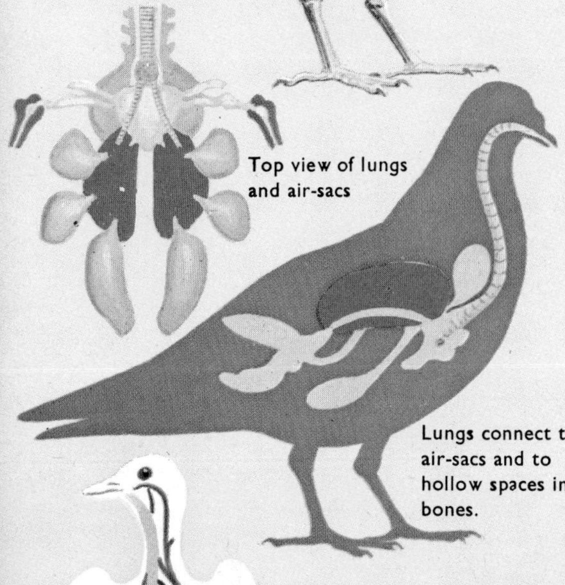

Top view of lungs and air-sacs

Lungs connect to air-sacs and to hollow spaces in bones.

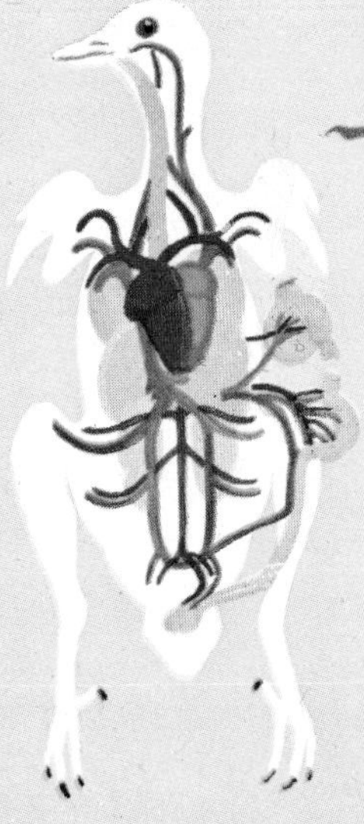

A bird's four-chambered heart separates enriched arterial blood from the venous blood containing carbon dioxide. A bird's heart beats rapidly in response to the high energy needs of its body.

SKELETON. The bird's skeleton is lighter than the skeleton of any other vertebrate. The long, round bones are hollow with thin internal struts, instead of being filled with marrow. This reduces weight without sacrificing strength.

Where flexibility is not important, bones are fused together to give compactness and strength. Parts of the spine and of the ribs are fused into the rigid frame of the body.

The most specialised part of a flying bird's skeleton is its breastbone, which has a strong, upright keel in its centre. The keel is the anchor for the flying muscles, which are the bird's strongest and largest muscles. Other powerful muscles are those that support the tail and give the legs and toes their strength.

The large bones of the wings which support the bird in flight are not fused, but the small wrist and hand bones are. Some finger bones have disappeared. In the leg the shin bones are fused, and the foot and ankle bones have become almost one unit. The only really flexible part of the bird is its neck. All these skeletal adaptations help the bird to fly.

Penguins literally "fly" underwater, using their short wings as flippers and their webbed feet as rudders.

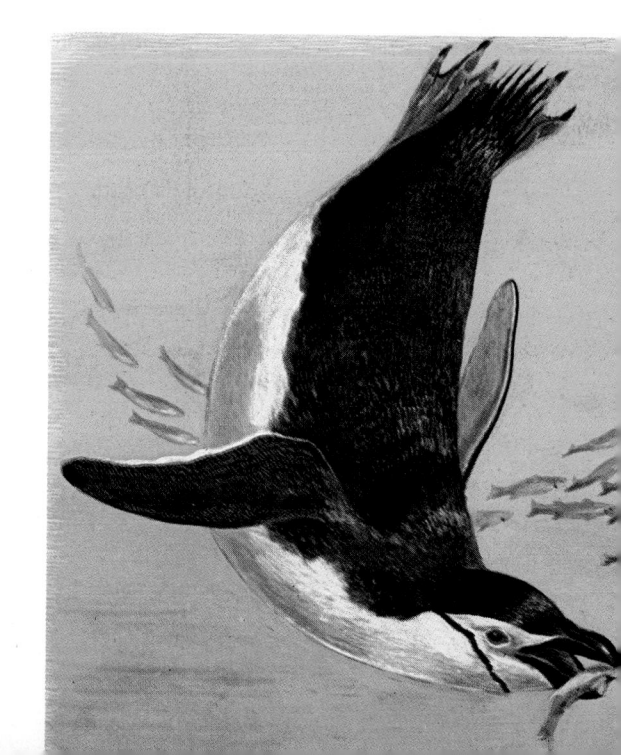

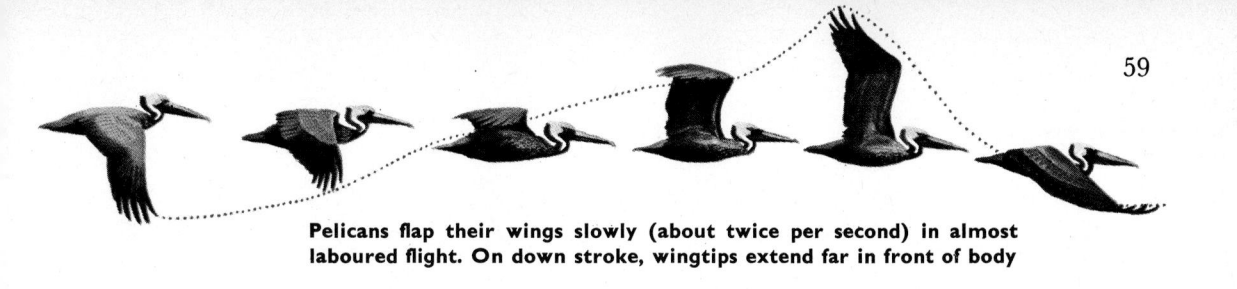

Pelicans flap their wings slowly (about twice per second) in almost laboured flight. On down stroke, wingtips extend far in front of body

BREATHING. Birds breathe with lungs, just as mammals do, and the motion of their wings in flight helps to pump the air in and out. Air is taken into their lungs, into some hollow bones, and also into a number of thin-walled air-sacs connected to their lungs by tiny transparent tubes. These sacs are located in various parts of the body, sometimes directly under the skin. The number of air-sacs varies in different speces and with different uses.

In all birds, the air-sacs increase the amount of oxygen available. They give birds extra lightness. They also give birds extra breath for long notes when they sing. In some cases, the air-sacs act as a barrier against cold and heat. Air-sacs also help water birds to float.

DIGESTIVE SYSTEM. A small bird spends much of its time eating. An adult Scarlet Tanager eats a third of its own weight in insects each day. Young birds are often fed more than their own weight daily, but much of this weight of food is really water. A bird uses 90 per cent of the food it eats. It takes a small bird only one or two hours to digest what it eats.

A bird usually swallows its food whole. It has no teeth for chewing. The food is first held in its elastic throat, which sometimes has a special storage-sac, called the crop, where digestion starts. From there the food passes through an upper stomach, which adds digestive juices to it, and then into the lower stomach, or gizzard. The gizzard is a strong, muscular sac which, in seed-eating birds, also contains grit, tiny stones, or pebbles in the case of some large birds. The gizzard automatically squeezes in and out, rubbing the food between the grit or pebbles to grind it up.

From the gizzard the food passes into the looped, tube-like small intestine, where it is absorbed and enters the blood-stream. The unusable part of the food passes

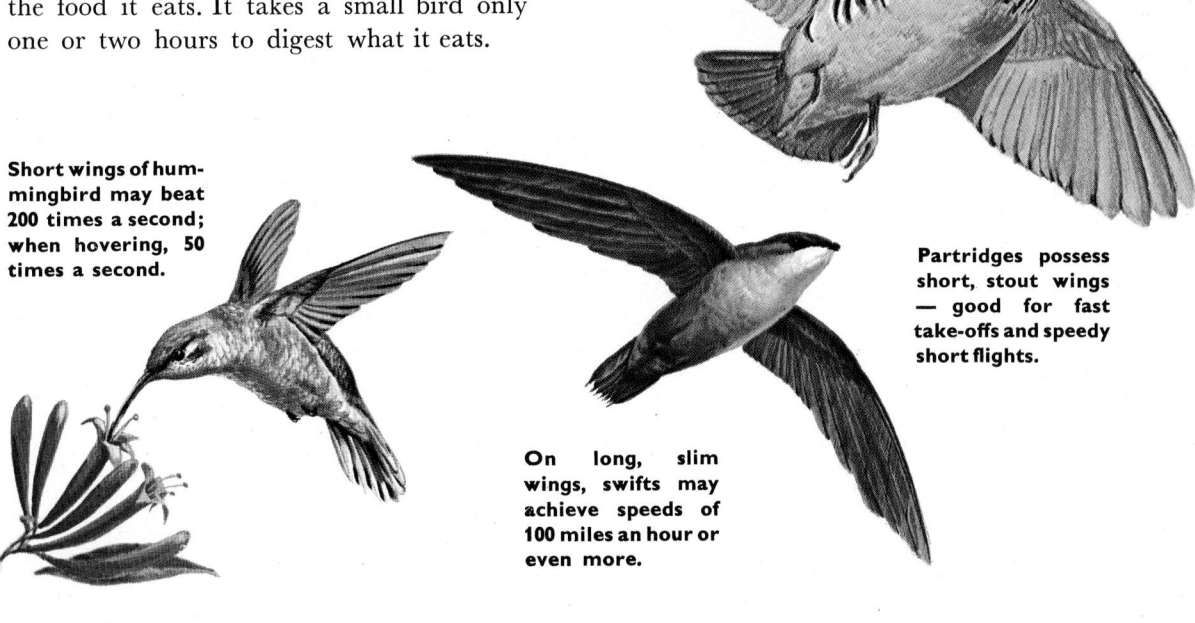

Short wings of hummingbird may beat 200 times a second; when hovering, 50 times a second.

On long, slim wings, swifts may achieve speeds of 100 miles an hour or even more.

Partridges possess short, stout wings — good for fast take-offs and speedy short flights.

from the small intestine to the large intestine and out through the opening of the pipe-like cloaca. A bird has only this one opening through which all waste-matter passes.

HEART. A bird's heart, like a mammal's, has four chambers, instead of three as in amphibians and most reptiles. This ensures sending only oxygen-rich blood from the lungs to the body.

Birds' hearts beat more quickly than those of other animals. They pump the

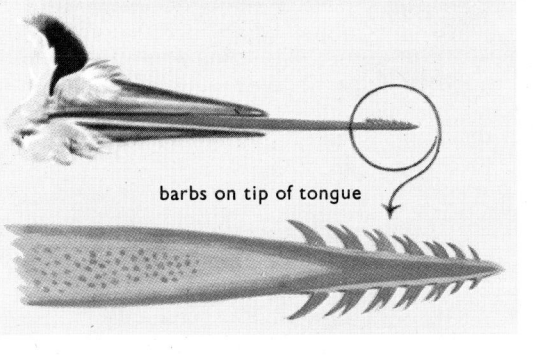

barbs on tip of tongue

Woodpecker's long, barbed tongue reaches into burrows and holes to spear grubs, borers, or other insects which it eats.

DEVELOPMENT OF A CHICK
(diagrammatic)

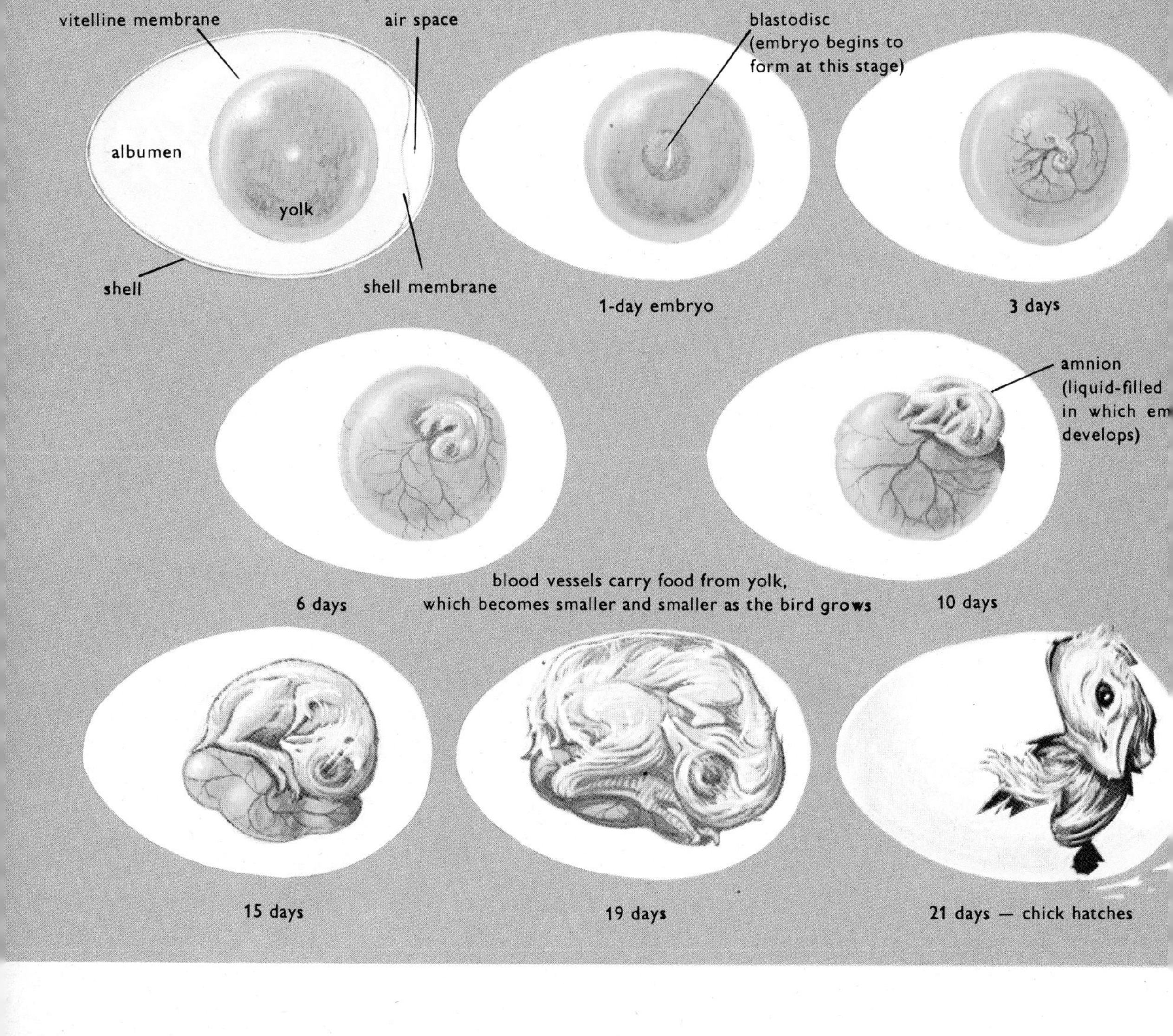

vitelline membrane

air space

blastodisc (embryo begins to form at this stage)

albumen

yolk

shell

shell membrane

1-day embryo

3 days

amnion (liquid-filled in which em develops)

6 days

blood vessels carry food from yolk, which becomes smaller and smaller as the bird grows

10 days

15 days

19 days

21 days — chick hatches

As a Cardinal comes in for landing, its body swings up (1) and its tail drops and spreads to cut down the speed (2). The bird's feet swing out to meet the branch (3) and the remaining forward motion carries the bird to an upright position (4).

birds' blood faster to supply the extra energy needed for flight. Birds that fly a great deal, or those that live at high altitudes, have bigger hearts for their size than other birds.

Birds also have higher body temperatures than other animals. A human has a fever if his temperature rises above 99 degrees F., but birds have a normal temperature of 105—110 degrees F. This burns their food more rapidly and gives them the energy needed for flying.

BILLS. Birds use their bills to get food, to defend themselves, to build nests, and to clean their feathers. The shape of a bird's bill is related to the kind of food it eats and the way in which it finds its customary food.

Sparrows and chickens have cone-shaped bills. The sharp point is for picking up seeds, and the rest of the bill is shaped for crushing them. Beaks of the well-named Crossbills prise open pinecones easily.

Woodpeckers have stronger bills and more muscular necks than most birds. A woodpecker uses its bill like a carpenter's adze or chisel to chop out fat grubs that bore under the bark and in the trunks of trees. When it opens a tunnel, the woodpecker sticks out its extraordinarily long tongue, which has hook-like bristles at its tip, and draws out the grub.

Nightjars have beaks and mouths evolved to trap insects. Their bills are tiny, but they can open their mouths in an enormous gape that is bigger than their heads. Bristles on either side make the trap still larger. These birds fly at night with their mouths

Grebes carry their precocial chicks on their backs.

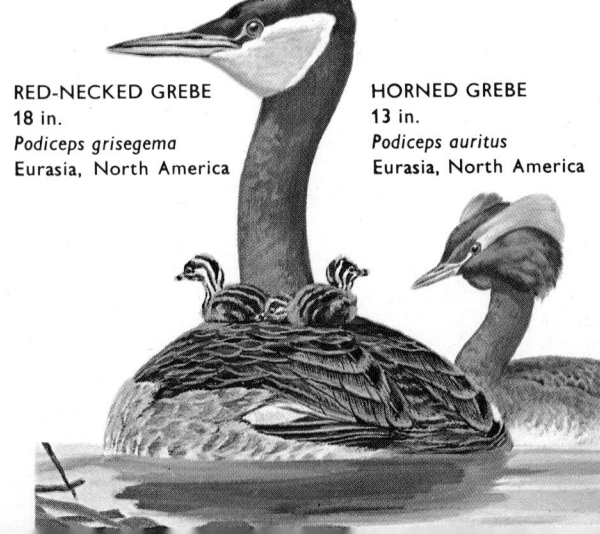
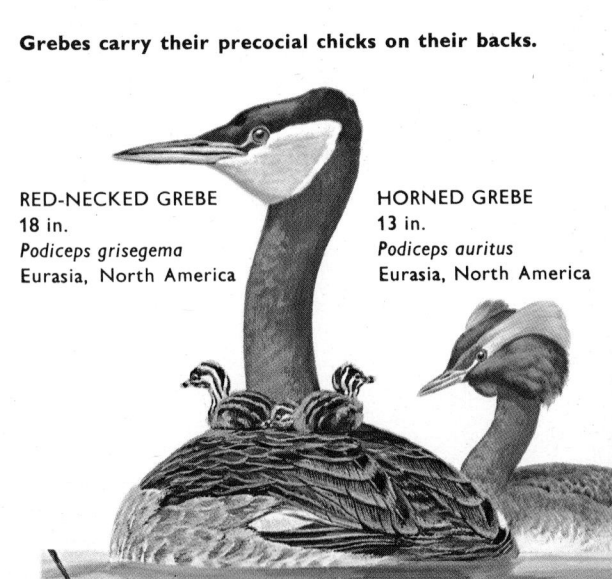

RED-NECKED GREBE
18 in.
Podiceps grisegema
Eurasia, North America

HORNED GREBE
13 in.
Podiceps auritus
Eurasia, North America

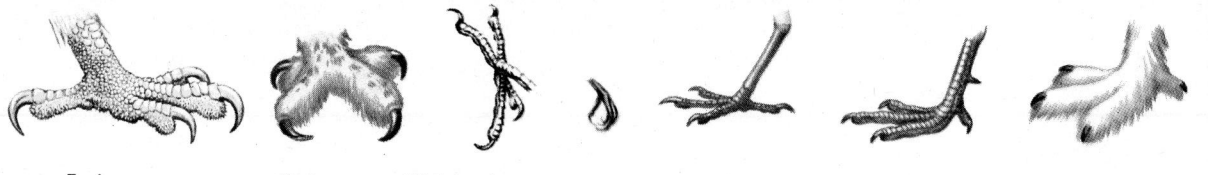

| Eagle: grasping | Owl: grasping | Woodpecker: climbing | Hummingbird: perching | Robin: perching | Pheasant: walking | Ptarmigan: walking in snow |

wide open to scoop in flying insects.

Humming-birds' long, slender bills are mainly for sipping nectar from flowers. They are also used for catching tiny insects.

Dabbling ducks have broad, flat bills for scooping up mud, in which they find worms and small animals, water-plants and weed seeds. The sieves on either side of the tongue and the lower bill strain out the sand and water.

The Black Skimmer skims over the top of the water with its lower bill just under the surface to catch the tiny fish it eats. Its lower bill is longer than the upper bill and is knife-sharp to make this food-catching easy.

Herons, terns, anhingas, kingfishers and loons all have spear-shaped bills for catching fish. Some of these birds fly above the water and watch for fish swimming below them. Some watch from a perch over the water, some from the water's edge, and others while swimming underwater. They seize the fish with lightning speed.

Hawks, eagles, and other birds of prey, have a sharp hook on the upper bill for tearing to pieces the meat they hold in their talons.

Parrots have a beak that is both a nut-cracker and a fruit spoon. They can raise the upper part of the bill quite high, which gives them power to crush seeds. The bill has nothing to do with the parrot's ability to imitate human speech.

FEET. Birds' feet are covered with scales, similar to the scales on reptiles. This may be evidence that birds are distantly related to reptiles.

Birds walk, perch, swim, grab, scratch and fight with their toes. Their toes have become the strong landing gear of the flyer, the equally strong grip of the percher or climber, the powerful talons of the hunter, and the paddles of the swimmers. Toes are therefore the most important parts of the feet. On the ends of their toes, all birds have claws, which are hard growths like toenails, but stronger.

Most birds have four toes — three in front and one behind. No bird has five toes, but a few have only three. Most of these are running birds that have lost the hind toe. Examples are bustards, emus and rheas. One bird, the Ostrich, has only two toes.

A few birds — parrots, cuckoos and toucans, for example — have two toes in front and two behind. This is usually found in species which spend their life

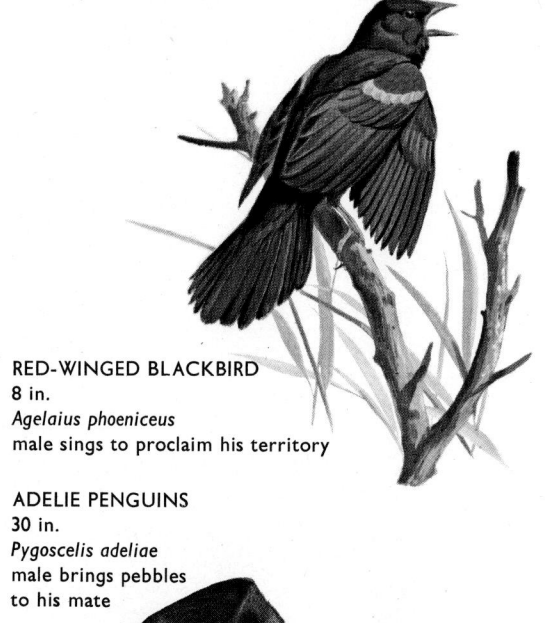

RED-WINGED BLACKBIRD
8 in.
Agelaius phoeniceus
male sings to proclaim his territory

ADELIE PENGUINS
30 in.
Pygoscelis adeliae
male brings pebbles
to his mate

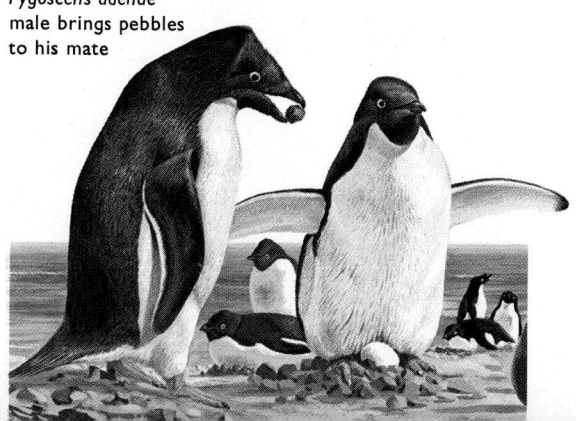

Jacana:
walking on lily pads

Cassowary:
walking

Coot:
swimming

Duck:
swimming

Pelican:
swimming

Greenshanks:
wading.

perching in trees. Ospreys and owls can move one of their three front toes around to the back, to grasp prey.

Birds' feet, toes and claws, like their bills, are many different shapes. Swimming birds have toes with webs, or half webs, between them for pushing water or for steering, and they have short claws for scratching in mud. Perching birds have toes that curl around a branch or a twig. Their slender, sharp-pointed claws also help them to cling to the perch. Some ground birds have long toes, but most running birds tend to have short toes, and may lose the hind toe altogether.

Climbing birds have toes with strong hook-like claws that can fit into tiny cracks, so that the birds can cling to bark or to a crevice in stonework. Hunting birds have powerful toes with strong piercing claws. These are the talons with which they grab their prey.

Wading birds have very long, flat toes which support them in soft mud, and their legs are so long they can walk in water and keep their feathers dry. One group of wading birds, the Jaçanas, have toes made for walking on water-lily leaves. They are long, very slender, and widespread. The claws and toes together on each foot of the Tacana are almost as long as the body of the bird itself.

Kingfishers have front toes partly joined, making a broad foot, which probably aids a bird that perches but hardly ever walks. Two groups of birds — colies (or mouse-birds) from Africa, and swifts — can turn all their toes forward to make a strong hook, from which they hang while resting or sleeping. Swifts hang rightside-up; but colies hang upside-down, like bats.

Some birds have feathered toes. Those of the Ptarmigan help it to walk on soft snow, while similar feathering helps the desert Sandgrouse to walk on sand. Most owls have feathered toes, but this is most marked in northern, and particularly Arctic, species, in which it may act as insulation against the cold.

Herons, nightjars, frigate-birds, and a

Red-bellied Woodpecker chisels a nesting hole in a tree.

Cliff Swallow builds a gourd-like mud nest.

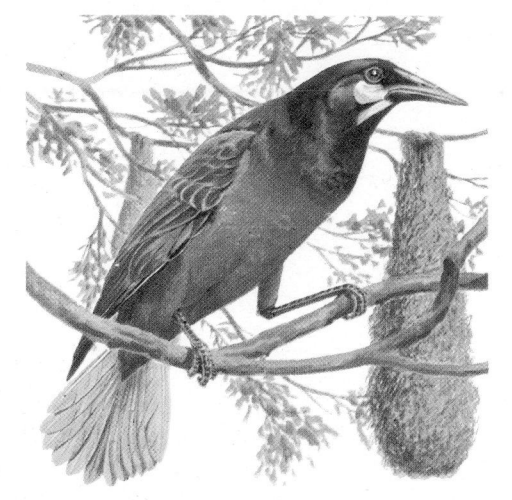

Wagler's Oropendola builds a hanging baggy nest.

few others, have a saw-toothed edge on their middle claws. This seems to be used by these birds when they are preening their plumage.

A few kinds of birds, such as pheasants, chickens, peacocks and turkeys, have a bony projection, or spur, between the toes and the heel. Strong and sharp, the spur serves

A fledgling Common Cuckoo of Europe has hatched from an egg laid by its mother in the nest of a Lesser Whitethroat, a much smaller bird.

COMMON CUCKOO
Cuculus canorus
fledgling

LESSER WHITE
THROAT — 5 in.
Sylvia curruca
Temperate Eurasia

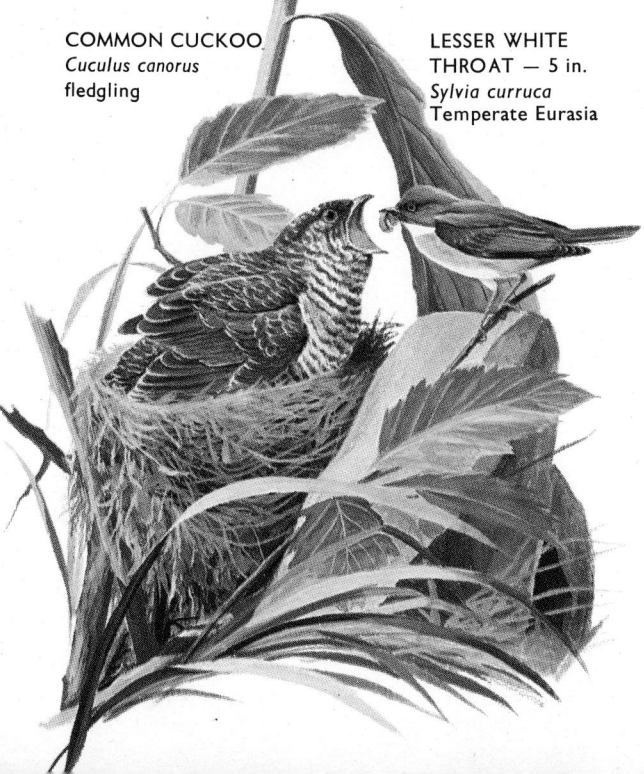

the bird as a weapon of defence. A spur is a special outgrowth and not a misplaced toe.

MATING AND CARE OF YOUNG. Most birds form pairs, and both parents help in the task of rearing the young. The difficult process of selecting a mate is aided by displays, usually performed by the male, which indicate that he is ready to breed. A female in breeding condition will respond to his display and join him, and in this way a pair is formed. In his display, a bird will endeavour to look as conspicuous and as unlike his normal self as possible. Some birds adopt strange postures and leap or move in unusual ways, and some perform spectacular flights. Birds with crests, ruff, plumes, or bright patches of colour, erect their plumage in such a way that these become conspicuous. Special calls or song are used by many species.

Some birds, such as ducks and geese, may pair while still in winter flocks, others wait until they have a nesting territory before advertising their presence to a potential mate. Many migrant visitors to the British Isles, such as warblers, do this, announcing possession by loud song. Still others wait until they have a nest before looking for a mate, and both the Weaverbirds and the homely Starling come into this category. The Starling announces his possession of a nest hole to any passing female by flipping his wings outwards and uttering a piercing whistle.

Then again, some birds do not form pairs. In certain gamebirds, and in that brightly ornamented wader the Ruff, the males all come together in one place and compete with each other in conspicuousness of posture, plumage or calls. The females visit the display ground and choose a mate, but nest and rear the young alone. In the *Phalaropes*, and a few other species, the female is more brightly coloured and does the courting, her more sober mate incubating the eggs and tending the young.

Some birds bring gifts when courting. Male terns bring fish to their intended

mates. Adelie Penguins bring pebbles.

Scientists believe that cranes and geese mate for life, but many birds select a new mate each year. A wild turkey gobbler has a harem of many turkey hens.

When they begin to search for mates, or after they have found them, birds start to make a nest to hold the eggs. Each species builds the same type of nest and in the same kind of place where it was hatched and raised. Most hawks nest high in trees, finches in low bushes, geese on the ground, and petrels in holes or burrows under the ground. House Martins hang their nests on the sides of cliffs or houses. Sand Martins burrow into banks. Woodpeckers nest in holes they chisel in trees; Bluetits, Pied-flycatchers, and even Tawny Owls, all of which nest in hollow trees, can be persuaded to use bird-boxes.

Terns and penguins nest in big colonies, sometimes many thousands of them crowded on to one strip of land. Some birds, such as Sociable Weavers and Quaker Parakeets, build their nests side by side in a tree, to form one huge structure.

Nest-building may be done by the mated pair together, by the male alone, or by the

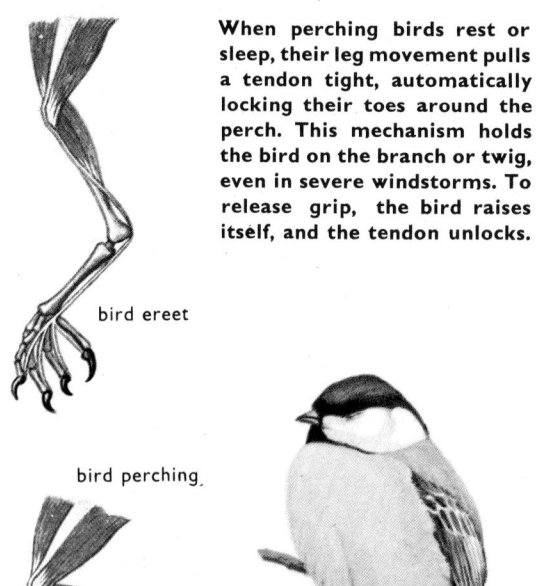

When perching birds rest or sleep, their leg movement pulls a tendon tight, automatically locking their toes around the perch. This mechanism holds the bird on the branch or twig, even in severe windstorms. To release grip, the bird raises itself, and the tendon unlocks.

bird ereet

bird perching

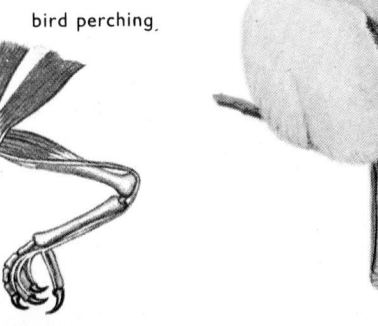

EGGS VARY WITH THE SPECIES

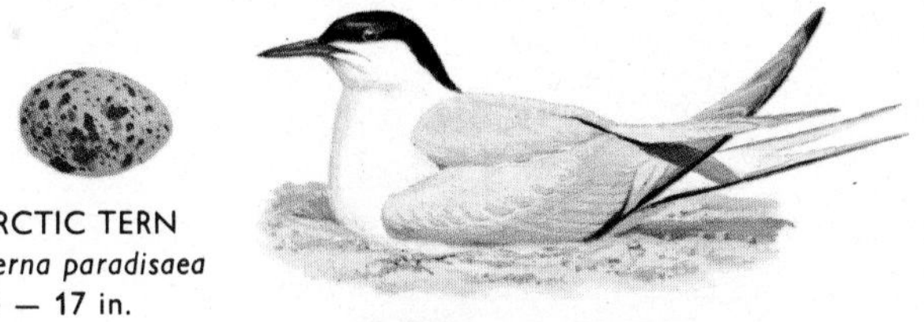

ARCTIC TERN
Sterna paradisaea
14 — 17 in.

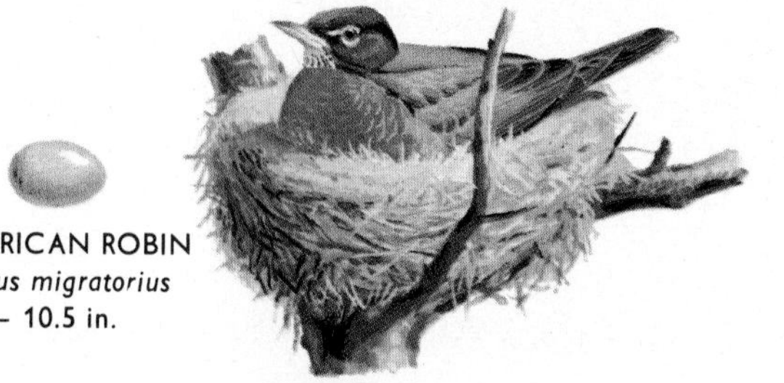

AMERICAN ROBIN
Turdus migratorius
8.5 — 10.5 in.

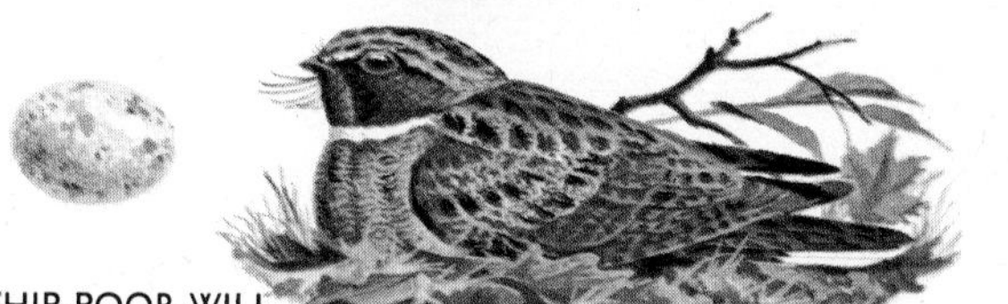

WHIP-POOR-WILL
Caprimulgus vociferus
9 — 10 in.

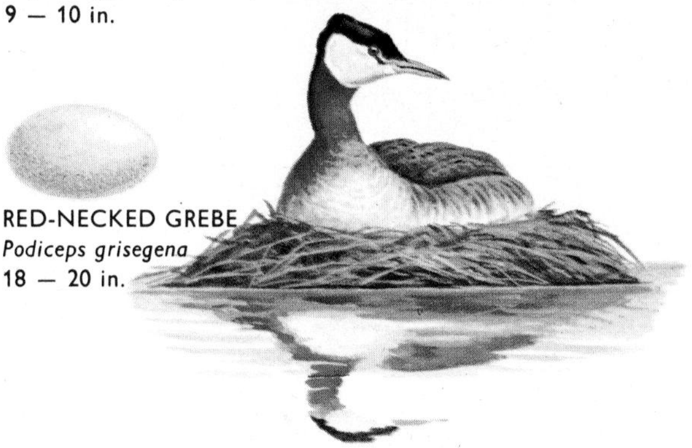

RED-NECKED GREBE
Podiceps grisegena
18 — 20 in.

LITTLE BEE-EATER
Melittophagus pusillus
6.3 in.

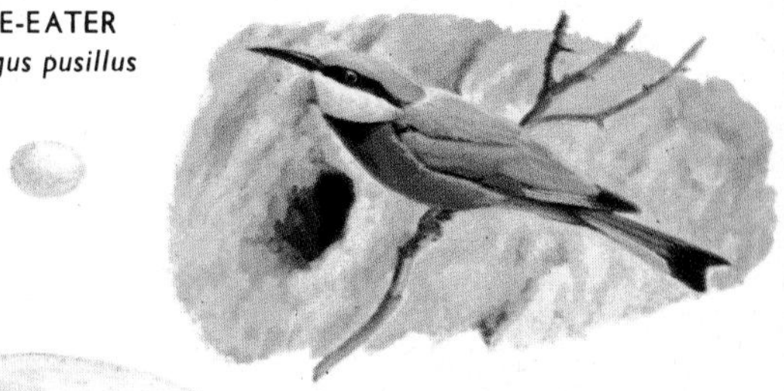

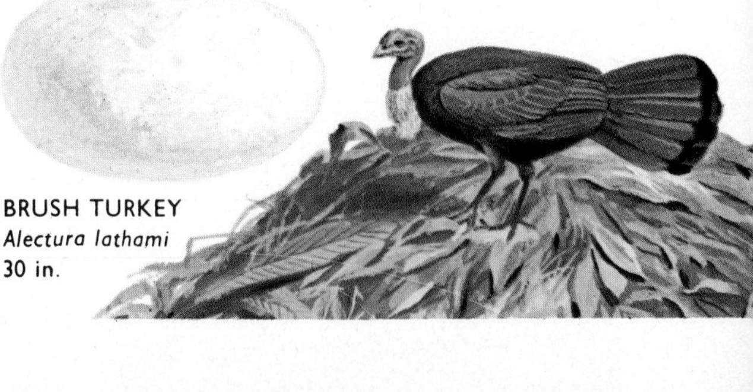

BRUSH TURKEY
Alectura lathami
30 in.

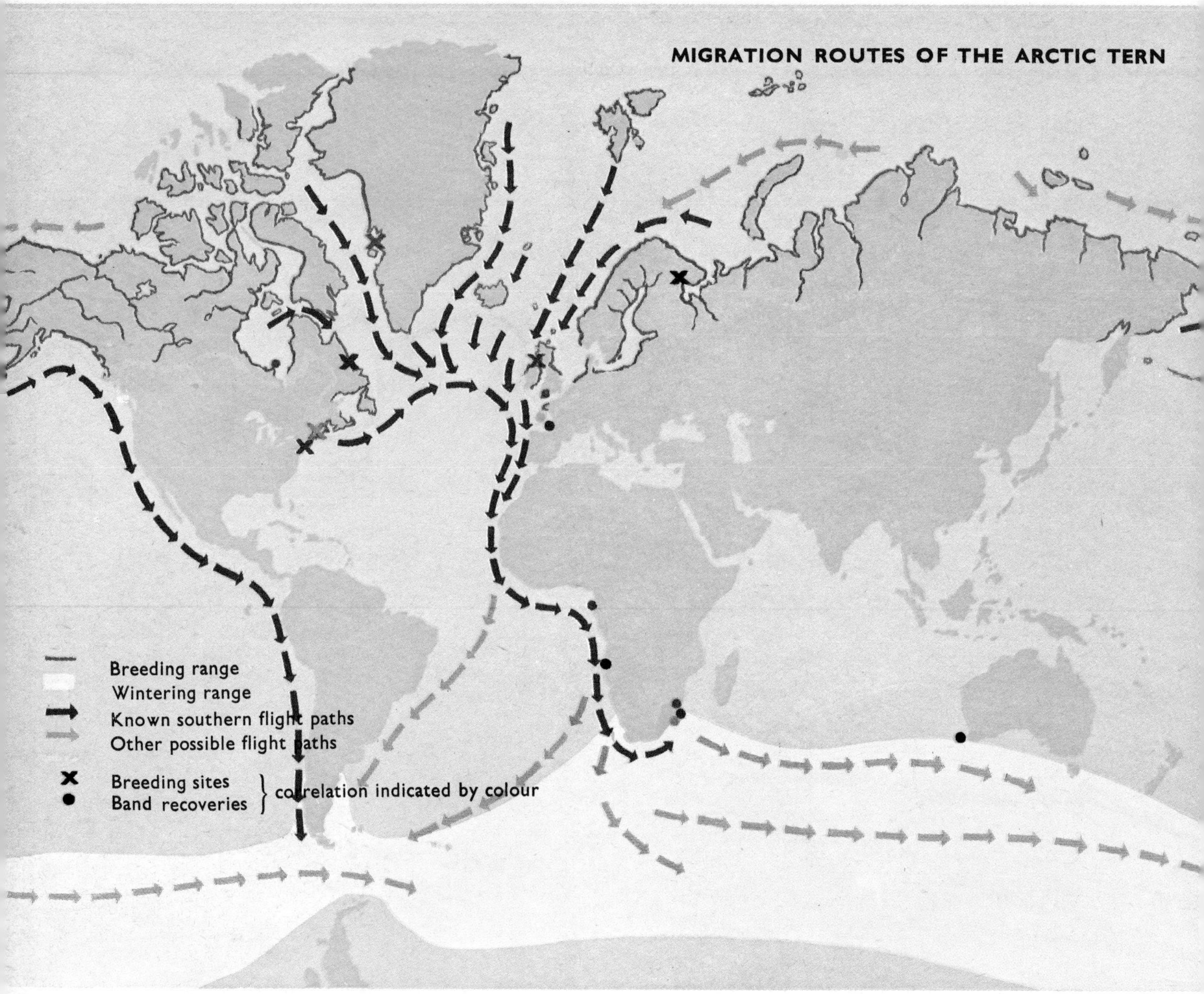

MIGRATION ROUTES OF THE ARCTIC TERN

Breeding range
Wintering range
Known southern flight paths
Other possible flight paths

✕ Breeding sites
● Band recoveries } correlation indicated by colour

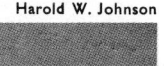

female alone. Sometimes one does all the building while its mate brings the material. Generally a nest is made by gathering twigs, stems and leaves, and weaving or plastering them together.

After the nest is started, the bird sits

Arctic Tern travels about 24,000 miles a year on migration flights from the nesting grounds to its wintering area.

Harold W. Johnson

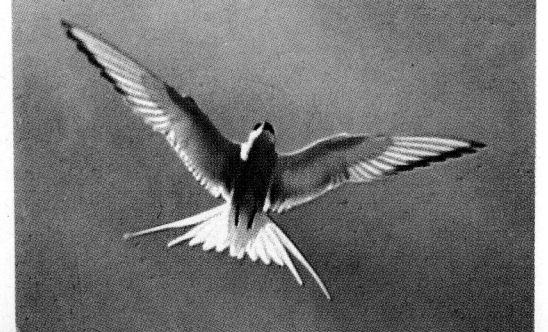

in it many times a day, and turns and presses to form the hollow centre. When the nest has been roughly shaped, it is lined with softer materials, such as grass, feathers, thistledown or animal hair.

Weaver-birds and Troupials make complicated nests by twisting strips of materials round twigs and weaving others around them with their beaks. Some Thrushes plaster their nest-lining with mud mixed with rotten wood.

Terns make hollows in the sand by turning around in one spot. They add only a few shells or plant stems. Swifts make a glue of saliva for cementing their nests. Nightjars lay their eggs on the ground, making no nest at all.

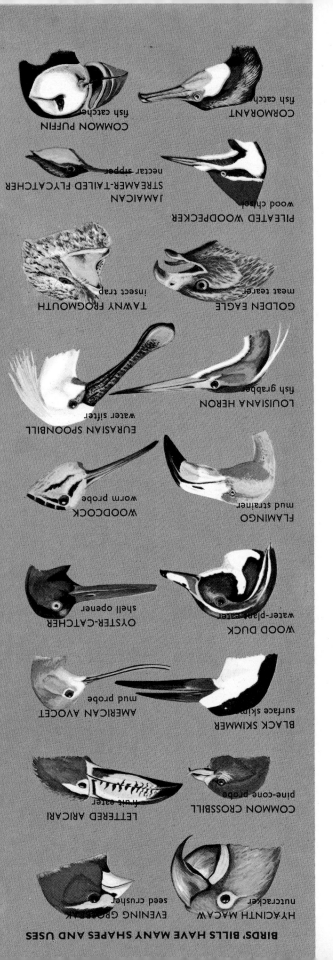

BIRDS' BILLS HAVE MANY SHAPES AND USES

COMMON PUFFIN — fish catcher
CORMORANT — fish catcher
JAMAICAN STREAMER-TAILED FLYCATCHER — nectar sipper
PILEATED WOODPECKER — wood chisel
TAWNY FROGMOUTH — insect trap
GOLDEN EAGLE — meat tearer
EURASIAN SPOONBILL — water sifter
LOUISIANA HERON — fish grabber
WOODCOCK — worm probe
FLAMINGO — mud strainer
OYSTER-CATCHER — shell opener
WOOD DUCK — water-plant eater
AMERICAN AVOCET — mud probe
BLACK SKIMMER — surface skimmer
LETTERED ARAÇARI — fruit eater
COMMON CROSSBILL — pine-cone probe
EVENING GROSBEAK — seed crusher
HYACINTH MACAW — nutcracker

When a nest is completed, the female starts laying eggs. The egg of a bird starts to grow inside the female in a knobbly organ called the ovary. The ovary takes proteins, fats and other substances from the blood to make the yolk. Then the yolk is wrapped in a thin tissue called the vitelline membrane.

The living egg cell with its capsule of food (the yolk) breaks loose from the ovary and enters the funnel-shaped top of the oviduct (egg tube). As it passes down the oviduct, the yolk becomes surrounded by albumen (egg white) and is then covered by another two thin skins, the shell membranes. Near the end of the oviduct a hard, limy shell forms around the egg. At this time, colour is deposited over the shell, unless it is to be plain white.

Now the egg is ready to be laid. Most birds lay one egg each day at a regular time. The Song Sparrow, for example, lays one egg early every morning until she has the four or five eggs from which she can raise a family.

For an egg to produce a baby bird the yolk must enclose a fertilised ovum. When birds mate, the sperm of the male enters the female's cloaca. Some of the sperm swim up the oviduct. One sperm fertilises the egg cell (ovum) at the top of the oviduct before the albumen is added.

The living cells inside the egg must be carefully tended. If the egg gets too cold or too hot, the embryo inside will die; so one or both parent birds make certain that the eggs are never exposed to strong sun in the heat of the day or to the cool air of the night. They brood the eggs, warming them with the body, until the embryo chicks, living on the yolks, have grown large enough to hatch. Sometimes one bird does all the incubating; sometimes both take turns, depending on the habits of the species.

The number of eggs a female lays is called a clutch. A wild bird's clutch may be anywhere from one to more than fifteen eggs. Petrels always lay one egg. Plovers

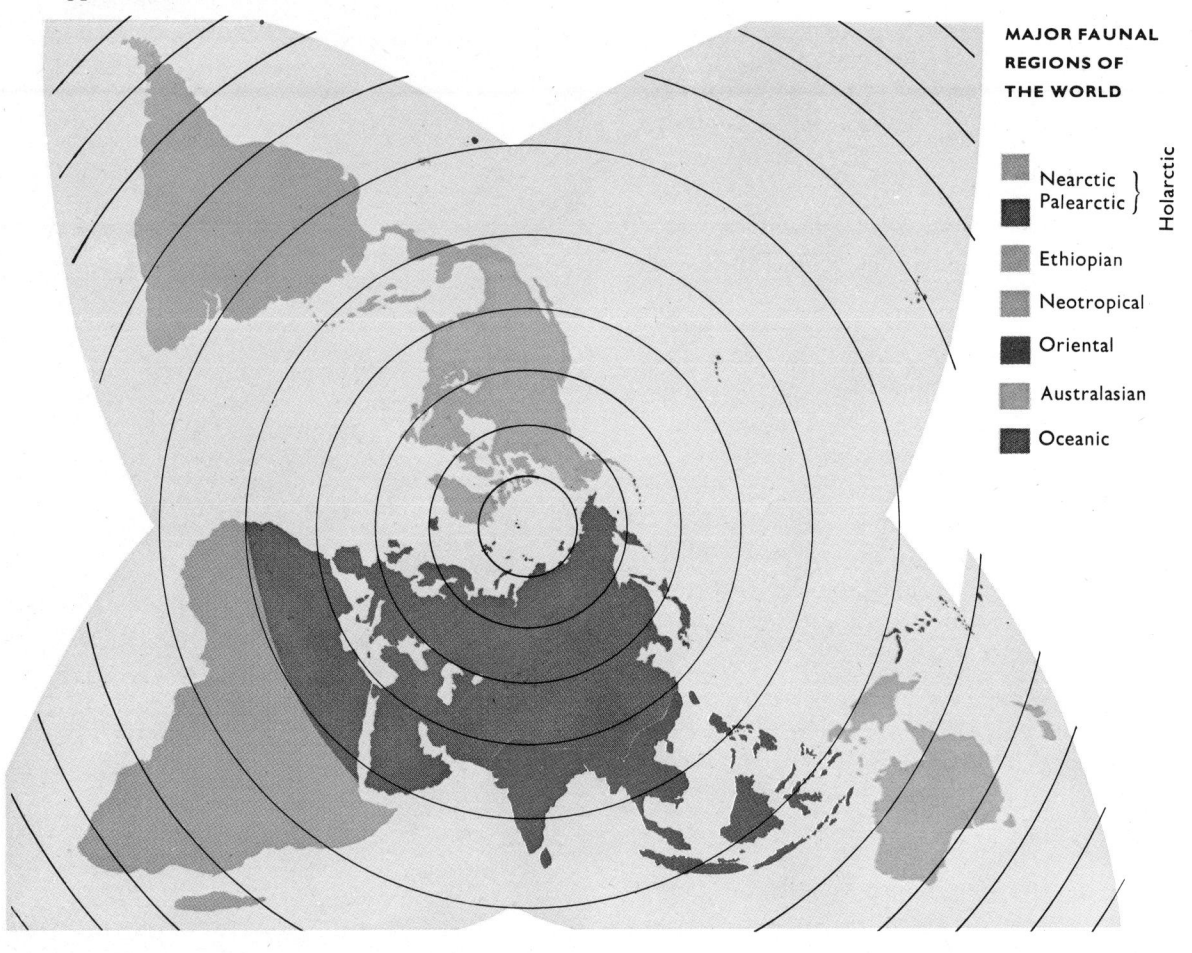

MAJOR FAUNAL
REGIONS OF
THE WORLD

Nearctic }
Palearctic } Holarctic

Ethiopian

Neotropical

Oriental

Australasian

Oceanic

always lay four. In many species the number of eggs in a completed clutch varies. One Mallard duck may lay a clutch of only eight eggs, and another lay a clutch of fifteen eggs.

Eggs are usually oval in shape, so that the clutch fits together neatly in the nest.

EMPEROR PENGUIN — 48 in.
Aptenoides forsteri
Shores of Antarctica

KING PENGUIN
38 in.
Aptenoides patagonicus
Falklands, sub-antarctic islands

Auks, which nest on cliffs, lay pear-shaped eggs that rotate instead of rolling, and are therefore not likely to fall off narrow rock-ledges.

Eggs of Owls and Kingfishers are almost round and usually white. So are the eggs of many other birds that nest in holes. Wild birds' eggs are mainly dull coloured — browns, soft blues and greens, or speckled — so that they cannot be easily seen. Buff and brown speckled eggs, such as those of Plovers, laid on bare sand or gravel, are hidden by their protective colouring.

Usually, but not always, small eggs hatch more quickly than large eggs. The tiny $\frac{1}{2}$-inch eggs of Wrens hatch in about 11 days. The barnyard chicken's eggs hatch in 21 days. The 1-pound, 5-inch egg of the Kiwi takes 77 days.

Just before the chick is ready to hatch, a horny growth called the "egg tooth"

develops on the top of its beak. The egg tooth is hard enough to cut the shell. The chick squirms within the egg and chips with the egg tooth until the shell cracks from the inside and finally breaks open at its widest part. Parent birds do not help to break the shell, but they often carry the pieces of shell away when the chick is free. The egg tooth drops off a day or so after the bird hatches.

Some birds hatch without feathers or with very few feathers. They are unable to see or stand and are completely helpless. These young are called altricial (al TREE shall). All they can do at first is open their mouths so that the parents can place food in them.

Altricial nestlings are "brooded" — kept warm under a parent's feathers — until they grow enough feathers to keep themselves warm. They are fed and cared for by the adults until they leave the nest, and sometimes even after they have learned to fly. All perching birds are altricial, as are hawks, owls, eagles and some sea birds, such as pelicans.

Other birds come out of the egg covered with down feathers and are able to run or swim or both. They leave the nest almost immediately. These young are called precocial (pre KO shall). Parents of these birds usually lead them away from the nest the day they hatch. Ducks and geese take their active young to the water. Quail and grouse hide theirs in thick cover. These chicks help to feed themselves immediately. Some know what to eat as soon as they hatch; others have to be taught by the parent birds. The young of some sea birds are fed by their parents until they learn to fish for themselves. Grebe parents carry their chicks on their backs while swimming, and the young birds watch them catch fish and water insects. The parent grebe turns its head over its shoulder and pops the food into the young birds' mouths.

Almost all chicks, both altricial and precocial, are protected and guarded by the parent birds until they have grown their flight feathers. Some are cared for by both parents; others by only one parent. Most precocial chicks are brooded only at night, when it is very cold, in the rain, or once in a while when they are tired.

Some parents feed the young birds with insects, worms, berries or fish just as they were collected. Others half-digest the food in their crops and then put the semi-liquid food into the chicks' mouths. Anhingas, herons and penguins are examples of birds that feed their young this way on regurgitated food. Pelicans and a few other kinds of birds open their mouths and let the young reach into their crops to get the food.

American cowbirds and European cuckoos do not build nests of their own. When ready to lay an egg, the female cowbird or cuckoo finds the nest of a warbler, a sparrow, or some other small bird, and lays her egg there. Then she flies away, leaving foster parents to incubate the egg and raise her chick.

U. S. Dept. of Interior — Fish & Wildlife Service
A duck is banded as part of a research programme to learn more about migration routes and habits.

After young birds learn to fly and to care for themselves, some stay in family groups. Others leave the parents or the parents leave them. A few young birds assemble in flocks by themselves during the first weeks of early autumn. Most of them join flocks of older birds. All birds spend these weeks eating and resting, storing fat for the autumn migration and getting ready for the change of season.

The end of the breeding cycle comes when all the young birds are independent.

MIGRATION. Many birds cross continents and oceans each autumn and spring, travelling between their summer nesting grounds and their winter homes. For years men could not discover how birds found their way, what routes they took, where they went, or how fast they travelled.

What routes birds take, and where and how fast they go, have been discovered by putting numbered rings on the legs of many kinds of birds. Two Arctic Terns, marked with numbered rings in Labrador in 1927 and 1928, did not leave their nesting grounds until after August 15th. On October 1st, one was picked up in France; on November 14th, the other was recovered in South Africa — 11,000 miles from its nest. This showed the wintering area, the route taken to reach it, and migration travelling time for Arctic Terns. This was the first time facts replaced guesswork on the Arctic Tern's routes.

The same scientist who marked the Arctic Terns banded a Lesser Yellowlegs, a shore bird, on Cape Cod on August 28th, 1935. Six days later this same bird was killed 1,900 miles away on Martinique, an island in the West Indies. This was the first proof that a migrating bird may travel more than 300 miles a day.

In recent years, scientists have learned a lot about how birds find their way. They navigate just as ancient sailors did before the compass was invented, for birds use the sun and stars to guide them. Experiments have proved that birds get lost only on foggy or cloudy days or nights, when they cannot see the sky. On dark, stormy nights birds fly into high buildings and lighthouses and are injured and killed. Thousands of night-flying birds have died when they hit masts and beacons.

Scientists are now studying the effects of radar beams on birds. Sea birds, picked up by a powerful radar beam, stop flying

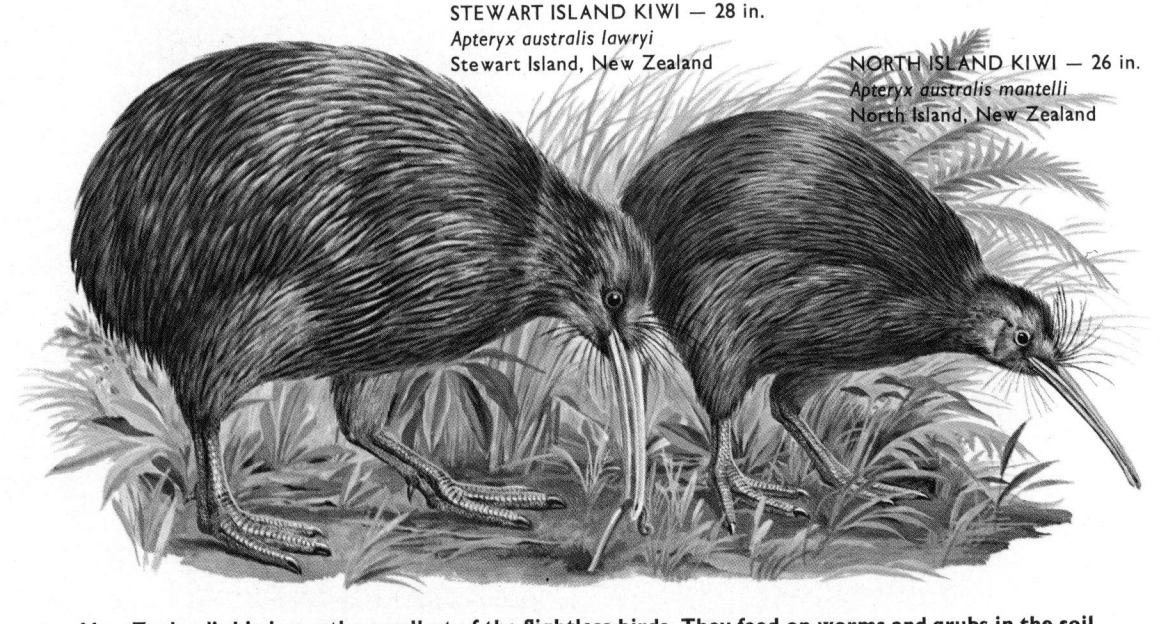

STEWART ISLAND KIWI — 28 in.
Apteryx australis lawryi
Stewart Island, New Zealand

NORTH ISLAND KIWI — 26 in.
Apteryx australis mantelli
North Island, New Zealand

New Zealand's kiwis are the smallest of the flightless birds. They feed on worms and grubs in the soil.

and drop to the water when they cannot escape from it.

Everything about birds shows that they are adapted to fly, yet some birds, over a period of millions of years, have lost this ability.

As these flightless birds changed their way of life, their bones and muscles changed too. They became heavier than their flying relatives; their bones became filled with marrow; they all nested on the ground or in burrows. Some of them became walkers or runners, and some became swimmers. Many flightless birds did not survive man's exploration and settlement of the world.

Birds that walk or run instead of flying tend to lose their flying muscles, and also the upright keel of the breastbone where those muscles attach. Since their flat breast-bones look like rafts instead of keeled boats, we call them "ratite" birds — from the Latin word *ratis*, meaning raft. (Birds with keels are called "carinate" birds — from the Latin word *carina*, meaning keel). Their wings are small and useless, but their legs are strong and heavy, their toes flat and hard. The Ostrich and the Kiwi are examples of ratite birds.

The wings of flightless birds that became swimmers changed into paddles or flippers, their feet into swim-fins or rudders. Since they still used their flying muscles (for swimming), they did not lose either those powerful muscles or the keel. Penguins and the Great Auk are examples of this.

Some flightless running birds that open their wings when they run, perhaps for balance, still have a keel. Their wings are small and weak, but their legs and feet are stout and strong. The Kagu is a nearly flightless running bird of New Caledonia.

Some birds have become flightless in the recent past. This most frequently occurs in the case of birds isolated on islands where they have no enemies, and it has happened most often to species of Rails. Such birds also tend to become larger and heavier.

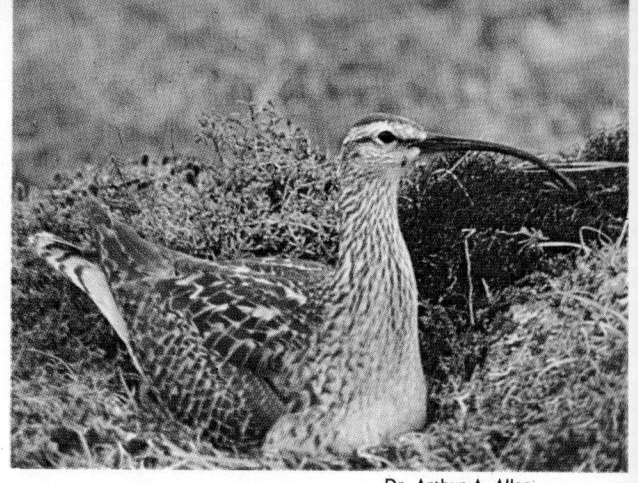

Dr. Arthur A. Allen

Bristle-thighed curlew flies 5,500 miles twice yearly, nesting on the tundra of Alaska within the Arctic Circle and wintering on islands in mid-Pacific.

One almost flightless bird known all over the world was made so by man, and all because chicken is a favourite dish. Certain kinds of domestic chickens are raised for their meat, rather than their eggs. For many years poultry-raisers have been breeding only the birds with the largest and most tender breasts, thighs and legs. Gradually these birds have become heavier, until now their wings can barely support them. Turkeys, pigeons and ducks have also been changed as the result of becoming domestic birds; they have been selectively bred to satisfy market demands. All are still capable of flight, however, and must be penned or have their wings clipped to prevent them from taking advantage of their freedom. (See DODOS; EMUS; OSTRICHES.)

HILL MYNAH — 13 in.
Gracula religiosa
India to Malaya

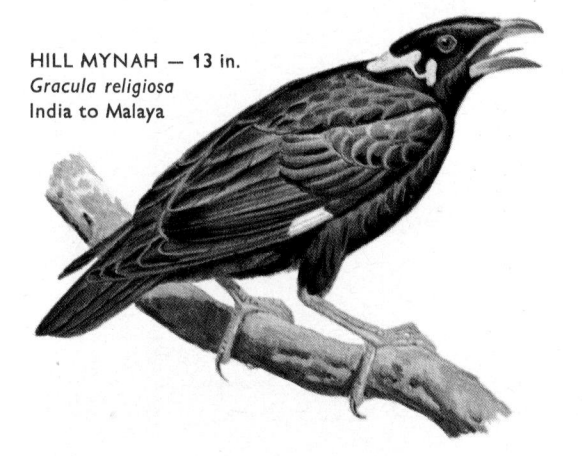

Hill Mynah is the best of the cage-bird mimics.

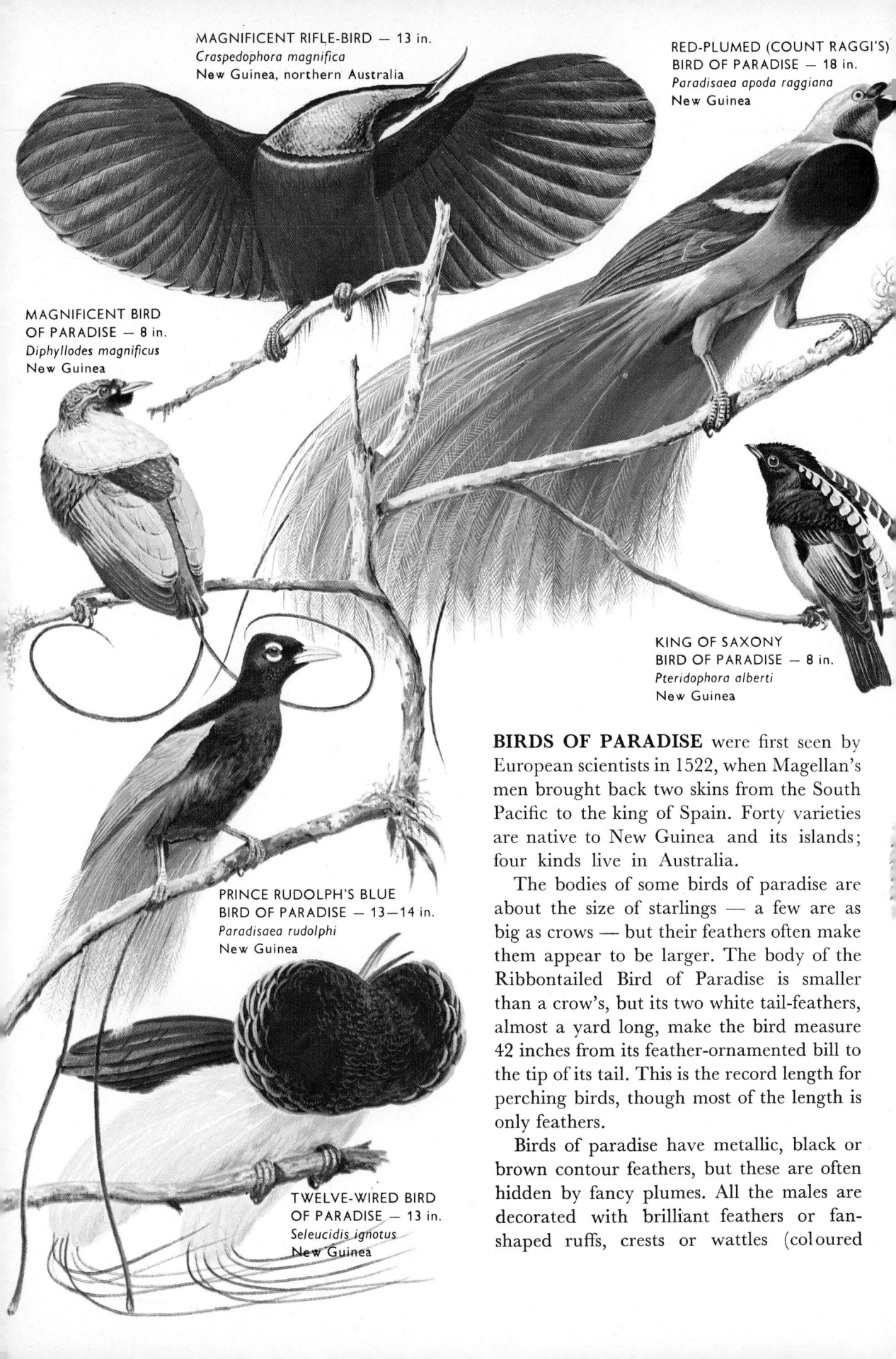

MAGNIFICENT RIFLE-BIRD — 13 in.
Craspedophora magnifica
New Guinea, northern Australia

**RED-PLUMED (COUNT RAGGI'S)
BIRD OF PARADISE — 18 in.**
Paradisaea apoda raggiana
New Guinea

**MAGNIFICENT BIRD
OF PARADISE — 8 in.**
Diphyllodes magnificus
New Guinea

**KING OF SAXONY
BIRD OF PARADISE — 8 in.**
Pteridophora alberti
New Guinea

**PRINCE RUDOLPH'S BLUE
BIRD OF PARADISE — 13—14 in.**
Paradisaea rudolphi
New Guinea

**TWELVE-WIRED BIRD
OF PARADISE — 13 in.**
Seleucidis ignotus
New Guinea

BIRDS OF PARADISE were first seen by European scientists in 1522, when Magellan's men brought back two skins from the South Pacific to the king of Spain. Forty varieties are native to New Guinea and its islands; four kinds live in Australia.

The bodies of some birds of paradise are about the size of starlings — a few are as big as crows — but their feathers often make them appear to be larger. The body of the Ribbontailed Bird of Paradise is smaller than a crow's, but its two white tail-feathers, almost a yard long, make the bird measure 42 inches from its feather-ornamented bill to the tip of its tail. This is the record length for perching birds, though most of the length is only feathers.

Birds of paradise have metallic, black or brown contour feathers, but these are often hidden by fancy plumes. All the males are decorated with brilliant feathers or fan-shaped ruffs, crests or wattles (coloured

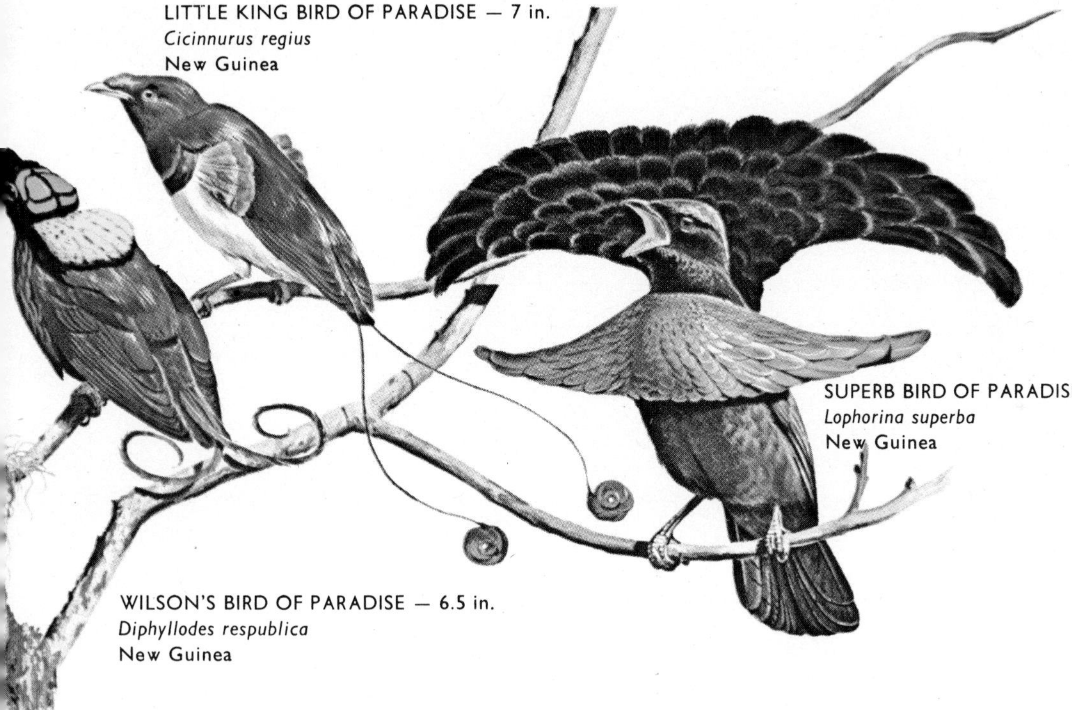

LITTLE KING BIRD OF PARADISE — 7 in.
Cicinnurus regius
New Guinea

SUPERB BIRD OF PARADISE — 9.5 in.
Lophorina superba
New Guinea

WILSON'S BIRD OF PARADISE — 6.5 in.
Diphyllodes respublica
New Guinea

skin), or tails of such bright hair-like feathers that they resemble a fountain when displayed. Females, quiet and retiring, are no gayer than ordinary perching birds; but the males show off — noisily. Some are acrobats in the air and on their perches; some dance in the trees and on the ground.

No wonder the islanders called these the "birds of the gods". No wonder local head-hunters decorated themselves with their feathers, and women all over the world did the same until laws protected the birds.

The Little King Bird of Paradise has jewel-tipped, wiry tail-plumes, blue skin on its legs, and green, red and yellow feathers over its head and back.

The Blue Bird of Paradise is a trapeze-artist. He hangs upside-down by his toes, and his gold-tipped, blue plumes shower around him like a fine-spread fan of colour.

The King Bird of Paradise is a dancer. Perched on a branch, he opens two emerald-tipped buff fans on either side of his white-plumed breast. He throws his long, wiry, green-tipped tail-plumes above his head, puffs out his green collar and his scarlet throat, and calls noisily to attract an audi-

ence. Then he sways himself and his tail ornaments to and fro and waves his fans in time to his loud and unmelodious song.

BISON *(Bison bison)*, also called Buffaloes (see BUFFALO), once roamed North America from the Atlantic Ocean to the Rocky Mountains in vast herds — an estimated total of 60 million animals. They were most abundant on the western plains of North America, where they were essential to the Indians' way of life, providing food, clothing, shelter and fuel. By 1885, nearly all the Bison had been wastefully slaughtered. Many

Disguised as animals, these Indian hunters are approaching bison that would otherwise flee.
American Museum of Natural History

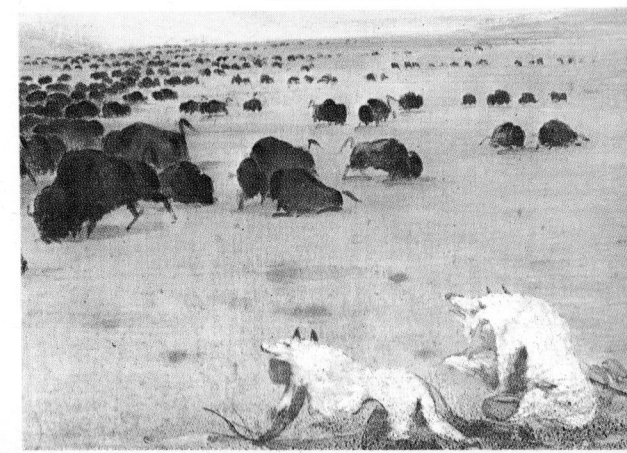

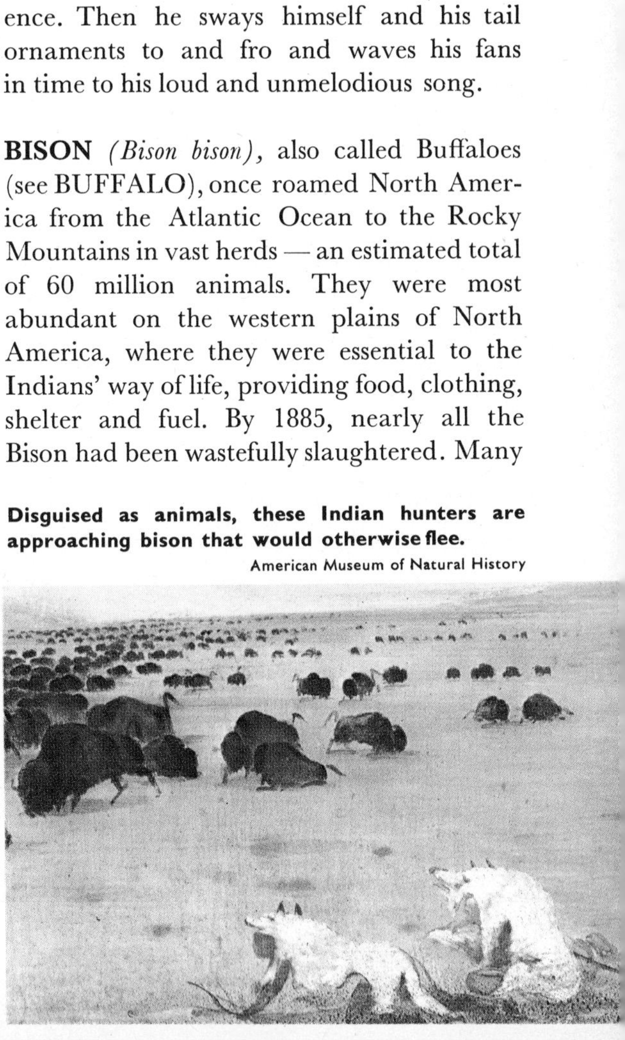

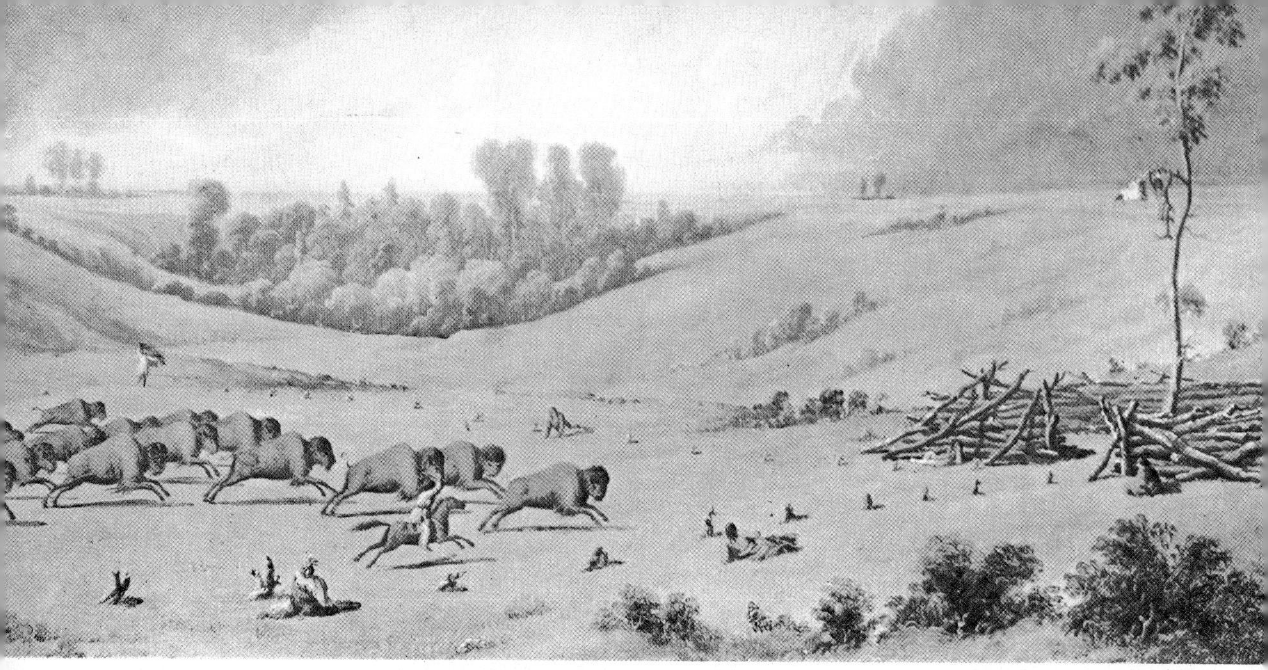

Royal Ontario Museum (Canada)

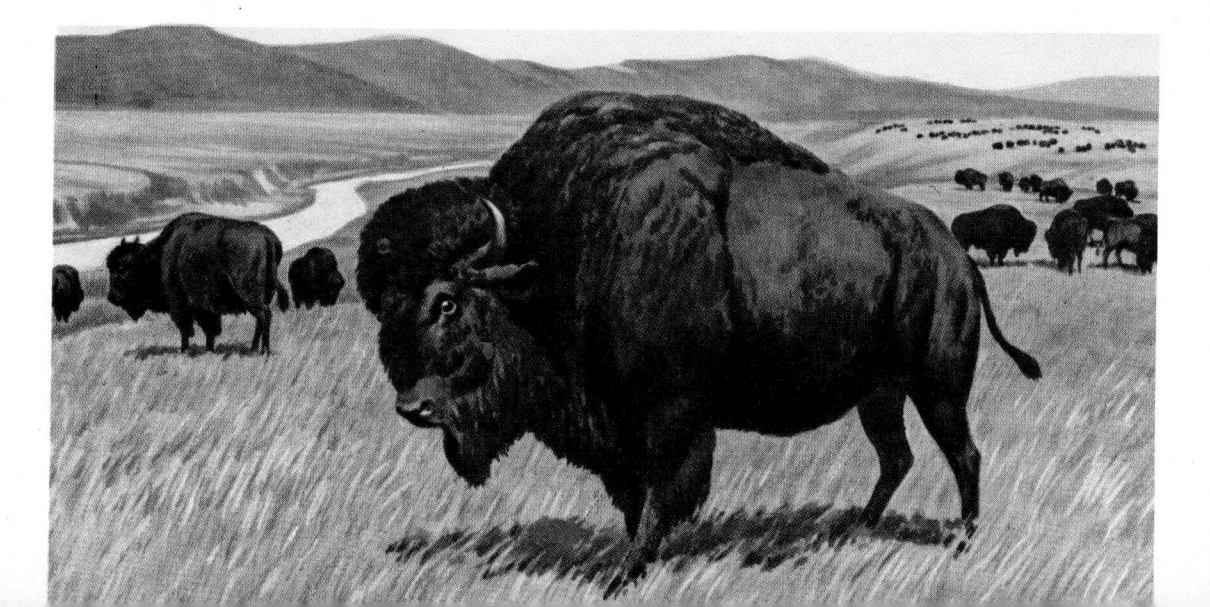

American Indians built corrals into which bison (buffalo) were driven for easy slaughter.

were killed entirely for sport, or purely to obtain their tongues and a few choice cuts as delicacies for the table. From the few survivors, which were protected on reservations, substantial numbers have developed again. These massive mammals have large, shaggy heads and curved horns. A bull American Bison may weigh more than a ton and stand six feet high at its humped and woolly shoulder.

Wisent, or European Bison *(Bison bonasus)*, slightly larger than the American Bison but with a smaller mane, were exterminated as wild animals in the middle 1920s. About

American Bison herds were once seemingly endless on the western plains of the United States, but over a period of about 50 years they were virtually exterminated as a wild species. Today, herds are on government lands, and their population is controlled. The prairies that once fed the American Bison have since become grain fields or extensive range country for beef cattle.

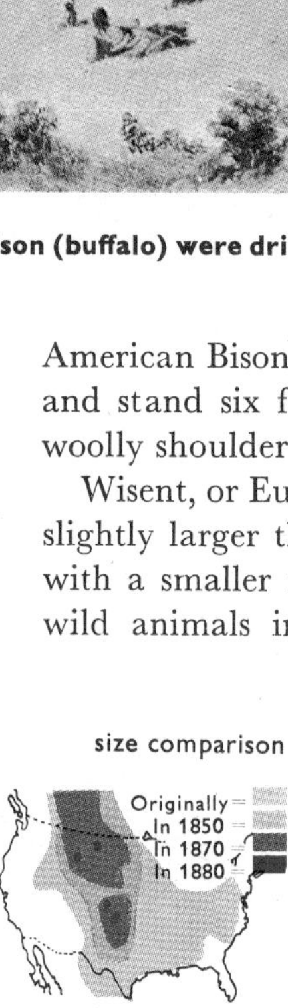
Originally
In 1850
In 1870
In 1880

size comparison

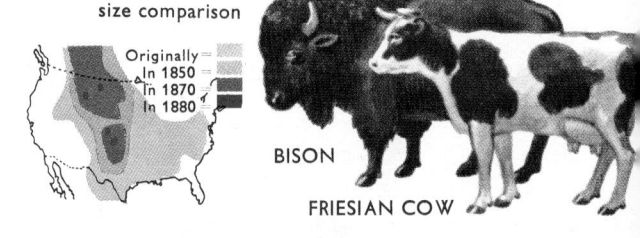

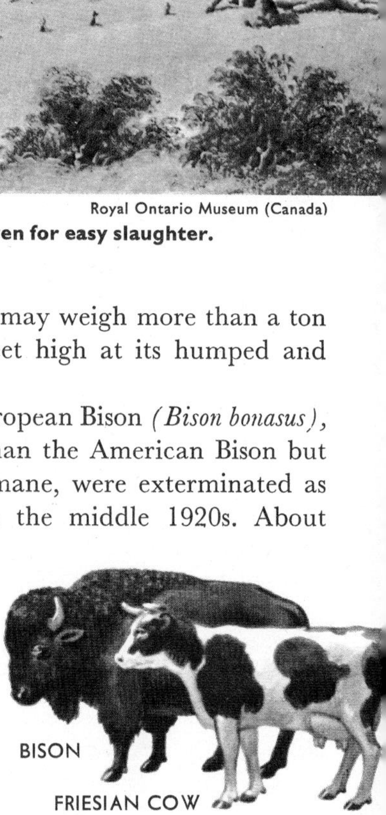
BISON
FRIESIAN COW

45, mostly from Lithuania, were preserved in zoos, and from these there are now more than a hundred of this vanishing species, all of the northern race. Like the American Bison, the Wisent can be bred with cattle.

BITTERNS, members of the heron family, are of world-wide distribution in temperate zones. Marsh birds, they stay in the reeds and flags of the swamps, both on their breeding and their wintering grounds.

When alarmed, bitterns stand absolutely still, their necks extended and bills pointing straight up. Turned so that their brown-striped throats face the danger, they blend perfectly with the background of marsh grass or cat's-tails. They seem to believe themselves invisible — and to most eyes they are. They look like another clump of brown, dried-up reeds.

Bitterns have powderdown feathers that are used to clean their necks and heads of the slime and the oil of their favourite food — eels. Bitterns rub their heads in the powderdown until they look as though they are covered with flour. Later they scratch off the powder, and the slime with it. Then they dress their feathers with oil from their preen gland, located in the back, just in front of the base of their tailfeathers.

Bitterns make a rough platform nest of dried reeds, straw and brush. Often this rests on the broken stems and stubs of old swamp-grass near open water. The nest is always built up, sometimes as much as 18 inches above the water level, to keep the four or five eggs dry. Bitterns nest alone.

The Common Bittern of Europe is rarely seen, skulking in reed-beds, but many people know its call. When breeding, it calls with a soft booming — a sound like someone blowing across the mouth of a bottle — but loud enough to carry a mile or more on a calm day. This bird is golden-brown with a black-barred pattern, while the American Bittern, shown here, is darker with a black

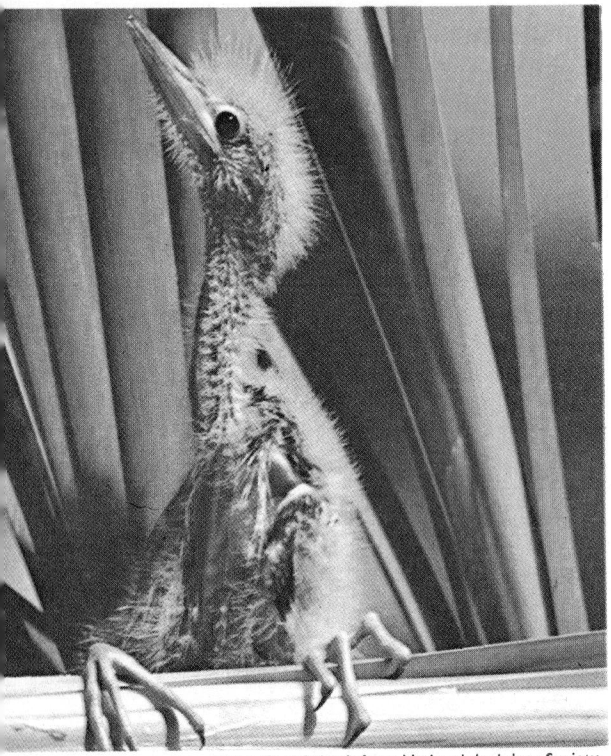

Helen Cruickshank from National Audubon Society

Least Bittern, still in down feathers, assumes the "freeze" position that adults use in hiding in reeds.

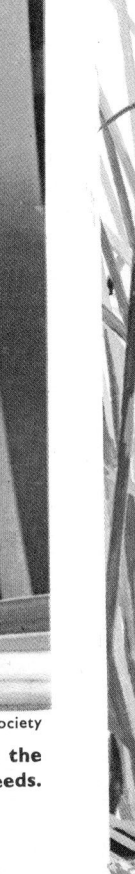

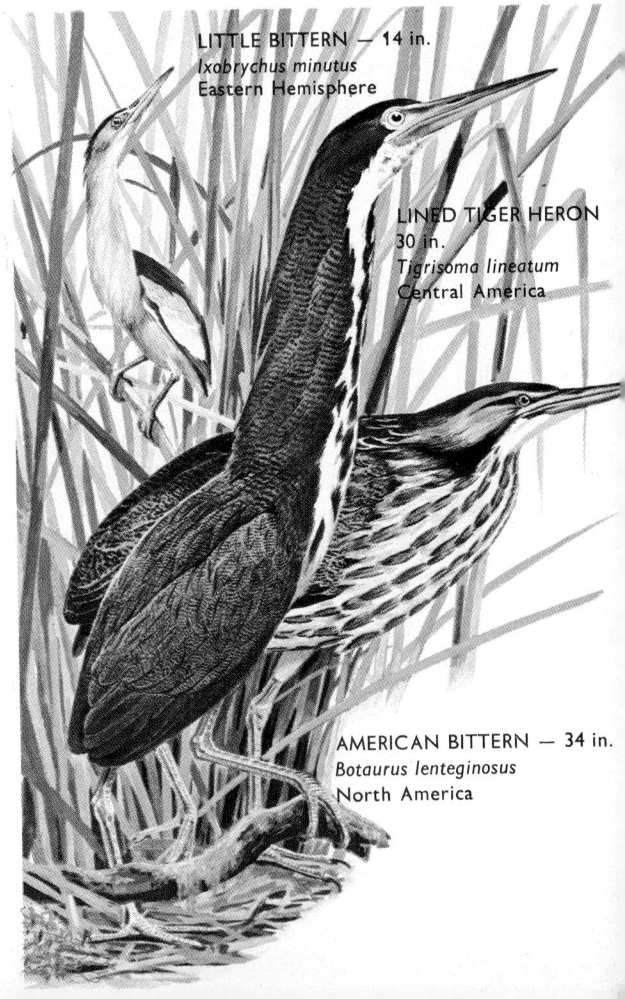

LITTLE BITTERN — 14 in.
Ixobrychus minutus
Eastern Hemisphere

LINED TIGER HERON
30 in.
Tigrisoma lineatum
Central America

AMERICAN BITTERN — 34 in.
Botaurus lentiginosus
North America

cheek-patch. Its call is a far-carrying thumping sound, like a wooden mallet driving a stake into the ground.

Least Bitterns silently climb from reed to reed, not touching the ground. Shy birds, they migrate at night. Their call is soft and somewhat like a cuckoo's. Least Bitterns nest from southern Canada into Central America.

BIVALVES, or Pelecypods, are molluscs with two valves, or shells, united at the hinge by a horny strap and interlocking teeth. Members of the large group occur in all seas and from inter-tidal zones to great depths. Many species — about 20 per cent of the total — live in fresh water. Powerful muscles open and close the two halves of the shells, which enclose the soft parts of the animals. When danger threatens, the shells are pulled tightly together. When the shells gape open, water is drawn into the gills through slits in the mantle or through siphons. The shell, built of layers of lime obtained from the water and from food, is secreted by the fleshy mantle. Oxygen, for respiration, and also food are taken from water circulated through the gills. The gills are primarily food-strainers; however, most

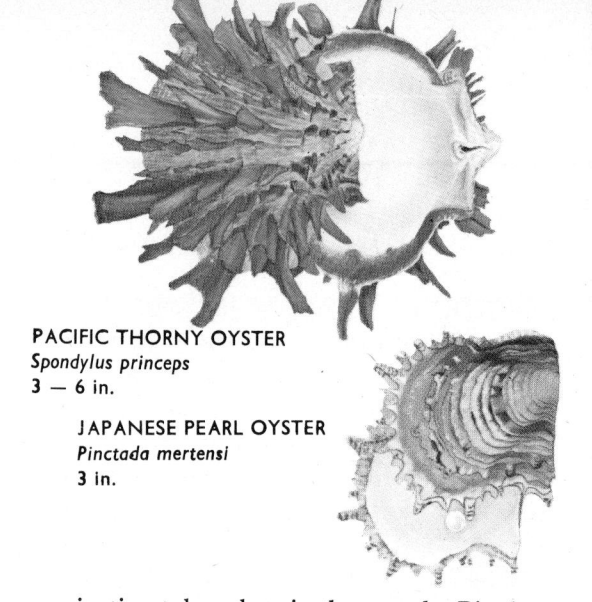

PACIFIC THORNY OYSTER
Spondylus princeps
3 — 6 in.

JAPANESE PEARL OYSTER
Pinctada mertensi
3 in.

respiration takes place in the mantle. Bivalves have no heads. They are sometimes referred to as the "acephala" (or "headless") animals.

Some bivalves swim by alternately opening and closing their valves. Others live in mud or sand, pulling themselves about by contractions of the foot. Still others bore into wood and rock, and may even attach themselves to hard objects by "cementing" one of their shells to the surface, or by anchoring themselves by horny threads.

Oysters are the source of an important fishery in many countries and have been cultivated or farmed in Europe since Roman times (see OYSTERS). Other bivalves are also important as food (see CLAMS; SCALLOPS); still others are destructive (see SHIPWORMS). Bivalves are the main source of pearls and mother-of-pearl. They range in size from a fraction of an inch to the Giant Clam, which may weigh 500 pounds.

The oldest fossil bivalves are found in rocks 450 million years old. Their shells dissolved during the process of fossilisation, however, and only moulds or casts of most early bivalves are known. Throughout most of the Paleozoic Era, bivalves continued to be widespread, but are rather unimportant fossils. The oldest fresh-water bivalves are found in Devonian rocks (350 million years old) from Ireland and New York. In rocks of Pennsylvanian age (250 million years old), freshwater bivalves are so distinctive that they have been used throughout Europe to

ANATOMY OF A BIVALVE

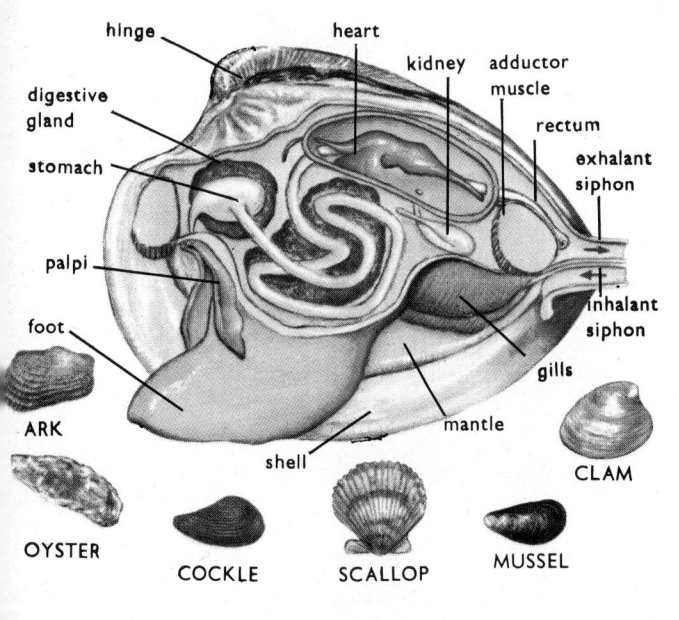

hinge
heart
digestive gland
kidney
adductor muscle
stomach
rectum
exhalant siphon
palpi
foot
inhalant siphon
gills
ARK
mantle
shell
CLAM
OYSTER
COCKLE
SCALLOP
MUSSEL

identify the coal-bearing strata of their age.

Pelecypods increased markedly in numbers and variety during the Mesozoic period. A few Paleozoic forms persisted, but many Mesozoic types were new. They remained abundant in Cenozoic times, and are today a common and widespread group of great commercial value.

BLACKBIRD is a common name for a number of species in which the male is all black. In Europe — and also in New Zealand, where it has been introduced — the Blackbird is a member of the Thrush family. The male is dull black with a golden bill, while the female is dark brown, more tawny on the breast, with a dull orange bill. The Blackbird is famous for its song, a slow lazy whistling phrase that is sufficiently low-pitched and melodious to sound like music to the human ear and to be easily imitated. The song phrases are varied and usually end on a slightly harsh note.

Originally, the Blackbird was a thrush frequenting thickets and the edge of woodland, feeding mainly on open turf or dead leaves under trees and bushes; but farmland, hedgerows, and suburban gardens with open lawns and scattered trees and shrubs, offered ideal conditions for the bird, and it has greatly increased in numbers. Although the Blackbird is a welcome visitor to most people, its fondness for ripe fruit makes it unpopular with some.

The Blackbird builds a bulky cup-nest of dried stems and leaves lined with mud, and then adds an inner lining of finer grasses. In this the four or five brown-speckled blue eggs are laid. At most seasons the soft clucking note of alarm, accompanied by flirting of the wings and tail, is a common sound; when the young emerge, however, the loud chinking alarm-call is a much more frequent sound from the anxious parents. Several broods are produced each year. Nests are often built in sheds or on the ledges of buildings, as well as in more usual places, such as bushes and trees.

In the northern part of the area it ranges,

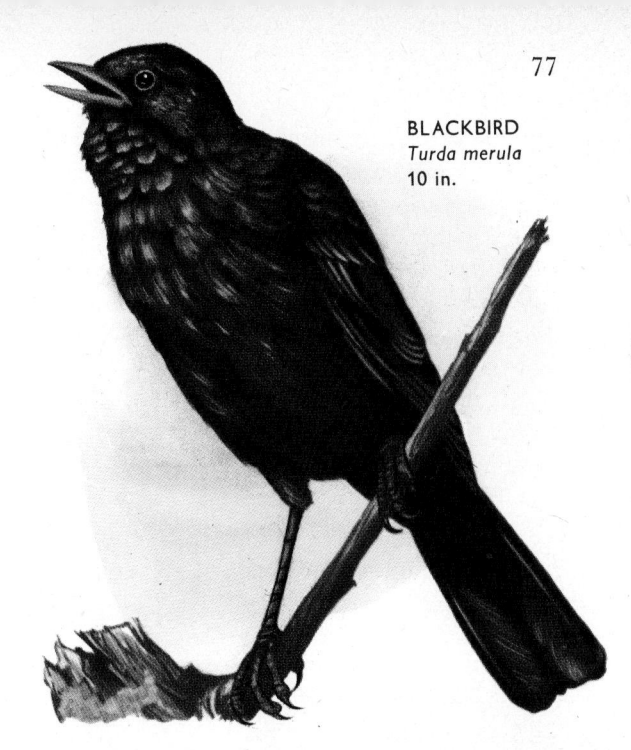

BLACKBIRD
Turda merula
10 in.

Scandinavia, the Blackbird is a summer visitor, but further south the bird is a resident, and may rely on man for some of its winter food.

In America, the name Blackbird is given to a group of species belonging to the Troupial family. These are glossy, starling-like birds, mostly nesting in reedbeds and swamps; again, the male is black and the female brown, but in some species the male has patches of vivid scarlet on the wings, while yet another has a yellow head and breast. These birds lack the song of the European Blackbird and have, instead, squeaky whistles and gurgling calls.

BLACK WIDOW SPIDERS (*Latrodectus mactans*) are probably the most notorious of all spiders. Most of their bad reputation is undeserved, however. Black Widows, like most spiders, are timid and will not bite unless molested. Even when its web is disturbed, a Black Widow tries to hide, rather than coming out to attack. These

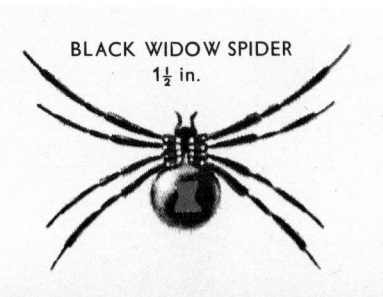

BLACK WIDOW SPIDER
1½ in.

spiders are widely distributed in the United States, but are most common in the southern and western States.

The name Black Widow comes from the belief that the female always eats the male after mating. In fact, she does this only if she is hungry. Other female spiders eat their mates, too, and in rare cases the males eat the females.

Black Widow females have a red hourglass-shaped mark on the underside of their abdomen. Males, less than half the size of females, do not have red hourglass marks. Most people bitten by females become ill, but fatalities are rare. (See SPIDERS.)

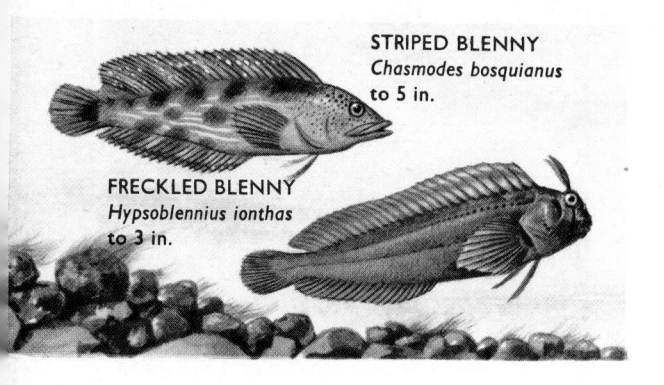

STRIPED BLENNY
Chasmodes bosquianus
to 5 in.

FRECKLED BLENNY
Hypsoblennius ionthas
to 3 in.

BLENNIES are a group of small fishes which range from arctic to tropical waters. Several species live in streams in Europe.

Of the Blennies living in cold waters, the Gunnel, or Butterfish *(Pholis gunnellus)*, is the largest. It occurs on both sides of the North Atlantic and reaches a length of 6-12 inches. In the breeding season, the female deposits a batch of eggs, which she rolls into a ball about $\frac{1}{2}$ inch in diameter. The male and the female then take turns to guard the eggs until they hatch.

Most Blennies live in shallow water. They are very agile and difficult to catch, and can use their fins much like legs, propping themselves up to view their surroundings. Some come right out of the water, or else leap from pool to pool when the tide is out.

Blennies of the tropics are brightly coloured, and often have long anal and dorsal fins. The related Scaled Blennies, or Klip-

fishes (family *Clinidae*), are found mainly in the Southern hemisphere. Most of them bear their young alive.

The Viviparous Blenny, or Eelpout *(Zoarces viviparus)*, is a coastal species, widely distributed in Northern Europe. It has long been known to scientists and was first described in 1624. Unlike the majority of fishes, the female Eelpout has a single roe, or ovary (two in most fishes). The eggs are fertilised internally, and there the eggs develop and hatch. The young are born after about four months, and an 8-inch female may give birth to about forty young.

BLIND SNAKES are slender, cylindrical burrowing snakes that do not have distinct necks. Members of two primitive families — the *(Leptotyplopidae)* (more commonly called Thread Snakes), and *Typhlopidae* — comprise the group, which occurs in the warmer parts of the world, except Australia, Europe and Madagascar. Their very smooth round body scales are uniform in shape, instead of those on the belly being larger, as characterises most snakes. In most blind snakes, the head scales are large and fit tightly to the skull. As their minute eyes are buried under the skin, these snakes see very poorly or are totally blind. Their short tail ends abruptly, often with a tiny conical or flattened spine, which has given rise to the belief that these snakes carry a sting in their tails. The Thread Snakes bear vestiges of hind limbs and only the lower jaw is toothed, whereas the other members of the group have teeth in the upper jaw and no trace of limbs.

Blind snakes dig earthworm-like burrows in loose soil just beneath the surface.

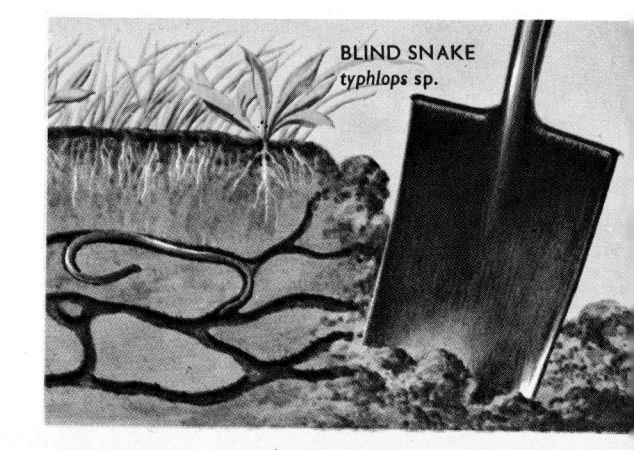

BLIND SNAKE
typhlops sp.

One species gives birth to its young, but all others lay eggs. Adults vary in length from 4 to 30 inches.

All blind snakes are subterranean burrowers. Sometimes they crawl about on the surface after dark. Their cylindrical body shape, tail spine, smooth body and buried eyes are useful adaptations for burrowing. Termites and ants are their chief food, and, since they swallow only small insects, the bones in their skull and jaws are not independently movable, as are the same bones in snakes that swallow bulky prey. Sometimes only the soft abdomen is swallowed, and later the emptied "shell" is then spat out.

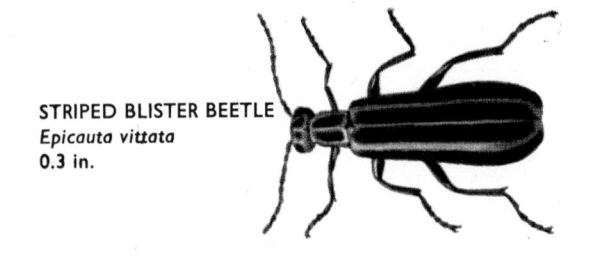

STRIPED BLISTER BEETLE
Epicauta vittata
0.3 in.

BLISTER BEETLES *(Meloidae)* are round-bodied and of medium size, with soft, flexible outer wings. Some species secrete a substance (cantharidin) which causes blistering when it contacts human skin. Some kinds, such as the Striped Blister Beetle, are pests of potatoes and other crops.

Blister beetles have a complex development in which there are several larval stages that differ from each other in appearance. The tiny larvae that hatch from the eggs have legs, and crawl about rapidly. These larvae feed on the eggs of grasshoppers or those of bees. Sometimes the larvae that feed on bees' eggs will attach themselves to a bee and ride to the nest. These larvae moult several times, eventually becoming sluggish, legless and worm-like. Finally they pupate and transform into adults.

BLUEFISH *(Pomatomus saltatrix)*, said to be the most bloodthirsty fish in the sea, are swift swimmers that travel in large schools. When they overtake schools of weakfishes or herrings, they literally "chop" their way

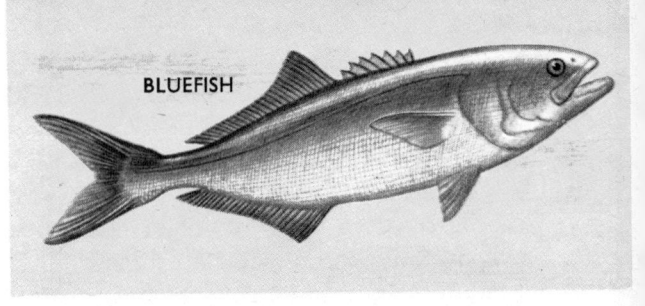

BLUEFISH

through, cutting the fish to pieces with their sharp teeth and churning the sea into a bloody froth. Bluefish are excellent sporting fish and are also good to eat. Small bluefish (1 to 3 pounds) are called "snappers". The average size for adults is about 5 pounds. Catches that weigh 15 to 20 pounds are exceptional, although Bluefish that weighed more than 30 pounds were reported in years gone by. Bluefish are found in the Atlantic from Nova Scotia to Brazil, but off the coast of Europe. They also live in the Mediterranean and the Indian Ocean.

BOAS form a family *(Boidae)* of large snakes that includes pythons as well as true boas (see PYTHONS). All are constrictors, living mostly on warm-blooded prey killed by suffocation. The snake wraps around its prey and squeezes until, by pressure on the ribs, the victim's breathing and heart action cease. This family contains giant constrictors that reach a reputed length of 37 feet or more; most of the species are in the 6-12 foot range, and a few never exceed $2\frac{1}{2}$ feet. A few records exist of large pythons having killed and swallowed adult human beings. Any boa over nine feet long is potentially dangerous to man.

Boas are typically snakes of the tropics, although the Rubber Boa *(Charina bottae)* extends barely to Canada in western North

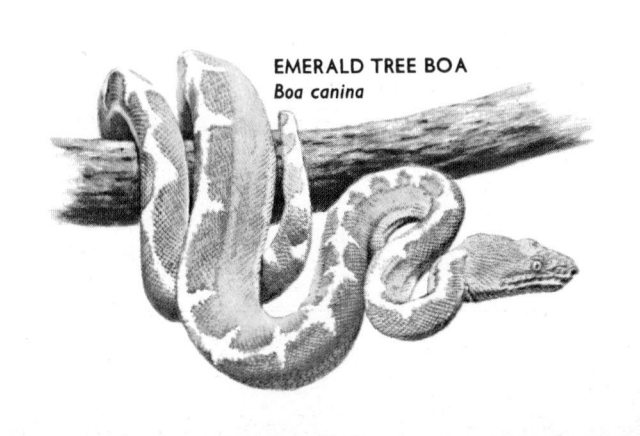

EMERALD TREE BOA
Boa canina

America. Most live in human areas, and those that inhabit semi-arid regions are most active in the rainy season. Most boas have small, useless hind limbs and bony girdles for the attachment of legs. These are often evident only as spurs and are better developed in males than in females. Their ventral scales are wide, but not as wide as in more highly evolved snakes. Their eyes have vertical pupils, an adaptation for activity at night or dusk, and their jawbones are long and stout, a development that helps in swallowing large prey. They can lift their snout when they bite, so that the upper jaw in effect is hinged not only at the lower jaw but also about its own middle. Most boas have small head scales, and the eye is always covered by a scale of its own size. Body scales are usually smooth. Contrary to Kipling's fanciful jungle tales, boas have tender and delicate snouts and are not able to use them as a battering ram.

Largely because of their size, boas are popular as pets because they are easy to feed and are docile. After a time in captivity, these snakes rarely bite. All have teeth, however, and their bites can be painful.

True boas of some 35 species occur in both hemispheres. All normally give birth to their young, but certain ones, like the Boa Constrictor *(Boa constrictor)*, occasionally lay eggs that hatch in a few days. The great, river-dwelling South American Giant Anaconda *(Eunectes murinus)* is the largest of the boas. Positive records are available for 25 feet; acceptable, but actually unverifiable, records exist for lengths up to 37 feet, and plausible reports go to 45 feet and more. Anacondas live in water, which favours their growing larger than land-dwelling snakes.

The Boa Constrictor, the species common in zoos, seldom exceeds 12 feet, but a reliable record of 18 feet exists. Caribbean boas *(Epicrates* spp.) of the West Indies, Central and South America, reach a length of 14 feet. Tree boas *(Boa* spp.) of Central and South America reach a length of eight feet, and include the beautiful Emerald Tree Boa that is very similar to the Green Tree Python of New Guinea. All other boas are small. These include: dwarf boas *(Ungaliophis* spp.) of Central America; two species of rosy boas *(Lichamura* spp.) in the South-western United States and adjacent

COOK'S TREE BOA
Boa cooki

Tree boas eat birds, eggs, small mammals and insects.

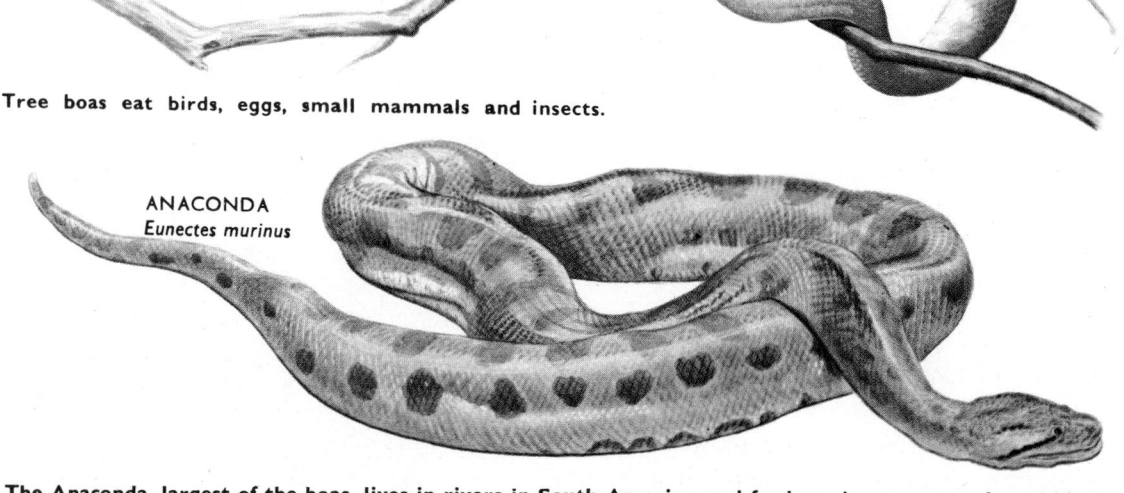

ANACONDA
Eunectes murinus

The Anaconda, largest of the boas, lives in rivers in South America, and feeds on large mammals and birds.

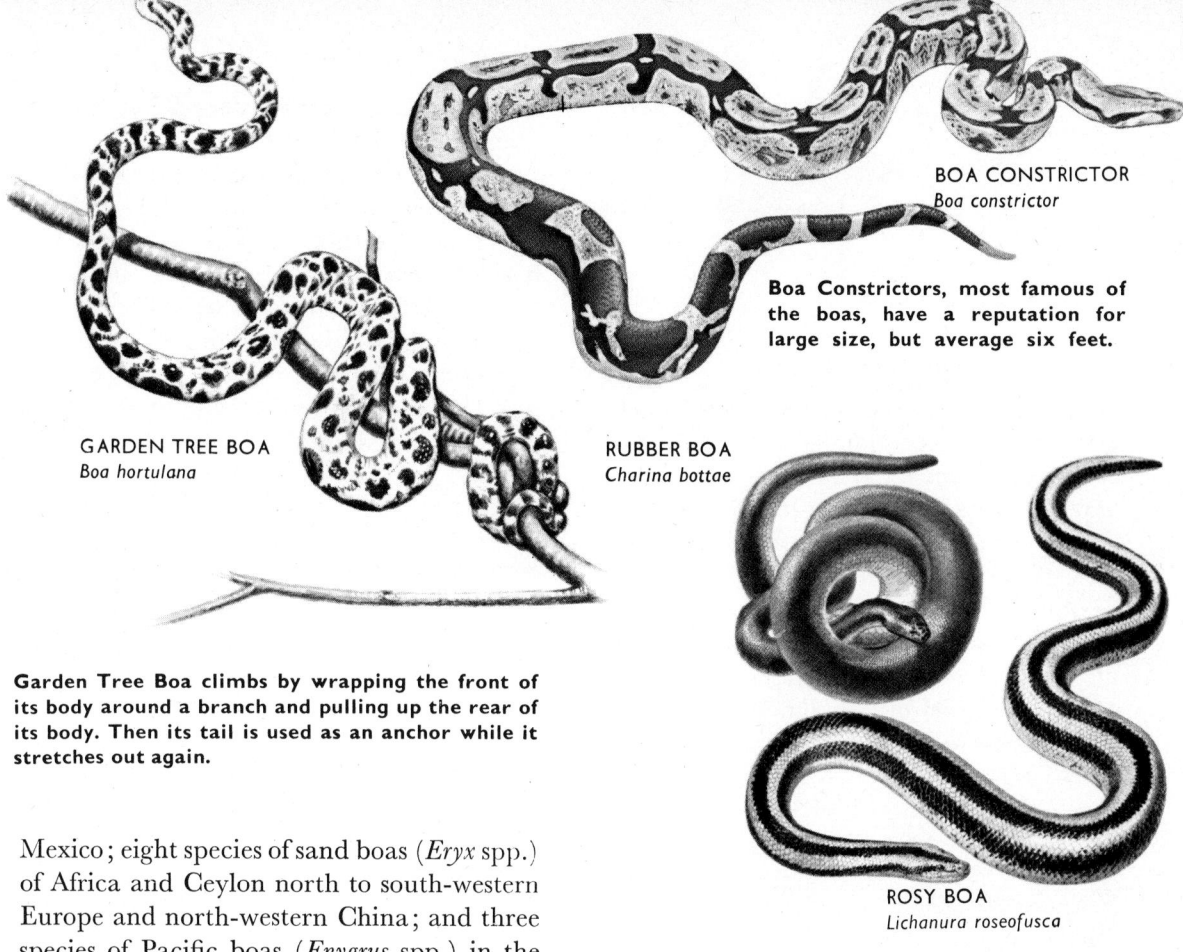

BOA CONSTRICTOR
Boa constrictor

Boa Constrictors, most famous of the boas, have a reputation for large size, but average six feet.

GARDEN TREE BOA
Boa hortulana

RUBBER BOA
Charina bottae

ROSY BOA
Lichanura roseofusca

Garden Tree Boa climbs by wrapping the front of its body around a branch and pulling up the rear of its body. Then its tail is used as an anchor while it stretches out again.

Mexico; eight species of sand boas (*Eryx* spp.) of Africa and Ceylon north to south-western Europe and north-western China; and three species of Pacific boas (*Enygrus* spp.) in the East Indies. Few are longer than three feet.

Pythons are similar to boas in appearance, but differ in skull structure, distribution and habits. They are egg-layers and live only in Africa, Asia, Australia; 21 known species.

Two boas *(Bolyeria* and *Casarea)* occur only on Round Island, close to Mauritius. These are the only boas that lack evidence of hind limbs and pelvic girdles, even internally. Furthermore, they are the only snakes in the world with the upper jawbone (maxilla) split in two parts.

Nine species of brown boas (*Tropidophis* spp.), smallest of all boas, occur in the West Indies and northern South America. Boas of the West Indies live on the ground; South American brown boas (*Trachyboa*) in trees.

BOLL WEEVILS (*Curculionidae*) are the most destructive of all insect pests that attack cotton. It has been estimated that, in America, it destroys the equivalent of 400,000 bales annually. The beetle entered the United States from Mexico about 1892. As adults, these small weevils eat leaves and buds of newly-sprouted cotton plants. The female deposits a single egg in a cavity eaten in a bud. Later in the season, eggs are also deposited in the bolls, or seed-pods. The larvae feed inside the bolls, and in about two weeks transform into pupae in the feeding cavity. A life cycle may be completed in two to four weeks. (See WEEVILS.)

adult

BOLL WEEVIL
Anthonomus grandis
0.3 in.

larva in boll

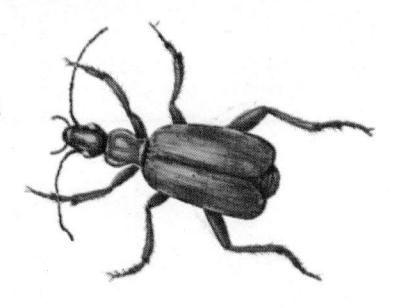

BOMBARDIER BEETLE
Brachinus sp.
0.25 in.

BOMBARDIER BEETLES are a group of ground beetles *(Carabidae)* that are unique in being able to eject a fine spray from the tips of their abdomens. The spray is visible, appearing as a small puff of smoke, and there is a slight "pop" when it is released. The tip of a bombardier beetle's abdomen is very flexible, so that the beetle can actually aim at its attacker. The beetle usually does not "fire" until touched or grabbed, and the sudden ejection of the liquid makes the attacker release its hold, freeding the beetle.

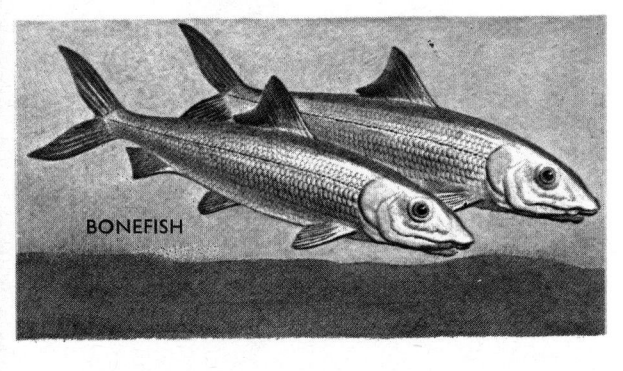

BONEFISH

BONEFISH *(Albula vulpes)*, sometimes known as Ladyfish, are slim, silvery fish found in warm seas throughout the world, but absent from the Eastern Atlantic. With their projecting snouts, they root in the sand and mud to get shellfish, shrimps and other animals for food. The lower jaw is "underslung", much like that of the anchovy.

Bonefish are popular with sport fishermen off the Bahamas. Most weigh less than

5 pounds, but a record fish of just over 18 pounds was caught in Hawaii.

The Bonefish is a primitive member of the great group of herring-like fishes. Another primitive member of this group is the Ten-pounder *(Elops saurus)*, a beautiful, silvery fish found in warm seas.

The larvae of the Bonefish and the Ten-pounder are quite unlike the adult. They are long and ribbon-like, and resemble the leptocephalus of the European Eel.

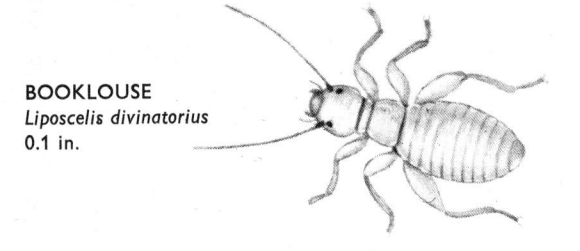

BOOKLOUSE
Liposcelis divinatorius
0.1 in.

BOOKLICE are tiny insects that feed on paper, glue, and other starchy substances. They are commonly found in rooms that have not been used for a long time and frequently damage books in libraries. Other kinds are pests in museums, grain mills and warehouses. Still other members of this order *(Psocoptera)* live under bark, in leaf litter, or in the nests of animals.

BOOMSLANGS, or Bushsnakes *(Dispholidus typus)*, of South Africa are one of the few deadly poisonous snakes that have fangs in the rear of the mouth. Their venom acts primarily on the blood and blood vessels, breaking down cells so that victims die from lack of oxygen. Bushsnakes have caused at least half a dozen deaths, among them that of the world-famous herpetologist Karl P. Schmidt. They are about three feet long,

TEN-POUNDER

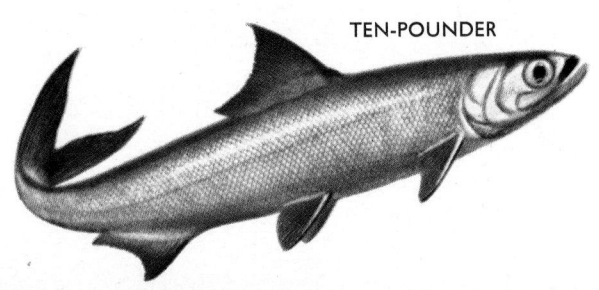

BOOMSLANG

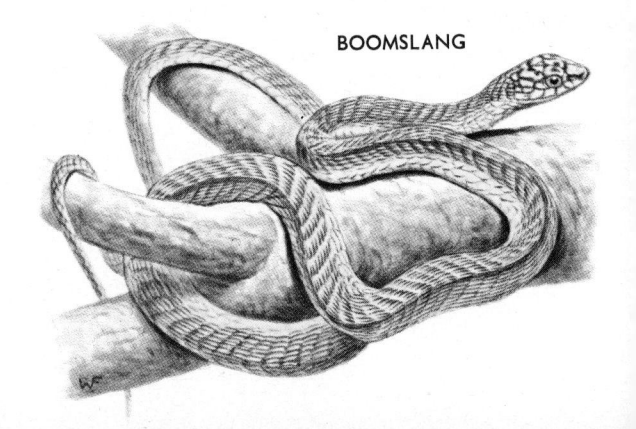

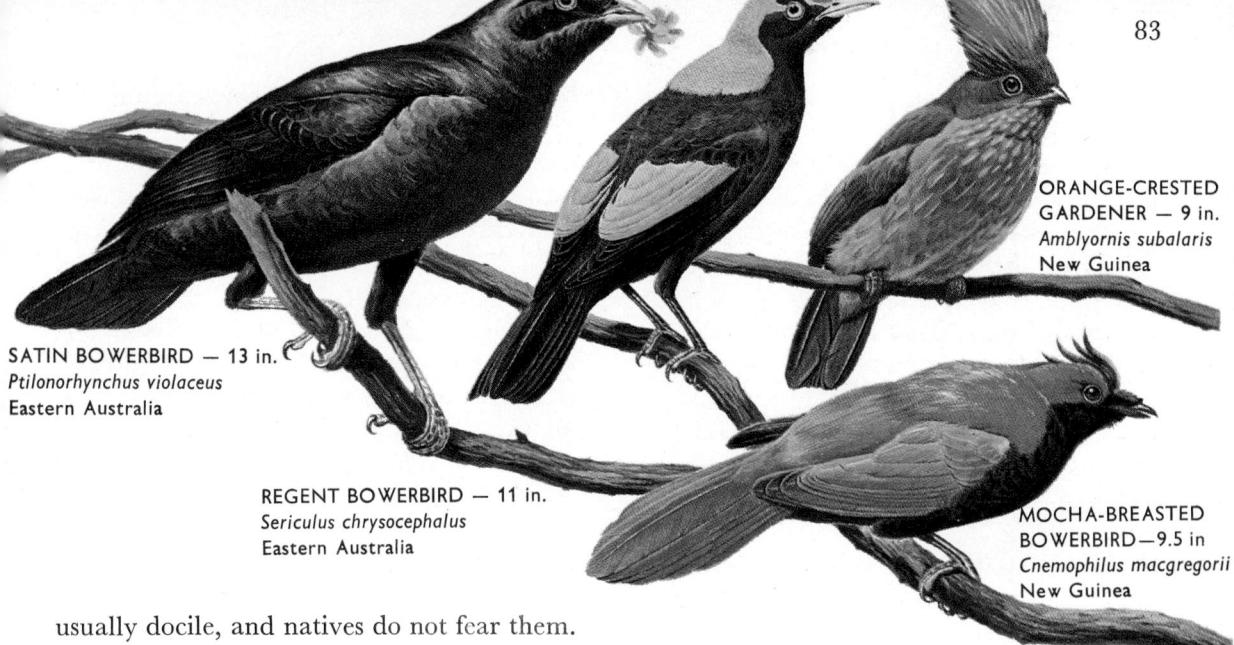

ORANGE-CRESTED
GARDENER — 9 in.
Amblyornis subalaris
New Guinea

SATIN BOWERBIRD — 13 in.
Ptilonorhynchus violaceus
Eastern Australia

REGENT BOWERBIRD — 11 in.
Sericulus chrysocephalus
Eastern Australia

MOCHA-BREASTED
BOWERBIRD—9.5 in
Cnemophilus macgregorii
New Guinea

usually docile, and natives do not fear them. They are rapid climbers and subsist on a diet of frogs, lizards, birds and mice.

BOWER-BIRDS, less gaudy relatives of birds of paradise, live in New Guinea and Australia. The males build strange display structures which they decorate with many bright, conspicuous objects — flowers, broken china and glass, shells, and bits of moss. These are called "bowers", and in them the males dance to attract a mate. Some bowers are elaborately woven, and are so beautifully made that the first explorers who saw them thought they were the playhouses of native children. Male bower-birds do not help the female in incubating the eggs or in the care of the young.

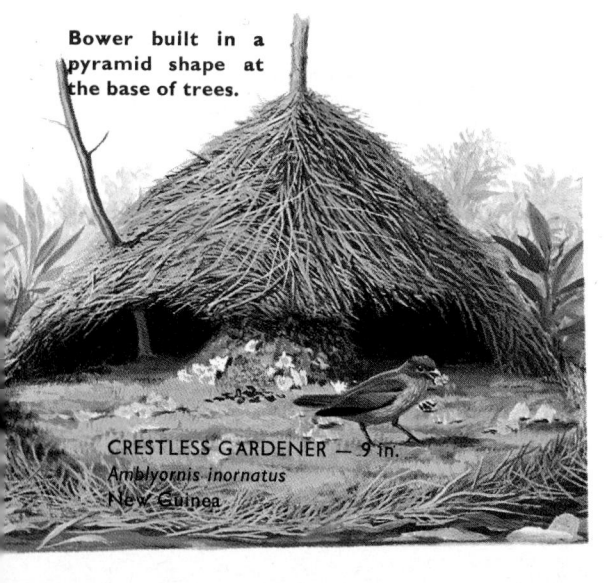

Bower built in a pyramid shape at the base of trees.

CRESTLESS GARDENER — 9 in.
Amblyornis inornatus
New Guinea

BOWFINS (*Amia calva*) are primitive freshwater fish, the only living representatives of a group once much more common. Sometimes they are referred to as "living fossils".

Bowfins — also called Dogfish, Mudfish and Grindle — live in lakes and ponds in the southern and mid-western United States. They are thick-bodied and olive to greenish in colour. Males have on each side, immediately in front of their tail, a large black spot ringed with bright orange or yellow. Fins of the males turn green during the mating season.

Male bowfins build nests by chewing off plants and fanning away the debris to clear a circular place in the mud. Several females

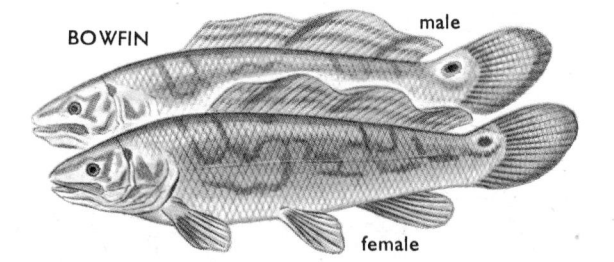

BOWFIN

male

female

may lay their eggs in this nest. Then the male fertilises the eggs and guards them, driving away intruders. After the eggs hatch, the young fish stay in a tight school, and the male continues to watch over them until they are three or four inches long. Often his

brood may consist of a thousand young.

Bowfins can breathe air through their mouths; often they rise to the top of the water and take in gulps. They have numerous blood vessels in their airbladders which serve as "lungs".

Bowfins sometimes weigh more than 15 pounds and may be three feet long, but most of them are less than half this size.

BOX TURTLES (*Terrapene* spp.) are North American land dwellers that can completely close their shells by means of a hinge in the lower surface. Box turtles usually hibernate by burrowing into the soil below the frost line. The turtles mate early in the spring, and the female lays four or five eggs in a cavity dug in loose soil. The young hatch in the autumn, or may overwinter in the egg and hatch the following spring.

Box turtles eat insects, carrion, succulent vegetation — whatever is most available when they are hungry. At times they feed on toadstools and mushrooms, and they are not susceptible to their poisons. The poisons from these fungi are stored, at least for a time, in their flesh, however, and will poison man or any other predator that eats the turtle.

BREAM. As is often the case, the common name is applied to two quite different groups of fishes — one freshwater, and the other marine. Freshwater bream are members of the great carp family *(Cyprinidae)*. The Silver Bream, sometimes called White

Bream, is a deep-bodied species found in Europe north of the Pyrenees and Alps, and extending eastwards into Siberia. In England, it is found in east-coast streams from Yorkshire to Suffolk, occurring only in slow-running rivers or lakes. It attains a weight of about $1\frac{1}{4}$ lbs.

The Common Bream (or Carp Bream, or Bronze Bream) resembles the Silver Bream, but has more branched rays in the anal fin — 23-29, as against 19-24. This fish is common in Ireland, and in England is found mainly in the south-east, including the Thames. It is much favoured by anglers.

The Common Bream and the White Bream are known to form a hybrid, and both species will hybridise with the Roach and the Rudd. The hybrid Bream-Rudd is well known to fishermen of Lough Erne, who call it the "White Roach".

Sea Breams, or Porgies, (family *Sparidae*), are deep-bodied fishes, with a single dorsal fin consisting of both a spiny and a soft-rayed portion. They usually have powerful canine or incisor teeth in the jaws, and they may also have strong molar (or grinding) teeth. There are about a hundred species, mostly in tropical and temperate seas, but some have become adapted to very cold water, and a few venture into fresh.

Included in this family are the Mussel-crackers, which prey on various kinds of shellfish, including oysters. One species, the South African *Cymatoceps nasutus*, is the largest of all the sparid fishes, reaching a weight of 100 pounds.

Around the coasts of Britain several species of Sea Bream are landed by fishermen, but the most commonly caught is the Common Sea Bream *(Pagellus centrodontus)*. It is caught in deep water in the Atlantic, but appears to enter the Channel and North Sea during the summer, occasionally wandering as far north as Norway. The Spanish Bream *(Sparus bogaroveo)* is another Mediterranean species which is sometimes caught off British coasts.

In Australia, one of the most important commercial fishes is the Sea Bream *(Chrys-*

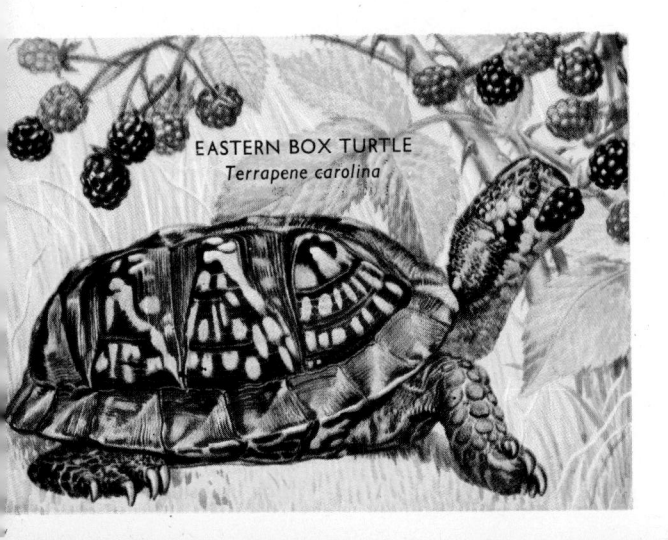

EASTERN BOX TURTLE
Terrapene carolina

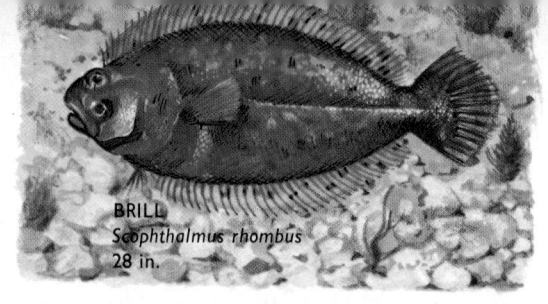

BRILL
Scophthalmus rhombus
28 in.

ophrys guttalatus), and a closely related spe-cies is caught in great numbers in the seas off Japan.

BRILL *(Rhombus laevis)* is a flatfish closely related to the Turbot, but whereas the latter grows to about 3 feet the Brill is a smaller species and rarely exceeds 2 feet. The Brill also has small, smooth scales, whereas the Turbot is scaleless.

The Brill is common all round the British Isles, where it favours medium depths of up to 30 or 40 fathoms on a muddy or sandy bottom. Like the Turbot, it lives chiefly on other fish.

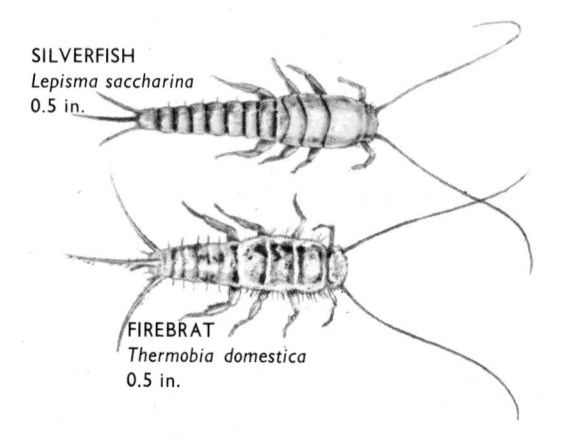

SILVERFISH
Lepisma saccharina
0.5 in.

FIREBRAT
Thermobia domestica
0.5 in.

BRISTLETAILS are small to medium-sized wingless insects with three bristle-like appendages at the end of their abdomen. Most kinds are found in damp places, such as under bark and stones, in leaf-mould, or similar habitats. Bristletails have chewing mouth-parts, and most of them feed on decaying plant material. The order *Thysa-nura*, to which they belong, includes the most primitive of all insects.

Two species — the Silverfish and the Firebrat — are common in dwellings and at times become serious pests. They feed on bookbindings, wallpaper paste, clothing or other starchy substances. Silverfish are generally found in damp locations, as in basements. The brownish or mottled Fire-brat lives in warm, dry places — around stoves or furnaces, for example. Both are about half an inch long, and their bodies are covered with small scales. They are quite active.

BRITTLE (SERPENT) STARS are active, slender-armed echinoderms belonging to the class *Ophiuroidea* (see ECHINODERMS). All their essential organs are contained in the small, circular bodies. In contrast, the vital organs of a starfish occur also in its thick arms. Many of these animals can drop off their arms if disturbed, later growing new ones — hence the name brittle star. Because they crawl about in a snake-like manner, they are also called serpent stars.

Brittle stars use their long, agile arms in crawling; one arm always trails behind. Some can even swim to a minor degree. Some live among rocks and seaweeds, where they are very difficult to see. Others lives beneath rocks, coming out only at night to feed on clams, shrimps and other small animals. Most brittle stars do not have common names and are known only by their scientific name. One of the largest of this type in eastern waters is *Ophiomyxa*

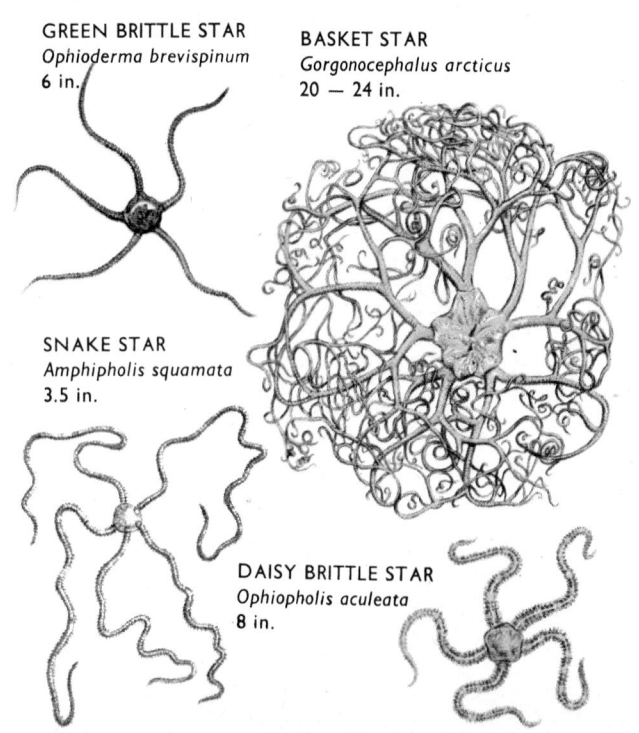

GREEN BRITTLE STAR
Ophioderma brevispinum
6 in.

BASKET STAR
Gorgonocephalus arcticus
20 — 24 in.

SNAKE STAR
Amphipholis squamata
3.5 in.

DAISY BRITTLE STAR
Ophiopholis aculeata
8 in.

flaccida, often rather brightly coloured. A large, active West Indian species *(Ophiocoma echinata)* has numerous large spines on the sides of its arms. Snake-skinned brittle stars *(Ophioderma),* many of them beautifully coloured, occur on both the Atlantic and Pacific coasts, the Pacific species attaining a span of seven inches.

Mud brittle stars, one of the commonest animals in muddy bottoms, may burrow several inches into the bottom with only the tips of their arms visible above the surface. Many are very fragile. An Atlantic species *(Amphioplus coniortoides)* becomes so numerous in places that their arms overlap.

Arms of basket stars, a type of brittle star, are branched repeatedly. *Astrophyton muricatum,* a basket star of the West Indies and Florida, may have over 8,000 tips. This species, like *Gorgonocephalus caryi* of the Pacific, clings to seaweeds, rocks or horny corals on the bottom, and feeds on large planktonic animals that become trapped in the network of their arms. In the West Indies, sometimes three or four basket stars are found on a single Sea Whip.

BROCKETS *(Mazama* spp.) and Pudus *(Pudu pudu)* are the smallest of all deer. They live in South and Central America.

Some brockets measure less than 19 inches in height at the shoulders when full grown. Pudus, which live in Chile, are only 13 inches high at the shoulders and weigh less than 25 pounds. Some are reddish in colour; others are dark brown. They never seem to live far from water and swim well. Both Brockets and Pudus have spike-like antlers. Their small size and short antlers aid them in slipping through jungles. Though active early and late in the day, they are shy and rarely seen. (See DEER.)

BROWN-TAIL MOTHS belong to the same family *(Lymantriidae)* as the Gypsy Moth. They were introduced to the United States from Europe. The caterpillars feed on a variety of trees and shrubs, such as apples, oaks and cherries, but not on evergreens. The caterpillars spend the winter in nests made of several leaves tied to twigs with silk. As many as 500 tiny caterpillars may occupy one nest. As soon as the buds open in the spring, the caterpillars begin eating the new leaves. Full-grown caterpillars are about $1\frac{1}{2}$ inches long. Adults emerge from the pupae in about two weeks, and as soon as they mate, females lay clusters of 200 to 400 eggs on the underside of leaves. The eggs hatch during late summer.

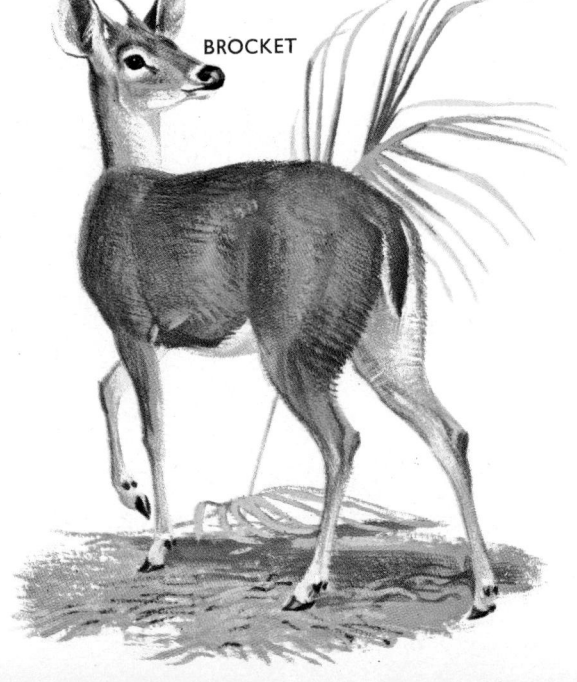

BROCKET

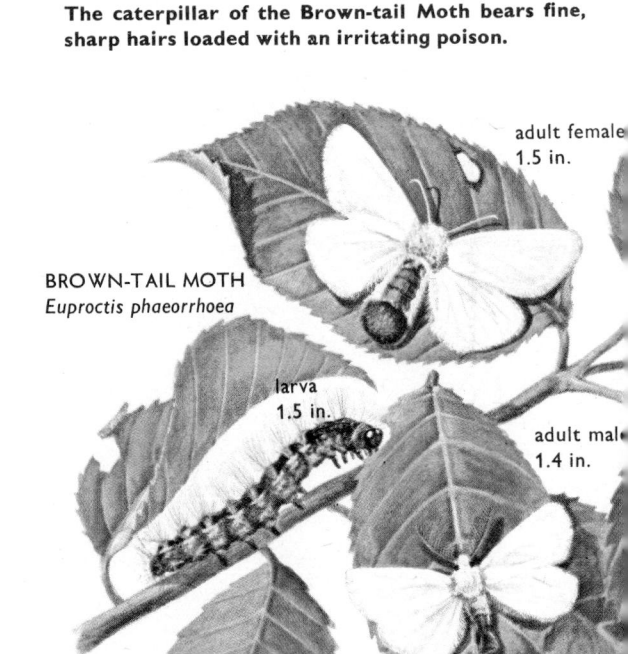

The caterpillar of the Brown-tail Moth bears fine, sharp hairs loaded with an irritating poison.

adult female
1.5 in.

BROWN-TAIL MOTH
Euproctis phaeorrhoea

larva
1.5 in.

adult male
1.4 in.

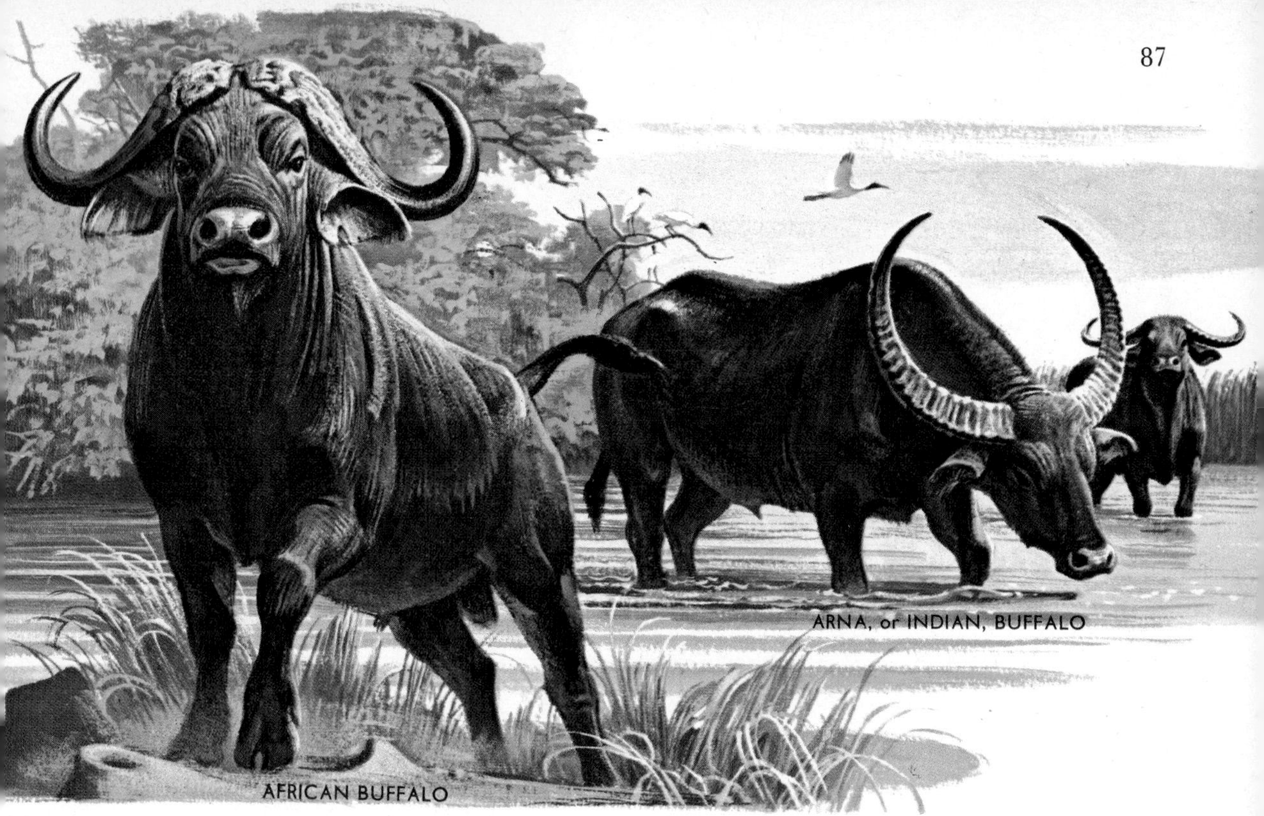

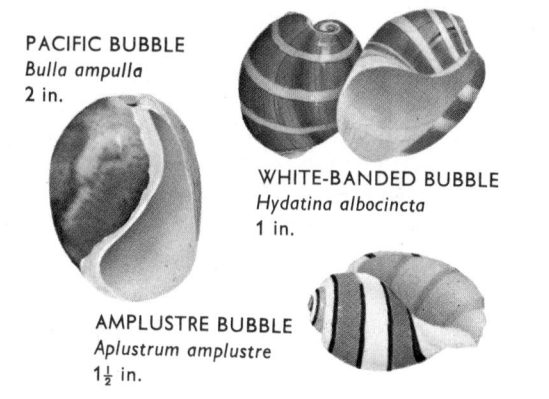

ARNA, or INDIAN, BUFFALO

AFRICAN BUFFALO

PACIFIC BUBBLE
Bulla ampulla
2 in.

WHITE-BANDED BUBBLE
Hydatina albocincta
1 in.

AMPLUSTRE BUBBLE
Aplustrum amplustre
1½ in.

BUBBLE SHELLS are often seen on beaches. The name is used for members of two families *(Hydatinidae* and *Bullidae)* of closely related molluscs in which the shell forms a final, large, open whorl over the rest of the shell and hides both ends. True bubbles are rather heavy; paper bubbles have very fragile shells and are seldom found whole on our beaches.

Most bubble shells live in warm, shallow waters, but some occur at great depths. A few live in cold northern seas. They are found on open sandy or muddy bottoms and in marine grass beds, where they feed largely on the organic debris or small animals that live on the bottom. In life the shell is not seen because it is covered by the living animal, which looks like a ball of dark jelly. The animal crawls about on a large flat "foot". Most bubble shells are drab, but a few are glossy and colourful.

BUFFALO is the proper name for such Old World animals as the Water Buffalo (Indian Buffalo) and the African Buffalo. Water Buffaloes *(Bubalus bubalis)* are natives of India, Ceylon and Indo-China, where they have been domesticated for centuries. They have been introduced to such places as Egypt and the Philippine Islands. Water Buffalo prefer dense, grassy jungles along large rivers. They frequently submerge their bodies in the water with only their heads exposed. Large herds of Water Buffalo feed during early morning and early evening. During the day they hide in the grass, where they chew their cuds and sleep. The African Buffalo, or Cape Buffalo *(Syncerus caffer)*, lives in the open grassy areas near large rivers in southern and central Africa. It

cools itself by wallowing in muddy pools and, when frightened, takes refuge in thorny thickets. The African Buffalo has larger ears than the Water Buffalo. Its ears are heavily fringed with hair. (See BISON.)

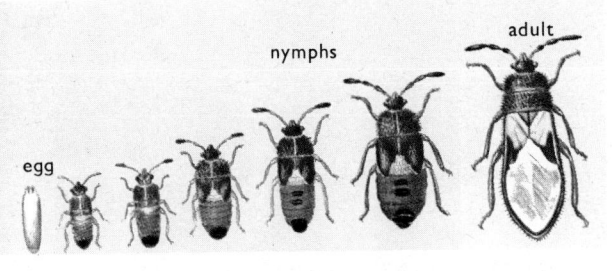

CHINCH BUG (*Blissus leucopterus*) — Metamorphosis

BUGS belong to the order *Hemiptera*. This name means "half wing", and was given to these insects because at least the apical half of their front pair of wings is usually thickened. Their hind wings are completely membranous. Bugs have sucking mouth-parts, and many kinds injure plants by sucking out the fluids. Some feed on the blood of mammals, including man; others prey on harmful insects. Most bugs are land dwellers, but some kinds live in water.

Bugs develop by simple metamorphosis (egg, nymph, adult). The young, or nymphs, usually look much like the adults, but they are often a different colour and their wings are still in the "bud" stage. After the last moult, the wings expand to full size.

Among the harmful species is the Chinch Bug, which causes an enormous amount of damage to grasses and cereals in America.

The Water Boatman *(Notonecta)* is familiar among the aquatic bugs, propelling itself on the surface of quiet waters by means of its oar-like legs. (See index for bugs described separately.)

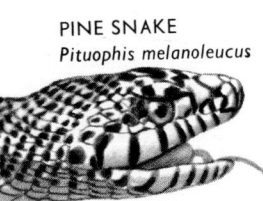

PINE SNAKE
Pituophis melanoleucus

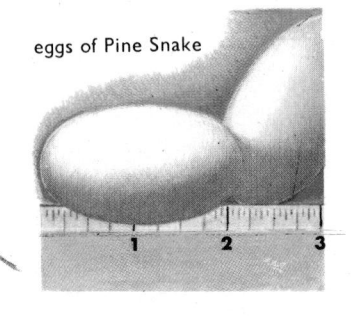

eggs of Pine Snake

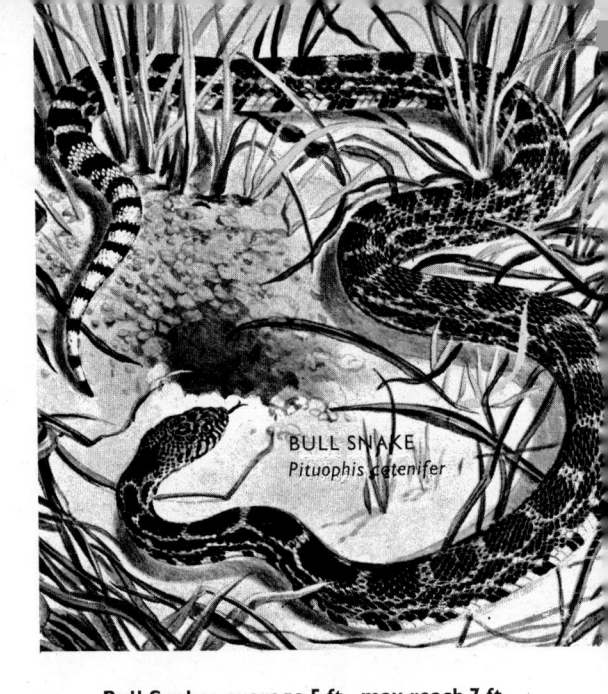

BULL SNAKE
Pituophis catenifer

Bull Snakes average 5 ft., may reach 7 ft.

BULL-SNAKES (*Pituophis* spp.) of about four species range from Guatemala through most of Mexico and the United States to extreme southern Canada. Many farmers value these snakes, for their food consists almost exclusively of rats and mice. The snakes are totally harmless. They may attempt to bite when first caught, but tame quickly and become good pets.

Bull-snakes that live north of central Mexico have a pointed snout with a protruding scale on its tip. Above ground they constrict their prey; underground they push the prey against the side of the burrow until it is suffocated. Bull-snakes reach a length of about eight feet. When first startled, they rear back and make a loud, rattling hiss by forcing air out rapidly and vibrating a gristly flap over their windpipe.

BUMBLE-BEES *(Bombidae)* are large, noisy bees that live in colonies. Most kinds are black and yellow. They have long tongues and can pollinate such flowers as red clover that bees with shorter tongues cannot.

Nest-building bumble-bees have three castes: workers, males (or drones) and queens. A queen often starts a new nest in a deserted mouse runway or burrow. There she places a small mound of pollen and honey, and builds a circular wall of wax on

its top. She deposits eggs in this cell, then caps it with more wax. At first the larvae feed on the pollen and honey. Later the queen feeds the larvae through a small hole that she cuts in the cell. When the larvae are ready to pupate, they spin small, oval cocoons. Bees that develop from these first eggs are all workers, which are much smaller than the queen. They take over all the duties of the colony except egg-laying. The males and females do not emerge until later. In late autumn, all the workers and males die, but the queens crawl into hollows of trees, under debris, or into holes in the ground, and live through the winter. They form new colonies again in the spring.

In one group of bumble-bees there are no workers. These bumble-bees invade nests of other bumble-bees and lay their eggs in their brood cells. Often they kill the queen. Their larvae are fed by the workers of the invaded colony. Eventually they pupate, hatch, and fly away in search of other bumble-bee nests.

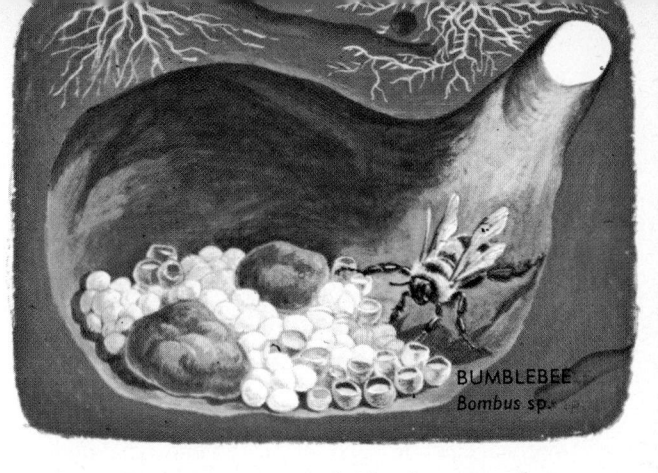

BUMBLEBEE
Bombus sp.

Egg cells and pupae are tended by the mature bees.

BUNTINGS are a large family of finch-like birds. In most species the male has brightly-coloured plumage during the breeding season, but the female is drabber in colour — usually streaky brown. The birds shown below are Eurasian buntings, and those given overleaf are American species. It has recently been claimed that the Chaffinch and Brambling are buntings, but this view is not accepted by all ornithologists. The Brambling is included in the second illustration. Buntings build cup nests and feed their

Adult buntings and sparrows eat seeds, but they feed their nestlings exclusively on insects.

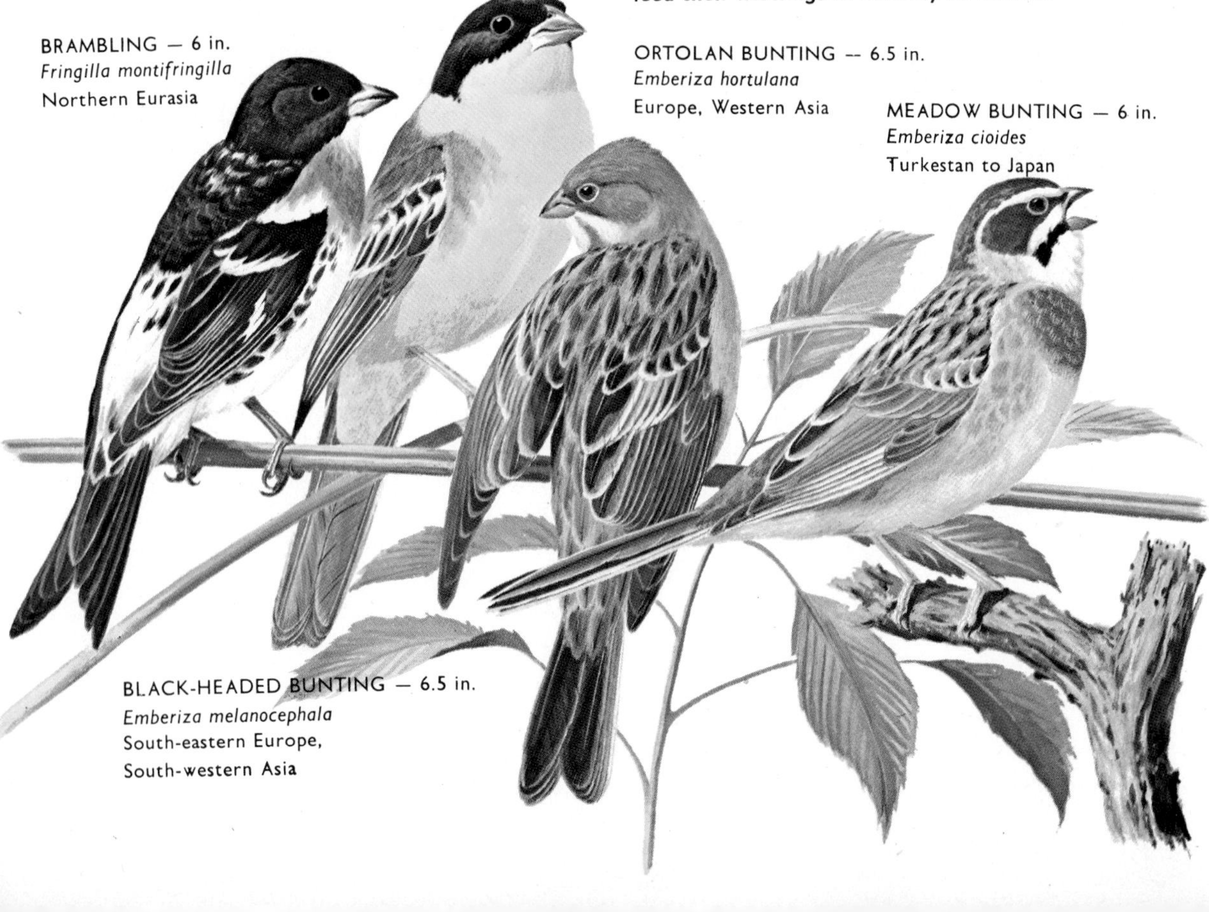

BRAMBLING — 6 in.
Fringilla montifringilla
Northern Eurasia

ORTOLAN BUNTING -- 6.5 in.
Emberiza hortulana
Europe, Western Asia

MEADOW BUNTING — 6 in.
Emberiza cioides
Turkestan to Japan

BLACK-HEADED BUNTING — 6.5 in.
Emberiza melanocephala
South-eastern Europe,
South-western Asia

young almost entirely on insects, though the food of the adults is mostly seed.

The largest number of bunting species are found in the Americas, and in addition some 30 species occur in Eurasia and Africa. These latter are rather similar to one another. The male is conspicuously coloured and has a simple song-phrase. These birds are found in different habitats with, apparently, one species to each — the yellow-headed Yellowhammer in hedgerow and heath, the Rock Bunting on rocky slopes, the Reed Bunting in marshes, the Ortolan in cultivated areas, the Snow Bunting in rocky Arctic areas and bare mountain-tops further south, and the Lapland Bunting in the Arctic tundra. Of these, the Snow Bunting has become conspicuously different, the summer male being white with black on back, wings and tail. In the other species, it is only the head-colouring that changes noticeably, usually to some pattern of black, chestnut and white.

In the Americas, the Bunting family

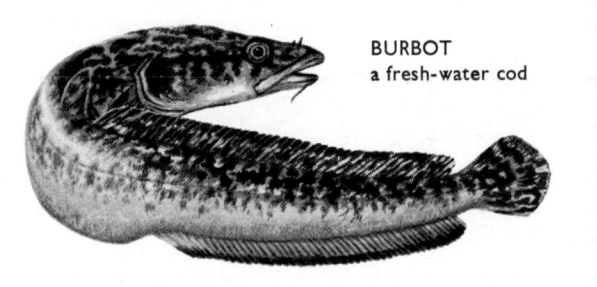

BURBOT
a fresh-water cod

lated to true sparrows of the eastern hemisphere. These are small, streaky-brown birds showing a great variety of colour and pattern on head and breast. There are a number of others, like those shown here, which are very brightly and boldly coloured.

This family includes the big, heavy-billed Cardinals with their scarlet colour; and it ranges from birds as big as thrushes to the tiny Grassquits, which are no bigger than Waxbills. It includes the Towhees, which behave like thrushes, and the American Grosbeaks, which seem to replace the larger finch species of Europe. Some of these birds have quite elaborate and musical songs.

BURBOT (*Lota lota*) are the only freshwater members of the cod-like fishes. The Burbot is found in northern Europe and also North America. In Britain, it occurs south of Durham, but not in Scotland or Ireland.

Burbot are slimy fishes somewhat resembling the catfishes, but with a single barbel under the chin. The largest specimen recorded weighed about 12 pounds.

Burbot are winter-spawning fishes, the young appearing in early spring. They make no nest, but deposit the eggs on the bottom. The larvae hatch out in about four weeks and resemble those of the Ling.

The adults are greedy fishes and will snap at almost anything that moves near them. They have even been known to swallow small rocks. The stomach stretches to accommodate large amounts of food.

Burbot are caught in fair numbers in the Great Lakes of America. They are active in winter, and are often speared or caught on hook and line by ice fishermen. They have been taken at depths of up to 700 feet.

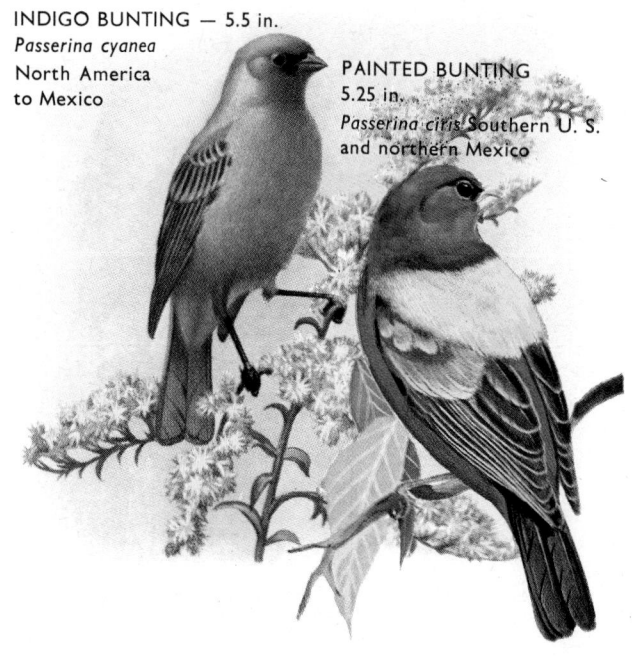

INDIGO BUNTING — 5.5 in.
Passerina cyanea
North America
to Mexico

PAINTED BUNTING
5.25 in.
Passerina ciris Southern U. S.
and northern Mexico

contains a great number and variety of species. There is a large group of what are called sparrows, although they are not re-

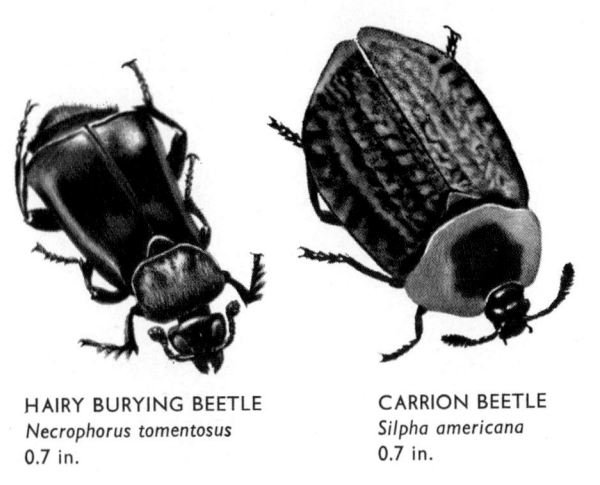

HAIRY BURYING BEETLE
Necrophorus tomentosus
0.7 in.

CARRION BEETLE
Silpha americana
0.7 in.

BURYING BEETLES and Carrion Beetles *(Silphidae)* are usually found around dead animals, although some live on plants.

Many carrion beetles *(Silpha* spp.) have very flat bodies and can easily crawl under a dead animal's carcass. Burying beetles *(Necrophorus* spp.) do not have flat bodies. Sometimes the beetles bury the carcasses of such animals as rats and mice. Actually the beetles dig more or less at random and undermine the carcass as they work under and around it, and the carcass may eventually sink below the surface. The beetles lay their eggs on it and the larvae feed there.

Other members of this family are found on fungi, some live in ant-nests, and a few kinds are pests of crops.

BUSHMASTER
bulkiest of the poisonous vipers

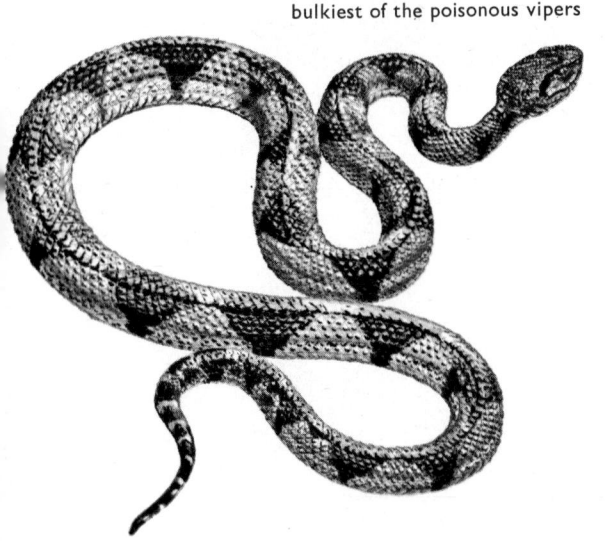

BUSHMASTERS *(Lachesis mutus)* are pit-vipers (see VIPERS) which occur in the tropical rain forests of Central and South America. In total bulk, the Bushmaster is the largest of all the New World venomous snakes, reaching a reputed length of 13 feet. The Bushmaster is not commonly encountered and, like some other highly dangerous snakes, is rather docile and even-tempered. It has small scales on its head, heavily-ridged scales on its body, and a rather high spine down its back. Females lay about 12 eggs and brood them until they hatch; it is the only American viper that lays eggs.

BUSTARDS are large birds that live on all the continents of the Eastern Hemisphere. There are 23 members in this family. Shaped like geese, but with longer necks and legs,

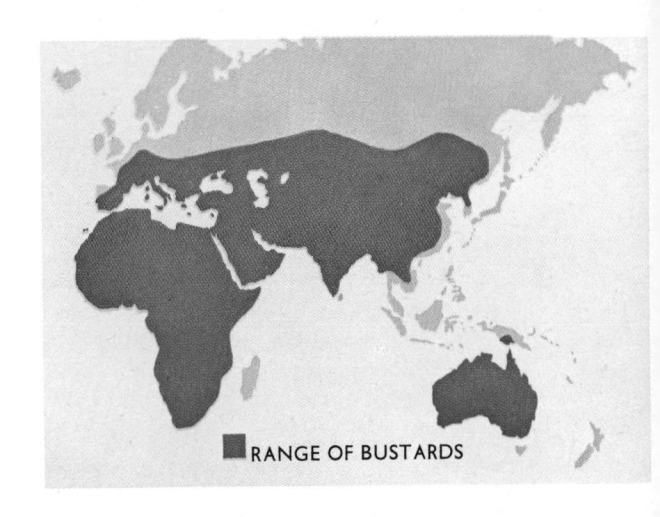

RANGE OF BUSTARDS

they are good runners. They have three long front toes and no hind toe. Unusual among birds they have no preening gland. The colouring of bustards makes them almost invisible when they are motionless in their open plains habitat. The European Great Bustard is three feet tall, weighs as much as 37 pounds, and is one of the world's heaviest flying birds. Taller is the Kori Bustard, is found in southern and eastern Africa.

All bustards are good to eat — hence they are rare near human settlements. The Great Bustard had been destroyed in Britain by about 1833. Occasional individuals may wander

to the British Isles from Europe.

Although bustards are primarily vegetarians, in some parts of Africa farmers value and protect bustards because they eat locusts and other harmful insects. Kori Bustards may permit the Carmine Bee-eater, a smaller bird, to ride on their back. The beeeater catches grasshoppers and other insects that jump out of the bustard's path.

KORI BUSTARD
Choriotis kori
54 in.

GREAT BUSTARD
Otis tarda
40 in.

BUTTERFLIES and MOTHS form one of the largest orders of insects — the *Lepidoptera,* which contains more than 100,000 species. The large size and striking colours of many of the species make this group one of the most popular with collectors.

Butterflies are distinguished from moths by their clubbed antennae. Moths have various types of antennae, but usually not clubbed. Moths ordinarily fly at night; butterflies during the day. Most butterflies have slender bodies; moths are generally thick-bodied. Most moths have a spine-like structure (frenulum) at the leading edge of the hind wing; butterflies do not.

A few members of the *Lepidoptera* do not have wings (see BAGWORMS), but most have two pairs, covered with overlapping scales that flake off like coloured powder when the insects are handled. Their bodies and legs are also covered with tiny scales. Moths and butterflies have sucking mouthparts as adults, and feed mainly on nectar.

Lepidoptera undergo a complete meta-

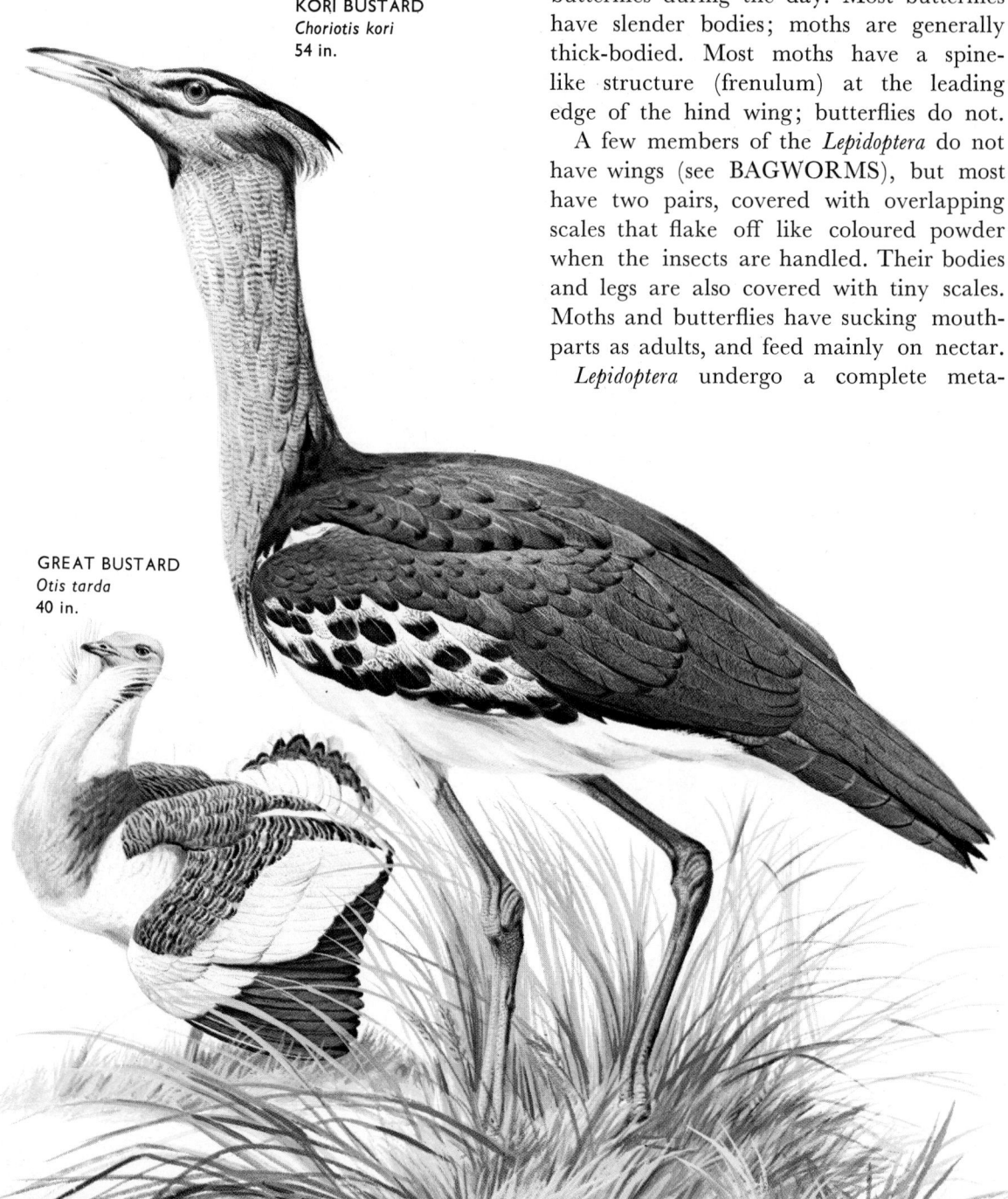

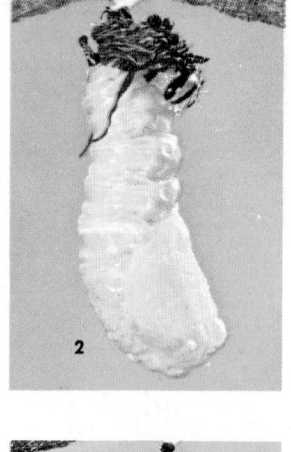

1

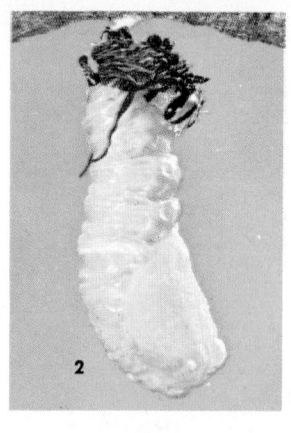

2

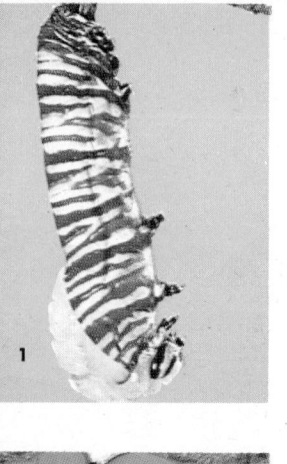

3

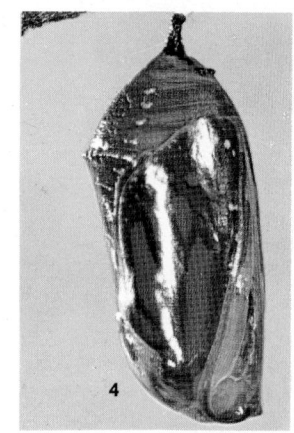

4

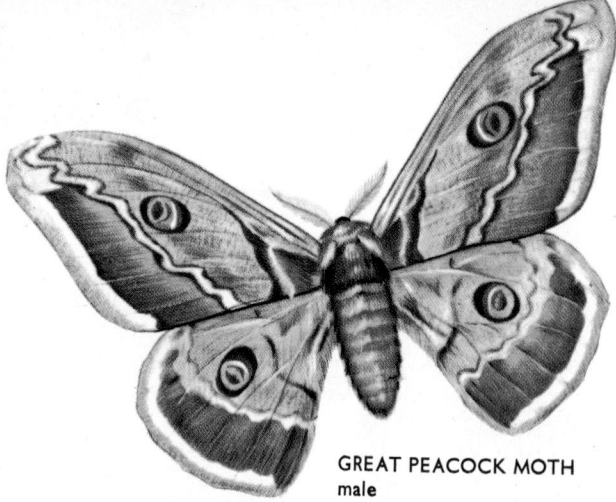

GREAT PEACOCK MOTH
male

abdominal segments, are fleshy and not jointed. They have at their tips several tiny hooks. Some caterpillars have very small legs, or, rarely, none at all. Caterpillars have chewing mouth-parts, and most kinds feed on plants. Some eat leaves;

METAMORPHOSIS OF A BUTTERFLY: The caterpillar of a Monarch Butterfly fastens itself to a twig by a few strands of silk (1). Hanging head down (2), it transforms into the chrysalis (or pupa) stage as the skin of the caterpillar splits and drops off. Inside the smooth, hard shell of the chrysalis (3 and 4), the pupa transforms into a butterfly which emerges (5 and 6) in about two weeks. The butterfly's wings must stiffen and dry (7) before it can fly away.

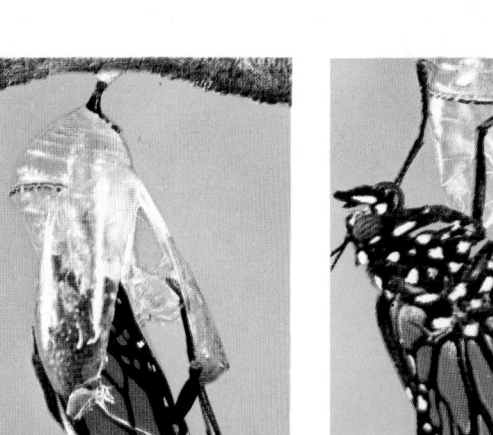

5

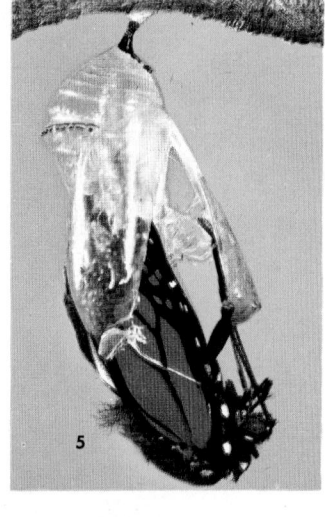

6

All photos by Herbert Lanks — Monkmeyer

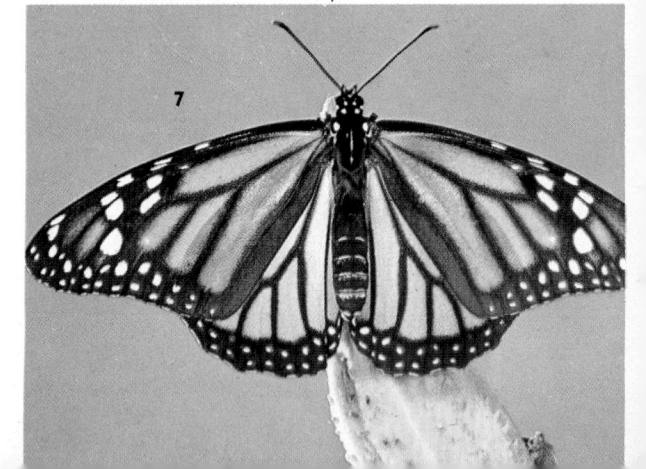

7

morphosis — egg, larva, pupa and adult. Females of some kinds deposit their eggs singly, while others deposit them in small groups. Usually the eggs are glued to the type of plant on which the larvae feed, although some species scatter their eggs at random. A few lay eggs in plant tissues and Tent Caterpillars cover their egg-masses with a hard protective coating.

Larvae of most butterflies and moths are called caterpillars. Typically the larvae are cylindrical and have one pair of legs on each of the three thoracic segments. Thoracic legs have joints and a little claw at the end; prolegs, ordinarily found on

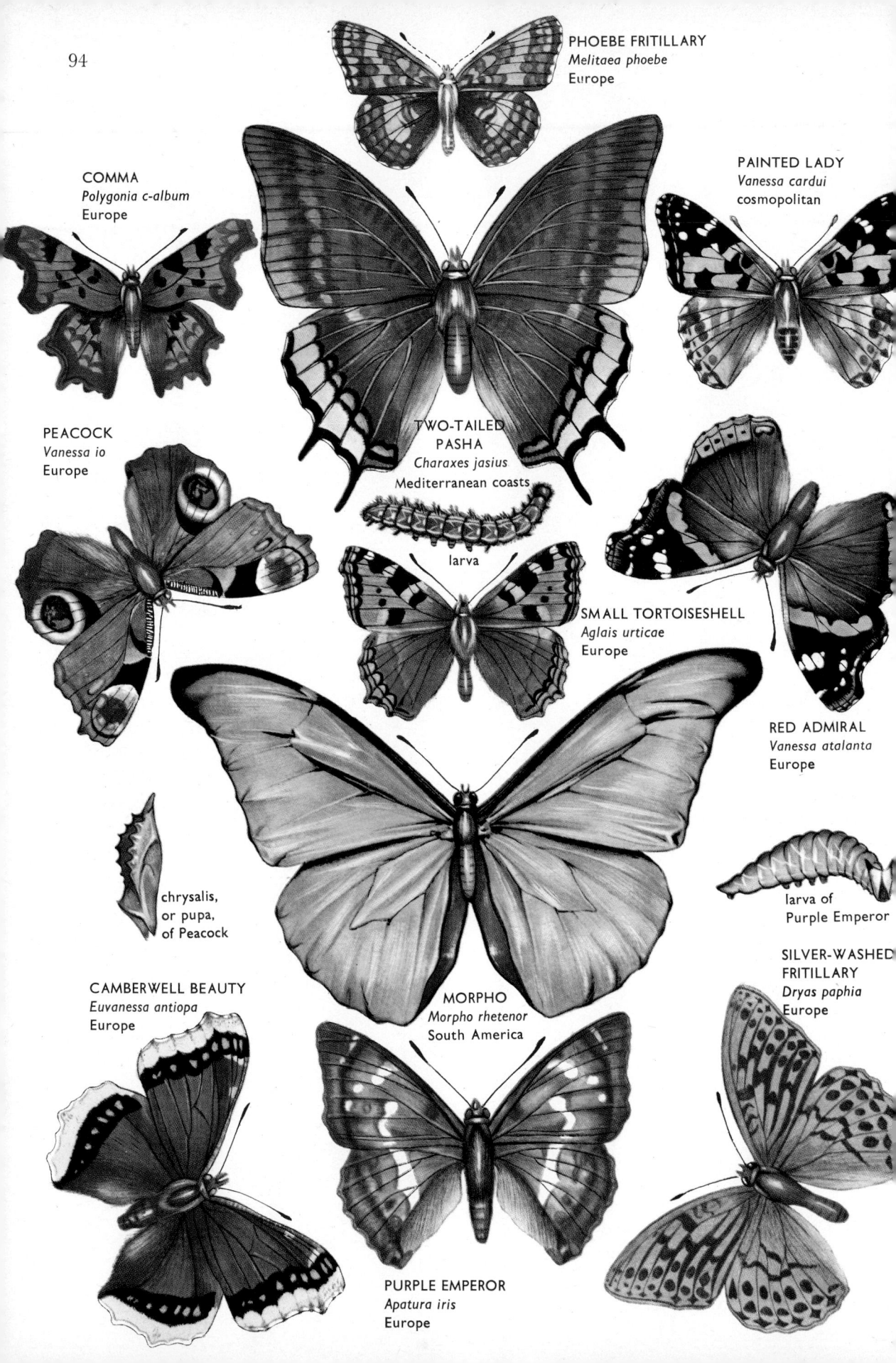

94

PHOEBE FRITILLARY
Melitaea phoebe
Europe

COMMA
Polygonia c-album
Europe

PAINTED LADY
Vanessa cardui
cosmopolitan

PEACOCK
Vanessa io
Europe

TWO-TAILED
PASHA
Charaxes jasius
Mediterranean coasts

larva

SMALL TORTOISESHELL
Aglais urticae
Europe

RED ADMIRAL
Vanessa atalanta
Europe

chrysalis,
or pupa,
of Peacock

larva of
Purple Emperor

SILVER-WASHED
FRITILLARY
Dryas paphia
Europe

CAMBERWELL BEAUTY
Euvanessa antiopa
Europe

MORPHO
Morpho rhetenor
South America

PURPLE EMPEROR
Apatura iris
Europe

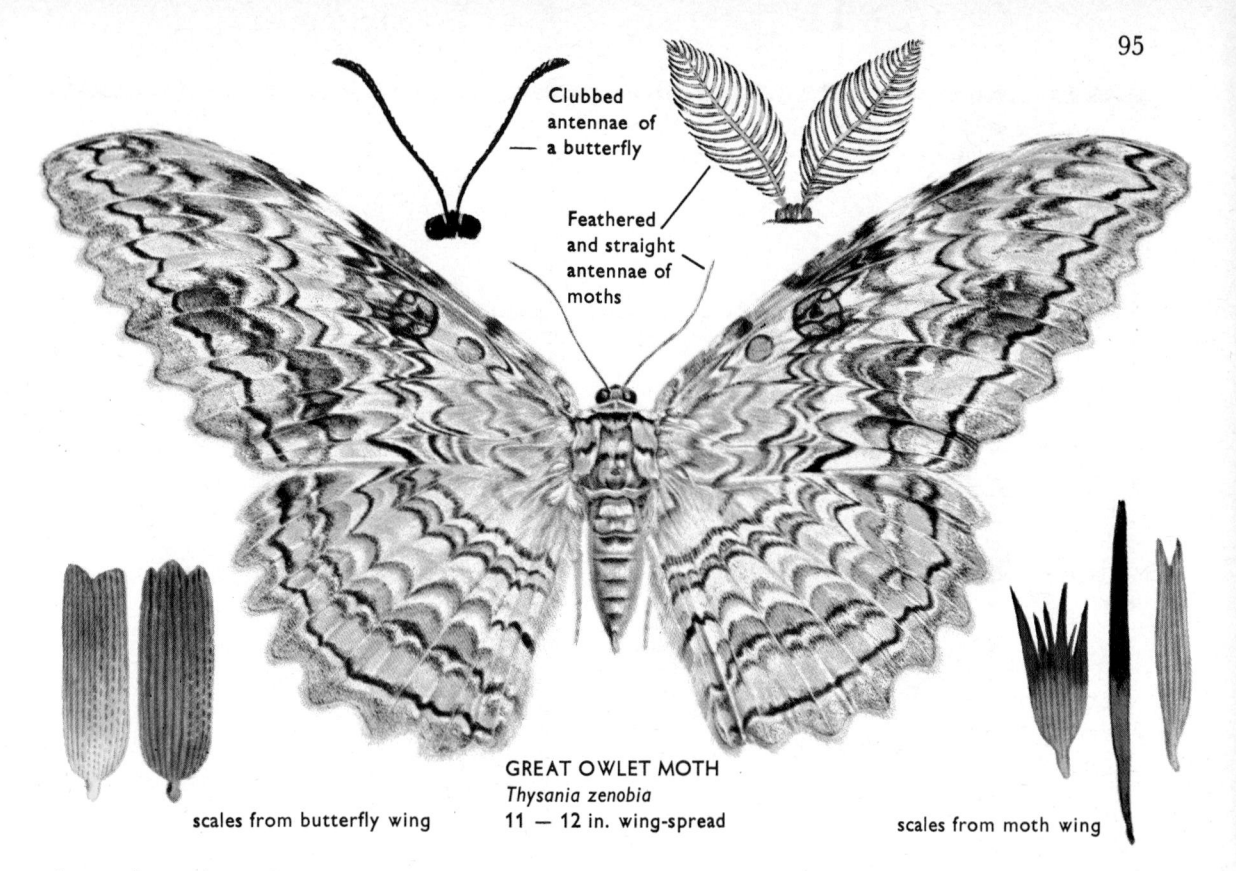

Clubbed antennae of a butterfly

Feathered and straight antennae of moths

GREAT OWLET MOTH
Thysania zenobia
11 — 12 in. wing-spread

scales from butterfly wing

scales from moth wing

others, bore into fruit or stems, or feed on roots, stored products or fabrics. Many cause heavy damage to crops.

Some caterpillars have unusual shapes or are covered with warts or spines, and many have striking colour patterns. In most, these structures and colours help to protect the caterpillars from enemies.

The green Puss Moth caterpillar is a fearsome object. On the thorax it bears several conspicuous protuberances, while behind the moth carries a pair of long telescopic processes. They are completely harmless, however. Other caterpillars are coloured like bark and resemble slender twigs when they motionless. Swallow-tail caterpillars possess a Y-shaped organ, normally retracted into the prothorax. When disturbed the caterpillar extends this organ through a slit and, at the same time, releases a powerful scent.

Many caterpillars rely on spines for protection. An irritating liquid is often released when these barbed and hollow spines are broken off in a wound, and a painful rash commonly results.

Usually only the terminal segments of the abdomen can be wriggled in moth and butterfly pupae, but in some groups the legs are partly free. Many caterpillars transform into pupae inside a cocoon made of silk produced by glands that open through a spinneret located on the lower lip. The silk is secreted as a liquid, but hardens as soon as it strikes the air. Nearly all young caterpillars spin silk continuously as they move about. This gives them good traction for crawling. Caterpillars of the Ermine moths and others make large web shelters in which they communally feed. Some caterpillars make a shelter by tying a few leaves together with silk. Caterpillars that bore in plants often line their tunnels with silk. Most butterflies have naked pupae, called chrysalids and usually fixed to a branch or leaf by a terminal pad of silk, and often by a silken girdle also.

Adult moths and butterflies vary in size from tiny moths with wing-spans of about 0.1 of an inch to the large Atlas Moth with a wing-span of 10 to 12 inches. (See index for species described separately.)

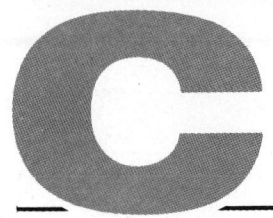

C

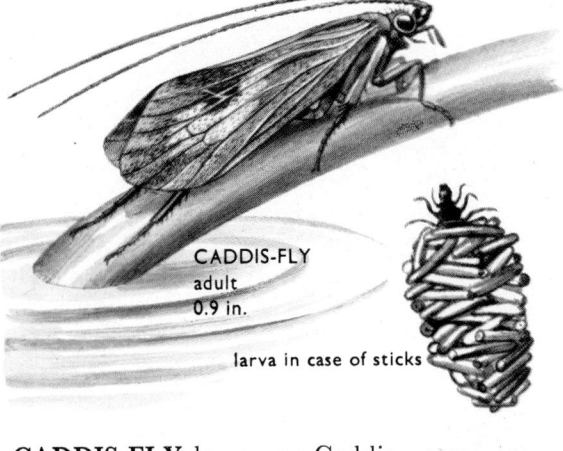

CADDIS-FLY
adult
0.9 in.

larva in case of sticks

CADDIS-FLY larvae, or Caddis-worms, are found in lakes, ponds and streams. Many kinds live in cases made of sand, pebbles, leaves, and twigs held together with silk; others spin cases entirely of silk. Many species can be identified by the kind of materials used and by the shape of their case. Most larvae drag their cases behind them as they crawl along, feeding on the bottom. Some caddis-flies do not build any protection; others spin silken nets in which they catch their food, just as spiders do. Most caddis-fly larvae are plant-eaters, others are carnivorous. They are eaten by many kinds of fishes. After a time the larvae transform into pupae and then into adults, some of which are hairy and look much like moths. Females of a few species do not have wings. Most kinds fly at night, and may collect in large numbers around lights. Caddis-flies belong to the order *Trichoptera*.

CAECILIANS (pronounced See-SILL-yans) form a primitive order of amphibians (see AMPHIBIANS). About 100 species live in the wet, tropical regions of the Americas,

Africa, south-eastern Asia, and the Seychelles Islands. They look so much like earthworms that they are easily mistaken for them. Except for a few species that live in water, caecilians spend their entire life burrowing in the soil; hence they are rarely seen or collected.

As is true of many other burrowing animals, caecilians have lost their sight. Their eyes are covered either with bone or with skin. They have no eardrums or middle ear structure, and so they are not able to hear airborne sounds. They can detect vibrations in the ground, however. Caecilians have a soft, feeler-like structure that can be extended at will from a tiny pit between the nostril and eye on each side of the head. This "tentacle" is used to taste food.

The largest caecilian measures about $4\frac{1}{2}$ feet in length; the smallest only $3\frac{1}{2}$ inches. Most are about a foot long. Some are very slender; others are thick. Some lay eggs; others bear live young. They are believed to eat small animals, such as worms, spiders and ants.

CALICO SHELLS (*Macrocallista* spp.) are large, showy shells much sought after by collectors, and commonly washed ashore.

CAECILIAN
Siphonops annulatus

gilled larva
on egg-sac

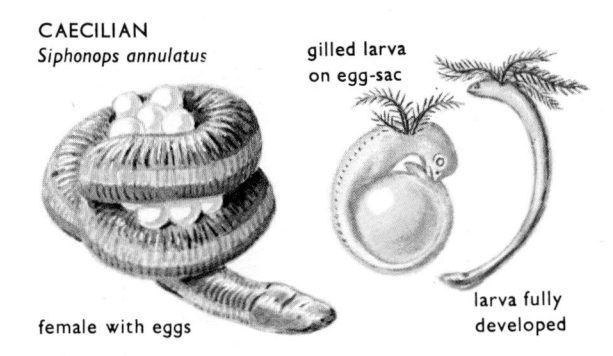

female with eggs

larva fully
developed

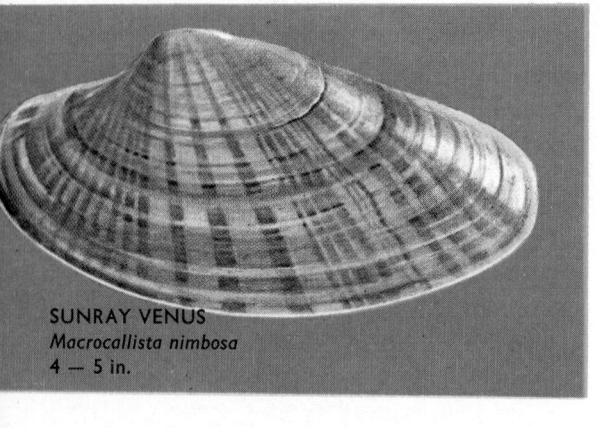

SUNRAY VENUS
Macrocallista nimbosa
4 — 5 in.

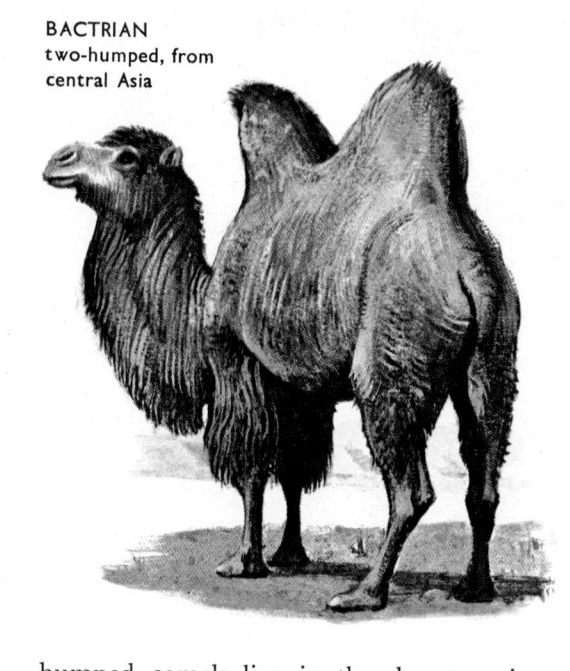

BACTRIAN
two-humped, from
central Asia

The Sunray Venus, which grows up to five inches in length, has a glossy surface with a thin, papery protective covering. It is marked on the outside with radiating rays of varied colours, while the inside is usually lavender or pinkish. It is common along the shores of southern Florida and the Gulf Coast, where it lives on shallow, sandy bottoms, burrowing below the surface. It reveals its hiding place by the slit-like holes it leaves in the sand. The Sunray Venus is commonly eaten by sea-gulls. The birds pull the shells out of the sand and crack them open to reach the soft meat.

CAMELS are of two kinds: the two-humped, or Bactrian *(Camelus bactrianus)*, and also the one-humped, or Dromedary *(Camelus dromedarius)*. Two-humped camels are found from China to Turkestan; one-

humped camels live in the desert regions of Arabia and Egypt. At present, camels exist only in domestication, except for small remnants of wild herds in the Gobi Desert. Camels have served man as beasts of burden for countless centuries. They were one of the first hoofed animals ever to be domesticated. The Koran, bible of the Moslems, calls the camel an example of God's wisdom because of its importance to desert people. Heavily loaded with 400 to 600 pounds, camels can travel 30 miles in a single day. They run by swinging both legs on one side forward at the same time, not alternating sides as horses do.

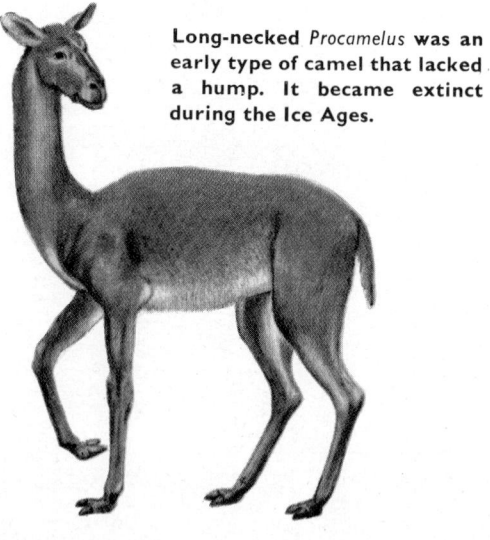

Long-necked *Procamelus* was an early type of camel that lacked a hump. It became extinct during the Ice Ages.

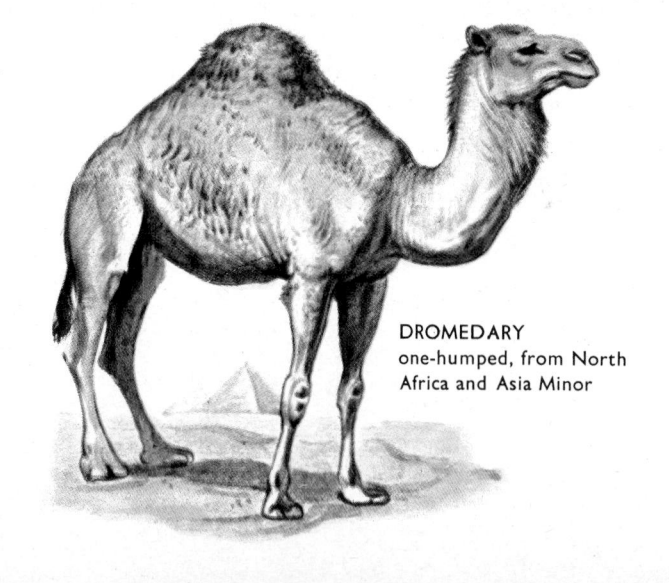

DROMEDARY
one-humped, from North Africa and Asia Minor

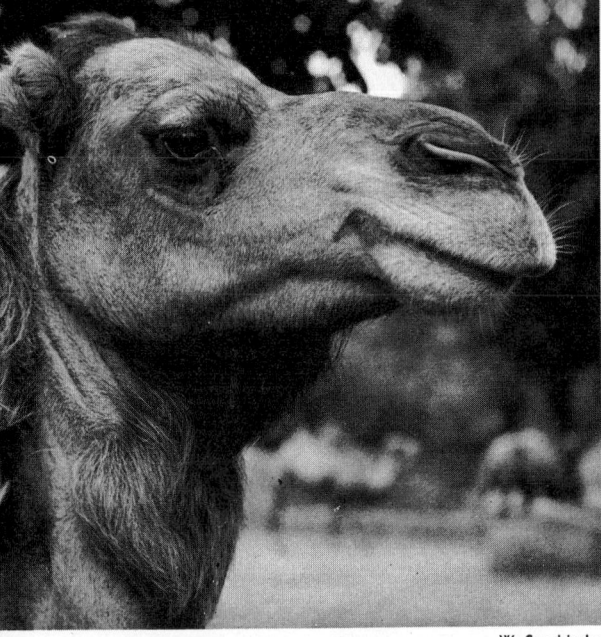

Camels have been servants of man for many centuries, but they remain defiant and ill-tempered.

Camel flesh and milk provide food and drink; their skins are tanned to make leather. Recent research has shown that camels do not store water in their stomach, but absorb large quantities throughout the body tissues. Their humps are stored fat. Heavy fringes of hair around their eyes and nostrils protect them from flying sand, and their broad feet help them to move easily through the sand of the deserts. Camels eat tough desert plants and chew their cuds like cows. Their stomach is three-chambered. Camels may live to an age of 25 years.

CANARIES are small domesticated finches that originally lived wild in the Canary Islands. Spanish sailors captured them there and took them to Europe as house-pets. By the seventeenth century, canaries were established as cage birds in Europe.

Canaries are seed-eaters. They are one of the few cage birds which have been

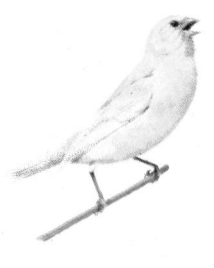

Pet canaries, descendants of wild finches of the Canary Islands, are hardy little cage-birds.

selected until a strain has been produced that will breed readily in artificial nests in small cages. Although some other birds, such as the Greenfinch, will breed readily in cages, most birds prefer the greater space of an aviary.

In Germany, particularly in the Harz Mountains of northern Germany, canaries are bred chiefly to be singers. Young birds are trained by putting them with an older singer, called a "campanini". Males become the best singers. A singer may be a "roller", which has a song that consists of low, soft notes and long trills, or a "chopper", which has a loud, vigorous song.

In England, canaries are bred primarily for their colour and body shape. The most popular breeds are the slender Yorkshire and the plumper Norwich. Another well-known breed is the Crested Norwich.

CAPYBARAS (*Hydrochoerus hydrochoeris*) are closely related to Chinchillas and Guinea-pigs. Pig-sized rodents of South America, they weigh as much as 100 pounds. These largest of all rodents live peacefully and quietly in family groups of a dozen or more. They are commonly found in marshes or along rivers or lakes, feeding on aquatic plants. Sometimes they graze in fields with cattle. When attacked by a jaguar they often jump into the water to escape, for they are excellent swimmers. Contented Capybaras make low clicking noises or sharp whistles.

Capybaras are more agile in water than on land.

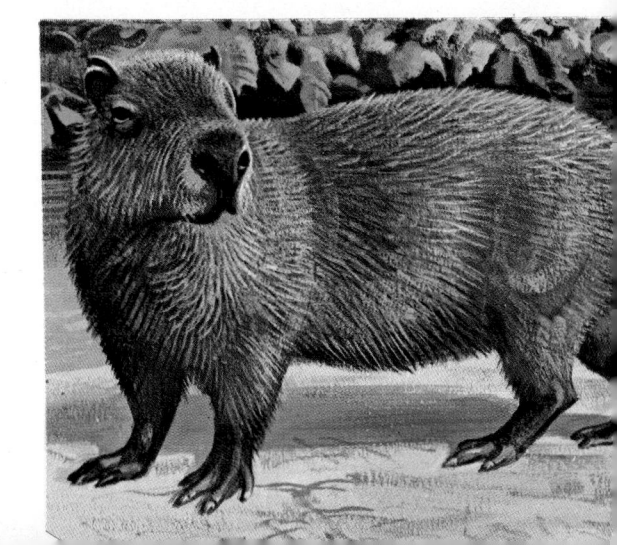

CARIBOU, or Reindeer (*Rangifer tarandus*), are large — weighing up to 300 pounds — wild deer of the Northern Hemisphere. Those native to northern Europe and Siberia are usually known as Reindeer and have been domesticated. In North America they are called Caribou. Both male and female Caribou and Reindeer have antlers, although the female's are slightly smaller. Highly sociable animals, Caribou and Reindeer travel in large herds and may migrate hundreds of miles. In the treeless arctic tundra lands where Caribou and Reindeer live, the only source of food during the winter is a lichen called Reindeer Moss. They use their sharp hoofs to break through the snow and ice to get these lichens, and also eat grasses, sedges, and the leaves of willows and birches. Insects, disease and lack of food plague the herds. They are attacked by wolves and hunted by Eskimos. Reindeer pull sleighs and provide milk, meat, and skins for clothing.

CARP (*Cyprinus carpio*) have been cultivated like farm animals in China for a long time — perhaps 4,000 years, some believe. During this long period, many techniques have been tried to make the fishes grow larger and more quickly. In China, the home of carp culture, the fish are often fed on silkworm pupae, and mulberry bushes line the banks of the ponds. The Chinese early discovered that carp fry, taken from the rivers, would grow well in ponds; later carp culture spread abroad.

The carp was not introduced into England until about 1500, but it soon became a popular food fish and was kept in the "stew ponds" of the monasteries and large manors. Izaak Walton, the patron saint of anglers, called the Carp the "queen of rivers: a stately, good, and very subtle fish". In England, Carp of 20-25 pounds are caught on rod and line, and the record was a fish of 33 pounds.

In many parts of Asia, and especially in China, the Carp is the most important of all food fishes grown in ponds. By inten-

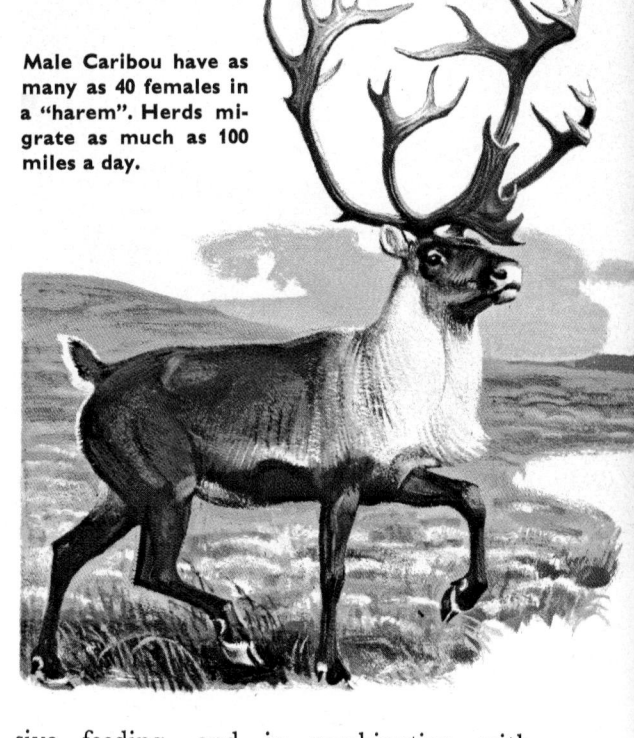

Male Caribou have as many as 40 females in a "harem". Herds migrate as much as 100 miles a day.

sive feeding, and in combination with other species of carp, the Chinese ponds may yield as much as 3-6,000 pounds of fish per acre in a year. In eastern Europe, there are Carp farms in many countries, and in the Soviet Union the Carp has been farmed successfully as far north as the 60th parallel. In England, and in Western European countries with an Atlantic coastline, fish culture itself is of minor importance compared with the great sea fisheries.

There are three main varieties of the Carp: the Mirror Carp has a few large scales along the body, whereas the Leather Carp has no scales at all; the ordinary Carp, with a complete series of scales on the body, is often referred to as the Scaled Carp. There are also other varieties, some different in colouration. One of these is quite golden, like the Goldfish. The Scaled

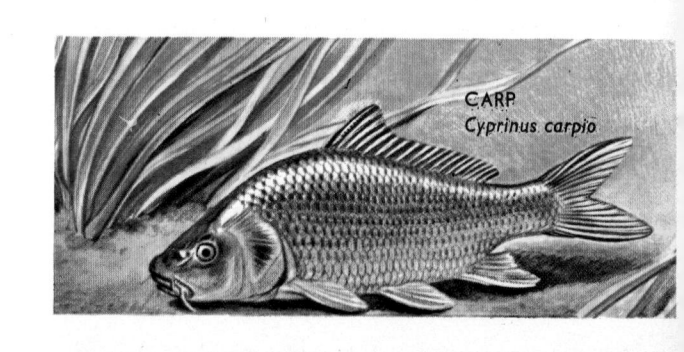

CARP
Cyprinus carpio

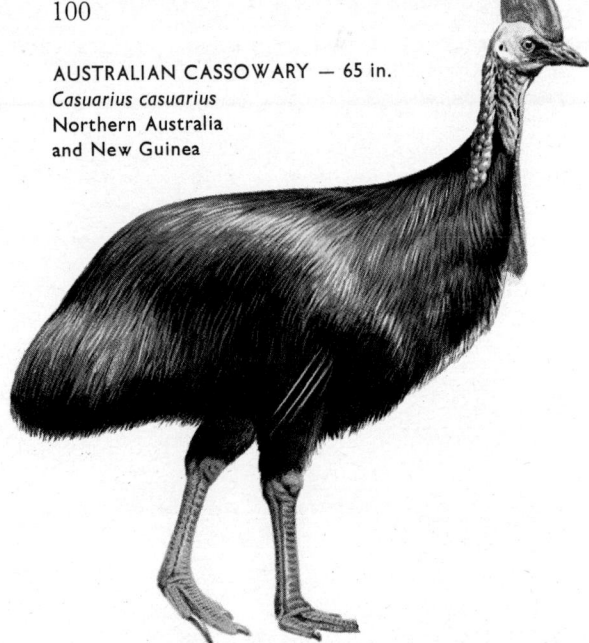

AUSTRALIAN CASSOWARY — 65 in.
Casuarius casuarius
Northern Australia
and New Guinea

Carp and Mirror Carp grow better and are more resistant to disease than others.

The Carp belongs to one of the most important of all families of freshwater fishes, the *Cyprinidae*. The cyprinids are found in Europe, Asia, Africa, and North America, but not in South America. In Asia many of the larger species are used as pond fish. In India, the Catla *(Catla catla)* is an important food fish. It feeds on decayed vegetation as well as microscopic plants and small animals. An important Chinese species is the Grass Carp *(Ctenopharyngodon idellus)* which, as its name implies, feeds mainly on grass. In fact the Grass Carp will feed on almost any plant material and is even reported to have eaten old boots. The Black Carp feeds chiefly on snails. The Bighead feeds on the minute animal and plant life in the pond water. By combining several species of carp in a pond, the fish farmer is able to use the food resources more efficiently.

In Britain, important cyprinid fishes are the Barbel *(Barbus barbus)*, Chub *(Leuciscus cephalus)*, Roach *(Rutilus rutilus)*, and the Bream *(Abramis brama)* (the Goldfish and Minnow are dealt with separately). Closely related to the Goldfis is the Crucian Carp *(Carassius carassius)*, a rare species in Britain, but reported from the Thames.

CASSOWARIES of the Australasian jungles are timid birds, but dangerous enemies. On the inside toe of each foot is a very long, sharp claw. With this, by means of powerful kicks, the Cassowary protects itself and has killed men when attacked. It uses the bony casque on its head to push aside underbrush as it runs through the forest. Much of its range is unexplored.

The Cassowary is a big, flightless, almost wingless bird, similar to an Ostrich but with shaggier feathers, heavier legs and a shorter neck. It feeds on fruit, berries, leaves and seeds. The call is a deep, booming grunt.

CATBIRDS received their name from their mew-like call-notes. Excellent mimics, they belong to the same family as the Mockingbird and the Thrashers (see MOCKING-BIRDS). Catbirds are known from central Canada south to Panama, the Bahamas and Cuba, where some of them winter. Their voices and fearless behaviour attract human attention. They have very sweet songs, but often interrupt themselves to imitate other birds. They eat some fruit, but balance this with many insects.

CATFISHES belong to the sub-order *Siluroidea*. They are usually easy to identify because the majority have barbels, or

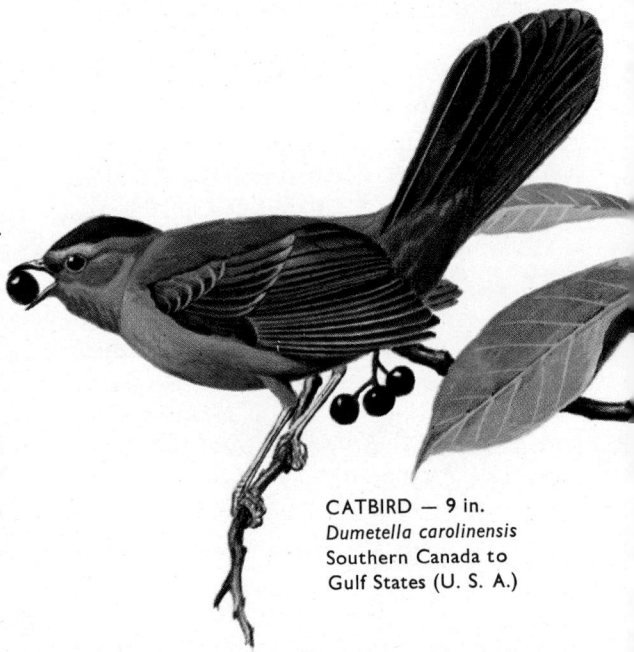

CATBIRD — 9 in.
Dumetella carolinensis
Southern Canada to
Gulf States (U. S. A.)

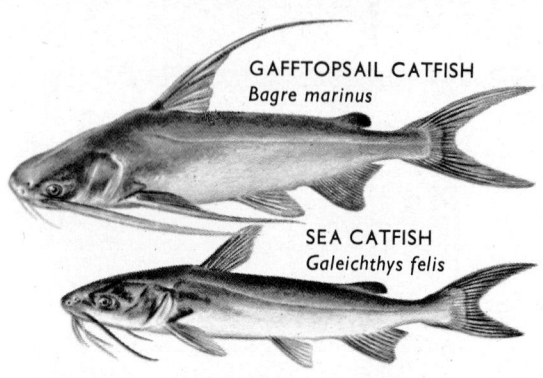

GAFFTOPSAIL CATFISH
Bagre marinus

SEA CATFISH
Galeichthys felis

feelers, near the mouth. Catfishes lack scales, but one large group have series of bony plates on the body. Often the first ray of the dorsal and pectoral fins is spiny, and in certain cases these spines bear poison glands. One of the most dangerous of catfishes in this respect is a marine species of the Indo-Pacific region, *Plotosus anguillaris,* because it is reported that death can follow wounds from the sharp fin spines and the subsequent injection of venom.

The Armoured Catfishes are found in South America. In the doradids, there is a single row of bony plates along the body. These plates are ornamented with hooks and other projections. In the callichthyids and loricariids the armour is smooth, the first group having two rows of plates usually, the second being covered entirely by plates. Some of the Armoured Catfishes are popular aquarium fishes, — especially species of *Corydoras,* which are small and peaceable. The Naked Catfishes, which lack bony plates on the body, are found not only in South America, but also in North America, Europe, Africa and

Asia. Some, like the Wels of the Danube *(Siluris glanis),* grow to an enormous size — up to 13 feet, it is said. Wels were introduced into England in the last century and are caught from time to time in the south-east. The Sea Catfishes are remarkable for their very large eggs, as big as marbles in some cases, and for the fact that the eggs are held in the mouth of the male until shortly after the larvae have hatched. During this time, the male cannot feed.

The freshwaters of Africa contain a varied assortment of catfishes. Some species of *Clarias* grow to a large size and are important in the fisheries of the lakes and rivers. They are able to gulp air at the surface and to absorb the oxygen by means of a spongy organ in the gill chamber. An extraordinary African species is the Electric Catfish *(Malapterurus electricus).* Large specimens of about 4 feet can produce a shock of about one hundred volts. The Ancient Egyptians knew this fish well, and it features in certain tomb paintings. Another interesting African species is the Upside-down Catfish, which swims on its back. The normal colour pattern in this fish is reversed, the belly being much darker than the back.

There are about 50 species of catfishes in North America, several of which are important sport fishes. The best of these is the Channel Catfish, which, unlike most other species prefers clearer streams. It may reach 50 pounds in weight. The smallest members of the North American catfishes are the Madtoms and Stonecats. They live

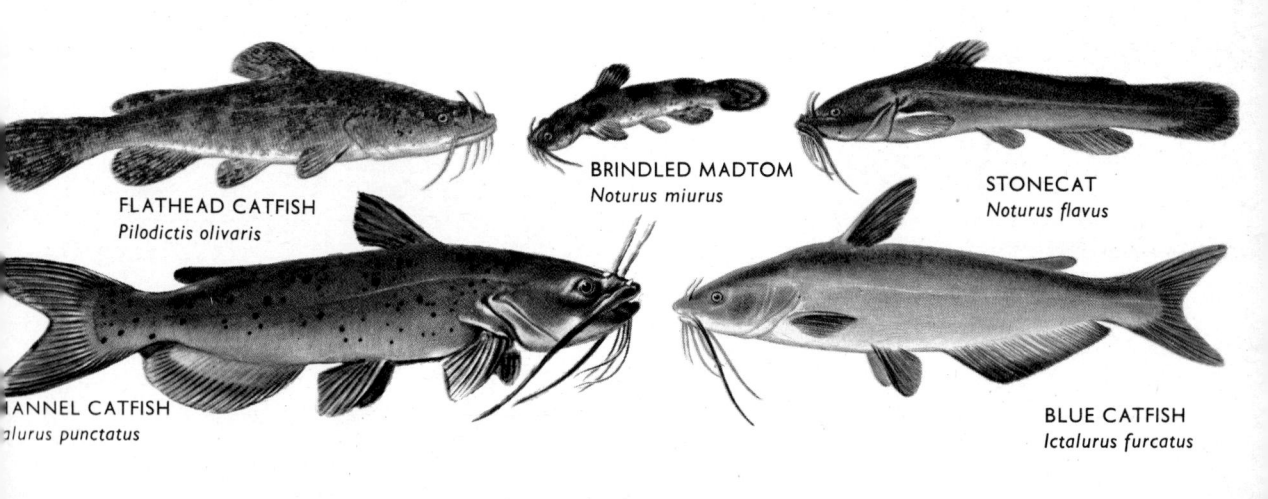

FLATHEAD CATFISH
Pilodictis olivaris

BRINDLED MADTOM
Noturus miurus

STONECAT
Noturus flavus

ANNEL CATFISH
alurus punctatus

BLUE CATFISH
Ictalurus furcatus

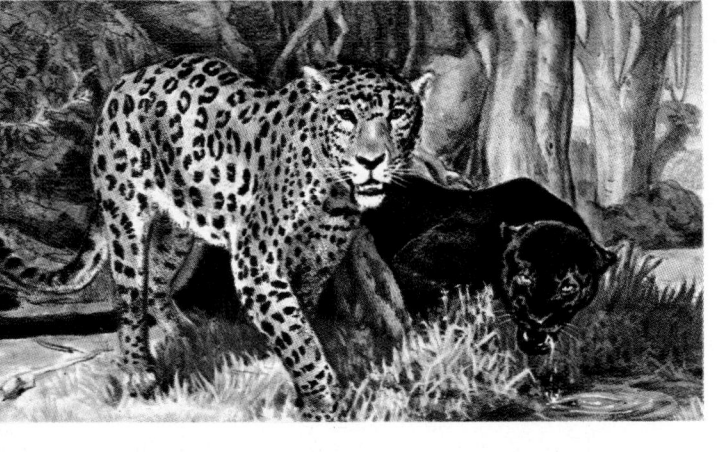

The Leopard is the largest of the spotted cats, some males weighing as much as 150 pounds.

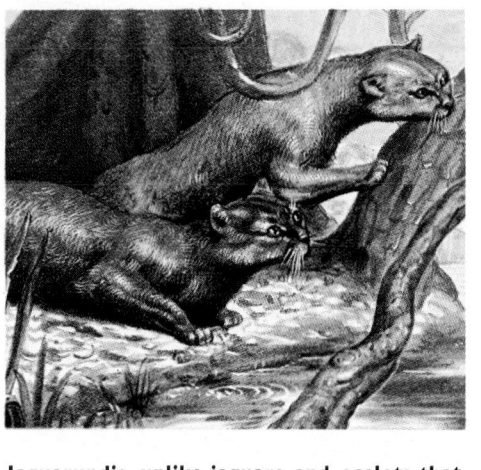

Jaguarundis, unlike jaguars and ocelots that live in the same area, are never spotted.

in fast, clear waters and are often caught for bait. They are armed with sharp spines and poison glands, and can inflict painful wounds. In fact, it is wise to handle all catfishes with a certain amount of care.

One of the smallest of the catfishes is the Candiru *(Vandellia cirrhosa)*. These fishes, only $2\frac{1}{2}$ inches in length, are parasitic, entering the gill chamber of larger fishes, and feeding on the gill filaments and blood. In South America, where they occur, they have the reputation of entering the urogenital openings of men and women while bathing, and they are thus greatly feared by people there.

Some catfishes are not slippery-skinned and scaleless as are typical catfishes. Instead, they are covered with sharp, horny plates much like those of the sturgeon. The Armoured Catfish of South American rivers is an example. Apart from an African catfish that can produce electric shocks to stun its prey, and a Nile species that always swims upside-down a certain species of the Amazon comes out of the water and wriggles along the bank. Another is long and slim, like a gar, and still another has a pointed, fox-like snout. Many kinds can grunt, squeal and growl, and there is one kind of catfish that can mew like a cat. Many of these small but strange catfishes make interesting aquarium pets.

CATS, a large family of flesh-eating mammals, range in size from the common House Cat and Lynx to Tigers and Lions (see TIGERS and LIONS). Cats are found everywhere in the world, except Australia and the extreme polar regions.

There are three groups: small cats, which can purr but not roar; larger cats, such as Lions and Tigers, which can roar but not purr; and the Cheetah, or Hunting Leopard which differs from all the other cats in that it has no claw-sheaths (see CHEETAHS). Sabre-toothed Cats *(Smilodon spp.)*, which became extinct during the Ice Age, had very long canine teeth in their upper jaws.

Bobcats *(Lynx rufus)* have slightly tufted ears and bobbed tails. Only about three feet long, they occur throughout most of North America, where they prey on rabbits, squirrels, mice and birds. Lynxes *(Lynx*

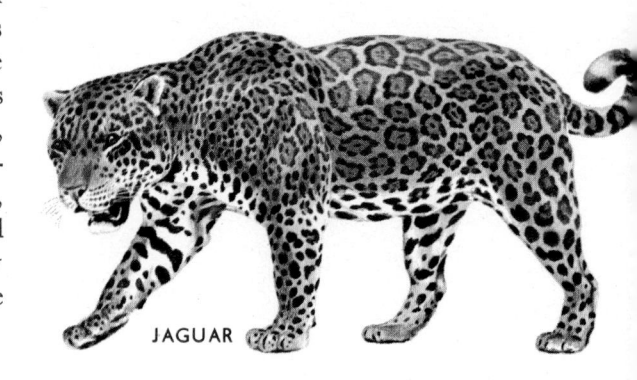

JAGUAR

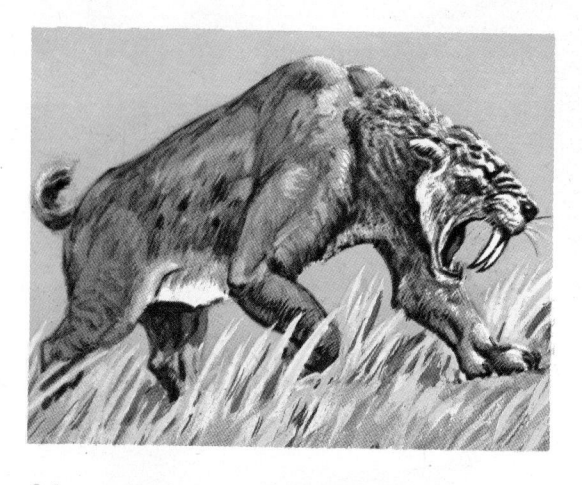

Sabre-toothed cats, extinct since the Ice Ages, had larger canine teeth than any other cat.

lynx), which are larger, paler versions of Bobcats, have longer ear-tufts and exceedingly broad feet, which enable them to walk on snow when other animals would sink. Lynxes are found in northern North America and in parts of mountainous Eurasia. Their principal food in North America is Snowshoe Rabbits. Their principal enemy is man.

Ocelots *(Leopardus pardalis)* are tropical American cats, about three feet long, their tails making up about one-third of this length. They are marked with a series of stripes around their heads and black rings over their bodies. Active mainly at night, Ocelots feed on birds and small mammals. They frequently climb trees to find their prey.

Jaguars *(Felis onca)*, the largest of all American cats, may weigh as much as 250 pounds. They look much like leopards and are more closely related to the Old World lions and tigers than to the New World Puma, or Mountain Lion. Jaguars live in the tropical jungles of Central and South America, occasionally straying north into the arid regions along the Mexican border. Sometimes they eat fish, but their principal food is other mammals, large or small. Jaguars often wait in trees and spring on their prey. They are the chief enemy of the Capybara (see CAPYBARA).

Jaguarundis *(Herpailurus jaguarundi)*, thin-bodied, long-tailed cats of the Central and South American tropics, occur in two colour phases — rusty red and speckled black.

Leopards, or Panthers *(Felis pardus)*, live in Africa, and also from Asia Minor eastwards to Malaya and Java, and north into Siberia. Famous for their cunning and savagery, they have also become notorious in some places as "man-eaters". Large males weigh less than 200 pounds; females are considerably smaller. Leopards eat deer, antelopes, porcupines, pigs, monkeys and other small mammals, sometimes dragging the carcass into a tree. Their coat patterns vary greatly. One of the most common variations is the Black Leopard, though this is rarely found in Africa. The Snow Leopard *(Uncia uncia)*, which has a beautiful, heavy, spotted coat of fur, is nearly as large as a true leopard. It lives in the high Himalayas and north to the Altai Mountains, where it preys heavily on ibexes, goats and other animals. The smaller, blotched Clouded Leopard *(Neofelis nebulosa)* lives in south-eastern Asia.

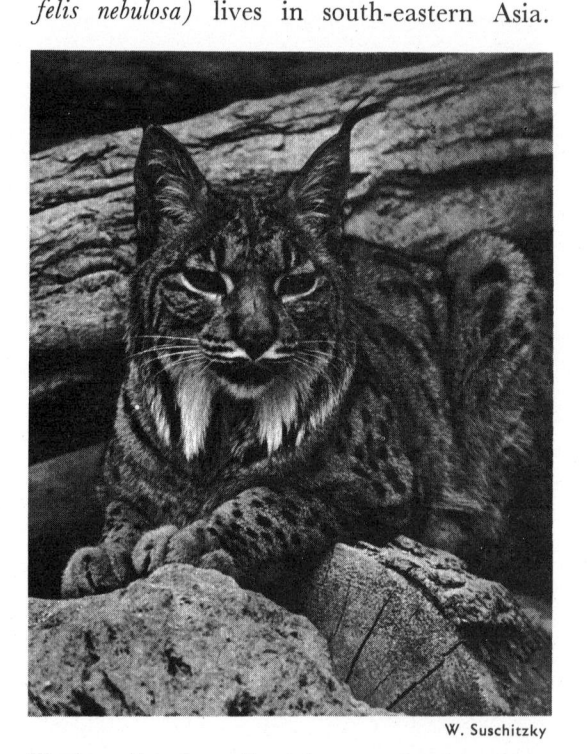

W. Suschitzky

The Lynx lives in northern forests and weighs about 20 pounds when fully grown.

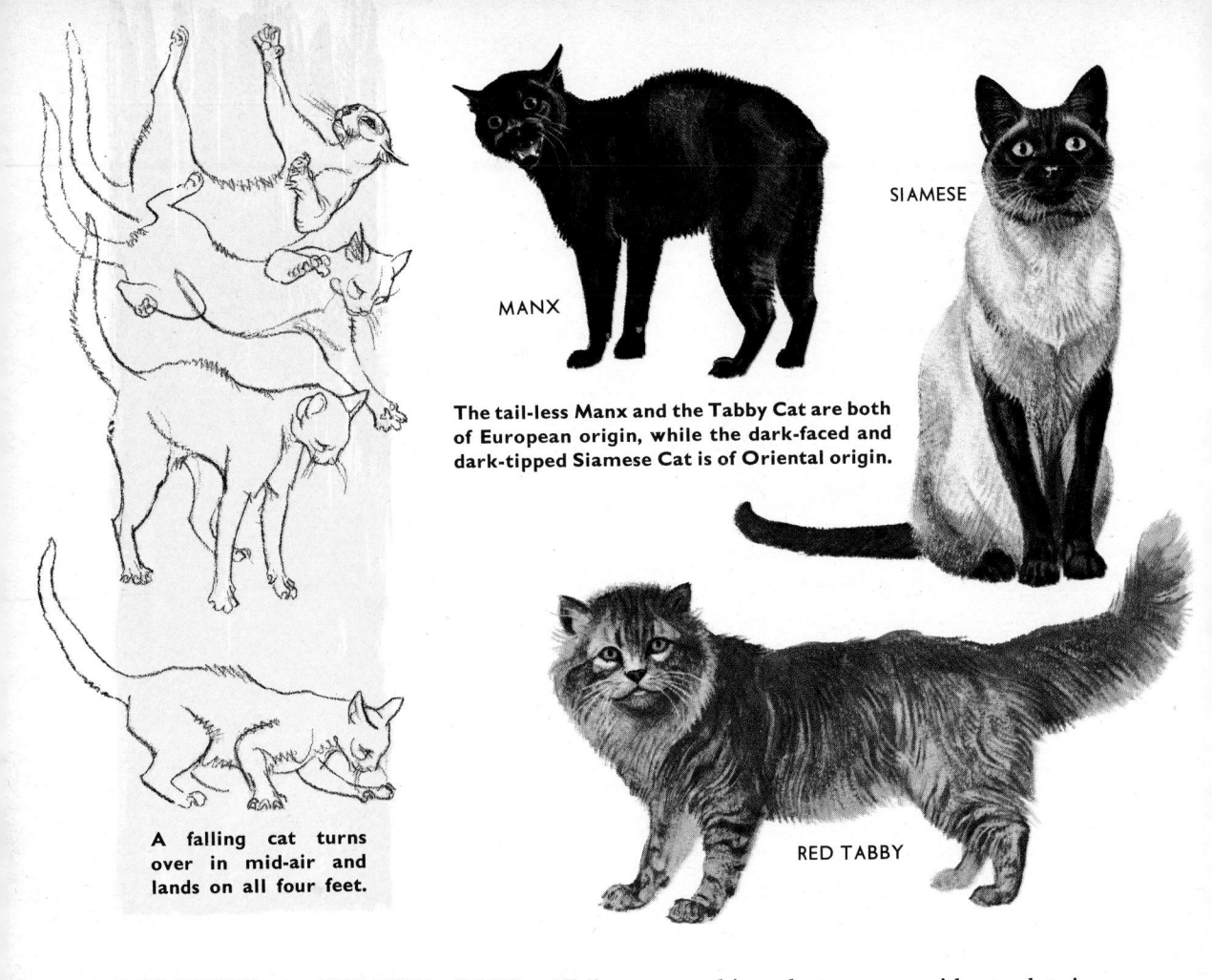

MANX

SIAMESE

The tail-less Manx and the Tabby Cat are both of European origin, while the dark-faced and dark-tipped Siamese Cat is of Oriental origin.

A falling cat turns over in mid-air and lands on all four feet.

RED TABBY

DOMESTIC (or HOUSE) CATS. *(Felis catus)* have been associated with man for much of recorded history, and were employed in ancient Egypt to help control rats and mice that infested stored grain.

More legends and superstitions are associated with cats than with any other animal pet. In ancient Egypt, cats were sacred. Thousands of cat mummies have been found in Egyptian tombs, some in tombs with their masters and others in special cemeteries containing only cats. Egyptians also had cat-headed goddesses. In the Middle Ages, cats were thought to be witches' helpers and sometimes were killed for engaging in witchcraft. In some European countries, however, the cat was so valued as a mouser that anyone guilty of killing one was fined. Cats are still considered to be very important today as mousers in grain-storage areas.

The iris of a cat's eye is slit-like in bright sunshine, but opens wide to let in more light at night. The retina of the eye reflects light in the dark. The eyes of most cats shine blue-green; but those of the Siamese Cat appear a ruby red.

Cats are meat-eaters and they have sharp, tearing teeth. They use their rough tongue to clean the meat from bones and also to comb their fur. In the wild, cats live chiefly on rodents, and birds make up only a small portion of their diet. When a cat is angry or scared, its fur stands erect.

There are many varieties of domestic cat and these fall into two main groups, long-haired and short-haired. Long-haired cats are also known as Persians or Angoras. Persians are short-legged, deep-chested and broad-shouldered, with a broad, round head and large, round eyes. Angoras are similar but have sharper features. Their long hair is noted for its rich gloss. These cats are named by the colour of their coat

and eyes. Copper or orange-eyed cats may be named Black, Blue, Orange, White, Blue Cream, Smoke, Red Tabby, Brown Tabby, Tortoiseshell or Blue Tortoiseshell. Those with green eyes are Chinchilla (or Silver), Shaded Silver or Masked Silver.

Short-haired cats are also divided into two main groups; domestic short-hairs and various foreign breeds. Like the long-haired cats, domestic short-haired cats are named according to their colours: Striped Tabby, Brown Tabby, Silver Tabby, Blue Tabby, Black, Blue, Orange, White, Tortoiseshell, and Tortoiseshell-and-white. Their eye colour ranges from green to orange.

Among the short-haired foreign breeds is the Abyssinian Ticked Cat, apparently descended from Egyptian ancestry. Small and graceful, this cat has a long head, large ears and small feet. Its coat is similar to a wild rabbit's — each hair is barred with

several colours, so that the cat has a reddish-brown undercoat with black ticking. Striping may also occur, and the eyes are green, yellow or hazel. The Abyssinian is rather shy, but pleasant and affectionate.

The Manx Cat, which originated on the Isle of Man, is easily recognised by its lack of a tail. Although there are other bobtailed cats, good Manx Cat specimens actually have a little hollow where the tail would ordinarily be. Manx Cats also have long hind legs and short backs, so that they seem to hop or bob along like rabbits. Their fur is also rabbit-like because it has a soft, thick undercoat. Contrary to the belief of many, however, the Manx Cat is not part rabbit. Manx Cats may be almost any colour. They are usually courageous and independent, but make good pets.

Siamese Cats are easily recognised by the unusual colouring of two main types:

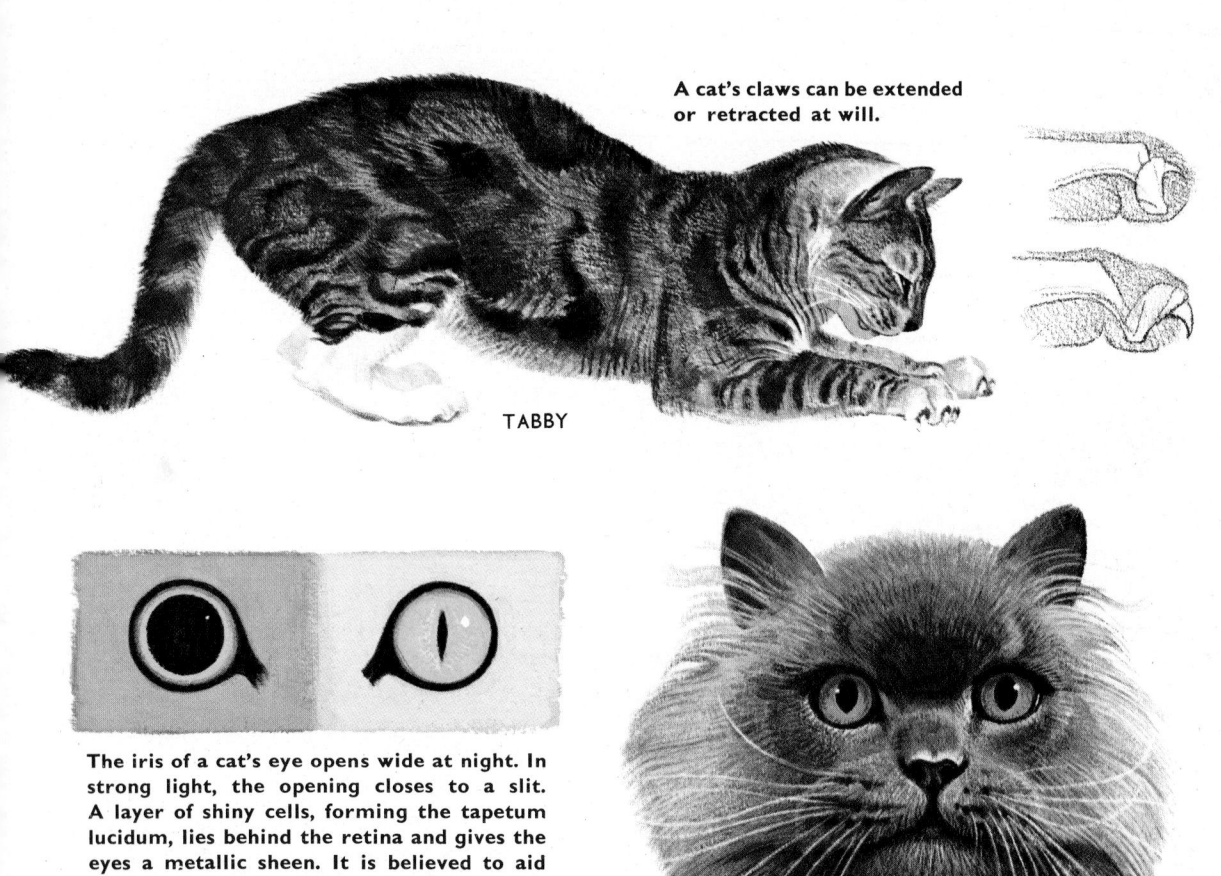

A cat's claws can be extended or retracted at will.

TABBY

The iris of a cat's eye opens wide at night. In strong light, the opening closes to a slit. A layer of shiny cells, forming the tapetum lucidum, lies behind the retina and gives the eyes a metallic sheen. It is believed to aid vision in weak light and causes the cat's eyes to seem to glow when shined upon with a light at night.

BLUE PERSIAN

blue-point and seal-point. The marking patterns are similar for both. A Siamese Cat is usually a light fawn or tan, shading to cream on its underparts. Its tail, legs, ears and face mask are distinctly darker. Seal-point Siamese Cats are generally a rich, deep brown, although the body colour is sometimes a paler shade of brown. Blue-points are marked with a delicate shade of grey-blue, and the body colour usually stays fairly creamy. Body shading seems to vary with the health, age and ancestry of the cat. Siamese Cats have slanted eyes of a deep sapphire blue. Their bodies are slim and muscular, and their tails long and tapered. They have rather narrow heads and small feet. It is said that these cats were used as watch animals in Siam. It is true that they are very active, love to climb, and give loud calls that sound more like a crying baby than a cat. Siamese Cats are probably the most popular of the show breeds.

The slightly smaller Burmese Cat, another of the short-haired breeds, is less well-known than the Siamese Cat, but makes a gentle, friendly pet. Its glossy coat is a deep brown, shading to lighter brown on the underbody. An individual with a slightly kinked tail is not uncommon.

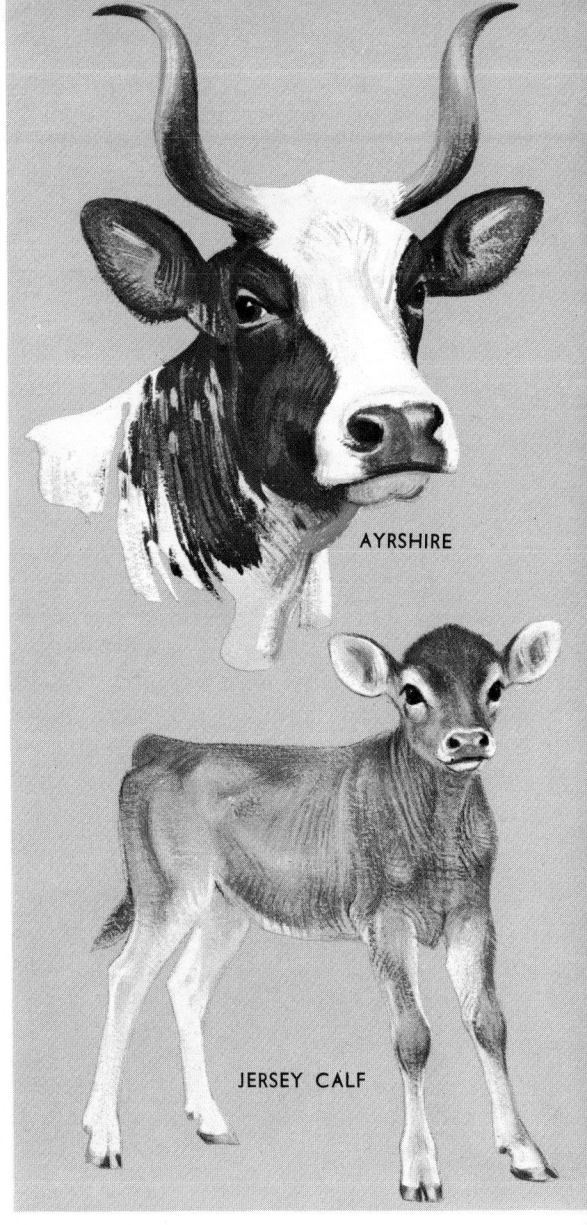

AYRSHIRE

JERSEY CALF

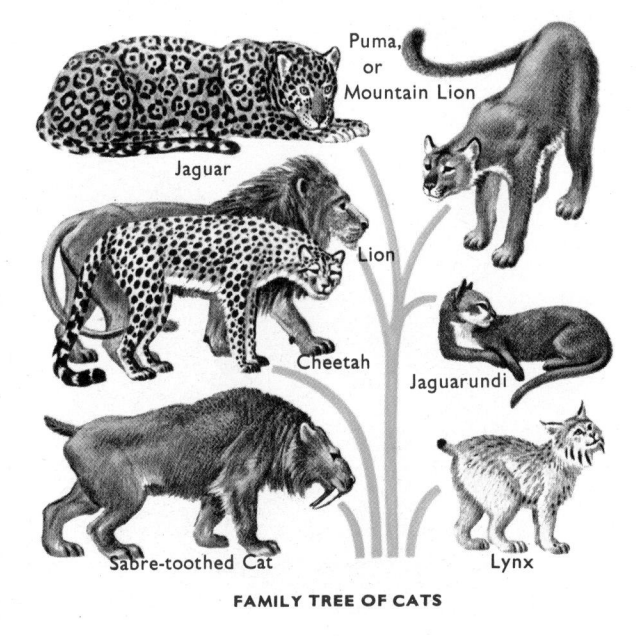

FAMILY TREE OF CATS

Jaguar

Puma, or Mountain Lion

Lion

Cheetah

Jaguarundi

Sabre-toothed Cat

Lynx

CATTLE have served man since prehistoric days as beasts of burden and as suppliers of milk, meat, and leather. Some of the earliest written records concern the sale of cattle.

There are many breeds of cattle developed for milk production, beef or as dual-purpose animals. Most modern breeds of cattle belong to the species *Bos taurus*.

The Zebu, or Brahman *(Bos indicus)*, of Asia has been introduced to America. Texas Longhorns of the Western United States are descendants of Andalusian cattle brought to America by the Spaniards. The early cattle industry in the western United States made famous the Texas

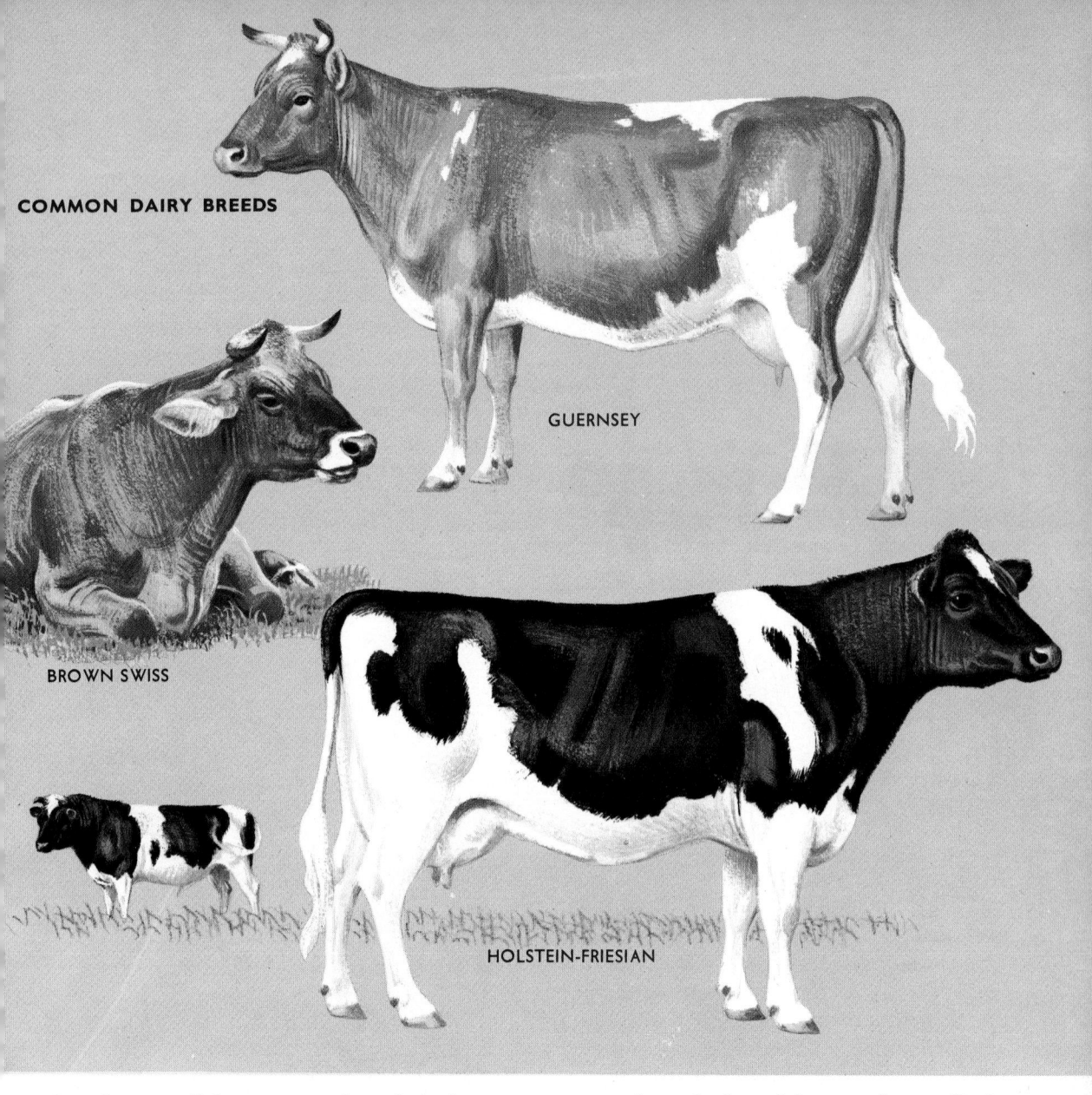

COMMON DAIRY BREEDS

GUERNSEY

BROWN SWISS

HOLSTEIN-FRIESIAN

Longhorns. Calves were branded in a spring round-up, and cattle were driven to market in the autumn. Large round-ups and cattle drives ended in the 1890s as fencing of western lands eliminated open ranges, but annual round-ups for branding still go on.

Red Polls are beefy, red, hornless cattle from England. In the United States, this dual-purpose breed is not as popular as the Milking Shorthorn.

Brahmans from India are also dual-purpose cattle and are easily distinguished from other breeds by their humps, drooping ears, saggy skins and broad horns. They are various shades of fawn and tan. Brahmans can withstand hot weather and are not as bothered by insects as other breeds.

Cattle swallow their food quickly and store it in the paunch, or rumen, the first of the four compartments in the stomach. Later the food passes into the second stomach, or reticulum, where it is rolled into little balls, or cuds. When the animal is resting, it coughs up these cuds and chews them more thoroughly. This time they pass into the third and then into the fourth stomach, where digestion takes place. Bacteria in the stomach aid in digesting the cellulose in stems of grass or hay.

Ayrshires are sturdy dairy cattle, bred originally in Scotland. They are usually red-and-white spotted, with a dark muzzle and a white switch of hair at the end of the tail. One strain is polled, or hornless, but most Ayrshires have long horns. Their butter-fat is produced in small, easily-digested globules.

Brown Swiss, possibly the oldest breed of dairy cattle, came from Switzerland.

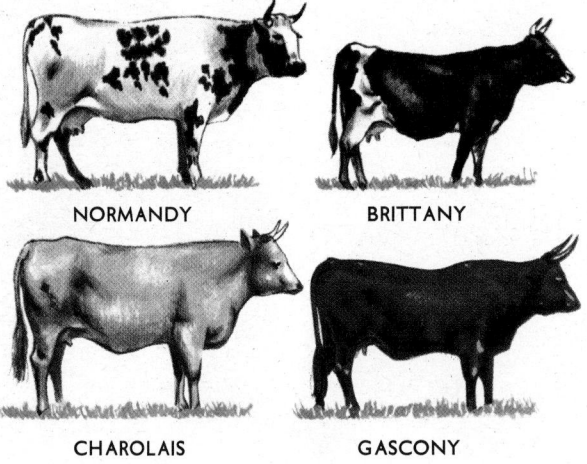

NORMANDY   BRITTANY

CHAROLAIS   GASCONY

Their colour ranges from grey to brown, with light hair on the underbody, muzzle, eyes and spine. Often their nose, tongue, switch and horn-tips are black. Brown Swiss are so strong and gentle that they are sometimes used in their native land as work animals. They are well adapted to hilly land.

Holstein-Friesians are large, black-and-white spotted cattle that originated in the Netherlands. They are the most popular dairy cattle in the United States. Holstein-Friesians produce the most milk, but it does not have such a high butter-fat content as the milk of other breeds.

Guernseys came from the island of Guernsey, in the English Channel, off the north-western coast of France. Their colour ranges from pale tan through orange to reddish-brown, often with white markings. The skin under their hair is yellow, the muzzle often buff, and the switch white. Guernsey milk is very yellow and contains rather

large fat globules, ranking next to the milk of Jerseys in richness.

Jersey cattle came from the island of Jersey, also in the English Channel. Their colour may be any shade of fawn, grey or mahogany-brown, with occasional white markings. Usually the muzzle and tongue are grey, the switch black. The hair around the muzzle is often pale. Although Jerseys are the smallest of the dairy cattle breeds, they produce the richest milk, with more than 5 per cent butter-fat. They are the best-tempered dairy breed.

Herefords are large, sturdy meat or beef breed cattle from England. They are red-and-white on the face, underbody, throat and top of the neck. They are said to be able to find their own food on the open

BRAHMAN

SHORTHORN

SANTA GERTRUDIS

range better than most breeds. A hornless, or polled, strain has been developed.

Aberdeen Angus are smooth-haired, jet-black, hornless beef cattle that were developed in Scotland. They are about the same size as Herefords.

Galloways, also from Scotland, resemble Angus cattle in being hornless and black; their hair is much longer, however. They are not as popular as other beef breeds.

Shorthorns, which originated in England, may be red, white, red-and-white, or roan (red-and-white hairs mixed together). Shorthorns are the largest of the beef breeds. Hornless Shorthorns have been developed.

Santa Gertrudis is a new breed developed in the United States. The animals are about five-eighths Shorthorn and three-eighths Brahman, having inherited the red colour and beefy body of the Shorthorn, and the hardiness and heat resistance of the Brahman. The Brangus, a breed now being developed, is a Brahman-Angus cross.

Dual-purpose cattle are used for both milk and meat. Milking Shorthorns are a dual-purpose breed. Their colouring is the same as the Shorthorn, but they are not quite as beefy and compact. Milking Shorthorns also produce much more milk.

CAVE ANIMALS live their life in a world of darkness, high humidity, moderate temperature, and absence of air currents. Rain, snow and excess heat are unknown in caves. Green plants cannot grow in darkness, so the only plant food available in caves is such blown-in or washed-in debris as dead leaves and wood on which molds and fungi grow. These, in turn, support fungus-eating beetles. Springtails

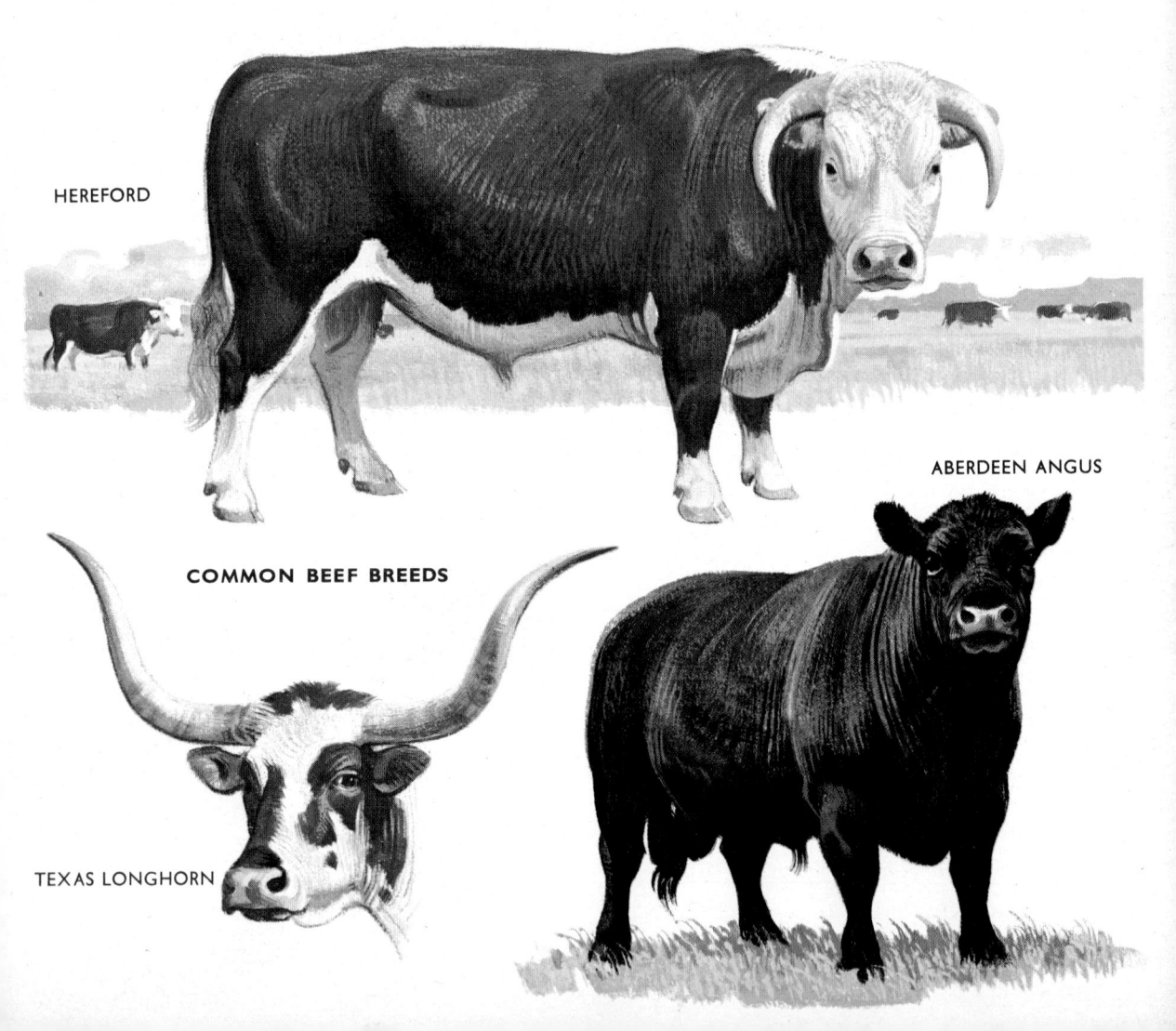

HEREFORD

COMMON BEEF BREEDS

ABERDEEN ANGUS

TEXAS LONGHORN

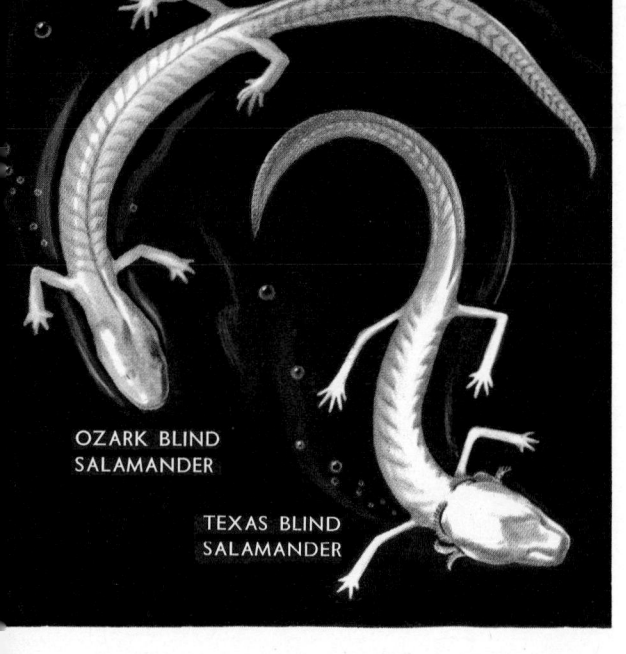

OZARK BLIND
SALAMANDER

TEXAS BLIND
SALAMANDER

**Ozark Blind Salamanders (Typhlotriton Spelaeus)
are born with eyes, but lose them. Texas Blind Salamanders (Typholomolge rathbuni) are born blind.**

and mites live on bat guano (excrement),
and also on food carried in by seepage
or ground water. Since food is usually
scarce in caves, living things are not abundant, and most cave animals are smaller
than their nearest relatives that live outside.

Most cave animals are white or nearly so.
Some kinds of cave fishes and beetles have
traces of colour, and spiders are fairly
dark. Many cave animals are blind, or
have only very small eyes.

Cave salamanders, members of the two
families *Proteidae* and *Plethodontidae,*
are colourless, but the blood showing through
their thin skin gives them a pinkish cast.
They are also blind, and many have a thin,
starved look. Found only in Yugoslavia,
Austria and the south-eastern United States,
all cave salamanders are water-dwellers,
most of them keeping and using their
gills throughout their lives.

Most species of one group of cave salamanders exist in springs. Their skin is
pigmented, and they have functional eyes.
Like other cave salamanders, however,
they never transform completely. They
reproduce as larvae. It is a short step from
life in these springs to life in underground

water channels which have springs as
their surface openings. What forms of
life these underground "rivers" may conceal
quickens the imagination.

Salamanders that live in underground
water have extremely slender bodies and
limbs. This may be a consequence of the
environment in which they live, for artesian
waters contain virtually no food. Apparently
these salamanders rarely eat, and the small
amount they do eat lasts them a long time.
European artesian salamanders have been
kept in captivity for *years* without taking
any visible food. Seemingly these animals
can subsist by absorbing into their bodies
the organic matter dissolved in the water.

Such animals as bears, badgers, muskrats,
foxes and bats may spend much of their
lives in caves but are not confined to them.
Bats spend as much as three-fourths of
their lives hanging upside down in caves,
some of which may harbour many thousands
of these flying mammals. (See BATS.)

CEPHALOPODS are the most highly
developed of all molluscs and of invertebrates in general. The Chambered Nautilus, most primitive of the cephalopods,
lives only in the Indo-Pacific, and the
Cuttlefish, with its chalky internal shell,
does not occur in the Western Hemisphere.
Cuttlebone (the shell of a cuttlefish) is
widely used in the diet of cage birds.

Octopuses and squids belong to this
group. They are peculiar among molluscs

**Blind, colourless fish live in the limestone caves of
the central Mississippi Basin.**

Janet L. Stone

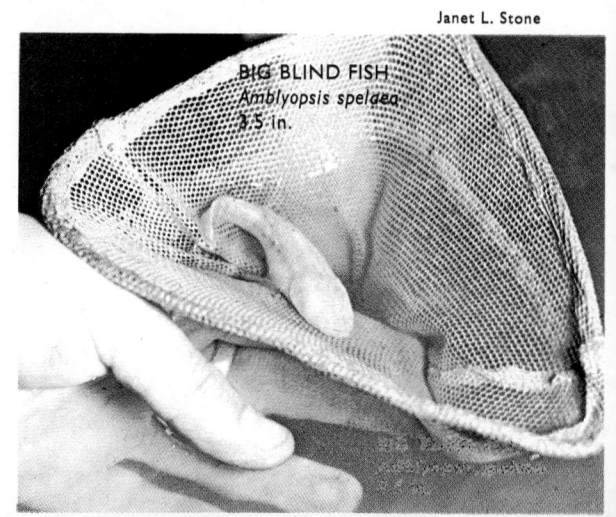

BIG BLIND FISH
Amblyopsis spelaea
3.5 in.

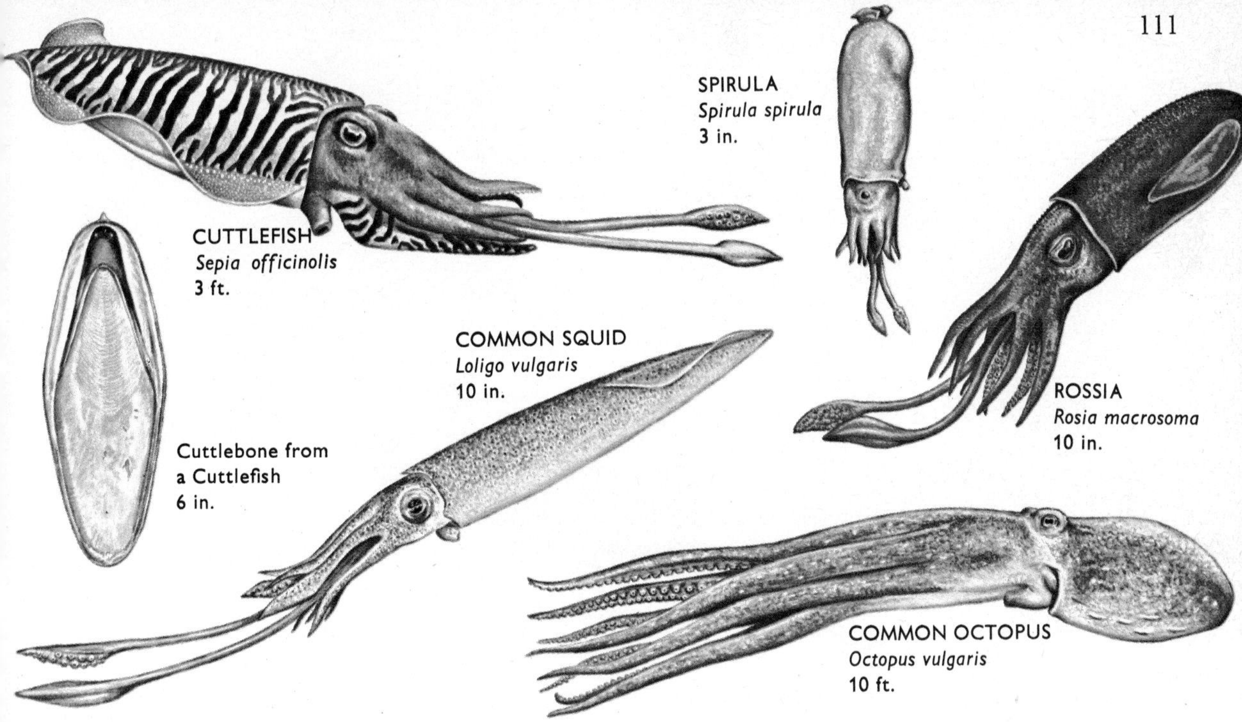

SPIRULA
Spirula spirula
3 in.

CUTTLEFISH
Sepia officinolis
3 ft.

Cuttlebone from
a Cuttlefish
6 in.

COMMON SQUID
Loligo vulgaris
10 in.

ROSSIA
Rosia macrosoma
10 in.

COMMON OCTOPUS
Octopus vulgaris
10 ft.

because their foot has become eight or ten long arms, or tentacles, surrounding their heads. Each arm bears numerous large suckers for grasping prey. Their well-developed brains are protected by a partial cranium, and their eyes are the most highly developed among the invertebrates, rivalling the eyes of man.

A squid's shell has been reduced to a thin, delicate shell under the skin on its back; this is called a "pen". An octopus has no shell at all. Squids swim by jet propulsion; water enters the mantle cavity

all around the head, and then is forced out by muscular contraction through the funnel, or siphon. Squids also can swim slowly by using the triangular fins formed from their mantle. Octopuses can swim slowly by jet propulsion, but normally crawl along the bottom as they hunt for clams, crabs and lobsters. Squids feed on fishes, shrimps, and also on other squids.

Cephalopods are both shore and open-ocean dwellers, some living at great depths. They range in size from about half an inch in length to the Giant Squid *(Architeuthis princeps)*, the largest known invertebrate.

Cephalopods are among the most common of marine animals, and are highly prized as food by such sea mammals as sperm whales and porpoises — and also by man. They are eaten by people in many countries. Over 60 per cent of the fishery harvest in Japan, the leading fishing country of the world, is of one species of squid, *Todarodes pacificus*. (See OCTOPUS; SQUID.)

CHAMELEONS *(Chamaeleo* spp.) are the strangest of all lizards. Some 85 species are found in Africa and Madagascar; one occurs in southern Spain and Palestine; one in India and Ceylon; and two in Arabia. Both the

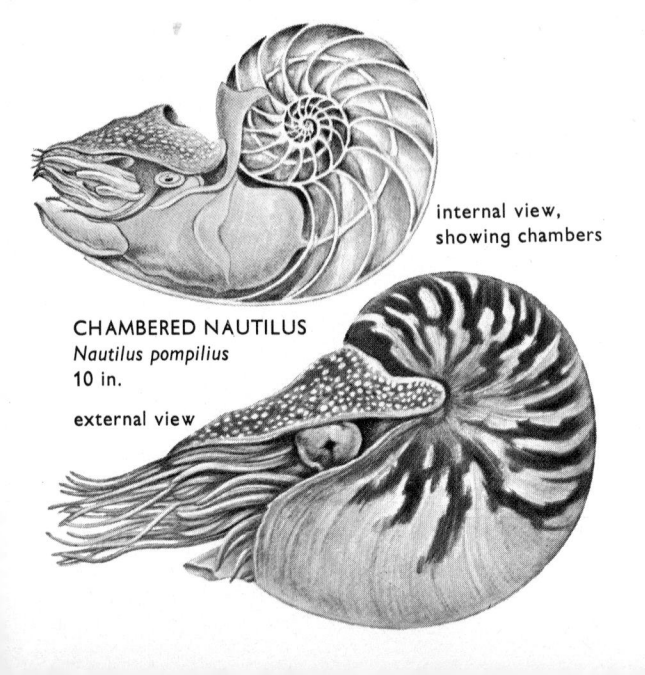

internal view,
showing chambers

CHAMBERED NAUTILUS
Nautilus pompilius
10 in.

external view

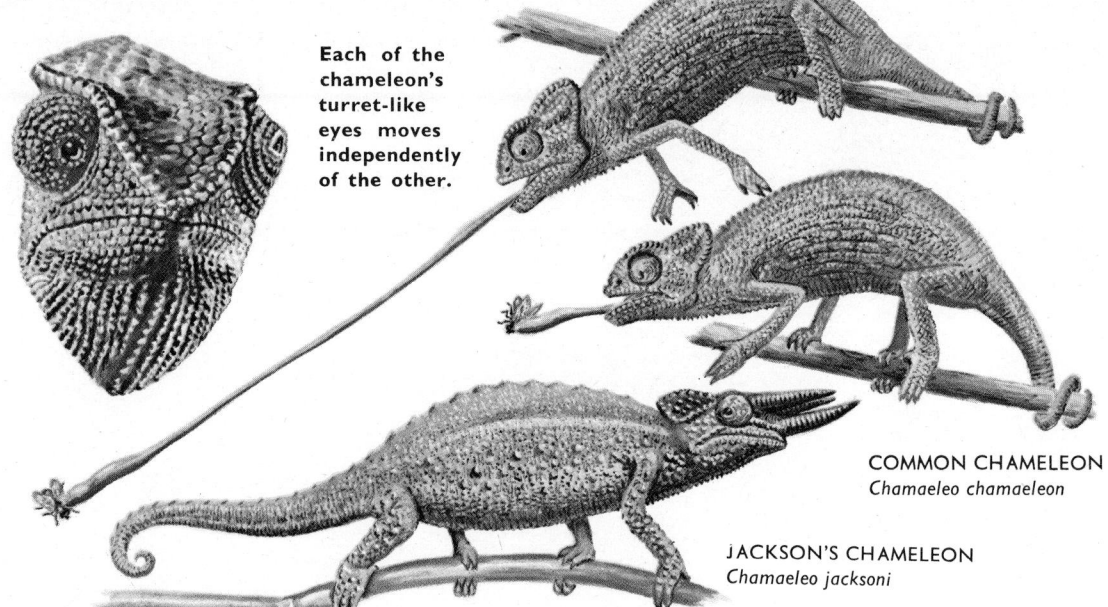

Each of the chameleon's turret-like eyes moves independently of the other.

Photo Gobin-Viollet

COMMON CHAMELEON
Chamaeleo chamaeleon

JACKSON'S CHAMELEON
Chamaeleo jacksoni

The Common Chameleon lives in North Africa and part of Spain. Jackson's Chameleon comes from tropical East Africa.

longest (2 feet) and the shortest (1½ inches) occur on Madagascar.

True chameleons can change colour among greens, browns, reds, yellows, white and black. They can also shift their colour pattern. Common American Anoles, sometimes described as "chameleons", are able to change only between green and brown (see ANOLES). True chameleons possess highly manoeuvrable. turret-like eyes, very long tongues and long, grasping tails.

Chameleons are the sloths of the reptile world. They walk with an odd, excruciatingly slow gait, moving their arms and legs slowly and one at a time. From time to time they rock their bodies, simulating fluttering leaves. Their fingers and toes are fused — three on one side and two on the other — forming a secure clamp for climbing the trees, vines and bushes in which most chameleons live. A few African species occasionally walk on the ground.

All reptiles can move their eyes independently, but this can be seen easily only in chameleons. Chameleons' eyelids are almost completely fused, with only a small hole in the centre when their eyes are open; the hole moves as the eye moves.

A chameleon's tongue is a slender sac with a sticky enlargement at its tip. Insects are caught on the tip when the tongue is "shot" at them. This happens when muscles contract around the fluid-filled sac and squirt the tongue forward so quickly that the eye can hardly follow the movement. Their target is rarely missed. The tongue can be extended to a greater length than the lizard's head and body. A different set of muscles snaps the tongue back, and the insect is swallowed.

When a male meets a male, he turns his body broadside to his competitor, and at the same time displays his colours, inflates his throat and opens his mouth slightly. Rarely is there any real physical contact. Males of some species have horns or flaps on their snouts, or elsewhere on their heads. These, too, seem to be used to attract females or to intimidate other males.

A few kinds of chameleon bear their young alive, but most lay their eggs in laboriously dug nests in the ground or in rotten wood.

CHAMOIS *(Rupicapra rupicapra)* are goat-like mammals that live in the Pyrenees, Alps and other high ranges of southern Europe. Chamois are so sure-footed that they can climb or descend steep rocky slopes with

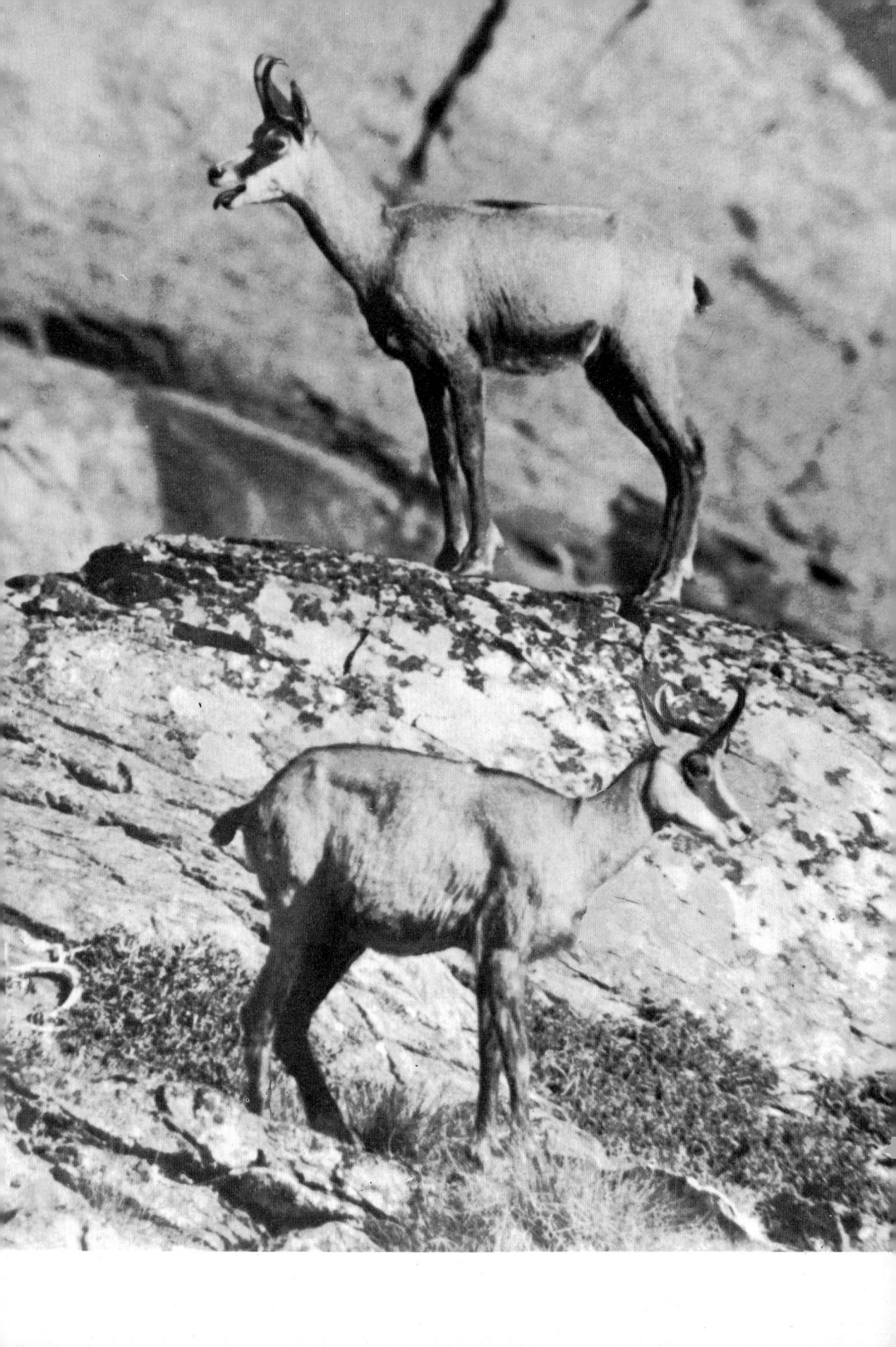

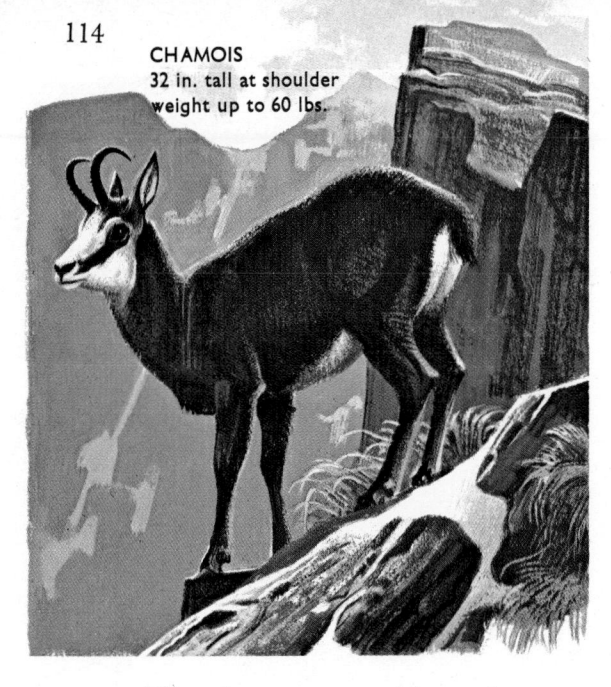

CHAMOIS
32 in. tall at shoulder
weight up to 60 lbs.

call is described as a barking howl. The structure of the foot differs somewhat from other cats, for cheetahs cannot completely retract their claws (see CATS). The fastest of all land mammals, they are said to be able to run at up to 70 m. p. h. in short sprints.

Cheetahs live in open country from southern Asia to Africa. These large cats (about 100 pounds) feed mainly on antelopes, which they catch with a swift, rushing attack. They are easily tamed and trained as hunting animals. A cheetah trained for hunting is taken into the field with a hood over its eyes. When antelopes are sighted, the hood is lifted, and the cheetah is turned loose to run the antelope down. Cheetahs are frequently called Hunting Leopards.

Cheetahs live together and usually hunt in pairs at sunrise and sunset. It is said that they never attack man.

ease. They leap across wide ravines, or stand safely on pinnacles barely large enough to accommodate their feet. Both male and female Chamois have small, rounded horns. Their shaggy coats of brown fur protect them from the cold of the high mountains. In summer they live near the tree line, feeding on lichens and alpine plants. In winter groups of Chamois move down the mountains to browse in the forests.

The soft leather made from their hides is called "chamois" or "shammy". Many other kinds of soft leather are now called chamois. Because the Chamois has become so rare, it is now protected in Switzerland.

CHEETAHS *(Acinonyx jubatus)*, the most unusual members of the cat family, have very long legs, a small head and short fur. Their

CHICKENS. Domestic chickens *(Gallus domesticus)* apparently originated in southern Asia from the Jungle Fowl, thousands of years ago. Bantams and fighting cocks are much like their ancestors.

By selective breeding, a great variety of birds, differing in shape, colour and size, have been produced. Different birds have been required for egg-laying, for meat, for fighting, or just to please the eye. Some have very long tails, and some have topknots and silky feathers. For show purposes, chickens are divided into classes. Classes are divided into breeds, which are groups that agree with size and shape specifications. Breeds are further divided into varieties. Thus the

Adult Cheetahs can be trained to hunt or tamed to be affectionate pets.

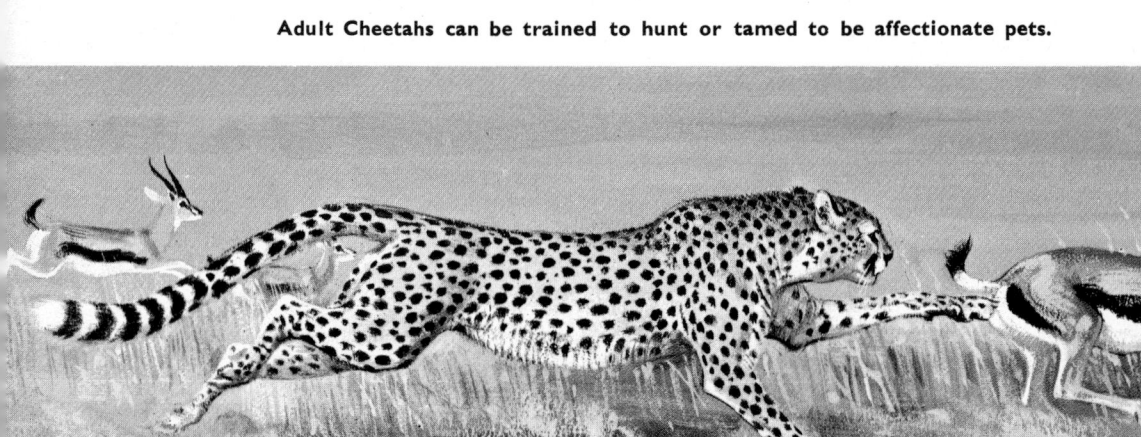

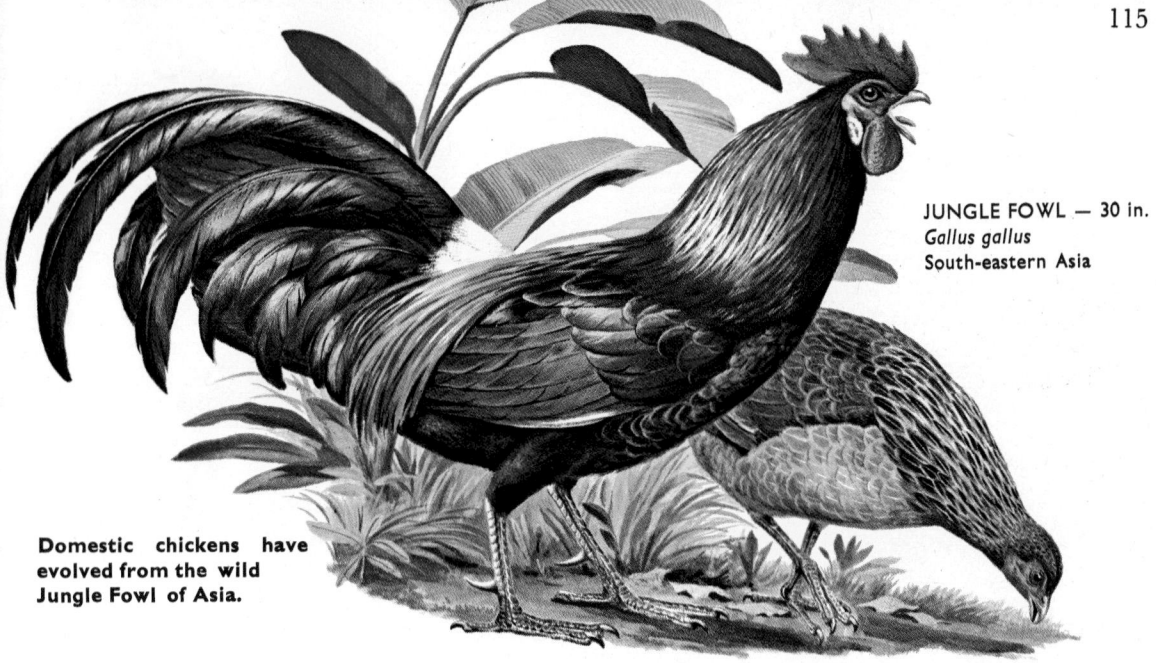

JUNGLE FOWL — 30 in.
Gallus gallus
South-eastern Asia

Domestic chickens have
evolved from the wild
Jungle Fowl of Asia.

Leghorn breed includes such varieties as White Leghorns, Buff Leghorns, Black Leghorns and Silver Leghorns.

In exhibition shows, chickens are judged on colour, size and shape. Hens are judged also on their ability to produce eggs, and roosters on their ability to transmit good production characteristics to their offspring.

Domestic chickens are being changed continually by selective breeding, to improve their usefulness either for meat or as egg-layers. In 1940, the average hen laid 100 eggs a year; in 1955, 150 eggs. Today, a hen may lay as many as 300 eggs in a year.

A five-pound hen needs approximately 90 pounds of food a year to keep her body weight uniform and to lay well. Improved feeds that make chickens grow faster, plus mechanical methods used while raising the birds and in preparing them for market, have lowered the cost of producing chickens and their eventual cost to consumers.

In captivity, hens in a flock arrange themselves in a "pecking order". The hen at the top can peck all the other hens, the one next in rank may peck all but the leader, and so on down the line. A rooster has "pecking rights" over all the hens. (See POULTRY.)

CHIMPANZEES *(Pan troglodytes)* are apes native to the forests of tropical Africa. A large adult male weighs about 150 pounds and stands five feet tall. Females are smaller. The Chimpanzee's body is more sparsely haired than that of the Orang-utan. Because of their human-like expressions and intelligence, Chimpanzees are used in the study of behaviour and diseases. They can learn many tricks and soon master skills that require a degree of reasoning.

While Chimpanzees are principally vegetarians, feeding on fruits, leaves and nuts, in captivity they soon learn to eat almost the same foods as man. They are tree-dwellers and build their nests in branches several

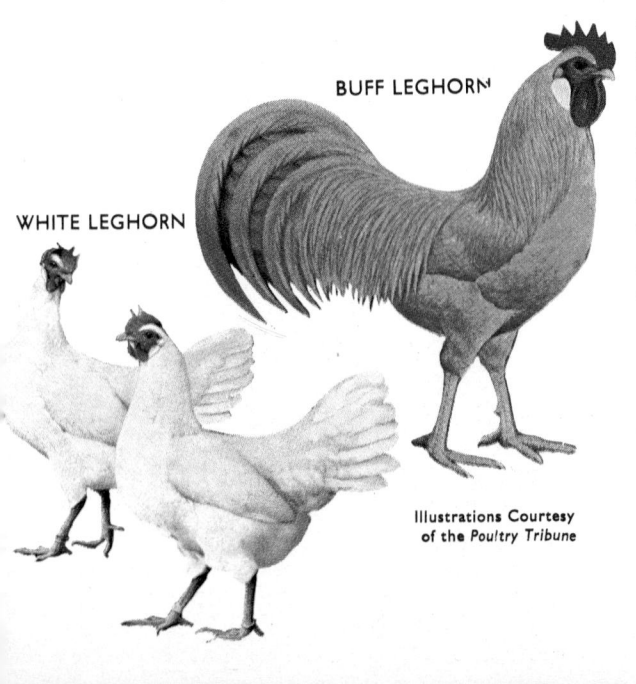

BUFF LEGHORN

WHITE LEGHORN

Illustrations Courtesy
of the *Poultry Tribune*

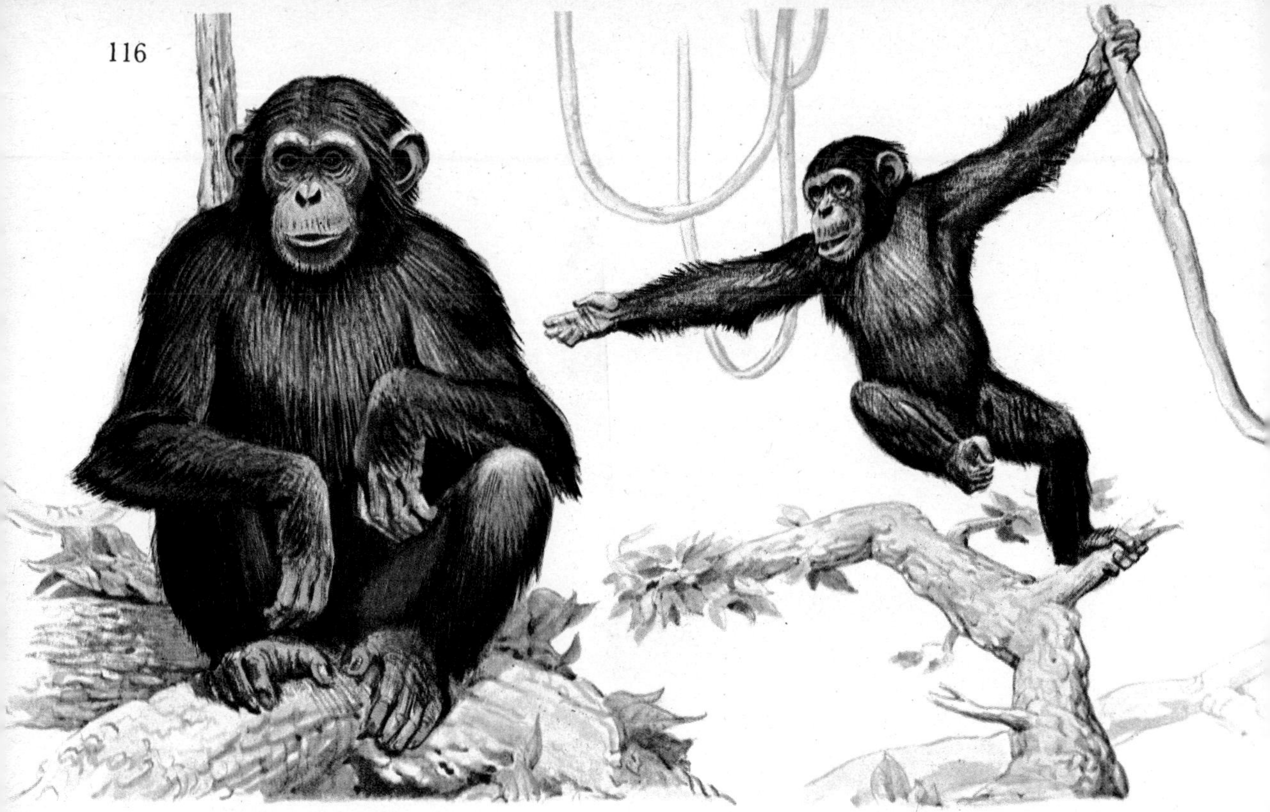

feet above the floor of the forest.

Chimpanzees use their long arms and large feet, with thumb-like first toes, to climb about in trees. They can walk erect, but usually move on all-fours, using the knuckles of their hands as well as their flat hind feet for support. Chimpanzees travel in loosely-organised groups, and communicate with a simple "language" of sounds which express their feelings.

CHINCHILLAS *(Chinchilla laniger)* are small, silky-furred rodents native to the South American Andes and the coastal mountains west of the Andes. Chinchillas live in burrows and rocky crevices as high as 11,000 feet. Because of their valuable fur, they have been hunted for more than a century and are now extinct in many parts. Wild animals become more rare each year, although they are now protected by laws.

Chinchillas are also raised on fur farms in many parts of the world. The fur of a Chinchilla is extremely fine and soft, but since the animals are so small (not over 12 inches in length), it takes many pelts (100 or more) to make a coat. This is one of the reasons why chinchilla coats are so costly.

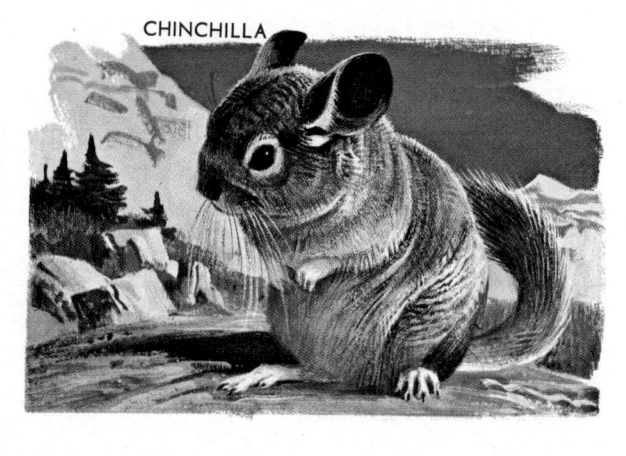

CHINCHILLA

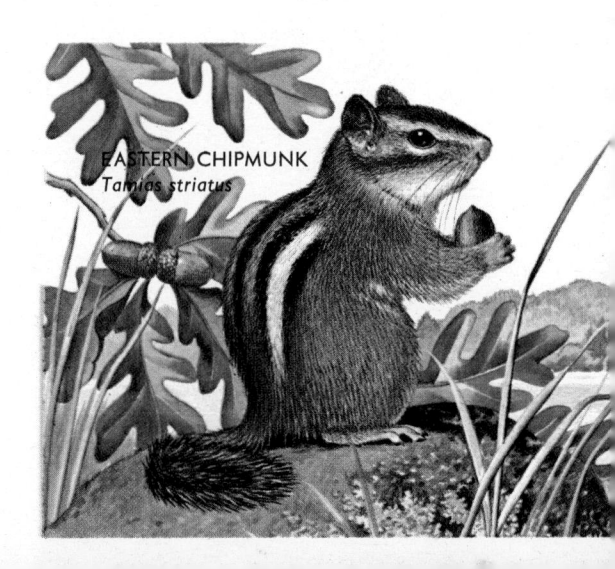

EASTERN CHIPMUNK
Tamias striatus

CHIPMUNKS are small, brightly coloured, striped squirrels found throughout most of North America. All chipmunks feed on nuts and seeds, but now and then make a meal of insects, mushrooms or birds' eggs. They stuff their cheek pouches with food and carry it to a safe place to eat or store it. Some kinds hibernate during periods of extreme cold.

The Eastern Chipmunk *(Tamias striatus)* is often seen scampering along logs or through thickets in woodlands of the eastern United States and Canada. Only rarely does it climb shrubs or trees. It builds its nest in a chamber at the end of a long, shallow burrow. Like all chipmunks, it is active by day. Many other kinds of chipmunks live in western North America. A few, such as the Lodgepole *(Eutamias speciosus),* spend a great deal of time in trees.

Asiatic chipmunks are much like those of western North America, living principally on the ground. Their fur is sometimes sold.

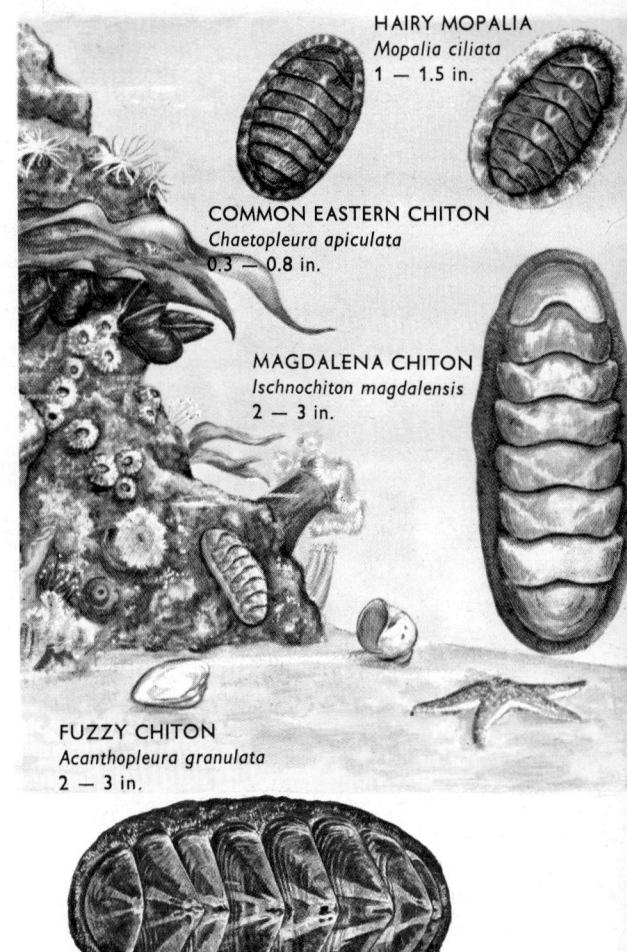

HAIRY MOPALIA
Mopalia ciliata
1 — 1.5 in.

COMMON EASTERN CHITON
Chaetopleura apiculata
0.3 — 0.8 in.

MAGDALENA CHITON
Ischnochiton magdalensis
2 — 3 in.

FUZZY CHITON
Acanthopleura granulata
2 — 3 in.

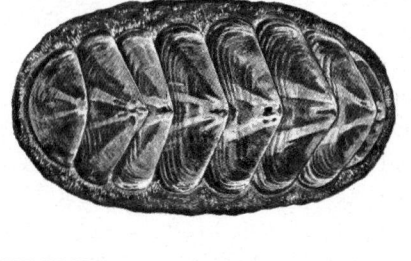

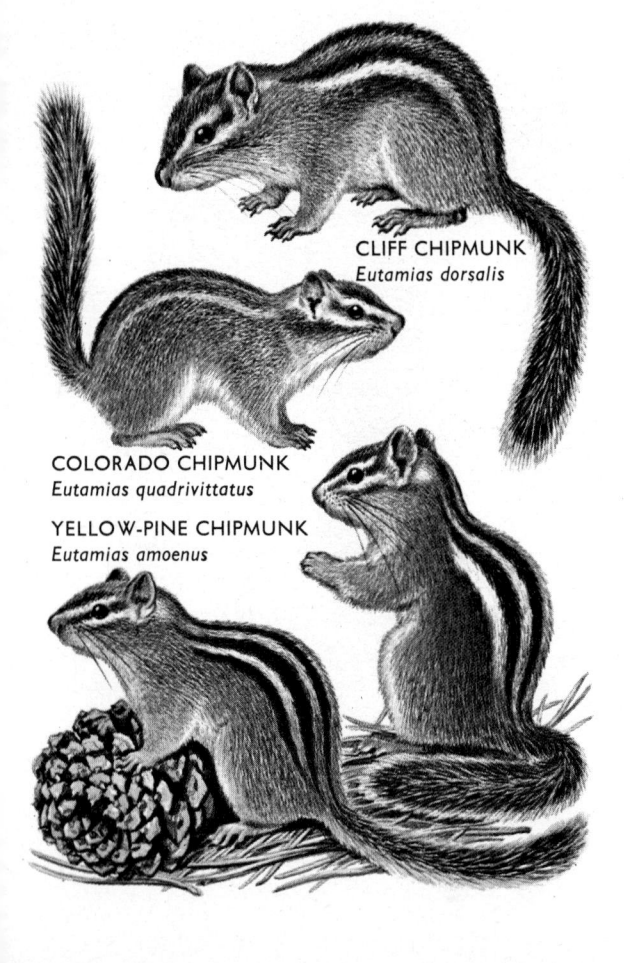

CLIFF CHIPMUNK
Eutamias dorsalis

COLORADO CHIPMUNK
Eutamias quadrivittatus

YELLOW-PINE CHIPMUNK
Eutamias amoenus

CHITONS are primitive molluscs of the class *Amphineura*. Their jointed shells are composed of eight overlapping plates connected by a tough, gristly girdle. Most chitons live on rocks, to which they are tightly attached by a tough, muscular foot. They may fasten themselves above the tide-mark, in tide-pools, or beneath the surface. Often they hide under rocks during the day. Chitons feed mainly on algae, which they scrape from the surface of the rocks with their file-like radula, or rasping organ. Chitons vary in length from less than an inch to nearly a foot. They are most numerous along the Pacific Coast, but also occur from New England to Florida and in the West Indies. In some areas they are very common and in some countries are

eaten. Their plates are often used in making jewellery. They are world-wide in distribution. (See MOLLUSCS.)

CICADAS *(Cicadidae)* are insects that are more often heard thon seen. Each of the more than 1,500 species in the world has a distinctive song by which it can be identified, and, except for a few species, the song is produced only by males. Often loud and continuous, the noise is made by contracting muscles that cause two oval, ribbed structures (tymbals) to buckle and vibrate. These are located one on each side of the body in cavities, usually covered by a plate which is called an operculum.

Some cicadas are less than an inch long, but many kinds are two inches or more in length and have wing-spans of three or four inches. They are the largest members of the order *Homoptera*. Their big eyes protrude from their large, somewhat flattened heads. Both pairs of membranous wings are held roof-like over their abdomens and extend beyond its tip.

Female cicadas lay their eggs in slits cut in twigs of trees and shrubs with their dagger-like ovipositors. Sometimes these slits are so numerous that the growing tips of the twigs die, seriously injuring the plant. In four to six weeks the eggs hatch, and the newly-hatched nymphs drop to the ground, where they burrow into the soil. They form a small

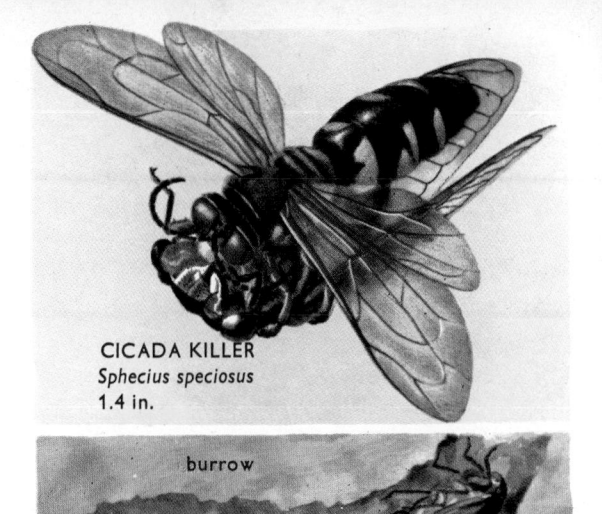

CICADA KILLER
Sphecius speciosus
1.4 in.

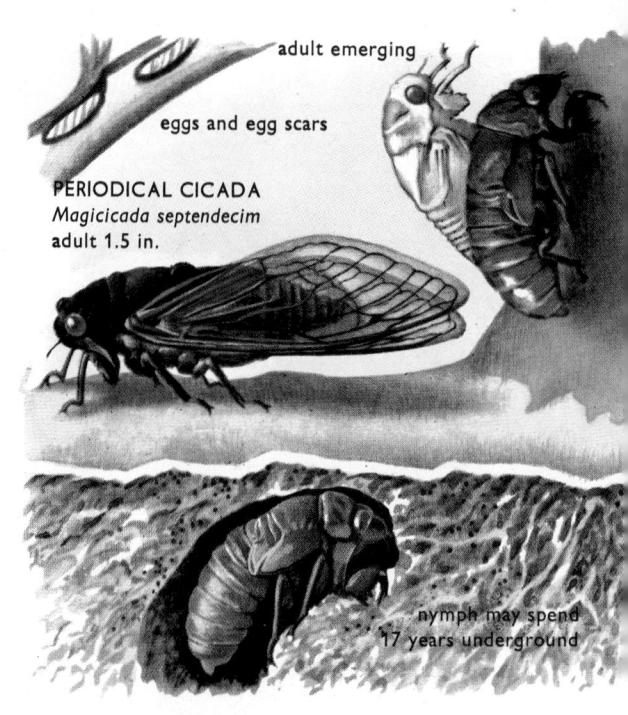

burrow

Cicada killer dragging a second victim into its underground burrow.

adult emerging

eggs and egg scars

PERIODICAL CICADA
Magicicada septendecim
adult 1.5 in.

nymph may spend
17 years underground

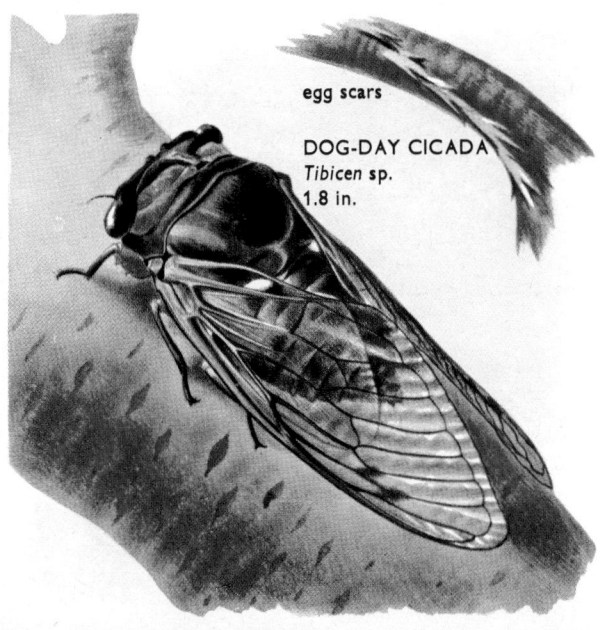

egg scars

DOG-DAY CICADA
Tibicen sp.
1.8 in.

cell around a rootlet from which they suck the sap. This feeding usually does not have a noticeable effect on the plant. When the nymph is full grown, it burrows to the surface and emerges. Often it makes mud tubes as much as two or three inches high around this hole, then crawls up the trunk of a tree or a shrub where it clings to the bark. Soon the nymph's skin splits down the middle of its back, and an adult slowly

work its way out. Several hours may pass before the wings have hardened and it is ready to fly.

The Dog-day Cicada, or Harvestman, usually completes its life cycle in two years. The Periodical Cicada, found only in eastern North America, requires 17 years and is often called the Seventeen-year Locust. Some broods in the south-eastern United States complete their cycle in 13 years, however. Early settlers probably referred to cicadas as locusts because they appeared in swarms, like the locust plagues of the Old World.

CIVETS (*Civettictis* spp.; *Viverra* spp., and others) are carnivorous mammals of southern Europe, Africa and Asia. Most kinds can secrete a strong defence scent, called civet.

Civets eat mice, birds, small game animals, and occasionally insects or fruit. Most civets are the size of cats or smaller, and many are good climbers. Genets (*Genetta* spp.) are a group of civets about the size of minks. Because of their colour and spotting, they are sometimes called leopard tigers, or spotted genets. The noisy Binturong is also a civet (see BINTURONG).

The best-known member of the family is the Mongoose (*Herpestes* spp.), which eats rats and snakes, and for this reason is welcomed around houses in its native India. It is also found in Africa. In 1872 the Mongoose was introduced to Jamaica, to control rats. It did not eliminate the rats, but it did multiply rapidly and became a pest itself, destroying native birds and poultry.

CLICK BEETLES (*Elateridae*). If a click beetle on a plant is touched, it generally feigns death by folding its legs and dropping to the ground. More often than not it lands on its back. After remaining still for a short time, the beetle arches its body so that only its front and rear parts touch the ground. Then, with a snap, the beetle straightens out and is flipped into the air. This process is repeated until the beetle lands on its feet. The flipping is accomplished by a special device on the under-surface of the beetle. A short spine beneath the thorax normally rests in a groove, but when the beetle arches its body, the spine is raised out of the groove. When the beetle straightens its body, the spine snaps back into the groove and causes the insect to be thrown into the air.

Most click beetles are black, brown or grey. A few are metallic, and some tropical species have red or green luminous spots. Some click beetles are found on flowers and foliage; others live in decaying wood.

The wireworm group of larvae are hard, smooth, brownish in colour and cylindrical. They burrow in the ground and feed on seeds and roots. Many are pests on corn and small grains, or potatoes and other root crops. Some live in the soil for as long as six years before transforming into pupae. Adults often live for as long as a year, spending the winter in burrows in the ground.

The Eyed Elater, one of the largest of the click beetles, may measure an inch and a half in length. It has two large black eye-spots on its thorax; the larvae live in decaying wood and feed on other insects.

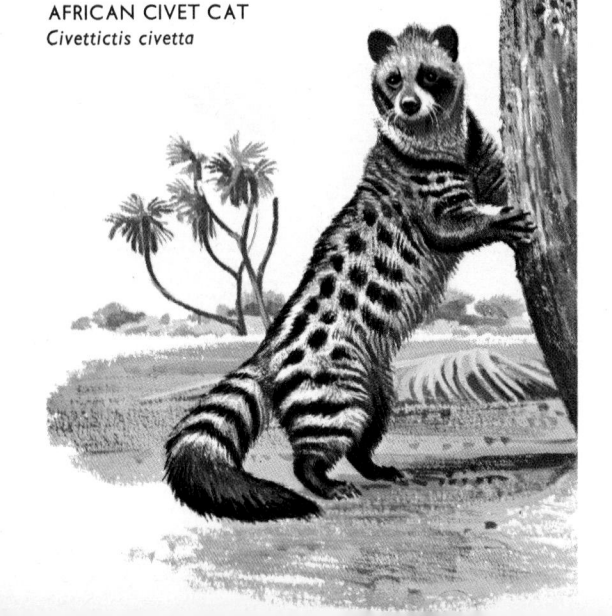

AFRICAN CIVET CAT
Civettictis civetta

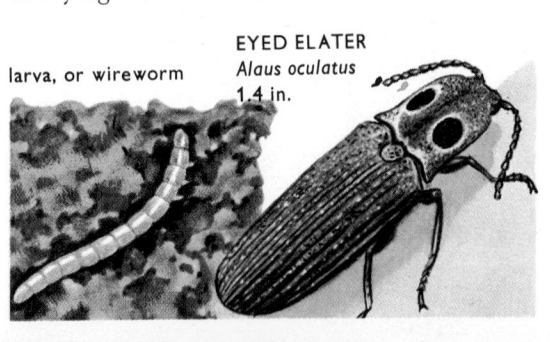

EYED ELATER
Alaus oculatus
1.4 in.

larva, or wireworm

CLOTHES MOTH larvae *(Tinaeidae)* feed on fabrics made of animal products, such as wool, felt, mohair and fur. They also eat animal and fish meals, dead insects, animal bristles, and feathers. Materials stored for long periods, particularly in dark places, are most likely to be damaged by these moths.

Adult clothes moths are harmless, taking only liquid nourishment, if any. They are usually not more than half an inch in wing-spread and are dull tan in colour. Females lay their eggs in the fabrics on which the larvae feed. In about a week the eggs hatch, and the very active larvae start feeding immediately. When full grown, the larvae are only about a third of an inch long. The entire life cycle may be completed in as short a time as two months, or may require as long as four years.

Webbing Clothes Moth larvae spin silken webs in the tunnels they eat through fabrics. Casemaking Clothes Moth larvae make oval cases in which they live, carrying the cases with them as they crawl.

Clothes moth larvae seldom eat synthetic fabrics, such as rayon or nylon, or those made of plant fibres, such as cotton.

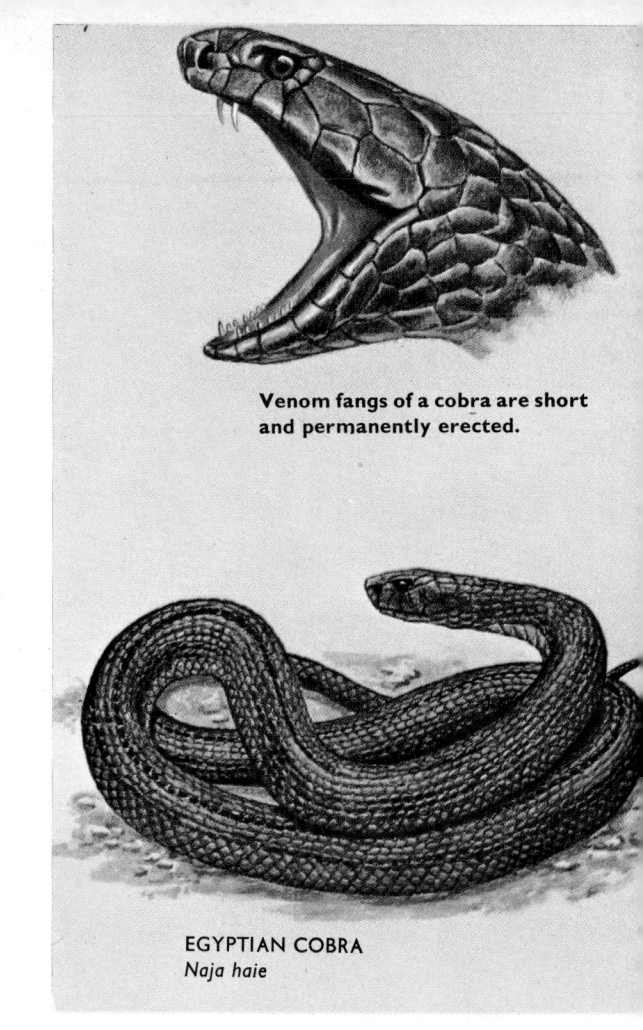

Venom fangs of a cobra are short and permanently erected.

EGYPTIAN COBRA
Naja haie

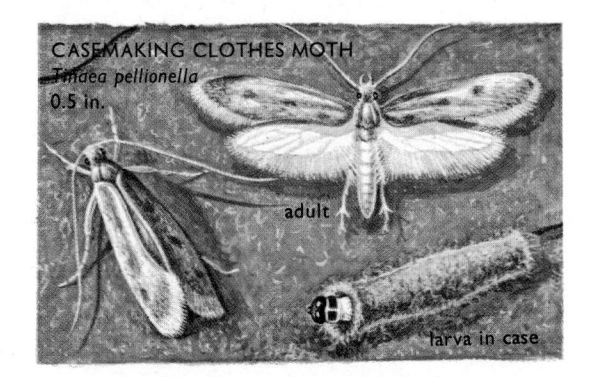

CASEMAKING CLOTHES MOTH
Tinaea pellionella
0.5 in.

adult

larva in case

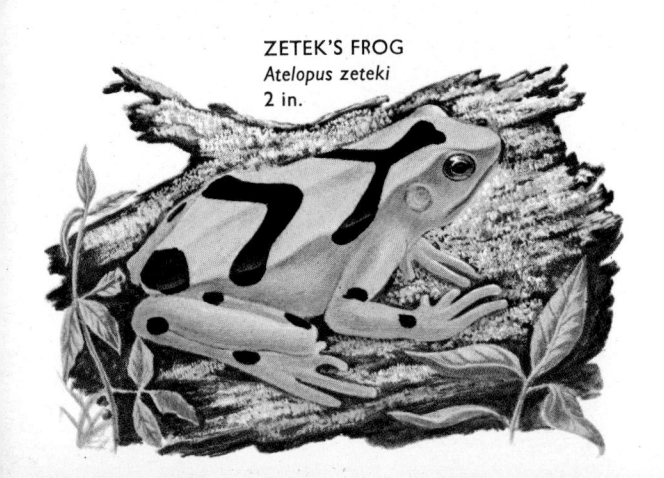

ZETEK'S FROG
Atelopus zeteki
2 in.

CLUB-FOOTED TOADS, members of the family *Atelopidae,* are small ground toads that live in the tropical rain forests of southern Central America and also northern South America. Best known are members of the genus *Atelopus,* which are brightly coloured and have poisonous skin secretions that make them inedible by small predators. These toads boldly expose themselves during the day and are easily captured. Indians of Central America use the skin secretions as arrow poisons.

Shielded toads *(Bachycephalus)* possess a large, bony plate in the skin that covers most of their back and is attached to the backbone. The purpose or value of this unusual bony growth is unknown.

COATIMUNDIS, Coatis, or Chulas *(Nasua narica),* live in South and Central America, ranging north through Mexico into Arizona. They look much like raccoons, and are

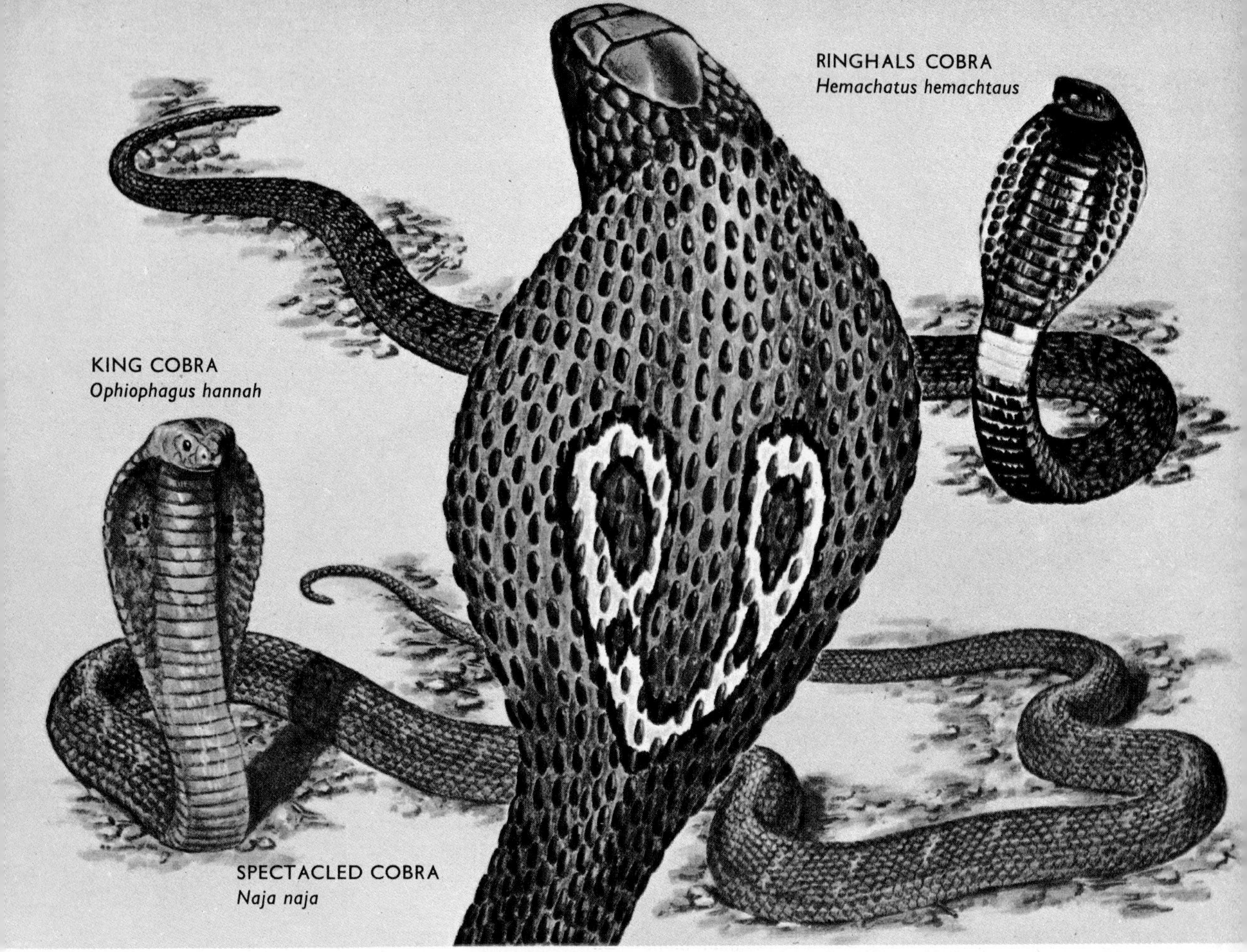

RINGHALS COBRA
Hemachatus hemachtaus

KING COBRA
Ophiophagus hannah

SPECTACLED COBRA
Naja naja

members of the same family. Coatis have long, short-haired tails with indistinct black rings. Their pointed snouts are long and flexible. Like raccoons they are inquisitive and mischievous. They usually travel during the day, in bands of 30 or more, moving about noisily as they forage for insects, worms or grubs, which they dig from the soil with their sharp, straight claws. Some

Coatimundis are ground dwellers, but climb ably.

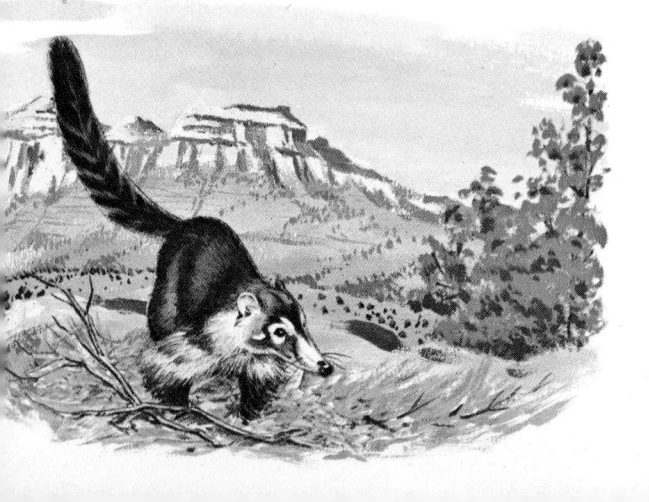

individuals, usually old males, become anti-social or solitary in habits and remain separate from the bands; they are often called "Solitarios". If captured while young, Coatis become good pets.

COBRAS are best known for the ability to spread their hoods. When alarmed, a cobra raises the front of its body, bends its head at a sharp angle to point towards the object of interest, and lifts the long, backward-projecting ribs just behind its head. This flattens the body and spreads the skin in the neck region. Cobras strike downwards and forwards, rather than straight forward as vipers do. A cobra's recovery from a strike is slightly slow, so that a mongoose or other enemy can grab the snake before it can defend itself. A mongoose is not able to kill a viper in the same manner. It is not immune to the venom of either type of snake, although it has some resistance.

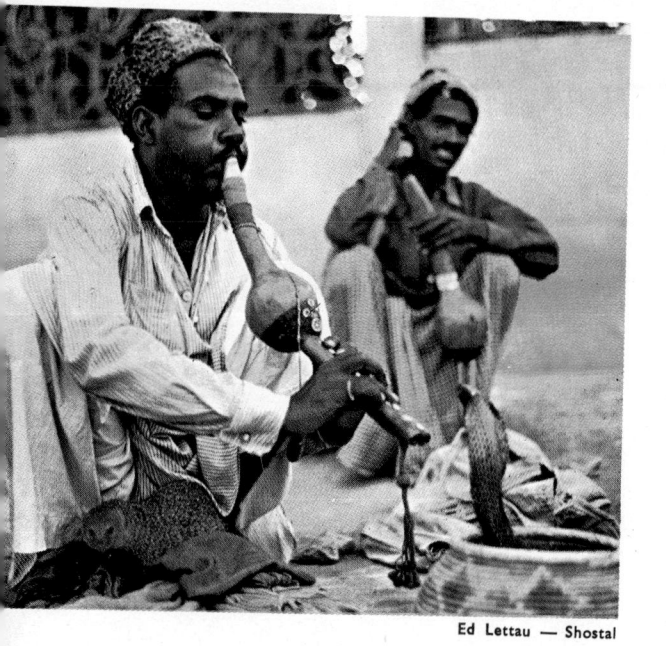

Ed Lettau — Shostal

A Pakistani snake-charmer sways his body and arms as he plays his flute to "charm" the deadly cobra in the basket. His rhythmic movements are watched closely by the snake, which is deaf to the sounds.

A dozen species of cobras occur in Africa, southern Asia, the Malay Archipelago, and the Philippines. Largest is the King Cobra (*Ophiophagus hannah*), which reaches a length of 18 feet and is one of the very few snakes to construct a nest. The Spectacled Cobra (*Naja naja*) has on the back of its hood a peculiar design, like a pair of arched spectacles held upside down. The design shows only when the hood is spread and is not perfect in all individuals. Other species of cobras do not have hood patterns. Several African cobras can squirt venom from specially modified fangs when they hold their mouth open slightly. These "spitting" cobras (*Hemachatus* sp. and some *Naja* spp.) deliberately aim for the eyes and are usually accurate up to 8 or 10 feet. The venom is excruciatingly painful and may cause blindness, if not promptly washed out. The Egyptian Cobra is believed to be the snake used by Cleopatra to commit suicide.

Indian Cobras are famous for their roles in snake-charming acts. The charmer plays a flute in front of a basket of snakes, and the snakes rise with spread hoods swaying in harmony with his music. All snakes are probably deaf to airborne sounds, so the cobras really move as the charmer moves. They spread their hoods instinctively to threaten the enemy, and usually cannot see well enough in the bright light to strike. Even when they do strike during the day, they often keep their mouths closed, or sometimes the charmer sews them shut. A charmer often takes a chance and the he risks death unless he has developed an immunity to cobra bites.

Only one cobra bite in ten is fatal; but cobras and closely-related kraits (*Bungarus*) cause as many as 30,000 deaths every year in India. Kraits are slender, banded snakes with an exceedingly potent venom. Like cobras, they are active mostly at night, and most deaths result when snakes are accidentally stepped on in the dark. Both these snakes are often almost docile during the day and do little to defend themselves. Cobras and kraits lay eggs, and the females brood and guard the nest. (See CORAL SNAKES, SEA SNAKES and MAMBAS.)

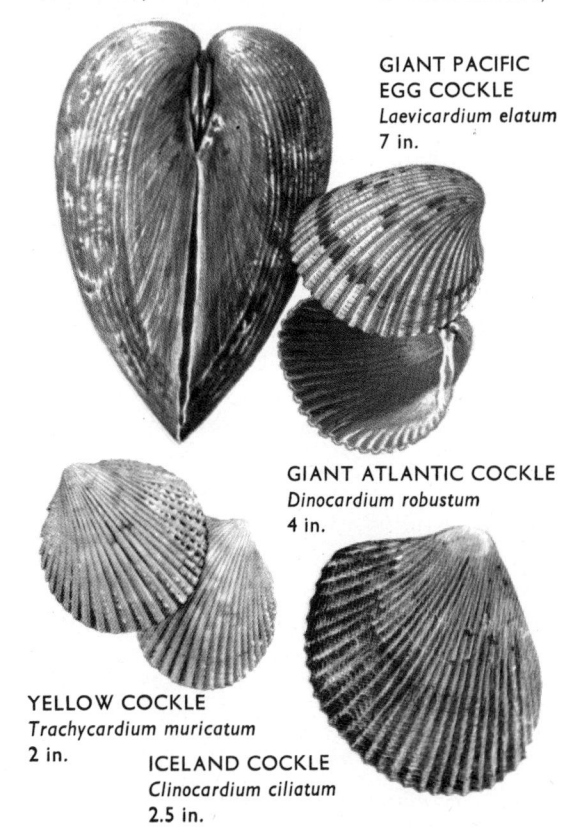

GIANT PACIFIC
EGG COCKLE
Laevicardium elatum
7 in.

GIANT ATLANTIC COCKLE
Dinocardium robustum
4 in.

YELLOW COCKLE
Trachycardium muricatum
2 in.

ICELAND COCKLE
Clinocardium ciliatum
2.5 in.

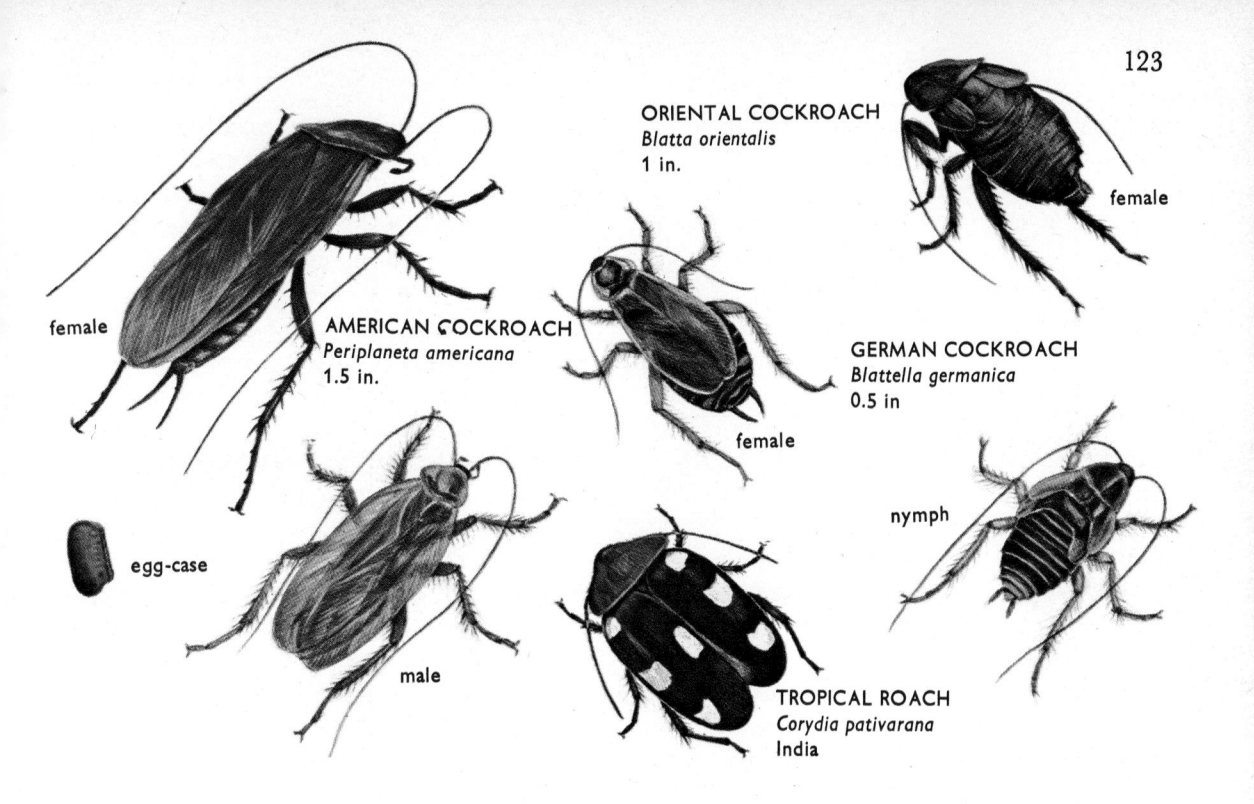

ORIENTAL COCKROACH
Blatta orientalis
1 in.

female

female

AMERICAN COCKROACH
Periplaneta americana
1.5 in.

GERMAN COCKROACH
Blattella germanica
0.5 in

female

egg-case

nymph

male

TROPICAL ROACH
Corydia pativarana
India

House-infesting cockroaches probably originated in the tropics but have been spread around the world. Most of the beautifully coloured tropical roaches subsist on vegetation, as do the wood roaches of temperate regions.

COCKLES, or Heart Shells, are inflated, heart-shaped bivalves that usually have strong radiating ribs on their shells. They live, buried only a few inches below the surface in sand or mud, in shallow water. Largest of the Atlantic species is the rather brightly coloured Baking Shell, or Giant Atlantic Cockle *(Dinocardium robustum)*, common along southern Atlantic beaches. The Prickly Cockle *(Trachyimdium egmontianum)* and Yellow Cockle *(Trachycardium muricatum)* occur from the Carolinas southward. The Yellow Cockle's valves have smooth sides and a toothed margin. Nuttall's Cockle *(Clinocardium nuttali)* occurs along the Pacific Coast from the Bering Sea to San Diego. Egg Cockles are thin-shelled, smooth members of the group. They measure from $\frac{1}{2}$ to 2 inches in length, and may be brightly coloured with rose, yellow or purple. They occur mostly in mud or sand in shallow water. Morton's Cockle *(Leuvicarodium mortoni)* is eaten by wild ducks and other waterfowl. The Common Cockle *(Cardium edule)* of Europe is a popular food.

COCKROACHES *(Blattidae)* are among the most primitive and most ancient of insects. Their fossil remains are found in rocks 200 million years old. Most of the more than 3,000 species live in tropical regions and are rarely seen. About 70 species occur in North America. A few are obnoxiously abundant in and around dwellings in temperate climates. They may contaminate food, since they often walk or live in filth.

Cockroaches have very flat bodies and long, slender legs, well adapted for running. The front of their thorax is expanded into a flattened plate that nearly covers the head. Cockroaches depend largely on running to escape enemies, but many kinds can also fly. Generally secretive, they hide in cracks and crevices and under bark or stones, coming out to feed at night. They eat a wide variety of substances, including glue in book-bindings and on stamps.

Cockroaches enclose their eggs in a hard, or membraneous, capsule, or sac. Females of some species carry this attached to their abdomen until the eggs are about to hatch.

Others drop it in some protected place for incubation. Depending on the species, the eggs hatch in from two weeks to three months. Young cockroaches, or nymphs, look much like the adults but have undeveloped wings. Some species moult only six to eight times and become adults in about six weeks. Others moult twelve times or more, and require as long as a year and a half.

The German Cockroach, or Croton Bug, has spread from Europe to nearly all parts of the world and is a small cockroach. The much larger American Cockroach, a native of tropical America, is found now in most warm regions of the world. The Oriental Cockroach, also common in dwellings, prefers damp places around water-pipes or in basements. Dark brown to nearly black and about an inch long, it is sometimes known as the Waterbug. Females are nearly wingless, and the wings of males are shorter than their abdomen.

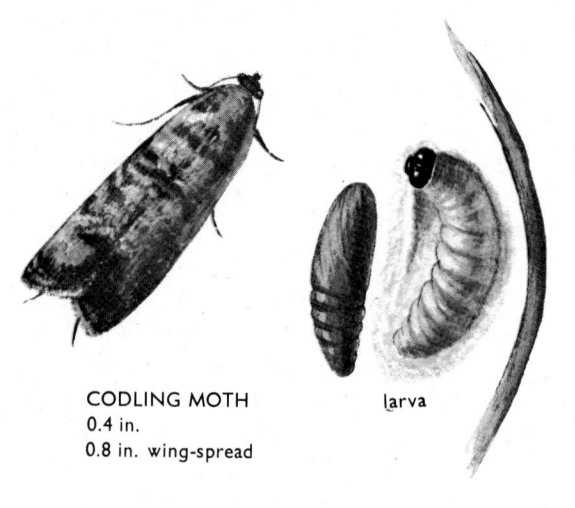

CODLING MOTH
0.4 in.
0.8 in. wing-spread

larva

CODLING MOTHS *(Enarmonia pomonella)* are one of the most destructive insect pests that attack apples. A native of Europe, the Codling Moth has spread to all apple-growing regions of the world. Winter is passed as a full-grown larva in a silken cocoon, usually spun under loose bark or in some similarly protected spot. In spring the larva transforms to the pupal stage, and within a few weeks the adult moth emerges. It is small and greyish with brown markings. Females lay their circular, flat eggs on apple

leaves and fruit. If the weather is warm, many eggs are laid, and damage for that season is great. If the temperature remains below 55 degrees Fahrenheit, few eggs are laid. As soon as the eggs hatch, the larvae begin feeding on leaves. Soon, however, they chew into the young apples and, typically, tunnel towards the core, where they feed on the pulp and seeds. When fully grown, they burrow out of the fruit and spin a cocoon in cracks in the bark or under debris on the ground. Fruit-growers can control this pest effectively with present-day insecticides.

COD, and cod-like fishes, belong to the *Gadidae,* an important family since many species play a part in the fisheries of the Northern Hemisphere. The cod-like fishes occur mainly in cold and temperate waters, and with one exception are marine. They are caught with large trawling nets which are dragged across the bottom, but also with lines, seines and gill-nets.

The most important member of the family is the Cod itself *(Gadus morhua),* which occurs on both sides of the Atlantic. There is also a species in the northern Pacific which is equally abundant. The Cod is the largest member of the family, reaching a weight of over 200 pounds and a length of 6 feet. Cod caught commercially are usually much smaller — about 25 pounds, at most. The cod-fishing industry is a very old one, perhaps chiefly because of the good keeping quality of dried and salted cod. Salt cod is still a common item in the diet of Latin Americans. Cut in strips for broiling, small

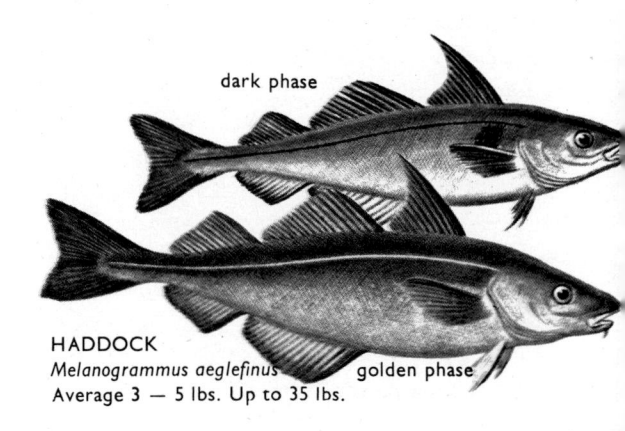

dark phase

HADDOCK
Melanogrammus aeglefinus
Average 3 — 5 lbs. Up to 35 lbs.

golden phase

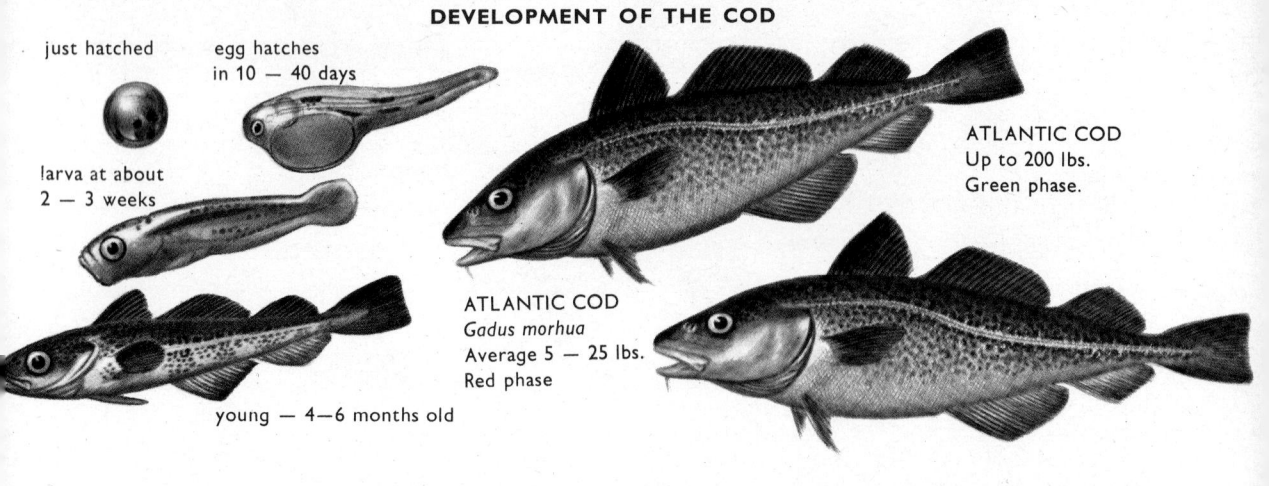

DEVELOPMENT OF THE COD

just hatched

egg hatches
in 10 — 40 days

larva at about
2 — 3 weeks

ATLANTIC COD
Up to 200 lbs.
Green phase.

ATLANTIC COD
Gadus morhua
Average 5 — 25 lbs.
Red phase

young — 4—6 months old

cod are called "scrod". Oil extracted from the liver is rich in vitamins A and D.

The Haddock *(Melanogrammus aeglefinus)* is much like the Cod in appearance, but has a large blotch behind the pectoral fin and lacks the speckled pattern on the flanks. It is a smaller fish, reaching about 35 pounds, but like the Cod is found on both sides of the Atlantic. Haddock also have a black lateral line running from the gills to the tail, whereas the lateral line is light in cod. The average haddock weighs less than 5 pounds, and those of 2 pounds or less are sometimes known as "scrog".

Hakes are also important cod-like commercial fishes. The Hake *(Merluccius merluccius)* of the Mediterranean and Eastern Atlantic, a typically deep-water species, has a maximum weight of about 20 pounds. Closely related is the Silver Hake, found chiefly in the Western Atlantic from Newfoundland south to the Bahamas, but also in European waters. The South African Hake *(M. capensis)* is the most important of all the commercial fish of that region. It is caught in waters as deep as 1,800 feet.

Other important members of the cod family are the Whiting, the Pollack, the Ling, the various species of Rockling, and the Torsk. The Whiting ranges from Norway to the Mediterranean, and inhabits shallower water than do other members of the family. Young Whiting occur in large numbers close to the shore. In British waters, the Pollack *(Gadus pollachius)* is most abundant

on the west and south-west coasts. In the western Atlantic, the name Pollack is applied to another species, *Gadus virens,* which is known in England as the Coalfish. The Ling has an elongated body and is covered with small scales. It is a valuable commercial fish, up to 7 feet in length.

Some of the cod-like fishes produce an enormous number of eggs. The female cod, for example, produces as many as four or five million in a season. The eggs float freely in the sea, where they are fertilised by the male. The young, which hatch in about two weeks, drift with the currents until they are an inch or so in length and can swim freely.

COELACANTH (meaning hollow-spined; pronounced SEA-la-canth). In December, 1938, a biologist found a strange fish in a catch of sharks brought to the port of East London on the south-east coast of Africa. Closer scrutiny revealed that this unusual fish belonged to a group believed to have become extinct about the time of the dinosaurs — some 60 million years ago. Fossil records indicate that land-dwelling vertebrates developed from primitive, lobed, finned fishes of this sort.

A £100 reward was offered for another specimen. None turned up during the years of World War II, but in 1952 another was discovered off the Comoro Islands, near the coast of Madagascar. There the natives had been familiar with these fish for years.

Coelacanths are ugly, oily fish. They are

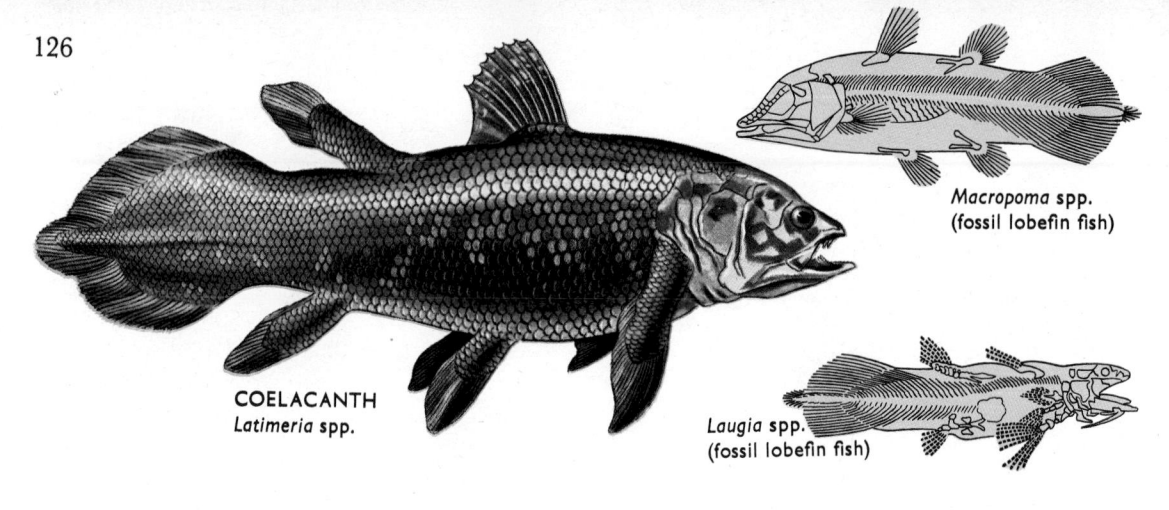

Macropoma spp.
(fossil lobefin fish)

COELACANTH
Latimeria spp.

Laugia spp.
(fossil lobefin fish)

Coelacanths are truly "living fossils". All members of this ancient group of lobefinned fishes were believed to have been extinct for millions of years. They were known only from fossils, until a living representative was unexpectedly netted off the coast of South Africa in 1938.

covered with heavy scales. The largest specimen captured so far weighed 130 pounds, but the native fishermen say they have caught 200-pounders in years gone by. Coelacanths live in deep waters, ranging from 500 feet downwards. None of them has remained alive long after being brought to the surface. Alive they are steel-blue in colour. Soon after death, the blue fades to brown and their eyes become dull. Their fins are fringed and are on fleshy stalks. From these fins, it is believed, were developed the simple legs used by vertebrates in

their first invasion of the land.

Coelacanths are the most ancient living animals with backbones; hence, they aid our understanding of animal life today.

COELENTERATES are small to large invertebrate animals that live either singly or in colonies. All coelenterates have a hollow, central body cavity that serves for digestion and circulation. The mouth is surrounded by tentacles equipped with stinging cells (nematocysts) that are used to capture prey. One group, the jellyfishes, are gelatinous animals with simple mouths and large body cavities (see JELLYFISH). Others, like stony corals, grow attached to the bottom, their soft bodies protected by heavy, limy "skeletons" (see CORALS). Another group, the hydroids, form plant-like branching colonies (see HYDROIDS).

Nearly all coelenterates live in the sea: some in arctic waters, others in tropical seas; some in the shallow tidal zone, others in the dark depths.

In corals and attached hydroids, the animals are called polyps (see illustration), and the free, drifting or swimming stages are called the medusae. These reproduce sexually and yield ciliated larvae (planulae) that drift or swim for a while in the sea before fastening to the bottom.

Coelenterates are inedible, but some, are commercially important, and a few, such as the Sea Nettle, the Portuguese Man-of-War, and the Stinging Coral, may be harmful or even dangerous. Their stinging organs (nematocysts) are hollow cells in

LIFE CYCLES OF HYDROID COELENTERATES

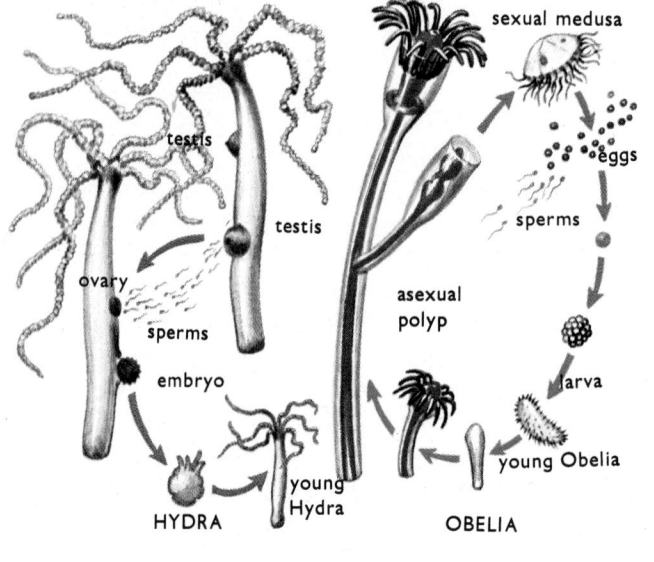

testis

testis

ovary

sperms

embryo

young Hydra

HYDRA

asexual polyp

sexual medusa

eggs

sperms

larva

young Obelia

OBELIA

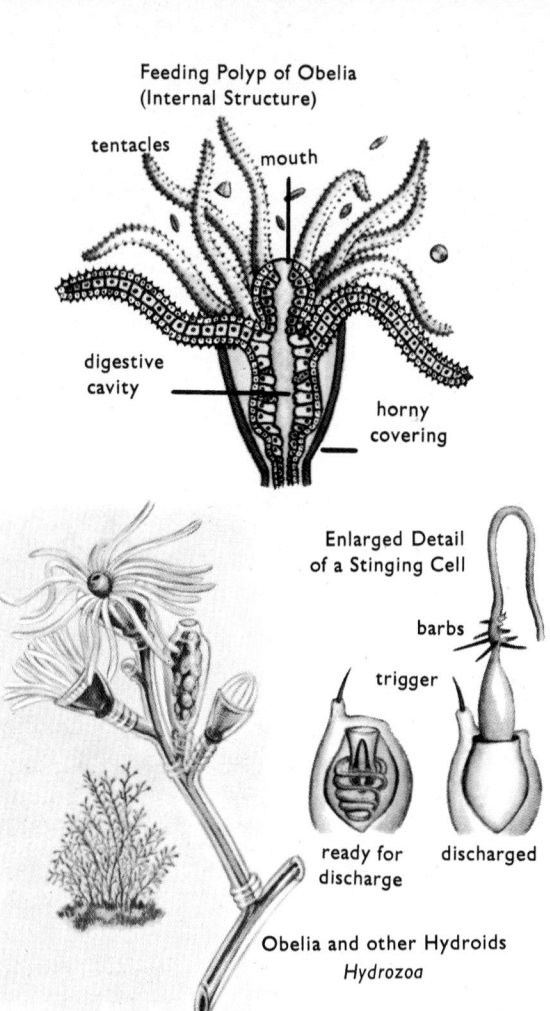

Feeding Polyp of Obelia
(Internal Structure)

tentacles

mouth

digestive cavity

horny covering

Enlarged Detail of a Stinging Cell

barbs

trigger

ready for discharge

discharged

Obelia and other Hydroids
Hydrozoa

which are coiled threads bearing hooks and spines. These cells lie at the surface of the tentacles and on other parts of the body. When touched, they discharge, the coiled threads shooting out and penetrating the victim. At the same time they secrete a poison which paralyses or kills the prey.

Coelenterates are split into three classes, based partly on their type of life history. Those belonging to the class *Hydrozoa* alternate between a polyp and a small

CLASSES OF COELENTERATES

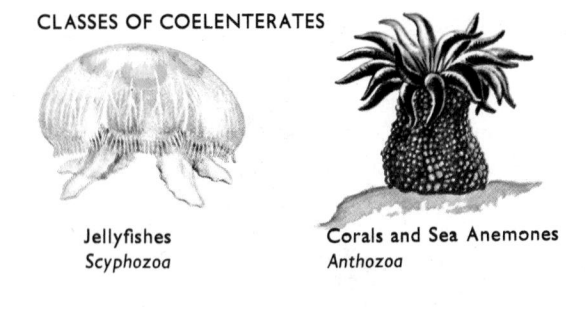

Jellyfishes
Scyphozoa

Corals and Sea Anemones
Anthozoa

medusa stage. *Scyphozoa* have a large medusa and a small polyp, and *Anthozoa* have polyps only. (see COMB JELLIES).

COLORADO POTATO BEETLES (*Leptinotarsa decemlineata*) were first discovered in Colorado and neighbouring areas feeding on the sand-bur, a plant related to the potato. Settlers took the potato west with them. The beetles readily took to the potato and gradually spread eastward, reaching the Atlantic coast about 50 years after their discovery along the upper Missouri River. Very little was known about insect control in those days, and entire potato crops were often destroyed. Colorado potato beetles are now found throughout continental U.S.A, except for parts of Florida, California and Nevada and are also serious pests in Europe.

When potato plants are not available, Colorado potato beetles feed on tomato, tobacco, egg-plant, cabbage, or other plants. Adults spend the winter in the ground. Soon after emerging, females deposit up to 500 orange-coloured eggs in clusters on the underside of leaves. Soon afterwards the adults die. The eggs hatch in about a week, and the larvae start to feed. They grow

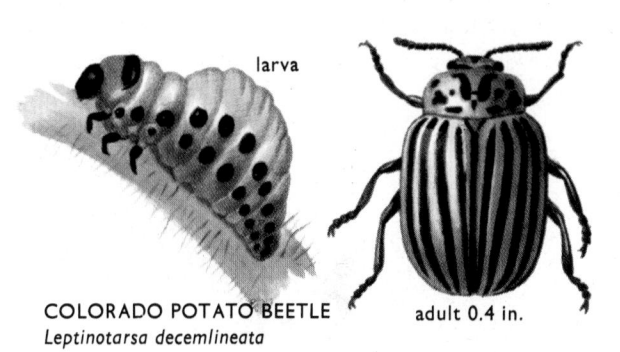

larva

COLORADO POTATO BEETLE
Leptinotarsa decemlineata

adult 0.4 in.

rapidly, and in about four weeks are nearly half an inch long. Then they burrow to pupate. Adults emerge in five to ten days.

COLUBRID SNAKES, At least 75 per cent of all species of snakes belong to the "typical" snake family — *Colubridae*. Most familiar harmless snakes are members of this family, but the family contains many specialised types. Among the most unusual

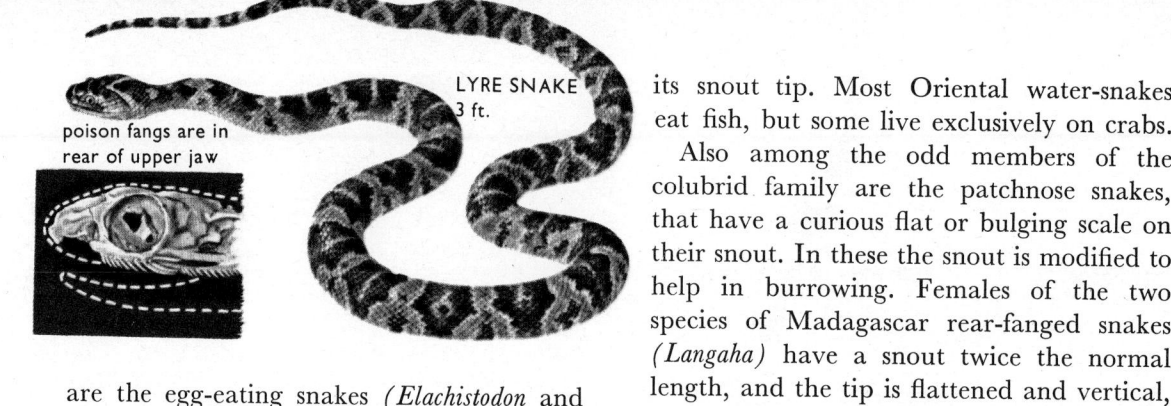

LYRE SNAKE
3 ft.

poison fangs are in
rear of upper jaw

are the egg-eating snakes *(Elachistodon* and *Dasypeltis)* of India, East Pakistan and Africa. A $2\frac{1}{2}$-foot egg-eating snake can swallow an egg three times the diameter of its body. As soon as the egg reaches the snake's neck region, it is cracked open by enlarged enamel-like projections on the underside of the backbone. The contents of the egg run into the snake's stomach, and the shell is spat out. (See SNAKES.)

The more primitive slug-eating snakes *(Aplopeltura* and *Pareas* of India, and *Sibon, Sibynomorphus* and *Dipsas* of the New World) are tree-dwellers that live almost entirely on a diet of slugs and snails. They have only a few widely-spaced teeth and no fangs.

A group of Oriental water-snakes is distinctive in having valves over the two nostrils, preventing the entrance of water. One kind *(Herpeton)* has flaps that fit over its snout tip. Most Oriental water-snakes eat fish, but some live exclusively on crabs.

Also among the odd members of the colubrid family are the patchnose snakes, that have a curious flat or bulging scale on their snout. In these the snout is modified to help in burrowing. Females of the two species of Madagascar rear-fanged snakes *(Langaha)* have a snout twice the normal length, and the tip is flattened and vertical, resembling a leaf. The Barred Tree Snake *(Chrysopelea pelias)* of the East Indies can lift its ribs to spread loose skin along the sides of its body, and then glide through the air from high in the trees to lower vegetation or to the ground.

Some colubrid snakes are venomous. Their fangs, always in the rear of the jaw, are only slightly enlarged, and the venom flows along a groove in the front of the fang into the bite wound. (All other venomous snakes have hollow fangs.) This method of injection is inefficient, so poisonous colubrids hold prey in their mouths for as long as half an hour until the venom takes effect. Their poison, generally mild, affects primarily the nervous system; there is little swelling. (See BOOMSLANG; BULLSNAKES; KING-SNAKES; RAT-SNAKES; WATER-SNAKES; WHIP-SNAKES.)

COMB JELLIES, or Ctenophores, are closely related to jellyfishes. They are jelly-like in consistency and round, oval, ribbon-like or lobed. They swim by means of eight rows of combs (tiny threads, or cilia) that beat rhythmically. A transparent "blister", or dome, at the upper end houses the balancing organ. This consists of a small grain of silica balanced on several fine hairs.

Most comb jellies live in the surface waters of the sea, but a few species dwell in the deeps.

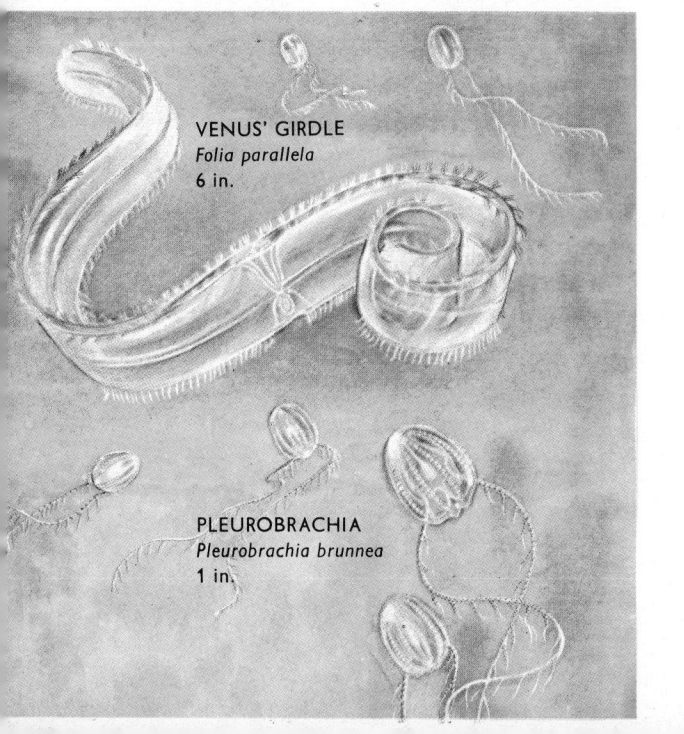

VENUS' GIRDLE
Folia parallela
6 in.

PLEUROBRACHIA
Pleurobrachia brunnea
1 in.

Pleurobrachia, a large species of comb jelly.

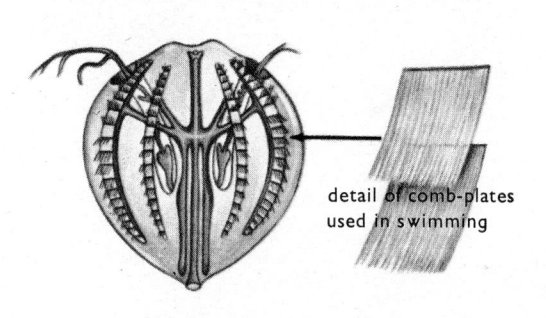

detail of comb-plates
used in swimming

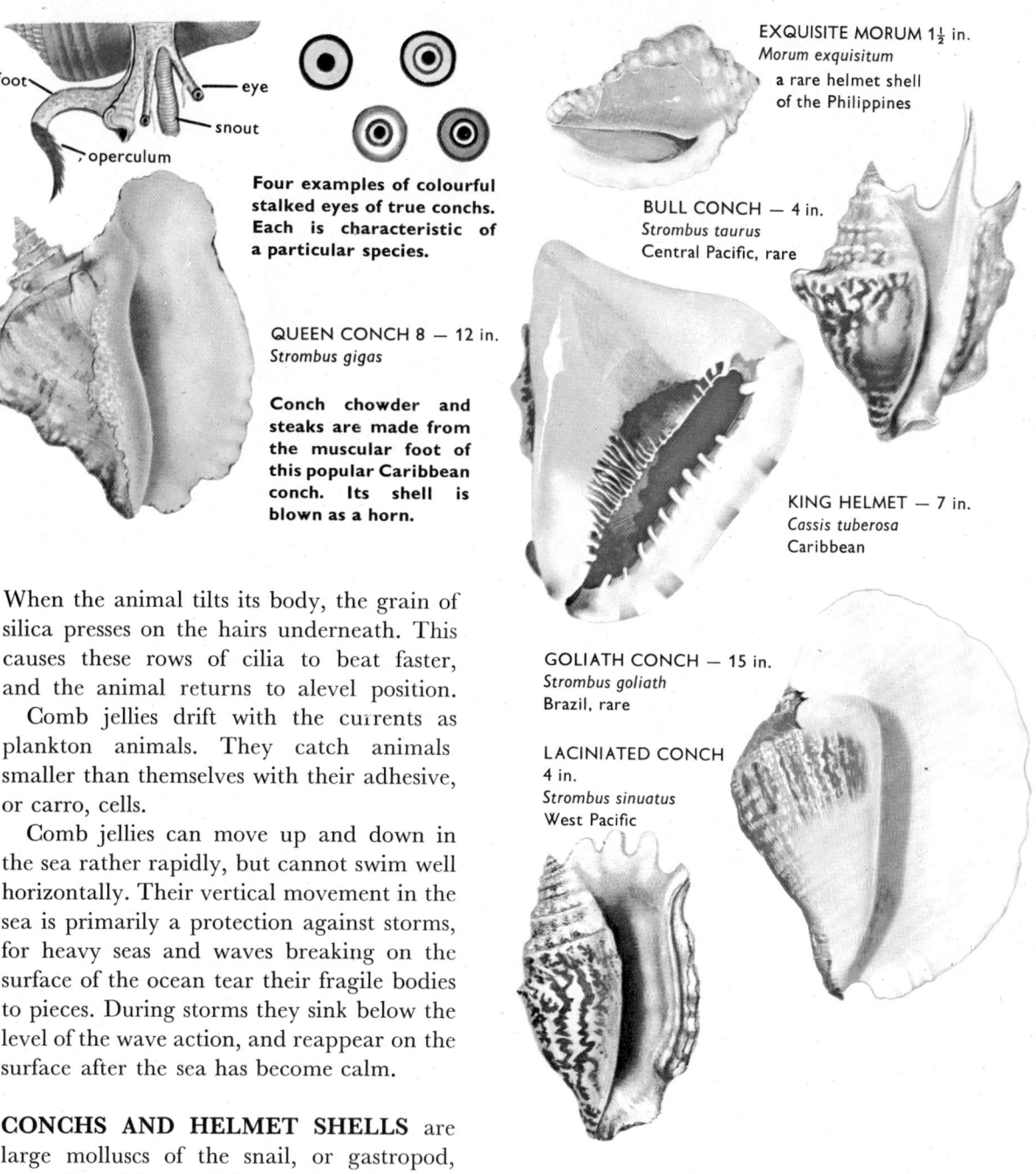

foot — eye — snout — operculum

Four examples of colourful stalked eyes of true conchs. Each is characteristic of a particular species.

QUEEN CONCH 8 — 12 in.
Strombus gigas

Conch chowder and steaks are made from the muscular foot of this popular Caribbean conch. Its shell is blown as a horn.

EXQUISITE MORUM 1½ in.
Morum exquisitum
a rare helmet shell of the Philippines

BULL CONCH — 4 in.
Strombus taurus
Central Pacific, rare

KING HELMET — 7 in.
Cassis tuberosa
Caribbean

GOLIATH CONCH — 15 in.
Strombus goliath
Brazil, rare

LACINIATED CONCH
4 in.
Strombus sinuatus
West Pacific

When the animal tilts its body, the grain of silica presses on the hairs underneath. This causes these rows of cilia to beat faster, and the animal returns to alevel position.

Comb jellies drift with the currents as plankton animals. They catch animals smaller than themselves with their adhesive, or carro, cells.

Comb jellies can move up and down in the sea rather rapidly, but cannot swim well horizontally. Their vertical movement in the sea is primarily a protection against storms, for heavy seas and waves breaking on the surface of the ocean tear their fragile bodies to pieces. During storms they sink below the level of the wave action, and reappear on the surface after the sea has become calm.

CONCHS AND HELMET SHELLS are
large molluscs of the snail, or gastropod, class. Found in tropical seas throughout the world, they occur in waters off Florida, in the West Indies, and from the Gulf of Lower California to Panama.

Conchs (*Strombus* spp.) live in shallow sand and on grass flats. They feed on organic debris and algae, and lay their eggs in gelatinous strings in the sand. The large Queen Conch of Florida and the West Indies makes an excellent chowder, and

may produce pearls, varying from pink through rose and yellow to almost black.

Helmet shells (*Cassis* spp., and other genera) are mainly predators, feeding on sea-biscuits and sand-dollars. Their shells are used by the Italians for carving cameos. Shells are sent to Italy for this use from various places in the Indian Ocean. Sometimes the whole shell is carved. Some cameos carved from helmet shells are vari-coloured.

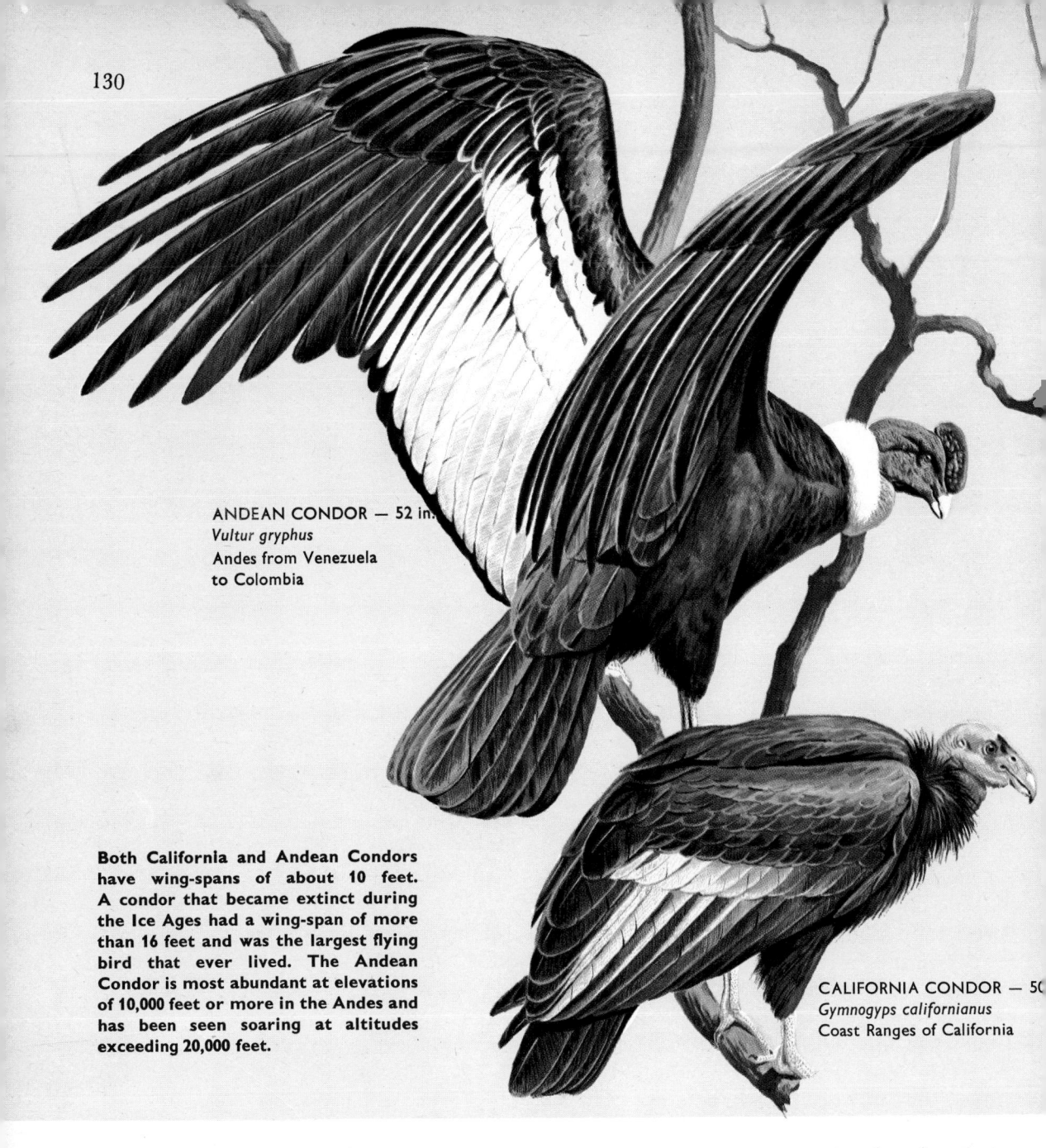

ANDEAN CONDOR — 52 in.
Vultur gryphus
Andes from Venezuela
to Colombia

Both California and Andean Condors have wing-spans of about 10 feet. A condor that became extinct during the Ice Ages had a wing-span of more than 16 feet and was the largest flying bird that ever lived. The Andean Condor is most abundant at elevations of 10,000 feet or more in the Andes and has been seen soaring at altitudes exceeding 20,000 feet.

CALIFORNIA CONDOR — 5(
Gymnogyps californianus
Coast Ranges of California

CONDORS are members of the *Cathartidae*, the family of American vultures. They are the largest of the birds of prey. They feed on carrion, and may gorge when food is plentiful. The great wing-spread is designed for soaring, with little effort, on air-currents until food is seen on the ground below.

Enormous birds and wonderful flyers, California Condors eat carrion but also catch some living prey, diving with great power. They do not breed until they are five years old and then not every year. Only one egg is laid, so it is no wonder that the species has been reduced to perhaps 50 birds, even though they are protected by law. They live in the coastal mountains of southern California southward into Baja California.

Andean Condors of South America are still fairly plentiful and are held in such esteem that several gold coins bear their name and have Condors engraved on them. They are the largest flying birds. The male has a display with neck arched, and a call like the throbbing of a remote engine.

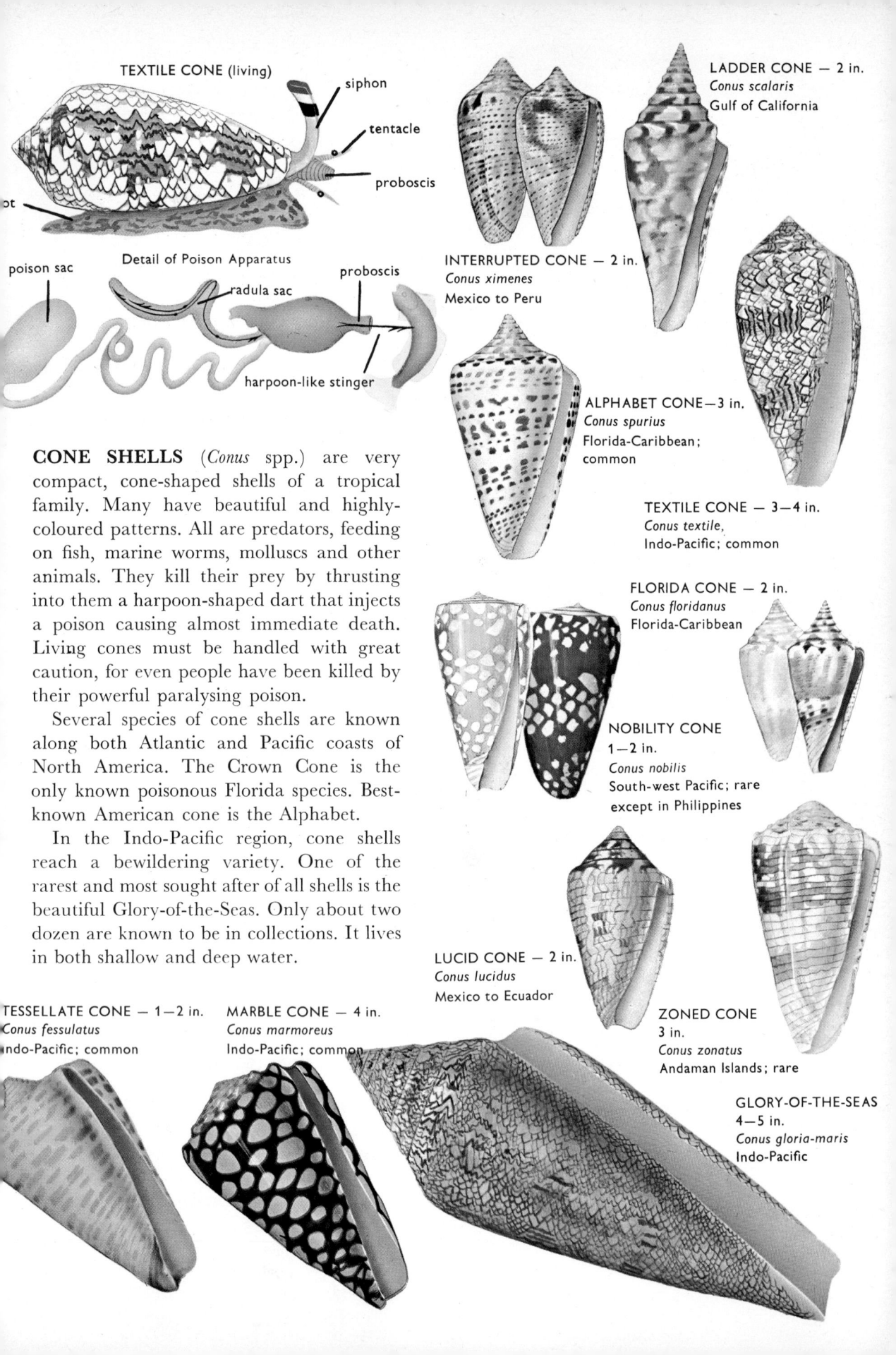

TEXTILE CONE (living)

siphon
tentacle
proboscis
...ot
poison sac

Detail of Poison Apparatus

radula sac
proboscis
harpoon-like stinger

LADDER CONE — 2 in.
Conus scalaris
Gulf of California

INTERRUPTED CONE — 2 in.
Conus ximenes
Mexico to Peru

ALPHABET CONE—3 in.
Conus spurius
Florida-Caribbean;
common

TEXTILE CONE — 3—4 in.
Conus textile,
Indo-Pacific; common

FLORIDA CONE — 2 in.
Conus floridanus
Florida-Caribbean

NOBILITY CONE
1—2 in.
Conus nobilis
South-west Pacific; rare
except in Philippines

LUCID CONE — 2 in.
Conus lucidus
Mexico to Ecuador

ZONED CONE
3 in.
Conus zonatus
Andaman Islands; rare

GLORY-OF-THE-SEAS
4—5 in.
Conus gloria-maris
Indo-Pacific

CONE SHELLS (*Conus* spp.) are very compact, cone-shaped shells of a tropical family. Many have beautiful and highly-coloured patterns. All are predators, feeding on fish, marine worms, molluscs and other animals. They kill their prey by thrusting into them a harpoon-shaped dart that injects a poison causing almost immediate death. Living cones must be handled with great caution, for even people have been killed by their powerful paralysing poison.

Several species of cone shells are known along both Atlantic and Pacific coasts of North America. The Crown Cone is the only known poisonous Florida species. Best-known American cone is the Alphabet.

In the Indo-Pacific region, cone shells reach a bewildering variety. One of the rarest and most sought after of all shells is the beautiful Glory-of-the-Seas. Only about two dozen are known to be in collections. It lives in both shallow and deep water.

TESSELLATE CONE — 1—2 in.
Conus fessulatus
Indo-Pacific; common

MARBLE CONE — 4 in.
Conus marmoreus
Indo-Pacific; common

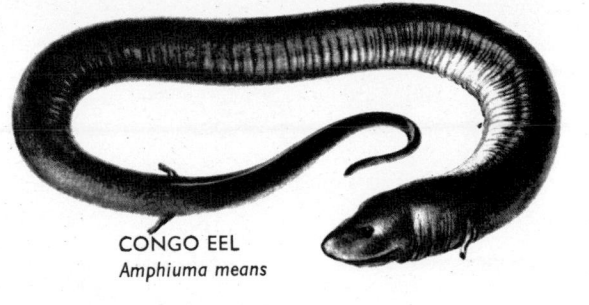

CONGO EEL
Amphiuma means

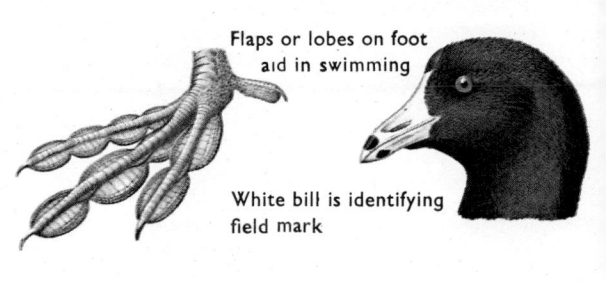

Flaps or lobes on foot aid in swimming

White bill is identifying field mark

CONGO EELS (*Amphiuma* spp.) are long, slender, round-bodied and extremely slippery amphibians derived from the salamandrids. Their legs are so short that they are useless for walking. Congo eels have no more than three toes on each extremity, and often only one. Two species occur in the south-eastern United States. Both reach a length of 40 inches. They are the largest salamanders in North America.

Congo eels live their entire lives in lakes, ponds and slow-moving streams. When very young they have external gills, but these are soon lost. Adults have lungs, but also breathe through their skin.

Females lay their eggs in depressions on land but near water. They remain nearby to protect the eggs until they hatch. The larvae immediately wriggle into the water, where they complete their development. Adults eat crayfish mainly but also consume such smaller animals as worms, insects, fishes, snakes and frogs. They can bite savagely.

COOTS, members of the rail family, are birds of lakes, rivers and fresh-water marshes. They are known all over the world. They gather in flocks in winter and feed together, but in spring they separate into pairs and take up territories, for which they fight fiercely with sharp-clawed feet and bill.

Coots dive and swim, and patter over the water with their feet when they take to the air. Their breeding routine is similar to that of Moorhens, their close relatives (see GALLINULES). The young birds swim as soon as they hatch. Coots are usually wary, but in a bird sanctuary are sometimes as tame as domestic ducks.

CORALS are coelenterates of the class *Anthozoa*. The "true", or stony, corals have "skeletons" of lime, which is extracted from the sea water by special cells in their bodies. Some grow as massive, solid structures; others as large, branched coral trees or as delicately-branched and fragile colonies. In

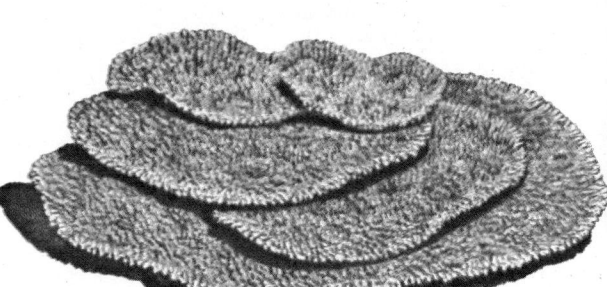

STONY COLONIAL CORAL
Acropora surculosa
Australia

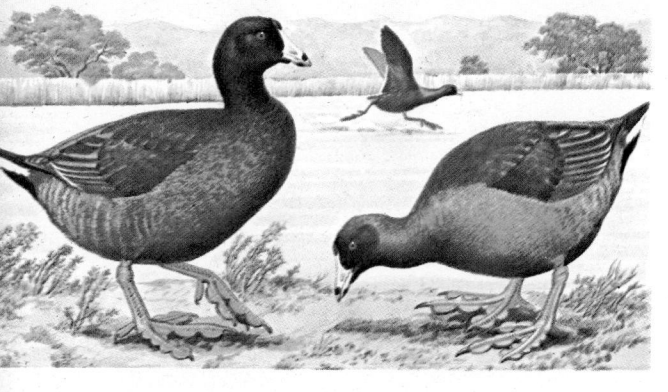

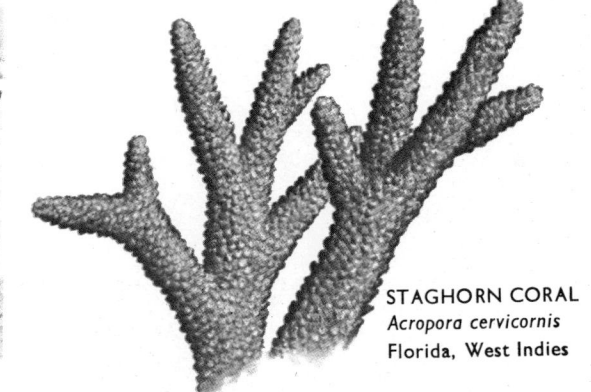

STAGHORN CORAL
Acropora cervicornis
Florida, West Indies

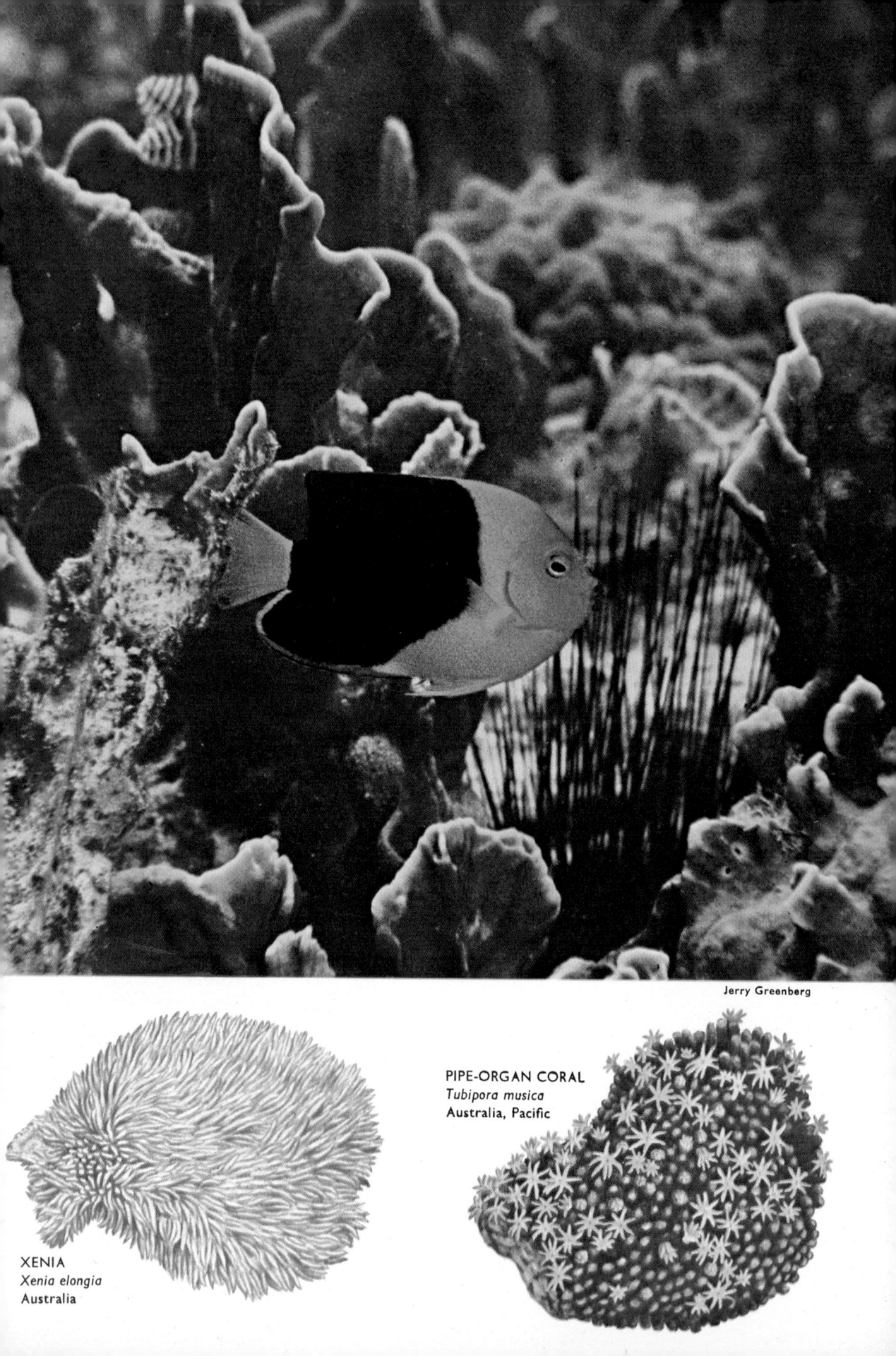

Jerry Greenberg

PIPE-ORGAN CORAL
Tubipora musica
Australia, Pacific

XENIA
Xenia elongia
Australia

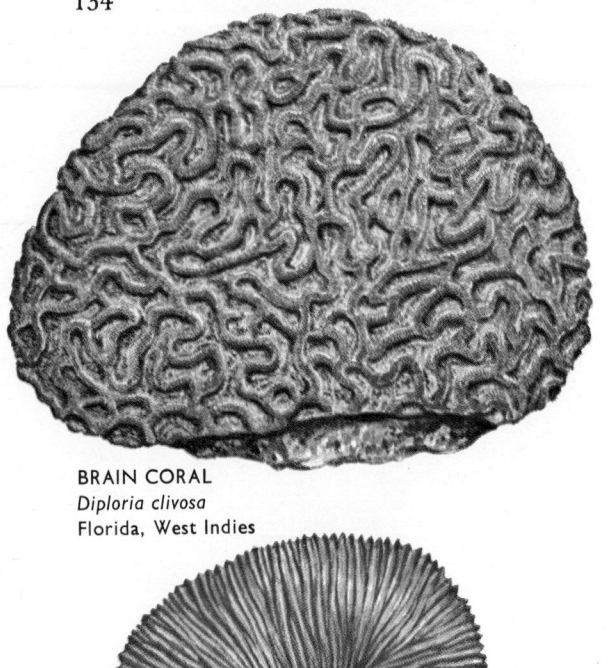

BRAIN CORAL
Diploria clivosa
Florida, West Indies

MUSHROOM CORAL
Fungia fungites
Australia

Corals feed mostly at night, capturing plankton with their short tentacles. Many other kinds of marine organisms live with corals, and skin-divers find reefs rewarding places to explore. Cuts from living coral are painful and often slow to heal.

CORAL SNAKES. The name Coral Snake is applied rather indiscriminately to a number of often quite unrelated species that have "warning" colours of red, black, yellow or white arranged in alternate rings round the body. True Coral Snakes, however, are confined to the Americas *(Micrurus, Micruroides* and *Leptomicrurus)*. All are venomous and secretive, and feed mainly on other snakes, and the majority when alarmed indulge in the curious defence behaviour of "head mimicking", by erecting the tail with tip curled over, and at the same time hiding the head under the coils of the body.

The family *Elapidae,* to which the coral snakes belong, includes the Cobras, Mambas, Kraits and Sea Snakes. All have fixed front fangs and all are poisonous. Not all are deadly to man, although the most poisonous of all snakes are members of this family. The venom is composed mostly of poisons that affect the nervous system, causing paralysis.

Some 60 species (almost half the total in the family) live in Australia. In fact, about 80 per cent of Australian snakes belong to the family *Elapidae,* and therefore are poi-

addition to stony corals, there are horny corals (see SEA FEATHERS and FANS) that have only spicules of lime in their tissues. Colonial stony corals that form reefs and atolls thrive only in warm, shallow tropical waters. Some corals live in cooler or in deeper water, but these are small and solitary; they do not bud or form reefs.

Over 50 species of reef corals — among them Brain, Staghorn, Star and Rose corals — are found along the Florida Keys and in the West Indies. Diving corals may be brightly coloured, but most kinds are drab yellows and browns. Their snowy-white skeletons, left after the soft animals are bleached away, are popular as souvenirs of the sea. Corals have little commercial value other than as curios, though their role in the life of the seas is important. Large quantities of corals are shipped every year from the Great Barrier Reef and the Bahamas for the curio trade.

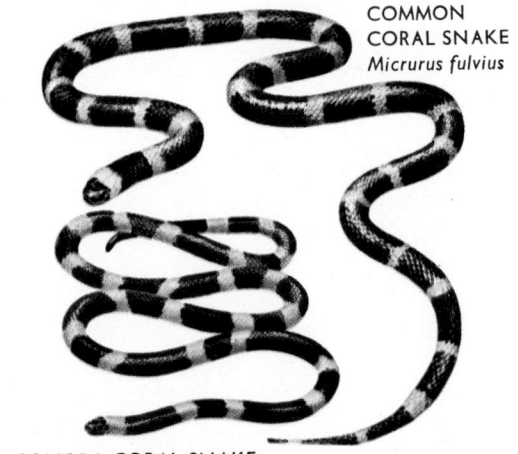

**COMMON
CORAL SNAKE**
Micrurus fulvius

SONORA CORAL SNAKE
Micruroides euryxanthus

sonous. Several have a notoriously powerful venom, and some are especially vicious. The Taipan *(Oxyuranus)* is the largest, reaching a length of 11 feet. The Tiger Snake *(Notechis)*, most dangerous because it is the most common, reaches a length of only six feet; drop for drop it has the most potent venom of any snake in the world. The Black Snake *(Pseudechis)* is another dreaded, six-foot species with a terrible temper, and the

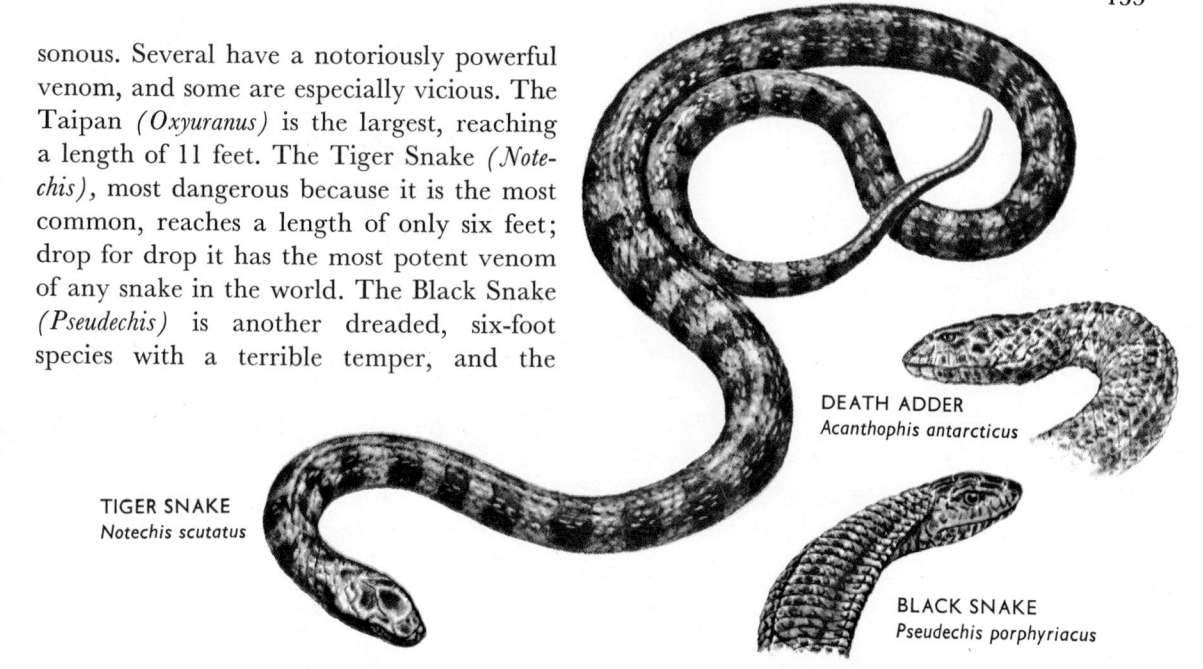

DEATH ADDER
Acanthophis antarcticus

TIGER SNAKE
Notechis scutatus

BLACK SNAKE
Pseudechis porphyriacus

Brown Snake *(Demansia)* is worse. The Brown Snake lays eggs; all others give birth to their young. The Death Adder *(Acanthophis)* closely resembles true vipers because of its big, triangular head and thick, short body. Like other coralline snakes, however, the Death Adder has fixed front fangs.

Most ornate are the Oriental coral snakes *(Calliophis* and *Hemibungarus)* and painted snakes *(Maticora)*, found from south-eastern Asia through the East Indies. All are brightly coloured. Painted snakes are striped above, and have tremendous venom glands that extend a third the length of the body. (See COBRAS; MAMBAS; SEA SNAKES.)

CORMORANTS, world-wide in distribution, are fish-eating birds of both fresh and salt water. They dive for their food from the top of the water, not from the air. Because of their ability to catch fish underwater, cormorants have been trained by men to fish for them. Rings, loose enough for breathing but too narrow for swallowing, are placed around the birds' necks. The birds are released in the water and allowed to fish until they make a catch, which their keeper then retrieves. After a bird has caught five or six fish, it is allowed to swallow a fish as a reward. Cormorant fishing was practised in China years ago and it still occurs in Japan.

All the cormorants of the Northern Hemisphere are blackish birds. They resemble crows; the name cormorant, in fact, is a corruption of the Latin for "sea crow". Some are called shags, a name usually given to those species which have slender, upstanding crests. More than half of the 30 species

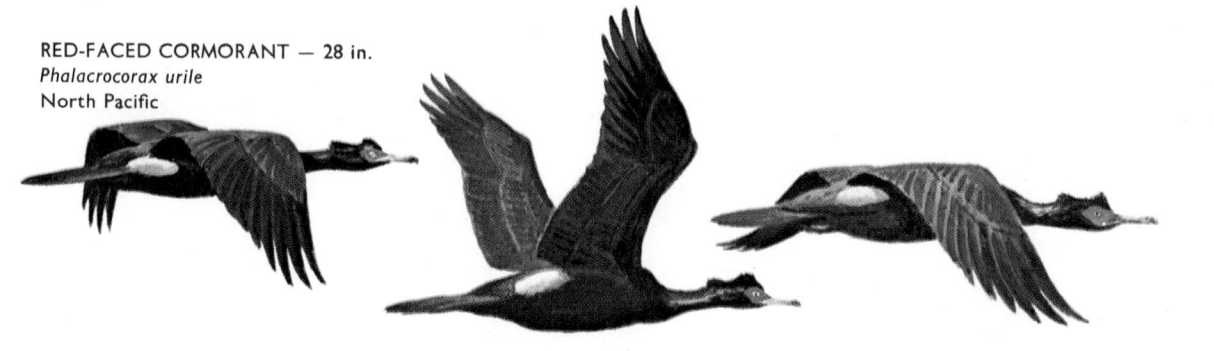

RED-FACED CORMORANT — 28 in.
Phalacrocorax urile
North Pacific

of cormorants live in the Southern Hemisphere, and many of these species have white bellies. Cormorants fly with their neck stretched out very much like geese.

COWRIES (*Cypraea* spp.) are small marine gastropods, and their shells are among the most popular of all sea-shells with the

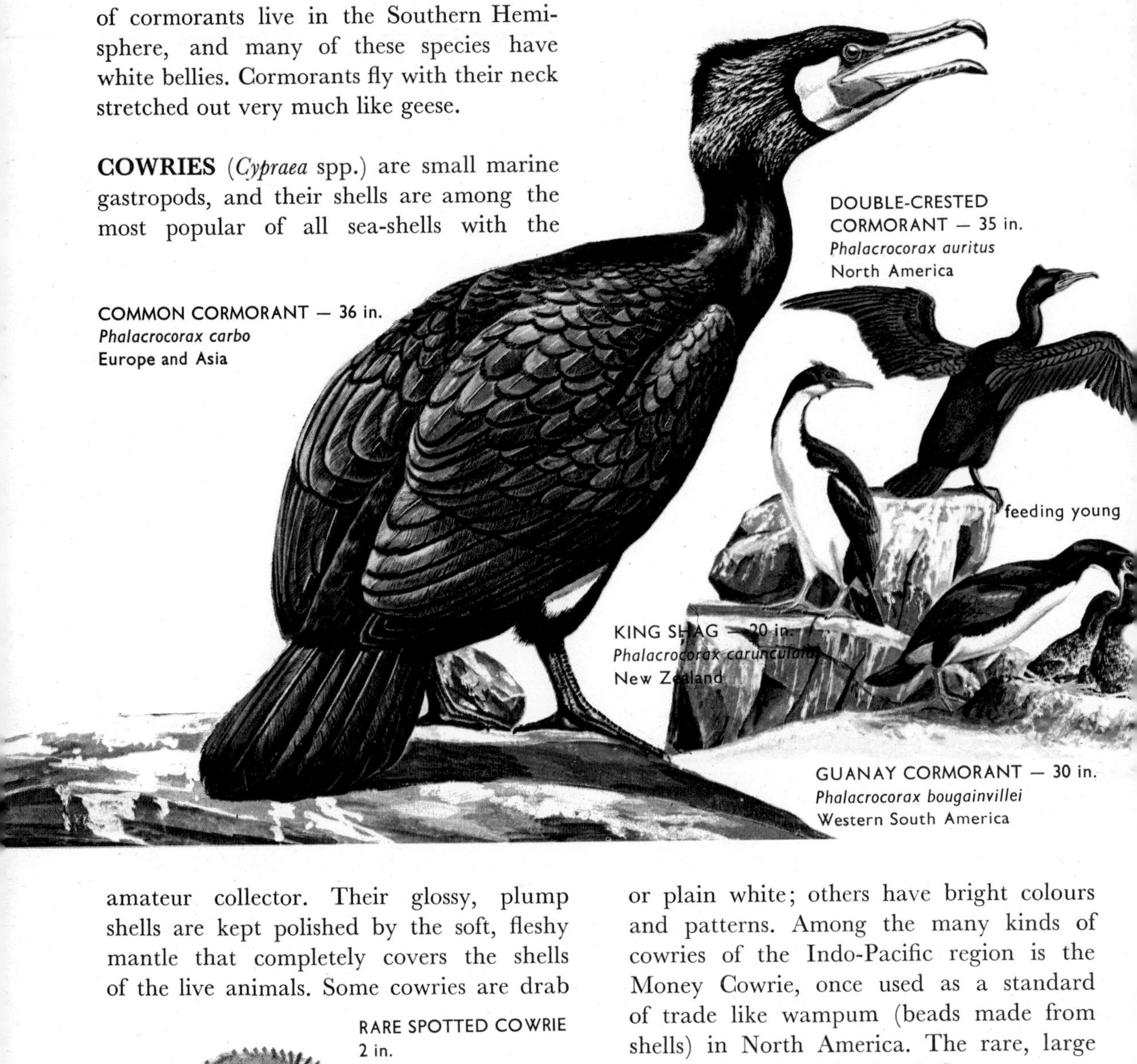

COMMON CORMORANT — 36 in.
Phalacrocorax carbo
Europe and Asia

DOUBLE-CRESTED
CORMORANT — 35 in.
Phalacrocorax auritus
North America

feeding young

KING SHAG — 20 in.
Phalacrocorax carunculata
New Zealand

GUANAY CORMORANT — 30 in.
Phalacrocorax bougainvillei
Western South America

amateur collector. Their glossy, plump shells are kept polished by the soft, fleshy mantle that completely covers the shells of the live animals. Some cowries are drab or plain white; others have bright colours and patterns. Among the many kinds of cowries of the Indo-Pacific region is the Money Cowrie, once used as a standard of trade like wampum (beads made from shells) in North America. The rare, large Golden Cowrie of the South Seas was worn as a badge of office by chiefs. Shells of young cowries are very delicate and easily

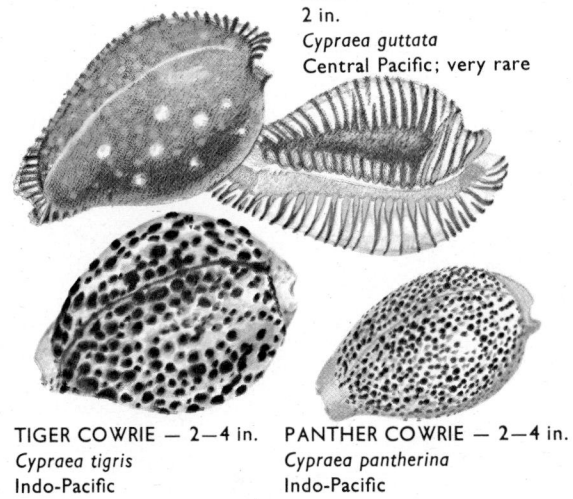

RARE SPOTTED COWRIE
2 in.
Cypraea guttata
Central Pacific; very rare

TIGER COWRIE — 2—4 in.
Cypraea tigris
Indo-Pacific

PANTHER COWRIE — 2—4 in.
Cypraea pantherina
Indo-Pacific

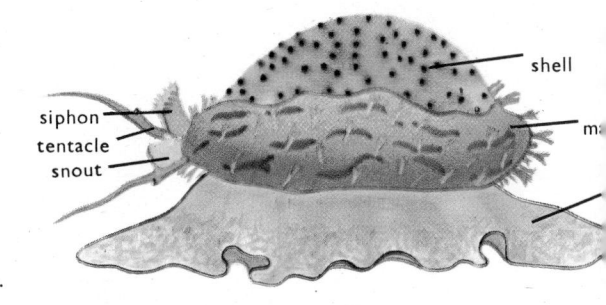

shell

siphon
tentacle
snout

ma

The fleshy mantle covers part of a cowrie's shell.

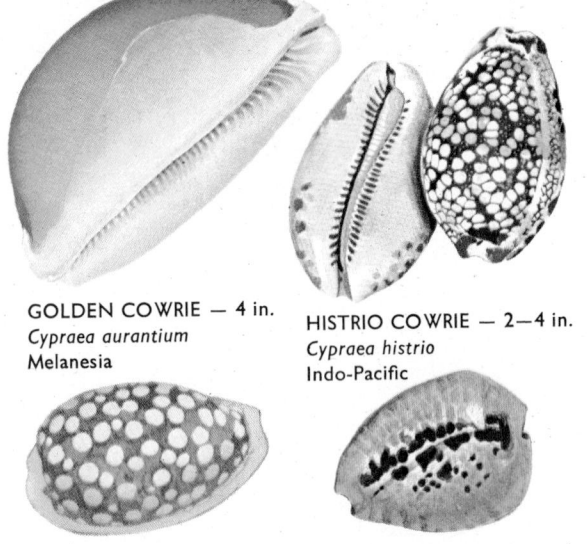

GOLDEN COWRIE — 4 in.
Cypraea aurantium
Melanesia

HISTRIO COWRIE — 2—4 in.
Cypraea histrio
Indo-Pacific

SIEVE COWRIE — 1 in.
Cypraea cribraria
Indo-Pacific; rare

MOUSE COWRIE — 2 in.
Cypraea mus
Venezuela

flies do not bite, however. Some adult crane-flies feed on the nectar of flowers, but little is known about the feeding habits of most species. Some larvae or maggots are aquatic; others live in mud or sand. Most feed on decaying vegetation, though some are predaceous. Larvae of a few

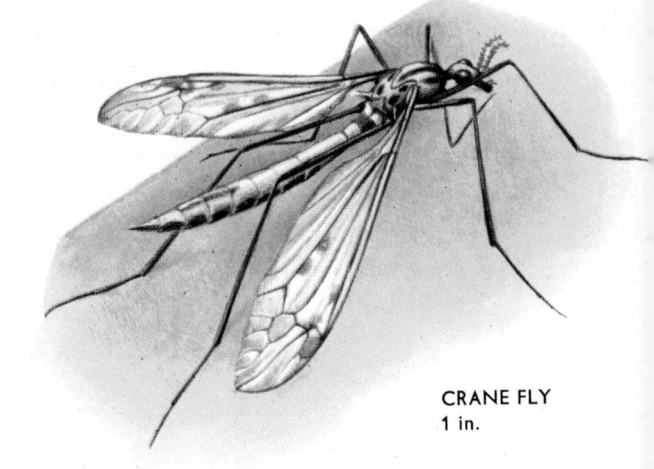

CRANE FLY
1 in.

broken, but when mature they are thick and strong. Cowries, along with the closely-related Trivias, are mostly shallow, warm-water species. The Common Cowrie is found on the British coast. The Deer Cowrie is one of the largest cowries in the world.

CRANE-FLIES (*Tipulidae*) are normally found in damp areas where there is heavy vegetation. Many are attracted to lights and are often mistaken for mosquitoes. Crane-

species damage pastures by feeding on the grass roots. These are called "leather-jackets", because of their tough integument.

CRANES are large, long-necked, long-legged, dignified birds, some as tall as men. They live in North America, Europe,

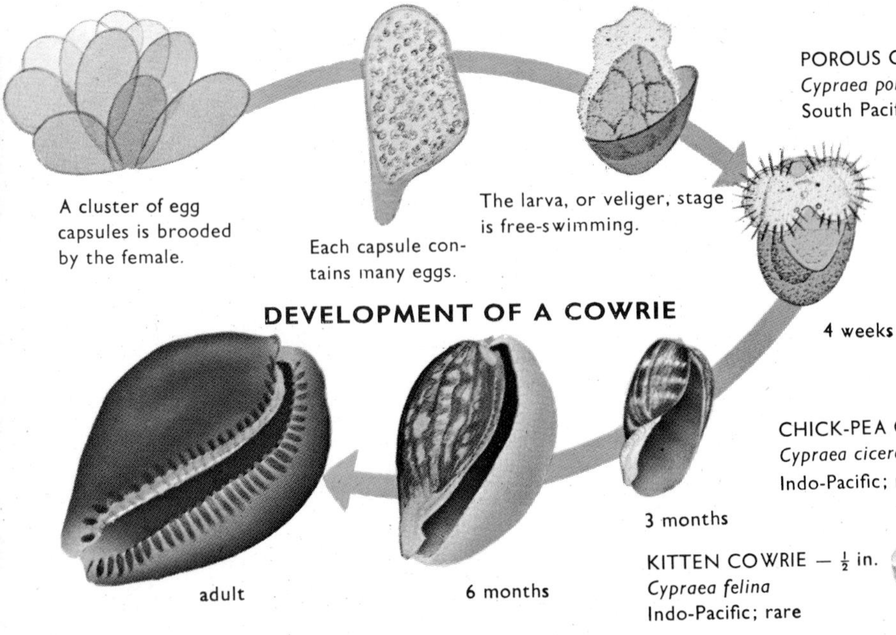

A cluster of egg capsules is brooded by the female.

Each capsule contains many eggs.

The larva, or veliger, stage is free-swimming.

DEVELOPMENT OF A COWRIE

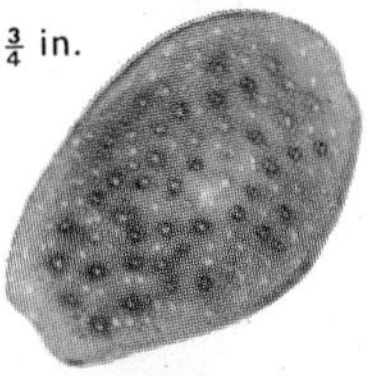

4 weeks

POROUS COWRIE — ¾ in.
Cypraea poraria
South Pacific; rare

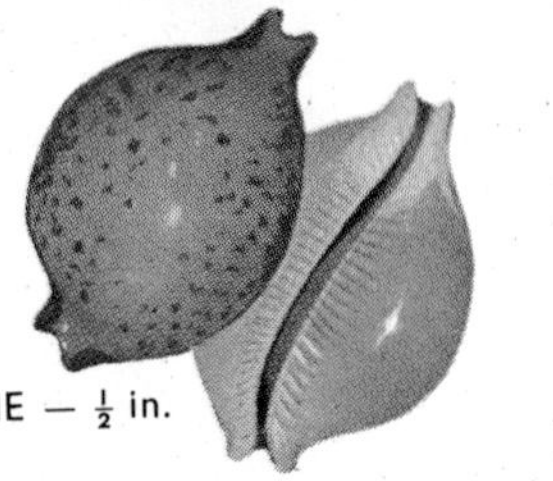

CHICK-PEA COWRIE — ½ in.
Cypraea cicercula
Indo-Pacific; not common

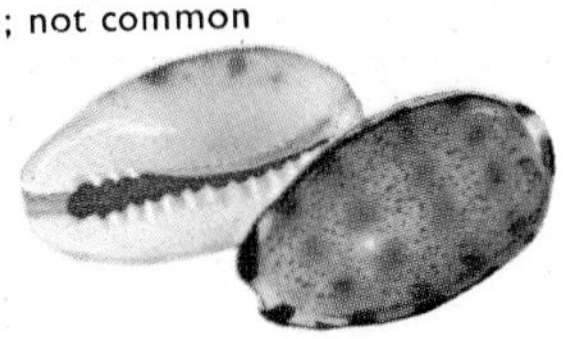

3 months

KITTEN COWRIE — ½ in.
Cypraea felina
Indo-Pacific; rare

adult

6 months

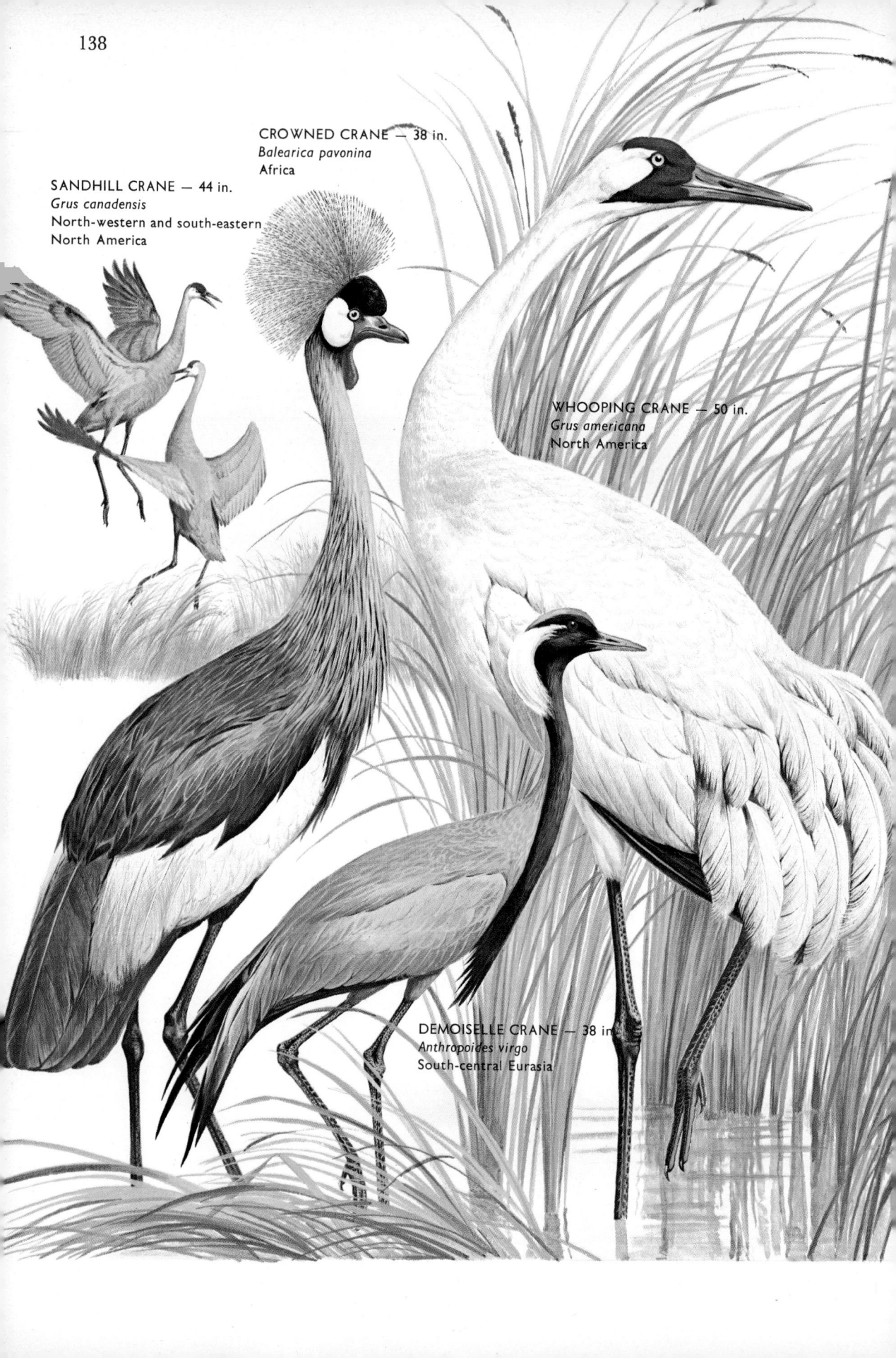

138

CROWNED CRANE — 38 in.
Balearica pavonina
Africa

SANDHILL CRANE — 44 in.
Grus canadensis
North-western and south-eastern
North America

WHOOPING CRANE — 50 in.
Grus americana
North America

DEMOISELLE CRANE — 38 in.
Anthropoides virgo
South-central Eurasia

Asia, Africa and Australia. Their peculiar windpipes are very long and curled around like trumpet tubes, and with these they make their loud trumpeting sounds. Cranes fly with their necks straight out in front of them and their feet trailing straight behind. Many have bare spots on their heads where the skin is bright red.

Although cranes are usually stately and sedate, they occasionally dance. After walking around stiff-legged and bowing to each other, the dancers leap in rhythm six or more feet into the air. At the same time they trumpet loudly, juggle sticks in their bills, and throw bits of grass over their heads. This dance may be performed at any time of the year. Whole flocks of migrating cranes on a resting ground sometimes hold a dance before flying on. Cranes migrate by day. Some cranes fly over mountains 14,000 feet high.

Each species of crane has different breeding habits, but all collect a mound of mud or vegetation for a nest, and none lays more than three eggs or less than two.

Demoiselle Cranes, smallest members of the crane family, are migratory birds that live in Europe, Asia and Africa. Their plumes of soft white feathers behind each eye make them easy to identify. They breed in captivity and can be seen in many zoos.

Sarus Cranes of India are the tallest and largest cranes. They do not migrate. Mated pairs of Sarus Cranes never leave each other. Legend says that when one is killed, the other dies of a broken heart. They can be tamed and kept loose in the gardens of homes, where they are efficient watchdogs, squawking loudly when people approach.

Sandhill Cranes are the only cranes that breed in the south-eastern part of the United States. Breeding colonies in Florida are now rigidly protected. Sandhill Cranes also breed on the western plains.

Whooping Cranes, once game birds, furnished food for settlers of the western plains of the United States and for those who crossed the country in covered wagons. Thousands of these great white birds for-

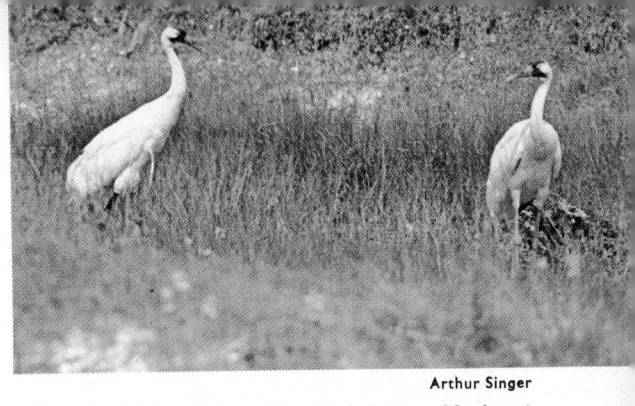

Arthur Singer

Whooping Cranes winter in the Arkansas National Wild-life Refuge, Texas, but are seldom photographed as in the picture above.

merly bred and migrated all the way from central Canada through the northern United States. They wintered south to parts of Mexico. Their whooping, trumpeting call could be heard for miles and was a familiar sound a century ago. Today, only about 42 (1961) Whooping Cranes are left in North America. The National Audubon Society, and the governments of Canada and the United States, are trying to save these wonderful birds.

CRAYFISH (*Cambarus* spp.) are small (3 to 6 inches in length) crustaceans that resemble lobsters. Some of the many species occur only in swift streams, others only in still waters, and yet others in wet meadows or marshes, where they dig burrows as much as three feet deep to reach the water level. The burrow is usually topped with a hollow "chimney" made of mud pellets removed in the digging.

CRAYFISH
Potamobius pallipes
Britain and France

COMMON FRENCH CRAYFISH
Astacus fluviatalis
France — widely
cultivated for food

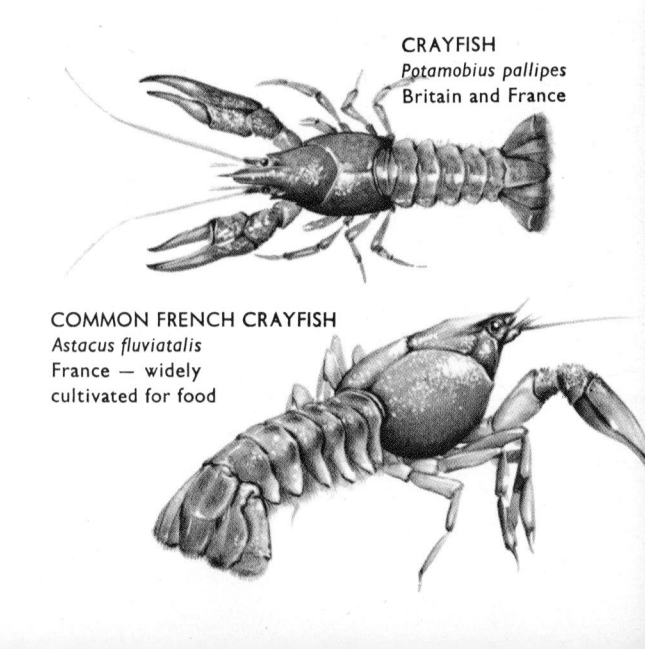

Crayfish have a hard outer skeleton, which is segmented on the legs and tail. The skeleton is shed and replaced as the animal grows. Young crayfish may moult several times a year until they attain full growth. The covering over a freshly-shed crayfish, including its legs and claws, is soft, and the animal usually stays in hiding until its new skeleton hardens.

A crayfish's two front legs end in pincer-like claws, which are used for catching food and for defence. Its remaining four pairs of legs are used for walking. Crayfish swim or dart backwards, by a flip of their strong, flattened, muscular tail.

Crayfish are mainly scavengers feeding on plant and animal debris. They also eat insect larvae, snails, worms, other crustaceans, small fish, and other animal matter. Burrowing species eat roots of plants. In turn, crayfish are food for fishes, frogs, turtles, snakes, water birds, and such mammals as raccoons.

CREEPERS, circumpolar in the Northern Hemisphere, are small birds with narrow, curved bills for probing for insects in cracks and under bark. They have long, sharp-clawed toes for climbing, and stiff tails to brace themselves against tree-trunks.

The Tree Creeper, as three very similar species, occurs over most of the Northern Hemisphere in woodland. It creeps up and spirals around trunks of tall trees. While it climbs, the Tree Creeper probes with its bill. When it gets to the first branches, the bird flies down and starts up the next tree. The Tree Creeper hides its nest under bark or uses any old woodpecker hole. The Wall Creeper is a bird of high mountains.

CRICKETS form an insect family (*Gryllidae*) of nearly 1,000 species. Most have long, tapering antennae, and hind legs adapted for jumping. Their wings, if present, are held flat over their abdomens, the edges bent sharply against their sides. Their "ears", or tympana, are located on their front legs. Females of most species have

CORAL-BILLED NUTHATCH — 5½ in.
Hypositta corallirostris
Madagascar

SPOTTED CREEPER — 5 in.
Salpornis spilonotus
Tropical Africa

STRIPE-HEADED CREEPER — 6 in.
Phabdornis mystacalis
Philippines

RED-BROWED TREE CREEPER — 5½ in.
Climacteris erythrops
Australia

Creepers are shy birds of the dense woodlands. They twitter as they feed, but their notes are very faint and are therefore seldom heard.

TREE CREEPER — 5 in.
Certhia familiaris
North America, Europe, Asia.

WALL CREEPER — 6½ in.
Tichodroma muraria
Central Eurasia

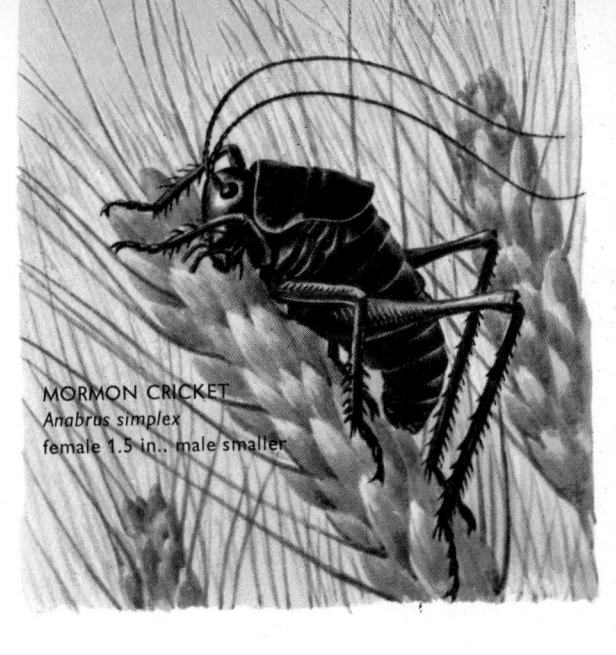

MORMON CRICKET
Anabrus simplex
female 1.5 in., male smaller

particularly long, slender ovipositors.

Only male crickets can sing, and the chirps are produced when their wings are held at an angle of about 45 degrees and rubbed together. On each wing is a rasping area, called the file, and a hardened area, called the scraper. The frequency of their chirps increases as the temperature rises.

Some crickets are said to be so sensitive to temperature changes that the actual temperature can be estimated by counting the frequency of their chirps. Similarly, it has been asserted that the number of chirps per minute can be predicted by reference to the temperature.

Field Crickets, the familiar black or brownish crickets, are often abundant in meadows and fields, and around dwellings or in gardens. Females lay slim, cream-coloured eggs in small clusters in the ground. The eggs are not glued together as are those of grasshoppers. In two to four months the nymphs develop into adults, moulting as many as twelve times during this period. Field Crickets occasionally become so abundant that they cause considerable damage to such crops as cotton, tomatoes, peas or beans. They will also eat holes in paper or in garments, especially those soiled with perspiration.

Tree Crickets are more often heard

Female cricket depositing eggs in the soil.

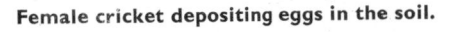

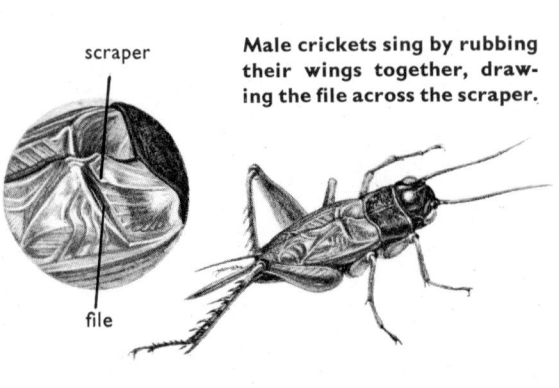

scraper

Male crickets sing by rubbing their wings together, drawing the file across the scraper.

file

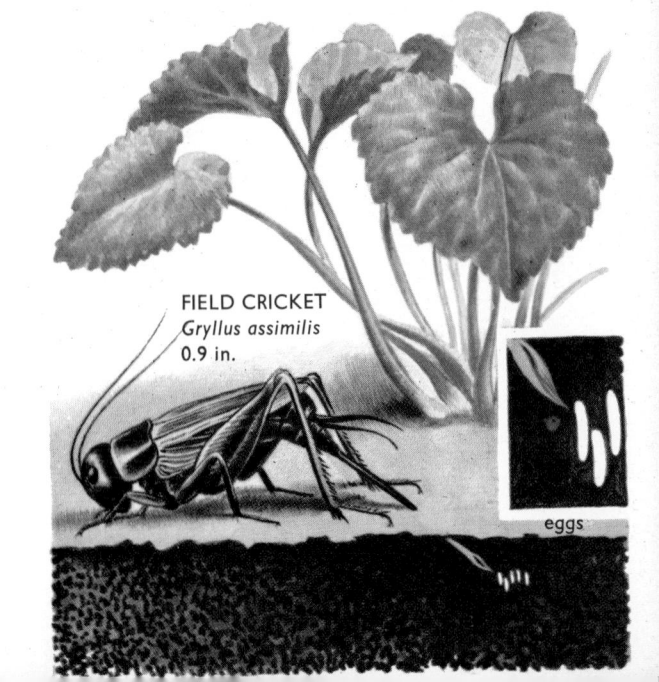

FIELD CRICKET
Gryllus assimilis
0.9 in.

eggs

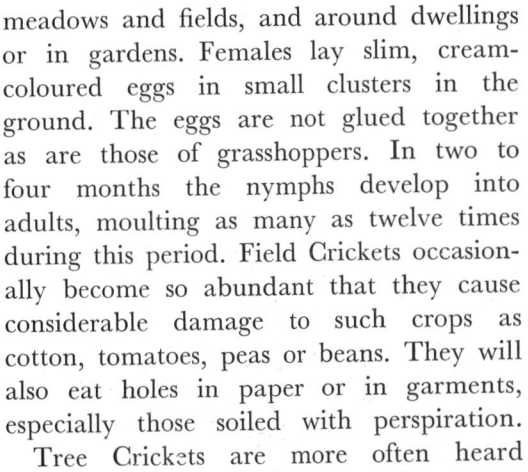

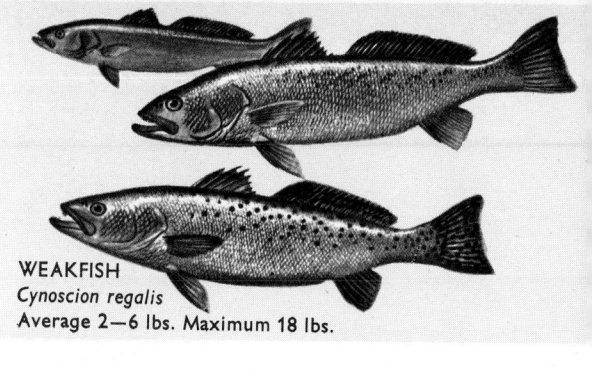

CAMEL CRICKET
Ceuthophilus sp.
0.8 in.

WEAKFISH
Cynoscion regalis
Average 2—6 lbs. Maximum 18 lbs.

than seen abroad. Usually pale green, these slender crickets live in shrubs and trees. Females sometimes do damage by their egg-laying habits, for each egg is deposited in a small hole in a twig. Often as many as 50 holes are made in a row, and the section of twig above the holes frequently dies as a result of the injury.

Mole Crickets are adapted for burrowing. Their broad, flat, front tibiae end in large tooth-like projections, and using these efficient diggers, Mole Crickets can burrow rapidly through moist soil. Sometimes they dig as deep as six inches.

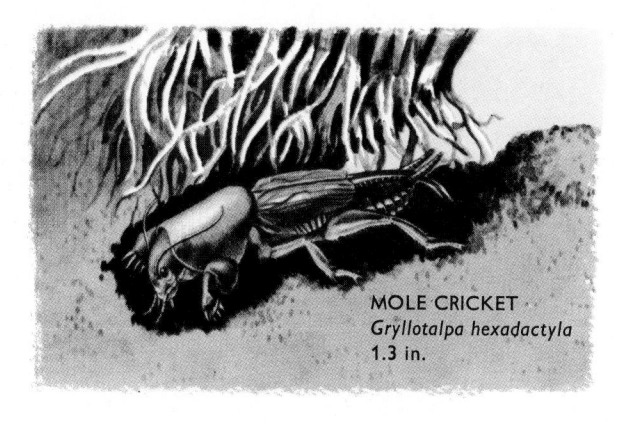

MOLE CRICKET
Gryllotalpa hexadactyla
1.3 in.

Paddle-like front legs are used to dig burrows.

CROAKERS, a family of about 160 species of salt-water fishes, live in shallow, warm water. Most are good to eat, some are important commercially. Besides their use as food, the livers of croakers are processed in some countries to extract their oil, which is as rich in vitamin A as cod liver oil.

These fish are called "croakers" because of the croaking, grunting or growling noises that most of them make as they swim. Some kinds continue to "croak" after they

are caught. They do this by vibrating special muscles in their abdomens. These muscles are attached to their large and many-branched air-bladders, which amplify the vibrations. Typically, only the males can make these noises, and apparently they do so to attract the females.

Only a single species is found in British waters — the Meagre, or Shade-fish (Sciaena equila) — and then only as an occasional visitor. The Meagre has a wide range, occurring also in South Africa and Australia. It reaches a length of about 6 feet.

There are a number of species in the Western Atlantic. The Red Drum, or Channel Bass (Sciaenops ocellata), has a black spot on the upper part of the caudal peduncle. The Black Drum (Pogonias cromis) is a larger species, sometimes reaching 150 pounds, and it is important commercially.

There are also some Croakers which lack an air-bladder. Known as Whitings along the American Atlantic coast, they are unable to produce the sounds made by other species of this family, and tend to sink when not swimming.

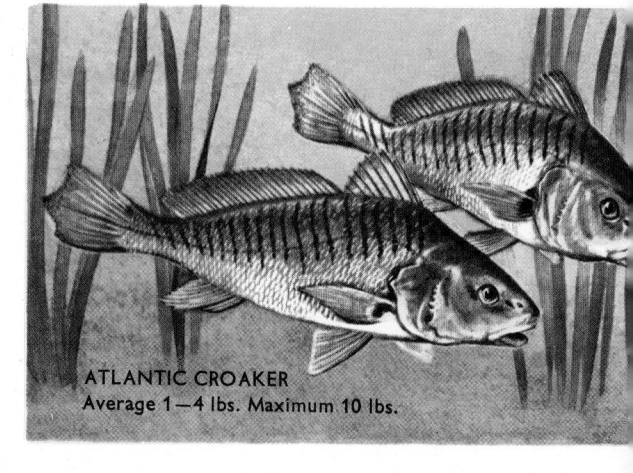

ATLANTIC CROAKER
Average 1—4 lbs. Maximum 10 lbs.

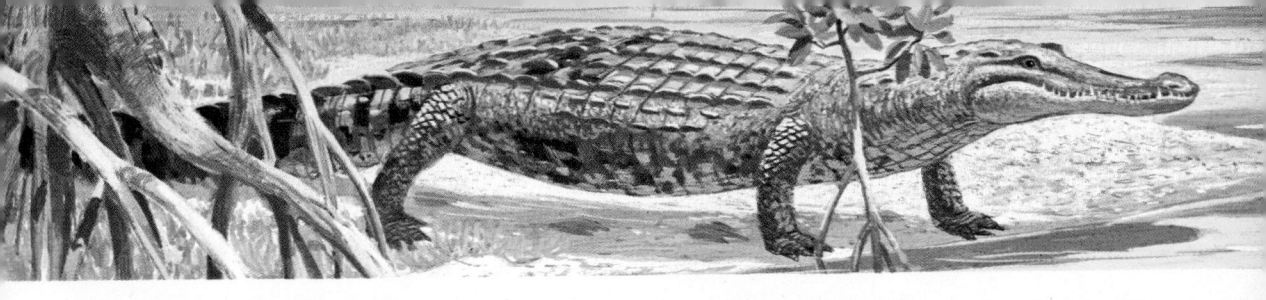

The American Crocodile occurs from northern South America through Central America to the southern tip of the Florida mainland.

CROCODILIANS were a widespread group of reptiles in ancient times, but only 23 species still exist. Their numbers were already greatly depleted before the appearance of man, who has rapidly reduced the few remaining crocodilians so that some species verge on extinction. Most living crocodilians are found in fresh water, and none are known to exceed 23 feet in length. Among extinct species were marine types that reached lengths of 35 or 40 feet and had skulls that measured 6 feet long.

All crocodilians — crocodiles, alligators, caimans and gavials — have long snouts and tremendous jaws. They look like oversized lizards, but have large horny plates over heavy bone, rather than thin scales. They are advanced over all other reptiles in having a four-chambered heart, like birds and mammals, and an air-breathing channel completely separated from the mouth, as in mammals. This permits them to hold and chew food underwater, while their nostrils are above the surface and breathing continues uninterrupted. Valves close up their nostrils and ear-openings, preventing the entry of water when they submerge. A semi-transparent third eyelid, beneath the other two eyelids, slides over the eye and protects it when open underwater. Crocodilians have teeth in sockets, like mammals, rather than attached to the sides or crests ot the jawbones. They are

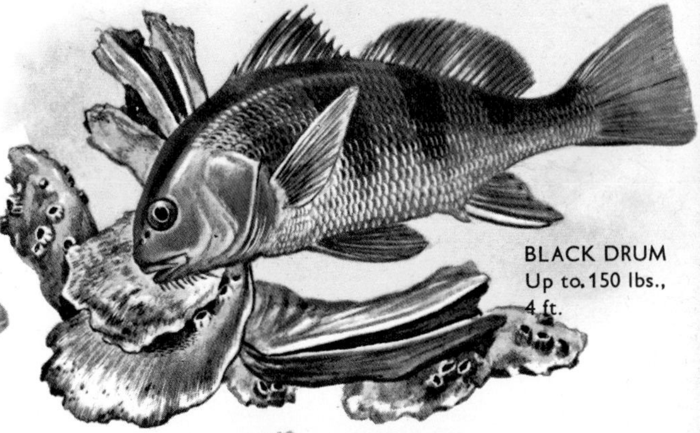

BLACK DRUM
Up to. 150 lbs.,
4 ft.

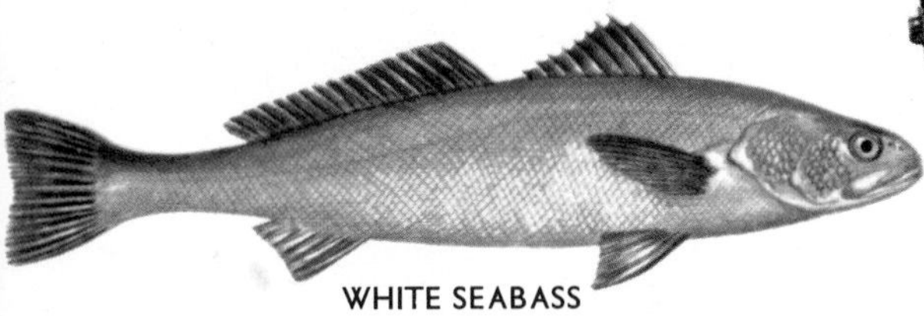

WHITE SEABASS
Average 5—25 lbs. Up to 80 lbs.

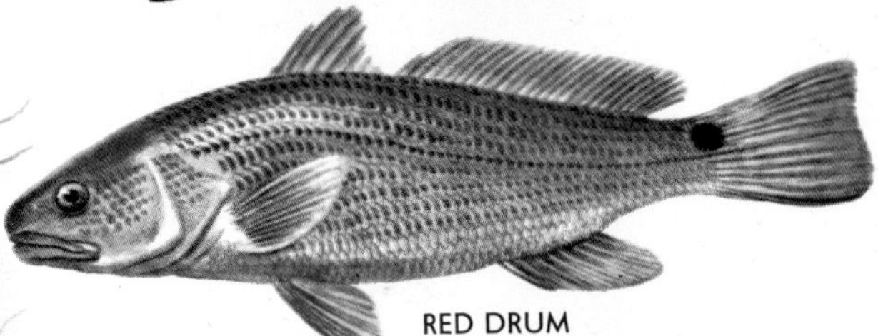

RED DRUM
Average 3—15 lbs. Maximum 85 lbs.

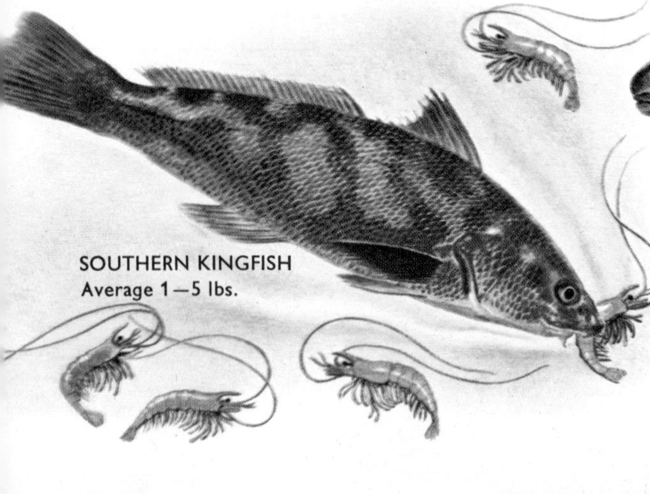

SOUTHERN KINGFISH
Average 1—5 lbs.

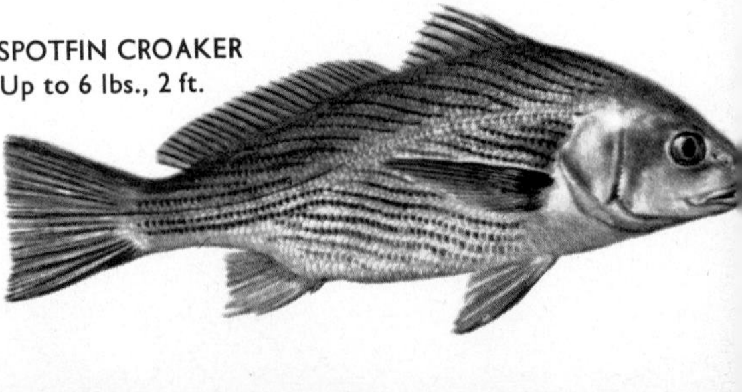

SPOTFIN CROAKER
Up to 6 lbs., 2 ft.

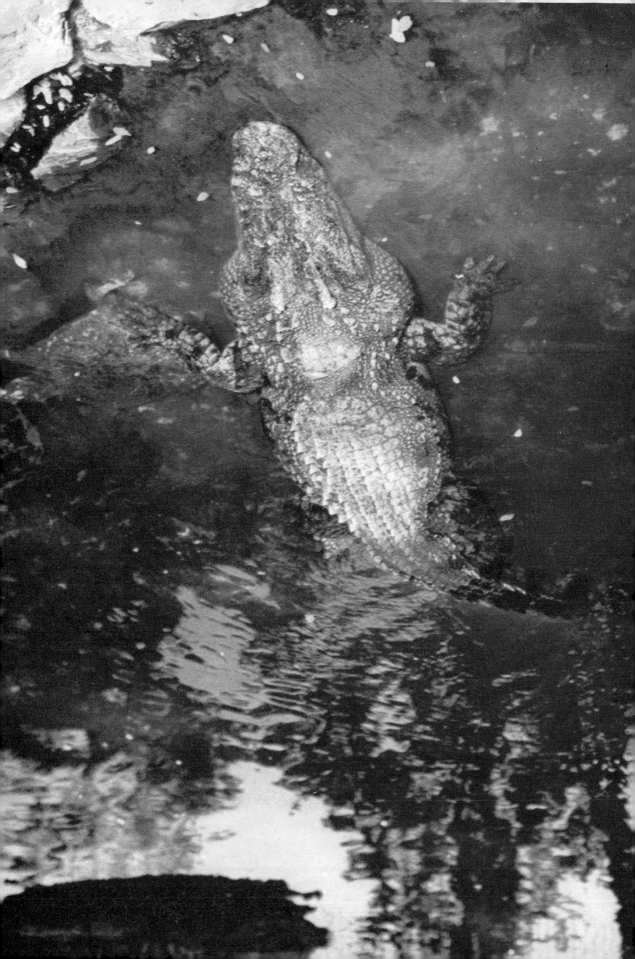

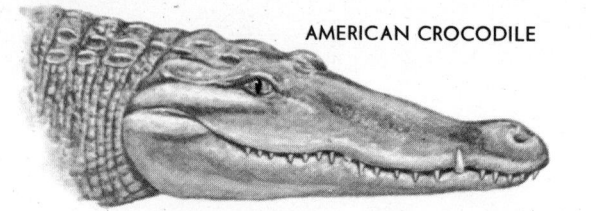

AMERICAN CROCODILE

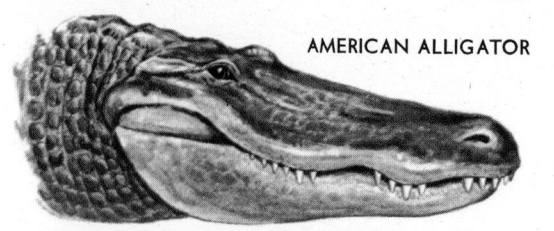

AMERICAN ALLIGATOR

The fourth tooth in the lower jaw of the narrow-snouted American Crocodile fits into a groove on the outside of the upper jaw; in the American Alligator, the fourth tooth of the lower jaw is concealed in a pocket in the broad upper jaw.

divided into three families — alligators and caimans, gavials, and true crocodiles. (See ALLIGATORS; GAVIALS.)

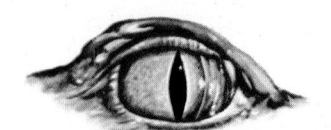

The eye of a crocodilian has a slit-like pupil, a protective inner lid, and glows at night in a beam of light directed at the animal.

True CROCODILES *(Crocodylus* spp.*)* of a dozen species are found in warm, brackish or salt waters around the world.

The Nile Crocodile, one of the two African species, has been famed for centuries as a fearsome creature that often attacks and eats children, and even adults. Like all other crocodilians, these crocodiles sun themselves on the banks, warming their sluggish bodies to a degree that permits them to move at astonishing speeds. Often while sunning they open their jaws and allow birds to enter their mouths, unharmed, to pick off leeches.

The American crocodile ranges from South America into Mexico and the southern tip of Florida, and reaches a length of at least 23 feet. It is often seen in coastal lagoons and in the broad mouths and channels of rivers entering the Caribbean Sea. The narrow-snouted American Crocodile is notoriously vicious compared to the relatively docile American Alligator. Three other species of crocodiles occur in the Americas: one in Cuba, one in Central America, and the third in South America.

Crocodiles hunt their prey primarily at the water's edge, rarely pursuing animals out of water. They bite with tremendous force, and whip their tails with such power that they knock down animals that might otherwise escape. Crocodiles have such weak muscles for opening their jaws that a man can easily hold their jaws shut with one hand. Hunters are said to capture

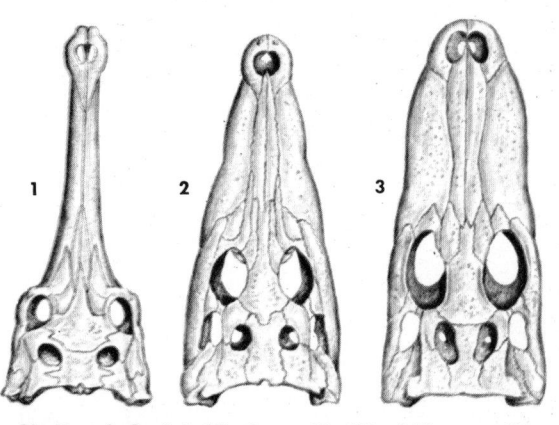

Skulls of Gavial (1), Crocodile (2), Alligator (3). The Alligator has a broader snout than the others.

crocodiles by holding in their hand a stout stick, pointed at both ends and fastened to a rope. When the crocodile snaps at the hunter's hand, it impales the stick in both jaws. Then the hunter hauls the animal on to land and kills it. The female Nile Crocodile lays her eggs in a hole dug in a sandy bank. Then she covers them and stays nearby on guard until they hatch. The Nile Crocodile is reported to reach a length of 28 to 30 feet, but no authentic records exceed 16 feet.

Six species of crocodiles occur in the Oriental region between south-eastern Asia and Australia. Most widespread is the Salt-water Crocodile that inhabits all the large streams, swamps and marshes of the East Indies, travelling from island to island.

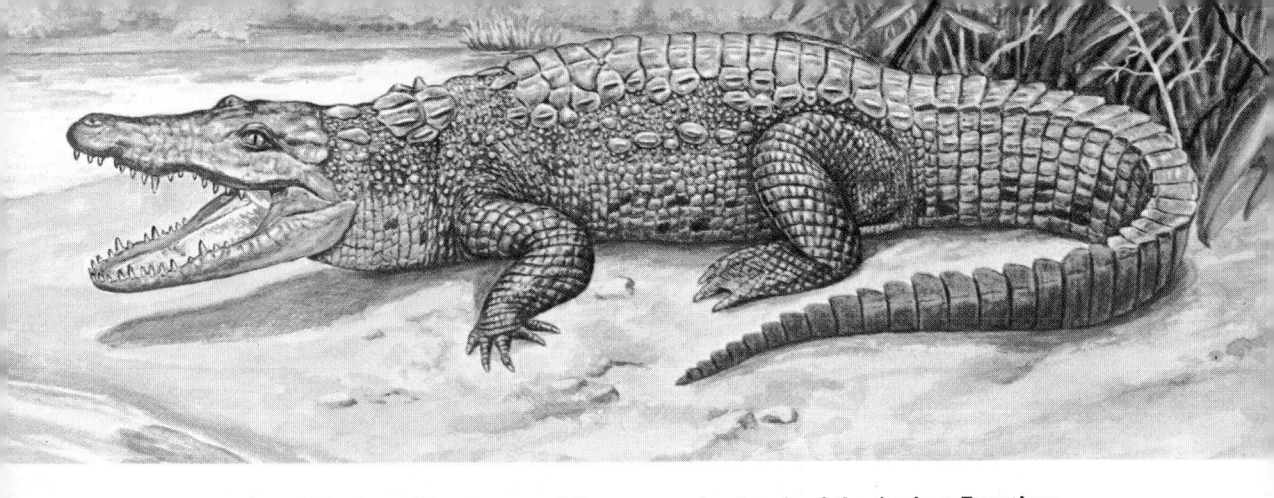

The Nile Crocodile was one of the many animal gods of the Ancient Egyptians.

It is much feared because of its large size (20 feet) and vicious, fearless temperament.

The Mugger, or Marsh Crocodile (13 feet), is found only in India. The Mugger is extremely common, but fortunately it is sluggish and rarely, if ever, attacks a human. In many parts of India, the Mugger is sacred. People walk among these big reptiles, even touching them without being harmed. Muggers are not known to live longer than 30 years, although there are incorrect reports of their living for centuries. Several other smaller crocodiles are found in various parts of the Orient.

Dwarf Crocodiles *(Osteolaemus)* of central Africa are the smallest known crocodilians. The largest on record measured only 3 feet 9 inches in length. These small crocodiles are unique in possessing bony plates on the underside as well as on the back.

CROWS belong to a family whose 100 members, found round the world, include jays, magpies, rooks, jackdaws and ravens.

They are intelligent, and in captivity they have a reputation for mischievousness.

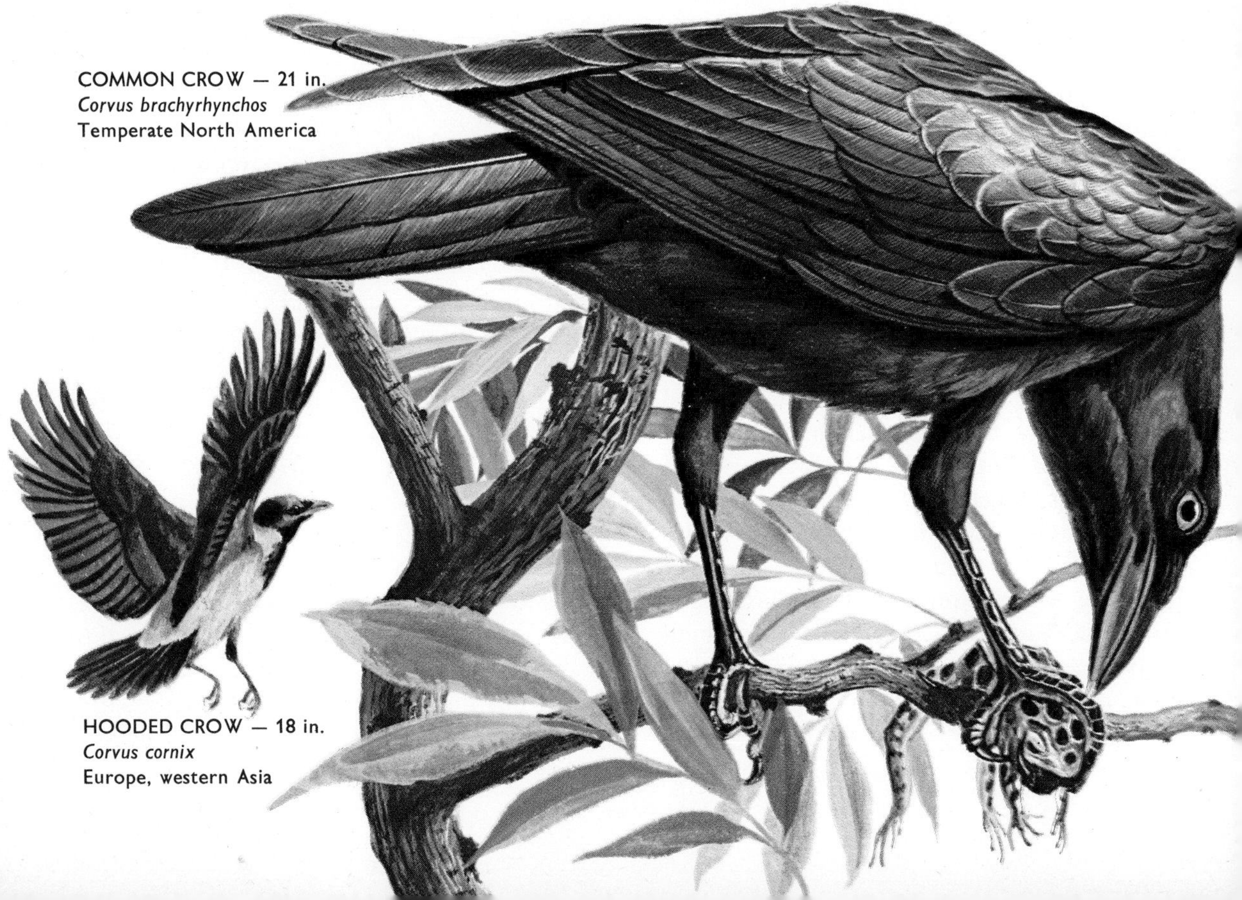

COMMON CROW — 21 in.
Corvus brachyrhynchos
Temperate North America

HOODED CROW — 18 in.
Corvus cornix
Europe, western Asia

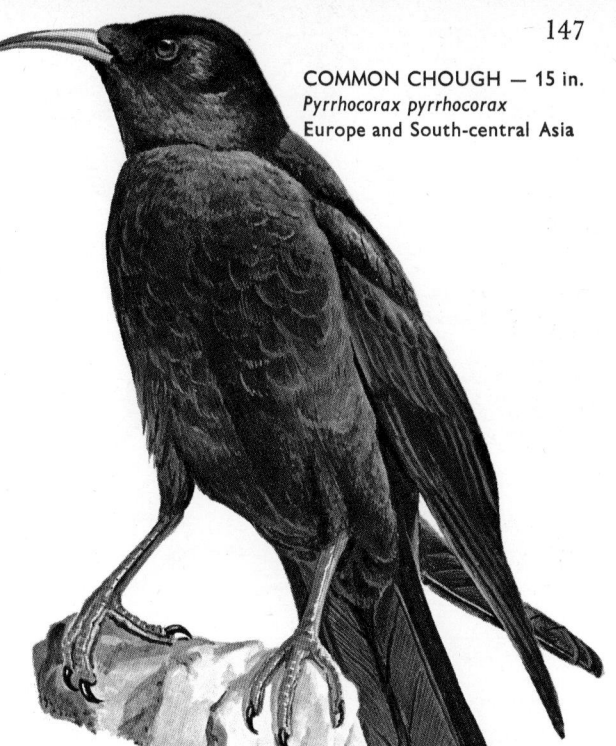

COMMON CHOUGH — 15 in.
Pyrrhocorax pyrrhocorax
Europe and South-central Asia

They learn to distinguish a man with a gun from one without, and in places where they are persecuted they become very wary and hard to approach. They are usually sociable birds, and many species flock in winter and share great communal tree-roosts. The Rooks and Jackdaws remain sociable when nesting and form colonies, the former in trees and the latter in holes. Magpies and Jays are less sociable, but they do gather in assemblies at the beginning of the breeding season, and displays occur.

Most Crows buid big well-constructed nests of twigs, usually at a considerable height above the ground in trees, but occasionally lower. Sometimes they nest in loose colonies. The female ordinarily lays five eggs and starts incubating when the first egg is laid. After the young are hatched, they keep their nest quite clean.

Taken as nestlings, crows make delightful pets, but annoy neighbours by stealing anything bright, loose and small enough to carry off in their beaks.

The Common Chough, shown here, is a specialised feeder. Its slender bill is used for probing deep into the turf of grassland, near the cliffs and rocky hills it prefers. It is a superb acrobatic flyer.

CRUSTACEANS, which belong to the *phylum arthropoda* (jointed-legged animals), have outer skeletons of chitin and lime. There are many different groups. Some are small; others are large. Some live in the sea, some in fresh water, others on land. They are known from mountain peaks and deserts to the depths of oceans. Many live as plankton in the sea, and some, like copepods, occur in countless millions.

Crustaceans have two pairs of antennae, which distinguishes them from all other arthropods. One pair is often much reduced in size, however. Because of their rigid moult covering, crustaceans do not grow continually as do most other animals. Instead, they stay the same size for a time, moult or cast off the old skeleton and emerge as soft-bodied animals. Their skeletons do

not harden for a few hours, and during this time the animals grow. More growth is impossible until the next moult.

Crustaceans such as copepods, which feed on diatoms (see PLANKTON), filter their almost microscopic food from the water. Other crustaceans may be active

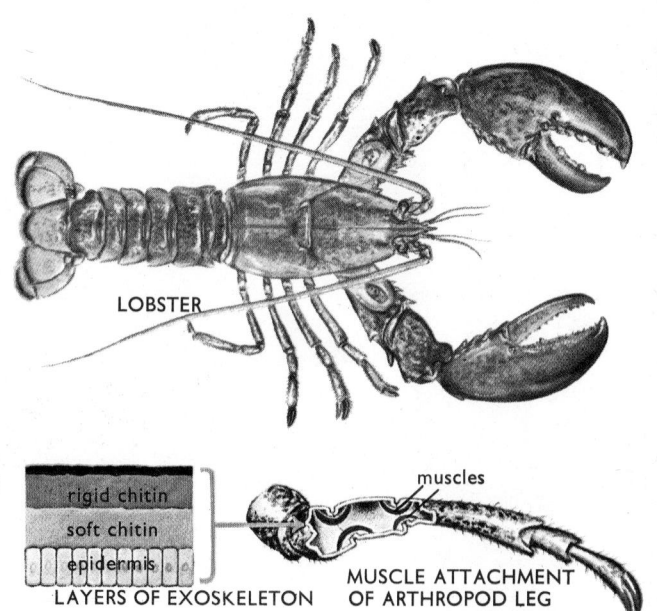

LOBSTER

rigid chitin
soft chitin
epidermis
LAYERS OF EXOSKELETON

muscles
MUSCLE ATTACHMENT OF ARTHROPOD LEG

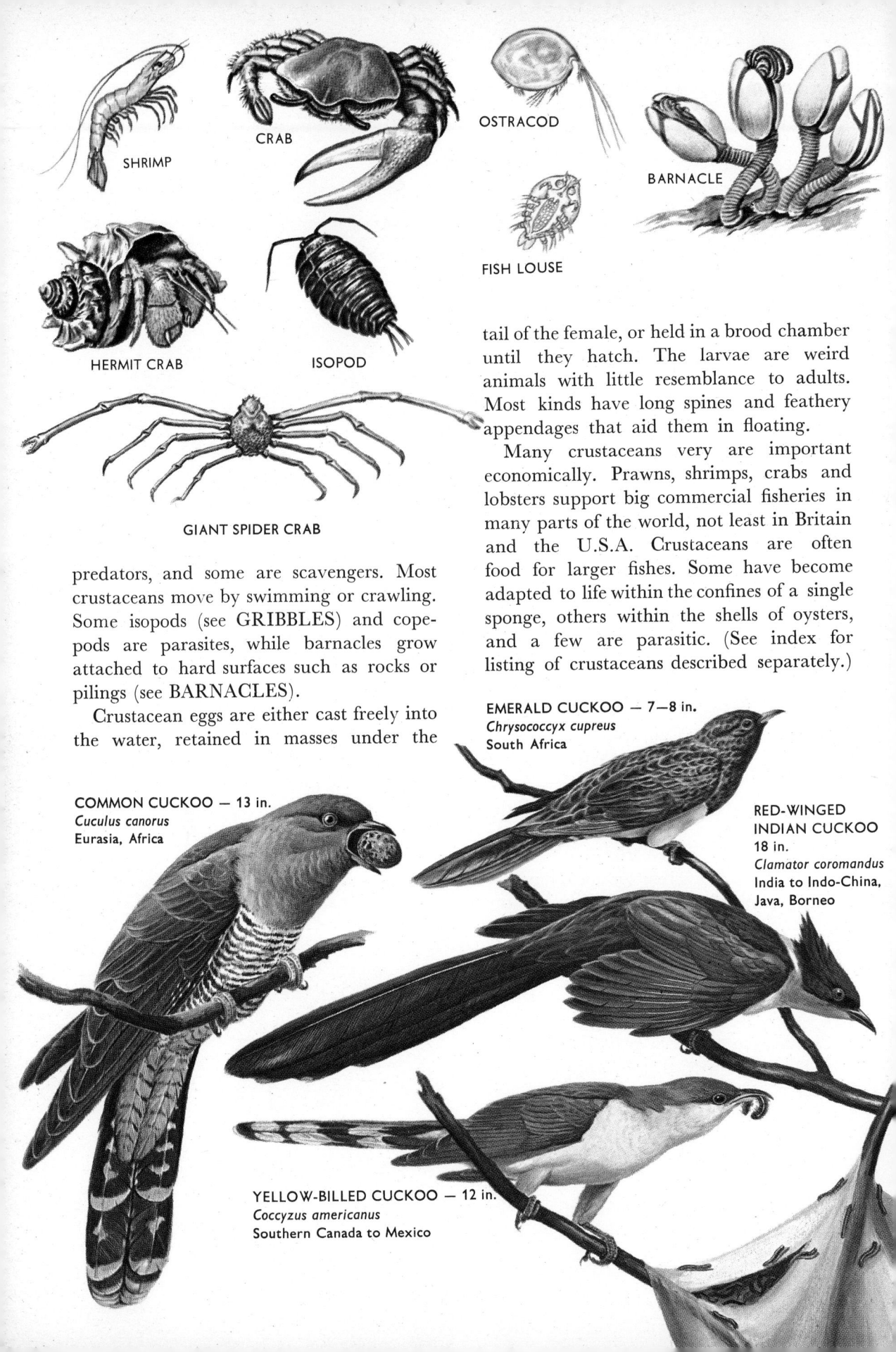

SHRIMP

CRAB

OSTRACOD

BARNACLE

FISH LOUSE

HERMIT CRAB

ISOPOD

GIANT SPIDER CRAB

predators, and some are scavengers. Most crustaceans move by swimming or crawling. Some isopods (see GRIBBLES) and copepods are parasites, while barnacles grow attached to hard surfaces such as rocks or pilings (see BARNACLES).

Crustacean eggs are either cast freely into the water, retained in masses under the tail of the female, or held in a brood chamber until they hatch. The larvae are weird animals with little resemblance to adults. Most kinds have long spines and feathery appendages that aid them in floating.

Many crustaceans very are important economically. Prawns, shrimps, crabs and lobsters support big commercial fisheries in many parts of the world, not least in Britain and the U.S.A. Crustaceans are often food for larger fishes. Some have become adapted to life within the confines of a single sponge, others within the shells of oysters, and a few are parasitic. (See index for listing of crustaceans described separately.)

EMERALD CUCKOO — 7—8 in.
Chrysococcyx cupreus
South Africa

COMMON CUCKOO — 13 in.
Cuculus canorus
Eurasia, Africa

RED-WINGED
INDIAN CUCKOO
18 in.
Clamator coromandus
India to Indo-China,
Java, Borneo

YELLOW-BILLED CUCKOO — 12 in.
Coccyzus americanus
Southern Canada to Mexico

CUCKOOS are a family with a world-wide distribution. The 127 species vary greatly in appearance and behaviour. They all tend to be slender, long-tailed birds. Some species are strong-legged runners, spending most of their time on the ground, where they chase and eat many small animals, including many reptiles. The Coucals of the Eastern Hemisphere and the Road-runner of America are birds of this kind. These species build the normal type of nest and rear their own young. The Yellow-billed and Black-billed Cuckoos of North America are examples of tree-haunters which also nest and rear their young in the normal way, but the Anis (see ANIS) nest communally and many species in the Eastern Hemisphere are parasitic. These birds lay their eggs in the nests of other birds, which then rear the young cuckoos. Each cuckoo species has a few particular host species which it parasitises, and the eggs often have a very close resemblance to those of the host. The Red-winged Cuckoo, shown here, parasitises Asiatic babblers and, like them, has a pale-blue, unmarked egg. The cuckoos of this genus, *Clamator*, are reared with the host's young.

The Common Cuckoo, whose call has given the family its name, has a more elaborate method. When it adds an egg to the nest, it removes one of the host's eggs, which it may swallow or drop. This probably helps to conceal the fact that an egg has been added to the clutch. In addition, it watches while the host is building and lays the egg at a time when it will hatch while the host has eggs or tiny young in the nest. The newly-hatched cuckoo squirms itself under eggs or nestlings one by one and heaves them right over the rim of the nest, leaving itself with the whole attention of the host pair. The fledgling cuckoo has an enormous appetite and a general-purpose food call, which may cause other birds besides its foster parents to turn aside and feed it. The conspicuous, unmistakeable call of these species has made it recognisable to people who hardly know one bird from another. It migrates south in winter, and its constant calling on return has made the cuckoo a welcome sign of Spring's arrival.

The Common Cuckoo parasitises small songbirds of all kinds. The Emerald Cuckoo parasitises small warblers and flycatchers in Africa. These cuckoos are not always successful. It is claimed that some birds will eject a cuckoo's egg from their nest or desert the nest entirely. The cuckoos are useful, since they are some of the few birds that will readily eat furry caterpillars.

CURLEWS, largest members of the sandpiper family, live on marshes most of the year but go to the uplands to nest. Their distribution is world-wide. All curlews have long legs, and long, down-curved bills with which they probe in mud and sand for shellfish, worms and insects. Like other sandpipers, they are wading birds and strong flyers, but also walk, run and swim.

Phot. Atlas-Photo — F. Merlet

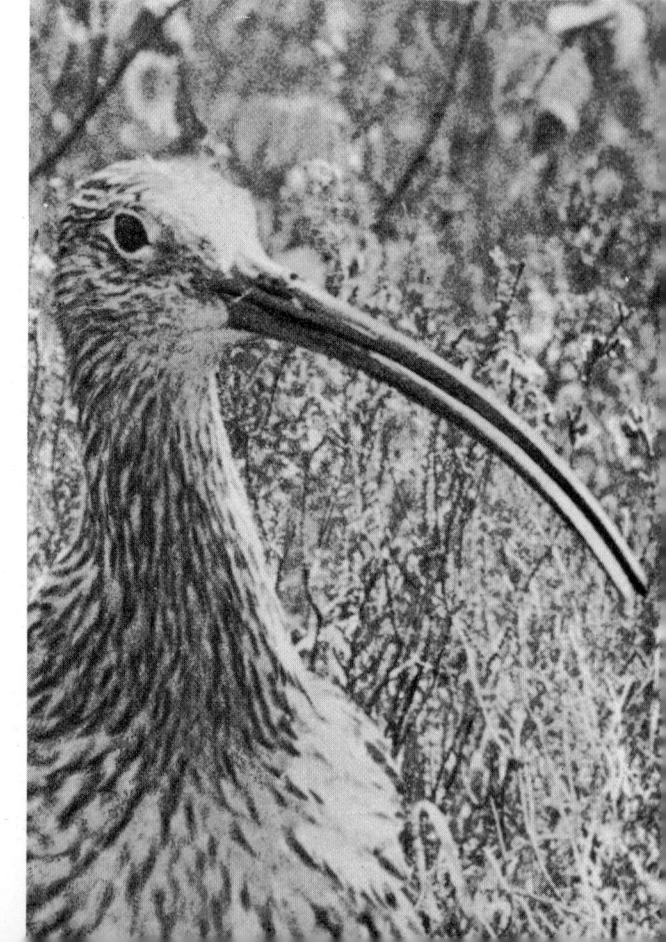

D

DEEP-SEA FISHES vary in colour according to the depth of the sea where they live. Blue and green, for example, are the dominant colours of fishes that live in the lighted zones. Below 600 feet, most fishes are silvery, transparent, or red. In deep sea (below 1,000 feet) most fishes are black.

The eyes of fishes that live at the lower limit of light penetration in the sea are larger than the eyes of fishes living near the surface. They no longer have cells for detecting colour (cones), but cells needed for detecting faint light (rods) are more numerous. Most fishes in the black depths of the sea have small eyes, and many have lost their eyes entirely, like cave-dwellers.

Many deep-sea fishes have luminous spots or stripes along their bodies, or have long, whiskery "feelers" with fringed or bulbous glowing tips. These help fishes to feel their way through the deep sea's eternal blackness. The lights also serve to attract or to identify mates, and to lure smaller fish within their grasp. Most of these fishes have huge mouths for catching and holding their prey, for fishes of the deep sea are, of necessity, flesh-eaters. They feed only on other fishes or on the dead and dying creatures that drift down to them from the lighted zone above. Some species have long, snake-like tails, which they apparently wrap around their prey; others have stomachs which stretch, permitting them to swallow fish as large as themselves.

(1) **Red Dory (Zenion roseus)**, 5 ft.; (2) **Ocellated Dory (Zenopsis ocellata)**, 2 ft.; (3) **Scorpion Fish (Setarches parmatus)**, 1½ ft.; (4) **Little Dory (Zenion hololepis)**, 3 in.; (5) **Red Sea Bass (Pronotogrammus vivanus)**, 8 in.

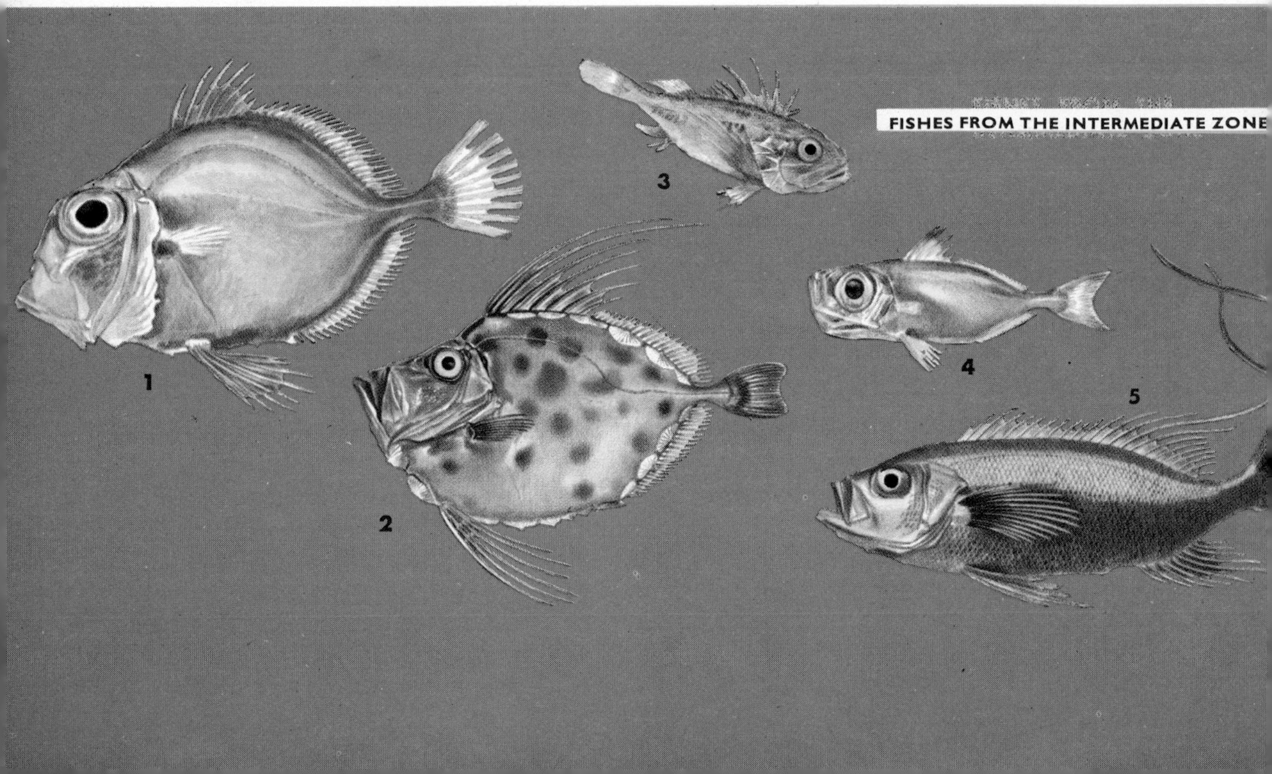

FISHES FROM THE INTERMEDIATE ZONE

DEER, found nearly everywhere in the world except in most of Africa and in Australia, are large-hoofed mammals. A few, such as the South American brockets and pudus (see BROCKET), are small. The Chilean Pudu *(Pudu pudu)*, for example, measures only about 13 inches high at its shoulders. With the exception of the Musk Deer and the Chinese Water Deer, all male deer have antlers. Female Reindeer and Caribou have antlers as well as the males. Most deer have coats of a brown colour; a few are spotted.

All deer are vegetarians, and many of them browse on shrubs or on the low branches of trees. Most deer are sociable, gathering in herds and often following a leader. Bucks usually have harems during the breeding season.

(1) Great Swallower (Chiasmodon), 5—7 in.; (2) Gulper (Eurypharynx), 8—10 in.; (3) Viper Fish (Chauliodus), 8—10 in.; (4) Hatchet-fish (Agyropelecus), 6—8 in.

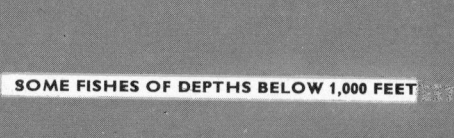

SOME FISHES OF DEPTHS BELOW 1,000 FEET

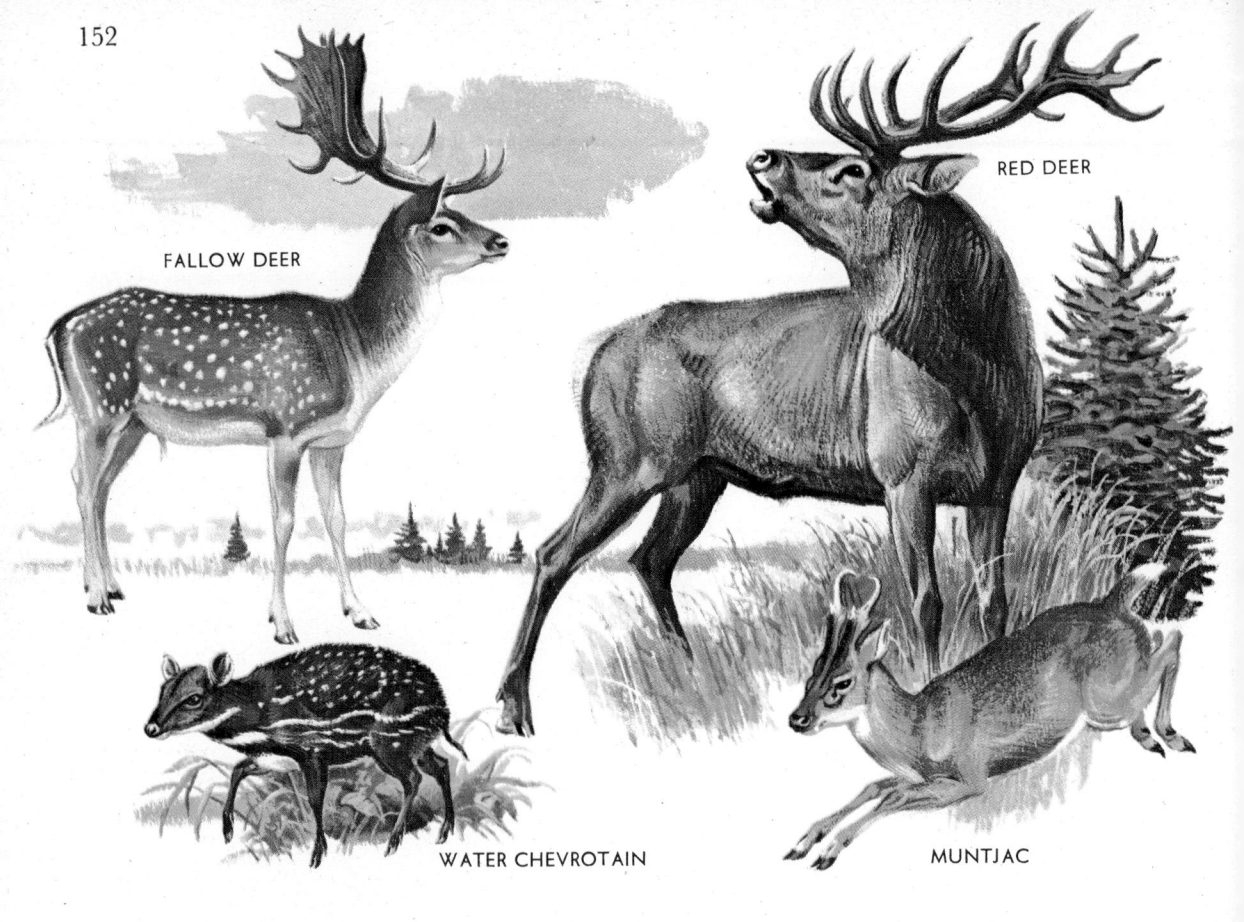

FALLOW DEER

RED DEER

WATER CHEVROTAIN

MUNTJAC

The Axis Deer *(Axis axis)*, which lives close to water in the grassy jungles of India and Ceylon, has conspicuous white spots on its reddish-brown coat. A full-grown Axis Deer may weigh 150 to 200 pounds, and herds may contain as many as 150. Males have long, sharp horns. Because the Axis Deer, or Chital, is so attractive, it has been introduced to many other parts of the world.

The Red Deer *(Cervus elaphus)* weighs from 200 to more than 500 pounds. Males are referred to as stags; females as hinds. Originally the Red Deer was found throughout Europe into western Russia and northern Africa, but after being hunted for hundreds of years, it has been exterminated in many areas. Only the noblemen were privileged to hunt these deer, as related in legends, such as those about Robin Hood. Specially-trained breeds of dogs, called staghounds, were used in the chase. Deer meat is called venison.

Barking deer, or muntjacs *(Muntiacus*

spp.*)*, are several species of small, 40-pound deer found in India and southern Asia. They make loud, sharp, barking sounds. Males have antlers like spikes, forked at their tips, and also have a pair of tusks in their upper jaws. These deer live in dense jungles, especially along streams. They travel alone or in pairs, not in herds. Although shy, they are killed by dogs, native wild-cats, and occasionally by human hunters. They walk in a stilted way and run with their heads held low.

The Marsh Deer, or Swamp Deer *(Blastocerus dichotomus)*, is the largest deer of South America. It lives in swamps and jungles of the low country along rivers. Large bucks may weigh more than 250 pounds. The Marsh Deer's coat is a rich red in summer, but becomes more brownish in winter. It hides in the thickets of wet grasslands, where the animal's colour conceals it; even the long antlers blend with the twigs of shrubs and small trees. Less afraid of man than any of the other large

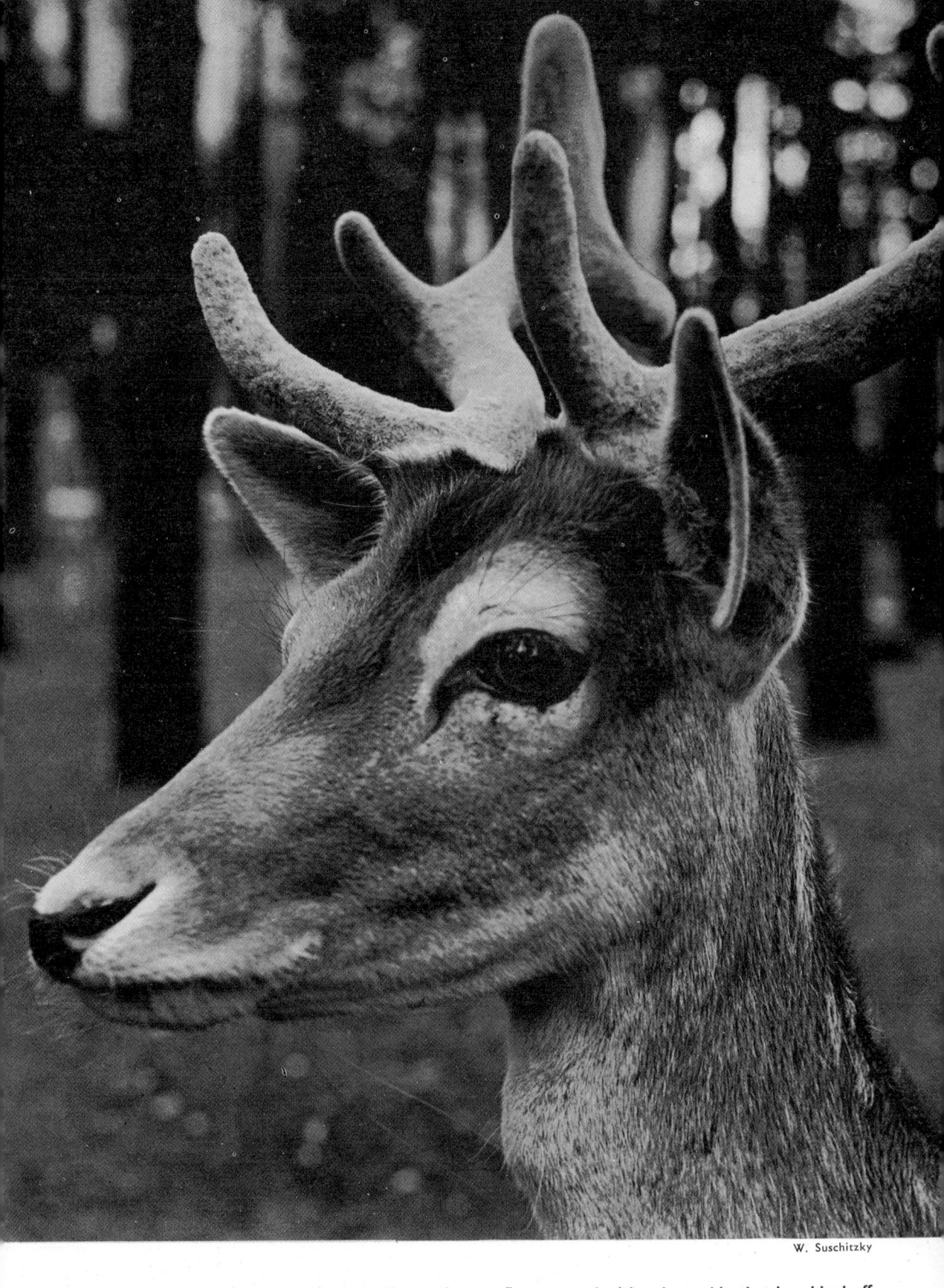

W. Suschitzky

Male Fallow Deer (stags) grow large, spreading antlers, at first covered with velvety skin that is rubbed off after the antlers are fully developed. The antlers on this young male are about half grown.

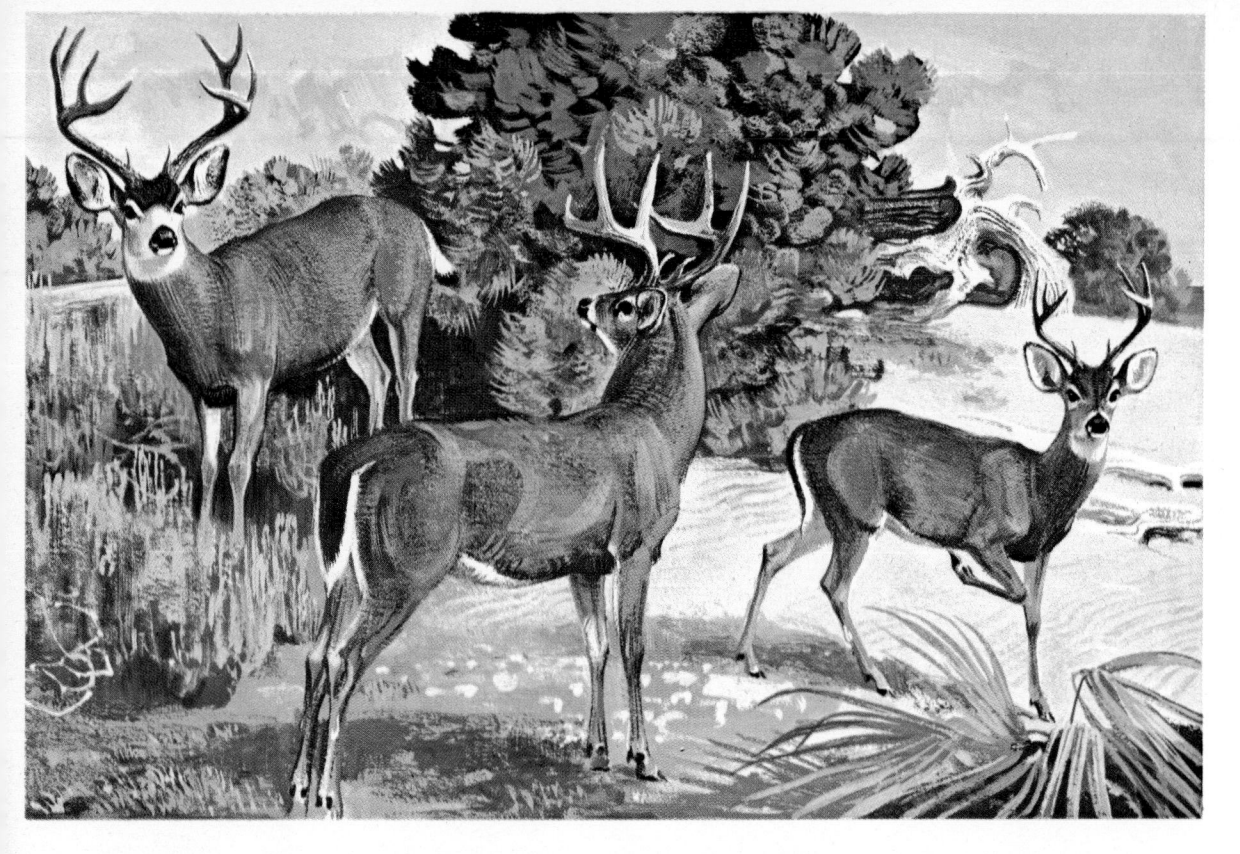

The Mule Deer (left) is a species of the western United States; the White-tailed Deer (centre) occurs mainly east of the River Mississippi. The small Key Deer (right), a sub-species of the White-tailed Deer, is found on the Florida Keys, a chain of islands at the tip of Florida.

South American mammals, this deer frequently grazes with cattle and horses, and sometimes wanders close to houses. This makes the Marsh Deer easy to kill, and it is hunted for its hide and meat.

The Fallow Deer *(Dama dama)*, recognised by the male's broad, flat antlers, generally has a brownish-red coat spotted with white dots. Some, however, are nearly white; others are dark brown and have no spots. The Fallow Deer lives in southern Europe and Asia Minor, and has been introduced to many areas, including New Zealand and Sweden, and it was brought to the British Isles by the Romans. This deer is an especially good jumper and can leap over high fences. It does well in a broad range of climates (from North Africa to as far north as Sweden) and also subsists on a great variety of foods, such as twigs of trees, nuts, grasses, or even hay. Often it grazes with domestic livestock.

The Mule Deer *(Odocoileus hemionus),*

a large deer of the western United States and Canada, has big ears like those of a mule — hence its name. Foraging herds of this deer are often quite large. They are easily distinguished from the White-tailed Deer by the black on their tail, their large whitish rump patch, and the peculiarly branched antlers. Large bucks may weigh as much as 200 pounds, rarely more; does are smaller. A variety of the Mule Deer that lives on the west coast of the United States is considerably smaller and has a large patch of black on its tail.

The White-tailed Deer *(Odocoileus virginianus),* found in the eastern and central United States, southern Canada, and southward into Central and South America, usually weighs less than 200 pounds, although occasional individuals weigh as much as 300 pounds. The underside of its tail is snowy white; the topside has a broad stripe of grey or brown down the centre and is bordered with white. When alerted,

the White-tailed Deer holds its tail erect so that the white shows like a flag. A White-tailed Deer's antlers bow forwards. This deer is found in the open woods and along the edges of forests. In some areas it was hunted so intensively that it was exterminated; but the White-tailed Deer has been

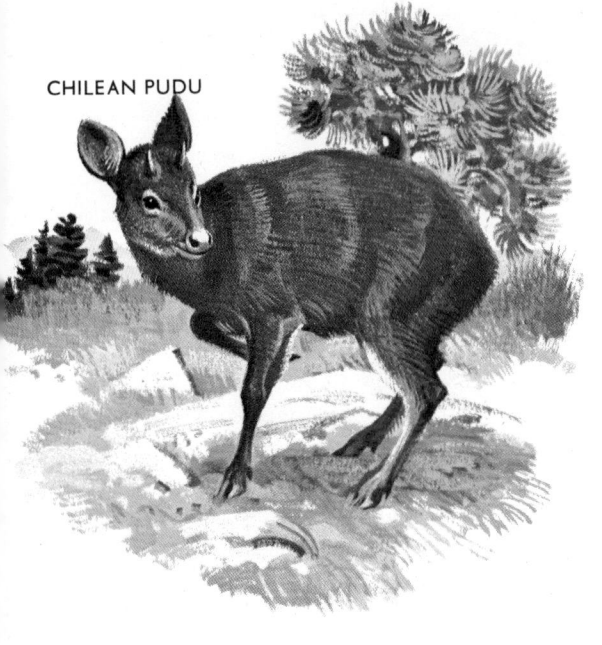

CHILEAN PUDU

reintroduced and, after a period of protection, it is now so abundant again that controlled hunting is permitted.

Key Deer (*Odocoileus virginianus clavium*) are dwarf White-tailed Deer, found only on the islands off the tip of Florida. They weigh as little as 50 pounds, and some are only two feet high at the shoulders. The Coues Deer (*Odocoileus virginianus couesi*), found in the south-western United States and central Mexico, is another dwarf White-tailed Deer.

The Musk Deer (*Moschus moschiferus*) is the most unusual member of the deer family. This small, antlerless deer lives in the high forests of central and eastern Asia. Males have long, dagger-like tusks which are used as protective weapons since these deer have no antlers. Males also have scent, or musk, glands (about the size of

an orange) just beneath the skin on the abdomen. The powerful musk taken from these scent glands is used as a base for many perfumes.

Mouse Deer (*Tragulidae* spp.), also called Chevrotains, are not deer, strictly speaking, through they are closely related to the deer family. "Mouse" refers to their small size, for they usually weigh less than 35 pounds and, in over-all size, some are not much larger than a rabbit. Males have long upper tusks. Mouse deer live in a variety of habitats from high mountains to lowlands in India, Malaya, Sumatra,

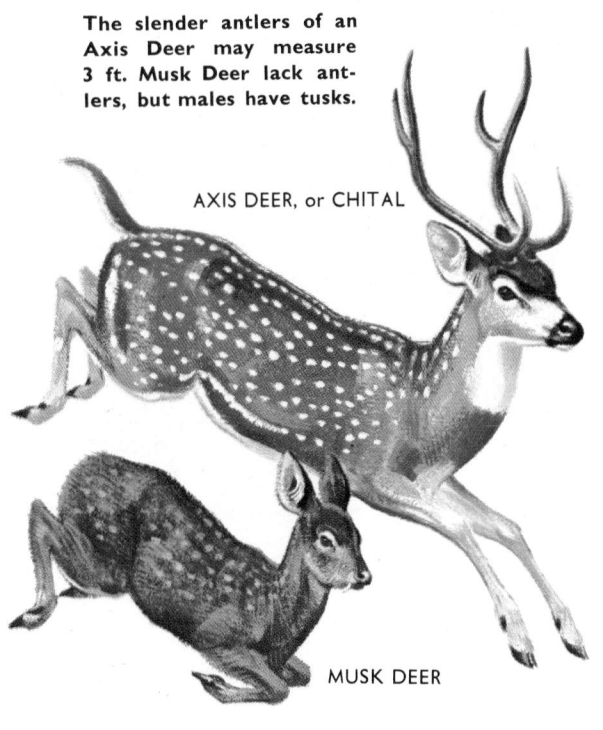

The slender antlers of an Axis Deer may measure 3 ft. Musk Deer lack antlers, but males have tusks.

AXIS DEER, or CHITAL

MUSK DEER

Java and Borneo. Water Chevrotains (*Hyemoschus aquaticus*) are found in the tropical forests of West and Central Africa. They are excellent swimmers, and jump into the water to escape when frightened. (See CARIBOU; MOOSE.)

DESMANS, relatives of the moles, spend as much time in the water as muskrats. They nest in burrows along stream banks and feed on frogs, snails, insects and fish. The

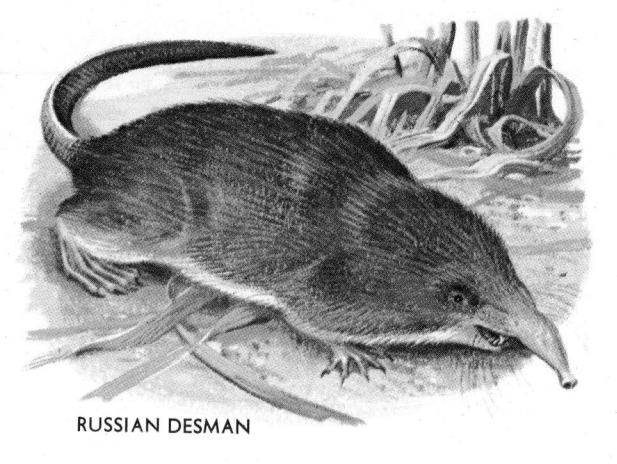

RUSSIAN DESMAN

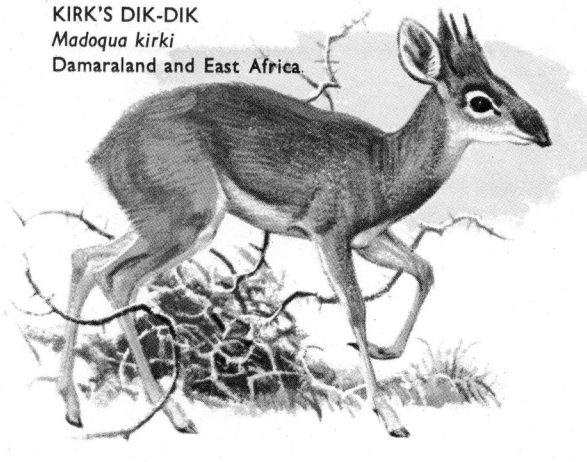

KIRK'S DIK-DIK
Madoqua kirki
Damaraland and East Africa

Desman has a tubular snout, like moles and shrews. Their partly-webbed feet help them in swimming. Russian desmans *(Desmana moschata)* have flat tails, used in swimming, and live by such rivers as the Volga and Don. A round tailed desman *(Galemys pyrenaica)* is found in the Pyrenees of France and Spain, and also in Portugal.

DIK-DIKS are a family of small antelopes that weigh only six or seven pounds and measure just over a foot at the shoulder. They often graze in pairs. Only males have horns. Most live in east Africa, with one species in Angola and south-west Africa. The Beira *(Dorcotragus megalotis)* is a large, reddish-grey dik-dik that lives in the mountain regions of Ethiopia and Somaliland. Salt's Dik-dik, or Beni Israel *(Madoqua saltiana)*, is found in Ethiopia and parts of the Sudan. Another member of the family is Kirk's Dik-dik, seen here.

DIPPERS are birds of fast streams, waterfalls and gorges in Europe, Asia, western North America and parts of South America. They do not migrate, and move from one area to another only if droughts, ice or floods drive them away from their home.

Walking on the rocky stream-bed, under the rushing water, dippers find insects, fish eggs and small molluscs. They swim and dip up and down in mountain torrents, and fly so low that they almost touch the water — so much their home that dippers often hide their nests behind waterfalls.

DIVERS are large goose-sized birds that spend almost all their time on or under water. They are perfectly adapted for this, being completely streamlined. The legs are used for propulsion and are set so far back that the bird can only stagger a few paces on land; it nests right at the water's edge, where it has no need to walk to the nest. The toes are flattened so that

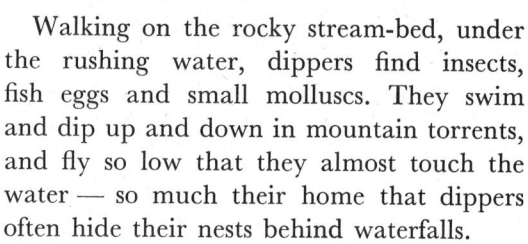

COMMON DIPPER — 7 in.
Cinclus Cinclus
Europe to Himalayas

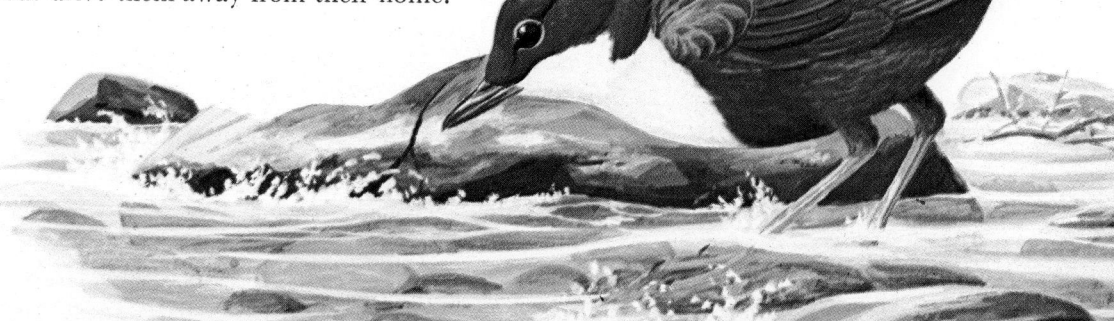

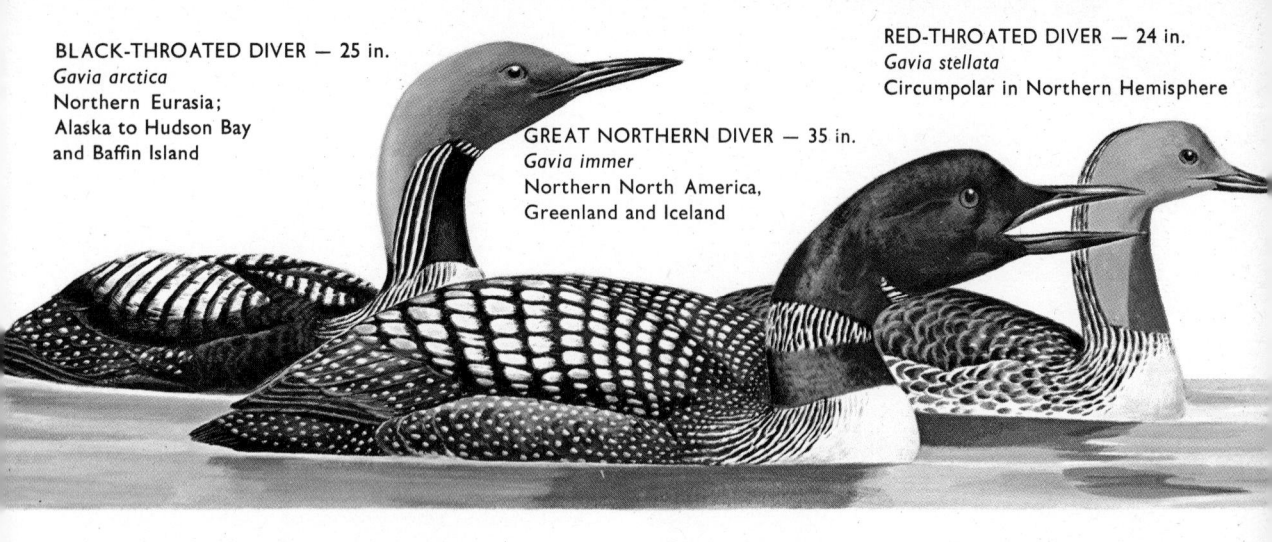

BLACK-THROATED DIVER — 25 in.
Gavia arctica
Northern Eurasia;
Alaska to Hudson Bay
and Baffin Island

GREAT NORTHERN DIVER — 35 in.
Gavia immer
Northern North America,
Greenland and Iceland

RED-THROATED DIVER — 24 in.
Gavia stellata
Circumpolar in Northern Hemisphere

they slide easily edge-on through the water, but can be turned broadside-on to give a hard thrust. The wings are small and curved, and fit tightly against the sides. A Diver cannot take off easily without pattering across the surface of the water; but, once in the air, its flight is very fast and direct, though without the power of rapid manoeuvring. Divers are fine swimmers, and can stay underwater for as long as five minutes, swimming almost a quarter of a mile in that time. They are known to descend to depths approaching 200 feet. Divers make no nest, but use a hollow by the water's edge — usually on a small island — without any concealment. They spend most of their non-breeding period at sea, often being seen just offshore.

There are only three species of Diver. The Red-throated Diver is the smallest. It nests on small lakes near the coast and often flies to the sea to feed. The Black-throated Diver is a bird of the larger lakes of northern Europe and Asia, breeding inland. The Great Northern Diver is another lake-nesting bird. The Siberian form has a white bill. All three have weird calls, but it is the last species which has the strange and hauntingly beautiful wails and maniacal laughter for which these birds are best known. All are birds of the colder parts of the north.

In America these birds are known as "loons", and this has been thought by some to refer to their crazy laughter, but in fact it is derived from the Scandinavian name and refers to their clumsy progress on land.

DODOS, extinct flightless birds, were giant pigeons weighing 50 pounds, at least seven times more than any pigeons capable of flight. They lived on Mauritius Island, in the Indian Ocean. The Portuguese discovered the island in 1507, and Dutch, French and English ships soon stopped there, too. Sailors killed the Dodos for food. Pigs and monkeys put ashore by the Portuguese multiplied rapidly; the monkeys ate the Dodo eggs, and the pigs killed off the parent birds.

Dodos nested on the ground. It is surmised that the female laid just one egg, but it is possible that she laid two. Nothing more is known of the Dodo's habits, for the bird survived only until 1681.

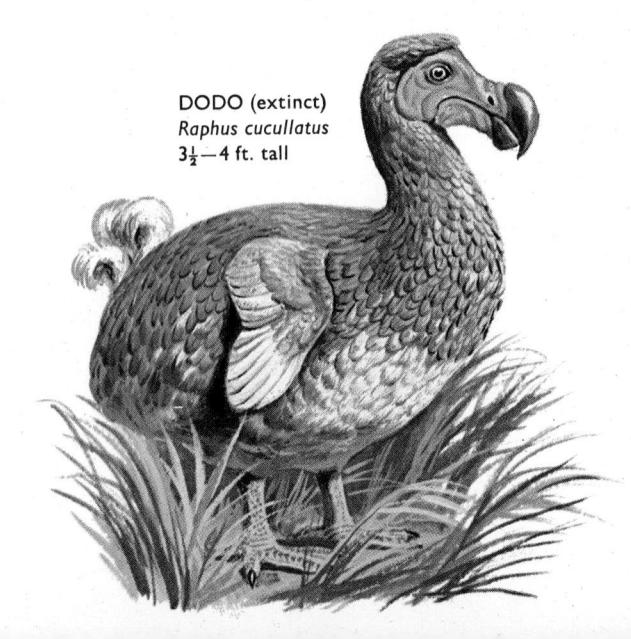

DODO (extinct)
Raphus cucullatus
3½—4 ft. tall

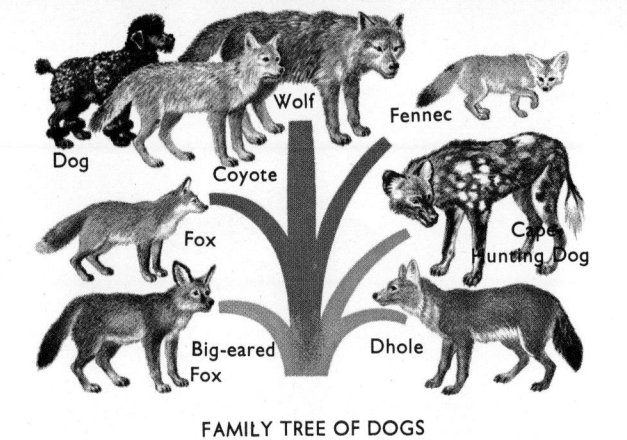

FAMILY TREE OF DOGS

DOGS, found in all parts of the world, are flesh-eating mammals with long tails, conspicuous ears and clawed feet. Dog is a name that often refers only to certain members of the dog family, particularly the domestic breeds. The variation in size and form among domestic dogs is greater than the variation between all the wild members of the family. Coyotes, wolves, foxes, and other dog-like animals, all quite similar in appearance, also belong to the dog family. (See FOXES; WOLVES.)

The Cape Hunting Dog *(Lycaon pictus)* of South Africa has especially long legs and a relatively thin body. It roams in packs, killing all kinds of game. As many as 30 dogs may run down a large antelope. When large game is not available, it eats smaller animals, such as rats and mice.

The Raccoon-like Dog *(Nyctereutes pro-cyonides),* found along the waterways in north-eastern Asia, has short, round ears, short legs, and a short, bushy tail ringed with colour. Its general appearance and habits are much like those of a raccoon. It feeds on water animals, such as frogs and fish, as well as on small rodents.

Dingos *(Canis familiaris dingo)* are the only carnivorous placental (that is, not marsupial) mammals native to Australia. These wild dogs resemble domestic dogs, but their pointed, erect ears cannot be laid down. They have very bushy tails, and instead of barking they yelp and howl mournfully. Some believe that the Dingo was once a domestic dog, and that it was carried to Australia by aborigines thousands of years ago. Dingos eat the native marsupial mammals, which they hunt largely at night and by methods similar to those of the Coyote. Dingos are hunted by sheep-farmers because damage the flocks.

The Coyote *(Canis latrans),* sometimes called the Prairie Wolf, is becoming rare on the western North American deserts where it was once abundant, but is extending its range eastward. The Prairie Wolf is smaller than a true wolf and has longer, more pointed ears. It feeds on rodents, rabbits, insects, fruit, game and poultry.

Jackals, found in most of Africa and southern Asia, eat rodents, birds, morsels left from the kills of lions, domestic livestock, and even fruits. They usually hunt in packs and at night. Most people consider jackals as pests. They are known for their cowardice, and when matched with a domestic dog

Sledges pulled by teams of husky dogs were once a principal means of transport in frozen Arctic lands.

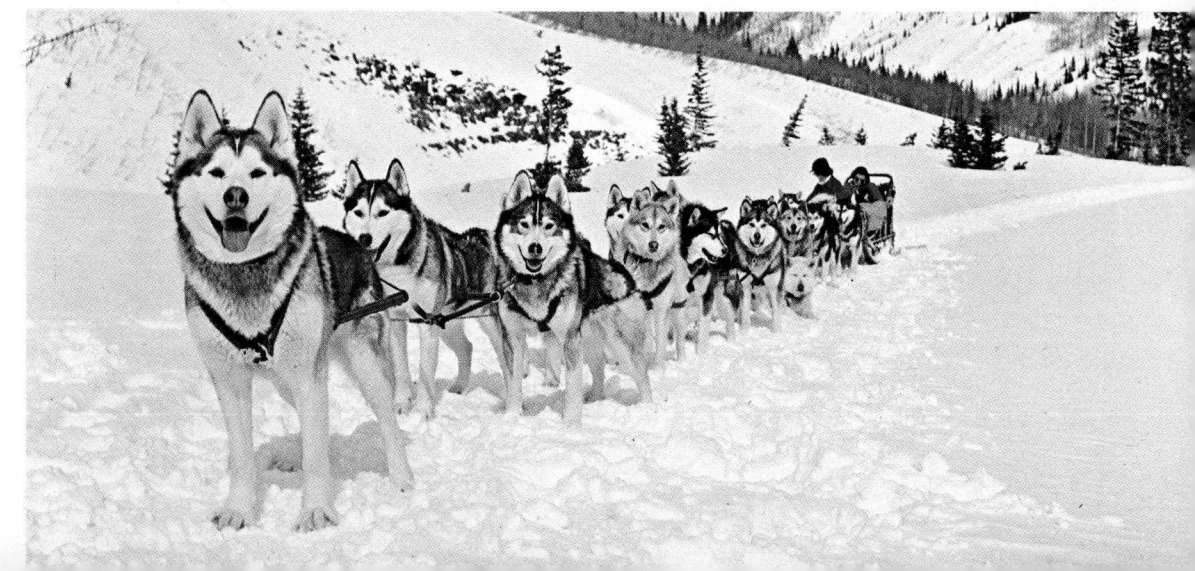

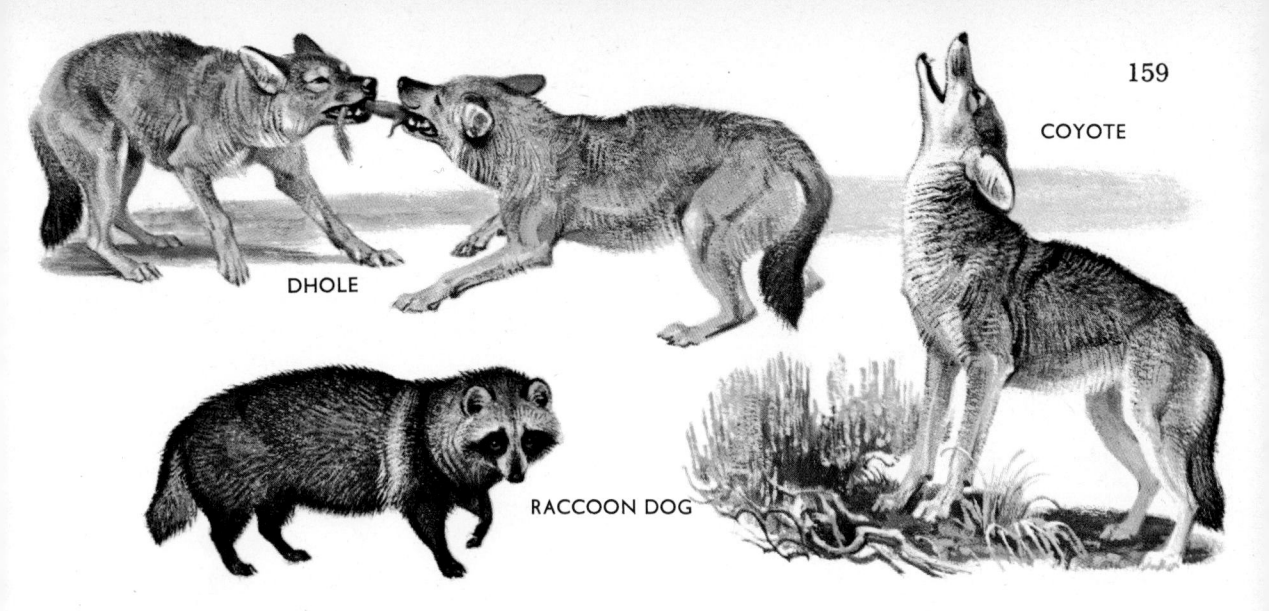

COYOTE

DHOLE

RACCOON DOG

of equal size, come off second best. Some calls are drawn-out wails; others are a series of long and short, sharp barks. The Black-backed Jackal *(Canis mesomelas)*, illustrated here, is found in most of southern Africa.

Dholes *(Cuon alpinus)*, sometimes called Red Dogs or Indian Wild Dogs, are found from central Asia to Korea and southward to Java. Similar in size to jackals, they are sociable animals and hunt during the day in packs of as many as 20. They are killers and will attack large antelopes, bears and, reputedly, even tigers. Dholes sometimes have nurseries where several females raise their young together.

All the dogs, wolves and coyotes of today are descended from a common ancestor shared with cats, weasels, bears and other carnivores. The earliest carnivores were a primitive group called Creodonts, known

only from fossils. They lived about 50 million years ago.

Wolves, jackals, dingos, coyotes and dogs are all so closely related that scientists have given them the same generic name, *Canis*. Differences between dogs, wolves, and coyotes are largely such external features as colour, hair length, size of body and limbs, and differences in skull and teeth.

Modern dogs are very similar to wolves and undoubtedly descended from wolf-like ancestors. Dogs and man became companions a very long time ago.

The recognised authority on the domestic dog in Britain is the Kennel Club. It has placed over 100 breeds in five categories, according to the use for which the breed is best suited and most often employed.

Sporting dogs are those used for hunting, and this category includes such breeds as

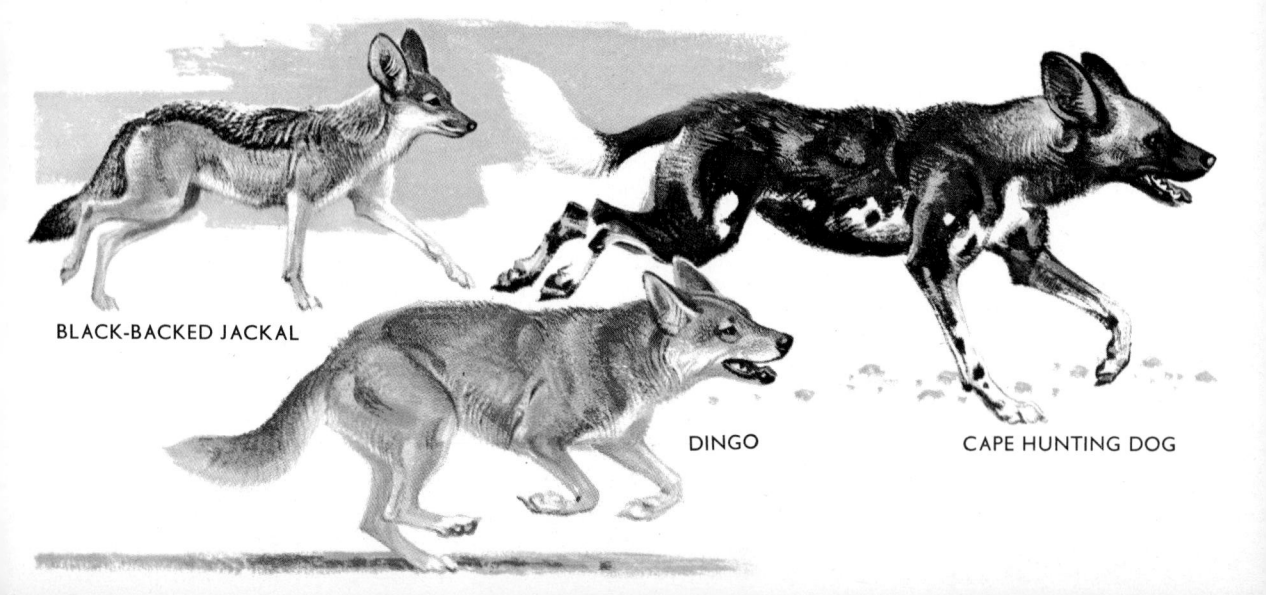

BLACK-BACKED JACKAL

DINGO

CAPE HUNTING DOG

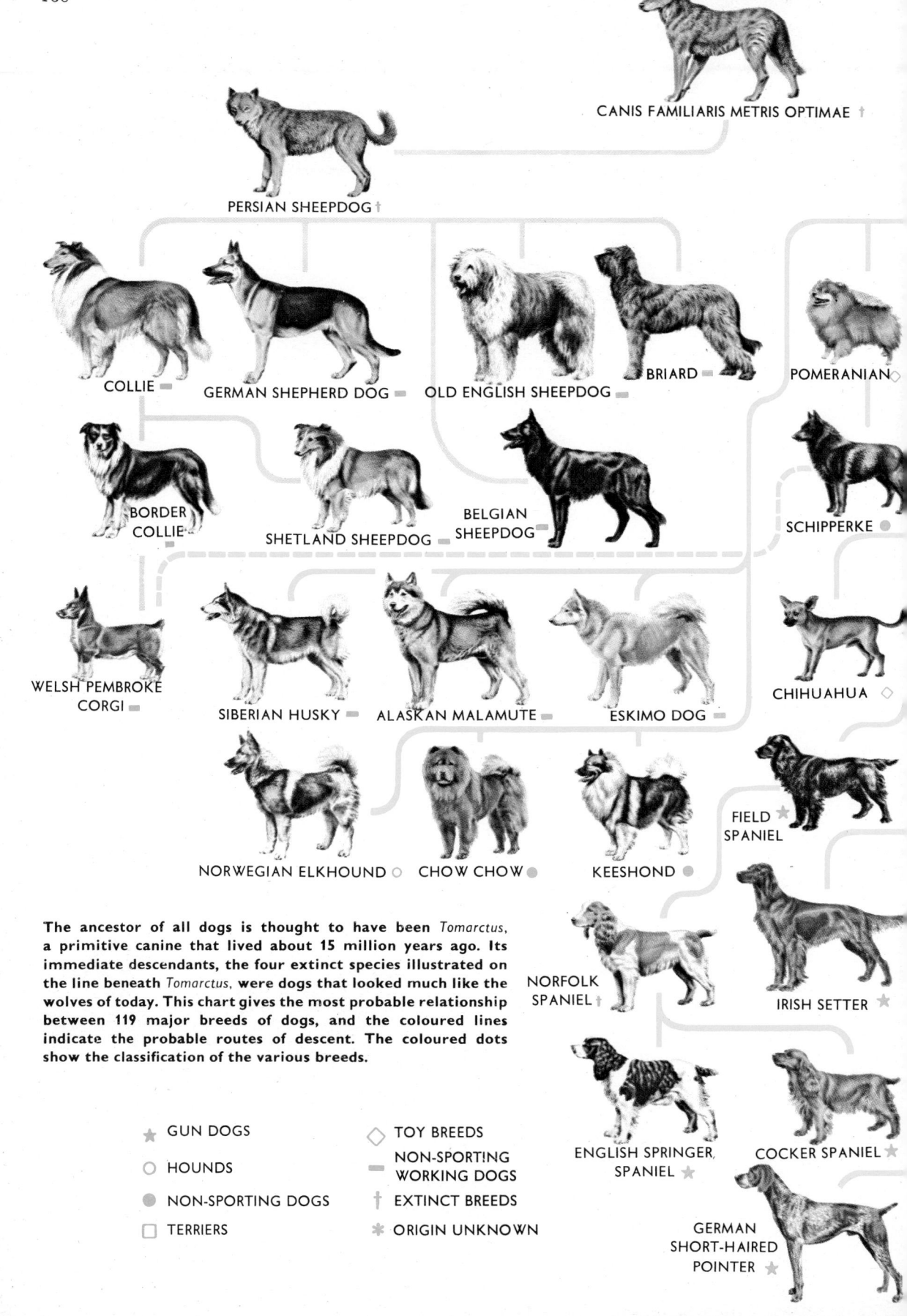

160

CANIS FAMILIARIS METRIS OPTIMAE †

PERSIAN SHEEPDOG †

COLLIE ▬   GERMAN SHEPHERD DOG ▬   OLD ENGLISH SHEEPDOG ▬   BRIARD ▬   POMERANIAN ◇

BORDER COLLIE ▬   SHETLAND SHEEPDOG ▬   BELGIAN SHEEPDOG   SCHIPPERKE ●

WELSH PEMBROKE CORGI ▬   SIBERIAN HUSKY ▬   ALASKAN MALAMUTE ▬   ESKIMO DOG ▬   CHIHUAHUA ◇

NORWEGIAN ELKHOUND ○   CHOW CHOW ●   KEESHOND ●   FIELD SPANIEL ★

The ancestor of all dogs is thought to have been *Tomarctus*, a primitive canine that lived about 15 million years ago. Its immediate descendants, the four extinct species illustrated on the line beneath *Tomarctus*, were dogs that looked much like the wolves of today. This chart gives the most probable relationship between 119 major breeds of dogs, and the coloured lines indicate the probable routes of descent. The coloured dots show the classification of the various breeds.

NORFOLK SPANIEL †   IRISH SETTER

ENGLISH SPRINGER SPANIEL ★   COCKER SPANIEL ★

★ GUN DOGS   ◇ TOY BREEDS
○ HOUNDS   ▬ NON-SPORTING WORKING DOGS
● NON-SPORTING DOGS † EXTINCT BREEDS
□ TERRIERS   ✳ ORIGIN UNKNOWN

GERMAN SHORT-HAIRED POINTER ★

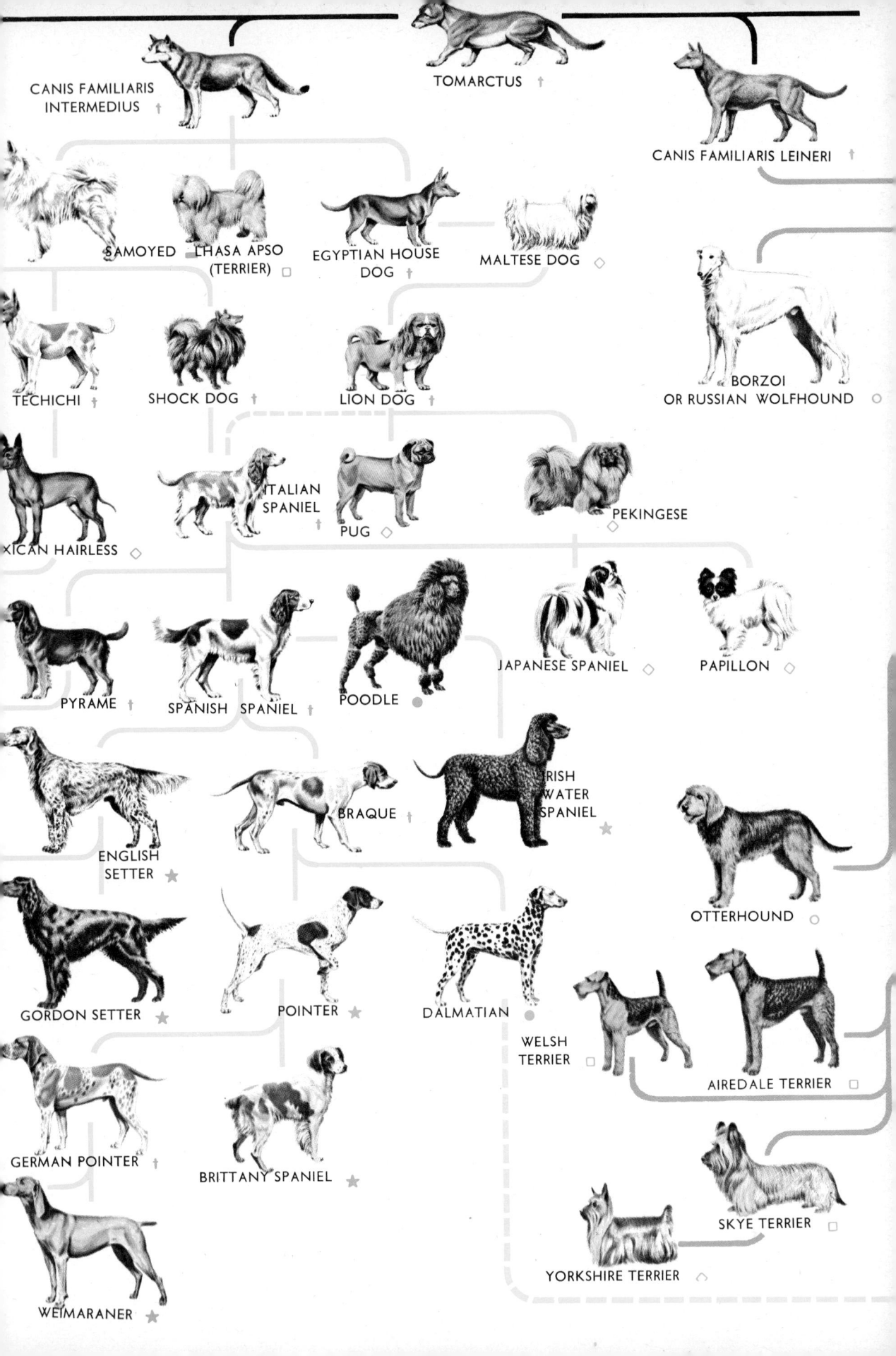

CANIS FAMILIARIS
INTERMEDIUS †

TOMARCTUS †

CANIS FAMILIARIS LEINERI †

SAMOYED

LHASA APSO
(TERRIER) □

EGYPTIAN HOUSE
DOG †

MALTESE DOG ◇

BORZOI
OR RUSSIAN WOLFHOUND ○

TECHICHI †

SHOCK DOG †

LION DOG †

MEXICAN HAIRLESS ◇

ITALIAN
SPANIEL †

PUG ◇

PEKINGESE

PYRAME †

SPANISH SPANIEL †

POODLE ●

JAPANESE SPANIEL ◇

PAPILLON ◇

ENGLISH
SETTER ★

BRAQUE †

IRISH
WATER
SPANIEL ★

OTTERHOUND ○

GORDON SETTER ★

POINTER ★

DALMATIAN ●

WELSH
TERRIER □

AIREDALE TERRIER □

GERMAN POINTER †

BRITTANY SPANIEL ★

YORKSHIRE TERRIER ◇

SKYE TERRIER □

WEIMARANER ★

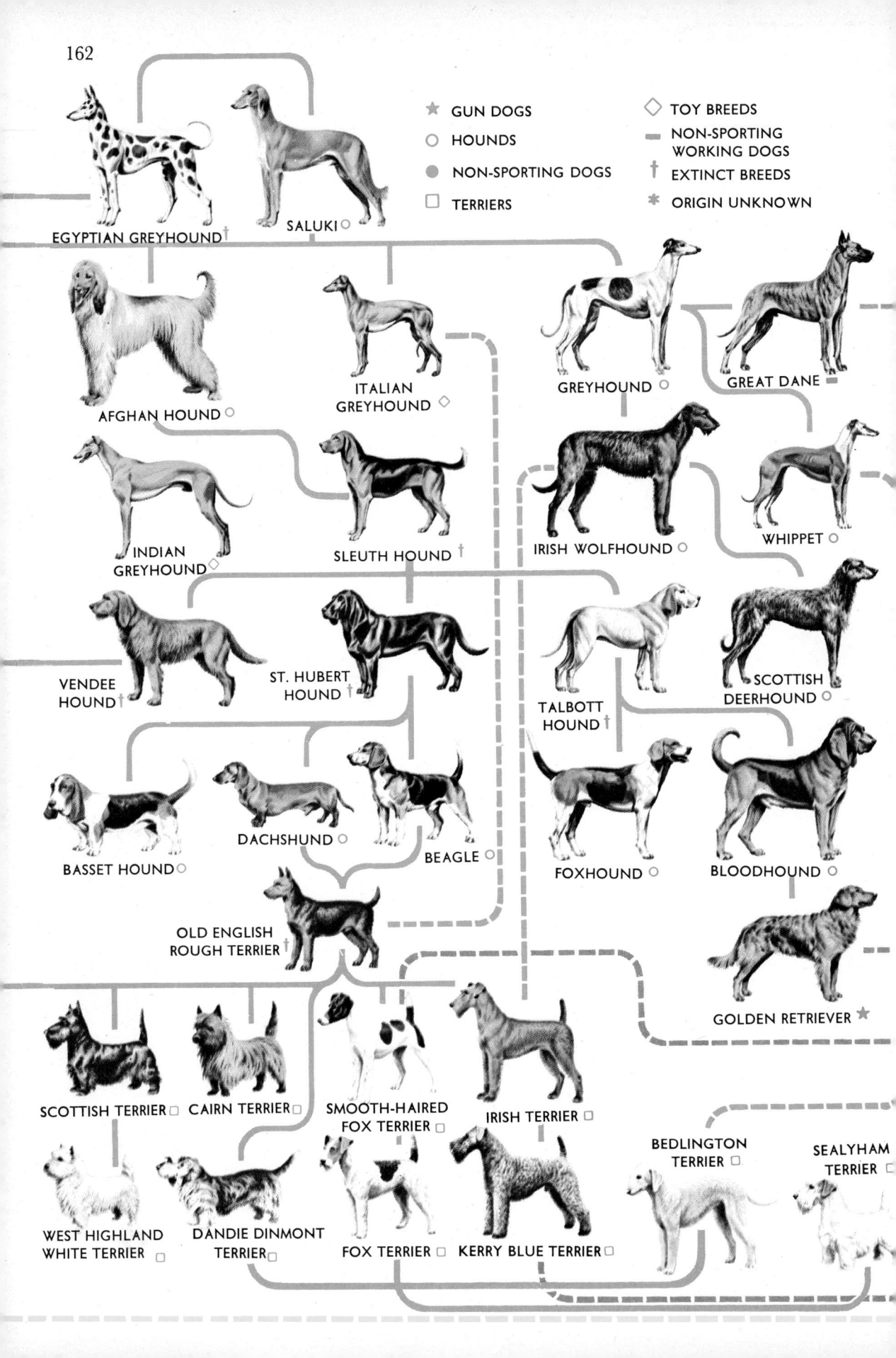

162

GUN DOGS
HOUNDS
NON-SPORTING DOGS
TERRIERS
TOY BREEDS
NON-SPORTING WORKING DOGS
EXTINCT BREEDS
ORIGIN UNKNOWN

EGYPTIAN GREYHOUND †

SALUKI ○

AFGHAN HOUND ○

ITALIAN GREYHOUND ◇

GREYHOUND ○

GREAT DANE ▬

INDIAN GREYHOUND ◇

SLEUTH HOUND †

IRISH WOLFHOUND ○

WHIPPET ○

VENDEE HOUND †

ST. HUBERT HOUND †

TALBOTT HOUND †

SCOTTISH DEERHOUND ○

BASSET HOUND ○

DACHSHUND ○

BEAGLE ○

FOXHOUND ○

BLOODHOUND ○

OLD ENGLISH ROUGH TERRIER †

GOLDEN RETRIEVER ★

SCOTTISH TERRIER □

CAIRN TERRIER □

SMOOTH-HAIRED FOX TERRIER □

IRISH TERRIER □

BEDLINGTON TERRIER □

SEALYHAM TERRIER □

WEST HIGHLAND WHITE TERRIER □

DANDIE DINMONT TERRIER □

FOX TERRIER □

KERRY BLUE TERRIER □

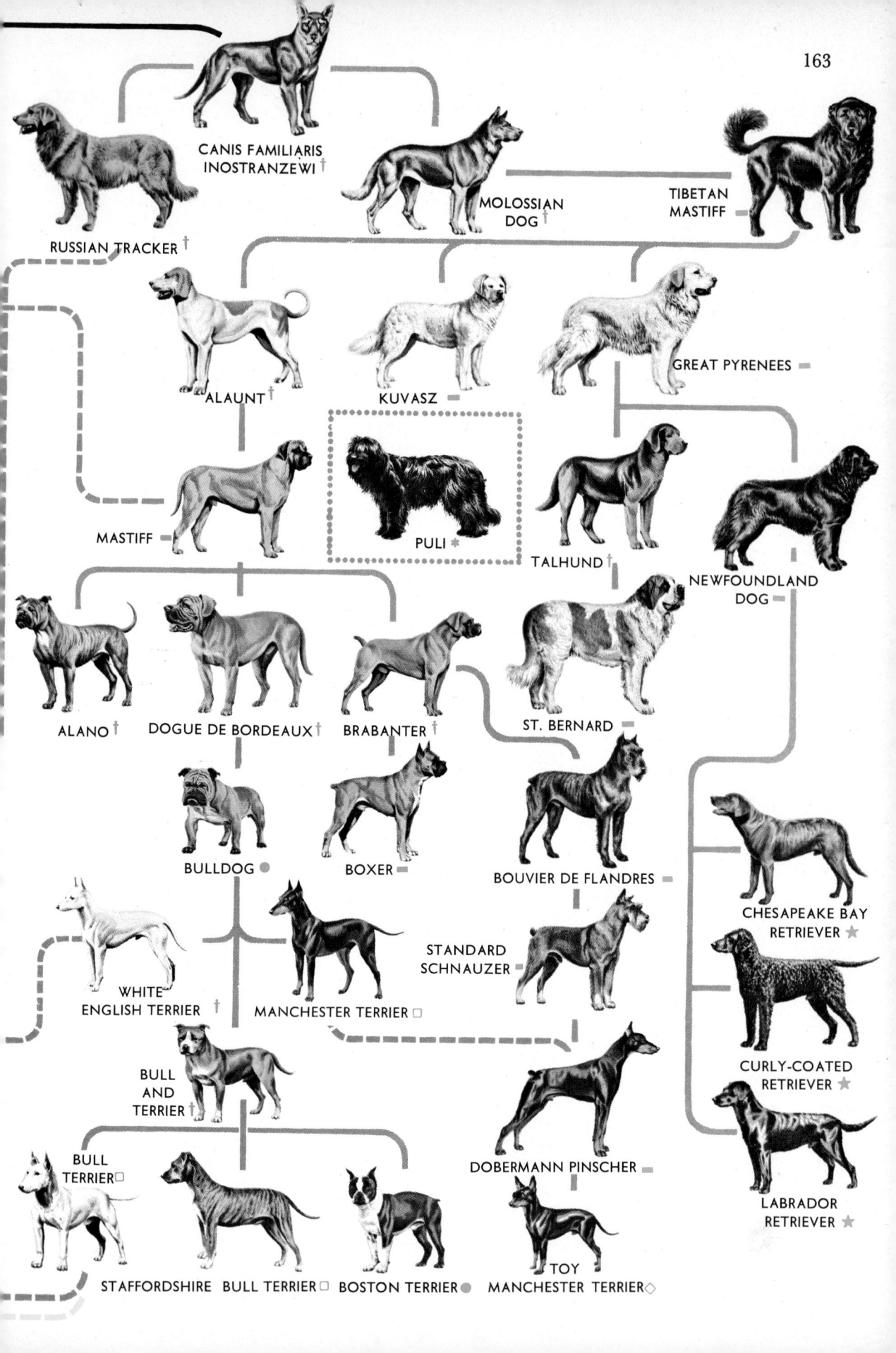

CANIS FAMILIARIS
INOSTRANZEWI †

MOLOSSIAN
DOG †

TIBETAN
MASTIFF

RUSSIAN TRACKER †

ALAUNT †

KUVASZ

GREAT PYRENEES

MASTIFF

PULI *

TALHUND †

NEWFOUNDLAND
DOG

ALANO †

DOGUE DE BORDEAUX †

BRABANTER †

ST. BERNARD

BULLDOG ●

BOXER

BOUVIER DE FLANDRES

CHESAPEAKE BAY
RETRIEVER ★

STANDARD
SCHNAUZER

WHITE
ENGLISH TERRIER †

MANCHESTER TERRIER □

CURLY-COATED
RETRIEVER ★

BULL
AND
TERRIER †

DOBERMANN PINSCHER

LABRADOR
RETRIEVER ★

BULL
TERRIER □

STAFFORDSHIRE BULL TERRIER □   BOSTON TERRIER ●

TOY
MANCHESTER TERRIER ◇

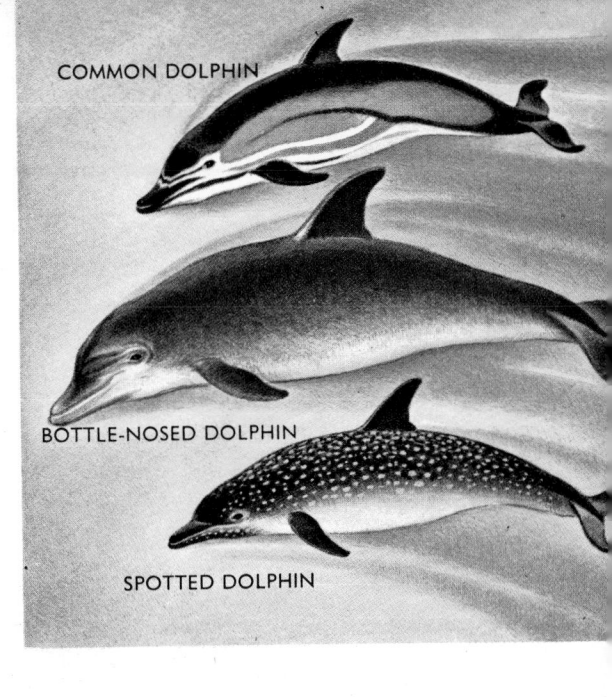

COMMON DOLPHIN

BOTTLE-NOSED DOLPHIN

SPOTTED DOLPHIN

Wolfhounds, Deerhounds, Greyhounds and Whippets — that is, breeds which hunt by sight or scent. Gundogs include Pointers, Setters, Retrievers and Spaniels. Terriers derived their name from the Latin word "terra", and this used to indicate dogs which go to earth after rabbits and badgers, but now also applies to the larger Terriers.

The Non-Sporting category consists of the Utility, Working and Toy groups. Bulldogs, Dalmatians and Poodles are three breeds in the Utility group. Boxers, Great Danes, Mastiffs and the Sheepdogs rank as Working dogs, together with Newfoundlands, Pyrenean Mountain Dogs, St. Bernards and the Welsh Corgis, of which there are two kinds — Cardigan and Pembroke. The Toy group includes Pekingese, Pomeranians, Yorkshire Terriers, Cavalier King Charles Spaniels and Chihuahuas.

DOLPHINS (*Delphinus delphis*) (also see PORPOISES) are small whales that have teeth. Generally the name dolphin is used for those with beaks. They suckle their

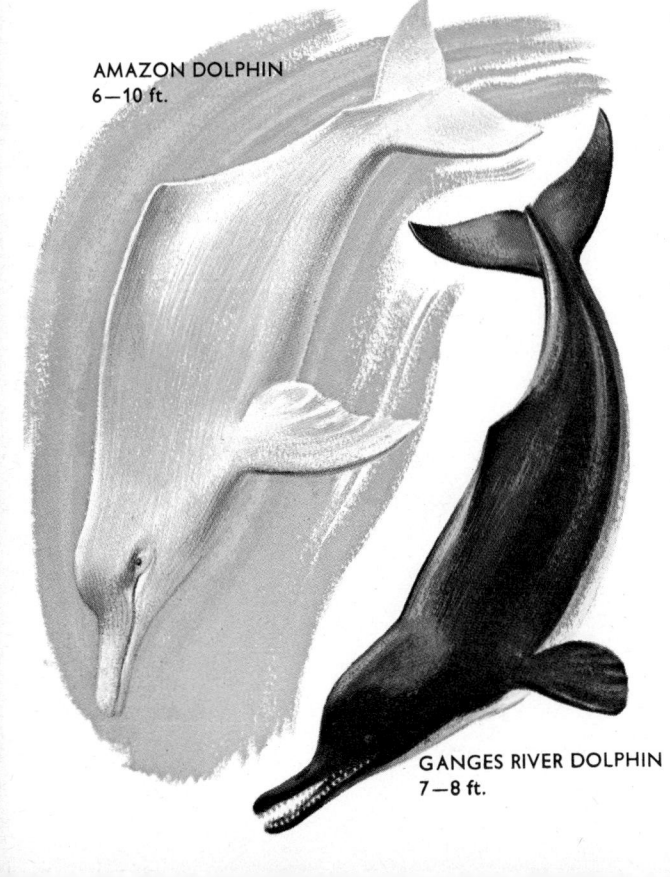

AMAZON DOLPHIN
6—10 ft.

GANGES RIVER DOLPHIN
7—8 ft.

young as all mammals do. Most kinds of dolphins feed on fishes, using their sharp teeth to catch and hold them.

Common Dolphins (*Delphinus delphis*), found in warm and temperate seas throughout the world, measure about eight feet long and have six-inch beaks. Sometimes they swim near shore, but they are also found far out at sea.

Bottle-nosed Dolphins (*Tursiops truncatus*), which reach a length of 12 feet, swim in schools (or groups) in both the Atlantic and Mediterranean. In the past, many were killed for their oil. Spotted Dolphins (*Stenella plagiodon*), so named because of the numerous white patches on their backs, occur all along the South American Atlantic Coast and in the Gulf of Mexico. Little is known about their habits.

Risso's Dolphin (*Grampus griseus*) measures up to 13 feet in length. It is an ocean animal and one of the largest of the dolphins. It has a bluntly-rounded head and no beak.

The Amazon Dolphin (*Inia geoffroyensis*) lives in the Amazon River and many of its tributaries. Sometimes the Amazon Dolphin is found in fresh water as much as 1,600 miles inland — actually in the foothills of the Andes Mountains. They change their colour from black or bluish-grey to whitish or flesh colour, depending on their surroundings, and feed on bottom-

dwelling fish of various sizes.

Ganges River Dolphins *(Platanista gangetica)* have nearly lost the use of their eyes, probably because the rivers they inhabit, such as the Ganges and the Indus, are so muddy that eyesight is of little or no use to them. They probe in the mud with their long snouts to find the crustaceans and fish which they eat. Like the dolphins of the Amazon, a Ganges River Dolphin never leaves its fresh-water home.

Chinese River Dolphins *(Lipotes vexillifer)* live only in Tung Ting Lake, some 600 miles up the Yangtze River, in China. Almost $7\frac{1}{2}$ feet long and weighing nearly 300 pounds, these pale-coloured dolphins are far removed from their original ocean habitat. They are nearly blind and use their long, sensitive beaks to probe the bottom of the lake for fishes.

DONKEYS *(Asinus asinus)* have been servants of man for many centuries. They were probably first domesticated in Egypt, where they submitted to the halter long before horses did. Donkeys are mentioned many times in the Bible, both as domestic

Lisl Steiner

and wild animals. A male donkey is a jack, and a female is a jenny. A mule is the offspring of a jack and a mare (female horse), and a hinny the offspring of a stallion (male horse) and a jenny. A burro is a small grey donkey. Burros were introduced to Mexico by the Spanish explorers.

Donkeys are small and easily cared for, yet they are strong and have great endurance. The average donkey is about eight hands (30 inches) high at the shoulder. In one region of France, however, they grow to be about twice as tall. Donkeys have a reputation for patience, and also for being slow, stubborn, and sometimes stupid. Often they are overworked and underfed. Wild donkeys, such as the Kiang and Onager of Asia, are swift animals and very difficult to capture. They are so independent that

Since time immemorial, the donkey has served man as a beast of burden.

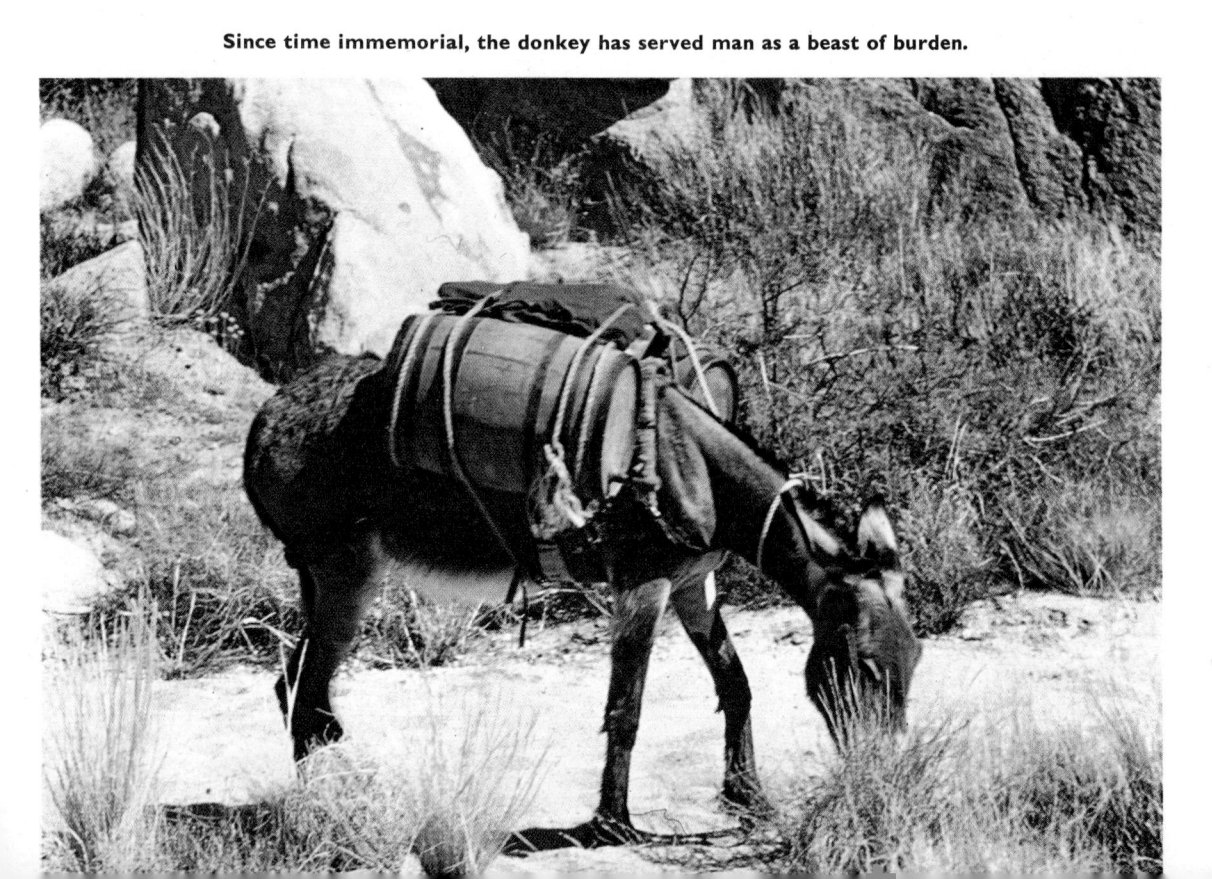

it is almost impossible to make them gentle.

Burros played an important role in the exploration and settlement of the western United States. They require less water than other pack animals and can live on weeds and thorny shoots. Burros were often companions chosen by prospectors in their search for silver and gold.

DORADOS, or **DOLPHINS** *(Coryphaena hippurus)*, are game fish that travel in schools. They are caught on trolled baits or lures, and often the first fish hooked is towed behind the boat so that others in the school will follow and be hooked, too.

Dorados strike hard and make long, fast runs, leaping and skittering across the surface. They are one of the fastest swimmers in the sea. They feed on flying-fishes, herrings, and other schooling fishes. The male Dorados have high, blunt foreheads. The females' foreheads slant. Both sexes are magnificently coloured, with long dorsal fins of a bluish-purple colour. Their bodies are green, dotted with blue; their sides yellow to orange; and their bellies white. Even more unusual is the way in which these colours ripple and change when the fish are caught. Romans placed live dorados in the centre of their banquet tables so that guests could watch these colour changes as the fish died. Dorados are good to eat.

Dorados, also popularly called dolphins, live in tropical seas throughout the world. They must not be confused with the small whale-like mammals named dolphins *(q. v.)*. Dorados are abundant off the coast of Florida, sometimes wandering a thousand miles north in summer; they are less common in the Pacific. Small dorados travel in schools, while large ones (up to six feet in length) are most commonly seen in pairs.

DORMICE have long, bushy tails and fluffy fur. They look like small squirrels and often climb trees to feed on nuts and fruits. Dormice put on extra fat before winter hibernation in nests in hollow trees,

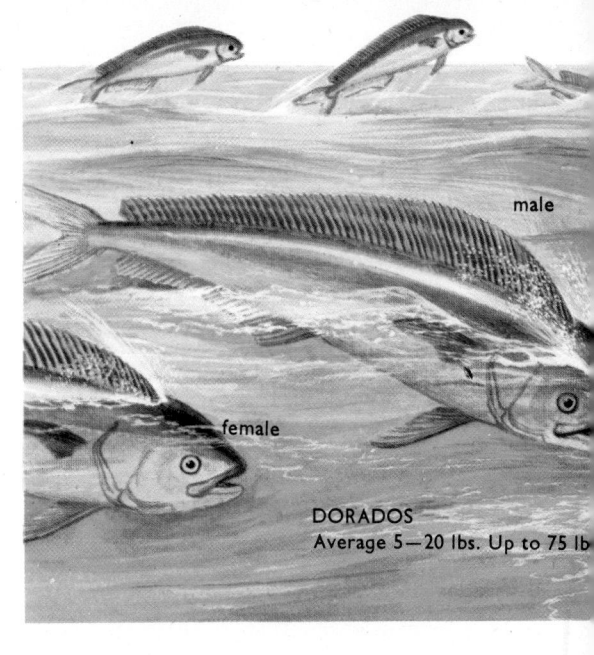

DORADOS
Average 5—20 lbs. Up to 75 lb

tree stumps, or piles of dead leaves.

Dormice measure less than 16 inches in length, and about half of this is taken up by their long tails. Several kinds live

EDIBLE DORMOUSE
Glis glis

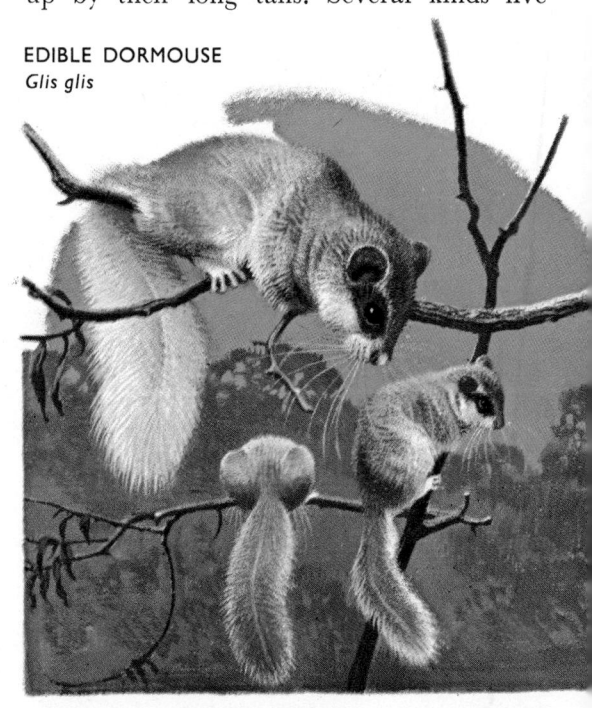

in Europe, Asia and Africa. Best known is the Edible Dormouse *(Glis glis)*, found from the Atlantic Ocean eastward across Europe into Russia. The European Dormouse was introduced from the continent into England in 1890, and has become established in several localities.

DRAGONFLIES and **DAMSELFLIES,** members of the order *Odonata,* are found wherever there are permanent bodies of fresh water. Nearly 5,000 species are known. Dragonflies, because of their larger size and rapid darting flight, are the more familiar. A dragonfly's hind wings are larger than its front wings; both pairs of wings are the same size in damselflies. Dragonflies have extremely large eyes, which tend to extend over the top of their heads; the eyes of damselflies, which have somewhat flattened heads, appear to be on projections. Dragonflies hold their wings extended outwards when at rest; damselflies hold their wings folded parallel to their body or tilted upwards.

Both dragonflies and damselflies lay their eggs in or near water. Some species swoop down and release their eggs as they dip the tip of their abdomen into the water. Another group flutters just above the surface of shallow areas, thrusting the tip of the abdomen into the sand to deposit their eggs. Damselflies of one group deposit their eggs in the tissues of plants above the water line, and the eggs do not hatch until the level of the water is high enough to submerge the stems the following season. Others lay their eggs in plant stems several inches below the surface of the water.

Nymphs of some species burrow into the sand on the bottom of ponds; others crawl over the vegetation. The long, hinged lower lip of nymphs can be extended rapidly, and prey is caught in the claw-like lobes at its tip. When not in use, the lip is folded beneath the head. Dragonfly larvae also have a series of gills in an enlargement at the end of their digestive tracts. They breathe by pumping water into and out of this chamber, and can also move rapidly by expelling the water from the chamber forcibly.

Most dragonfly and damselfly nymphs stay in the water for one year, but a few species remain in the nymph stage for two or three years. When ready to transform into an adult, a nymph crawls from the water, usually on to a plant or a stone,

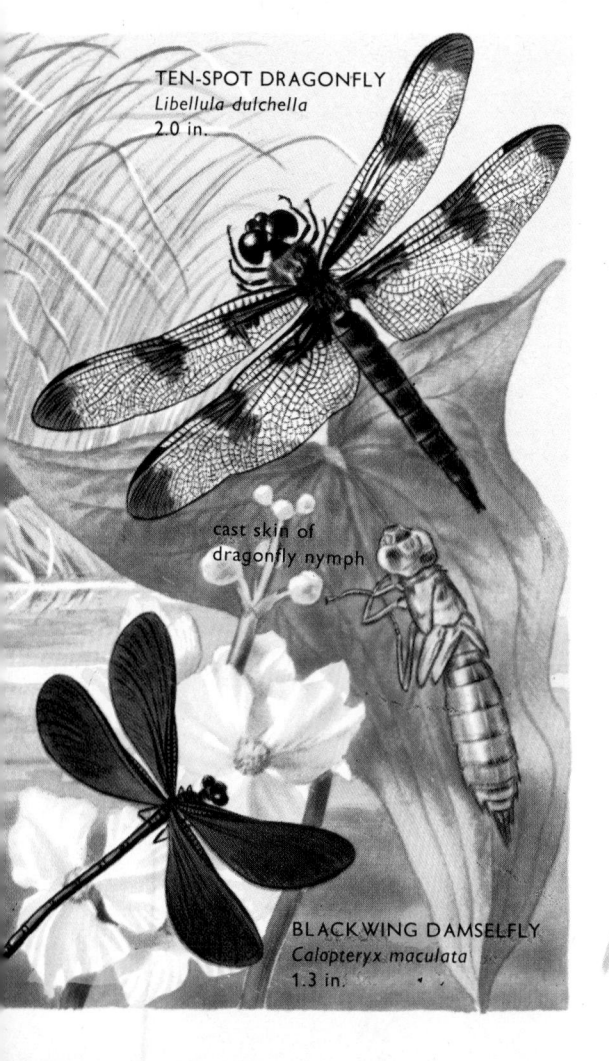

TEN-SPOT DRAGONFLY
Libellula dulchella
2.0 in.

cast skin of dragonfly nymph

BLACKWING DAMSELFLY
Calopteryx maculata
1.3 in.

BROWN ORTHETRUM
Orthetrum brunneum
wing-spread: 2.4 in.

cast skin of nymph

VIRGIN DAMSELFLY
Calopteryx virgo

adult

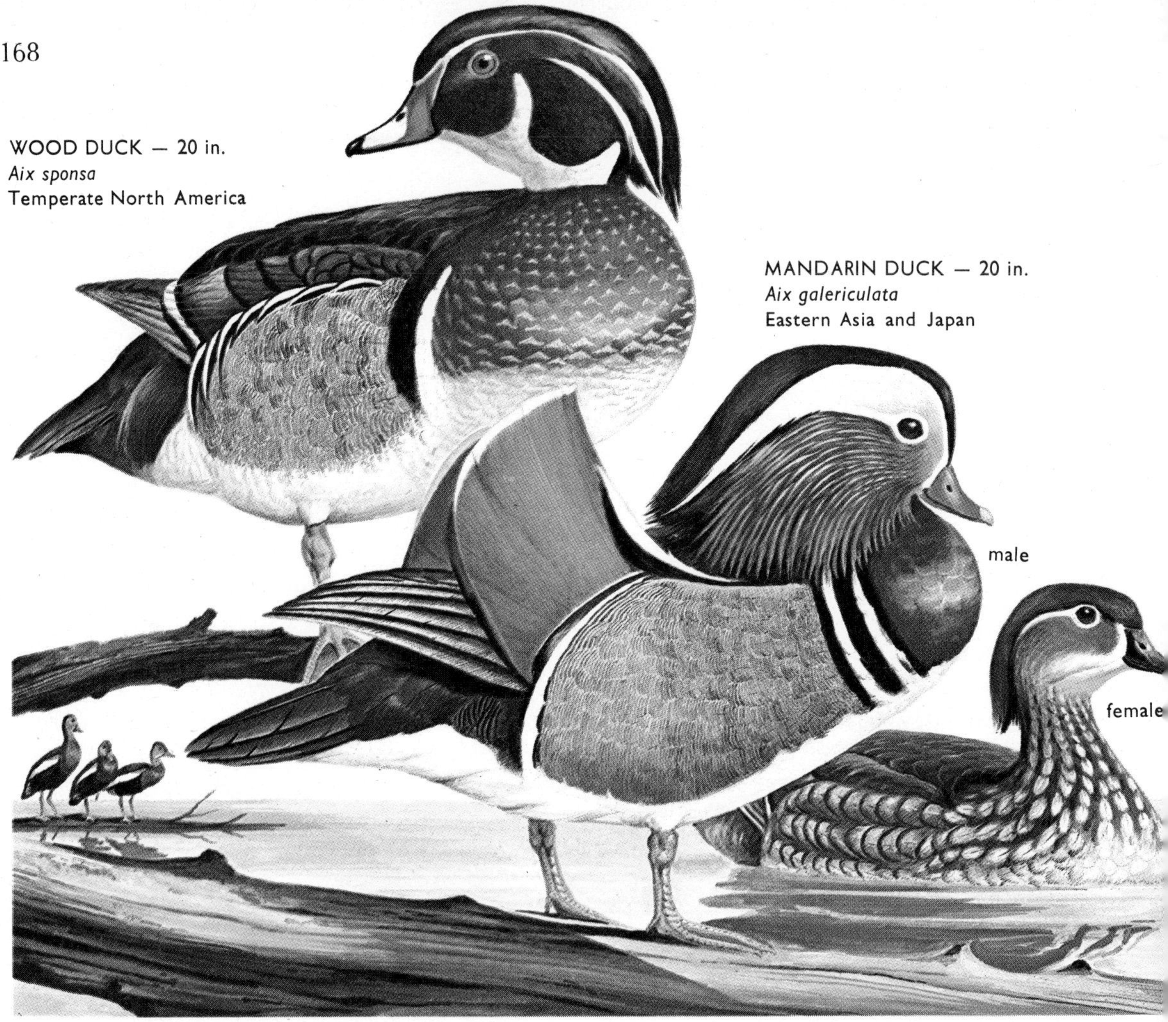

WOOD DUCK — 20 in.
Aix sponsa
Temperate North America

MANDARIN DUCK — 20 in.
Aix galericulata
Eastern Asia and Japan

male

female

and undergoes its final moult. Cast skins are often seen on plants at a pond's edge.

Both adults and nymphs are predaceous. Nymphs usually feed on small animals, but some of the large species attack small fish, and occasionally become pests in fish hatcheries. Adults find their prey — mostly mosquitoes, midges and other small insects — while flying over water. Although mostly sun-lovers, a few *Odonata* are night-flyers.

DUCKS are known to all peoples of the world. About 118 species of wild ducks have been described. All are water-birds with webbed feet, dense feathering, and mostly flat bills with strainer edges. They are clumsy on land, but move easily in the water. Differences in their colour patterns, called sexual dimorphism, make it easy to tell males from females in most species.

Great tracts of marshes and ocean, river

and lake-shore lands have been set aside as resting and breeding places for ducks. These sanctuaries benefit all wild-life.

In northern Europe and America, Eider Ducks are the basis of a profitable industry. Female Eiders pluck down feathers from

The female Eider Duck builds her nest of soft down feathers that she plucks from her breast.

Rutherford Platt

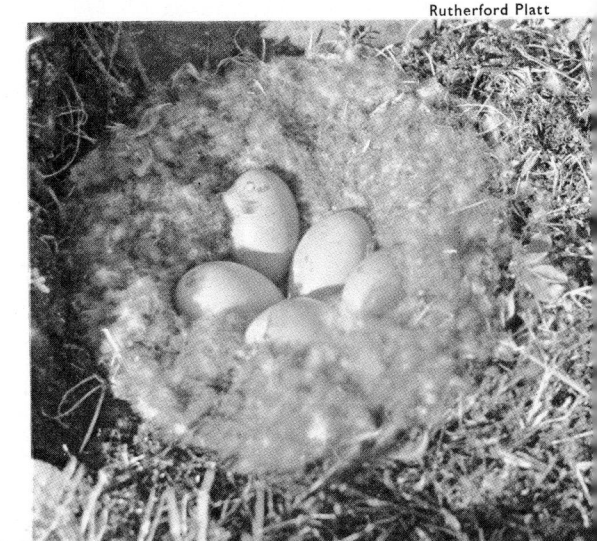

their breasts to line their nests. Men gather this down from nests, clean it, and use it to stuff pillows and quilts.

In Japan, where there are few domestic animals, wild ducks — mostly Mallards, Teals and Pintails — are an important source of protein food. For hundreds of years these birds have been netted every winter on the same small ponds. The number of ducks harvested each year is regulated by law, so that enough breeding birds fly north to ensure a steady supply of ducks for future years. Many of these ducks nest in Siberia.

Mallard Ducks were tamed in China centuries ago and are raised in thousands for eggs, meat and feathers.

In Colombia, South America, the fine Muscovy Duck, named after the Muysca Indians of Nicaragua, was tamed and bred in captivity by the Indians long before Columbus discovered America. Spaniards carried the Muscovy Duck to their other colonies and also to Europe.

In eastern Asia, Mandarin Ducks, mated for life, are symbols of wedded happiness. Like the Wood Ducks, they perch in trees and nest in holes or stumps.

The ducks have adapted themselves and spread into different habitats. The dabbling ducks are surface feeders that strain food through their bills — the Mallard is the best-known, but the Shoveller is the most striking, with its great flattened bill. The divers — such species as the Scaup and Goldeneye — find their food below the

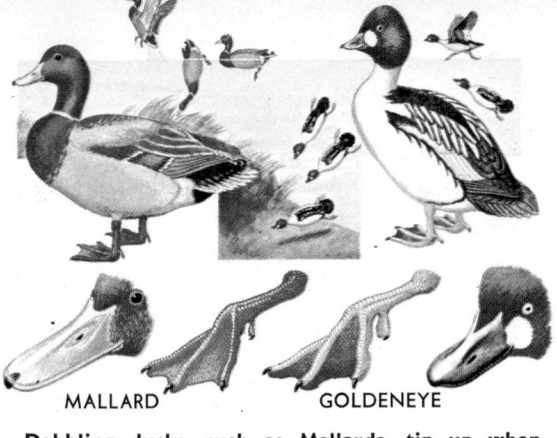

MALLARD   GOLDENEYE

Dabbling ducks, such as Mallards, tip up when feeding. Diving ducks, such as Goldeneyes, swim underwater completely.

surface. The Wigeon has a small goose-like bill, and uses it like a goose for grazing grasses and weeds. Eiders and Scoters are sea ducks, with heavy bills for dealing with the shellfish and crabs on which they feed.

The Smew is one of the small group of Sawbills. These have a slender bill with a sawtooth edge, and feed on fish which they pursue and seize under water with this bill.

The Common Shelduck is an estuarine species, finding its food on the mudflats, while the Ruddy Shelduck is often found in the semi-desert regions, well away from any water. The Tree Ducks, Wood Ducks and Mandarins are some of the duck species which occur in warmer forest regions and which frequently perch in trees. It is not only these species which nest in trees, for the Goldeneye uses holes high in trees in the pine forests of the North, often utilising the old holes of Black Woodpeckers.

Both the Harlequin and the Torrent Duck

River ducks eat vegetation. Salt-water ducks, such as mergansers, are fish-eaters; eiders prefer shellfish.

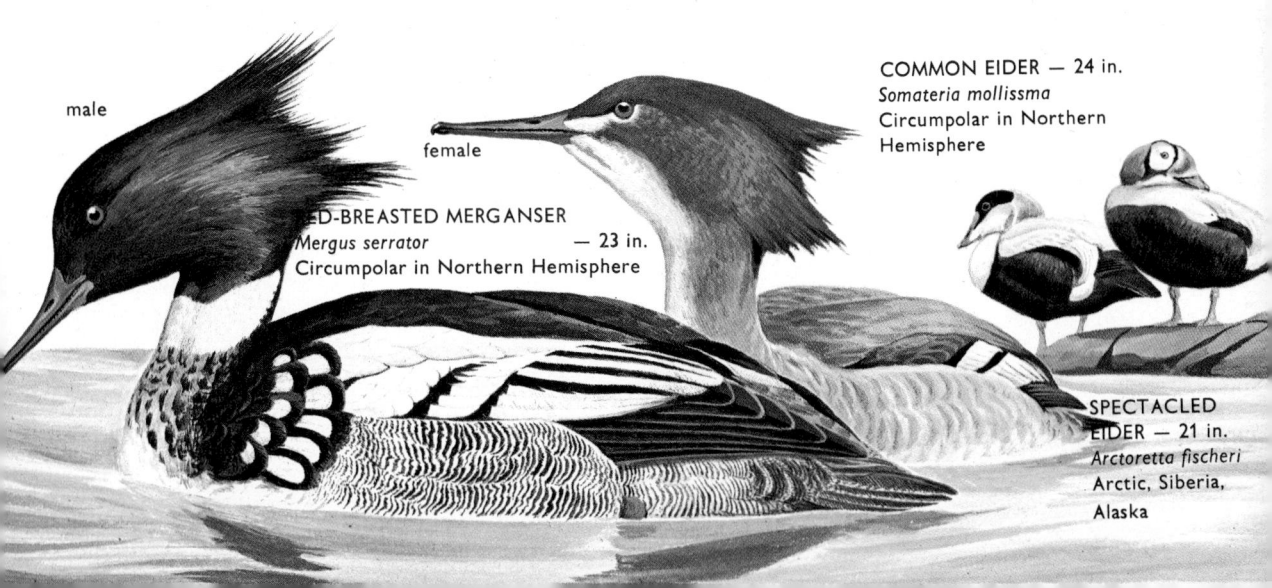

male

female

COMMON EIDER — 24 in.
Somateria mollissma
Circumpolar in Northern Hemisphere

ED-BREASTED MERGANSER
Mergus serrator   — 23 in.
Circumpolar in Northern Hemisphere

SPECTACLED EIDER — 21 in.
Arctoretta fischeri
Arctic, Siberia, Alaska

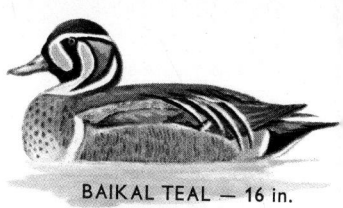

TORRENT DUCK — 17 in.
Merganetta armata
Andes of Colombia and Chile

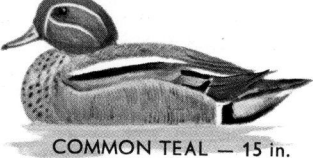

MALLARD — 28 in.
Anas platyrhynchos
Northern Hemisphere

BAIKAL TEAL — 16 in.
Anas formosa
Eastern Siberia

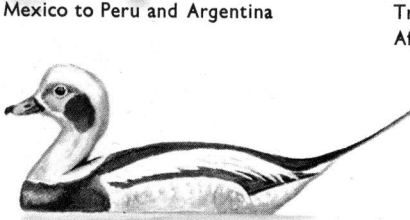

FLIGHTLESS STEAMER DUCK — 29 in.
Tachyeres pteneres
Tierra del Fuego

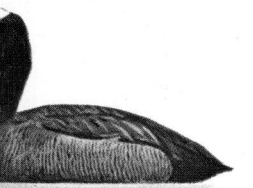

CINNAMON TEAL — 17 in.
Anas cyanoptera
North and South America,
Falkland Islands

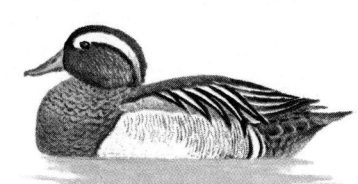

COMMON TEAL — 15 in.
Anas erecca
North America

MUSCOVY DUCK — 28–30 in.
Cairina moschata
Mexico to Peru and Argentina

WHITE-FACED TREE DUCK — 17–18 in.
Dendrocygna viduata
Tropical South America,
Africa, and Madagascar

GARGANEY TEAL — 15 in.
Anas querquedula
Eurasia

LONG-TAILED DUCK — 21 in.
Clangula hyemalis
Circumpolar in arctic
and sub-arctic regions

RUDDY DUCK — 17 in.
Oxyura jamaicensis
North America, West Indies,
northern South America

HARLEQUIN — 17 in.
Histrionicus histrionicus
North-eastern Siberia,
north-western North America,
Labrador, Greenland, Iceland.

Most species of ducks have a speculum, or colourful wing-patch, which helps in their identification.

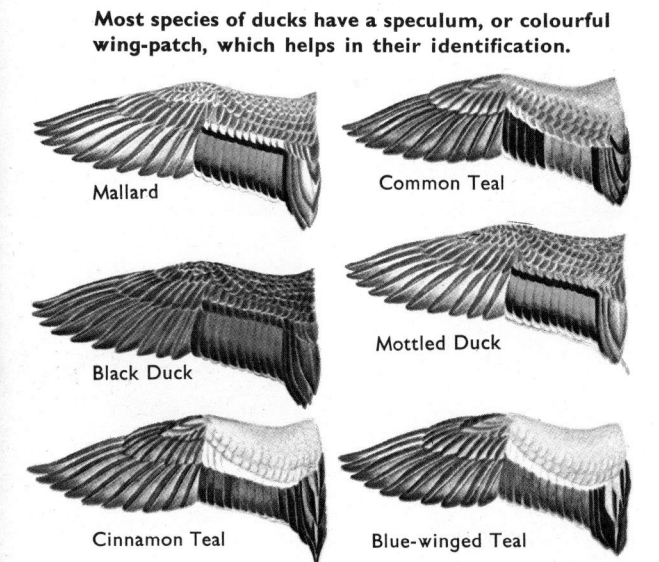

Mallard

Common Teal

Black Duck

Mottled Duck

Cinnamon Teal

Blue-winged Teal

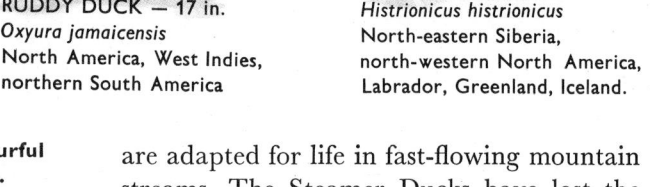

are adapted for life in fast-flowing mountain streams. The Steamer Ducks have lost the power of flight, and run along the surface, using feet and wings like paddles.

DOMESTIC DUCKS. All domestic ducks are closely related to one of two wild species — the Mallard of the Northern Hemisphere or the Muscovy of tropical America. The 118 species of wild ducks and the 12 domestic varieties are all swimming waterfowl, with short legs, fairly long necks, and webbed feet. Oil from a gland on the upper surface of the tail is spread by preening to all body feathers, to waterproof them.

Selective breeding for many centuries has

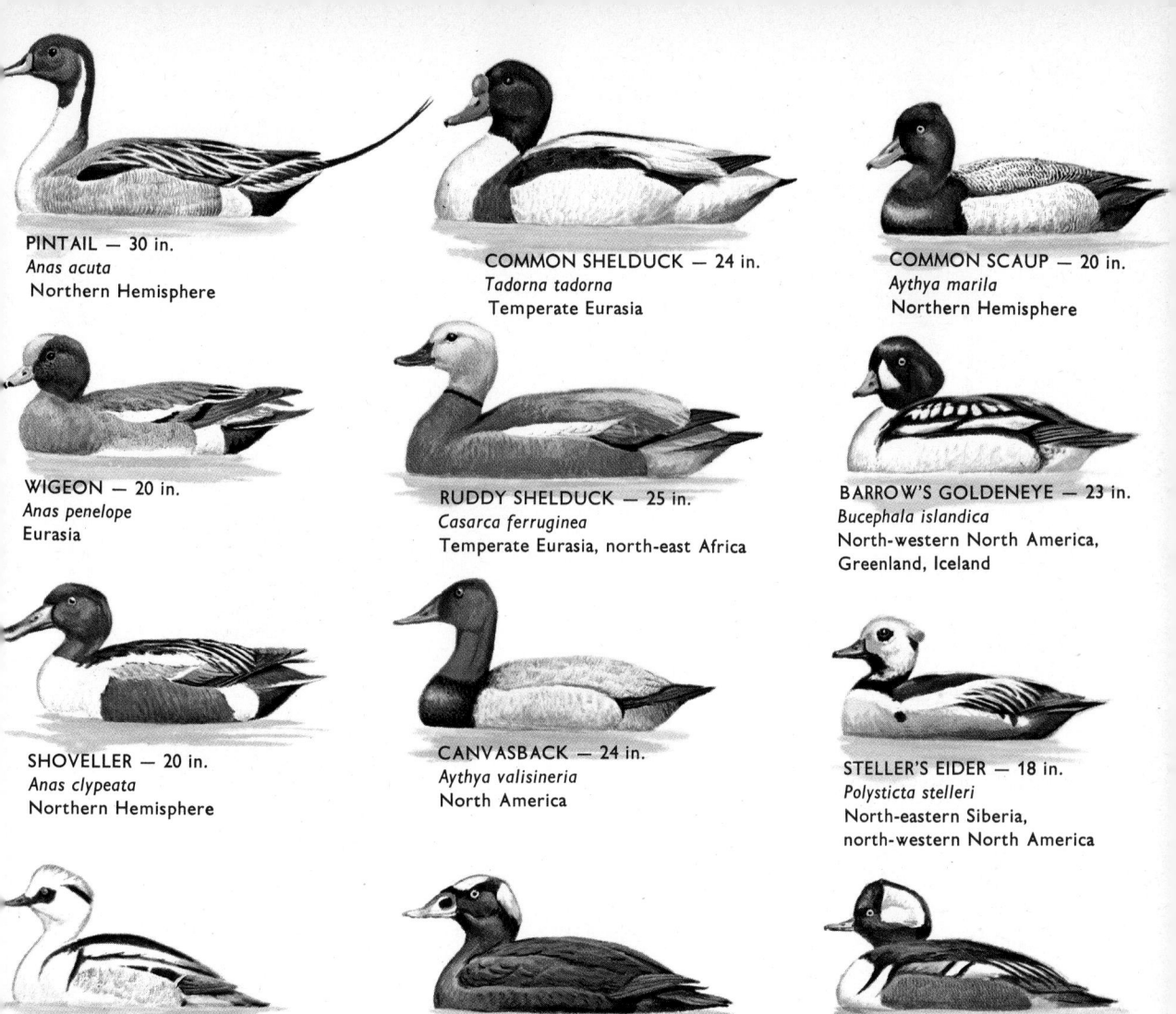

PINTAIL — 30 in.
Anas acuta
Northern Hemisphere

COMMON SHELDUCK — 24 in.
Tadorna tadorna
Temperate Eurasia

COMMON SCAUP — 20 in.
Aythya marila
Northern Hemisphere

WIGEON — 20 in.
Anas penelope
Eurasia

RUDDY SHELDUCK — 25 in.
Casarca ferruginea
Temperate Eurasia, north-east Africa

BARROW'S GOLDENEYE — 23 in.
Bucephala islandica
North-western North America,
Greenland, Iceland

SHOVELLER — 20 in.
Anas clypeata
Northern Hemisphere

CANVASBACK — 24 in.
Aythya valisineria
North America

STELLER'S EIDER — 18 in.
Polysticta stelleri
North-eastern Siberia,
north-western North America

SMEW — 16 in.
Mergellus albellus
Northern Eurasia

SURF SCOTER — 19 in.
Melanitta perspicillata
Northern North America

HOODED MERGANSER — 18 in.
Lophodytes cucullatus
Temperate North America

developed two main types of domestic ducks: those that are used for meat, and those that have a high egg production.

The White Pekin is a meat variety developed in China. Males often weigh as much as 9 pounds; females, about 8 pounds. The weight at marketing is usually $5\frac{1}{2}$ pounds, when the birds are most tender. The birds are about 12 weeks old at these stages and are called "green ducks", a description that refers to their age and tenderness and has nothing to do with their plumage. Duck meat is mostly dark, in contrast to the preferred light meat of chickens and turkeys.

Other meat varieties are the Aylesbury, Rouen, Cayuga, Buff, Swedish and Muscovy.

The most prolific egg-laying variety is the Indian Runner, though the Khaki Campbell has also gained some favour. Duck eggs are good to eat, but are suspect since they may be infected with bacteria if laid in wet places.

Some of the showy varieties of ducks kept for ornamental purposes are the Call Duck, East Indian Duck and Crested Duck.

Feathers of domestic ducks are valued as stuffing for pillows. They are not as desirable as eiderdown, the breast down of the female Eider Duck. Eiders nest in Greenland and Iceland, and two successive down linings are taken from each nest, a third lining being removed after the young have left the nest.

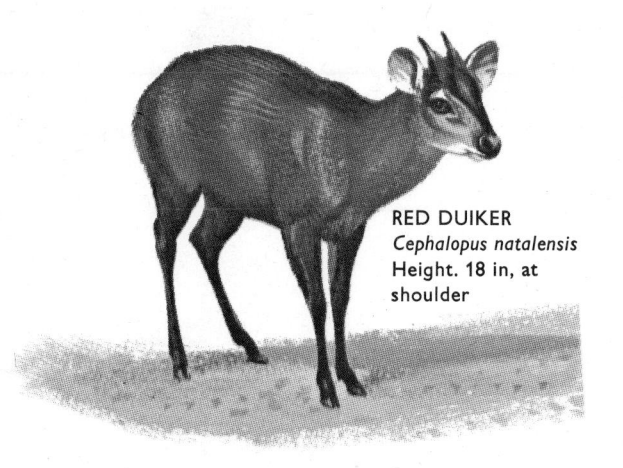

RED DUIKER
Cephalopus natalensis
Height. 18 in, at
shoulder

DUIKERS *(Cephalophus* spp.*)* are small African antelopes. Some are as large as goats; others no larger than hares. All live in forested or brush lands and are seldom seen. They have the peculiar habit of escaping pursuers by diving headfirst into the underbrush — Duiker, in fact, means "diver". Their horns are short, straight and spike-like, sloping backwards slightly. In some species, both sexes are horned. One kind has a reddish coat broken with prominent black stripes. Perhaps because of the habitat in which they live, they are not found in large herds, as are the better-known grassland-dwelling antelopes.

SCARABS
Canthon laevis
0.8 in.
At work.

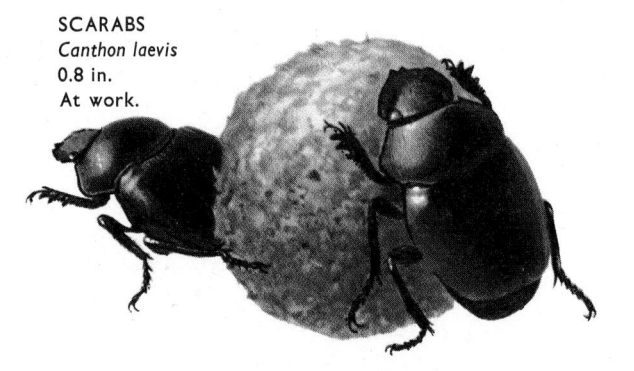

DUNG BEETLES and **SCARABS** *(Scarabaeidae)* are stout beetles that vary from a quarter of an inch to an inch and a half in length. Most species are dull, but some are bright metallic in appearance. Dung beetles live in cow pastures, or similar places where large animals graze. They dig holes and tunnels near or under piles of dung, and may bury several times their weight in dung during an evening. The beetles eat the buried dung and also lay their eggs on it. The dung then becomes food for their larvae.

Scarabs form balls from fresh dung and often roll them considerable distances. The ball may be as large as a golf ball, although the beetles are scarcely an inch long. After the ball is formed, the beetle pushes it with its hind legs, bracing itself against the ground with its front legs. Often two beetles

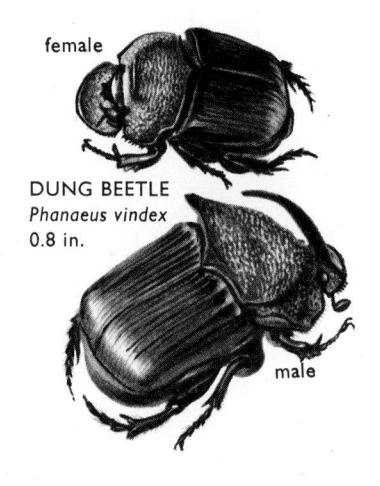

female

DUNG BEETLE
Phanaeus vindex
0.8 in.

male

work on the same ball. Eventually the ball is rolled into a depression, and then the beetles bury themselves with it. They feed on the dung until it is entirely consumed. Later in the season the dung balls are used for egg-laying. Each is buried separately with a single egg in it. The larva feeds inside the ball, eating all but a thin outer shell. Then it pupates, and an adult emerges later.

The Sacred Scarab, perhaps the most famous member of this family, was held in high esteem by the Ancient Egyptians. They believed that the ball of dung represented the earth, and that the beetle rolled the ball from sunrise to sunset, the beetle itself representing the sun; the sharp projections on its head were supposedly the rays of the sun, and the 30 segments of its six tarsi were the days of the month. Egyptians placed the Sacred Scarab in their tombs. They also carved precious stones in the shape of scarabs, and painted the beetle's picture on

many objects. Japanese Beetles and June Beetles are members of the same family (see JUNE BEETLES).

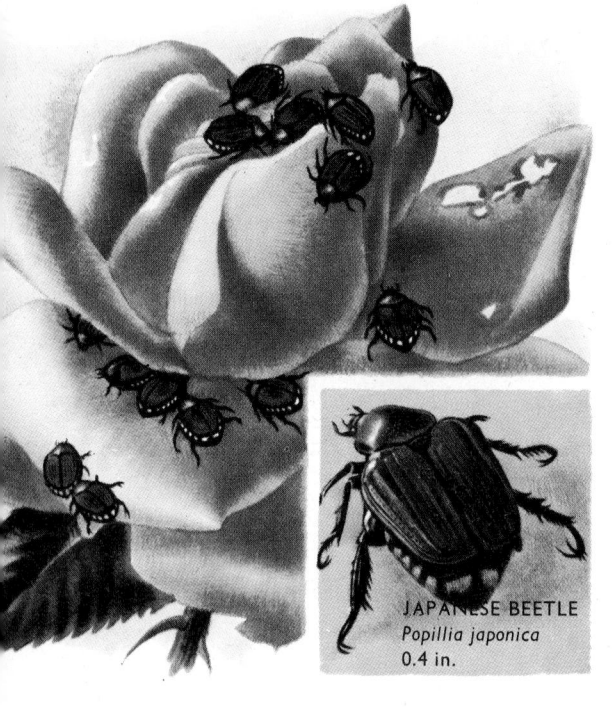

Members of the same family *(Scarabaeidae)* as June Beetles and Dung Beetles, Japanese Beetles are metallic, greenish-bronze, with a series of white spots at the tip and along the sides of the abdomen.

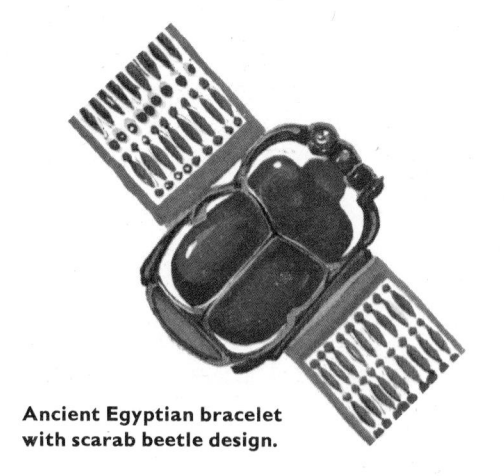

Ancient Egyptian bracelet with scarab beetle design.

DUSKY SALAMANDERS *(Desmognathus spp.)* occur in the eastern United States. There are about 11 species. Like their close relatives, the lungless salamanders (see LUNGLESS SALAMANDERS), they lack lungs and breathe through their mouth lining and moist skin. Most kinds measure two to six inches in length and live in or close to shallow mountain streams. The eggs are laid on land in protected depressions near water, or under stones in shallow water, and the larvae develop in the water. Adults transform completely; they have eyelids and no remnants of either gills or gill slits. Their

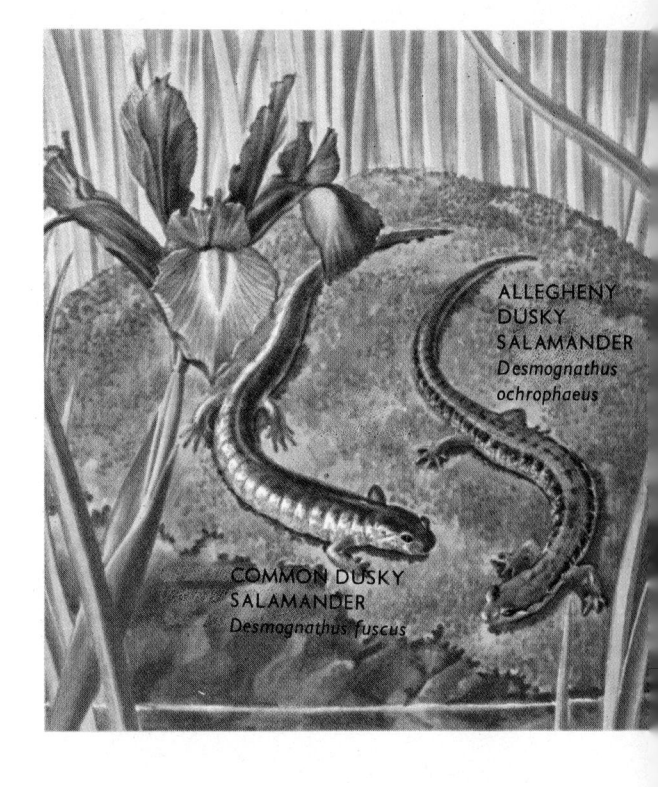

lower jaw is so nearly fixed in position that they open their mouths largely by an upward movement of their skull. Dusky Salamanders are most easily recognised by the peculiar narrowing of their heads from the level of their eyes forward, and by a slanted, often dim, white streak between each eye and the corner of the mouth. Their sides are deeply grooved, and their dark, mottled colours blend them well with the rocks and moss along the streams or pools where they live. Like other salamanders, they are often mistaken for lizards; but they have a moist rather than a scaly skin, and only four toes instead of five on each front foot.

E

EAGLES, members of the hawk family, inhabit all the regions of the world except New Zealand and Antarctica. They nest on rocky mountain crags, on cliffs above the sea, and in the tops of trees, using the same nest year after year. A pair of breeding eagles occupies a territory of several square miles. In Ohio, U.S.A., one pair of Bald Eagles used the same nest for 35 years. Annually, a little new material was added to this six-foot-wide tree-nest, and each year it served as a nursery for two eaglets.

Eagles catch and kill their prey with their powerful talons, swooping down from great heights with unbelievable speed. Sometimes they eat carrion, but usually take live prey. Eagles cannot lift anything heavier than themselves. With talons and beak they pull apart prey which is too heavy to carry, and often clean the catch — pluck chickens, skin rabbits, and take the heads off fish — before offering it to the nestlings. Stories of eagles stealing babies are not true. In Asia, eagles have been trained to hunt game.

Eagles, often called "King of the Birds", have been symbols of royalty and leadership in Europe since ancient times. The eagle was the emblem of the Roman legions. The

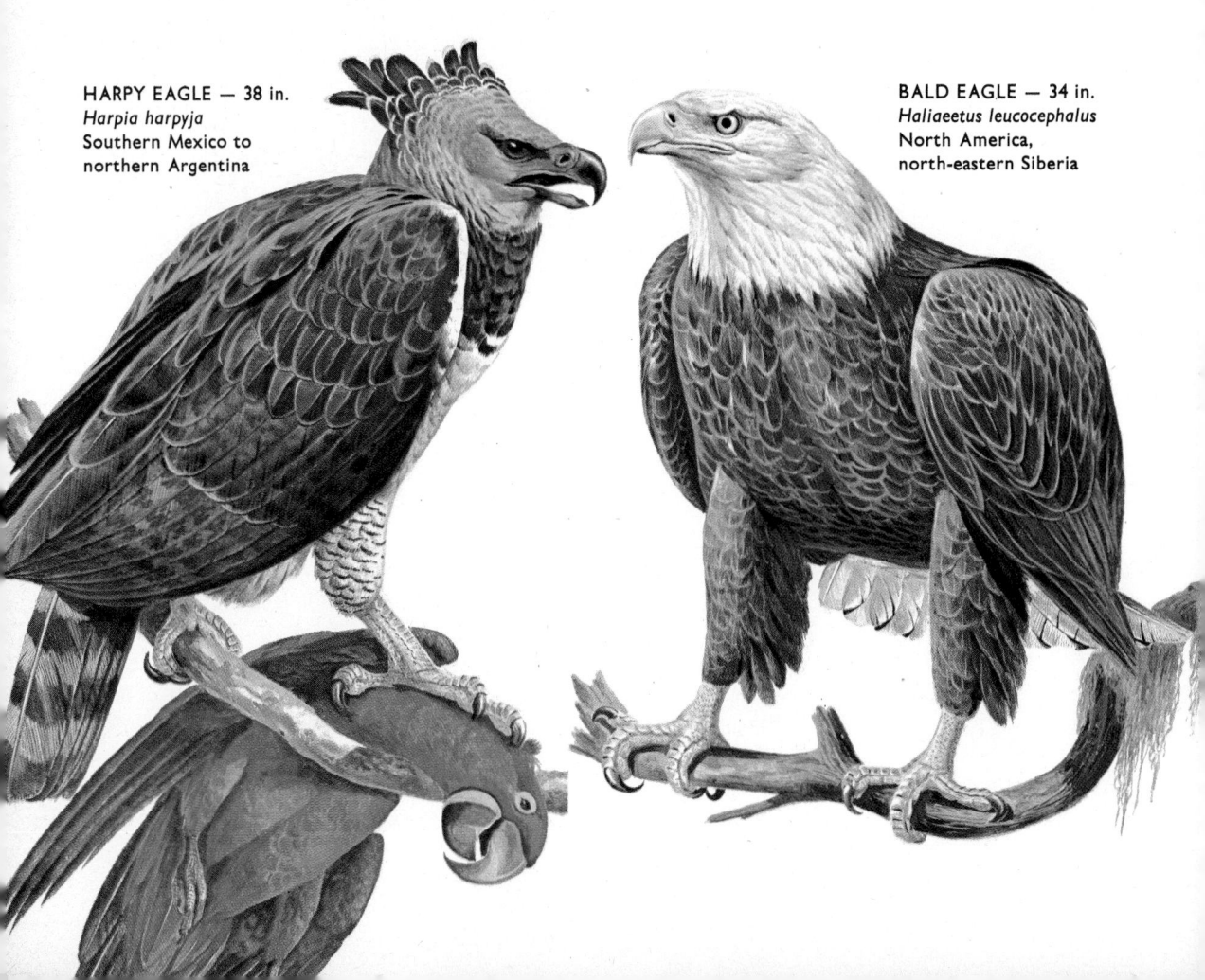

HARPY EAGLE — 38 in.
Harpia harpyja
Southern Mexico to
northern Argentina

BALD EAGLE — 34 in.
Haliaeetus leucocephalus
North America,
north-eastern Siberia

eagle's appearance of nobility and power has been interpreted in the same way both by primitive men and civilised nations.

Some American Indians believed that an imaginary super-eagle, called Thunderbird, caused the thunder and lightning. Eagle feathers could be worn only by braves who proved themselves by an act of courage.

The Bald Eagle is the national emblem of the United States and is pictured on the Great Seal. It is known for its powerful flight, its keen eyesight, and its habit of perching to watch the Osprey fish, and then swooping down to steal the catch.

The Golden Eagle breeds north to the arctic tundra, all over the Northern Hemisphere except Iceland. This bird was once kept in captivity by the Tartars, of Mongolia, who taught it to hunt for them.

The Bateleur Eagle, renowned for its acrobatic flight, sometimes eats small antelopes. The female lays only one egg a year.

The Harpy Eagle is a large eagle of

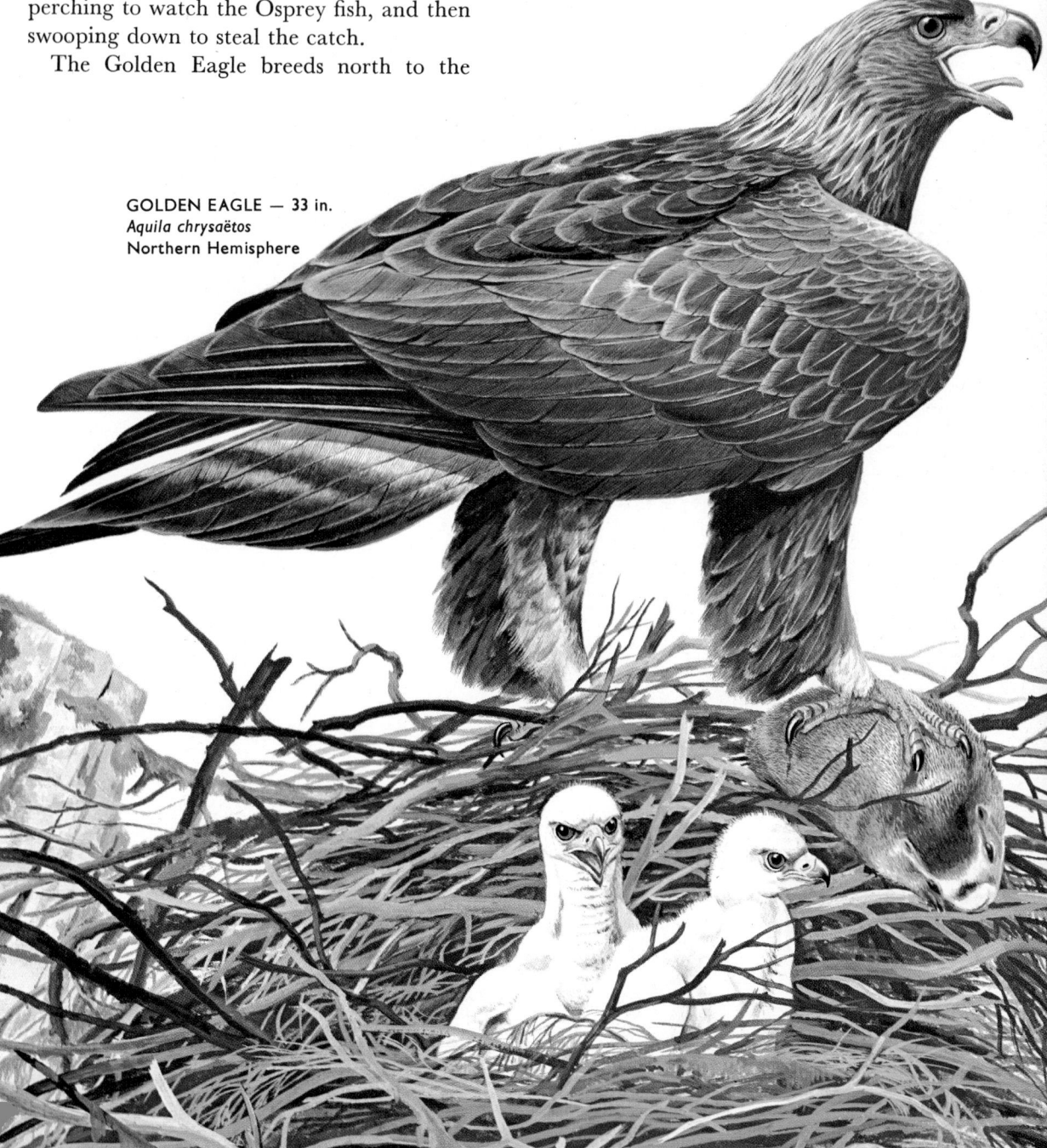

GOLDEN EAGLE — 33 in.
Aquila chrysaëtos
Northern Hemisphere

Mexico, and Central and South America. It has powerful talons, with which it attacks such prey as the macaws and monkeys.

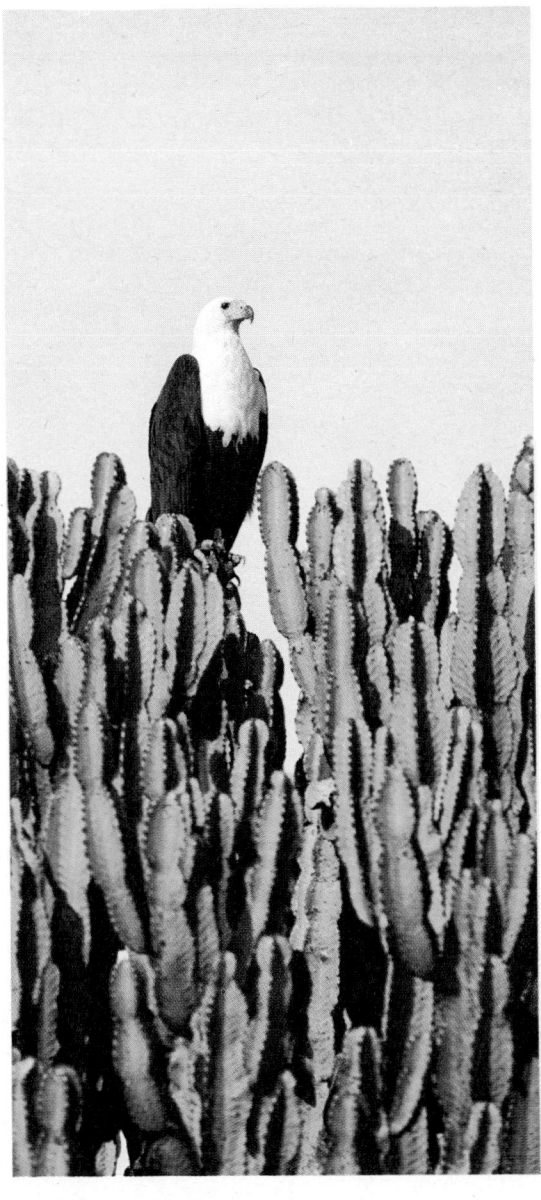

200 segments. They have a mouth at the forward end, but no other visible sense organs. Earthworms do react to changes in light intensity and to vibrations, however.

Each earthworm has both male and female organs, but is apparently incapable of self-fertilisation. After mating, each worm forms a cocoon that may contain as many as 28 eggs which hatch within three weeks.

Earthworms feed on organic debris in the soil. The tunnels dug by worms permit the entrance of both air and water, and piles of

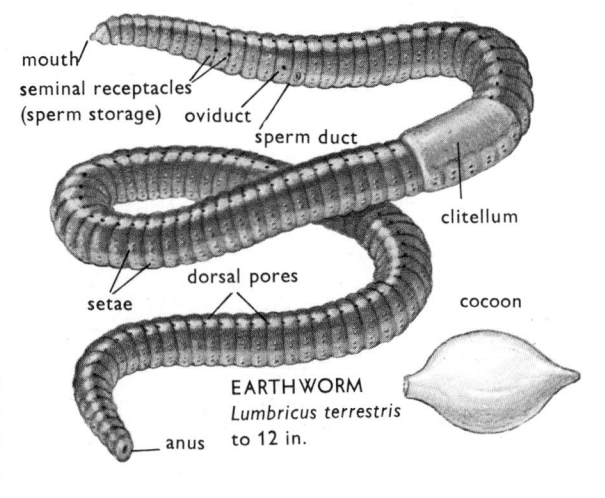

mouth
seminal receptacles
(sperm storage) oviduct
sperm duct
clitellum
setae dorsal pores cocoon
EARTHWORM
Lumbricus terrestris
anus to 12 in.

"castings" on the surface indicate worm activity. In a year, worms are capable of turning over tons of soil on an acre of land.

Most earthworms have a broad band of lighter tissue about a third of the way down the body from the head. Called the clitellum, this is the gland that secretes the material used to form the cocoon which encases the eggs.

EARTHWORMS belong to a group of more than 2,000 land-dwelling, segmented worms (see WORMS). The largest species, found in South America and Australia, measure over seven feet in length, but the common garden earthworms seldom reach six inches.

In appearance, earthworms are usually pink or dull red and are composed of nearly

EARWIGS (*Dermaptera*) are slender, chiefly nocturnal insects. Usually they have four wings. The first pair of wings are very short and leathery; the hind wings are pleated and carried folded under the front pair. At the end of the abdomen is a pair of large forcep-like structures with which an earwig can pinch. Occasionally one is seen carrying a dead insect along in these forceps. Most earwigs feed on plants, and they may cause

considerable damage to flowers and vegetables. Others are scavengers on dead animals, and a few are predators. Female earwigs deposit their eggs in a chamber in the ground, then guard them until they hatch.

ECHINODERMS are an ancient group of animals found only in the sea. Most kinds have a hard, limy outer skeleton armoured with spines. In fact, the word *echinoderm* is from the Greek word meaning "hedgehog skin". The bodies of echinoderms are divided into five parts. This is easily observed in starfish, which have five arms, and in the five sections of the shell of sea-urchins. Sand-dollars resemble flattened sea-urchins. Sea-lilies, or crinoids, also show this five-parted body organisation, but it is not as distinct in the soft-bodied sea-cucumbers.

Some echinoderms use their spines, or arms, for moving, but most use their tube feet. These soft tubes along their arms have suction cups at their tips and can be extended or pulled in. They operate by means of a unique water system found only in this group. Water canals run throughout their bodies, opening to the sea at one point.

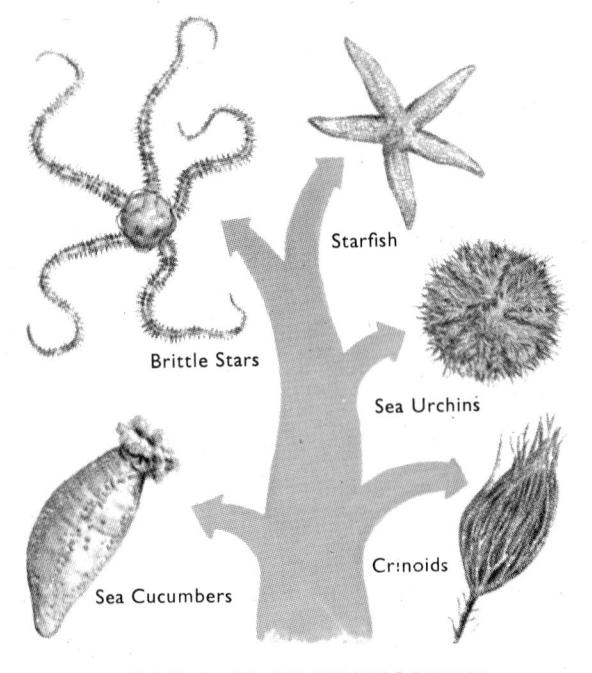

FAMILY TREE OF ECHINODERMS

Brittle Stars

Starfish

Sea Urchins

Sea Cucumbers

Crinoids

By a system of valves the animals can squeeze water into their tube feet and thus extend them, or draw water out and so shorten the feet. (See SEA-CUCUMBERS; SEA-LILIES; SEA-URCHINS and SAND-DOLLARS; STARFISH.)

EELS are fish with snake-like bodies. They have jaws, small, sharp teeth and no ventral fins. Often they do not have distinct pectoral

MOVEMENTS OF EEL LARVAE

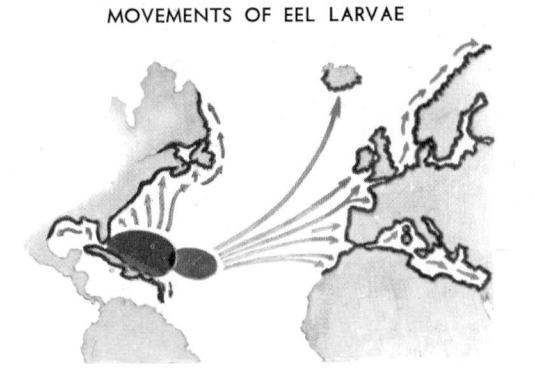

A: Breeding area — American Eel
B: Breeding area — European Eel

fins and tail fins, and their fins are soft and spineless. Some kinds have tiny scales covering their bodies; others are naked.

The journey of common fresh-water eels *(Auguilla* spp.*)* from America and Europe to the Sargasso Sea area of the Atlantic to lay eggs is a fascinating story (see FISHES).

Conger Eels, sometimes found in waters 600 feet deep, are among the largest of the marine eels. Some conger eels grow to a length of eight feet and may weigh as much as 100 pounds. They are common in the Atlantic Ocean and in most other seas.

Like other eels, congers are strong fish with sharp teeth. A large one is almost impossible to manage when caught.

More vicious than conger eels are the various morays *(Muraena* spp. and *Gymnothorax* spp.*)* that exist in tropical seas. A species that lives in the Pacific Ocean, off the coast of India, grows to a length of 10 feet. Morays are frequently encountered by skin-divers who explore coral reefs where the morays live. These eels lie hidden in coral

caves or crevices, or entwined about the coral, waiting for prey to come within reach. Often they wait with their mouths half open; many, morays, in fact, are unable

GREEN MORAY
Gymnothorax funebris
Up to 30 lbs., 6 ft.

SPOTTED MORAY
Gymnothorax moringa
Maximum of 3 ft.

CONGER EEL
Conger oceanicus
Up to 8 ft.

OCELLATED MORAY
Gymnothorax ocellatus
Maximum 2 ft.

Moray eels are common in tropical waters throughout the world and especially in the vicinity of coral reefs. Though ugly and dangerous to handle, they are good to eat.

to close their mouths completely.

Most eels move by swimming through the water in a snake-like manner. Other use sharp, horny tips on their tails to burrow tail-first into the sand or mud with astonishing speed. They leave only their heads sticking out, so that they can grab fish, crabs, or any other animals that come close. Many kinds of eels are brilliantly decorated with stripes and spots, and the young of one species of conger eel are a golden yellow.

The Worm Eels greatly resemble elongated worms. They have one lip (usually the upper) overlapping the other. The Snipe Eels are deep-sea fishes, with long needle-like jaws which cannot be closed.

Many of the Snake Eels, also found in the tropics, are more placid in temperament, and can even be picked up without fear of being bitten. Generally spotted, with dark patches on a yellowish or olive background, they prowl by crawling sluggishly along the bottom. Their snouts are unusually long compared to other eels, and they use them as probes to locate the shellfish, crabs and other sea creatures that they eat.

Large numbers of eels are caught commercially in nets or in baited traps. Less commonly they are taken on hook and line. In many countries eels are highly prized as food and bring a high price in the market. While they are often sold as fresh fish, some are preserved by smoking or pickling. The skins of eels were formerly used as coin purses and as sheaths for the queues of wigs.

Eel larvae are transparent and ribbon-like. While still small (less than 3 inches long) they swim from the Sargasso Sea, in the mid-Atlantic, either to Europe or to America, depending on the species (see map on page 177). Soon after entering fresh water, they become slimmer (glass eel) and later become dark miniatures of the adults (elver). After about five years in fresh water, the adults swim to the Sargasso Sea to spawn and then die.

WORM EEL
Myrophis punctatus

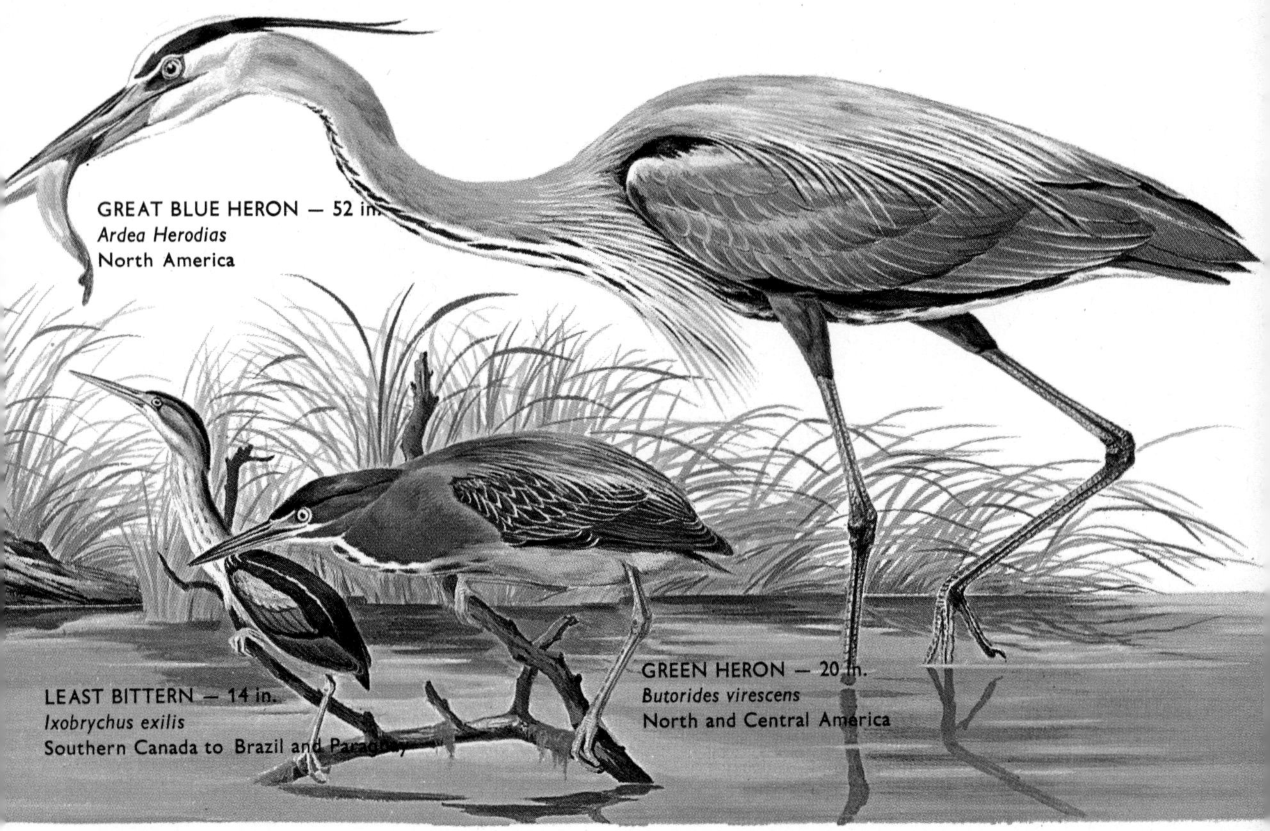

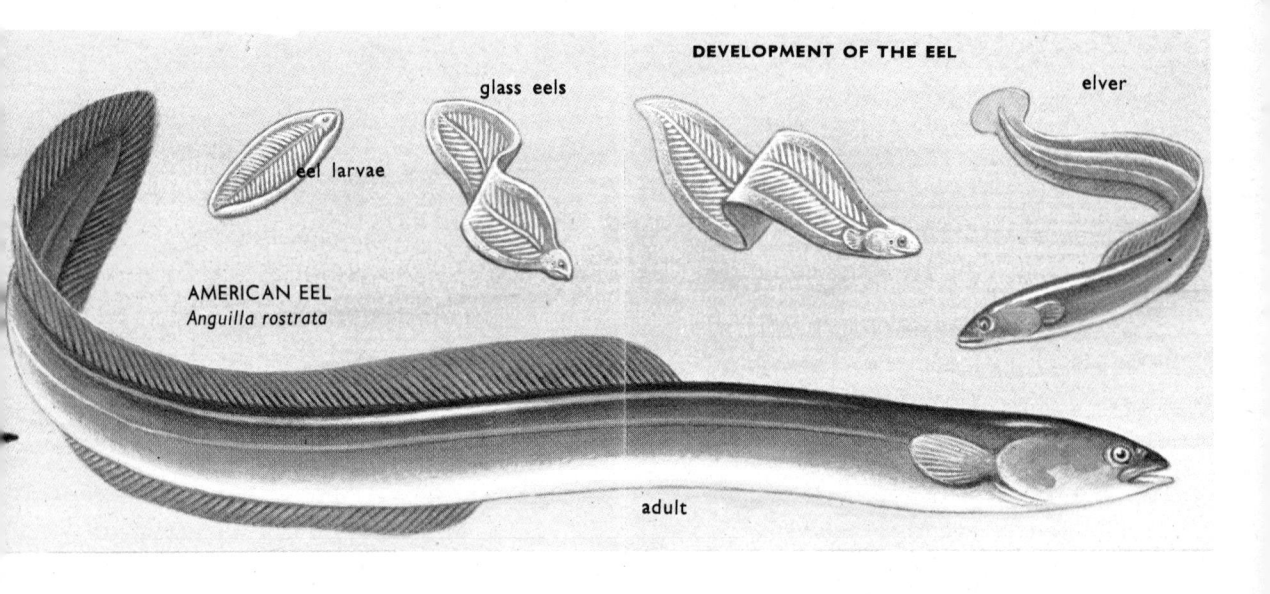

GREAT BLUE HERON — 52 in.
Ardea Herodias
North America

LEAST BITTERN — 14 in.
Ixobrychus exilis
Southern Canada to Brazil and Paraguay

GREEN HERON — 20 in.
Butorides virescens
North and Central America

EGRETS are members of the heron family (see HERONS). They have habits similar to herons, but sometimes nest on the ground. Their name comes from the French word, *aigrette,* for a head-decoration of feathers and gems. It was given to species of heron with handsome neck and shoulder plumes.

The magnificent courting plumage of the Snowy, Common and Reddish egrets nearly caused their extermination. Millions were killed each year until they were protected by law early in this century.

The Cattle Egret reached South America from Africa after 1900. No one knows how

DEVELOPMENT OF THE EEL

glass eels

eel larvae

elver

AMERICAN EEL
Anguilla rostrata

adult

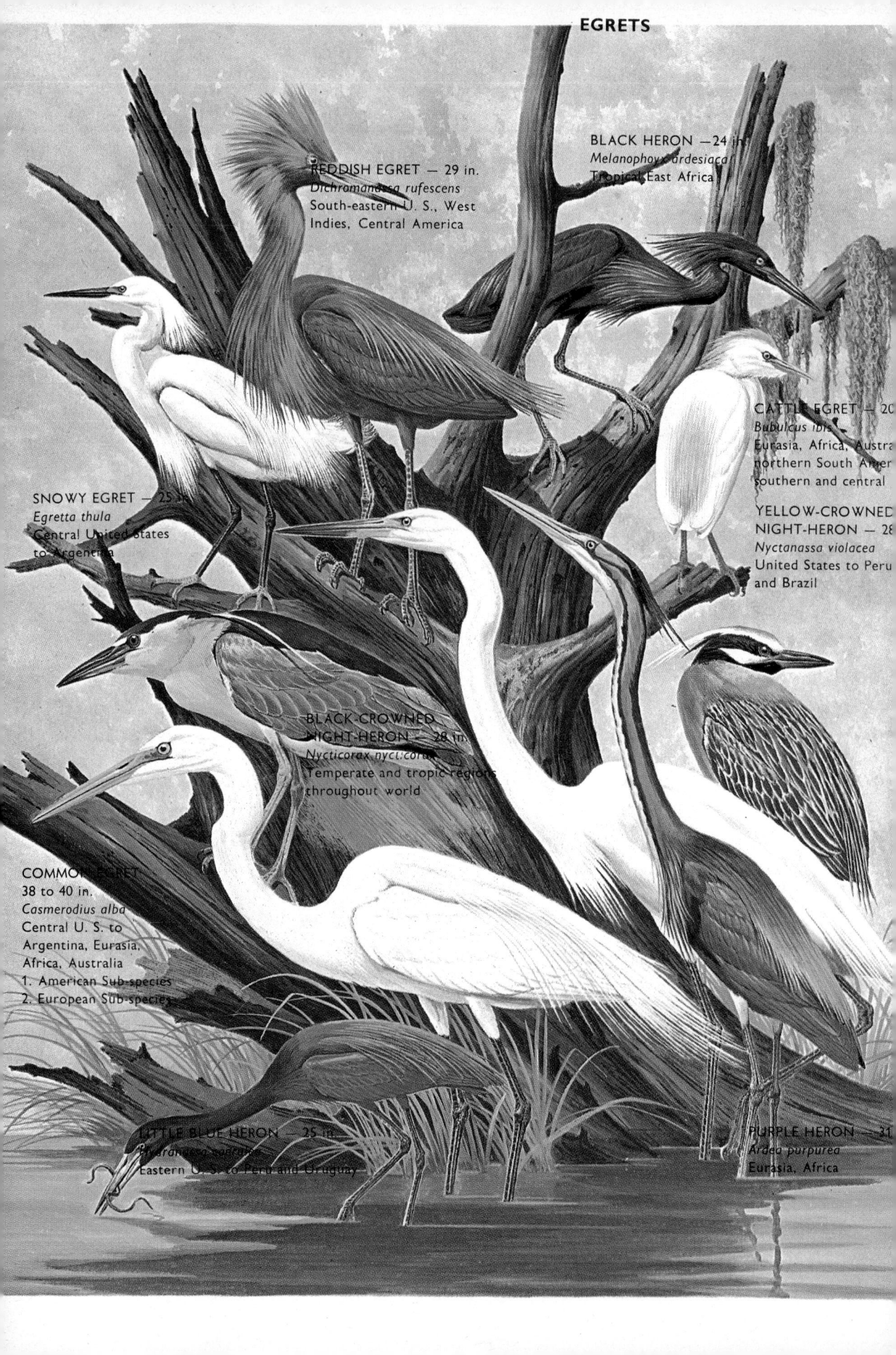

REDDISH EGRET — 29 in.
Dichromanassa rufescens
South-eastern U. S., West
Indies, Central America

BLACK HERON — 24 in.
Melanophoyx ardesiaca
Tropical East Africa

SNOWY EGRET — 25 in.
Egretta thula
Central United States
to Argentina

CATTLE EGRET — 20
Bubulcus ibis
Eurasia, Africa, Austra
northern South Amer
southern and central

**YELLOW-CROWNED
NIGHT-HERON — 28**
Nyctanassa violacea
United States to Peru
and Brazil

**BLACK-CROWNED
NIGHT-HERON — 28 in.**
Nycticorax nycticorax
Temperate and tropic regions
throughout world

**COMMON EGRET
38 to 40 in.**
Casmerodius alba
Central U. S. to
Argentina, Eurasia,
Africa, Australia
1. American Sub-species
2. European Sub-species

LITTLE BLUE HERON — 25 in.
Florida caerulea
Eastern U. S. to Peru and Uruguay

PURPLE HERON — 31
Ardea purpurea
Eurasia, Africa

this was achieved, as egrets do not ordinarily cross oceans. Recently the Cattle Egret spread into the United States and Australia, and is now common in cattle country. It has provided the scientists who study birds with an unrivalled opportunity to study the spread and adjustment of a newly-arrived species.

ELANDS (*Taurotragus* spp.) are large, cattle-like antelopes that live in Africa from the Sahara Desert southward. Both males and females have long, twisted horns. Large bulls have shoulder humps, and flaps on their throats, like Brahma bulls. Elands graze in herds in the open country along the edges of forests. When the grass dries, they feed on leaves. Sometimes they invade cultivated fields to feast on growing crops. Because of their large size (bulls may weigh a ton) and tasty flesh, they have long been hunted for their meat, and by big-game hunters for sport.

ELEPHANTS are huge beasts, the largest of all living land mammals. They have long trunks and nearly hairless bodies, and they walk with a peculiar, stiff-legged shuffle. Both males and females have long ivory tusks

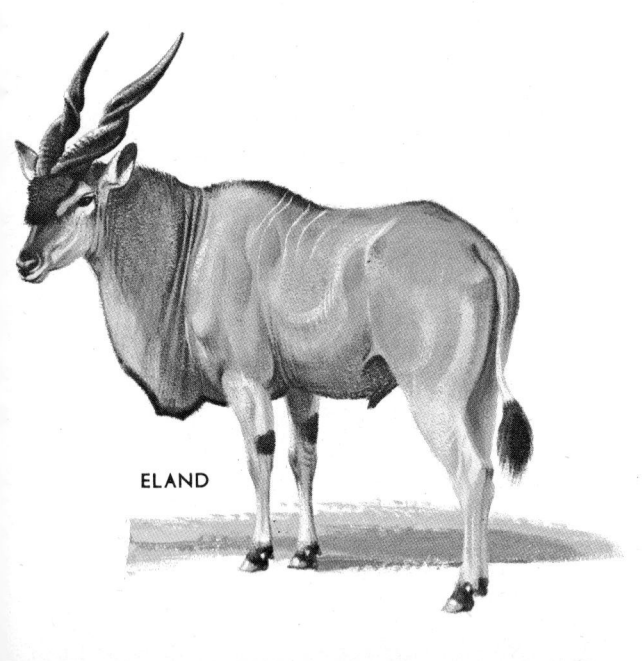

ELAND

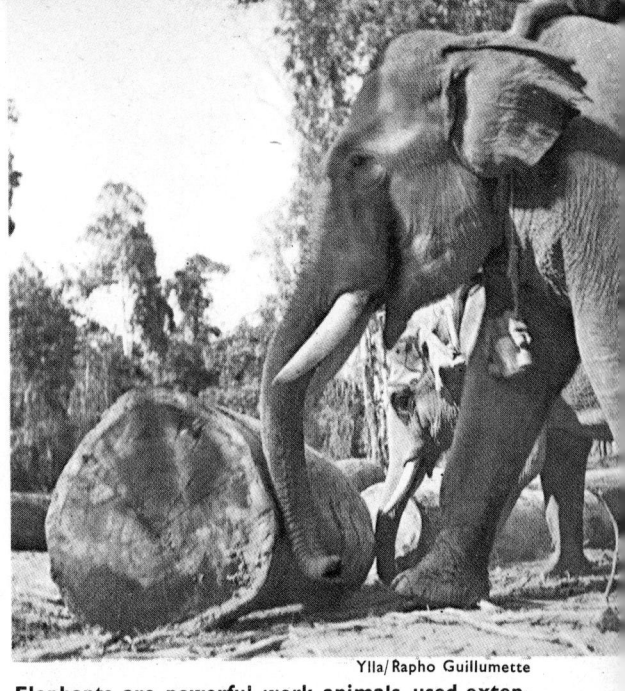

Ylla/Rapho Guillumette

Elephants are powerful work animals, used extensively in the important teak lumbering industry of India and Burma.

which are upper incisors. Tusks of the female Indian Elephant are commonly very short. Their molars, also huge, are long and flat, and consist of a series of plates which wear unevenly, making washboard-like grinding surfaces for crushing leaves, grasses, fruits and bark. Their nostrils are located at the ends of their trunks, and any water that is drawn in is soon blown out, either into their mouths or into the air. The forehead of the African Elephant (*Loxodonta africana*) is dome-shaped, or convex; that of the Indian (*Elephas maximus*) is concave, or hollowed.

Elephants usually live in well-organised herds. Under ideal conditions, elephants may live to be as much as 60 years old. Weird stories are told about where these animals go to die, since the remains of dead elephants are rarely found.

An elephant may eat nearly half a ton of food every day, so a herd soon consumes most of the vegetation over a large area of land. They make clearly-marked trails in their wanderings over hundreds of miles of jungle in search of food. In parts of Africa, well-worn elephant trails have been used in developing roads. Elephants also require a source of water for drinking, cooling their

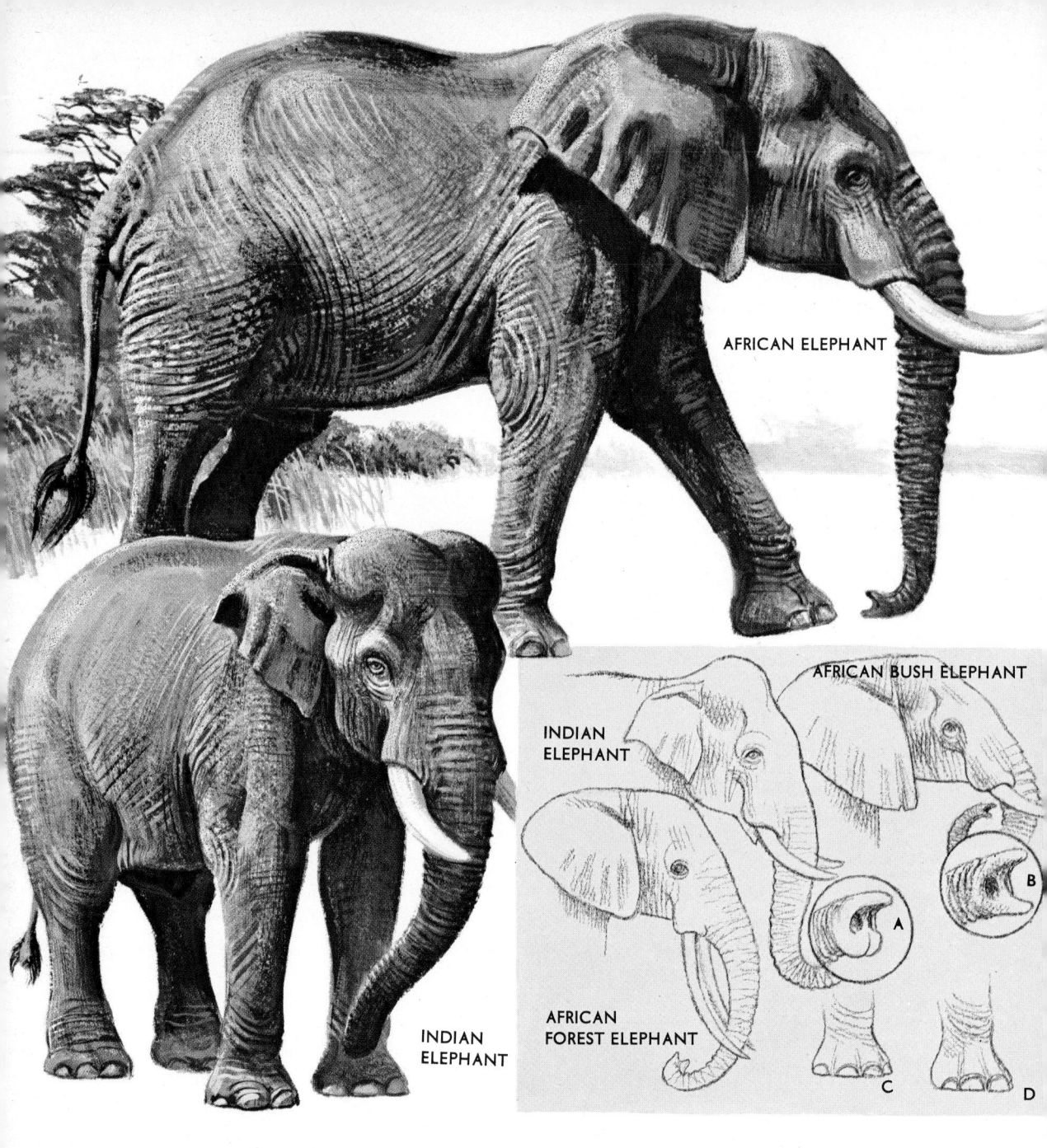

AFRICAN ELEPHANT

INDIAN ELEPHANT

INDIAN ELEPHANT

AFRICAN BUSH ELEPHANT

AFRICAN FOREST ELEPHANT

A

B

C

D

bodies, and washing off insect pests.

The African Elephant occurs throughout much of Africa, south of the Sahara. It has much larger ears than the Indian Elephant. A bull African elephant may stand almost 11 feet high at its shoulders and weigh more than four tons; its tusks may weigh as much as 200 pounds or more each. Females are smaller, usually less than nine feet high at the shoulders. The African Elephant has been trained and domesticated, but not like

An Indian Elephant has one "finger" on its trunk (A); the African Elephant has two (B). The Indian Elephant has 5 nails on its front foot, 4 on its back (C); the African, 4 nails on its front, 3 on back (D).

the Indian Elephant. Elephants have now been exterminated in many areas of Africa.

There are two forms of the African Elephant. The Bush Elephant, which lives in the open or in slightly wooded regions, is generally larger than the Forest Elephant.

The Indian Elephant, found from India eastward to Indo-China and south into Sumatra, has comparatively small ears, and is also smaller in over-all size than the African Elephant. Bulls usually measure less than nine feet in height at the shoulders, and average about three and a half tons in weight. Whereas the African Elephant is famous as a game animal and as the largest land mammal, the Indian Elephant is renowned as a working animal. These elephants have been trained to move heavy objects or to carry considerable loads on their backs. They are also used in ceremonial parades, to carry hunters in pursuit of the Bengal Tiger, and as beasts of war. Indian elephants are also trained for use in circuses. Their four basic tricks are to lie down, sit up, whirl around, and whirl around on their hind legs. Elephants from Ceylon often lack tusks, while those of Sumatra are smaller and have longer trunks.

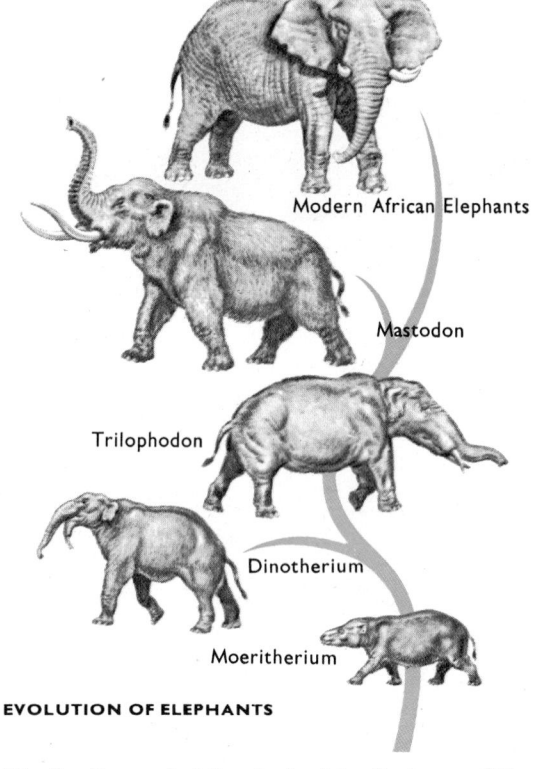

Modern African Elephants

Mastodon

Trilophodon

Dinotherium

Moeritherium

EVOLUTION OF ELEPHANTS

The fossil record of the elephant family is one of the most complete. The earliest ancestor of all was *Moeritherium*, a trunkless swamp-dweller that lived 50 million years ago.

EMUS, large, ostrich-like, flightless birds, were originally very plentiful in Australia, where they were hunted by the natives for food. European settlers did not like their meat, and so did not molest them. Until 1919, when farmers complained that the Emus trampled their wheat, this "King of Australian Fauna" was protected. In 1932, the Australian government sent a military unit with machine-guns to make war on the birds. From June, 1945, to June, 1949, when the government paid one shilling for each dead Emu, citizens killed 70,814 birds. Efforts are now being made to establish sanctuaries where Emus can live unmolested in the wild. They thrive in captivity.

Emus nest in open areas near trees or bushes. Females have nothing to do with the incubation of the eggs or the protection of the young. No one knows how many females lay eggs in one clutch. The male, on its own, incubates the eggs for 58 to 63 days, and protects the 7 to 12 young birds that are able to feed themselves as soon as they hatch. Males can only grunt; females utter loud, echoing booms. Emus are fast runners, said to be capable of speeds up to 30 miles an hour. They usually travel in small flocks, but always pair off in the breeding season.

The Emu, which may weigh as much as 120 pounds, is second in size only to the Ostrich.

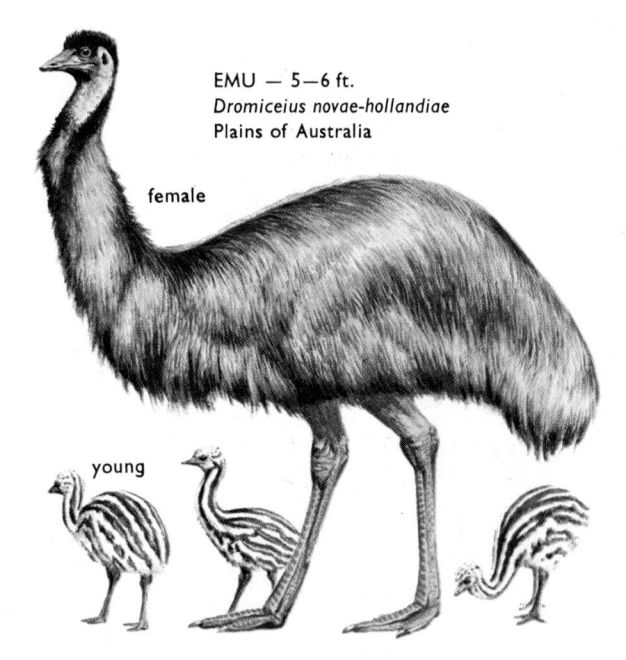

EMU — 5—6 ft.
Dromiceius novae-hollandiae
Plains of Australia

female

young

F

FALCONS are one of the major groups in the *Falconiformes*. They differ in having long, pointed wings and long, thin, wedge-shaped tails. Like the hawks, falcons are predators. They have a strong, sharp, hooked bill and needle-pointed talons.

The Gyrfalcon, largest of the falcons, makes its home in the Arctic regions of North America, Europe and Asia. It may measure 22 inches in length, with a 4-foot wing-spread, and weigh 4 pounds. It feeds on northern grouse and rodents.

The Peregrine Falcon is nearly world-wide in distribution. It dives on its prey, usually small birds, as fast as 175 m.p.h. The prey is then retrieved from the ground.

The American Sparrow Hawk is a representative of the widespread Kestrel group. Males of this group are more grey than the russet female. As with most hawks, the female is the larger bird.

Falcons were once in great demand for the sport of falconry. The birds were trained to kill when released, and then to return to their human owner. Falconry flourished in the Middle Ages, but has dec'ined now.

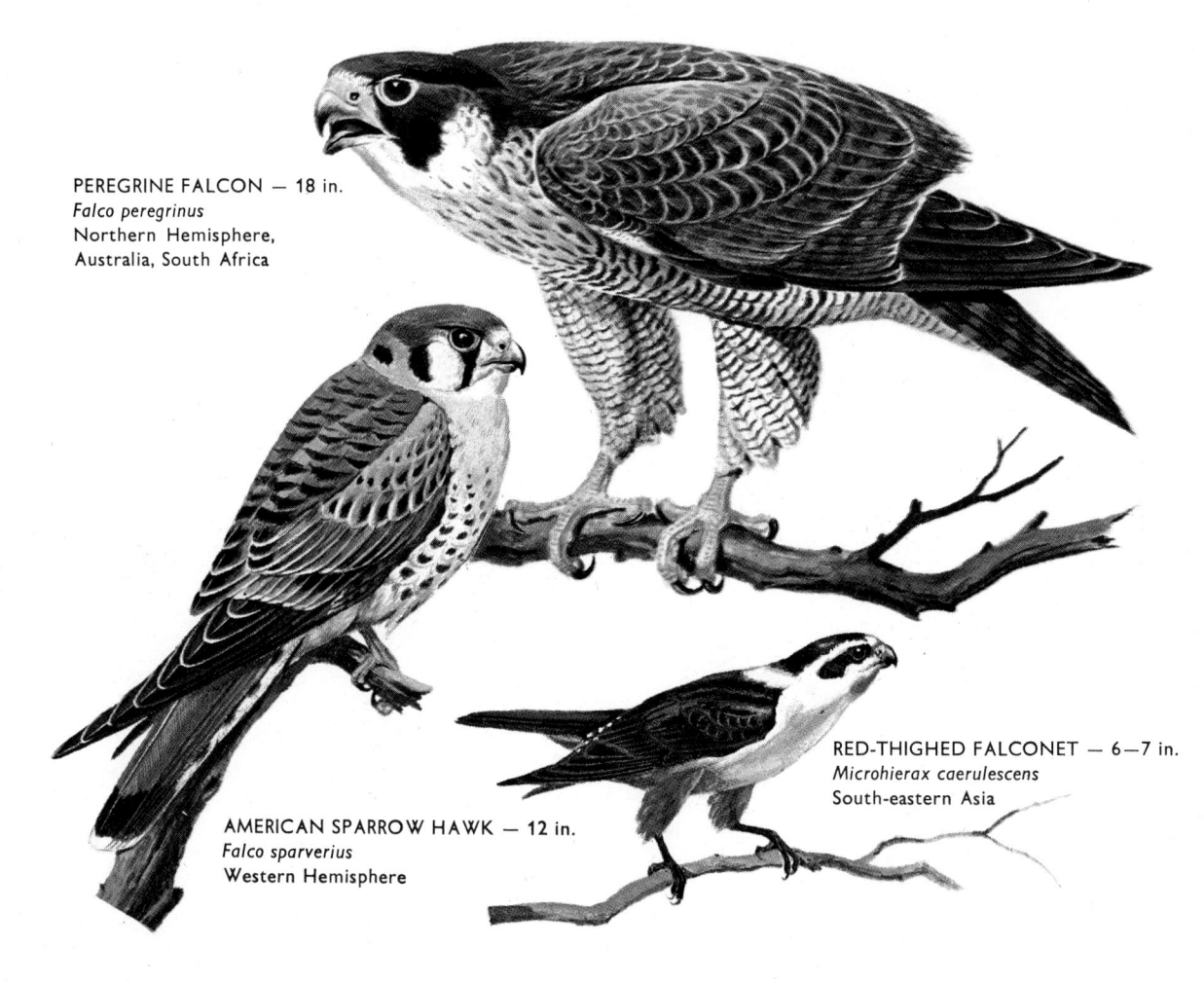

PEREGRINE FALCON — 18 in.
Falco peregrinus
Northern Hemisphere,
Australia, South Africa

AMERICAN SPARROW HAWK — 12 in.
Falco sparverius
Western Hemisphere

RED-THIGHED FALCONET — 6—7 in.
Microhierax caerulescens
South-eastern Asia

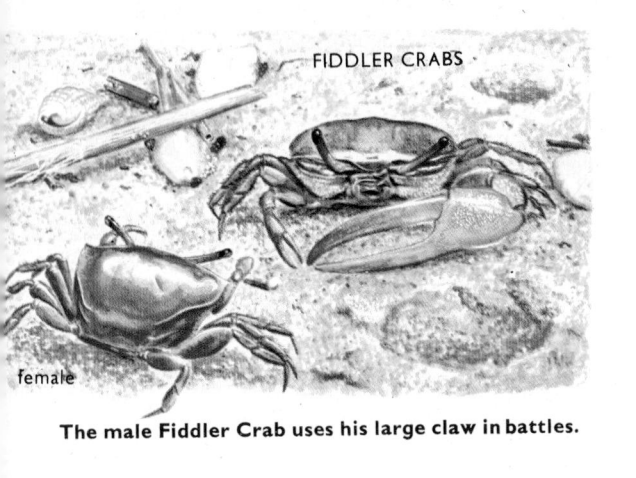

FIDDLER CRABS

female

The male Fiddler Crab uses his large claw in battles.

them of dead and decaying material. They dig their holes by rolling the mud into pellets and carrying them out of the burrow, which may be as much as three feet long.

FINCHES, members of the *Fringillidae,* are small, chunky birds with cone-shaped bills for eating seeds. Some species have delightful songs. A greenish-yellow wild finch brought from the Canary Islands in the early 1500s was the ancestor of caged canaries (see CANARIES). Finches occur all over the world. They lay from two to six eggs, in a cup-shaped nest.

FIDDLER CRABS *(Uca pugnax)* are commonly seen at low tide on low, muddy shores, where their small burrows may honeycomb the beach. They seldom measure more than two inches in width. Females have two small, inconspicuous claws, but males have one huge claw, which they hold up and move as a fiddler does his bow; at mating time they may be brightly coloured.

Fiddlers feed on organic debris on the bottom. As scavengers, they occupy an important place in the mud-flats by ridding

FIREFLIES are long, soft-bodied beetles *(Lampyridae)*. They ordinarily fly only at night, hiding in vegetation during the day. The heads of most species are completely covered by a thin extension of the thorax. Females of many species are wingless and greatly resemble their larvae. Both are luminescent and are frequently referred to as "glow-worms". Their light-producing organs are located on the abdomen, sometimes on only one segment and sometimes

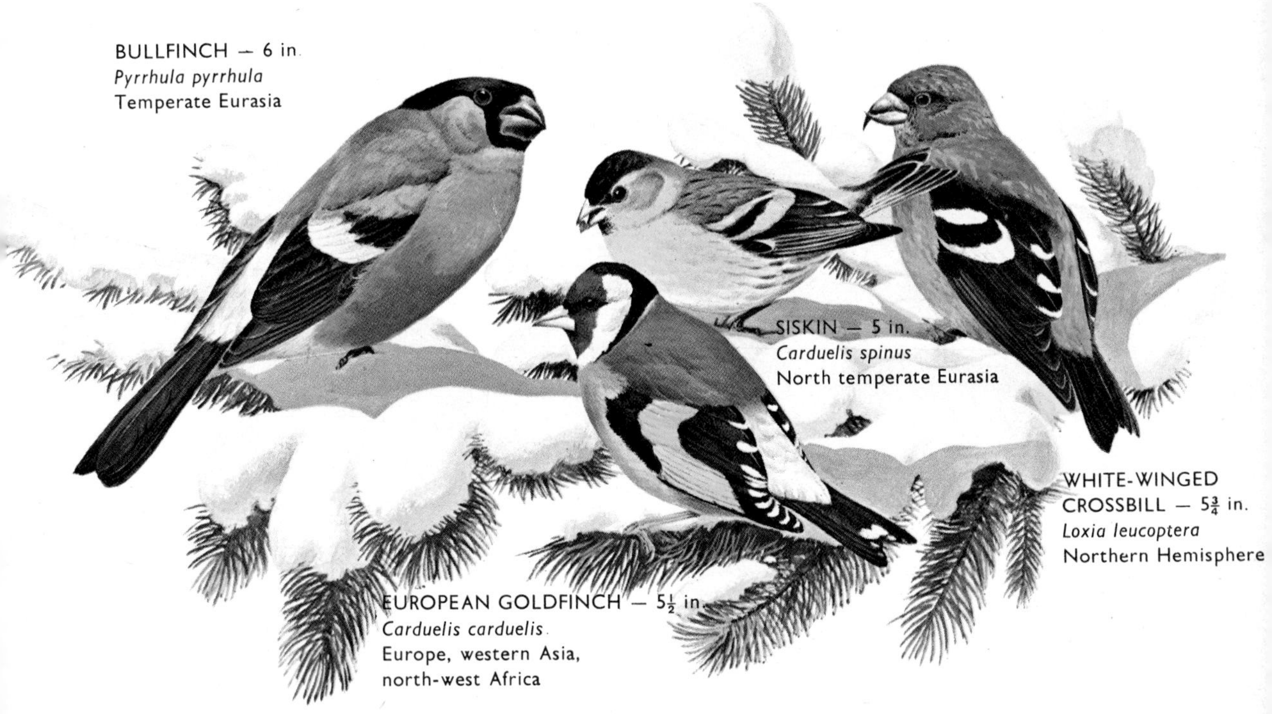

BULLFINCH — 6 in.
Pyrrhula pyrrhula
Temperate Eurasia

SISKIN — 5 in.
Carduelis spinus
North temperate Eurasia

WHITE-WINGED
CROSSBILL — 5¾ in.
Loxia leucoptera
Northern Hemisphere

EUROPEAN GOLDFINCH — 5½ in.
Carduelis carduelis
Europe, western Asia,
north-west Africa

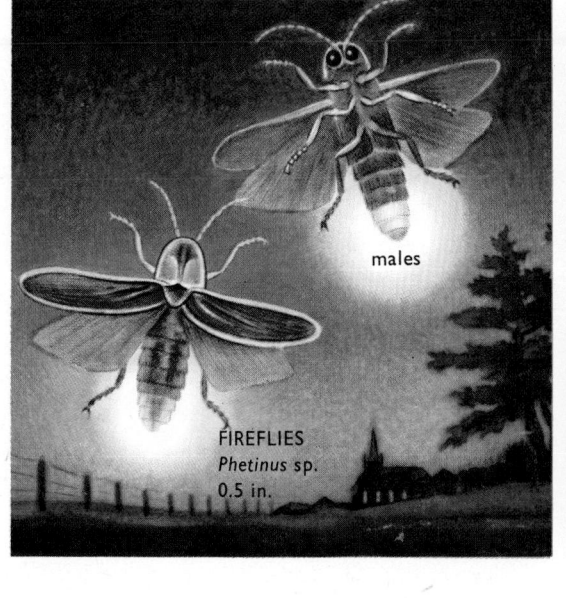

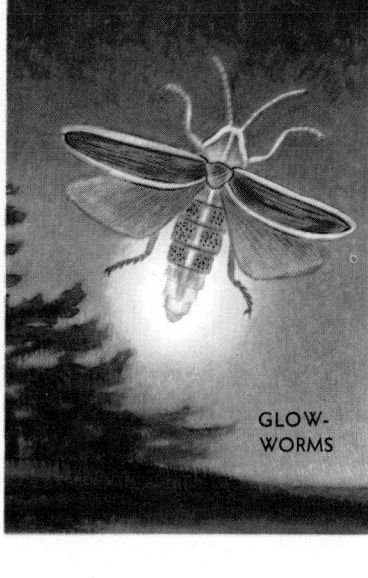

FIREFLIES
Phetinus sp.
0.5 in.

males

GLOW-
WORMS

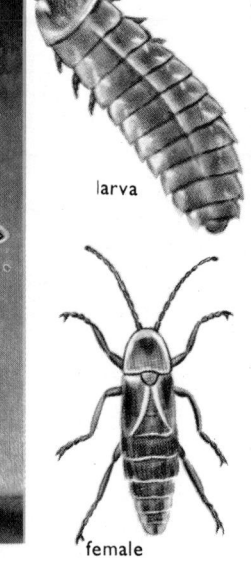

larva

female

on several. The male of our common species, *Lampyris noctiluca,* also produces a light, as larva and adult. In both sexes, the light is pale yellowish green, varying in intensity according to the insect's activities. It is not phosphorescent light.

FISHES are the only major group of vertebrates (or backboned animals) completely adapted for life in the water. A fish usually has fins and scales, and breathes by means of gills. Since its body temperature varies with the water temperature in which

it lives, the fish is referred to as a cold-blooded animal.

Fossil records reveal that fishes were the first backboned animals. They appeared more than 400 million years ago.

The earliest fish-like creatures, called ostracoderms, were covered with a heavy armour of horny plates and overlapping scales. These primitive fishes had no jaws and only poorly-developed fins; but ostracoderms did live in water — probably in fresh-water swamps — and they breathed by means of gills. They also had backbones made of cartilage.

Modern fishes — and there are more than 30,000 species — developed from fishes of this sort. They are placed in three main groups. The most primitive are the lampreys and hagfishes, direct offshoots of those ancient ostracoderms. Both are eel-like and have no scales, jaws or paired fins.

Sharks, rays and skates, which form the second group, are not bony fishes. They have skeletons of cartilage, not bone. This ancient group developed in the sea about 300 million years ago. They have tooth-like scales and several slits opening to their gills. Bottom-dwelling sharks and rays also have a single opening, called a spiracle, on each side of their head, just behind their eyes. This spiracle is the organ used for taking in

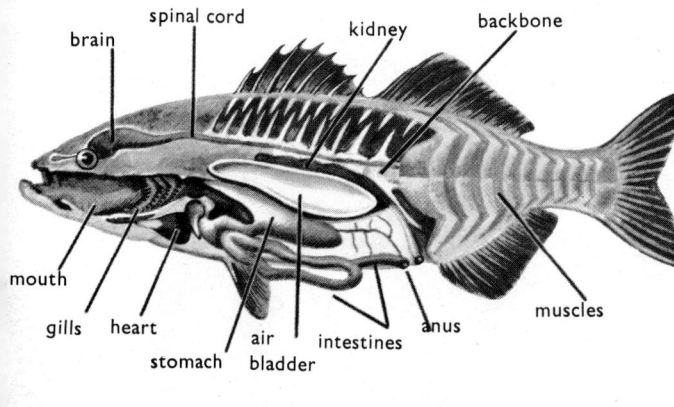

brain
spinal cord
kidney
backbone
mouth
gills
heart
stomach
air bladder
intestines
anus
muscles

INTERNAL ANATOMY — A typical bony fish, the Striped Bass, is used here to illustrate the fish's simple digestive system, the position of the two-chambered heart, air bladder, kidney, and other internal structures. Note the broad, W-shaped muscles with which the fish is equipped.

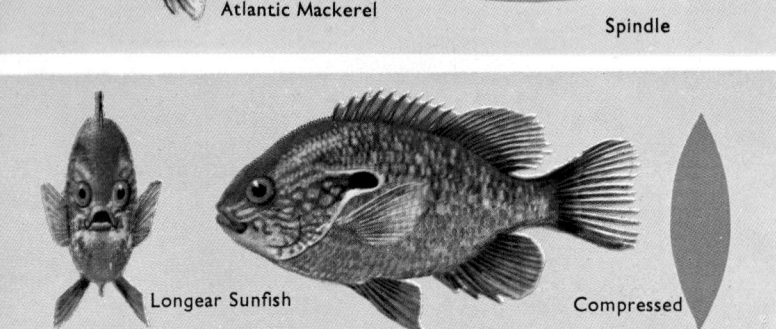

Atlantic Mackerel

Spindle

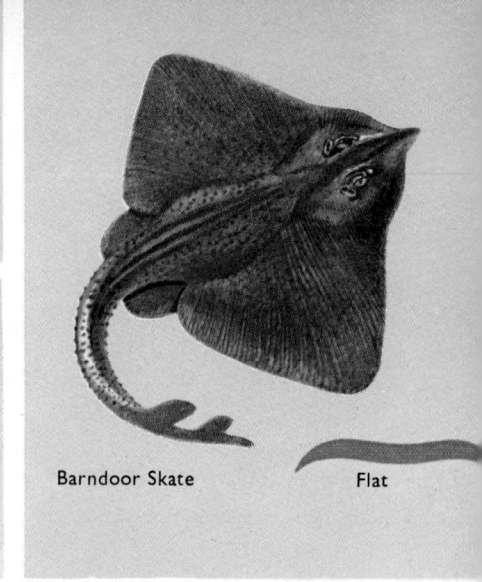

Barndoor Skate

Flat

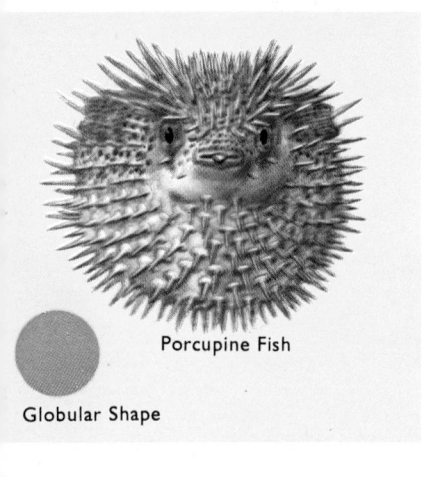

Longear Sunfish

Compressed

Porcupine Fish

Globular Shape

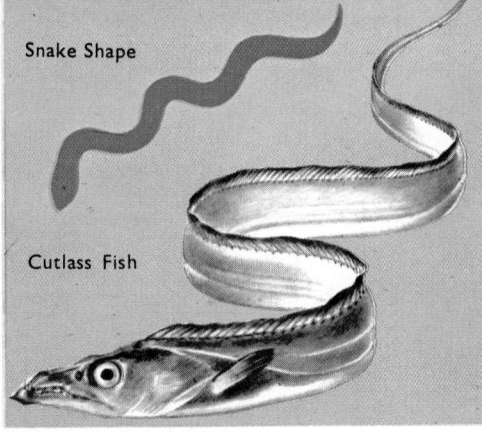

Snake Shape

Cutlass Fish

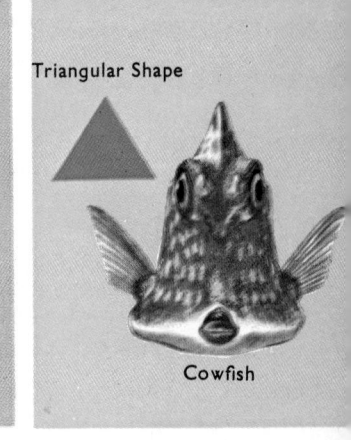

Triangular Shape

Cowfish

water when the fishes breathe.

Most of our present-day fishes have skeletons of bone. They make up the third group — the bony fishes. To this group belong the basses, herrings, salmons, catfishes, mackerels — the kinds most familiar to us. The majority of bony fishes are covered with overlapping scales. They have a single operculum, or gill cover, on each side of the head, and their fins are strengthened by bony rays.

Man's interest in fishes began long before any written records. Early man caught fishes for food. He trapped them in shallow pools and learned to catch them with his hands. Later, he made spears and nets; and finally — no one knows how long ago — he learned how to make a hook and catch fish with bait.

Fishes are one of the most important food resources in the world. About 30 million metric tons are harvested from fresh and salt waters every year. Commercial fishermen

EXTERNAL ANATOMY — Pectoral and ventral fins are paired — one fin on each side, like our arms and legs. Dorsal, caudal, and anal fins, located on the midline of the body, are not paired. Most fishes are covered with scales and have a visible lateral line.

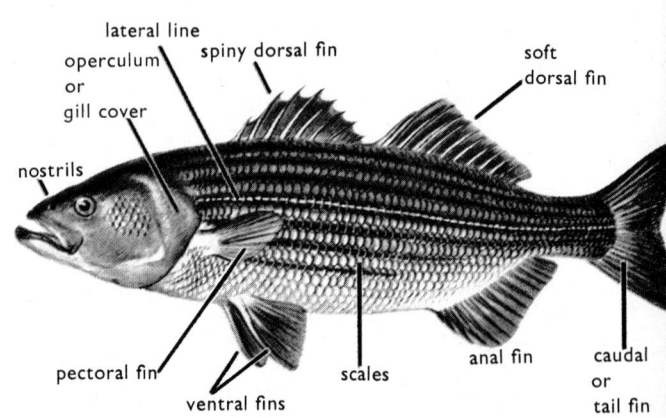

lateral line
operculum
or
gill cover
nostrils
spiny dorsal fin
soft
dorsal fin
pectoral fin
ventral fins
scales
anal fin
caudal
or
tail fin

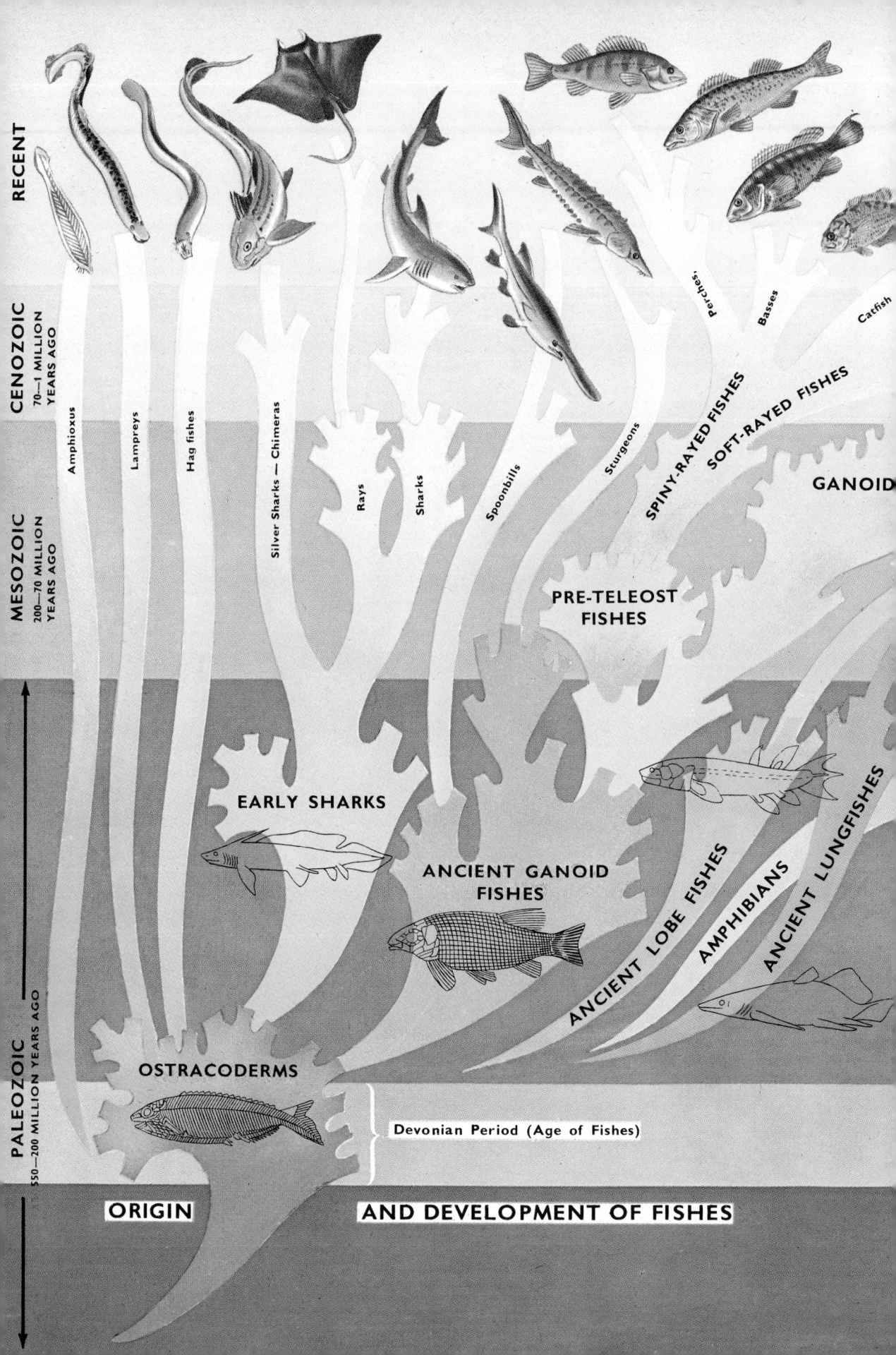

RECENT

CENOZOIC
70—1 MILLION
YEARS AGO

MESOZOIC
200—70 MILLION
YEARS AGO

PALEOZOIC
550—200 MILLION YEARS AGO

Amphioxus

Lampreys

Hag fishes

Silver Sharks — Chimeras

Rays

Sharks

Spoonbills

Sturgeons

Perches

Basses

Catfish

SPINY-RAYED FISHES

SOFT-RAYED FISHES

GANOID

PRE-TELEOST
FISHES

EARLY SHARKS

ANCIENT GANOID
FISHES

ANCIENT LOBE FISHES

AMPHIBIANS

ANCIENT LUNGFISHES

OSTRACODERMS

Devonian Period (Age of Fishes)

ORIGIN   AND DEVELOPMENT OF FISHES

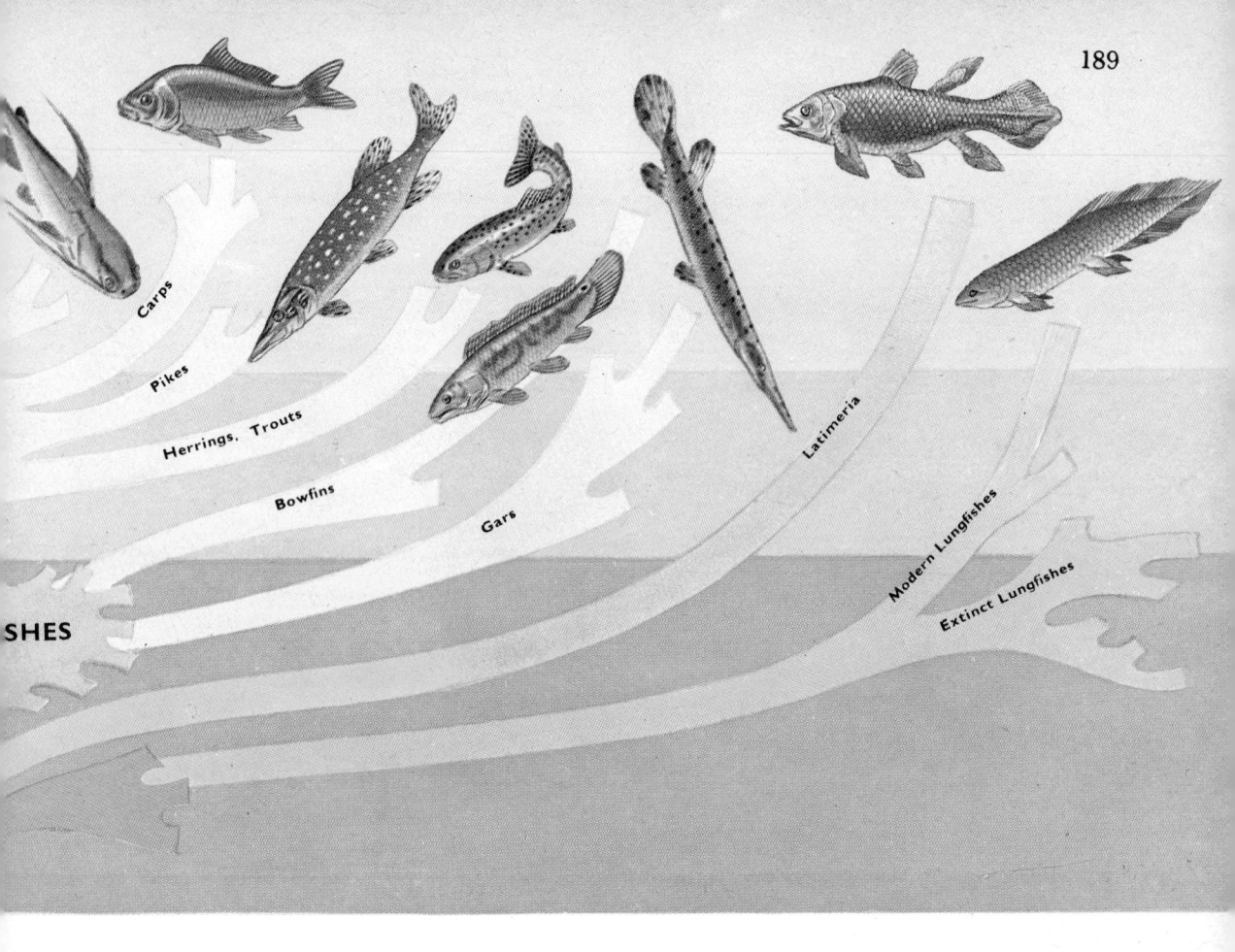

Carps

Pikes

Herrings, Trouts

Bowfins

Gars

Latimeria

Modern Lungfishes

Extinct Lungfishes

SHES

now use inventions, such as radar, to help them make their catches. Some are eaten fresh, many are tinned or frozen, others are salted or smoked. Some kinds are processed for animal foods, to get oils for use in paints, or as sources of vitamins A and D.

SIZES. Tiny gobies that live in fresh-water lakes in the Philippine Islands are the smallest fishes in the world. They are the smallest backboned animals. Even when full grown, they still measure less than half an inch long. Men catch these little fish in fine-meshed nets and sell them in the markets to be baked into fish-cakes. It takes nearly 15,000 of these gobies to weigh a pound!

At the opposite extreme are monstrous Whale Sharks that roam the warm oceans. These giants may measure as much as 50 feet in length and weigh more than 15 tons. Whale Sharks, despite their size, are not dangerous. They feed mainly on plankton (see PLANKTON).

In fresh water, sturgeons rank as the largest fish. Russia reports catches of sturgeons that weigh as much as a ton and a half. Sturgeons that weighed more than 1,000 pounds were once caught in the Snake River, western United States, where half that size is rare now (see STURGEON).

Next in size among fresh-water fishes are giant catfish. The Wels, found in the Danube and other rivers of Europe, tips the scales at 400 pounds or more. The Pla Bük, a catfish that lives in Siam, weighs more than 500 pounds. Many kinds of fresh-water fishes exceed 100 pounds in weight. Alligator Gars of the lower Mississippi and its tributaries may weigh over 300 pounds. Paddlefish from there may weigh several hundred pounds (see CATFISH; PADDLEFISH.)

Most giant fishes, however, live in the sea. Of these, one of the most unusual is the Ocean Sunfish, or *Mola mola*. Known to weigh as much as a ton, this strange fish appears to be all head, for its fins are set far

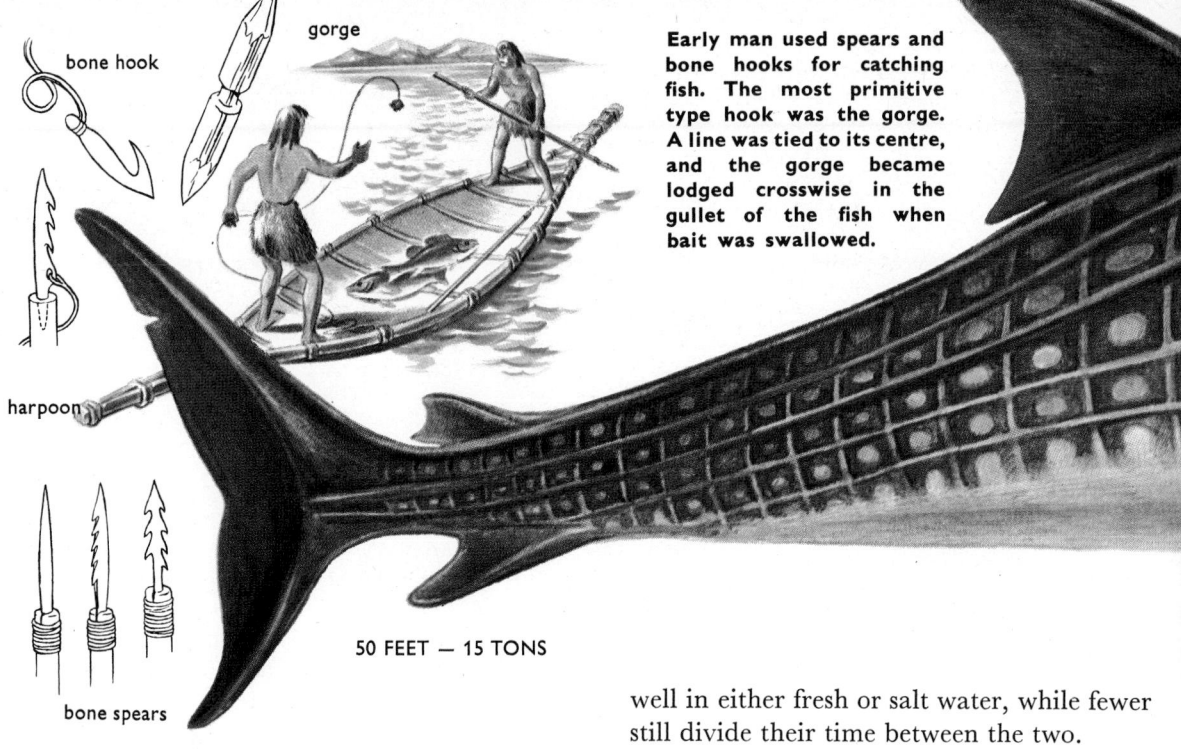

bone hook

gorge

harpoon

bone spears

Early man used spears and bone hooks for catching fish. The most primitive type hook was the gorge. A line was tied to its centre, and the gorge became lodged crosswise in the gullet of the fish when bait was swallowed.

50 FEET — 15 TONS

back on its broad, almost tail-less body. Basking Sharks reach a weight of five tons. Mantas may also weigh a ton or more. There are several species of sharks, tunas and marlins that may attain a weight of more than 1,000 pounds (see MARLINS; OCEAN SUNFISH; RAYS; SHARKS; TUNAS).

If food is plentiful, a fish grows rapidly at first. Its growth slows down after it becomes mature, but the fish continues to increase in size slightly every year as long as it lives. In warm waters fish grow more rapidly than in cold waters, largely because there are more months in the year during which they can feed. For this reason, a three-year-old bass in the southern United States may weigh more than a bass of twice that age from a northern lake or stream.

WHERE FISHES LIVE. Salt waters cover about 71 per cent of the earth's surface. In addition, there are numerous lakes and streams on land areas. Despite this abundance of water, each kind of fish is in some way best suited for life in a certain type of water, and even in a particular area.

Some kinds of fishes can live only in salt water; others only in fresh. Some do equally well in either fresh or salt water, while fewer still divide their time between the two.

Some fishes spend their lives swimming close to the surface in the blue waters of the open sea. Others are found only in dark waters two miles or more deep. But the greatest variety is found in shallow, tropical seas. As many as a thousand species may live in only a few square miles of coral sea, while an area the same size in a cold, northern sea may harbour no more than a dozen kinds.

In contrast, the number of individuals of one kind of fish found in cold seas may be astonishingly large.

Tropical seas contain the greatest variety of fishes. Cold seas, however, are richer in individuals of a species. This is due primarily to seasonal upwellings of water that mix into the sea the rich nutrients spread over the bottom. As the sun warms the water and light reaches depths darkened during the long winter months, the sea "blooms" with plankton — tiny plants and animals that are the basic food of all fishes. Those few kinds of fishes that are adapted to life in cold waters have little competition for this abundance of food, and so they feed in these vast pastures of the sea and become fat and plentiful (see PLANKTON).

In fresh water, too, some kinds of fishes can live only in cold, swift streams, while

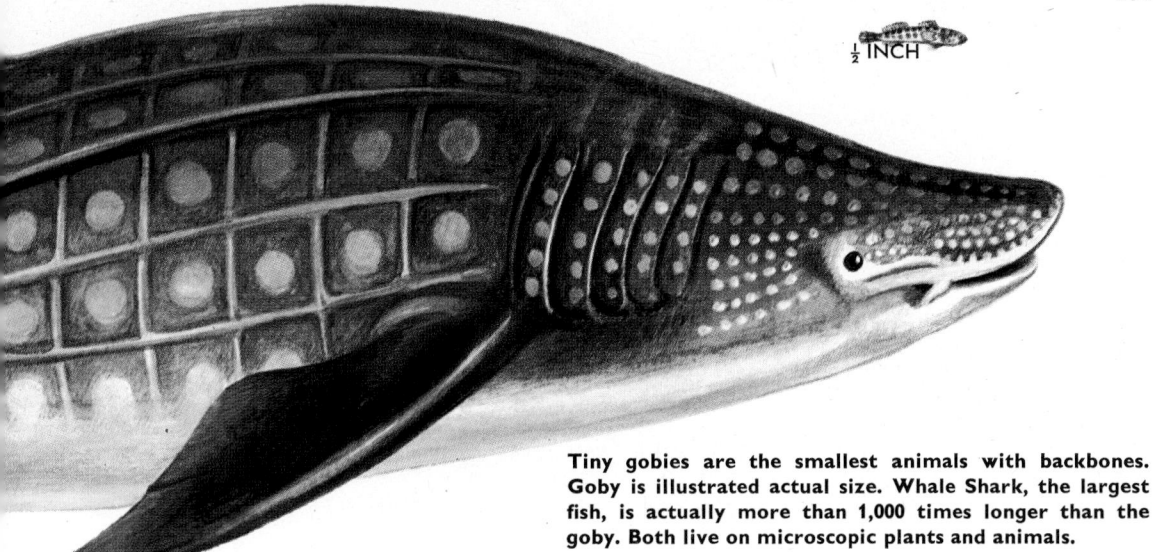

Tiny gobies are the smallest animals with backbones. Goby is illustrated actual size. Whale Shark, the largest fish, is actually more than 1,000 times longer than the goby. Both live on microscopic plants and animals.

others are confined to warm, sluggish rivers or stagnant pools. As in the sea, the greatest number of species is found in warm waters, but the schools of a single kind of fish are generally larger in cold waters.

Some species live in strange places. There are fresh-water fishes that thrive in hot springs where the temperature of the water is seldom less than 100 degrees Fahrenheit. Others, blind and colourless, live in the total darkness of cave waters. Blind gobies of

the Pacific hide beneath rocks, clinging to them as tightly as snails. A little South American catfish lives in the gill chambers of larger fishes; it chews on their gills and feeds on the blood that oozes out. There is a fish that lives in the gut of the sea-cucumber, and another that spends its life darting about in the midst of the dangerous tentacles of the Portuguese man-of-war. A colourful fish of the West Indies makes its home inside the shell of a living conch.

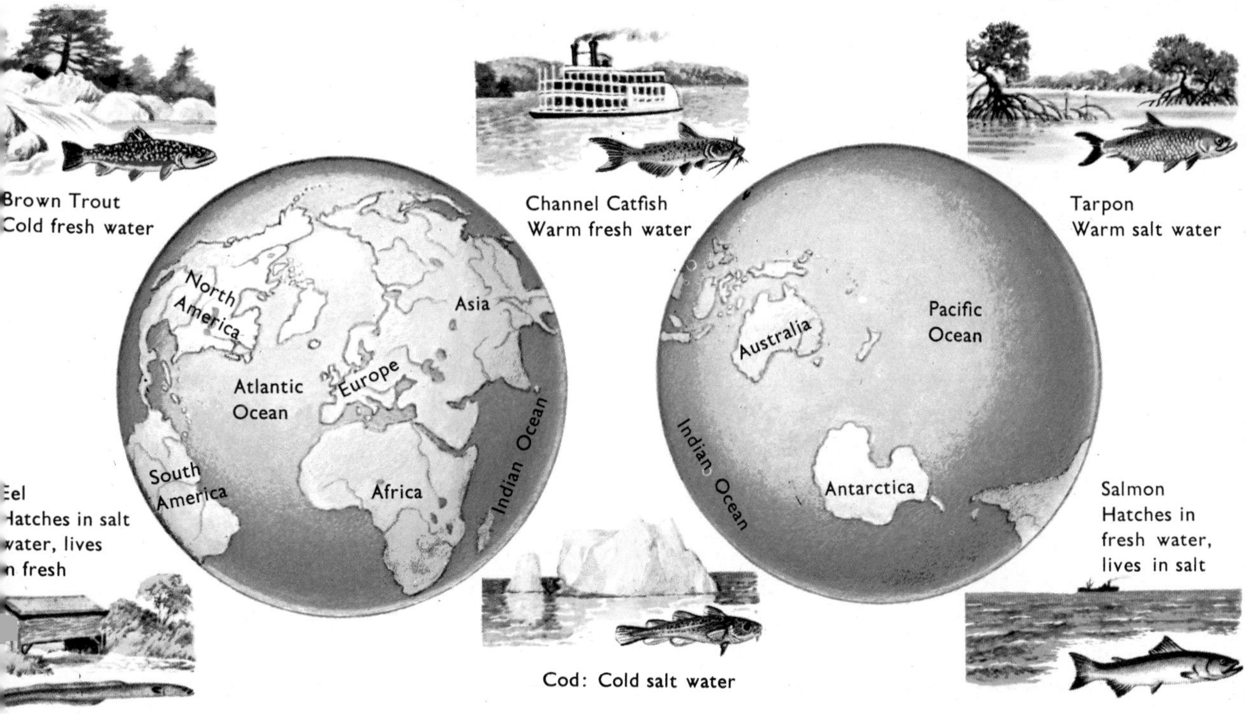

Brown Trout
Cold fresh water

Channel Catfish
Warm fresh water

Tarpon
Warm salt water

North America

Asia

Atlantic Ocean

Europe

Australia

Pacific Ocean

Indian Ocean

South America

Africa

Indian Ocean

Antarctica

Eel
Hatches in salt water, lives in fresh

Salmon
Hatches in fresh water, lives in salt

Cod: Cold salt water

still others hold on to rocks with suckers.

Sea-horses are unusual sights when out of their natural surroundings, but are really hard to see among the waving, feathery seaweeds where they normally live. Sargussum fishes are virtually invisible in the floating masses of brown sargussum weeds where they make their homes.

Males of one kind of deep-sea angler fish

A hooked Atlantic Sailfish thrills game fishermen by leaping high and "tail-walking" across the surface.

Four-winged Flying fish skims along the surface of the sea, sometimes for distances of a quarter of a mile, before plunging into the water again.

Some fishes bury themselves in the sand or mud, to hide from enemies or to lie in wait for prey. Some burrow in head-first, others tail-first. Flat-bodied fishes wriggle back and forth until the sand and mud, stirred up by their efforts, settles over them. There is a small fish that literally "swims" through soft mud, almost as easily and rapidly as other fishes move through water.

There are fishes that are found only in the raging torrents of mountain streams. Some, slim and pencil-like, creep about in the holes and crevices beneath rocks. Others have adhesive discs on their bellies, and

are dwarfs compared to their mates. Early in their lives they fasten themselves to a female's body, and then grow attached there. The tissues of the two fishes fuse, and the male loses its ability to carry out many of its normal functions. For the rest of his life, the male is a parasite on the female, which may eventually weigh a thousand times more than her parasitic mate.

Remoras have sucking discs on top of their head. With these they fasten themselves to sharks, turtles or other creatures. Ancient myths credit remoras with the ability to hold back ships at sea; hence, one of their common names is Ship-holder.

Some fishes die almost immediately, if they are taken out of the water. Others, such as the African Lungfish, live out of water for many months in protective cocoons. Eels travel overland, crawling through wet grass.

Flat-fishes jet-propel themselves upwards from the bottom by squirting water through the gill-opening on their underside.

Fishes swim fast by wagging their bodies rapidly from side to side. Long, slim fishes, such as the eel at right, also swim in this manner. Their wriggling bodies make "S" shapes as a snake's does.

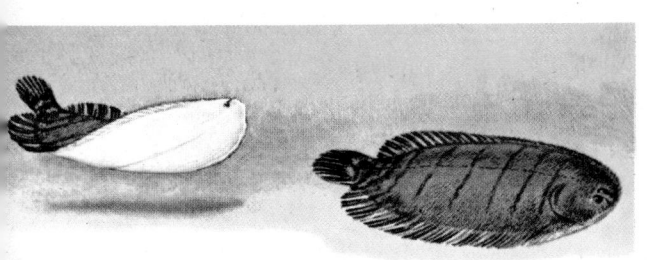

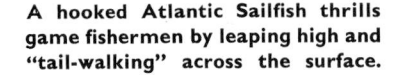

Gobies and blennies skip along the rocks from one tidal pool to another. The Climbing Perch, a strange fish found in Asia, prowls for hours among roots and over mud flats in search of food. Even when the Climbing Perch is in the water, it must surface from time to time to gulp air in order to survive.

HOW FISHES SWIM. Long, eel-like fishes swim by wriggling their bodies, much as a snake does when it crawls rapidly. Their bodies make a series of flowing "S" shapes as they move through the water.

Other fishes use only their fins for swimming. Rays, for example, undulate their broad and wing-like pectoral fins and appear to fly through the water. They are among the most graceful creatures in the sea. Trunkfishes, their bodies immovable in their shell-like outer covering, also swim, awkwardly, by using only their fins.

Almost all fishes can employ jet propulsion to give them a fast start. They do this by expelling the water forcefully from their gills. This shoots them forward. Flat-fishes often use this method for making a fast get-away. They seem to explode from the bottom,

imitated by designers of boats, aeroplanes and cars in trying to achieve greater speeds.

These fishes derive their driving power from the mass of W-shaped muscles that extend from their gill covers to their tails. These muscles are the part of the fish that we eat; they are the familiar flakes or chunks that separate from each other easily after a fish is fried or baked.

The typical fish swims by moving its whole body from side to side. This is actually the same kind of movement used by long-bodied, eel-like fishes; but fishes with short bodies make incomplete "S" shapes that cannot be distinguished easily. These fishes use their fins only as brakes or for steering. Their fins also help them to "stand still", for the water forced from their gills as they breathe tends to push them forward.

Among the fastest fishes in the sea are the mackerels, tunas, sailfishes and marlins. Many of these swift swimmers can fold their

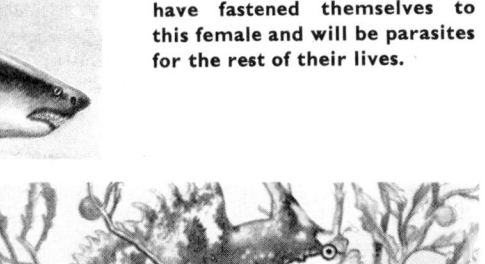

males

Four male Ceratioid Anglerfish have fastened themselves to this female and will be parasites for the rest of their lives.

Remoras have a powerful suction disc formed from their first dorsal fin. They ride through the sea attached to sharks and other creatures.

and, by the time the stirred up debris has settled, they are out of sight.

Ordinarily, of course, you think of one of the sleek and streamlined, fast ocean swimmers when you think of a fish. Coated with slime to help reduce the friction, its torpedo-shaped body can slip through the water with little resistance. This is the shape

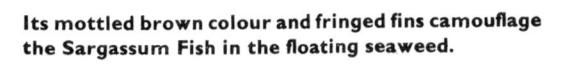

Its mottled brown colour and fringed fins camouflage the Sargassum Fish in the floating seaweed.

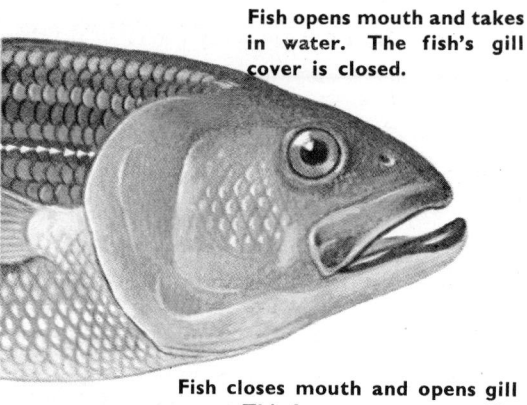

Fish opens mouth and takes in water. The fish's gill cover is closed.

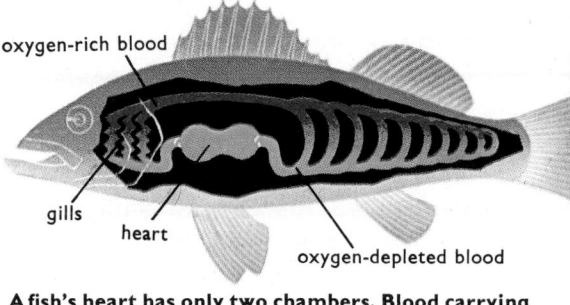

oxygen-rich blood

gills

heart

oxygen-depleted blood

A fish's heart has only two chambers. Blood carrying oxygen from gills, which serve the same function as lungs of higher animals, moves through body at a lower pressure (less rapidly) than with more efficient four-chambered heart possessed by the warm-blooded animals.

Fish closes mouth and opens gill cover. This forces water over gills.

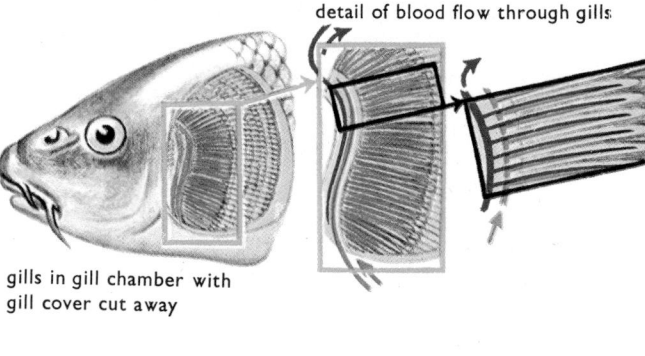

detail of blood flow through gills

gills in gill chamber with gill cover cut away

dorsal fins into grooves on their backs, so that even the slight resistance of these thin and knife-like fins is eliminated when they are travelling at top speed.

Many fishes jump, to escape being caught by some other fish that is chasing them or to hurdle barriers in their paths. Others, such as mullets, appear to jump for the sheer joy of it. Many kinds jump when hooked, and these make the most thrilling catches.

Some fishes make their jumps by surging up from deep water. Others swim close to the surface, then suddenly turn their noses skyward and give a powerful thrust with their tails, in order to attain enough speed to take to the air. Sail-fishes can leap more than 10 feet. Flying-fishes glide as far as a quarter of a mile along the surface of the sea.

Once it was believed that a fish's tail-fin was essential to its swimming. Tails do vary greatly in size and shape, and many fishes get a great amount of driving force from their tails, but experiments have demonstrated that a fish can swim even after its tail-fin is cut off. If all its fins are cut off,

a fish can continue to swim, though steering and keeping itself upright become difficult.

Sharks, which have poor control of their fins, can swim swiftly in a straight line, but have difficulty in stopping or turning, as do bony fishes with large, heavy pectoral fins.

Many fishes have unusual ways of swimming, too. Sea-horses, for example, swim in a "standing up" position. They get their swimming power from the wavelike motion of their dorsal fins. An African catfish swims upside down. Needle-fishes and halfbeaks skitter across the surface with the front halves of their bodies held high out of the water, and their tails still submerged, wagging rapidly. Other members of the same family swim with their heads down and their tails up.

A fish's remarkable air-bladder, which sometimes serves as a lung and sometimes as a sound amplifier, also assists the fish in swimming. By varying the amount of gas contained in its air-bladder, a fish can adjust its body weight to equal the weight of water its body has displaced. The effect of

this is to make the fish have almost no weight at all; it neither floats nor sinks, but remains suspended at whatever level it desires; all its energy can be used for swimming. Flat-fishes, such as flounders, have no air-bladders, so they sink directly to the bottom. Sharks also have no air-bladders. They tend to sink, too, but the abundance of oil in their livers makes it easier for them to float.

HOW FISHES BREATHE. Fishes breathe oxygen, like other living creatures. The small amount of oxygen dissolved in the water is absorbed into their blood through their gills.

Watch a fish in an aquarium. It opens and shuts its mouth constantly, as though drinking in gulps of water. Each time the fish opens its mouth, water flows into its mouth cavity. The gill covers, located on each side of its head, just behind the eyes, remain closed while its mouth is open. The mouth is then closed, and the water is forced out through the gill openings, passing over the gill filaments on the way. Other fishes depend on their swimming to cause water to flow over their gills, and such fish will die if they do not continue swimming.

The circulation of water through a fish's mouth and out of its gill openings is easily observed by putting a drop of food colouring into the water just in front of the fish's mouth. The coloured water disappears as it is drawn into the fish's mouth. A moment later it is forced out through the gill openings.

When the fish is resting, it gulps water slowly; but if it begins to swim, or becomes excited, the fish opens and shuts its mouth more rapidly, using oxygen at a faster rate, and needs to get more of it — the fish is, in fact, "breathing hard".

Each gulp of water passes over the fish's gills. These are much-divided, thin-walled filaments where blood vessels lie close to the surface. The gills of a living fish are bright red, because of the numerous blood vessels.

In these gills an exchange of gases takes place. This is part of the process called respiration. Carbon dioxide, waste material released by the cells of the fish's body and carried by the blood, is given off by the gills. At the same time, dissolved oxygen in the water is absorbed into the blood and transported to the fish's body cells. A fish's gills expose so great a surface area, and are so efficient, that 75 per cent of the oxygen contained in the water is removed during the brief time the gills are bathed in each gulp of water. By contrast, we withdraw less than 25 per cent of oxygen available to us in each breath.

Different fish need different amounts of oxygen, and this often determines the sort

Rays undulate their broad pectoral fins and appear to fly through the water.
Eels form an "S" shape.

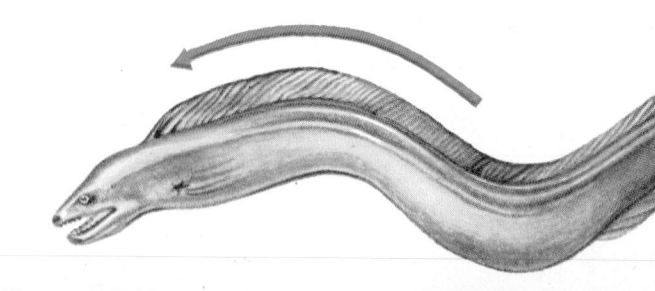

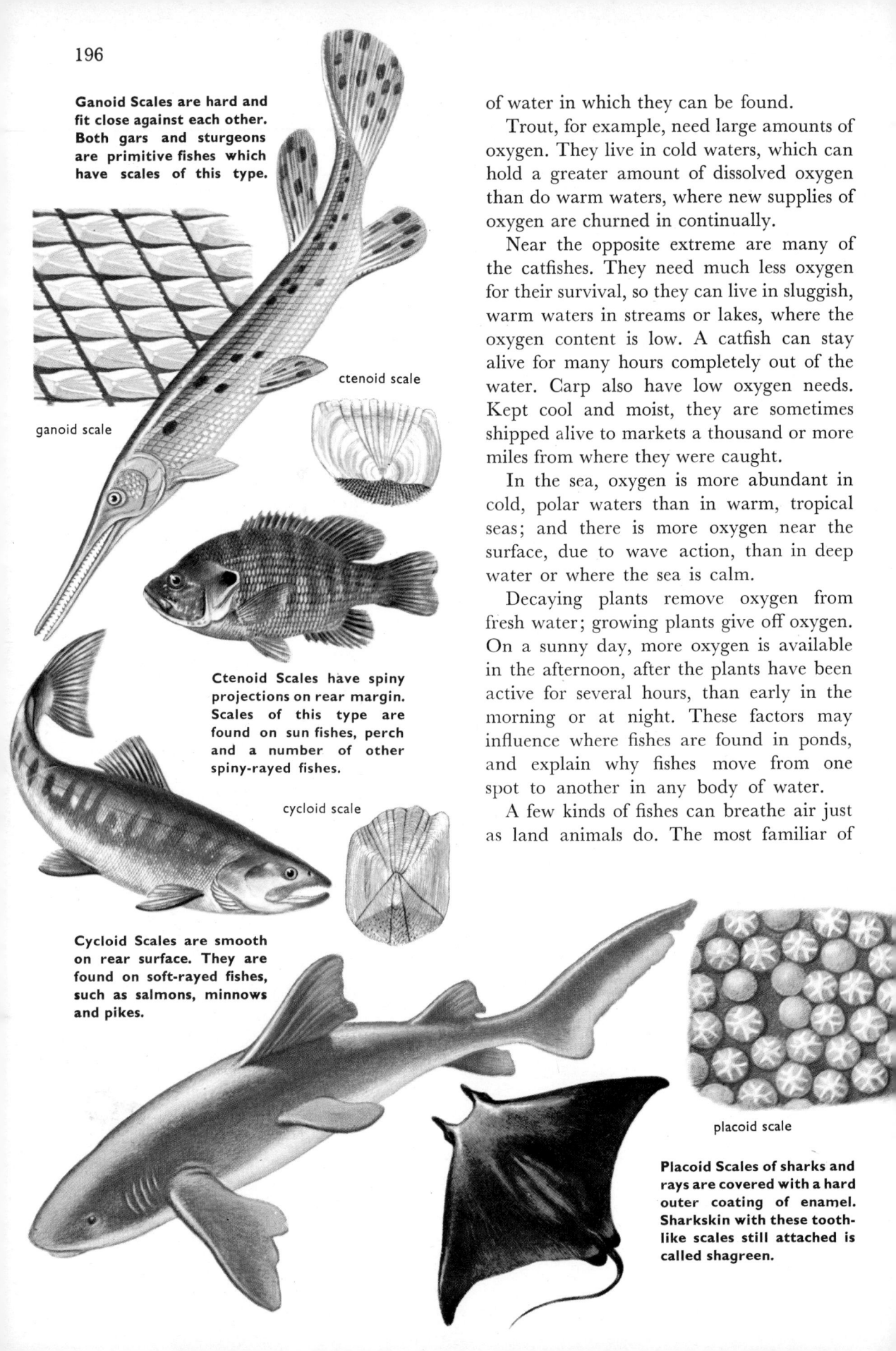

Ganoid Scales are hard and fit close against each other. Both gars and sturgeons are primitive fishes which have scales of this type.

ganoid scale

ctenoid scale

Ctenoid Scales have spiny projections on rear margin. Scales of this type are found on sun fishes, perch and a number of other spiny-rayed fishes.

cycloid scale

Cycloid Scales are smooth on rear surface. They are found on soft-rayed fishes, such as salmons, minnows and pikes.

placoid scale

Placoid Scales of sharks and rays are covered with a hard outer coating of enamel. Sharkskin with these tooth-like scales still attached is called shagreen.

of water in which they can be found.

Trout, for example, need large amounts of oxygen. They live in cold waters, which can hold a greater amount of dissolved oxygen than do warm waters, where new supplies of oxygen are churned in continually.

Near the opposite extreme are many of the catfishes. They need much less oxygen for their survival, so they can live in sluggish, warm waters in streams or lakes, where the oxygen content is low. A catfish can stay alive for many hours completely out of the water. Carp also have low oxygen needs. Kept cool and moist, they are sometimes shipped alive to markets a thousand or more miles from where they were caught.

In the sea, oxygen is more abundant in cold, polar waters than in warm, tropical seas; and there is more oxygen near the surface, due to wave action, than in deep water or where the sea is calm.

Decaying plants remove oxygen from fresh water; growing plants give off oxygen. On a sunny day, more oxygen is available in the afternoon, after the plants have been active for several hours, than early in the morning or at night. These factors may influence where fishes are found in ponds, and explain why fishes move from one spot to another in any body of water.

A few kinds of fishes can breathe air just as land animals do. The most familiar of

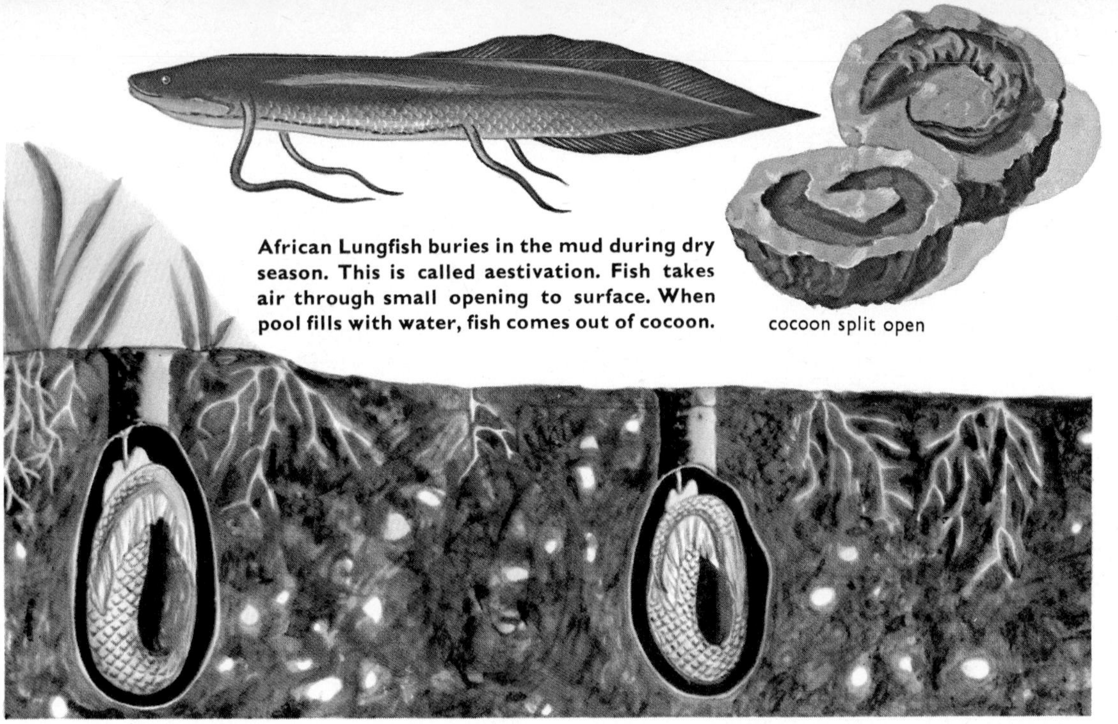

African Lungfish buries in the mud during dry season. This is called aestivation. Fish takes air through small opening to surface. When pool fills with water, fish comes out of cocoon.

cocoon split open

these are the lungfishes, living in the tropics of Africa, South America and Australia. Their "lungs" are their air-bladders, richly supplied with blood vessels.

When a lungfish needs oxygen, it comes to the surface and gulps in a new supply, taking it directly from the air. A lungfish will actually drown if it stays under water.

In dry seasons, the stagnant pools where lungfishes live dry up. The African Lungfish burrows into the mud at the bottom and secretes a slimy, protective coating over its body. A small air-hole connects with the surface through the mud-casing over it, and through this the lungfish continues to breathe air. When the rains come again and the pools fill with water, the lungfishes wriggle out of their strange cocoons.

SCALES. A typical fish's body is covered by a protective coat of scales which usually overlap each other like roof-tiles. On the outside of these scales there is a thin, tight-fitting membrane containing glands that secrete slime. The slime may help to reduce the friction of the fish's body as it moves through the water, and it also provides a barrier to disease organisms that might attack the fish. It is this slime that makes a fish slippery and hard to hold.

The total number of scales on a fish's body remains the same throughout its life. New scales are added, however, to replace any that are lost, and each scale increases in size as the fish grows larger. Periods of rapid growth or lack of growth are recorded on the scales as ridges and spaces. These are like the annual rings in the trunk of a tree.

Biologists learn much about a fish's past history by studying its scales. For one thing, they can determine its age, since the seasons of abundant food and fast growth are easily distinguished from the periods of food shortage and slow growth. These usually correspond to summer and winter, a pair of rings equalling one year's growth. Between these most prominent lines there are smaller lines that reveal other events in the fish's life. An expert fish-scale reader can tell at what age the fish spawned for the first time,

Shark's spiny scale resembles a tooth in structure. Each scale is covered with enamel and has a pulp cavity. The shark's teeth are similar.

TEETH OF SHARK

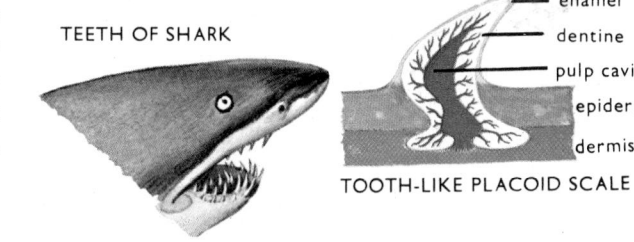

enamel

dentine

pulp cavity

epidermis

dermis

TOOTH-LIKE PLACOID SCALE

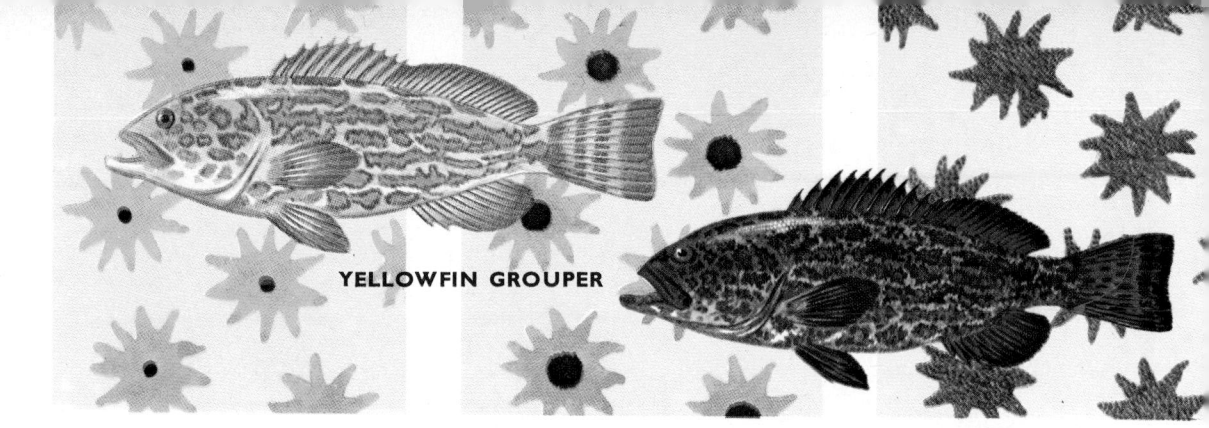

YELLOWFIN GROUPER

With the pigment pulled to the centre of its star-shaped chromatophores (left), this Yellowfin Grouper is a light colour. To the right, the pigment has spread throughout the cell so that the fish is dark.

how often it has migrated, if it has been sick, and which years have been its best. The age of fishes scale-less can be determined by counting similar growth rings in certain bones—but, to do this, the fish must be killed. A few scales, however, can be removed from a fish without harming it seriously.

Counting rows of scales, and the number of scales in rows, on the fish's body is also a method used to tell one species from another. Often two young fish of the same size will look much alike, but a scale count will reveal that they are different species. For example, the Ballan Wrasse has more than 40 scales, the Corkwing has less.

Fishes do not have scales when they first hatch from the egg, but their scales begin to grow within a few weeks. Most catfishes never grow scales; they remain "naked", or smooth-skinned, throughout their lives, protected by their slippery skins — which are often tough and leathery — and by the

A flounder matches its background by varying the size of the white and dark patches on its body. A blinded flounder is unable to make these changes.

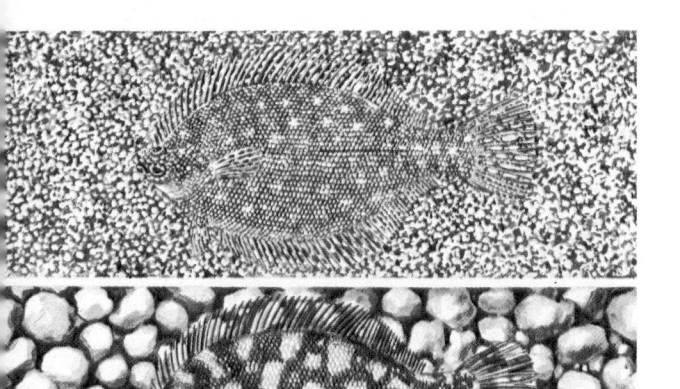

sharp spines in their fins. Paddlefish have no scales. Sculpins have only a few, which are greatly modified. Mackerels have very tiny scales. Swordfish have scales when they are young, then lose them as their "bills" develop. Trout have tiny scales covered by their thick skin. Eels, too, have widely separated scales that are buried deep in their skin. In contrast, a Tarpon's large, silvery scales may measure several inches across.

Fish scales are of several different types. Most bony fishes have the familiar thin, shingle-like scales. Some of these have stiff spines along their rear margins; other scales have smooth rear margins.

Garfishes — primitive modern fishes — are covered with hard, almost bony scales. Those of a sturgeon are enlarged and shell-like, so that they form ridges of armour along the sturgeon's back and sides.

Sharks have still another type of scale; they are enamel-coated and have a dentine core, similar in structure to our teeth. Sharkskin, with these small, hard scales still attached, is called shagreen; it was once used to make non-slipping covers on knife and sword handles and as sand paper.

COLOURS. The familiar silvery colour of a fish's scales is due to a deposit of guanine, a by-product of protein digestion. In some fishes this deposit is heavy and almost chalky white. In others the crystals act as prisms, breaking up the light that strikes them and producing metallic, iridescent hues. The pigment colours, blacks, greens, yellows, reds, and their various combinations — are

made by special cells, called chromatophores. These numerous star-shaped cells are scattered throughout the fish's skin.

By varying the concentration of pigment in these cells many kinds of fishes can change their colours to suit their moods or to match their surroundings. The pigment in a chromatophore cell can shrink until only a small spot is visible. At other times the pigment expands and fills the whole cell.

Sometimes these colour changes take place rapidly. They can occur as a fish swims from one type of background to another, or a fish may flush with colour at the sight of an enemy, as some male tropical fishes do when they see another male. Often the colours seem to ripple as they change from one colour to another. This may happen when a fish has just been caught and is brought into the boat. This sort of colour change is often seen in dolphins, caused apparently by fright or shock (see DOLPHINS).

When a fish is angry, its colour generally becomes darker. When it is frightened, its colours become paler, and it is also more pale than usual when it is ill.

Colour changes are often brought about by sight, for a blinded fish is unable to make colour changes to match its environment.

During winter, fish grow very slowly, and so "growth rings" on scales are close together. They are almost a solid line. In summer, fish grow rapidly, and rings are far apart. By counting the number of winter rings, we can determine the fish's age.

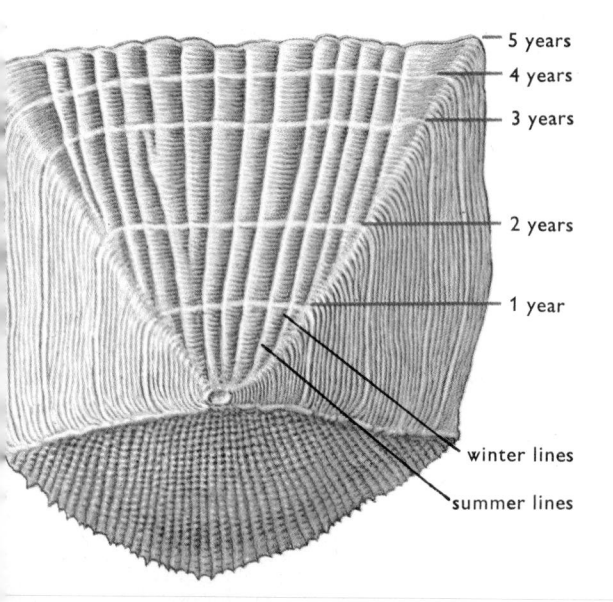

- 5 years
- 4 years
- 3 years
- 2 years
- 1 year
- winter lines
- summer lines

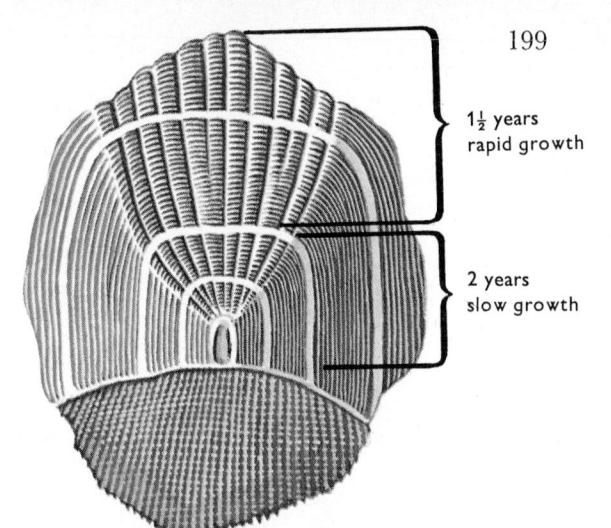

1½ years rapid growth

2 years slow growth

Scale from a 3½-year-old salmon shows how salmon grew slowly during its two years spent in fresh water, then grew much more rapidly in the sea.

This is demonstrated by flounders. Blinded, a flounder remains the same colour, no matter on what background it is placed. Normally, however, a flounder is able to match its surroundings with remarkable accuracy. Over a sand bottom it becomes a yellowish-brown hue but when it moves over a dark-coloured bottom, its colour changes to almost black — and, most remarkable, if the flounder swims over an area mottled with dark and light, it becomes spotted too. Experiments show that flounders can almost achieve the square-checked pattern of a chess board. Nor are the flounders restricted to black, brown and white; some can become reddish, yellow, or green.

Normally a flounder is white on its underside, for all its pigment cells are located on the top surface, but a flounder put in a glass-bottomed aquarium, with lights shining through from below, also acquires pigmentation on its belly side.

SENSES. Most fishes are near-sighted. Since light does not penetrate far in water, distance vision would be of little use to the ordinary fish. But at close ranges a fish can see clearly.

The lens in the human eye is slightly curved and equipped with special muscles which can change its shape so that the eye can be focused on objects that are close or far away. But the lens in a fish's eye is almost

Archer Fish are accurate marksmen at distances up to four feet.

Barbels, or whiskers, around a fish's mouth are used as tasters or feelers in finding food.

cod

sturgeon

catfish

drum

Lateral lines, distinctively shaped and of various lengths, are important sensory organs.

spherical, and since its shape cannot be changed, its focus is pre-set for seeing nearby objects. Some fishes do have muscles attached to the lens, so that it can be moved back and forth to get a sharper focus.

Light rays travel at a greater speed in air than in water, which is more dense. Therefore, the rays are bent as they pass at an angle from the one medium to the other. A man must remember this when shooting a fish with a bow and arrow, or when casting a lure directly to a fish, for the fish is really closer than it appears to be. The light rays are not bent as they travel from the water to a point directly overhead, so that viewed from straight above, the fish is located exactly where it appears to be.

Also because of the bending of the light rays, the fish looks from water at objects in air through a sort of circular window. The circle's outer edge is formed where light rays strike the surface at an angle great enough for them to be bent back into the water again. Objects just within the fish's range of vision appear around the edge of this window, while those directly overhead appear in its centre.

One of the oddities in the fish world is the Four-eyed Fish, which lives in the shallow water of muddy streams in Central America. Its bulbous eyes, located on top of its head like a frog's, are always half in the water and half out of the water. It really has only two eyes, but they function as four because of their internal structure.

The lens in the Four-eyed Fish's eye is egg-shaped rather than spherical. When

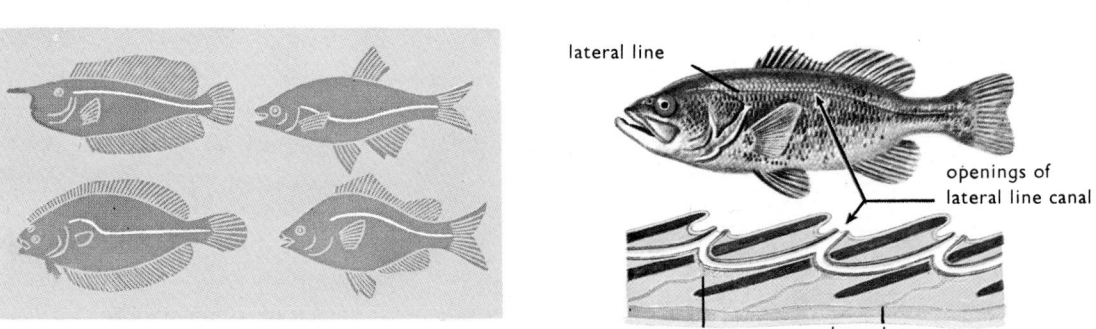

lateral line

openings of lateral line canal

sensory organ

lateral nerve

LONGITUDINAL SECTION OF LATERAL LINE

the fish looks under the surface of the water, light rays pass through the entire length of this lens. The Four-eyed Fish's vision in water is as near-sighted as that of any other fish, but when it looks out into the air, light passes through the shorter width of the lens. This gives the fish good distance vision in the air.

Most fishes have no true eyelids. Their eyes are constantly bathed in water, and so they have no need for eyelids to keep their eyes moist, which is the principal function of our eyelids.

Some sharks, however, have a semi-transparent membrane which moves across the eyes. This slides over the shark's eyes to protect them from sand, mud, or other debris stirred up as it feeds on the bottom. It is known as a nictitating membrane.

Experiments have demonstrated that fishes are able to recognise colours. Black bass, for example, quickly learn to distinguish the colour red when it is associated with food. Then, in order, they learn green, blue and yellow. There is a good possibility that some fishes may prefer one colour to another, or that water conditions will at times make one colour more easily recognised than at others.

Archer Fish are outstanding examples of fish that have excellent vision. They shoot

their prey by hitting them with drops of water squirted forcefully from their mouth. At distances up to four feet, they are deadly accurate and can knock spiders from their webs, hovering insects from the air, or frogs on the bank.

The eyes of fishes that live in the dark depths of the ocean are frequently greatly reduced in size. Fishes that inhabit the dusky regions of the sea, generally have enlarged eyes so that they can utilise even the small amount of light that is available. Some of these fishes have, by comparative size, larger eyes than any other backboned animals, and fishes that live in the perpetual darkness of cave waters, either have very small eyes or no eyes at all.

Since it has no eyelids, a fish cannot

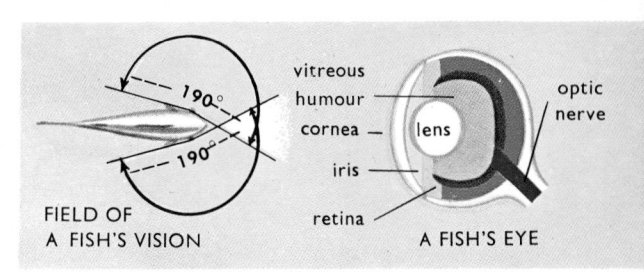

Fish's eyes on sides of head give it good vision towards rear and at sides, and a small area (shaded white) of binocular vision straight ahead.

Fish looks through a circular "window" on the surface of the water, since light rays that strike surface are bent back (dotted line) into the water again when they strike surface at enough angle. Everywhere beyond the point of refraction the surface appears opaque.

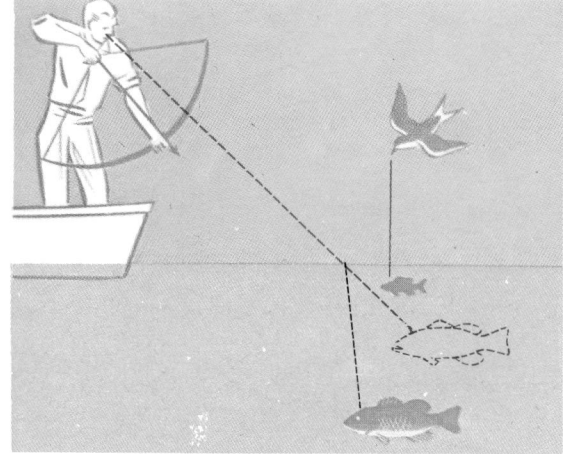

Fish appears to be along dotted red line, due to bending of light rays as they pass at an angle from water to less dense air. Light rays travelling directly to bird overhead are not bent.

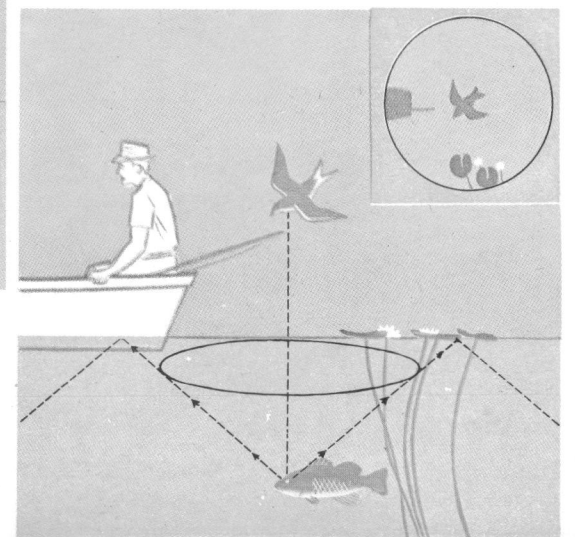

shut its eyes when it goes to sleep, and many fishes do sleep, or rest, at quite regular intervals. Schools of perch, for example, scatter every night, and the fish drop down to the bottom individually to rest. At daylight they assemble in schools again. Other fishes lie on their sides when they sleep. Some "stand up", or lean against rocks, or crawl into crevices. One eccentric fish dives into the soft bottom head-first when it wants to take a nap. A tropical parrot-fish secretes a mucous blanket all round itself at night, often spending an hour every evening preparing its "bed".

Fishes that have poor vision may make up for this drawback by having a better developed sense of taste or smell. Bullheads, for example, have taste buds distributed over their whole bodies. If a morsel of food is held near a bullhead's tail, it immediately begins opening and shutting its mouth, for it has tasted the food through its tail and is ready to eat.

Sharks also depend on their good sense of smell to locate their food, and will sometimes follow traces of an odour for long distances through the sea to its source.

The nerve-endings for the sense of smell are located in the fish's nostrils. These are blind openings at the end of the fish's nose and are not used at all for breathing. Exceptions are the stargazers, which spend much of their time buried in the sand or mud. Their mouths cannot be used to channel water over their gills; instead, they use their nostrils.

Most fishes are also able to hear sounds and can detect vibrations in the water. They learn to come to a particular spot to be fed when certain sounds are repeated day after day at feeding time. Thus, the ringing of a bell, the playing of the same music, or the sound of a man's voice, may soon become associated with food. Yet a fish has no external ears or ear openings. It does have, internally, small ear bones, and since sound waves travel better in water than in air, a fish can hear noises even though it has no external ear to help capture the vibrations.

The fish's lateral line contains sensory cells which open to the outside through pores. Through its lateral line the fish can determine the direction of currents of water, detect the presence of nearby objects through variation in water pressure, and also sense vibrations. This ability is useful to a fish in navigating at night or in murky waters, in keeping schooling fish together, and also in finding food or escaping enemies.

Finally, some fishes are far from being quiet creatures. They can make rasping, grunting, squeaking or squealing noises. Some make noises by rubbing together special bone extensions of the vertebrae. Other noises are made by vibrating muscles that are connected to the air-bladders

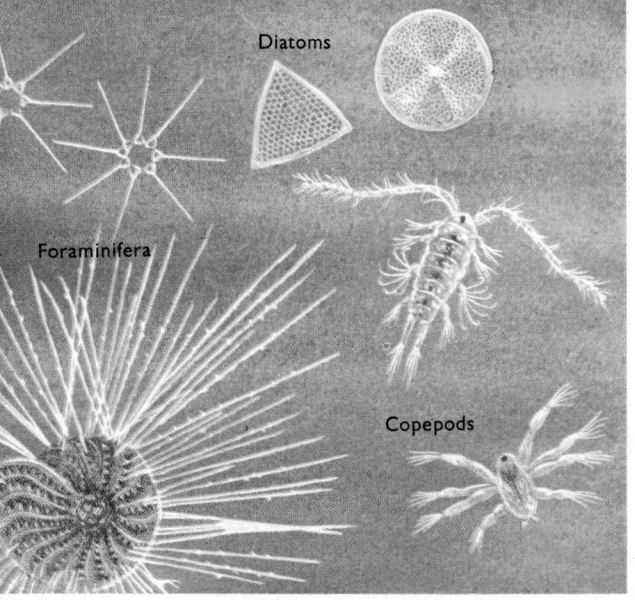

The plankton at left is magnified many times, for most of these tiny plants and animals are microscopic in size. As a basic food of fishes and other aquatic animals, they are the most important life in any body of water.

Plankton   Copepod   Smelt   Mackerel   Tuna

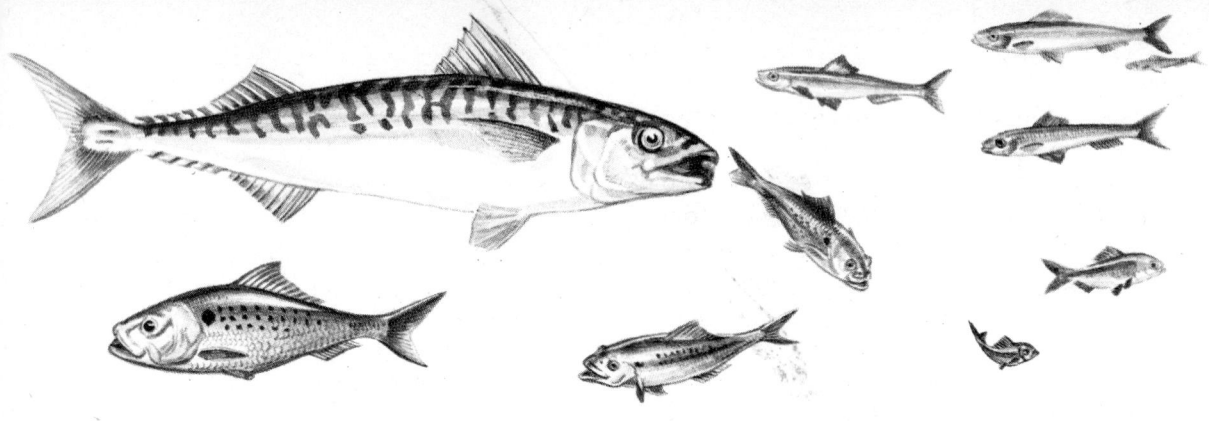

which amplify the vibrations. Still other fishes grind their teeth, their mouth cavities serving as the sound-box to amplify the noise. Sound-detecting devices lowered into the sea to pick up engine noises of submarines or other ships during World War II were frequently "jammed" by the noises of schools of fish. Many fishes make noises when they are caught.

WHAT FISHES EAT. Most fishes are flesh-eaters. They feed on smaller fishes or other aquatic animals. These, in turn, feed on still smaller creatures. Finally, the smallest plants and animals, those consisting of only a single cell, become food, too. These tiny plants and animals are the first step in the food chain.

These small plants and animals which float about in the water are called plankton. When conditions are right, billions of them — several tons to the acre — may be found in a body of water. Sometimes they "bloom" so abundantly that they colour the sea for hundreds of square miles. Similar blooms in small fresh-water lakes or ponds may use up all the oxygen and kill the fish.

These tiny bits of life, invisible to the naked eye, are the basic food of all fishes.

The illustration at the bottom of page 202 shows a simple food chain in the sea. Plankton is eaten by small crustaceans; these are eaten by successively larger fish. In the illustration, the plankton indirectly adds to the meal of a tuna and arrives at our table. Biologists estimate that it probably takes as much as five tons of plankton to be converted finally to one pound of tuna (see PLANKTON).

Some large fishes feed directly on these small plants and animals. Paddlefishes detect swarms of these tiny creatures with their sensitive snouts. Herrings strain them from the sea through their sieve-like gill-rakers. Bottom feeders sift them from the bottom oozes. Even giant Whale Sharks and Basking Sharks feed on plankton.

A plant-eating fish usually has a long, coiled intestine, perhaps ten times the length of the fish itself. Plant food is more difficult to digest than meat and requires longer processing. A flesh-eating fish has a short digestive tract, often shorter than the total length of its body.

Fish-eating fishes generally have mouths that fairly bristle with teeth. Many even have teeth on their tongues. Yet a fish does not chew its food as we do; it swallows its

Egg-shaped lens of the Four-eyed Fish permits fish to see in the air as well as in the water.

food whole, using its teeth only to grab and to hold the food, or to tear off chunks.

Some fishes have "teeth" in their throats, called pharyngeal teeth. These grinders are connected to the bony arches over their gills and are used to mash up plants or other food before it passes on into the fish's stomach.

Catfishes, which eat both living and dead foods, have numerous small teeth, and their strong jaws get a vice-like grip on anything that comes between them. Most fishes have medium-sized teeth which are large enough to catch and hold fish smaller than themselves. The Pike, however,

is a real "tiger" of fresh waters. It has a big mouth and numerous large, pointed teeth. These fishes will attack prey of any size. In salt water, sharks and barracudas are among the best equipped to attack prey their own size or larger.

The Eagle Ray is also called Clam Cracker, because of its flat, powerful teeth which crush the shells of oysters, clams, and other molluscs to get at the animals inside.

The teeth of tropical parrot-fishes are fused into sharp, powerful beaks, like a parrot's, used to bite off chunks of living coral. Butterfly fishes, pipe-fishes, and trumpet-fishes have long, tubular snouts which can be poked into coral crannies to suck out food. Swordfish, and other "billed" fishes, have no teeth. Parasitic Sea Lampreys have rasping, sucking mouths with which they bore holes in other fishes and suck out their body fluids.

Several kinds of fishes, such as the Torpedo Ray and the stargazers, have organs which can produce electricity to shock and stun prey, and also frighten attackers.

Nearly every body of water contains a few kinds of fishes that eat only plants, a larger number that eat only fishes or other aquatic animals, and a few kinds that are scavengers. An exception is the deep sea, where almost all fishes are carnivorous (see DEEP-SEA FISHES).

SPAWNING. There are a number of fishes which build nests in which to lay their eggs. A good example is the North American Bluegill Sunfish. As is often

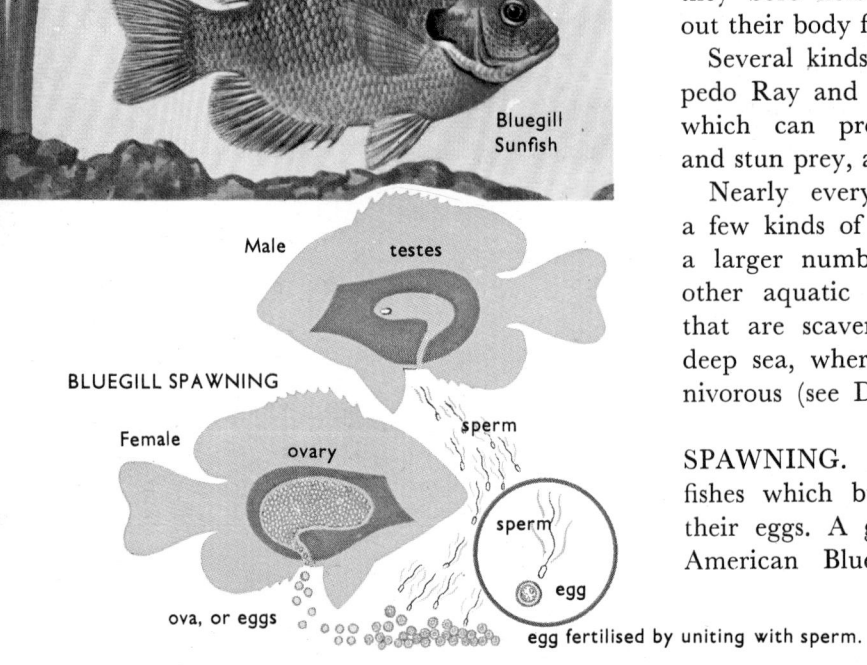

Bluegill Sunfish

BLUEGILL SPAWNING

Male — testes

Female — ovary

sperm

sperm

egg

ova, or eggs

egg fertilised by uniting with sperm.

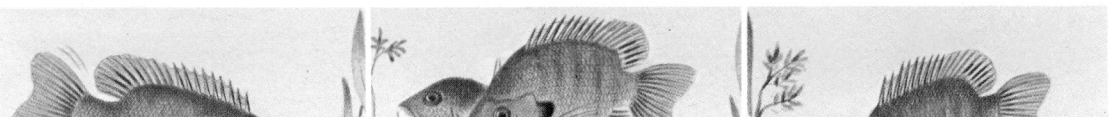

Male fans saucer-shaped nest . . . then squirts milt over eggs as they are laid . . . and guards until they hatch.

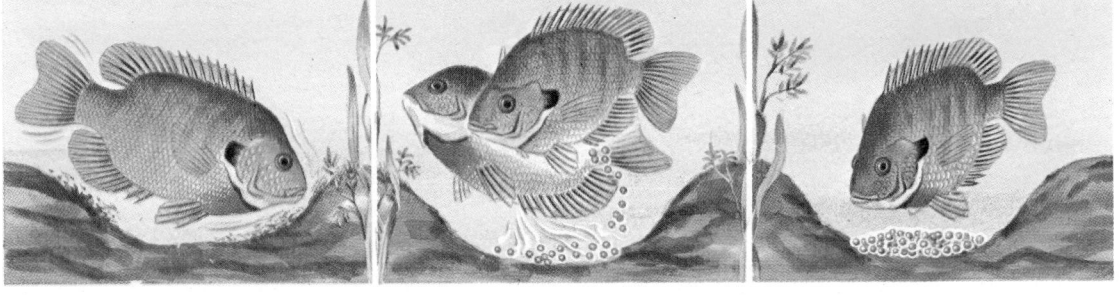

the case, it is the male which builds the nest and cares for the young.

Bluegills generally spawn in groups, each male selecting its own spot and fanning the area with its fins. As the fish fans, it turns its body first in one direction and then in the other, until, after much wriggling and sweeping, it has swept a saucer-shaped depression of silt and debris.

When the nest is complete, the male entices a female over the nest to lay her eggs. Average-sized females lay about 5,000 eggs; larger females may deposit as many as 50,000, often visiting several nests during a season. The male discharges milt (sperm) over the eggs as they are laid.

Each egg that unites with a sperm is fertilised and begins to grow, the tiny embryo receiving its nourishment from the egg's yolk.

Only the male stays at the nest. Frequently he fans the eggs, which prevents sand or silt from settling over them. His sweeping also stirs the water surrounding the eggs; and if any inquisitive creatures come too close to the nest, the male chases them away.

In about a week, the exact time depending on the temperature of the water and other factors, the eggs hatch and the nest becomes a swarming mass of tiny bluegills. The male continues to stand guard for several more days until the young finally venture to swim away. Then the male leaves, too.

Trout also build nests, but unlike the Bluegill, they do not guard their eggs. The female is the nest-builder. In a gravel area of stream rapids, she begins stirring and sweeping to make a depression in the bottom. The sediment moved by her fins and body washes away in the swift current.

After the hole has become several inches deep, the female lays her eggs there, and her mate fertilises them. Then the female swims upstream, just beyond the edge of the nest, and begins dislodging more rocks and pebbles. These wash into the hole until it is filled. The trout continue to work their way upstream, making more

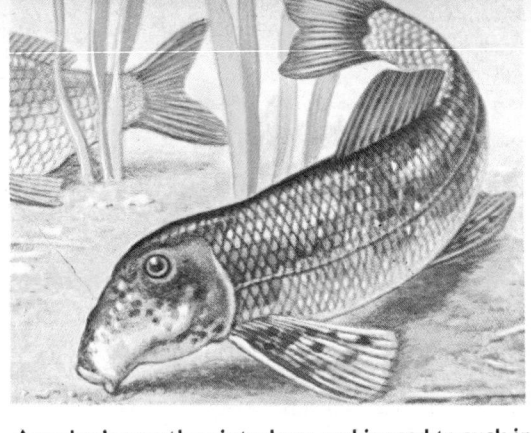

A sucker's mouth points down and is used to suck in bottom oozes.

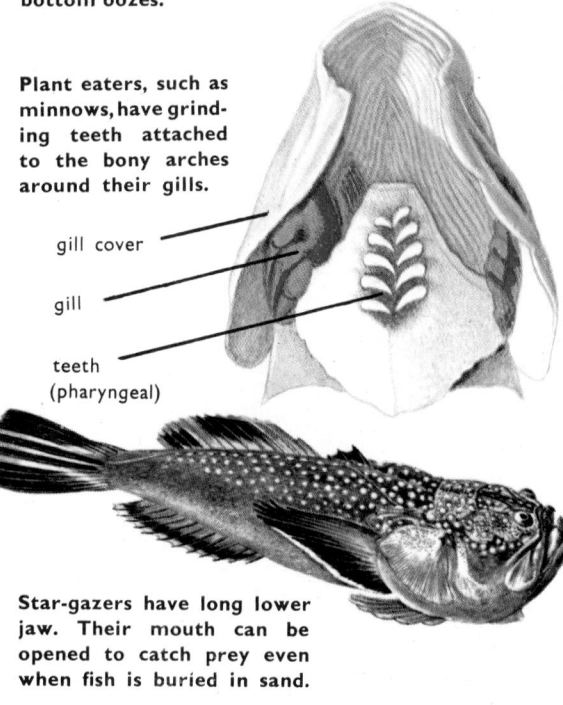

Plant eaters, such as minnows, have grinding teeth attached to the bony arches around their gills.

gill cover

gill

teeth (pharyngeal)

Star-gazers have long lower jaw. Their mouth can be opened to catch prey even when fish is buried in sand.

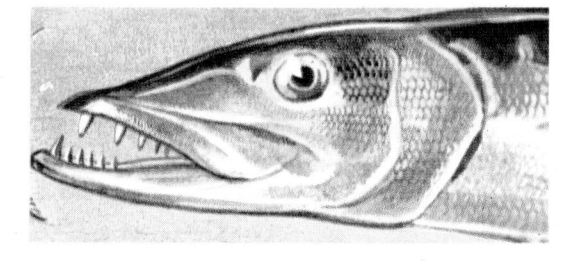

Barracuda's mouth is filled with long, sharp teeth, equipping this fish to hold prey of any size.

Barbels on sturgeon's snout drag along bottom. When it detects a morsel of food, the sturgeon sticks out its tube-like mouth and sucks it in.

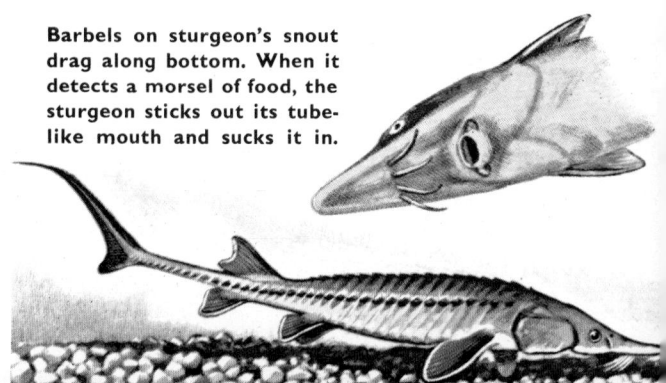

nests as they go. After several weeks or months, the eggs left in the nests hatch. The young trout, with yolk-sacs still in evidence, squirm out of the loose gravel.

Not all fishes build nests, of course, but some kinds give their eggs and young really unusual treatment. Sea Catfish males, for example, carry the eggs in their mouths, which serve as brood pouches. Even after the eggs have hatched, the males continue to carry the young fish in their mouths. As they grow larger, the young catfish spend more and more time outside, but if they are frightened, they dart inside to hide. Finally, when they are about two inches long, they leave the male and do not return. Then, for the first time since he began incubating the eggs, the male can eat a meal.

Many kinds of tropical fishes dig burrows in which they lay their eggs. A female South American catfish carries her eggs attached to a spongy adhesive disc on her belly. Sticklebacks make nests of sticks and debris, like a bird's nest, and the males will defend them with their lives.

Male Gourami fish blow bubbles which rise to the surface and form a floating raft, the bubbles stuck together with a mucus secreted by the fish. Then the female lays her eggs beneath the nest, and her mate picks them up and blows them up into bubbles, where they float about until they

hatch. The watchful male stays underneath the raft and chases away any intruders. Siamese Fighting Fish also deposit their eggs in bubble rafts.

Some fishes hide their eggs in shells, or beneath rocks or sticks, and others attach them to the bottom. Perch lay long strings of eggs which they stretch about in the underwater vegetation. Male seahorses carry their eggs and young in belly pouches, like opossums or kangaroos.

Fishes that build nests and protect their eggs and young do not lay as many eggs as those that give their eggs and young no attention at all. A female carp may lay several million eggs during a spawning season. Many of these eggs never hatch because they become covered with silt or debris, or are eaten by other fishes or aquatic creatures, but enough hatch to assure there being an abundance of carp.

Cods and mackerels also lay millions of eggs, discharging them into the open sea. Female sturgeon often carry more than a million eggs at a time, the weight of the eggs being as much as 25 per cent of the fish's total weight. Sturgeon eggs, salted and processed, are highly prized as caviar.

Still other fishes give birth to living young. The females carry the eggs inside their bodies until they have hatched, and then the young are born. Some sharks nourish their developing young by an

The male sea catfish uses its mouth as a brood pouch for the female's eggs. After the eggs hatch, the male continues to carry the young for several weeks.

Trout bury their eggs in loose gravel. When eggs hatch, the young trout squirm through the pebbles and swim along the bottom.

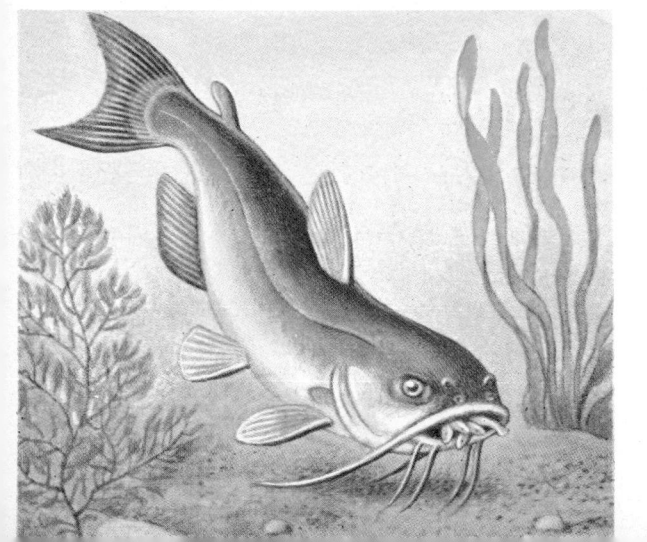

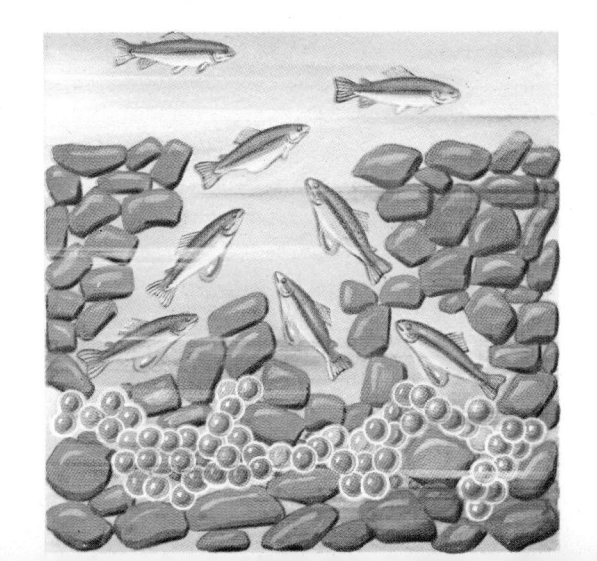

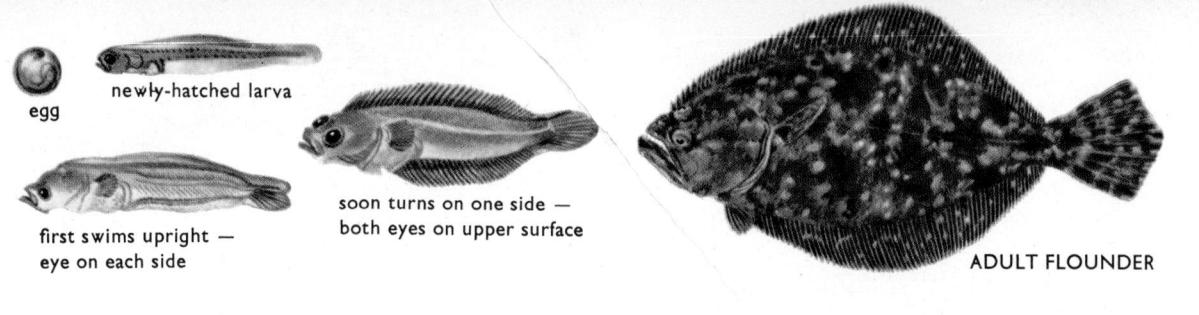

egg

newly-hatched larva

first swims upright — eye on each side

soon turns on one side — both eyes on upper surface

ADULT FLOUNDER

attachment of blood vessels similar to the placenta of mammals.

Fishes that give birth to their young produce the fewest number. Exceptions are the salt-water rock-fishes. A female rock-fish may give birth to as many as 30,000 young at a time. Less than an inch long when born, these tiny fish are at first nearly transparent, and they float about in the sea, carried along by the currents. Several weeks pass before young rock-fish

they transform into the parasitic adult stage, larvae of the Sea Lamprey live for as long as five years as burrowers in the soft mud on the bottom of fresh-water streams. Baby Bluegills, in contrast, begin to look like their parents within a few weeks after they emerge from the egg.

Under natural conditions few fishes ever die of old age. As soon as age weakens them, they become food for other fishes, or for some fish-eating bird, reptile or

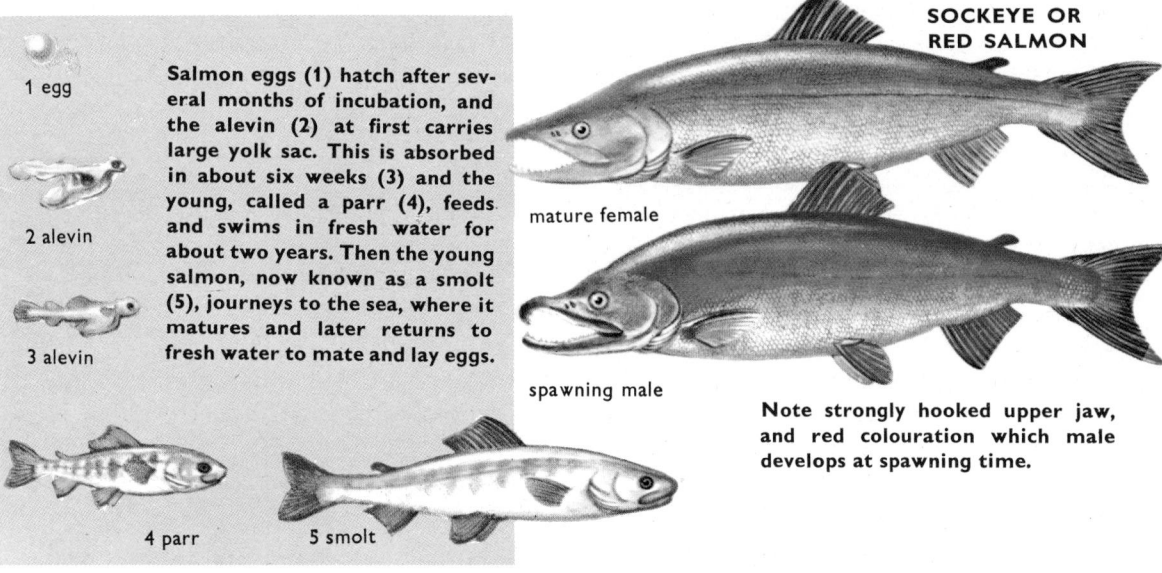

1 egg

Salmon eggs (1) hatch after several months of incubation, and the alevin (2) at first carries large yolk sac. This is absorbed in about six weeks (3) and the young, called a parr (4), feeds and swims in fresh water for about two years. Then the young salmon, now known as a smolt (5), journeys to the sea, where it matures and later returns to fresh water to mate and lay eggs.

2 alevin

3 alevin

4 parr

5 smolt

SOCKEYE OR RED SALMON

mature female

spawning male

Note strongly hooked upper jaw, and red colouration which male develops at spawning time.

acquire colour and begin to look at all like their parents.

Typically, a newly-hatched fish, called a larva, still carried with it an undigested supply of yolk from the egg. Its paunchy stomach makes it look much like a tadpole, but this built-in food supply gives it a day or two to adjust to the outside world, before it must begin hunting food for itself.

How long it takes for a young fish to mature varies greatly with the species, and also with the temperature of the water and the amount of food available. Before

mammal. It is known, however, that some kinds of fishes live past the age of 50 years. There are reliable records for eels and for the Wels, a giant European catfish. In the United States, a Carp that lived more than 60 years was reported.

Young flat-fishes make one of the most unusual transformations as they become adults. A young flat-fish begins life by swimming in an upright position like any other fish; its eyes are located one on each side of its head. Within a few days, however, the little fish begins to lean to one side.

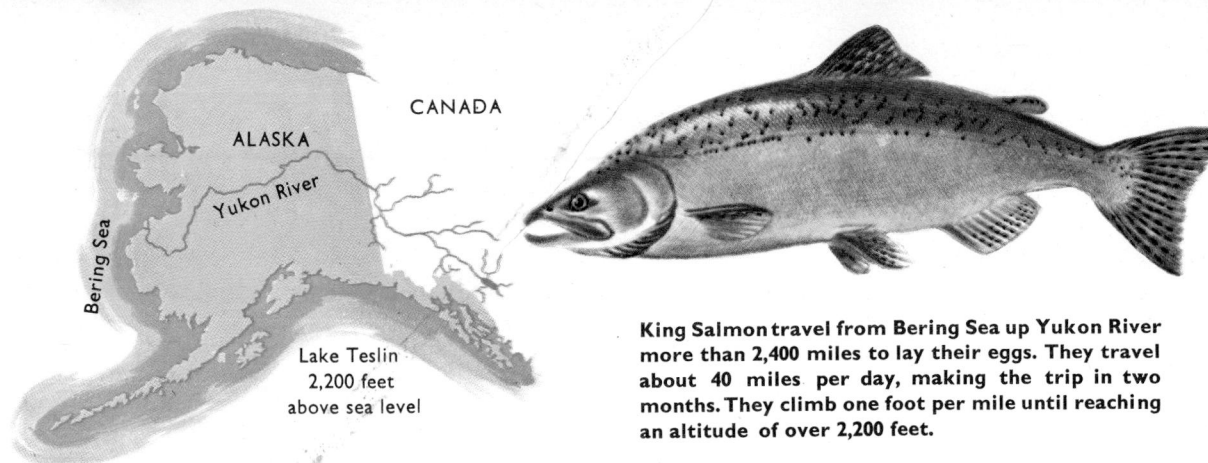

King Salmon travel from Bering Sea up Yukon River more than 2,400 miles to lay their eggs. They travel about 40 miles per day, making the trip in two months. They climb one foot per mile until reaching an altitude of over 2,200 feet.

Some kinds of flat-fishes always lean to the left, others always to the right. The eye on the side towards which the fish is leaning begins to move towards the opposite side of the fish's head. Within a few weeks, the flat-fish is lying completely on its side, and the eye is in a position close to the other eye.

The life stories of fishes, from the time the adults spawn until the eggs hatch and the young fish are mature, are filled with examples of adaptations which aid survival.

DAILY AND SEASONAL MOVES.

A fisherman knows that, in summer, he can catch certain fish in a lake or a pond early in the morning or late in the evening, when they are feeding in the shallows; but during the heat of the day, they stay in the cool, deep water far from shore.

Fishes do move from place to place to find food or to make themselves more comfortable. Some kinds never travel far from where they hatch. Others journey thousands of miles to find food or lay eggs.

King Salmon, for example, may swim more than two thousand miles from the ocean to the headwaters of mountain streams to lay their eggs. As soon as they

Grunion spawning on the sand at peak of tide.

Richard A. Boolootian

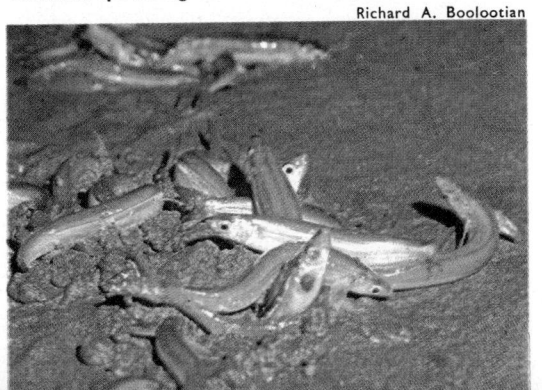

have spawned, they die, too exhausted to make the return trip to the sea.

Shad, sturgeons and smelts also travel from salt water to fresh water to spawn. American and European eels reverse the trip, however; they journey from fresh water to salt water to lay their eggs.

For many centuries people had no idea where eels spawned. All sorts of tales were told about how eels came into being. One belief was that they came from horsehairs that fell into the water. Finally, a Danish naturalist worked out the true story.

American and European Eels both spawn in nearly the same area of the Atlantic Ocean, at the edge of the Sargasso Sea. There each female lays millions of eggs, which the males fertilise. It is believed that both adults then die in the sea.

Newly-hatched eels are thin, transparent and leaf-like. Young eels, or glass-fish, do not at first resemble their parents. Soon they begin drifting along with the ocean currents towards fresh water.

Young American Eels drift towards North America, while the European Eels swim towards Europe — yet neither has ever seen its "home" before, and they have no guides to show them the way. For American Eels this is a trip of about 1,000 miles; for European eels, 3,000 miles or more. It takes nearly three years for the baby European Eels to make their journey, but American Eels get home in about a year. Astonishingly, the growth rates of the two species are so different that the young of each have developed to about the same

size when they reach their "home" waters.

At the mouths of rivers, the young eels develop thicker bodies and have begun to look very much like adults. At this stage they are called "elvers".

Males stay at the mouths of rivers and in coastal waters; females continue to swim upstream. Occasionally they crawl out of the water and slither through the wet grass to get from one stream to another, or to a lake or a pond. Eventually they settle down in a body of water where they feed and grow. Females may grow to a length of three feet or more in their fresh-water homes; males rarely become more than a third as long.

After several years, eels lose their greenish-yellow colour. They fade until almost white, and are then known as Silver Eels. At this stage they are ready to begin their trip to the sea to lay their eggs (see EELS).

FLAMINGOES are colourful birds that are most abundant in the tropics of Europe, Asia, Africa and America. They nest in shallow ponds, building a mound of mud on which to lay their eggs, or, rarely, two eggs. All the eggs of a colony hatch at about the same time. Males help in incubating the eggs.

Flamingoes are thought to be distantly related to geese, and make the same honking sounds. Newly-hatched flamingo chicks are downy white with short legs, and look like baby geese until their legs grow.

Flamingoes feed with their heads and bills upside down. The birds move forward, dragging the upper bill in the silt, while the tongue creates a suction that draws the marine organisms, on which the bird feeds, into the bill. The lower bill is held still, while the upper bill, joined to the skull by a flexible plate, moves slightly.

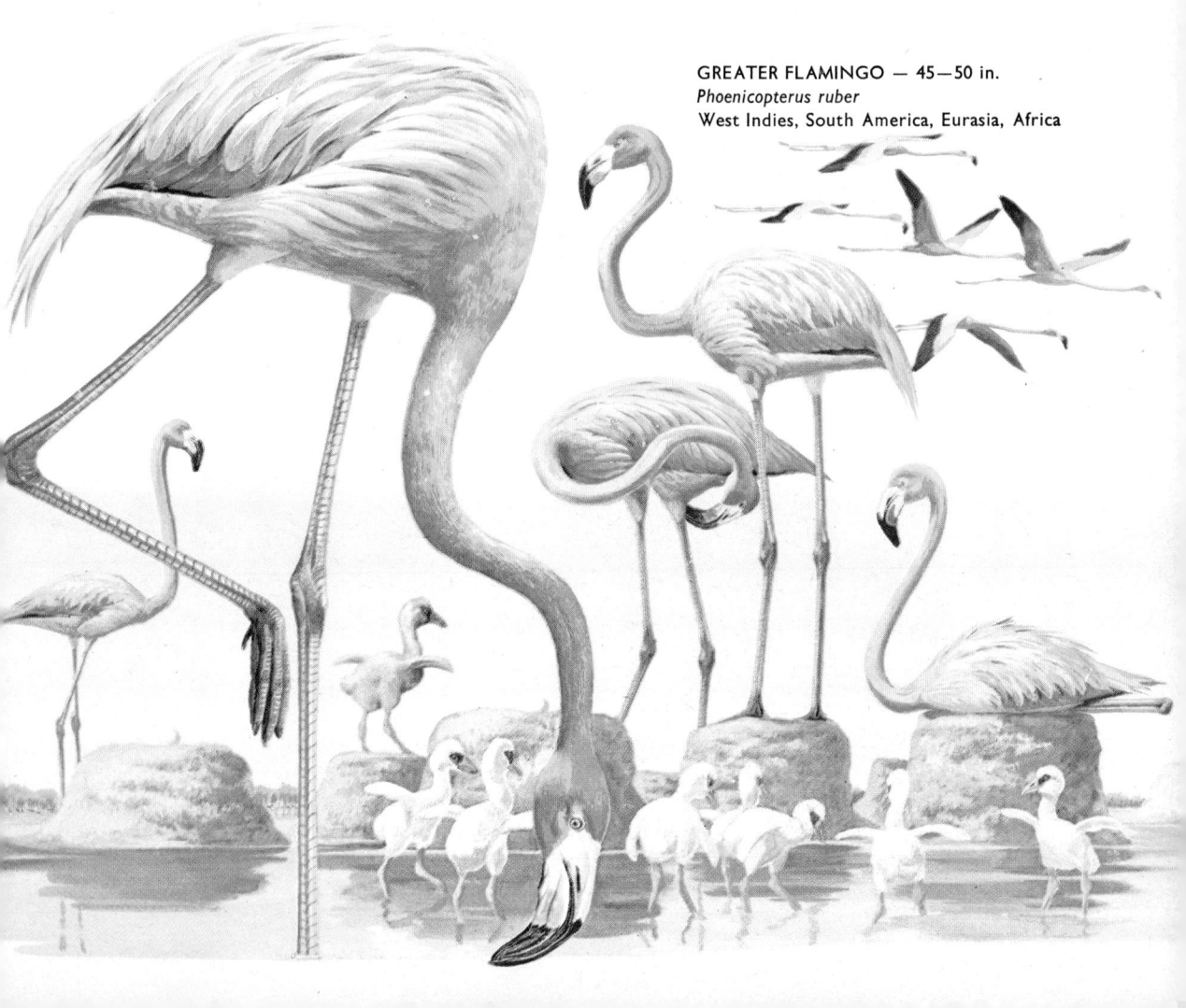

GREATER FLAMINGO — 45—50 in.
Phoenicopterus ruber
West Indies, South America, Eurasia, Africa

Flamingoes find their food in saline water and, because of this, are found only on salt coastal lagoons or in the saline lakes of desert regions. The Greater Flamingo feeds mainly on minute crustacea, while the Lesser Flamingo of Africa feeds on the blue-green algae found in such lakes. When possible these birds visit fresh water daily to drink and bathe. Few birds compete with them for their particular food, and on suitable lakes Flamingoes can be found to be present in enormous flocks.

The Greater Flamingo has the widest distribution, being found in India, Africa, the Mediterranean, South America, and the Caribbean region. The Lesser Flamingo is confined to Africa, where it occurs on the soda lakes of the Great Rift Valley. There are two other species, the Andean Flamingo and James Flamingo, both confined to the lakes of the Andes.

FLAT-FISHES look like typical fish when they first hatch from the egg. Soon, however, they begin to lean to one side. The eye on the underside begins to migrate to the top surface, and the "blind" side loses its pigment and becomes pale or white. In some species, even the mouth twists upward. After several weeks the flatfish has completed this remarkable transformation which fits it for a one-sided existence.

More than 500 species make up this important group of ocean fishes, distributed throughout the world. Some species come close to shore or move into bays in summer, then return to deep water in winter. A great many kinds are valued as food fish, and millions of pounds are harvested annually. Some are caught for sport.

Most flat-fishes are small and live in shallow to moderately deep waters. There they lie close to the bottom, darting up occasionally to grab fish, crustaceans, worms, or other creatures on which they feed. Female flat-fish lay numerous eggs (one halibut may contain two million eggs, for example) which float until they hatch.

The Plaice, with eyes on the right side and orange spots on the body, is the most important of the British flat-fishes. Related to the Plaice are the Lemon Sole, the Dab and the Flounder. One of the largest of the flat-fishes is the Atlantic Halibut (*Hippoglossus hippoglossus*), which in the eastern Atlantic reaches as far south as the Bay of Biscay. Halibut are reported to attain a weight of 700 lbs and to live to an age of forty years. They are active swimmers and spend less time than other flat-fishes

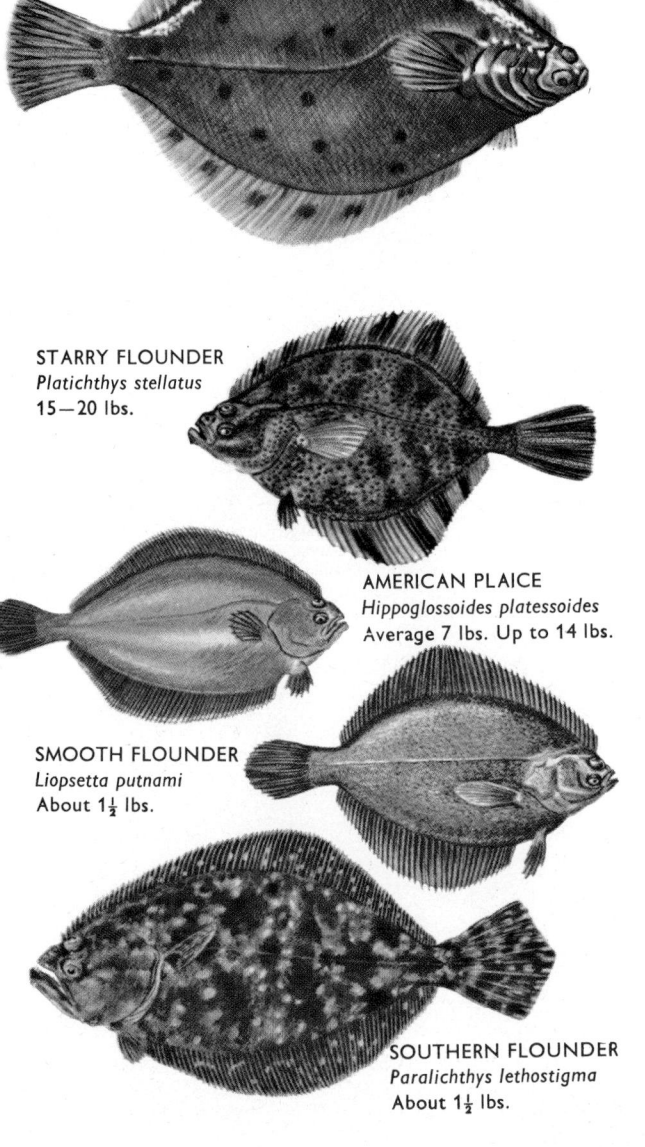

PLAICE (European)
Pleuronectes platessa
Up to 8 lbs.

STARRY FLOUNDER
Platichthys stellatus
15—20 lbs.

AMERICAN PLAICE
Hippoglossoides platessoides
Average 7 lbs. Up to 14 lbs.

SMOOTH FLOUNDER
Liopsetta putnami
About 1½ lbs.

SOUTHERN FLOUNDER
Paralichthys lethostigma
About 1½ lbs.

waiting for prey to come to them.

The Sole *(Solea solea)* is one of the best flavoured of the British species. It is caught in large numbers by trawlers — more frequently at night than by day, since it is nocturnal in its habits. The term "sole", however, is rather loosely applied to a number of flat-fishes.

One of the most unusual features about flat-fishes is their ability to change their colours for the purpose of matching their environment (see FISHES).

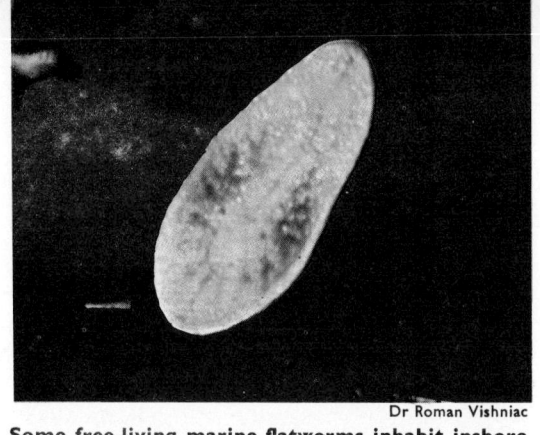

Some free-living marine flatworms inhabit inshore waters; others drift with the plankton in the open sea, far from land.

FLAT-WORMS are members of the *phylum Platyhelminthes*, which includes free-living flat-worms (turbellarians), parasitic flukes, and tapeworms. Free-living flat-worms live under rocks, among seaweeds, or in growth on pilings. Flat-worms are so thin they are extremely hard to pick up except with a knife blade. Some swim near the surface at night and are attracted to lights.

Marine flat-worms have broad, thin bodies with only one opening to the exterior. A number of them grow to more than six inches in length. Some flat-worms eat animals of various kinds, and because their bodies

are so thin and nearly transparent, they are often coloured by the food they eat. Flat-worms are sometimes brightly coloured, and may be spotted or striped. All have the ability to grow new parts (regenerate) when their bodies are damaged.

Liver flukes, which are mainly parasitic, reach a length of five or six inches. A salt-water ray caught on the Pacific Coast had one species in its body cavity, another in its mouth cavity, and a third on a copepod (a class of crustacea) which was itself a parasite on the ray. They are commonly found on the gills of fishes. Generally sac-like, they have one sucker surrounding their mouth and sometimes another in the middle of the body.

Swimmer's itch is caused by the larvae of a kind of flat-worm. They usually bury themselves in the skin, especially beneath a bathing suit, and may cause severe itching for several days. In this case, the intermediate host is a snail that releases the flat-worm larvae in visible clouds.

FLEAS, small wingless insects of the order *Siphonaptera,* feed on the blood of warm-blooded animals. The body of a flea is flattened from side to side (compressed) and is covered with spines that project backwards. Both features allow the flea to move freely between an animal's hairs.

An infested animal may have many thousands of fleas on its body at one time. Although fleas feed on blood, they often spend much of their time off their host's

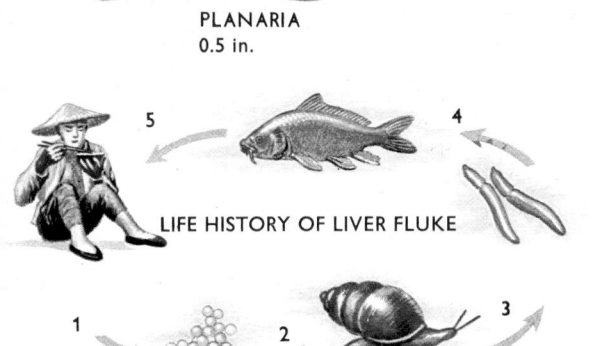

PLANARIA
0.5 in.

LIFE HISTORY OF LIVER FLUKE

Planaria is a free-living, fresh-water flatworm. Liver flukes are parasitic. Their eggs (1) are spread through wastes to water where they hatch into tiny larvae that infest snails (2). After a period of development, tailed larvae (3) leave the snail and bore through the skin and into the muscles of a fish (4). The larvae are transmitted to man or other animals through eating raw or poorly cooked fish (5).

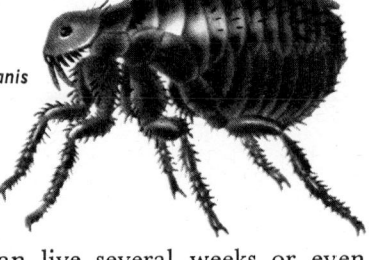

DOG FLEA
Ctenocephalides canis
0.1 in.

body, and can live several weeks or even longer without food. They leave the host to lay their eggs in cracks in the floor or in tiny crevices. Usually within two weeks the eggs hatch. Flea larvae are white, wormlike creatures without legs and less than a quarter of an inch long. They crawl about actively and feed on dried blood from the droppings of adult fleas and on other organic debris. The larval stage usually lasts two to four weeks, but if conditions are not favourable, it may last for several months. Then they spin silky cocoons, to which dust or other dirt sticks so that the cocoons are hard to see. The pupal stage lasts as long as the larval stage.

There are nearly 1,000 kinds of flea, and most live in the tropics. Fleas are important not only because of the discomfort they cause by biting man and his pets, but also because they can transmit plague (sometimes called "black death") and endemic typhus. Flea-bites itch because of a substance in the

This model of a House Fly's head shows numerous facets in the compound eyes and the sponging mouthparts.

American Museum of Natural History

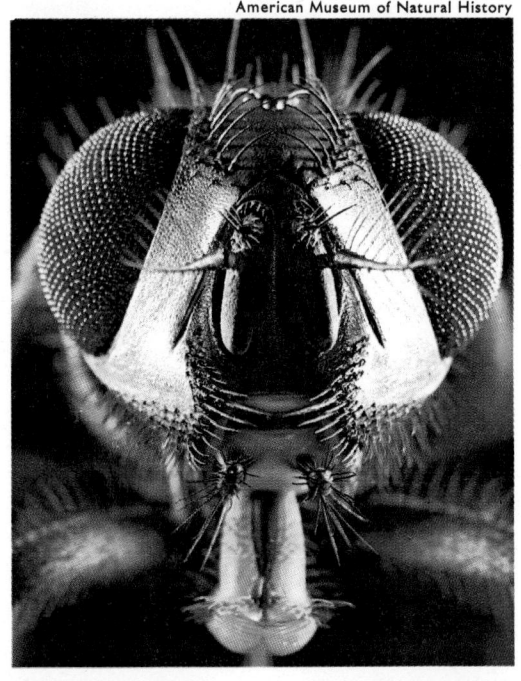

flea's saliva that prevents the victim's blood from coagulating.

Tropical "chigoe" fleas bury their heads in the flesh of their hosts, and may cause festering sores. They are common in the West Indies and South America. They are not the same as the chigger mite, or redbug, which is a common pest in the southern and central United States of America (see MITES).

FLIES, members of the order *Diptera*, never have more than one pair of wings, and nearly all have a pair of slender, knobbed structures — called halteres — in place of the second pair of wings. "Fly" is often used as a part of the name of many other insects — butterfly, stonefly, mayfly, and dragonfly are examples. But in these

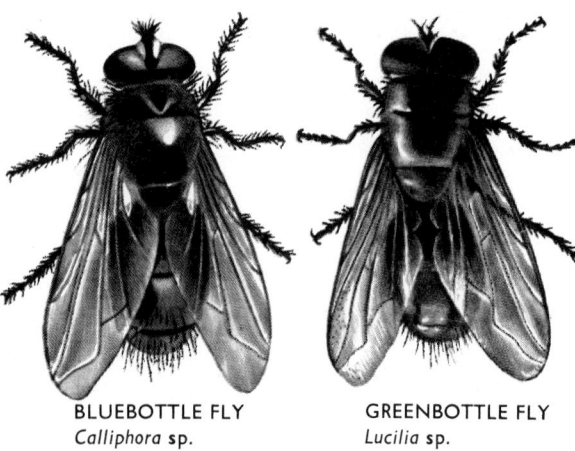

eggs larva pupa adult
LIFE CYCLE OF A HOUSE FLY

BLUEBOTTLE FLY
Calliphora sp.
0.5 in.

GREENBOTTLE FLY
Lucilia sp.
0.5 in.

"fly" is used as part of the name to form a single word. When "fly" is written as a separate word — as in flower fly or soldier fly — the insect in question is a true fly. There are many species of fly. Only the *Coleoptera* (beetles), *Lepidoptera* (moths, butterflies), and *Hymenoptera* (bees, wasps, ants) are more abundant.

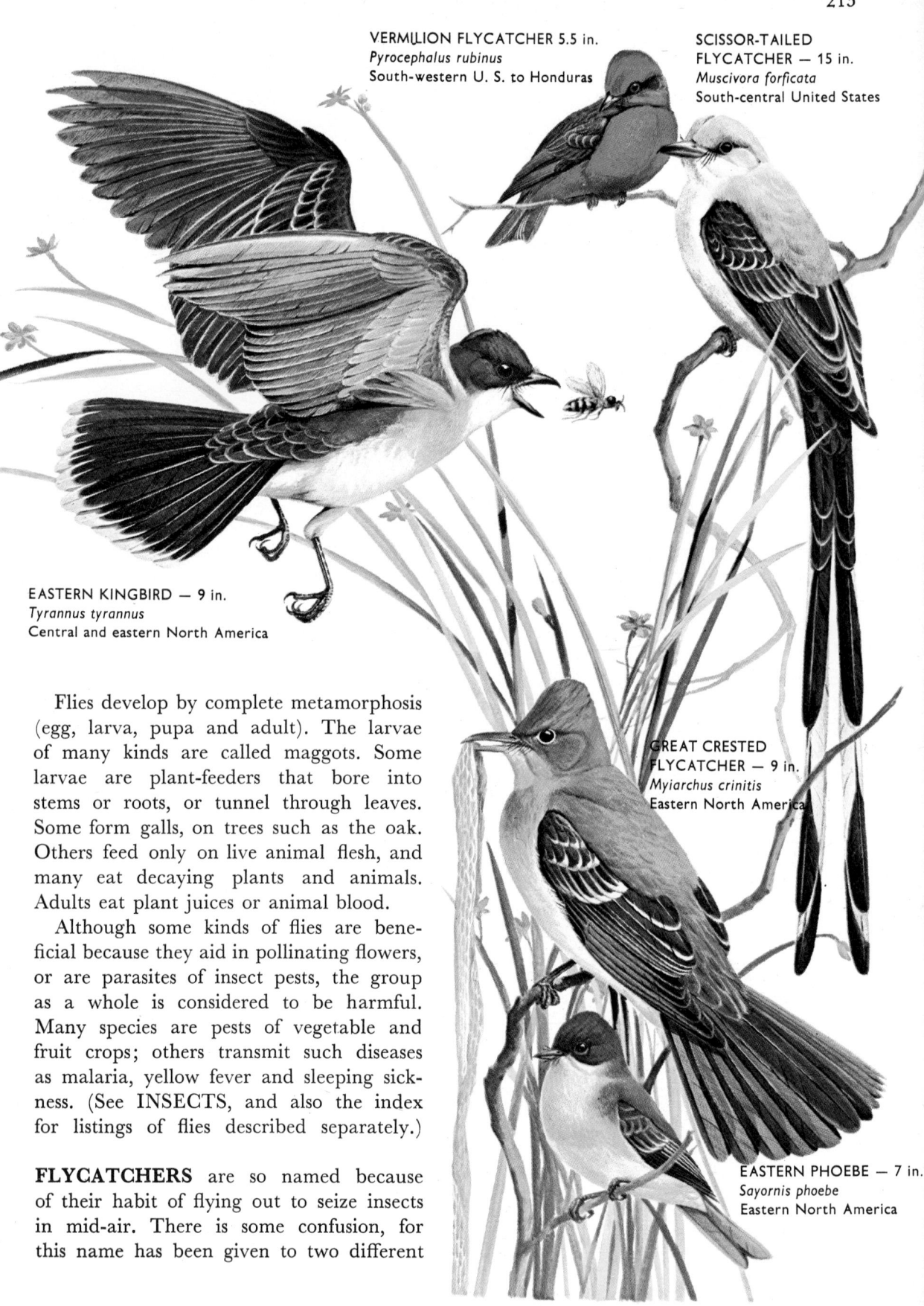

VERMILION FLYCATCHER 5.5 in.
Pyrocephalus rubinus
South-western U. S. to Honduras

SCISSOR-TAILED
FLYCATCHER — 15 in.
Muscivora forficata
South-central United States

EASTERN KINGBIRD — 9 in.
Tyrannus tyrannus
Central and eastern North America

GREAT CRESTED
FLYCATCHER — 9 in.
Myiarchus crinitis
Eastern North America

EASTERN PHOEBE — 7 in.
Sayornis phoebe
Eastern North America

Flies develop by complete metamorphosis (egg, larva, pupa and adult). The larvae of many kinds are called maggots. Some larvae are plant-feeders that bore into stems or roots, or tunnel through leaves. Some form galls, on trees such as the oak. Others feed only on live animal flesh, and many eat decaying plants and animals. Adults eat plant juices or animal blood.

Although some kinds of flies are beneficial because they aid in pollinating flowers, or are parasites of insect pests, the group as a whole is considered to be harmful. Many species are pests of vegetable and fruit crops; others transmit such diseases as malaria, yellow fever and sleeping sickness. (See INSECTS, and also the index for listings of flies described separately.)

FLYCATCHERS are so named because of their habit of flying out to seize insects in mid-air. There is some confusion, for this name has been given to two different

groups of birds which show this behaviour, one in the Eastern and one in the Western Hemisphere. The eastern birds are members of the *Muscicapidae,* and are related to the thrushes and warblers with which they are often grouped. The western birds are members of the specialised family of Tyrant-flycatchers, or *Tyrannidae.*

The eastern flycatchers are very like the thrushes and warblers, but are usually recognisable by large, dark eyes, a rather upright perching stance, and rather short legs. Since they usually fly from one perch to another, the legs are little used. They have keen sight and can manoeuvre rapidly, often flying out from a perch to seize a passing fly, turning rapidly and returning to the perch again in a single rapid movement. The bill is usually short and slightly broad, and the gape is often fringed with bristles which help to trap the insect.

The best-known of these birds is the little brown Spotted Flycatcher that nests right into the sub-arctic regions in summer. It builds a cup nest in a hollow against a tree-trunk or in a broken branch, but is equally happy to nest in the ivy on the side of a house. The Pied Flycatcher is less widespread but known to many people. The black-and-white patterned male has a pleasant little song and, since it is a hole-nester, will build in a garden nest-box.

Some of the Asiatic species are much more colourful and patterned in blue and chestnut, or yellow and black.

These flycatchers do not, as a whole, show great ornamentation, but the Paradise Flycatchers of Asia and Africa have elongated crests and long tails that may be twice the bird's length. They are boldly patterned in chestnut, white and blue.

Another distinct group of eastern flycatchers are the Fantailed Flycatchers of Asia and the East Indies, and also Pacific regions. These have large, fan-shaped tails that are in almost constant motion as the birds move through the trees. These are birds of relatively weak flight, with small feet; but one species, the Willie Wagtail of Australia, is long-legged and much more of a ground bird. It nests round farmsteads and is regarded with some affection.

The American Tyrant-flycatchers are a more varied group. Some are small warbler-sized species, while others are larger birds with heavy, hook-tipped bills, more like shrikes or kingfishers. For the most part they are famed for being conspicuous, noisy and aggressive. Many of the smaller species will unhesitatingly attack and drive off predators much larger than themselves. The Kingbirds of the genus *Tyrannus,* common in North America, have earned their name by the way in which they harry and drive away birds, such as crows and hawks, far larger than themselves.

Although their main diet is insects, some tropical species also take berries, and the larger species will take reptiles and amphibians, while the Derby Flycatcher has also been known to take fish. Like the eastern true flycatchers, these birds tend to have broad bills and bristles at either side of the gape. Long tails again appear in these western birds, but in this case they are usually very long forked tails. Such tails would appear to aid the birds in performing sudden halts in mid-air, rapid turns, and such-like manoeuvres.

A feature of many of these species is a crest of feathers that can be erected when the bird is excited, to reveal brightly-coloured feathers concealed by the duller ones on the crown. Such hidden crest feathers are usually coloured in bright yellow or red. Most fantastic of these crests is that of the little drab Royal Flycatcher, who, when excited, erects a large spread fan of scarlet feathers tipped with blue; which is set across the head facing forwards, like a great cocked hat. At other times it is folded back and will pass unnoticed.

Another gaudy species is the widespread Vermilion Flycatcher, the male of which is vivid scarlet over the underside and head.

Some of the more drably-coloured species make themselves known by the persistent use of the voice. Both the Wood Pewee

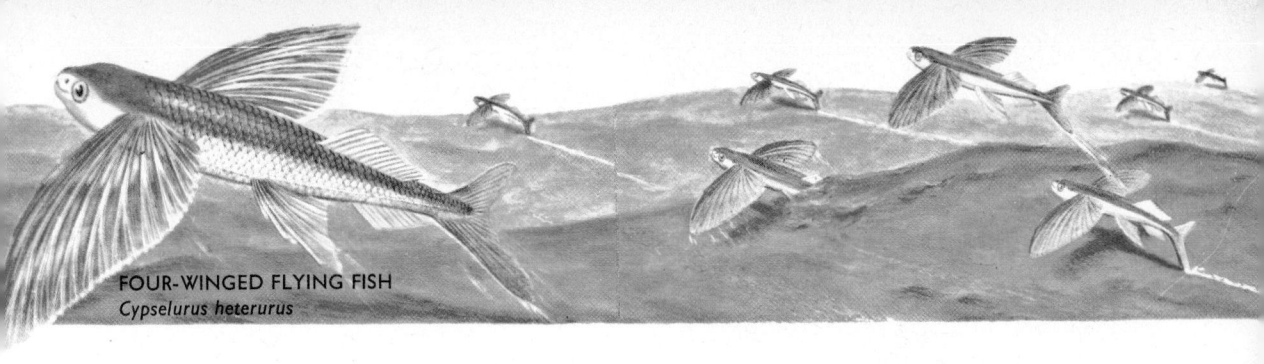

FOUR-WINGED FLYING FISH
Cypselurus heterurus

and the Phoebe of North America are flycatchers which are named after the calls which they repeat incessantly. Both are soberly coloured and would otherwise pass unnoticed in the trees. Apart from calls of this type, few of these western Tyrant-flycatchers have real songs, being more primitive species with a rather simple syrinx.

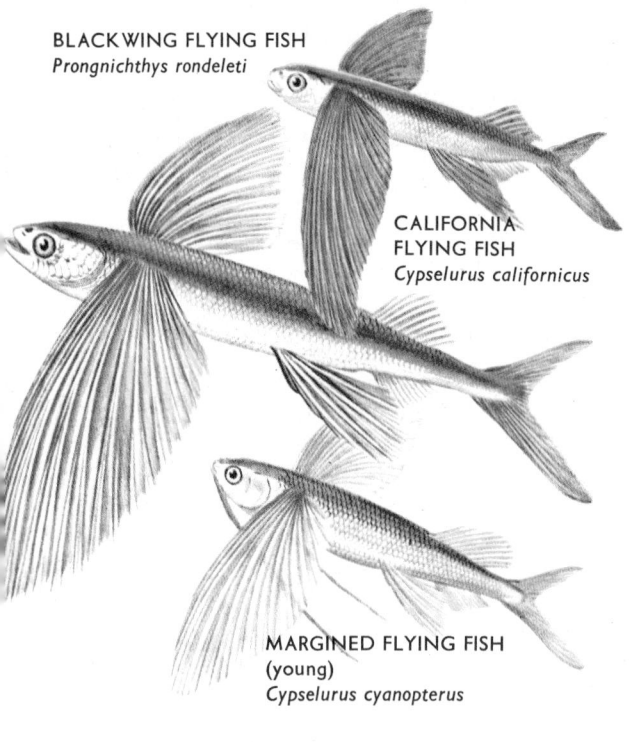

BLACKWING FLYING FISH
Prongnichthys rondeleti

CALIFORNIA FLYING FISH
Cypselurus californicus

MARGINED FLYING FISH
(young)
Cypselurus cyanopterus

FLYING FISHES (*Cypselurus* spp.) are small fishes that live close to the surface in the deep waters of warm seas. They feed on smaller fishes and are, in turn, important food for larger surface feeders, such as tunas, mackerels and dolphins. To escape, they swim rapidly along the surface, turn upwards suddenly and shoot into the air. Occasionally they "fly" for long distances. More often they are airborne for only a few

seconds at a time in glides of 50 yards or less. The broad pectoral fins, in some species the pelvic fins, too, are their wings. California Flying Fish reach a length of 18 inches; most species are less than 12 inches long.

FLYING LEMURS (*Gynocephalus* spp.) are found in the tropical forests from Malaya to the Philippines. They do not appear to have any relationship to true lemurs, despite their name. They are not capable of true flight, as are bats, but are excellent gliders. By spreading the thin membrane between their neck, legs and tail, they can sail 200 feet or more from one tree to another, losing only about a foot of altitude for every five feet of the glide. These soft-

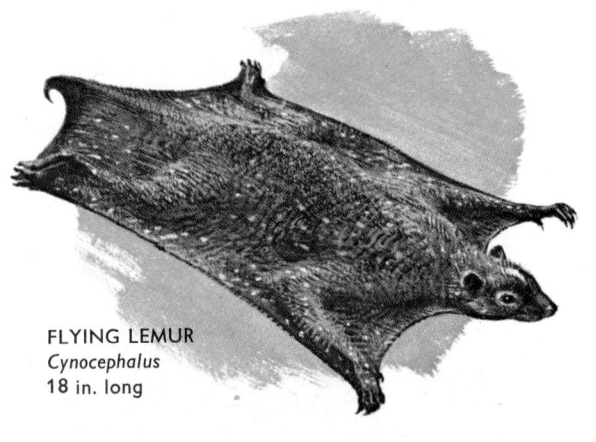

FLYING LEMUR
Cynocephalus
18 in. long

furred, almost cat-sized animals — also called Colugos — are nearly helpless on the ground and are unable to stand erect. Adults are shades of brown or grey; some are dappled with small, white spots. Their nearly naked ears are pinkish.

FLYING LIZARDS (*Draco* spp.) are slender 10-inch tree lizards of the agamid family. About 40 species live in the jungles of the

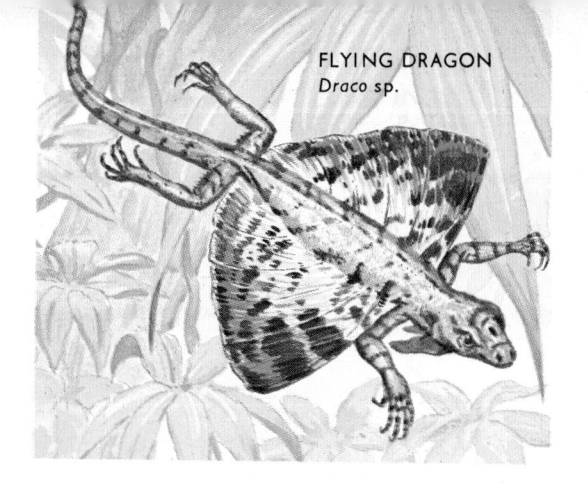

FLYING DRAGON
Draco sp.

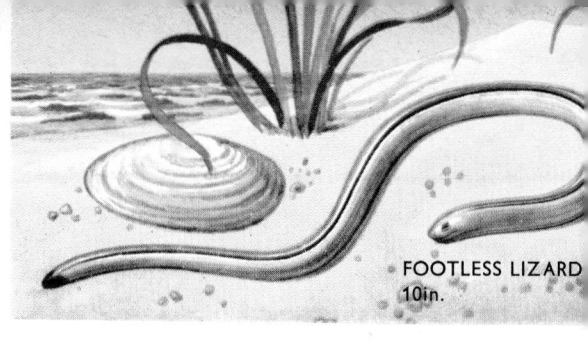

FOOTLESS LIZARD
10in.

Loose folds of skin stretched over extra-long ribs make the gliding "wings" of these Asiatic lizards.

East Indies and south-eastern Asia. They have wide flaps of skin stretched between their front and hind legs, and several long ribs also project into the webs to give them support. When the flaps are spread wide, the lizards can glide from high in a tree to the ground, or to a lower spot on other trees or vegetation. They do not flap these "wings", but are expert gliders. The flaps are brightly coloured, but the remainder of the body is drab. Because these lizards do not live well in captivity, they are not often seen in zoos. (see LACERTIDS).

FOOTLESS LIZARDS *(Anniella pulchra)* of western North America, in California and Baja California, are smooth-scaled, earless and completely limbless lizards that live in sandy soils. Often they burrow in the top few inches where they find their insect food by smell or touch. Their eyes are greatly reduced and covered with small, movable lids.

FOXES are all about the same size and are all members of the dog family. All foxes feed on small mammals and birds, occasionally on fruits and insects. They hunt at night and usually dig burrows in which they rear their young, commonly four to a litter. When contracted, the pupil of a fox's eye is elliptical, like a cat's, rather than round, as in domestic dogs and wolves. Foxes, unlike dogs, are mainly nocturnal in their habits, although they sometimes hunt during the day when they are pressed to find food, as for a litter of cubs in the early spring.

The Red Fox *(Vulpes vulpes)*, found in northern Europe, Asia and North America, lives in brushland or along the forest edges. Several colour forms occur: black, silver (hairs black with white tips), and "cross" (a reddish pelt striped with black). All these can be found in a single litter of young,

Cross, Silver and Black Foxes are colour phases of the Red Fox. The Grey Fox is a separate species.

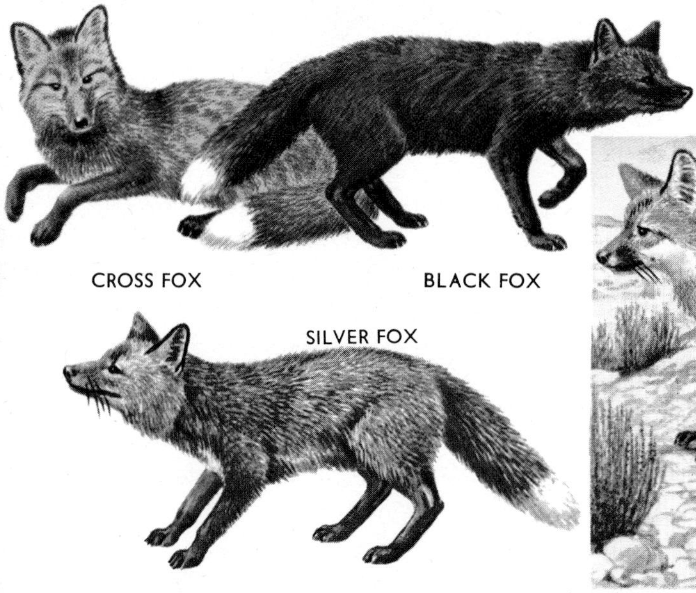

CROSS FOX

BLACK FOX

SILVER FOX

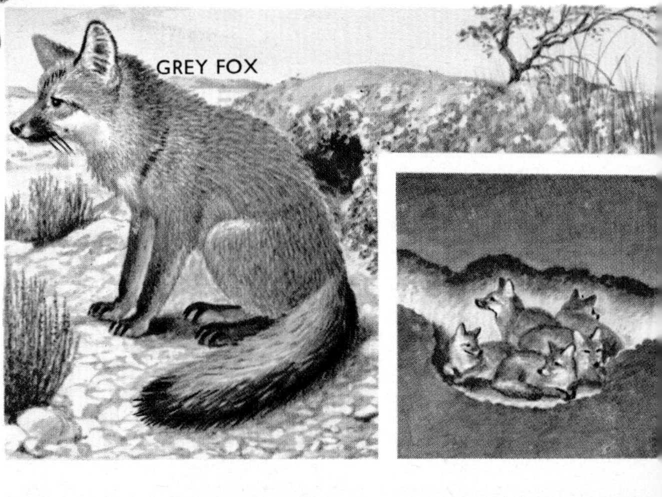

GREY FOX

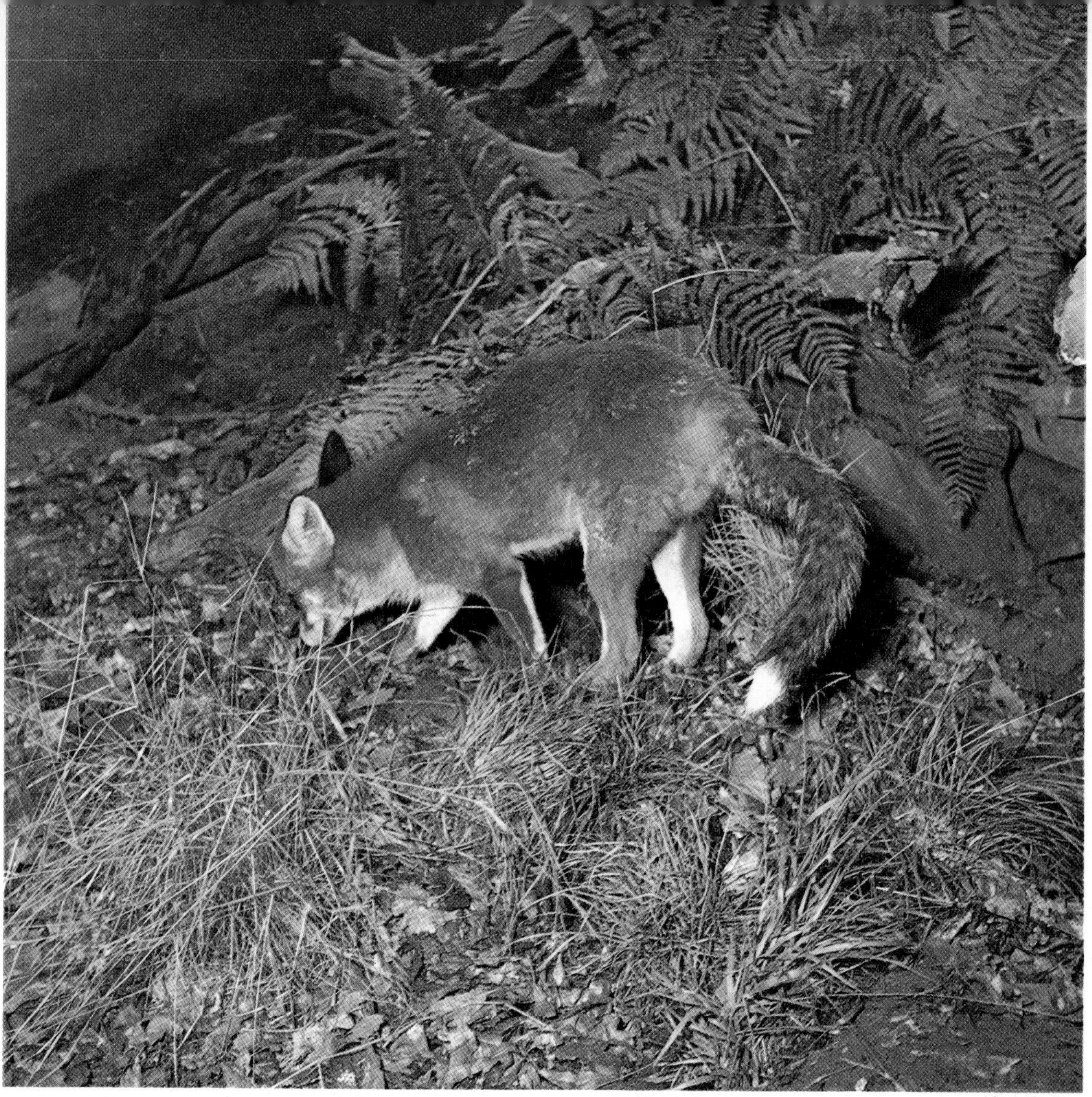

Adult European Red Fox caught by the camera in its natural surroundings.

though red is the normal colour. "Silver Fox" was a very popular fur for many years, and since this colour phase is not common in nature, "silvers" were bred on fur farms. The Red Fox is noted for its cunning and has been hunted for sport for hundreds of years, by horse and hound, tracking in the snow, trapping, and other methods. These foxes eat mostly mice, but they may become pests by making raids on poultry. Males usually stay with their mates and assist in feeding and rearing the young, which are born blind and helpless. In warm climates, the young are born in the spring, are ready to leave the family by autumn, and mature by the following spring.

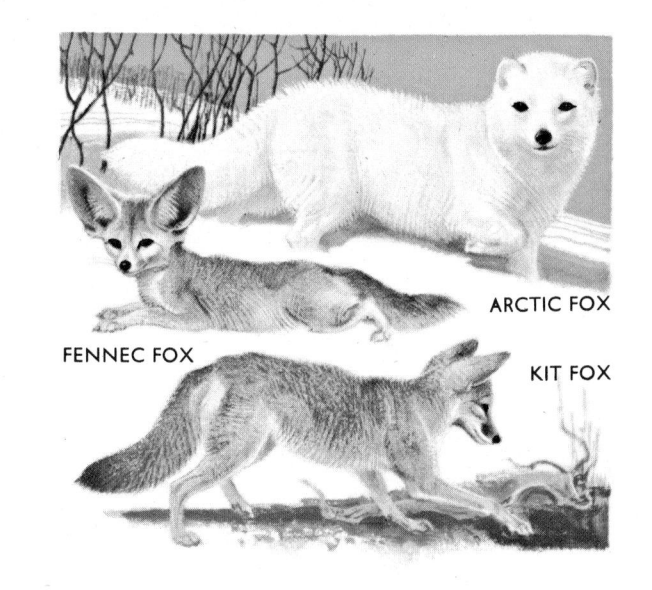

ARCTIC FOX

FENNEC FOX

KIT FOX

This Great Frigate-bird will chase the Brown Booby until it drops its fish, which the marauder will then grab for itself.

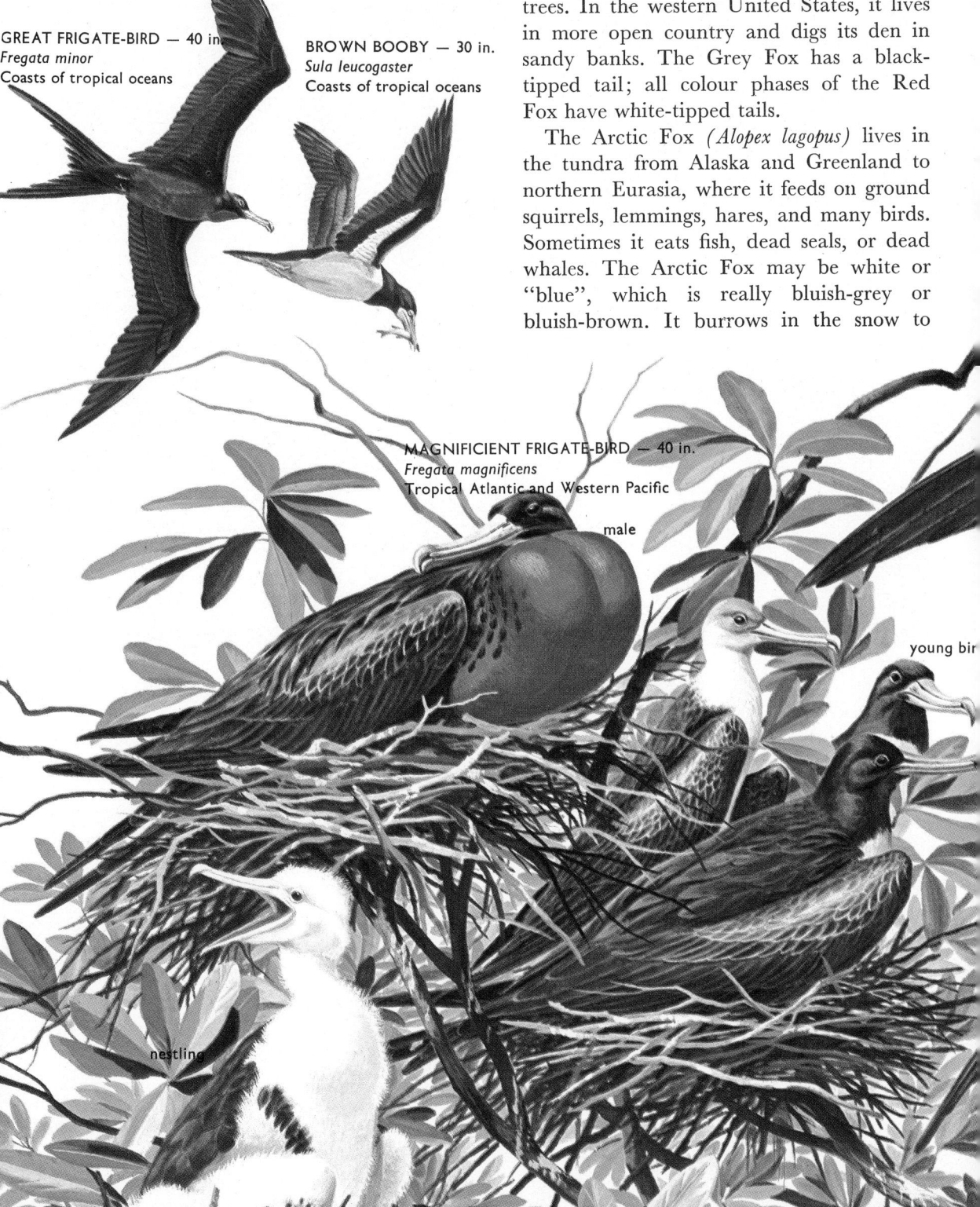

GREAT FRIGATE-BIRD — 40 in.
Fregata minor
Coasts of tropical oceans

BROWN BOOBY — 30 in.
Sula leucogaster
Coasts of tropical oceans

MAGNIFICIENT FRIGATE-BIRD — 40 in.
Fregata magnificens
Tropical Atlantic and Western Pacific

male

young bird

nestling

The Grey Fox *(Urocyon cinereoargenteus)* is common throughout most of the United States southward into northern South America. In the eastern United States, it lives in wooded areas and occasionally climbs trees. In the western United States, it lives in more open country and digs its den in sandy banks. The Grey Fox has a black-tipped tail; all colour phases of the Red Fox have white-tipped tails.

The Arctic Fox *(Alopex lagopus)* lives in the tundra from Alaska and Greenland to northern Eurasia, where it feeds on ground squirrels, lemmings, hares, and many birds. Sometimes it eats fish, dead seals, or dead whales. The Arctic Fox may be white or "blue", which is really bluish-grey or bluish-brown. It burrows in the snow to

make a temporary den for rearing young.

The Kit Fox *(Vulpes macrotis)*, a small, big-eared member of the fox group, lives in the deserts of the south-western United States and also in Mexico. Exceedingly shy and a fast runner, the Kit Fox can endure extreme desert heat and needs little water. The Swift Fox *(Vulpes velox)*, which has short ears, is closely related to the Kit Fox. Years ago the Swift Fox was abundant on the prairies of the central United States and southern Canada, and was commonly found with the great herds of Bison; now it is rare. The Fennec Fox *(Fennecus zerda)*, also much like the Kit Fox in appearance, has exceptionally long ears, is small in size, and has a bushy tail. It lives in the deserts of northern Africa and Arabia.

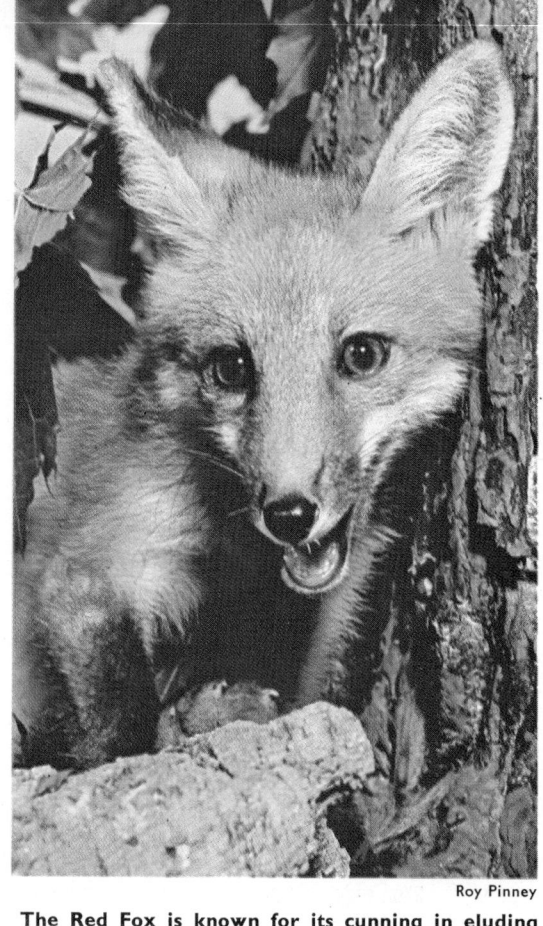

Roy Pinney

The Red Fox is known for its cunning in eluding hunters and their dogs. Though heavily hunted, it has become more abundant in many areas.

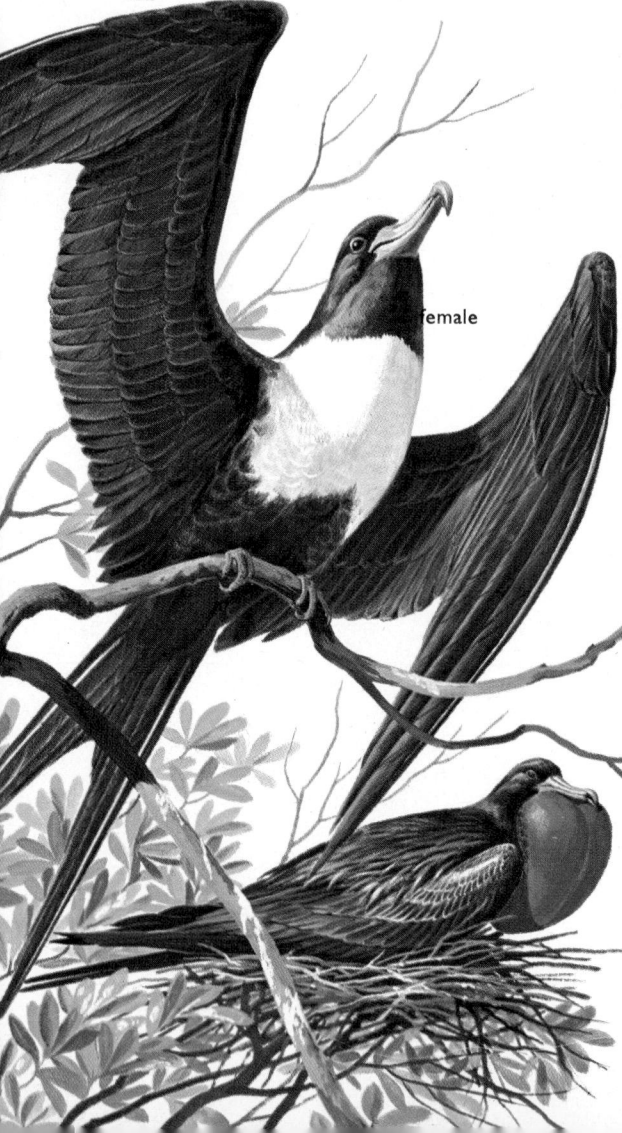

Female

FRIGATE-BIRDS are skilled flyers. Sea birds of the tropics, they stay in the air most of the time. Frigate-birds' legs are so short and their wings so long, it is difficult for them to rise from land and nearly impossible for them to take off from the sea. When they alight, it is always on a tree, buoy, or similar elevation. They capture fish by swooping or hovering just over the water, or by stealing from gulls, pelicans or other sea birds. During courtship and nest-building, male birds inflate their orange throat pouches, which then turn red, and keep them puffed up for hours. Females lay a single egg in the frail nest built by the male. The newly-hatched chicks are covered with thick, white down. This beauty lasts only a short time, and the moment their long wings begin to grow, they become awkward, droopy creatures.

220

FROGS and **TOADS** are amphibians that do not have tails when mature. They are called anurans, which in Greek means "without a tail". Most toads have rough skin; frogs generally have smooth skin.

Frogs and toads are abundant in almost all moist, warm habitats throughout the world. They cannot live in salt or brackish waters. A few kinds spend their entire lives in water, but most come out on to the land frequently, and often for long periods. In semi-arid regions, toads and frogs are found near whatever water is available, or in burrows. They emerge only at night.

No other backboned animals have the unusual body form or strange method of movement that marks frogs and toads. Their long and powerful hind legs, used for jumping, are much larger than their front legs, which catch the body's weight when they land. In kinds that crawl rather than jump, such as the European Green Toad, both pairs of legs are the same size.

Other body changes also help absorb the shocks of leaping and landing. For example, the pelvic girdle, which receives the jolt of the hind legs in the leap, is greatly enlarged. It extends forward almost half the length of the body. The tail bones are fused into a solid shock-absorbing bar, which lies in the middle of the pelvic girdle. There are only six to ten free bones in the backbone, the smallest number in all vertebrates. The chest region is encased in a greatly enlarged pectoral girdle. Most frogs and toads have stout projections on

FAMILY TREE OF FROGS AND TOADS

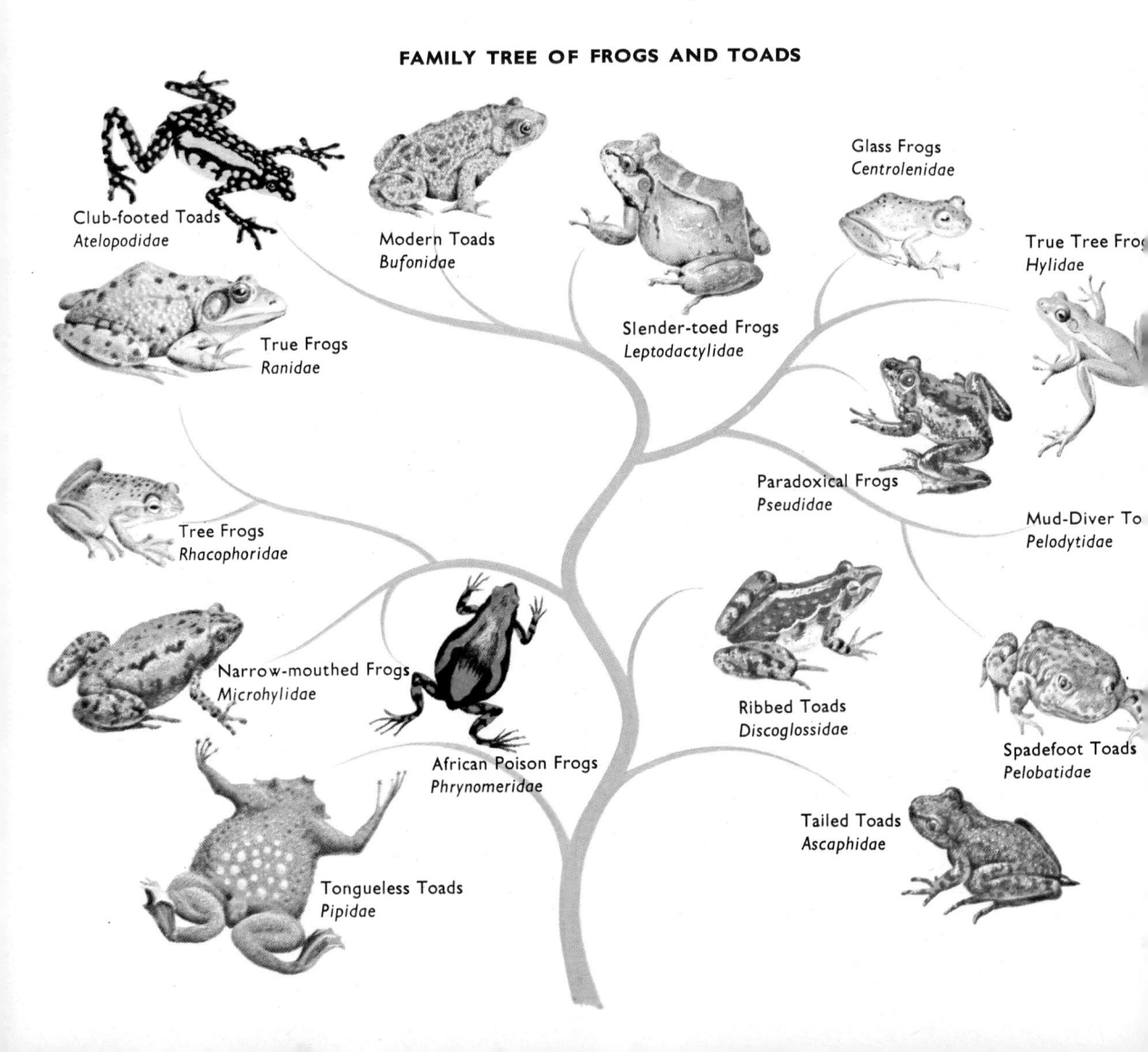

Club-footed Toads
Atelopodidae

Modern Toads
Bufonidae

Glass Frogs
Centrolenidae

True Tree Frog
Hylidae

True Frogs
Ranidae

Slender-toed Frogs
Leptodactylidae

Paradoxical Frogs
Pseudidae

Mud-Diver To
Pelodytidae

Tree Frogs
Rhacophoridae

Narrow-mouthed Frogs
Microhylidae

African Poison Frogs
Phrynomeridae

Ribbed Toads
Discoglossidae

Spadefoot Toads
Pelobatidae

Tailed Toads
Ascaphidae

Tongueless Toads
Pipidae

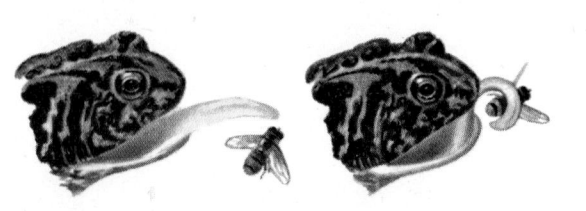

Frogs and Toads catch their insect prey by means of their sticky tongue, which can be flipped out quickly.

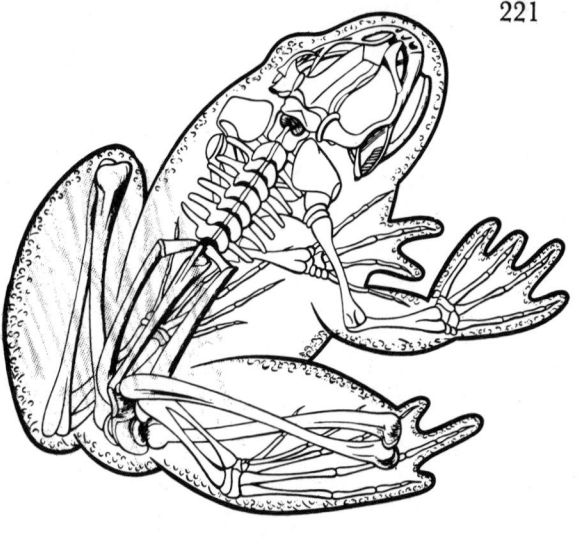

each side of the vertebrae but no ribs, which would break easily in landings.

Completely aquatic frogs and toads have small eyes, and have also lost their eyelids; most frogs and toads, however, have large eyes, and not only eyelids but also transparent rims on their large lower lids. They can look out through these thin membranes even when their lids are closed.

Frogs and toads feed mostly on worms, insects, spiders, and other small animals. Occasionally they eat small mammals or birds. Most kinds react only to moving objects, which they catch by flipping out their sticky tongue. In most kinds, the tongue is attached at the front of the mouth, allowing the greatest possible reach. Some aquatic frogs and toads have no tongue, and in others the tongue is attached at the rear of the mouth. Frogs and toads, like other carnivorous animals, have relatively short intestines, less than twice the length of their body. Vegetarian animals have much longer intestines.

Frogs and toads, both the adults and the tadpoles, are eaten by wading birds,

Skeleton of frog shows the long bones in its powerful hind legs and the large pelvic girdle which receives the shock of the landing. Note the small number of vertebrae in the backbones with stout rib-like projections and the skull, which joins the backbone without any neck whatever.

small mammals, snakes and fishes.

Frogs and toads usually breed in warm, wet weather in spring. Those that live in dry regions breed whenever the rains come; this may be in summer or autumn. When no heavy rains fall, they may even skip a season. Those that live in water breed

Frogs lay their eggs in a jelly-like mass. Each fertilised egg develops an embryo. After a period of time, a tadpole hatches from each egg and clings to vegetation by adhesive suckers under its mouth. At first the tadpole has branched outer gills, but soon these gills are grown over by skin. After a period of growth, the hind legs appear, then the front legs. At this stage the tadpole looks like an adult frog, although it still has a stubby tail when it emerges on land. Soon the tail is absorbed.

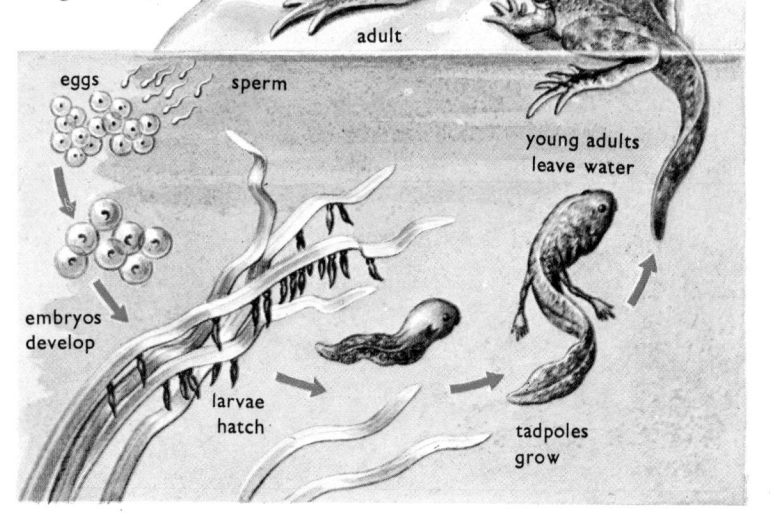

adult

eggs   sperm

young adults
leave water

embryos
develop

larvae
hatch

tadpoles
grow

when the temperature of the water is warm enough.

At the proper time, the males seek the nearest water of suitable depth; then they inflate their throat pouches with air and start "calling", by forcing the air out over their vocal cords. Each kind of frog or toad has a distinctive call, which directs females and other males to the breeding site. A chorus of males calling at a breeding spot may be almost deafening to anyone nearby. Each male clasps in his forelegs the first female that comes within reach. Then, as the eggs are laid a few at a time, he squirts over them a small jet of sperm-bearing fluid. In only one group of frogs is internal fertilisation carried out (see TAILED TOADS).

All female frogs and toads produce two streams of eggs, one from each ovary, but in only a few types do these remain as two

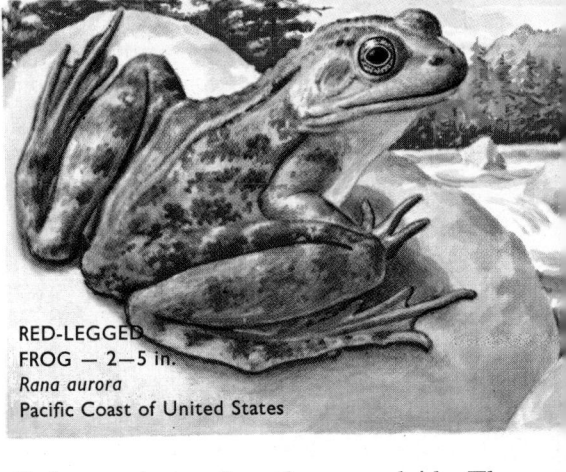

RED-LEGGED FROG — 2—5 in.
Rana aurora
Pacific Coast of United States

distinct strings after they are laid. They form a mass under water or a film on the surface. Some frogs lay eggs on moist land.

Each egg hatches into a larva, or "tadpole". The larva has adhesive organs, one on each side below its mouth, for attaching to underwater objects. It also has large

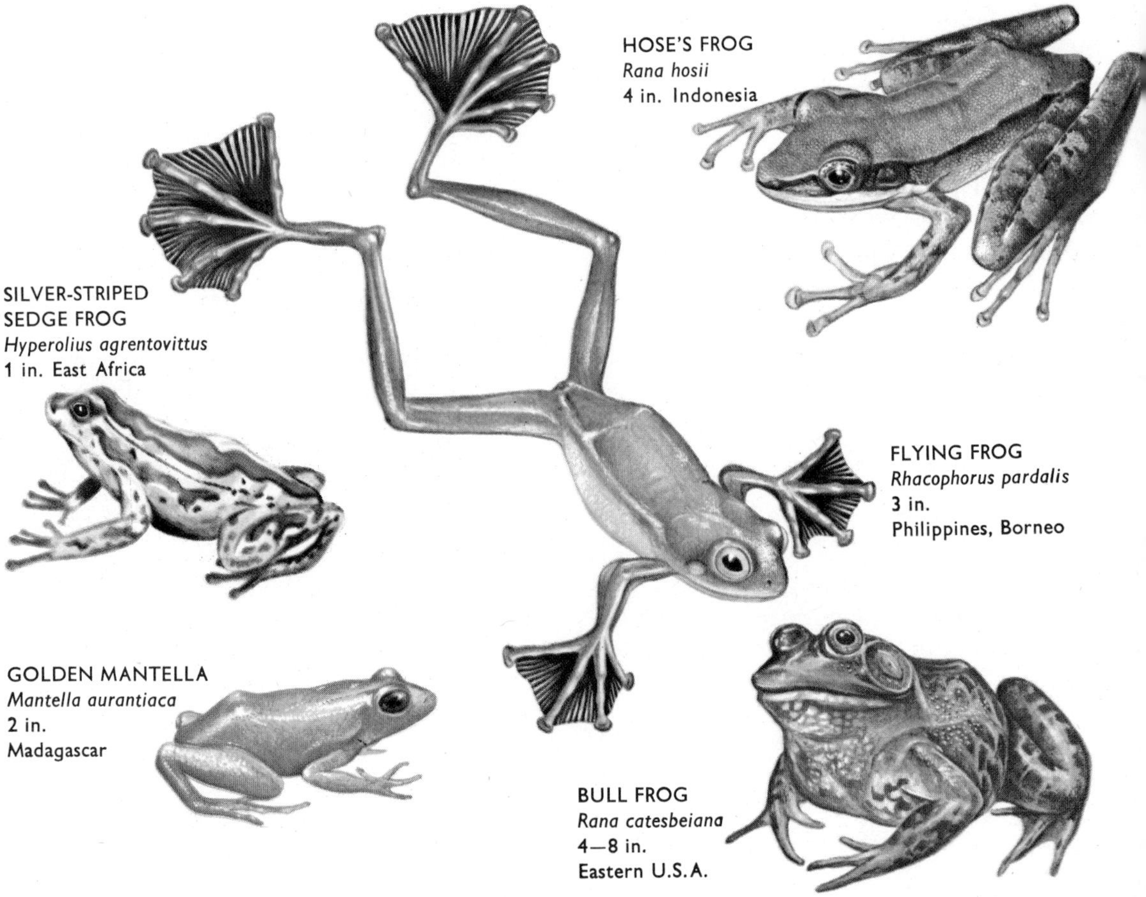

HOSE'S FROG
Rana hosii
4 in. Indonesia

SILVER-STRIPED SEDGE FROG
Hyperolius agrentovittus
1 in. East Africa

FLYING FROG
Rhacophorus pardalis
3 in.
Philippines, Borneo

GOLDEN MANTELLA
Mantella aurantiaca
2 in.
Madagascar

BULL FROG
Rana catesbeiana
4—8 in.
Eastern U.S.A.

external gills, just behind its head. The external gills soon disappear and are replaced by internal gills, similar to those of fishes. Water drawn into the mouth passes into the gill chamber and emerges from one or two small openings located on the tadpole's side or, in some cases, on its belly.

Tadpoles feed on algae and other small plants which grow on underwater surfaces. Their "scrapers" are tiny projections on the flexible disc around their small, horny jaws. Unlike their flesh-eating parents, tadpoles have long, coiled intestines.

When a tadpole starts to "transform" into the froglet (imago) stage, its mouth disc disappears and its jaws lose their horny rims. Hind legs appear at the base of its tail, which then shortens. Eventually front legs appear. Small changes in the pattern and texture of the skin also occur before the froglet becomes a completely tail-less adult.

Frogs of the family *Ranidae* are the most common ground-dwelling frogs of Europe and North America, but some members of the family are tree frogs, and others are narrow-mouthed, baggy-bodied burrowers.

Members of the genus *Rana* are the typical frogs of North America, Africa, Europe and Asia. Generally they are long-legged, slender-bodied and smooth-skinned, with the toes joined by a web of skin. The largest species is the Goliath Frog *(Rana goliath)* of the Cameroon region of Africa; it can attain the size of a small terrier, and feeds on crabs. Another but considerably smaller crab-eating frog, *Rana cancrivora,* which occurs in the flooded rice fields, ditches and ponds of S. E. Asia, will frequently invade brackish water, and its tadpole too can survive similar saline conditions. Other frogs, like the European Common Frog and the Edible Frog, penetrate brackish parts of the Baltic.

Ten species of *Rana* occur in Europe and Asia, and several have a vast distribution; the Common Frog, for instance, reaches from Europe's Atlantic coast to Japan.

Both the American Bullfrog *(Rana catesbeiana)* and the European Edible Frog *(Rana esculenta),* as well as smaller, related

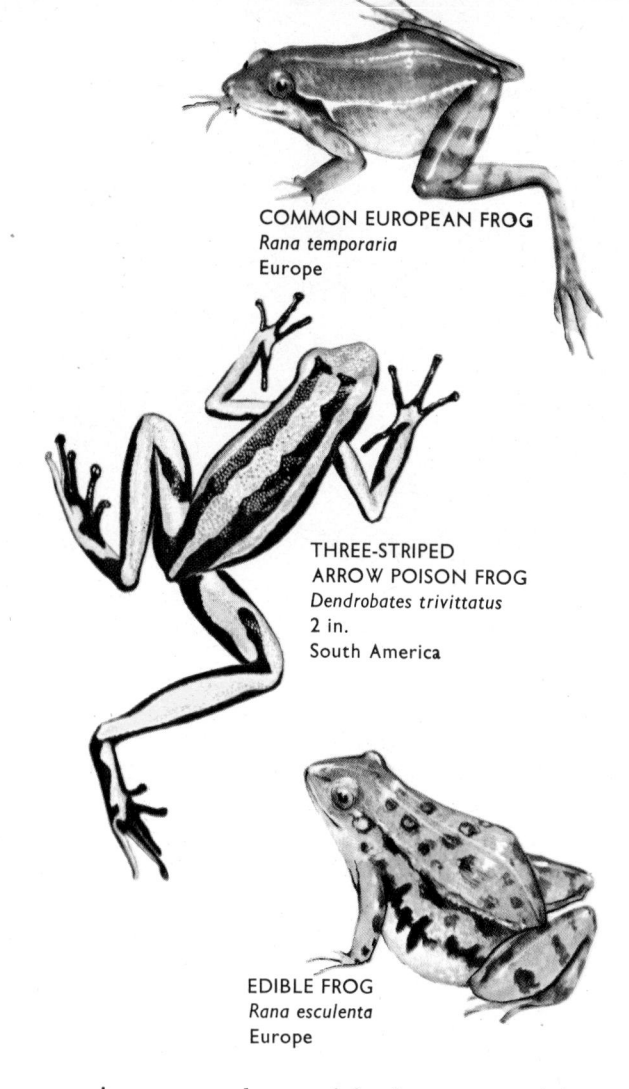

COMMON EUROPEAN FROG
Rana temporaria
Europe

THREE-STRIPED
ARROW POISON FROG
Dendrobates trivittatus
2 in.
South America

EDIBLE FROG
Rana esculenta
Europe

species, are used to satisfy the commercial demand for frogs' legs. The market is supplied by professional frog hunters, who dazzle the frogs with lights and then net, spear, or fish for them with rod and line.

The Hairy Frog *(Trichobatrachus)* of the French Cameroons is an unusual African species. Adult males have long, hairlike strands of skin on their hind legs and the rear sides of their body. The function of these strands, absent in females and also in young males, is not known, but they are believed to be useful in respiration. Mature African frogs *(Arthroleptis)* have very long third fingers; females do not. When annoyed, a fat-bodied, narrow-headed African frog *(Hemisus)* puffs up its body and arches its back, and then stretches its legs, bending down its head in a menacing manner.

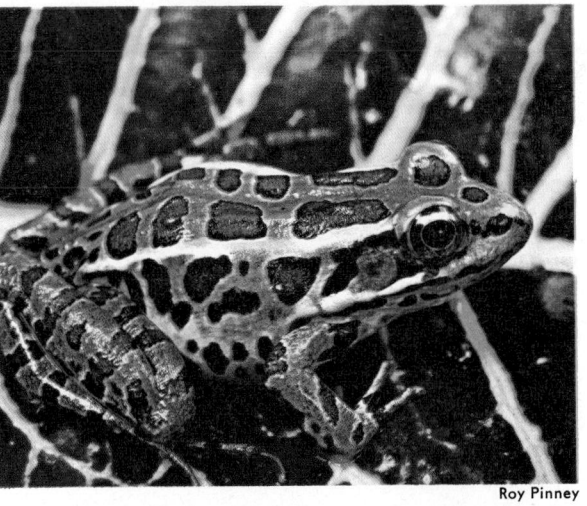

Roy Pinney

Leopard Frogs have three or four different calls, each communicating a specific meaning to other frogs in the neighbourhood.

Another member of this genus carries its eggs in a pouch on its belly, and the tadpoles do not emerge until they are well developed. Still another lays eggs in a depression in the ground, digging an escape tunnel to a nearby source of water for the newly-hatched larvae.

Poison Frogs *(Dendrobates)*, of both Central and South America, have a very powerful skin poison which is used by natives on the tips of their darts and arrows. The poison will kill large animals almost instantly. These frogs lay their eggs in small pools of water in hollow trees or logs, where the larvae also develop. The tadpoles have strong mouth discs, with which they attach themselves to adults that hop into their pools, so that they can leave as "passengers". Then they release themselves when the frog hops into some water again, travelling in

this piggyback fashion from pool to pool.

Rhacophorids *(Rhacophorus* spp.*)* are a large group of frogs that have expanded tips on their fingers and toes. Found in southern Asia, Africa and Madagascar, and on the

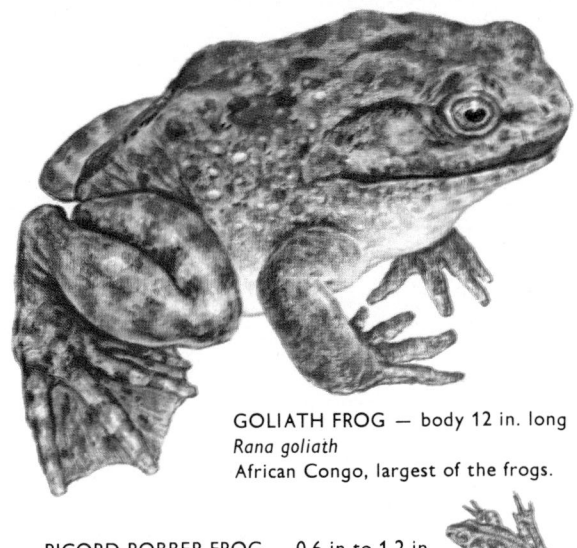

GOLIATH FROG — body 12 in. long
Rana goliath
African Congo, largest of the frogs.

RICORD ROBBER FROG — 0.6 in to 1.2 in.
Eleutherodactylus ricordi
Florida; smallest North American frog.

large islands of the East Indies, these frogs usually live in trees and lay their eggs on the leaves a few feet above water. They beat the gelatine surrounding the eggs into a frothy mass with their hind legs. In a short time the eggs hatch, and the larvae drop into the water, where they complete their development to become air-breathing adults.

Some species lay their eggs on land, just above the water level of a stream or a pond. They also beat their eggs into a froth, and the larvae develop in the froth until rains

SPOTTED FROG
Rana pretiosa
3—4 in.
North-west Pacific

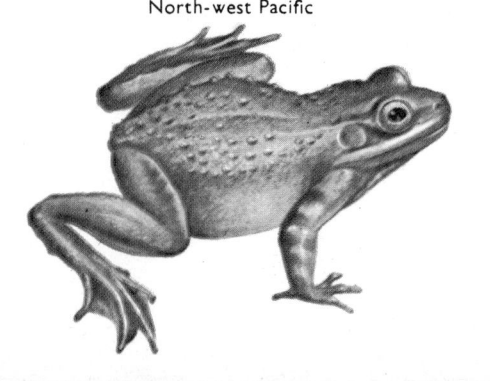

PICKEREL FROG
Rana palustris
2—3 in.
U.S.A. and Canada

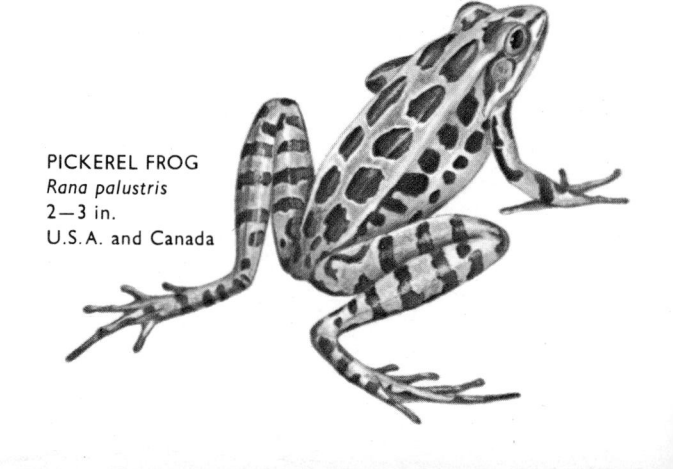

raise the level of the water and they can swim free. Sometimes these frogs make mistakes and lay their eggs too late, too soon, too far from water, or in a place where they are exposed to the sun.

Some rhacophorids have large, fully-webbed feet and hands. In leaping they spread these webs and sail long distances.

About one hundred species of African frogs also belong to the family Rhacophoridae. These are among the most beautifully marked frogs in the world. Some lay their eggs on leaves in trees, but most kinds lay their eggs in water, or on land at the water's edge. The female of one kind *(Leptopelis)* holds her eggs in her mouth until the froglets are ready to emerge. During this time, of course, she does not eat. When disturbed, some frogs of this genus "play 'possum", by opening their mouth and putting their hands over their head. (See AMPHIBIANS; TOADS; TREE FROGS; and consult index for listing of frogs and toads described separately.)

FRUIT FLIES *(Drosophilidae)* will usually be found flying around fermenting or decaying substances, in which they breed. They are small brownish or yellowish flies, and have a deliberate, hovering flight. The females eventually settle on the selected material to lay their eggs, from which the grubs develop. These flies are also attracted to vinegar, cider and pickles, and some breed in decaying fungi. In fact, fermentation is almost bound to attract them, whether in factories, homes or out of doors.

During the last war, a cosmopolitan species *(Drosophila repleta)* established itself in London. It has a black and brown mottled thorax. Besides preferring the high temperatures of kitchens, it likes white surfaces. The grubs develop in decomposing vegetables, and thus it rapidly became a nuisance in canteens and cafés.

One widespread species *(Drosophila melanogaster)* is commonly used in studies of heredity, because it is easily reared and completes its life cycle in about 10 days.

Some members of another family, Trypetidae, are called the Large Fruit Flies. Some are very destructive to fruit crops. For instance, in the Mediterranean area, the larvae of *Ceratitis capitata* feed in cherries, oranges, peaches, plums and other fruit.

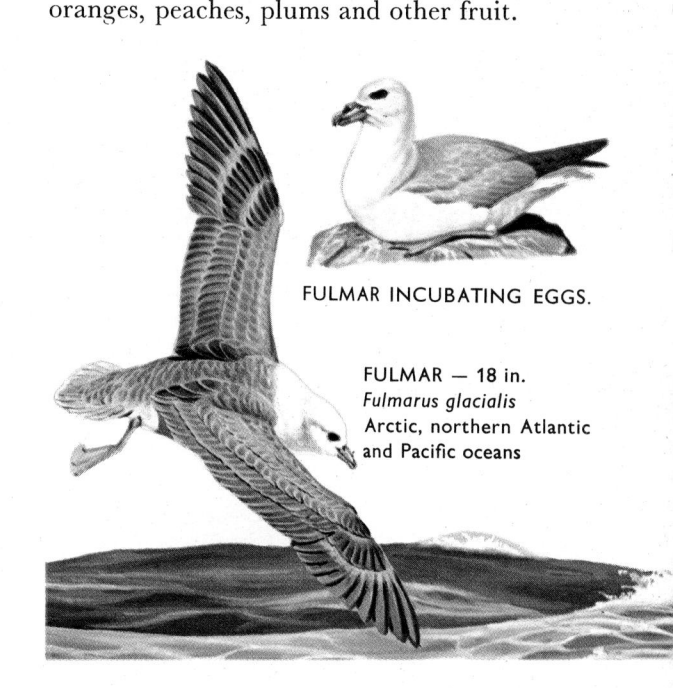

FULMAR INCUBATING EGGS.

FULMAR — 18 in.
Fulmarus glacialis
Arctic, northern Atlantic
and Pacific oceans

Fulmars favour gliding but are strong flyers.

FULMARS are tube-nosed petrels of the Arctic and North Atlantic oceans. They follow fishing-boats, whaling ships and sealers, and eat the waste thrown overboard. They land only to nest in large colonies on sea-cliffs. Females lay one egg on a bare ledge. When annoyed or alarmed, nesting fulmars squirt out a stream of oil. The young are fed by regurgitation.

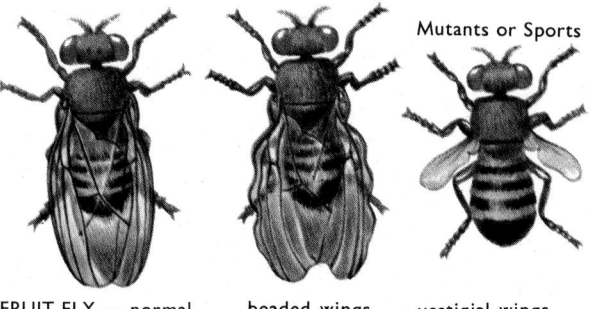

Mutants or Sports

FRUIT FLY — normal
Drosophila melanogaster
0.2 in.

beaded wings   vestigial wings

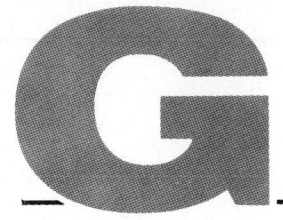

GANNETS are goose-sized seabirds of the Pelican family. They feed on fish, which are captured by diving. Gannets are highly specialised as high-divers. The body is torpedo-shaped, with tapering head and bill, and tapering tail. The bird sights the fish as it flies, and plummets down vertically with closed wings from a height of up to 100 feet, raising a great plume of spray as it hits the water. The air-sacs under the skin cushion it against the shock of impact. It has no visible nostrils and breathes through the edges of the bill. The eyes are close-set for accurate distance judgement.

Gannets spend the year out at sea, coming to island or cliff colonies to breed. They nest in close ranks, with each bird just beyond a bill-thrust of the next; the birds fight fiercely for nest-sites. Gannets have no brood patches, and incubate the single egg by covering it with the webbed feet, before lowering the body on to it. The fluffy white young become dark brown, flecked with white, in the first plumage, and take three years to attain adult plumage.

The strikingly white plumage of the adult bird is visible a long way off at sea, and when one bird dives, others may be attracted to the shoal of fish in the same way that vultures follow one another to a carcase.

The other species related to the Gannet are usually known as Boobies. They are birds of tropical seas, nesting on uninhabited islands, and encounter man so little that they are absurdly unafraid. This lack of fear and a rather stupid manner, caused sailors to give them their apt name. In behaviour, the Booby is rather similar to the Gannet, but the Red footed Booby nests on bushes on islands, and not on bare, open rocks.

GAVIALS (*Gavialis gangeticus*) are crocodilians that live in the Indus, Ganges and Brahmaputra rivers of India. Harmless to man except when attacked, the long-snouted Gavial feeds on fish, and perhaps

All members of this family have thick skins, with air-sacs just under the surface that act as cushions, or shock-absorbers, when the birds strike the water.

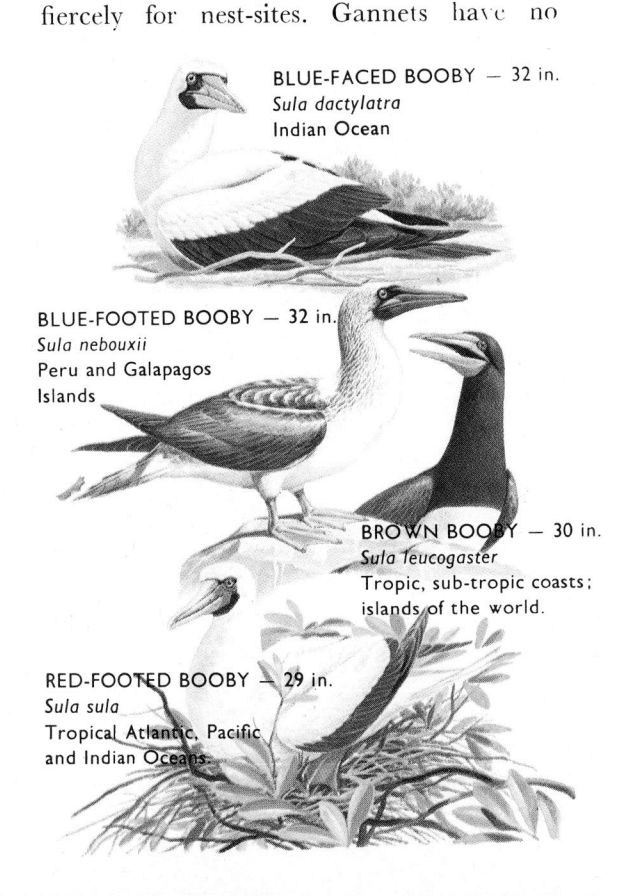

BLUE-FACED BOOBY — 32 in.
Sula dactylatra
Indian Ocean

BLUE-FOOTED BOOBY — 32 in.
Sula nebouxii
Peru and Galapagos Islands

BROWN BOOBY — 30 in.
Sula leucogaster
Tropic, sub-tropic coasts; islands of the world.

RED-FOOTED BOOBY — 29 in.
Sula sula
Tropical Atlantic, Pacific and Indian Oceans

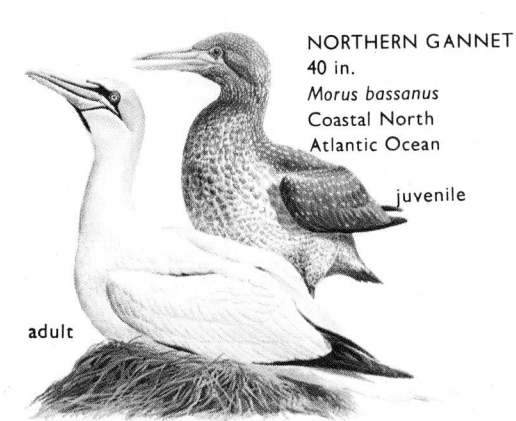

NORTHERN GANNET
40 in.
Morus bassanus
Coastal North Atlantic Ocean

juvenile

adult

occasionally carrion. It may reach a length of 28 to 30 feet; but the official record was 23 feet (see CROCODILIANS).

GAZELLES, fleet-footed antelopes, live in open country, and literature abounds with expressions which acknowledge the speed and gracefulness of these animals. Males have larger horns than females.

The Goitred Gazelle *(Gazella subgutturosa)*, which lives in Persia and Central Asia, is so called because, in the breeding season, the male's neck swells to almost twice normal size; this swollen area resembles a goitre. The Goitred Gazelle is not very large, averaging only about 26 inches at its shoulders, but it runs very swiftly. Males have beautiful lyre-shaped horns. This antelope forages on grass and on the thick leaves of succulent desert plants.

Grant's Gazelle *(Gazella granti)*, found in eastern Africa, may weigh as much as 150 pounds. Both sexes have long horns. Herds of these gazelles are common around waterholes. Thomson's Gazelle *(Gazella thomsoni)*, also found in East Africa, is reddish in colour but has distinctive black-and-white markings. Thomson's Gazelle has been a much-hunted game animal for many years in Kenya and Tanganyika.

Gerenuks *(Lithocranius walleri)*, of eastern

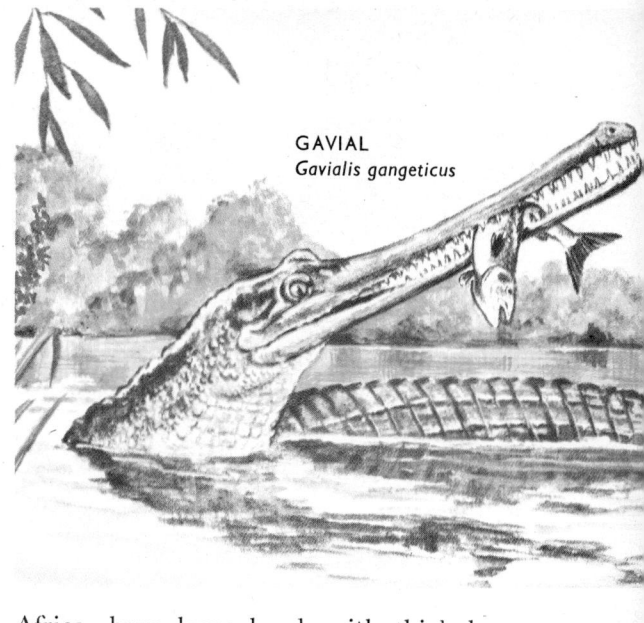

GAVIAL
Gavialis gangeticus

Africa, have large heads with thick horns on very long, thin necks. They stand on their hind legs to reach up for leaves.

Herds of many thousands of Springboks *(Antidorcas marsupialis)* were once common in South Africa, but are now much rarer. They are found as far north as Angola. Like Impalas *(Aepyceros melampus)*, these animals are good jumpers and can leap as much as eight feet high. Impalas, which stand only about three feet tall at their shoulders, are found in South and East Africa. In horizontal jumps, they can span 35 feet.

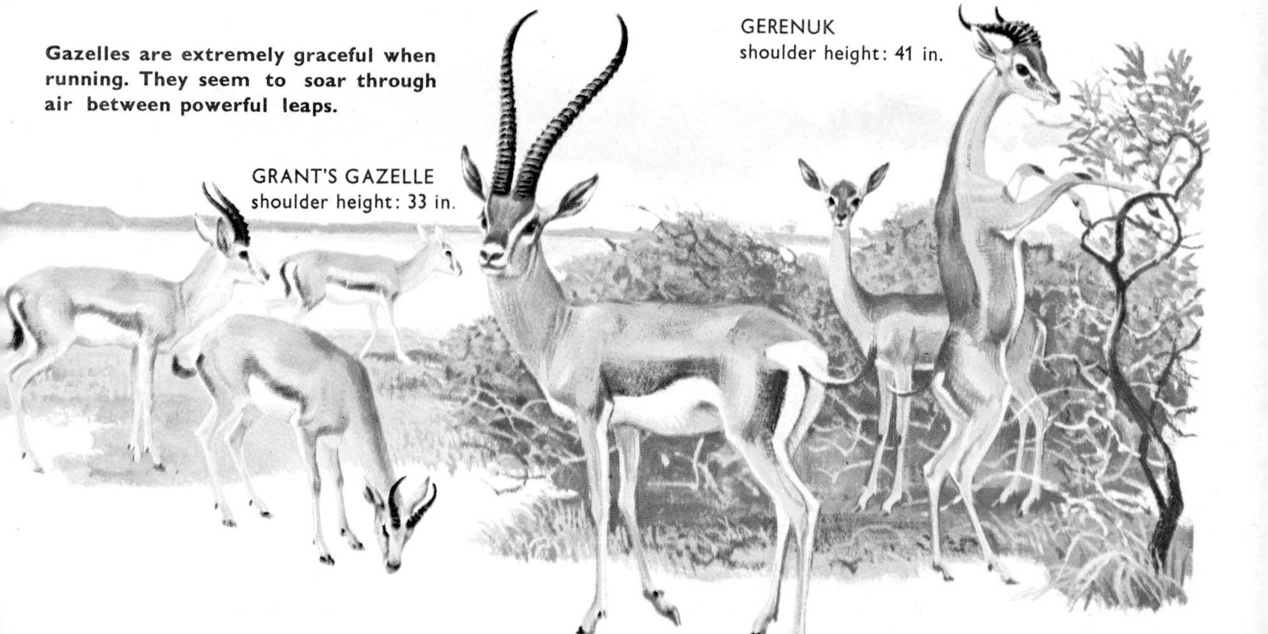

Gazelles are extremely graceful when running. They seem to soar through air between powerful leaps.

GERENUK
shoulder height: 41 in.

GRANT'S GAZELLE
shoulder height: 33 in.

GECKOS, most primitive of living lizards, are small to medium-sized and world-wide in distribution. Most species are active only at dusk or at night. A few kinds are common around dwellings, where they congregate on walls and ceilings, and especially around lights, to catch insects.

All geckos — some 450 species of three families — have very tender, easily torn skin which lacks bony scales. Tails of all except two species of south-western Asia are delicate and easily broken off. A new tail grows quickly, however, and a partial break often results in a branched tail. The largest species measure 14 inches in length; the shortest is a dwarf gecko *(Sphaerodactylus elegans)*, only 1½ inches long.

Dwarf geckos live in the West Indies and in Central and South America. This is the only group of geckos without a voice. Some have a single, round pad at the tip of each finger and toe; others have no pads. Unlike most other geckos, the pupil of the eye in dwarf geckos is usually round or broad oval, rather than lobed and vertical. They are active in daylight, but not in bright sun. No dwarf geckos occur natively as far north as the United States, but two species introduced from the West Indies are established in southern Florida.

Eye-lidded geckos are the most primitive of their kind. Ground geckos *(Coleonyx)*, which live in the south-western United States and southward through Central America, are the only members of this group in the Western Hemisphere. The four other forms occur in Africa and south-eastern Asia. All have eyelids, much like most other lizards, and slender fingers and toes without pads. None of the other geckos have movable eyelids and most others have pads on their hands and feet. Eye-lidded geckos usually lay two eggs, as do most other geckos, and they utter long, drawn-out rattles unlike the single croaks uttered by other geckos.

Both ground and dwarf geckos have long, slender, round tails. In some kinds, the tail is swollen at the base so that it is carrot-shaped, although usually this shape is associated with regenerated tails. In one a knob occurs at the tip of the tail. Many have flattened tails, sometimes fringed with projecting scales on each side. Others have thin, fleshy lobes or broad, leaf-like expansions which help in gliding flights from high trees. Geckos that are gliders also have fringes along the sides of the body.

Some 400 species belong to the family of "true" geckos. The large lower eyelid is fused with the small upper one and has in the centre a transparent scale (a "brille" or "spectacle"), through which the lizard can see. Snakes have the same sort of spectacle.

True geckos have distinct voices. Geckos are, in fact, the only lizards that really have voices. The sound produced is a single croak, though sometimes of two distinct parts. The very name gecko is an attempt to convey the sound made by the common House Gecko *(Hemidactylus mabouia)* of

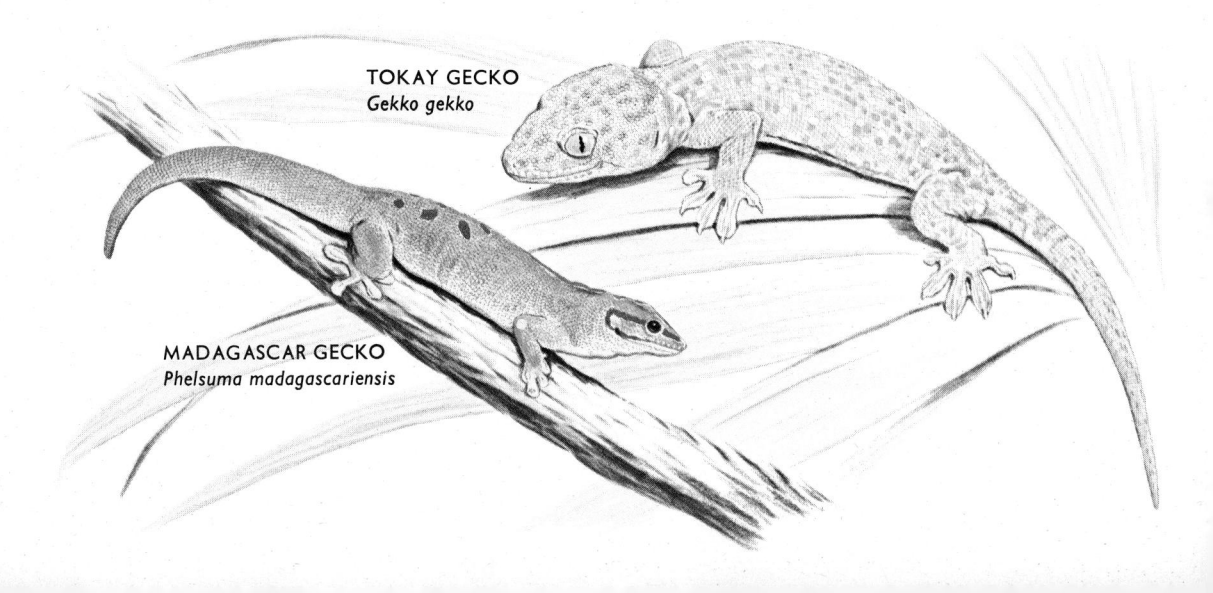

TOKAY GECKO
Gekko gekko

MADAGASCAR GECKO
Phelsuma madagascariensis

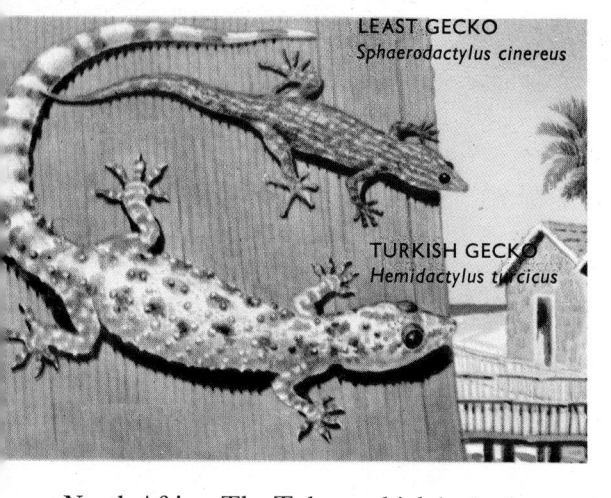

LEAST GECKO
Sphaerodactylus cinereus

TURKISH GECKO
Hemidactylus turcicus

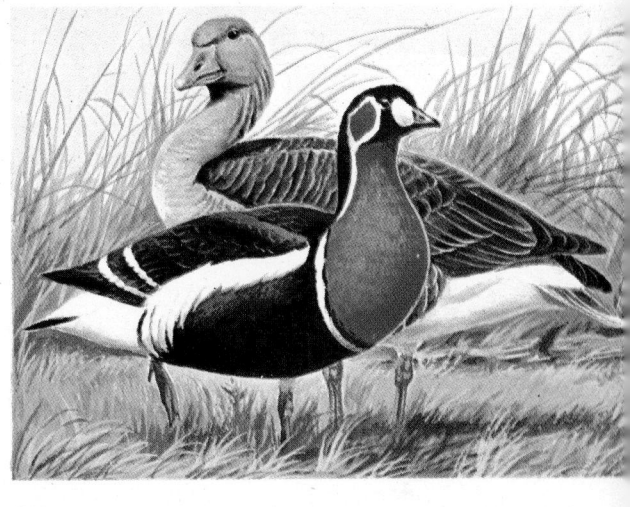

GREY-LAG GOOSE
35 in.
Anser anser
Eurasia and Iceland

RED-BREASTED GOOSE
22 in.
Branta ruficollis
North-central Siberia

North Africa. The Tokay, which is the largest of the geckos, gives a loud cry. In the sand-dunes of south-western Africa, the abundant Garrulous Geckos *(Ptenopus garrulus)* emerge in the early evening and create a din.

True geckos are active in late afternoon, and after dark or in open shade. Their eyes are so sensitive to light that they can see in nearly total darkness. The pupil is slit-like instead of round, and the edges of the slit are lobed so that three or four pinhole-sized openings remain along the vertical line when the slit is closed. This gives a sharp focus on objects located both near and far. Geckos

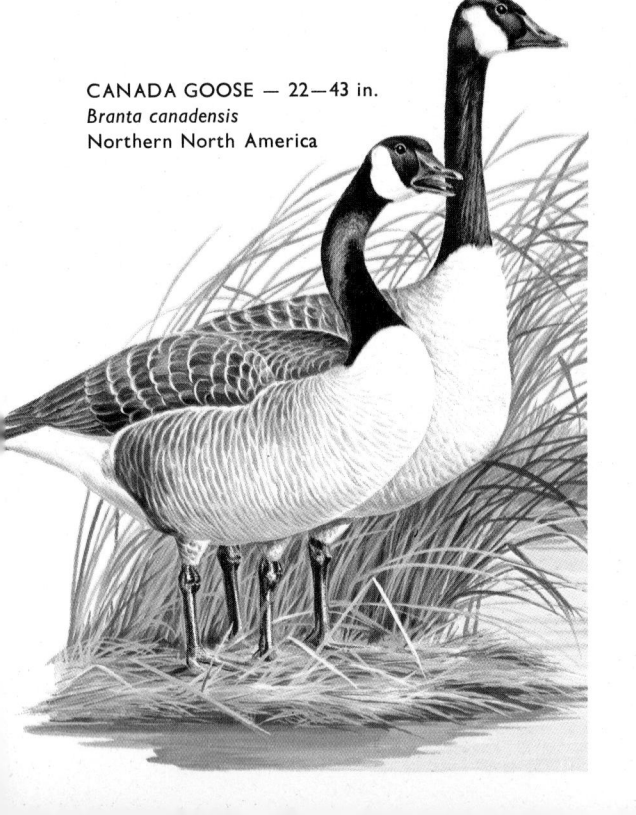

CANADA GOOSE — 22—43 in.
Branta canadensis
Northern North America

of Madagascar, African Banana Geckos, and some other forms differ in being active during the day and in having round pupils.

Most true geckos have a fairly large pad on each finger and toe. These pads are responsible for the extraordinary ability of geckos to walk on ceilings, walls and other smooth surfaces. Though seemingly smooth, the pads are coated with many thousands of tiny hooks that catch on tiny irregularities.

True geckos lay eggs, typically two. These are stuck to tree-bark, window-shutters, or in other hidden spots. The eggs are more or less round, white, and hard-shelled. A few New Zealand geckos give birth to young.

GEESE belong to the same family as ducks and swans. They are larger than ducks, with thicker bills and longer necks and legs.

Geese spend much of their time on land. They crop at grass and other plants like grazing cattle. They also eat grain and roots, including root vegetables. In lakes and ponds and along the coast, they tip-dive for aquatic plants. In migration, geese fly in V-formation, very high when the weather is fine, honking to each other as they go. The flock is made up of family groups.

Brent Geese, smaller than other kinds, are circumpolar in distribution. They breed

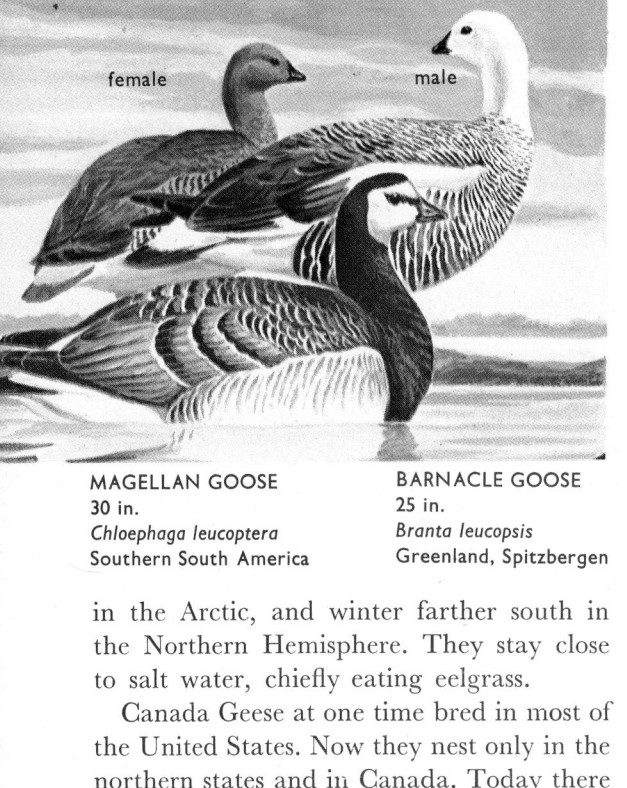

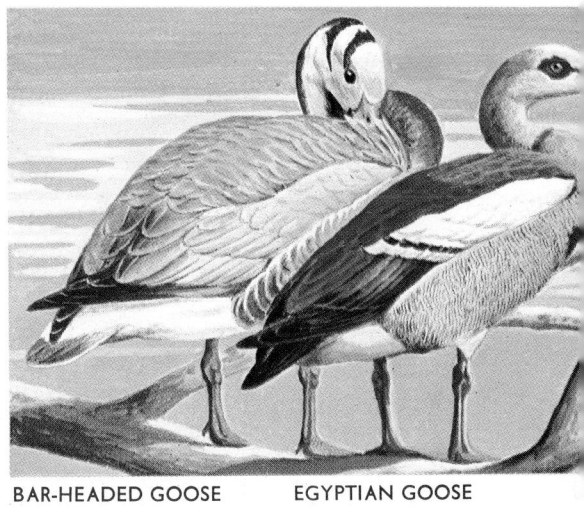

MAGELLAN GOOSE	BARNACLE GOOSE	BAR-HEADED GOOSE	EGYPTIAN GOOSE
30 in.	25 in.	30 in.	28 in.
Chloephaga leucoptera	*Branta leucopsis*	*Anser indicus*	*Alopochen aegyptiaca*
Southern South America	Greenland, Spitzbergen	Highlands of central Asia	Nile Valley through Africa

in the Arctic, and winter farther south in the Northern Hemisphere. They stay close to salt water, chiefly eating eelgrass.

Canada Geese at one time bred in most of the United States. Now they nest only in the northern states and in Canada. Today there are few Canada Geese compared to the tremendous flocks described in colonial times.

Grey-lag Geese of Europe and Asia are the only wild geese that still breed in the British Isles. They are the ancestors of the tame geese from which such breeds as the Embden and Toulouse Geese have been produced by selection. The Chinese Goose

has been derived from a different species, the wild Swan Goose of Asia.

Grey Geese are confined to the Northern Hemisphere, but in the Southern Hemisphere there are several relict forms. The Magpie Goose of Australia is such a bird, adapted to life in extensive swamps. The Cape Barren Goose has a peculiar limited distribution on islands off Australia. In South America, there is a group of species of what are called Sheld-geese. The Magellan

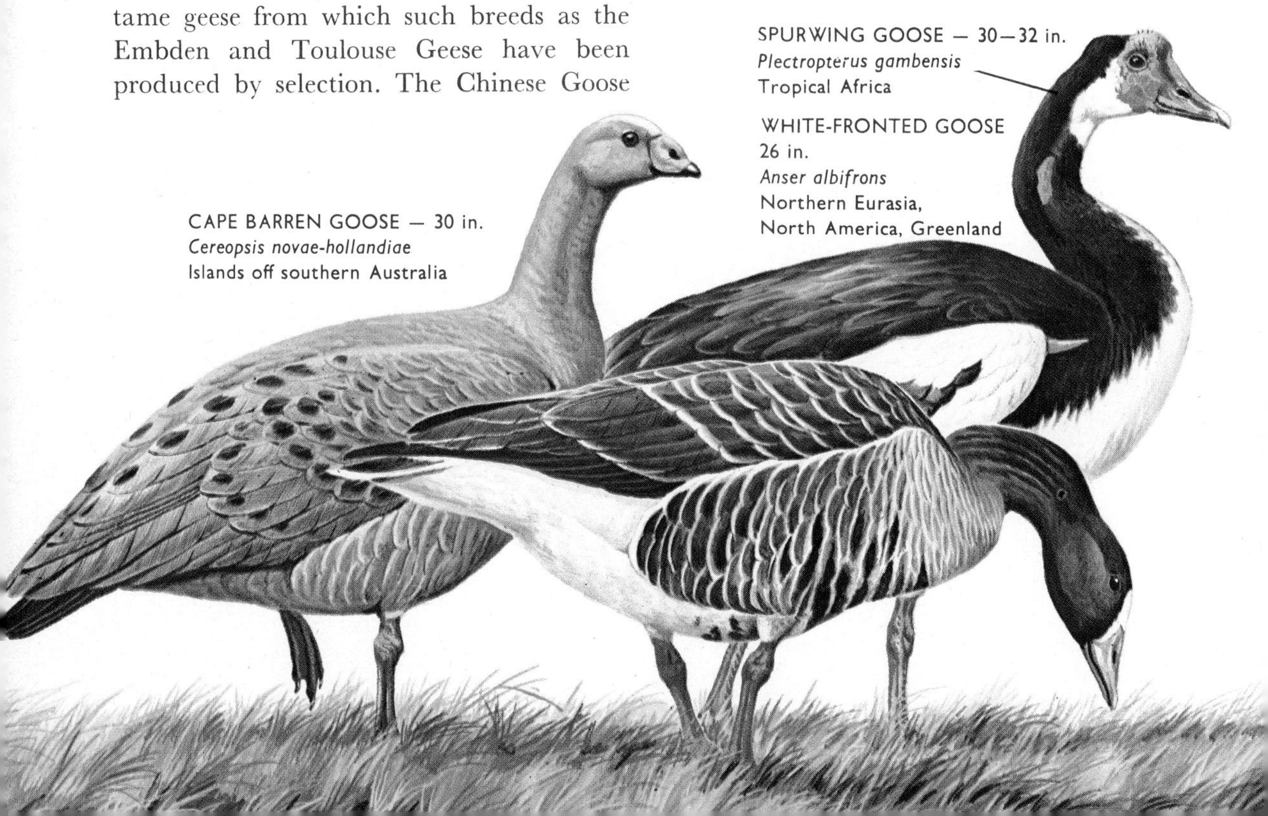

SPURWING GOOSE — 30—32 in.
Plectropterus gambensis
Tropical Africa

WHITE-FRONTED GOOSE
26 in.
Anser albifrons
Northern Eurasia,
North America, Greenland

CAPE BARREN GOOSE — 30 in.
Cereopsis novae-hollandiae
Islands off southern Australia

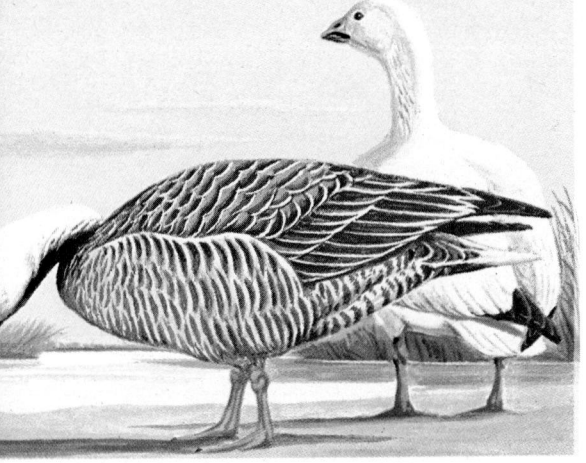

EMPEROR GOOSE
26 in.
Philacte canagica
Alaska and eastern Siberia

SNOW GOOSE
28 in.
Chen caerulescens
Northern North America

Goose is one of these. They have long, slender necks and small bills, and are grazing birds. In spite of their name they are considered to be related to the Shelducks, as is the Egyptian Goose, while the Spur-winged Goose is a relative of the Wood-ducks. The Nene Goose of Hawaii is a species saved from extinction by being bred in captivity. It is a bird, not of sea-coasts, but of lava-flows, and has become long-legged, with reduced webs on the feet. It is related to the Canada Goose.

DOMESTIC GEESE. Geese were probably tamed as long ago as the Stone Age or Bronze Age. When Roman legions invaded Germany, they found tame white Embden Geese and took them back to Rome. They plucked the birds several times a year and used the feathers for bedding. Goose was the traditional feast-day meal in Europe before the turkey was introduced from America.

Geese are raised for their meat and eggs, as well as for their feathers. They are usually marketed when they are about three months old. At this age they are called "green geese" and weigh about 14 pounds.

Geese are customarily kept in flocks, usually led by a gander (male). Geese usually mate for life, although a gander may be mated with as many as five females.

GHOST CRABS *(Ocypode quadrata)* have light, sand-coloured shells. They are found on sandy beaches of America's Atlantic coast from New Jersey (U.S.A.) to South America. Ghost Crabs dig small burrows near the grass line above the high-tide mark, and come out to forage on sea-wrack in the late evening and at night. About six to eight inches wide, and with one large and one small claw, they can run extremely fast and are hard to catch, except with a rake or some other long-handled implement. If blocked off from its burrow, a Ghost Crab will dash into the water, where it is generally seized by a fish. The crab is called a "ghost" because its quick movements and protective colouration make it hard to see. Ghost Crabs are closely related to Fiddler Crabs; both are crustaceans (see CRUSTACEANS; FIDDLER CRABS).

GIBBONS *(Hylobates, Symphalangus)* are small apes that spend nearly all their time high in trees (see APES). Their muscular arms are so long that, when they stand erect, their fingertips touch the ground. Their scientific name, *Hylobates*, means "tree walkers". Gibbons can swing through the branches of trees with speed and grace, sometimes dropping dozens of feet to catch a branch, and then swinging up again to a higher one. Since they use their arms for locomotion, gibbons use their feet to hold objects as they swing from branch to branch. Young gibbons wrap themselves around their mother's waist like a belt as she moves through the trees. All gibbons

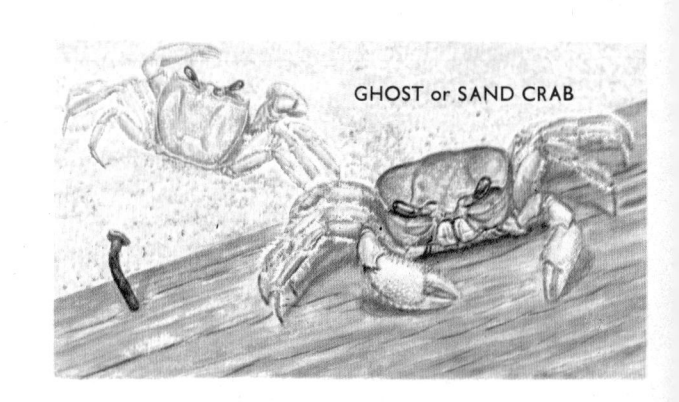

GHOST or SAND CRAB

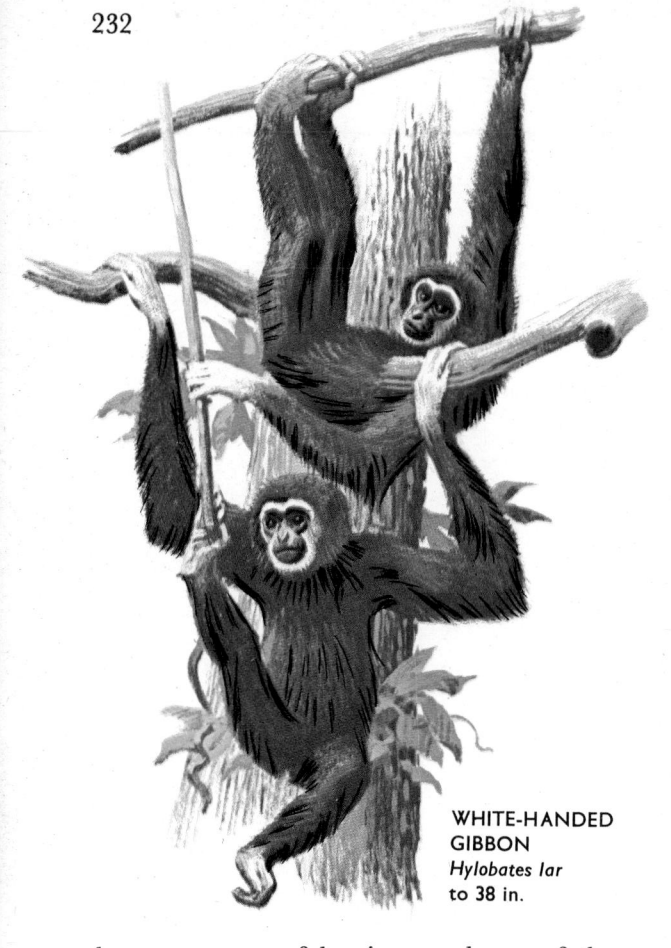

WHITE-HANDED
GIBBON
Hylobates lar
to 38 in.

have very powerful voices, and one of the noisiest is the Hoolock *(Hylobates hoolock)*.

Gibbons live in family groups which consist of the male and female and their offspring of several ages. The young are carefully reared and trained by both parents. All Gibbons are found in the Orient, and among the most common are the White-handed Gibbon *(Hylobates lar)* and the Siamang *(Symphalangus syndactylus)*.

GILA MONSTERS, or Beaded Lizards *(Heloderma* spp.*),* are the only poisonous lizards in the world. Their beaded skins make them easily identified. Each bead-like bump contains a small bony core. They have fairly short, blunt, club-like tails in which food reserves are stored. A well-fed Gila (pronounced *Heel-uh*) Monster has a heavy, fat tail; a lizard starved for a month or more has a more slender tail.

One species, first found near the Gila River in Arizona, lives in the desert regions of the south-western United States and north-western Mexico. The only other species, known as the Mexican Beaded Lizard, lives in forested coastal regions of Mexico southward almost to Guatemala. The Gila Monster is mostly pink or light yellow, with irregular, scattered patches of black or dark brown, and four or five dark rings on its tail. The Mexican species is mostly black or dark brown, with irregular, scattered patches of pink or light yellow, and six or seven tail rings. The Mexican Beaded Lizard reaches a recorded length of 32 inches; no Gila Monster above 20 inches is on record.

These lizards eat eggs of ground-nesting birds and reptiles, and also eat small birds and mammals, especially the young. Most flesh-eating animals are fast-moving, but these lizards are sluggish and incapable of running down anything that is not virtually helpless. They snap their jaws with astonishing quickness and flip their bodies to change direction quickly. They use smell more than sight to find food, frequently sampling ground odours with their tongues.

Large salivary glands in the lower jaw — and sharp, conical, grooved teeth of both jaws — are the venom apparatus. Each tooth is deeply grooved down its front and back edges. The poisonous saliva is released into the mouth and seeps into the bite wound by flowing along the grooves. Gila Monsters have very powerful jaws.

GILA MONSTER
Heloderma suspectum

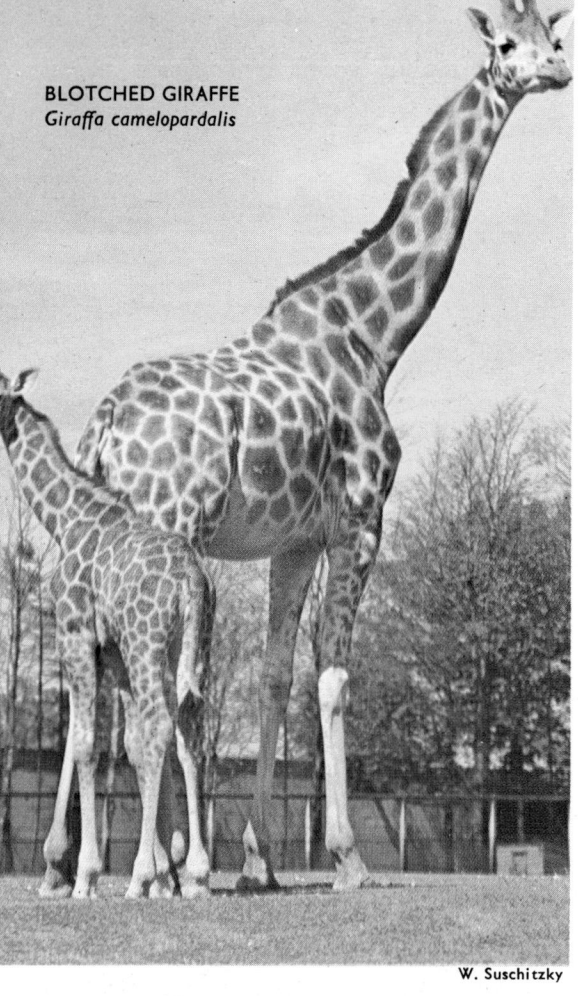

BLOTCHED GIRAFFE
Giraffa camelopardalis

W. Suschitzky

Although they appear to be defenceless, and will run from danger whenever possible, giraffes have sharp hoofs and, when pressed, will kick with great power.

GIRAFFES *(Giraffa camelopardalis)* are the tallest animals in the world. Large males may stand more than 18 feet high. Giraffes live in herds, commanded by bulls, in the comparatively open country of Africa. They feed mainly on leaves and branches, which they pluck with their long (as much as 18 inches), sensitive tongues. Giraffes can go for fairly long periods of time without drinking. When they do stop for water, they spread their front legs wide apart so that their long necks can reach the water. The several varieties of Giraffe are distinguished by differences in coat patterns and by the number of "horns", or bony knobs, on the top of their skulls. Both males and females have these "horns", which are covered with skin and tufts of hair. Some have a third horn, situated between their eyes and in front of the other pair. Giraffes move both front and hind legs on the same side simultaneously as they run, giving them a peculiar gait, like camels. Their vocal cords are degenerate, hence their voices are weak.

Blotched Giraffes, found throughout much of eastern and southern Africa, are the most common kind. Reticulated Giraffes, which live in Somaliland and northern Kenya, have reddish-brown spots outlined by narrow white lines.

GLASS FROGS, members of the family *Centrolenidae,* are found in Central and South America. The undersides of their delicate, jewel-like bodies are so transparent that their white or green leg and arm bones show through clearly, with red blood vessels running along them. The heart and other internal organs are also visible. Their upper surfaces are an opaque, bright green. Unlike all other frogs, this group has fused ankle bones. All of the three genera in the family are tree-dwellers and are related to the true tree frogs (see TREE FROGS).

GLASS LIZARDS *(Ophisaurus* spp.*)* are able to break off any part of their tail into one or several pieces at the slightest disturbance. Since the tail is several times as long as head and body, it appears that the body has broken into pieces. The wriggling pieces of tail decoy an enemy while the lizard

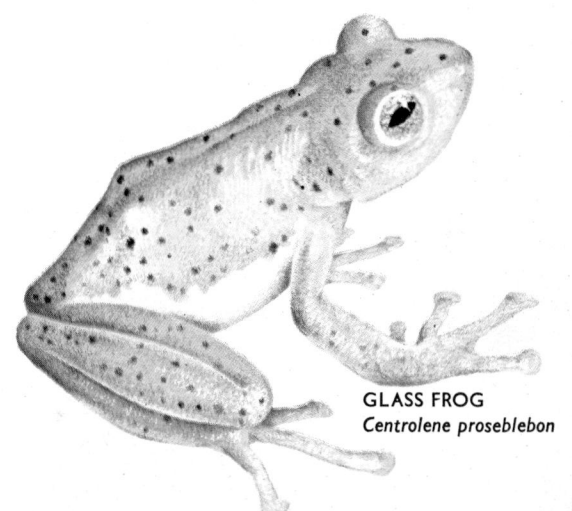

GLASS FROG
Centrolene proseblebon

escapes. The pieces never grow together, despite the belief that they do, but a new tail grows rapidly from the old stub.

The Scheltopusik, of south-eastern Europe, grows to a length of nearly four feet, and its body is nearly three inches thick. The Scheltopusik eats mice, snakes, and other large animals. Smaller kinds eat insects.

All glass lizards lack legs, although a reduced bone structure of legs is still present internally. They also have ear openings and eyelids, distinguishing them from snakes.

GNUS *(Connochaetes* spp.*)*, also known as Wildebeests, are strange-looking antelopes of the veld — the grass country of southern and eastern Africa. Their heavy horns curve outward and upward like meat-hooks. Chin whiskers and bushy, horse-like tails add to the odd appearance of gnus. Their sad-looking faces are especially broad, like those of the Bison, and their hair appears to be closely clipped, in the style of a horse. Gnus usually travel in large herds, or troops. Easily alarmed, the herd charges off noisily,

The White-bearded Gnu of East Africa is a sub-species of the Brindled Gnu, or Blue Wildebeest (Connochaetes taurinus) of East and South Africa. The smaller Whitetailed Gnu (Connochaetes gnu), the only other species, occurs in South Africa, but not in the wild state and only on farms.

W. Suschitzky

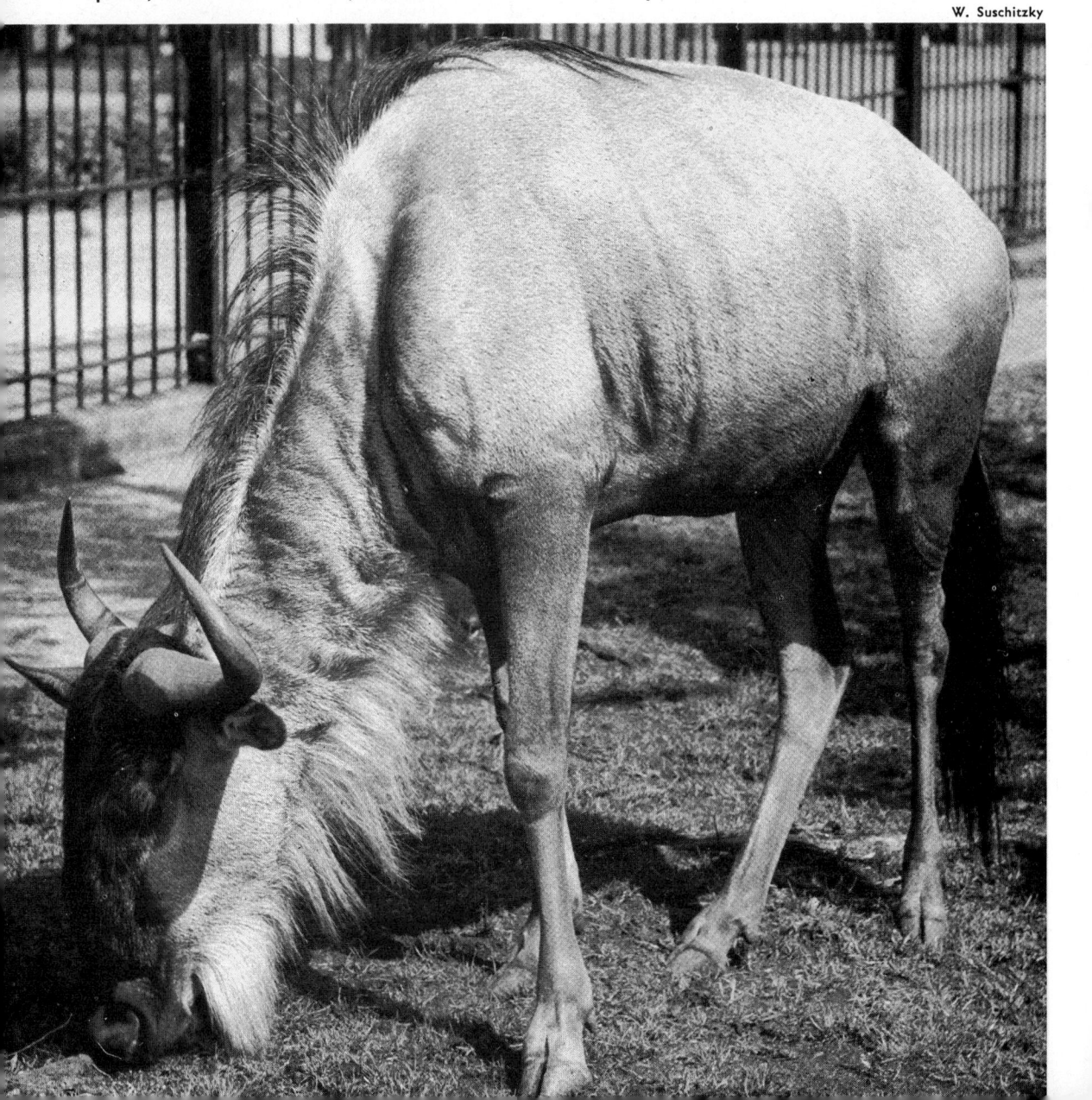

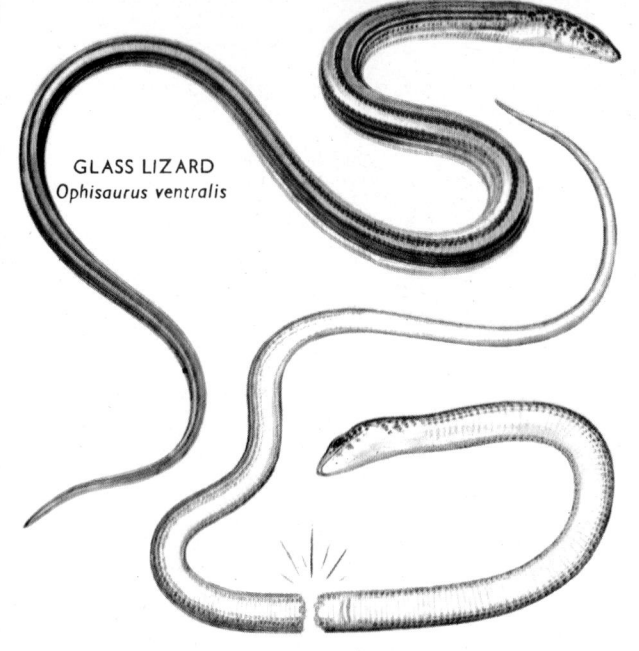

GLASS LIZARD
Ophisaurus ventralis

jumping and kicking. Frequently, the fleeing troop stops suddenly as a unit, wheels around, and faces the intruder. As gnus need a constant source of water, they are most common around water-holes. They rest during the middle of the day, and feed in the morning and evening. Gnu is the Hottentot name for this animal — Wildebeest (wild ox) is the Dutch settlers' name for it.

GOATS. Most male goats have beards and a strong "goaty" odour. Both sexes have horns, but those of the male are larger.

Ibexes *(Capra ibex)* are the wild goats of Europe, North Africa and parts of Asia, living in mountainous areas of steep cliffs and rocky slopes. They are difficult to approach because they take alarm at the slightest sign of danger. A protected colony of Ibexes still survives in the Italian Alps. Some people believe our domestic goats may have been derived from the Ibex.

Tahrs *(Hemitragus* spp.*)* are goat-like animals that exist on the lightly-forested, steep slopes of the Himalayas. They have short, heavy horns, no beards, and thick coats to withstand the rigorous weather of the high altitudes. Other Tahrs are found in southern India and Arabia.

Markhors *(Capra falconeri),* found in the mountainous areas from northern India to southern Russia, have twisted or spiral horns up to three feet in length. Males have large, shaggy beards. Their name means "snake-eater". They graze in glades, and resort to forests only to escape insect pests.

DOMESTIC GOATS. The Domestic Goat *(Capra hircus)* has been of use to man since the New Stone Age. Farmers in Ancient Egypt used goats to trample seed into the ground after it was sown. In some areas of the south-western United States, goats are highly valued because they can clear brushland. A goat will eat all the leaves and twigs it can reach, even standing on its hind legs to get those that are high overhead. When the twigs and leaves are all eaten, the goat eats bark, and the following year it eats new shoots. As soon as the sun can reach the soil exposed in this manner, grass grows. Land cleared by goats can then be ploughed and planted with crops, or it can be used for pasture.

The Cashmere Goat has not been successfully raised anywhere in the world except in Kashmir and Tibet. A fine coat of

The large herd below is in the Georgian Mountains of southern Russia.

George Hunter — Annan Photo Features

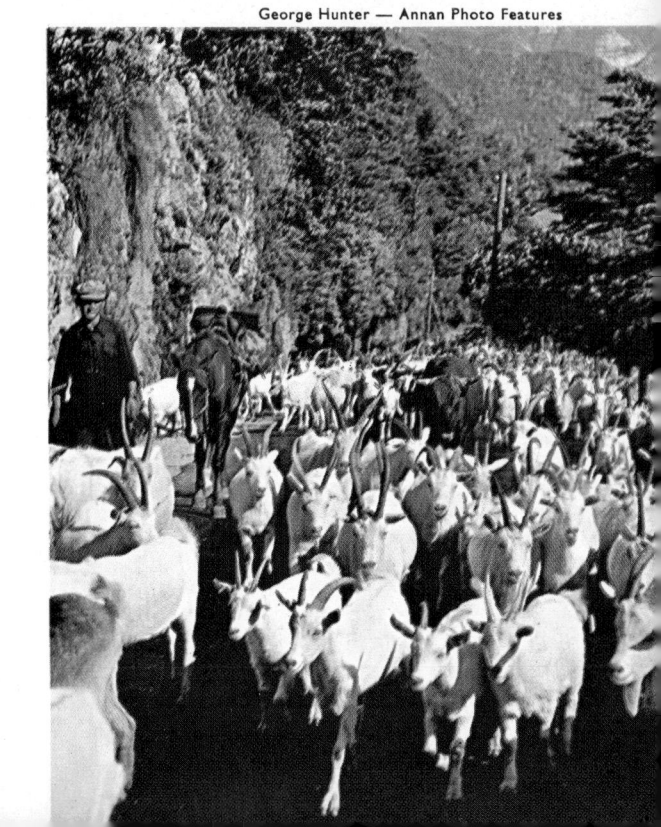

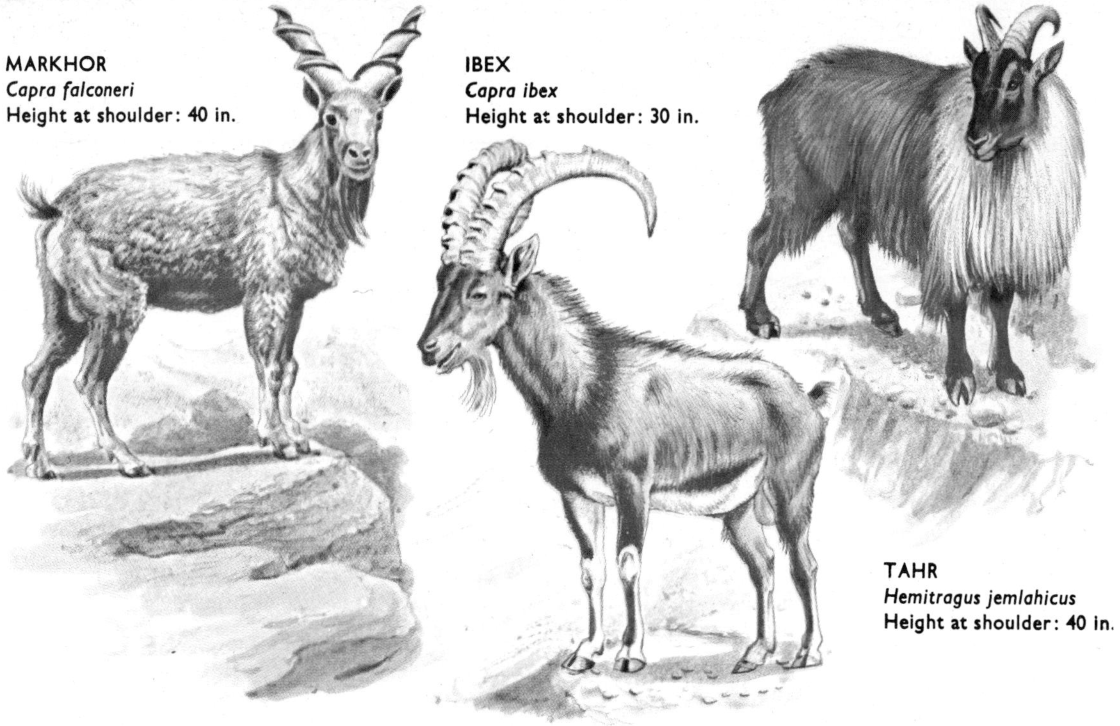

MARKHOR
Capra falconeri
Height at shoulder: 40 in.

IBEX
Capra ibex
Height at shoulder: 30 in.

TAHR
Hemitragus jemlahicus
Height at shoulder: 40 in.

The wild relatives of the domestic goats live in rugged mountain country, travelling in small bands.

wool, called "pashm", is produced by this goat. The wool is combed out several times a year, but one goat may produce only two or three ounces of wool a year. Because there is so little cashmere, it is very expensive, and often mixed with other woollen fibres.

Goats' milk has a small, soft curd, and can be drunk by many people who cannot tolerate cows' milk because of stomach trouble or allergies. A goat that gives from two to four quarts of milk a day for a period of six to ten months is a good milker. Goats have been milked for as long as two years without giving birth to further kids.

Goat-meat tastes much like mutton and is marketed as "chevon".

Goats, like sheep and cattle, have hoofs and a four-chambered stomach.

GOBIES are a family *(Gobiidae)* of fishes that frequent shallows and tidal pools in all seas and also in fresh water. They are most abundant in the tropics. Some species are extremely small. The smallest back-boned animal is a goby that lives in fresh-water streams of the Philippine Islands. Several kinds are important as food, and in Asia and

Africa these are reared in pools and fattened in special ponds. The family includes blind species inhabiting dark, cool cave-waters.

Typically the ventral fins of gobies are joined, or nearly so, to form a sucking disc which helps them cling to the wave-washed rocks along the shore. Some gobies burrow in the mud. Others spend long periods out of water, crawling about over the wet rocks and sandflats. By using oxygen in the water trapped in their large gill-chambers, they can stay out of the water for several hours.

Gobies make good, interesting aquarium pets. Unlike blennies, many of which move rapidly with an eel-like motion, gobies swim by darting from rock to rock. Males, usually brighter coloured than the females, make nests, and then try to lure a female (or several) to lay eggs there. When courting, they spread their fins to show dazzling colours that change with the fish's mood. Often they fight other males in defending their nesting sites, viciously protecting their nests and eggs. (See FISHES; BLENNIES.)

RIVER GOBY
Gobius fluviatilis
2—3 in.

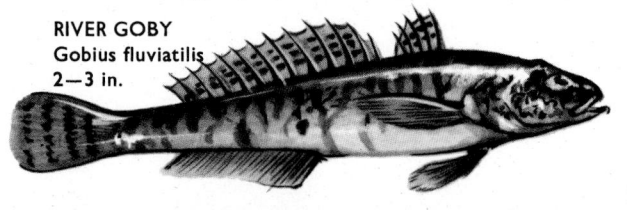

GOLDFISH *(Carassius auratus)* are native to the temperate regions of Asia, and in the wild are brown or silver. The bright yellow-orange of the common aquarium variety is the result of selective breeding. Goldfish fanciers have developed more than 100 varieties. Some of the common names under which the fish are sold are Comet, Fantail,

Through centuries of selective breeding, mainly in Japan and China, the Common Goldfish has been changed from its original drab grey or silvery colour to varieties that are bright red, orange, white, black or calico. Prized types have unusual fin shapes and protruding, or "telescope", eyes. Goldfish can be kept in small aquariums, but do best when kept in larger outdoor pools.

Shubunkin and Fringetail. Colour varies from near white, through yellow, to orange or black. Black specimens are called Moors.

Breeders have developed varieties with large heads (Lionheads); with large, bulging eyes (Telescopes and Celestials); and with very long, lacy tails (Japanese Fringetails). Calico goldfish are those with scales not entirely pigmented.

Goldfish are extremely hardy fish, which has made them favourites for aquariums the world over (see AQUARIUMS).

GOPHER is a name for several kinds of American rodents, but it refers only to the pocket gophers, which are members of the family *Geomyidae*. Ground squirrels are rodents which are sometimes called gophers, too (see GROUND SQUIRRELS).

Pocket gophers are found mainly in the western United States and Mexico, although a few kinds live in the south-eastern United States. Pocket gophers spend most of their time in underground burrows; hence they are sometimes confused with moles. They have rather large, functional eyes, however, and also short noses, and their fur is thinner than that of moles. They feed on stems and roots of plants, rather than on insects, and carry their food in cheek pouches, which form the "pockets" from which they get their name; these pouches open outside the mouth.

Pocket gophers have strongly-clawed front feet, and are constantly digging tunnels to

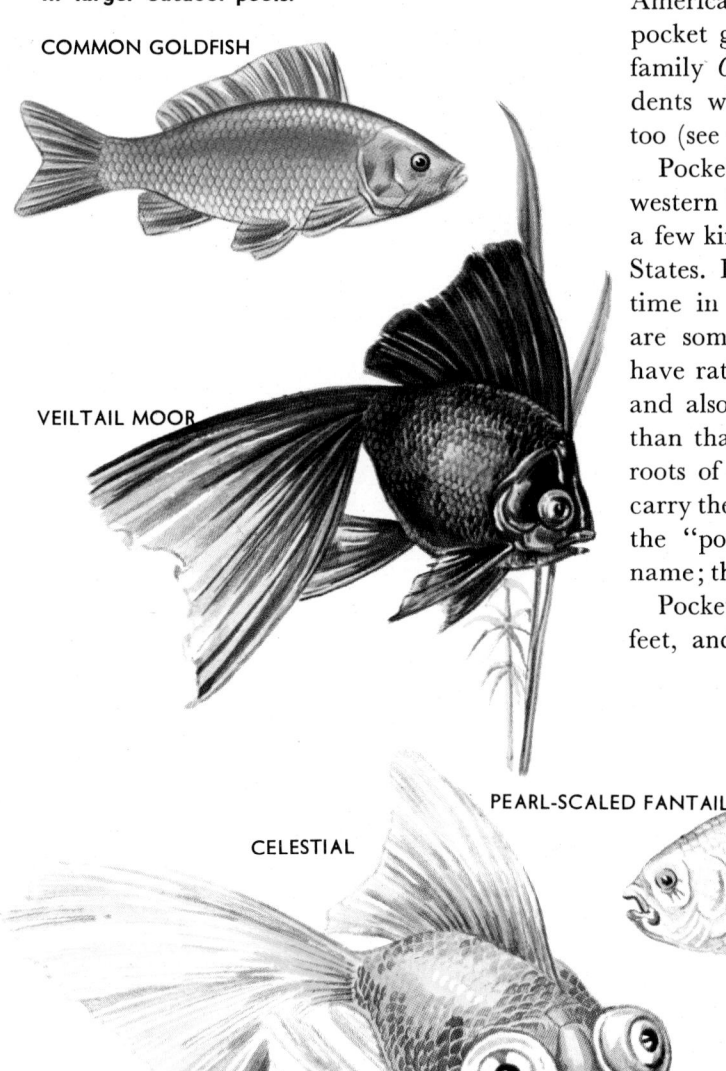

COMMON GOLDFISH

VEILTAIL MOOR

CELESTIAL

PEARL-SCALED FANTAIL

SHUBUNKIN

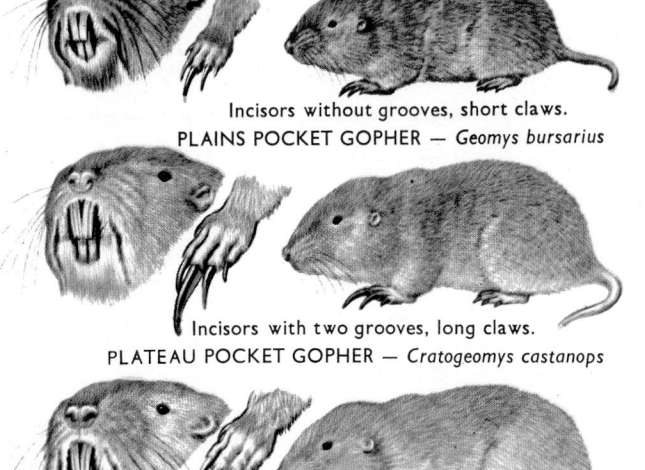

WESTERN POCKET GOPHER — *Thomomys bottae*

Incisors without grooves, short claws.

PLAINS POCKET GOPHER — *Geomys bursarius*

Incisors with two grooves, long claws.

PLATEAU POCKET GOPHER — *Cratogeomys castanops*

Incisors with one groove, long claws.

find new sources of food. They seldom come to the surface, and when they do, they quickly fill their burrow with soil so that it is again sealed off from the outside. Their short, nearly naked tail serves as a "feeler" for directing them as they back up along the tunnels. Each gopher occupies its own burrow system, except when seeking a mate.

The common pocket gopher of the southeastern United States is *Geomys bursarius*, while the many species of the western United States are mostly members of the genus *Thomomys*.

GORILLAS (*Gorilla gorilla*), largest of the apes, are peaceable animals, despite their size. A large male may stand over five feet in height and weigh more than 500 pounds. Adults are very powerful. They have been known to bend two-inch steel bars and to tear large limbs from trees. Unless trapped or frightened, they apparently make no attempt to molest man.

Gorillas live in the forested areas of central Africa, from the lowlands far up into the mountains. Mountain-dwelling gorillas generally have black coats, while those that live in the lowlands often have rusty-grey coats. They live together in family groups,

including young of different ages. Their "homes" are platforms of sticks and branches built in trees a few feet above the ground. Gorillas are active during the day, spending much of their time on the ground, and walk on all-fours, using their long arms for support. They will climb trees to eat fruit or leaves, however. At night they sleep in nests, generally at the foot of a tree. Little is known about the habits of these interesting animals in their native haunts.

GRASSHOPPERS and their sounds are familiar to nearly everyone. The more than 10,000 species of grasshopper can be divided into two broad groups: shorthorn grasshoppers, or locusts (*Acrididae*), which have antennae shorter than their body; and longhorn grasshoppers (*Tettigoniidae*), which have antennae longer than their body. Shorthorn grasshoppers usually make their sounds by rubbing the femur of their hind leg against a hardened area on the front wing. Longhorn grasshoppers rub their front wings together. Each species produces a song as distinctive as the calls of birds.

Many of the shorthorn grasshoppers, or locusts, are brown or dark. The Rocky

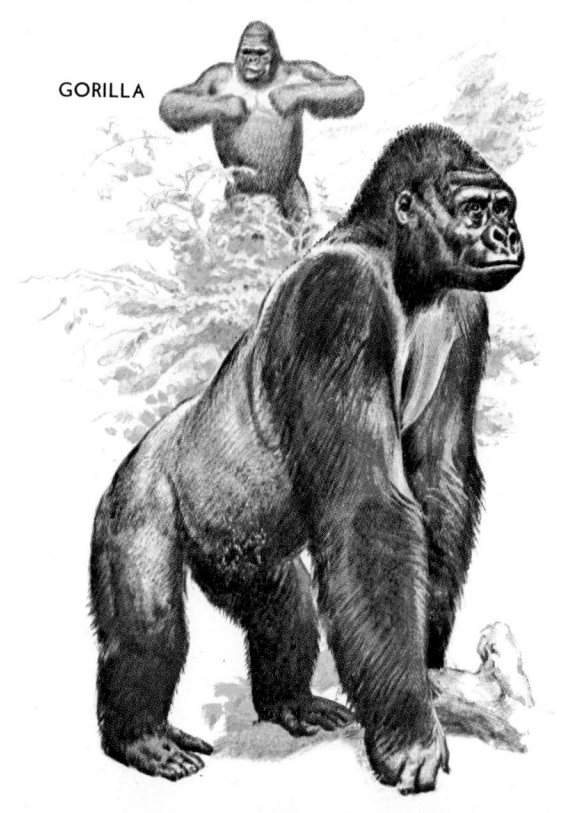

GORILLA

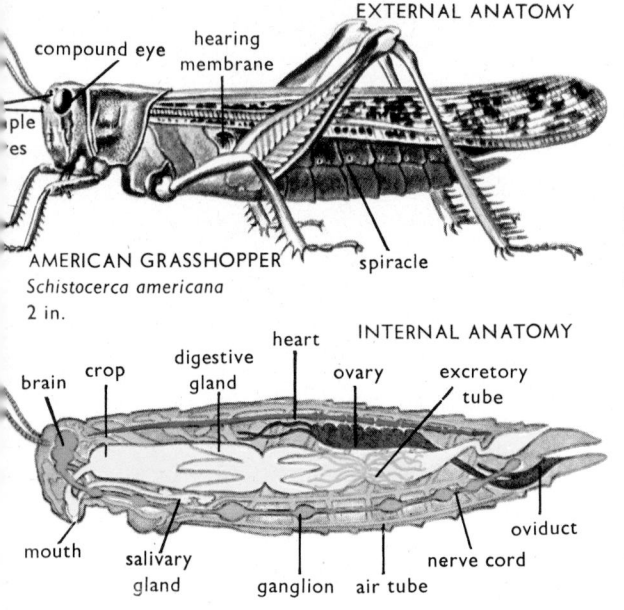

EXTERNAL ANATOMY

compound eye
hearing
membrane
ple
es

AMERICAN GRASSHOPPER
Schistocerca americana
2 in.

spiracle

INTERNAL ANATOMY

heart
digestive
gland
brain
crop
ovary
excretory
tube

mouth
salivary
gland
ganglion
air tube
nerve cord
oviduct

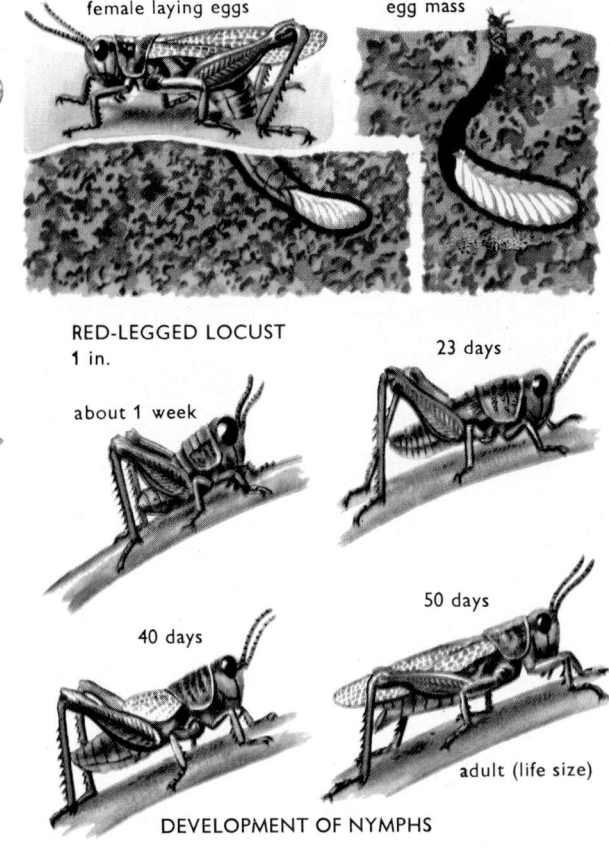

female laying eggs

egg mass

RED-LEGGED LOCUST
1 in.

about 1 week

23 days

40 days

50 days

adult (life size)

DEVELOPMENT OF NYMPHS

Mountain Locust and the Red-legged Locust are members of this group. Sometimes these grasshoppers become very abundant and then migrate in tremendous swarms, destroying nearly all plants in their path. Locust plagues have been recorded since the beginning of history and are one of the world's major insect problems.

Most locusts deposit their eggs in the ground, but some lay their eggs in logs or stumps. The eggs are laid in the autumn, in a mass held together by a glue-like substance. The eggs hatch in the spring, and the nymphs feed and moult during the summer, becoming adults in late summer or early autumn. Some species pass the winter as nymphs or adults and lay eggs in spring.

Band-winged locusts have bright-coloured hind wings. The hind wings of the Carolina Locust, a member of this group, are black edged with yellow. The Coral-winged Locust's hind wings are red or coral coloured. Their wings make a crackling noise in flight.

Longhorn grasshoppers are usually green. Some deposit their eggs in the ground. Others insert their eggs in leaves or stems, or place them in rows on the surface. The Great Green grasshopper (*Tettigonia viridissima*) is the largest longhorn in Britain. In the southern half of the country, its noisy sounds cannot fail to attract attention.

GREBES are squat-bodied diving birds, found in all parts of the world on fresh water. A few species haunt the sea-coasts when not breeding, but typically they are birds of ponds and lakes. Like the divers they are streamlined for movement underwater, with the feet set so far back for propulsion that movement on land is difficult. The toes of the feet are lobed to give a better thrust. The wings are small and narrow, and grebes cannot take flight easily; once airborne, however, their flight is rapid and direct.

They escape danger by diving and swimming away under water, where they can travel faster than on the surface. The plumage forms a waterproof insulating layer and was once sold as "grebe fur".

The display plumage takes the form of ear-tufts, and ruffs of narrow feathers that can be erected when they are required; at other times, however, these lie flat and do not spoil the grebe's streamlined shape. The Little and Pied-billed Grebes lack these

adornments. Such plumes are most highly developed in the Great Crested Grebe, and when a pair display, they often rear up to face each other, erect the ear-tufts and ruff, and solemnly shake their heads.

The nests are usually floating mounds of rotting weeds, anchored by growing reeds or rushes. The white eggs are often covered with nest material, if the parent leaves them, and they become stained brown. The young birds can swim and dive as soon as they are hatched. When tired, they are carried on the backs of the parents, their small, striped heads showing between the wings.

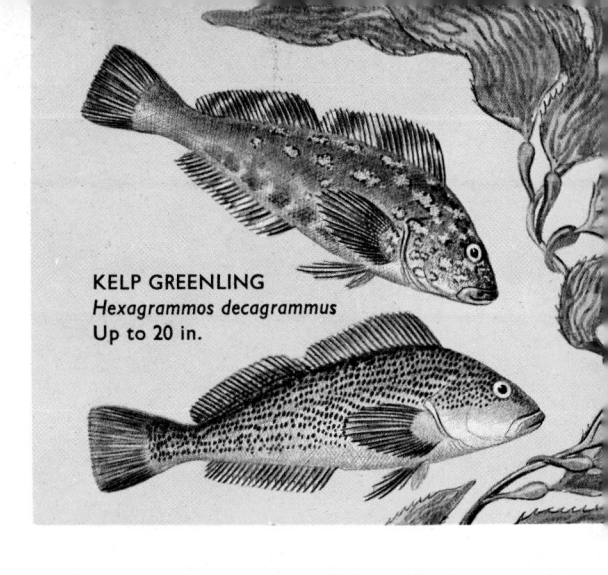

KELP GREENLING
Hexagrammos decagrammus
Up to 20 in.

GREENLINGS (*Hexagrammos* spp.) are fish that live in the cold waters of the Pacific from central California northward to Alaska. The several species are easily identified by their long dorsal and anal fins, and by the presence of more than one lateral line. All species live fairly close to shore, in kelp beds or among rocks. Most species are brown or olive, with bright spots of blue, orange or red. Greenlings never get large (20 inches in length; two or three pounds in weight), but they furnish good sport for fishermen. Those that feed on kelp often have green flesh.

GREENSNAKES (*Opheodrys* spp.) are slender, harmless snakes (18 to 30 inches in length) found either on the ground or in

bushes. They are accomplished climbers, and often "freeze" in position in the green foliage, where they are almost impossible to see, so well are they camouflaged. Their food consists of insects, spiders, and other small invertebrates. They do not feed well in captivity.

The Smooth Greensnake, the smaller of the two species found in North America, has smooth scales. The Rough Greensnake has a strong ridge (keel) down the middle of each dorsal scale. They both occur in the United States and Central America. Both species lay eggs. Those of the Smooth Greensnake develop for such a long period in the body of the female that they sometimes take only three days to hatch after being laid, and never more than 23. The eggs are laid in the ground, under debris, or in rotten wood.

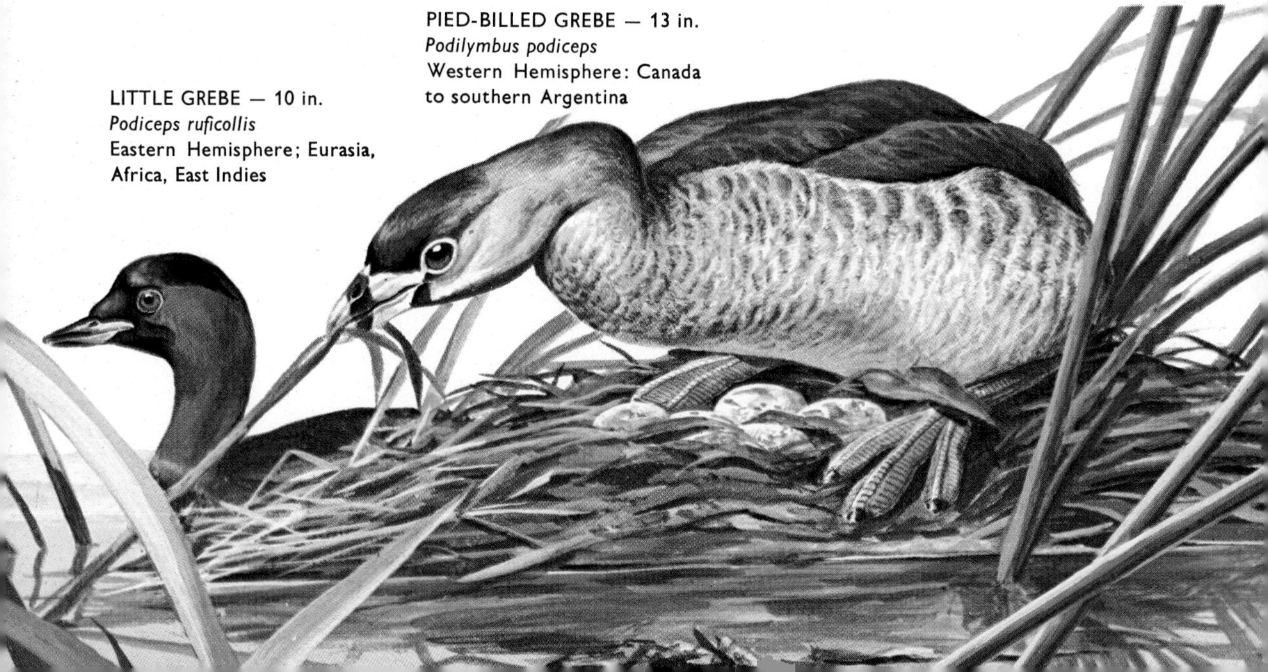

PIED-BILLED GREBE — 13 in.
Podilymbus podiceps
Western Hemisphere: Canada to southern Argentina

LITTLE GREBE — 10 in.
Podiceps ruficollis
Eastern Hemisphere; Eurasia, Africa, East Indies

GROUND BEETLES *(Carabidae)* are one of the largest groups of beetles. Most of the some 25,000 species in the family are long-legged, flat-bodied, and dark in colour. They live under stones, logs, or other ground debris, coming out at night to feed. Nearly all ground beetles can run rapidly. Most of them feed on other insects, but some feed on snails and a few on plant material. The larvae, also predaceous, are elongated and have sharp mandibles. Most larvae exist in habitats similar to those of the adults.

Caterpillar Hunters *(Calosoma)* are the largest and most brilliantly coloured of the ground beetles. They feed primarily on caterpillars and search quite actively for them in trees. A European species of this genus *(C. Sycophanta)* was introduced to the United States to help control the Gypsy Moth and the Brown-tailed Moth.

Fiddle Beetles *(Mormolyce)*, of south-eastern Asia, are three to four inches long and very flat, with slender heads. The flared wing-covers of these unusual beetles extend beyond the sides of their abdomen, like the shape of a violin. These beetles are arboreal.

Bombardier beetles are also members of this family (see BOMBARDIER BEETLES).

GROUND SQUIRRELS are a group of rodents that belong to the same family *(Sciuridae)* as tree squirrels. They live underground in burrows, but are active on the surface during the day collecting food, which they store temporarily in pouches in their cheeks. Ground squirrels are also called spermophiles, and in parts of Asia they are known as susliks. Found throughout most of North America, south-eastern Europe, Asia and parts of Africa, ground squirrels feed principally on plants, including grasses, seeds and nuts. In farmed areas, ground squirrels may be serious pests of crops; and on pasture or grazing lands, their burrows are a hazard to livestock. The animals may also be carriers of diseases, such as tularemia. Ground squirrels multiply rapidly, with each litter of 8 to 12 young. Many species hibernate in winter (see MAMMALS).

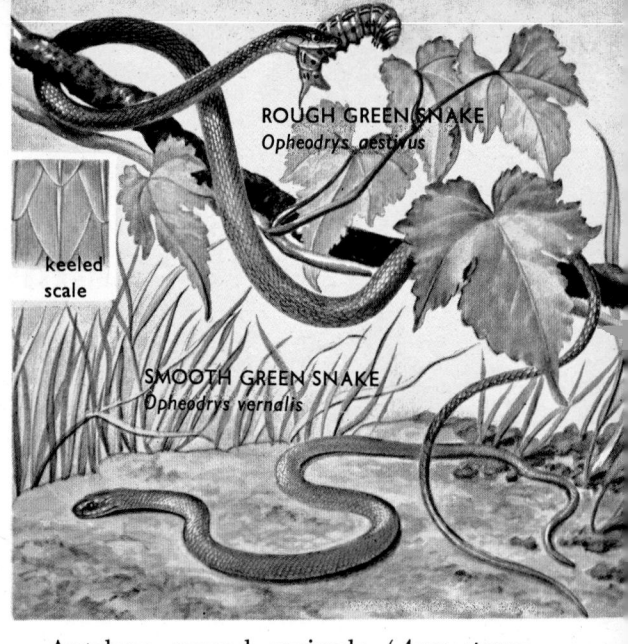

ROUGH GREEN SNAKE
Opheodrys aestivus

keeled scale

SMOOTH GREEN SNAKE
Opheodrys vernalis

Antelope ground squirrels *(Ammospermophilus* spp.) live in the hot deserts of the south-western United States. Their short tail is white underneath, like that of an antelope. They eat cactus apples, which are good sources of water. They eat the seeds and stems of other desert plants and some insects, such as grasshoppers and grubs.

Golden-mantled ground squirrels *(Callospermophilus* spp.)*, of the pine forests of the western United States and Canada, resemble the chipmunk because of the stripes and the reddish mantle around the head; but they do not have stripes on their face as chipmunks do. In addition to seeds and nuts, they frequently eat mushrooms and insects. They hibernate in winter.

Rock ground squirrels *(Otospermophilus*

Caterpillar Hunters hibernate in winter as adults, and thus may survive for several seasons.

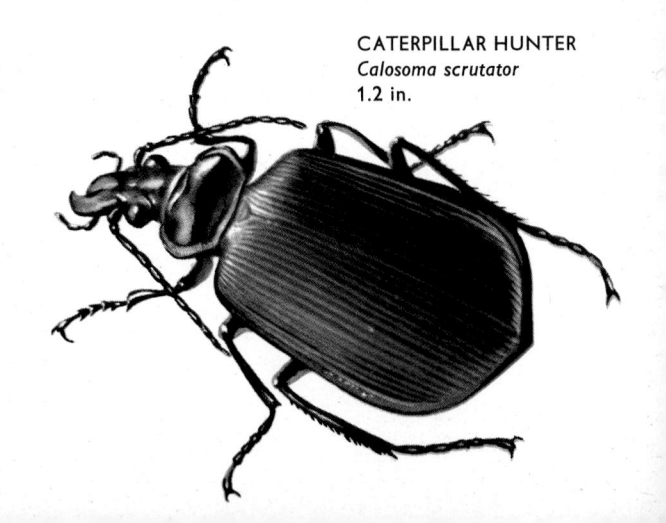

CATERPILLAR HUNTER
Calosoma scrutator
1.2 in.

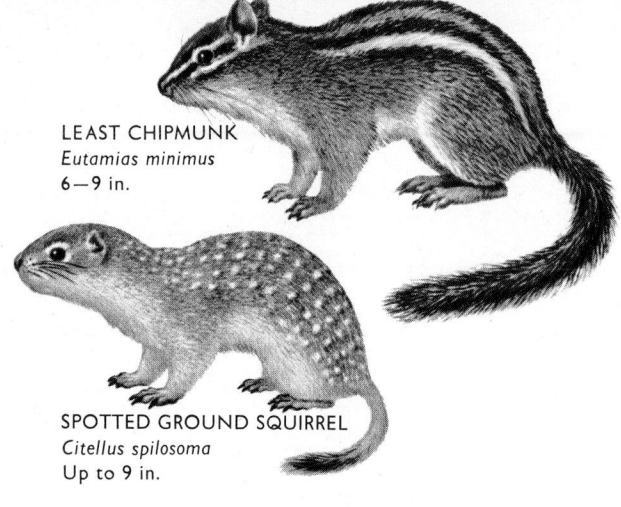

LEAST CHIPMUNK
Eutamias minimus
6—9 in.

SPOTTED GROUND SQUIRREL
Citellus spilosoma
Up to 9 in.

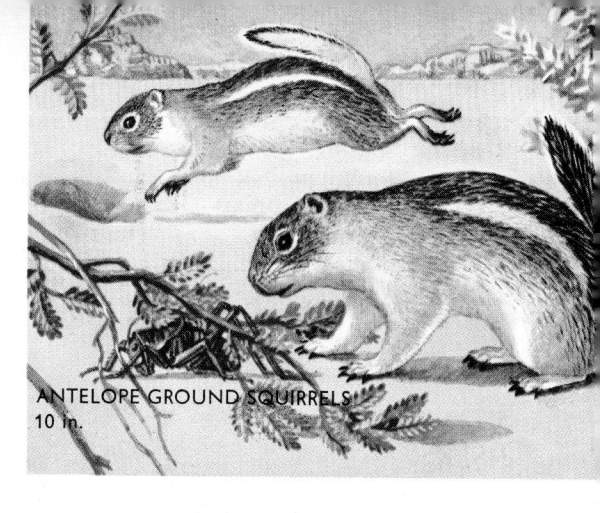

ANTELOPE GROUND SQUIRRELS
10 in.

Chipmunks, and other ground squirrels, belong to the same family as tree-dwelling squirrels; the principal difference lies in their contrasting habitats.

spp.), are found in rocky places from the deserts to mountain tops of the western United States and Mexico. They hide in the cracks and crevices, and are frequently seen perched on boulders, either sunning themselves or surveying the countryside for enemies. When alarmed, they give loud whistles. Rock ground squirrels have large cheek pouches in which they store food.

Thirteen-lined ground squirrels (*Spermophilus tridecemlineatus*) are most abundant in central U.S.A., where they live in the open prairie country and are frequently seen on lawns and golf courses. Brownish animals with yellowish stripes, they are often seen running across roads or sitting up alongside their burrow. The burrow does not have a mound in front. They eat and store seeds and feed on insects or, occasionally, on the eggs of ground-nesting birds.

European ground squirrels (*Citellus* spp.) live in the sandy wastes and treeless country (steppes) of Eurasia. They are large ground squirrels and are good diggers. Like other ground squirrels, they have high-pitched whistles to warn of approaching danger (see GOPHER; MARMOTS).

GROUSE are non-migratory, chicken-like birds that live in forests of the Northern Hemisphere. Grouse eat buds, seeds, berries and, during the breeding season, insects.

The courtship dance is spectacular. The Black and the Sage Grouse are shown in display postures. Both have communal display grounds, on which the males come together to perform and where the females come to find a mate. The Capercaillie, also shown displaying, is the largest grouse, almost turkey-size, and the male struts up and down emitting odd crackling and popping sounds. The Ruffed Grouse makes a drumming noise with its wings, alone on a log in woodland. The Red Grouse of

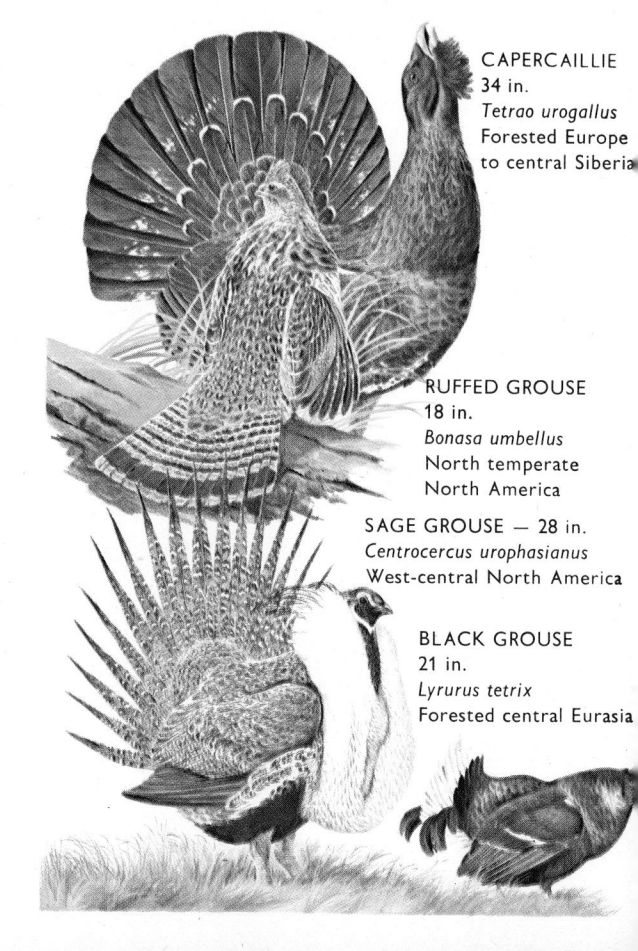

CAPERCAILLIE
34 in.
Tetrao urogallus
Forested Europe
to central Siberia

RUFFED GROUSE
18 in.
Bonasa umbellus
North temperate
North America

SAGE GROUSE — 28 in.
Centrocercus urophasianus
West-central North America

BLACK GROUSE
21 in.
Lyrurus tetrix
Forested central Eurasia

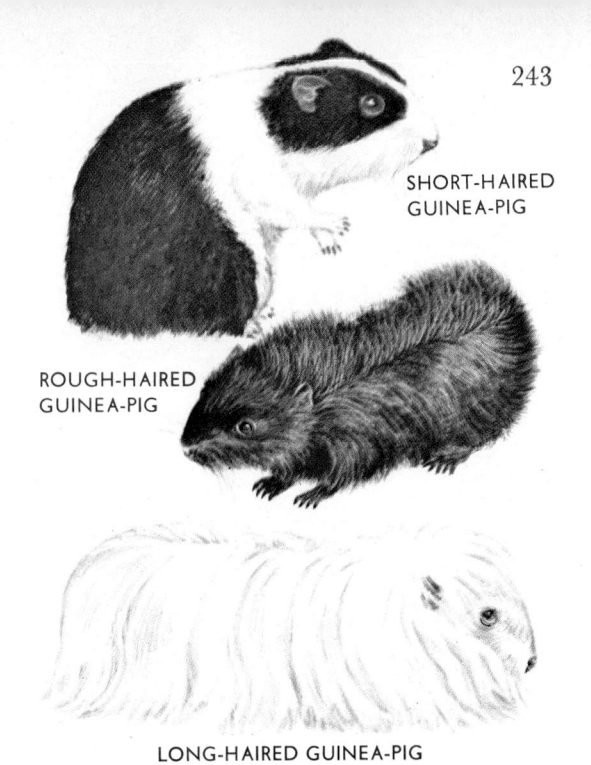

SHORT-HAIRED GUINEA-PIG

ROUGH-HAIRED GUINEA-PIG

LONG-HAIRED GUINEA-PIG

Guinea-Pigs have two or three litters a year, each with from 2 to 8 offspring weaned in three weeks.

the heather moors also cackles and struts in display, but spends more time with the hen, helping her to bring up the family.

Species living in pine-woods often feed on the buds and needles of the trees, and the Capercaillie is said to taste of resin at times. The females build a nest on the ground, lay six to sixteen eggs, do all the incubating, and raise the downy young alone. Males often mate with more than one female. After breeding, grouse move in family coveys, sometimes in larger flocks. They fly swiftly for short distances, their wings moving so rapidly that they whirr.

GUINEA-FOWL are wild chickens from Africa. Seven species live in different parts of the continent. Domestic guinea-fowl, descendants of birds brought from Africa centuries ago, are raised for food and as pets all over the world. Some guinea-fowl species have tufts of bristly quills or bony growths on their bare heads. Their breeding habits in the wild are not known.

GUINEA-PIGS, or Cavies *(Cavia porcellus)*, are short-haired, tailless rodents from the mountains of South America. The Incas

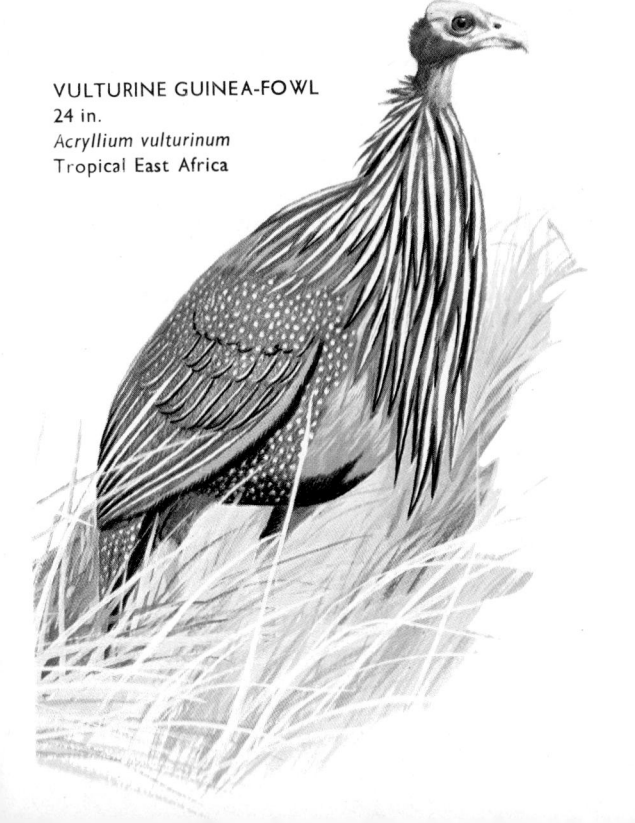

VULTURINE GUINEA-FOWL
24 in.
Acryllium vulturinum
Tropical East Africa

domesticated the species 2,000 years ago. A white strain has proved more popular than the original brown, and a large proportion of guinea-pigs are varicoloured, usually brown and black on white.

Although Indians of South America still use guinea-pigs for food, they are most valuable to the rest of the world as laboratory animals. They are susceptible to many of the diseases that afflict the human race and serve as test animals for possible remedies. Their rapid rate of reproduction and simple vegetarian diet make them easy and inexpensive to raise and maintain.

Guinea-pigs make gentle, friendly pets and seldom bite. They are hardy, need little cage space, and require no special treatment. Short-haired breeds need less attention than long-haired breeds. The low level of intelligence of guinea-pigs keeps them from becoming more popular as pets.

GULLS are sea-birds known in every land from the arctic to the antarctic. They are strong flyers, alternating leisurely wing-beats with soaring, but they seldom go far out of sight of land. They do not dive, but

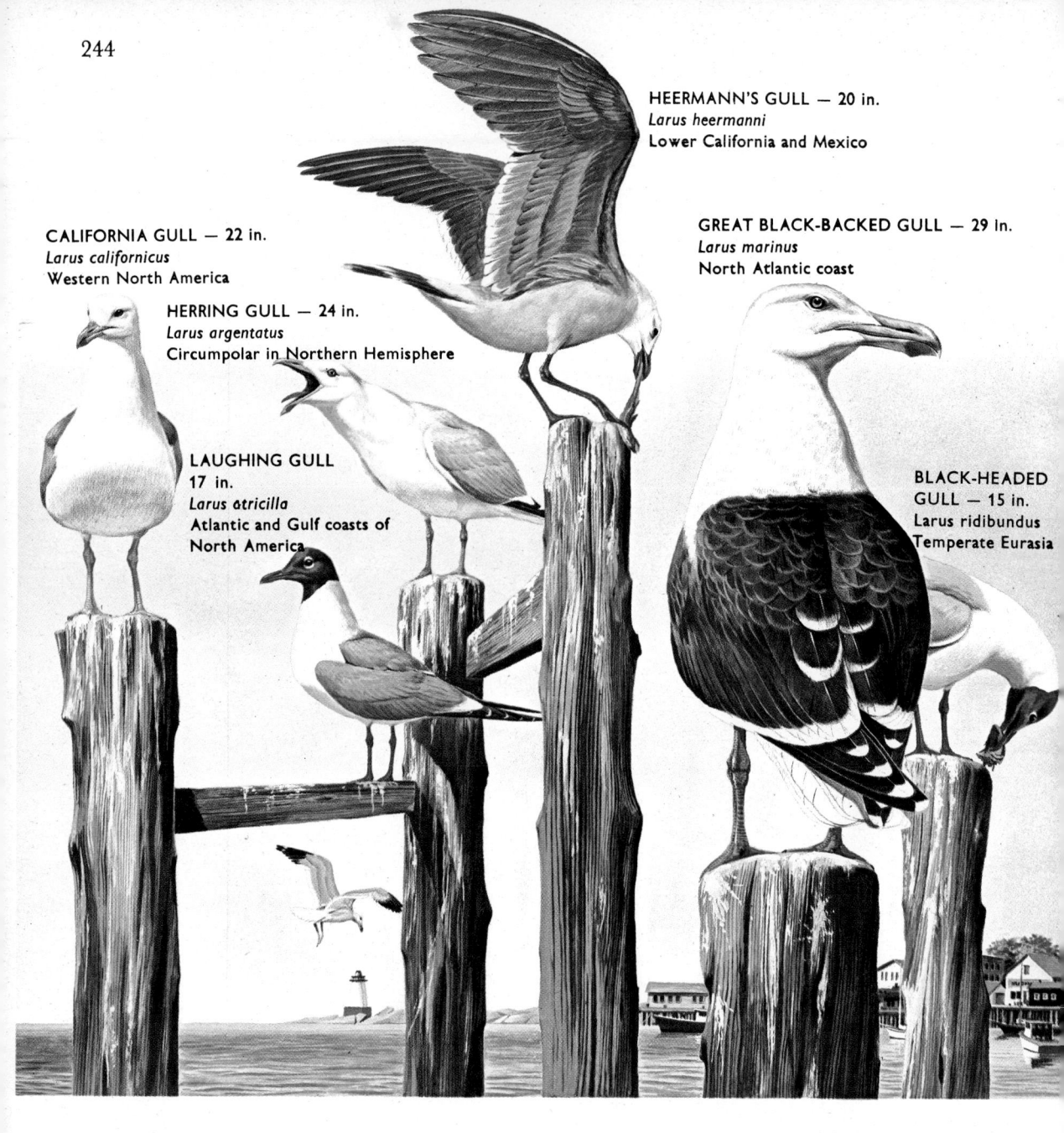

HEERMANN'S GULL — 20 in.
Larus heermanni
Lower California and Mexico

CALIFORNIA GULL — 22 in.
Larus californicus
Western North America

GREAT BLACK-BACKED GULL — 29 In.
Larus marinus
North Atlantic coast

HERRING GULL — 24 in.
Larus argentatus
Circumpolar in Northern Hemisphere

LAUGHING GULL
17 in.
Larus átricilla
Atlantic and Gulf coasts of
North America

BLACK-HEADED
GULL — 15 in.
Larus ridibundus
Temperate Eurasia

they swim, run and walk well. Songless, they make noisy, raucous screams.

Gulls are sociable birds and often nest in colonies. Both parents incubate the eggs and feed the young by regurgitation. Some young gulls develop adult plumage during the first year, but most require two or three years to lose brown hues of the young.

Many gulls are scavengers, keeping our harbours and beaches clean. If a gull swallows something that cannot be digested, it is cast up from the stomach in the form of a pellet, the bones and hard part of shellfish being so treated.

Gulls drink salt water when they cannot get fresh, and so would often have too much salt in their systems, if they did not have a mechanism for eliminating it. Glands in their heads remove the surplus salt, and it drips from their nostrils as brine.

The Great Black-backed Gull is the largest of these birds. With its large size and heavy bill, it is not only a scavenger but will also kill other birds. It lives on

rocky coasts of the North Atlantic, replaced in the south by the Domican Gull.

The Black-headed Gull is one of the small species. It nests in colonies on inland marshes, finding much of its food in winter around rubbish-tips or by following the plough, and may never go to the sea. They have slender bills and catch many insects in mid-air, at the time of year when they emerge on their mating flight.

The Herring Gull, circumpolar in the Northern Hemisphere, is one of the commonest gulls. It has increased in numbers by feeding on garbage and waste during the winter, when natural foods are scarce. Abundant along the coasts, the Herring Gull also wanders inland to lakes, rivers and ponds. The Herring Gull is fond of shellfish. It opens cockles and mussels by dropping them from the air on a hard surface. If the first drop does not break the shell, it is picked up and dropped again from a greater height. The Herring Gull has learned that cement highways and flat roofs on beach cottages are fine places on which to crack shellfish.

Skuas, or Jaegers, are primitive gulls known as "robbers of the sea". They survive by killing smaller birds and animals, and stealing food from birds too big to kill. They nest near colonies of other birds so that they can feed themselves and their young on their neighbours' eggs and chicks. If their own young stray too far from the nest, the parents sometimes eat them, too. In the Antarctic, Skua Gulls prey on colonies of Adelie Penguins. Skuas fly farther from land than other gulls. The Great Skua is the only bird in the world that nests in both the Arctic and Antarctic.

GYPSY MOTHS *(Lymantriidae)* belong to a group in which the males are attracted over considerable distances by the scent of newly-emerged females of their own species. A male of the Gypsy Moth is known by experiment to have flown over two miles to reach a mate. The hairy caterpillars feed on deciduous trees. The species was introduced into North America about 1868, and has now become a serious pest of shade and foliage trees on that continent. A vast sum has been expended there on its control.

Females lay 300 to 500 eggs in hair-covered masses on stones, tree-trunks, and a number of other objects. The eggs are usually laid during July and August, but do not hatch until the following April. After about six weeks of feeding ravenously on nearly any green tree or shrub, the caterpillars are fully grown and ready to pupate. Each spins a loose cocoon on a tree or other object and transforms into the pupal stage. Within a few weeks, the adult moths emerge. Females are heavy-bodied and only fly very short distances.

The Brown-tail Moth, a member of the same family, was also introduced from Europe to the United States and also damages deciduous trees (see BROWN-TAIL MOTHS).

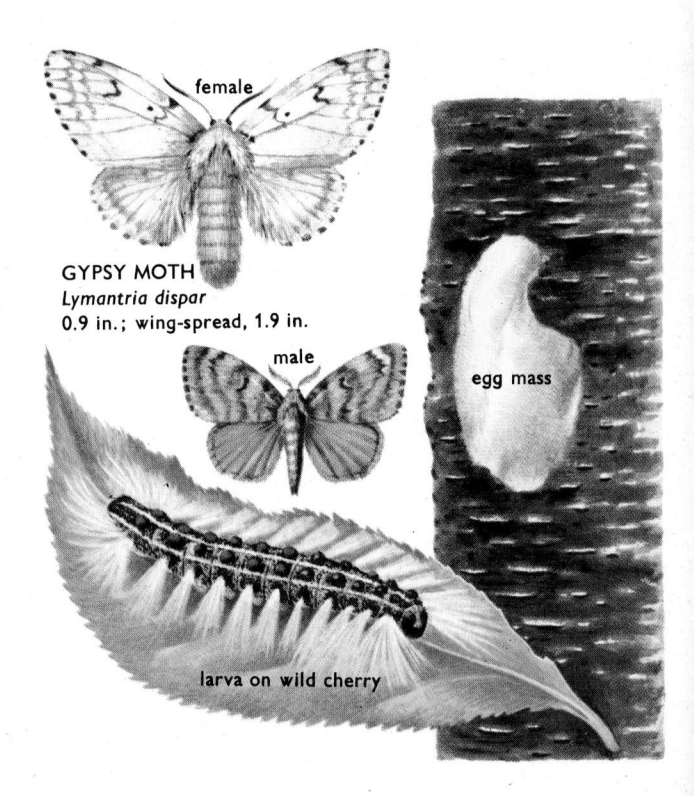

GYPSY MOTH
Lymantria dispar
0.9 in.; wing-spread, 1.9 in.

female

male

egg mass

larva on wild cherry

H

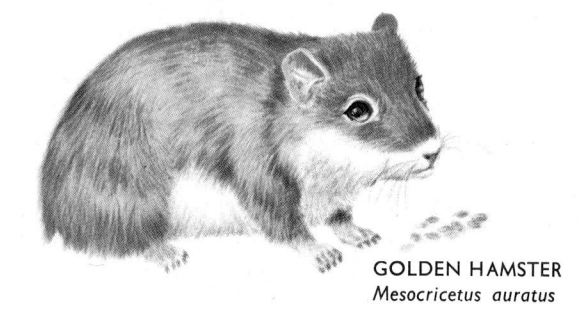

GOLDEN HAMSTER
Mesocricetus auratus

HAMSTERS *(Cricetus* spp.*)* are small, furry rodents. Several species occur in Europe and northern Asia, but the one kept as a pet and as a laboratory animal is the Golden Hamster. All the captive animals are believed to be descendants of a few specimens caught near Aleppo, Syria, and taken to Israel in 1930.

In the wild, hamsters are burrowers, living on grain which they carry in cheek pouches. In captivity, they do well in wire cages with wood-shavings or torn paper.

Females are usually about seven inches long, slightly larger than males. When kept in the same cage, a pair of hamsters often fight, and the female is capable of killing the male. Their incisors inflict deep wounds.

The animals breed readily in captivity, with several litters a year and as many as thirteen young in each litter. One pair of hamsters could increase the population by 100,000 hamsters in one year, if all their descendants lived and had young.

HARES *(Lepus* spp.*)* are long-legged, high-jumping members of the rabbit family. They give birth to young that are well-furred, have their eyes open, and can run about almost immediately. Included in this group are the European Hare, the Arctic Hare, the Snowshoe Hare, and jackrabbits. Many

of the northern hares moult in the spring and again in autnmn, to get their brown summer and white winter pelages. These colours make the hares match the seasonal colour changes of their surroundings, and so help to protect them. The white winter coat is much heavier than the brown summer coat. Hares have very long feet and heads,

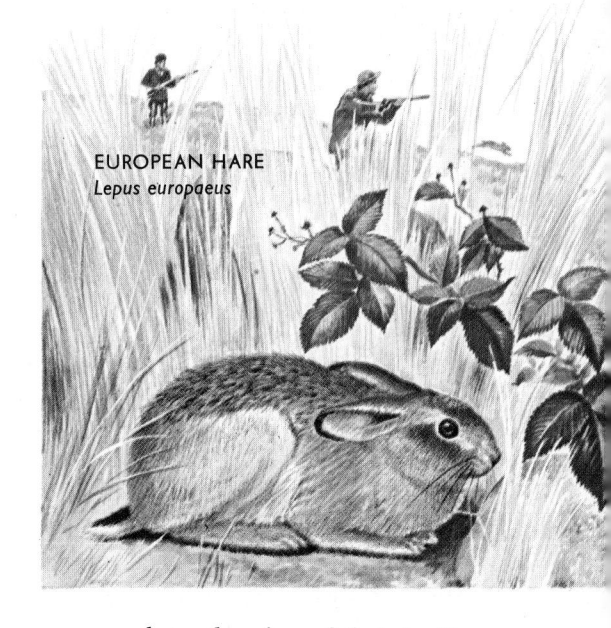

EUROPEAN HARE
Lepus europaeus

compared to the size of their bodies.

Hares fight among themselves by kicking with their powerful hind legs and by biting. Their only defence against the many animals that feed on them is speed. Some species can leap 20 feet in one bound, and all can change direction between jumps to confuse and to throw off close pursuers.

The Arctic Hare *(Lepus arcticus)* is large, weighing as much as 10 pounds. Found in the northern polar regions around the world, it lives on snow and ice for most of the year; it has heavily-furred feet, as well as thick fur covering its body. The

Arctic Hare eats grasses and the leaves of shrubs, as well as the bark of stunted trees. In turn, it becomes food for many predators, such as wolves, foxes, owls and lynxes.

The European Hare *(Lepus europaeus)*, unlike most American hares, does not get a white winter coat. It lives in the more temperate regions of Europe and Asia, from the British Isles eastward through European Russia. This hare has been imported into south-eastern Canada and the north-eastern United States. It is usually active in the early hours of morning and the late afternoon, but may also forage for a good portion of the night. The European Hare lives on the surface, not in burrows like the rabbit. Males fight each other and jump about before mating in spring.

The Snowshoe (or Varying) Hare *(Lepus americanus)* is a middle-sized hare of northern forests of North America. It is sometimes called the Snowshoe Rabbit, and goes through cycles from years of extreme abundance and over-population to times of scarcity. When these hares are plentiful, they are preyed on by lynxes, owls and wolves. "Varying" refers to their seasonal change in colour from a brown summer coat to a winter coat that is almost totally white. "Snowshoe" refers to their wide, heavily-furred feet, which give them good footing on the ice and in negotiating soft snow.

The Alpine Hare *(Lepus timidus)* of Eurasia, often called the Blue Hare, also adopts a white coat in winter. It occurs in Scotland and Ireland: in Ireland, its coat does not always become white, or sometimes only partially so.

HAWK-MOTHS — see **SPHINX-MOTHS**.

HAWKS, found throughout the world, are fierce, strong birds. Daylight hunters with keen eyesight, powerful talons and arched beaks, they are wholly carnivorous. Usually mated for life, each year's family stays together well into the winter. Males are smaller than their mates. Both parents feed and protect their altricial young.

Most hawks have blunt-tipped, broad wings, like the Goshawks, Sparrow-hawks, Red-shouldered and Cooper's Hawks. These hawks catch their prey by swooping suddenly and rapidly from cover, surprising their prey. Marsh Harriers glide low over the ground, pouncing on their quarry.

Falcons are hawks with long, narrow, pointed wings. They dive from great heights with such speed that they seem to appear out of nowhere. Kestrels and Merlins are

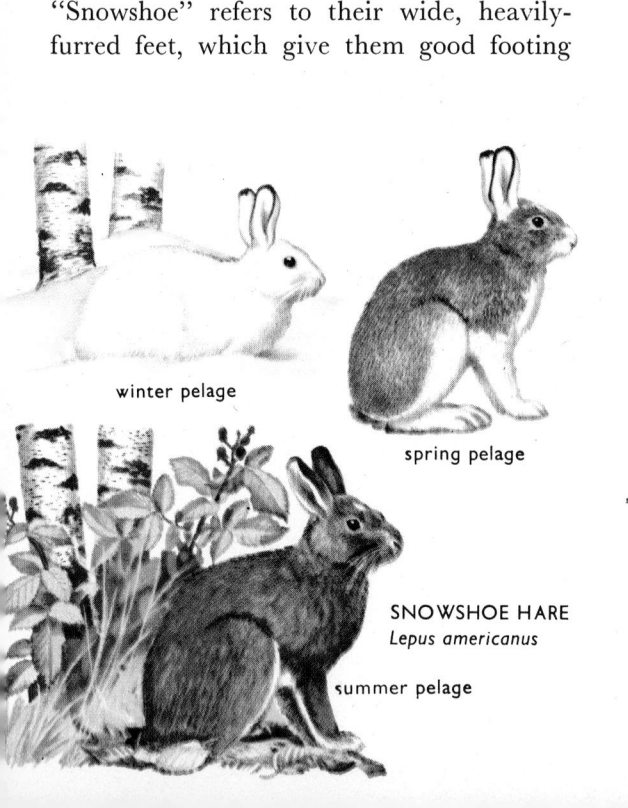

winter pelage

spring pelage

SNOWSHOE HARE
Lepus americanus

summer pelage

HEN HARRIER — 24 in.
Circus cyaneus
Temperate Northern
Hemisphere, circumpolar

RED-THIGHED FALCONET — 6—7 in.
Microhierax caerulescens
South-eastern Asia,
India to China

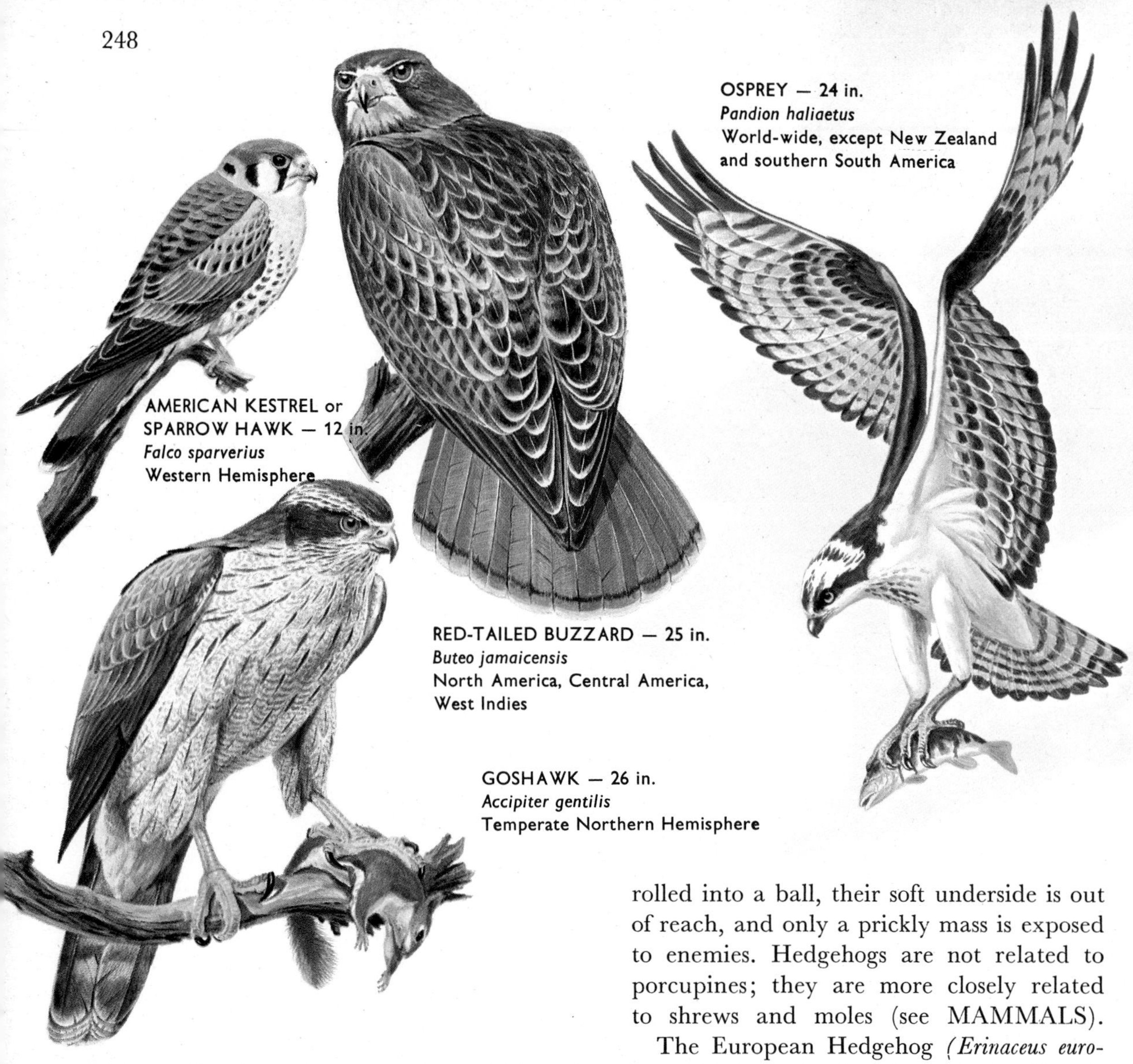

AMERICAN KESTREL or
SPARROW HAWK — 12 in.
Falco sparverius
Western Hemisphere

OSPREY — 24 in.
Pandion haliaetus
World-wide, except New Zealand
and southern South America

RED-TAILED BUZZARD — 25 in.
Buteo jamaicensis
North America, Central America,
West Indies

GOSHAWK — 26 in.
Accipiter gentilis
Temperate Northern Hemisphere

falcons. The finest hunter in the world is the Peregrine Falcon, often called the Duck Hawk. Sportsmen train falcons to hunt game for them (see FALCONS). The American Kestrel is known as the Sparrow-hawk, causing confusion with the European Sparrowhawk, which is not a falcon.

Buzzards soar high overhead and drop down to feed on carrion or small, helpless creatures. Ospreys, or Fish Hawks, dive to the surface of the water to seize fish, which are their only food (See OSPREYS).

HEDGEHOGS are covered with small spines, sometimes called quills, that protect them from attackers. The spines are densest and largest on the back and sides. When rolled into a ball, their soft underside is out of reach, and only a prickly mass is exposed to enemies. Hedgehogs are not related to porcupines; they are more closely related to shrews and moles (see MAMMALS).

The European Hedgehog (*Erinaceus europaeus*) is about the size of a squirrel. When it hibernates, or when frightened, the hedgehog rolls into a tight ball with its feet tucked in close to the body. It feeds on insects, small mice, snakes, and is very fond of eggs.

Tenrecs, of which there are several genera (*Centetes, Hemicentetes* and *Ericulus*) are found in Madagascar, off the southern coast of

HEDGEHOG

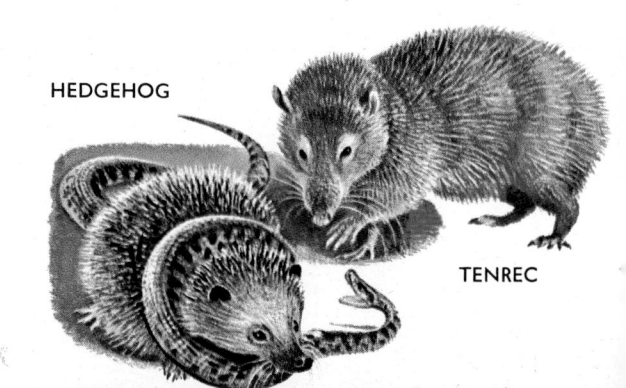

TENREC

Africa, and are related to hedgehogs. Some are no larger than mice, and have small tails or none at all. Some tenrecs have thick coats of spines. They feed mainly on insects.

HERMIT CRABS have large, soft, unprotected abdomens. Most of these crabs protect their abdomens by making their homes in empty mollusc shells. An Indo-Malayan hermit crab lives only in joints of bamboo, however, and others use old pipe bowls and pieces of tubing, which offer them protected living quarters.

Hermit crabs are often rather comical looking, as they drag their homes awkwardly along the bottom. Their borrowed shells become too small as they grow, so the crabs search for unoccupied shells of a larger size. They move alongside, quickly crawl out of the old shell, and tuck themselves into the new home. Hermit crabs start life as free-swimming larvae, but soon settle to the bottom, where most of them live as scavengers.

Petrochirus bahamensis, largest Atlantic species, sometimes lives in shells of full-grown conchs. Common Pacific hermit crabs belong to the genera *Pagurus* and *Paguristes. Coenobita clypeatus,* a hermit crab of the West Indies and Florida, lives on dry land.

The Robber Crab *(Birgus latro),* of the Indo-Pacific area, is a powerful hermit crab that climbs coconut trees, and cuts down

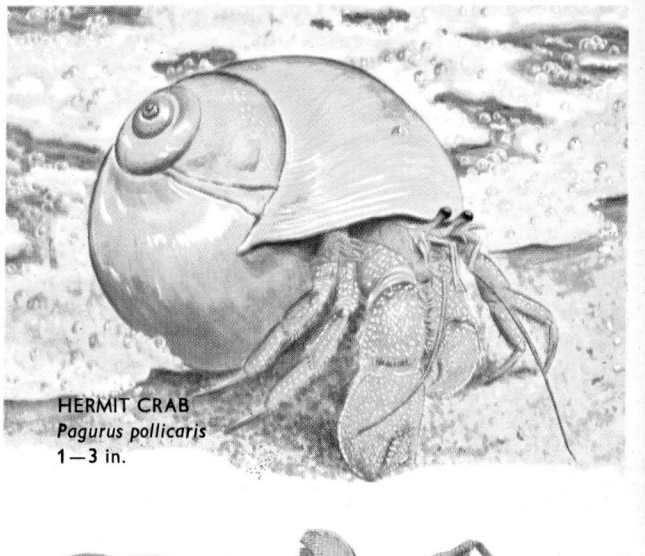

HERMIT CRAB
Pagurus pollicaris
1—3 in.

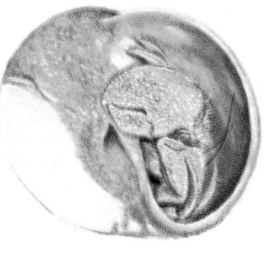

Hermit Crab in shell

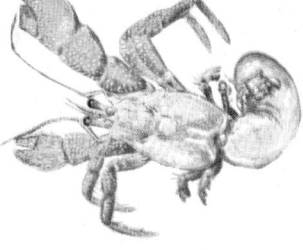

Hermit Crab out of shell,
showing soft abdomen

the nuts and eats them. Hunting Robber Crabs by torchlight is exciting, for the large, sharp claws of these big crabs make them dangerous opponents. Because they are so destructive to coconut plantations, these large crabs are destroyed whenever possible.

The European Hedgehog rarely ventures forth in daylight hours, and it hibernates in winter.

Roy Pinney

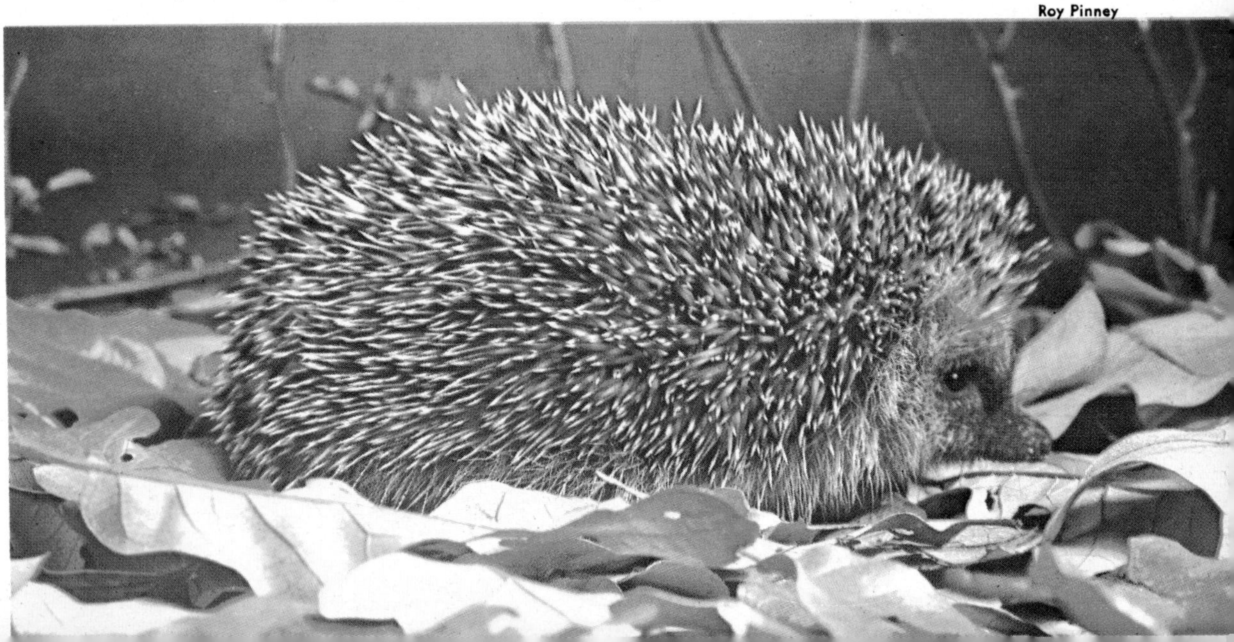

HERONS, scattered over the world in temperate and tropic zones, are long birds with long bills, necks, wings and legs. They fly with their legs sticking straight out behind them and their bills straight out in front, but with their necks folded in an "S" against their shoulders. Herons flap their wings so hard in taking off that it looks as though climbing into the air is hard work. When they level off, however, their flight is easy and graceful. Herons are solitary feeders, but they roost and migrate together in flocks.

Herons nest in groves of trees. After some years, the heron guano and rotting fish over-fertilise and kill the trees, and the birds move to a new place. Heron chicks are fed by regurgitation. When the three to six young leave the nest, they exercise by climbing among the branches and, if alarmed, they will disgorge their last half-digested meal on any intruder below.

The Common Heron of Eurasia, with its counterpart the Great Blue Heron of North America, is the largest species of the Northern Hemisphere, with a wing-span of up to six feet. The still larger Goliath Heron occurs in Africa. The Night-Herons are nocturnal feeders, flying out to feed at dusk. The Green Heron, with its wide distribution from Asia to America, is one of the smallest species. The long head plumes of most species are erected in display.

The adult Green Heron is dark with iridescent neck feathers. Young birds are striped.
Helen Cruickshank from National Audubon Society

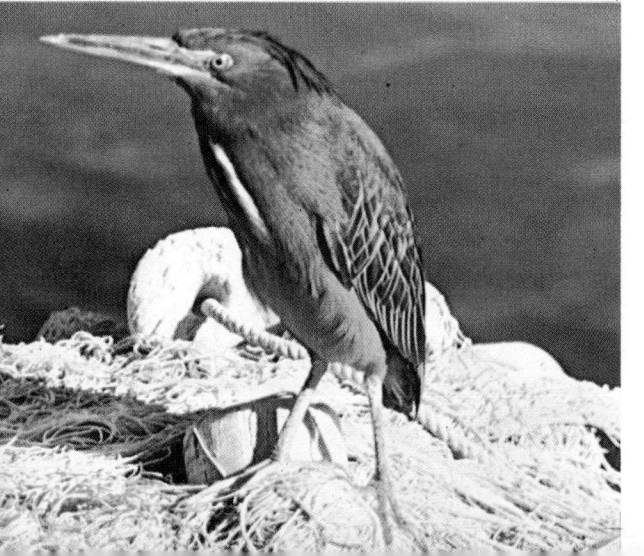

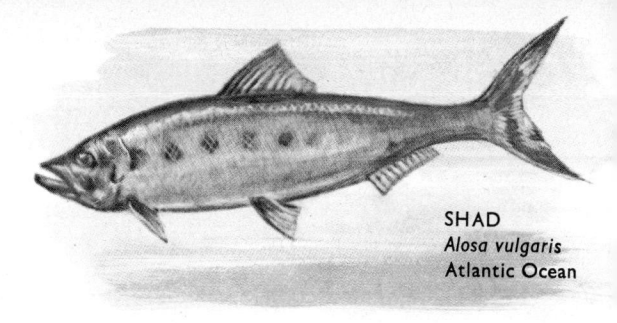

SHAD
Alosa vulgaris
Atlantic Ocean

HERRINGS, together with the anchovies, form the most important single group of fishes used as food by man. They are important commercially, and form a major part of the diet of many other food fishes.

There are nearly two hundred species of herring-like fishes included in the family *Clupeidae*. Most are small, hardly reaching a foot in length and occurring mainly in tropical waters, often in large shoals. In some cases, the shoals may cover 10 or 20 square miles. The clupeid fishes are easily recognised by the characteristic herring-like mouth and a sharp keel along the belly, formed by a series of scutes. Most are silvery when alive, and dark blue or green along the back; sometimes there is a series of black spots along the sides of the body.

The Herring *(Clupea harengus)* occurs in the cooler waters on both sides of the Atlantic. There is also a related form in the northern part of the Pacific. The European Herring has been fished by man for hundreds of years. The fishery dates back to the days when sailing ships took on board barrels of salted or smoked herring for their long sea voyages. Wars were often fought over herring fishing-grounds, so important was the industry.

The Herring are caught in gillnets by trawlers drifting over the fishing-grounds. The smaller, immature fishes, pass through the net, so there is no danger of taking them before they have had a chance to breed. Unlike most commercial fishes in British waters, the Herring has demersal rather than floating eggs, the eggs being laid on the bottom or on seaweed.

Another important group of herring-like fishes are the Shads. The Allis Shad *(Alosa alosa)* and the Twaite Shad *(Alosa finta)* occur in Britain, but they cannot

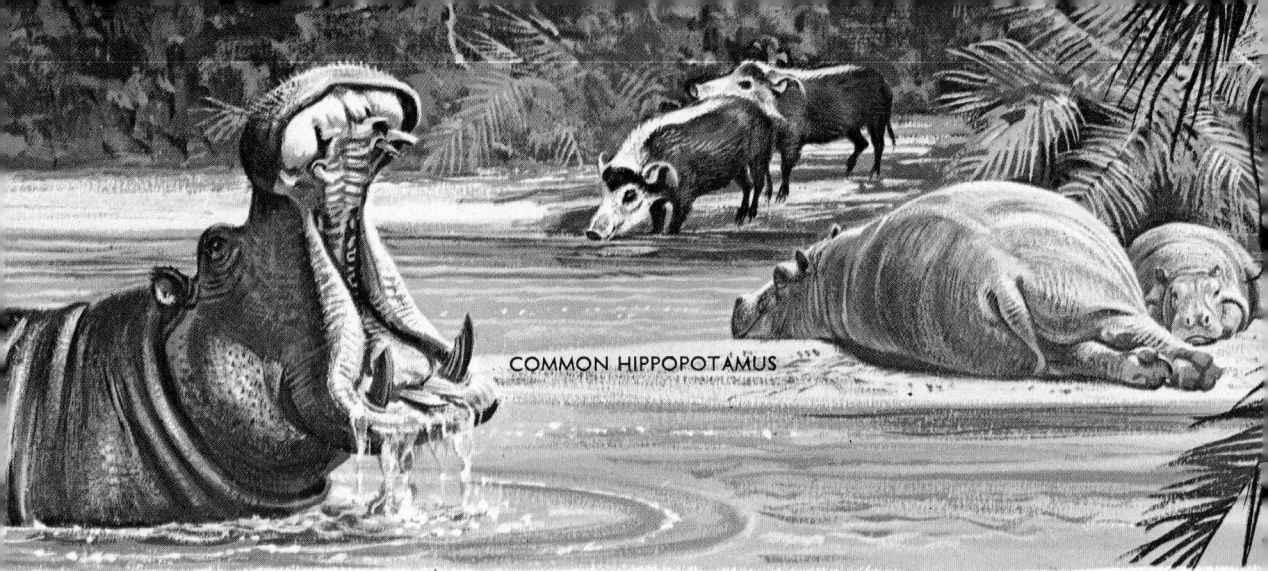

Hippos, despite their bulk, can swim fast. They rest during the day and forage at night.

compare with the Menhaden *(Brevoortia spp.)*, which are caught in millions off the Atlantic coast of America; no other fish is caught in such quantities. However, the Menhaden is not caught for its flesh, but for the oil which can be extracted from it. In India there is an important fishery for the Hilsa *(Hilsa ilisha)*. Like most Shads, the Hilsa is anadromous, ascending rivers to spawn during the breeding season.

The name Sardine is used all over the world for small herring-like fishes, and especially those suitable for canning. However, in Europe the true Sardine is the species *Sardina pilchardus,* the adults of which are known as Pilchards. Often labelled "Sardine" are young Herrings or small Sprats *(Sprattus sprattus)*. The great sardine fisheries are those of the Mediterranean, where the fishes are attracted by bright lights on dark nights, and then surrounded by a net and hauled in. In the Black Sea are the Kilka fisheries for a local variety *(Clupeonella spp.)*.

HIPPOPOTAMUSES *(Hippopotamus amphibius)* are large, smooth-skinned mammals that live in the deeper rivers of Africa. They sometimes reach a weight of 8,000 pounds. Hippopotamuses normally live in small groups of from four to a dozen; they are excellent swimmers. During much of the day, they stay on sandbars, or half submerged. At night they come out on land to feed on vegetation, particularly the grasses and reeds along the edge of the water. Occasionally, they invade cultivated fields and destroy crops. Awkward and ponderous, they can gallop when necessary.

Hippopotamuses were formerly found in nearly all rivers and lakes deep enough to permit them to submerge completely. Much hunted for their fat, flesh and hides, they have been eliminated from many of their original haunts. In captivity they may live

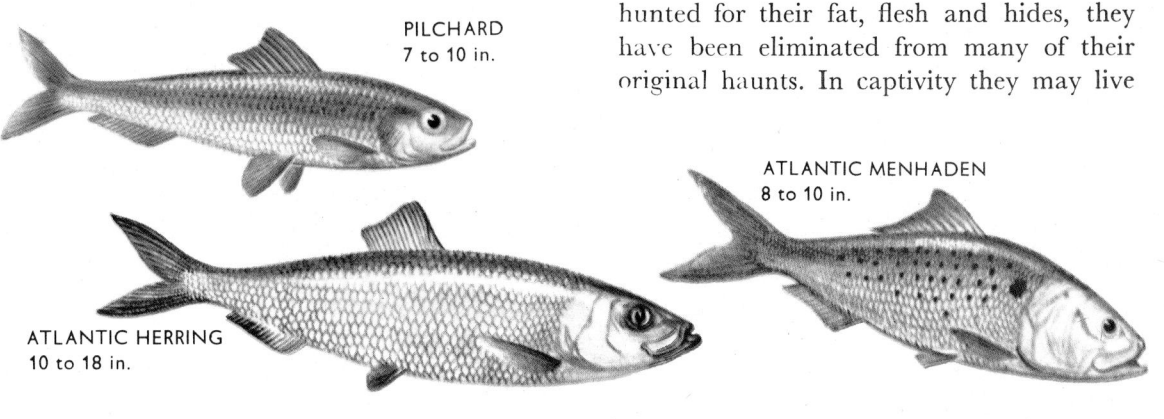

PILCHARD
7 to 10 in.

ATLANTIC MENHADEN
8 to 10 in.

ATLANTIC HERRING
10 to 18 in.

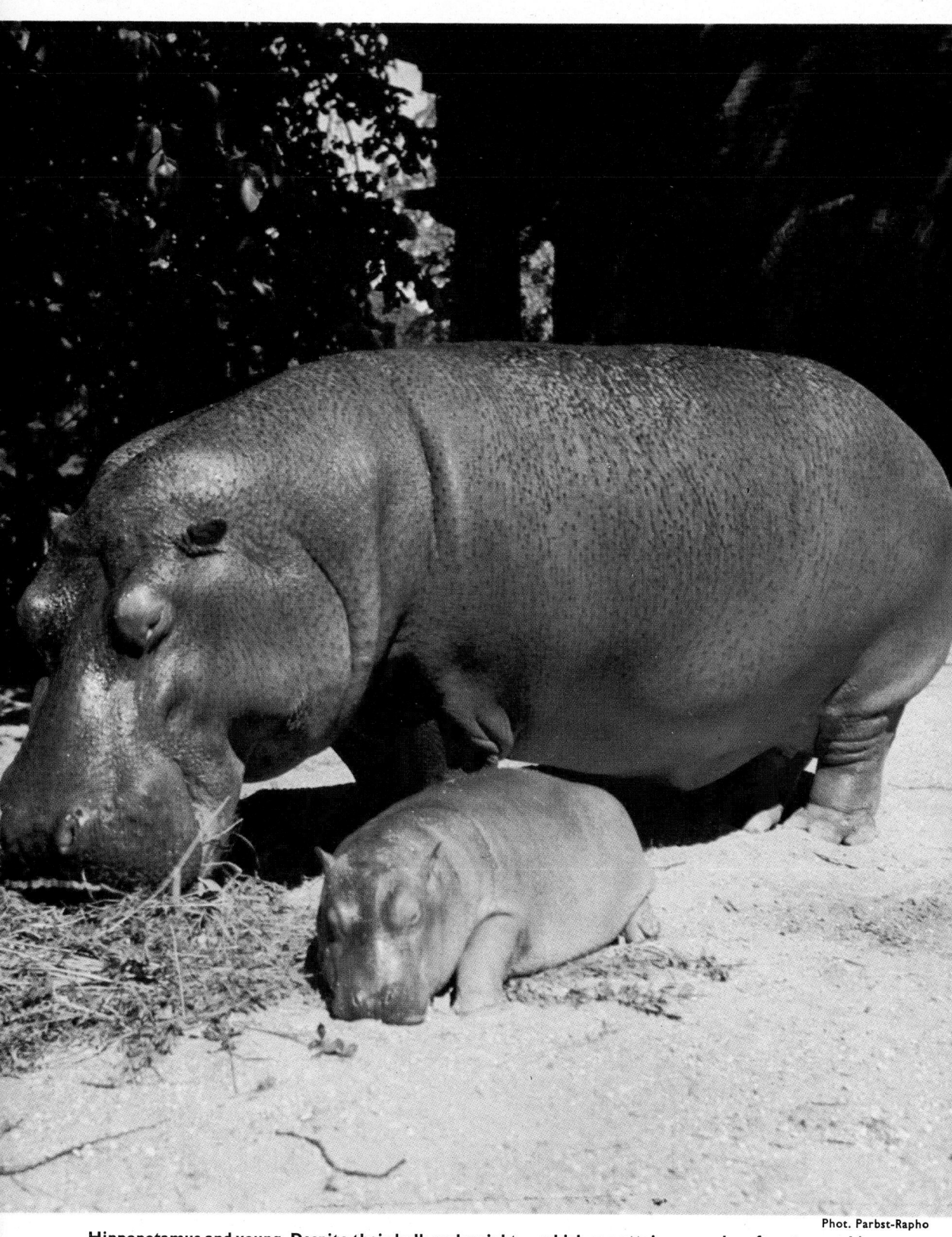

Phot. Parbst-Rapho

Hippopotamus and young. Despite their bulk and weight — which can attain as much as four tons — hippos can swim rapidly. They spend the day resting, almost entirely submerged in rivers and lakes, with only their eyes and nostrils above the surface. Then, at night, the animals land to forage for their food.

for a period of at least 50 years.

Pygmy Hippopotamuses *(Choeropsis liberiensis)*, found in western Africa, are only about a quarter the size of the large hippos. They spend less time in the water and are also less sociable than other hippos.

Hippopotamuses appear to have normally placid dispositions. Nevertheless, many cases have been recorded of apparently unprovoked attacks by the creatures.

HOATZINS are most unusual birds that live in small river colonies of the jungle of the Amazon Basin, in South America. The birds nest in small trees, usually over the water. Their main food is the leaf of a water plant that grows beneath the trees.

An outstanding peculiarity of the Hoatzin is that its newly-hatched chicks, which are born completely featherless, have two functional claws on each wing. These are used to great advantage, for the young birds clamber about in the branches, even falling into the water and climbing back up to the nest. The claws disappear in two or three weeks, and the adults show no trace of them.

Another peculiarity of the Hoatzin is the huge size of the two-compartment crop, in which leaves on which it feeds are stored and digested. Fully one-third of the bird's body is taken up by this organ, which displaced the breastbone and flying muscles; because of this the birds are poor flyers.

These characteristics of the Hoatzin have led scientists to consider it a primitive bird, although it is now suspected that it may be the result of more recent specialisation.

HOGS and Pigs are even-toed, hoofed mammals with long snouts. Many kinds have long tusks that stick out beyond their lips. In addition to the domestic pigs, a number of wild hogs and pigs are found throughout the world, on every continent except Australia. All tend to live in groups and to indulge in mud-baths.

The Warthog *(Phacochoerus aethiopicus)* is a strange-looking African hog with warty bumps on its scooped-out face. It has large tusks (the upper pair much longer than the lower), small eyes, and a bulky, nearly hairless body. The Warthog usually sleeps in a hole, often using one dug by the Aardvark (see AARDVARKS). Strangely, the

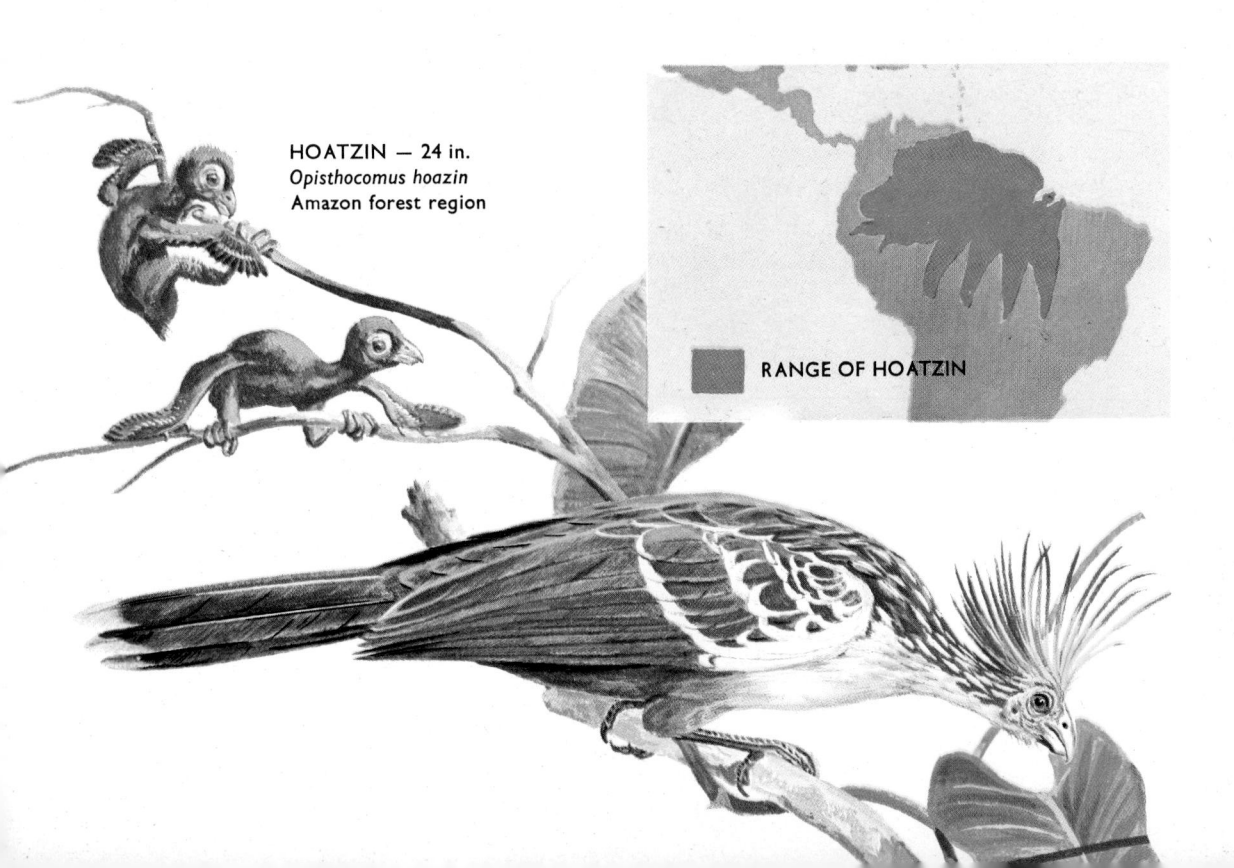

HOATZIN — 24 in.
Opisthocomus hoazin
Amazon forest region

RANGE OF HOATZIN

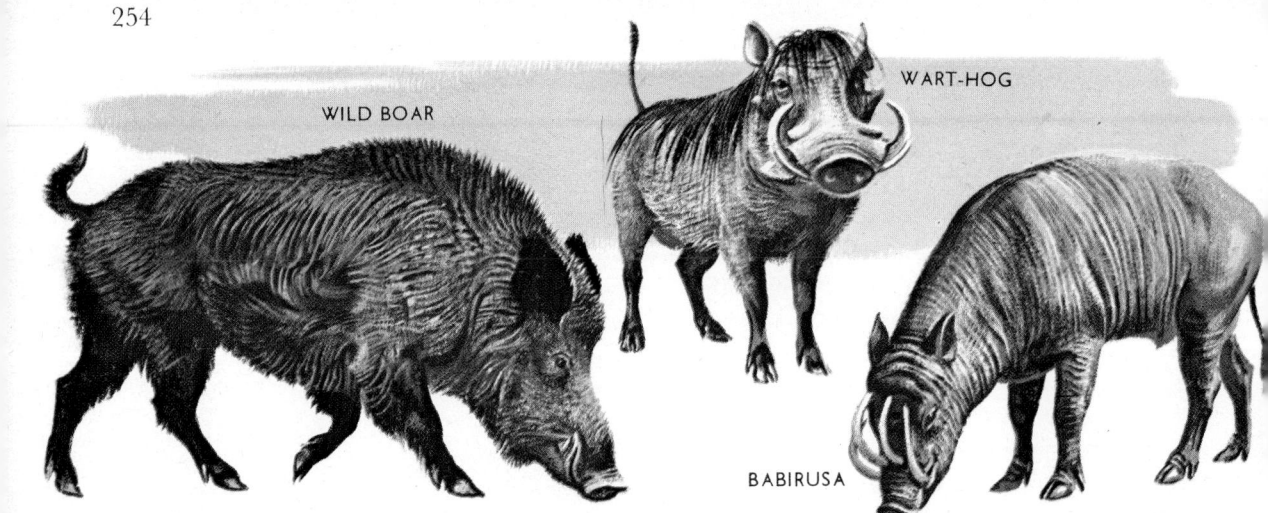

WILD BOAR

WART-HOG

BABIRUSA

Warthog enters the hole by backing in, so that it always faces any intruder. It attacks quickly, goring with its formidable tusks. The Warthog feeds mostly by day — principally on grasses, but also on other vegetable matter. It takes frequent mudbaths. When frightened, the Warthog runs into the brush with its tail held straight up.

The Red River Hog, or Bush Pig *(Potamochoerus porcus)*, has a very distinctive, bright reddish colour, a white mane and eye-rings, and long ear-tufts. In central and southern Africa, this hog occurs in small groups, but it feeds largely at night and is not commonly seen. It has a bad temper and is easily provoked to attack.

The Wild Boar *(Sus scrofa)* of Europe and Asia is the probable ancestor of domestic pigs. This Wild Boar still occurs wild in many parts of its range. It tends to keep to the forests, generally sleeping by day and rooting in search of food at night. Females give birth to their litters in nests of branches on the surface of the ground.

The Babirusa *(Babyrousa babyrussa)* is the most grotesque of all pigs. The male's tusks, as much as 17 inches in length, grow upward through the skin of his upper lip, then turn back over the forehead. Tusks from the lower jaw grow upward alongside. Females do not have long tusks. The Babirusa's tusks are probably symbols of strength to other males. Babirusas live in Celebes and the island of Buru. Because their long tusks suggest the antlers of local deer, they are sometimes called Pig Deer. They travel in groups as they root through the jungle in search of food. Good swimmers, Babirusas sometimes move from island to island in their foraging.

HONEYBEES *(Apis mellifera)* are one of the few insects ever domesticated. They produce honey and beeswax for the use of mankind and also act as pollinators of flowers, fruits, vegetables and field crops.

A colony of honeybees may contain as many as 80,000 individuals. With other social insects, a colony is made up of three casts: workers, drones (males) and a queen. Commonly seen are the workers, which also make up the bulk of the colony. Drones, larger and heavier-bodied than workers, are usually present in the early summer. The queen is also larger than the workers, but is more slender than drones.

A new colony of honeybees is formed in a different manner to that of other social insect such as bumblebees or ants. The old queen leaves the hive and takes with her a large number of workers. A newly-hatched queen is left in possession of the remaining portion of the original colony. Usually the "swarm", consisting of the old queen and workers, gathers on a branch or some other structure some distance from the old colony. Then scouts from the swarm search for a new home, which is often in a hollow tree. As soon as the site is selected, the swarm moves in and the workers begin

building combs for storage of food and for production of new individuals. The comb is made of wax produced by younger workers. It is secreted by glands that open on the underside of the abdomen. A sheet of comb is made of two sets of six-sided cells opening in opposite directions and tilted upward slightly. Two sizes of cells are made. Cells that contain the brood of workers are the smaller of the two, and this size is also used for pollen storage. Large cells are for drone brood. Honey is also stored in this size of cell. The queen lays a single egg in the bottom of each brood cell. Unfertilised eggs develop into drones, fertilised eggs into workers. The eggs hatch in three days, and the larvae are fully grown within a week. Workers then put a wax cap over the cells, and the full-grown larvae inside each cell spin a silken cocoon and pupate. Adults emerge in 10 to 15 days.

Queens require about a week less in which to develop than do either workers or drones. Queen brood cells are very large

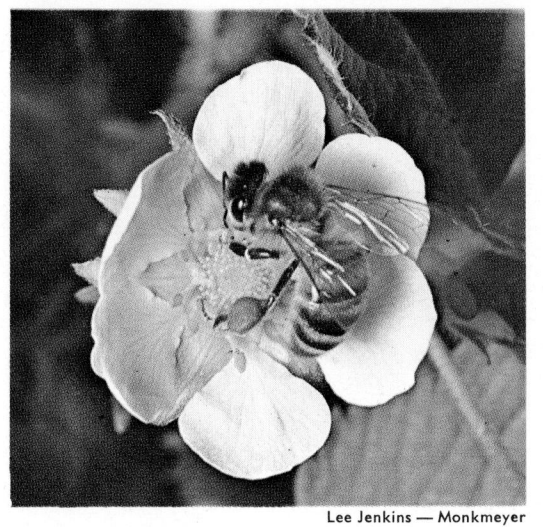

Lee Jenkins — Monkmeyer

Honeybees carry pollen from one flower to another, thus fertilising them by cross-pollination. Note the filled pollen baskets on the legs of the Honeybee on a strawberry blossom above.

and are usually fastened to the edge of a comb. The larva that hatches in the queen cell is fed royal jelly throughout its development. The larva would not develop into a

Workers are the most abundant members of a colony of bees. These busy workers on the comb of their hive are tending the young, building new comb, or filling cells with honey or pollen and capping them with wax.

Ross E. Hutchine

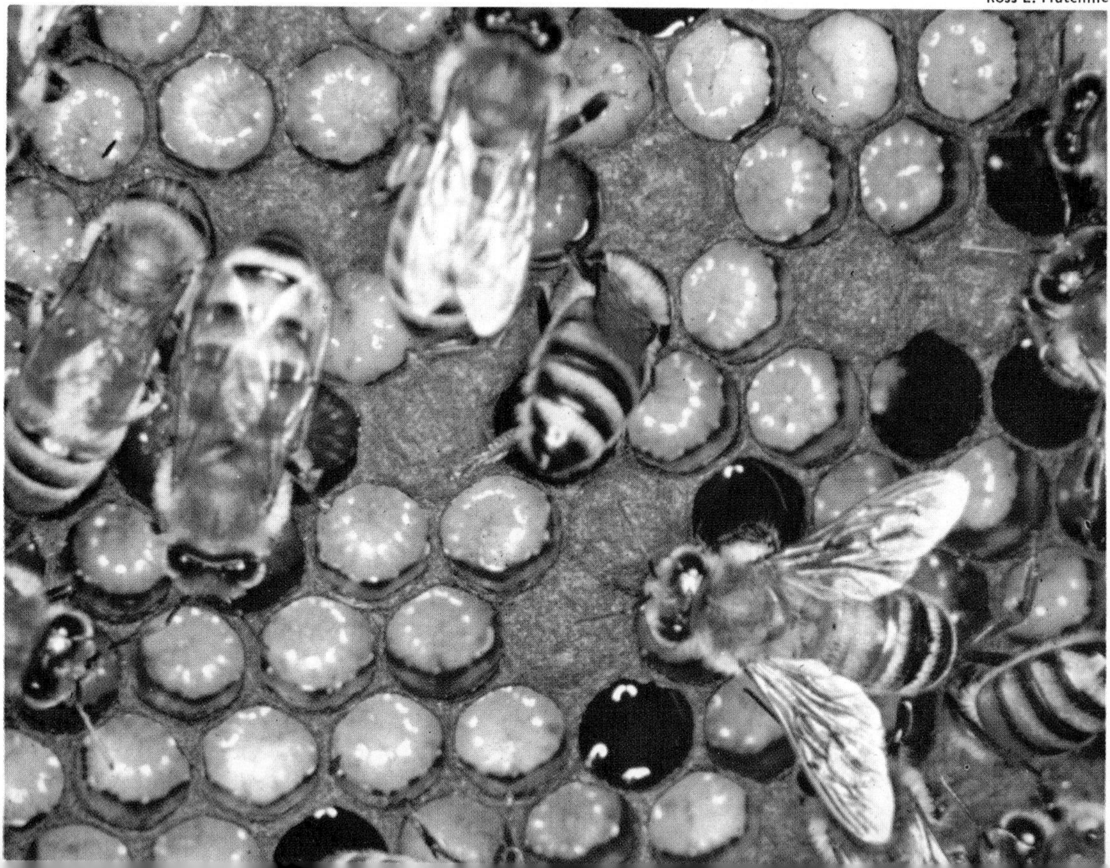

CASTES OF THE HONEYBEE

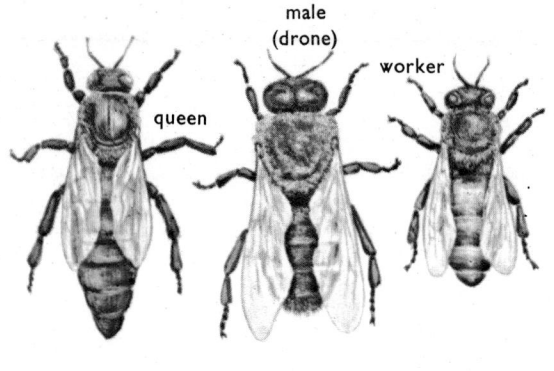

queen — male (drone) — worker

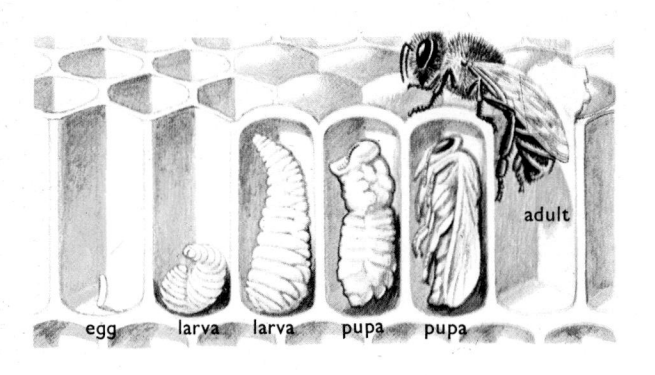

egg   larva   larva   pupa   pupa   adult

Worker bees are produced in cells the same size as those in which pollen is stored. A larva becomes fully grown in about five days. It spins a thin, silken cocoon inside the cell, which is capped with wax by workers. In about two weeks, a young bee emerges, chewing through the cap to escape.

queen without this special diet.

A queen mates only once and remains fertile throughout her life. She may lay as many as 2,000 eggs a day for as long as she lives, which is usually three to five years.

For several days, newly-hatched larvae are fed royal jelly, a special food produced by the workers. After that, the diet is changed to honey and pollen. The egg from which a queen develops is laid in a larger cell than those in which workers develop. Worker bees live only a few weeks during the busy honey-collecting season, but for as long as six months in winter.

Honeybees can communicate with each other to indicate the abundance of food, its direction, and its distance from the colony. When a worker finds a nectar source, it fills its crop and returns to the hive. If the source is within a hundred yards, the worker performs the "round" dance on the surface of one of the combs. This is really a series of figure-eight loops. The worker's dance excites the other workers, and they touch the dancer with their antennae. In this way, they identify the scent of the flower. The round dance does not indicate direction, only that the food source is close, but the vigour of the dance is in direct proportion to the amount of food that has been found.

If the food supply is some distance away, the worker does a "tail-wagging" dance. In this dance the worker moves its abdomen from side to side as it makes its figure-eight pattern. The farther the food is from

COMMUNICATION DANCES OF THE HONEYBEE

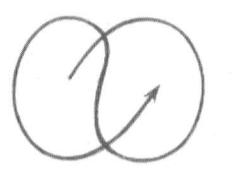
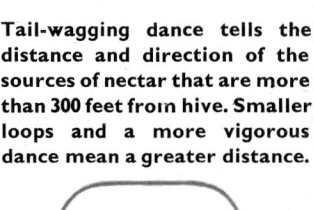

Round dance tells that food is near — within 300 feet. Other workers follow dancer, trying to get the scent of the flower.

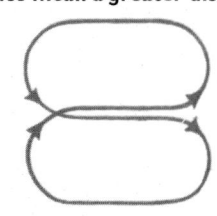

Tail-wagging dance tells the distance and direction of the sources of nectar that are more than 300 feet from hive. Smaller loops and a more vigorous dance mean a greater distance.

the colony, the smaller the loops and the faster the wagging of the abdomen. Direction is indicated with respect to the position of the sun. If the food is in the opposite direction of the sun, the worker makes a straight

line downwards between the loops of the figure eight. If the food is towards the sun, the bee makes a straight line towards the top of the comb. As the position of the sun changes, the angle of the dance also changes.

Honeybees are kept chiefly for their honey, but the bees are even more valuable as pollinators of flowers. It is estimated that about 85 per cent of all fruit and vegetable crops are pollinated by insects, chiefly honeybees. The colour and flavour of honey depends on the kind of flowers from which the bees collect nectar. Clover honey is especially prized, but most honey sold in shops is a blend of different kinds. Some honey is sold in a section of the comb, just as it comes from the hive.

Honey and bees have been mentioned by writers since ancient times. In fact, the first book on bee-keeping was written by Virgil, the poet. However, it was not until 1841 that scientific bee-keeping began with the advent of the modern type of hive, with movable frames for the combs and a chamber for surplus honey. A Russian named Proko-povitsch was the inventor. Up to then straw skeps were used as hives, and before removing the honey, burning brimstone was used to smoke out the bees, which were usually killed in the process. Since then improvement after improvement has taken place, up to the present day. The best time to stock a hive is in the spring. A swarm may be bought by weight. A good swarm should weigh about five pounds and is made up of about 25,000 bees. This is the best way for a novice to stock the hive.

The common hive-bee *(Apis mellifera)* is not a native of Britain, but has been introduced from the Continent. It has, in fact, been introduced for bee-keeping purposes into almost every country in the world.

Samson's riddle *(Judges, 14 : 14)* — "Out of the eater came forth meat, and out of the strong came forth sweetness" — followed his removal of honey from a lion's body. Bees would certainly not nest in a putrefying carcass, but it may be that Samson found the dried skeleton.

DIRECTION DANCES

Having described the discovery of nectar, the worker indicates direction as follows: a straight line towards the top of the comb, between the loops, when the food is towards the sun . . .

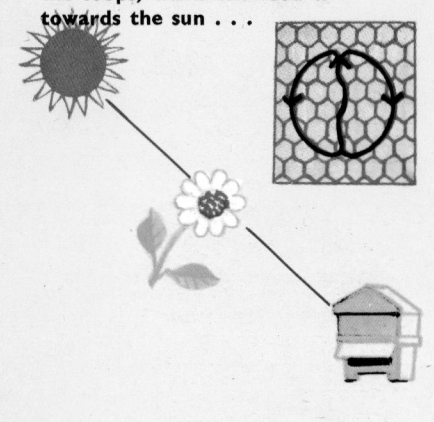

. . . and a straight line downwards, between the loops, when location of the food is away from the sun.

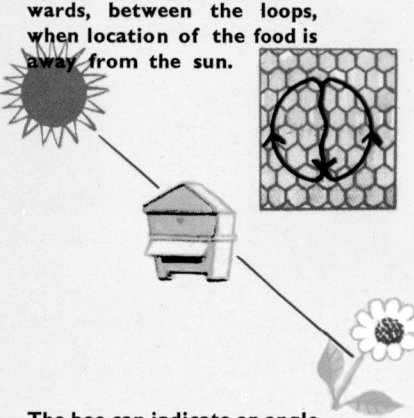

The bee can indicate an angle between the sun and the nectar, by changing the angle of its direction dance in relation to a vertical line drawn from top to bottom of the comb.

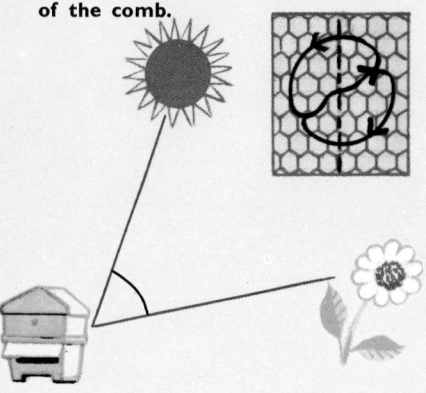

The Great Hornbill is a fruit-eater. Other members of the family eat insects, and some feed on lizards, snakes and small mammals.

GREAT HORNBILL — 60 in.
Buceros bicornis
India to Indo-China and Sumatra

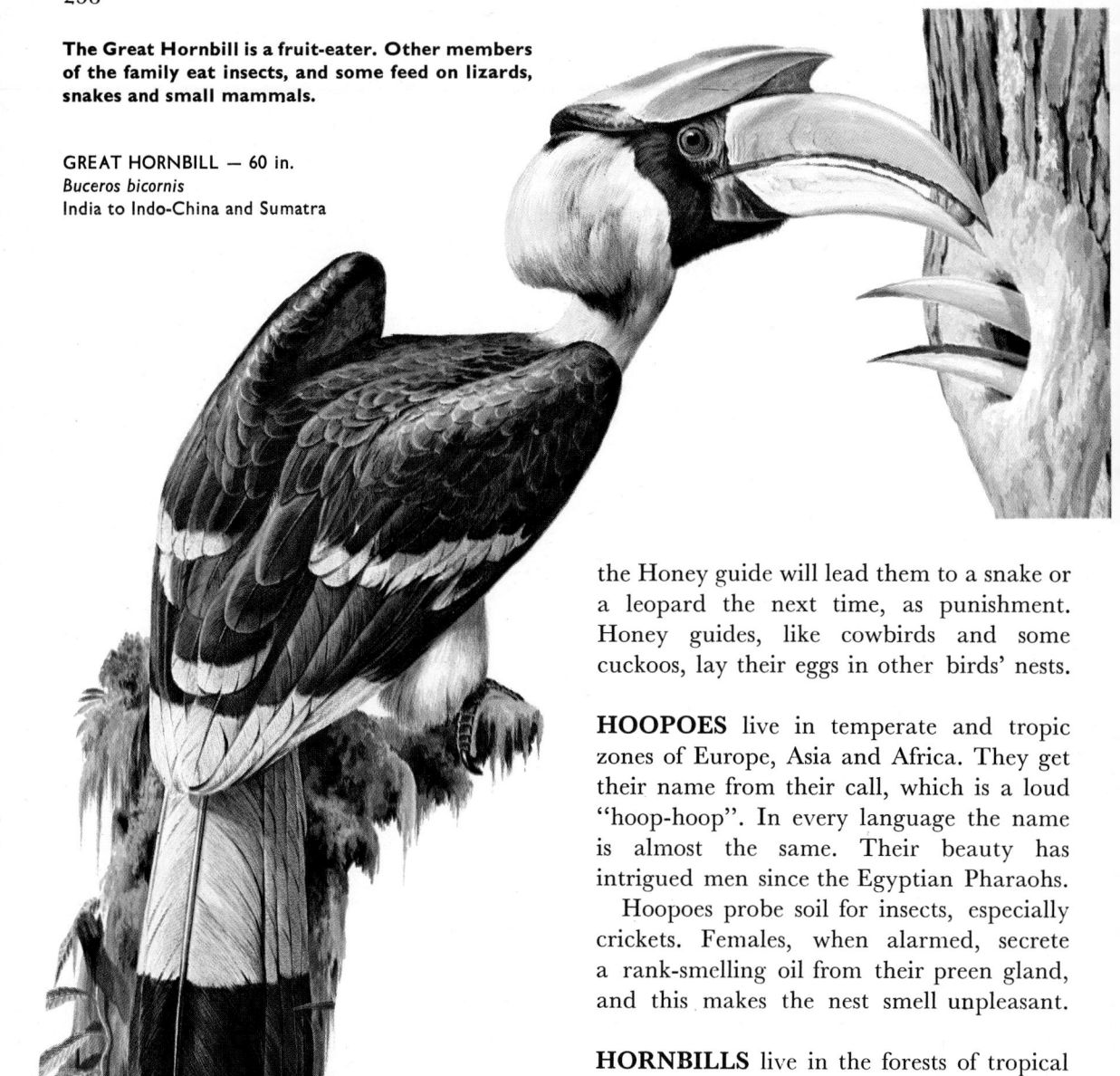

the Honey guide will lead them to a snake or a leopard the next time, as punishment. Honey guides, like cowbirds and some cuckoos, lay their eggs in other birds' nests.

HOOPOES live in temperate and tropic zones of Europe, Asia and Africa. They get their name from their call, which is a loud "hoop-hoop". In every language the name is almost the same. Their beauty has intrigued men since the Egyptian Pharaohs.

Hoopoes probe soil for insects, especially crickets. Females, when alarmed, secrete a rank-smelling oil from their preen gland, and this makes the nest smell unpleasant.

HORNBILLS live in the forests of tropical Asia and Africa, and on many islands in the South Pacific. They have large bills and horny growths on their head. Some of the 45 different kinds are no longer than crows.

The Great Hornbill, of the islands of the Far East, is one of the largest of the family. Its ornamental casque is hollow; that of the Helmeted Hornbill is partly solid ivory. Hornbills nest in hollow trees. When the female enters the hole to lay her eggs, the birds build a wall of mud or clay across the entrance. The female remains imprisoned for several months until the eggs hatch. During this time, the male feeds her through a tiny slit in the wall.

HONEY GUIDES eat beeswax, bee larvae and honey, but they cannot open bees' nests without help. African natives and Honey Badgers know this, and when they hear a honey guide calling, they follow it through the forest. This sparrow-like bird guides them to the bees' nest and waits for them to open it. The Africans believe that, if they do not open the hive and leave some honey,

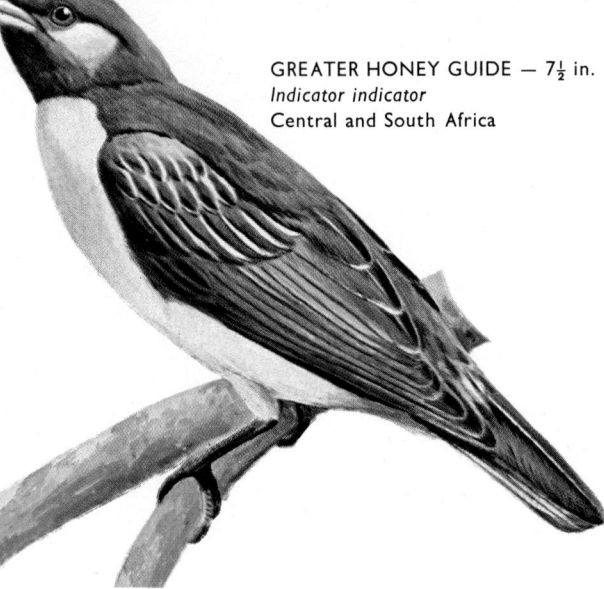

GREATER HONEY GUIDE — 7½ in.
Indicator indicator
Central and South Africa

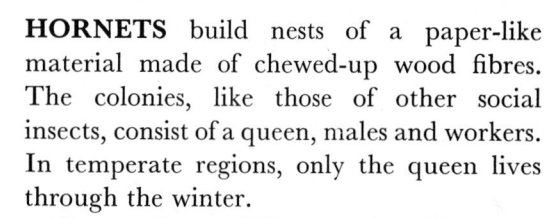

HOOPOE — 11 in.
Upupa epops
Eurasia, Africa

HORNED TOADS *(Phrynosoma* spp.*)* range throughout western North America and southward into Mexico, and are actually lizards and members of the iguanid family (see IGUANAS). Some species are very common; others are extremely rare. The tail of some dwarf species is reduced to a mere nub. Some lay eggs; others give birth to their young. Their horns, distinctively arranged in different species, look formidable but are not significant in combat. Some species inflate their body when disturbed or angry; others flatten themselves. They tame quickly and make good pets.

HORNETS build nests of a paper-like material made of chewed-up wood fibres. The colonies, like those of other social insects, consist of a queen, males and workers. In temperate regions, only the queen lives through the winter.

Hornets hang their nests from branches or from the eaves of buildings. In each nest there are one or more combs which contain larvae, eggs and pupae. These combs are fastened one above the other, and are surrounded by the several layers of paper that form the nest's outer shell. The only entrance is a small hole near the bottom.

Roy Pinney

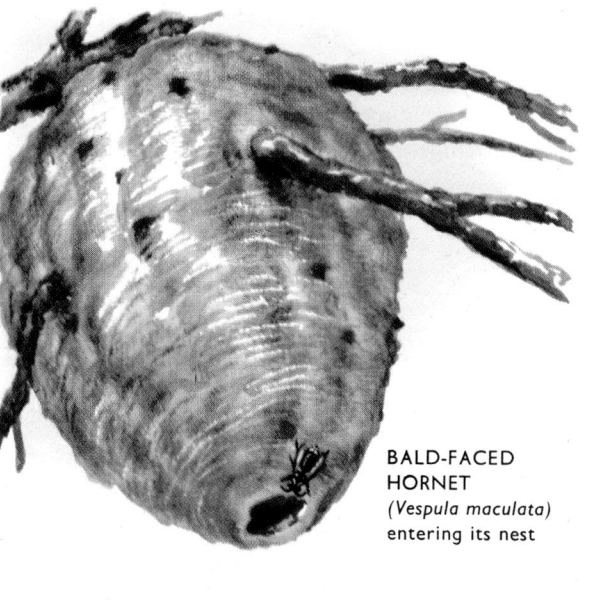

BALD-FACED HORNET
(Vespula maculata)
entering its nest

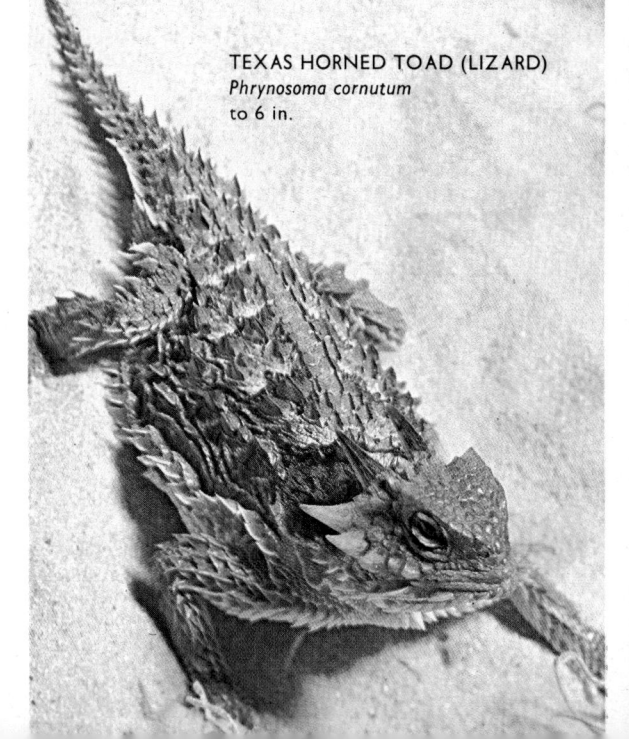

TEXAS HORNED TOAD (LIZARD)
Phrynosoma cornutum
to 6 in.

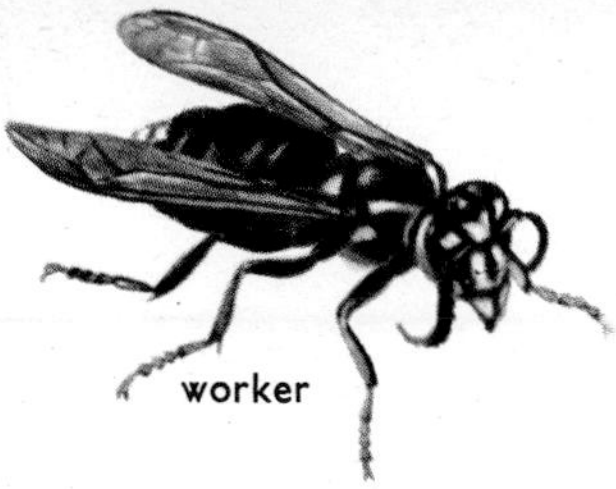

worker

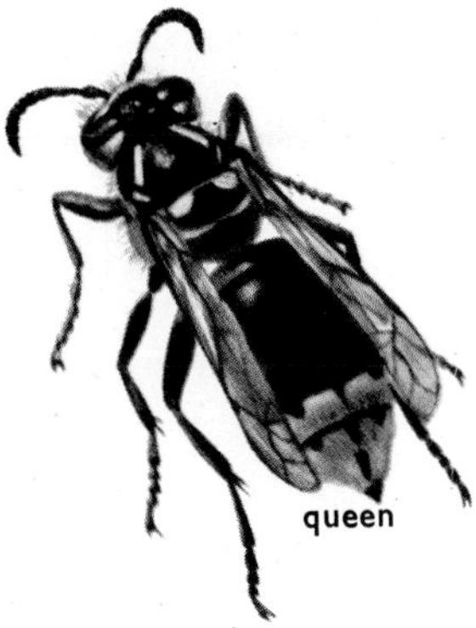

queen

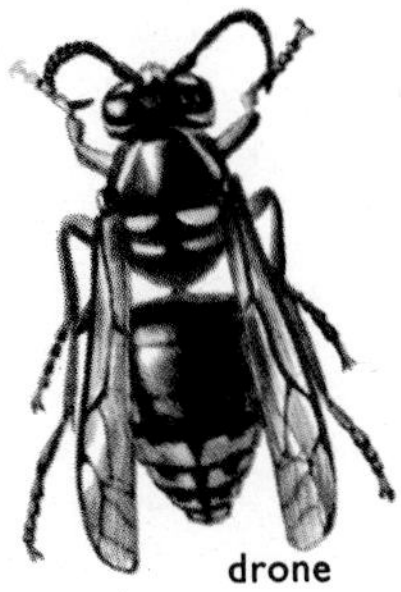

drone

HORNET CASTES

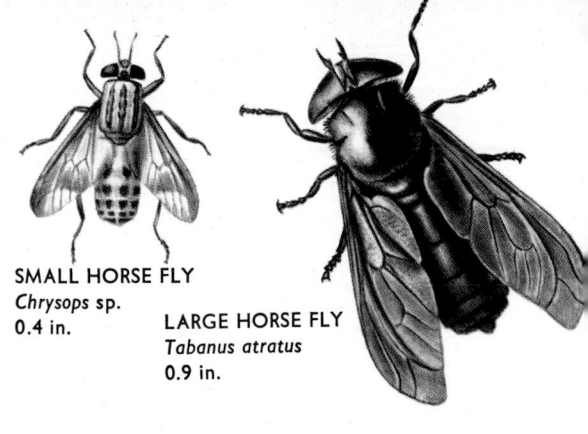

SMALL HORSE FLY
Chrysops sp.
0.4 in.

LARGE HORSE FLY
Tabanus atratus
0.9 in.

In each colony there may be several thousand hornets, mostly workers.

The common American Bald-faced Hornet is large, with black and yellow markings. It constructs a nest up to a foot in diameter, and is extremely vicious when disturbed.

Animals disturbing the nest of large hornets have been fatally stung by the fierce hordes that fly out in defence of their home.

One of the largest hornets in the world is the Himalayan *Vespula ducalis*, whose queens are up to $1\frac{3}{4}$ inches long, with a wing-spread of over 3 inches.

Hornets feed mostly on nectar, fruit juices, and the fermenting liquids of decaying fruit. Often, they prey on other insects and spiders, or chew on the carcasses of dead animals, as food for their larvae (see WASPS).

HORNSHELLS are small, rather drab molluscs that live in shallow water and in intertidal regions. Their long, spiral shells leave distinctive trails on sand and mud-flats. Most kinds eat plants. A large number of species in several different groups are found along Atlantic and Pacific beaches of North America. Tiny hermit crabs use their shells as temporary homes. The family *(Cerithiidae)* is abundant in the tropics.

HORSE FLIES *(Tabanidae)* are medium to large sized flies ($1/4$ to 1 in.) consisting of about 3,000 species. Males are primarily pollen and nectar feeders, but the group is best known for the blood-sucking habits of the females. The larger horse flies usually have clear or uniformly dusky wings. The smaller horse flies often have banded wings. These flies characteristically have large eyes occupying most of the area of the head. The eyes of many species are banded with iridescent colours. These colours do not last when the flies are killed, so are not seen in specimens in collections. Some horse flies lay their eggs in masses on stems of plants growing in swamps or other damp areas. As soon as they hatch, the larvae burrow into the mud, where they feed on other mud-dwelling larvae or on earthworms. Other

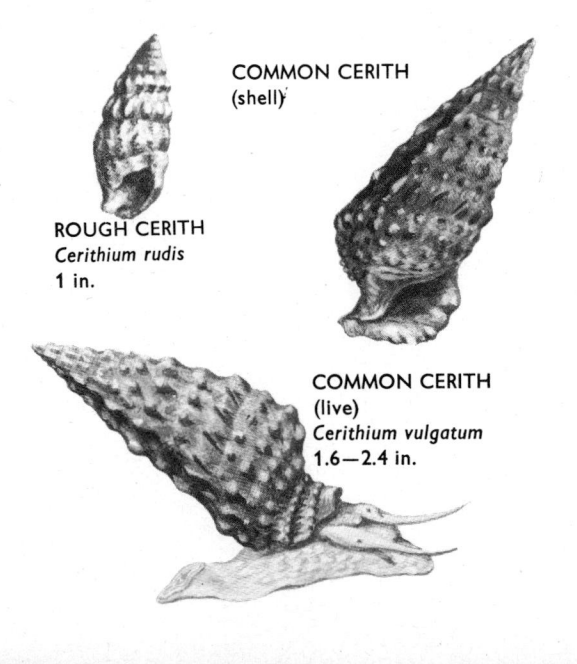

COMMON CERITH
(shell)

ROUGH CERITH
Cerithium rudis
1 in.

COMMON CERITH
(live)
Cerithium vulgatum
1.6—2.4 in.

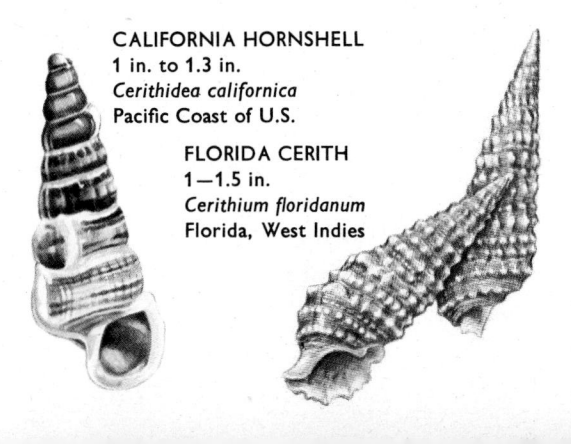

CALIFORNIA HORNSHELL
1 in. to 1.3 in.
Cerithidea californica
Pacific Coast of U.S.

FLORIDA CERITH
1—1.5 in.
Cerithium floridanum
Florida, West Indies

species prefer drier places. The larval stage lasts for two to fifteen months.

Many female horse flies bite painfully and are persistent once they find a victim. Cattle suffer torments from them.

HORSES *(Equus caballus)*. All modern breeds of horses are descendants of wild horses that once lived in Europe and Asia. From this one species, various breeds have been developed over the centuries. Their wide range of characteristics are a result of cross-breeding to bring out desired features.

The Arabian Horse, one of the most famous of many breeds developed in the arid country of the Arabian Peninsula, probably had shown some natural refinements over its ancestral stock even before man learned to domesticate animals. Its breeding has placed the emphasis on speed, with size and bulk being sacrificed to obtain swiftness and stamina. On mounts of Arabian blood,

Mohammedan conquerors achieved their remarkable victories in the Middle Ages.

While the Arabian Horse was developing in semi-desert country, another breed was taking shape in the rich grazing lands of northern Europe, particularly in the fertile marshland of what is today the Netherlands and Belgium. These horses were considerably larger, slower and more powerful than the light Arabians. They became known as the

Horse chariots, pulled by one to four horses, were used first in war, and then for work and pleasure. The chariot below is on an Italian coin of about 500 B.C.

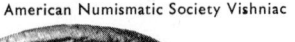
American Numismatic Society Vishniac

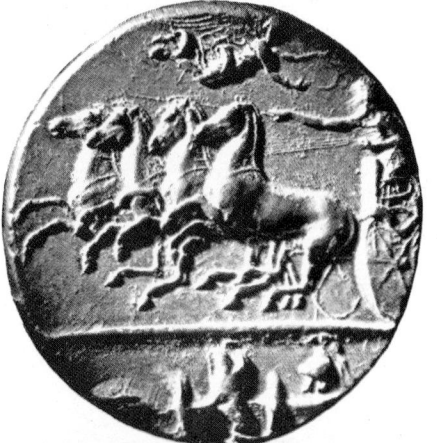

The Przewalski, or Mongolian Wild Horse, from Central Asia is the only remaining wild species of horse. The Tarpan, of Europe, is now extinct. Other so-called wild horses, such as mustangs of the western United States, are descendants of domesticated horses that have returned to the wild.

Catskill Game Farm, Photo by F. W. Davis

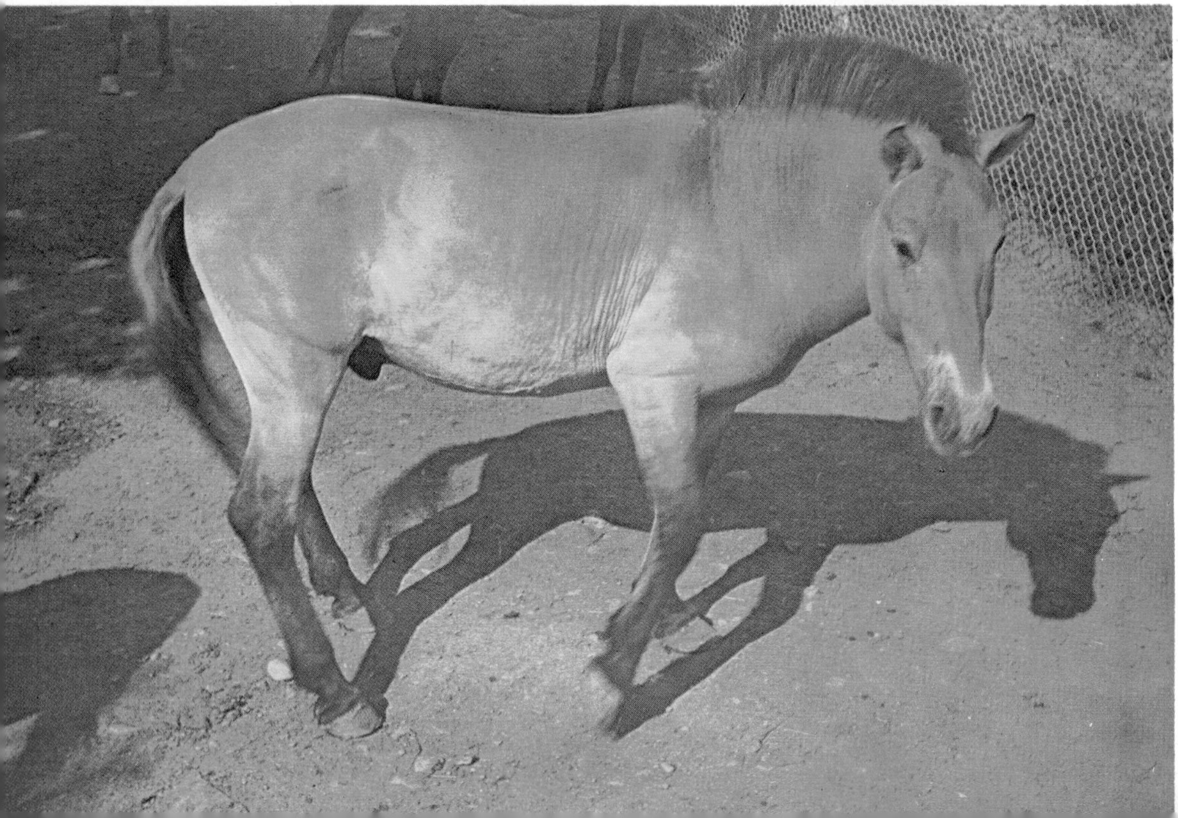

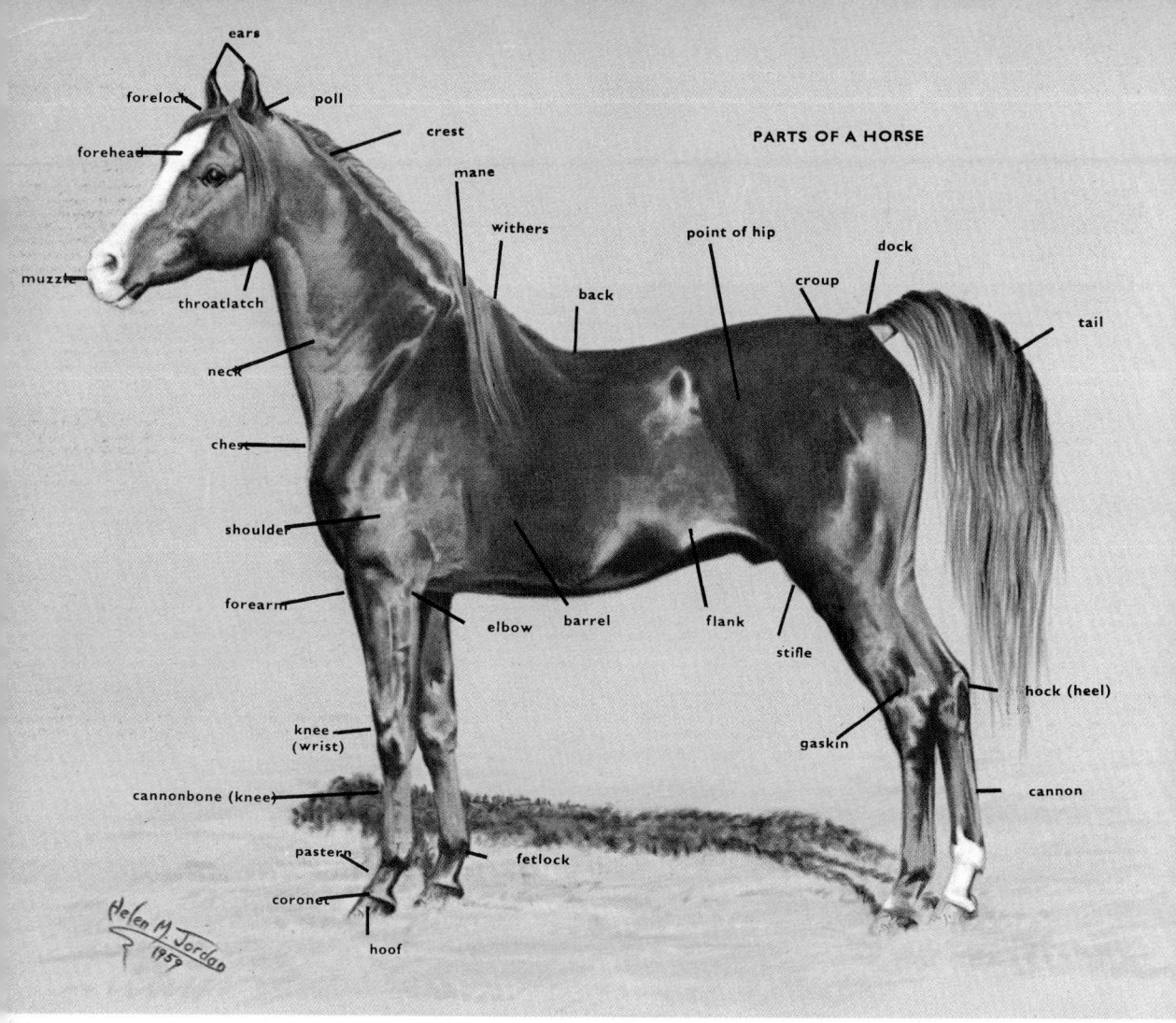

PARTS OF A HORSE

ears
forelock
poll
forehead
crest
mane
withers
muzzle
throatlatch
neck
chest
shoulder
forearm
elbow
barrel
knee
(wrist)
cannonbone (knee)
pastern
coronet
fetlock
hoof
point of hip
croup
dock
tail
flank
stifle
hock (heel)
gaskin
cannon

Helen M. Jordan 1959

Portrait by Helen M. Jordan of Jordan Arabian Farms

The structure, or conformation of the horse's body is important in judging classes and breeds in horse shows.

Great Horse, and were the powerful chargers of the armoured knights. These animals carried weights of as much as 400 pounds of man and metal into enemy battle-lines. Later, they were developed into the draft horse breeds (the Percheron, Belgian and Shire) of the nineteenth century.

In the remainder of Europe and Asia, a more generalised type of horse prevailed. It lacked both the bulk of the Great Horse and the speed of the Arab. In addition, several recognisable breeds of ponies (see PONIES) evolved in areas where food was scant and where small size was a valuable factor in survival. The Asiatic Pony, still another strain, became important in the history of modern horses. This was the steed of the westward-moving barbarians — from the Celts who annoyed early Rome, to the Golden Hordes of Kublai and Jenghiz Khan. Its great stamina was one of the animal's most valuable traits.

The westward movement of the Arabs introduced the Arabian Horse to all parts of North Africa and to Spain. Some individuals were taken to other parts of Europe by the Crusaders, who also introduced the Great Horse to the Near East. The Asiatic Pony, in its turn, reached Russia and Austria with the invading Mongols. The breeds were crossed by men who sought to develop a mount with the best qualities of each, and the resulting breeds differed from each other and from both parents by some recognisable feature or features. Bloodlines of desirable types were guarded by breeding the horses

only with those animals that showed the same sought-after trait. In this manner many breeds were developed.

Each breed has been developed to satisfy a purpose. Breeds now designated as heavy work, draft, or cold-blooded, are descendants of the Great Horses. Light horses — also called saddle or warm-blooded horses — were first developed for speed. Other breeds were formed from them in subsequent centuries for such purposes as pulling carriages and sulkies, ease in riding, or general utility use. Intelligence, responsiveness and courage were personality traits sought in every breed.

The Arabs were probably the first horse-breeders, and certainly few people have been as devoted to their steeds as these desert people. The knights of Europe may well have been second in attention to the art, but it is considered that modern horse-breeding began late in the seventeenth or early in the eighteenth century, when the Thoroughbred Horse was developed in England.

The Thoroughbred Horse was derived from two basic stocks. One was the general saddle horse then in common use, lacking both breed name and standardised characteristics. The other was the Arabian Horse imported from Mohammedan lands. Charles II, reigning from 1660 to 1685, had a stable of Barbs, the term used to designate Arabian horses raised in Barbary, the present Algeria and Tunisia. The Byerly Turk (1689), the Darley Arabian (1706), and the Godolphin

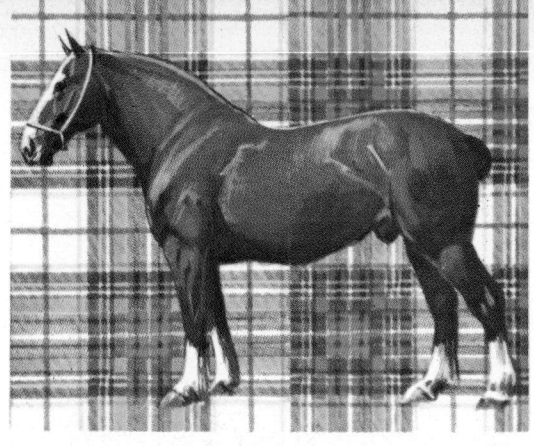

The Clydesdale, from Scotland, is smaller than other draft horses, and is also more spirited and handsome.

Barb (1724), further standardised the breed, and all Thoroughbreds of today can be traced to one or more of these remarkable horses. The chief use for the Thoroughbred is in racing and as a saddle horse.

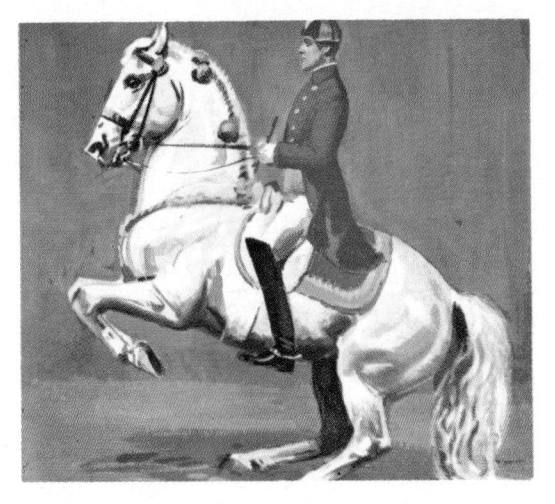

A white Lippizan performing the levade, one of the difficult steps executed by these well-trained horses.

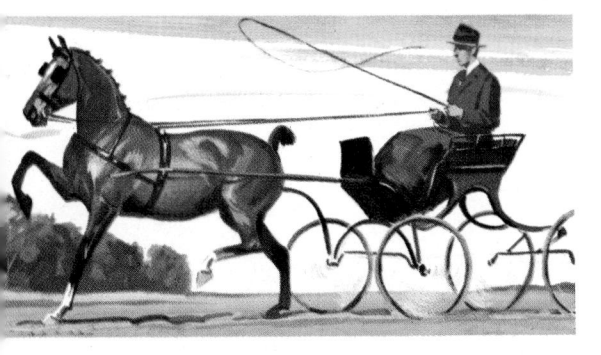

The Hackney, a small harness horse, was developed, like the Thoroughbred, from the Darley Arabian.

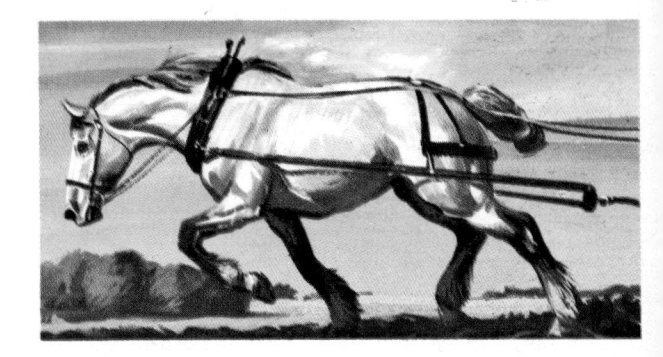

The Percheron, a draft horse bred in France, was once the most popular work animal in the U.S.A.

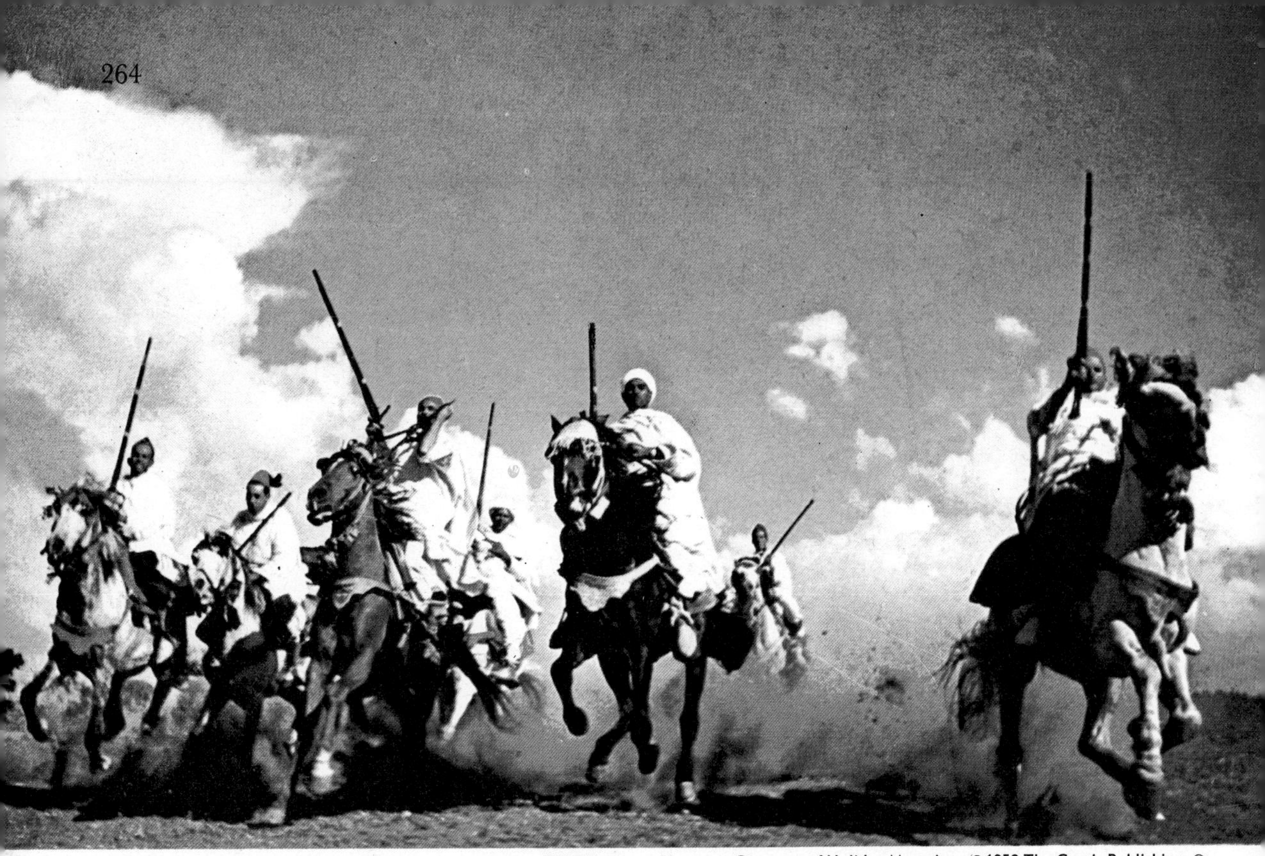

Elliot Erwitt — Magnum; Courtesy of Holiday Magazine; ©1958 The Curtis Publishing ©

The Arabian was developed centuries ago as the swift steed of desert warriors, and still exists as a pure breed. Most light horses of today have an Arabian bloodline in their ancestry.

A rival claimant for the title of oldest of the modern breeds is the American Quarter Horse. Early colonists in Virginia developed a small, rather stocky horse from saddle horses brought with them. These were crossed with mustangs acquired from the Indians, and the most notable quality of the horse developed from this cross was its great speed for short distances. Its name is derived from the quarter-mile race tracks that were then popular. The Quarter Horse was later mixed with the western mustang, descendant of the Spanish horse, to develop the cow-pony that became the dependable mount of the cattlemen of the West.

The Hackney was developed in England as a harness horse, rather than for racing. It was used for pulling the nobility's carriages in the eighteenth century. The Hackney has a high-stepping gait and a showy appearance that makes it a favourite show horse. It is too spirited for a saddle mount.

The Shire, from the marshy English counties of Lincolnshire and Cambridgeshire, is the largest of all horses. Stallions weigh over a ton. Although developed as a cavalry horse, the Shire is used now only as a heavy work animal on farms.

The Clydesdale, from Scotland, resembles the Shire but it is less bulky and has a more flowing gait. Always used as a farm horse, it is noted for its willingness and spirit.

The Suffolk, or Suffolk Punch, is short-legged compared to most draft breeds and lacks the "feathered" hocks that other

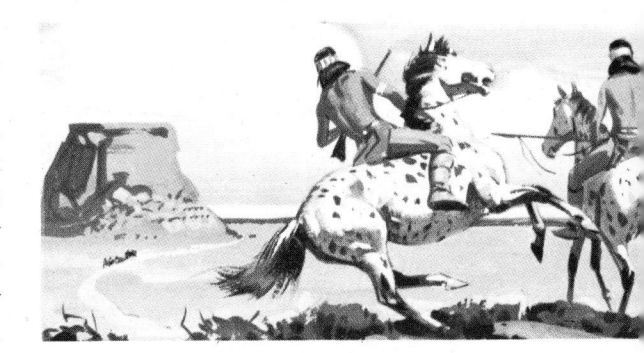

The Appaloosa, probably developed from mustangs, was the horse of the Nez Perce Indians.

This skeleton shows some of the horse's adaptations for speed. Each foot has only one toe, ending in a broad, flat hoof. Because other bones of the lower leg are also elongated, the so-called "knee" on the horse's front leg corresponds in bone structure to our wrist; the "hock" on its hind leg, to our ankle.

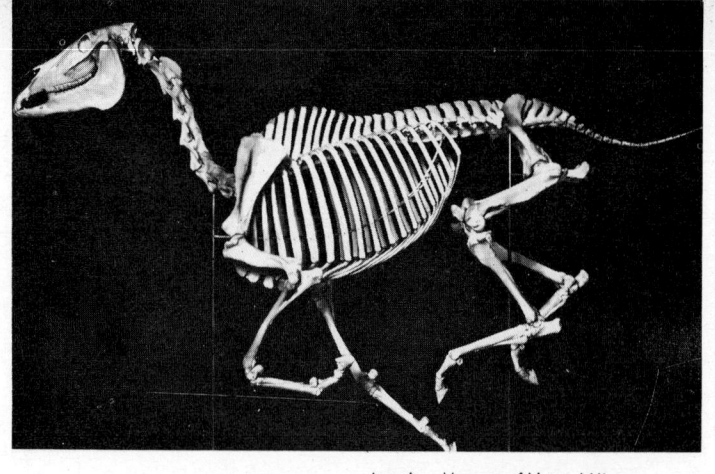

American Museum of Natural History

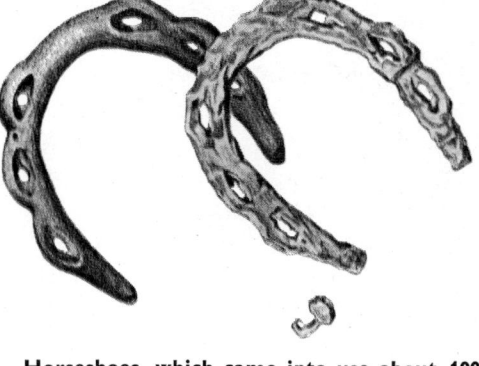

Horseshoes, which came into use about 100 B.C., made it possible for horses to run on pavement, cobblestones, or over any rough terrain, without splitting their hoofs. The shoes shown here are Roman (left) and Norman (right).

British breeds have. It is tremendously popular as a farm animal in the Suffolk region, but is not well known elsewhere.

Developed in France, in a region south of Normandy and south-west of Paris, the Percheron is somewhat smaller than British breeds, and has a very thick body and unfeathered hocks. Most Percherons in the United States are black; Frenchmen prefer the same breed of horse in grey.

The Belgian, a predominantly roan or chestnut horse, was developed in the lowlands of the Scheldt and Meuse rivers. It is so heavy-bodied that it appears shortlegged compared to other draft horses.

The Lippizaner was developed by the command of Emperor Maximilian II of Austria in 1565, and has been bred carefully ever since. Snow-white stallions of this breed are trained to perform difficult movements and paces for show performances.

There are many breeds of horses, from such countries as Norway, Russia and Turkey. New breeds have been developed to meet new conditions and fresh needs.

A newborn horse of either sex is called a foal. It is known as a yearling after its first birthday and until its second. Until the fourth year, a male is called a colt, and a female is a filly. Male horses are called stallions, and the de-sexed males are geldings. Females are called mares.

Every horse can walk, trot and run. These are called the natural gaits, and many horses are also natural pacers. In walking, a horse lifts its hoofs and moves them forward one by one. In the trot, the diag-

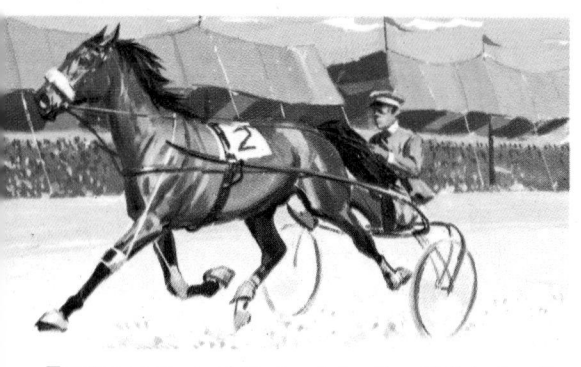

Trotters are carefully bred in the U.S.A. for the American sport of trotting, shown here.

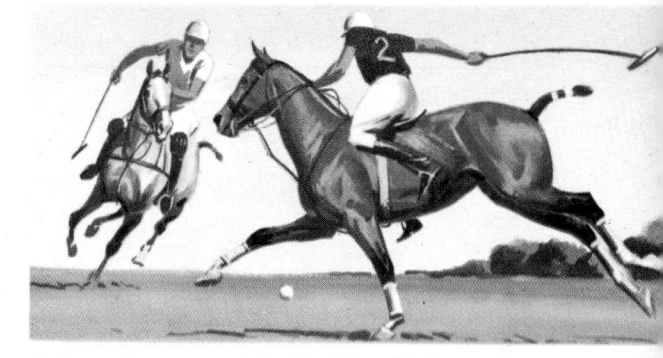

Polo ponies are specially bred for this increasingly popular English sport, which originated in India.

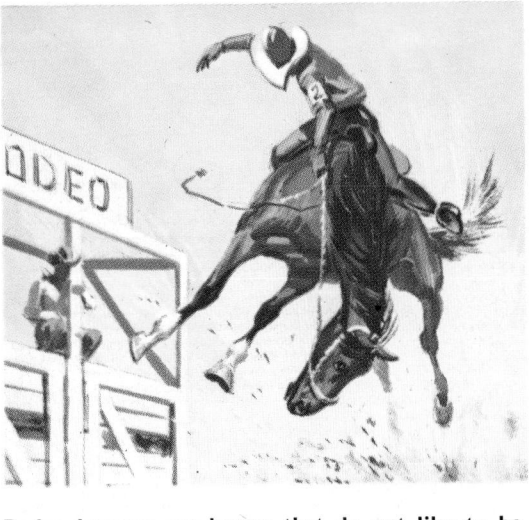

Rodeo broncos are horses that do not like to be ridden. They toss, turn, twist and leap to throw the rider. A bucking bronco is really valuable in a rodeo only, because it has such a bad disposition.

in pleasure riding, racing, hunting, polo, exhibitions, rodeos and parades. Horses are still useful, too, in mounted police work, and to some degree in agriculture.

HORSESHOE CRABS, or King Crabs (*Limulus polyphemus*), are not actually crabs or even crustaceans. They are members of the class *Arachnida*, to which spiders also belong. Horseshoe crabs grow to a length of 12 inches. They are found along the Atlantic Coast of North America, from Nova Scotia to Florida, and also occur in south-eastern Asia and in the Philippine Islands.

Protected by its spiked and armour-plated body, the Horseshoe Crab lives in shallow water, eating worms and other soft-

onally opposite hoofs strike the ground at the same time, left fore and right rear, then right fore and left rear. In the pace, hoofs on the same side work in unison. The gallop is the running gait, with a one-two-three rhythm, in which the first beat is one hind foot, the second is the other hind foot and one front foot, and the third is the remaining front foot. The horse then has all four hoofs off the ground for an instant, and the series begins again with one hind hoof.

The other common gaits, for which training is necessary, are the amble, the canter, the running walk and the rack. The amble is a slow pace, with a one-two-three-four beat as the hoofs strike the ground one by one. In the canter, the horse goes through the same motions as in a gallop, but at a slower rate and with less leg motion. The running walk is a slower version of the trot, in which the legs take great strides at a steady six to eight miles an hour. The rack is a fast four-beat gait that is strenuous for the horse, but easy on the rider. Each hoof strikes the ground in sequence. The beat is a definite, fast one-two-three-four.

The age-old partnership of man and horse continues, even though the horse's role as a major means of transportation has ended. Machinery cannot replace the horse

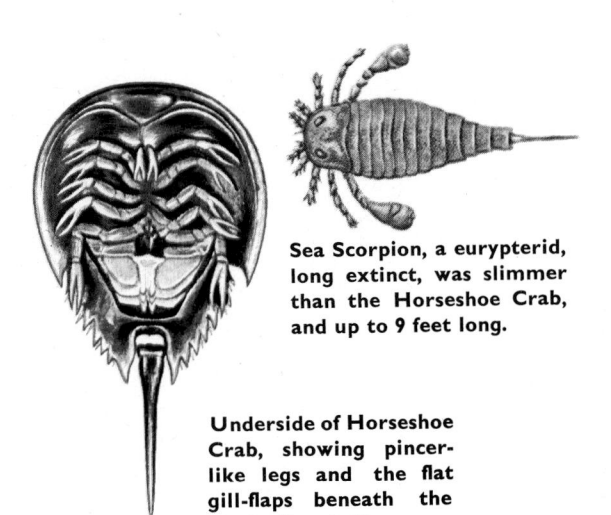

Sea Scorpion, a eurypterid, long extinct, was slimmer than the Horseshoe Crab, and up to 9 feet long.

Underside of Horseshoe Crab, showing pincer-like legs and the flat gill-flaps beneath the protective shell.

bodied animals. Females lay their eggs during the summer in shallow depressions in the sand. Newly-hatched larvae do not have tail spikes, but the young, which burrow beneath the surface, leave easily recognised broad trails. The Horseshoe Crab has no commercial value.

Because they are descendants of a very ancient group, Horseshoe Crabs are called "living fossils". The extinct Eurypterids, their closest relatives, lived with them in the Paleozoic seas about 500 million years ago. Eurypterids died out before the end of the Paleozoic era.

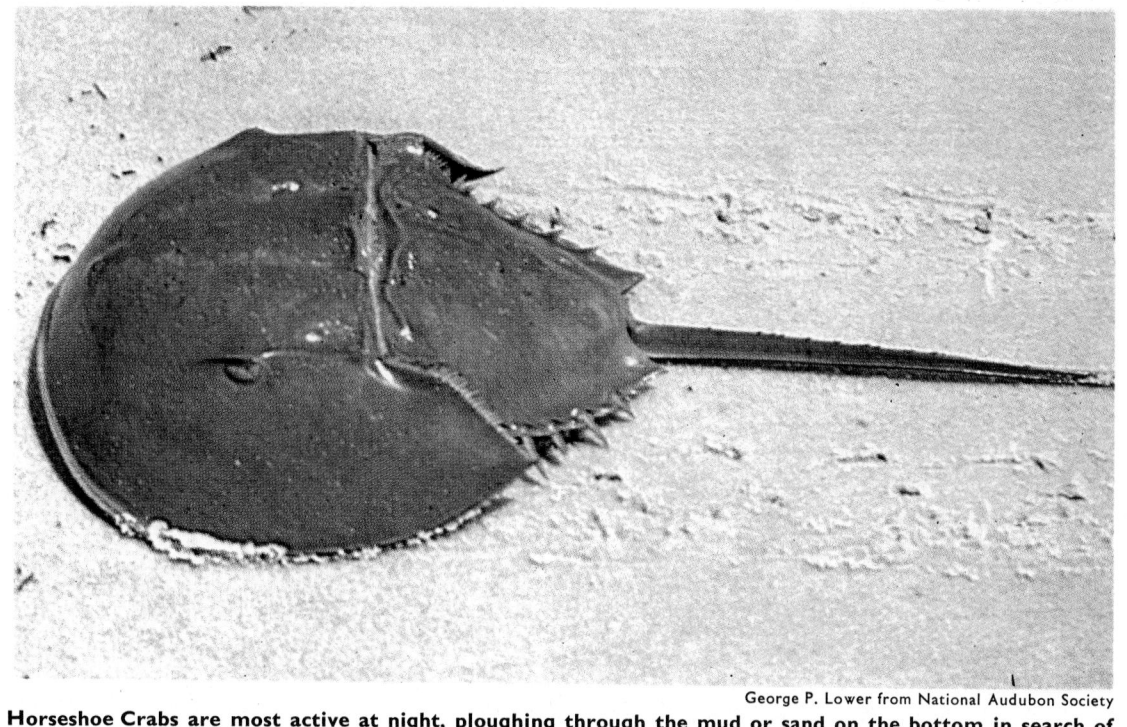

Horseshoe Crabs are most active at night, ploughing through the mud or sand on the bottom in search of seaworms and other animals for food. Many are found along the beaches in spring or summer at mating time. The female lays her eggs in the sand at the high-tide mark, and the male then fertilises them.

HOUNDS are sporting dogs that hunt by sight or scent for rabbits, foxes, and other game animals. Some are swift runners; others trail their quarry slowly.

The Greyhound is such an old breed that it is mentioned in Egyptian hieroglyphics. Its name is almost synonymous with speed, and although greyhounds were originally hunting dogs, they have become popular race animals. Greyhounds are long-legged and lean, with slightly arched barks. They have long tails and rather short ears. Their short hair may be almost any colour, despite the breed's name.

The Whippet, which looks like a miniature Greyhound, is bred for racing and has been called the "poor man's race-horse". Although a Whippet may weigh only 15 to 30 pounds, it can run as fast as 35 miles per hour.

The Borzoi, or Russian Wolfhound, has been employed as a coursing hound in Russia since the thirteenth century. After thorough training, the Borzoi is ideal for hunting wolves; it is large (75 to 100 pounds), lean and graceful. The Russian Wolfhound has a long, narrow head, small ears and long, wavy hair, which is usually white marked with yellow, tan, grey or black.

The English Foxhound was bred spe-

The Borzoi, or Russian Wolfhound, is a swift and graceful hound noted for its good disposition.

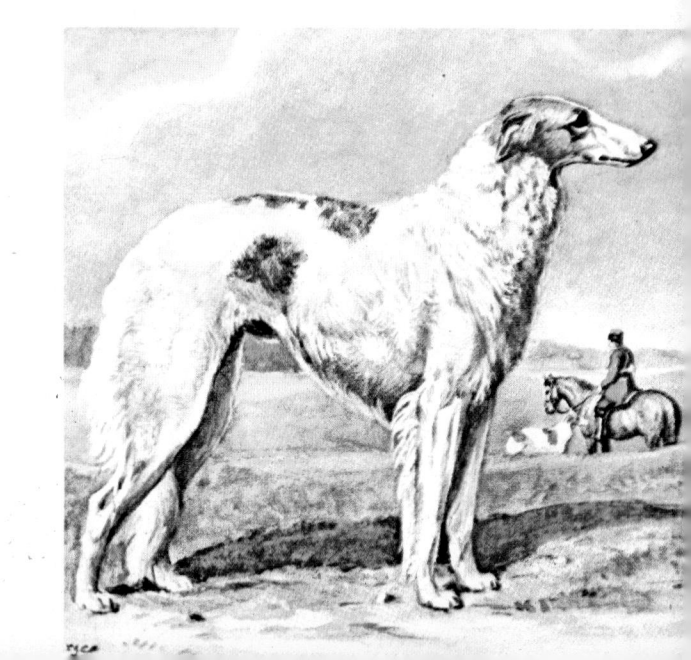

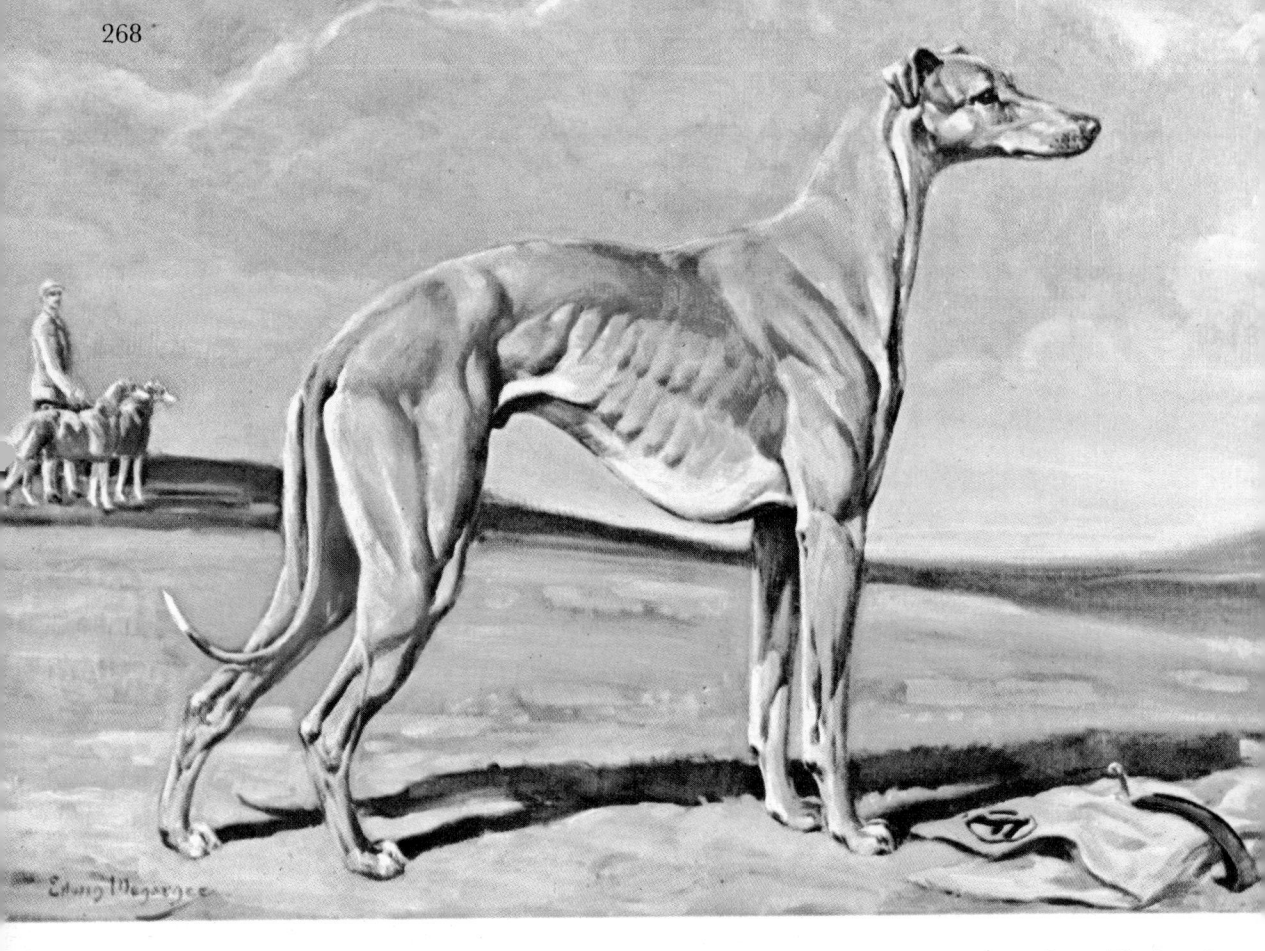

The Greyhound, the swiftest of dogs, has been clocked at speeds of more than 35 miles per hour. The breed was originally developed for hunting rabbits and deer, and is still bred at the present time, with speed in mind, for the modern pastime of Greyhound racing.

cifically to hunt foxes, and a good pack of these hounds is very much a part of the sport of "riding to hounds". English Foxhounds are sturdy and fast and, of course, have keen noses. They have short, sleek hair, rather long, drooping ears, and a long tail. Most are white, with large brown and black markings on the head and back.

The American Foxhound's lineage can be traced back mainly to the English Foxhound, which it resembles in general appearance. American Foxhounds, however, are usually smaller, and are bred both for hunting in packs and for hunting alone.

The Basset was developed in France for trailing game, but has become more popular in the United States since World War 11 as a pet. A Basset may weigh as much as 40 pounds. It has short legs, large, floppy ears, and a melancholy facial appearance.

The Dachshund is now a popular pet, but was originally a hunting dog. It has a long, muscular body and extremely short legs, developed so that it could squirm down the holes of badgers (*dachs* in German). Dachshunds have long tails and medium-length, drooping ears. There are three coat variations: wire-hair, long-hair, and smooth-hair. Dachshunds may be solid brown, or black with small tan markings.

The Irish Wolfhound, a very old breed, is the tallest of all dogs. When the Celts sacked Delphi in the second century, they brought their great Wolfhounds with them. Though used as war dogs and hunting dogs, Irish Wolfhounds make wonderful pets. Lean and long-legged, they have a narrow head with small, partially-erect ears. Their rather long hair is wiry, and grows thick around their eyes and muzzle, like eyebrows and a beard.

Wolfhounds are usually grey, but may be brindle, fawn, or solid red, black or white.

The Scottish Deerhound, like the Borzoi and the Greyhound, has been known for centuries in its native land as a hunter of such swift game as deer. In the United States, this breed has been used in pursuit of wolves, coyotes and rabbits. These dogs are large (85 to 110 pounds), long and muscular. Their long, rough coats are usually dark blue-grey.

The Beagle, popular both as a hunter and as a pet, is a medium-sized dog weighing about 30 pounds. It has a long, erect tail and drooping ears. Beagles are lively and have keen noses. Their coats are short and flat; most are white, with large brown and black markings on their head and back.

Bloodhounds have such a good reputation for trailing by scent that their "testimony" is accepted in courts of law. Their name, however, means that this breed has been "blooded" (kept pure) for many years. Bloodhounds are traditionally used in hunting fugitives, but are nevertheless very docile and friendly. They are large (about 90 pounds), muscular dogs with thin, loose skin that hangs in folds and wrinkles. Their ears are long and drooping. Bloodhounds are black, tan or red, with a white marking on the chest, feet or tail. (See DOGS.)

HOUSE FLIES (*Muscidae*) are probably as familiar as any other insect, and a great deal more abundant, particularly in hot weather, than most people would like.

House flies lay their eggs in a cluster of 100 or more, each female producing as many as 20 clusters. Usually the eggs are deposited in animal manure, but decaying animal and vegetable matter is also used. The eggs hatch in twelve hours to three days, depending on the temperature, and the larvae, or maggots, feed for five to ten days, and then pupate; adults emerge in about a week. It is actually possible for a house fly to go through a complete generation in a period of less than two weeks.

The House Fly does not bite and is consid-

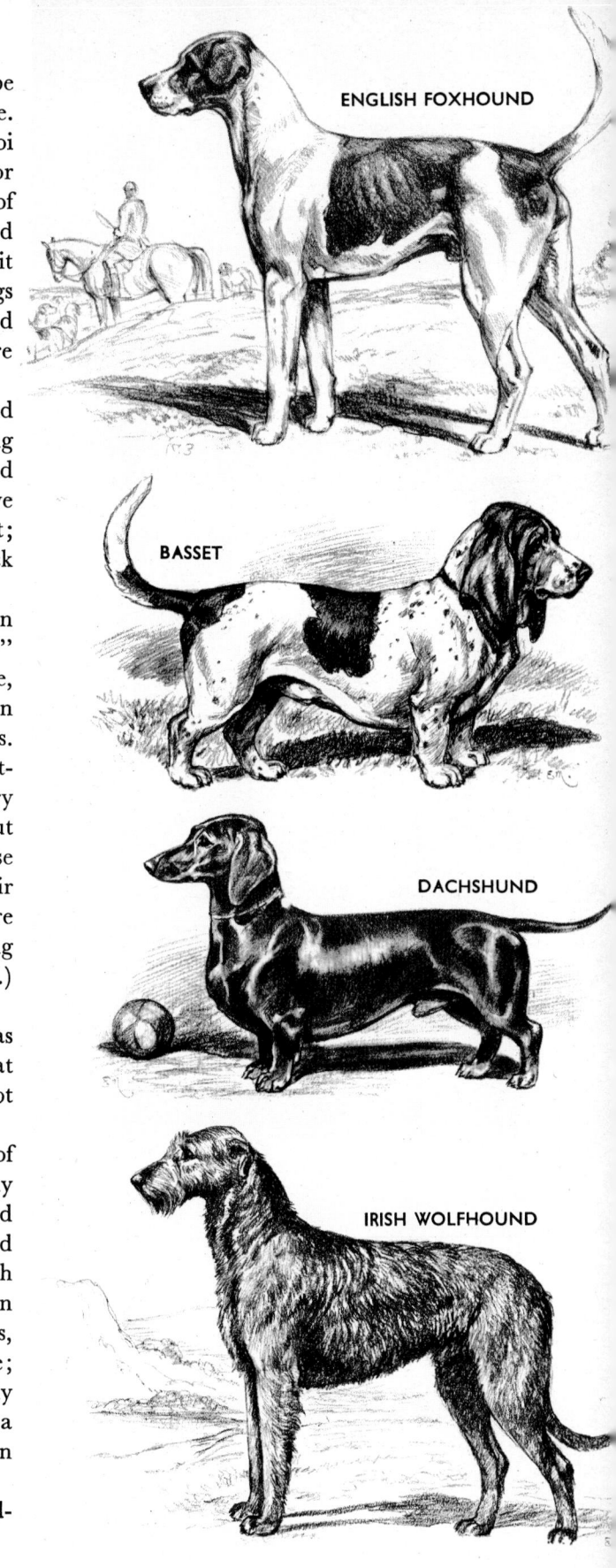

ENGLISH FOXHOUND

BASSET

DACHSHUND

IRISH WOLFHOUND

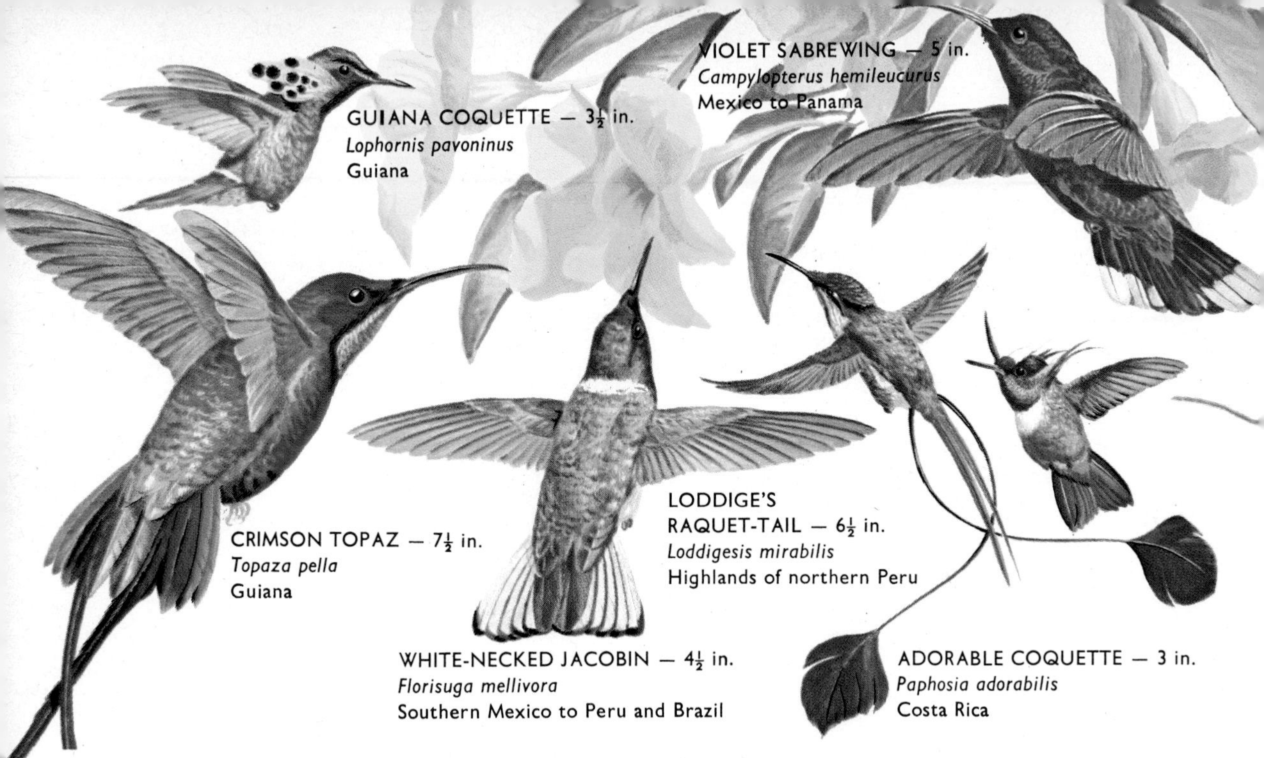

GUIANA COQUETTE — 3½ in.
Lophornis pavoninus
Guiana

VIOLET SABREWING — 5 in.
Campylopterus hemileucurus
Mexico to Panama

CRIMSON TOPAZ — 7½ in.
Topaza pella
Guiana

LODDIGE'S
RAQUET-TAIL — 6½ in.
Loddigesis mirabilis
Highlands of northern Peru

WHITE-NECKED JACOBIN — 4½ in.
Florisuga mellivora
Southern Mexico to Peru and Brazil

ADORABLE COQUETTE — 3 in.
Paphosia adorabilis
Costa Rica

ered by many people to be only a nuisance. In fact, however, the House Fly is a carrier of diseases — typhoid, anthrax, cholera, and many others. A house fly lands on a dead animal, sewage or garbage, and then on the food on your table. Disease organisms are carried on the many hairs on its legs and body. (See FLIES.)

HUMMING-BIRDS are New World creatures with marvellous colouring, astounding flight, and peculiar feeding habits. Their brilliant feathers gleam as if gold underlies the vivid greens, reds, yellows, purples and blues of their ornamental feathers.

Humming-birds have a tiny, squeaky song; the humming is made by their wings,

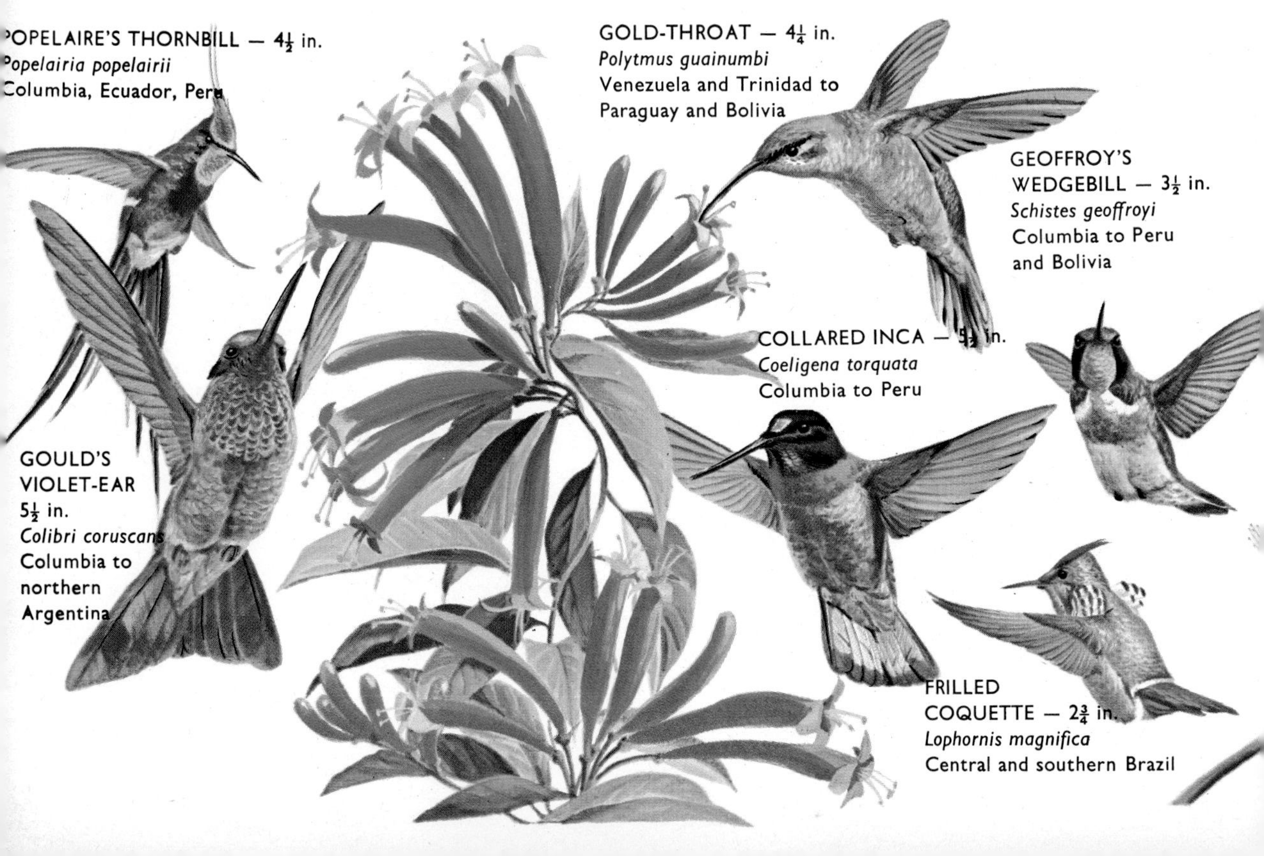

POPELAIRE'S THORNBILL — 4½ in.
Popelairia popelairii
Columbia, Ecuador, Peru

GOLD-THROAT — 4¼ in.
Polytmus guainumbi
Venezuela and Trinidad to
Paraguay and Bolivia

GEOFFROY'S
WEDGEBILL — 3½ in.
Schistes geoffroyi
Columbia to Peru
and Bolivia

COLLARED INCA — 5½ in.
Coeligena torquata
Columbia to Peru

GOULD'S
VIOLET-EAR
5½ in.
Colibri coruscans
Columbia to
northern
Argentina

FRILLED
COQUETTE — 2¾ in.
Lophornis magnifica
Central and southern Brazil

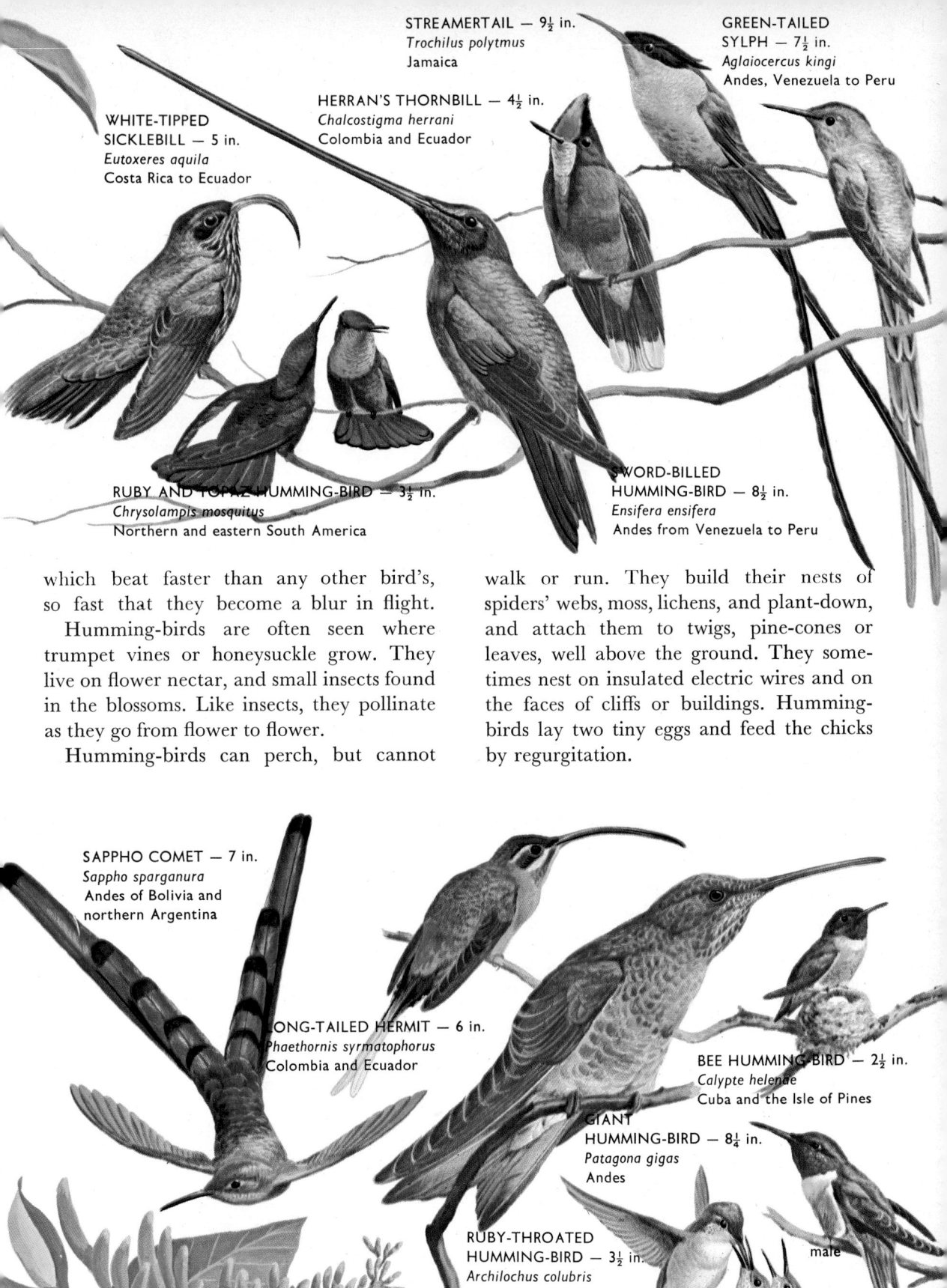

STREAMERTAIL — 9½ in.
Trochilus polytmus
Jamaica

GREEN-TAILED
SYLPH — 7½ in.
Aglaiocercus kingi
Andes, Venezuela to Peru

HERRAN'S THORNBILL — 4½ in.
Chalcostigma herrani
Colombia and Ecuador

WHITE-TIPPED
SICKLEBILL — 5 in.
Eutoxeres aquila
Costa Rica to Ecuador

RUBY AND TOPAZ HUMMING-BIRD — 3½ in.
Chrysolampis mosquitus
Northern and eastern South America

SWORD-BILLED
HUMMING-BIRD — 8½ in.
Ensifera ensifera
Andes from Venezuela to Peru

which beat faster than any other bird's, so fast that they become a blur in flight.

Humming-birds are often seen where trumpet vines or honeysuckle grow. They live on flower nectar, and small insects found in the blossoms. Like insects, they pollinate as they go from flower to flower.

Humming-birds can perch, but cannot walk or run. They build their nests of spiders' webs, moss, lichens, and plant-down, and attach them to twigs, pine-cones or leaves, well above the ground. They sometimes nest on insulated electric wires and on the faces of cliffs or buildings. Humming-birds lay two tiny eggs and feed the chicks by regurgitation.

SAPPHO COMET — 7 in.
Sappho sparganura
Andes of Bolivia and
northern Argentina

LONG-TAILED HERMIT — 6 in.
Phaethornis syrmatophorus
Colombia and Ecuador

BEE HUMMING-BIRD — 2½ in.
Calypte helenae
Cuba and the Isle of Pines

GIANT
HUMMING-BIRD — 8¼ in.
Patagona gigas
Andes

male

RUBY-THROATED
HUMMING-BIRD — 3½ in.
Archilochus colubris
Eastern United States
and southern Canada

female

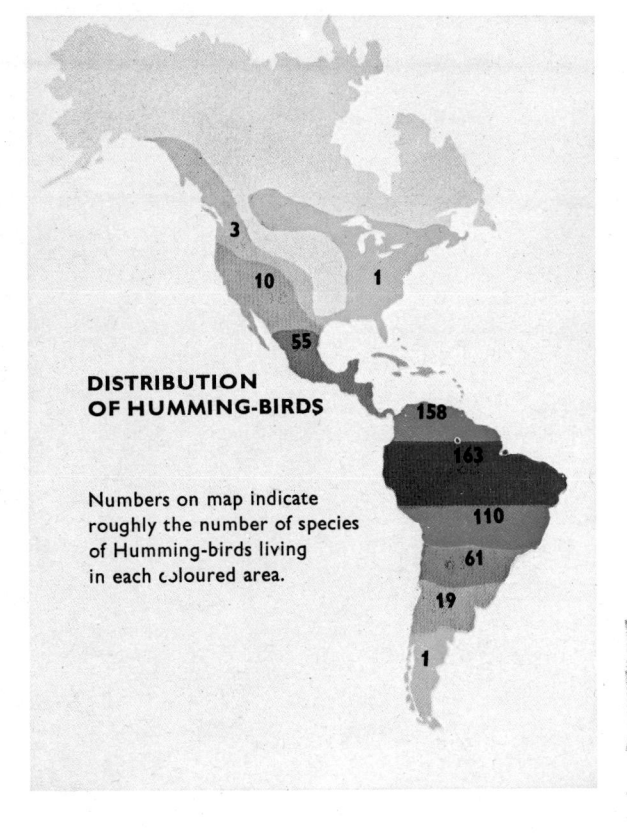

DISTRIBUTION OF HUMMING-BIRDS

3
10
1
55
158
163
110
61
19
1

Numbers on map indicate roughly the number of species of Humming-birds living in each coloured area.

bird's naked chicks look like caterpillars. It cannot nest in some parts of California because the introduced Argentine ants kill and eat the young birds.

The Swordbilled Humming-bird has a bill longer than its head and body. The Raquet-tail is as ornamented as a bird of paradise. Other humming-birds have fin-like feathers on the side of their heads, making them look as though they had an extra pair of wings.

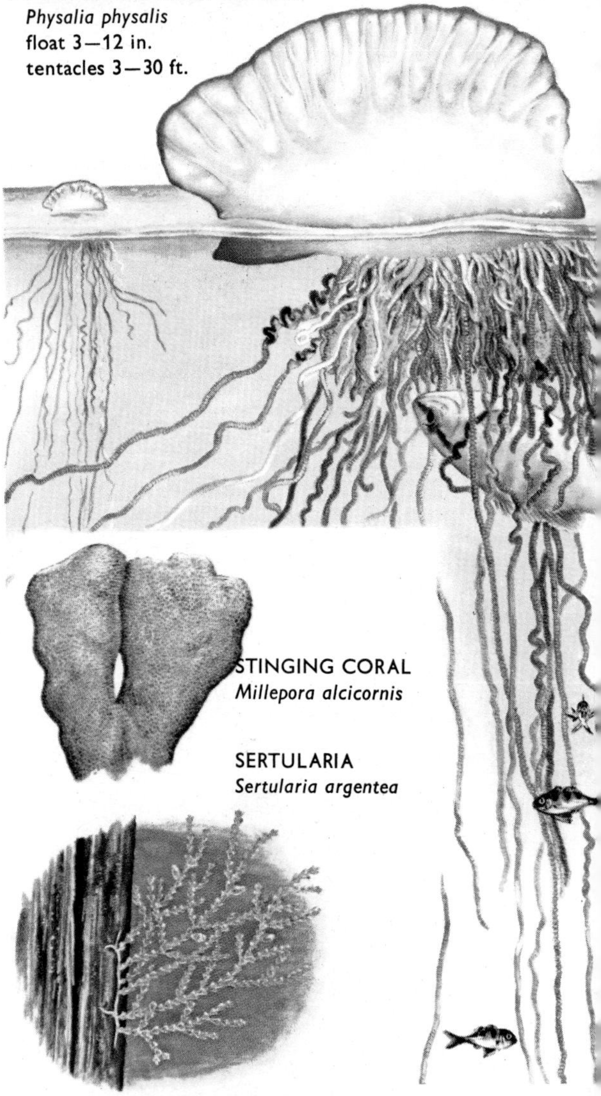

PORTUGUESE MAN-OF-WAR
Physalia physalis
float 3—12 in.
tentacles 3—30 ft.

STINGING CORAL
Millepora alcicornis

SERTULARIA
Sertularia argentea

The 319 species of humming-bird, most of them in the tropics, include the tiny $2\frac{1}{2}$-inch Bee Humming-bird, the smallest bird in the world. Its wee nest is only three-quarters of an inch in diameter. Largest is the Giant Humming-bird of the high Andes; it attains a body length of $8\frac{1}{2}$ inches.

The Ruby-throated Humming-bird, the only member of the family in eastern North America, was first described by Thomas Morton in 1632. It is always attracted to anything red, and has been known to investigate a red nose in the same way it does a flower. Red sugar water will bring Ruby-throated Humming-birds to a window sill.

The Rufous Humming-bird goes farther north than any other. It summers along the west coast of North America, from California to Alaska, and migrates to Mexico in winter.

The Anna Humming-bird stays in California throughout the year. It is fond of the orange groves in the southern part of the State and likes to bathe in dew. Until their feathers grow, the Anna Humming-

HYDROIDS are coelenterates of the class *Hydrozoa*. On dock pilings, rocks, coral reefs and seaweeds, the thick growths of

colonial marine hydroids sometimes look like ferns. Adults, which may be branched or unbranched, produce tiny jellyfishlike young (medusae) that seldom grow very large. Medusae reproduce sexually, forming larvae (planulae) that attach themselves to the bottom and grow into the hydroid colonies by budding.

Tentacles of hydroids are armed with stinging cells, called nematocysts, used to capture prey. Their powerful stings may be painful to swimmers who rub against them. Common northern forms are *Tubularia* and *Obelia;* and *Sertularia* is found in tropical waters all over the world.

Stinging (Fire) Coral *(Millepora),* closely related to the hydroids, has a massive, limy skeleton with tiny polyps, each armed with stinging cells. Stinging corals form leaf-like colonies, often encrusting the dead skeletons of Sea Feathers.

The Portuguese Man-of-War *(Physalia physalis)* is the most famous of the hydroids.

SPOTTED HYENA
Crocuta crocuta
length 5 ft.

STRIPED HYENA
Hyaena hyaena
length 4—5 ft.

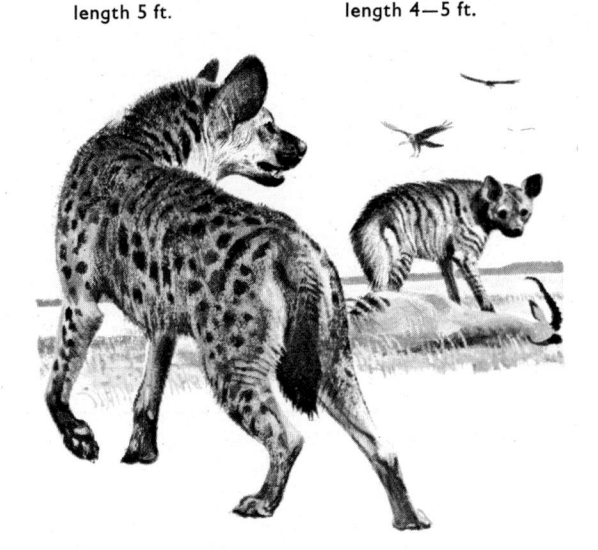

HYENAS *(Hyaena* spp. and *Crocuta)* are strange-looking, dog-like animals that live almost entirely on picked-over scraps left by other carnivores; they are scavengers of the feasts that other animals have enjoyed.

Ordinarily they are cowardly, but, when very hungry, packs of hyenas may attack other animals.

Hyenas have large heads, low hind quarters and a generally ungraceful appearance. They make a variety of noises which have been described as cries, cackles, barks and laughs. They are often called Laughing Hyenas. Hyenas eat the bones of the large antelopes and buffaloes, crushing them with their powerful teeth and strong jaws. They also have strong digestive fluids to break down these bones in their stomachs. Striped Hyenas are found from India to North Africa; Brown Hyenas in southern Africa; Spotted Hyenas, the largest of the group, in most of central and southern Africa.

HYRAXES *(Procavia, Heterohyrax* and *Dendrohyrax* spp.) are about the size of rabbits, but have very short ears. They are related to the gigantic rhinoceroses and elephants, yet they look like rodents and behave much like goats. Hyraxes live along cliffs and rocky slopes. They have blunt nails, hoofs, and can climb almost vertical cliffs, leaping up and down steep slopes with great ease. Some kinds even live in trees, where they feed on the leaves. Tree hyraxes usually live singly; most others live in colonies. Hyraxes are found throughout most of Africa, and also in part of the Arabian Peninsular.

Though small and shy, hyraxes have a reputation for fearlessness when cornered. Their upper incisors are sharp and capable of making deep wounds in an adversary.

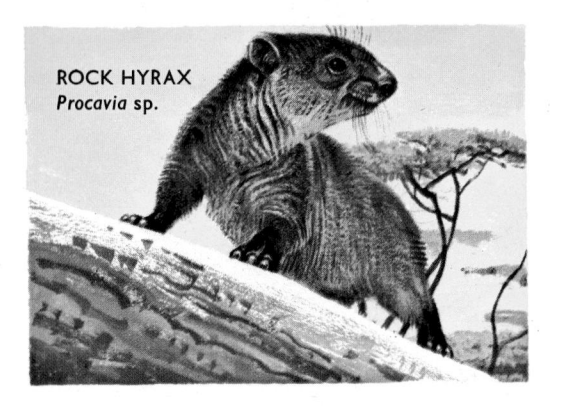

ROCK HYRAX
Procavia sp.

IBISES are large birds that inhabit the warmer parts of all large land masses in the world. Relatives of storks and herons, they also have long necks, long legs, and the same sort of flight, but they hold their necks straight out in flight and have short tails. Their long, curved bills are excellent for probing in mud for worms, insects, larvae and shellfish. Ibises nest in colonies similar to heronries (see HERONS).

The Glossy Ibis of the Western Hemisphere is so named because of the metallic sheen of its feathers.

Ancient Egyptians believed the Sacred Ibis was the creator that hatched the "world egg". Later it was associated with Thoth, Egyptian god of wisdom, who had a man's body and an ibis's head. The birds were sometimes kept in captivity; then, when one died, its body was mummified and placed in a temple. The Sacred Ibis is very rare in Egypt today.

The Scarlet Ibis from Central and South America is one of the most beautiful members of the family. At one time it was hunted for its colourful feathers.

The White Ibis is plentiful from the southern United States to Venezuela and Peru. Some of its colonies are enormous, as many as 50,000 birds nesting together.

ICHNEUMONS, or Ichneumon Flies *(Ichneumonidae)*, are large parasitic wasps. Several thousand species are known. Nearly all groups of insects are parasitised by ichneumons. Each ichneumon species, however, is fairly limited in the number of host insects it will attack, and most of them parasitise only immature stages.

Among the largest are species of the genus *Rhyssa*, some of which are two inches long and have ovipositors four inches long. They parasitise the burrowing larvae of wood-wasps (see SAWFLIES).

When a female ichneumon finds a tree infested with a wood-wasp larva, she drills a hole into a burrow with her ovipositor and

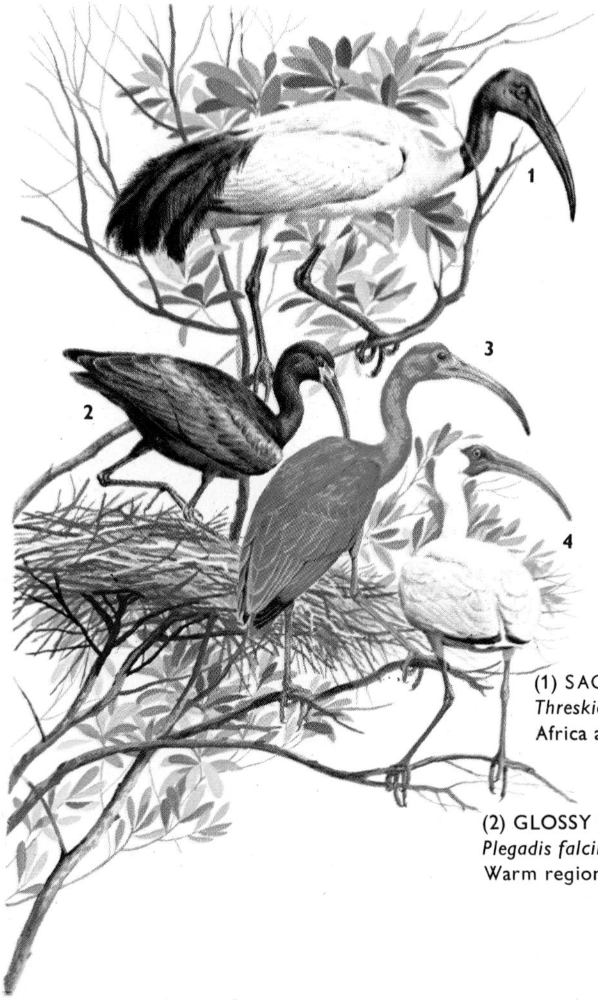

(1) SACRED IBIS — 30 in.
Threskiornis aethiopica
Africa and Madagascar

(3) SCARLET IBIS — 24 in.
Eudocimus ruber
Tropical South America

(4) WHITE IBIS — 27 in.
Eudocimus albus
Southern United States, West Indies, Central and northern South America

(2) GLOSSY IBIS — 22 in.
Plegadis falcinellus
Warm regions throughout the world

ICHNEUMON FLY
Megarhyssa atrata
1.4 in

the Galapagos. Only seven species occur in the Old World, and on Fiji and Tonga islands. All except the smallest species in this family are prized for food.

Anoles are the largest group (see AN-OLES). In the Old World, the place of the iguanids is taken by the strikingly similar agamids (see AGAMIDS).

Largest is the Green Iguana *(Iguana),* which reaches a length of more than $6\frac{1}{2}$ feet. About two-thirds of the creature's length is its long, whip-like tail, which the lizard may use as a lash to defend itself. When a Green Iguana is startled in a tree, it often drops to the ground with a crash and dashes off through the underbrush. If the lizard is over water, it drops with a loud splash and swims away in a snake-like manner, holding its legs against its sides.

Black Iguanas *(Ctenosaura)* of Central America have shorter, thicker tails than do Green Iguanas. Their tails are ridged with sharp spikes, making them more formidable.

Ground Iguanas *(Cyclura),* of the West Indies, are about the same size as Black Iguanas, but live in natural caves or in

deposits an egg in or near the larva. The wood-wasp larva becomes food for the ichneumon fly larva that hatches from the egg.

IGUANAS are members of the largest lizard family *(Iguanidae)* in the New World. There are over 400 species of iguanids, which occur from southern Canada to southern Chile and Argentina, in the West Indies, and on most islands in the Pacific, including

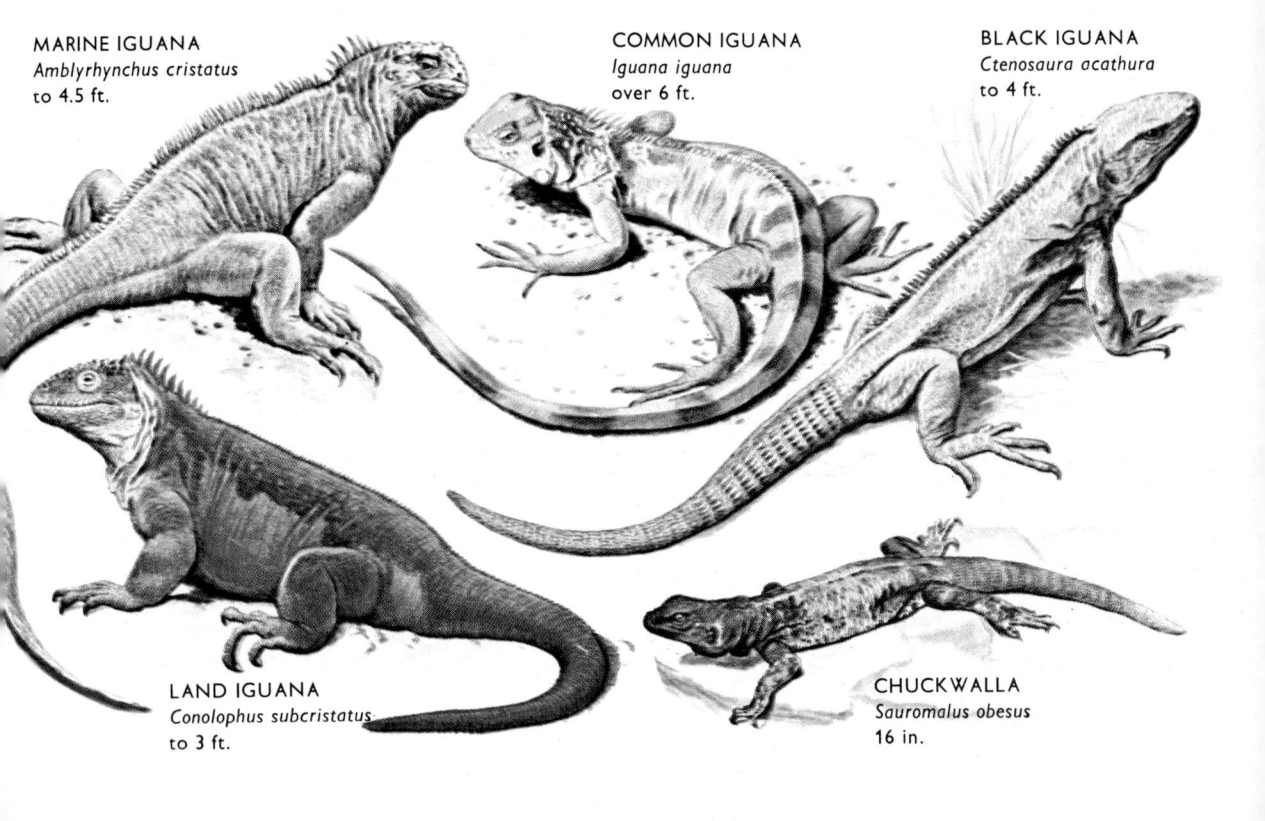

MARINE IGUANA
Amblyrhynchus cristatus
to 4.5 ft.

COMMON IGUANA
Iguana iguana
over 6 ft.

BLACK IGUANA
Ctenosaura acathura
to 4 ft.

LAND IGUANA
Conolophus subcristatus
to 3 ft.

CHUCKWALLA
Sauromalus obesus
16 in.

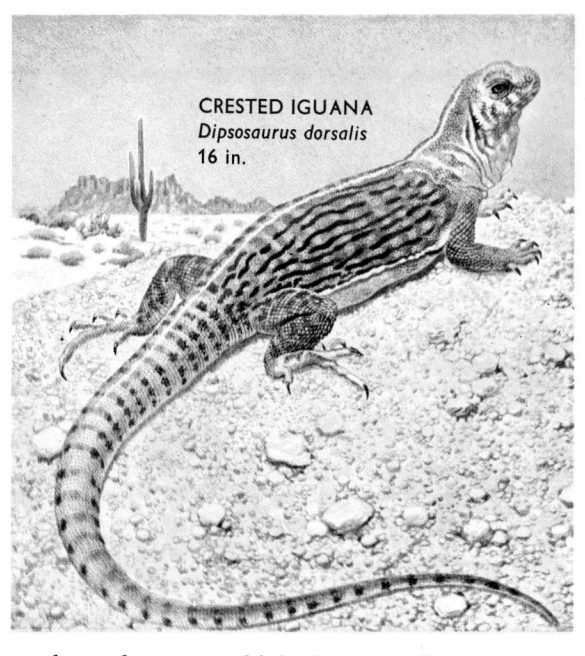

CRESTED IGUANA
Dipsosaurus dorsalis
16 in.

large burrows which they dig. Some species of Ground Iguanas have become extinct in the past 200 years. Bole Iguanas *(Enyaliosaurus)* are smaller — not over about $1\frac{1}{2}$ feet — and their tails are heavily spined. They are found only in hollows of trees and are extremely wary.

Two kinds of iguanas live in the Galapagos Islands. A five-foot species *(Amblyrhynchus)* lives on rocky shores and is one of the very few lizards with a marine existence; it eats marine algae. A three-foot species *(Conolophus)* eats cacti. The only iguanids occurring outside the New World are the three-foot Fijian Iguana, a tree-dwelling species nearing extinction, and two Madagascan forms.

The fat-bodied, short-tailed Chuckwallas *(Sauromalus)* and the more slender, long-tailed Crested Lizards *(Dipsosaurus)* are the only members of this iguanid group found in the United States of America. Both are restricted to south-western desert regions. Chuckwallas (12 in.) live among boulders, venturing away only to feed. Crested Lizards (16 in.) are ground-dwellers, running swiftly from bush to bush in relatively open desert country. Chuckwallas wedge themselves in rock crevices by inflating their lungs. Indians, who prized them for food, used pointed sticks in order to puncture

their lungs and then extract them.

Most iguanids lay their eggs in the ground or in rotten wood. A few bear their young alive, and all "bob" their bodies when they detect danger. They do this by pumping the front of the body up and down, and at the same time flattening the body and throat.

INSECTS. About 80 per cent of the known kinds of animals are insects. About 900,000 species of insect have been described and named, and new ones are being discovered at a rate of about 7,000 per year. Over 20,000 are listed in the British Isles.

Calculating the number of individual insects is impossible — even for a relatively small area. Considering the great number of

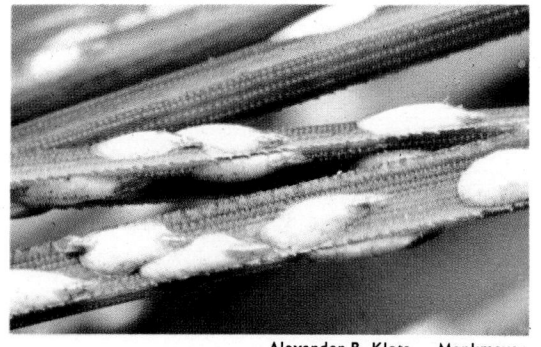

Alexander B. Klots — Monkmeyer

Among the smallest insects of importance are the scales. Many kinds are so modified in body form, that they are hard to recognise as insects. These whitish Pine Needle Scales are very small.

different kinds and their very high rate of reproduction, any such figures are tremendous. For example, a female Cabbage Aphid has about 40 offspring, each of which can mature and have offspring in about two weeks. If all these offspring lived and multiplied for 16 generations (normal duration of the breeding season), there would be in a single season . . .

1,560,000,000,000,000,000,000,000 . . . aphid descendants from the original female. Some termite queens lay one egg every two seconds, twenty-four hours a day. Migrating butterflies have been seen in such large numbers that 1,250,000 flew across a zone 250 miles long every minute — and con-

tinued at that rate for 18 days! Locust swarms have been reported that averaged half a mile in height, and that were 100 miles wide and 300 miles long. The total number of locusts in this gigantic swarm was estimated at 124,000,000,000.

Insects also vary greatly in size and shape. Some beetles and midges are much smaller than the head of a pin — smaller even than the largest of the one-celled animals. At the opposite extreme are stick insects (*Phasmidae*), more than 12 inches long, and many moths with wing-spreads up to 12 inches. Several kinds of beetle measure up to six inches in length.

The largest insects that ever existed were the now extinct Protodonata, relatives of modern dragonflies. One fossil specimen of this group had a wing-span of 30 inches. These giant insect-eating insects soared over coal-forming swamps some 250 million years ago. In those same swamps were cockroaches almost identical to species alive today, though no larger.

Most living insects, however, are small in size compared to most familiar animals with backbones. Smallness is of advantage, since

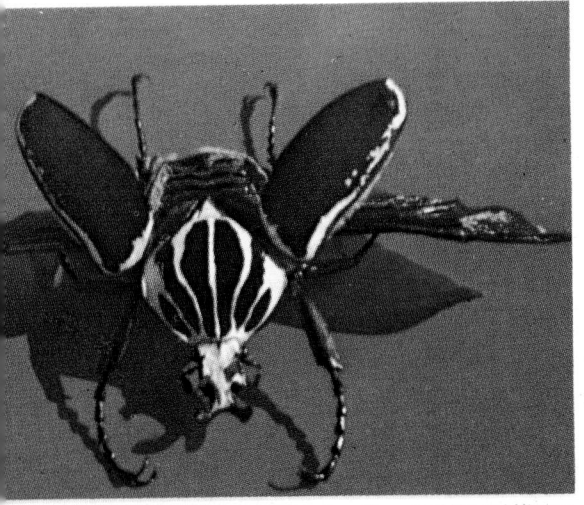

Alice Gray, American Museum of Natural History

Goliath Beetles of Africa are the bulkiest of insects, measuring more than 5 inches long and 2 inches wide.

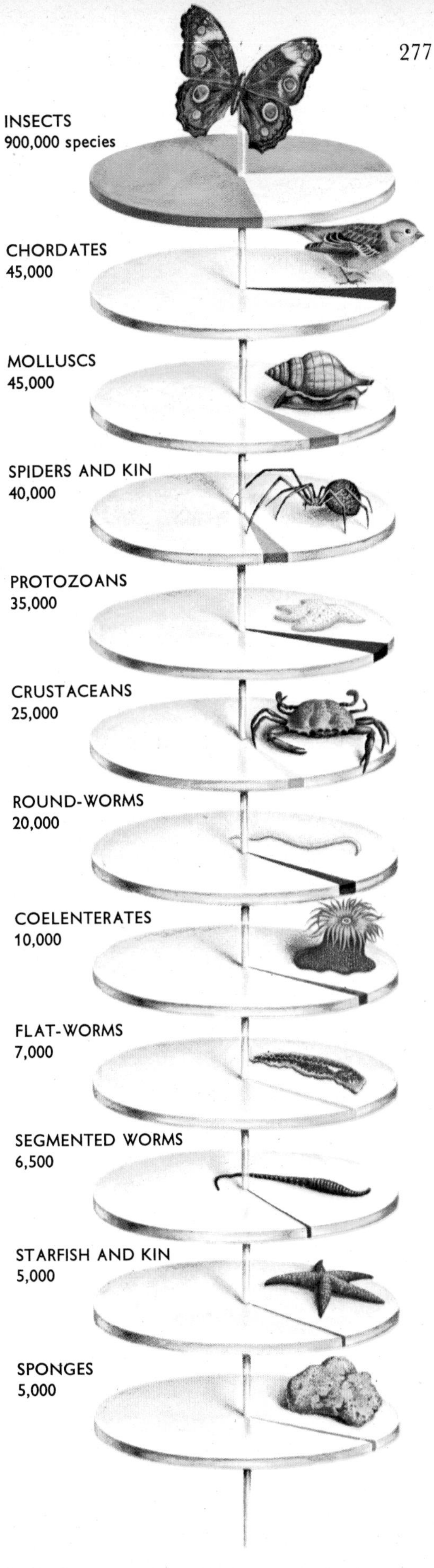

In number of species, insects are far more abundant than all the other major groups of animals combined. Many new species are named yearly.

INSECTS
900,000 species

CHORDATES
45,000

MOLLUSCS
45,000

SPIDERS AND KIN
40,000

PROTOZOANS
35,000

CRUSTACEANS
25,000

ROUND-WORMS
20,000

COELENTERATES
10,000

FLAT-WORMS
7,000

SEGMENTED WORMS
6,500

STARFISH AND KIN
5,000

SPONGES
5,000

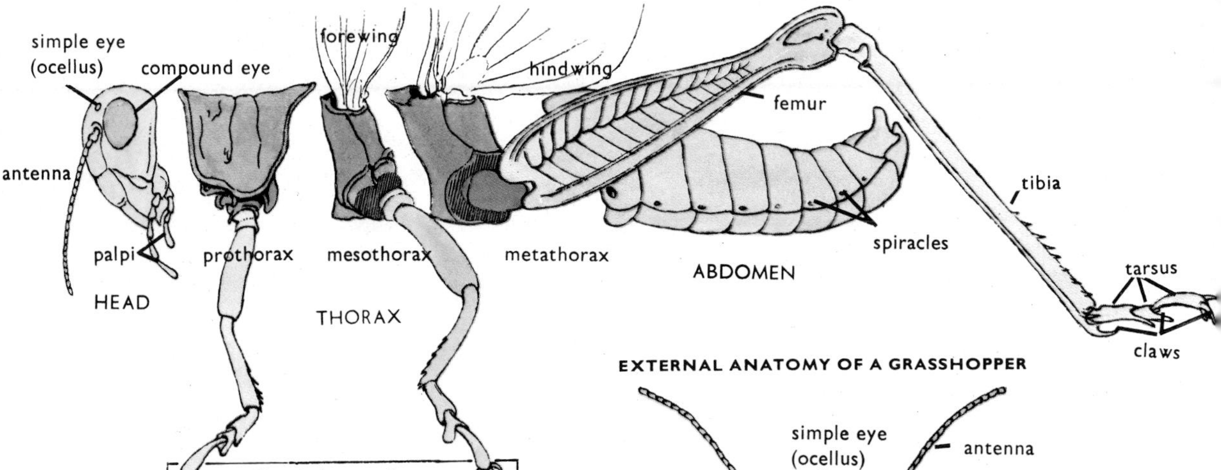

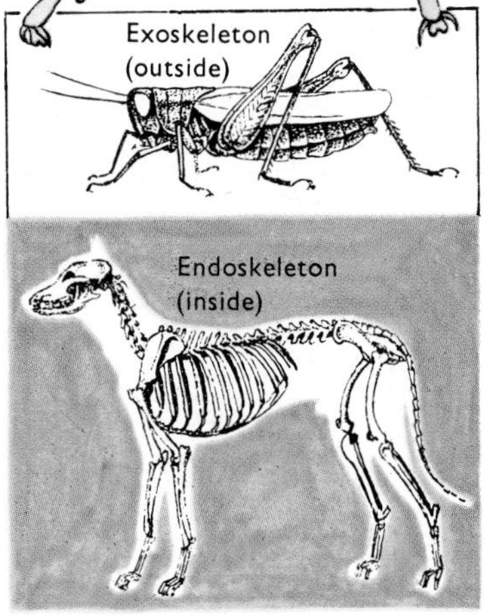

EXTERNAL ANATOMY OF A GRASSHOPPER

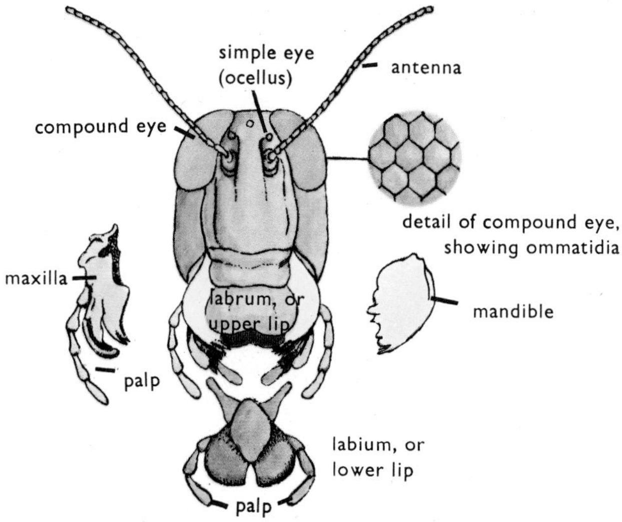

simple eye (ocellus)

compound eye

antenna

palpi

HEAD

prothorax

mesothorax

metathorax

THORAX

forewing

hindwing

femur

spiracles

ABDOMEN

tibia

tarsus

claws

Exoskeleton (outside)

Endoskeleton (inside)

compound eye

simple eye (ocellus)

antenna

detail of compound eye, showing ommatidia

maxilla

labrum, or upper lip

mandible

palp

labium, or lower lip

palp

large numbers can feed on a small food supply, and hiding places, prohibitive to many larger predators, can be occupied. Their limitation in size is largely governed by their method of breathing.

Fossil insects are found in rocks 300 million years old, and even these oldest-known insects were so well developed that they already had wings. Because of their rather delicate structure, insects are rare as fossils. The oldest are primitive, wingless species found in a Devonian rock of Scotland. Best known are the earliest known dragon-flies and cockroaches from rocks of the Pennsylvanian age.

During their millions of years on Earth, insects have become adapted to nearly every type of habitat. They are found at an altitude of over 16,000 feet in the Andes Mountains of South America. Others, blind and colourless, live in caves several hundred feet beneath the earth's surface, and it is usual for springtails to jump over the snow in mid-winter or on mountain snowfields.

Insects that live in crevices high in the mountains are not able to survive temperatures above 80 degrees Fahrenheit. At the opposite extreme are insects found in hot springs where the temperature of the water reaches 120 degrees. Others live in the fluid at the base of the leaves of carnivorous pitcher-plants, surviving in juices that con-

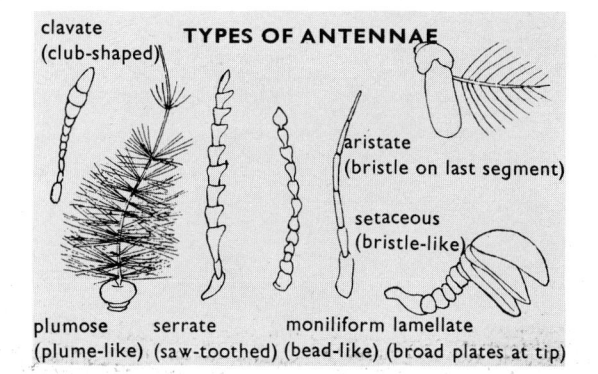

TYPES OF ANTENNAE

clavate (club-shaped)

aristate (bristle on last segment)

setaceous (bristle-like)

plumose (plume-like)

serrate (saw-toothed)

moniliform (bead-like)

lamellate (broad plates at tip)

Honeybee
chewing, lapping

Butterfly
for sucking nectar

Thrips
rasping, sucking

Mosquito
piercing and sucking

TYPES OF MOUTH-PARTS

House Fly
sponging

sume other insects, and some live in pools of petroleum. Insects are found in every livable place on Earth, even in many places that seem impossible of supporting life.

The fantastic success of insects is due to their adaptability to almost every type of environment; their capacity for flight, resulting in a wide distribution; their external skeleton, giving them the mechanically strongest type of structure known, the tube; their small size, which gives them advantages in food supply and hiding places; and, finally, their rapid rate of reproduction. THE INSECT'S BODY. An insect's body is supported by an outer covering (usually hard), called an exoskeleton. Skeletons of backboned animals — fishes, amphibians, birds and mammals — are on the inside of the body and are called endoskeletons. An insect's exoskeleton has many hardened areas connected to each other by membranes which help to make the insect's body flexible. The insect's exoskeleton has also external ridges, or projections, that give the body additional strength and also serve as points of attachment for muscles.

An insect's segmented body is divided into three regions: head, thorax and abdomen. On the insect's head are its antennae, eyes and mouth-parts. The antennae are a pair of structures usually located between the eyes or somewhat below them. In most insects the antennae are used as feelers; in others they are organs of smell or of hearing. Each antenna consists of at least three segments, but usually many more. Antennae vary greatly in size and shape — from the small hair-like antennae of dragonflies to the long thread-like antennae of longhorn grasshoppers.

An insect has two types of eyes. Most obvious are its large, compound eyes. These are made up of a number of facets that are individual lenses for each eye unit (omatidium). Some insects may have as many as 20,000 units in each compound eye. Most insects also have simple eyes, or ocelli. These are usually located on the upper region of the head, between the compound eyes. Ocelli are sensitive to changes in light

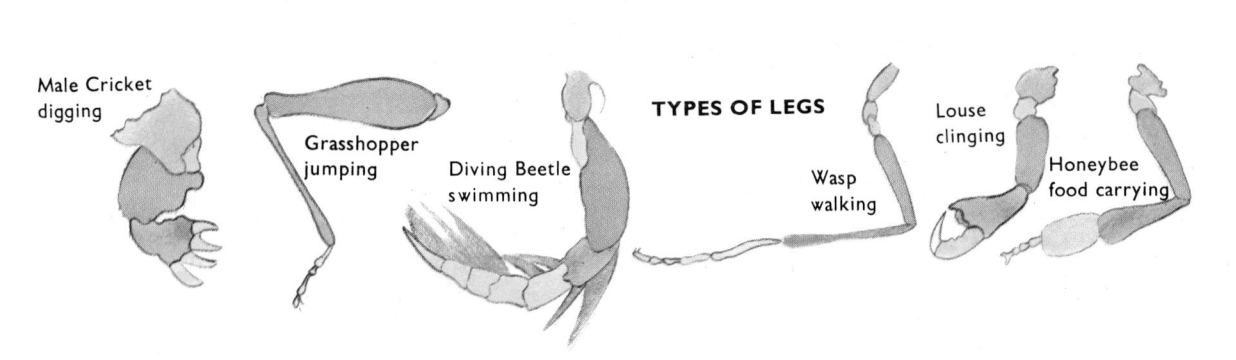

Male Cricket
digging

Grasshopper
jumping

Diving Beetle
swimming

TYPES OF LEGS

Wasp
walking

Louse
clinging

Honeybee
food carrying

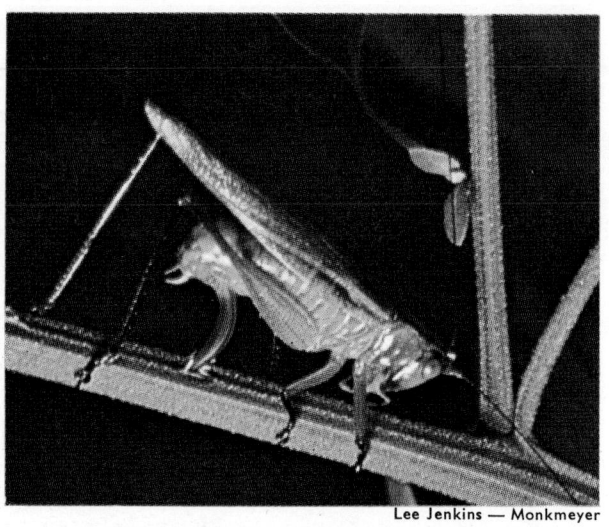

Lee Jenkins — Monkmeyer

Female meadow grasshoppers, found mainly in moist meadows, have sword-like ovipositors.

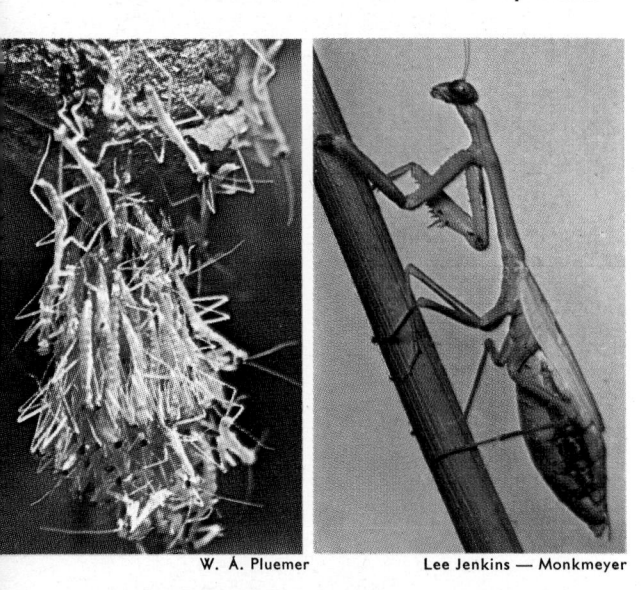

W. A. Pluemer   Lee Jenkins — Monkmeyer

This female praying mantid has a swollen abdomen and is about to lay her eggs. She will spin an egg-case from which many young will hatch in the spring.

intensity, and thus inform the brain of distant objects, while at closer range the compound eyes give precise vision.

Mouth-parts of insects vary greatly. Their components are most easily seen in an insect with chewing mouth-parts, such as a grasshopper. They include an upper lip (labrum) and a lower lip (labium). Most important are the paired jaws (mandibles), used to chew the food. They are generally very hard and have several projections,

or "teeth", along their inner edges. An insect works its jaws from side to side, rather than up and down. Some insects use their mandibles for fighting. An insect's second pair of jaws, or maxillae, are more complicated. Each bears a palp, usually slender, that is used as a feeler, or as an organ of taste or smell. On the floor of the mouth is a tongue-like structure, through which the salivary glands usually open.

Some insects have mouth-parts for piercing tissues and sucking fluids. Mosquitoes and aphids have mouth-parts of this type. Butterflies and moths also have sucking mouth-parts, but they form a long hollow tube through which nectar and water are sucked. Some insects, such as the House Fly, have sponging mouth-parts. These insects feed on nectar, or use their saliva to dissolve such solids as sugar, and then sponge up the resulting solution. Thrips have rasping and sucking mouth-parts. They scrape plant tissues, then suck up the liquids that seep out. Bees also have combination-type mouth-parts, and thus are able to chew or to lap up liquids.

The thorax, the insect's second body region, bears its wings and legs. The thorax is divided into three parts: prothorax, mesothorax and metathorax. Each part is made up of four hardened plates. An insect also has three pairs of legs, and these are divided into distinct segments. Legs of insects are modified in various ways for different functions. A cockroach's legs are suited for running; a grasshopper's hind legs for jumping; and a praying mantis's front legs for grasping prey. Mole crickets use their broad front legs for digging. Many insects carry food in their legs, and others use their legs for swimming. When an insect walks or runs, it first moves the middle leg of one side, then the front and hind legs on the opposite side of its body. Then it repeats this movement with its other three legs. Thus the insect always has three legs on the ground, forming a firm tripod.

Typically insects have two pairs of wings, which are outgrowths of their body wall.

SIDE VIEW

heart

blood vessel

brain

mouth

anus

digestive tract
(red)

nerve
ganglion

gastric
caeca

nerve
cord

digestive tract

blood vessel

**INTERNAL ANATOMY
OF A GRASSHOPPER**

spiracle

air tube (tracheole)

nerve cord

CROSS SECTION

NERVOUS SYSTEM

ganglion   nerve   brain

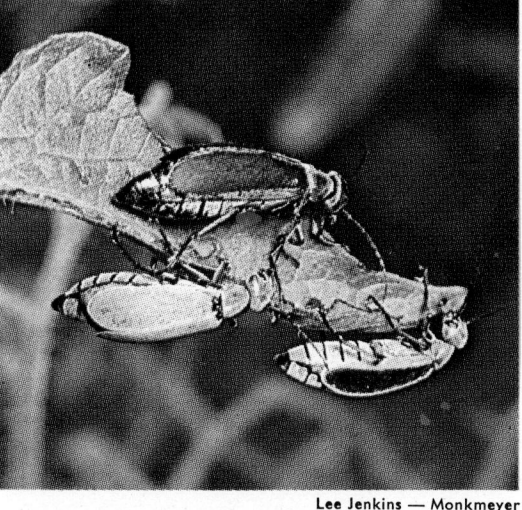

Lee Jenkins — Monkmeyer

**Blister beetles secrete a fluid causing skin to blister.
Their dried bodies are used in medicines.**

Usually the wings are membranous and contain a series of veins.

Each segment of the insect's abdomen, its third body region, consists of two plates — one on top and one below. The sides are usually membranous. An insect's abdomen also bears the organs of reproduction. Females of some kinds have strong ovipositors for depositing their eggs in the ground or even in wood. Some insects have tail-like structures, called cerci, positioned at the end of the abdomen.

INTERNAL ANATOMY. Insects have the same organ systems as most other animals. Although an insect is small, its body may contain from several hundred to several thousand muscles, which are complex in arrangement and very efficient. Many insects can lift several times their own weight, and some are able to move their wings more than 1,000 times a second.

An insect's digestive system begins with its mouth-parts, where the food enters. Food then passes to the first region of the digestive tract, or foregut, where some digestion takes place. In some insects this region also serves as a food storage area. In the next region, the midgut, the digested food is absorbed into the blood. Lastly, in the hindgut, water is removed from the food wastes, which then pass out of the body.

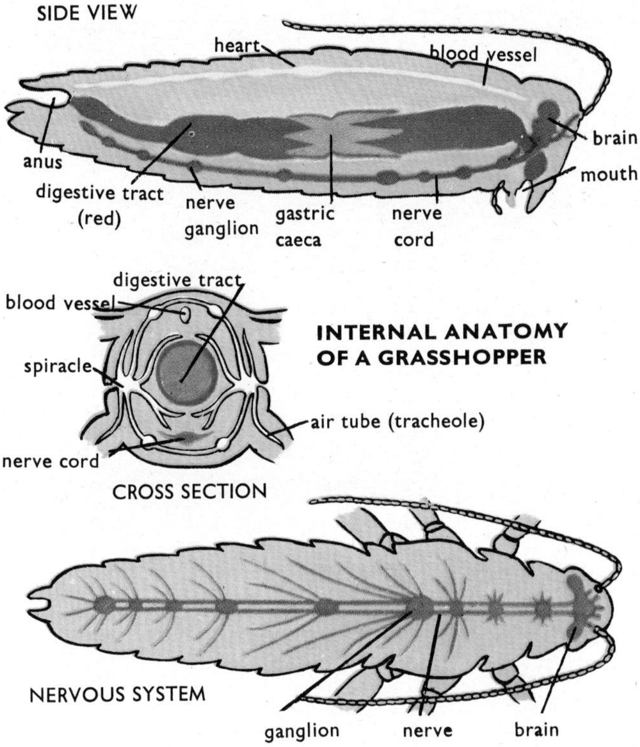

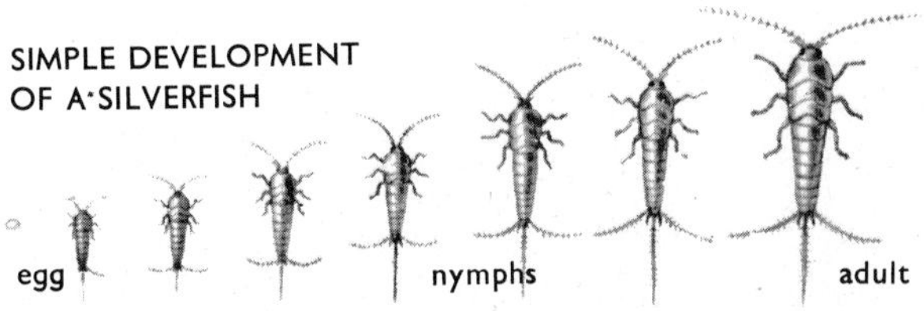

SIMPLE DEVELOPMENT
OF A SILVERFISH

egg   nymphs   adult

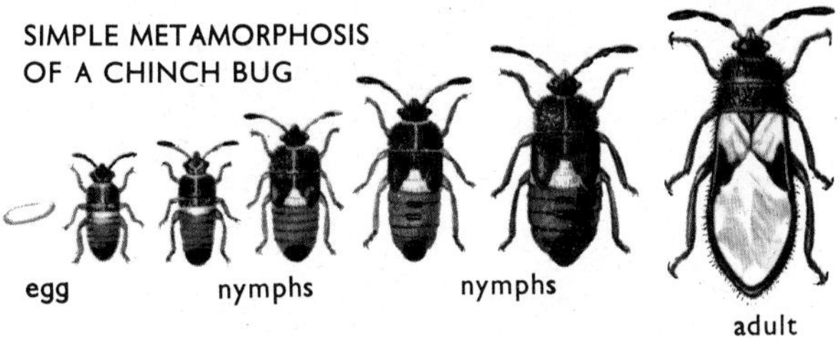

SIMPLE METAMORPHOSIS
OF A CHINCH BUG

egg   nymphs   nymphs   adult

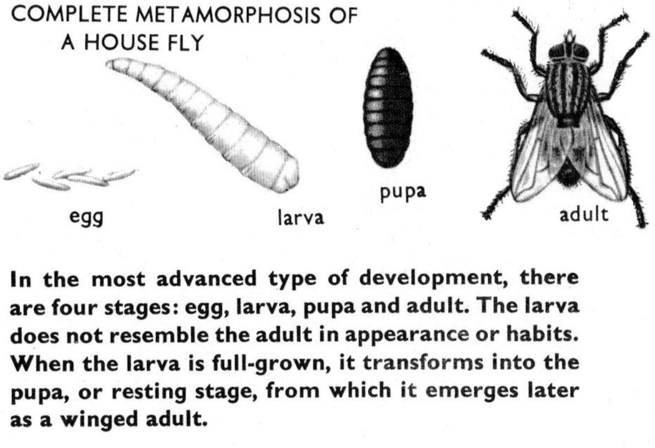

COMPLETE METAMORPHOSIS OF
A HOUSE FLY

egg   larva   pupa   adult

**In the most advanced type of development, there
are four stages: egg, larva, pupa and adult. The larva
does not resemble the adult in appearance or habits.
When the larva is full-grown, it transforms into the
pupa, or resting stage, from which it emerges later
as a winged adult.**

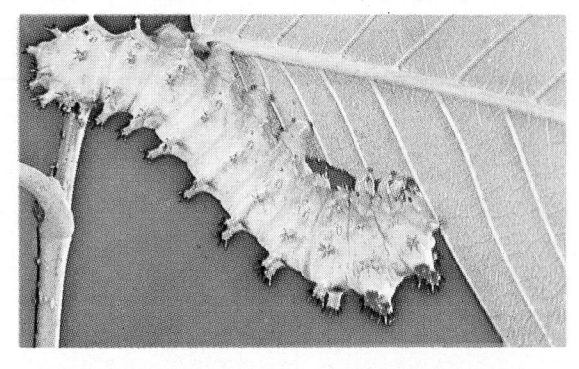

The moth's larva, or caterpillar, feeds on leaves.

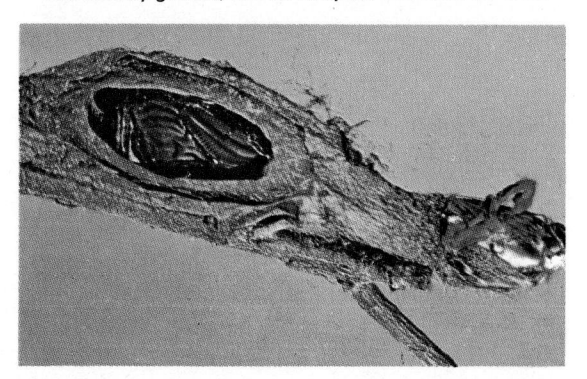

When fully grown, the larva spins a cocoon on a leaf.

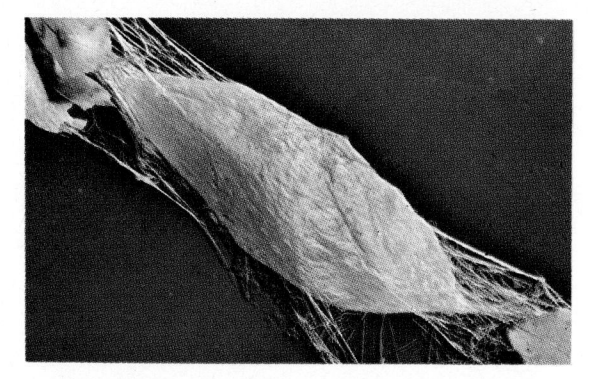

Inside, the pupa changes and emerges as an adult.

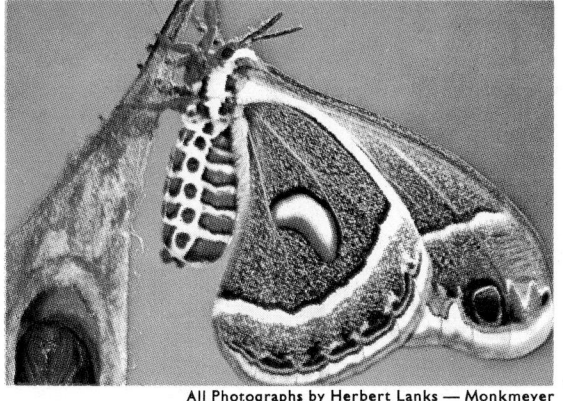

All Photographs by Herbert Lanks — Monkmeyer

Insects have a simple excretory system which consists of thin tubes (Malpighian tubules) connected to the front end of the hindgut. Waste products in the blood are taken up by these tubules and passed out of the body through the hindgut.

An insect's circulatory system consists of a single blood vessel located just under the upper surface of the body. This tube is divided into two parts: the front is called the aorta, and the rear is called the heart. The heart pumps the blood, and the aorta carries it forward to the head region, where it flows out into the body cavity. The blood circulates through the body cavity, and is drawn into the heart again through openings along its sides. Since the blood is not confined to blood vessels and circulates throughout the insect's body cavity, this type of circulatory system is termed an open one.

Insects breathe through a system of tubes that carry the air to cells of the body. The main tubes are called tracheae, and open to the outside through spiracles. These vary in shape and size, and usually have some sort of closing device. There may be from one to ten pairs of spiracles along the sides of an insect's body. Inside the body, the tracheae branch several times, and end finally in tiny tubes, called tracheoles, deep in the insect's body tissues. Dragonfly nymphs and some other insects do not have functional spiracles. They have gills that contain a fine network of tracheae in which the exchange of gases takes place.

An insect's highly developed nervous system consists of a brain, and a nerve cord that runs through the lower part of its body. This consists of two cords that connect paired nerve centres, or ganglia. Typically there is one nerve ganglion in each body segment. Often the ganglia are fused. The brain normally controls activities stimulated by sense organs in the head region — such as the antennae and the

The moth spreads and dries its wings before flying away to find a mate, starting the cycle again.

eyes. Many activities in other parts of the body are regulated by ganglia in the thorax and abdomen, however.

HOW INSECTS DEVELOP. All insects develop from eggs. Most insects lay their eggs in places where the newly-hatched young can find food as soon as they emerge. In certain plant lice and flies, the eggs are held inside the female until they hatch, then the larvae and nymphs are born alive.

Some insects produce only one egg at a time, and only a few during their lifetime; others produce thousands. Usually, though not always, those insects that make no special provisions for their young produce the most eggs. Mud-dauber wasps, for

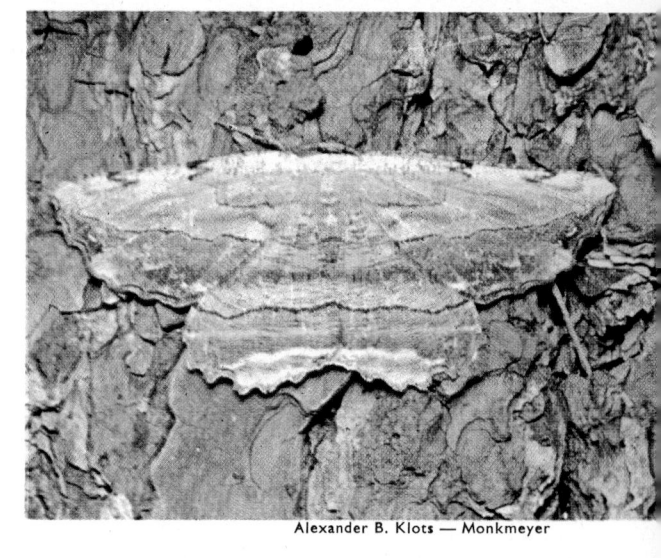

Alexander B. Klots — Monkmeyer

The pattern and colour of this measuring-worm moth conceal it against the bark of a tree. In a related group of moths, the front wings are dull in colour, while the hind wings are bright. The bright colours are hidden when the moth comes to rest, disappearing so suddenly that a pursuer loses track of the moth. Other moths have transparent wings, and in conseuence the background on which they rest shows through.

Eye-spots are believed to discourage predators by making an animal appear to be much larger and more formidable than it really is. These eye-spots are on the thorax of a butterfly's caterpillar.

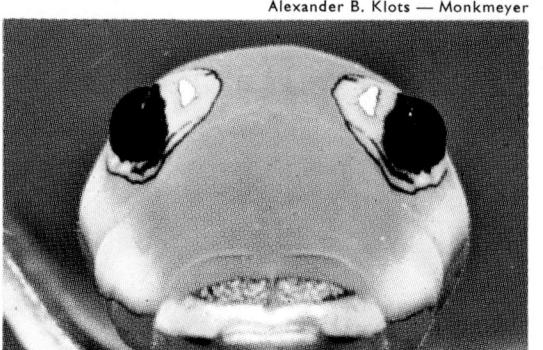

Alexander B. Klots — Monkmeyer

One of the most familiar examples of mimicry is the Viceroy's resemblance to a Monarch. The Monarch is not eaten by birds or other predators because it is distasteful, and so the Viceroy benefits from its mimicry. Often a distasteful species has many imitators. Similarly, some harmless flies look like stinging types of bees or wasps, and cockroaches and beetles that live in ant-nests resemble their hosts.

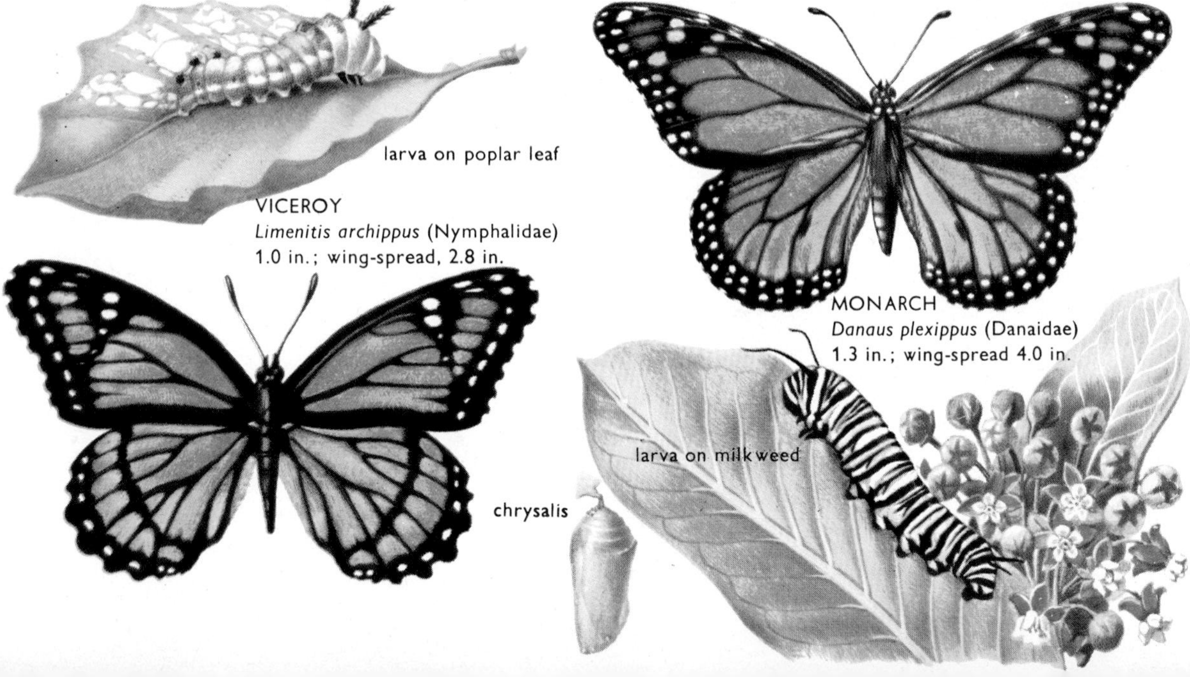

larva on poplar leaf

VICEROY
Limenitis archippus (Nymphalidae)
1.0 in.; wing-spread, 2.8 in.

MONARCH
Danaus plexippus (Danaidae)
1.3 in.; wing-spread 4.0 in.

larva on milkweed

chrysalis

example, lay only a single egg in each mud-cell of their nests. In each cell they place an insect, or a spider which has been paralysed by their sting; this serves as food for the larva when the egg hatches. Many moths and flies that do not provide food for their young deposit large numbers of eggs.

Insects lay their eggs in many kinds of places and in a variety of ways. Insects that eat leaves generally lay their eggs on the kind of leaves the young will eat. The Tomato Hornworm Moth, for example, lays each egg on the leaf of a tomato or a tobacco plant. The female Gypsy Moth lays a large mass of eggs, covered with hairs and scales, on tree trunks. Cockroaches produce hard egg-cases, each containing many eggs. The male giant water bugs (*Belostoma*) carry the eggs on their backs, where they are deposited by the female. Lacewings attach their eggs to leaves or to other objects by long silk stalks. This prevents its newly-hatched young from eating all the eggs near it. Grasshoppers and some other insects lay their eggs in the ground. Tree crickets, tree-hoppers, and some plant bugs, cut slits in plant stems with their sword-like ovipositors, and then lay their eggs inside. The slits leave scars on the stem and, depending on their size, may seriously and permanently damage the plant.

The process of change through which an insect goes in developing from egg to adult is called metamorphosis.

Young insects vary greatly in appearance when they hatch from the egg. Those that resemble the adult insect are called nymphs. If the adult has wings, they appear as small pads on the thorax of the nymph. If the adult has compound eyes, the nymph has compound eyes, too. Both stages usually have the same type of mouth-parts and eat the same kinds of food. After a period of growth and shedding several times, the nymph becomes an adult. This is called *simple metamorphosis*. Nymphs of some insects that undergo simple metamorphosis develop in water, although the adults live on land. These nymphs are called naiads. They do

Cockroaches shun light, and scamper into a dark corner or beneath an object when a light is turned on (1), while a moth is drawn to a light (2). When disturbed, the Plum Weevil feigns death by falling on to its back and pulling its legs in close to its motionless body (3).

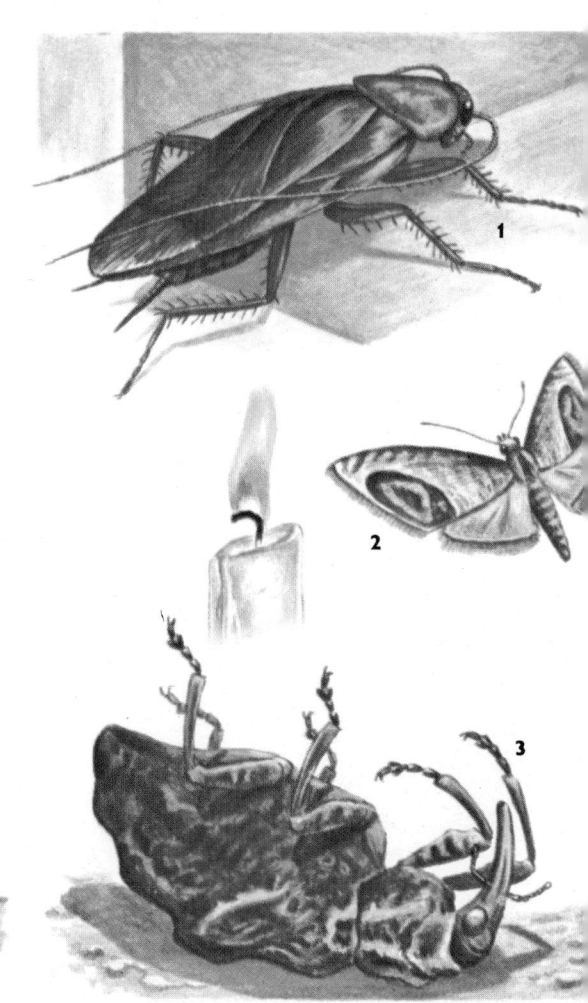

A fly's wings continue to vibrate until its feet contact an object, then they stop. Both reactions are entirely automatic.

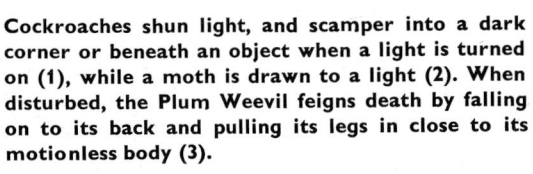

not eat the same food as the adults, as do the nymphs of the land-dwellers.

Immature stages of other insects look quite different from the adult, and are not usually found in the same type of habitat. In these the development is said to be by *complete metamorphosis*. Those in the first stage after the egg are worm-like and are called larvae. Many larvae have special names. Those of moths and butterflies are called caterpillars, fly larvae are termed maggots, and some beetle larvae are called grubs.

Since its exoskeleton is fairly rigid, the growth of an insect is step-like rather than uniform. Each step is preceded by a process called moulting, in which the thin outer covering of the exoskeleton is shed, and also the linings of the foregut and hindgut, and the lining of the tracheae. Just before moulting, an insect usually stops feeding and becomes inactive. At this time a new outer covering forms under the old one. The old covering then splits along the middle of the back, and the insect crawls out. At first it is quite pale and soft. Usually, within 24 hours, normal colour develops and its covering hardens.

In some groups of insects, such as the Blister Beetles and the Twisted-winged Parasites, the larvae differ in appearance and habits at different stages in their life history. This complex type of development is referred to as *hypermetamorphosis*.

Still another stage occurs in those insects that undergo complete metamorphosis. This is called the pupa, or is often referred to as the "resting stage" because the insect moves very little and does not feed during this period. This is a very active stage, even though the activity cannot be seen. It is at this time, for example, that the caterpillar becomes a butterfly, a maggot changes into a fly, and a grub becomes a beetle.

There are three types of pupae. In the type found in the development of butterflies and moths, and also in some flies, the developing insect's legs and wings are glued to the surface of its body. In another type, which occurs in the pupae of beetles,

The behaviour pattern of digger wasps is so inflexible that, if any step is interrupted, the wasp starts the cycle from the beginning again. In one group of digger wasps, the female paralyses her prey and then digs her nest. In another the prey is not hunted until the eggs hatch and the larvae are in need of food. The kind of digger wasp illustrated here digs her nest (1), then closes its entrances and goes in search of prey.

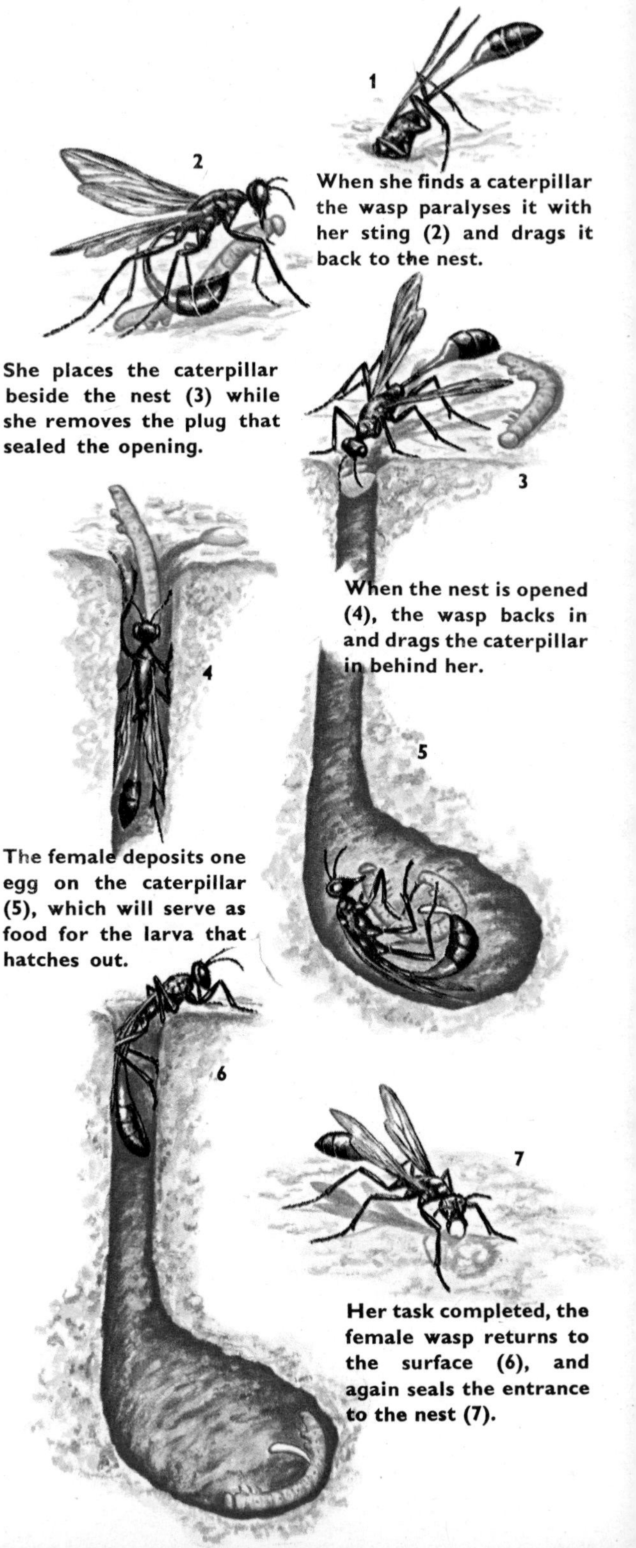

When she finds a caterpillar the wasp paralyses it with her sting (2) and drags it back to the nest.

She places the caterpillar beside the nest (3) while she removes the plug that sealed the opening.

When the nest is opened (4), the wasp backs in and drags the caterpillar in behind her.

The female deposits one egg on the caterpillar (5), which will serve as food for the larva that hatches out.

Her task completed, the female wasp returns to the surface (6), and again seals the entrance to the nest (7).

286

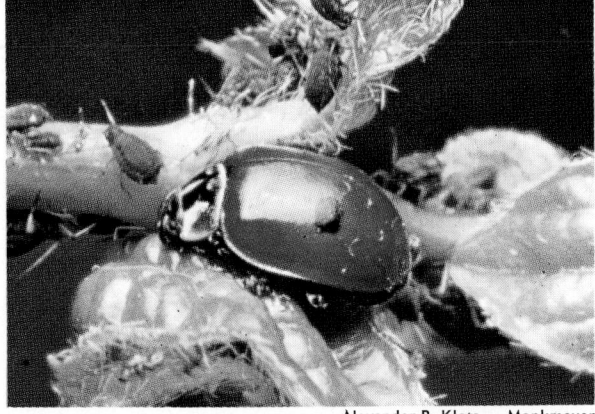

Alexander B. Klots — Monkmeyer

This two-spotted Ladybird is feeding on aphids, or plant lice. Smaller, darker species of these beetles feed primarily on mites, scales and mealy-bugs. Ladybirds are sometimes collected, and then turned loose in crop and orchard areas to help control aphid pests. Each adult ladybird beetle may consume as many as a thousand aphids during its life.

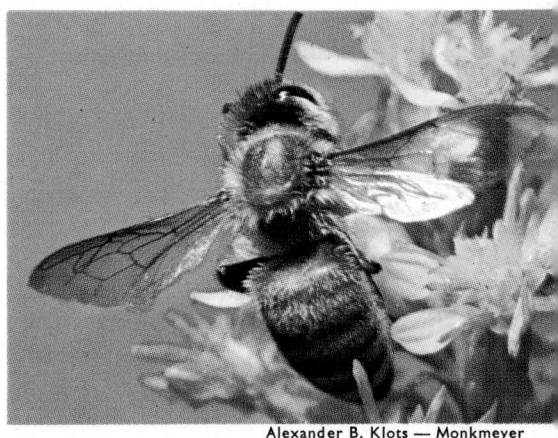

Alexander B. Klots — Monkmeyer

Honeybees are valuable to man as cross-pollinators of flowers. These include not only the many flowers planted as ornamentals, but also most of our garden and vegetable crops. It is estimated that for each Pound's worth of honey and wax obtained from honeybees about twenty Pounds' worth of seeds and fruits have been produced by pollination.

the legs and wings are free, though they are folded close to the body. The pupa looks much like the adult, but is pale in colour. Some flies have pupae that are similar in appearance to those of beetles, but they are covered by the hardened outside covering of the last larval stage.

Many pupae are protected by coverings, or cocoons, as they develop. Moth and butterfly larvae spin silky cocoons before they go into the pupa stage. Other insects make cocoon cases of sand, bits of wood, or

other debris cemented together. Some kinds make burrows in the ground, or in fallen logs or trees, and bees and wasps make cocoons of wax.

Finally the adult stage is reached. This is the only stage in the development of insects that has fully-developed wings. Often insects live as adults for only a few days, just long enough to mate and produce eggs — thus starting the development cycle again. HOW INSECTS SURVIVE. Many insects escape enemies by running rapidly or

Bagworms infest both evergreen and deciduous trees, stripping them of foliage and killing them.
Lee Jenkins — Monkmeyer

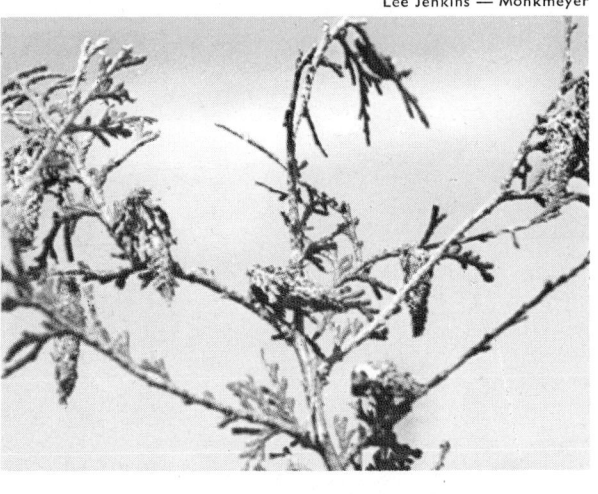

Termite workers spend their lives in dark, damp tunnels which they cut through wood as they feed.
Lee Jenkins — Monkmeyer

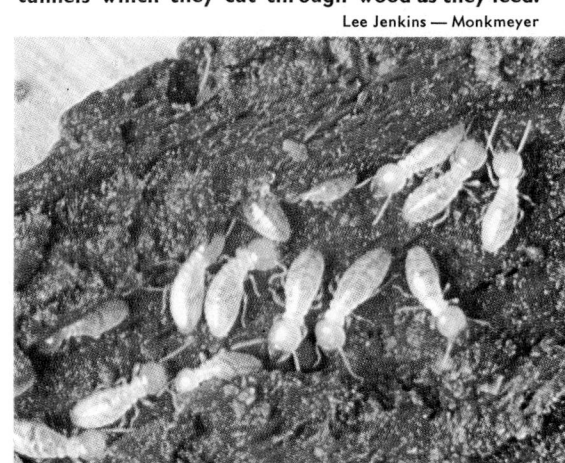

by flying. Others are protected largely by shape or colouration, or by actions.

Some have remarkable resemblance to the background on which they are found. Stick insects are good examples. Often people are surprised to see a "stick" suddenly come to life and walk away. Many moths are coloured like the bark on which they rest during the day. Some grasshoppers blend perfectly with certain kinds of soil, or are coloured to look like the vegetation on which they feed.

Most bees, wasps and ants can sting, but insects that do not have efficient stingers also produce venoms. The caterpillar of the Saddle-back Moth is one of several that have hollow hairs which contain venom. If these hairs are broken off in a wound, they may cause a severe rash. Some beetles secrete a "blistering" fluid, and many kinds of bugs give off undesirable odours which are distasteful to birds or other predators.

Some insects live in protective cases that resemble their surroundings. Bagworms, for example, live in bags covered with pine needles. Caddisworms build stick- or pebble-coated cases which are carried with them as they crawl about. Casemaking Clothes Moths make their portable cases of bits of fabric or plaster, and nymphs of some predaceous bugs and flea larvae are covered by lint or dust.

Perhaps the most interesting of insect protective devices is mimicry. In one type an otherwise defenceless insect, such as a fly, resembles a wasp or some other insect that can defend itself, and thus is probably avoided by predators. Similarly there are kinds of bugs that look like ants.

In another type of mimicry, insects may resemble each other, although both have other protective devices. Many wasps resemble each other, and some tasteful butterflies will mimic distasteful butterflies, thus escaping animals that might eat them. For this ruse to work, it is essential that the model be much commoner than the mimic.

INSECT BEHAVIOUR. An insect does not think what it is going to do when it is chased

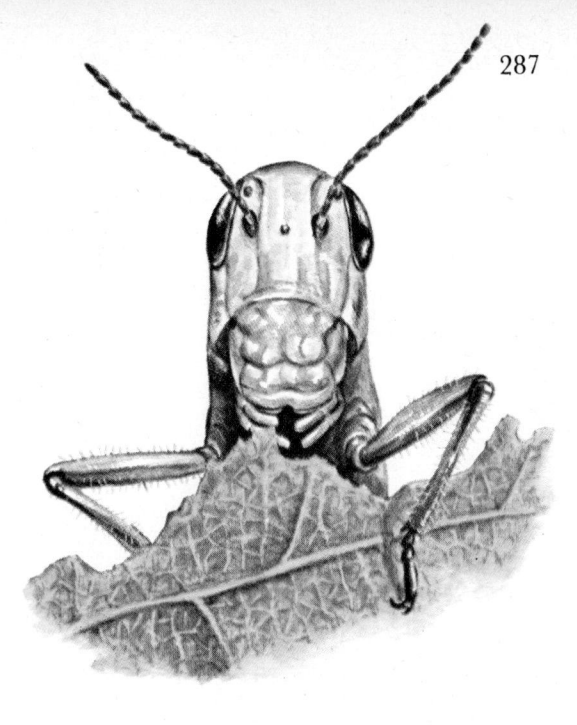

Grasshoppers and other insect pests with chewing mouth-parts can be killed with stomach poisons. These are insecticides that are sprayed or dusted over the surface of the plants or other substances on which the insects feed.

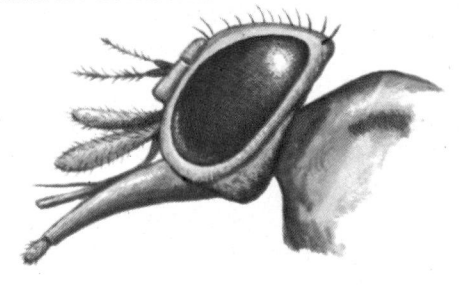

Horn-flies and other insects with sucking mouth-parts feed on the fluids of plants and animals. They are killed with contact poisons, which are sprayed or dusted directly on to their body, or with poisons that are drawn in with the fluids as they feed.

or touched. Its reaction is largely automatic. Its actions are triggered by signals or impulses that travel over definite patterns, and these are, for the most part, inherited. They are "built into" the insect, and so all insects of the same species react in the same way to the same sort of stimulus.

Many responses are "towards" or "away from" the stimulus. Thus, such night-flying insects as moths fly towards a light. Cockroaches and bedbugs avoid a light. Such things as changes in temperature, direction of wind or water currents, and odours, also bring about definite reactions.

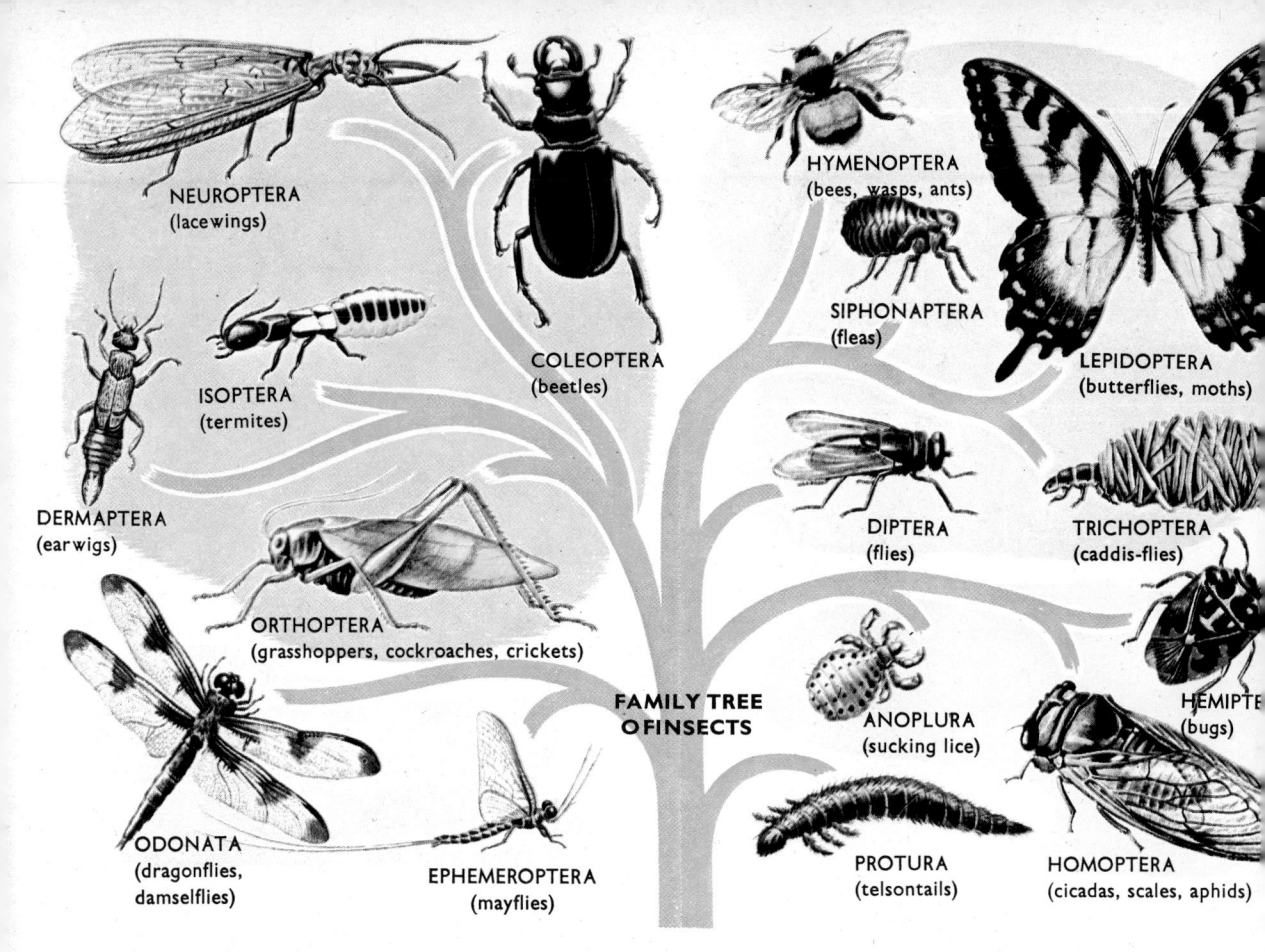

NEUROPTERA
(lacewings)

COLEOPTERA
(beetles)

ISOPTERA
(termites)

DERMAPTERA
(earwigs)

HYMENOPTERA
(bees, wasps, ants)

SIPHONAPTERA
(fleas)

LEPIDOPTERA
(butterflies, moths)

DIPTERA
(flies)

TRICHOPTERA
(caddis-flies)

ORTHOPTERA
(grasshoppers, cockroaches, crickets)

FAMILY TREE
OF INSECTS

ANOPLURA
(sucking lice)

HEMIPTE
(bugs)

ODONATA
(dragonflies,
damselflies)

EPHEMEROPTERA
(mayflies)

PROTURA
(telsontails)

HOMOPTERA
(cicadas, scales, aphids)

This family tree of insects shows the probable relationships of the most important orders of insects. The coloured backgrounds show the most closely related groups of orders. The four largest orders are: Coleoptera (beetles), Diptera (flies), Lepidoptera (moths, butterflies), Hymenoptera (bees, wasps, ants).

Probably the most studied of all insect reactions is reflex activity. Some insects — and particularly flies — begin to fly automatically when their feet are not in contact with some solid object. Other insects begin to fly, or will spread their wings, when a stream of air strikes their head. When a cockroach is lifted from the ground, its legs begin to move in a way to turn the cockroach rightside up — even though it isn't upside down. Some insects respond to being touched, or to other disturbance stimuli, by "playing dead". Many species of weevils, for example, release their hold on the plant on which they are feeding if the plant is jarred or vibrated, although being shaken by the wind does not produce this response. Some stick insects remain motionless for long periods of time if exposed to light, for these insects feed and move about at night.

Many types of insect behaviour are more complex, involving several steps. Laying eggs, making cocoons and mating are among these more complicated types of behaviour. Some species of digger wasps, for example, first dig a burrow and then close it. Next they hunt a caterpillar and sting it. They carry their prey to the burrow, and put it down beside the sealed-up entrance. After that they open the burrow, pull the paralysed caterpillar down inside, and deposit an egg on it. Finally they leave the burrow and close its entrance. These steps are usually performed in the same sequence, and, if interrupted at any stage, the wasp starts again from the very beginning.

Most insect behaviour appears to be so inflexible that the pattern can never be changed or adjusted to varying conditions. In some, however, a degree of variation may be possible: wasps that ordinarily take only a certain kind of spider will utilise others if

their normal prey are not available.

An insect's age sometimes determines its type of behaviour, too. For example, during the first two or three days of its adult life, a worker bee cleans the hive and comb. Next the bee spends about a week feeding honey and pollen to the old larvae. For another week she feeds the newly-hatched larvae with a honey and saliva mixture. Following this she builds a comb and begins to take foraging trips into the field. Finally, and until her death, she does nothing but gather honey and pollen. These stages of behaviour are brought about by changes in the bee's physiology with age.

Although insects cannot reason, they are capable of some learning. Honeybees learn to recognise certain landmarks and use them as a guide. By shocking them with an electric current, scientists have been able to condition various beetles to avoid either a rough or smooth surface. The insect learns after 40 to 50 trials. Cockroaches, ants, and a few other insects, have been tested in their ability to run various mazes. Ants appear to learn most readily. In no insects, however, is learning an important element of their behaviour.

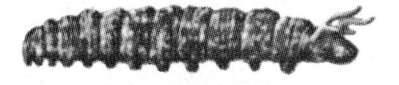

Peripatus, **a primitive worm-like creature resembling an earthworm, is believed to resemble the ancestor of insects and of all other arthropods. These rare animals live in tropical regions throughout the world.**

PRINCIPAL ORDERS OF INSECTS. Insects are members of the phylum Arthropoda ("joint-legged" animals). All animals in this phylum have segmented bodies and paired, jointed legs. They shed their outer covering (exoskeleton) as they grow. Their digestive tract is tubular and relatively straight, and their circulatory system is "open". With few exceptions, all breathe by means of tracheae and spiracles.

Other members of the phylum Arthropoda are such animals as shrimp and crayfish (class *Crustacea*), millipedes (class *Diplopoda*), centipedes (class *Chilopoda*), *Peripatus* (class *Onychophora*), and spiders, ticks and scorpions (class *Arachnida*). Insects form the class *Insecta*, and are distinguished from other members of the phylum by having three body regions, three pairs of legs, one pair of antennae, and usually two pairs of wings. The class *Insecta* is the largest in the phylum and is divided into 26 orders.

Many members of these orders are discussed in separate entries in this book. Because of the great number of insect species, most of the entries describe families of insects, although important and interesting species in each family are also treated. (See the index for listings of insects.)

IO MOTHS belong to the large silkworm moth family *(Saturniidae)*. Smaller than most members, their wing-spread seldom exceeds three inches. Females, slightly larger than males, have brownish front wings; males have yellow front wings. Both have eye-spots on their wings. Io caterpillars are bright green, with a red-and-white stripe along each side. They also have clumps of stinging spines that cause a burning rash where they touch the skin. The caterpillars feed on leaves of many kinds of trees, and also on grasses.

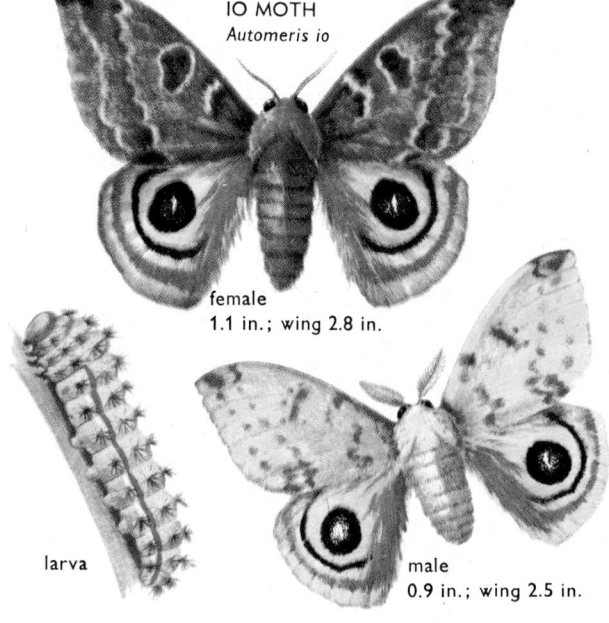

IO MOTH
Automeris io

female
1.1 in.; wing 2.8 in.

larva

male
0.9 in.; wing 2.5 in.

J

JAÇANAS *(ya-sa-NA)* were named by the Tupi Indians of the Amazon region of South America. Their name means "lily-pad jumper", for these birds have exceedingly long toes and can walk on floating reeds or leaves, without sinking in.

All jaçanas are boldly coloured. One that lives in Asia has a pheasant-like tail; one in Africa has a golden collar. The bright-winged American Jaçana sometimes occurs as far north as Texas. Like all jaçanas, it uses the thorn-like spur on each wing for fighting.

Jaçanas' nests are built on floating vegetation, and sometimes both nest and eggs drift from one side of a lake to the other. The eggs are wet most of the time, and the chicks can swim as soon as they hatch.

JACKS (or Horse Mackerel) are surface-living fishes belonging to the family *Carangidae*. They vary greatly in shape and size, but most are fast swimmers and provide sport for fishermen. Typically, they have streamlined bodies and two spines in front of the anal fin.

The Horse Mackerel *(Trachurus trachurus)* of British waters is not unlike the Common Mackerel in appearance, but can be distinguished by the plate-like scutes along its lateral line which are keeled towards the

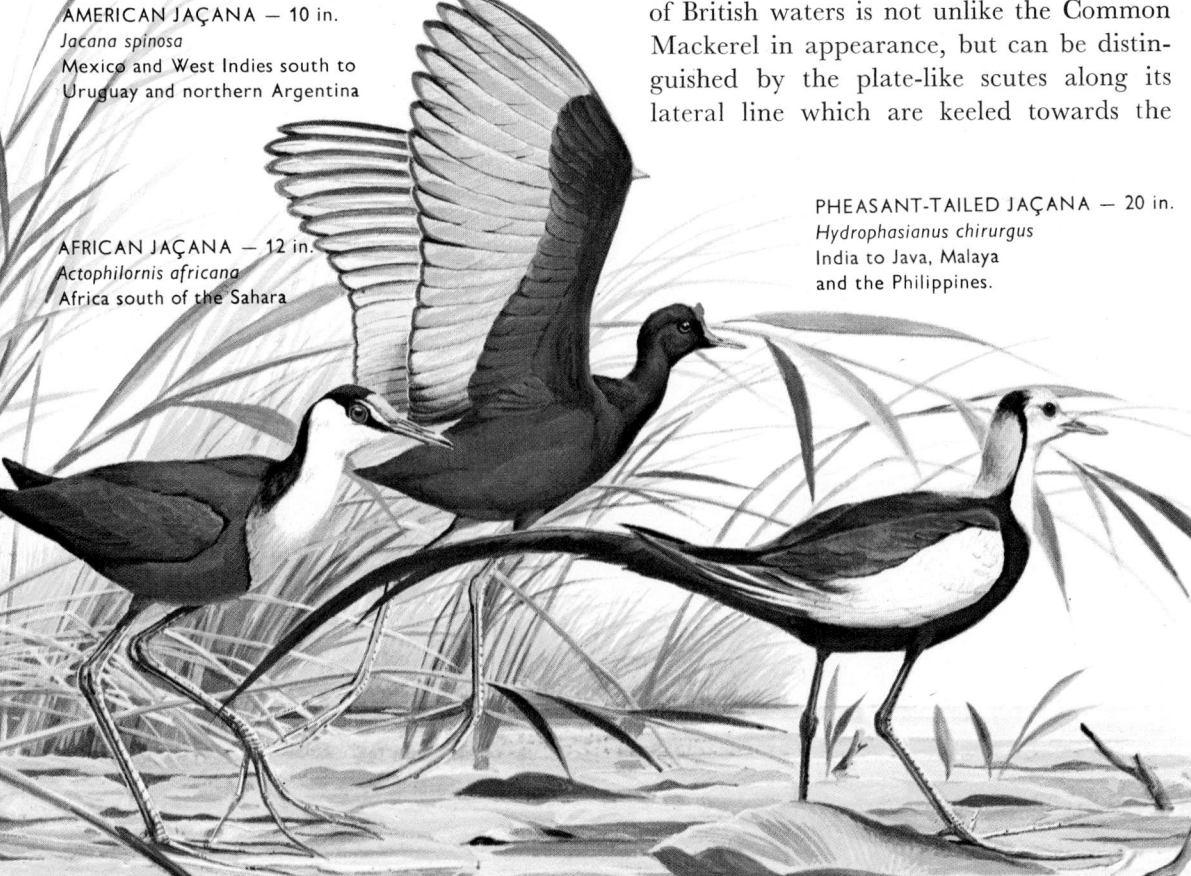

AMERICAN JAÇANA — 10 in.
Jacana spinosa
Mexico and West Indies south to
Uruguay and northern Argentina

AFRICAN JAÇANA — 12 in.
Actophilornis africana
Africa south of the Sahara

PHEASANT-TAILED JAÇANA — 20 in.
Hydrophasianus chirurgus
India to Java, Malaya
and the Philippines.

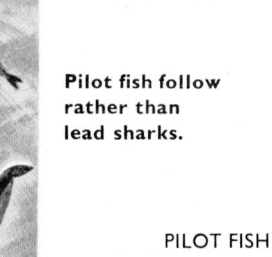

Pilot fish follow
rather than
lead sharks.

PILOT FISH
Naucrates ductor
Average 1—2 ft.

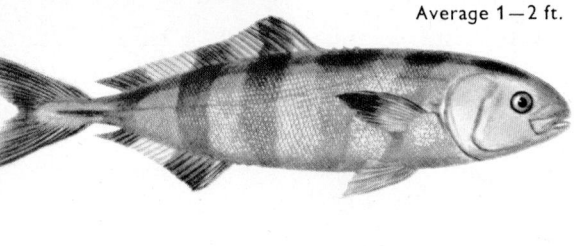

forehead and long filaments on the dorsal and anal fins. They are given their name because they feed with their tails up and their head down on the bottom. The Threadfin (*Alectis* spp.) also have long trailing filaments from the fins, but these shorten as the fish becomes larger.

LOOKDOWN
Selene vomer
8—10 in. Average ½—2 lbs.

MOONFISH
Vomer setapinnis
8—10 in. Up to 2 lbs.

tail. Young Horse Mackerel swim with the Mediterranean Sombrero Jellyfish (*Cotylorhiza*), taking refuge under the bell at the sign of danger.

The Pilot Fish (*Naucrates ductor*) is another carangid fish found off the shores of Britain. It is known for its habit of accompanying ships, and large fishes such as sharks. Known as Pompilus to the ancients, it was supposed to lead lost ships, fish or even swimmers to safety. In fact, the Pilot Fish merely swims alongside its host in order to pick up scraps of food.

Along the Pacific coast of America, from California to Chile, one of the most popular fishes with fishermen is the Yellowtail (*Seriola dorsalis*), a fast and streamlined fish. Yellowtails often drive smaller fishes, on which they feed, on to the rocks or sandy beaches, after herding them into shallow water.

Some Jacks have deep and compressed bodies, much like Angel fishes. The Lookdown (*Selene vomer*) has a high, slanting

JACK MACKEREL
Trachurus symmetricus
1—5 lbs.

POMPANO
Trachinotus carolinus
18 in. Average 1—2 lbs.

PERMIT
Trachinotus falcatus
1 ft. Average 1—3 lbs.

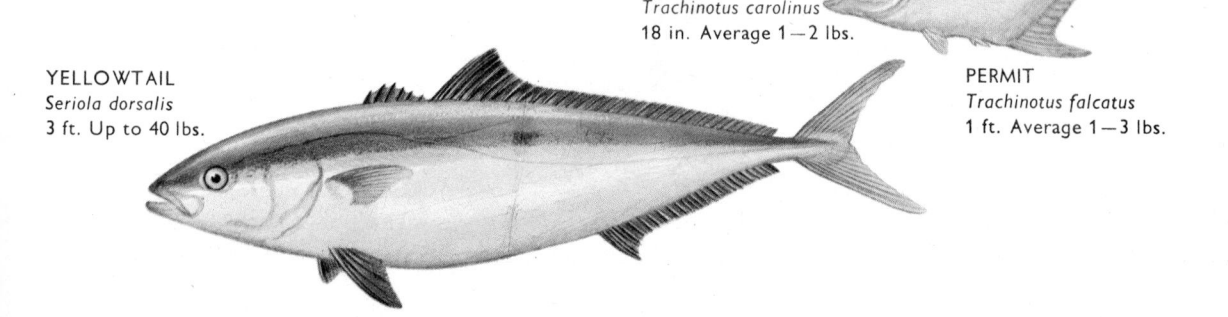

YELLOWTAIL
Seriola dorsalis
3 ft. Up to 40 lbs.

The deep-bodied Pompano (*Trachinotus carolinus*) is a valuable species caught along the Atlantic coast of North America. It grows to 18 inches in length and provides considerable sport, but is a wary fish.

JAYS, members of the crow family, are smaller and brighter than most crows, and their bills and feet are weaker. They are noisy birds, calling to one another and mobbing predators with harsh, raucous cries. In captivity, they learn to mimic.

Noisy at other times, they become silent during the breeding season, and do nothing to draw attention to their well-hidden nests. They protect their eggs and young bravely. Male jays are naturally quarrelsome, and become fearless when their homes are threatened. They chase off larger birds and squirrels. Even cats may flee in terror from a jay's pecking attack.

Jays, like squirrels, hide acorns and other food for use in winter. Anything they can steal from the tents of campers, or from picnic tables, is included in their omnivorous diet. They also eat eggs and young of smaller birds.

The Common Jay lives across Europe and Asia from the British Isles to Japan, and it likes oak forests. The Blue Jay inhabits south-eastern Canada and the eastern United States. The Scrub Jay lives in the western United States and Florida. Stellar's Jay inhabits western North America.

JELLYFISHES are mainly free-swimming gelatinous coelenterates of the class *Scyphozoa* (see COELENTERATES). Common species are cup-shaped, disc-like, or almost round. Their mouths on the underside of their bodies are often surrounded by large flaps or long tentacles. At the outer rim

Jays are usually regarded as noisy pests, prized for their colourful plumage but disliked for their fondness for the eggs of other birds.

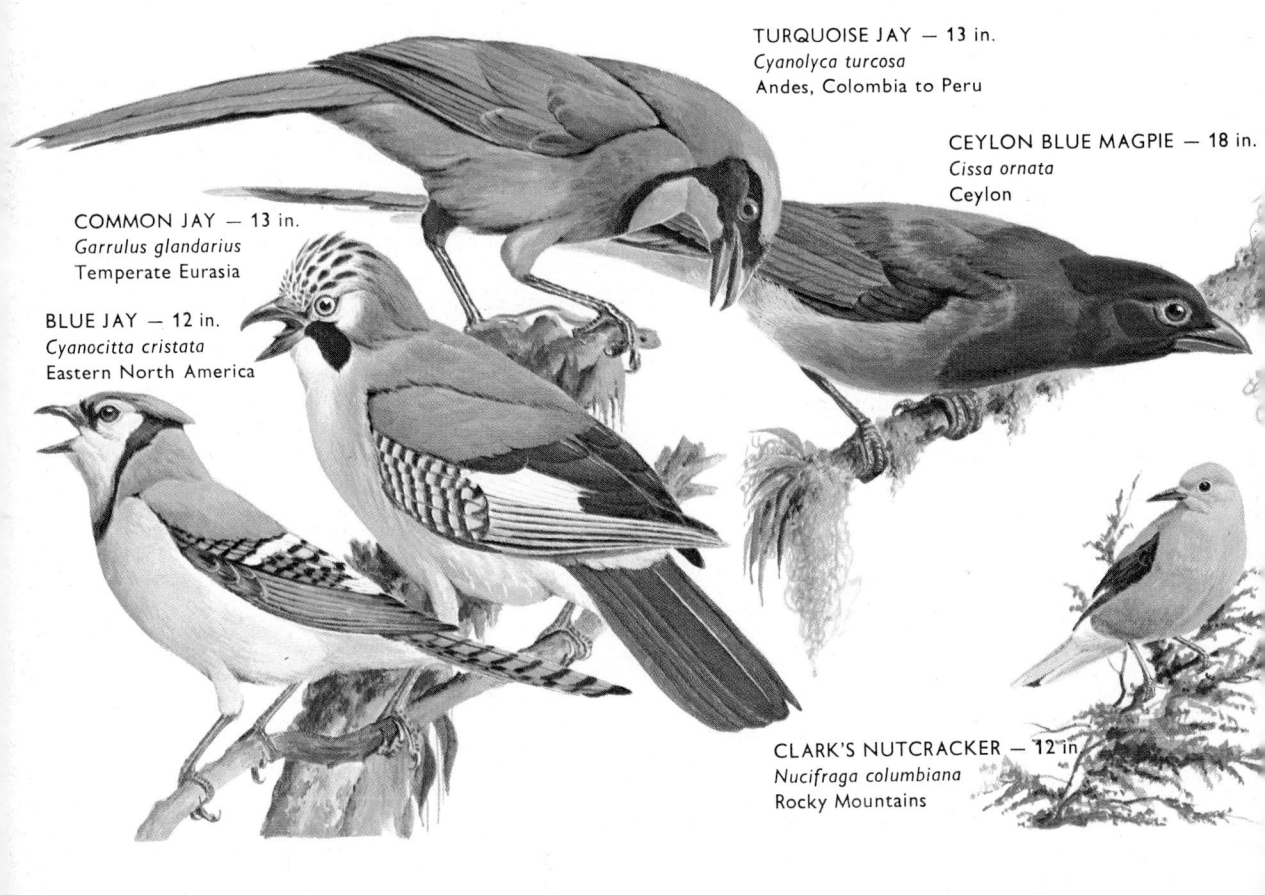

TURQUOISE JAY — 13 in.
Cyanolyca turcosa
Andes, Colombia to Peru

CEYLON BLUE MAGPIE — 18 in.
Cissa ornata
Ceylon

COMMON JAY — 13 in.
Garrulus glandarius
Temperate Eurasia

BLUE JAY — 12 in.
Cyanocitta cristata
Eastern North America

CLARK'S NUTCRACKER — 12 in.
Nucifraga columbiana
Rocky Mountains

293

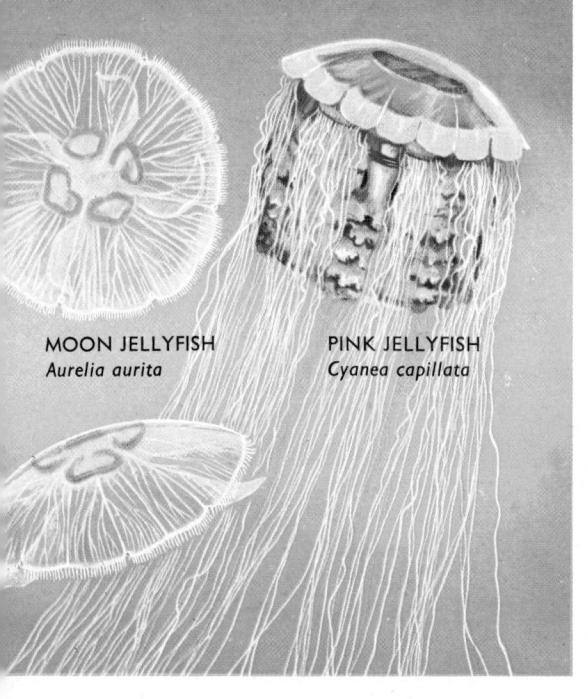

MOON JELLYFISH
Aurelia aurita

PINK JELLYFISH
Cyanea capillata

Fossils of jellyfishes are known from rocks of Cambrian age. Usually only a disc-like impression of their body is found. Less commonly, almost complete specimens are preserved, as in the Solenhofen limestone of Bavaria, in southern Germany.

JUNE or MAY BEETLES (BUGS) *(Scarabaeidae)* are cockchafers commonly seen buzzing around lights during early summer. Most species are brownish and heavy-bodied. Adults feed at night on the leaves of many kinds of trees. During the day they stay in burrows in the soil. Females lay their eggs in the ground in pastures, lawns, or fields of corn or other grain. The larvae, called "white grubs", feed on tender roots of grasses and other plants, often doing considerable damage. These beetles also

of the body are fine tentacles with stinging cells. A jellyfish reproduces sexually. The larvae settle to the bottom and bud off new medusae. Jellyfish are largely plankton feeders, but they also eat small shrimps, crabs and fishes.

Many jellyfishes are small. The *Lunuche* of tropical waters provide an example. Others attain a large size. *Aurelia* grows to 12 inches in diameter; *Cyanea,* the giant of the clan, attains a body diameter of 8 feet and its tentacles a length of 100 feet. Some jellyfishes, such as *Chiropsalmus* of Japan and the Philippines, give painful, dangerous stings with their tentacles, and whole beaches along north-eastern North America are sometimes closed to bathers because of swarms of the jellyfish *Dactylometra.* The Cabbage Head Jellyfish *(Stomolophus)* has no tentacles around its bell. The Upside-down Jellyfish *(Casiopeia)* lies on the bottom in tropical waters; its mouth-flaps are shaped like clusters of grapes, each ball containing cultures of algae which it "farms" in the bright sunlight. Large jellyfishes offer protection to numerous small fishes that cluster under their bell.

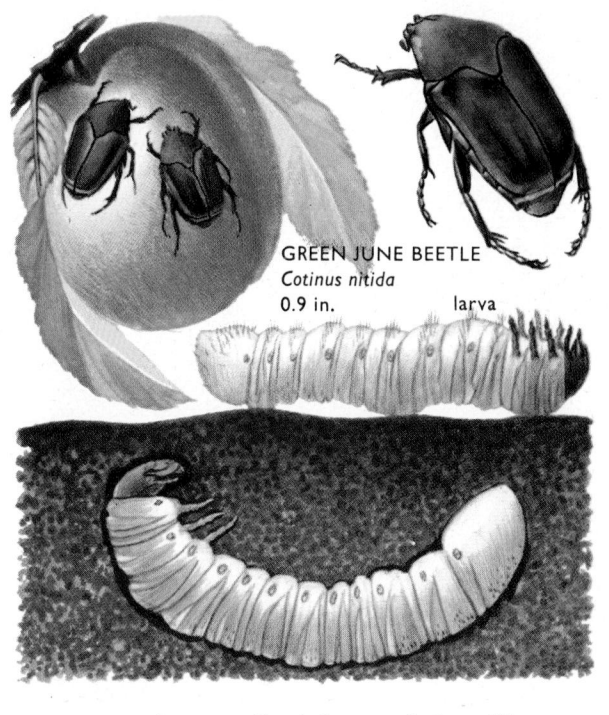

GREEN JUNE BEETLE
Cotinus nitida
0.9 in.   larva

serve as intermediate hosts of the Giant-Thorn-headed Worm, an intestinal parasite of hogs. The hogs root out and eat the beetles in infested pastures. Some June beetles require as long as four years to complete their life cycle — others only a year; a three-year cycle is most common. (See DUNG BEETLES.)

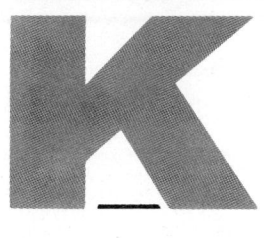

K

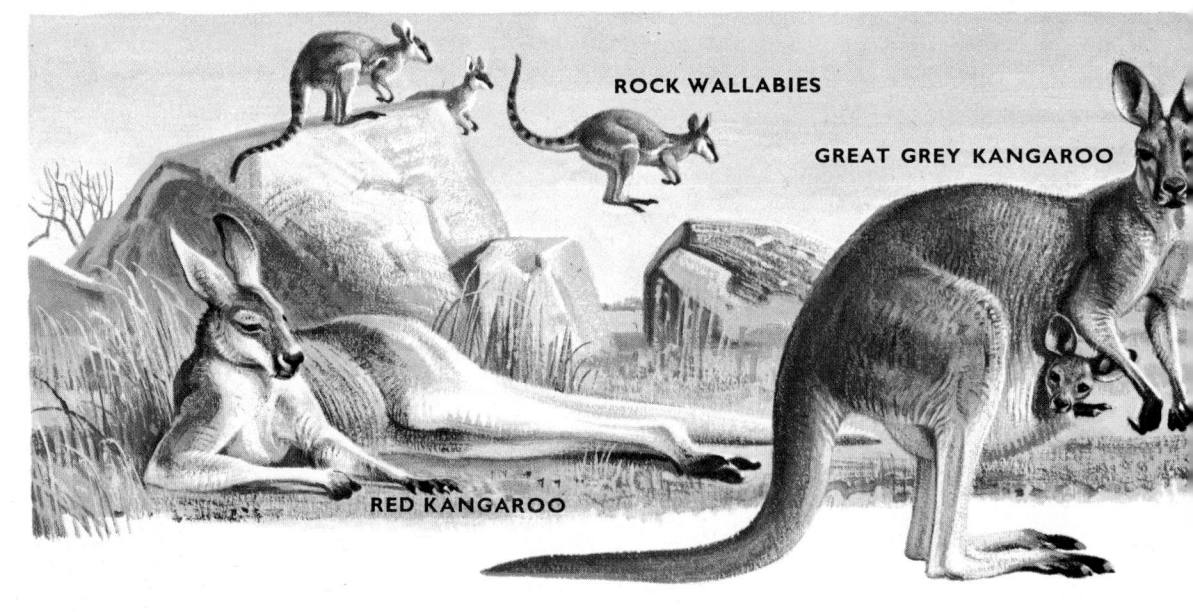

ROCK WALLABIES

GREAT GREY KANGAROO

RED KANGAROO

When danger threatens, Kangaroos hold their front legs close to their body and bound rapidly over the ground on their powerful hind legs. Kangaroos are sometimes hunted for food and fur.

KANGAROOS are large, pouched, jumping mammals from Australia and New Guinea. They range in size from no larger than rats to the Great Grey Kangaroo (*Macropus giganteus*), over 7 feet in length and 200 pounds in weight. Kangaroos feed principally on grasses and leaves. They have long hind feet, short front feet, and long, round tails that act as counterbalances.

The Great Grey Kangaroo occupies much of Australia's open forest. This shy, usually friendly and docile animal may travel at speeds up to 25 miles an hour, with jumps covering a distance of 15 to 20 feet. Ordinarily it travels more leisurely, with jumps of less than 10 feet. The male, larger than the female, is called a "boomer".

The Red Kangaroo (*Macropus rufus*) is almost as large as the Great Grey Kangaroo. In Australia these two kangaroos frequently live together in groups known as "mobs". Wallaroos, or Rock Kangaroos (*Osphranter robustus*), live in rocky areas.

Wallabies (*Wallabia thylogale*), the most common kangaroos seen in captivity, vary in size and also in colour. Some are light grey, others dark red or brown. The Rock Wallabies (*Petrogale* spp.) inhabit rough, hilly regions.

Tree kangaroos (*Dendrolagus* spp.), using their long tails for support, and possessing

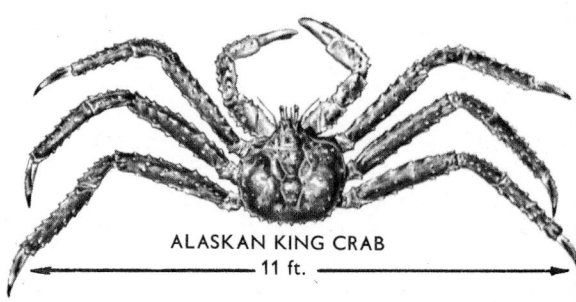

ALASKAN KING CRAB
— 11 ft. —

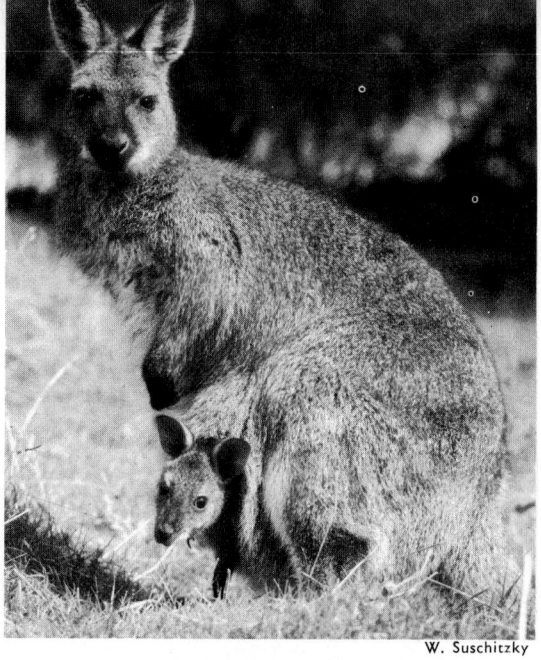

W. Suschitzky

A mother wallaby carries her young in her pouch for about four months after its birth. This baby, or "joey" as it is often called, is old enough to spend much of its time outside.

examples. These kingfishers nest in burrows dug in stream banks. They like to sit on a favourite perch above the same fishing hole daily, and wait for a fish to swim within striking range. When the birds catch a fish that is too big to swallow, they sit with its tail hanging out of the beak until digestion makes room for it to slide down their short throats. The Kookaburra of Australia, famed for its weird laughing cries, is a dry-country bird that snatches snakes and lizards. Other kingfishers, such as the Indian Three-toed, the White-throated and the Grey-headed are insect-eaters. The insect-

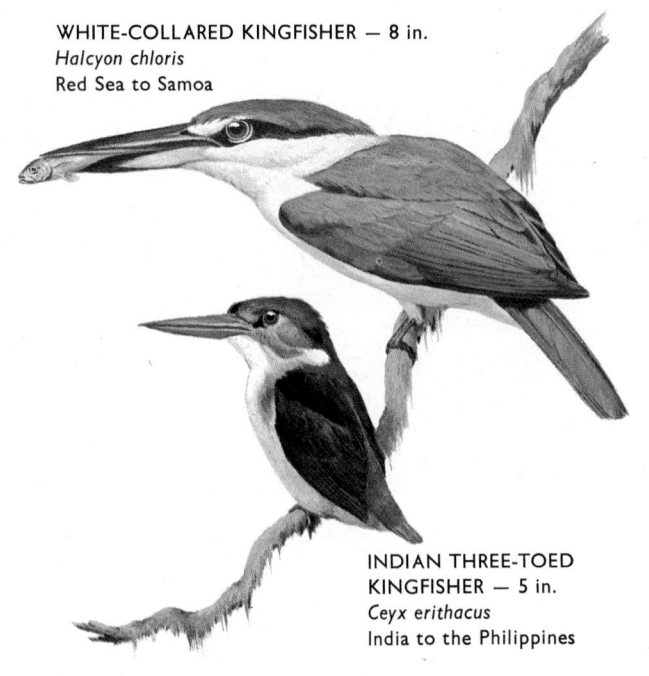

WHITE-COLLARED KINGFISHER — 8 in.
Halcyon chloris
Red Sea to Samoa

INDIAN THREE-TOED KINGFISHER — 5 in.
Ceyx erithacus
India to the Philippines

strong claws, are adapted to live in trees, eating the leaves. Some of these forest-dwellers reach a length of 4 feet; nearly half of this length is tail. During the day, many sleep in hollows or crotches of trees.

Rat Kangaroos (*Potorous* spp.) feed on tubers and grass, and are often pests of cultivated crops. These small kangaroos use their tails to carry bundles of grass to their nests, and they run on all four legs.

KING CRABS (*Paralithodes camtschatica*) are large crustaceans that resemble spider crabs but are actually related to the hermit crabs. They attain a spread of three to four feet across their claws. King crabs live in deep water off Alaska, Japan and in the Bering Sea. They are harvested in large numbers for crab meat, as are the "centolla", a related species of southern Chile and the Straits of Magellan. The legs of king crabs are so large that only a few sections will make a full meal.

KINGFISHERS are found the world over. Those with slender black bills are usually fish-eaters. The Common White-collared and the Belted Kingfishers are typical

eating Kingfishers tend to have broader and shallower red bills. Because of their food, they may occur away from water.

KING-SNAKES (*Lampropeltis* spp.), of some 15 species, are colubrid snakes found in the Americas. They are famed primarily for their habit of eating other snakes, even poisonous ones. They are not wholly immune to snake venom, but are immune enough to survive most bites. Poisonous snakes as well as others are afraid of king-snakes and seek only to escape. When cornered, poisonous

snakes do not try to bite, but ward off attacks by keeping a loop of the thick part of their body towards the king-snake, so that it cannot secure a swallowing hold. King-snakes also eat lizards and small mammals, killing their prey by constriction. The snakes they eat are not always dead when swallowed, however, for snakes are not easily killed by constriction. A king-snake always works its jaws to the head of the snake it is swallowing, and if the prey is still struggling at that time, the king-snake often stretches its victim to break the spinal cord. King-snakes tame quickly in captivity and make excellent pets. Because rats and mice are favourite foods, king-snakes are valuable to farmers. The snakes follow the rodents into burrows. The Scarlet King-snake is similar in colour to coral snakes; but each band of yellow is bordered by black, while in coral snakes each band of black is bordered by yellow. (See COLUBRID SNAKES.)

KITES are members of the hawk family. Most of them, like the Black Kite, are narrow-winged, weak-footed, swift-flying scavengers. The Everglade Kite has broad wings for low, steady flight over the Florida marshes when hunting for snails *(Pomacea),* its only food. The Brahminy Kite is a scaven-

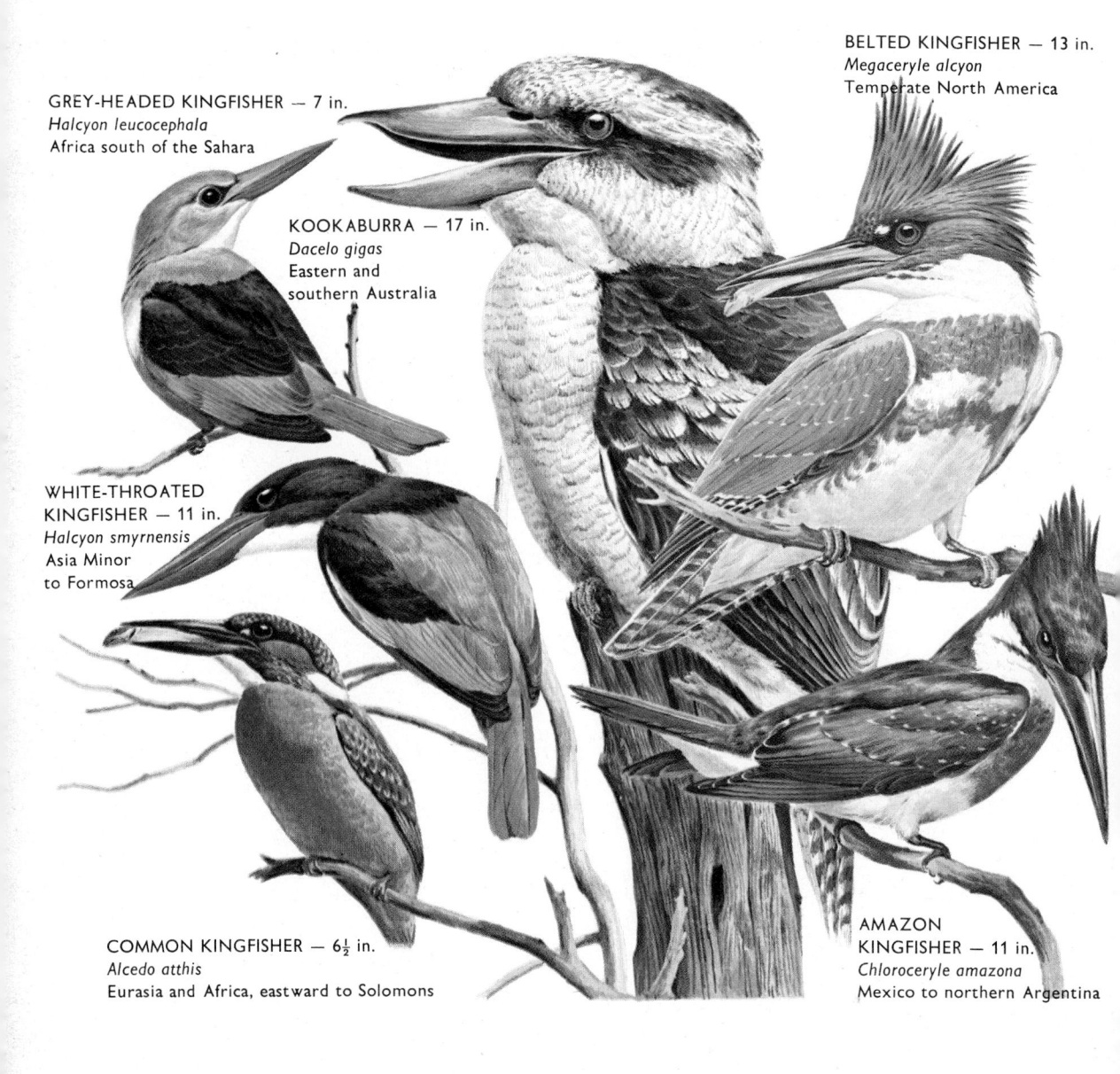

GREY-HEADED KINGFISHER — 7 in.
Halcyon leucocephala
Africa south of the Sahara

KOOKABURRA — 17 in.
Dacelo gigas
Eastern and
southern Australia

BELTED KINGFISHER — 13 in.
Megaceryle alcyon
Temperate North America

WHITE-THROATED
KINGFISHER — 11 in.
Halcyon smyrnensis
Asia Minor
to Formosa

COMMON KINGFISHER — 6½ in.
Alcedo atthis
Eurasia and Africa, eastward to Solomons

AMAZON
KINGFISHER — 11 in.
Chloroceryle amazona
Mexico to northern Argentina

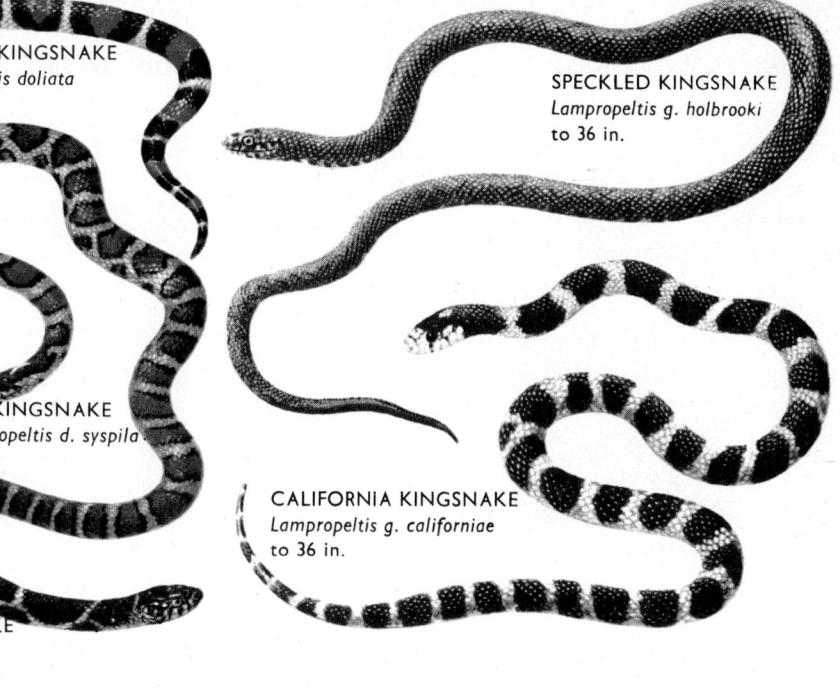

SCARLET KINGSNAKE
Lampropeltis doliata
18 in.

SPECKLED KINGSNAKE
Lampropeltis g. holbrooki
to 36 in.

RED KINGSNAKE
Lampropeltis d. syspila
30 in.

CALIFORNIA KINGSNAKE
Lampropeltis g. californiae
to 36 in.

COMMON KINGSNAKE
Lampropeltis getulus
30—48 in.

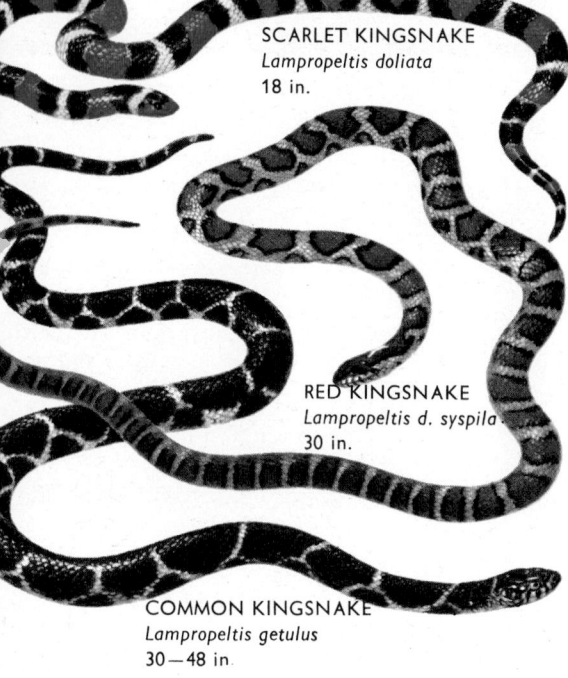

ger near the coast, but it will also hunt insects and small animals, covering the ground in low flight like a Harrier.

KIWIS — chicken-sized, flightless birds of New Zealand — live in boggy, wet forests. They hide by day and come out to feed at night. They are easy prey for cats, dogs, weasels and man. They are flightless, with hair-like feathers and proportionately very large legs and feet. The eyes are tiny, but the bill is long and sensitive at the tip,

EVERGLADE KITE — 18 in.
Rostrhamus sociabilis
Florida, Cuba and southern
Mexico to eastern Argentina

BRAHMINY KITE — 18 in.
Haliastur indus
India to Solomon Islands
and Australia

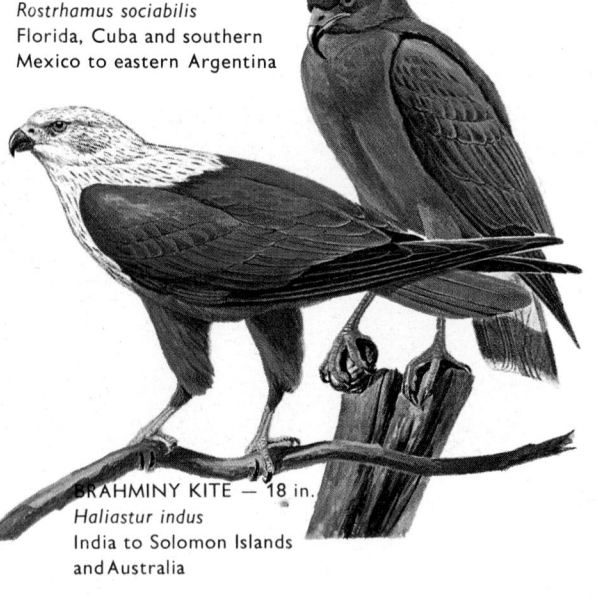

enabling the bird to detect worms deep in the ground. The egg is enormous, compared with the size of the bird.

KOALAS (*Phascolarctus cinereus*) are miniature, bear-like marsupial mammals of Australia. They weigh less than 30 pounds and have large, bushy ears, prominent, wide eyes, and short, woolly fur. Koalas feed entirely on the oily, tough leaves of eucalyptus trees, in which they live. They carry supplies of these leaves in their cheek-pouches to their nests. Until they are about two months old, the young are carried in the mother's pouch; later, they ride on her back. Koalas are almost as symbolic of Australia as kangaroos.

A mother Koala carries her baby on her back.

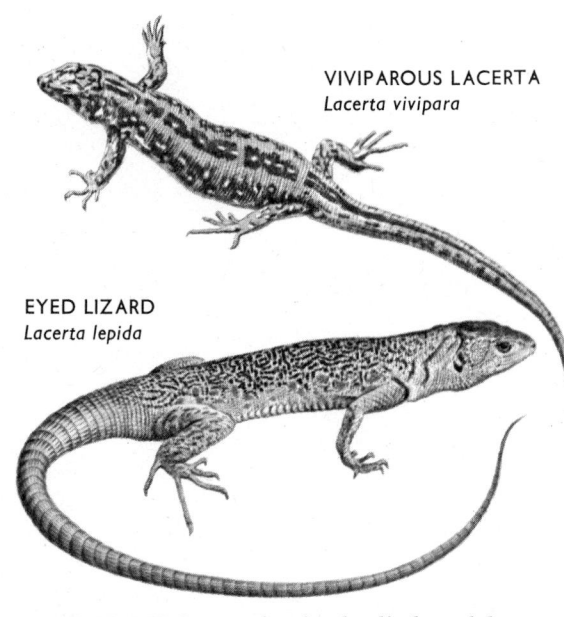

VIVIPAROUS LACERTA
Lacerta vivipara

EYED LIZARD
Lacerta lepida

LACERTIDS are slender-bodied and long-tailed lizards, consisting of about 150 species, found in Africa, Europe and Asia. One is found in the East Indies; none occurs in the Western Hemisphere. Largest living species is the Jewelled Lacerta *(Lacerta lepida)* of Spain. It reaches a length of $2\frac{1}{2}$ feet, more than twice as long as the average for the family. Large species feed on lizards, snakes, mice or other large prey, while the smaller ones eat insects, spiders or other small animals. None is vegetarian. All have strong legs and are similar in body shape. The large scales on the head cover flat, bony plates which are fused with the skull. Males rise on their legs and hunch the back when they meet, and generally charge into a biting, rolling combat, tearing skin and drawing blood until one retreats.

The Viviparous Lacerta *(Lacerta vivipara)* of northern Eurasia is the only lizard that occurs north of the Arctic Circle, where its activity is limited to three months of the year. It is also the only lacertid that bears its young alive, for the climate is too cold for eggs to hatch from incubation by the sun. In the Pyrenees Mountains of Spain, where even the high altitudes are relatively warm, this lizard lays eggs like other members of the family.

The Tiger Lizard *(Nucras delalandi)* of Africa protects itself from being swallowed by snakes by seizing one hind leg in its

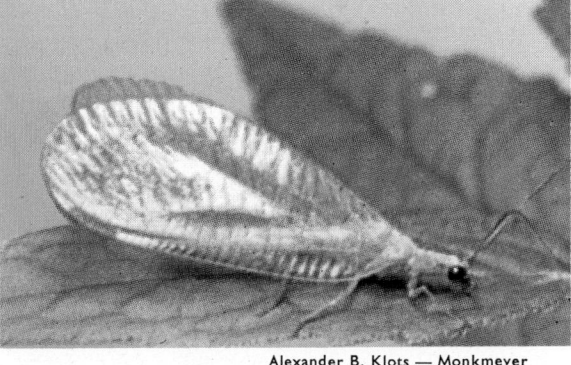

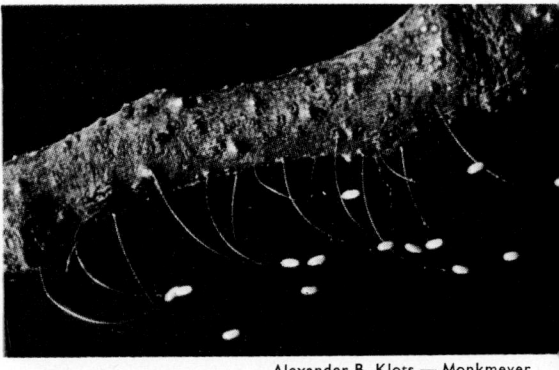

The female lacewing, a close relative of the Ant Lion Fly, lays her eggs on stiff, hair-like stalks that project about half an inch below the twig or leaf.

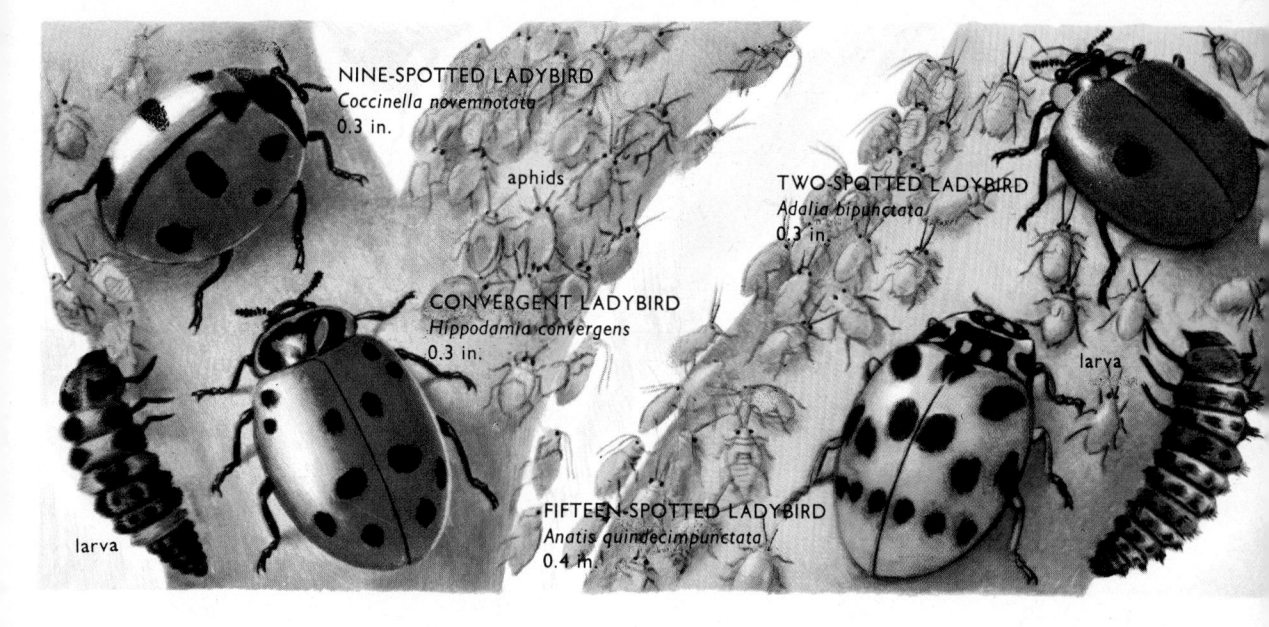

NINE-SPOTTED LADYBIRD
Coccinella novemnotata
0.3 in.

aphids

TWO-SPOTTED LADYBIRD
Adalia bipunctata
0.3 in.

CONVERGENT LADYBIRD
Hippodamia convergens
0.3 in.

larva

larva

FIFTEEN-SPOTTED LADYBIRD
Anatis quindecimpunctata
0.4 in.

jaws and forming a circle with its body. Then the snake can find no free end to swallow.

Fringe-tailed lizards of the West African forests are capable of gliding flight. The large scales projecting from the sides of the tail, coupled with the animal's ability to flatten the body, are believed to be responsible for this unusual behaviour in a lizard. In one genus, a fringe of projecting scales along the toes acts as sand-shoes, and enables the lizards to run rapidly in loose sand.

LACEWING FLIES (*Neuroptera Planipennia*). These slender, soft-bodied insects (see page 26) have four gauze-like wings with a very complex system of veins, but are very weak flyers. The head bears a pair of long, thread-like antennae and a pair of glistening eyes. These insects often enter houses to hibernate. A common species, *Chrysopa carnea*, gradually changes from green to brown during hibernation; when Spring comes along, however, it reverts to its original green colour.

The eggs of the Green Lacewings are laid on long stalks on plants, but the eggs of Brown Lacewings are without stalks. The larvae of Lacewings have large, curved jaws and are all voracious predators, feeding on aphids and other small insects. Some Green Lacewing larvae cover their bodies with debris to conceal themselves from

enemies. The larvae spin globular, silken cocoons from a spinneret at the anal end of the body.

Species of *Sisyra* allied to the Brown Lacewings are found on the banks of slow-moving rivers and lakes. The larvae of *Sisyra* live as parasites in fresh-water sponges.

Some very remarkable forms are found among these insects. Adults of the family *Nemopteridae* have greatly-elongated and ribbon-like hind wings, and a long head. *Pterocroce storeyi* is found in caves in Egypt and Palestine, and has a remarkably elongated neck which is equal in length to the rest of the body.

Closely related to the Lacewings are the Ant Lion Flies, whose larvae, the Ant Lions, excavate pits in which they sit with only their large jaws protruding, awaiting the ants on which they prey.

LADYBIRDS (*Coccinellidae*) are, with the exception of a few species, extremely beneficial, for both adults and larvae feed on such pests as aphids and scale insects. Their name can be traced to the Middle Ages, when these beetles were dedicated to the Virgin and at that time were called Beetles of Our Lady. Most of the nearly 5,000 species of ladybirds (or ladybird beetles) are less than a quarter of an inch long.

They are oval to circular in shape, strongly convex above, and very flat beneath. Most are orange or red with black dots, but some are black with red or orange dots. Ladybird larvae are long, with tapered bodies usually covered with small bumps, or spines. Most are combinations of black, red, orange or blue.

Ladybirds lay their eggs on plants in or near colonies of aphids or other insects on which they feed. Each female can lay several hundred eggs during her lifetime. Because many species require only four to six weeks to complete development, there can be several generations a year. Ladybirds spend the winter as adults.

Sometimes ladybirds are sold to owners of orchards and plantations, to help control aphids. Many species have been intro-duced to foreign countries to feed on such pest insects. In 1888, Vedalia, an Australian ladybird, was imported to the U.S.A., to control the Cottony-cushion Scale (see SCALE INSECTS). Within two years, this scale insect was under control, and has been held in check ever since.

LAMPREYS belong to a most primitive group of fishes, the class *Agnatha* (without jaws). The skeleton is of cartilage, and there are no scales and no paired fins. They also lack jaws and have a circular sucking mouth, with horny teeth and rasping tongue.

Of the two British species, the Sea Lamprey is the larger, reaching 3 feet in length, on both sides of the Atlantic. The Sea Lamprey enters rivers to breed, removing stones from the river-bed to make a nest. The parents usually die after spawning. The young, properly known as ammocoetes, are blind, toothless and worm-like, and do not change into the adult form for 4 to 6 years.

The Sea Lamprey feeds as a parasite on other fishes. When the American Great Lakes were opened to the sea by canals, Sea Lampreys swam is and, in 30 years, destroyed the huge lake fisheries.

The Lampern is a smaller species *(Lam-*

RIVER LAMPREY (LAMPERN)
Lampetra fluviatilis
10—24 in.

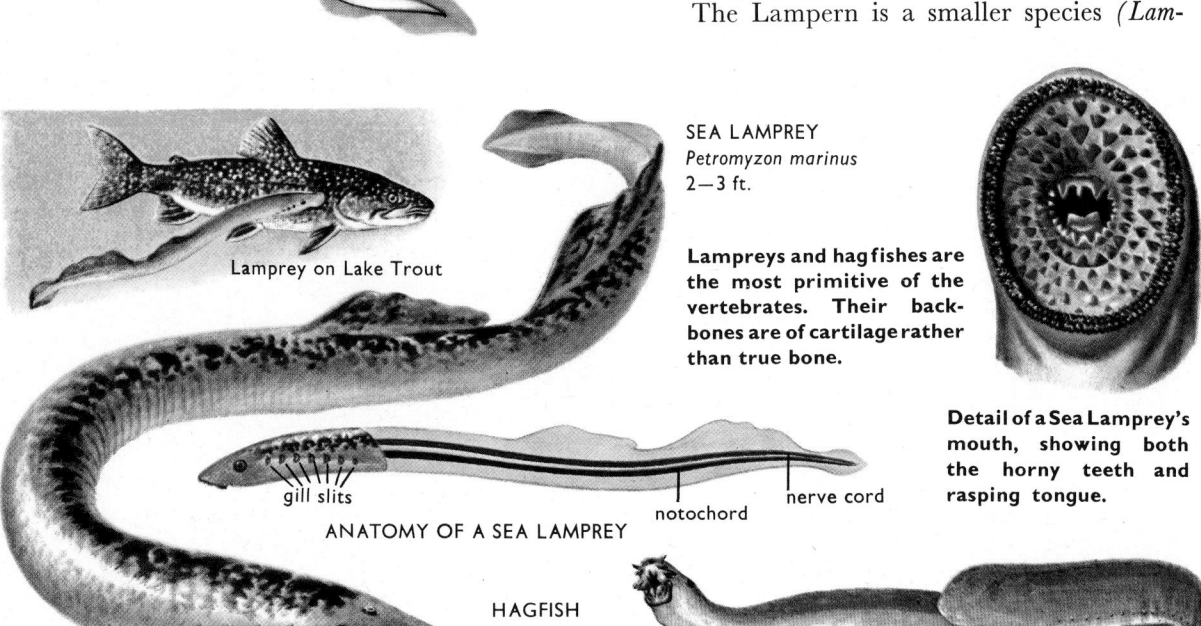

Lamprey on Lake Trout

SEA LAMPREY
Petromyzon marinus
2—3 ft.

Lampreys and hagfishes are the most primitive of the vertebrates. Their backbones are of cartilage rather than true bone.

Detail of a Sea Lamprey's mouth, showing both the horny teeth and rasping tongue.

gill slits

ANATOMY OF A SEA LAMPREY

notochord

nerve cord

HAGFISH
Myxine glutinosa
2—3 ft.

petra fluviatilis) which grows to about 16 inches. Like the Sea Lamprey, it ascends rivers to spawn, and the ammocoetes spend 3 to 5 years before changing into adults.

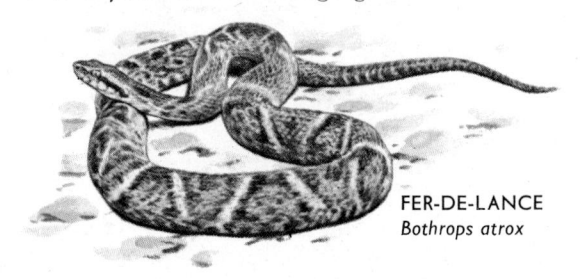

FER-DE-LANCE
Bothrops atrox

The Fer-de-lance is abundant in Central and South America, where it is greatly feared because of its vicious disposition and powerful poison. Its Spanish name, Barba Amarilla, refers to its yellow chin.

LANCEHEADS. About 35 American species *(Bothrops)* and 25 Asiatic species *(Trimeresurus)* of these pit-vipers are known. A few Old World species lay eggs, but all others give birth to their young. All except one species that lives in Ceylon have small head-scales. Most lanceheads live on the ground, but species in Asia and America are arboreal. Some have upturned snouts or short horns. Largest is the widely distributed (Mexico to northern South America) Fer-de-lance, or Barba Amarilla, which reaches a length of 8 feet. Several other South American species are nearly as large. All lanceheads have a powerful venom; most live primarily on birds and mammals. A South American species that feeds almost exclusively on birds has almost purely neurotoxic (nerve) venom. Females of another South American species are believed to be able to produce young without fertilisation by males, a process called parthenogenesis. (See VIPERS.)

LAND CRABS are found mainly in Florida and the West Indies. They occur from muddy or sandy, swampy areas near the sea to dry pine lands, and even on mountain slopes in Jamaica and Haiti. The Blue Land Crab *(Cardisoma guanhumi)*, with its long claw outstretched, may measure nearly 18 inches across. Mountain crabs are smaller.

The Blue Land Crab is a serious pest in the low farmlands of south Florida, where it is common. It eats young peppers, tomatoes, lettuce and cabbage plants. Farmers trap

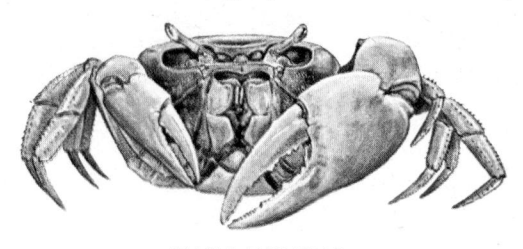

BLUE LAND CRAB

or poison the crabs, but in the Bahamas and West Indies, these crabs are prized as food, and are preferred to salt-water crabs. Blue Land Crabs live in large, slanted burrows where they stay during hot, dry weather to keep their gills damp.

Land crabs go to sea to spawn, and so great migrations occur during spring and autumn months. Vast herds are seen (or heard) at night, crawling with a rustling, clicking sound across roads, fields and lawns in their urge to reach the sea. A smaller land crab *(Gecarcinus)* of the Florida Keys and West Indies will climb obstacles in its path, and has even been found on roof-tops. (See HERMIT CRABS.)

LARKS are birds of Europe, Asia and North Africa. Only one member of the family, the Horned Lark, occurs in America.

SHORE LARK — 6½–7 in.
Eremphila alpestris
Eurasia, North Africa, North America, Mexico, Colombia

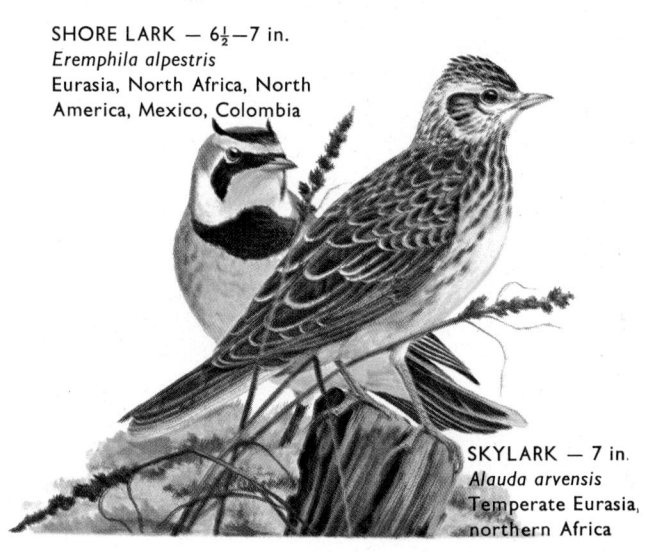

SKYLARK — 7 in.
Alauda arvensis
Temperate Eurasia, northern Africa

All larks nest on the ground, but do most of their singing and courting while flying.

The Skylark, and to a lesser extent the Woodlark of Europe, are famous for the beauty of their long and varied songs, sung as the bird soars overhead. They are ground-nesters, the former in bare, open places, the latter on woodland fringes. The Shore Lark is so named because, in Europe, it appears during winter from its northern breeding grounds, to feed along the beaches.

LEAF-HOPPERS *(Cicadellidae)* are a family of more than 2,000 species, many of which cause considerable damage to crops. Most leaf-hoppers are small, and only a few are as much as half an inch long. They are slender and have triangular-shaped heads. Two rows of spines extending along the tibia of their hind legs distinguish them from similar insects. Many are green or dull in colour, but some are attractively marked.

Leaf-hoppers feed on nearly all types of plants, from grasses to trees. Some will feed on a variety of plants, but most species are quite limited in their tastes. In addition to the damage done by their feeding, many leaf-hoppers spread diseases among plants.

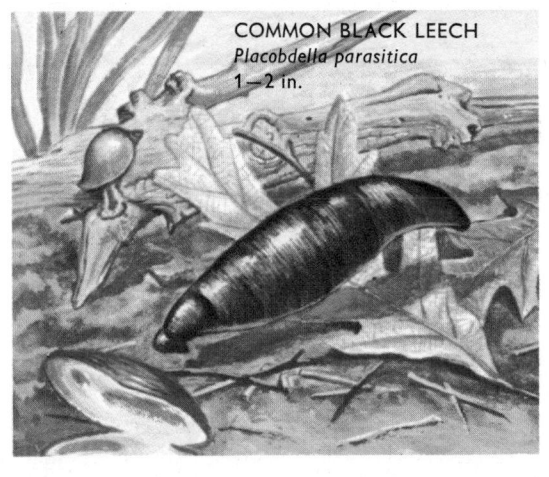

COMMON BLACK LEECH
Placobdella parasitica
1—2 in.

LEECHES are segmented (or annelid) worms, members of the same phylum as earthworms (see EARTHWORMS). Most species are either predators or parasites on other animals, although some kinds feed as scavengers on the remains of plants and animals. The majority of the nearly 300 species live in fresh water. A few kinds live in the sea, and some are found in moist soil. In Asia, tropical land-dwelling leeches *(Haemadipsa* spp.) sometimes enter the respiratory tracts of animals and make breathing difficult for their victim.

Best known of the leeches are the blood-

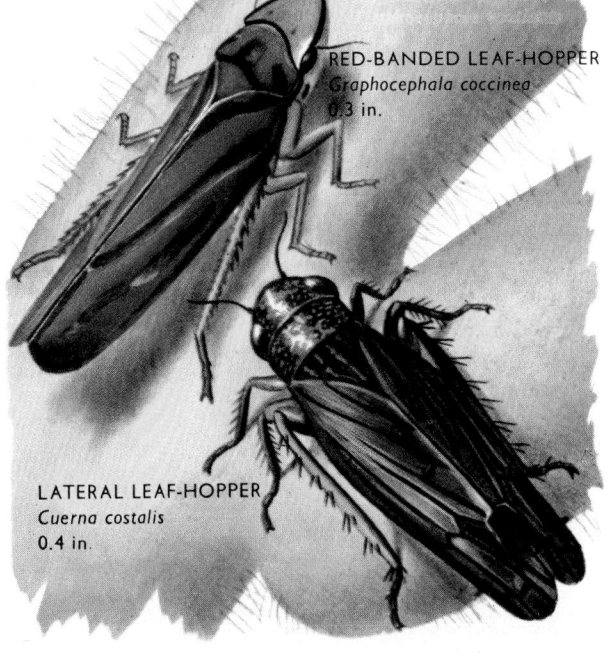

RED-BANDED LEAF-HOPPER
Graphocephala coccinea
0.3 in.

LATERAL LEAF-HOPPER
Cuerna costalis
0.4 in.

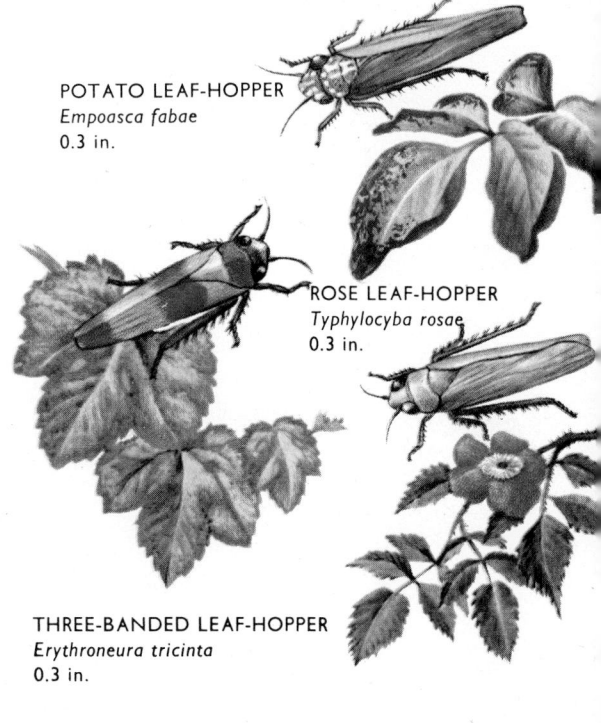

POTATO LEAF-HOPPER
Empoasca fabae
0.3 in.

ROSE LEAF-HOPPER
Typhlocyba rosae
0.3 in.

THREE-BANDED LEAF-HOPPER
Erythroneura tricinta
0.3 in.

suckers. By means of suckers at their head and tail end, they fasten themselves to a host creature, such as an insect, worm or other animal. Then they pierce a hole through its skin and, with their muscular pharynx, pump out the animal's blood. Often they take in several times their own weight, before they stop feeding and drop off their

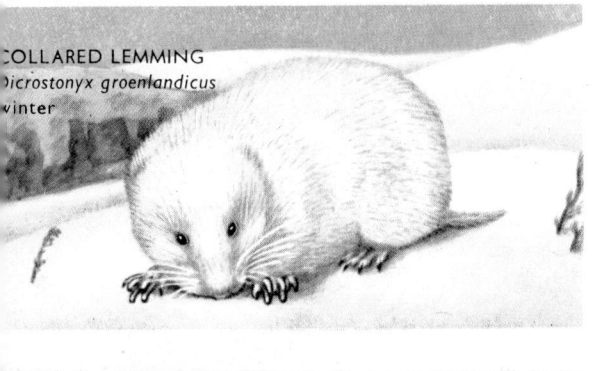

COLLARED LEMMING
Dicrostonyx groenlandicus
winter

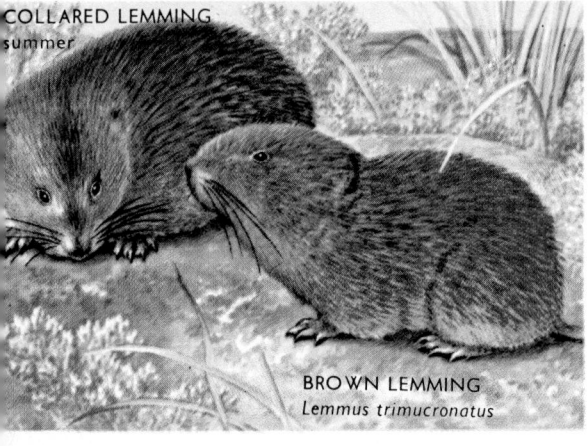

COLLARED LEMMING
summer

BROWN LEMMING
Lemmus trimucronatus

host to digest the meal.

Leeches were once used extensively by the medical profession in blood-letting, or the removal of blood from patients who were believed to suffer from an excess. In progressive countries this practice has now been stopped, but the enzyme (hirudin) secreted by the leeches to keep the blood of their victims from coagulating in the bite wound is still used for a similar purpose in some types of surgery. The European leech used for this purpose was *Hirudo medicinalis,* an average-sized leech (1 to 4 in). Among the common leeches found in fresh waters in North America are species of *Placobdella* and

Macrobdella. They feed on the blood of snails, crustaceans, turtles, fishes and other animals, and will attach themselves to waders or swimmers. Largest of the leeches is the North American Horseleech *(Haemopis grandis),* which reaches a length of 18 inches.

LEMMINGS *(Lemmus* and *Dicrostonyx* spp.*)* are small burrowing rodents that live in the tundra and stunted forests of northern polar regions. They feed on mosses, sedges, grasses and bark. One to several litters of young are raised each year in a nest at the end of a burrow. In winter, the Collared Lemming of North America moults into an all-white coat. The greatly-enlarged nails on the third and fourth fingers of its front feet are shed each Spring. Collared Lemmings provide food for northern fur-bearing animals.

The Brown Lemming does not get a white winter coat. The Common Lemming of Norway is often written about because of its strange migrations, or "marches to the sea". Lemming populations rise and fall in definite cycles (generally every four years), and at the peak of a population rise, a forced march or movement in search of new territory and food occurs. During the march, the lemmings are eaten by many predators. When they come to water, they try to swim across; being unable to reach the far side of large bodies of water, however, they die of exhaustion. This has given rise to the legend that lemmings "commit suicide" by trying to migrate across the Atlantic Ocean.

LEMURS are primitive primates found nowhere in the world except the island of Madagascar. They have large eyes, broad hands, and dense, woolly fur. Some look like squirrels with long pointed noses. Lemurs live in trees, rarely coming to the ground. They eat vegetation, fruit, insects and birds' eggs.

Mouse lemurs *(Cheirogaleus* spp.*),* the smallest of the lemurs, are only about 12 inches long. They live in the tops of tall forest trees, where they make nests like those of birds, or in tree hollows. Mouse lemurs feed on fruits, insects and honey.

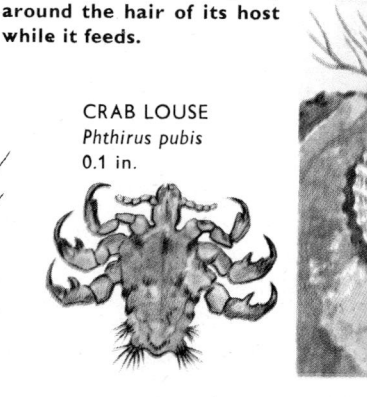

AYE-AYE
A true lemur
of Madagascar

The Aye-Aye *(Daubentonia madagascariensis)*, a most unusual lemur about the size of a cat, has a long, bushy tail and a very thin, wire-like middle finger on each hand. This sensitive finger is used for tapping on branches to locate insect grubs inside, and then to dig them out.

LICE, small wingless insects, are divided into two distinct orders: biting lice *(Mallophaga)*, found mostly on birds; and sucking lice *(Anoplura)*, found on mammals. There are more than 3,000 species in these orders.

Most biting lice are less than 1/20 of an inch long, though some are about 1/5 of an inch long. They feed on hair, feathers, scales and skin, and do not live long if not on a host. Though not considered to be disease-carriers, biting lice irritate their host and cause a run-down appearance.

Biting lice that live on birds have two claws at the end of their tarsi. When the bird ruffles its feathers and exposes these lice, they run rapidly to hide. The few kinds of biting lice found on mammals have a single claw, used to cling tightly to hairs. These lice do not move around much.

Most important of the several species of biting lice that live on chickens are the Chicken Head Louse and the Chicken Body Louse. Chickens infested with these lice become weak and lay fewer eggs.

Sucking lice draw blood from their host. Like biting lice that live on mammals, sucking lice have a single claw on the end of each leg. The claw closes against a projection so that it can be locked tightly around a hair.

Man is a host for three different kinds of sucking lice: Head, Body and Crab lice. Head Lice are usually found in the fine hair of the head, though occasionally they wander to other parts of the body. Body Lice actually live on clothing, rather than on the body, and they deposit their eggs (or nits) along seams in clothes, rather than on hairs. The Crab Louse, considerably different in appearance from the other two lice which inflict them-

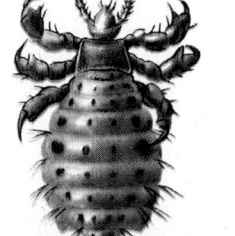

A louse locks its claw tightly around the hair of its host while it feeds.

CRAB LOUSE
Phthirus pubis
0.1 in.

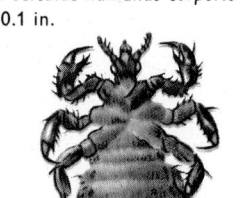

SHORT-NOSED
CATTLE LOUSE
Haematopinus eurysternis
0.1 in.

BODY LOUSE
Pediculus humanus corporis
0.1 in.

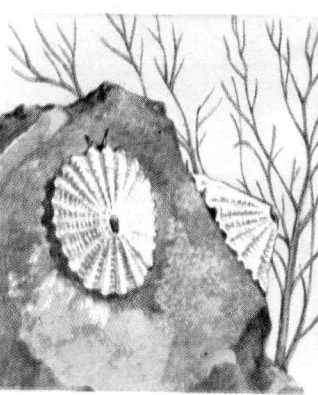

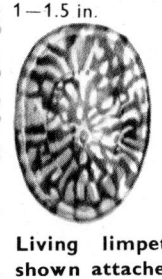

ATLANTIC PLATE LIMPET
Acmaea testudinalis
1—1.5 in.

Living limpets shown attached to a rock.

selves on humans, lives on the parts of the body where coarse hair grows. This louse is found almost exclusively on members of the Caucasian race. Body Lice transmit trench fever (a disease that was serious among soldiers during World War I), epidemic

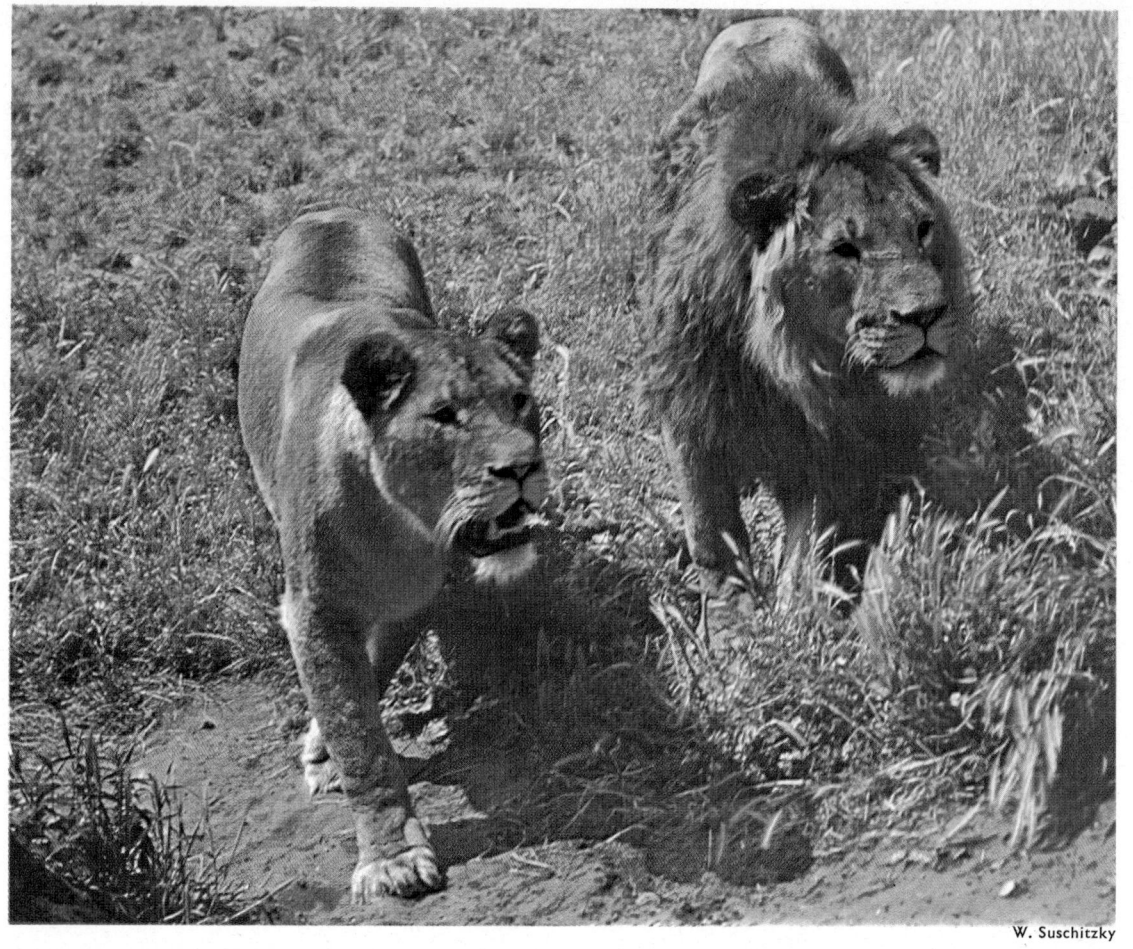

W. Suschitzky

Lions usually live in open country, in high grass regions where grazing animals abound. A pair or a family join in the stalk, but it is most often the female who bursts from cover to pounce on the prey.

typhus, and a form of relapsing fever. These diseases spread rapidly when people live in crowded or unclean conditions. Lice also transmit diseases among rats, dogs, rabbits, horses, cattle sheep and goats.

LIMPETS are cup or cone-shaped shells of the families *Fissurellidae* and *Acmaeidae*. They live closely attached to rocks, or occasionally to algae. Some are inter-tidal; others live in deep water. They are found in both the Atlantic and Pacific, mainly in warm waters, and feed on algae scraped from the rocks. All limpets begin life with coiled shells, but flatten out when they settle on rocks. The shells of Keyhole limpets have a hole at the top, and may be partly or entirely covered by a soft mantle. Most limpets return to

their "home" at low tide or when not feeding. Their shell edge leaves a tell-tale oval scar on the rocks where they rested.

LIONS *(Felis leo)* have great strength and majestic beauty. Large males weigh as much as 500 pounds and usually have a bushy mane; females are maneless and weigh up to 300 pounds. The newly-born cubs, unlike their parents, are spotted; these spots, some of which are so close together that they look like stripes, usually disappear in about six months. In most parts of Africa and Asia, lions prefer the open, grassy plains, rather than the dense, tropical forests. Lions feed at night, principally on such large animals as antelopes, buffaloes and zebras, They usually lie in wait near a water hole; then, when

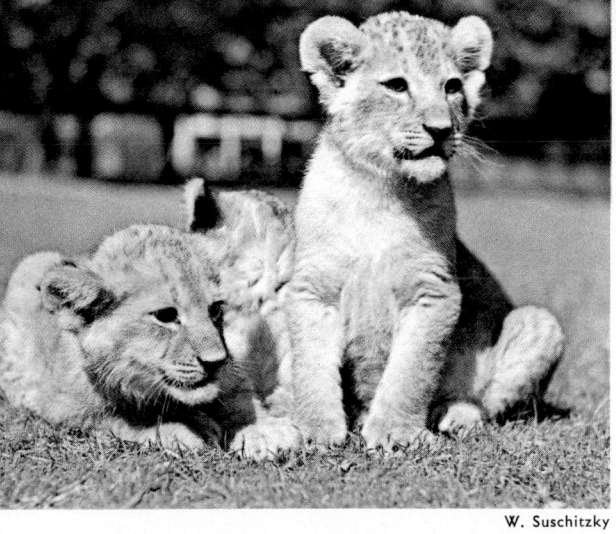

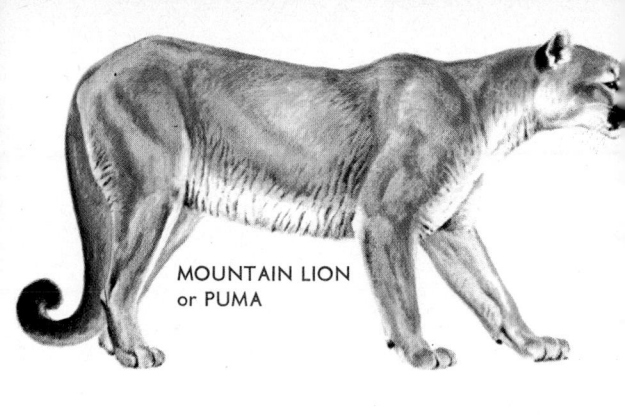

MOUNTAIN LION
or PUMA

Mountain Lions wait along game trails, often on branches from which they drop on their prey. They prefer deer, but also eat small animals.

W. Suschitzky

Lion cubs play and purr like large kittens, but tend to become savage as they grow older.

an animal gets close, they rush at it and strike with their paws, frequently breaking the quarry's neck. Except during the breeding season, when fighting is common, Lions live peacefully in family groups, or in groups of adults. These groups are called "prides".

Mountain Lions *(Felis concolor)*, sometimes called Cougars or Pumas, live in North and South America. Their inability to roar separates them from the true lions, tigers and leopards of the Old World. Mountain Lions weigh between 100 and 200 pounds, and are capable of killing animals as large as sheep, deer and cattle. They live in rocky areas, and climb trees only when closely pursued or

when lying in wait for prey. They normally fear and avoid man. Their range in North America has been greatly reduced.

LIZARDS. About 2,800 species of lizard are found all over the world. There are almost as many different kinds of snake, members of the same order of reptiles, but lizards are far more abundant in number of individuals. In many warm regions, lizards seem to be everywhere. Salamanders, which are amphibians, are sometimes mistaken for lizards. Salamanders, however, have smooth skins instead of scaly skins; also they never have more than four fingers on their front legs, while the majority of lizards have five (see SALAMANDERS; SNAKES).

Lizards are also more varied in form than

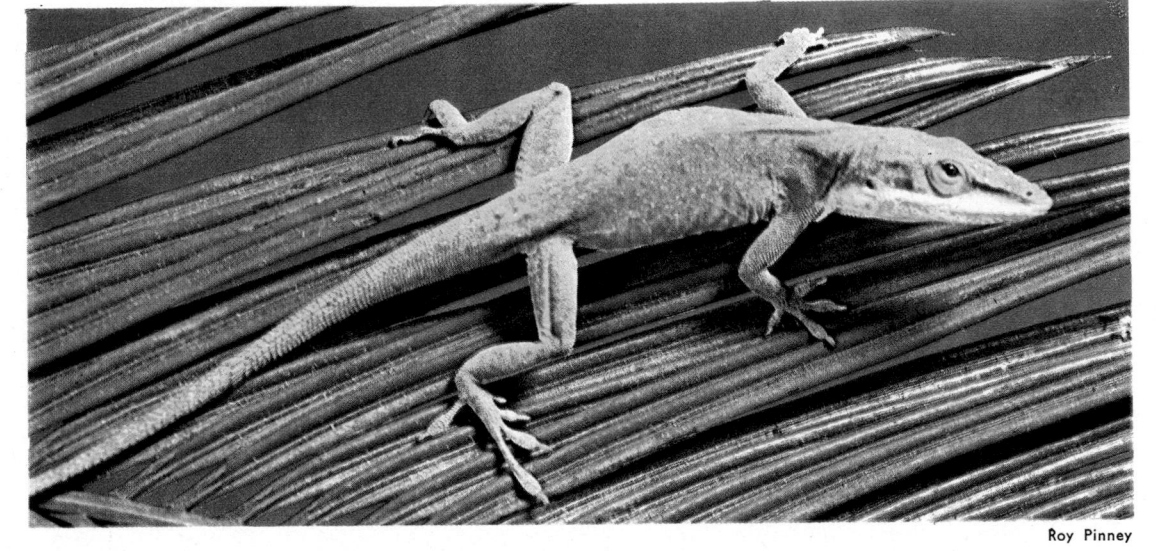

Roy Pinney

Anoles, or American Chameleons, make good pets. They eat only live food, such as insects or grubs.

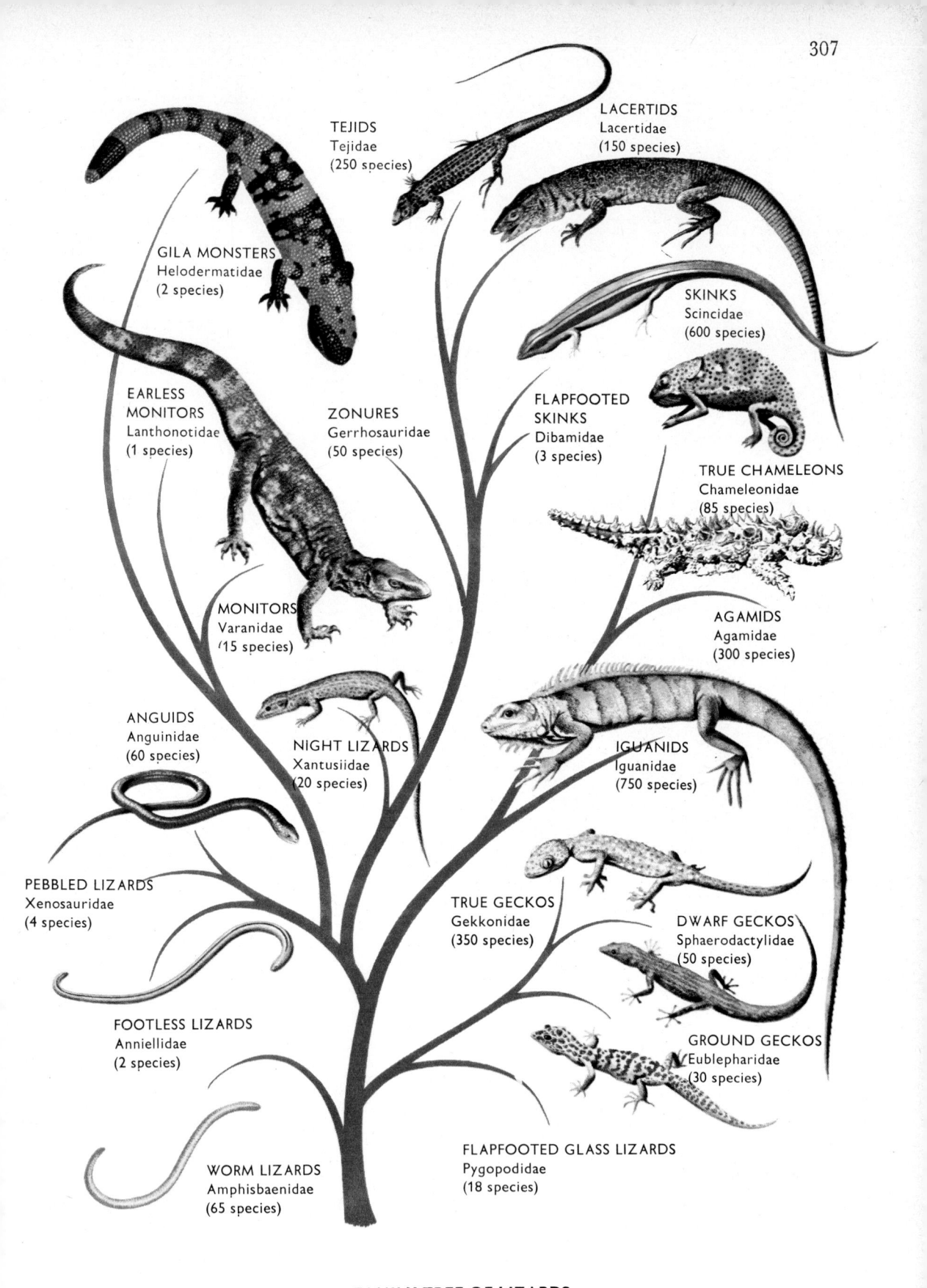

TEJIDS
Tejidae
(250 species)

LACERTIDS
Lacertidae
(150 species)

GILA MONSTERS
Helodermatidae
(2 species)

SKINKS
Scincidae
(600 species)

EARLESS
MONITORS
Lanthonotidae
(1 species)

ZONURES
Gerrhosauridae
(50 species)

FLAPFOOTED
SKINKS
Dibamidae
(3 species)

TRUE CHAMELEONS
Chameleonidae
(85 species)

MONITORS
Varanidae
(15 species)

AGAMIDS
Agamidae
(300 species)

ANGUIDS
Anguinidae
(60 species)

NIGHT LIZARDS
Xantusiidae
(20 species)

IGUANIDS
Iguanidae
(750 species)

PEBBLED LIZARDS
Xenosauridae
(4 species)

TRUE GECKOS
Gekkonidae
(350 species)

DWARF GECKOS
Sphaerodactylidae
(50 species)

FOOTLESS LIZARDS
Anniellidae
(2 species)

GROUND GECKOS
Eublepharidae
(30 species)

WORM LIZARDS
Amphisbaenidae
(65 species)

FLAPFOOTED GLASS LIZARDS
Pygopodidae
(18 species)

FAMILY TREE OF LIZARDS

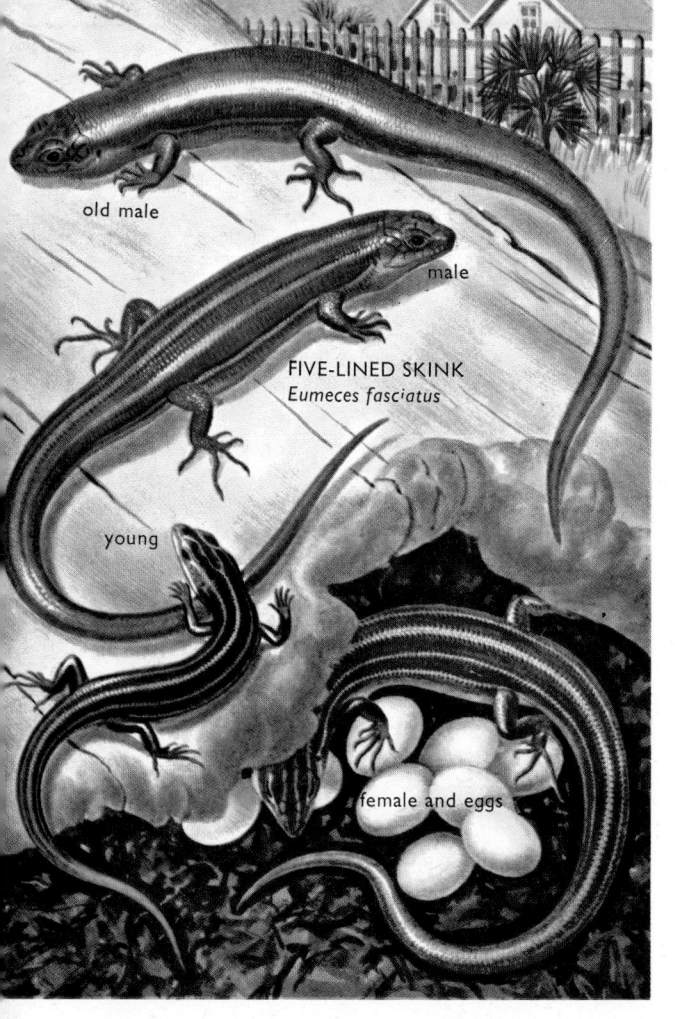

old male

male

FIVE-LINED SKINK
Eumeces fasciatus

young

female and eggs

A female skink broods her clutch of 6 to 18 eggs, but does not take care of the young after they have hatched. Young skinks have a bright blue tail.

are snakes. In the 21 lizard families (as compared to 14 snake families), there are such variable types as slender, long-tailed racers; earthworm-like burrowers; stump-tailed, short-bodied rock-dwellers; and the

spiny, pancake-shaped desert species.

Fossil lizards known from the Jurassic period — about 130 million years ago — resembled currently living ones. Exceptions were mosasaurs and their kin, which lived in the sea and reached a length of at least 20 feet. Monitors are believed to have evolved from these giant sea-dwelling lizards (see MONITORS).

Most lizards eat insects and small mammals. A few kinds, with powerful crushing teeth somewhat like our molars, feed on snails or crabs, and some eat only plants.

A few kinds give birth to their young, but most lizards lay rather soft-shelled eggs, in moist soil or under litter. Geckos often lay their eggs, which are generally hard-shelled and do not dry out, in a crevice in wood or among rocks. Lizards continue to grow slowly as long as they live. They seldom reach 10 years of age (54 is the maximum known), and some kinds live only about 10 months.

A few kinds of lizard can bite severely, but gila monsters are the only poisonous lizards. No lizards attack man unless provoked. Most run and hide at the slightest movement, and are so wary that they cannot be approached closer than several feet. A few kinds that live around dwellings may become tame enough to be caught by hand. Some live well in captivity; but others will struggle until they die of exhaustion.

A lizard's tail is as useful as one of its legs. For some kinds, the tail serves as a balancer. This is especially true in the case of basilisks and others that run on their hind legs, with the front of their body held high (see BASILISKS). Others use the tail to grasp twigs or rocks while climbing. A tail may be shaped or coloured to help camouflage the

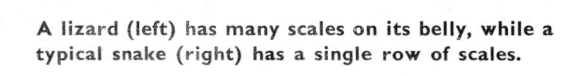

A lizard (left) has many scales on its belly, while a typical snake (right) has a single row of scales.

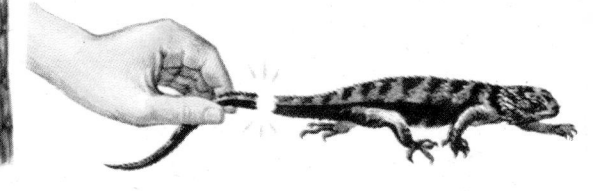

Some lizards can re-grow their tail, which they break off in struggling to get free from an enemy.

lizard, or it may be waved over the body to expose a bright underside, serving as a warning or deceptive device. Fat stored in the tail is used in winter hibernation, and the tail of some lizards seems capable also of absorbing moisture. Spiked or club-like tails are effective weapons of defence. Some tails are so short that they are scarcely visible nubbins; others are slim, and several times the length of the lizard's body.

Most lizards can break off their tail at will. The break usually occurs at the point where the tail is grasped or struck a blow. The dismembered tail wriggles conspicuously, hold ing the enemy's attention while the lizard slips away. Muscles tighten around blood vessels at the breaking point so that there is little loss of blood. A new tail, slightly different in shape and colour pattern, soon grows from the stump. It can be shed also.

In the breeding season, male lizards defend their home territories from other male lizards of the same species, but may allow young males or females to enter. They stay with the same mate for at least one season or more.

Some lizards are able to change their colour. In most the change is limited to becoming slightly lighter or darker, and there is no change in the colour pattern. A light colour reflects heat and light and helps to protect the lizard from the sun's rays. Lizards become darker to absorb the rays or to blend with a dark background. Active lizards in shade are usually dark; those in the sun — or asleep — are light. Anoles — the so-called American of false chameleons (see ANOLES) — change from green to brown, but only true chameleons of Africa and adjacent lands readily change their pattern as well as colour in response to heat, light and mood. A "purple rage" can be an accurate description of these chameleons (see CHAMELEONS).

LOBSTERS are large crustaceans related to shrimps. Young lobsters look like small shrimps and swim freely in the open sea. Soon they settle to the bottom and become scavengers, developing two enormous claws,

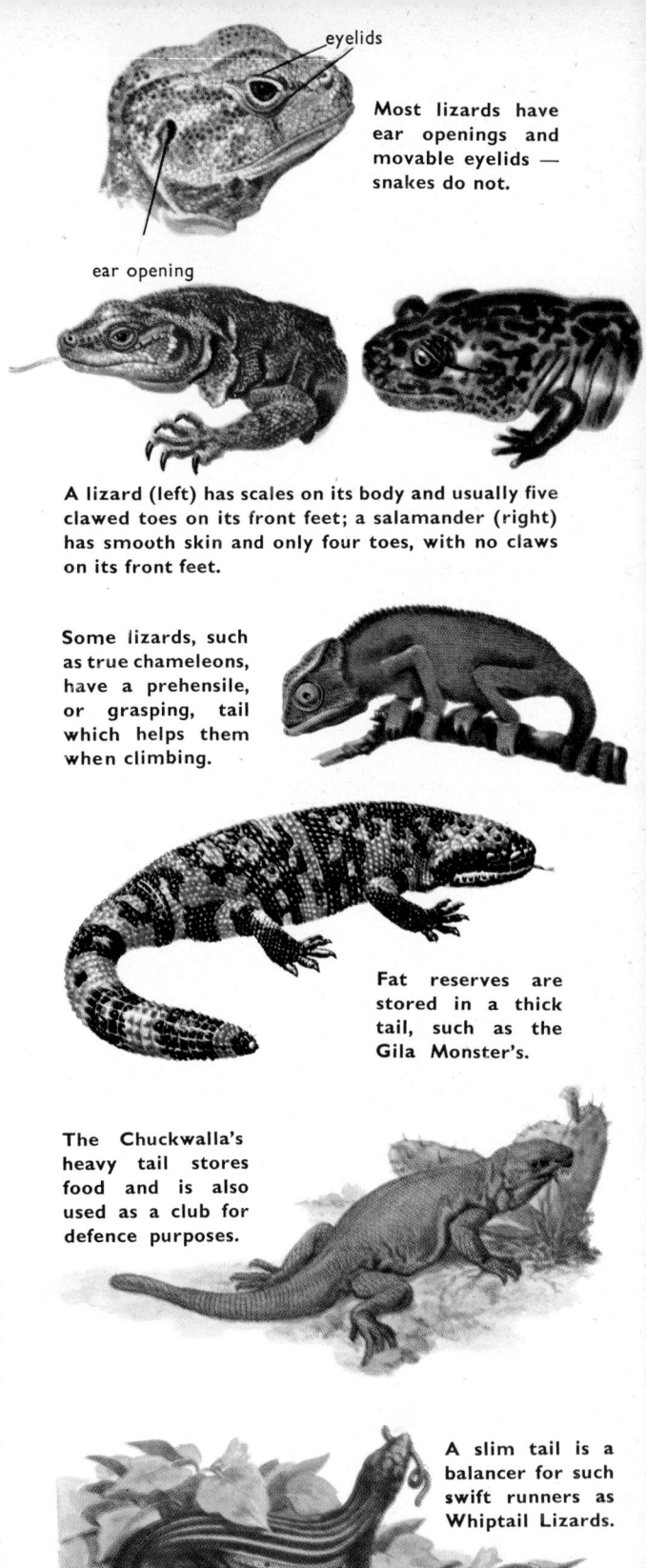

eyelids

ear opening

Most lizards have ear openings and movable eyelids — snakes do not.

A lizard (left) has scales on its body and usually five clawed toes on its front feet; a salamander (right) has smooth skin and only four toes, with no claws on its front feet.

Some lizards, such as true chameleons, have a prehensile, or grasping, tail which helps them when climbing.

Fat reserves are stored in a thick tail, such as the Gila Monster's.

The Chuckwalla's heavy tail stores food and is also used as a club for defence purposes.

A slim tail is a balancer for such swift runners as Whiptail Lizards.

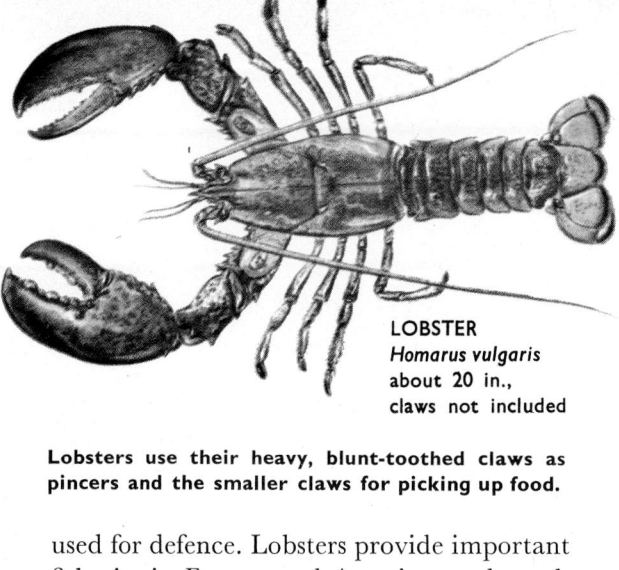

LOBSTER
Homarus vulgaris
about 20 in.,
claws not included

Lobsters use their heavy, blunt-toothed claws as pincers and the smaller claws for picking up food.

used for defence. Lobsters provide important fisheries in Europe and America, and reach market size in about five years. The Common Lobster *(Homarus gammarus)* and the Norway Lobster *(Nephrops norvegicus)* of Europe are found from Norway to the Mediterranean, the latter being smaller and an occupant of deeper water. The American Lobster *(Homarus americanus)* lives in the Atlantic from Labrador to the Carolinas. It may

SPINY LOBSTER
8—16 in.

The edible part of a Spiny Lobster is the tail muscle; in true lobsters, the claws also provide meat.

reach a weight of 35 pounds. Those caught in wooden traps weigh about three pounds and have a better flavour than larger ones. Spiny (or rock) lobsters *(Panulirus spp.)* are called crawfish in Florida and the West Indies. Only distantly related to the American Lobster, they do not have claws, but their spiny antennae help to protect them from enemies, and they also have spiny shells. Their thin, transparent larvae often drift for several months with the plankton. One

species of spiny lobster is found on the California Coast; several species are found off Florida and in the Caribbean.

The Spanish Lobster *(Scyllapides sculptus)*, a near relative, is awkward-looking and rather helpless, except for the protection provided by its heavy shell.

LORISES are primitive primates related to lemurs. Sluggish nocturnal creatures, they live in tropical forests from southern Asia to the Philippines. Two closely related forms occur in Africa. Most of their time is spent amongst lower branches.

The Slow Loris *(Nycticebus coucang)* from south-east Asia is a sluggish, stockily-built, woolly animal, about a foot and a half long. Active at night, it feeds on a wide variety of plants, fruit and animals, particularly insects. The Slender Loris *(Loris tardigradus)* of Ceylon and India moves slowly through the lower branches of bushes and trees. Only about five inches long, it has slender arms and legs and large eyes.

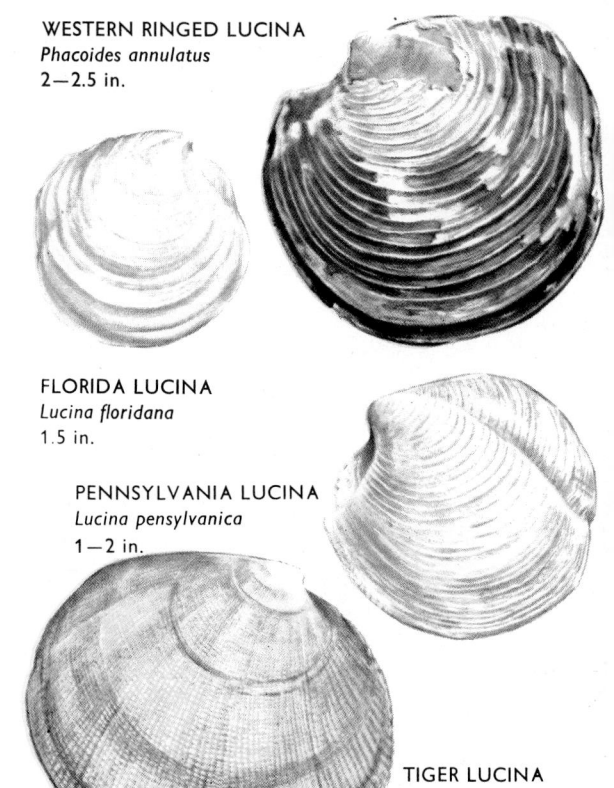

WESTERN RINGED LUCINA
Phacoides annulatus
2—2.5 in.

FLORIDA LUCINA
Lucina floridana
1.5 in.

PENNSYLVANIA LUCINA
Lucina pensylvanica
1—2 in.

TIGER LUCINA
Codakia orbicularis
2.5—3.5 in.

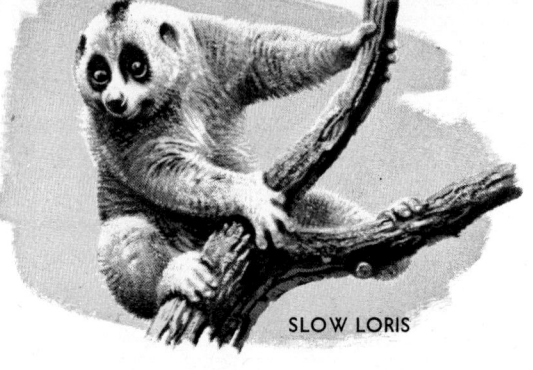

SLOW LORIS

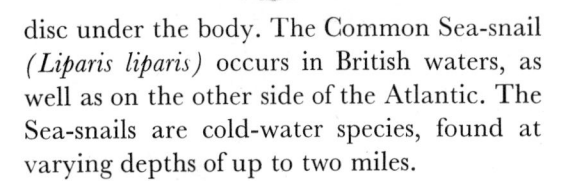

cocoon

LUNA MOTH
Actias luna
0.8 in.;
wing-spread, 3.2 in.

larva

LUCINAS are small to large (3½ in.) bi-valved molluscs with rather flattened shells that have a circular outline. While the shells are mostly white or chalky, they may sometimes be yellowish. The Tiger Lucina has a streak of bright red near its hinge. Most lucinas live in shallow sand or mud, but some live at depths of 100 fathoms or more. The sculpture of their shells varies. In some it consists of concentric lines or ridges; others have radial ribs or lines, or deep radial grooves or folds. Lucinas are unusual among bivalved molluscs in retaining the eggs in the gill chamber until they hatch. Their shells are common in warmer regions on both Atlantic and Pacific coasts along sandy shores.

LUMPSUCKER *(Cyclopterus lumpus)*. This fish occurs on both sides of the Atlantic, reaching a length of about two feet. It belongs to a family of fishes which have the ventral fins modified to form a sucker, by which they can attach themselves to rocks. The eggs are laid in shallow water and are guarded by the male. For this reason, the name Seahen is sometimes given to this fish.

The Sea-snails are related to the Lumpsuckers, and have the same kind of sucking

disc under the body. The Common Sea-snail *(Liparis liparis)* occurs in British waters, as well as on the other side of the Atlantic. The Sea-snails are cold-water species, found at varying depths of up to two miles.

LUNA MOTHS *(Saturniidae)* have pale-green wings with a purplish band along the leading edge. Their narrow hind wings end in long, slender tails. Larvae of Luna Moths feed on leaves of hickory, walnut, persimmon, and other trees in hardwood forests of eastern North America. Cecropia, Polyphemus and Io moths are other large moths that belong to the *Saturniid* family.

LUNG-FISHES are the remnants of an ancient group of fishes, now represented only by a species in Australia, one in South America and four in Africa. The first has

African Lungfish are shipped alive to zoos wrapped in their cocoons. The cocoons are dug from the mud and corded together during shipment. The fish breathe through a small hole in the cocoon's wall.

New York Zoological Society Photo

SEA-SNAIL
under 6 in.

LUMPSUCKER
to 20 in.

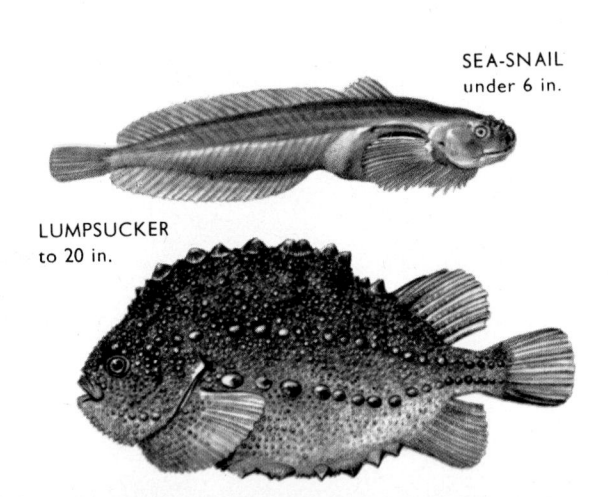

only a single lung, but the others have two lungs, and can remain buried in mud during dry periods. The African Lung-fish builds a cocoon in the mud, with a short breathing tube from the fish's mouth to the outside. African Lung-fishes have been kept for four years out of water. During this time, the fishes absorb muscle tissue for food.

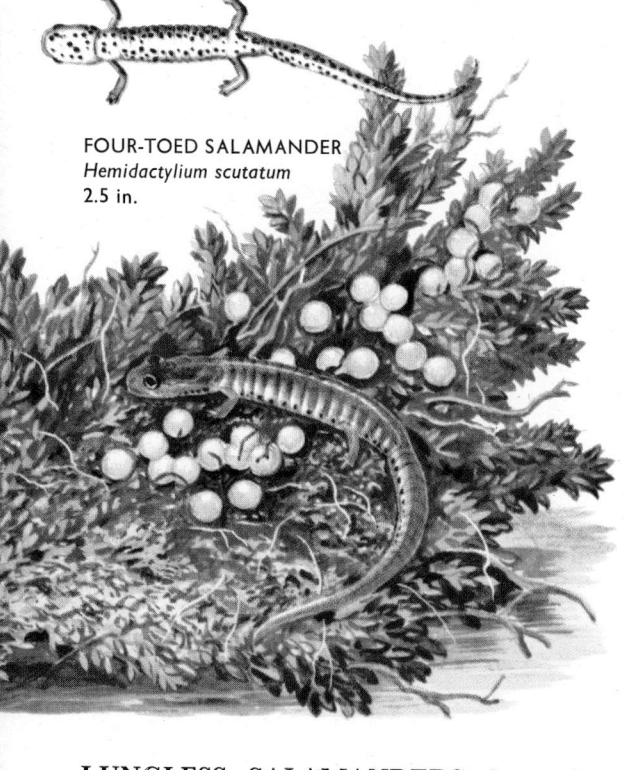

FOUR-TOED SALAMANDER
Hemidactylium scutatum
2.5 in.

LUNGLESS SALAMANDERS form the largest salamander group. About 125 species — half the known kinds of salamander — belong to this family, *Plethodontidae,* found mainly in North and Central America. Three species occur in north-western South America, and two in Sardinia, Italy and France. All members of the family have a "nasolabial" groove — a fine groove in the skin between the nostril and the lip. Larvae do not have this groove, and sometimes it can be seen in adults only by using a lens.

The lack of lungs adapts these salamanders to life in swift mountain streams, the habitat in which the family apparently developed. With lungs they would be buoyant, and it would be difficult for them to maintain their position in the flowing water. The many species that now live in other places have never redeveloped lungs. An adult lungless salamander breathes through its skin and also through the soft membrane that lines its mouth. To breathe it lifts and lowers the floor of its mouth rapidly, often as many as 120 times per minute. This draws in air, then forces it out again.

Many lungless salamanders have stalked, mushroom-shaped tongues. Tongues of others broad and lack stalks, but both kinds are attached at the front of the mouth.

Lungless salamanders are generally small or average in size. Included in the group is the smallest of all salamanders — a species that measures less than an inch in length when full-grown. The giant of the clan reaches a length of $11\frac{1}{2}$ inches.

Following a courtship session, the males deposit sperm packets, or spermatophores, which are picked up by females. Eggs are laid separately, not in strings or cords.

Some species, such as the Red Salamander (*Pseudotriton ruber*), spend their entire lives in water. They attach their eggs underneath

RED SALAMAND
Pseudotriton rube
5 in.

PURPLE SALAMANDER
Gyrinophilus porphyriticus
5 in.

RED SALAMANDER
(young)

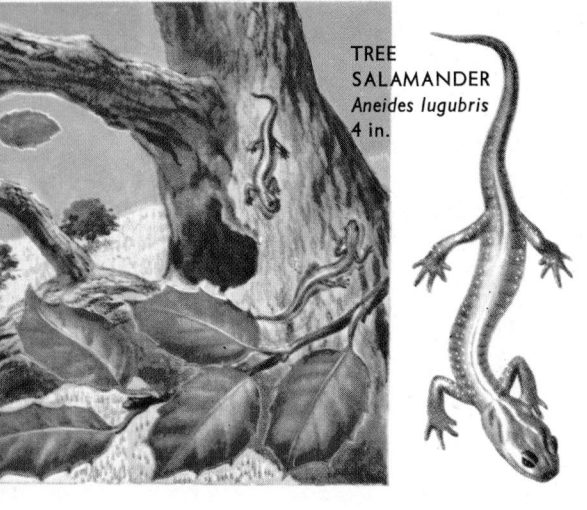

TREE
SALAMANDER
Aneides lugubris
4 in.

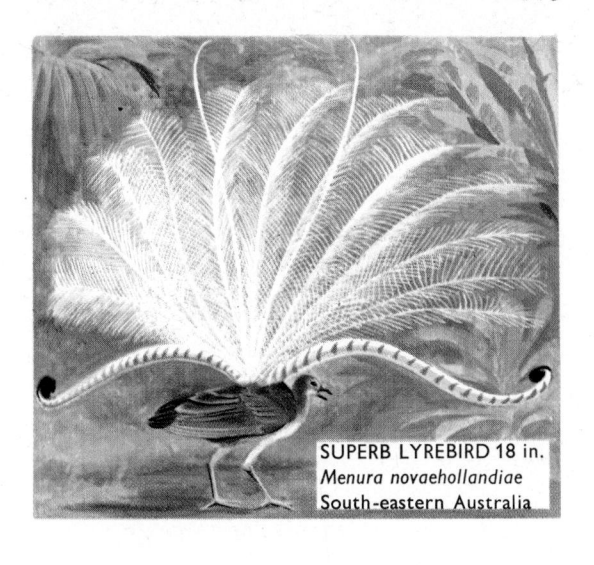

SUPERB LYREBIRD 18 in.
Menura novaehollandiae
South-eastern Australia

stones, leaves, or other underwater objects, and the larvae develop in the water. Other types, such as the Purple Salamander *(Gyrinophilus)*, live on land but return to water to lay their eggs. Still others, like the Four-toed Salamander *(Hemidactylium)*, live on land and also lay their eggs on land. Their hatchlings wriggle into the water, where they go through a gilled larval stage. In some land-dwelling types, such as the Red-backed

Salamander *(Plethodon)*, the larval stage is passed in the egg, which is laid on land, and an imago hatches. Tree salamanders lay their eggs in hollows in trees, in water pockets in the leaves of air plants, in the fold of banana-plant leaves, or in rotten logs and stumps.

The strangest salamanders in this family are the blind forms which live in limestone caves in the United States. They are flesh-coloured and semi-transparent, although the juvenile Grotto Salamander, which lives in mountain streams, is dark and does not lose its pigment until it moves, in its adult life, into the caves. With the exception of the Grotto Salamander, the adult blind salamanders retain the larvae's bright-red gills.

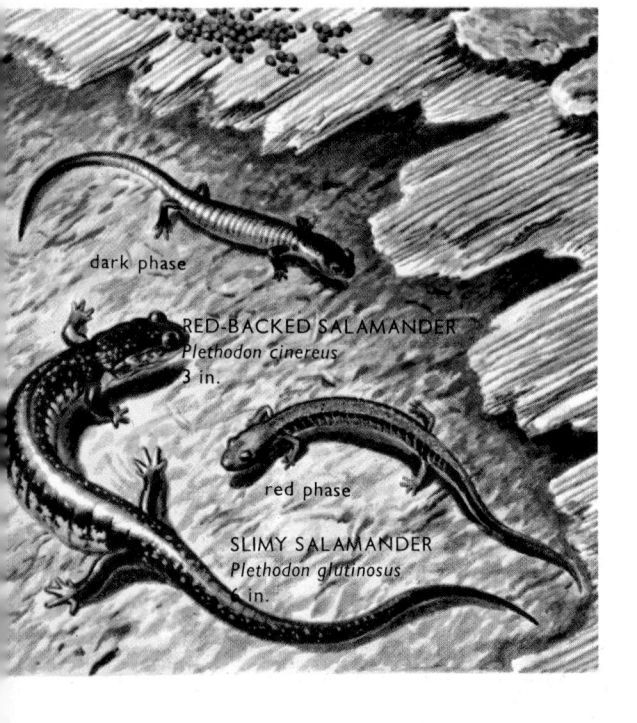

dark phase

RED-BACKED SALAMANDER
Plethodon cinereus
3 in.

red phase

SLIMY SALAMANDER
Plethodon glutinosus
6 in.

LYRE-BIRDS live only in South Australia, and it is only the males that have beautiful tails. These grow in June and are shed when the breeding season is over in October. Two outside plumes form the frame of the "lyre". Between them are fourteen stiff, hair-like feathers. The picture shows these as they are spread in song.

Lyre-birds are chicken-sized. They build domed nests on or near the ground. Lyre-birds live in dense mountain forest. They are very shy and hard to see, but easy to hear. The song is loud, musical, and very varied. If they live near to farms, they sometimes imitate pigs, cocks, or babies crying.

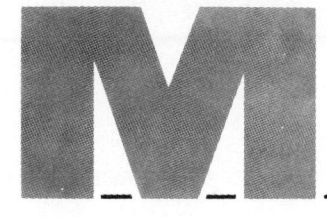

MACKEREL belong to the family Scombridae, a family of fast-moving fishes which includes such important food fishes as the Tunas. The mackerel-like fishes are highly streamlined, with a crescent-shaped tail and a series of small finlets behind the dorsal and anal fins. The tail is more rigid than in other fishes, the rays overlapping the last vertebra, and this gives the tail more driving power.

Most mackerels feed on herrings and other small fishes. The Atlantic Mackerel *(Scomber scombrus)* is an exception, for it feeds largely on small crustacea, and other members of the plankton drifting in the surface layers. The Mackerel strains its food from the water by means of its gillrakers. The female lays as many as 500,000 eggs. These float at first, but later slowly sink. Mackerel are migratory

fishes, spending the winter in deeper water and reappearing in the summer, very thin, having fed little during the winter.

A less common species in British waters is the Spanish Mackerel *(Scomber colias)*, which is distinguished from the Atlantic Mackerel by its less distinct black markings on the back, and fewer dorsal spines (9—10, as against 11—12).

In the Western Atlantic, there are several important mackerels in addition to the two mentioned above. In America, members of the genus *Scomberomorus* are known as Spanish Mackerels, or Kingfish, and reach a length of 5 feet, and there are important fisheries for them on the Atlantic coast of America.

The Wahoo *(Acanthocybium solandri)* is a more widespread species, occurring also in

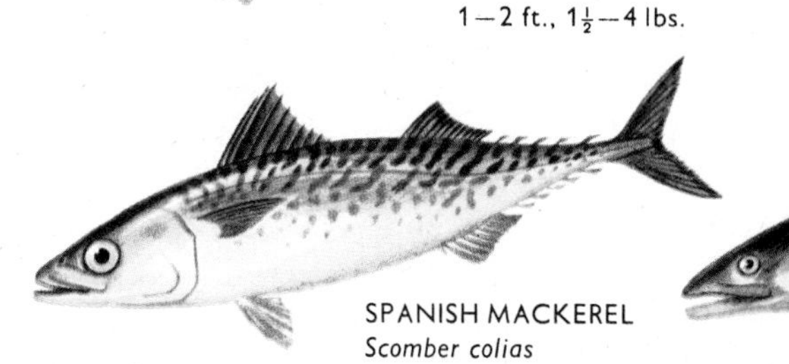

ATLANTIC MACKEREL
Scomber scombrus
1—2 ft., 1½—4 lbs.

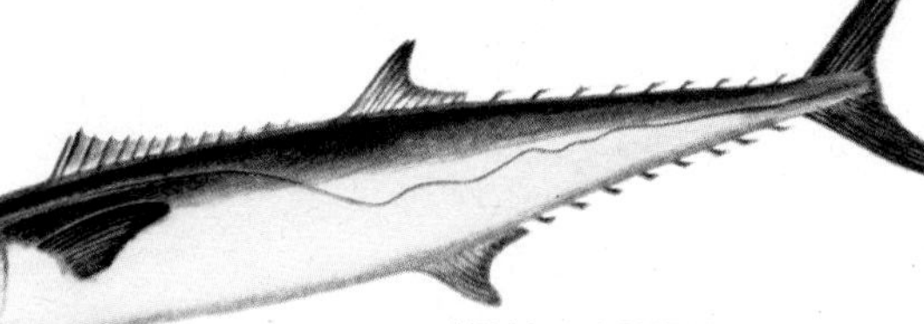

PACIFIC MACKEREL
Scomber diego
15—24 in., to 6 lbs.

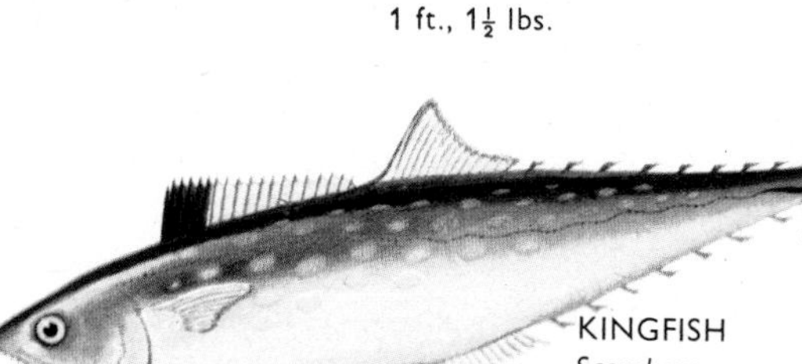

SPANISH MACKEREL
Scomber colias
1 ft., 1½ lbs.

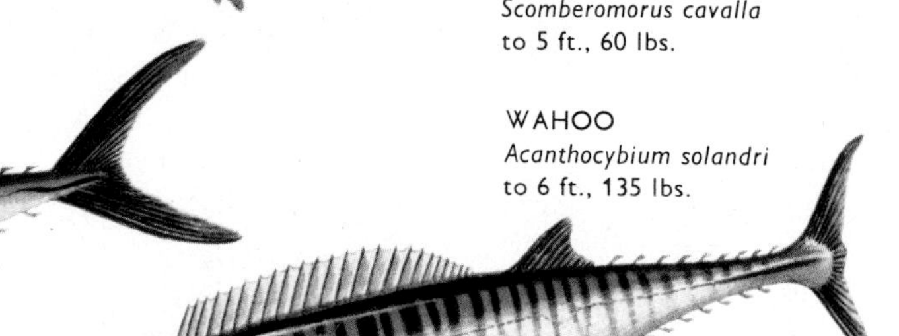

KING MACKEREL
Scomberomorus cavalla
to 5 ft., 60 lbs.

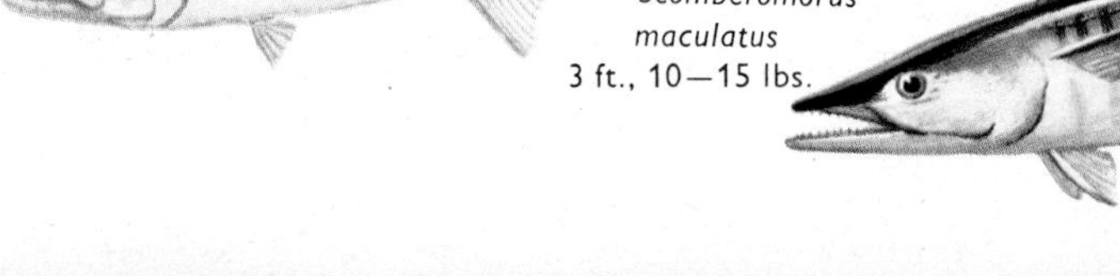

KINGFISH
Scomberomorus maculatus
3 ft., 10—15 lbs.

WAHOO
Acanthocybium solandri
to 6 ft., 135 lbs.

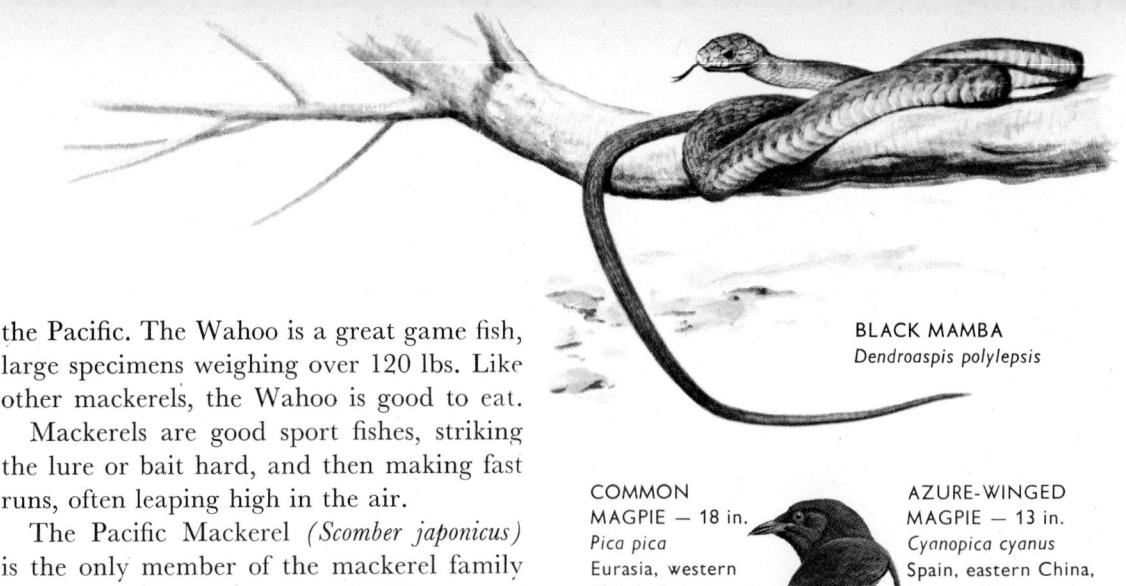

BLACK MAMBA
Dendroaspis polylepsis

the Pacific. The Wahoo is a great game fish, large specimens weighing over 120 lbs. Like other mackerels, the Wahoo is good to eat.

Mackerels are good sport fishes, striking the lure or bait hard, and then making fast runs, often leaping high in the air.

The Pacific Mackerel *(Scomber japonicus)* is the only member of the mackerel family found abundantly along the Pacific coast of North America. It ranges from Mexico northward to Alaska, following warm water and the smaller schooling fishes on which it feeds. Largest runs off the coast of California are in autumn. Commercial fishermen net millions of pounds of these mackerels, which are also becoming increasingly popular catches with sport fishermen.

MACKEREL SHARKS. The two species in this family, the Mako *(Isurus oxyrhincus)* and the Great White Shark *(Carcharodon carcharias)* are the fastest swimmers of their kind. They are compact and cigar-shaped, and pursue fast-swimming mackerel, herring, and, in the case of the Great White Shark, seals and sea-lions. The Mako averages 6 feet, but has been known to reach 12. It weighs from 150 to 1,200 pounds. The Great White Shark averages close to 10 feet and 800 pounds, but has been recorded at 36 feet and 7,100 pounds. Both are considered dangerous. (See SHARKS.)

MAGPIES, members of the crow family, resemble jays in habits and behaviour, but have much longer tails. With their slender, long tails and rather short wings, they are adapted for slipping through thickets and tree branches, rather than for open country. They usually have cup nests, but the Common Magpie adds a thin dome of twigs. Their food is very varied, and most species have a bad reputation where eggs and nestlings are concerned. On the ground, they

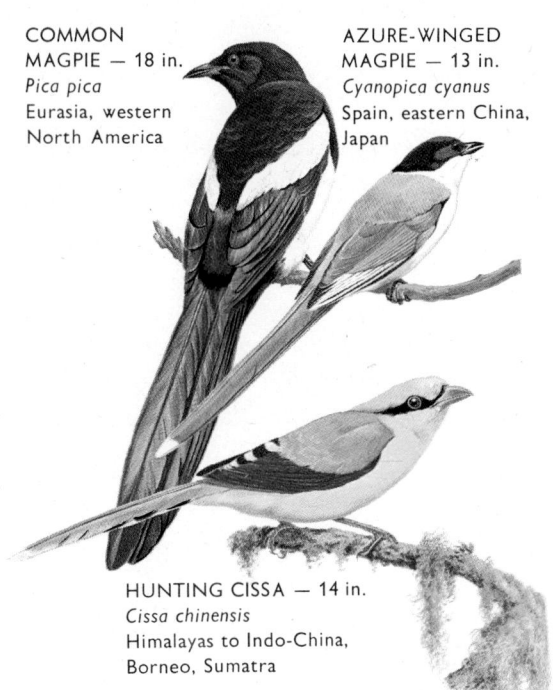

COMMON
MAGPIE — 18 in.
Pica pica
Eurasia, western
North America

AZURE-WINGED
MAGPIE — 13 in.
Cyanopica cyanus
Spain, eastern China,
Japan

HUNTING CISSA — 14 in.
Cissa chinensis
Himalayas to Indo-China,
Borneo, Sumatra

hop and run with tail held rather high, giving them a slightly comical air. The only Magpies in North America are black and yellow-billed forms of the Common Magpie. The Azure-winged Magpie is a species with an odd relict distribution. It is found in Spain, and occurs in Eastern China and Japan, but nowhere in between.

Some eastern Magpies have finer tails, those of the Blue Magpies being twice the length of the body and arched; while the Racket-tailed Magpies are small birds with long tails that widen to a paddle shape at the tip.

MAMBAS *(Dendroaspis spp.)* of Africa are often said to be the most deadly of all snakes. The Black Mamba, largest of the five species,

reaches a length of 14 feet. All mambas are tree-dwellers and have a powerful venom. When startled, a mamba often opens its mouth wide. No more than three or four people are known to have survived a bite from one of these snakes. They are reputedly vicious, but most tales of their ferocity are grossly exaggerated. All mambas have a single, fang-like tooth at the front of each lower jaw, just below the poison fangs of the upper jaw. Mambas belong to the same family as coral snakes and cobras (see CORAL SNAKES; COBRAS; SEA SNAKES).

MAMMALS. Many biologists consider mammals to be the most successful of all animals. Their large brains and superior intelligence account for much of this success. Mammals range in size from 115-ton Blue Whales, the largest of all animals, to tiny Pygmy Shrews, less than an inch long and a tenth of an ounce in weight when full grown. An enormous variety of mammals are known; they live everywhere in the world from open seas to river-banks, and from equatorial deserts to arctic wastelands.

Most people can tell a mammal when they see one, but it is not easy to find clear-cut characteristics that distinguish all mammals from all other animals. For example, mammals are the only animals with hair, yet some, such as whales and dolphins, have only a few hairs. Mammary glands, which supply the young with milk, are found only in mammals, but monotremes (spiny ant-eaters and the Platypus) have only milk-producing pores.

Mammals are often called "animals", but they are only one of about 50 classes of animals. Some mammals are called "beasts",

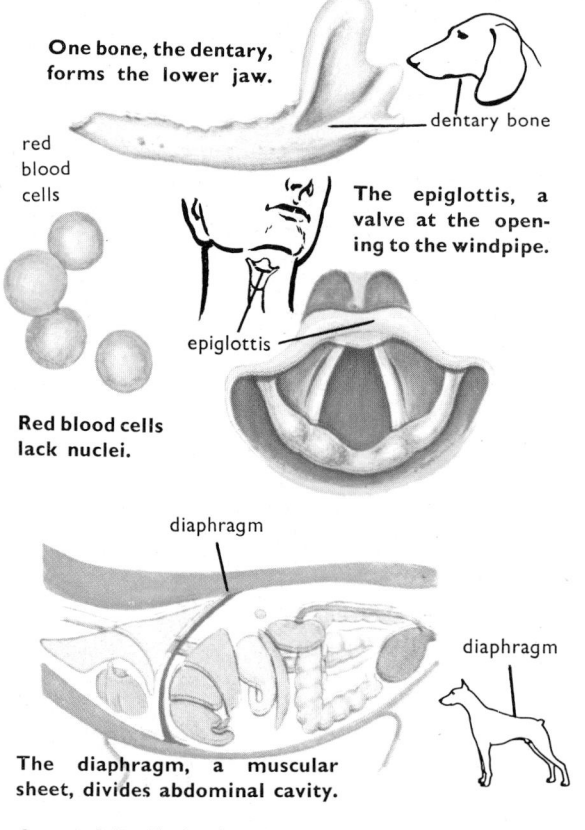

One bone, the dentary, forms the lower jaw.

dentary bone

red blood cells

The epiglottis, a valve at the opening to the windpipe.

epiglottis

Red blood cells lack nuclei.

diaphragm

diaphragm

The diaphragm, a muscular sheet, divides abdominal cavity.

Some of the distinctive characteristics of mammals.

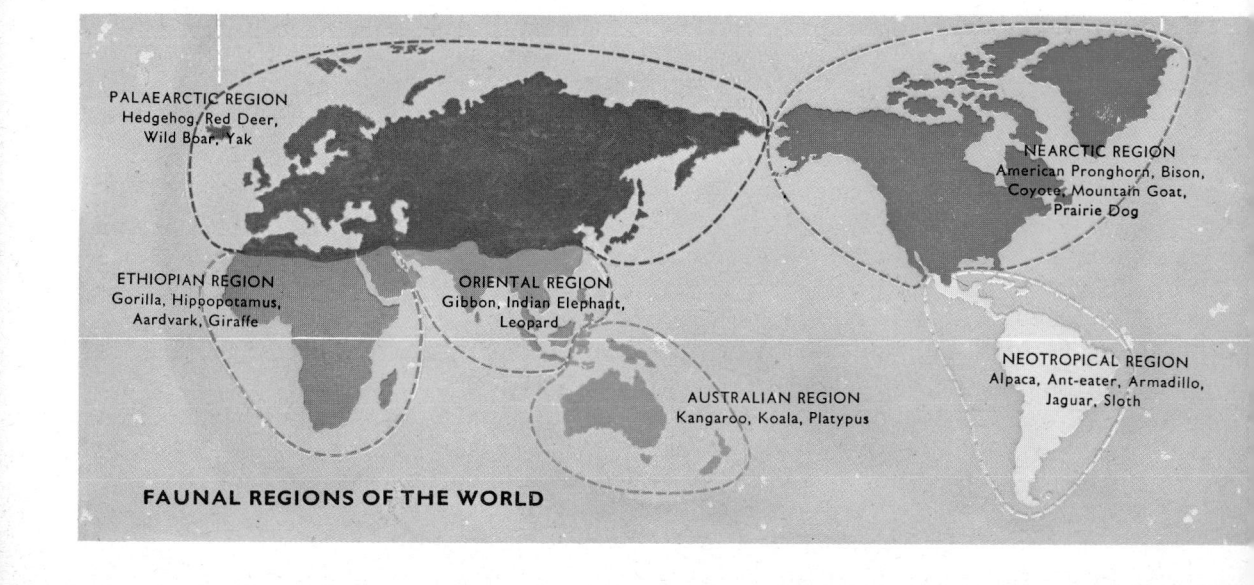

PALAEARCTIC REGION
Hedgehog, Red Deer, Wild Boar, Yak

NEARCTIC REGION
American Pronghorn, Bison, Coyote, Mountain Goat, Prairie Dog

ETHIOPIAN REGION
Gorilla, Hippopotamus, Aardvark, Giraffe

ORIENTAL REGION
Gibbon, Indian Elephant, Leopard

NEOTROPICAL REGION
Alpaca, Ant-eater, Armadillo, Jaguar, Sloth

AUSTRALIAN REGION
Kangaroo, Koala, Platypus

FAUNAL REGIONS OF THE WORLD

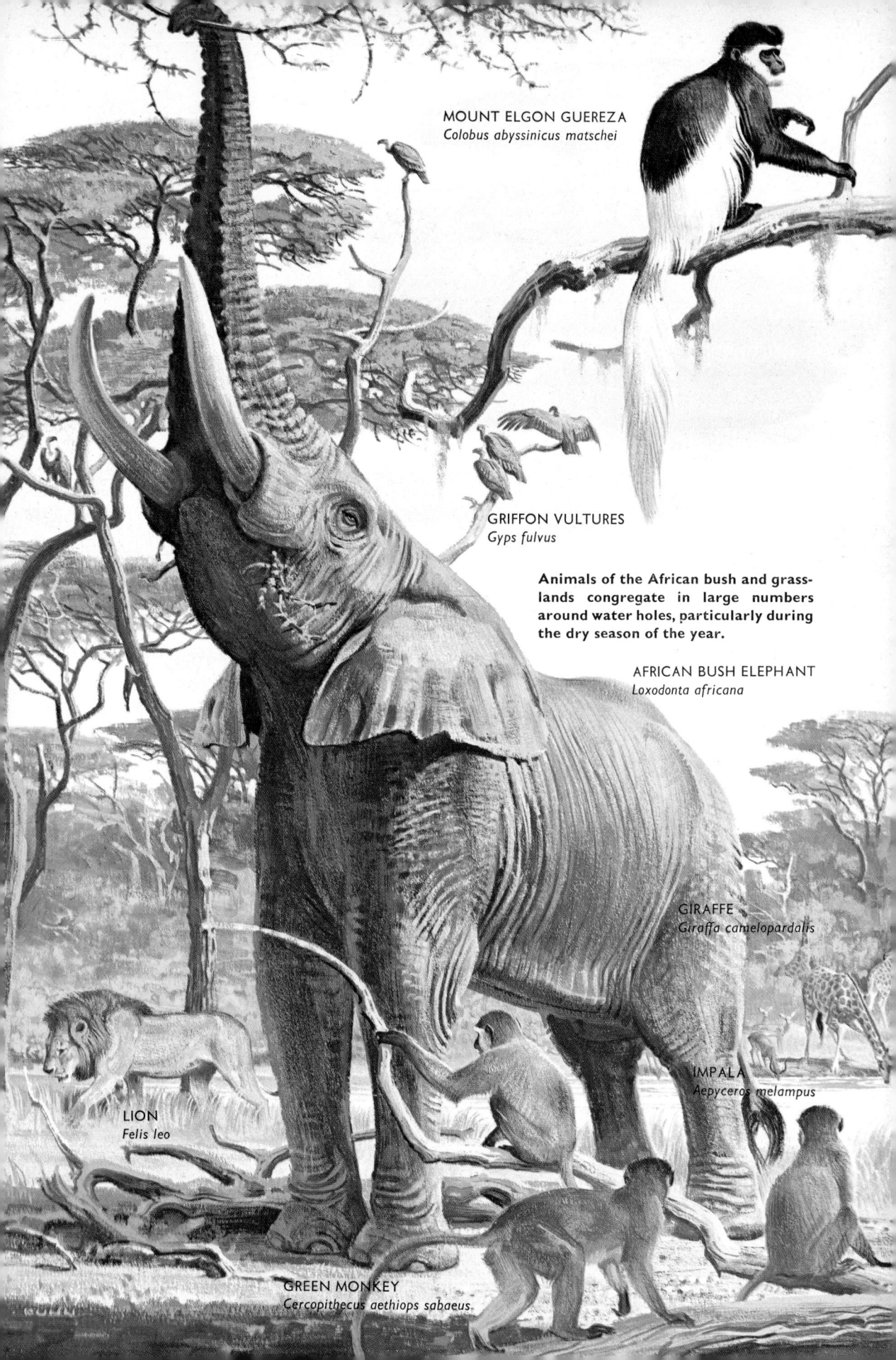

MOUNT ELGON GUEREZA
Colobus abyssinicus matschei

GRIFFON VULTURES
Gyps fulvus

Animals of the African bush and grass-lands congregate in large numbers around water holes, particularly during the dry season of the year.

AFRICAN BUSH ELEPHANT
Loxodonta africana

GIRAFFE
Giraffa camelopardalis

IMPALA
Aepyceros melampus

LION
Felis leo

GREEN MONKEY
Cercopithecus aethiops sabaeus

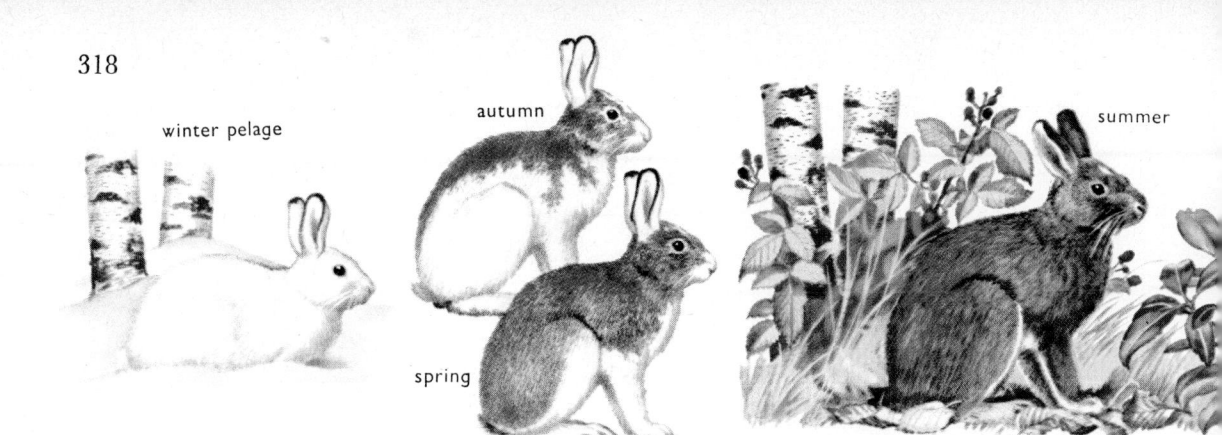

Seasonal changes in the pelt of the Varying Hare, or Snowshoe Rabbit.

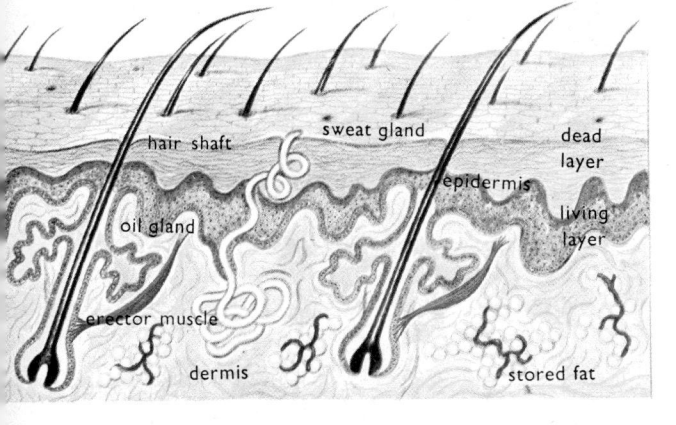

Human skin is similar to that of other mammals. Some mammals have horns, claws, hoofs or nails as skin appendages that form from skin cells.

but this name hardly applies to such mammals as mice, men or whales. "Quadruped" is another name often used for mammals, but it refers only to those that are four-footed. Bats and whales are not four-footed, though their ancestors were.

Some of the obvious features that make mammals different from other animals are: hair; mammary glands; sweat glands; oil glands; three small bones in the middle ear; with a few exceptions, seven neck bones; teeth of different shapes; and a highly developed brain. Mammals also have a valve (epiglottis) guarding the opening to the windpipe; only one bone (dentary) in the lower jaw; and a muscular sheet, or diaphragm, which varies the size of the chest cavity (see illustration).

Mammals differ from birds by having hair and never feathers, in not laying eggs (except monotremes), nearly always in having teeth (birds do not), and in other ways. Mammals

that fly (bats) do not have a large keel on the breastbone, as birds do (see BIRDS).

Mammals differ from reptiles by having hair, not found in reptiles, by not laying eggs (except monotremes), and by being warm-blooded. Mammals also have a four-chambered heart, a single bone in each half of the lower jaw, and teeth of different kinds. Reptiles have none of these.

HAIR and FUR. Mammals are the only animals that have hair. Even those with little or no hair as adults, such as elephants and whales, have some hair before birth.

Each hair is a single shaft growing from a tiny pocket in the skin. The exposed part of the hair is dead. Hence, cutting hair does not cause pain, but pulling a hair by its roots injures living cells and is painful.

After a time the cells at a hair's root stop growing. Soon the hair loosens and is pushed out by a hair coming in from below. In this way hairs are lost (moulted) and replaced by new ones. People who have pet dogs or cats know how regularly they "shed".

Hair or fur colour is due to pigments deposited in the hair. The exact colour is determined by two pigments — either yellow or brown, which may be so heavily deposited that it appears to be black. Colours vary according to where these pigments are deposited in the hair, by the nature of the surface (cuticle) of the hair, and by how much of each pigment is present. Some hairs are of several colours along their length. Most rodents have hairs of this sort, called

"agouti" hairs. Sometimes hairs may lack pigment completely, as in albinos.

Most mammals moult twice a year. In autumn they change to a thick winter coat; in spring, to a lightweight summer coat. This is most obvious in mammals that change their colour, such as the Ermine.

When a mammal's coat, or pelage, changes from one colour to another, the change is not due to a new pigment within the hairs. Since the hairs are dead, their colour cannot be altered after the pigments have been deposited. Only by a moult can a mammal change its hair colour. This occurs gradually over a period of weeks or months.

Moult is brought about principally by changes in the length of day, not by temperature. As days get shorter, there is less light. This indirectly affects the pigment deposited in the developing hair cells. In the Ermine, for example, each new hair has the white winter colour instead of summer brown. When days get longer, the process reverses.

Mammals, as a group, have several kinds of hair. Underhair (or underfur), commonly called wool, is the most abundant. The most valuable furs consist entirely of underfur. Overhair, or guard hairs, are longer, stiffer, and more pointed. They protect the underfur.

Other hairs may be specialised, such as the facial bristles, or whiskers, of cats. These hairs, which serve as "feelers", have sensitive nerve endings at their roots. Some hairs, such as those in a horse's tail, grow to great length and are rarely shed.

Some hairs are so changed that they no longer look like hairs. Spines or "quills", of porcupines and spiny ant-eaters are specialised hairs. The horn on the snout of rhinoceroses is really made of many hairs closely pressed together, as are the "horns" of the Pronghorn.

Biologists can tell some species of mammals from others by their hair structure, particularly by the pattern of the scales on the hairs' outer surface.

SPECIAL GLANDS. Mammary glands are found only in mammals — in fact, it is from the name of these glands that we get the word "mammals". In most mammals, the mammary glands occur in two rows running along the sides of the abdomen.

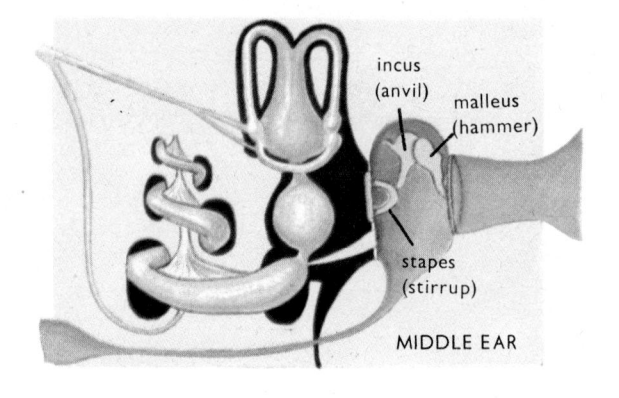

incus (anvil)

malleus (hammer)

stapes (stirrup)

MIDDLE EAR

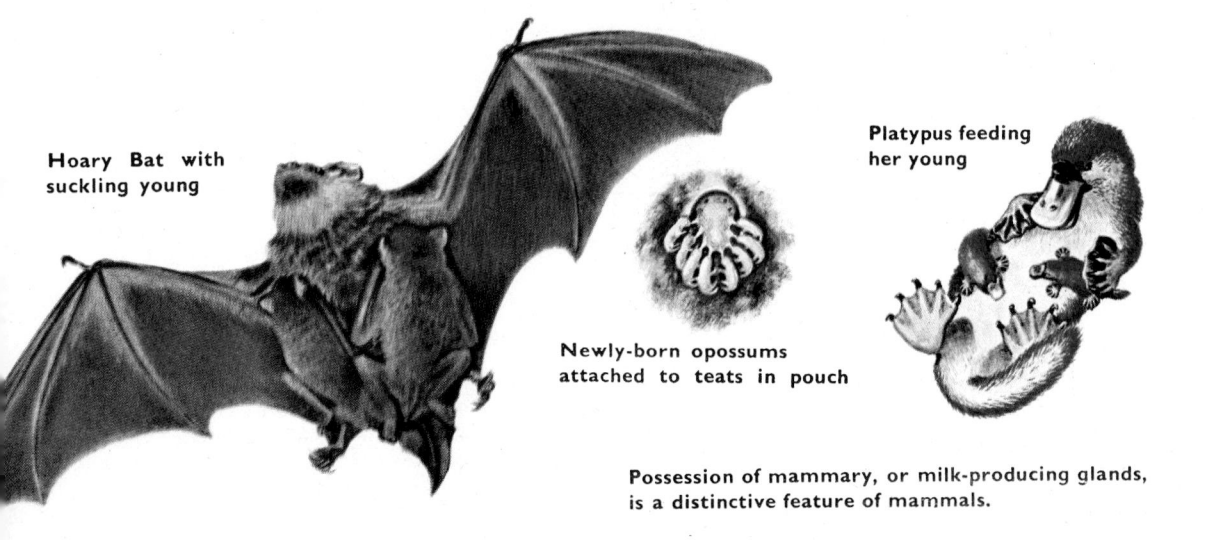

Hoary Bat with suckling young

Platypus feeding her young

Newly-born opossums attached to teats in pouch

Possession of mammary, or milk-producing glands, is a distinctive feature of mammals.

These are called the milk lines, or milk ridges. Numerous glands empty through the same openings into nipples, which may occur anywhere along the milk line, depending on the kind of mammal. For example, opossums may have as many as 15 nipples; some rats have six pairs; bats, whales, elephants, horses and humans have only one pair.

In most large, four-legged mammals, particularly hoofed mammals, the mammary glands are located far to the rear. Often they are close together, forming an enlarged area called an udder. In the pouched mammals, or marsupials, mammary glands are usually located in a pouch on the abdomen. The developing young enter this pouch and become attached to the nipples. In monotremes, milk is secreted from milk pores on to patches of hairs in cup-like hollows near the openings. The young lap up the milk from these hollows and the hairs around them.

Sweat glands are found in most mammals. These simple, tubular glands secrete a watery material on to the surface of the skin. Its evaporation cools the animal. Sweat also contains salt and other wastes from the body.

Oil (or sebaceous) glands are also found with the hairs. These glands secrete an oil that lubricates the skin and hair.

Scent glands give many kinds of mammals their characteristic smell or odour. Some scent glands produce odours which attract other mammals of the same kind; this may bring males and females together for mating. Other mammals, such as skunks and weasels, have repellent odours.

SKELETON. A mammal's skeleton puts it in the same great group (the vertebrates) with fishes, frogs, reptiles and birds. Compared to most other backboned animals, mammals have fewer bones, especially in the skull. For example, there is only one bone — the dentary — in the lower jaw. Nearly all mammals have seven bones (vertebrae) in their neck. This is true of long-necked giraffes and of short-necked whales. You have 206 bones in your body; much the same number of bones as in a mouse or an elephant.

Mammals — and only mammals — have three bones in the middle ear. These three bones (called the stirrup, anvil and hammer) transmit sound waves from the eardrum through the middle ear to the inner ear.

Horns and antlers, used for protection or to help get food, are special outgrowths. Horns are not branched, and form as a horny material, similar to your fingernails, over bony cores growing out from the skull. They

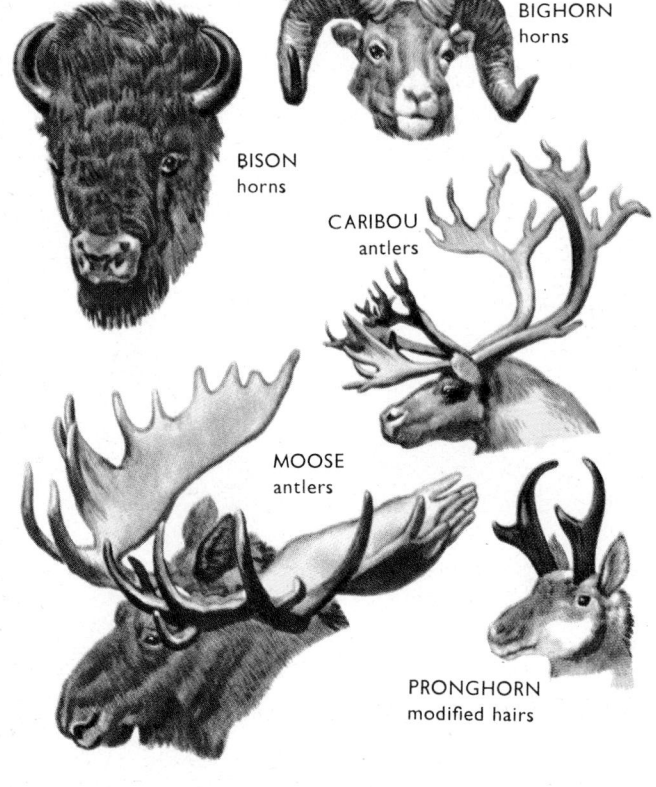

BIGHORN horns

BISON horns

CARIBOU antlers

MOOSE antlers

PRONGHORN modified hairs

STRUCTURE AND GROWTH OF ANTLERS

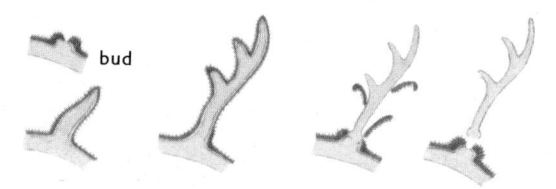

bud

antler in velvet   antler losing velvet   shed antler

Antlers begin as buds on the surface of the skull. They grow outwards as spongy tissue that calcifies, or hardens, into bone when fully developed. Velvet, a soft covering over the growing antler, contains a net of blood vessels. Antlers are shed close to the skull, each leaving a base from which a new antler will develop the following year.

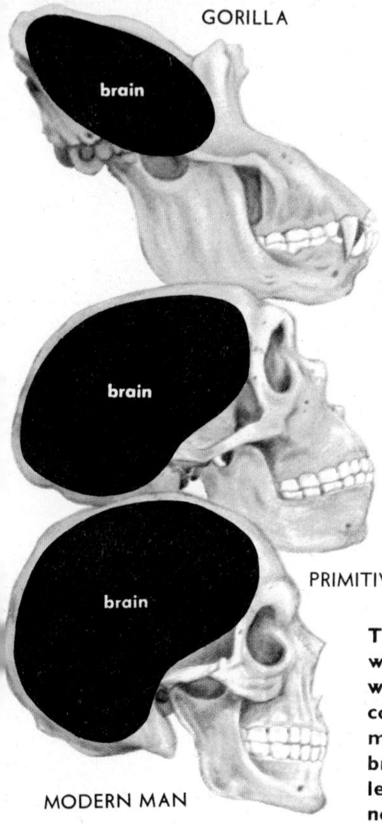

GORILLA

brain

brain

PRIMITIVE MAN

brain

MODERN MAN

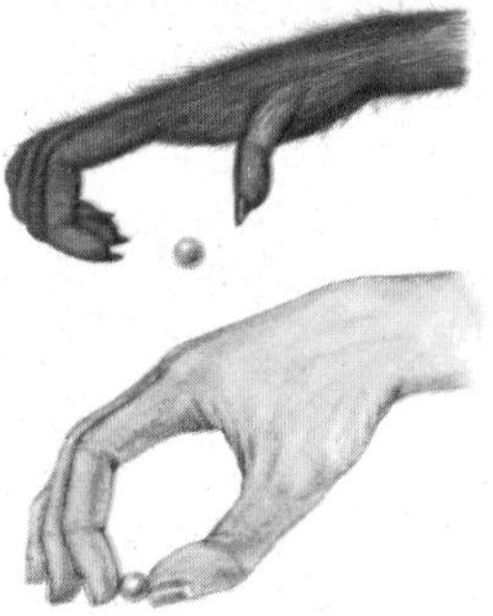

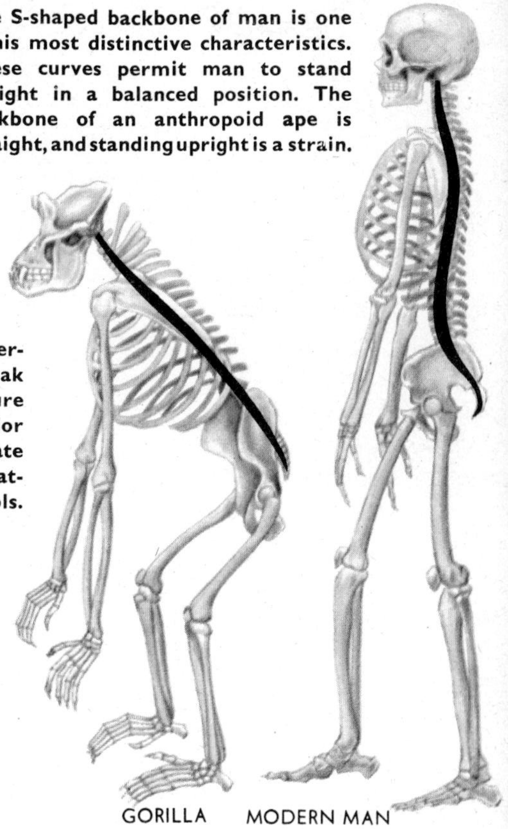

The S-shaped backbone of man is one of his most distinctive characteristics. These curves permit man to stand upright in a balanced position. The backbone of an anthropoid ape is straight, and standing upright is a strain.

The opposable thumb, a characteristic of all primates, reaches its peak of development in man. This feature provided man with a superior ability to grasp and to manipulate objects, and thus contributed greatly to his skill in the use of tools.

These skulls compare modern man with an extinct, primitive man and with the gorilla, a less advanced but contemporary primate. Modern man has a larger cranial capacity or brain volume. His brow ridges are less prominent; his lower jaw does not protrude in the same way.

GORILLA   MODERN MAN

increase in size each year and are not shed. Cows, sheep, goats, bison and antelopes have hollow horns of this type. Giraffes also have stubby horns which are covered with skin throughout their life.

Antlers are solid, bony growths from the skull, and they are shed each year. New antlers are formed annually under a layer of living skin, called velvet. When antlers reach their full growth for the year, the skin dies and peels off, leaving the bony antlers exposed. With a few exceptions, all male deer have antlers; females lack them, except for the Caribou and Reindeer.

TEETH. Mammals have four kinds of teeth: incisors, canines, premolars, and molars. Birds have no teeth, and reptiles have only one kind. Most mammals have two sets of teeth during their lives — milk teeth and permanent teeth. All except the molars appear first as milk teeth, then are pushed out and replaced by a permanent set. There

is only one set of molars, however. Marsupial mammals are exceptions, for they have only one set of teeth during their lives. Several kinds of mammals — spiny ant-eaters and pangolins, for example — have lost their teeth in the course of evolution, though their

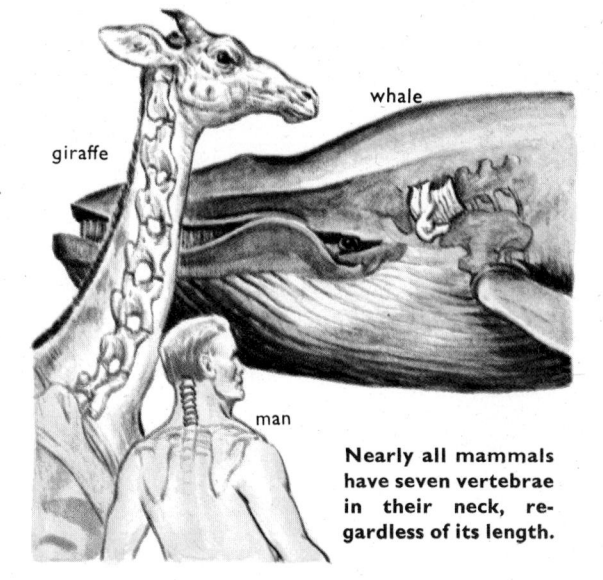

Nearly all mammals have seven vertebrae in their neck, regardless of its length.

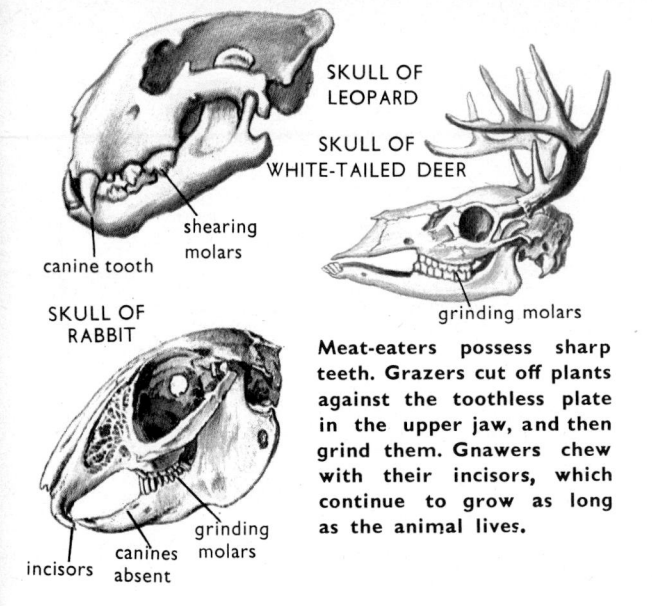

SKULL OF
LEOPARD

SKULL OF
WHITE-TAILED DEER

shearing
molars

canine tooth

grinding molars

SKULL OF
RABBIT

grinding molars

incisors

canines
absent

Meat-eaters possess sharp teeth. Grazers cut off plants against the toothless plate in the upper jaw, and then grind them. Gnawers chew with their incisors, which continue to grow as long as the animal lives.

direct-line ancestors definitely had teeth.

Since different kinds of mammals have different numbers of incisors, canines, premolars or molars, a "dental formula" can be determined for each kind of mammal. This helps zoologists to identify and classify mammals. When all teeth are present, an adult human being has in the upper jaw four incisors, two canines, four premolars and six molars. Thus, in *each half* of the upper jaw, are two incisors, one canine, two premolars and three molars. This is written in a dental formula as 2-1-2-3.

A typical tooth consists of dentine, or "ivory", covered by a layer of very hard enamel. Frequently, a material called cement covers the roots and the sides of the tooth.

Some teeth continue to grow throughout the life of the mammal. This is true of the gnawing incisors of rodents and rabbits, and

also the tusks of elephants. These teeth never wear out as long as the mammal lives.

The teeth of mammals are adapted to special uses. Some are elongated into fangs, as in the Sabre-toothed Cat and the Musk Deer. Some teeth are thin and blade-like for cutting, as in most meat-eating mammals. Others are flattened for grinding, as in mammals that feed on grass and leaves.

BRAIN Mammals have better-developed brains than any other animals. Two parts, the cerebrum and the cerebellum, are so greatly enlarged that they actually make up most of the volume of the brain.

The cerebrum is wrinkled and convoluted, except in primitive mammals such as the monotremes, marsupials, moles and shrews, and some rodents. These cerebral furrows increase many times the total surface area of the cerebrum. Its outer covering, or cortex, is the brain's grey matter and is most complex in monkeys, apes and man. Nerve endings for intelligence or learning are located in this grey matter. The cerebrum also controls memory, the senses and voluntary actions.

The enlarged cerebellum, or hindbrain, located just in front of the spinal cord, controls muscular co-ordination and balance, which are involuntary or automatic actions.

In general, the larger the brain compared to the total size of the mammal, the more intelligent the mammal is.

REPRODUCTION. The tiny egg of the mammal is retained within the body of the

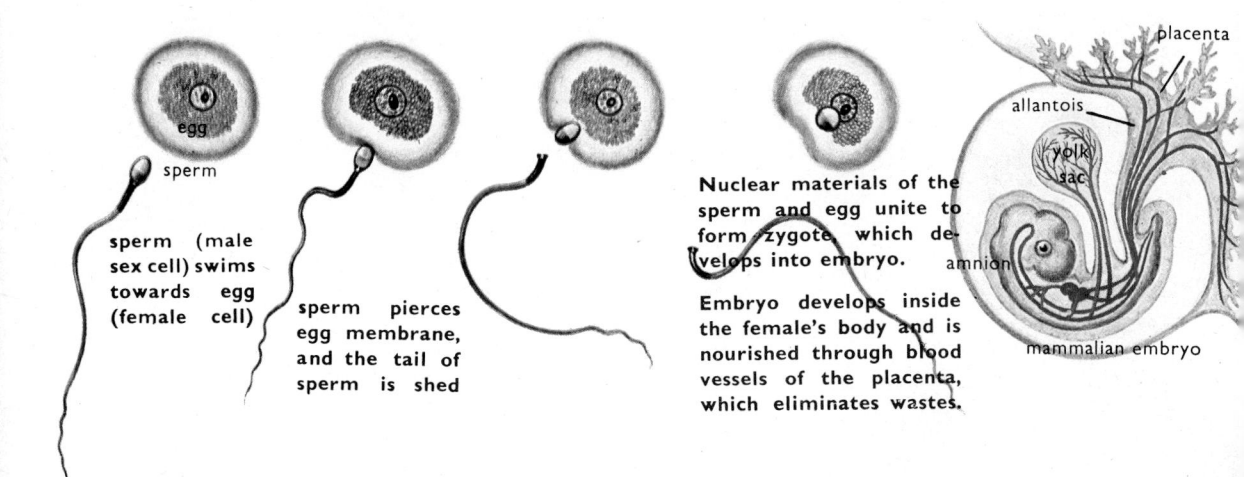

egg

sperm

sperm (male sex cell) swims towards egg (female cell)

sperm pierces egg membrane, and the tail of sperm is shed

Nuclear materials of the sperm and egg unite to form zygote, which develops into embryo.

Embryo develops inside the female's body and is nourished through blood vessels of the placenta, which eliminates wastes.

placenta

allantois

yolk sac

amnion

mammalian embryo

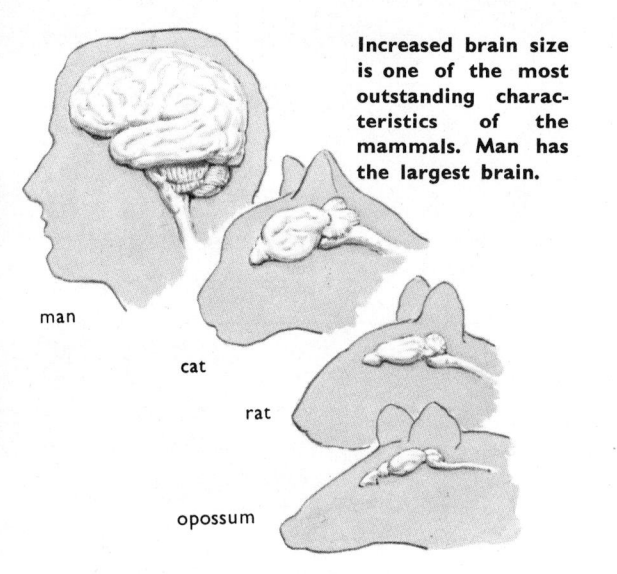

Increased brain size is one of the most outstanding characteristics of the mammals. Man has the largest brain.

man

cat

rat

opossum

female. The male introduces sperms into the female, and one sperm unites with the egg, fertilising it. The egg then grows to form an embryo within the uterus. In most mammals the embryo has a placenta, through which it receives nourishment. When it is born, the mammal may still be weak and helpless. For a time after its birth, a young mammal is fed milk secreted by the female's mammary glands. Young mammals are cared for until able to care for themselves.

In only one group, the monotremes, the egg develops externally. Monotremes' eggs are covered with a leathery shell, like the eggs of many reptiles.

The young of pouched mammals, or marsupials, are born after a short period of development within the uterus. Immature young crawl along the abdomen to the pouch, or marsupium, where each attaches by its mouth to a nipple. There they continue to develop while they suckle in the pouch.

The time required for a mammal to develop and be born is called its gestation period, sometime quite short. Opossums, for example, are born in 9 to 13 days. Elephants take as long as 22 months.

Many mammals give birth to only a single young. Bats, whales, elephants and monkeys are examples. Others have twelve or more young at birth, as do opossums, pigs, and certain mice and rats. Some armadillos always have four young, all of the same sex.

Care given to the young reaches its peak in the apes and, most notably man. Many mammals build elaborate dens and nests in which they rear their offspring. Beavers, tree squirrels and foxes are examples. A few, like most bats, provide no homes at all. Some mammals keep the young together in a family group during a training period. After a time, some mammals drive their young away from the "home" and force them to fare for themselves.

HIBERNATION. Mammals are "warm-blooded" animals. Their body temperatures do not go up and down with the temperature of their surroundings, as do the body temperatures of reptiles, amphibians and

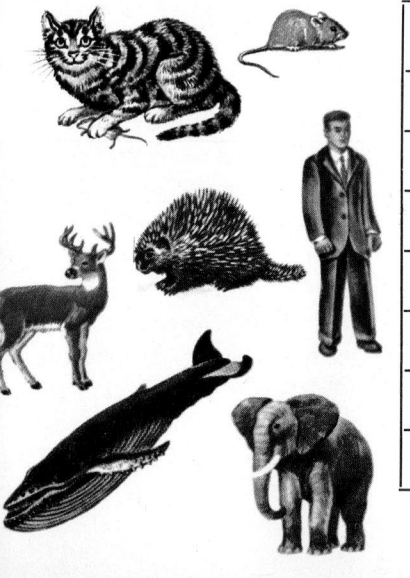

	Period of Development Before Birth	Average Number of Young
HOUSE MOUSE	19 days	5—7
HOUSE-CAT	2 months	4—6
PORCUPINE	2 months	2—4
DEER	8 months	1—3
MAN	9 months	1
WHALE	10—12 months	1
INDIAN ELEPHANT	22 months	1

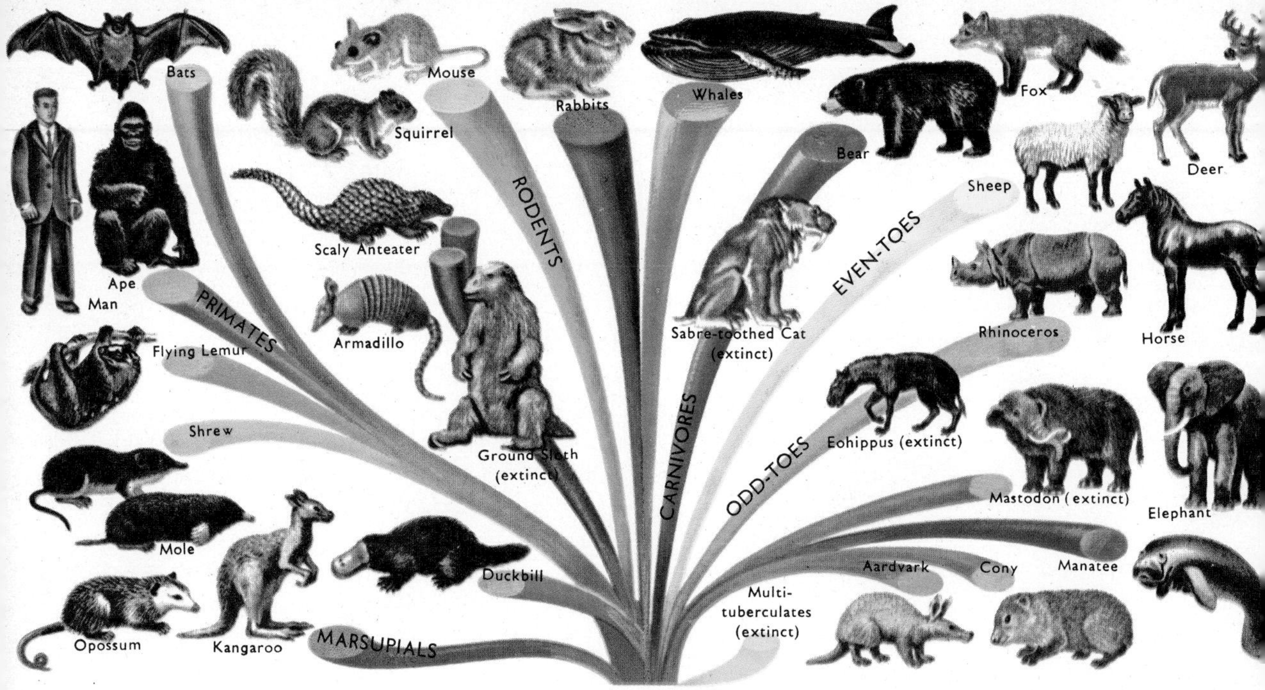

The illustration at the top shows a family tree of mammals with labeled animals: Bats, Mouse, Rabbits, Whales, Fox, Squirrel, Bear, Deer, Sheep, Scaly Anteater, RODENTS, EVEN-TOES, Man, Ape, Armadillo, Rhinoceros, Horse, Flying Lemur, PRIMATES, Sabre-toothed Cat (extinct), CARNIVORES, ODD-TOES, Eohippus (extinct), Shrew, Ground Sloth (extinct), Mastodon (extinct), Elephant, Mole, Aardvark, Cony, Manatee, Duckbill, Multituberculates (extinct), Opossum, Kangaroo, MARSUPIALS.

FAMILY TREE OF MAMMALS

All mammals are believed to be descended from a reptilian ancestor. Major modifications of this ancestral stock include hairy skin, warm blood, live birth of the young, and the development of mammary glands.

fishes. Most mammals have a constant temperature of about 98 degrees Fahrenheit. Man's body temperature is 98.6 degrees.

Certain mammals, however, can permit their body temperatures to drop close to the temperature of their surroundings. This

	Heartbeat	Breathing Rate	Temperature
Normal	80 per min.	25 per min.	97°F
Hibernation	4 per min.	1 in 5 min.	37°F

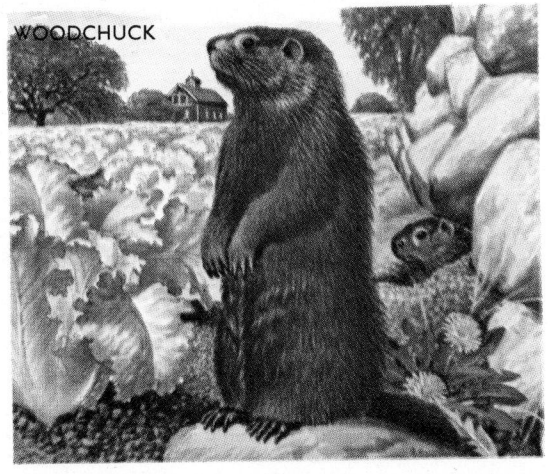

WOODCHUCK

Woodchucks are true hibernators; their heartbeat, breathing rate and temperature decrease, as above.

occurs during hibernation, a period of "deep sleep" during the cold weather.

Hibernation is really more than a deep sleep. While the animal's temperature is lowered, all of its body processes are also slowed down, including its heartbeat and its rate of breathing. A woodchuck's heart normally beats about 80 times per minute; in hibernation, about 4 times per minute. A woodchuck's average rate of breathing is 25 to 30 times per minute; in hibernation it takes only 1 breath every 5 minutes. Its normal temperature is 97 degrees Fahrenheit, in hibernation, about 37 degrees.

Mammals that hibernate do so for a good reason. In winter, the food they eat is not available. If these mammals were active in winter, they would die of starvation. Insect-eating bats of temperate zones can find no insects during the cold winter months. They must either migrate far enough south, where insects are active all the winter, or go into hibernation. By hibernating, they reduce the speed at which they use fat stored in their bodies.

In the weeks before an animal goes into hibernation, it stores large quantities of

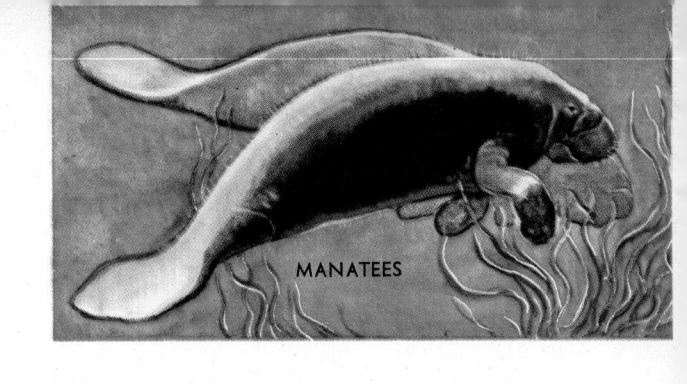

MANATEES

fat in its body. Then, as the time of hibernation approaches, the animal becomes less and less active. Most rodents that hibernate make special chambers in the ground. They roll up into balls inside nests of fur, grass or leaves in these underground chambers. In all hibernating chambers, whether nests in the ground or in caves, it has to be cool, but the temperature must remain above freezing. Temperatures below freezing cause the formation of ice crystals in the blood, and result in death.

Among mammals that are true hibernators are woodchucks, jumping mice, dormice, certain ground squirrels, hamsters, hedgehogs, and those bats that do not migrate south in winter. No carnivores, including bears and raccoons, are known to hibernate. These animals may become inactive in winter, but they do not truly hibernate. Their body temperatures are not greatly lowered, and their rate of breathing and heartbeats remain about the same as normal.

MANATEES, or Sea Cows (*Trichechus* spp. *)*, are large, nearly hairless aquatic mammals. They move sluggishly, feeding on water plants in the shallow coastal waters of bays, lagoons, and estuaries in tropical parts of the Atlantic Ocean. Manatees can remain below water for about 4 minutes, then they must surface to breathe. The forelegs are modified into flippers or paddles; the hind legs

Bears sleep in winter, but are not true hibernators.

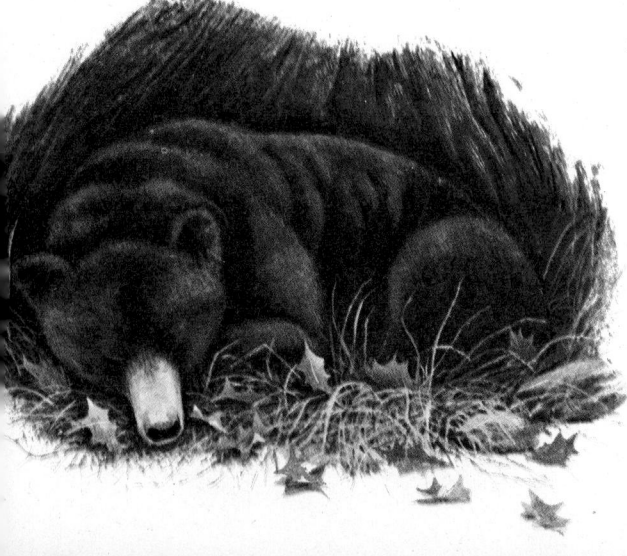

are entirely absent, bodies end in a broad, flat tail. Manatees may be 6 feet long and weigh as much as 400 pounds. Their single young is born in a sheltered lagoon, and it can swim almost immediately.

Dugongs *(Dugong dugon)* are sea cows that live in the Red Sea, — the Indian and western Pacific oceans. They feed on seaweed. The males have tusks up to 10 inches long. Dugongs, despite their ugly appearance, are the animals believed to have been responsible for the mermaid myth.

MANTIS SHRIMPS are not related to true shrimps. In fact, they do not resemble any other crustaceans. Their peculiar front claws are armed with long, curved spines. These claws cannot pinch, but are used to

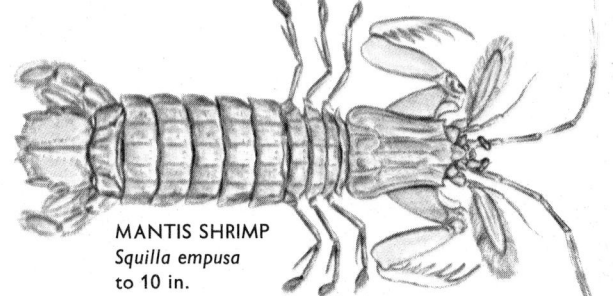

MANTIS SHRIMP
Squilla empusa
to 10 in.

impale or to cut in two small shrimps and fish. Mantis Shrimps are the most voracious of all invertebrate predators. Because of their striking ability, they are often called "thumb splitters" and are dangerous to handle. Some reach a length of only 2 to 3 inches and crawl or glide about among rocks and clumps of seaweed. Others grow to a length of 12 inches or more and live in deep, round holes. Due to their slinking movements, the mantis shrimps are sometimes likened to tigers. They lurk with

the head and claws outstretched, waiting for unwary creatures to come close. Common Atlantic species are *Pseudosquilla ciliata*, *Squilla empusa* and *Lysiosquilla scabricauda*. *Pseudosquilla bigelowi* lives in shallow water in the Pacific. The larvae are eaten by fish.

MARLINS and Sail-fishes belong to the same family and are easily recognised by their "spears". Swordfish *(Xiphias gladius)* — also "billed" fish — belong to a related family. The long extensions of their snouts are round in marlins and sail-fishes, and flattened like the blade of a sword in the Swordfish. Occasionally, an angered fish will ram a boat or some other object in the sea. They have been known to drive their sharp bills through planks three or four inches thick. Marlins and sail-fishes have sharp, thorn-like scales. Swordfish have no scales as adults.

These large fish are sought by sport fishermen. When hooked, they surge from the sea in leap after leap, shaking violently as they try to get free. Battles with these big fish may last hours, as the fish will

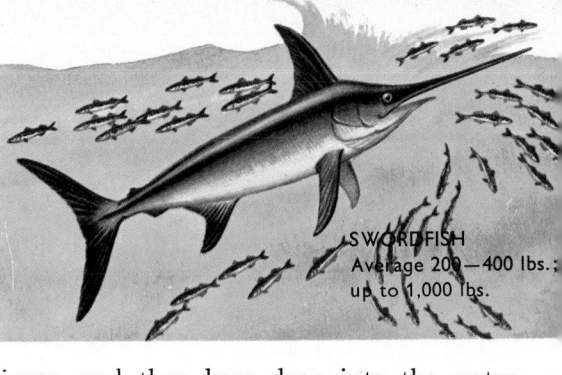

SWORDFISH
Average 200—400 lbs.;
up to 1,000 lbs.

jump and then bore deep into the water.

One method of distinguishing these three fishes is by their dorsal fins. If the fin is high and about the same height as its full length, it is a sail-fish. If the fin consists of a single, tall lobe, it is a swordfish.

White Marlins *(Makaira albida)* live in the Gulf of Mexico, and abundantly in the Atlantic as far north as Massachusetts; the smallest of the marlins, they rarely weigh more than 125 pounds. Blue Marlins *(Makaira nigricans ampla)* are much larger. They are found in the same territory, but are more common in the Caribbean, farther south. Many also occur off the coast of Europe and Africa. Specimens weighing 2,000 pounds have been netted.

The Striped Marlin *(Makaira audax)* occurs in the Pacific, off the coasts of the United States, Japan and China. The Black Marlin *(Makaira nigricans)* is even larger. A 1,560-pound Black Marlin was caught off the coast of Peru, but they are more common, in the Antipodes.

Sail-fishes are found both in the Atlantic and the Pacific. These are the most beautiful of the "speared" fishes. Pacific Sail-fishes *(Istiophorus greyi)* average 100 pounds in

COMPARISON OF BILLS AND DORSAL FINS

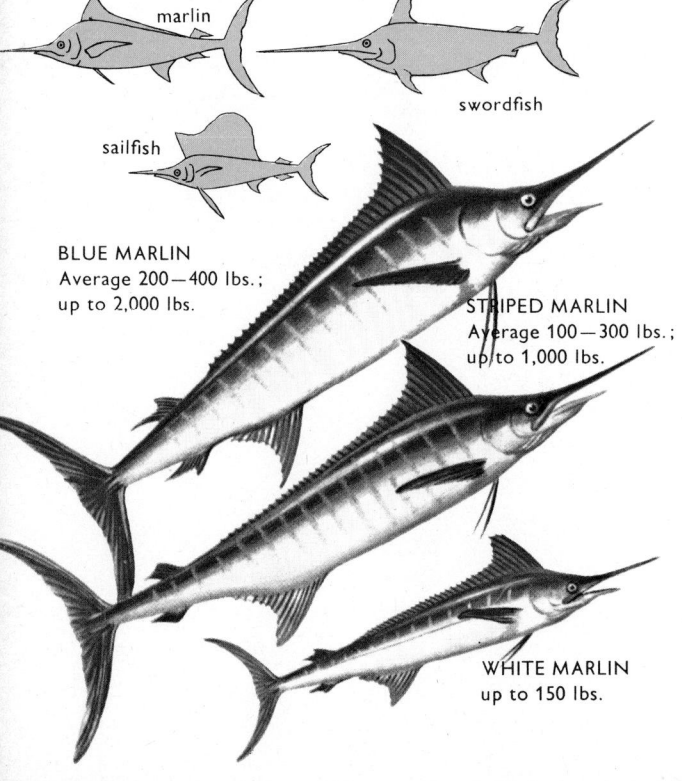

marlin

swordfish

sailfish

BLUE MARLIN
Average 200—400 lbs.;
up to 2,000 lbs.

STRIPED MARLIN
Average 100—300 lbs.;
up to 1,000 lbs.

WHITE MARLIN
up to 150 lbs.

MARMOT
Marmotta marmotta

weight, twice as much as the Atlantic Sail-fish *(Istiophorus albicans)*. These fishes often swim close to the shore, commonly in pairs. For this reason they are seen more often than the marlins, which are open-sea dwellers. Like marlins, sail-fishes are caught by trolling small fish as bait or by using large-sized artificial lures. When tra-velling fast, sail-fishes fold their high dorsal fin into a slot on their back.

Swordfish roam deep, hot seas through-out the world. Their great "swords" are nearly a third as long as their bodies, and their high dorsal fins protrude from the water as they cruise along close to the surface. Commercial fishermen also fish for Swordfish, which are highly prized as food. They are usually taken by a harpoon, rather than a hook and line.

MARMOTS are very large ground squirrels. They feed on grasses or grains, and either dig burrows themselves or use burrows made by other animals. They are active above the ground during daylight hours. In winter they usually hibernate.

The Yellow-bellied Marmot *(Marmota flaviventris)*, which has yellowish fur on its belly, occurs in the mountains and mountain valleys of the north-western United States; it prefers rocky areas. The Hoary Marmot *(Marmota caligata)*, so-named because the tips of its hairs are frosted with white, lives

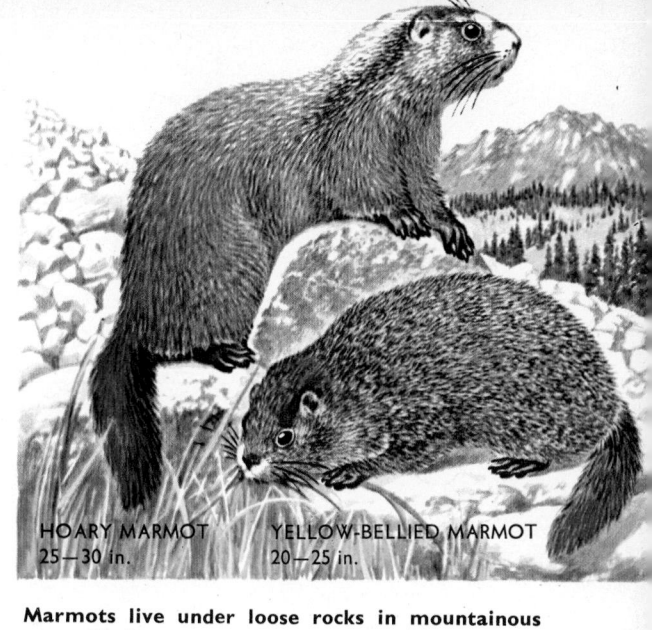

HOARY MARMOT
25—30 in.
YELLOW-BELLIED MARMOT
20—25 in.

Marmots live under loose rocks in mountainous areas. Their calls are shrill, piercing whistles.

from the north-western United States north-ward into Canada and Alaska.

The Woodchuck, or Groundhog *(Marmota monax)*, is native to the eastern United States and much of Canada. It often sits erect on the mound at the entrance to its burrow. Woodchucks are leanest when they emerge from hibernation in early spring. Two to six young are born in April or May. These must be sufficiently fat by late autumn to be ready to hibernate for four months or longer.

Marmots also live in the mountainous regions of Europe and Asia. The Alpine Marmot occurs in the Alps eastward into Siberia, the Bobak Marmot in the Hima-layas, and still others in Mongolia. (See GROUND SQUIRRELS; MAMMALS; and SQUIRRELS.)

MARTENS *(Martes spp.)* have long been sought for their exceedingly valuable fur. Related to the weasels, martens spend much time running and leaping through the trees with great agility. Their range in the New and Old World is closely correlated with pine forests. Most species are about two feet long. They feed on small birds and rodents, and the Red Squirrel is their most common prey. Sables from Siberia are closely related to martens.

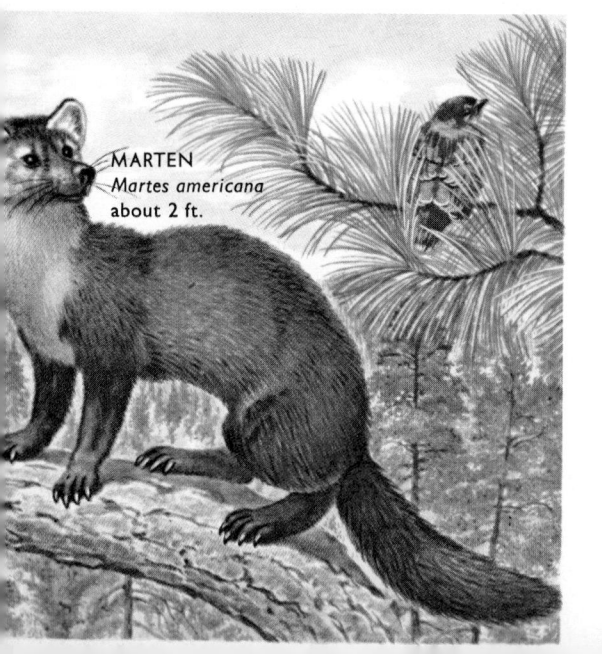

MARTEN
Martes americana
about 2 ft.

MAYFLIES *(Ephemeroptera)* are small to medium-sized insects with delicate wings that contain many veins. Their triangular-shaped front wings are large, their hind wings much smaller or absent. Adults have greatly reduced mouth-parts and do not feed during their short lives. In some the legs are so greatly reduced that they are useless, and the insects spend their whole life flying. Some live as adults for only a few hours or days.

Swarms of many hundreds of adult mayflies are often seen on their mating flights near bodies of water. Females usually lay their eggs at dusk. Some scatter a few eggs at a time on the surface of the water; others drop their eggs in a mass. Females of some species crawl under the water and deposit their eggs beneath stones.

Most mayfly nymphs have three long tails and a series of gills along the sides of their body. Nymphs of nearly all of the 1,000 species feed on vegetation and take up to three years to complete development. When prepared to transform, a

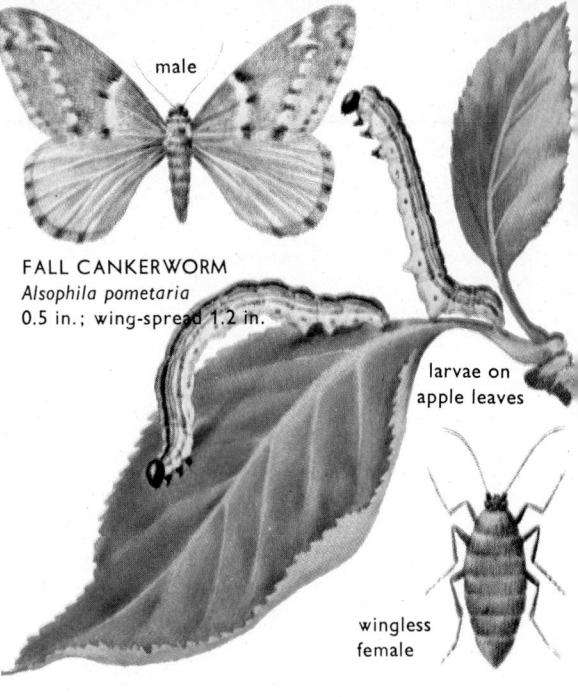

FALL CANKERWORM
Alsophila pometaria
0.5 in.; wing-spread 1.2 in.

male

larvae on apple leaves

wingless female

Mayfly nymphs are abundant in fresh-water lakes and streams, providing important food for fishes.

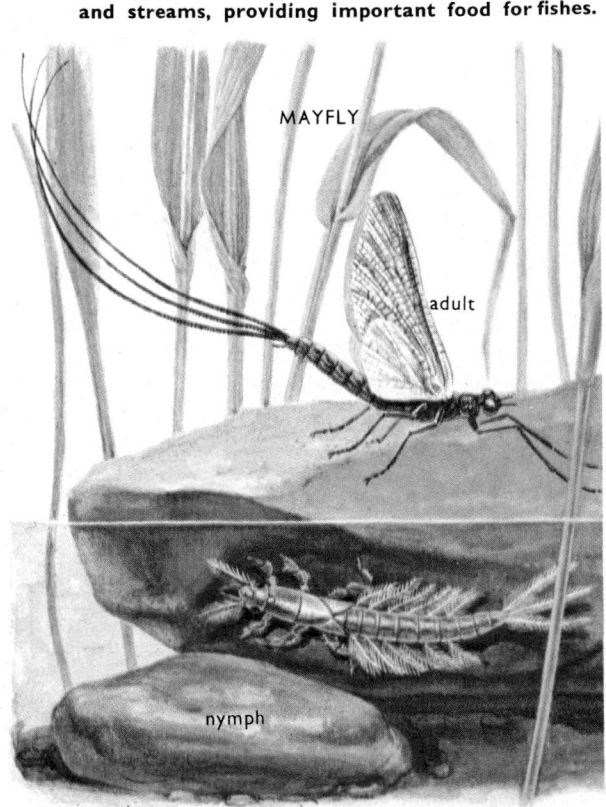

MAYFLY

adult

nymph

nymph crawls out of the water and emerges from its skin as a winged form called a subimago. Usually, within 24 hours, the subimago moults again to become an adult. These are the only insects that moult after their wings are functional.

MEASURING-WORMS are named for their peculiar type of locomotion. These caterpillars have the typical three pairs of thoracic legs, but usually have only two or three pairs of prolegs, and these are located at the end of the abdomen. The caterpillars crawl by lifting the hind end of their body and placing it close to the front. The middle of the body forms a loop. Then they let go with their thoracic legs and move the front end of the body forward. This "looping" type of movement can be done rapidly. When they are disturbed, some measuring-worms hold on with their prolegs and stretch their body out rigidly so that they look like twigs, which they also resemble in colour.

Moths of most of the several thousand species of measuring-worms range in size from $\frac{1}{2}$ to $1\frac{1}{2}$ inches across their wings. They are generally shades of brown or grey, often delicately patterned. The family *(Geometridae)* contains many destructive

species, such as canker-worms. Two notable species, the Spring Canker-worm and Fall Canker-worm, are common in the United States. Both attack a number of kinds of fruit and shade trees and have similar life histories. The Spring Canker-worm, spends the winter in the pupa stage; the Fall Canker-worm winters in the egg stage. Females of both species are wingless.

A common British species is the Winter Moth, the larvae of which attack the foliage of fruit trees in Spring. The females are wingless and it is to prevent them from crawling up the trunks to lay eggs on the leaves that the trunks of fruit trees are grease-banded in the autumn.

MEXICAN CONE-NOSED TOADS (*Rhinophrynus*)

are swollen-bodied, short-legged, three-inch toads that live in the grassy, tropical lowlands of Mexico. On their large hind feet are big, callous-like projections used for digging burrows, for these toads live almost exclusively underground. They are rarely seen, except during and after heavy rains, when they emerge and congregate about flood waters. There the males sing with a curious loud call. Their heads are narrow and pointed, their bodies large and flabby, like round bags of water. Their food consists of termites and ants. The tongue of Mexican cone-nosed toads is attached at the rear of the small mouth, as in mammals and birds. An African toad (*Werneria*) also has its tongue attached at the rear of its mouth, but the tongue of all other frogs and toads is either absent or is attached at the front of the mouth. (See AMPHIBIANS; FROGS; TOADS.)

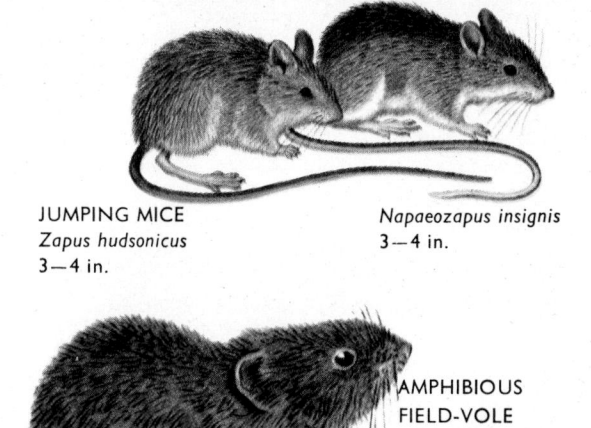

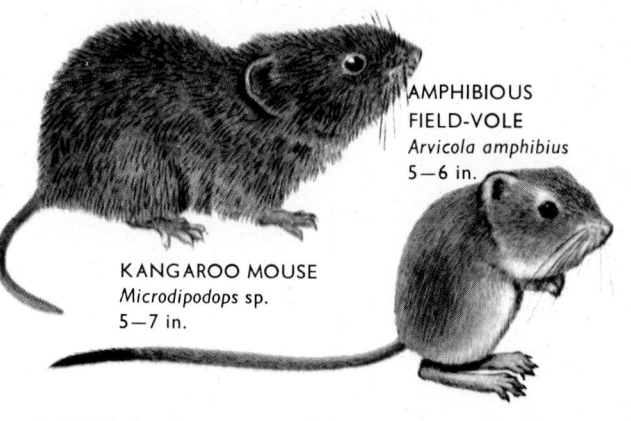

JUMPING MICE
Zapus hudsonicus
3—4 in.

Napaeozapus insignis
3—4 in.

AMPHIBIOUS FIELD-VOLE
Arvicola amphibius
5—6 in.

KANGAROO MOUSE
Microdipodops sp.
5—7 in.

MICE is the name given to a multitude of small rodents. Some kinds live in houses; others on the ground, under the ground, or even entirely in trees. Nearly all feed on such vegetable matter as grasses, seeds and fruits. A few eat insects, and many will feed on meat when it is available.

White-footed mice (*Peromyscus* spp.) are probably the best known wild mice in North America. There are many kinds, found from deserts to heavily-wooded areas and only rarely in houses. Slightly larger than house mice, they have much larger eyes and whitish hair on their feet and underparts. They nest in logs, trees, under rocks, or in similar protected spots, sometimes entering houses in winter. They may have more than one litter a year. Several species of field mice found in Europe and Asia are similar in appearance and habits to the North American white-footed mice, though not closely related.

Meadow mice, or voles (*Microtus* spp.), occur throughout the Northern Hemisphere. They have short tails, dense fur, and short ears. Large numbers of young are born each year in several litters. They eat grass, and also use grass to build their nests. When abundant — several hundred mice per acre — they damage fields and orchards.

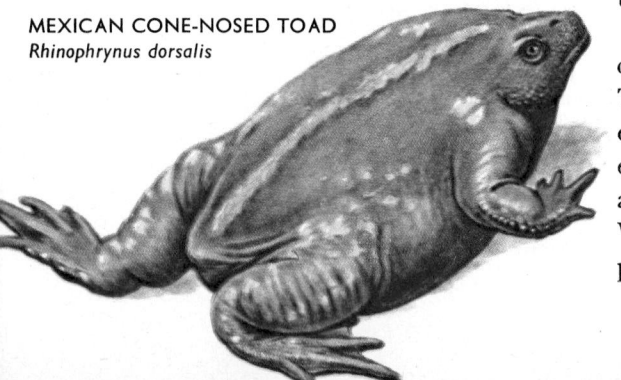

MEXICAN CONE-NOSED TOAD
Rhinophrynus dorsalis

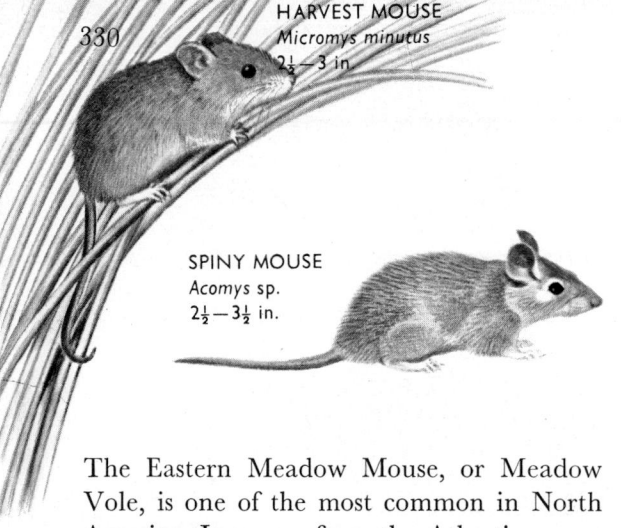

HARVEST MOUSE
Micromys minutus
2½—3 in

SPINY MOUSE
Acomys sp.
2½—3½ in.

The Eastern Meadow Mouse, or Meadow Vole, is one of the most common in North America. It ranges from the Atlantic across the northern United States and Canada into Alaska, and prefers grassy fields or woodland prairies. A similar species is the Field Vole, which ranges from England across Europe to eastern Siberia.

Both the desert kangaroo mice *(Microdipodops* spp.*)* and the forest jumping mice *(Zapus* and *Napaeozapus* spp.*)* have long, powerful hind legs and are good jumpers.

Spiny mice *(Acomys* spp.*)* of Africa and India have spines like porcupines. Although only the size of a house mouse, these animals are walking pincushions. Their fragile, naked tails are often broken off when these mice are caught by hand.

The House Mouse *(Mus Musculus)*, which has a nearly hairless tail, has been carried around the world by man. This mouse, and the several house-dwelling rats, cause untold damage annually to foods and materials. Albinos — white mice — are valuable research animals.

MIDGES are a large group of very small true flies *(Diptera)*. One family (Cecidomyiidae) contains many species that form galls. Some members of this family live in fungi or under bark; others, such as the Hessian Fly, are pests of crops. Biting midges, or punkies (Ceratopogonidae), are sometimes nicknamed "no-see-ums", because of their small size. Many species of midges suck blood from insects; others bite man or other warm-blooded animals. Their bites may itch more than bites of

mosquitoes or deer-flies, for instance.

Most midges belong to the family Chironomidae. Many species look like mosquitoes but do not bite. Large swarms of these midges may be a nuisance, however. Their larvae are aquatic, although a few kinds do live in decaying vegetation or under bark. Species are found in nearly every type of fresh water, from still, polluted ponds to clear, fast stream. Many are bright red and these are called "bloodworms". Often they are so abundant that they are important in the balance of life in fresh waters. They convert large quantities of plants into animal protein, and are eaten by predatory insects or by small fishes which are then eaten by larger fishes.

MILLIPEDES are slim, cylindrical arthropods that have two pairs of legs on most of their body segments. Some are only 1/10 of an inch long; others as much as four inches. Usually found under stones and logs, or in other damp habitats, most species eat decaying vegetation. A few

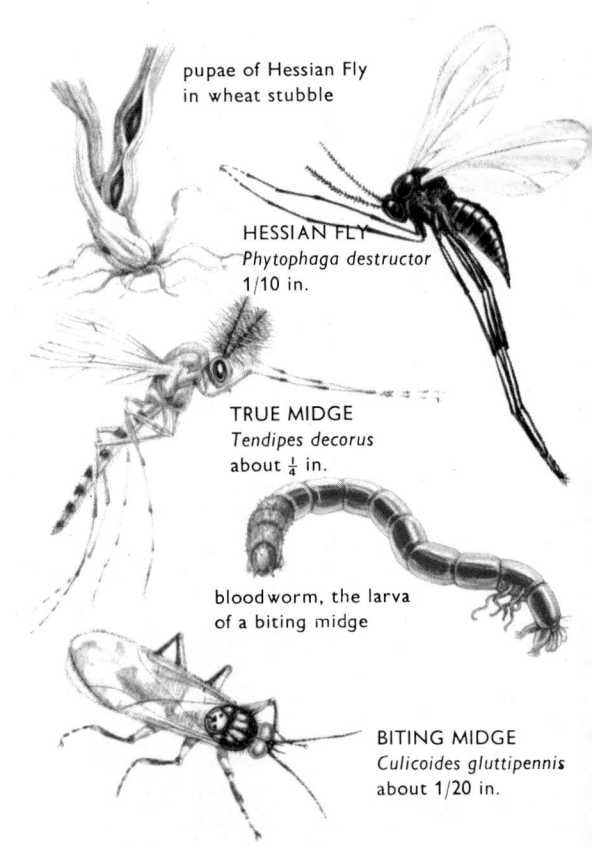

pupae of Hessian Fly
in wheat stubble

HESSIAN FLY
Phytophaga destructor
1/10 in.

TRUE MIDGE
Tendipes decorus
about ¼ in.

bloodworm, the larva
of a biting midge

BITING MIDGE
Culicoides gluttipennis
about 1/20 in.

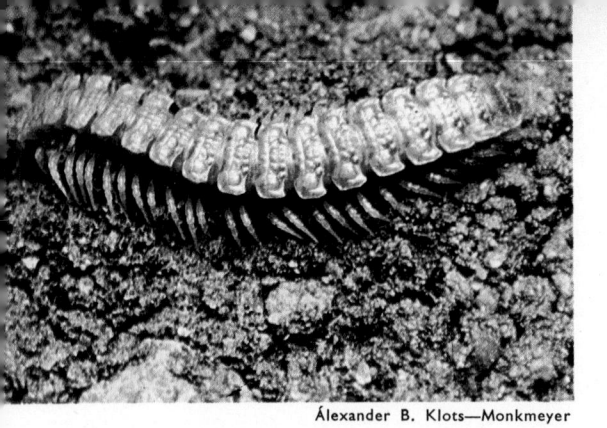

Slow-moving millipedes may have as many as 200 pairs of legs; their name means "thousand-legged".

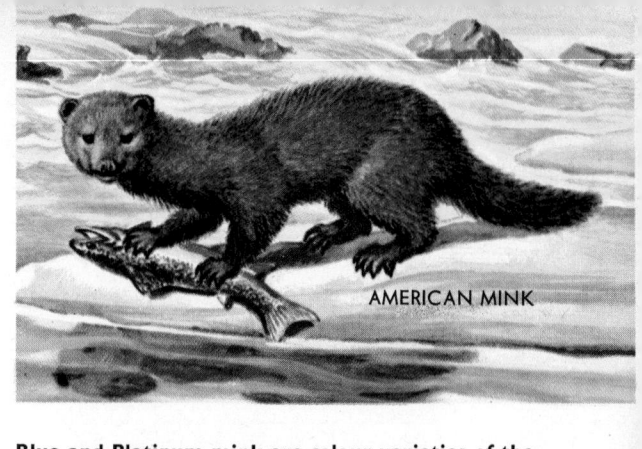

Blue and Platinum mink are colour varieties of the American Mink raised on fur farms.

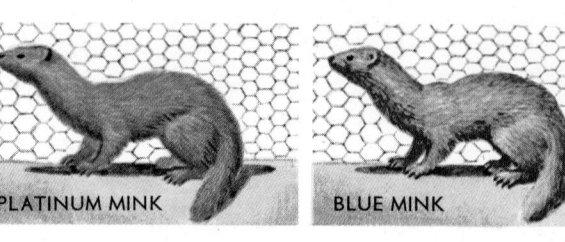

feed on living plants and occasionally become pests. Many millipedes release a foul-smelling fluid when handled, but they do not bite man. (See ARTHROPODS.)

MINK are weasel-like animals with exceedingly fine fur coats. Males are about 25 inches long, females somewhat smaller. Active at night, mink are rarely seen by man, but their presence is revealed by their tracks and droppings. They feed on frogs, musk-rats, fishes, birds, and all kinds of small animals which live along waterways. Mink have been trapped for many centuries and raised on fur farms, to obtain particular colours of fur. The value of their fur has greatly reduced the number of wild mink. European Mink occur from western France across Europe to western Siberia. American Mink are found in woods near waterways throughout North America, except in the south-western United States.

MINNOW. In Europe the name Minnow is given to a small fish of the carp family, *Phoxinus phoxinus*. It resembles a miniature Chub or Dace, but has many more scales along the flanks (80—100). It is one of the commonest and best known of British freshwater fishes. It is not found in Northern Scotland or in Spain and Portugal, but otherwise occurs throughout Europe and extends even to some of the Siberian rivers.

The Minnow is one of the smallest of the freshwater fishes in England, rarely exceeding 4 inches in length. Nowadays, it is used mainly for bait, but was formerly eaten; at a banquet for King Richard II, the menu included 7 gallons of minnows.

In England, the Minnow spawns from May to July, and at this time the males develop whitish tubercles on the head. The fishes spawn in shallow water over sand or gravel, congregating in large shoals. The eggs are small and adhesive.

The family of carp-like fishes, the Cyprinidae, contains about 1,200 species, many of which are quite small. The cyprinids have no teeth in the jaws, but a series of teeth in the throat which are used to grind the food. They have no true fin spines. The group seems to have arisen in southern Asia and then spread to Northern Asia, Europe, Africa and North America. It does not occur in South America, nor in Australia or Madagascar.

Some of the smaller cyprinid fishes are familiar to aquarists. Many of the Barbs *(Barbus* spp.) are popular aquarium fishes, although they do not usually show the variety of colours found in other groups.

The minnow-like fishes are important, not as a direct food for human consumption, but as the food of other larger fishes which are commercially valuable.

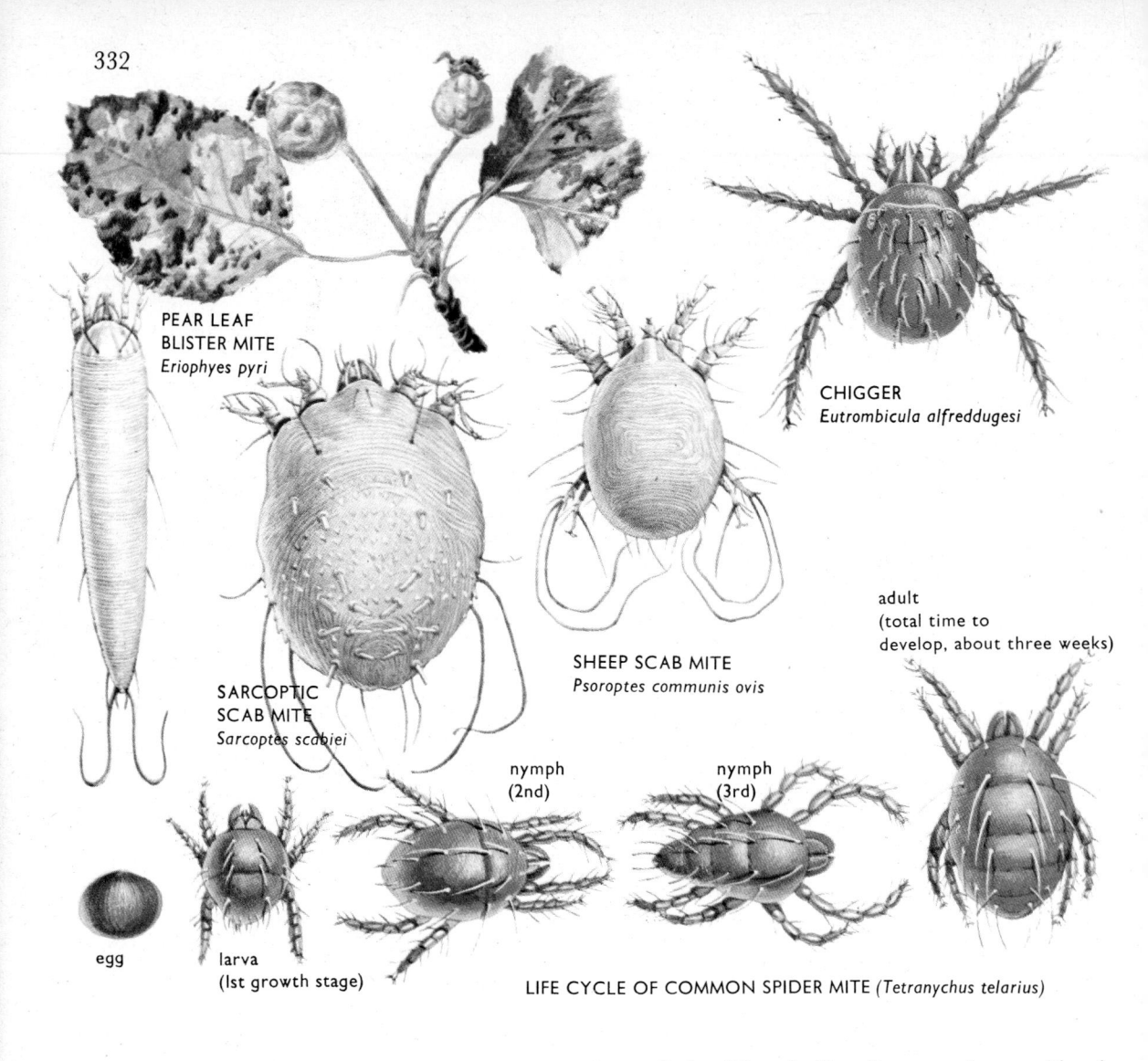

PEAR LEAF
BLISTER MITE
Eriophyes pyri

CHIGGER
Eutrombicula alfreddugesi

SARCOPTIC
SCAB MITE
Sarcoptes scabiei

SHEEP SCAB MITE
Psoroptes communis ovis

adult
(total time to
develop, about three weeks)

nymph
(2nd)

nymph
(3rd)

egg

larva
(1st growth stage)

LIFE CYCLE OF COMMON SPIDER MITE *(Tetranychus telarius)*

MITES are not insects, but members of the class Arachnida, as are spiders, ticks and scorpions (see SCORPIONS; SPIDERS; TICKS). Like other members of this class, they have four pairs of legs — rather than three as insects do — and they do not have antennae. But their bodies are not divided into two definite regions, as are those of spiders. Most mites are so small that they can be seen only with the aid of a hand lens or a microscope. Some are long and slim; others are nearly globular.

Many mites live in the soil or in leaf-mould, decaying wood, or other debris.

MOCKING-BIRDS are closely related to wrens and thrushes. They are found in southern North America, Central America and the West Indies. In extensive parkland or small gardens, they sing beautifully, and also imitate the songs and calls of every bird they have ever heard. Mocking-birds sing all day and often at night, from tree-tops and roof-tops, from hedges and fence wires, and from the feeding-table where they come for raisins and suet.

When Mocking-birds build nests in shrubs and trees, they often make use of bits of wool and string. They raise two or three broods each year, often so near houses that they can be watched from a window or porch as they feed and care for their young. In the North, their natural diet is primarily insects during the breeding season. In the South, all the year round they eat seeds, fruits and berries.

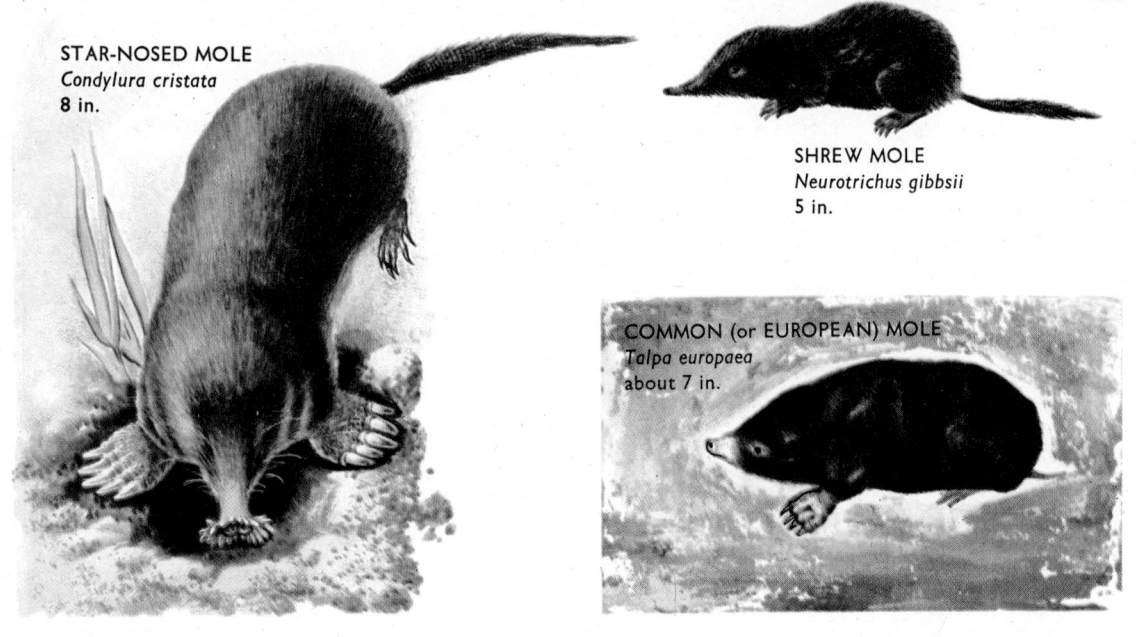

STAR-NOSED MOLE
Condylura cristata
8 in.

SHREW MOLE
Neurotrichus gibbsii
5 in.

COMMON (or EUROPEAN) MOLE
Talpa europaea
about 7 in.

MOLES are mammals closely related to shrews. They live in underground burrows and rarely come to the surface. Using their broad, powerful front legs for digging, they virtually swim through the soil. When they move backwards through their burrows, the tail serves as a sensitive feeler. Many kinds also use their noses as wedges or rams. Moles live in complete darkness; their eyes are poorly developed and small — or, in some, absent or covered with skin. Frequently they also lack ears. Their fur is very dense and fine.

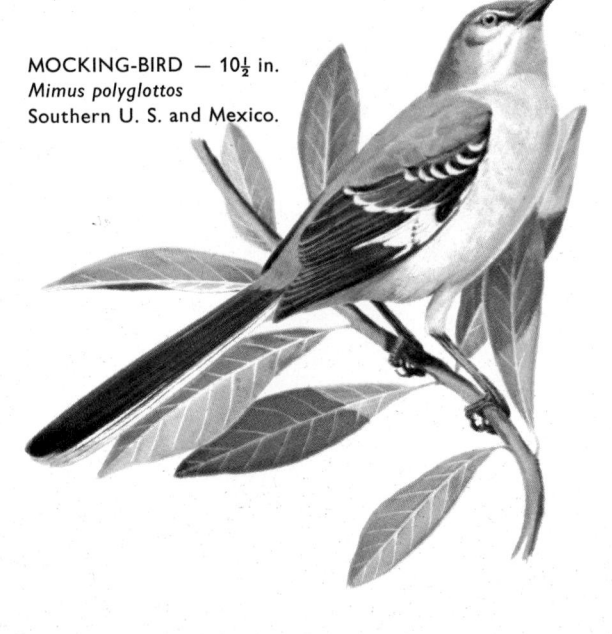

MOCKING-BIRD — 10½ in.
Mimus polyglottos
Southern U. S. and Mexico.

The Common (or European) Mole *(Talpa europaea)* feeds mainly on earthworms. It digs burrows marked by mounds of earth, and is found in much of Europe and Asia. A similar mole lives in the forests and grasslands of the eastern United States.

The Star-nosed Mole *(Condylura cristata)*, found in marshes and wet meadows of the north-eastern United States and south-eastern Canada, has a disc of flesh-coloured tentacles at the end of its elongated snout. These are apparently used as feelers to locate worms and grubs. This mole has a very long, thick tail.

The Shrew Mole *(Neurotrichus gibbsii)*, intermediate in size and structure between moles and shrews, has a long snout and quite evident eyes. It lives in leaf litter in forests of the western United States.

Golden Moles *(Chrysochloris spp.)* of southern Africa are a brilliant, metallic colour, and their feet are heavily clawed for digging. They feed principally on insects, but some kinds also eat lizards.

The Marsupial Mole *(Notoryctes typhlops)* of Australia looks like a mole but is, in fact, a marsupial, with a pouch in which it carries its young. Like true moles, it lacks functional eyes. It feeds principally on ants or their larvae.

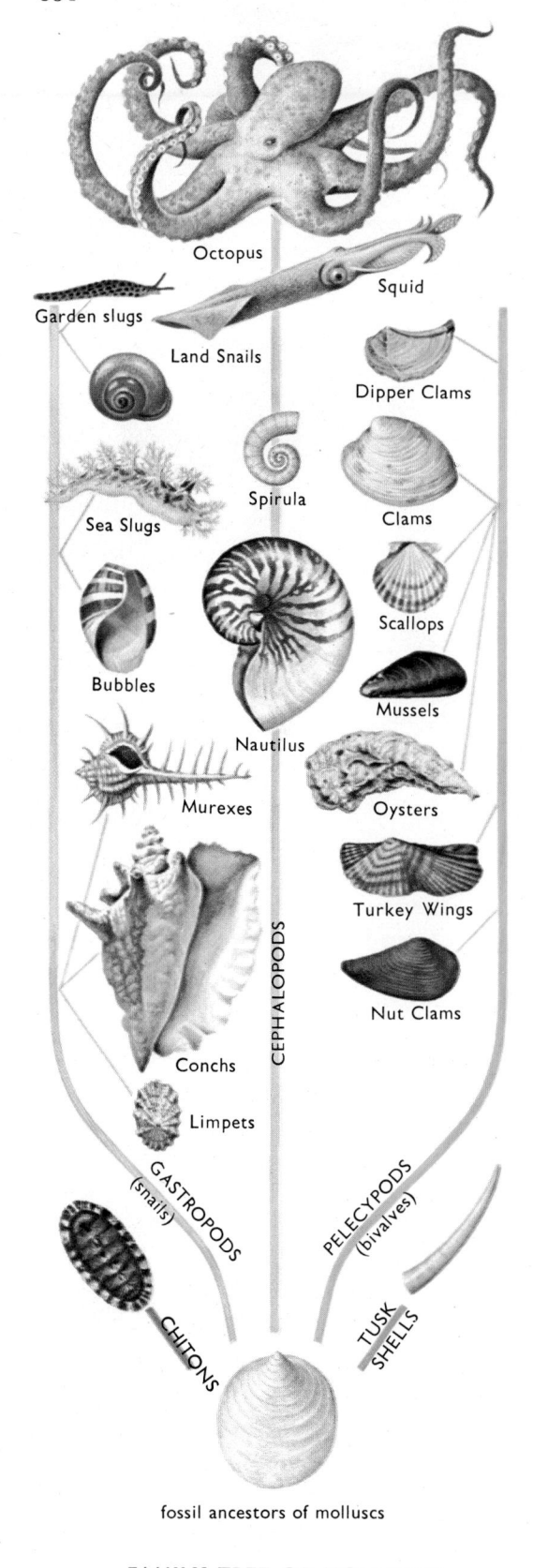

Octopus

Squid

Garden slugs

Land Snails

Dipper Clams

Spirula

Sea Slugs

Clams

Scallops

Bubbles

Mussels

Nautilus

Murexes

Oysters

Turkey Wings

Nut Clams

Conchs

CEPHALOPODS

Limpets

GASTROPODS (snails)

PELECYPODS (bivalves)

CHITONS

TUSK SHELLS

fossil ancestors of molluscs

FAMILY TREE OF MOLLUSCS

MOLLUSCS, represented by such animals as snails, clams, oysters and octopuses, are one of the largest groups of animals. They inhabit the seashore from the inter-tidal zone to great depths, and some, like sea-butterflies, swim or drift far out at sea with the plankton. Many kinds of bivalves and snails live in fresh water, and a few kinds of snail live on land. There are 45,000 species of mollusc, their fossils are found in rocks over 500 million years old.

Most molluscs have a limy outer skeleton, or shell, secreted by the soft mantle that covers their body. Some shells are straight tubes; others are coiled, others consist of two valves hinged together, or of a series of overlapping plates. In sea-hares, squids and octopuses, the shells either have become internal or have disappeared.

Some molluscs are carnivorous, preying on other shells. Others, such as oysters, are filter-feeders, straining plankton from currents of water that flow over their gills. Most molluscs crawl slowly about, scraping algae from the rocks with a band of teeth called the radula. Drawn back and forth by muscles, the radula functions much like a file or a wood rasp. In some, such as cone shells, the radula consists of poison darts used to kill prey.

Molluscs breathe with their gills and also their mantle. In bivalved molluscs the gills are used primarily for straining food, and the mantle for breathing. Few marine molluscs give their young any care. In many the eggs are simply shed into the water; others enclose their eggs in horny capsules, in which the young hatch and develop young shells before being liberated.

Molluscs are very important to man as sources of food (see OYSTERS). Their shells are made into buttons and jewellery; pearls and mother-of-pearl are obtained from some. The five classes of molluscs are separated on the basis of their shells, and the shape and structure of their swimming or crawling organ or foot. (See BIVALVES; CEPHALOPODS; CHITONS; SNAILS; TOOTH SHELLS).

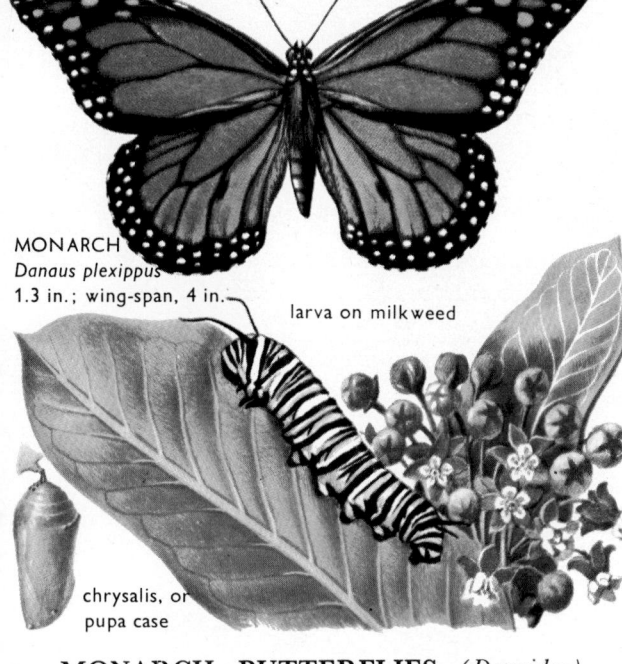

MONARCH
Danaus plexippus
1.3 in.; wing-span, 4 in.

larva on milkweed

chrysalis, or
pupa case

MONARCH BUTTERFLIES *(Danaidae)*

are often seen in swarms of hundreds of thousands, for the Monarch is one of the many butterflies that migrate. Some travel from Canada to Florida and back again, a distance of more than 2,000 miles. Great flocks move southward in autumn. Smaller numbers — only those few that survive — return in spring. Information about their migration paths, speed and similar data has been collected by tagging wings of the migrants with bits of white paper. The females lay their eggs on various kinds of milkweeds, which become food for the caterpillars. Both butterflies and caterpillars are distasteful to birds. A bird learns to recognise Monarchs and to avoid them. The Monarch is found in many parts of the world apart from North America.

The Viceroy Butterfly is a mimic of the Monarch and looks so much like it that it is rarely attacked, although the Viceroy is not distasteful. The larvae of the Viceroy Butterfly does not resemble the larvae of the Monarch.

MONITORS *(Varanus* spp.*)* are the giants

of the lizard world. The Komodo Dragon, found on the island of Komodo in the East Indies, reaches a length of ten feet and a weight of 300 pounds. Smallest of the 23 species is an eight-inch dwarf monitor of western Australia. Monitors are found only in the Old World, and half the present-day species occur in Australia. Almost as many are found in the East Indies, but only three occur in Africa.

All monitors look astonishingly alike. They have heavy bodies, strong legs and long tails. Their necks are fairly long, and their heads long and flattened. They flip out their long, forked tongues much as snakes do. The tongue picks up particles of scent and carries them to a special taste organ in the roof of the mouth. This enables the lizard to trail by scent.

Monitors are found in deserts and lush jungles. Some live in burrows, others in trees. Some live near fresh water, others near oceans. All monitors can swim well and do so frequently. They will eat any animal they can catch and overpower. When approaching prey, they draw their head back by curving their neck, and then strike like a snake. Those with strong crushing teeth eat snails and crabs. The Nile Monitor eats crocodile eggs dug from their nest. It lays its own eggs in termite nests. Other monitors lay their eggs in nests dug in the ground. Monitors bite when first captured, but they tame quickly and make good pets.

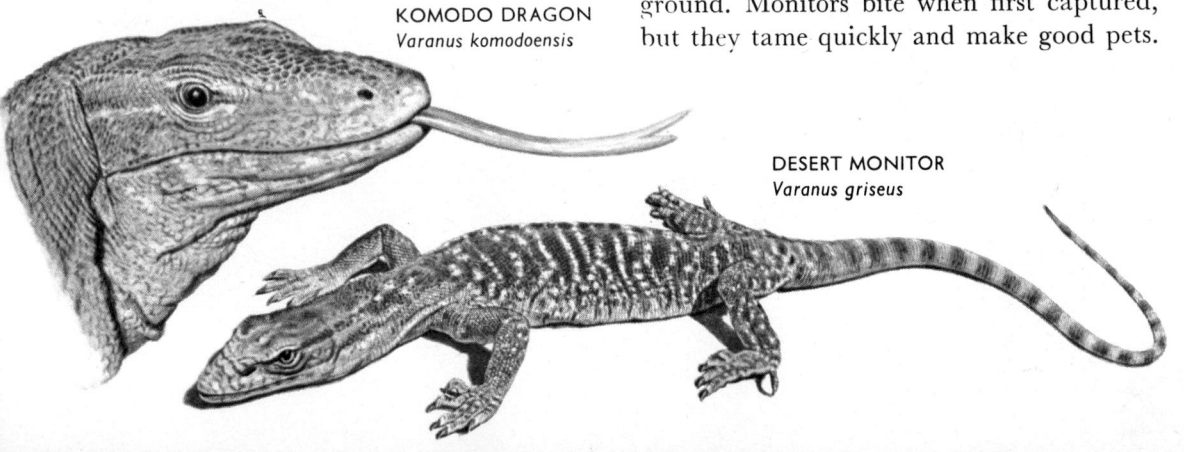

KOMODO DRAGON
Varanus komodoensis

DESERT MONITOR
Varanus griseus

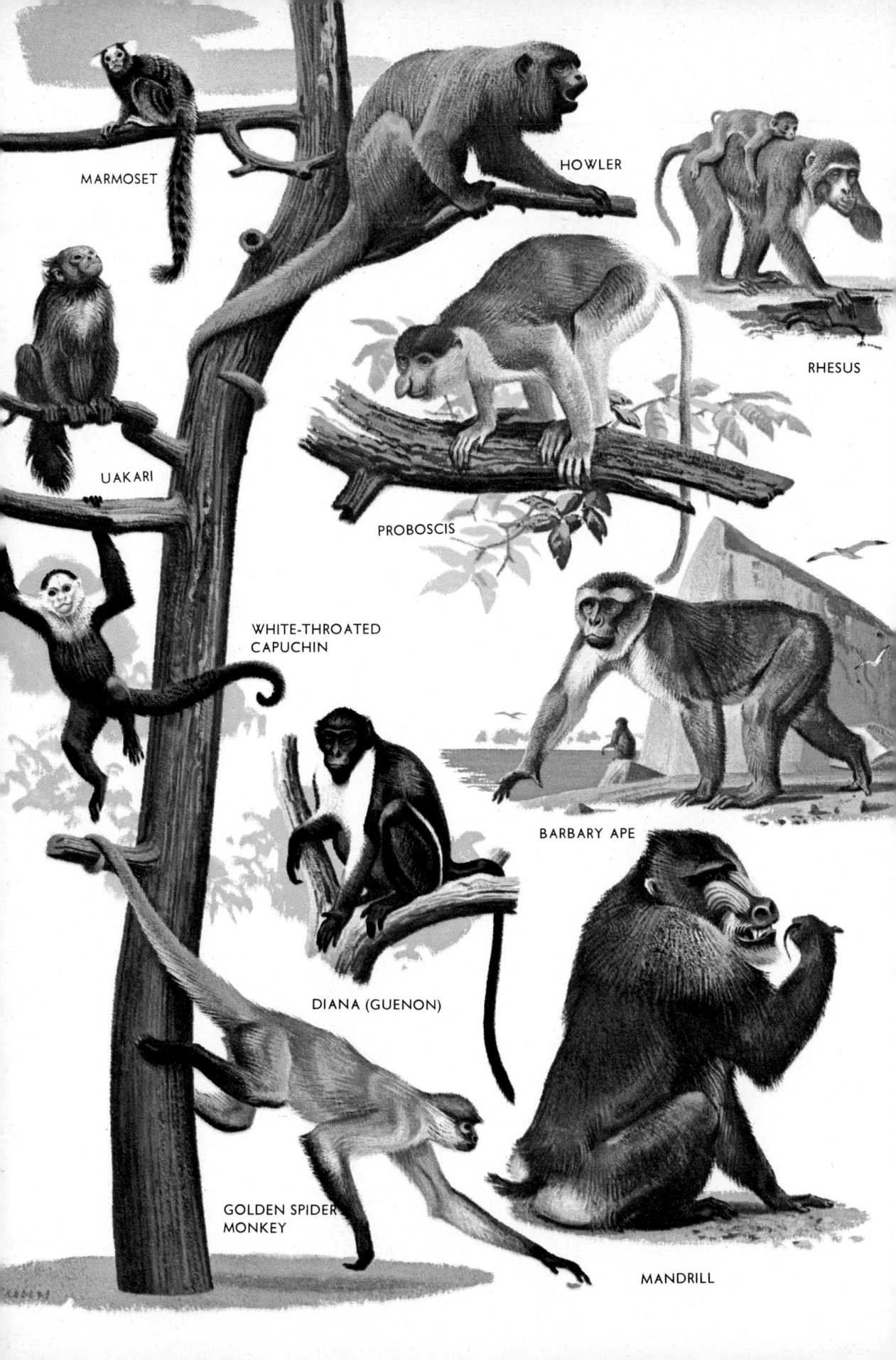

MARMOSET

HOWLER

RHESUS

UAKARI

PROBOSCIS

WHITE-THROATED
CAPUCHIN

DIANA (GUENON)

BARBARY APE

GOLDEN SPIDER
MONKEY

MANDRILL

MONKEYS are primates — the highest, or most intelligent, group of mammals. Commonly the word monkey refers to all primates except apes, man and lemurs — the highest and lowest members of the primate family. More precisely, the name monkey refers to small, long-tailed primates, as distinguished from apes and man, and excludes tarsiers, lemurs, and all other primates of lesser development. Most monkeys are tree-dwellers.

OLD WORLD MONKEYS. Old World Monkeys are found in Africa and Asia, and one kind has been introduced to Gibraltar. They may have either a short or a long tail, but the tail is not used for grasping. They have 32 teeth, and many kinds have cheek pouches in which they can stuff food to be eaten later. Their nostrils open downwards, as do those of the more advanced primates, the great apes and man.

Guenons (*Cercopithecus* spp.), the commonest monkeys of Africa, average about 20 inches in body length; their tails are slightly longer than their bodies. Most guenons live in small groups in tropical forests, where they feed on fruits, vegetation, insects and birds. Some have impressively long beards, which are frequently brightly coloured or white. Some of the many kinds are known as Diana Monkeys, Green Monkeys, Diadem Monkeys, Monas, Grivets, Vervets and Rolaways.

Military monkeys (*Erythrocebus* spp.) are ground-dwellers that look and behave somewhat like dogs. In the wild, they travel in large bands, and their red coats resemble uniforms. They are almost three feet from crown to rump and have tails about 25 inches long. While their gentle disposition and relative lack of destructive tendencies qualify them as good pets, their size demands a large exercise area and ample quarters.

Mangabey monkeys (*Cercocebus* spp.) of Central Africa are long-tailed and gentle. They do well in captivity and are noted for their amusing facial expressions. They resemble guenons, but their snouts are longer.

Rhesus Monkeys (*Rhesus* spp.), which measure about 2 feet in length, are often used for research and are also common in zoos. In the wild they live from southern China to India and Burma. Barbary Apes (*Simia sylvana*) which belong to the same large group (the macaques), are the only monkeys that live in Europe. They are natives of North Africa, but were established on the rocky slopes of Gibraltar by man.

Mandrills (*Mandrillus* spp.), their faces and buttocks marked with vivid purples and reds, are the most brilliantly coloured of all mammals. Found only in small groups in the forests of western Africa, they are a type of baboon. Much of their time is spent on the ground. They feed extensively on plant material, but sometimes kill and eat animals. Drills, less colourful relatives, have shiny black faces and pale pink buttocks. Mandrills have large heads with long snouts and deeply-furrowed cheeks. They have practically no tail.

Proboscis monkeys (*Nasalis larvatus*) are found only in Borneo. The males have noses that droop down almost below their chins. Females have smaller noses. Through their long noses these monkeys utter honking noises. They eat leaves and fruit. These monkeys pine in captivity, and little is known about their habits. Langurs (*Presbytis*) of Asia and Colobus monkeys (*Colobus*) of Africa are related to the Proboscis monkeys. (See APES, BABOONS, CHIMPANZEES, GIBBONS, GORILLAS, LEMURS, ORANG-UTANS, TARSIERS.)

NEW WORLD MONKEYS. Monkeys of the New World have long tails, often used for grasping, 32 (marmosets) or 36 teeth, no cheek pouches, and wide nostrils that open to the front or to the side, rather than downwards. They occur from Mexico through Central and South America.

Marmosets are small monkeys, of several genera, that have hooked claws instead of nails on all except their big toes.

Ring-tailed Monkeys, or Capuchins (*Cebus* spp.), range from Mexico through

Brazil. The name "ring-tail" comes from their habit of carrying the tail coiled over their back. These monkeys live in groups in the high tropical forests, where they feed principally on fruit, but occasionally eat eggs or insects. None of the several kinds are larger than a house cat. In captivity they make good pets.

Uakaris (*Cacajao* spp.) are strange-looking monkeys of the Amazon forests. Not much larger than house cats, they have nearly human-looking, naked, thin faces with chin whiskers, sunken eyes, and little hair on their heads. Uakaris are shy animals living in trees and feeding on fruit.

Spider monkeys (*Ateles* spp.) have long, slender arms, legs and tails, which accounts for their name. These monkeys move through the branches of the jungle forest nearly as adeptly as gibbons, and they rarely come to the ground. They carry their tails coiled over their backs. The single young at first holds on to the front side of the mother. Later it rides on her back, as she swings from branch to branch.

Howler monkeys (*Alouatta* spp.), also found in the Amazon region, are large forest-dwellers that growl and roar. Most howlers are black, but some are reddish-brown. All are sturdily built and thickly furred. Woolly monkeys (*Lagothrix* spp.), nearly as large as howlers, have dense, short hair over their bodies. They enjoy hanging from limbs by their tails.

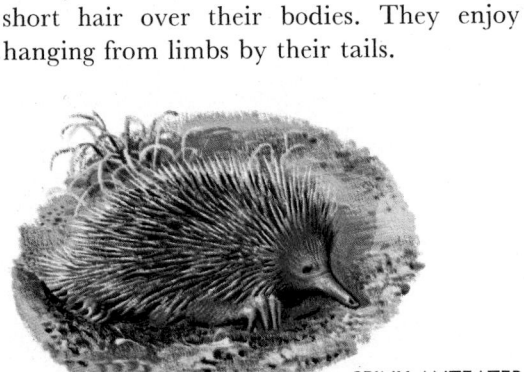

SPINY ANTEATER

MONOTREMES are the only mammals that lay eggs. They do not have true mammary glands, for their milk seeps from pores into pockets on the female's abdomen.

While monotremes are the most primitive of living mammals, they are also highly specialised in their adaptations and structures. Found only in Australia, New Guinea and Tasmania, monotremes include the Platypus, or Duckbill, and the spiny ant-eaters, or echidnas.

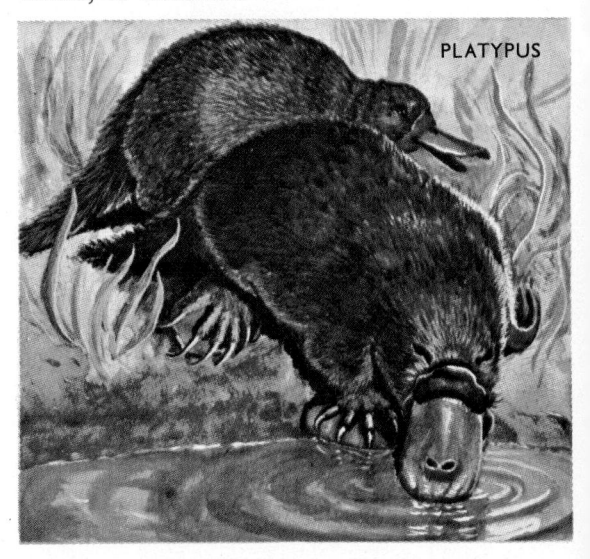

PLATYPUS

The Platypus (*Ornithorhynchus anatinus*), which measures nearly two feet in length, has a duck-like bill, a flat tail, and webbed feet. It is adapted for life in the water, where it feeds on shrimps, insects, worms, and molluscs by probing for them in the mud with its broad, soft bill. The Platypus digs a burrow as much as 60 feet long in a stream or lake bank, and at the end builds a nest of stems and leaves. The female lays one to three round, leathery eggs, about three-quarters of an inch in diameter. When hatched the young are only about three-fifths of an inch long. They remain in the nest until they have grown to about six inches. The male Platypus has large, curved spurs projecting backwards from each ankle, and these spurs are made more dangerous by a poisonous fluid which they discharge.

Spiny ant-eaters, or echidnas (*Echidna aculeata* and *Zaglossus* spp.), are slightly smaller than the Platypus and look entirely different. Their spines are actually enlarged hairs that can be raised and waved about. These animals can also roll up into a ball

to avoid enemies. They are powerful diggers and have little or no trouble opening termite or ant hills. Echidnas live in scrub lands and open forests, and are most active in the evening or at night. A single egg is laid and carried in a special pouch which develops on the female's abdomen in the

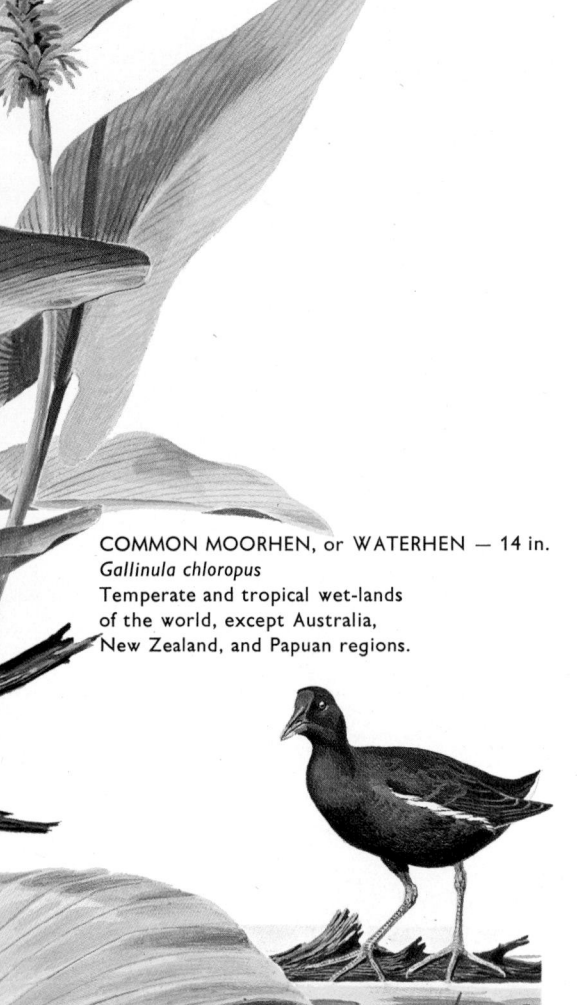

COMMON MOORHEN, or WATERHEN — 14 in.
Gallinula chloropus
Temperate and tropical wet-lands
of the world, except Australia,
New Zealand, and Papuan regions.

breeding season. The young animal is carried in the pouch until its spines develop and become annoying. By this time, it is about $3\frac{1}{2}$ inches long.

MOORHEN. This bird builds a nest of dried reeds lined with grass, wedged between growing weeds above the marsh water. The nest is edged with reeds broken off to

form a bristly fence all round, except for the entrance, a hole about three inches wide. The bird builds a reed walk, like a ship's gangway, from the entrance to the water below. The Moorhen is one of the Gallinules, fresh-water marsh birds found in warm-temperate and tropic zones throughout the world. Because they act and sound like chickens, in every language their common name includes "hen" or "chicken".

MOOSE *(Alces spp.)* are the largest of the deer and may weigh as much as half a ton. These animals of northern regions frequent marshy areas and nearby forests of fir and spruce. They feed on the leaves and bark of both conifers and broad-leaf trees, and also on aquatic plants. Because its neck is so short, a Moose can graze on low plants only by kneeling. Males shed their large, flat antlers each year; females do not have antlers. A flap of skin, known as the "bell", hangs beneath their throats. Females give birth to one (rarely two) young late in the spring. The calf stays with its mother for nearly a year. The European Elk is a member of the same genus, and is similar in appearance and habits.

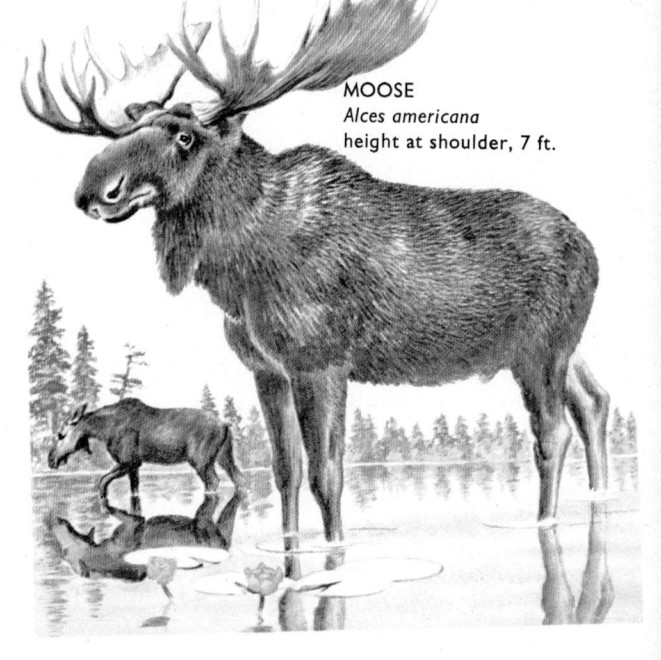

MOOSE
Alces americana
height at shoulder, 7 ft.

MOSQUITOES *(Culicidae)* inflict more direct harm to man than any other insects. More than 2,000 species are known, and they range from the arctic to the tropics. They are true flies of the order Diptera.

The wrigglers, or larvae, of some species develop only in fresh water; others only in salt or brackish water. They hatch from

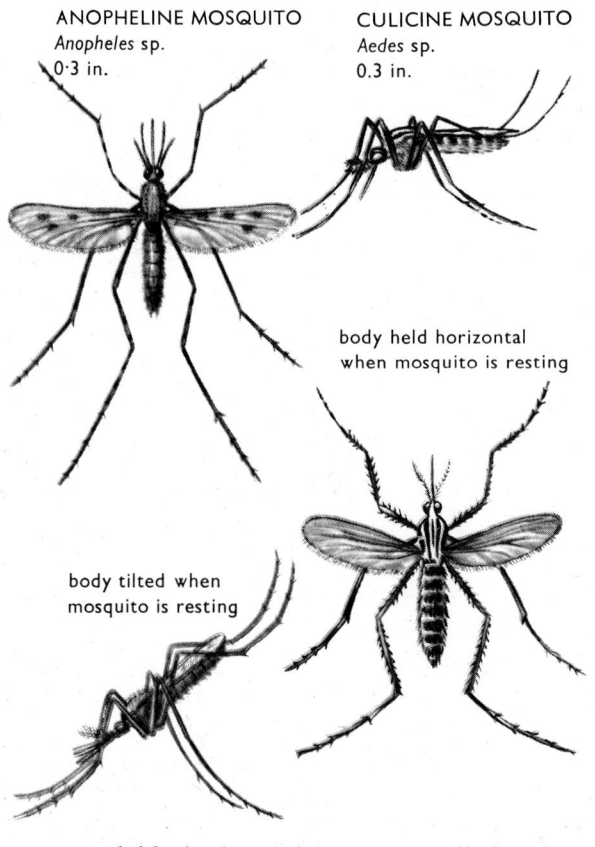

ANOPHELINE MOSQUITO
Anopheles sp.
0·3 in.

CULICINE MOSQUITO
Aedes sp.
0.3 in.

body held horizontal
when mosquito is resting

body tilted when
mosquito is resting

eggs laid singly or in masses, called rafts, on the surface of the water. Eggs may be laid in permanent bodies of water or in flooded lowlands. They can develop in clean or polluted water, in large or small pools. Each species usually has a preferred type of habitat. One kind lays its eggs in the water reservoirs at the base of the leaves of pitcher plants. Larvae of this mosquito (and those of a few other insects) are able to live in this water, although other insects that drop into the water are digested as food by the pitcher plant. Some mosquitoes of the tropics use water trapped at the base of leaves or in the hollows of

bamboo. Holes in trees, tin cans, old tyres — any standing water is suitable for the development of mosquitoes.

Most mosquito larvae feed on algae and other bits of organic material in water, but larvae of a few species feed on other mosquito larvae. Most mosquito larvae rise to the surface from time to time to breathe through tubes (siphons) at the end of their abdomen, but those of one group puncture stems of aquatic plants with their air-tubes and use the air inside the stems. The pupal stage lasts only a few days for mosquitoes, however, and adults mate shortly after they emerge. Males, identified by their feathery antennae, usually die soon after mating. Those that do remain alive for several days feed on nectar. Most females require a meal of blood before they lay their eggs.

Mosquito bites are irritating and may also transmit various diseases to man and his animals. Malaria, one of the most widespread diseases in the world, is caused by a tiny one-celled animal that invades red blood-cells. The disease organisms go through part of their development inside certain mosquitoes *(Anopheles maculipennis)*. When one of these mosquitoes bites a man or other warm-blooded animal, the parasites are transmitted to the new host. Yellow fever is transmitted mainly by *Aedes aegypti*. Filariasis, dengue, and encephalitis are among other diseases transmitted by mosquitoes.

Chemical controls of mosquitoes are effective but only temporary. Draining wet areas of land to eliminate breeding sites is a more permanent means of control, as is the use of certain surface-feeding fish that eat the larvae.

MOSS ANIMALS, or Bryozoa, are mainly marine animals that live on rocks, shells, boat bottoms, pilings, and other hard objects. Most are very small and live in large colonies; a few are solitary. Some grow in branching, fern-like colonies, but most kinds form thin, lace-like coatings

larvae (wrigglers) and pupae (tumblers)

eggs hatching

adult emerging

adult, 0.3 in.

LIFE CYCLE OF THE HOUSE MOSQUITO (*Culex pipiens*)

only a single layer thick. Branching colonies are usually drab, but encrusting species may be deep purplish black, yellow, bright orange, red, or green.

Bryozoa are very simple animals. They consist only of the lumpish body of the animal, a short and rudimentary digestive tract, and the tentacles. They do not have organised systems for their respiration, circulation, nor excretion. Specialised reproductive organs are also absent. Young are produced by simple budding off of new individuals, often in symmetrical patterns. Bryozoa also reproduce by means of eggs and sperm. Fertilised eggs form planktonic larvae that later settle on hard objects and grow into new colonies.

Each animal lives in a leathery or limy chamber with an opening through which the soft parts and tentacles are thrust. Many can close the entrance with a small trapdoor. The head is surrounded with a ring of tentacles covered with hairs, or cilia. These beat in unison, causing a current of water to flow to the mouth. The animals feed on small plankton and particles of detritus (debris) in the water.

Under a microscope, odd little structures resembling a bird's head on a long neck can be seen scattered over the surface of a bryozoan colony. These are called avicularia, and each has a beak that snaps at anything which comes near. They may be defensive, or for capturing large prey to use for growing bacteria.

Bryozoa are widespread in the sea and occur to moderate depths. They appear to have little direct value either as food or as refuge for other animals. They are a nuisance to boat-owners, especially in tropical waters, where their dense growths may slow down a boat fouled by them.

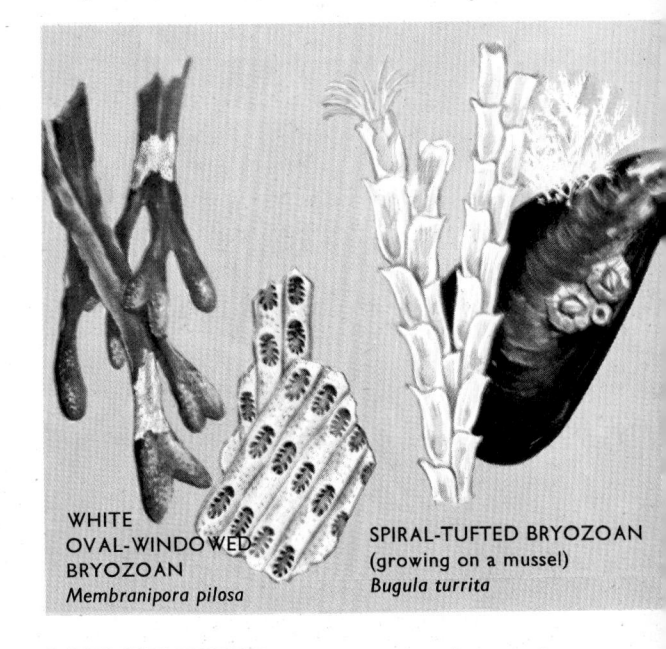

WHITE OVAL-WINDOWED BRYOZOAN
Membranipora pilosa

SPIRAL-TUFTED BRYOZOAN (growing on a mussel)
Bugula turrita

MUDSNAPPERS are two turtle species found in Mexico, Guatemala, and British Honduras. They resemble mud-turtles from above, but are similar to snappers from below. The Smooth Mudsnapper (*Claudius*) has a very narrow bridge on the lower shell, or plastron. The bridge is not much larger in the Keeled Mudsnapper (*Staurotypus*), which is rather long and slender. It has three high ridges down its arched top shell, or carapace. The Smooth Mudsnapper is almost as broad as it is long, and rather flat. Both are like mud- and musk-turtles (See MUD-TURTLES; MUSK-TURTLES; TURTLES.)

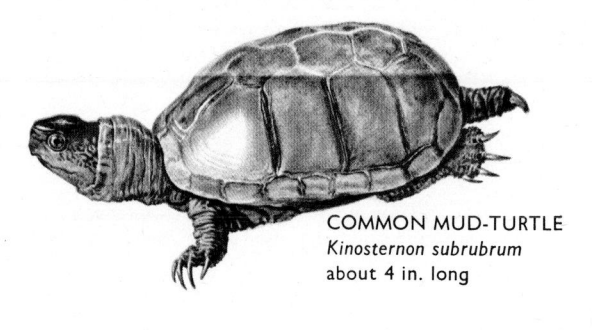

COMMON MUD-TURTLE
Kinosternon subrubrum
about 4 in. long

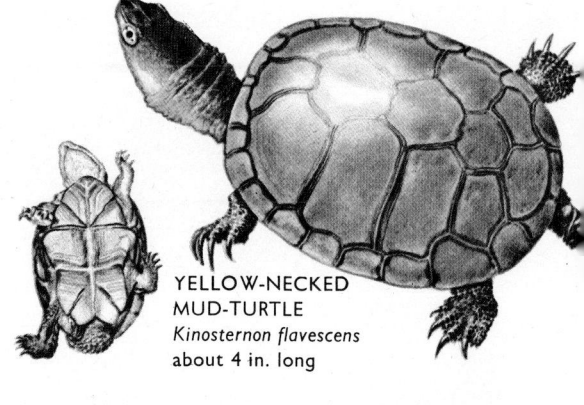

YELLOW-NECKED
MUD-TURTLE
Kinosternon flavescens
about 4 in. long

The lower shell, or plastron, is hinged and can be drawn snug against the upper shell.

MUD-TURTLES (*Kinosternon spp.*), — of some 16 to 20 species, — range from New England and Arizona southward through Brazil. The smallest are little more than three inches long, the largest about eight inches. All are dark slate above and brownish beneath. Along with musk-turtles, they belong to a group known as "aromatic turtles", because of the rather strong odour they give off when first captured. After a time in captivity they no longer produce the odour, even when handled. Some males have a heavy spine at the tip of their tail. Mud-turtles eat carrion, and also insects, crayfish and other small animals. Females lay their eggs in moist soil or in rotten wood. They live in a wide variety of habitats — from small temporary pools to lakes and streams.

MULES are a cross between two species — a male donkey and a female horse. The offspring of a female donkey and a male horse is called a Hinny. A mule cannot have young. In the past, in some countries, kings and nobles rode beautiful, spirited mules rather than horses. Today mules are used as sure-footed pack animals and make good mounts in rough, mountainous country. Mules are usually not large or heavy enough to compete with big draft horses, nor are they as fast or as spirited as fine riding horses. They do better than horses, however, in areas where good food is not abundant, for like goats they can live on brush. Although mules are considered more intelligent than either of their parents, they are also more stubborn.

MULLETS (*Mugil spp.*) are often referred to as Grey Mullets, to distinguish them from the Red Mullets, which are members of quite a different group of fishes. Grey Mullets are streamlined fishes which are abundant in warm seas throughout the world. They have two dorsal fins, the first with hard rays. Usually they are found in shallow water, where they grub around in mud or sand for food. The stomach is

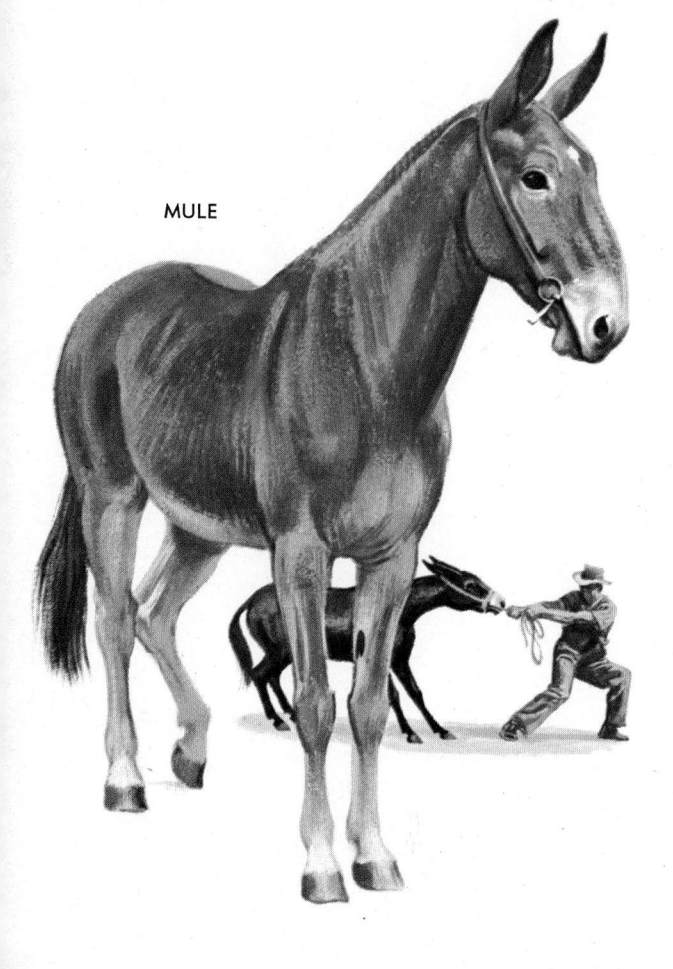

MULE

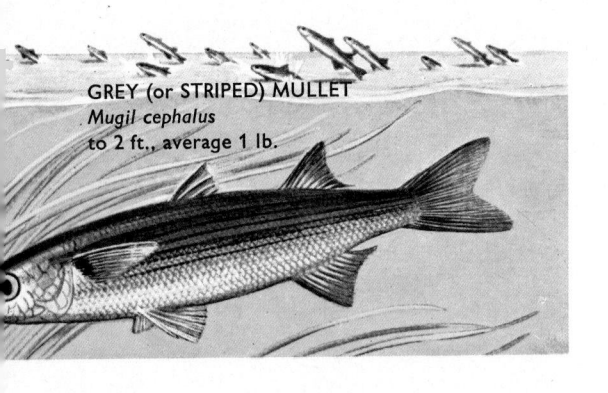

GREY (or STRIPED) MULLET
Mugil cephalus
to 2 ft., average 1 lb.

muscular, somewhat like the gizzard of
a bird, and the gut is extremely long,
enabling them to grind up and digest algae
and other aquatic plants.

Off the west coast of England, Mullets
appear in early summer and leave again
in the autumn. They are sometimes caught
with seine nets, but are great jumpers,
leaping over the net as it is pulled in.

The Red Mullet *(Mullus surmuletus)* belongs to the family Mullidae. It has two
long barbels under the chin. It makes

excellent eating and was a popular dish
in Roman times.

MUREX, or Rock Shells *(Murex* spp.*)*,
are favourites of shell-collectors because
of their beautiful sculpture of fluting, spines
and lacy projections. Nearly a thousand
species of these sea-snails are currently
known, and the most elaborate occur in the
tropics. Some, such as Hidalgo's Murex
of the West Indies, being very rare, are
especially prized by collectors. Many live
among rocks and coral reefs, but some

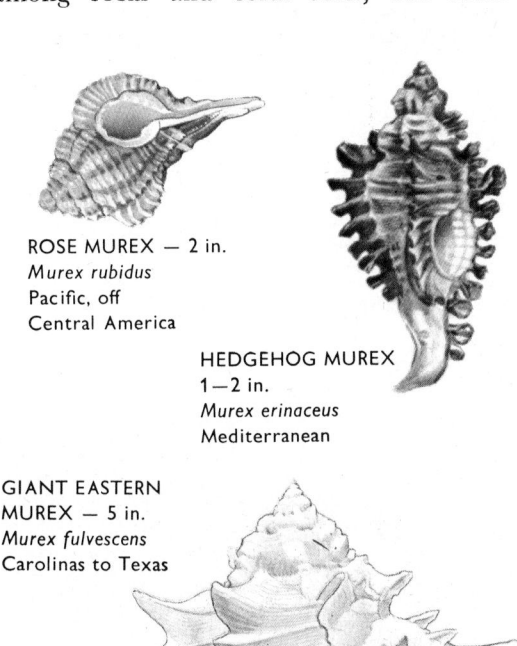

ROSE MUREX — 2 in.
Murex rubidus
Pacific, off
Central America

HEDGEHOG MUREX
1—2 in.
Murex erinaceus
Mediterranean

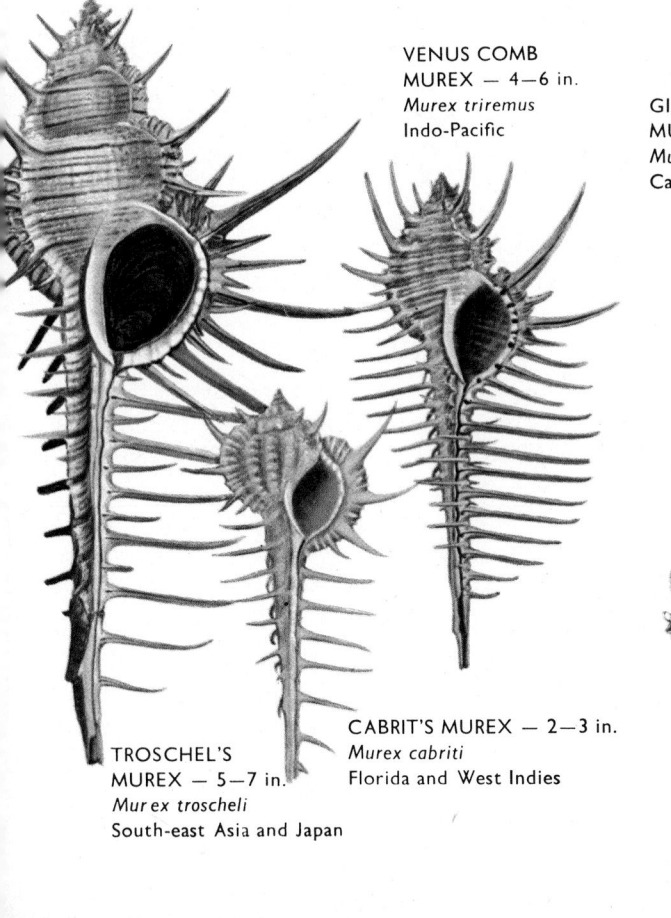

VENUS COMB
MUREX — 4—6 in.
Murex triremus
Indo-Pacific

GIANT EASTERN
MUREX — 5 in.
Murex fulvescens
Carolinas to Texas

TROSCHEL'S
MUREX — 5—7 in.
Murex troscheli
South-east Asia and Japan

CABRIT'S MUREX — 2—3 in.
Murex cabriti
Florida and West Indies

ROSE-BRANCH
MUREX — 3—4 in.
Murex palmarosae
South-East Asia

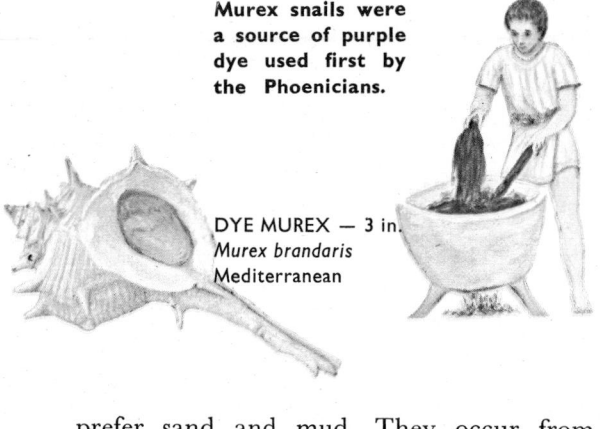

Murex snails were a source of purple dye used first by the Phoenicians.

DYE MUREX — 3 in.
Murex brandaris
Mediterranean

MUSK-OXEN *(Ovibos moschatus)* are long-haired, cow-like animals that manage to survive in barren, polar regions of North America and Greenland. Their long, heavy coats of coarse fur withstand the winds and snow of the tundra. In winter, Musk-oxen feed on mosses, lichens, and dead grass; in summer, they find fresh grass, and the shoots of dwarf willows and scrub pines. Musk-oxen live in herds of 10 to 35. To protect themselves against wolves, they form a circle with their heads outwards,

prefer sand and mud. They occur from shallow to deep water. These molluscs are carnivorous, feeding mainly on bivalve molluscs by drilling a hole through their shell. Largest North Atlantic species is the Giant Eastern Murex, which grows to a length of six inches. Some rock shells have a series of long, curved spines that may be good defence against predators. Murex shells lay their eggs in clusters.

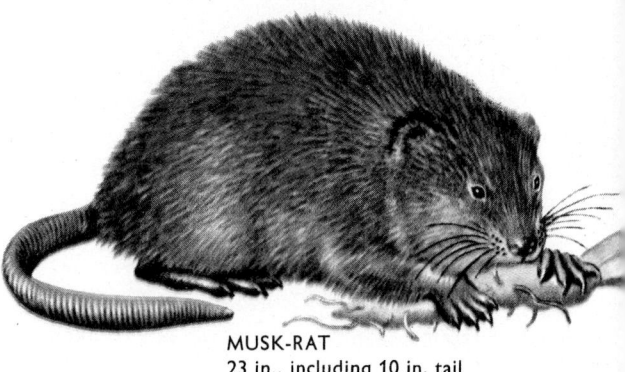

MUSK-RAT
23 in., including 10 in. tail

MUSK OX
Height at shoulder, 5 ft.

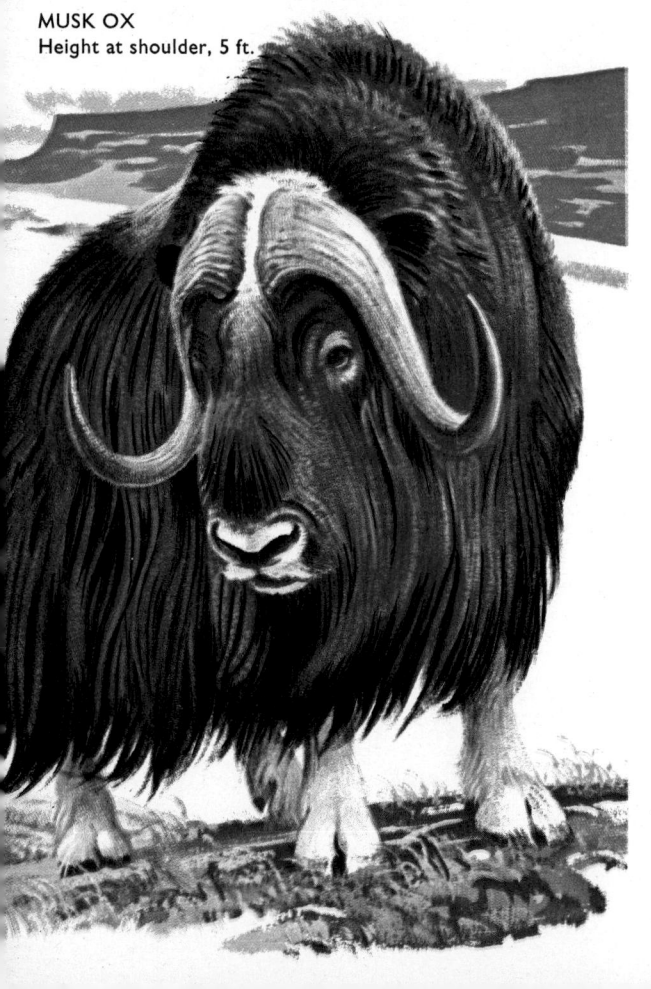

directed at the attackers. Both their horns, which are as much as two feet in length, and their sharp hoofs are effective weapons of defence. Partially successful attempts have been made to domesticate Musk-oxen. They are closer relatives to sheep than to cattle.

MUSK-RATS *(Ondatra zibethica)*, related to meadow mice, average about one foot in body length. The scaly tail, flattened from side to side (compressed), is used in swimming, as are the creature's partially webbed hind feet. Musk-rats live along ponds, lakes or streams. They build large houses of sticks, stems and roots in shallow marshes. The nest is located above the high-water level to keep it dry. Musk-rats feed principally on cat's-tail roots and stems, and on other aquatic plants; less frequently they eat clams and fish. They may have several litters of two to nine young each year. In America, more pelts of musk-rat are harvested annually than from all other fur animals combined.

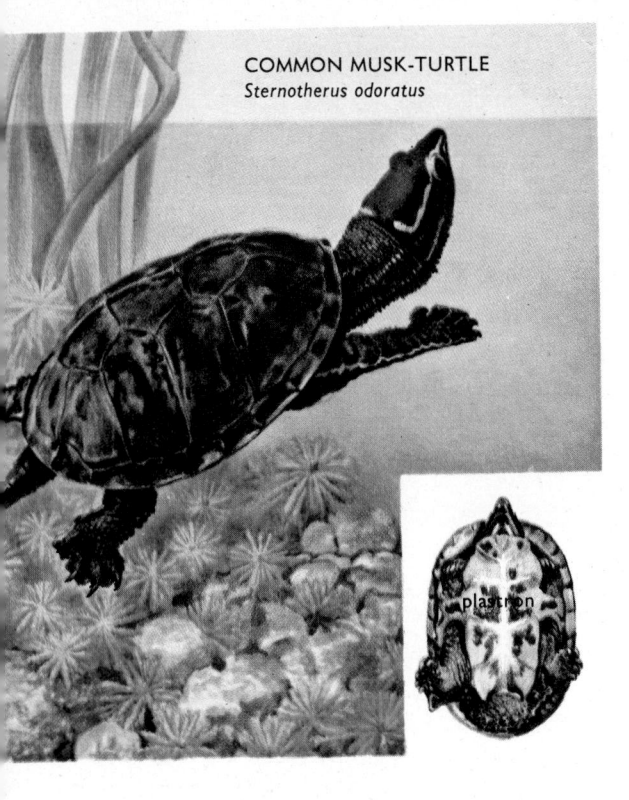

COMMON MUSK-TURTLE
Sternotherus odoratus

plastron

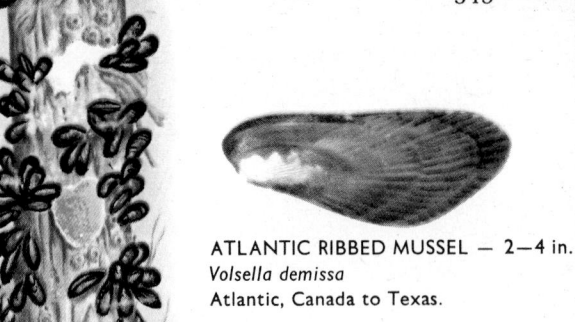

Blue Mussels
on piling

ATLANTIC RIBBED MUSSEL — 2—4 in.
Volsella demissa
Atlantic, Canada to Texas.

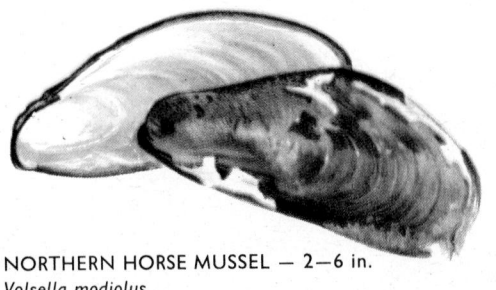

BLUE MUSSEL — 1—3 in.
Mytilus edulis
Europe and north-eastern America

NORTHERN HORSE MUSSEL — 2—6 in.
Volsella modiolus
North-eastern Atlantic

MUSK-TURTLES (*Sternotherus* spp.*) of some five species are found in the eastern United States. All are small (3 to 6 in.) and similar to mud-turtles, except that they have extensive areas of bare, whitish skin on the shell of the plastron. They are the most careless of all turtles in laying their eggs. The eggs are laid on the surface of the ground, or are feebly covered with leaves, or buried in rotten wood. Musk-turtles have a strong musky odour, and one species is often called the "Stinkpot".

MUSSELS are common, elongated, bival-ved molluscs that usually grow attached to rocks and pilings by bundles of tough threads secreted by a gland near the foot. They are found between the tides and at moderate depths. Some, such as Blue and Northern Horse Mussels of the Atlantic, and the Horse Mussel of California, form large clusters. Others, like the Yellow and Hooded Mussels, form great sheets of animals on exposed rocks. Date Mussels, of tropical Atlantic and California coasts, are shaped much like a date seed, and

burrow into dead coral or beach rocks. Mussels range in size from $\frac{3}{8}$ to 6 inches. Larger species are commonly eaten in Europe and are very popular. American mussels provide excellent food also, and are either steamed or roasted. Those from polluted water may harbour disease orga-nisms; mussels feed on plankton and may be poisonous at times, especially along the Pacific coast and in the Bay of Fundy.

MYNAHS (*Gracula religiosa,* and others*) are members of the starling family, and are native to India and adjacent parts of Asia. In their homeland, they are very bold, living near man and feeding largely on cultivated crops of fruit and insects. Mynahs are natural mimics and imitate whistles, phrases and miscellaneous sounds.

NARROW-MOUTHED FROGS, which belong to the family Microhylidae, are found in warm climates throughout the world. None lives north of the central United States nor in temperate areas of Europe and Asia. A dozen kinds occur in South America and about three dozen can be found in the Old World.

These frogs have narrow, pointed heads; short, flat legs; and swollen, often sac-like

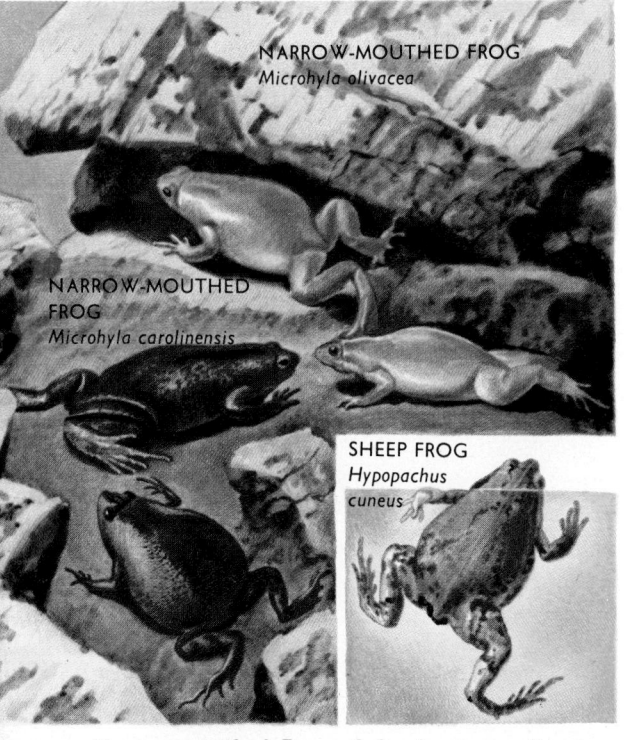

NARROW-MOUTHED FROG
Microhyla olivacea

NARROW-MOUTHED FROG
Microhyla carolinensis

SHEEP FROG
Hypopachus cuneus

Narrow-mouthed Frogs thrive in warm climates.

bodies. Most kinds are strong burrowers and dig under stones or logs, or directly into the ground. They are shy, like most other frogs and toads, and emerge only at night.

Most narrow-mouthed frogs specialise in eating ants. A few Old World species have expanded tips on their fingers and toes. These probably act like suction-cups for climbing trees and bushes.

Only two kinds are native to North America: a Narrow-mouthed Frog *(Microhyla)* and the Sheep Frog *(Hypopachus)*.

The toothless, burrowing Blaasops, or Rain Frogs *(Breviceps)*, of East and South Africa are fully terrestrial and complete their life cycle away from water, the larval stage being passed in the egg capsule and the eggs being laid in burrows. During mating, the male frog is "glued" to the back of the female and, if forcibly separated, the skin of the female is broken. These frogs emerge only after heavy rain and are generally to be found in ground close to termitaria; their diet consists of ants and termites.

Eggs of American and Asiatic narrow-mouthed frogs float on the surface of the water in a thin envelope of gelatine, which is flat on its top side. Each newly-hatched tadpole has on the underside of its head a pair of adhesive organs by which it fastens itself to objects. Its external gills are projections on the sides of its body, just behind its head. These disappear when internal gills develop, in hours or a few days.

African poison frogs *(Phyrnomerus)* belong to the same family. They are well-known for their strong skin poison and their brilliant red and black warning colours. When captured, these frogs secrete a milky, poisonous fluid that quickly becomes so gummy it is difficult to remove even by washing.

NEMATODES are roundworms, most of which are small or microscopic in size. The largest is the yard-long Guinea Worm,

a parasite of humans in tropical countries. Unlike leeches and earthworms, members of a different animal phylum, nematodes do not have segmented bodies.

Nematodes are among the most common of all forms of life in numbers of individuals. Some species live in soil, and others in fresh and salt water. Parasitic species live in the tissues of plants and animals. One acre of an infected cornfield may contain 500,000 nematodes in the top six inches of soil. A beetfield of the same size may contain as many as 12 million nematodes; 3,000 million nematodes per acre has even been recorded in especially rich soils.

Plant nematodes have sharp beaks, called stylets, with which they pierce the cell walls of roots, stems or leaves. They feed on the soft contents of the cells, and seriously infected plants develop symptoms known as root-knot, stem-and-bulb disease, and also others. Nematode-caused diseases are a major agricultural problem in many parts, and successful control measures have been developed only in recent years for some nematode pests.

Among the nematodes that are parasites in man are the intestinal roundworm

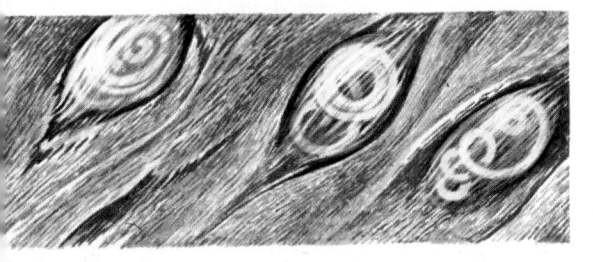

Trichinosis is a painful muscular disease. Trichina worms form cysts in muscle, shown (enlarged) above. Undercooked pork may contain the worms.

(Ascaris), trichina *(Trichinella)*, pinworm *(Enterobius)*, and hookworms *(Anclystoma)*. The heartworm *(Dirofilaria)* is transmitted to dogs by mosquitoes. Treatment for worms is usually with a drug that does not harm the host, but causes the worms to weaken so that they are carried out of the body with wastes. (See WORMS.)

NEWTS of about 60 species form the family Salamandridae, second largest family of salamanders. They occur in North America,

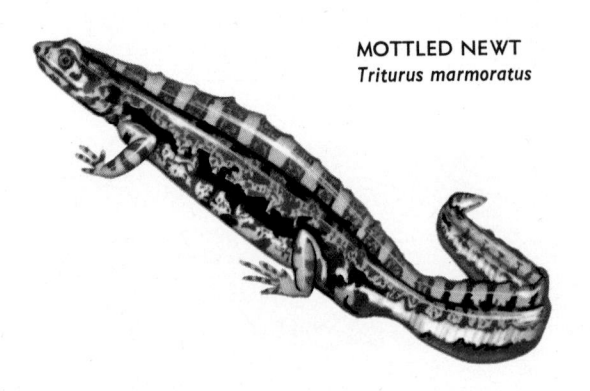

MOTTLED NEWT
Triturus marmoratus

LIFE CYCLE OF THE RED-SPOTTED NEWT
(Triturus viridescens)

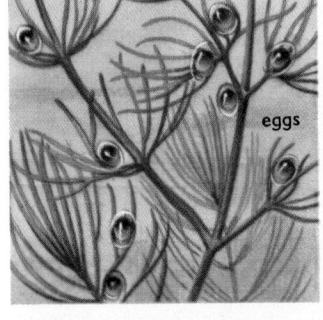

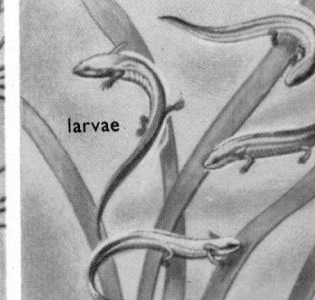

eggs

larvae

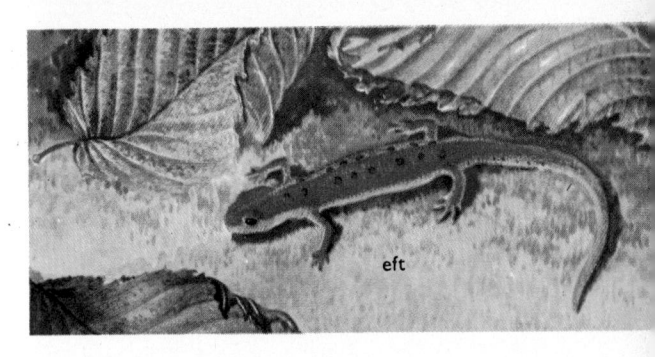

eft

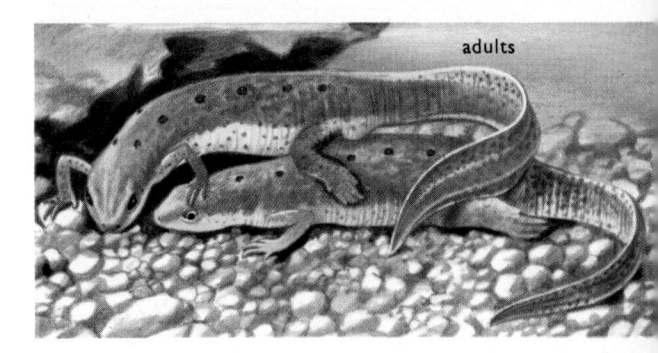

adults

348

throughout Europe, in Asia Minor, Algeria, and eastern Asia. Unlike lungless salamanders, newts do not have well-defined rib grooves, and also lack grooves between their nostrils and lips. All species have poisonous skin secretions, which in some are powerful

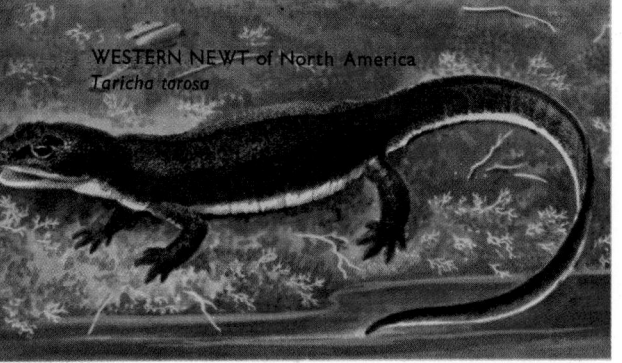

WESTERN NEWT of North America
Taricha torosa

and cause a sharp, burning sensation when they are touched.

A few larvae of newts do not transform but remain in the water, where they eventually become mature and breed; such a state is called neoteny and is quite common in the Alpine Newt *(Triturus alpestris)*.

The genus *Triturus* occurs only in Europe and West Asia, and three species extend into the British Isles; only one, the Common Newt *(Triturus vulgaris)*, is known from Ireland. The Warty Newt is the largest species and attains a total length of about six inches. During the breeding season, when all *Triturus* become fully aquatic and swim by means of a strongly-compressed tail, the males indulge in an elaborate courtship display, and some, like the Warty Newt, develop ornamental fringes to back and tail. After the breeding season, the fringe is absorbed. Eggs are laid singly, and are usually wrapped or enclosed by the female in the leaves of water plants.

The only known live-bearing (viviparous) salamanders occur in Europe. One, the Fire Salamander *(Salamandra salamandra)*, gives birth in the water to as many as 50 young larvae. It has been so-named because

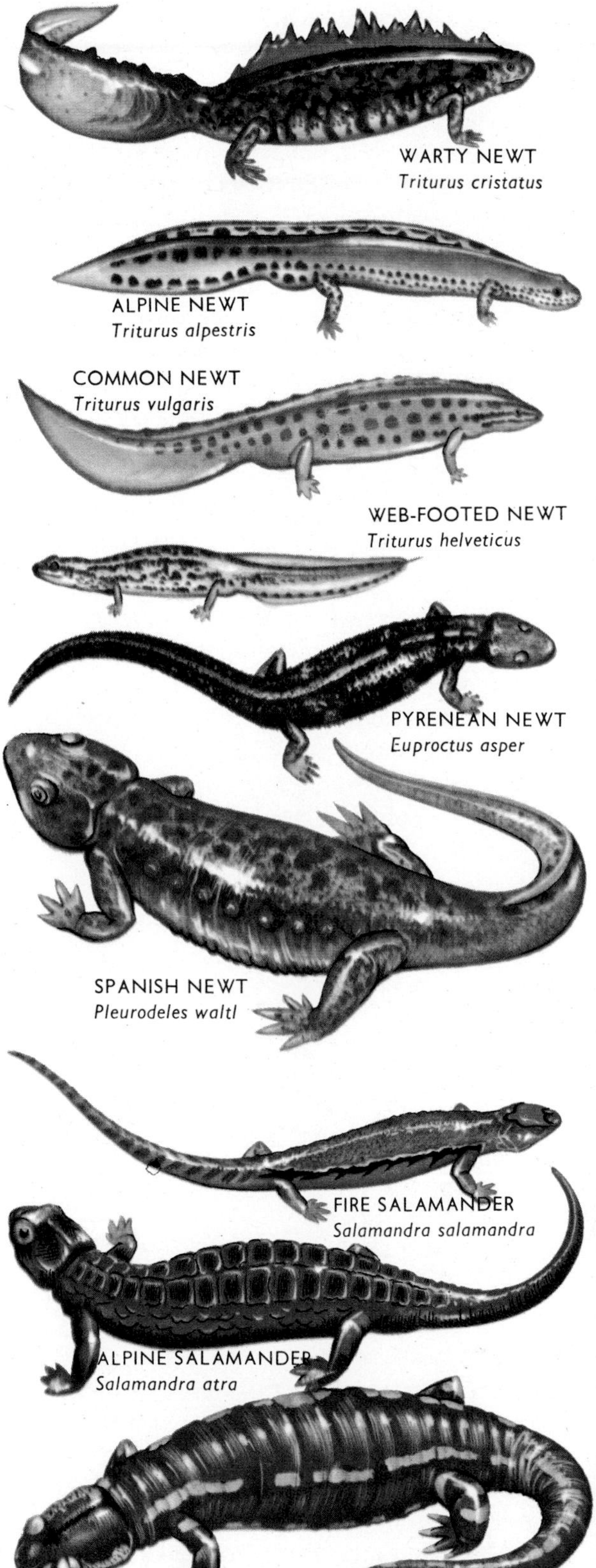

WARTY NEWT
Triturus cristatus

ALPINE NEWT
Triturus alpestris

COMMON NEWT
Triturus vulgaris

WEB-FOOTED NEWT
Triturus helveticus

PYRENEAN NEWT
Euproctus asper

SPANISH NEWT
Pleurodeles waltl

FIRE SALAMANDER
Salamandra salamandra

ALPINE SALAMANDER
Salamandra atra

SPECTACLED SALAMANDER
Salamandrina terdigitata

it is often forced from its hiding place in logs, or under their bark, when the wood is thrown into the fire. Because of this, it was once believed that salamanders were supernatural creatures, capable of living in fire. The Alpine Salamander *(Salamandra atra)* gives birth on land to two fully-transformed young. Many eggs are produced, but only two develop. The sharp ribs of the Spanish Newt *(Pleurodeles waltl)* project through its skin and pierce any animal that squeezes it.

NIGHTJARS are a family of night-flying, insect-eating birds, found in all parts of the world. They are slender-winged birds, possessing large eyes and a tiny bill with such a wide mouth that, when it gapes, the head seems almost to split in half. As night birds

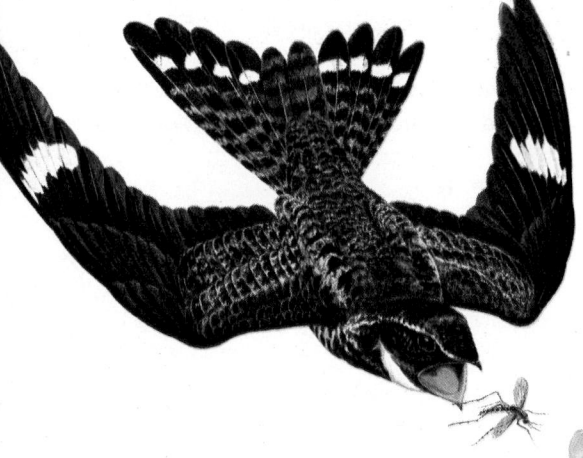

they are best known for their persistent songs. They feed by flying with the mouth wide open, snatching up insects in flight.

During the day, they rest on the ground or lengthwise on a tree branch. Their plumage is beautifully patterned and camouflaged, and often bears such a close resemblance to the dead leaf or bark background on which the birds rest that they pass as a piece of dead wood or a broken branch. The large, conspicuous eyes are kept closed to mere slits, even when the bird is wide awake. At night the eyes are fully open, and when the birds rest on open ground they reflect headlight beams.

Nightjars build no nest. They lay two eggs on the bare ground and sit closely, relying on their protective colouration, and only flying up at the last moment if danger threatens. Both parents take turns at incubating the eggs and feeding the young. In North America, the Common Nighthawk has taken to nesting on the flat roofs of town buildings in some places.

As night-flying birds, with cryptically coloured plumage, nightjars have little display plumage, and many species closely resemble each other. The most usual signal marks are white patches on wings and tail. One or two species have evolved unusual silhouettes. The Pennant-winged Nightjar has two wing-feathers prolonged into long streamers that trail behind the bird in flight, while the Standard-winged Nightjar has two similar feathers, but these are long, bare quills with large, rounded feathers at the ends. In flight, the bird looks as though it is being pursued by two smaller birds!

Most nightjars rely on the voice to make their presence known. The calls are usually

COMMON NIGHTHAWK — 9 in.
Chordeiles minor
Temperate North America

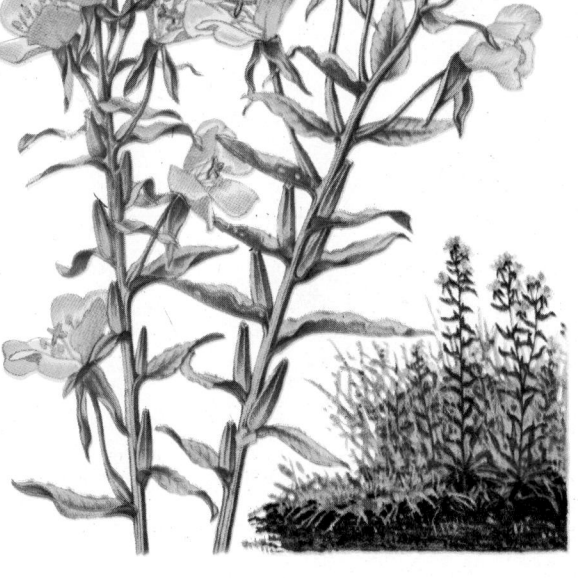

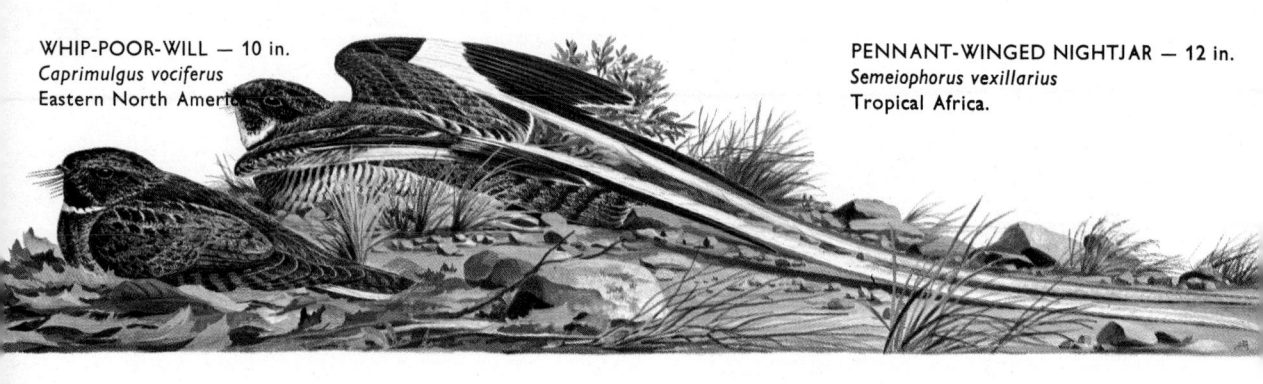

WHIP-POOR-WILL — 10 in.
Caprimulgus vociferus
Eastern North America

PENNANT-WINGED NIGHTJAR — 12 in.
Semeiophorus vexillarius
Tropical Africa.

either low-pitched churring or rapping sounds, or else whistling calls. The Common Nightjar emits a low-pitched churr like a distant engine. The sound carries on without a pause, and with only slight fluctuation in pitch, for very long periods.

Some nightjar calls resemble human phrases, and in this way the Whip-poor-will and Chuck-will's-widow of America have gained their names. The Common Night-hawk of North America is one of the few species which makes its call mechanically, diving from a height and making a buzzing sound with the wings at the end of the stoop.

Most of these birds feed on insects, but Chuck-will's-widow, with a two-inch gape on a twelve-inch body, has been found with small birds in its stomach. This is not too surprising, since some of the odder relatives of the nightjars — such as the large, owl-like Frogmouths — feed by swooping down and swallowing small mammals, reptiles and amphibians. Their need for large insects makes the nightjars summer visitors to most of the temperate regions.

NIGHT LIZARDS of about 15 species are found in the south-western United States, Mexico, Central America and Cuba. The largest is about six inches in length. All bear their young alive. They resemble the geckos and are probably closely related to them. Like most other nocturnal animals, their eyes have vertical pupils. The head is covered with large, smooth plates, the belly with rectangular scales, and the back and sides with granules and scattered, slightly enlarged nubbin-like scales. One type *(Xantusia)* lives under fallen stalks of yucca, or thin flakes weathered loose from granite rocks. Another *(Lepidophyma)* is found under bark of large dead trees and in crevices of limestone cliffs in the lowland jungles. Another *(Gaigeia)* is found limestone rocks in the pine belt of the high mountains of southern Mexico. Night lizards feed on insects.

NUTHATCHES are busy little birds that climb up and down tree-trunks looking for insects. They move up the trunk with their heads pointing up, and down and around with their heads pointing down. Their name comes from an old English verb meaning

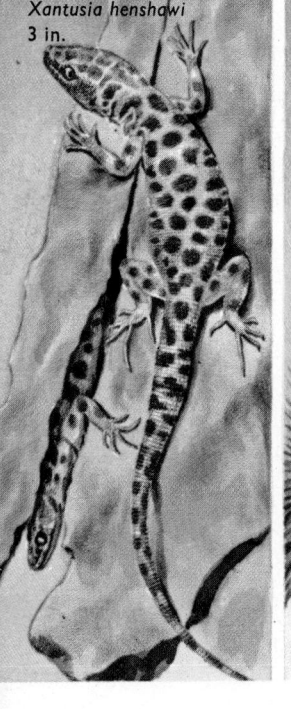

GRANITE NIGHT LIZARD
Xantusia henshawi
3 in.

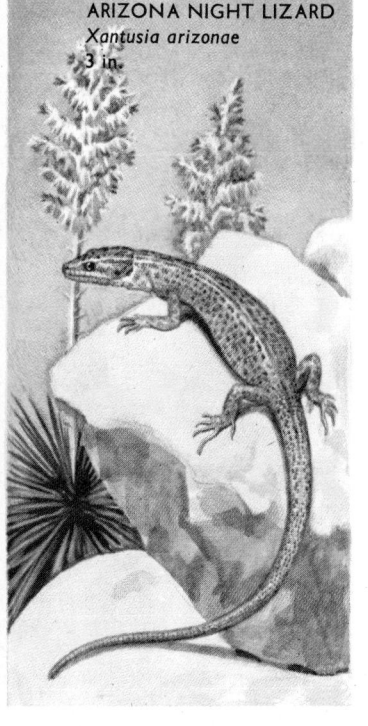

ARIZONA NIGHT LIZARD
Xantusia arizonae
3 in.

PYGMY
NUTHATCH
4½ in.
Sitta pygmaea
Western
North America

WHITE-BREASTED
NUTHATCH — 5½ in.
Sitta carolinensis
Southern Canada to Mexico

RED-BREASTED
NUTHATCH — 4½ in.
Sitta canadensis
Northern North America

VELVET-FRONTED NUTHATCH — 5 in.
Sitta frontalis
South-eastern Asia

"to chop with a hatchet", for European nuthatches push nuts or hard seeds into a bark crevice to chop them open with their strong bills. They build their nests in holes in trees, and the entrance is plastered up with mud to leave a hole just big enough for the adults to go in and out. The closely-related Rock Nuthatch climbs rocks, not trees, and builds its nest in a crevice, building over the entrance a cone of mud with the entrance hole at the tip. The nest cavity is lined with nest-material, and the male feeds the female while she incubates, and then helps her to feed the young.

The Red-breasted Nuthatch of North America seems to use a similar building technique, but nests among pines, and smears the nest entrance with resins. It feeds on pine seeds, and stores food for the winter.

Nuthatches are noisy birds at all times, and the European Nuthatch has a variety of loud whistling calls, and one spring song that sounds like a stone skimming over ice on a pond. They are inquisitive feeders and quite ready to try new foods at a bird-table.

NUTRIAS (*Myocastor coypus*) are large, brownish, round-tailed South American rodents that may weigh as much as 35 pounds. They are also known by such names as Coypu, South American Beaver, and Russian Rat. Much like Musk-rats in habits, though they may be active more often during the day, Nutrias are excellent swimmers, living in swamps or along waterways. They build nests by piling together vegetation, or sometimes by digging short burrows into riverbanks. They have become serious pests in some areas. Females may have as many as three litters every year, and the young are able to care for themselves within a few hours after their birth. A young female may bear young when she is eight months old.

Because of their fur, Nutrias have been introduced into many parts of the world, including Britain. Where they have escaped they have established themselves in the wild. Fur-farmers have produced a number of attractive mutant shades of Nutrias, but have so far failed to build a substantial enough interest in the fur to make raising the animals a profitable business.

NUTRIA
30—42 in. long

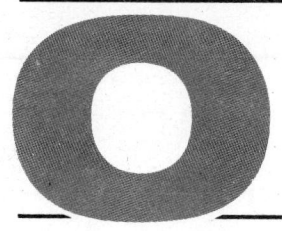

OCEAN PERCH *(Sebastes norvegicus)*, known in Britain as the Norway Haddock, occurs in deep water and bears live young. A related species *(S. marinus)* is a commerical fish along the American Atlantic coast.

OCEAN SUNFISH

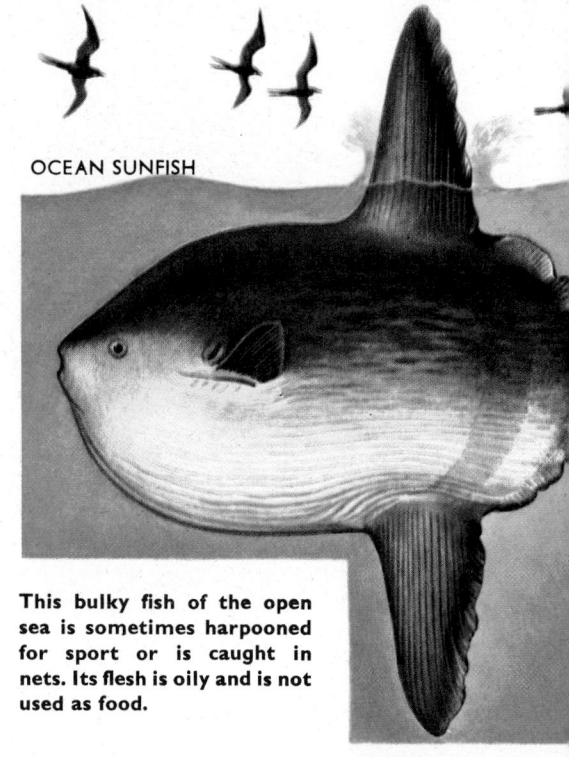

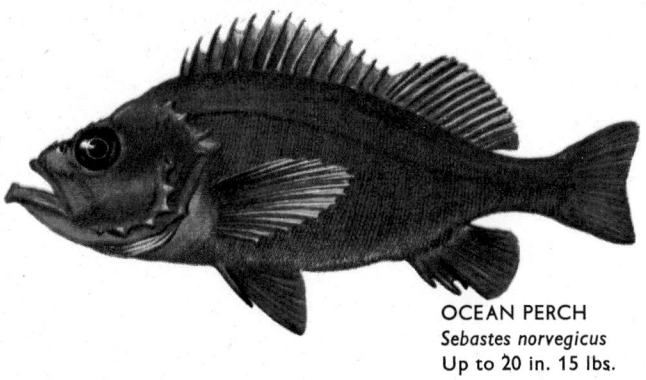

OCEAN PERCH
Sebastes norvegicus
Up to 20 in. 15 lbs.

OCEAN SUNFISH *(Mola mola)* is a giant-sized fish of warm, open seas, yet it is related to the puffers and porcupine fishes. It appears to be all head, hence it is also called Headfish. Possessing a small mouth and a horny beak it is known to reach a length of 11 feet and a weight of 2,000 pounds (averaging less than half this size). These great fish are often found in the open sea, floating on their sides, and are apparently helpless when they get into cold water.

This bulky fish of the open sea is sometimes harpooned for sport or is caught in nets. Its flesh is oily and is not used as food.

OCTOPUSES are round-bodied cephalopods that have eight sucker-equipped arms around their head. Secretive animals, they live in shallow to deep water, in holes or beneath rocks or corals, and feed on clams, crabs and lobsters. Octopuses crawl about on their arms or occasionally swim slowly by jet propulsion. Either for protection or when excited, they can change colours rapidly. The colours in a wide range flow over their heads like waves of light. Octopuses have been the subject of much study

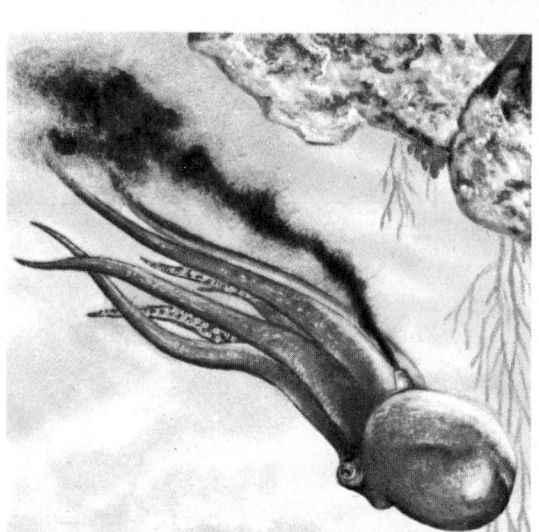

The ink ejected by the octopus may divert a possible predator by affecting its sense of vision or smell.

Most octopuses, like the female Common Octopus guarding her egg-clusters under a rock ledge, are bottom dwellers. A few species, such as the Paper Nautilus, wander over the surface of seas.

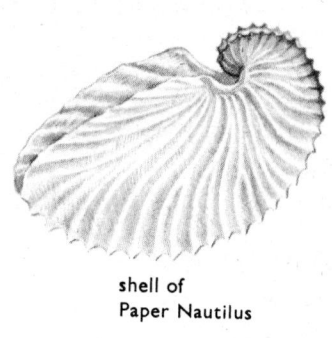

shell of
Paper Nautilus

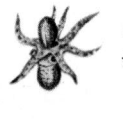

male
½ in.

COMMON OCTOPUS
Octopus vulgaris
Tentacle spread, up to 10 ft.

PAPER NAUTILUS
Argonauta argo

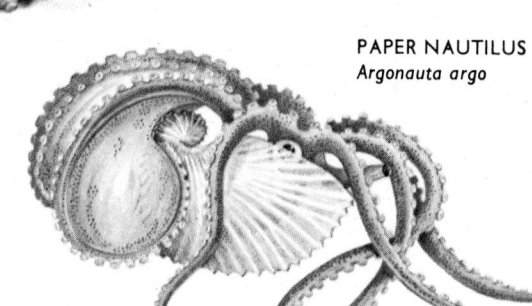

female
to 12 in.

because of their apparently intelligent behaviour. It has been demonstrated that they can learn and remember past actions.

The largest known octopus had an arm spread of 30 feet and came from the Pacific North-west. Reports of dangers from octopuses are greatly exaggerated, though the bites of few species are dangerous, due to a poison secreted into the wound. Eggs of shallow-water species are laid in grape-like clusters or in single layers under rocks. Newly-hatched young may resemble the adults or may drift in the plankton as larvae.

The Paper Nautilus (*Argonauta argo*) lives in the open sea, where it floats or swims on the surface. The female Paper Nautilus has a coiled shell about eight inches long, used as a float or egg-chamber.

Octopuses (*Octopus* spp.) are highly prized by many people as a table delicacy. Unlike squids, an octopus may use its ink like a smoke-screen to slip away from pursuers. (See CEPHALOPODS; SQUIDS.)

OKAPIS (*Okapia johnstoni*) are relatives of the Giraffe, but lack its very long neck and legs. They are only five feet tall and are not spotted. The males, like giraffes, have fur-covered horns on their forehead, and both sexes have long tongues and very flexible lips, useful for picking leaves from trees and bushes. Okapis are shy, living singly or in pairs in the densest parts of the damp Congo, in Central Africa. They feed at night. Okapis have horizontal, zebra-like stripes on their thighs, haunches, and the upper parts of their forelegs; the remainder of the body is dark reddish-brown. They have very long, broad ears. Okapis were not discovered

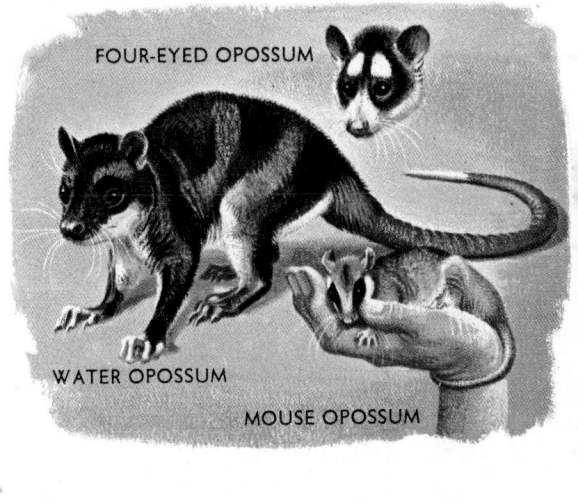

OKAPI
Height at shoulder:
5—5½ ft.

FOUR-EYED OPOSSUM

WATER OPOSSUM

MOUSE OPOSSUM

until just after the turn of this century, although they have long been known to the pygmies of the Congo, the animals' natural home. They have been brought to most of our larger zoos, but not much is known about the history and habits of the okapi.

OLIVE SHELLS (*Oliva* spp.) are beautifully coloured and marked shells that burrow just beneath the surface in sandy areas. The living shells are completely covered by the soft mantle, which gives the shells a glossy lustre. A good example is the Lettered Olive, or Panama Shell, found along the south-eastern coast of the United States and in the Gulf of Mexico; it is the largest (2 to 2½ in.) of the American species. Occasionally golden-coloured specimens of this and the Netted Olive are found. They are easily discovered by following their deep tracks, which are like tiny, ploughed furrows.

OPOSSUMS are marsupial mammals (see MAMMALS) found from South and Central America northward into central North America. In some kinds, the marsupium (or pouch) consists only of two folds of skin. In others it is a well-formed pouch. The young are born small and immature. They stay in the pouch, attached to the nipples of the female, until about a quarter grown.

Among the earliest fossil mammals discovered, there have been marsupials which closely resemble the present-day opossums of North America. The opossum group was once widespread, but failed to compete with more advanced placental mammals.

The Common, or Virginia, Opossum (*Didelphys virginiana*) occurs in South America and northward to California and through the eastern United States. It prefers forested areas, where it finds shelter in hollow trees or in burrows in the ground.

Living Olive Shell, showing foot and head extended and the mantle covering part of the outer shell.

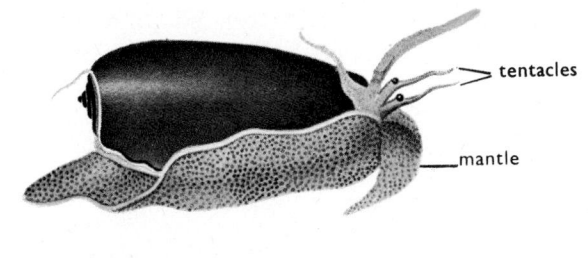

tentacles

mantle

ORANGE-MOUTHED OLIVE — 3 in.
Oliva sericea
Indo-Pacific   four colour variations

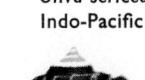

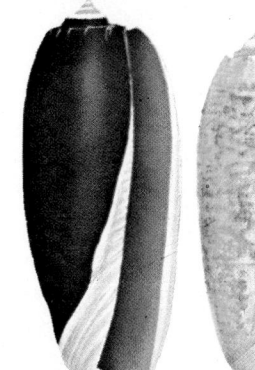

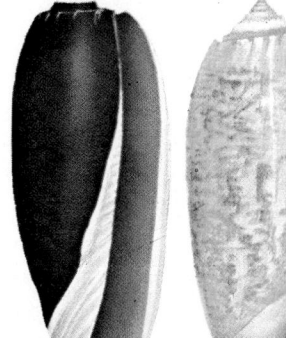

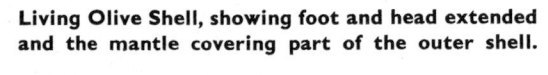

About the size of a large cat when grown, it has a long, scaly, almost bare tail, naked ears, a pointed face, and grasping feet. This opossum eats fruit, insects, small mammals or birds — nearly anything, living or dead. It avoids enemies by running, hiding, biting, or feigning death. Thirteen days after mating the young are born, each weighing less than 1/15th ounce. Not more than half-a-dozen of the twenty or so in a litter reach maturity. The young live in the mother's fur-lined pouch for nearly three months.

The Four-eyed Opossum (*Philander opossum*) has a set of light-coloured spots between and above its eyes. This tropical opossum, found in Central America, tropical Mexico and the northern regions of South America, is considerably smaller than the Common Opossum. Much of its time is spent in bushes and trees, where it hangs by its tail from branches. It has short, woolly fur.

Mouse opossums (*Marmosa spp.*) are mouse-grey in colour, and some kinds are not much larger than house mice. They feed on insects and fruits and are sometimes accidentally transported with large shipments of bananas. Females lack a pouch. The young are probably nursed in a nest which the mother builds in the trees.

The Water Opossum (*Chironectes minimus*) of South and Central America has entirely webbed feet, and full adaptation for water life. It inhabits burrows near waterways, where it hunts for crayfish, water insects and fish. The mother apparently carries her young in her pouch while she swims. Water opossums are smaller than the Common, or Virginia, Opossum.

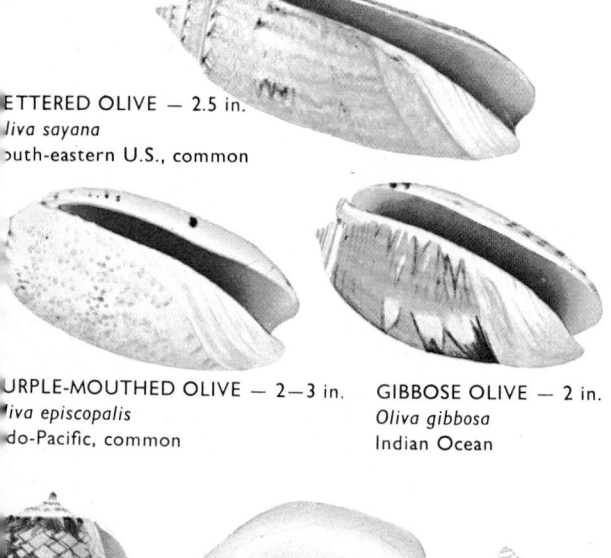

LETTERED OLIVE — 2.5 in.
Oliva sayana
South-eastern U.S., common

PURPLE-MOUTHED OLIVE — 2—3 in.
Oliva episcopalis
Indo-Pacific, common

GIBBOSE OLIVE — 2 in.
Oliva gibbosa
Indian Ocean

EAR OLIVE — 2 in.
Olivancillaria auricularia
Eastern South America

PURPLE DWARF OLIVE — 1.3 in.
Olivella biplicata
Pacific Coast of U.S.

TENT OLIVE — 3—5 in.
Oliva prophyria
W. Central America

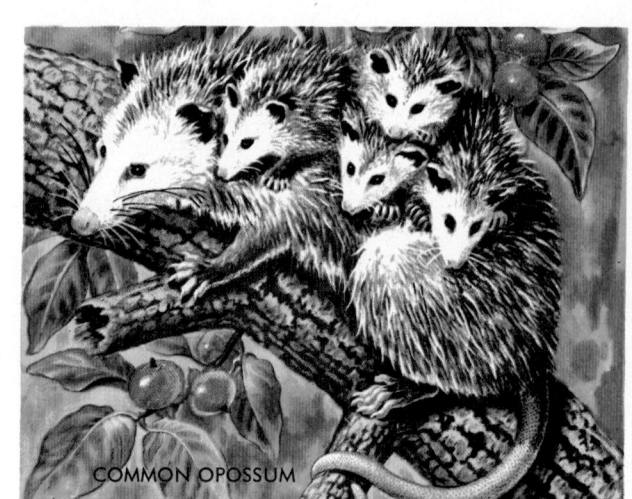

COMMON OPOSSUM

These young opossums clinging to their mother's back are nearly big enough to be independent.

ORANG-UTANS, or Orang-outangs (*Simia satyrus*), are apes with long, reddish hair, an immense arm span and powerful shoulders. Large males may weigh 200 pounds; females are smaller. Orang-utans live in the dense forests and jungles of Borneo and Sumatra, where they move about by slowly swinging from one large branch to another. They build sleeping-platforms in trees and feed mostly on fruits. A single young is born

after about a nine-month gestation period. Orang-utans probably live 15 to 30 years in the wild. (See PRIMATES.)

ORIOLE, like Flycatcher, is a name that has been given to two different groups of birds — in the Eastern Hemisphere referring to the family Oriolidae, and in the Western Hemisphere referring to the more brightly coloured members of the Icteridae.

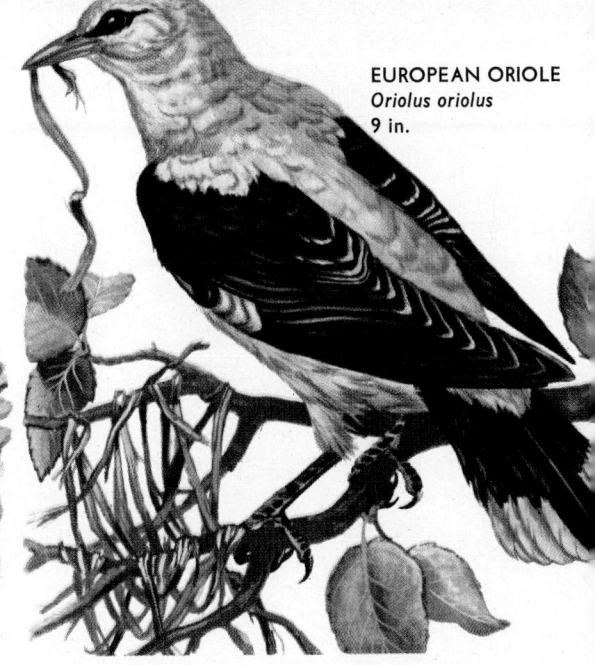

EUROPEAN ORIOLE
Oriolus oriolus
9 in.

orange and black. They are much more accomplished nest-weavers, and some species known as Hangnests weave long, pendant, bag-shaped nests, often in colonies. The nest of some species may be six feet long, but that of the Baltimore Oriole, will only be about six inches deep. Whereas the eastern oriole resemble thrushes, these American species are more reminiscent of the starlings, with tapering bills and rather close-set eyes.

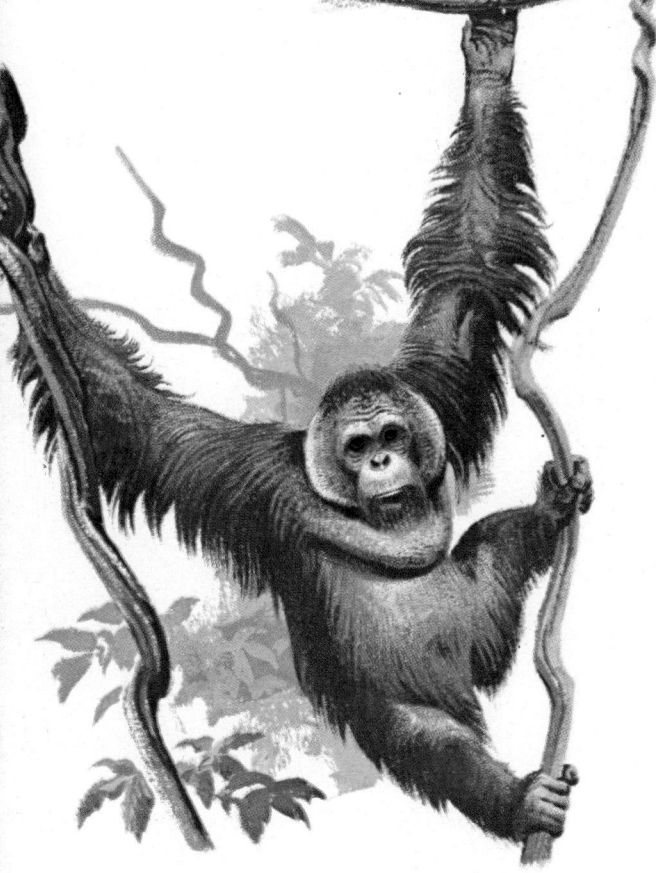

Orang-utans may have arm-spread of 7½ feet.

In the true Orioles, the males are usually yellow and black, although one shown here is maroon and black. Females and young are greenish like the Figbirds. They are mostly fruit-eaters, living in trees and making nests which are slung like a hammock between two twigs.

The western orioles are superficially similar, being boldly patterned in yellow or

OSPREY — 24 in.
Pandion haliaetus
Cosmopolitan, except for polar regions, New Zealand, and S. South America

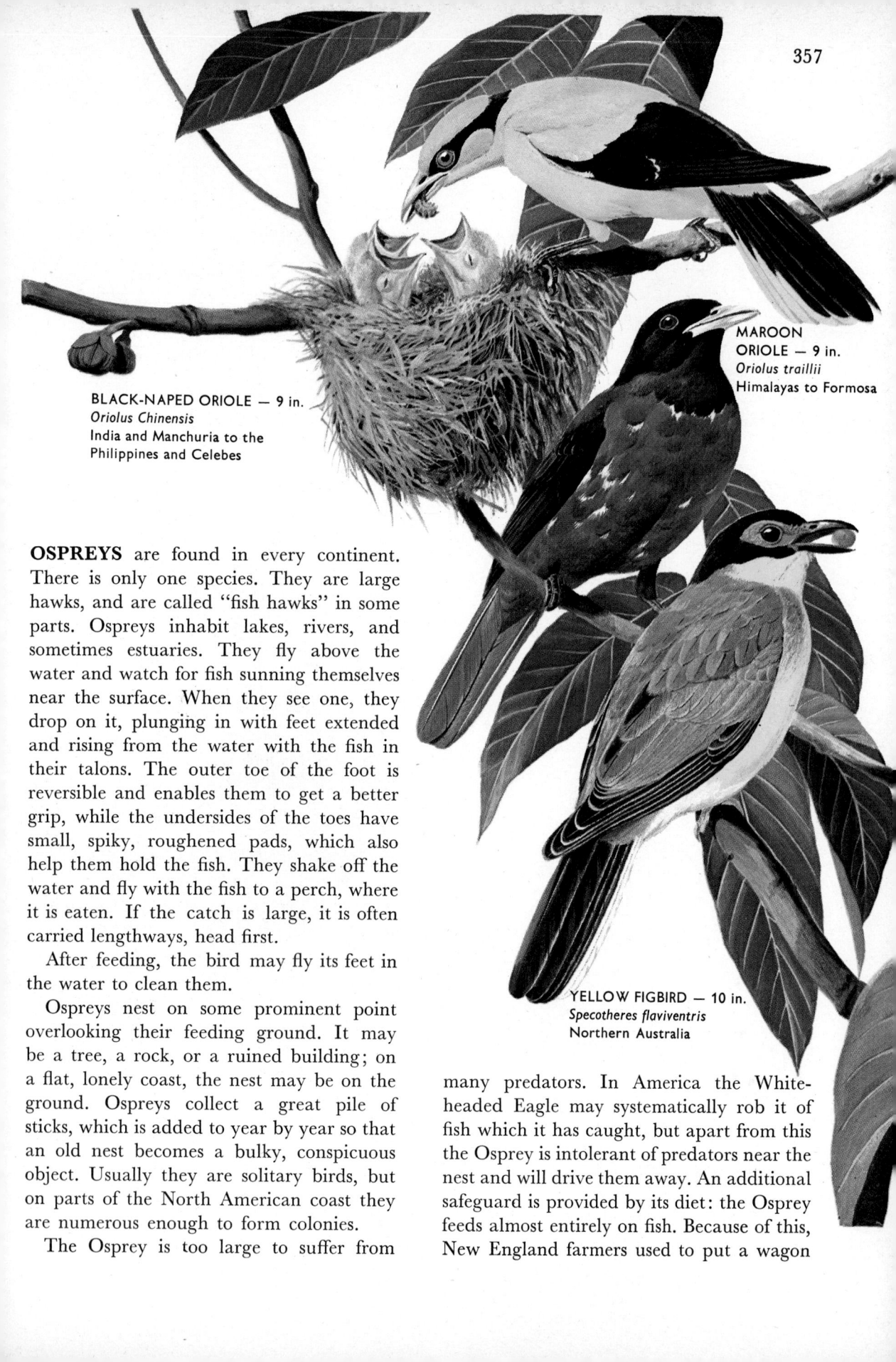

BLACK-NAPED ORIOLE — 9 in.
Oriolus Chinensis
India and Manchuria to the
Philippines and Celebes

MAROON
ORIOLE — 9 in.
Oriolus traillii
Himalayas to Formosa

YELLOW FIGBIRD — 10 in.
Specotheres flaviventris
Northern Australia

OSPREYS are found in every continent. There is only one species. They are large hawks, and are called "fish hawks" in some parts. Ospreys inhabit lakes, rivers, and sometimes estuaries. They fly above the water and watch for fish sunning themselves near the surface. When they see one, they drop on it, plunging in with feet extended and rising from the water with the fish in their talons. The outer toe of the foot is reversible and enables them to get a better grip, while the undersides of the toes have small, spiky, roughened pads, which also help them hold the fish. They shake off the water and fly with the fish to a perch, where it is eaten. If the catch is large, it is often carried lengthways, head first.

After feeding, the bird may fly its feet in the water to clean them.

Ospreys nest on some prominent point overlooking their feeding ground. It may be a tree, a rock, or a ruined building; on a flat, lonely coast, the nest may be on the ground. Ospreys collect a great pile of sticks, which is added to year by year so that an old nest becomes a bulky, conspicuous object. Usually they are solitary birds, but on parts of the North American coast they are numerous enough to form colonies.

The Osprey is too large to suffer from many predators. In America the White-headed Eagle may systematically rob it of fish which it has caught, but apart from this the Osprey is intolerant of predators near the nest and will drive them away. An additional safeguard is provided by its diet: the Osprey feeds almost entirely on fish. Because of this, New England farmers used to put a wagon

wheel on top of a high pole, so that an osprey would nest near the farm and protect the chickens. It has, however, an unfortunate habit of picking up a large variety of objects and using them as nest material.

OSTRACODS are small, bivalved crustaceans — the large group that includes lobsters, crabs, shrimps and barnacles. Ostracods live in salt and fresh water, and most of them are so small that they cannot be seen with the naked eye. In some parts of the ocean they exist in countless numbers. Ostracods eat both tiny plants and animals, dead or alive. Most kinds live or burrow on the sea floor, but others drift in the sea as plankton. Their flat body is completely enclosed by a shell of two valves, joined by teeth and muscles along a dorsal hinge-line; one valve often overlaps the other. (See CRUSTACEANS.)

Ostracod fossils are found in rocks from Ordovician to Recent in age, and in both marine and fresh-water strata. In some rocks they are very abundant. The wide distribution of ostracod fossils makes them useful in correlating rocks.

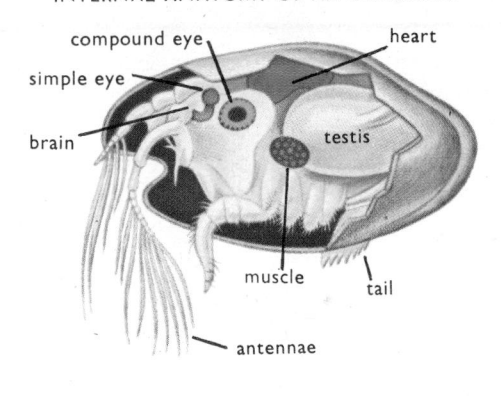

INTERNAL ANATOMY OF AN OSTRACOD

compound eye
simple eye
brain
heart
testis
muscle
tail
antennae

Ostriches have only two toes on each foot.

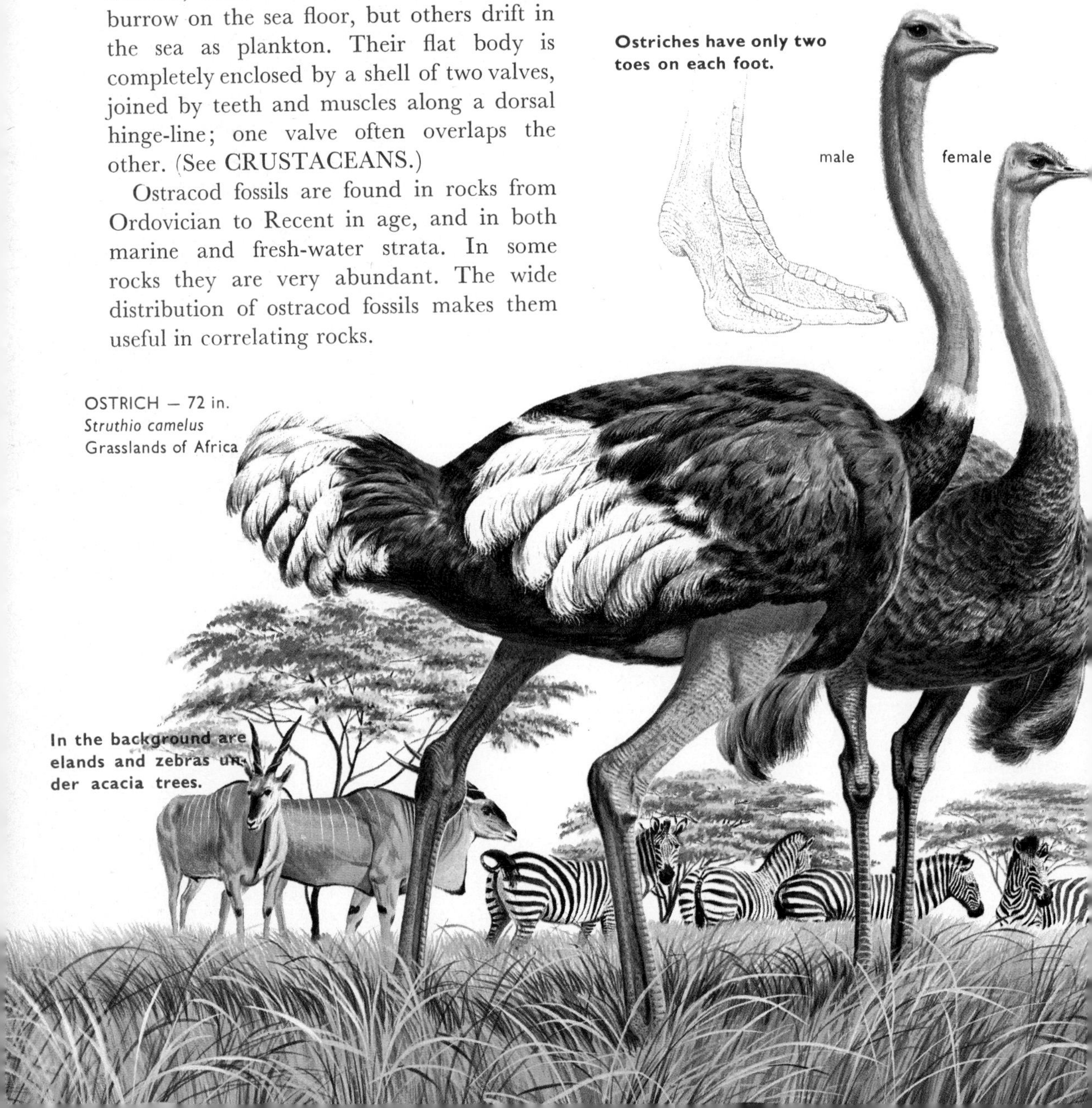

male   female

OSTRICH — 72 in.
Struthio camelus
Grasslands of Africa

In the background are elands and zebras under acacia trees.

OSTRICHES, best known of the flightless birds, are the largest living birds in the world. A male ostrich may weigh as much as 345 pounds. At one time ostriches lived in southern Europe, in Asia as far north as the Gobi Desert, and all through Africa. Today they survive only in the Sahara Desert and the dry tablelands of south-eastern Africa.

Men have hunted ostriches for thousands of years. Their meat was used for feasts and their plumes as ornaments. Their eggs were made into containers.

Ostriches are about eight feet tall. Their silhouettes against the sky can be seen for miles. Ostriches hide from their enemies by crouching flat on the ground, where their colouring makes them almost invisible, or seek safety by running; they do not bury their heads in the sand. Ostriches are wary and very shy, and have survived because of their alertness and their speed; they can run faster than their enemies — almost 40 miles an hour when in danger — and are fierce fighters. They have only two toes on each foot, but these are as heavy and hard as a horse's hoofs; their kick is so wicked that they can even defend themselves against lions. The Ostrich's voice produces a loud, booming roar, and it can also hiss.

Ostriches do well in captivity. They have been raised on farms for their plumes, and have even been taught to pull carts. Ostrich skins can be tanned to make leather, and are used in the manufacture of wallets, gloves, and similar items.

OTTERS are beautifully furred, weasel-like mammals adapted for life in the water. They have a streamlined body, small ears, a long, powerful, tapering, rudder-like tail, and webbed feet. Their short, dense fur is oily, and a layer of fat beneath the skin keeps them warm, despite cold water.

River Otters *(Lutra canadensis)*, though much less abundant now than formerly, still live in a few large, unpolluted rivers in Canada and the U.S.A. They feed on small fish, musk-rats, crayfish, insects, frogs, small birds, and mammals. Otters build "slides"

on stream-banks, and apparently enjoy sliding down the mud into the water. During winter, they frequently slide and tumble in the snow. In late spring, each female bears two or three pups, which remain with her while she teaches them to swim and hunt.

Otters that live in the Amazon River basin of South America, and another species found in Africa, are both larger than the River Otter of North America. They reach a length of almost five feet and may weigh as much as 60 pounds. Other small, fresh-water otters, all similar in appearance, are found from Europe, Asia and India, to as far east as Java, and also in tropical Africa.

Sea Otters *(Enhydra lutris)* live entirely in the sea, and only rarely come to land. They eat, sleep and give birth to their young at sea. Originally they were abundant in the Pacific coastal waters from California northward to Alaska, and southward from there to Japan. Excessive hunting for their valuable fur greatly reduced their numbers — almost to extinction. Sea Otters live in herds, and to keep from drifting apart during the night, while asleep, each one wraps itself in a ribbon of kelp or holds a strand under one arm. Then the whole herd floats with the tangled mass of seaweed. Sea Otters eat fish, abalones, sea-urchins, clams, and other marine animals. Breaking abalones (large molluscs) loose from their firm attachment to the rocks, or opening clam-shells, requires both

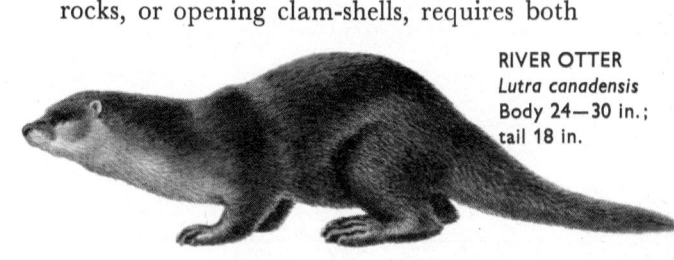

RIVER OTTER
Lutra canadensis
Body 24—30 in.;
tail 18 in.

Sea Otters can avoid drifting by holding on to kelp.

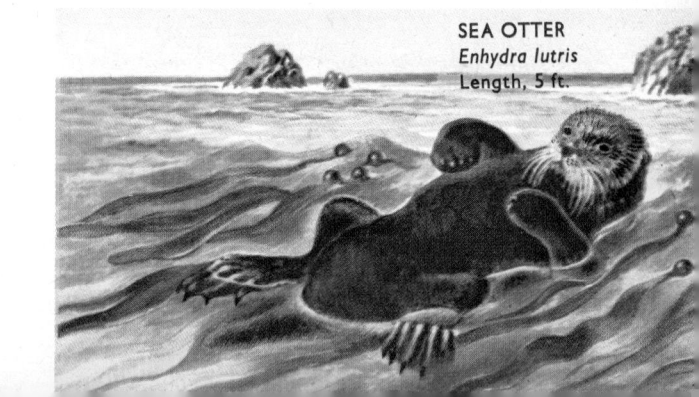

SEA OTTER
Enhydra lutris
Length, 5 ft.

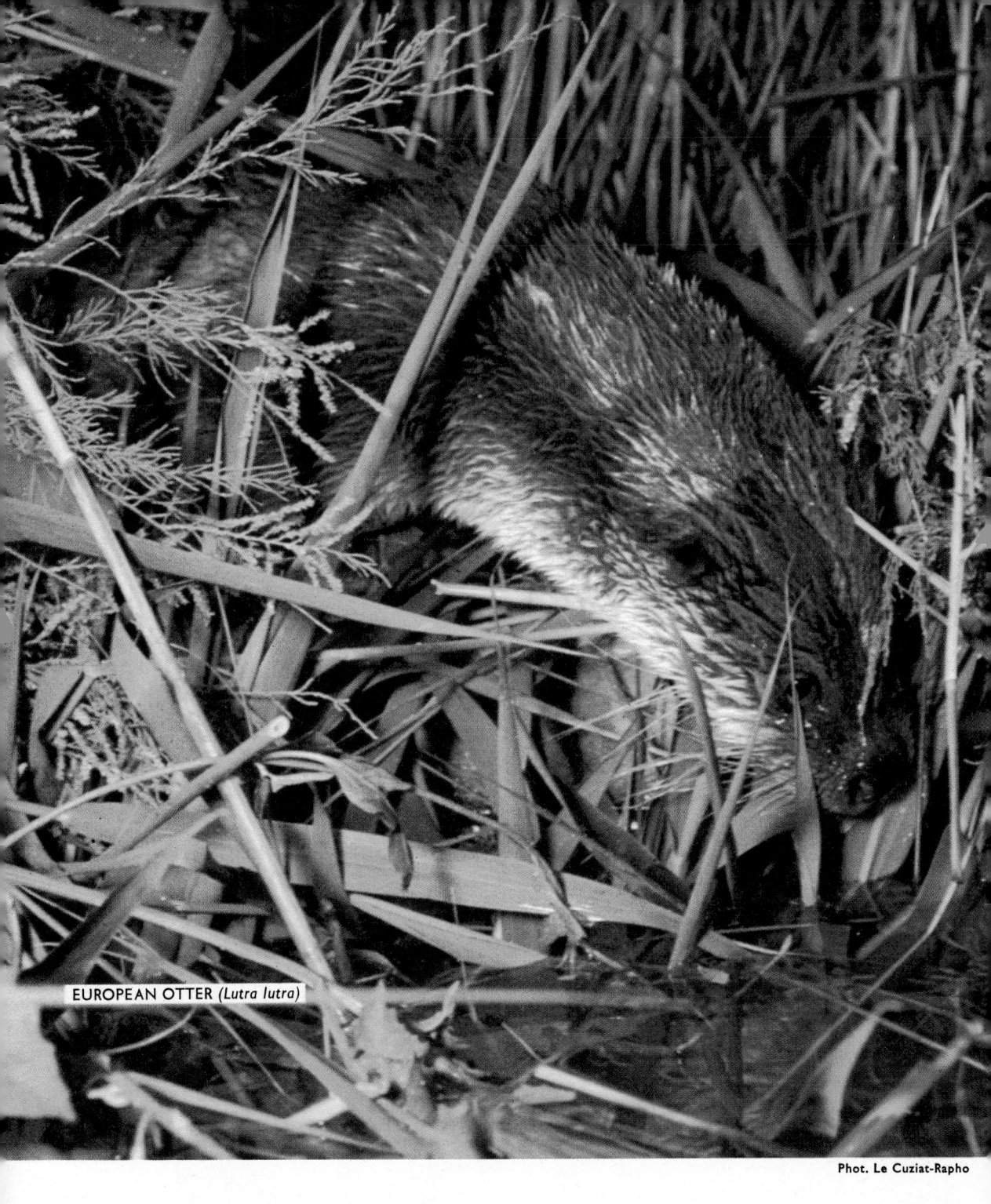

EUROPEAN OTTER *(Lutra lutra)*

Phot. Le Cuziat-Rapho

strength and cleverness. For example, a sea otter breaks a clam-shell by lying on its back, and then placing a large, flat rock on its stomach. Next the clam is laid on the rock, after which the sea otter strikes it with another rock. As the shell breaks, the sea otter scoops out the soft meat inside.

OWLS have very large eyes set in the front of a round head. As their eyes face forwards, and they cannot move their eyeballs, owls must turn their whole head to look around.

Owls have very soft, fluffy plumage that makes them seem larger than they are. Many have ear-like tufts of feathers on their head;

the legs, and sometimes the toes, are feathered. Owls have strong feet, with sharp claws with which they grab and kill prey.

Owls are found in all lands except Antarctica. They seldom migrate, but lack of food sometimes drives them to new hunting grounds. Most of them hunt during the night, but a few species hunt day, too. Owls can see in the light just as well as in the dark; they have an extra, transparent eyelid which protects their eyes from glare.

Owls eat small mammals, fish, reptiles, insects, and other birds. The owl's gizzard separates the indigestible bones, fur or feathers, and forms them into neat, smooth little balls called pellets, which the owl coughs up and spits out. An owl's nest can be found by looking for these pellets. By examining the bones and fur in the pellets, scientists learn what an owl eats.

All owls use little if any nesting material, and nest in a great variety of places — from a burrow in the ground to a deserted eagle's nest set high in a tree. They use hollow logs, empty crates, hollow trees and buildings. The females usually lay up to seven almost round, white eggs. In some species, the female does all the incubating, but the helpless young are always cared for by both parents.

Barn Owls live all over the world. They do

1 SPECTACLED OWL — 17 in.
Pulsatrix perspicillata
Mexico to Argentina

2 ELF OWL — 5½ in.
Micrathene whitneyi
Southern United States and Mexico

3 SNOWY OWL — 25 in.
Nyctea scandiaca
Circumpolar, in arctic tundra

4 AMERICAN EAGLE OWL
25 in. *Bubo virginianus*
Western Hemisphere from tree line to Patagonia, except West Indies

5 BARN OWL — 15 in.
Tyto alba
Cosmopolitan, except polar regions

6 AMERICAN BARN OWL — 10 in. *Otus asio*
Temperate North America and Mexico

7 FERRUGINOUS PYGMY OWL — 7 in.
Glaucidium brasilianum
South-west U. S. to Patagonia

8 BARRED OWL — 20 in.
Strix varia
Central and eastern North America and Mexico

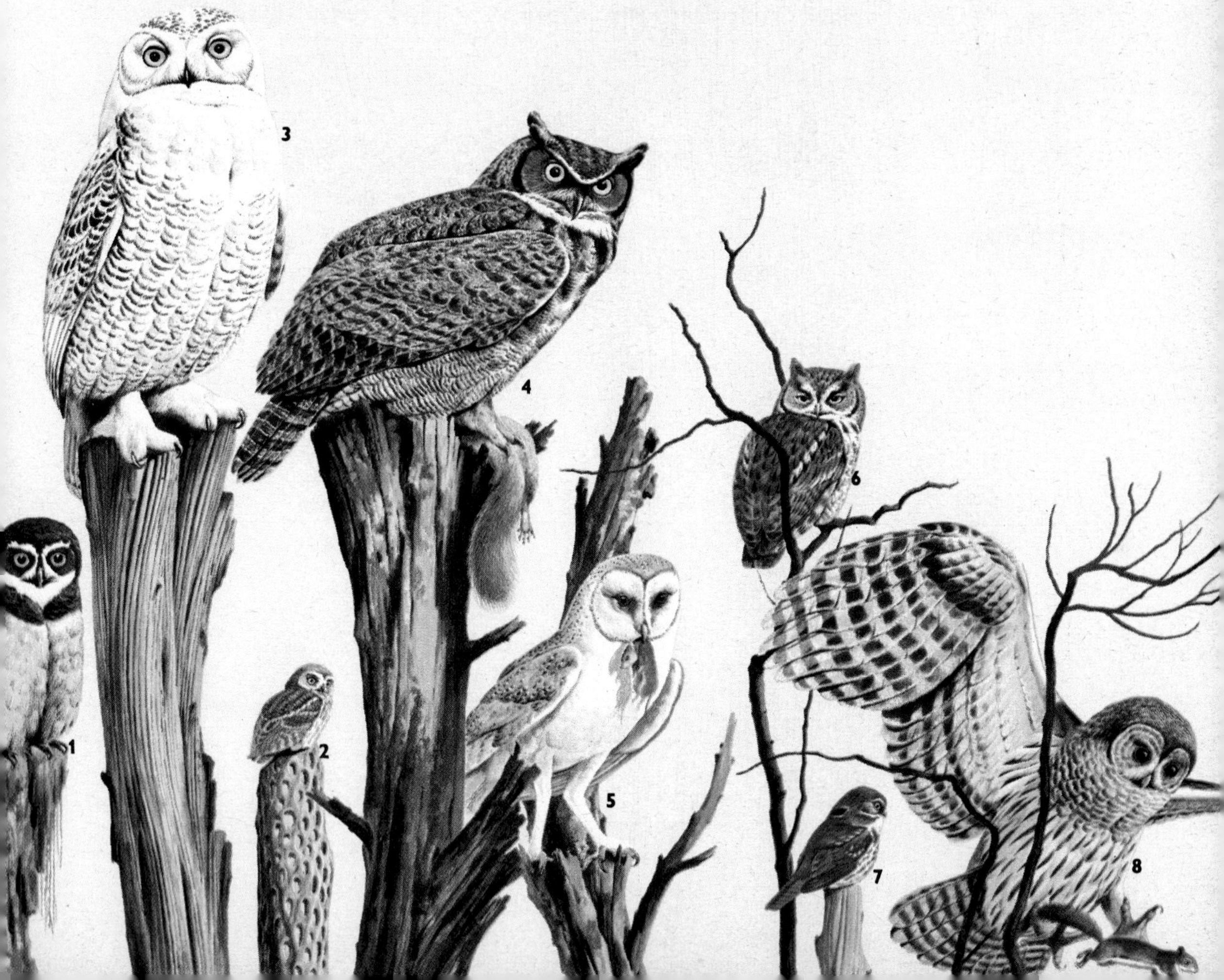

362

not build a nest; sometimes they use a nest deserted by crows or hawks, but more often lay their eggs in barns, sheds, church-towers, empty houses, or hollow trees. They hunt at night, as much by hearing as by sight, and can catch a mouse in complete darkness by detecting its faint rustlings.

Barn Owls utter cries and calls which have given them a false reputation as birds of ill omen. They live almost entirely on rodents, and control them far better than cats do.

Owls have a fine, downy surface to their

Atlas-Photo-Vienne

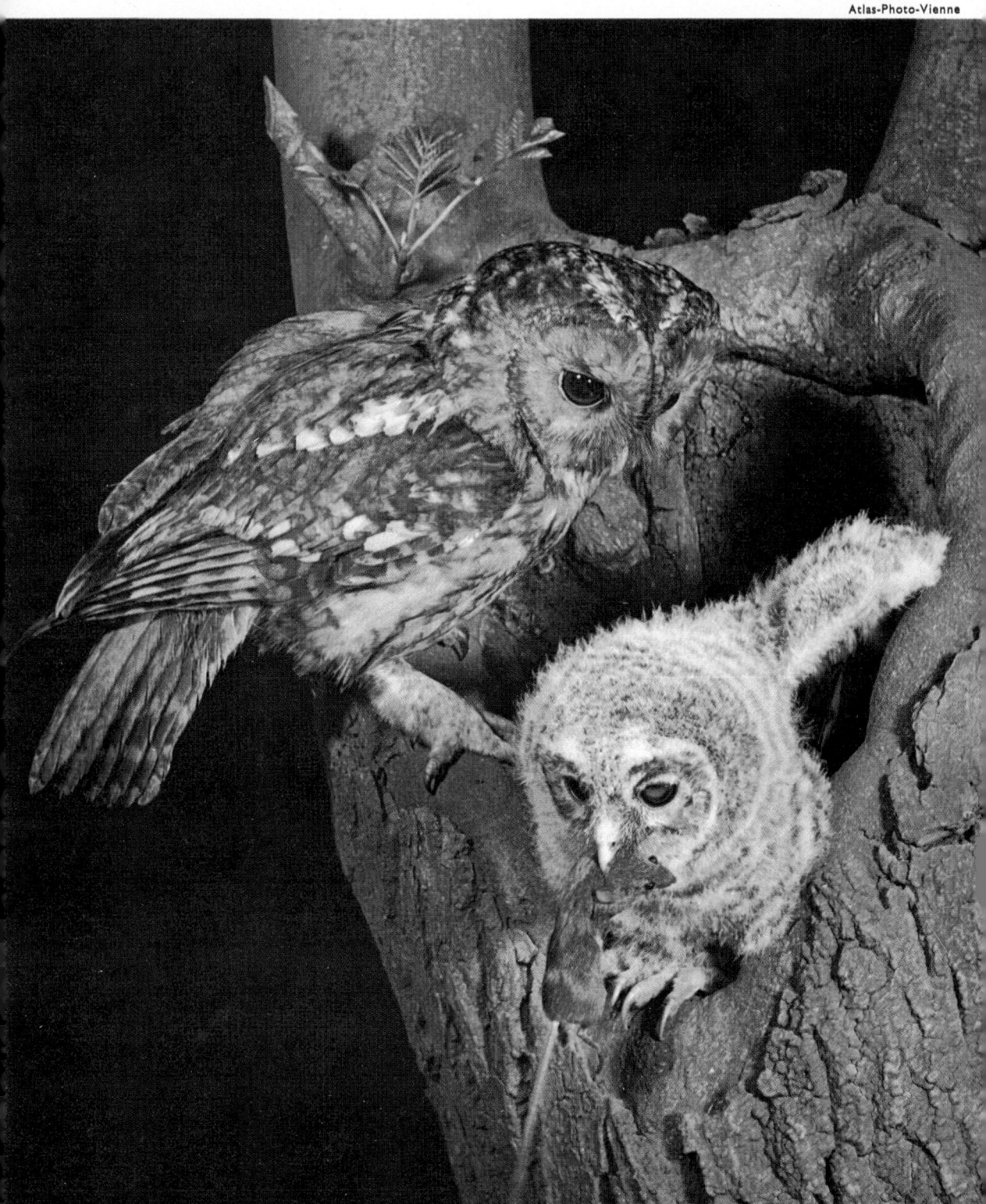

feathers, which makes their flight absolutely silent and gives their prey no warning. The only owl lacking this is the Fishing Owl shown in the illustration. This bird seizes fish from near the surface of the water, and thus has no feathering on the legs.

Most owls nest in tree or rock holes. The Little Owl will use a rabbit burrow, and the Burrowing Owl of the prairies (see illustration) digs its own burrow, four to eight feet long with a nest cavity at the end. Some species nest on the ground. The Snowy Owl is one such species, nesting on the tree-less arctic tundra and choosing a slight eminence. It feeds largely on lemmings, and when these are scarce the Snowy Owl erupts southwards in autumn, to appear in temperate regions.

Owls such as the Snowy and Short-eared varieties, which rely on lemmings or voles for food, have larger broods and rear more young in periods when their prey is plentiful. At other times broods are not only smaller but, in addition, the smallest members of them may not survive.

OYSTER-CATCHERS

OYSTER-CATCHERS are wading birds found in most parts of the world. At low tide they look for cockles, mussels and oysters along the sandy coasts. With their strong bills, they prize open the shells. Oyster-catchers nest on the sand or rocks above the high-tide line, carrying some material to the nest. The female lays from three to five eggs. Males and females look alike.

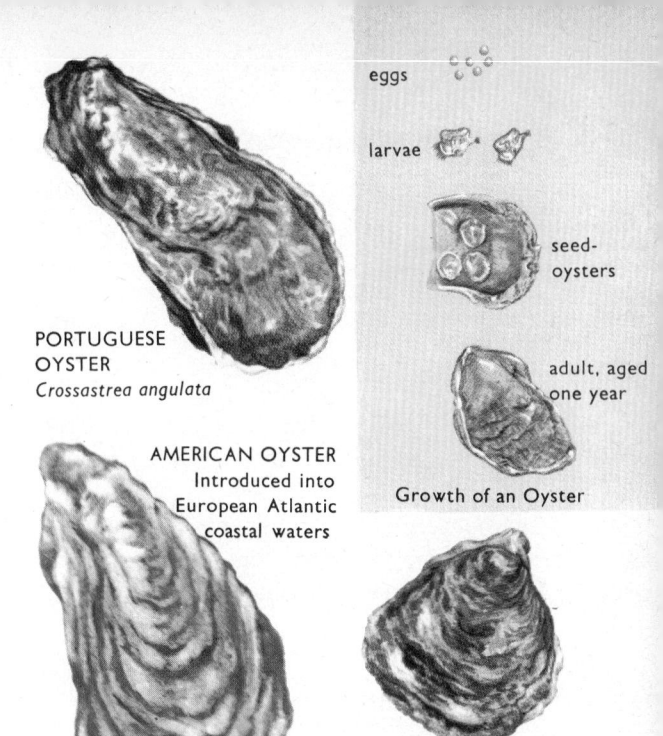

PORTUGUESE OYSTER
Crossastrea angulata

AMERICAN OYSTER
Introduced into European Atlantic coastal waters

eggs

larvae

seed-oysters

adult, aged one year

Growth of an Oyster

NATIVE OYSTER
Ostrea edulis

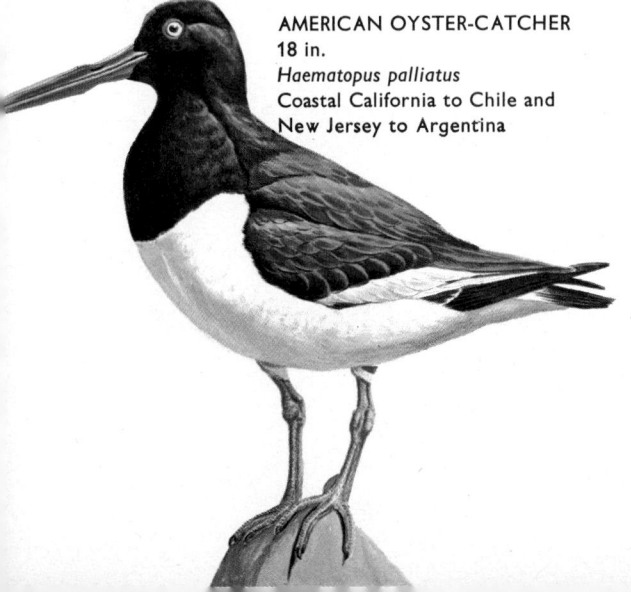

AMERICAN OYSTER-CATCHER
18 in.
Haematopus palliatus
Coastal California to Chile and New Jersey to Argentina

OYSTERS have been the delight of epicures since earliest times. Many species of oyster occur in temperate and warm seas, and most are small. There are about 100 species of oyster living today, and the edible varieties are divided into two groups. The first of these consists of round, flat types, represented in Europe by *Ostrea edulis* and along North America's Pacific coast by *Ostrea lurida*. The second group contains those of a long, cup-like shape; examples are provided by the Australian Oyster (*Ostrea commercialis*), Indian Oyster (*Ostrea cucullata*), Japanese Oyster (*Ostrea gigas*), and species inhabiting the Atlantic coast of the U.S.A. (*Ostrea virginica*), the Pacific coast of Central and South America (*Ostrea chilensis*), and coasts of France and Portugal (*Ostrea angulata*).

Oysters have been cultivated since the days of the Romans, and the industry is highly specialised in Britain, France and a number of other countries. In England, Colchester and Whitstable are renowned for their fisheries. Edible oysters do not secrete true mother-of-pearl, and the infrequent pearls they do produce are seldom valuable (see WING AND PEARL SHELLS).

P-Q

PADDLEFISH *(Polyodon spathula)*, also known as Spoonbills, belong to a primitive family of fresh-water fishes closely related to sturgeons. There are only two species in the world. One lives in the Yangtze-Kiang River of China; the other in the Mississippi

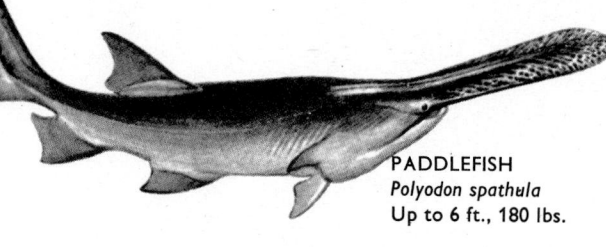

PADDLEFISH
Polyodon spathula
Up to 6 ft., 180 lbs.

River and its tributaries, U.S.A. They are netted by commercial fishermen.

These strange creatures are easily recognised by their long, flat snout, which may be nearly half the length of the fish's body. There are no scales on the Paddlefish, except for a small area on the tail. Paddlefish are good to eat, and their eggs, like the sturgeon's, make excellent caviar.

PANDAS — those strange-looking, attractive mammals that are such favourites in zoos — come from China and Tibet. They are closely related to raccoons, though they look more like bears.

The Giant Panda *(Ailuropoda melanoleuca)* weighs as much as 200 pounds and is sometimes six feet long. Largely white, the Giant Panda has black eyes, ears and legs. This bear-like animal lives in dense bamboo jungles at high elevations (up to 14,000 ft.).

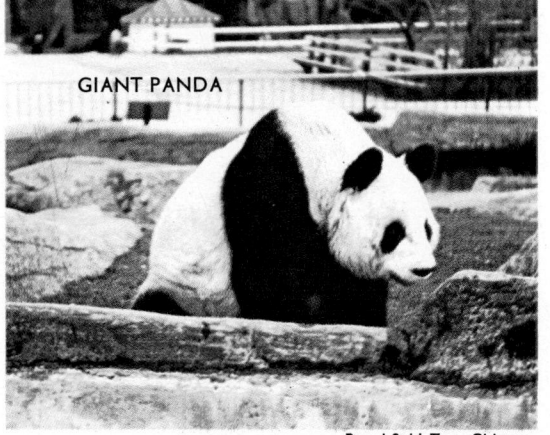

GIANT PANDA

Brookfield Zoo, Chicago

It feeds extensively on bamboo shoots, crushing them with its heavy teeth and powerful jaws. Much remains to be learned about its life history and natural habits.

The Lesser Panda *(Ailurus fulgens)*, which is about the size of a large house cat, has reddish-brown fur and a long, bushy, ringed

This 10-inch larva of the Paradoxical Frog shows both the tail and body of a tadpole and the legs of the adult.

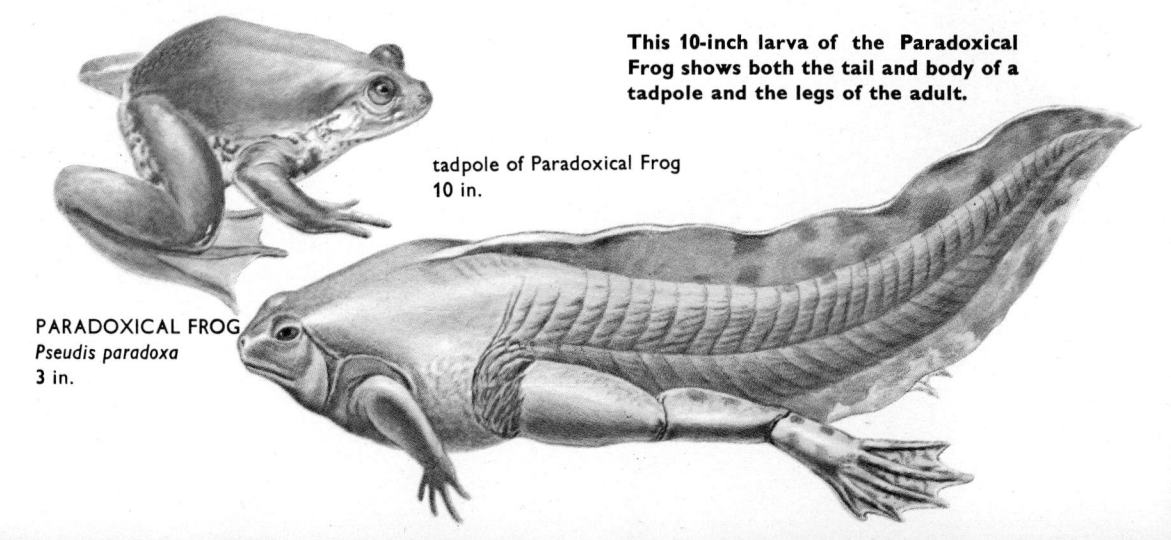

tadpole of Paradoxical Frog
10 in.

PARADOXICAL FROG
Pseudis paradoxa
3 in.

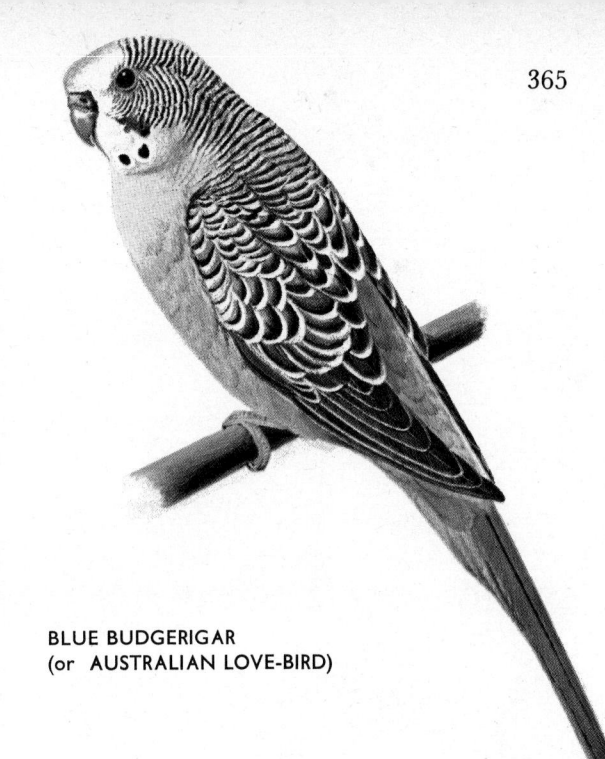

SAY'S PANDORA
Pandora trilineata
0.8—1 in.

GOULD'S PANDORA
Pandora gouldiana
0.8—1.4 in.

WESTERN PANDORA
Pandora filosa
1 in.

PUNCTATE PANDORA
Pandora punctata
2 in.

BLUE BUDGERIGAR
(or AUSTRALIAN LOVE-BIRD)

tail like a raccoon's. Much of its time is spent in the forest of the Himalayas. It feeds on insects, small mammals, and birds.

PANDORA SHELLS *(Pandora* spp.*)* are small shells ($1\frac{1}{4}$ to $1\frac{1}{2}$ in.) found burrowing in shallow to moderate depths. The shells are very flat or compressed, and usually thin. In some the valves are unequal — the right valve flat, the left convex. All have a characteristic arched shape, and they may be opalescent white to chalky in appearance.

PARADOXICAL FROGS *(Pseudis* spp.*)* in their tadpole stage look so much like fish that at one time it was believed that they were young fish. The tadpoles grow to five inches in length — twice as large as the adults — and develop a thick, muscular tail during the several years they spend as tadpoles. For many months the tadpoles of these South American frogs remain in a semi-transformed stage, with the fore and hind legs of an adult on the body and tail of a tadpole. The adults have movable thumbs to grasp underwater plants.

PARAKEETS are small members of the parrot family. Many species are found in tropical Africa, America and Asia, but the most popular pet is the Budgerigar, or Shell Parakeet (Budgie), from Australia.

The Shell Parakeet is about seven inches in length and has a long, tapering tail. This bird's colour in the wild is green with some yellow on the head. Colours of captive birds include green, yellow, blue and white.

While much of the bird's popularity is due to its colour, it is also greatly valued for its tameness, intelligence and ability as a mimic. It is very active and responds well to training. As many as 50 words and phrases have been taught to birds that have been kept apart from others of their species.

Parakeets are seed-eaters, and commercially prepared food consists of canary grass seed and various millets. Other suitable foods include sprouted oat seeds and also the yolks of hard-boiled eggs. Cuttlefish bone placed in the cage provides a source of needed calcium. Grit, to aid the gizzard in its grinding function, is also a requirement.

A well-mated pair of Budgerigars may produce many young. The birds are usually ready for breeding after they are a year old. At this time, the cere, a fleshy band over the bill, changes colour. The male's becomes bright blue; the female's dark brown, and often wrinkles and peels. The birds should then be furnished with a nesting-box.

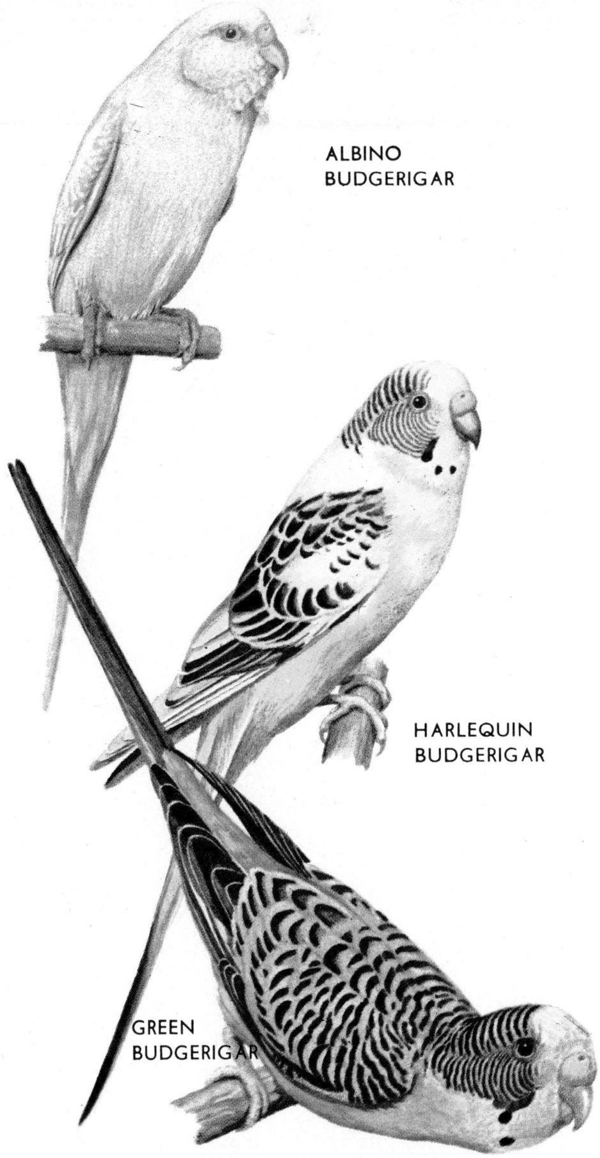

ALBINO
BUDGERIGAR

HARLEQUIN
BUDGERIGAR

GREEN
BUDGERIGAR

Budgerigars respond well to training. They are naturally inquisitive parakeets and appear to enjoy showing off their accomplishments. If they are rewarded, the birds will repeat their acts.

As many as six eggs are laid in a normal clutch. If they are left in the nest, incubation usually begins at once. It takes eighteen days for the eggs to hatch. The young birds are downy as nestlings, but soon resemble their parents. The head plumage of young birds is barred, but this changes to a solid colour as the birds mature.

Other parakeets, especially in India and Australia, compete with farmers for the harvests of orchards and fields. Some species are found only in limited areas of moun-

tainous islands between Australia and Asia, and a few species have never been raised in captivity at all.

Species which have green in their plumage, similar to the Budgerigar's, may also produce blue or yellow forms in captivity, since these two colours combine to produce green and can be separated by mutation.

PARROT-FISHES form a large family *(Scaridae)* of brightly-coloured tropical fish, found in all warm seas. They have been given their name because of their curious, fused teeth, which resemble the beak of a parrot. In colour, too, the parrot-fishes resemble parrots, with beautiful reds and greens and blues.

Their teeth are sharp and powerful, and are said to be capable of snipping wire in two. They feed on shellfish and other inhabitants of the coral reefs, removing pieces of coral as they feed, and passing these, too, down the digestive tract.

At night, certain parrot-fishes secrete an envelope of mucus round their bodies, but nobody yet knows what purpose this serves.

PARROTS. The parrot family includes the parrots, conures, macaws, cockatoos, the cockatiel, lories, lorikeets and parakeets. All have strong, curved, pointed beaks,

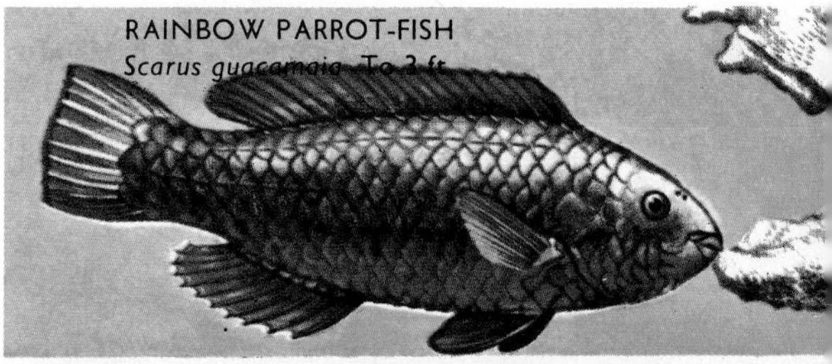

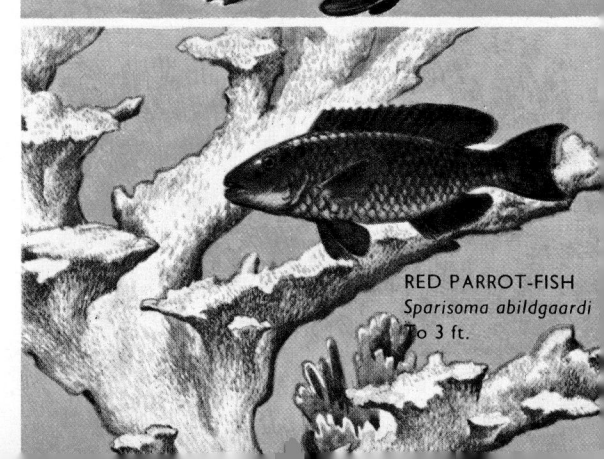

RAINBOW PARROT-FISH
Scarus guacamaia. To 3 ft.

RED PARROT-FISH
Sparisoma abildgaardi
To 3 ft.

with a hinged and movable upper mandible. Each foot has two toes turned forward and two turned backward. The birds perch on one foot and hold their food in the other. Both bill and feet are used in climbing.

Parrots are found in all tropical regions of the world. Since the fifth century B. C., when a Greek doctor described a gaudy bird that spoke the language of India, adventurers have brought parrots home from far countries. Ancient Romans kept the birds as pets, in ivory cages with silver bars. British sailors of the eighteenth century sometimes carried parrots, which they called "popinjays", on their shoulders. Two familiar parrots in fiction are Robinson Crusoe's parrot companion, and Long John Silver's bird that kept on saying "pieces of eight" in Robert Louis Stevenson's classic story entitled *Treasure Island*.

Parrots eat fruit, nuts, grain, buds, nectar, roots or small animals. New Zealand Kea occasionally eat fat from dead sheep carcases, and have been accused of attacking live sheep.

Breeding habits of at least half the parrot family are unknown. Certain lovebirds breed in captivity, but their nests in the wild have never been seen by scientists. Some parrots nest like woodpeckers, some like burrowing owls, some on cliff ledges. Others

build a loose platform, use second-hand nests of other species, nest in anthills, or establish themselves on the bare ground. Some live in jungles, some in open fields, some in desert, and some in high mountains. All of the parrot family are strong flyers, but

The largest and most colourful members of the parrot family are the macaws from the jungles of Mexico, Central and South America. All macaws have long, tapered and colourful tails.

SCARLET MACAW — 36 in.
Ara macao
Mexico to Bolivia

GOLD AND BLUE MACAW — 31 in.
Ara ararauna
Panama to Argentina

MILITARY MACAW — 30 in.
Ara militaris
Mexico to Panama

KEA — 18—19 in.
Nestor notabilis
South Island, New Zealand

HYACINTH MACAW — 34 in.
Anodorhynchus hyacinthus
Brazilian forests south of the Amazon

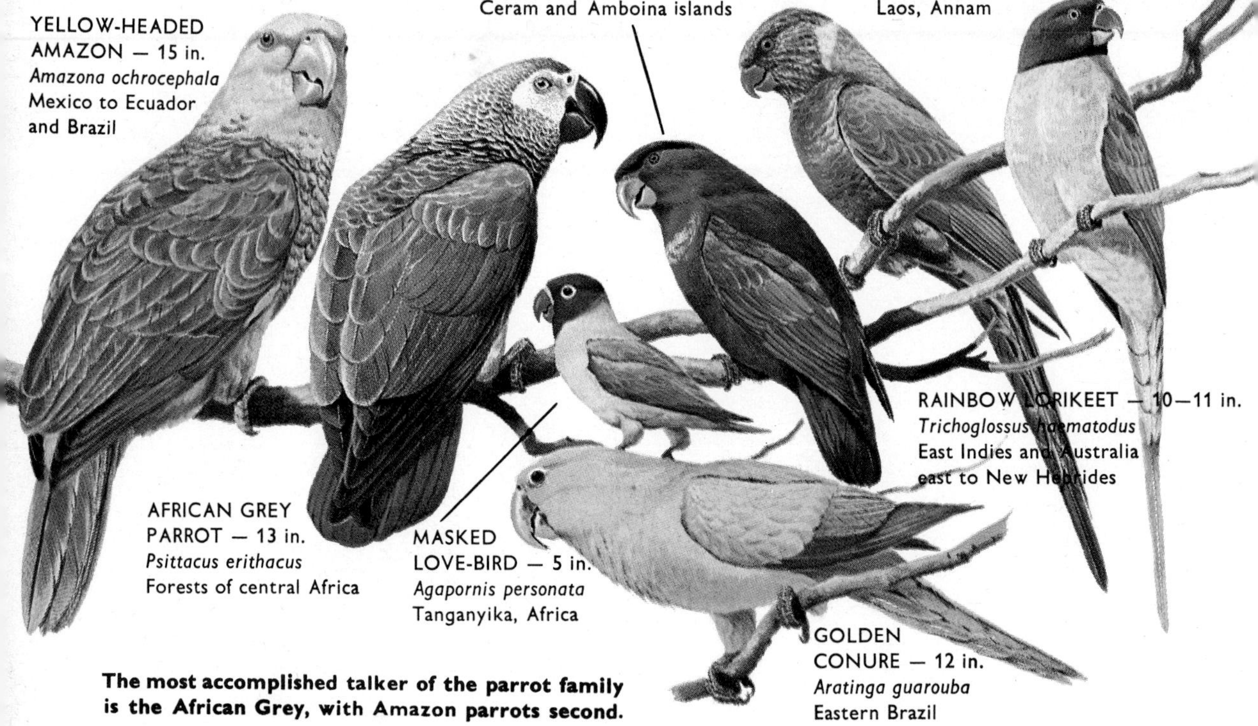

YELLOW-HEADED
AMAZON — 15 in.
Amazona ochrocephala
Mexico to Ecuador
and Brazil

BLACK-CAPPED LORY — 11 in.
Domicella domicella
Ceram and Amboina islands

SLATY-HEADED PARAKEET — 15 in.
Psittacula himalayana
North-west India to Thailand,
Laos, Annam

RAINBOW LORIKEET — 10—11 in.
Trichoglossus haematodus
East Indies and Australia
east to New Hebrides

AFRICAN GREY
PARROT — 13 in.
Psittacus erithacus
Forests of central Africa

MASKED
LOVE-BIRD — 5 in.
Agapornis personata
Tanganyika, Africa

GOLDEN
CONURE — 12 in.
Aratinga guarouba
Eastern Brazil

**The most accomplished talker of the parrot family
is the African Grey, with Amazon parrots second.**

for the flightless Kakapo of New Zealand.

Parrots mate for life, and both parents care for their birds. Except in the breeding season, parrots congregate in noisy flocks.

African parrots include such favourites as lovebirds (9 species) and the African Grey Parrot. Macaws, many species of Amazon parrots, and conures are native to Central and South America. Australia and the islands to the north of it are the home of the cockatoos, lories, lorikeets, and many of the parakeets. During geological periods when climates were warmer, parrots were more widely distributed.

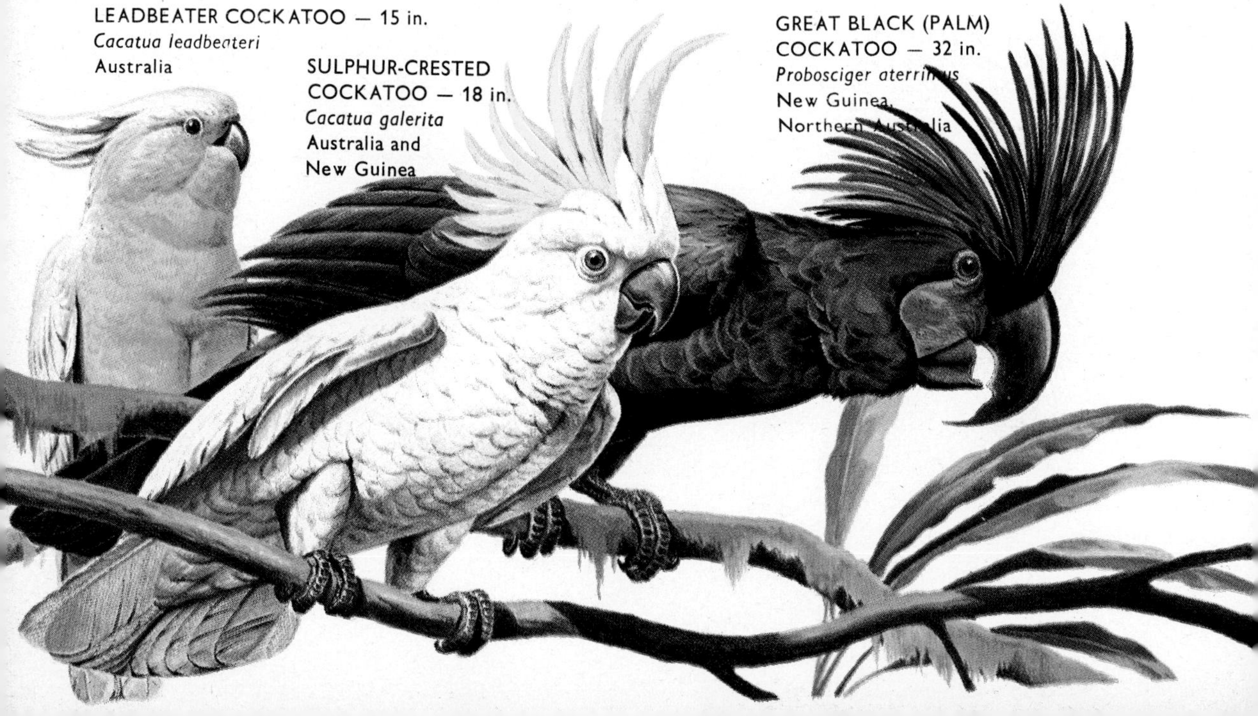

LEADBEATER COCKATOO — 15 in.
Cacatua leadbeateri
Australia

SULPHUR-CRESTED
COCKATOO — 18 in.
Cacatua galerita
Australia and
New Guinea

GREAT BLACK (PALM)
COCKATOO — 32 in.
Probosciger aterrimus
New Guinea,
Northern Australia

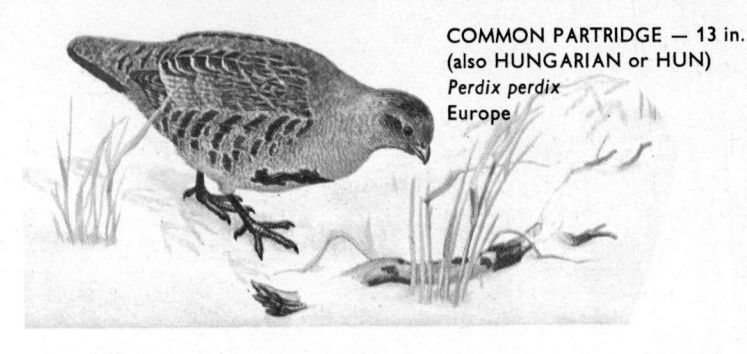

COMMON PARTRIDGE — 13 in.
(also HUNGARIAN or HUN)
Perdix perdix
Europe

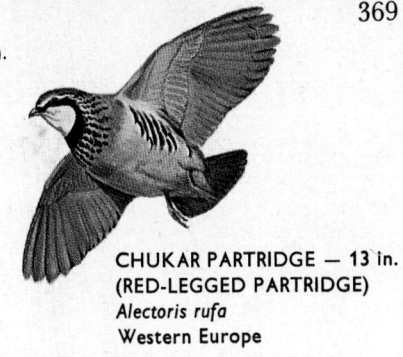

CHUKAR PARTRIDGE — 13 in.
(RED-LEGGED PARTRIDGE)
Alectoris rufa
Western Europe

PARTRIDGES are European game birds related to quail and pheasants. They are compact birds with short tails and rounded wings. When not breeding, they live in small flocks or coveys, usually consisting of the family party, and these break up into pairs to nest. All species are cryptically coloured on the upper parts, and any conspicuous colouring is on the throat, flanks and underside. They inhabit open places, and this makes them inconspicuous when they crouch at the approach of danger. If closely threatened, they explode into sudden flight at the last moment. The flight is swift, low and direct, whirring wings alternating with long glides.

In these birds, the male plays an active part in bringing up the family. In the case of the Red-legged Partridge, the female will lay two clutches of eggs, one of which she incubates herself, the other being incubated by the male; after hatching, the two lots of chicks are brought together and tended by both parents. The Red-legged Partridge and its relatives are more southerly birds, preferring drier soils.

PEAFOWL is the correct name for members of the pheasant family known as Peacocks and their more sombre mates, the Peahens. Males are a symbol of vain pride all over the world. The Peafowl's native home is from India and through Ceylon to Indo-China and Malaya.

Peafowl have been taken to ornament gardens and delight the eyes of many people in many lands. The Bible tells us that King Solomon brought Peacocks to Palestine about 950 B.C. Around 650 B.C., they were taken to China, where as "Kung ch'iang", Bird of Confucius, they became a symbol of fire and fortune. Nowadays, Chinese people use their feathers for fine embroidery work.

Alexander the Great brought the Peafowl to Europe. In ancient Rome and medieval England, Peacocks were roasted for feasts, and served with their feathers put back over them and their tails spread wide. Shah Jahan, builder of the Taj Mahal, had a throne decorated with gem-encrusted golden Peacocks. In India, wild peafowl are associated with royalty and the god Krishna. Today they are permitted to raid grain-fields unharmed.

In captivity, Peacocks are quarrelsome and will fight each other. Their call is a trumpeting scream. In the wild, they live in small flocks. The birds forage the ground for seeds and insects, but fly up to roost in trees at night.

The displaying Peacock fans his train, which is propped against the true tail.

COMMON PEAFOWL (male)
80—92 in., including train
Pavo cristatus
India and Ceylon

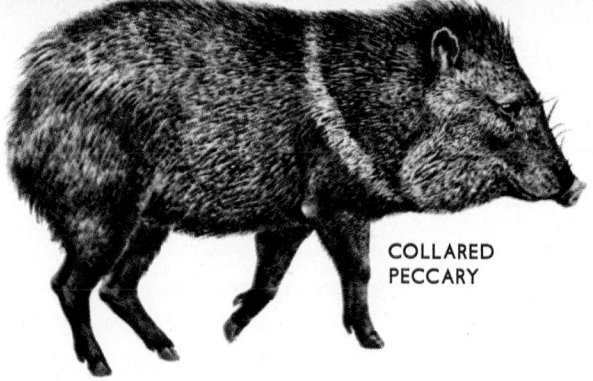

COLLARED
PECCARY

Peccaries, or wild pigs of the New World, defend themselves with their sharp tusks and pointed hoofs.

PECCARIES, often called Javelines, are pig-like mammals of the New World found in Central and South America northward into parts of the southern United States. Along the forest edges they forage in bands of from three to a hundred or more animals, eating fruits, roots, nuts and berries. Peccaries also eat small animals, including snakes. Adults weigh from 40 to 65 pounds.

The Collared Peccary (*Tayassu angulatus*) lives as far north as the deserts of the southwestern United States. Its name comes from the whitish or yellowish collar that extends around its throat. Collared Peccaries often take refuge in mine tunnels. Since they prey on rattlesnakes, miners welcome them. A musk gland, in the middle of the back near the rump, secretes a strong odour.

The White-lipped Peccary (*Tayassu pecari*) does not have a collar, but it does have a white area that extends from its chin nearly to its eye. Found in the tropical forests of Central and South America, it travels in bands that contain as many as a hundred animals.

PELICANS are a family of fish-eating water-birds known all over the warmer parts of the world. They have a six-foot wing-spread, very short legs, and webs between all four of their toes. They use the large pouches under their enormous bills to scoop up and hold fish.

Pelicans are graceful and beautiful when flying, but on land they wobble with the funny dignity of clowns. They take flight slowly, but once airborne have an easy, gliding flight. In landing, their large air-sac systems seem to give them buoyancy, and

The Brown Pelican (Pelecanus occidentalis) ranges the Atlantic Coast from North Carolina to Venezuela and the Pacific Coast from Canada to Chile. Younger birds are uniform greyish brown, and take three years to develop the mature plumage of dark red and white neck, yellow crown, and soft grey wing and body feathers.

Helen Cruickshank from National Audubon Society

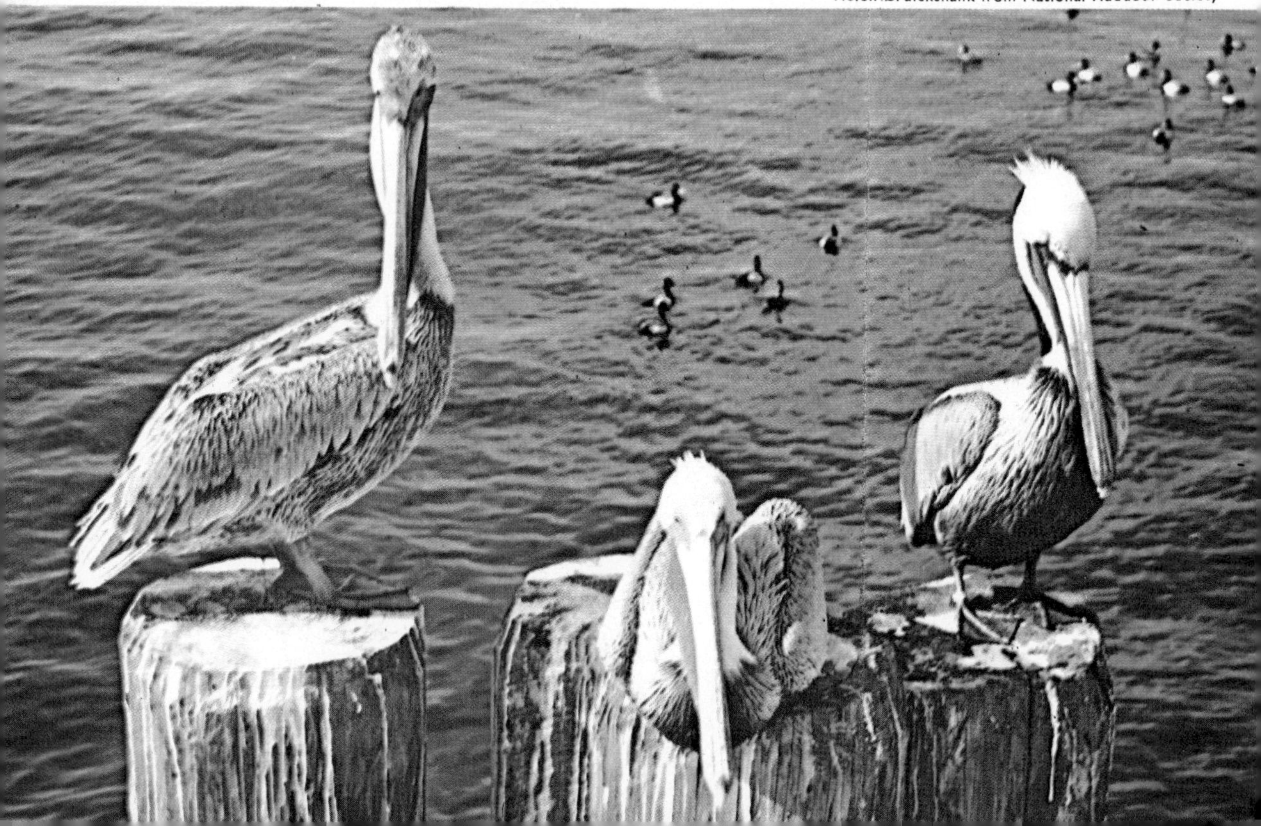

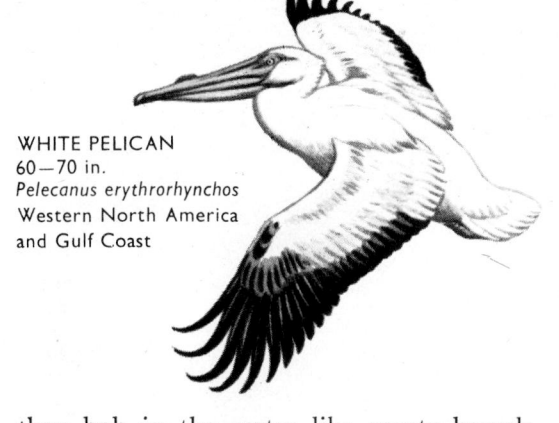

WHITE PELICAN
60—70 in.
Pelecanus erythrorhynchos
Western North America
and Gulf Coast

PENGUINS are flightless, swimming birds of the Southern Hemisphere. About 15 kinds live in the southernmost seas, and nest on the shores of Antarctica and on islands off Australia, New Zealand, South Africa and southern South America. They use their stiff, hard, paddle-like wings for "flying" under water, and they steer with their feet. On land, penguins either hop, or walk with a waddle. On ice, they slide along on their bellies. To get from the sea on to land or ice, they may leap four to six feet into the air.

they bob in the water like empty barrels.

White Pelicans feed largely in fresh water and often fish together on the surface. Forming a line, they drive the fish before them; then every bird dips up the fish at the same time, in a mad scramble. Brown Pelicans fish in salt water along the coasts, and hunt from the air. When they sight a school of fish, they plunge vertically down into the water, as gannets do, to seize them. The Brown Pelican has a heavy skull, with a spongy pad at the forehead. The skull of the White Pelican, which does not dive, is much lighter.

The Emperor Penguin, largest member of the family (4 foot high and 75 pounds in weight), breeds on the sea ice in the bitter cold and darkness of the antarctic winter. It is the only penguin in which the male does all the incubating. He goes without food for two months, while he holds the single egg on top of his feet to keep it off the ice and warm under the fold of his skin. When the chick hatches, the female returns from the sea to feed it, and then the male goes off to feed. Only

Penguins are flightless birds whose ancestors, some 100 million years ago, gave up mastery of the air for underwater hunting. Their swimming speed is more than 25 miles an hour, enough to permit them to prey successfully on fish. Their enemies are the Leopard Seal and the Killer Whale.

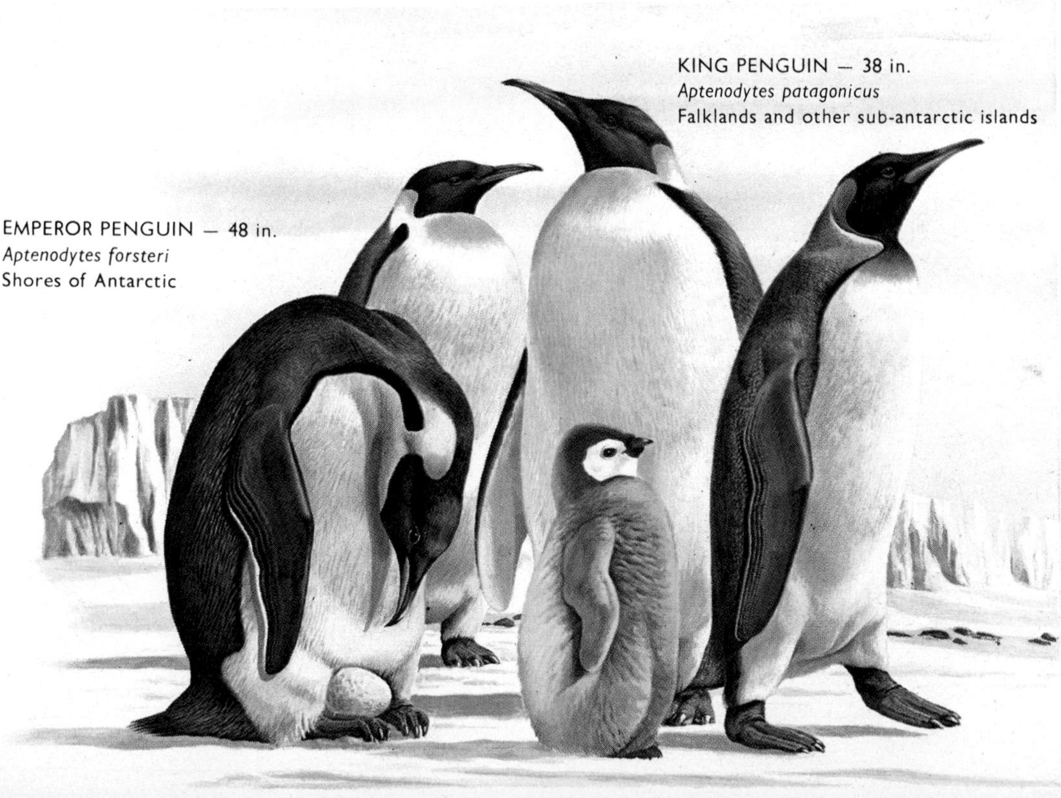

KING PENGUIN — 38 in.
Aptenodytes patagonicus
Falklands and other sub-antarctic islands

EMPEROR PENGUIN — 48 in.
Aptenodytes forsteri
Shores of Antarctic

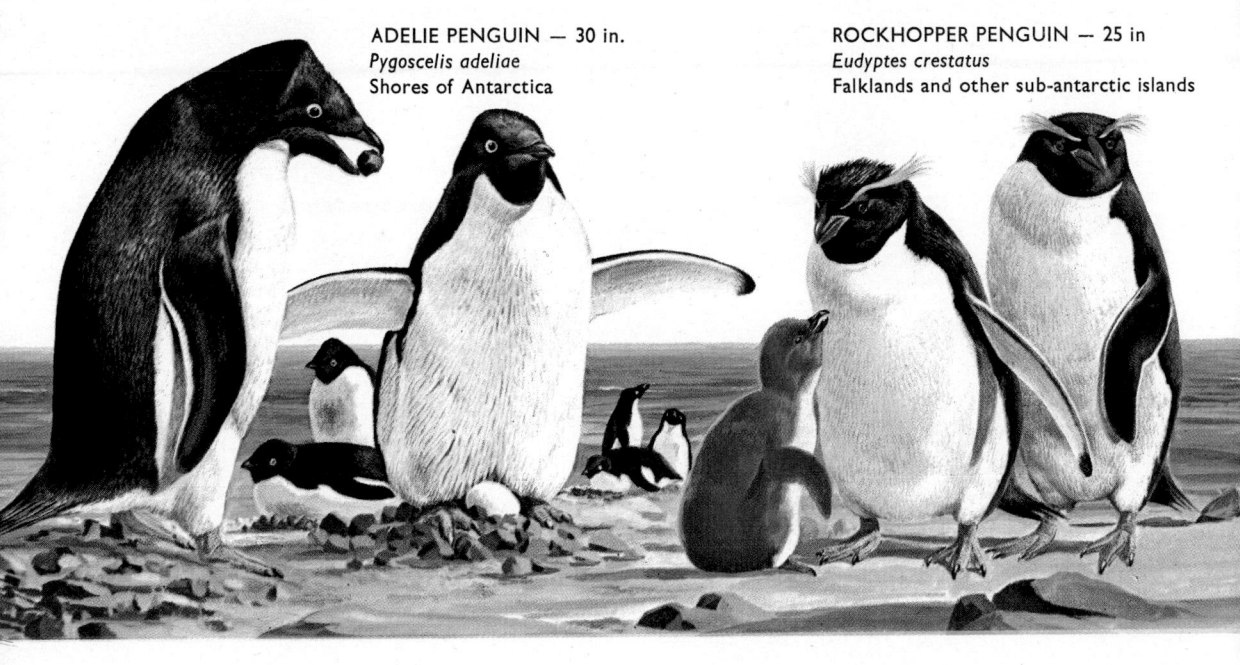

ADELIE PENGUIN — 30 in.
Pygoscelis adeliae
Shores of Antarctica

ROCKHOPPER PENGUIN — 25 in
Eudyptes crestatus
Falklands and other sub-antarctic islands

one other penguin, the King Penguin, holds its egg on its feet. Other penguins, nesting in warmer places, incubate in the normal bird way.

The Adelie Penguin also breeds in Antarctica, on the level patches of bare land along the coasts of this ice-covered continent. Its courting habits are very interesting. Expeditions to the Antarctic in the past few years have destroyed a number of the Adelie Penguin nesting-sites, to make landing-strips for 'planes and erect buildings.

Additionally, men with sledge-dogs have used the penguins for dog-food. If men kill too many breeding birds, and take away the places where the Adelie Penguins lay their eggs and raise their young, these birds may, like the Great Auk in the Arctic, vanish for ever.

The Little Blue Penguin of New Zealand, about 14 inches high, is the smallest member of the family. It nests underground, in burrows or rock crevices. The Galapagos Penguin lives farther north than any other. Its home is near the equator in the Galapagos Islands. No one has ever seen its nest, eggs, or chicks.

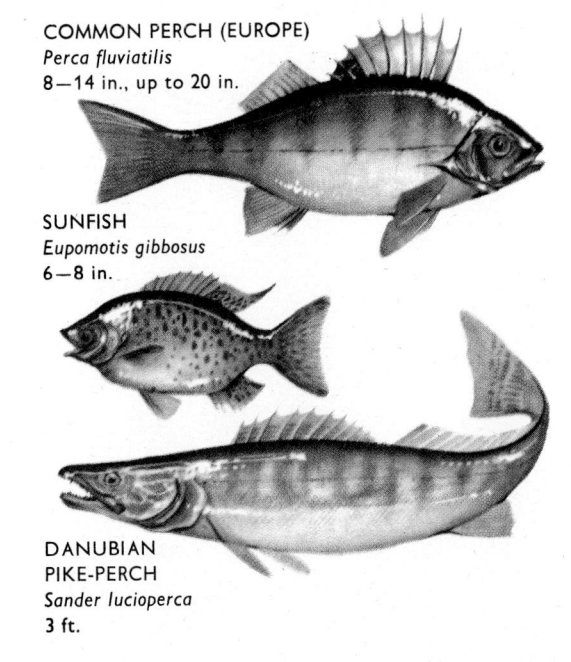

COMMON PERCH (EUROPE)
Perca fluviatilis
8—14 in., up to 20 in.

SUNFISH
Eupomotis gibbosus
6—8 in.

DANUBIAN
PIKE-PERCH
Sander lucioperca
3 ft.

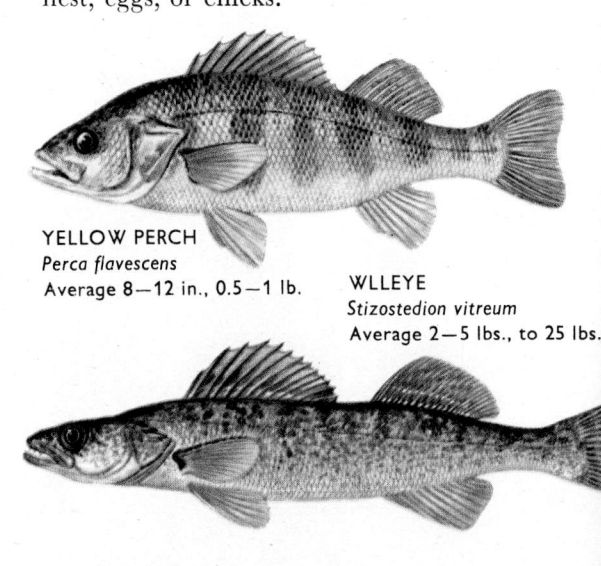

YELLOW PERCH
Perca flavescens
Average 8—12 in., 0.5—1 lb.

WLLEYE
Stizostedion vitreum
Average 2—5 lbs., to 25 lbs.

PERCHES are a large family of freshwater fishes, represented in Europe by the Perch (*Perca fluviatilis*). The Perch is not found in Spain or Portugal, but extends to the Caspian Sea and Lake Baikal in the east. In England, it is one of the best known of freshwater fishes. Large specimens weigh about 5 pounds, but a 10-pound fish has been reported.

Perch prefer slow-moving waters and lakes, where they rove in shoals, searching for the small fishes, worms or insect larvae on which they feed. In March to May, they congregate to spawn, laying strings of eggs along the bottom.

Closely related to the European Perch is the American Perch (*P. flavescens*). It, too, has prominent, vertical black bars on the flanks.

The Perch family contains two other groups of fishes. The first includes the Walleye, a valuable commercial species in the U.S.A. and the Pope, or Ruffe (*Acerina cernua*), which is found in England. The second group contains the Darters, which are only found in North America.

PERIWINKLES (*Littorina* and others) of about a dozen species, are common inter-tidal shells of both Atlantic and Pacific coasts of North America. Some live in tidal pools, clinging to the rocks. They feed on plant material. Prickly-winkles and Angulate Periwinkles often live high above the sea on grasses, tree-trunks and rocks. They have a leathery operculum that closes their shell. These creatures produce a mucus by which they cement themselves to rocks or plants during

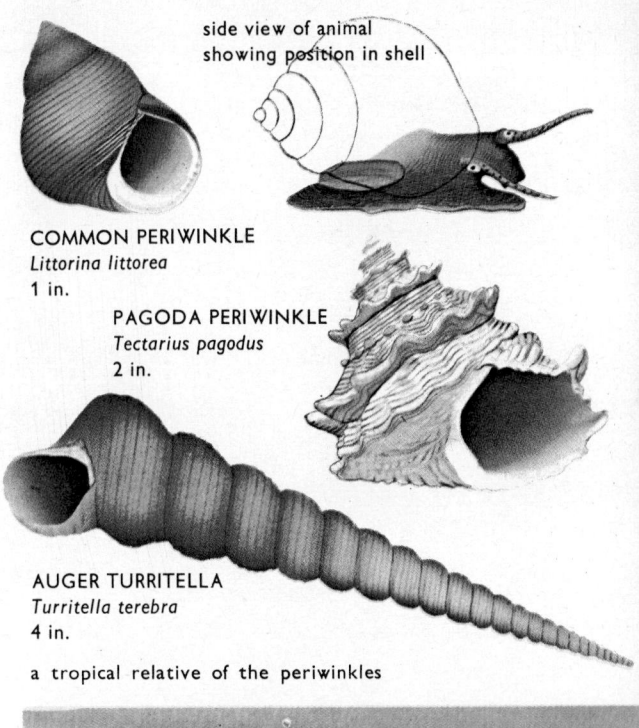

side view of animal showing position in shell

COMMON PERIWINKLE
Littorina littorea
1 in.

PAGODA PERIWINKLE
Tectarius pagodus
2 in.

AUGER TURRITELLA
Turritella terebra
4 in.

a tropical relative of the periwinkles

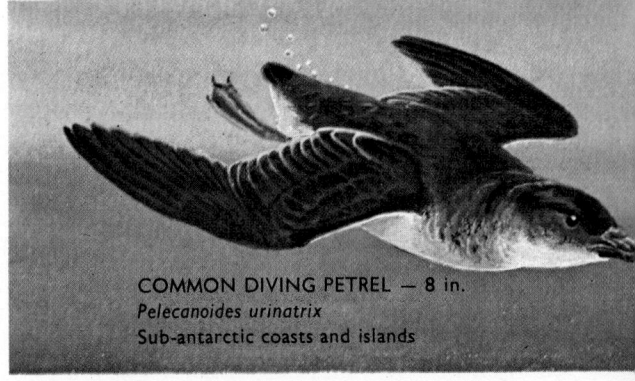

COMMON DIVING PETREL — 8 in.
Pelecanoides urinatrix
Sub-antarctic coasts and islands

Diving petrels catch fish or other food animals by swimming under water, like auks and penguins.

dry periods. The Common Periwinkle, introduced from Europe, is a favourite food in its native home. Periwinkles are often used as fish-bait.

PETRELS, dark sea-birds the size of blackbirds, live in all the oceans of the world. They feed on the surface, and flutter over the sea with their feet pattering on the waves. From this habit comes their name, meaning "little Peter", after the Saint who walked on water. Petrels often follow ships. Old sailors call them "Mother Carey's Chickens", because they brave

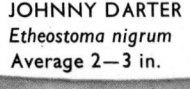

RAINBOW DARTER
Etheostoma caeruleum
Average 2—3 in.

JOHNNY DARTER
Etheostoma nigrum
Average 2—3 in.

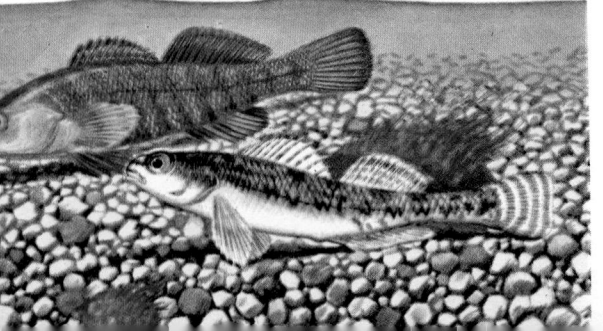

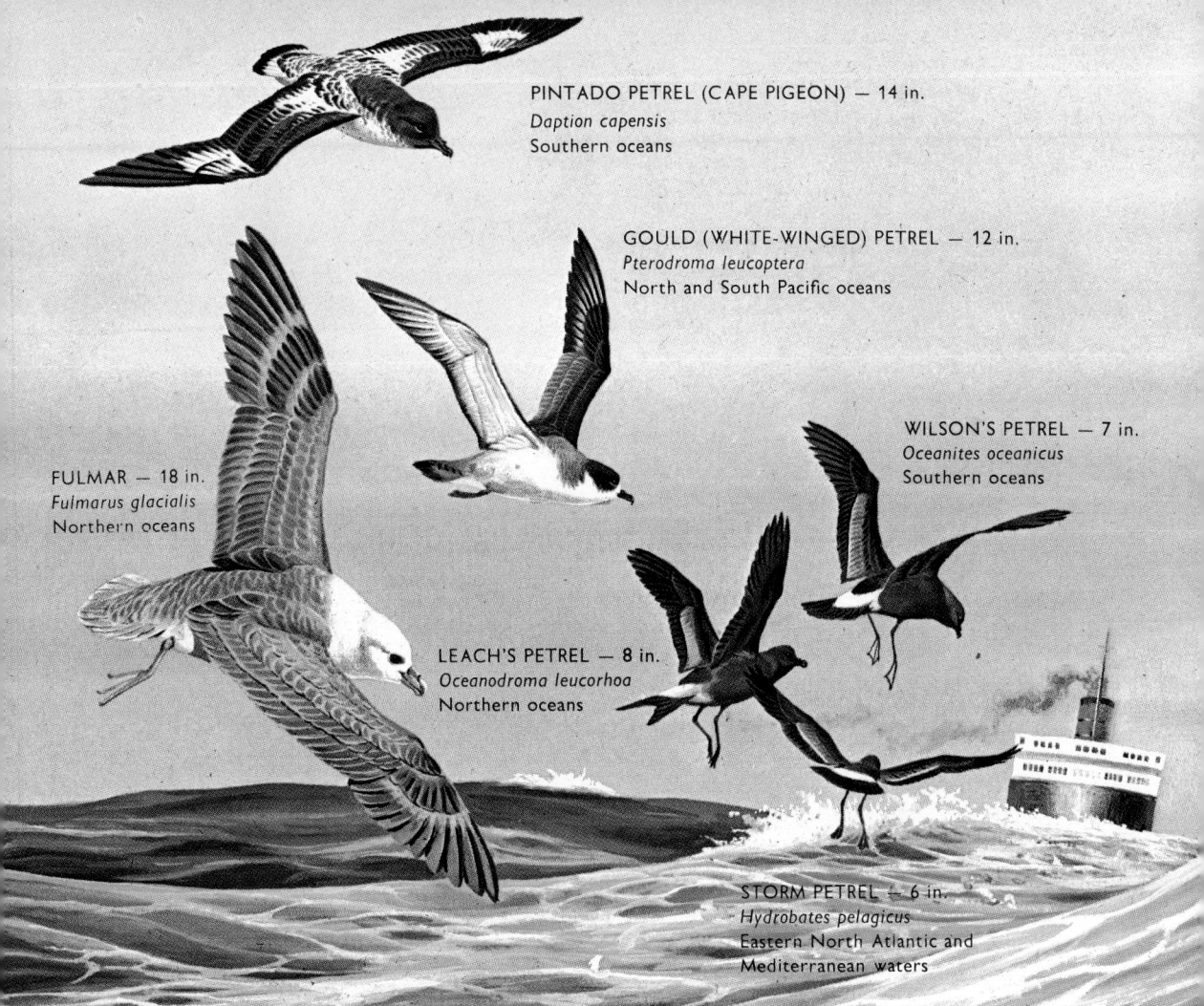

PINTADO PETREL (CAPE PIGEON) — 14 in.
Daption capensis
Southern oceans

GOULD (WHITE-WINGED) PETREL — 12 in.
Pterodroma leucoptera
North and South Pacific oceans

WILSON'S PETREL — 7 in.
Oceanites oceanicus
Southern oceans

FULMAR — 18 in.
Fulmarus glacialis
Northern oceans

LEACH'S PETREL — 8 in.
Oceanodroma leucorhoa
Northern oceans

STORM PETREL — 6 in.
Hydrobates pelagicus
Eastern North Atlantic and
Mediterranean waters

Petrels are sometimes called the swallows of the sea, because the loose flocks in wheeling, dipping flight resemble flocks of swallows. All petrels are dark above and much smaller than the Fulmar (see FULMAR). The Fulmar can often be seen flying with a flock of Petrels.

storms fearlessly as though protected by Mother Carey, a sailor's name for the Virgin Mary. Petrels have tubular noses like albatrosses. When frightened they spit a smelly oil, so seamen sometimes call them "Stink-pots".

On the breeding grounds, petrels incubate their one egg quietly all day, while their mates feed far out at sea. At night they relieve each other at the nest, which, in most species, is a burrow under the ground. Many petrels cannot walk on land, and have to shuffle along, using their wings as crutches. A petrel shares the burrow of the primitive Tuatara, or Sphe-

nodon, of New Zealand (see TUATARA).

Wilson's Petrel nests on the islands and shores around Antarctica in the southern summer. When the weather gets cold, the bird migrates to the north, and spends June to September as far away as the Atlantic coasts of the British Isles and New England. In the Eastern Hemisphere, this petrel does not cross the equator, but spends the same months wandering about the South Pacific and the Indian Ocean.

Leach's Petrel breeds in the far north. In winter, it goes south to the equator, both in the Pacific and the Atlantic. One of the common followers of ships is the

smaller Storm Petrel, which breeds on islands of the North Atlantic coast.

PHALANGERS (*Petaurus, Petauroides,* and *Acrobates* spp.) are a group of mammals native to the Australian region, where most kinds are known as "possums". Phalangers eat nectar, foliage, insects and other small animals.

Flying phalangers, the best known members of the phalanger family, are "gliders" and not true flying animals. They look and act very much like North American flying squirrels. During the day they sleep in their nests of leaves in hollow trees. At night they become active, gliding from the top of one tree to the base of another, and then climbing to its top and repeating the performance.

Cuscuses *(Phalanger* spp.*)*, another kind of phalanger, have small ears and a partially naked, scaly tail about two feet long — as long as the body. These sluggish, cat-sized tree-dwellers curl their tails around limbs to help them in climbing. They are found

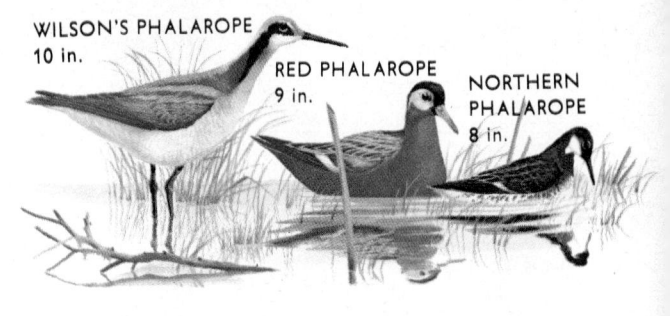

WILSON'S PHALAROPE 10 in.

RED PHALAROPE 9 in.

NORTHERN PHALAROPE 8 in.

from Celebes to Australia and the Solomon Islands. The Honey Opossum, or Honey Mouse *(Tarsipes spenserae),* of south-western Australia has a long snout and a long, hair-tipped tongue which it uses to lap up the nectar and pollen from flowers. These mouse-sized phalangers move from place to place to find flowers in bloom.

PHALAROPES are small, circumpolar seabirds related to snipes and sandpipers. They breed on the arctic tundra or the western plains of North America, and then go far out to sea, where they feed on small animals floating on the water. Whalers called phalaropes "whale birds" because

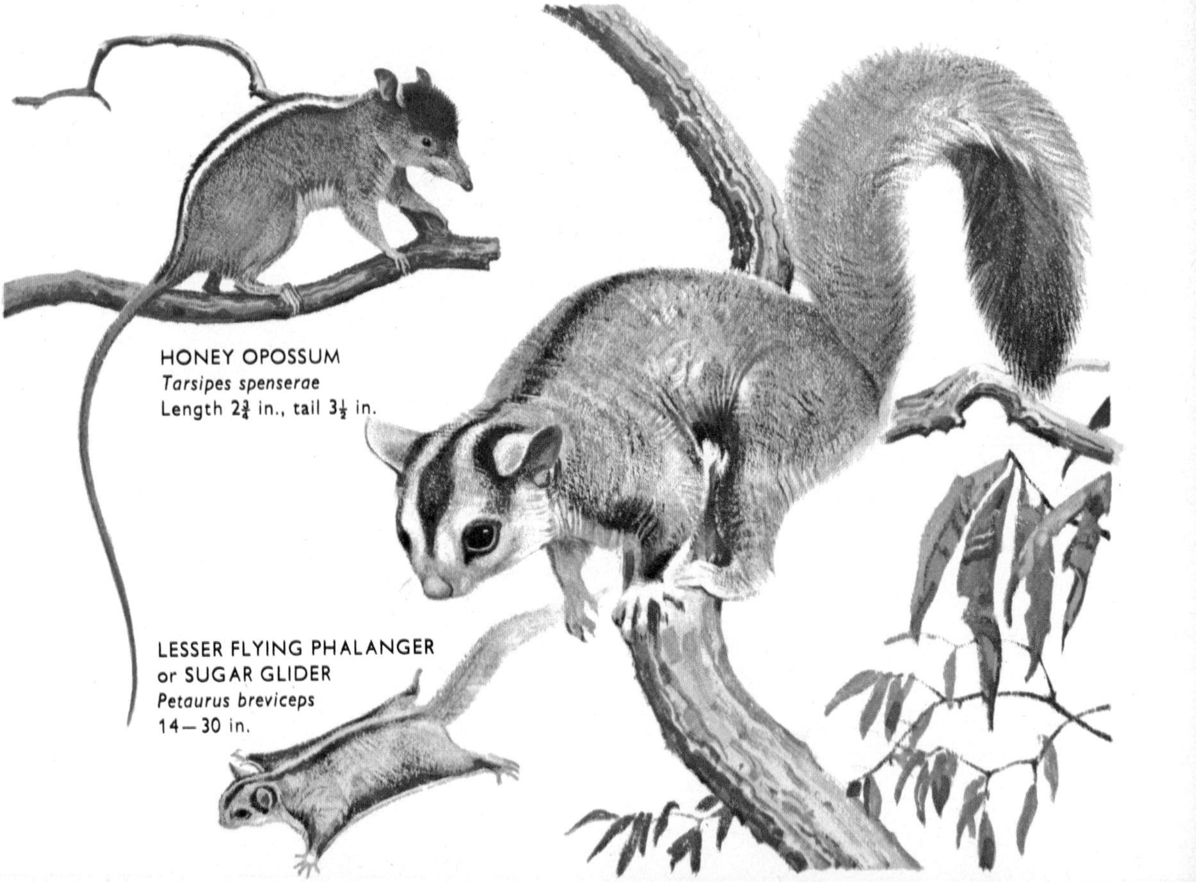

HONEY OPOSSUM
Tarsipes spenserae
Length 2¾ in., tail 3½ in.

LESSER FLYING PHALANGER
or SUGAR GLIDER
Petaurus breviceps
14 — 30 in.

ROCK DOVE — 13 in.
Columba livia
Southern Eurasia,
North Africa

they feed on the same plankton as whales and are found with them.

Phalaropes are graceful little birds and very tame, but the males are the original henpecked mates! Females are larger, are more brightly coloured, have louder voices, do all the courting, and select the nesting-site. After the male has hollowed out the

nesting-cup, the female stays in it only long enough to lay the three to four eggs. Then off she goes, leaving her mate to incubate the eggs, and look after the newly-hatched chicks; these, however, are precocial (i.e., able to feed themselves immediately they emerge from the egg).

PHEASANTS are natives of Asia. The Ring-necked Pheasant is found across Asia and Europe, where it is said to have been introduced, and is now naturalised in North America. The majority of pheasant species are birds of forest and scrub. Most have very long tails, and the plumage is boldly coloured in the males, often with vivid, metallic sheens.

Pheasants are polygamous, and the male takes no part in the nesting and care of the young. The male displays to a female by circling round her and spreading out his

Pheasants are closely related to domestic chickens and turkeys. They adjust well to captivity and to a diet of grains. Like chickens and turkeys, pheasants are excellent eating.

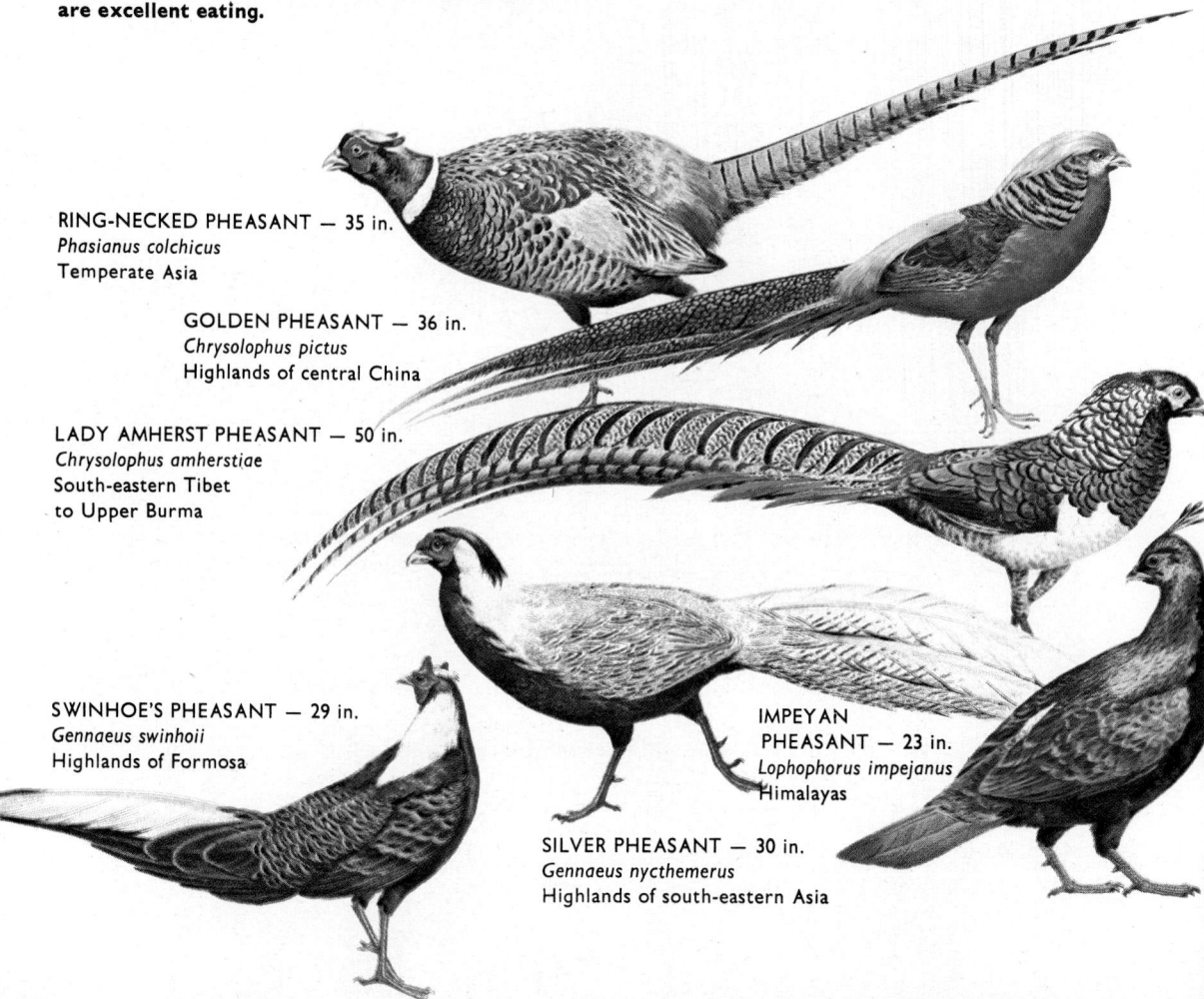

RING-NECKED PHEASANT — 35 in.
Phasianus colchicus
Temperate Asia

GOLDEN PHEASANT — 36 in.
Chrysolophus pictus
Highlands of central China

LADY AMHERST PHEASANT — 50 in.
Chrysolophus amherstiae
South-eastern Tibet
to Upper Burma

SWINHOE'S PHEASANT — 29 in.
Gennaeus swinhoii
Highlands of Formosa

IMPEYAN
PHEASANT — 23 in.
Lophophorus impejanus
Himalayas

SILVER PHEASANT — 30 in.
Gennaeus nycthemerus
Highlands of south-eastern Asia

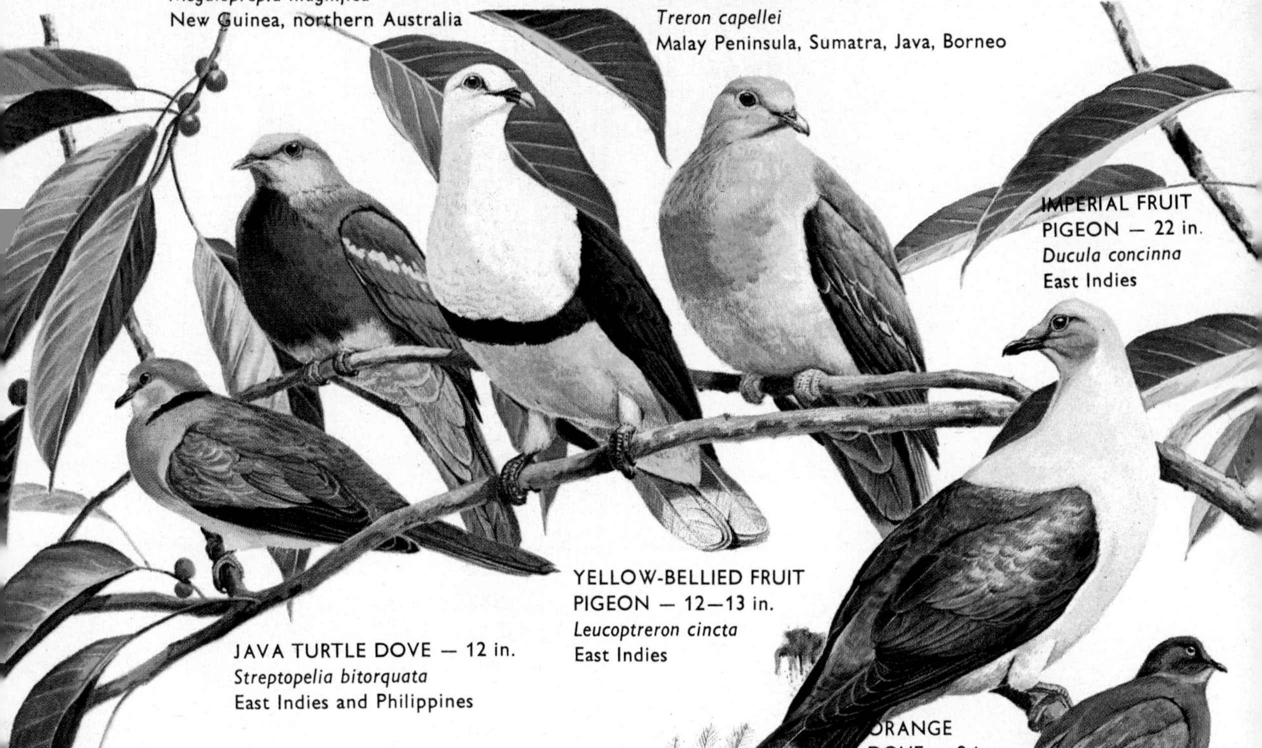

MAGNIFICENT FRUIT
PIGEON — 14 in.
Megaloprepia magnifica
New Guinea, northern Australia

LARGE GREEN PIGEON — 14 in.
Treron capellei
Malay Peninsula, Sumatra, Java, Borneo

IMPERIAL FRUIT
PIGEON — 22 in.
Ducula concinna
East Indies

JAVA TURTLE DOVE — 12 in.
Streptopelia bitorquata
East Indies and Philippines

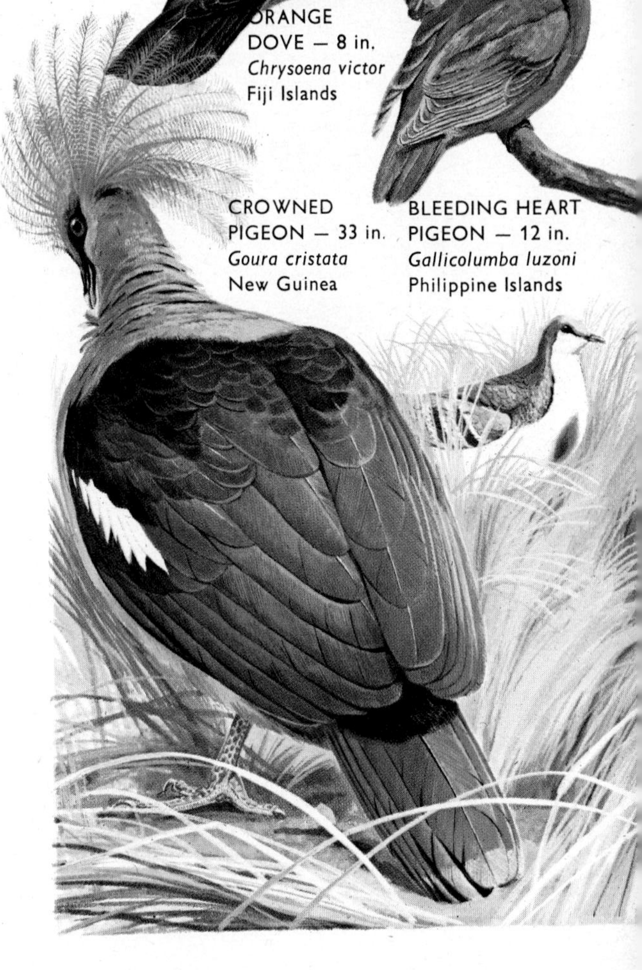

YELLOW-BELLIED FRUIT
PIGEON — 12—13 in.
Leucoptreron cincta
East Indies

ORANGE
DOVE — 8 in.
Chrysoena victor
Fiji Islands

CROWNED
PIGEON — 33 in.
Goura cristata
New Guinea

BLEEDING HEART
PIGEON — 12 in.
Gallicolumba luzoni
Philippine Islands

feathers to display his brightly coloured plumage. The Golden and Amherst Pheasants spread their capes on one side of the head, like a big coloured fan, and make a hissing sound.

PIGEON is an old French word that the Normans, when they invaded England, used for the birds which Anglo-Saxons called doves. Ornithologists usually speak of the pigeon family, but either name is correct. They occur all over the world, except in arctic regions.

Most wild pigeons live and nest in trees. Parent birds feed the newly-hatched young birds on "pigeon milk", which is produced as the skin inside their crops flakes off and liquefies. Chemists have analysed this liquid and found it similar to mammals' milk. When pigeons drink water, they suck it up; other birds fill their bill and tilt the head.

Our tame pigeons are derived from the wild Rock Dove which, unlike most species, is a cave-nester, and finds ledges on buildings or in pigeon-lofts equally appropriate. Most other species build flimsy platforms in

trees, or, in a few species, on the ground. Only one egg, or at most two, is laid.

The Barbary Dove is a domesticated variety of an African species of the ringed-necked doves. Another species, the Collared Dove, has suddenly spread right across Europe in the present century.

The fruit pigeons are birds of tropical regions, relying to a large extent on various fig trees for food. Unlike other pigeons they are mainly green in colour, but many are ornamented with bright patches.

Many species show iridescent patches or spots on the wings. Some are ground birds and resemble game birds, being plump-bodied, short-winged and short-tailed, with long, strong legs. Some are very tiny species, no larger than thrushes.

Largest of the pigeons is the Crowned Pigeon of New Guinea, larger than a chicken, with a fan-shaped crest of lacy feathers on its head.

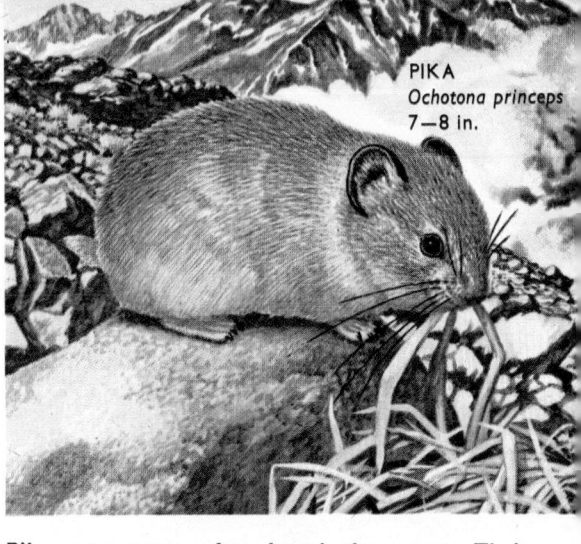

PIKA
Ochotona princeps
7—8 in.

Pikas are more often heard than seen. Their sharp, piercing whistle carries a long distance.

PIKAS (*Ochotona* spp.*) are rabbit-like mammals that live in the high mountains, often above the timber line, in Asia, and also western North America. They appear to have no tail at all, and are usually less than nine inches long when full-grown.

Note the gracefully-shaped body of this pike. It has a duck-like 'beak' and a large number of sharp teeth.

Phot. Kovaleff-Viollet

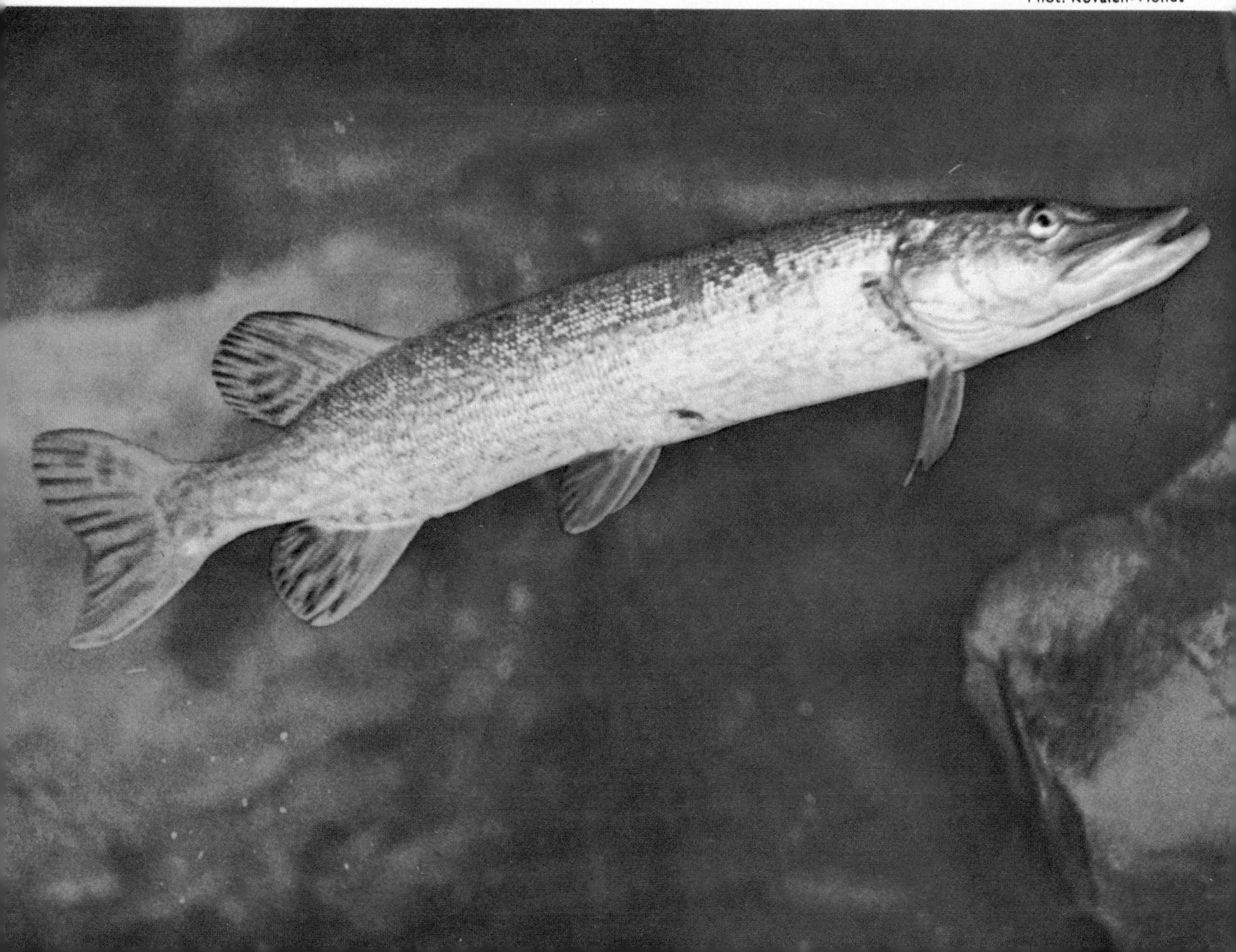

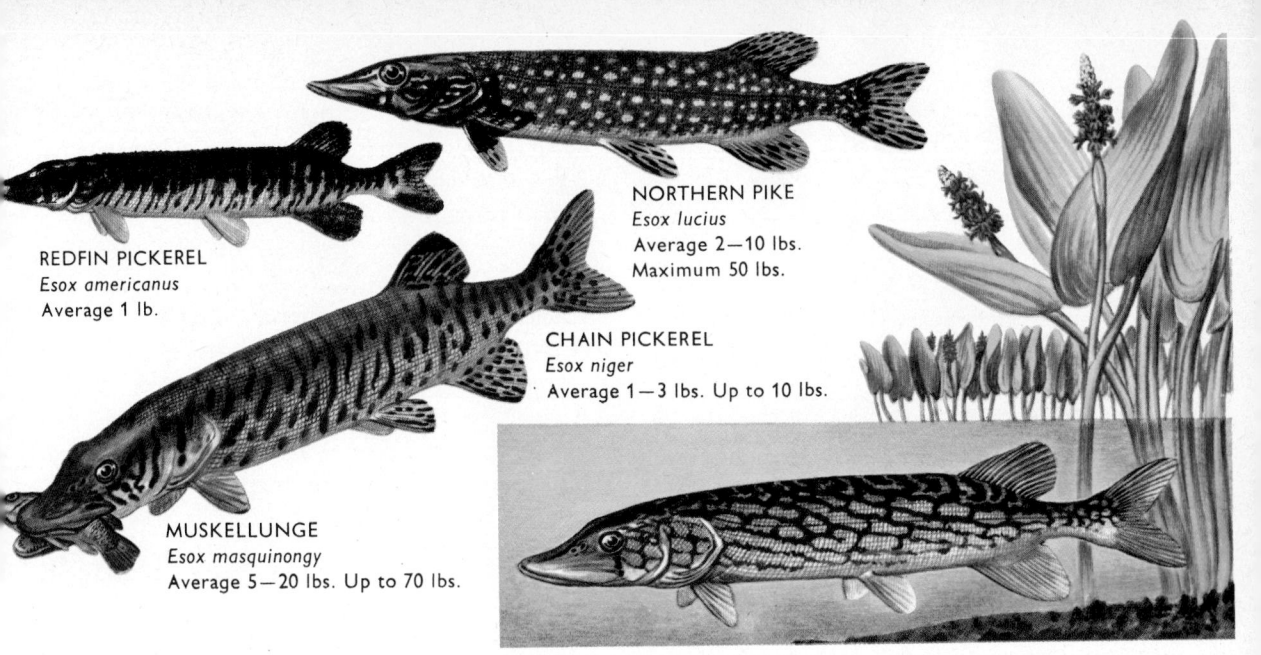

REDFIN PICKEREL
Esox americanus
Average 1 lb.

NORTHERN PIKE
Esox lucius
Average 2—10 lbs.
Maximum 50 lbs.

CHAIN PICKEREL
Esox niger
Average 1—3 lbs. Up to 10 lbs.

MUSKELLUNGE
Esox masquinongy
Average 5—20 lbs. Up to 70 lbs.

Their colours blend well with the rocks where they live, and although pikas are active during the daytime, they are usually difficult to see. Their sharp, whistled calls are one of the most common sounds in high mountain country. Pikas feed on grasses and bushes, and store dry grass in piles for use when no other food is available.

PIKE belong to a small family, the *Esocidae,* found in fresh waters in the Northern Hemisphere. The European Pike occurs throughout most of Europe (except Spain and Portugal), and also occurs in parts of Asia and in North America. It is easily recognised by its large mouth, armed with strong teeth, and it has the dorsal and anal fins set well back on the body. It prefers quiet, weedy waters, where it lurks in wait for prey, shooting out with a thrust of its powerful tail to seize a fish or frog.

Pike have a great reputation for ferocity, and have been known to attack and eat fishes of almost their own size. Pike of 35—45 pounds are not uncommon, and even larger fishes may be caught.

The Pike spawns in shallow water in spring. The eggs are scattered. In certain parts of the Baltic, off the coast of Sweden, Pike are known to spawn in the sea.

In North America, there are other species of Pike. The Pickerels are rather smaller fishes, but the Muskellunge *(Esox masquinongy)* may grow to a maximum weight of just over a hundred pounds. It is found in the Great Lakes region and is considered a fine sport fish. It has been known to form a hybrid with *Esox lucius,* and also with the two species of pickerel.

PIPE-SNAKES *(Cylindrophis* spp.*)* belong to a primitive snake family closely allied to the boas, and resembling them in having remnants of hind limbs and in their small plates on the under-surface of the body. All bear their young alive and are burrowers. Most pipe-snakes eat eels, snakes and lizards; one kind eats mice. They possess no fangs.

A group of 10 species that exist in south-eastern Asia, Ceylon and the East Indies have short tails, often reddish below. When disturbed, these snakes raise their tail and keep their head hidden under loops of the body in order to achieve maximum protection (see SNAKES).

PIPITS are small ground birds related to the wagtails. They are furtive and inconspicuous birds, with brown-streaked plumage, feeding on insects and nesting under a grass-tuft. Most have simple song flights,

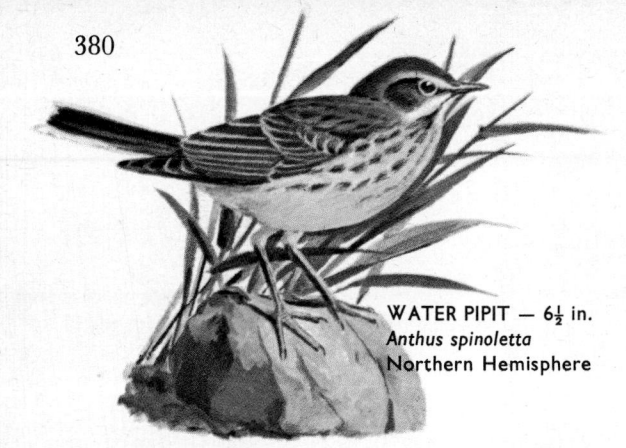

WATER PIPIT — 6½ in.
Anthus spinoletta
Northern Hemisphere

The Water Pipit nests in the arctic tundra and mountains. It feeds on insects.

rising up with a series of piping notes and parachuting down again while still singing. The Meadow Pipit is found in open grassy places; the Tree Pipit where there are scattered trees and bushes on open ground; and the Rock Pipit on open shores. The Water Pipit, shown here, is a mountain form of the latter.

PIT-VIPERS are venomous snakes that have a unique type of pit — on each side of the head, between the nostril and the eye — which is sensitive to heat and assists the snake in locating warm-blooded prey, especially during the night, when there is a marked temperature difference between such prey and their surroundings.

Over a hundred species of Pit-vipers are known — one-third in Asia, from the Caspian Sea to the Celebes, and the remainder in America. While most species are aboreal or terrestrial, the dangerous Water Moccasin, or Cottonmouth *(Ancistrodon)* — so called on account of the white lining to its mouth, which is exposed when the snake is alarmed and opens its jaws — is distinctly aquatic, and is a denizen of the swamps and rivers of the eastern United States. Other notoriously dangerous New World species are the South American Bushmaster *(Lachesis)* — the largest of the American vipers, with a length of 11 to 12 feet, and unique among them in laying eggs instead of bearing live young — and the Fer-de-Lance *(Bothrops)* and Rattlesnakes *(Crotalus)*.

The Malayan Temple Viper *(Trimeresurus)* is a docile creature, and is even protected by the natives. It is an arboreal form with a prehensile tail.

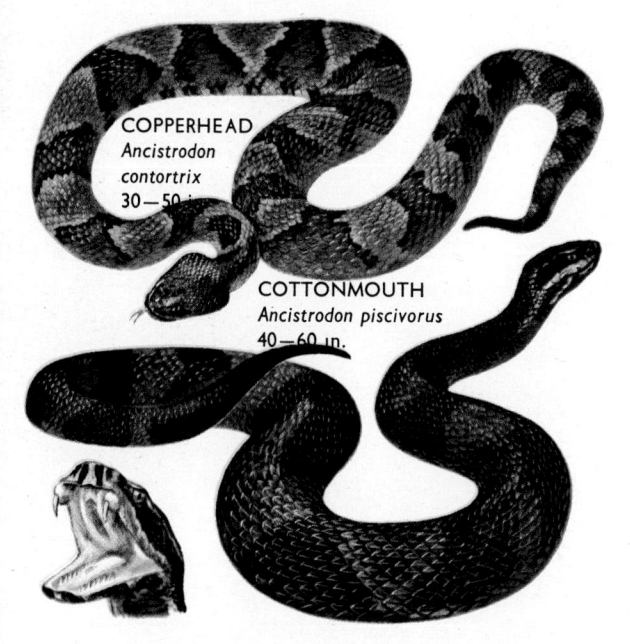

COPPERHEAD
Ancistrodon contortrix
30—50 in.

COTTONMOUTH
Ancistrodon piscivorus
40—60 in.

WATER MOCCASIN (COTTONMOUTH)
showing the white lining to its mouth

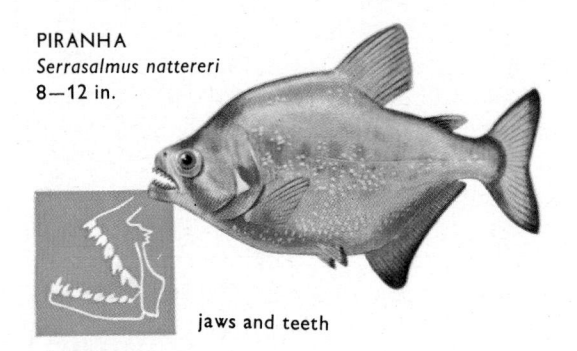

PIRANHA
Serrasalmus nattereri
8—12 in.

jaws and teeth

PIRANHAS *(Serrasalmus* spp.*),* also called Cannibal Fish, are small and ferocious fish that live in the Amazon River and other freshwater streams in tropical South America. Swift swimmers, they travel in schools and quickly descend on any wounded creature, following the faintest taste of blood in the water. Size makes no difference to these razor-toothed little fish, which rarely measure longer than 12 inches

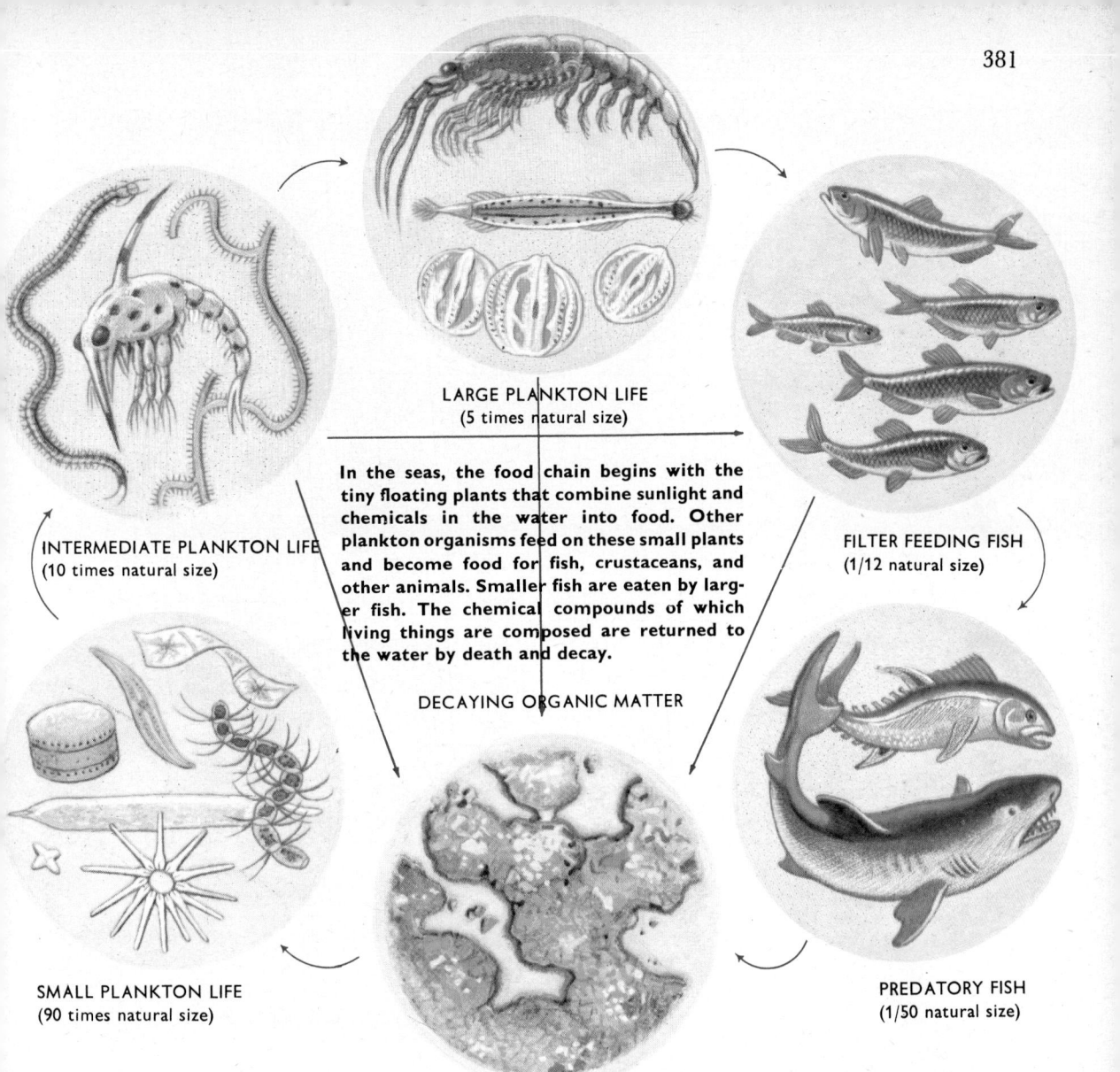

INTERMEDIATE PLANKTON LIFE
(10 times natural size)

LARGE PLANKTON LIFE
(5 times natural size)

FILTER FEEDING FISH
(1/12 natural size)

In the seas, the food chain begins with the tiny floating plants that combine sunlight and chemicals in the water into food. Other plankton organisms feed on these small plants and become food for fish, crustaceans, and other animals. Smaller fish are eaten by larger fish. The chemical compounds of which living things are composed are returned to the water by death and decay.

DECAYING ORGANIC MATTER

SMALL PLANKTON LIFE
(90 times natural size)

PREDATORY FISH
(1/50 natural size)

themselves. They can rip to shreds a horse or an ox as readily as some smaller animal. Stockmen, in regions where piranhas abound, often kill a sick or weakened animal in the herd to draw all the piranhas to one spot, while the other animals swim the river at another point in safety.

PLANKTON, a Greek word meaning wanderer, is the name used for the drifting life in the sea. Actually, most plankton can swim, and many species do so very rapidly. Because they are small, however, they are swept along by ocean currents and have little control over where they go. They

are collected for study under a microscope by towing conical nets of fine silk cloth slowly through the water. Among the most abundant of all marine life, plankton are the basic food of all other animals in the sea. Large animals can feed on plankton only if they have some type of filtering mechanism, but the largest creature in the sea — the Blue Whale — feeds by filtering plankton, as does the Basking Shark, which reaches a length of more than 30 feet. Many colonial animals, and many of those attached to the bottom, eat plankton, which they catch in their tentacles or in their filtering mechanism. Because plankton organisms

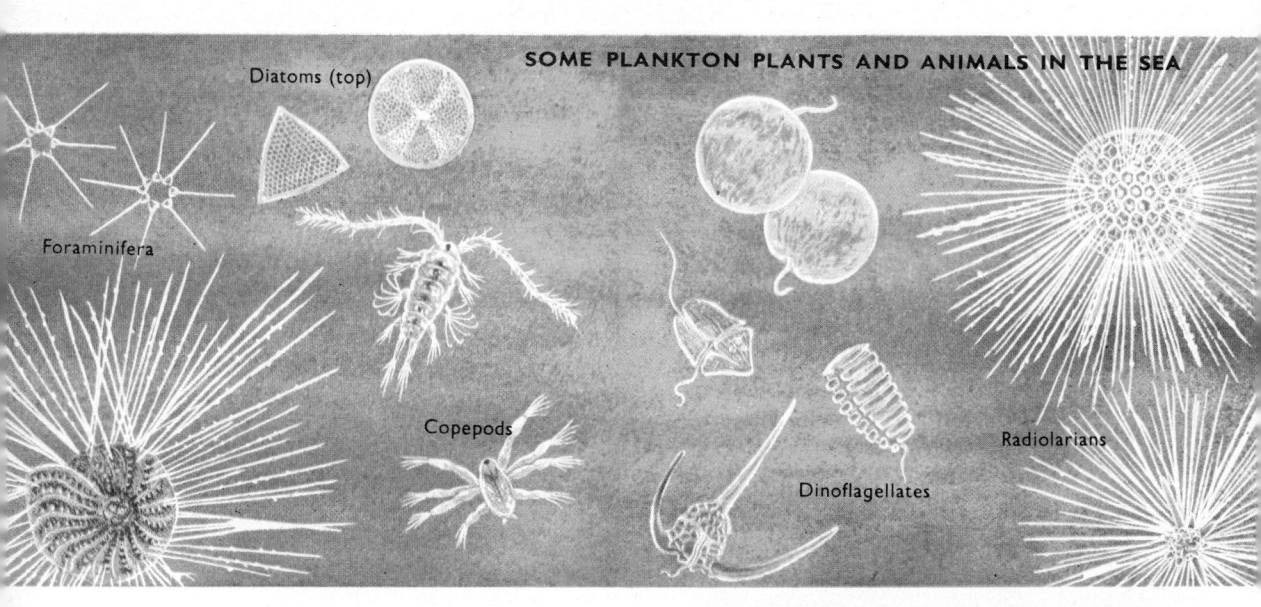

SOME PLANKTON PLANTS AND ANIMALS IN THE SEA

Diatoms (top)

Foraminifera

Copepods

Dinoflagellates

Radiolarians

are so abundant, many biologists believe they can be used for human food in the future, when better methods are developed for catching them.

Most plankton live only in the upper layers of the sea, since the animal types (zooplankton) depend on the plants (phytoplankton) for their food. Thus, microscopic plants consisting of only a single cell are the basis for all food in the sea. These tiny plants utilise the nutrient salts of the sea to

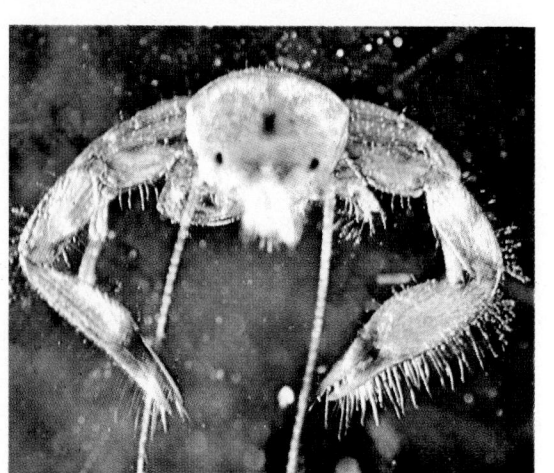

Dr. Roman Vishniac

The larva of the Porcelain Crab (10 times natural size) is one of many marine invertebrates found in zooplankton drifting with the sea currents.

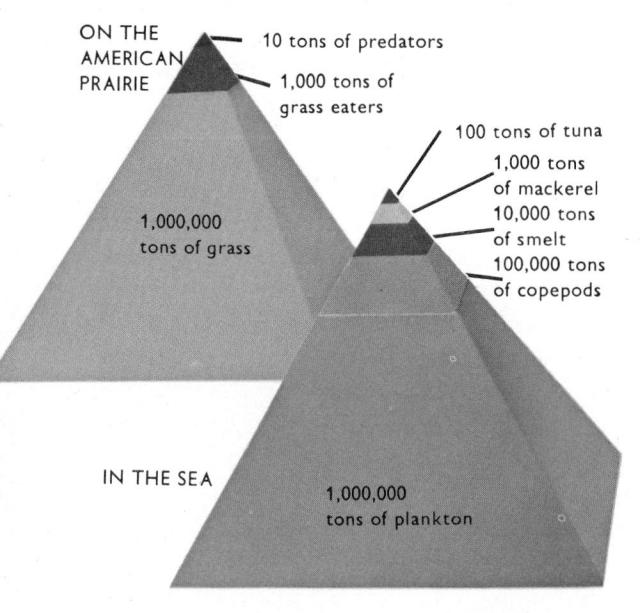

ON THE AMERICAN PRAIRIE

10 tons of predators

1,000 tons of grass eaters

1,000,000 tons of grass

100 tons of tuna
1,000 tons of mackerel
10,000 tons of smelt
100,000 tons of copepods

IN THE SEA

1,000,000 tons of plankton

Plankton is as important in the food chains of the sea as are the grasses to life on the American prairie.

manufacture food by photosynthesis. Multiplying by simple cell division at a very rapid rate, the phytoplankton increase to great numbers when there is sufficient food and sunlight. Sometimes these "blooms" actually colour the surface of the sea.

Of the many different kinds of phytoplankton, two groups are very important: diatoms and dinoflagellates. Diatoms are encased in a shell formed of silica, or glass. This shell consists of two parts that fit one inside the other, like the two halves of a pill-box. Because they need silica, which

is deposited in the sea largely by melting snow and ice, diatoms are more common in cold regions, to which they are better adapted. The silica shells make diatoms heavier than water, and so they often have long, thread-like projections, called flotation processes, to slow their sinking. Oil droplets in their bodies also aid them in staying near the surface where they can get sunlight. Unlike most plants, diatoms never form starches. Their food reserves are fat. Shells of diatoms form layers many feet thick on the bottom of the sea in some areas. These deposits are called diatomaceous ooze. Similar deposits on land are called diatomaceous earth, which has many industrial uses.

Dinoflagellates, the other major group of phytoplankton, are also microscopic. Their cells may be covered with two flagella, one in front and the other wrapped around the cell's middle. The flagella are used for swimming. Since some dinoflagellates can also take in food like animals, zoologists and botanists are undecided whether they are plants or animals. Those that manufacture their own food are important as a basic food in tropical waters.

PLOVERS are waders adapted to live on bare, open places. They have large, keen eyes and rather short bills. Plovers feed by moving with a series of short runs and pauses, suddenly tipping up as they pick up some small insect.

Best known is the Lapwing, or Peewit. With its green-glossed back, whispy crest, black-and-white wings and tail, and chestnut tail-coverts, this is the most colourful species. It is a bird of grassland, and in spring performs a crazy, tumbling flight, uttering the "peewit" call.

The Ringed Plover is a bird of the beach. The accompanying picture shows its colouring, but not the black band across a white breast. It nests in a scrape in the sand or shingle, and the eggs are so perfectly camouflaged that great care is needed to avoid treading on them.

Other plovers which nest elsewhere move

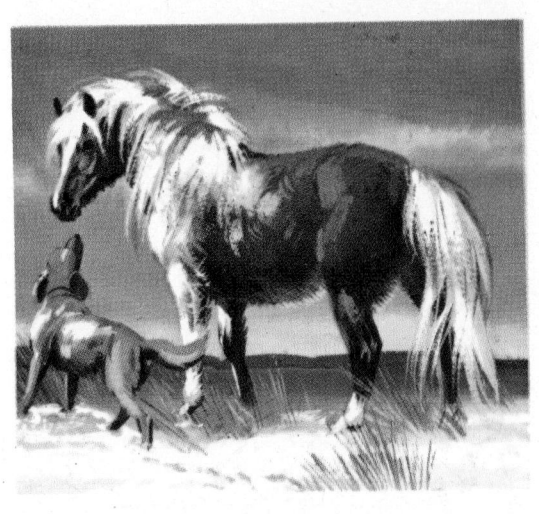

The Shetland Pony, though small, is exceptionally sturdy and has great endurance.

to the coasts in winter. Golden and Grey Plovers both occur. The plumage of the one is yellow-spotted above, while the other is marked with white. Both become black on the face, throat and underside in summer. The Golden Plover moves to high moorland to nest, and the Grey to arctic Tundra. Both have plaintive whistles as call-notes.

The rarer Dotterel is a plover of bare uplands, commoner towards the arctic, and elsewhere occurring only on the bare tops of mountain areas. It is extremely tame.

PONIES. The Celtic Pony, a small breed of horse from the British Isles and Scandinavia, was probably the ancestor of many breeds of pony. The Hackney Pony, a cross between the Welsh Pony and the Hackney Horse, is

Plovers feign injury in an attempt to draw predators away from their carefully concealed nests.

Edward Prins

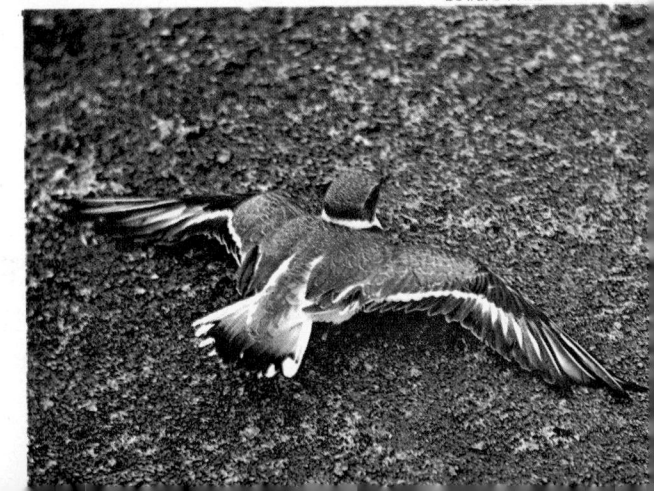

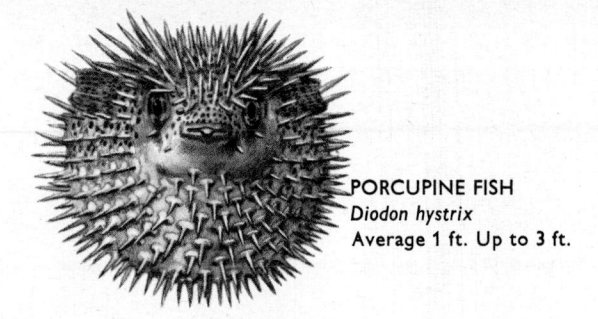

PORCUPINE FISH
Diodon hystrix
Average 1 ft. Up to 3 ft.

at least one breed developed by man. Small horses used in the game of polo are also called ponies, and in some areas the term pony refers to any small horse. The ponies of India are probably descendants of small horses taken to that country by conquerors from Northern Asia. The diet of the Mongol warriors of Jenghiz Khan consisted largely of fermented mare's milk (kumiss) and fresh mare's blood.

While horses are inhabitants of warm regions, the smaller ponies appear to have developed in colder climates. An example is the Shetland Pony, which originated on the Shetland Islands, north of Scotland, where the weather is cold and grass pastures are scant.

Although ponies have been used for such tasks as hauling coal in mines or carrying packs, they are used today almost exclusively as pets and as riding mounts for children.

PORCUPINE FISHES, closely related to puffers, can inflate their bodies to several times normal size. They then look like a ball; their fins almost disappear and, at the same time, the sharp spines over the body stand out stiffly. The fish becomes as formidable as a porcupine, hence the name.

Members of this family are widely distributed in warm waters. The Porcupine Fish (*Diodon hystrix*), for example, is found throughout the world. The Striped Burrfish (*Chilomycterus schoepfi*) is a native of the West Indies, sometimes straying to New England.

Natives of the South Seas once made war-helmets out of the skins of porcupine fish. In the Orient, inflated, dried skins were hung from wires as decorative lanterns, each lit by a candle placed inside.

PORCUPINES are large rodents with most of their hair modified into heavy spines or quills. These spines are easily pulled out,

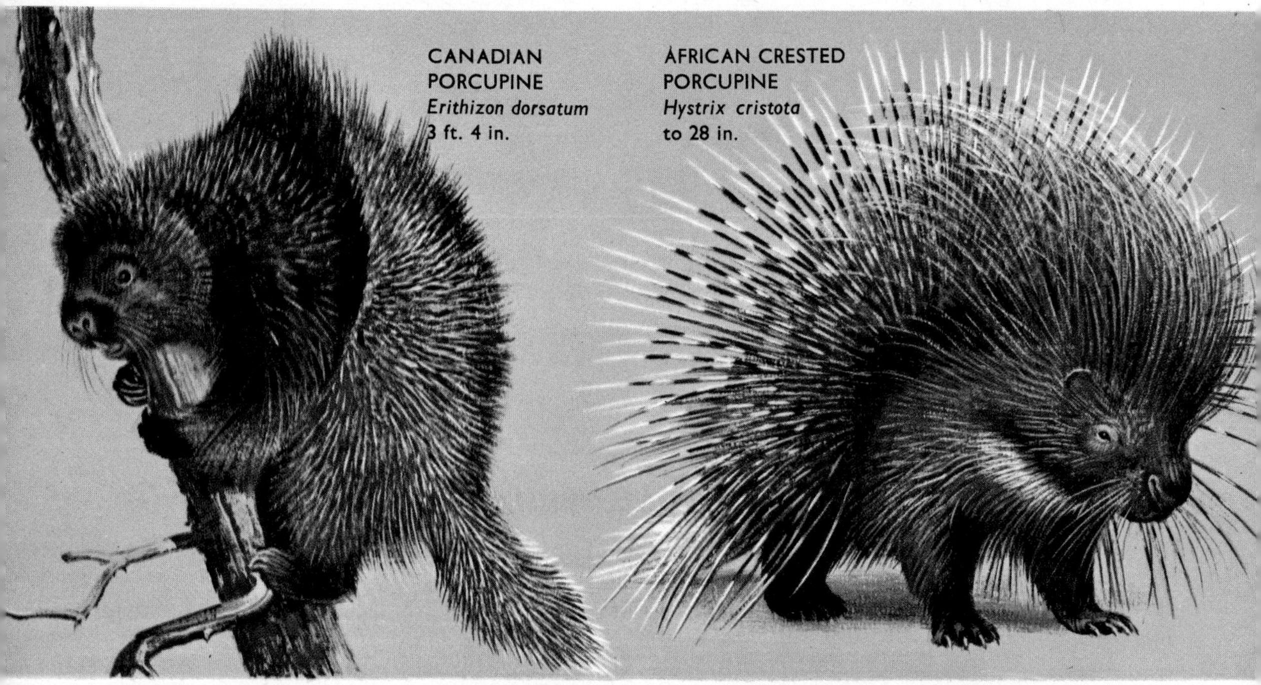

CANADIAN PORCUPINE
Erithizon dorsatum
3 ft. 4 in.

AFRICAN CRESTED PORCUPINE
Hystrix cristata
to 28 in.

Smaller predators are usually put to flight by threats or by a blow from a porcupine's quilled tail. The porcupine's defence against large animals is to erect its spines and back towards its adversary.

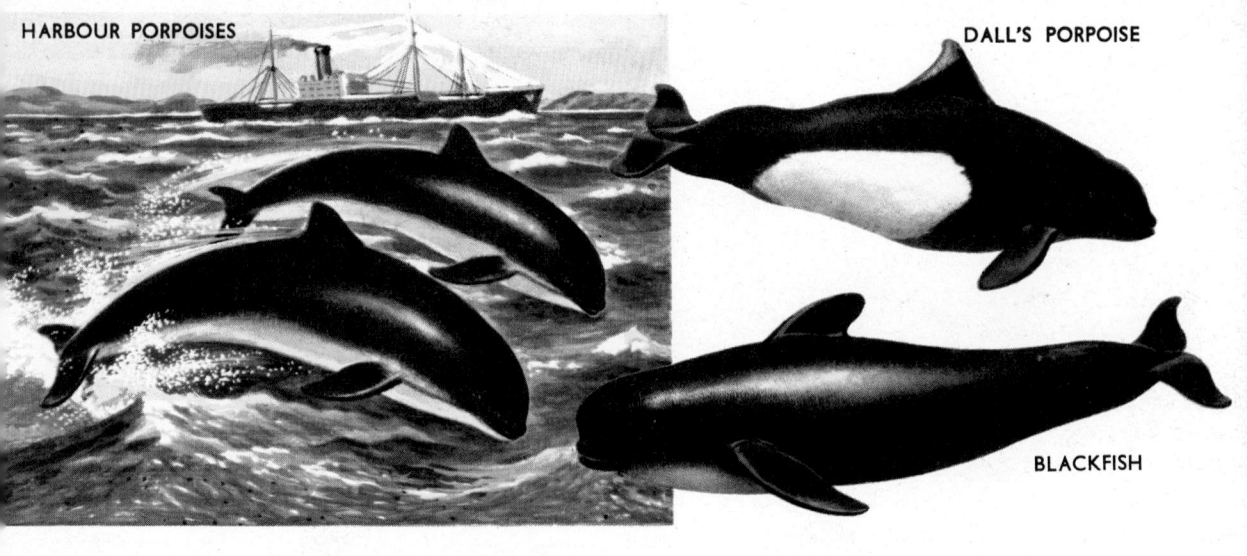

HARBOUR PORPOISES

DALL'S PORPOISE

BLACKFISH

Porpoises commonly swim in schools near the top of the water, arching their back above the surface at regular intervals to breathe through the "blowhole" located on the top of the head.

but they cannot be shot or thrown at enemies. Porcupines — particularly the Old World species — may warn potential attackers by rattling or vibrating their spines. North American porcupines *(Erithizon* spp.*)* have barbed spines, which are difficult to remove when lodged in a victim. If allowed to remain in the skin, they may work their way into the muscle beneath. Tree Porcupines frequently perch high in trees. They feed mainly on wood and bark, but may also eat seeds and fruits.

South and Central American porcupines *(Coendou* spp.*)* have a long, grasping (or prehensile) tail, which they wrap around branches and use as a fifth leg.

Old World porcupines live in parts of Africa, Asia, and south-eastern Europe. They nest in burrows and feed on roots, bulbs, and occasionally on bark. Crested Porcupines *(Hystrix* spp.*),* common in the Old World, have spines that may reach a length of two feet. These spines are longest on the porcupine's back, and give the appearance of a crest.

PORPOISES are small whales which live in all the oceans. They are smaller than dolphins, usually less than six feet in length, and do not have snouts, or beaks. Porpoises have low, triangular dorsal fins and oval flippers. Like dolphins, however, porpoises are among the most intelligent of all mammals.

Dall's Porpoise *(Phocaena dalli),* about six feet in length, is most common in the cold waters of the northen Pacific Ocean, off the coast of Alaska.

Harbour Porpoises *(Phocaena phocaena)* are common in both Atlantic and Pacific coastal waters. When they leap out of the water, their distinctive colours, black above and light below, are clearly visible. Harbour Porpoises feed mainly on fish and squids.

Blackfish *(Globicephala melaena),* also called Pilot Whales, are found in the Atlantic and Pacific Oceans; they reach a length of 28 feet. Blackfish commonly travel in schools, and their habit of closely following a leader, or pilot, has often brought misfortune to the entire school. For if the leader becomes stranded on a beach or sandbar, other members of the school follow and may be unable to get back to deep water again. Once beached, the whales are not capable of supporting the weight of their large bodies, and collapse of the lung cavity causes their death. Like all water-dwelling mammals, Blackfish come to the surface to breathe. The female gives birth to, and nurses, a single young (See WHALES.).

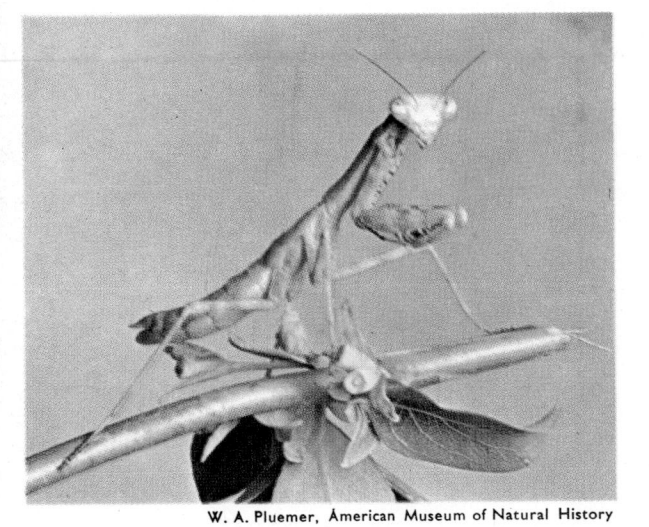

W. A. Pluemer, American Museum of Natural History

A Praying Mantid searches for food as soon as it hatches, and will eat its own brothers and sisters.

Praying Mantid eggs are laid in clusters. All the eggs hatch at the same time, and the young disperse.

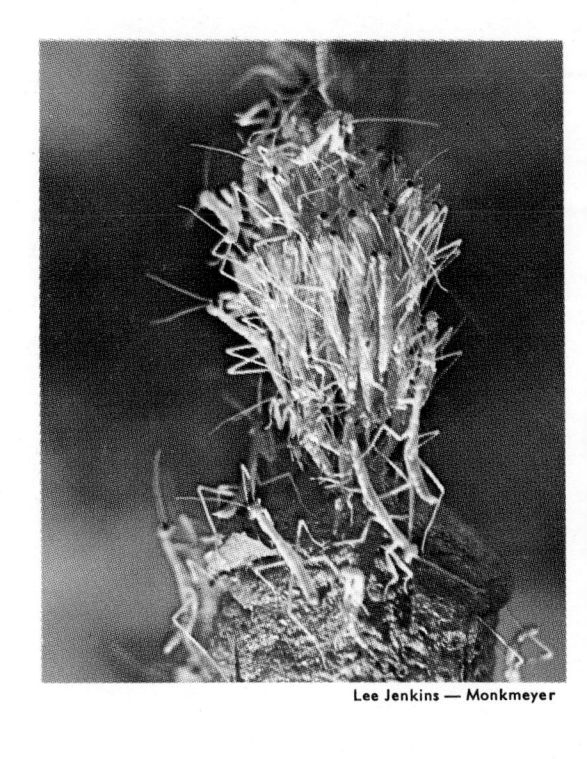

Lee Jenkins — Monkmeyer

PRAYING MANTIDS (*Mantidae*) are predaceous insects that belong to the order Orthoptera, along with grasshoppers, katydids, cockroaches, crickets and stick insects. There are several hundred species found largely in the tropics or sub-tropics. Most mantids are green or mottled, to resemble the vegetation in which they live. There they wait for their prey — mostly other insects, but occasionally small frogs or even lizards. At rest, a mantid holds the front of its body high and its large, sharply-spined front legs folded, so that it appears to be in a position of prayer. It remains motionless except for its head, which it turns back and forth while watching for prey to come within reach — then it lashes out quickly and grabs the hapless victim.

Mantids lay their eggs in masses, covered by a frothy material that soon dries. The egg-cases are usually attached to a twig or a stem. Occasionally they are sold to gardeners to establish a population of mantids to assist in controlling pest insects, but it is doubtful if such attempts really do much good. Mantids that live in temperate zones pass the winter in the egg-case. Newly-hatched mantids — several hundred from each egg-case — do not have wings and, though tiny, are as voracious as the adults. Males often fight and kill each other, the victor consuming his foe. Females may eat their mates. In the Orient, caged mantids are sold for fights, which continue until one of the contestants is dead.

PRIMATES. Man has assigned himself to an order of mammals called Primates. The lower primates are small quadrupeds that are mostly arboreal, but show some characteristics of their more highly evolved kin. These are the tree shrews, lemurs and tarsiers. The higher primates are the New World monkeys, the Old World monkeys, the Anthropoid apes, and man.

Primates are largely a tree-dwelling group, whose members possess long arms and legs, each of which has generally five digits (fingers and toes) and rather flattened nails. In many primates, grasping and manipulating is made easier by the thumb and, in some, the first toe, which works in an opposable direction to the remaining digits. Primates have good vision (their eyes

directed forward) and complex brains. They feed chiefly on fruits and seeds; some, including man, are also carnivorous.

The oldest primates were similar to living lemurs, and their fossils are found in rocks of the Paleocene period. They probably arose from some tree-dwelling insectivore ancestors, perhaps similar to the tree shrews living today.

Tarsiers are small primates with rat-like bodies, long tails, and jumping legs. They are tree-dwellers that live in the East Indies.

Monkeys, apes and men constitute the third group of primates and are known as anthropoids. Apes do not have a tail or cheek pouches, and include gibbons, siamangs, orang-utans, gorillas and chimpanzees.

Although all anthropoids are highly intelligent, man is conspicuously the most intelligent. The gap between man and other members of the group is one of degree and not of kind, however. It is chiefly in the development of certain parts of the body, especially of certain parts of the brain.

One result of man's peculiar anatomy and physiology is that, of all animals, he is the only important toolmaker. This is a useful definition of man in palaeontology. Tools and weapons are relatively common fossils.

They are called artifacts and are much more common, than are the remains of man himself. Tools are a way of identifying where the various fossil men lived and how far advanced they were. (See APES; CHIMPANZEES; GIBBONS; GORILLAS; LEMURS; MONKEYS; ORANG-UTANS; TARSIERS.)

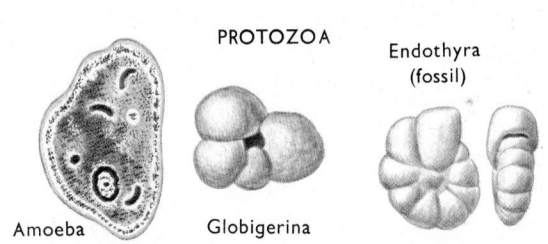

PROTOZOA

Endothyra (fossil)

Amoeba   Globigerina

Class Sarcodina: pseudopodia, or "false feet", used for locomotion and to capture food. Some kinds secrete shells of lime or silica. Some are parasitic.

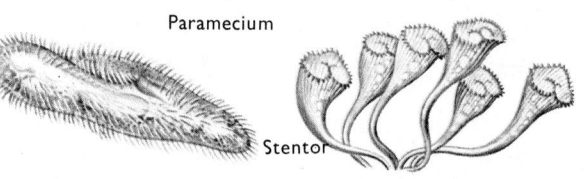

Paramecium

Stentor

Class Ciliata: locomotion by means of tiny "hairs", or cilia, covering the cell. Most are free-swimming; some are attached by a stalk.

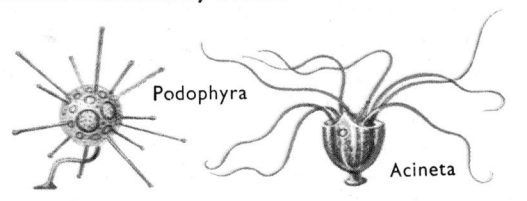

Podophyra

Acineta

Class Suctoria: move by means of a cilia when young, but are usually fixed in one place by a stalk as adults, capturing prey by means of their tentacles.

PROTOZOA means "first animals", a name given to microscopic one-celled animals that were undoubtedly one of the earliest forms of life. All of the necessary life functions are performed by these one-celled animals, many of which have developed fairly complex methods of feeding and locomotion. There are about 30,000 species of protozoans, distributed throughout the world in fresh and salt waters, in soils, or wherever there is moisture. Even a thin film of moisture is enough for their survival. Some kinds survive

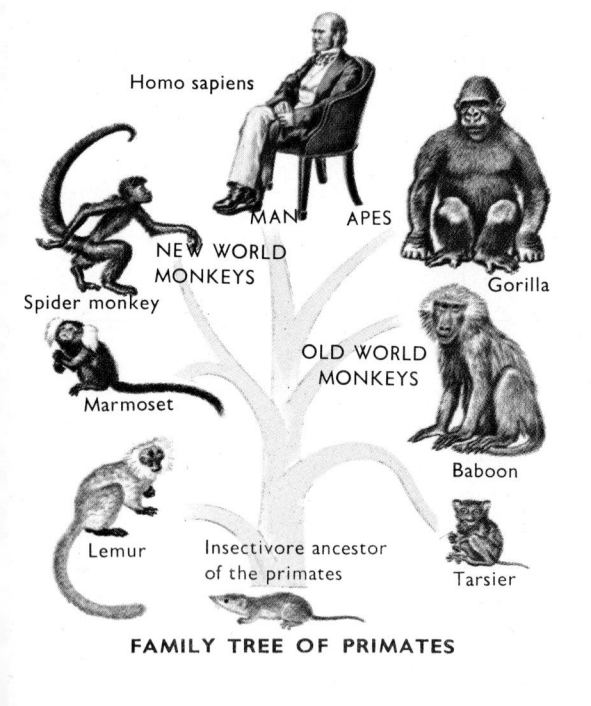

Homo sapiens

MAN   APES

NEW WORLD MONKEYS

Spider monkey

Gorilla

Marmoset

OLD WORLD MONKEYS

Baboon

Lemur   Insectivore ancestor of the primates

Tarsier

FAMILY TREE OF PRIMATES

periods of dryness by surrounding themselves with an impervious covering, called a cyst, from which they emerge and resume normal life processes when they become moist again.

Amoebas are among the best known of the one-celled animals. Nearly all of the species are microscopic, although a few are barely visible to the naked eye. These simple animals consist of a shapeless mass of protoplasm, and they move by a flowing of their protoplasm to form pseudopods, or "false feet". In this manner they take in food literally by surrounding it, or flow away from undigested wastes. They also move towards favourable surroundings and

MORE PROTOZOA

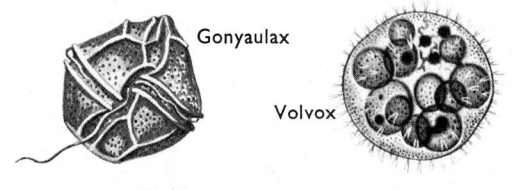

Coccidium

Porospora

Class Sporozoa: all members of this class are parasites, causing diseases of man and other animals. They lack organs of locomotion.

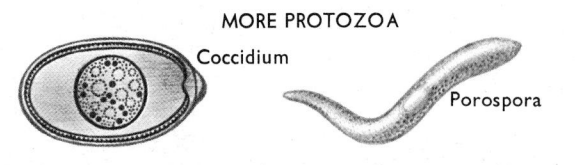

Gonyaulax

Volvox

Class Mastigophora: movement by means of one or more whip-like flagella. Some live as single cells; others are colonial. Also classified as plants.

away from conditions that are undesirable. Some members of this class (Sarcodina) are parasitic, causing dysentery in man and other animals. Many kinds, such as the foraminifera and radiolarians, secrete shells around themselves. Some are enormously abundant in shallow seas and in surface waters of oceans, forming a large part of the plankton (see PLANKTON). About one-third of the ocean floor is covered by an ooze consisting largely of the limy shells of *Globigerina*, a foraminifera.

The oldest fossil foraminifera described so far are from rocks of Cambrian age in Siberia. The Bedford Limestone of Indiana

consists almost entirely of the shells of a coiled foraminifera *(Endothyra)*.

The Pyramids of Egypt contain shells of large foraminifera. They were once thought to be the remains of lentils carried as food by the slaves who built the tombs.

Radiolarians have a spherical covering (capsule) of silica, often beautifully ornamented with delicate rods or spikes radiating from the central body sphere. Radiolarians live in great numbers today in the surface waters of warm oceans. Their tiny skeletons

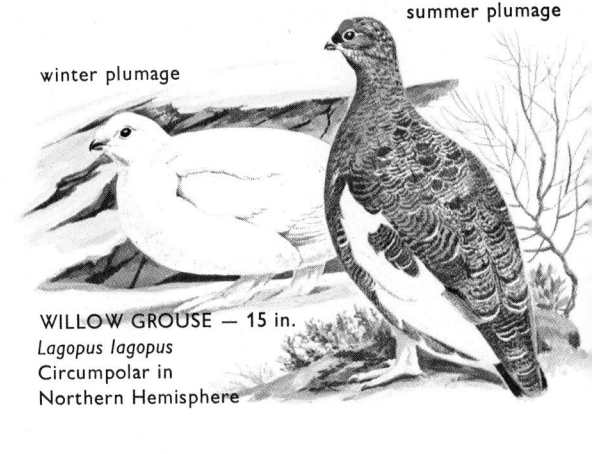

summer plumage

winter plumage

WILLOW GROUSE — 15 in.
Lagopus lagopus
Circumpolar in
Northern Hemisphere

form a deposit of ooze said to cover 2 million square miles of the ocean floor. Radiolarians are members of the class Sarcodina.

Another of the classes of protozoans is made up of the ciliated types (Ciliata), which move by means of hair-like projections (cilia) over their cell body. The cilia are used also to channel food into the cell. *Paramecium* is a familiar, free-swimming member of this group. Other types, such as *Stentor* and *Vorticella,* are attached by means of a stalk, as are members of still another class (Suctoria), which have cilia and are free-swimmers when young. Members of the class Sporozoa lack structures for locomotion, and all species are parasites causing such diseases as malaria in man, and fevers in cattle and other grazing animals. Protozoans of the class Mastigophora are known as flagellates, because they have one or more whip-like flagella that are used for locomotion. Among the common kinds are *Euglena*

and *Volvox*, a colonial type consisting of a hollow sphere composed of many single cells. Both kinds contain chlorophyll and are sometimes classified as plants.

PTARMIGAN, grouse of the northern tundra and brushlands, are circumpolar in distribution. They live on berries, buds, seeds and lichens. The Willow Grouse is the continental mountain form of the Red Grouse. The typical Ptarmigan is a bird of bare, northern mountain-tops; it is grey-brown in summer, and white in winter.

PUFFERS, also called Globefish, are much like porcupine fishes, but are not spiny. They can inflate their bodies quickly when in danger. Some gulp down water to make themselves swell; others take in air — then turn upside down and float to the surface (see illustration). When they deflate, which they can also do rapidly, they may belch noisily. Even baby puffers can inflate.

Puffers' teeth, like those of porcupine fishes, are fused to form a sharp, powerful beak used to crush crustaceans and shellfish. They can make a rasping noise by grinding their teeth. Some puffers are good to eat, but the flesh of others is very poisonous.

The Globefish *(Lagocephalus lagocephalus)* is a species which is occasionally drifted into British waters by warm ocean currents from the Atlantic. In the Western Atlantic, the Smooth Puffer, or Rabbitfish *(Laevigatus)*, is found from North Carolina southwards to the West Indies. It is the largest of the Puffers, reaching a length of two feet. It cannot inflate its body as much as other species. The Northern and Southern Puffers *(Sphaeroides maculatus* and *S. nephalus)* are smaller species of the Western Atlantic. When inflated, these puffers look like small balloons, and they bob about hel plessly on the surface.

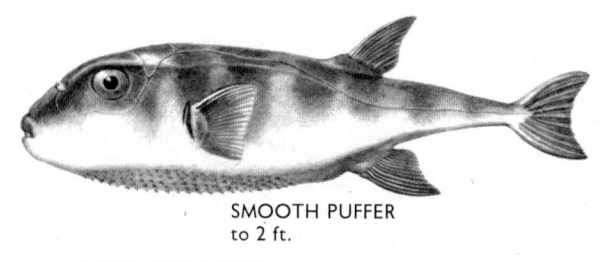

SMOOTH PUFFER
to 2 ft.

SOUTHERN PUFFER
(inflated)
Average 6—8 in.

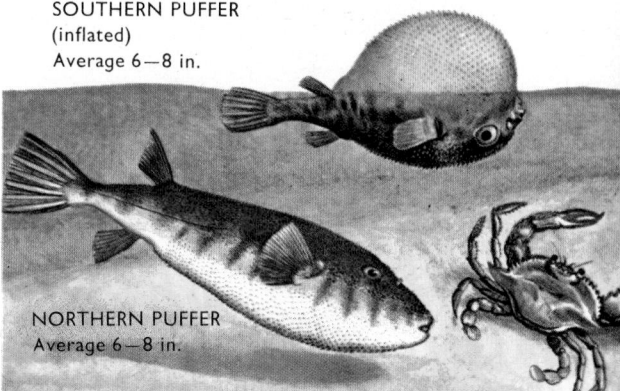

NORTHERN PUFFER
Average 6—8 in.

TUFTED
PUFFIN — 15 in.
Lunda cirrhata
Bering Sea and
North Pacific

COMMON PUFFIN — 12 in.
Fratercula arctica
North Atlantic coasts

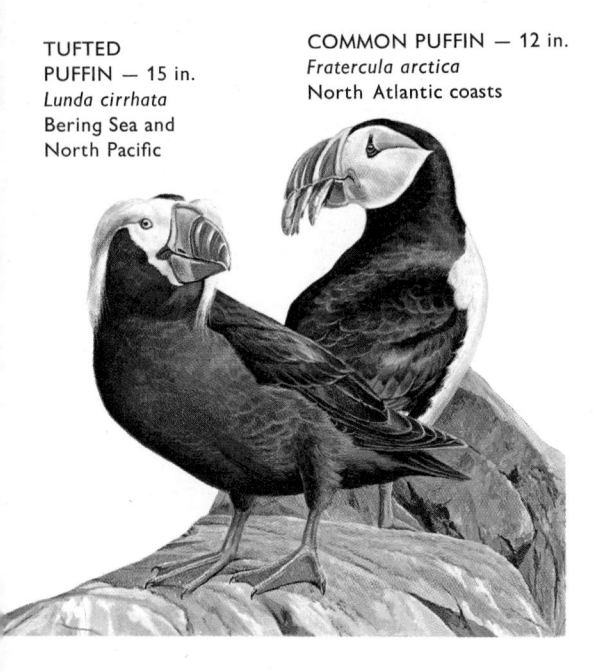

PUFFINS are the clowns of the auk family. During the breeding season, the large parrot-like bills of both sexes grow a bright sheath, and the insides of the mouth match the birds' scarlet feet. Facing one another, they do solemn bill-rapping displays. They nest in burrows which they dig with their feet. Puffins lay only one egg. They dive for fish and, when feeding their young, can carry a dozen small fish in their beak. Puffins lose the sheath over their bill and the colour in their mouth after the breeding season.

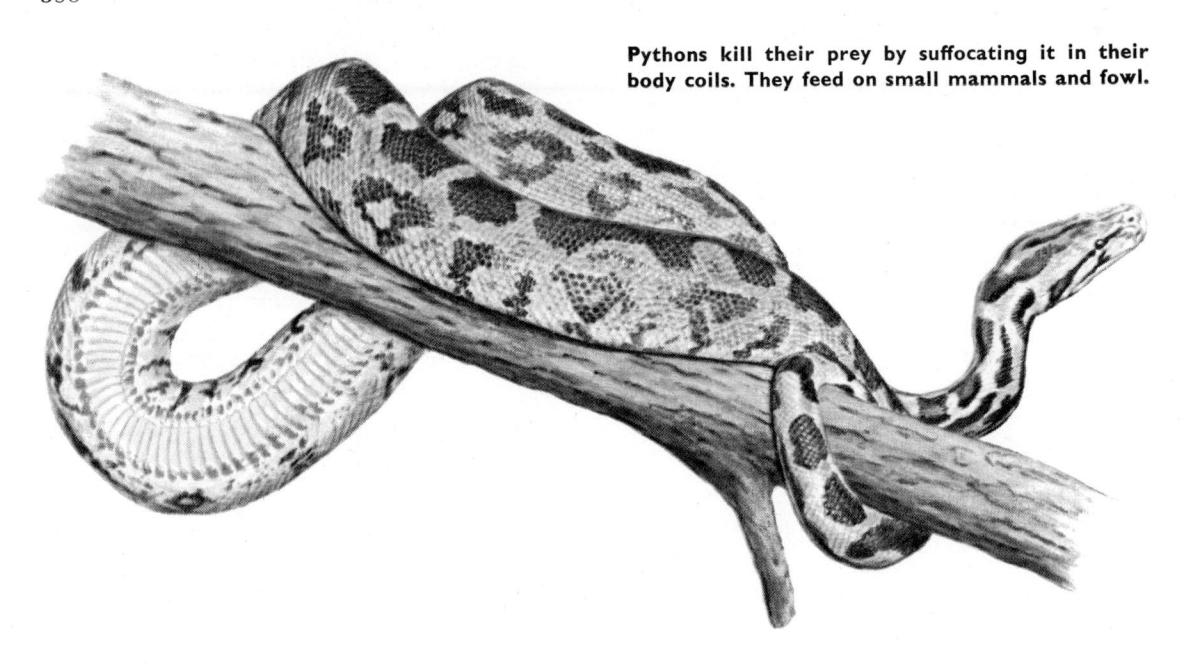

Pythons kill their prey by suffocating it in their body coils. They feed on small mammals and fowl.

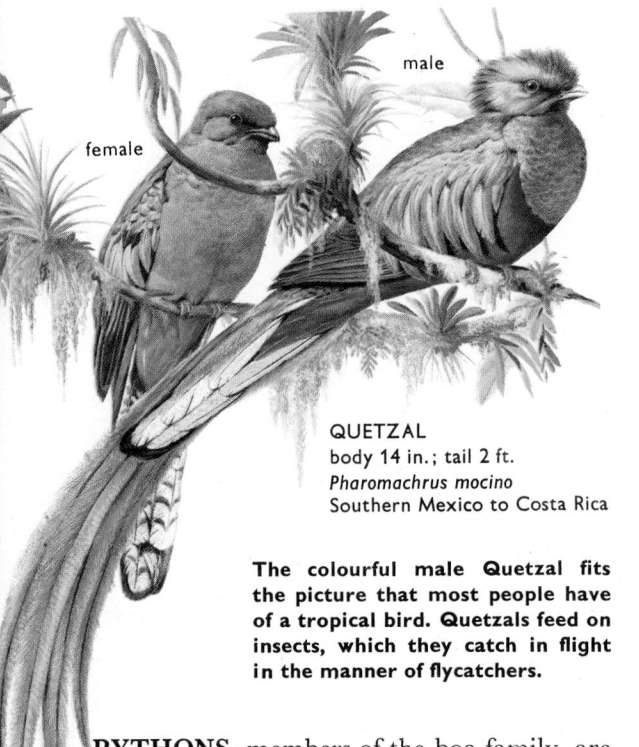

female

male

QUETZAL
body 14 in.; tail 2 ft.
Pharomachrus mocino
Southern Mexico to Costa Rica

The colourful male Quetzal fits the picture that most people have of a tropical bird. Quetzals feed on insects, which they catch in flight in the manner of flycatchers.

PYTHONS, members of the boa family, are Old World snakes of some 21 species. The females often brood their eggs, which may number as many as a hundred. Largest is the 30-foot Reticulate (or Regal) Python *(Python)* of south-eastern Asia, the East Indies, and the Philippines. One of the rock pythons *(Liasis)* found in Australia and

on Pacific islands attains a length of 20 feet. The Burrowing Python *(Calabaria)* of West Africa is only about three feet long. (See BOAS.)

QUAILS are small game birds related to the Partridges. The Common Quail, unlike most species, is a migrant, and for centuries large numbers have been slaughtered each year as the tired birds settle to rest in countries around the Mediterranean. They are skulkers, living and breeding in ground vegetation, and often the only indication of their presence is the monotonous "wet-my-lip" call of the male.

The Painted Quail is a widespread species, often kept and bred in captivity. It is a tiny bird, only the size of a sparrow, and the pairs keep together most of the time. They can creep through tiny runs in the grass as furtively as mice. They lay large clutches, and the chicks, when they first hatch, are no bigger than bumble-bees.

The many Quail species of North and Central America are larger birds, about thrush to partridge size, and take the place of such birds.

QUETZALS, beautiful birds of the highland cloud forests of Central America, are one of

about 30 species of trogons found in tropical regions around the world.

The Toltec Indians of Guatemala worshipped Quetzalcoatl, their god of the air, through the Quetzal, and used the males' brilliant long tail-feathers for their priests' ceremonial capes. They caught Quetzals and pulled out their tail-feathers, but never killed the birds.

The Spaniards who conquered the Indians did not follow this good example, and few

birds remain today, although they are now protected and are increasing in number. Guatemalans have made the Quetzal their national emblem. One of their largest cities is named after it, and instead of pounds or dollars Guatemalans have "quetzales" as their monetary unit.

Quetzals nest in holes in rotten tree-trunks. Both the males and females incubate. When the male sits on the eggs, he faces the entrance, and his two-foot tail stands against the back of the nest, curves against the roof, and sprays out of the door-hole; it looks like fern leaves high on the tree and hides the nest-hole. In addition to insects, they will also take small fruits snatched on the wing. The tail of the male is beautifully displayed as he hovers.

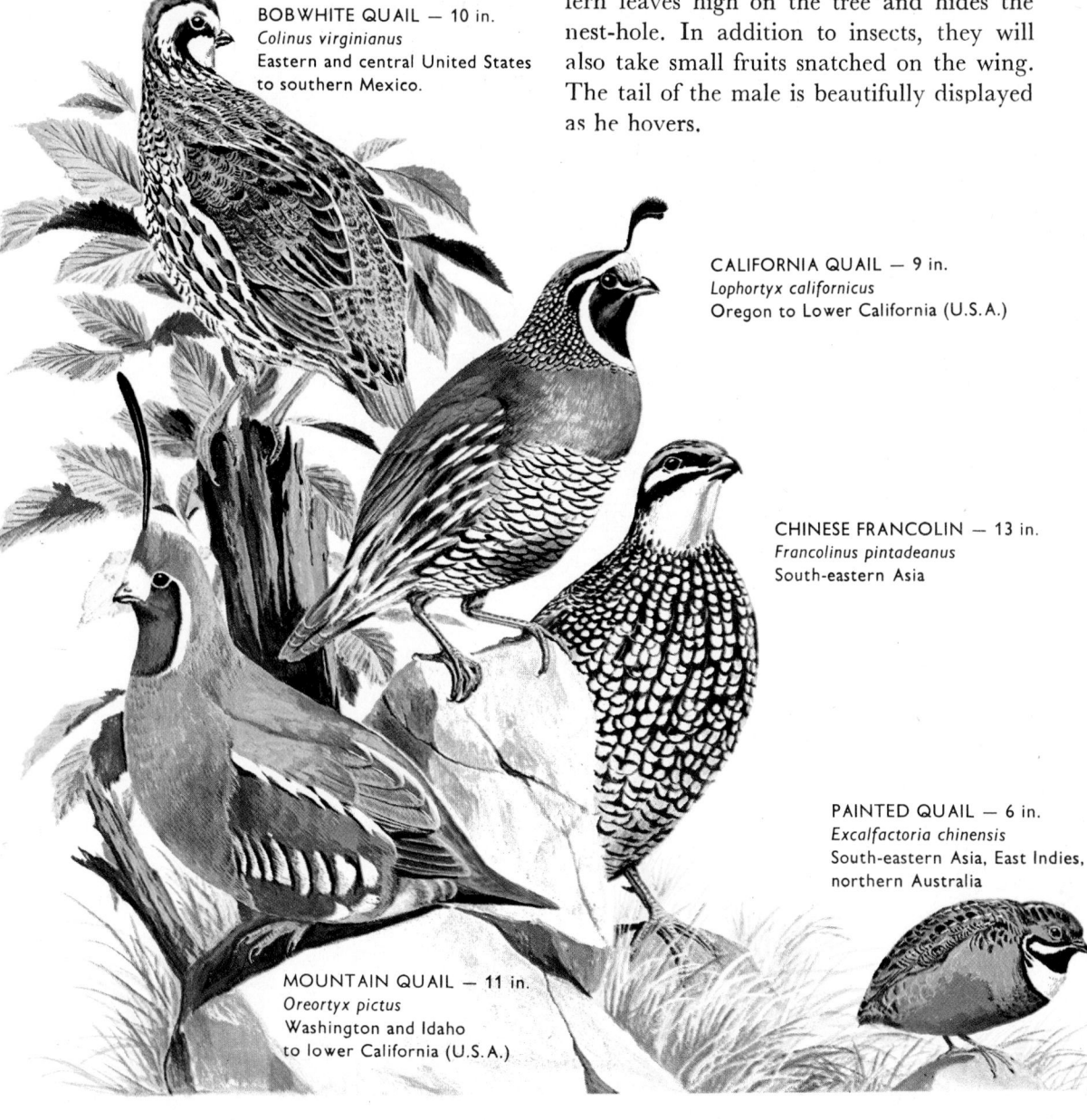

BOBWHITE QUAIL — 10 in.
Colinus virginianus
Eastern and central United States to southern Mexico.

CALIFORNIA QUAIL — 9 in.
Lophortyx californicus
Oregon to Lower California (U.S.A.)

CHINESE FRANCOLIN — 13 in.
Francolinus pintadeanus
South-eastern Asia

PAINTED QUAIL — 6 in.
Excalfactoria chinensis
South-eastern Asia, East Indies, northern Australia

MOUNTAIN QUAIL — 11 in.
Oreortyx pictus
Washington and Idaho to lower California (U.S.A.)

R

RABBITS are found in many parts of the world — even in Australia, where they were introduced by man. They have shorter legs than hares, and run rather than leap. Young are born helpless, naked and blind.

Cottontails *(Sylvilagus* spp.*)*, common almost everywhere in North America, have short legs, cottony tails, short ears and large, dark eyes. Their nests are frequently built in vacant burrows, or in the shelter of brush heaps or thickets. They feed on grasses and leaves and, in winter, on the bark of trees and shrubs. The Pygmy Rabbit, smallest of the cottontails, lives on the sagebrush flats of the western United States. Swamp Rabbits, slightly larger than other cottontails, live in the canebreaks of the south-eastern United States.

Domestic rabbits *(Oryctolagus cuniculus)* were derived from wild rabbits of Europe. These wild rabbits live in groups in a network of underground burrows, and well-beaten surface paths, called warrens. Rabbits have several litters of young each year, usually with two to eight young in each litter. A full-grown rabbit weighs almost six pounds. European rabbits were introduced to Australia early in the nineteenth century. They multiplied rapidly, and without carnivores

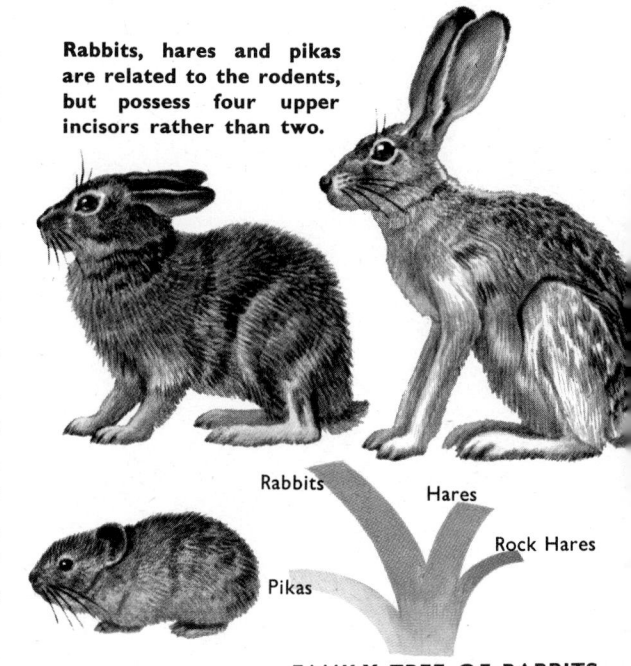

Rabbits, hares and pikas are related to the rodents, but possess four upper incisors rather than two.

Rabbits   Hares
                Rock Hares
Pikas

FAMILY TREE OF RABBITS

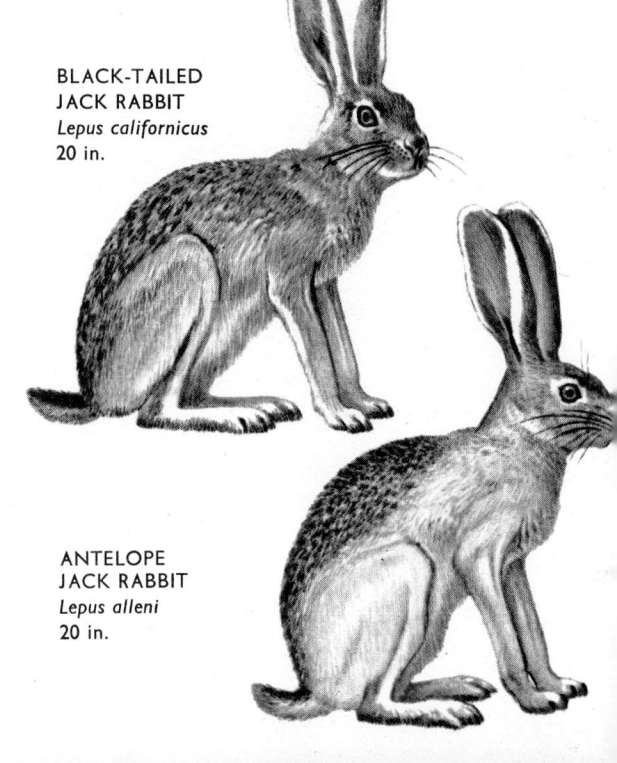

BLACK-TAILED JACK RABBIT
Lepus californicus
20 in.

ANTELOPE JACK RABBIT
Lepus alleni
20 in.

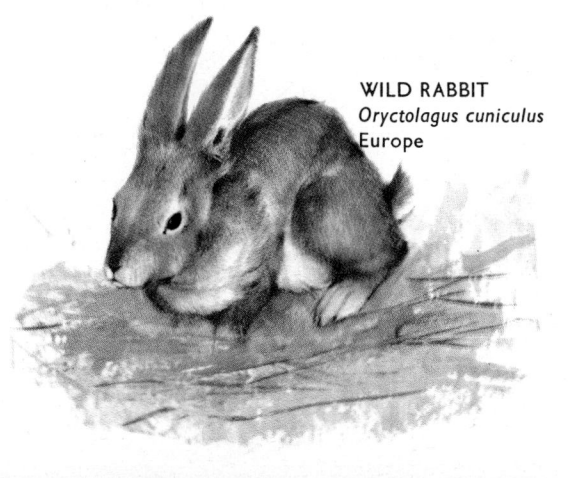

WILD RABBIT
Oryctolagus cuniculus
Europe

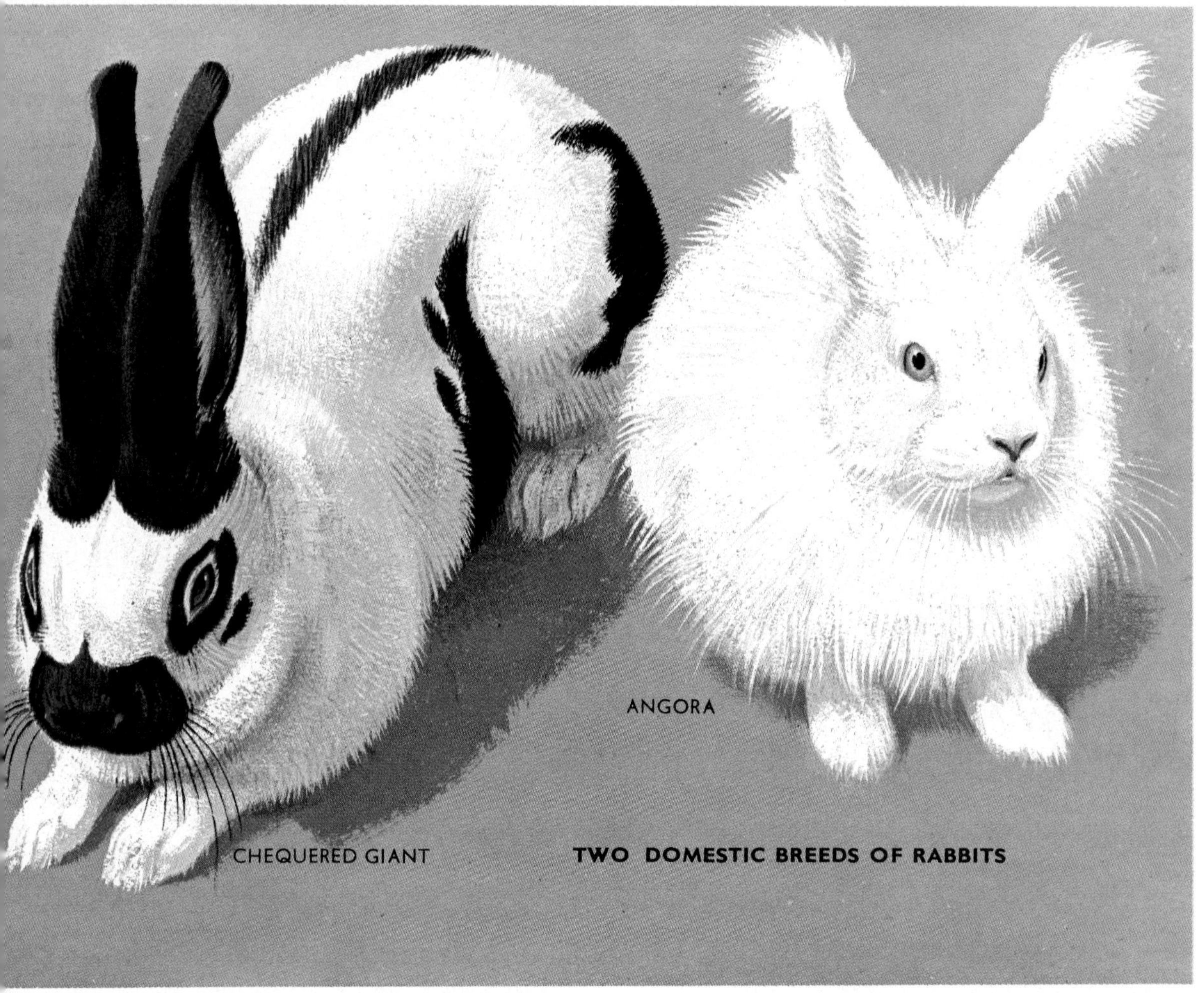

ANGORA

CHEQUERED GIANT

TWO DOMESTIC BREEDS OF RABBITS

Although raised primarily for the market, meat breeds also furnish valuable pelts. More valuable is the wool of the Angora Rabbit, which is clipped or plucked four times a year. One can produce 12 ounces of wool a year.

to prey on them, soon became over-abundant. They destroyed much of the native vegetation, which brought about soil erosion and turned fertile land into desert; this also upset the life of the native marsupials. Since then, the government has spent great sums of money to keep the rabbit population under control. Myxomatosis, a virus disease, has been responsible for reducing Britain's rabbit population of recent years.

Jack rabbits, which have extremely long ears, are not in fact rabbits at all, but hares *(Lepus* spp.*)*. They feed on almost every kind of vegetation and can get along with very little water. They are eaten by coyotes,

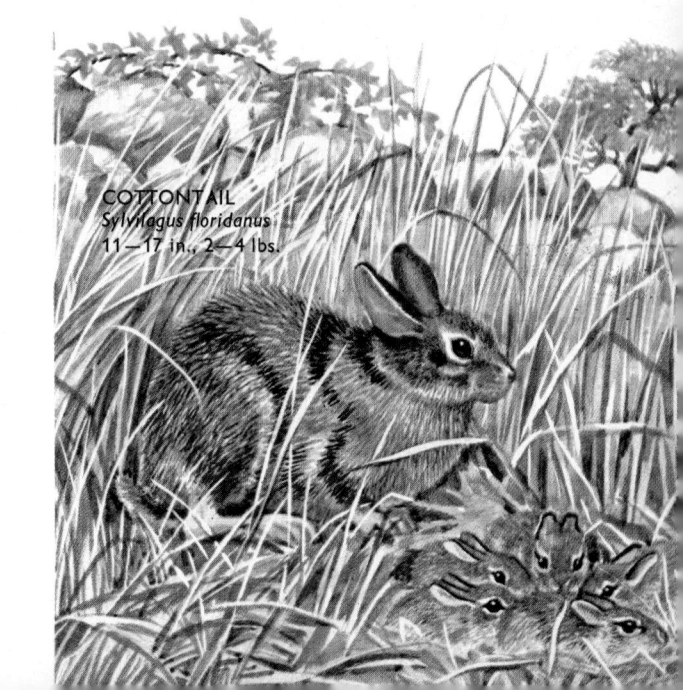

COTTONTAIL
Sylvilagus floridanus
11—17 in., 2—4 lbs.

foxes and badgers, and their young become food for owls and hawks. The Blacktailed Jack Rabbit, common in the deserts of the western United States, has exceedingly large, black-tipped ears. It reaches a weight of as much as seven pounds, and is capable of leaping along as fast as 40 miles per hour for long periods of time. The Antelope Jack Rabbit has pale sides and even larger ears.

RACCOONS *(Procyon lotor)* are flat-footed, black-masked, ringed-tailed mammals. Typically American, they range from southern Canada to Panama. The related Crab-eating Raccoon *(Procyon cancrivorous)* ranges as far south as Paraguay. Raccoons always live close to water, where they feed on such things as crayfish, insects, frogs, wild fruit, corn and rodents. In most areas, they make their den in hollow trees. These creatures have a habit of dipping their food in the water before eating. Raccoons have been trapped for many years to acquire their valuable fur; they are also hunted for sport, usually with dogs. Most weigh between 8 and 15 pounds but some reach 30 pounds. Full-grown raccoons can be dangerous when cornered, and have been known to kill raccoon hounds.

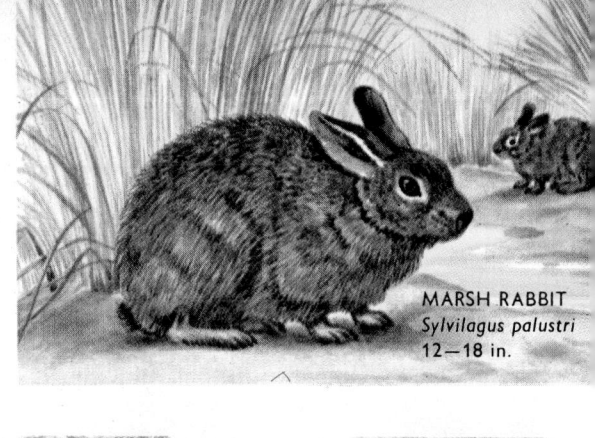

MARSH RABBIT
Sylvilagus palustri
12—18 in.

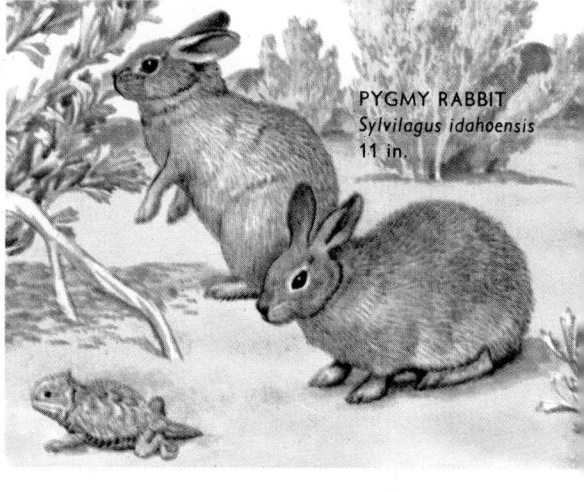

PYGMY RABBIT
Sylvilagus idahoensis
11 in.

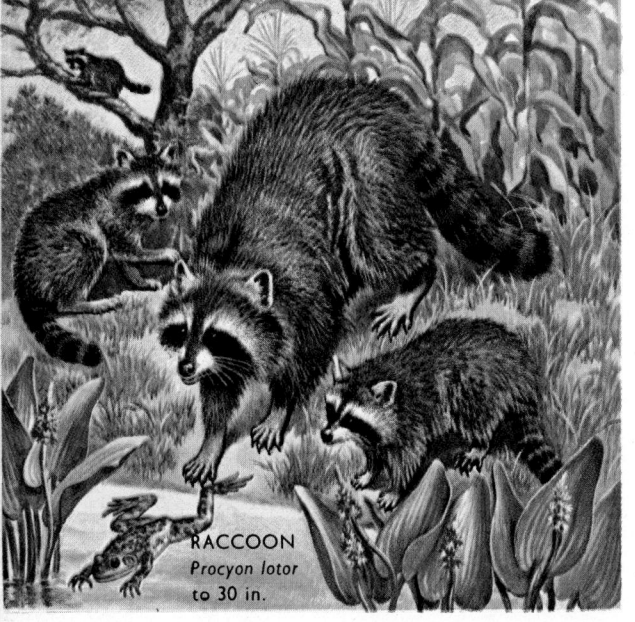

RACCOON
Procyon lotor
to 30 in.

RATFISH, or Chimaeras, are primitive fishes, in some ways intermediate between the sharks and the bony fishes. Like sharks, they have a skeleton of cartilage, lay eggs encased in horny capsules, and the males have a pair of claspers used for internal fertilisation. On the other hand, they have a single gill-opening like bony fishes — although the gill cover, or operculum, is not bony.

The Rabbitfish *(Chimaera monstrosa)* is recorded from British waters. It is one of the largest species, reaching 5 feet, and like most chimaeras occurs in deep water.

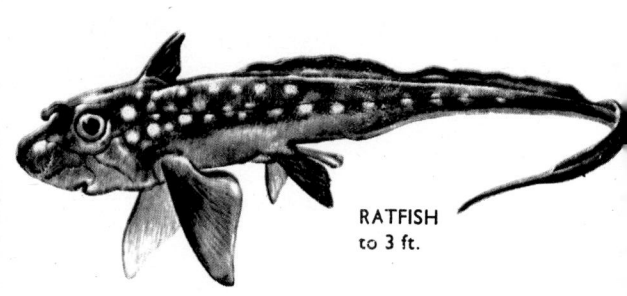

RATFISH
to 3 ft.

Chimaeras have long, pointed tails, as do many other deep-sea fishes. A sharp spine at the front of their dorsal fins can inflict a deep wound, and these spines may be poisonous. Males may use the fleshy knobs on their heads as claspers to hold the females when mating. Although their flesh is good to eat, these fish are repulsive-looking and are not used as food. Their reproductive and other internal organs are poisonous if eaten.

RATS are small rodents that are, in general, larger than mice. The terms "rats" and "mice" have no technical meanings, and there is no one group of rats or of mice. Rather, these are terms referring to size, and have no more clear-cut distinction than the difference between a pond and a lake.

Rats are highly successful because of their high reproductive rate, ability to subsist on almost any kind of food, and adaptability to a wide range of living conditions.

The best known rats are those of the genus *Rattus*. There are many kinds spread throughout the tropical and sub-tropical regions of the Old World. Some of these accompanied the European explorers and colonists to continents and islands all over the world. In many places, they have competed successfully with native species, sometimes exterminating them or forcing them into other habitats. Black Rats, *(Rattus rattus),* in combination with fleas, were responsible for the spread of the bubonic plague — the Black Death — that decimated human populations in Europe, Asia and parts of Africa in the Middle Ages.

Today, plague is found in only a few places in the world.

Some of these rats have been introduced and have become well established in North and South America. These are the Norway Rat *(Rattus norvegicus)* and the Black Rat, or Roof Rat. The Norway Rat has the larger body and shorter tail; the Black Rat is a good climber. Both of these rats live in close proximity to man — in his homes, barns and stores — and they feed on many of the same things that man eats. The destruction and contamination of foodstuffs by these rats have made man their chief enemy, while man's habit of storing food has made him the chief benefactor of these rodents.

Woodrats, or Packrats *(Neotoma* spp.*),* are as large or larger than the well-known Norway Rat; their tail is more hairy and their undersides white. Woodrats occur in North America from deserts to mountain tops. Many prefer to live in abandoned buildings; some have the habit of collecting objects and taking them to their nests. They pack away all kinds of things — hence their name — and nest in a variety of places: among the spines of cacti, in trees, or on

BLACK RAT
Rattus rattus
body, 7—8 in., tail, 8—9 in.

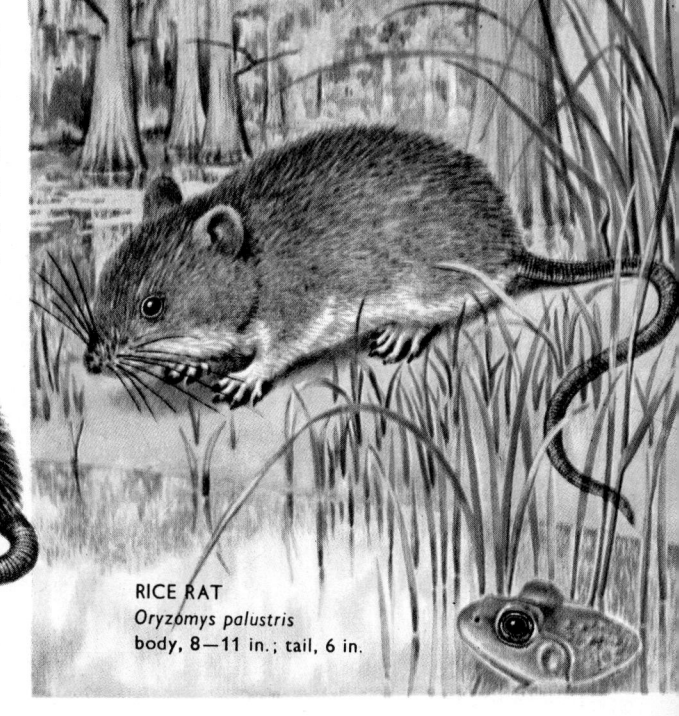

RICE RAT
Oryzomys palustris
body, 8—11 in.; tail, 6 in.

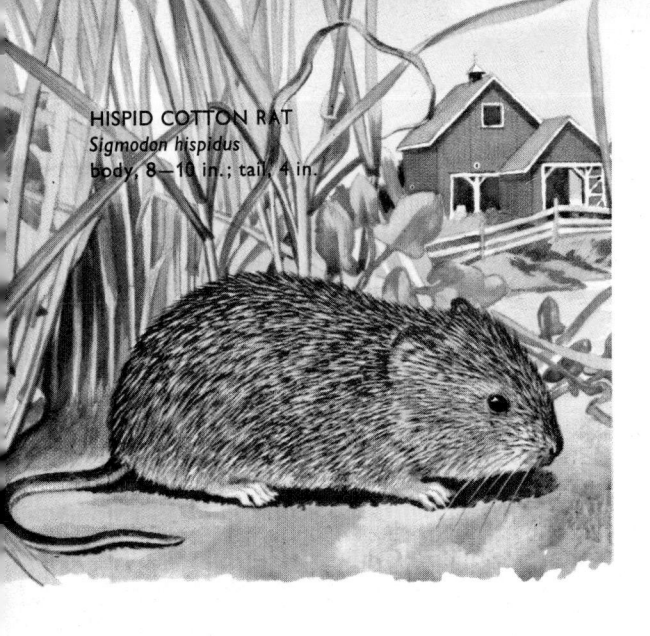

HISPID COTTON RAT
Sigmodon hispidus
body, 8—10 in.; tail, 4 in.

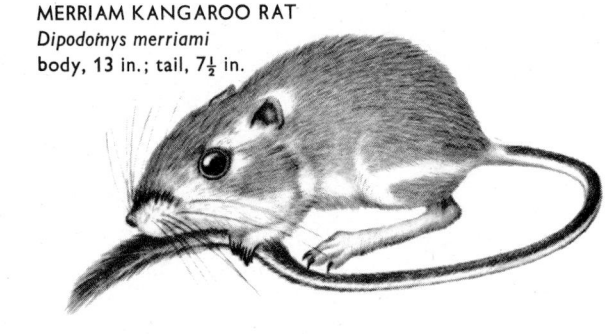

MERRIAM KANGAROO RAT
Dipodomys merriami
body, 13 in.; tail, 7½ in.

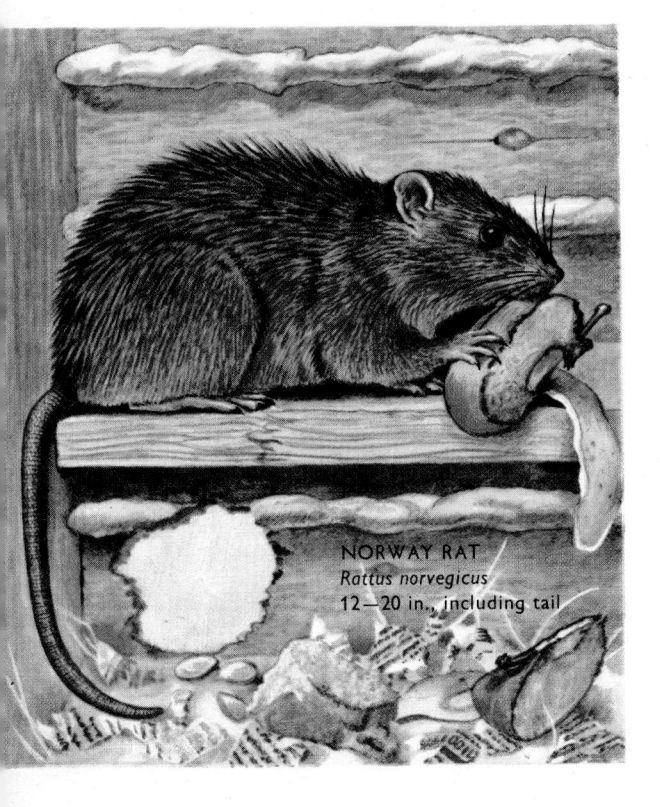

NORWAY RAT
Rattus norvegicus
12—20 in., including tail

mountain cliffs. All are nocturnal, spending the day in stick nests, which they build and rebuild over several generations.

The African Giant Rat *(Cricetomys gambianus)*, largest of all, measures between two and three feet in length, including its tail. Giant rats live in holes in the ground in the tropical forest. Active only at night, they feed principally on seeds and are rather docile when caught.

Mole rats live in ground burrows much like those of moles. Some kinds resemble moles even more, by having eyes greatly reduced — even completely covered with skin — very short tails, and front legs enlarged for digging. Most mole rats live in North Africa or Asia Minor. The Naked Mole Rat *(Heterocephalus glaber)*, is nearly hairless. It burrows in the hot sands of Somaliland and northern Kenya.

The hair of spiny rats *(Proechimys* spp.*)*, of South and Central America, is modified into short, sharp, spiny bristles which discourage predators. There are many kinds of spiny rats. They live in forests, usually near water, and seek shelter under boulders, stumps, fallen trees, and roots.

The Cotton Rat *(Sigmodon hispidus)* and the Rice Rat *(Oryzomys palustris)* are found in the southern United States. The Rice Rat lives in marshes, both fresh and salt water, and often invades rice fields. Cotton rats of several kinds live from mountains to lowlands, and are often pests in fields and gardens. They have a more rounded muzzle and a shorter tail than house rats.

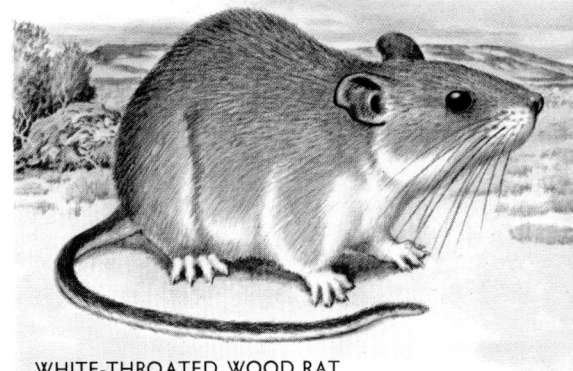

WHITE-THROATED WOOD RAT
Neotoma albigula 12—15 in., including 6½ in. tail

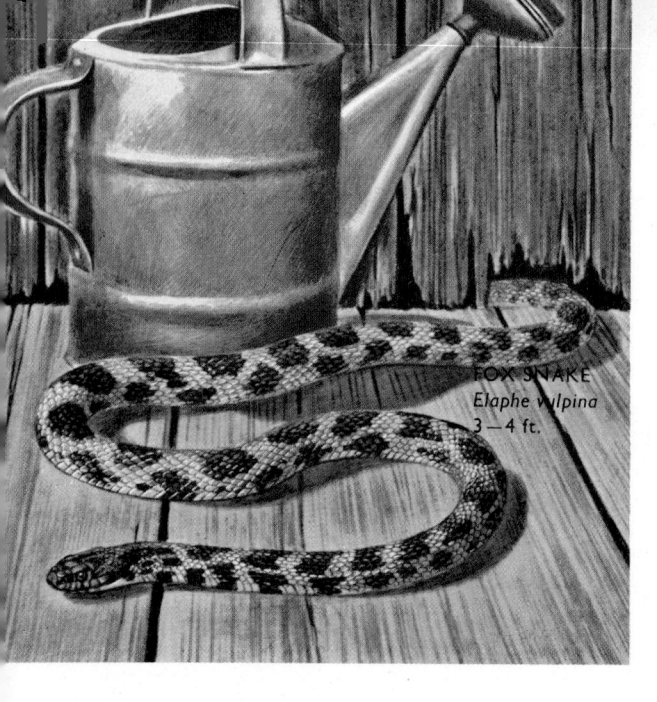

FOX SNAKE
Elaphe vulpina
3—4 ft.

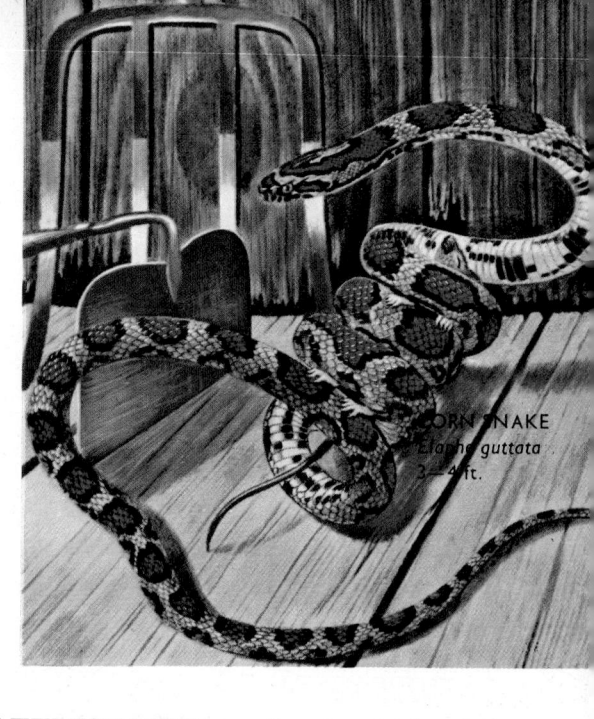

CORN SNAKE
Elaphe guttata
3—4 ft.

RATSNAKES are a non-venomous species, living both in America and Asia *(Elaphe* spp., *Ptyas* spp., and *Zaocys* spp.*)*. Some of the most colourful of all snakes — the Corn Snake and the Yellow Ratsnake, for example — belong to this genus. Most of these snakes tame easily and make excellent pets. Their food consists almost entirely of birds and their eggs, or rodents, but the Indian Ratsnake eats mainly frogs. They kill their prey by constriction. All ratsnakes have the habit of hissing, and vibrating their tail, when disturbed, and most ratsnakes are good climbers. The Black Ratsnake, or Pilot Black Snake, has a blotched colour pattern when young, but is nearly all black as an adult. It is sometimes mistaken for the slimmer, more nervous Black Racer.

RATTLESNAKES are found only in the Americas. There are about 30 species of "mailed" rattlesnake *(Crotalus)*, which have small head scales, and three species of pygmy rattlesnake *(Sistrurus)*, which have large head scales. Pygmy rattlesnakes occur only in the eastern and southern United States and central Mexico; the largest rarely exceeds $2\frac{1}{2}$ feet. All have a powerful venom potentially lethal to man, but few deaths are recorded, primarily because of the small amount of venom produced (see VIPERS).

"Mailed" rattlesnakes vary in size from

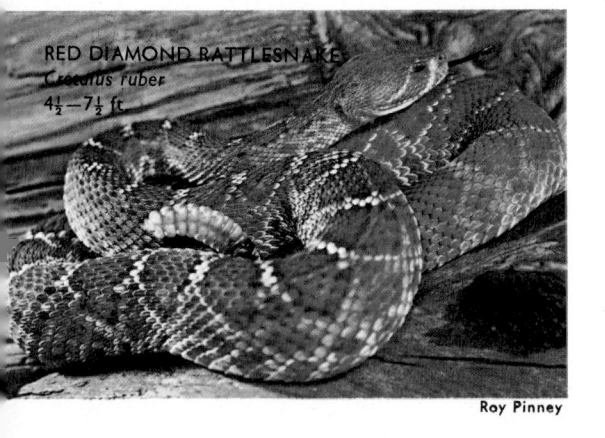

RED DIAMOND RATTLESNAKE
Crotalus ruber
$4\frac{1}{2}$—$7\frac{1}{2}$ ft.

Roy Pinney

PYGMY RATTLER
Sistrurus militarius
18—24 in.

head of
Pygmy Rattler

small species, $\frac{1}{2}$ feet to 2 feet in length, to the Florida Diamondback Rattlesnake, recorded at 8 feet 2 inches. Thirteen species of "mailed" rattlesnake occur in the United States. This makes the total number of poisonous snakes in the United States 19 (2 species of coral snake, 15 species of

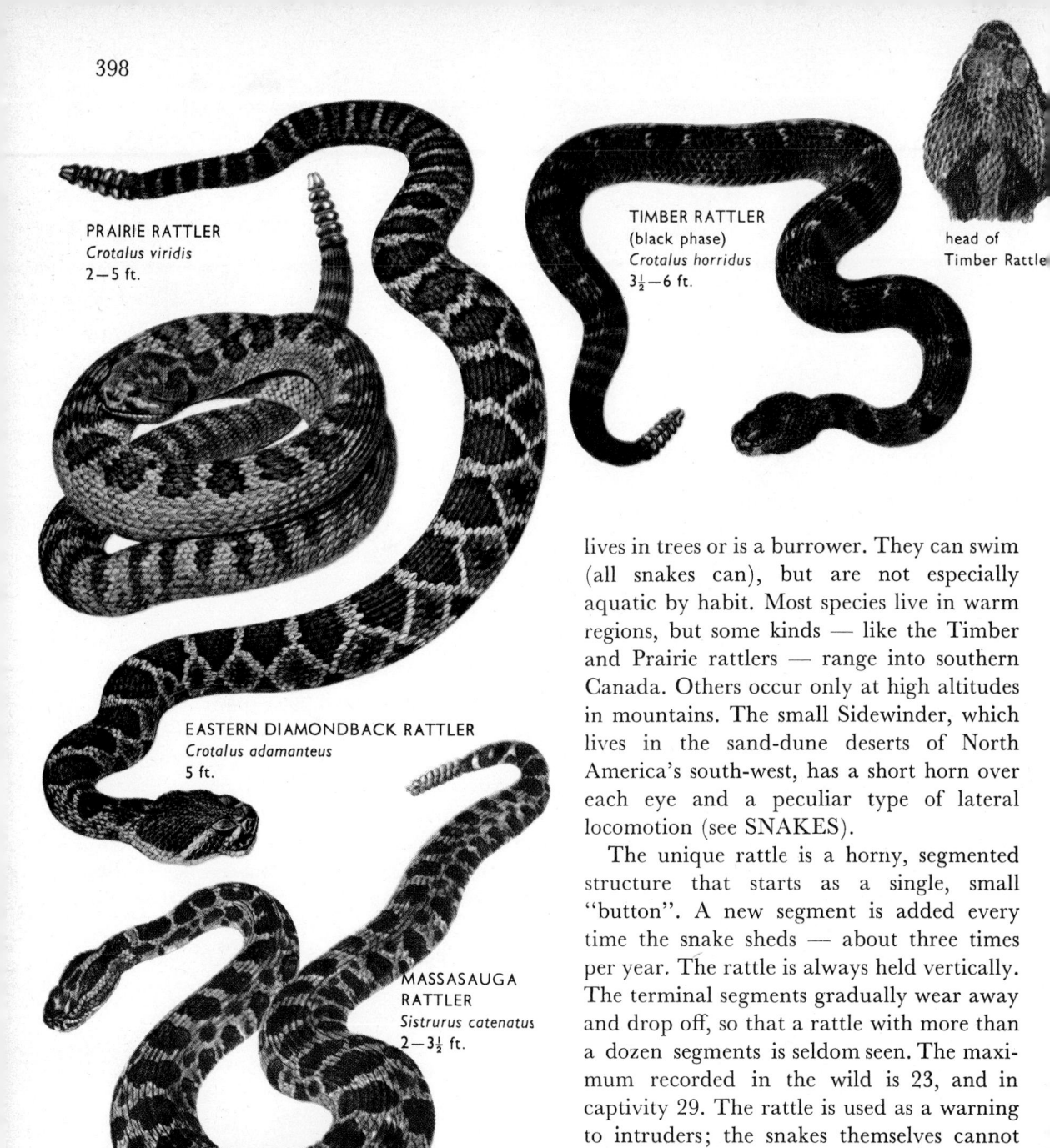

PRAIRIE RATTLER
Crotalus viridis
2—5 ft.

TIMBER RATTLER
(black phase)
Crotalus horridus
3½—6 ft.

head of
Timber Rattle

EASTERN DIAMONDBACK RATTLER
Crotalus adamanteus
5 ft.

MASSASAUGA
RATTLER
Sistrurus catenatus
2—3½ ft.

lives in trees or is a burrower. They can swim (all snakes can), but are not especially aquatic by habit. Most species live in warm regions, but some kinds — like the Timber and Prairie rattlers — range into southern Canada. Others occur only at high altitudes in mountains. The small Sidewinder, which lives in the sand-dune deserts of North America's south-west, has a short horn over each eye and a peculiar type of lateral locomotion (see SNAKES).

The unique rattle is a horny, segmented structure that starts as a single, small "button". A new segment is added every time the snake sheds — about three times per year. The rattle is always held vertically. The terminal segments gradually wear away and drop off, so that a rattle with more than a dozen segments is seldom seen. The maximum recorded in the wild is 23, and in captivity 29. The rattle is used as a warning to intruders; the snakes themselves cannot hear the sound — at least not by air vibrations. Many harmless snakes also wiggle the end of the tail nervously when alarmed; this makes a rattling sound, if the tail strikes some resonant object.

Rattlesnakes pass the winter in deep crevices, or "dens". They may travel miles to reach such a den, particularly in areas where suitable sites are scarce. How they locate the dens, year after year, is not known. At denning time, they "follow the leader", using the sense of smell to trail each other.

rattlesnake, plus the Cottonmouth and the Copperhead), rather than only four as is commonly stated. Timber, Prairie, Texas, Florida and Blackface Rattlesnakes are the most widely distributed and dangerous.

All rattlesnakes are ground-dwellers. None

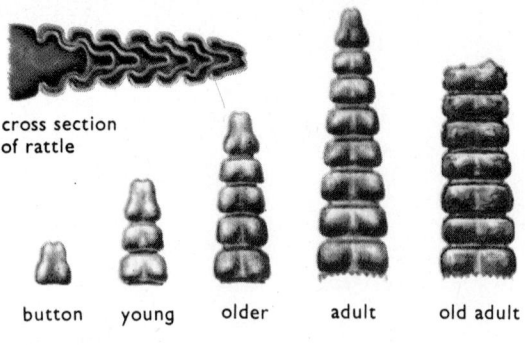

cross section
of rattle

button young older adult old adult

A rattlesnake may add several "buttons" to its rattle each year, one for every time it sheds its skin.

RAVENS, largest members of the crow family, have all the habits, good and bad, of their relatives. Their food, voices, nests and eggs are all similar, but female Ravens may lay as many as seven brown-splotched, greenish eggs, a few more than crows. The birds range widely in both Old and New Worlds; they live in mountains, in northern forests, and along sea-coasts.

Much larger than crows, ravens can be told apart in flight by their shallower and

more rapid wing-beats, tapered tail-tip, heavier bill, and long, spiky feathers about the throat, making the bird's head look heavier still. They are skilled in flight manoeuvres and will roll over on to their backs, then right themselves again, apparently just for the pleasure of it.

Ravens are famed chiefly for their intelligence and cunning, which has helped the birds to evade many of the traps which man sets for them. They take a wide range of food, including carrion.

RAYS, like sharks and ratfish, have skeletons of cartilage rather than bone. A typical ray's body is greatly flattened — although a few kinds, such as the giant Sawfish, have a long, slim, shark-like shape. The Swordfish, though it is similar in shape, is not related.

A ray's large and wing-like pectoral fins are joined broadly to its head and body. It swims by flapping these "wings", seeming to fly through the water. Many kinds of ray measure wider across their wings than from head to tail.

Rays breathe by drawing in water through their spiracles. These open one on each side of their head, just behind their eyes. The water passes over the gills and then out of

The Raven has a wing-spread of over four feet, a foot more than the crow. Its tail is longer and wider.

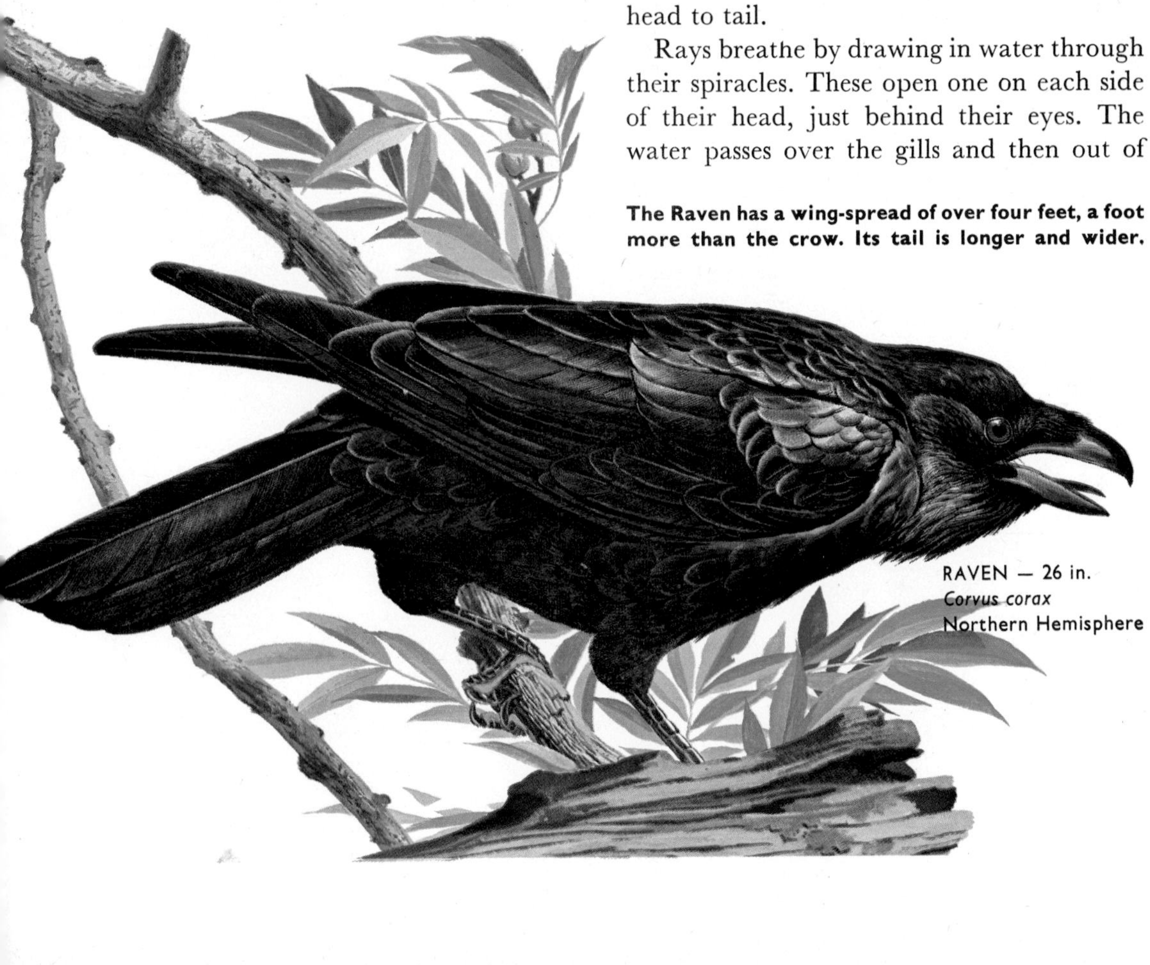

RAVEN — 26 in.
Corvus corax
Northern Hemisphere

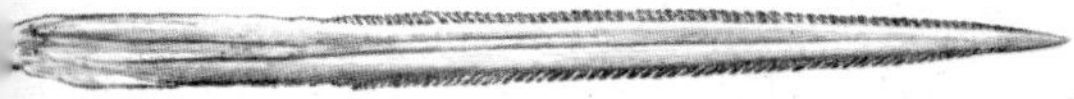

barbed spine of a Stingray

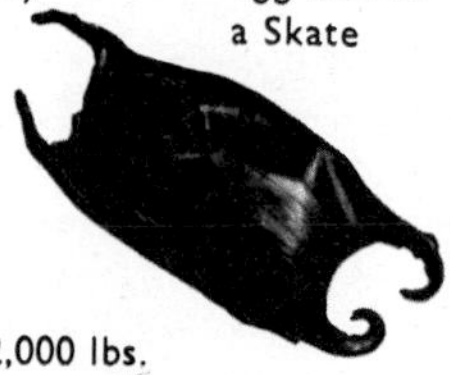

egg case of a Skate

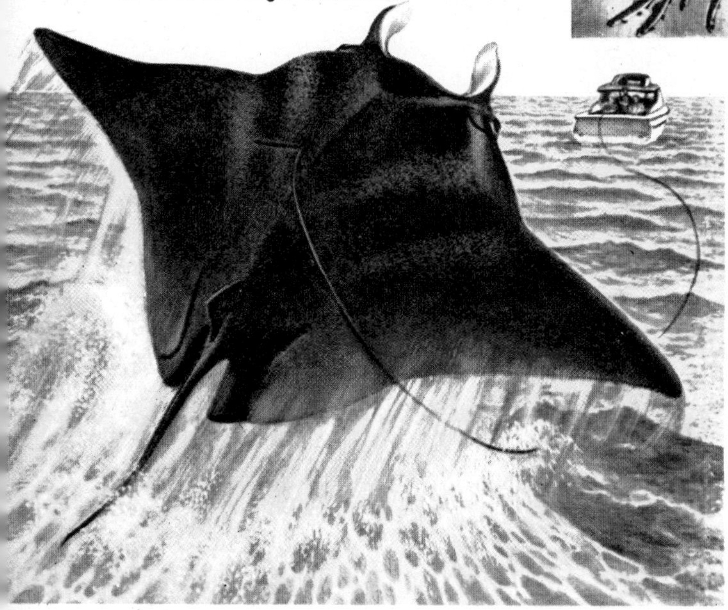

ATLANTIC MANTA
Manta birostris
20 ft. across wings; to 2,000 lbs.

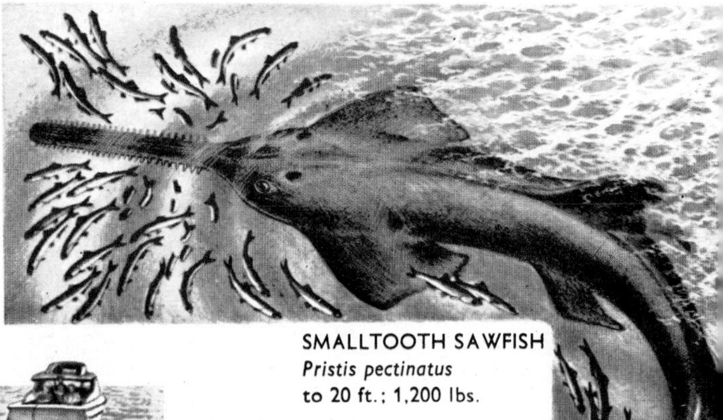

SMALLTOOTH SAWFISH
Pristis pectinatus
to 20 ft.; 1,200 lbs.

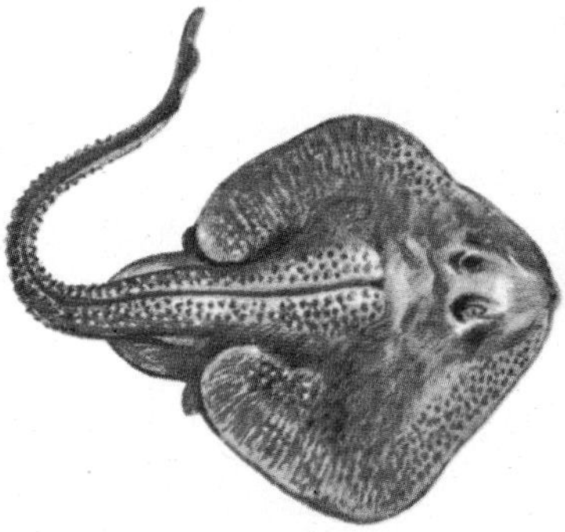

LITTLE SKATE
Raia erinacea
to 20 in.

the gill-openings. Since most rays live close to the bottom, the mouth, located on their underside, cannot be used to take in water for breathing, as with other fishes.

Some rays lay eggs in tough egg-cases called "sea purses"; others give birth to their young. It is believed that some kinds leap out of the water as each young is born.

The largest ray is the Manta (*Manta birostris*), also called Devil Ray and Devilfish. It roams the warm seas of the world, frequently basking on the surface, or leaping out of the water, to fall back with a resounding smack. A harpooned Manta can tow a boat for many miles before tiring.

On each side of the Manta's mouth there are formidable looking "horns". These are

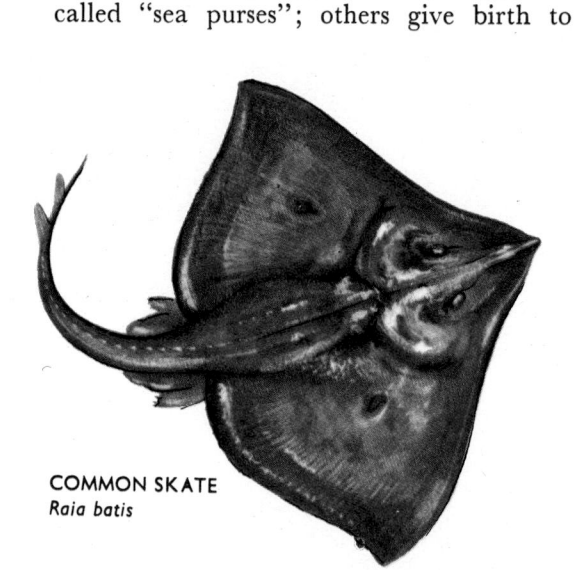

COMMON SKATE
Raia batis

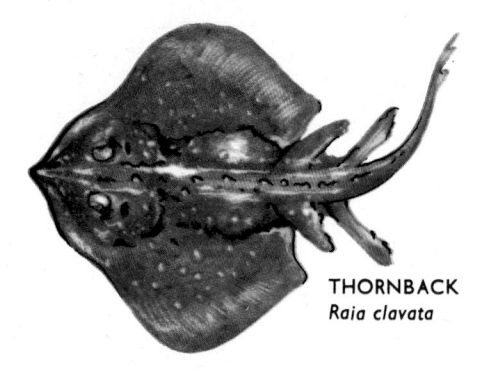

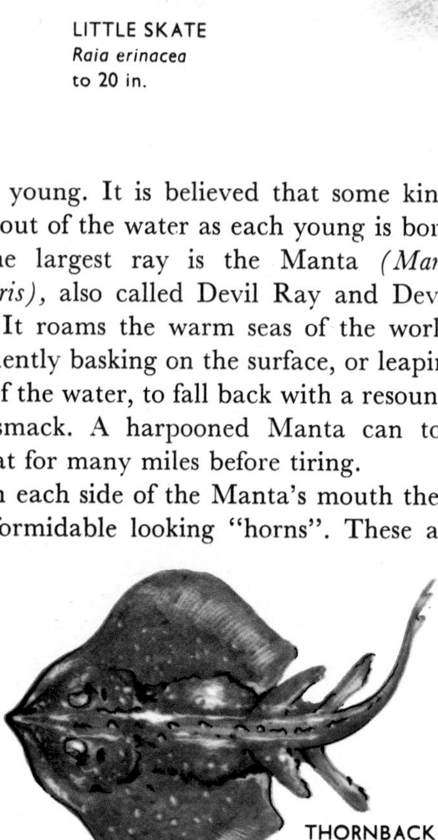

THORNBACK
Raia clavata

actually just flaps of flesh that help to channel fish and other creatures inside the Manta's mouth; its teeth are small. Mantas are harmless — although they can do damage with their huge wings when trying to escape.

Smaller, but more dangerous, are rays that can produce electricity. Torpedo rays *(Torpedo* spp.*)*, for example, can give a shock of 100 volts or more — enough to stun a man. Rays use this electricity to catch their prey; they wait sluggishly on the bottom until a fish swims near enough to be jolted. Special nerve and muscle organs on their disc-like bodies produce the electricity. If they are forced to give one shock after another, they become exhausted, and must rest and store up a new charge in their cellular batteries.

Stingrays *(Dasyatis* spp.*)* are also danger-ous. When disturbed, they lash their tail and can imbed the spine in an intruder's arm or leg. The mucus covering the spine's saw-toothed edge contains poison which makes the wound painful, and sometimes fatal. Primitive people used these "stingers" as heads for their spears or arrows.

Butterfly rays *(Gymnura* spp.*)* appear to be all wings. Their tail is short and spineless, and their head is not set off from the wide, flattened body.

Eagle rays *(Aetobatus* and *Myliobatis* spp.*)* have a shovel-shaped snout and also a long, whip-like tail. They use the snout to pry out clams, oysters, or other shellfish, from the bottom, then crush the shells with their flat and powerful teeth.

Most abundant in numbers and species

are bottom-dwelling skates *(Raja*s pp.*)*. There are more than 100 species. Skates spend most of their time lying on the bottom, often partly covered with sand or mud. If a fish comes close, they dart up suddenly and fold their body over it, holding the prisoner against the bottom until they can grab it in their jaws and swallow it. Frequently, skates are caught on hook and line, whereupon they prove their worth as fighters. Sometimes their "wings" are cut into strips and eaten; strips of skate wings are also used by fishermen as bait.

BARNDOOR SKATE
Raia laevis
to 5 ft.

ATLANTIC TORPEDO
Torpedo nobiliana
to 3 ft.

ATLANTIC GUITAR-FISH
Rhinobatos lentiginosus
Average 2 ft.

SMOOTH BUTTERFLY RAY
Gymnura micrura
to 6 ft. across wings

BLUNTNOSE STINGRAY
Dasyatis sayi
to 7 ft.

ROUND STINGRAY
Urolophis halleri
to 2 ft.

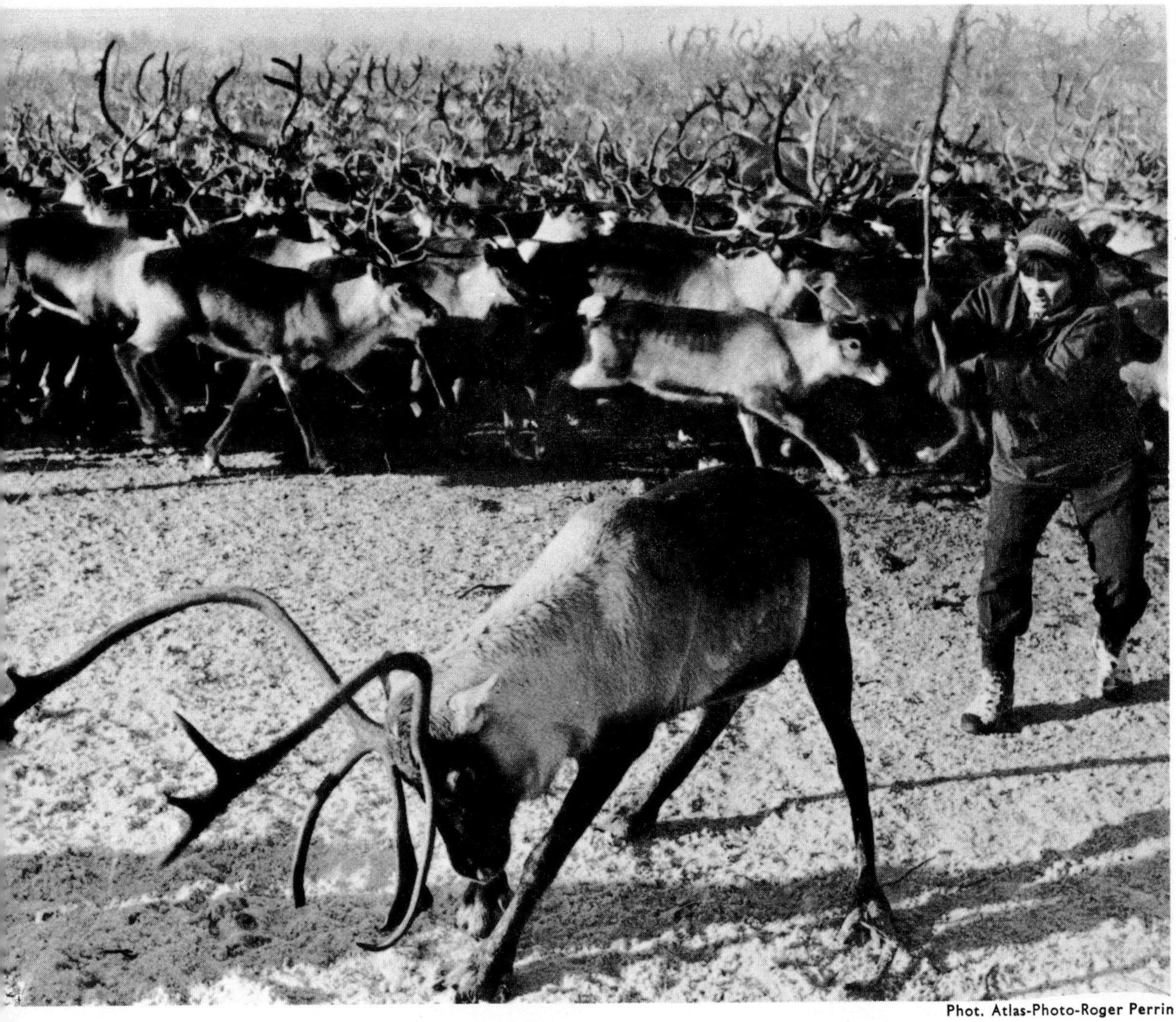

402

Phot. Atlas-Photo-Roger Perrin

Guitar-fish *(Rhinobatos lentiginosus)*, which are shark-like rays, have a disc-shaped body and a stout, shark-like tail. Their snout is generally long, like that of the Sawfish. Guitar-fishes, again like the Sawfish, are found in warm and tropical seas throughout the world. They are slow-swimming bottom feeders, often lying half-buried in sand or mud. Sawfish prowl shallow, inshore waters, feeding on small fish.

RAZOR SHELL — 6—7 in.
Ensis siliqui
Coasts of Europe

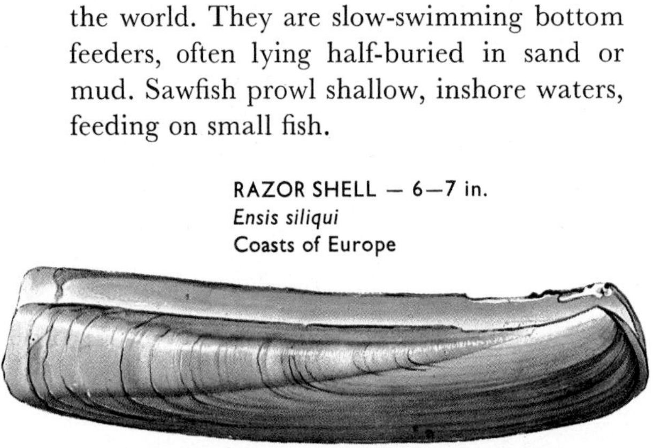

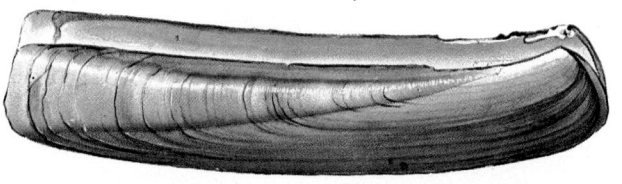

RAZOR-SHELLS, of the family Solenidae, are long, smooth-shelled clams found burrowing in shallow and inter-tidal sand flats on both Atlantic and Pacific coasts. They burrow by thrusting their long foot downward into the sand, anchoring it there by swelling its end, and then pulling the shell down with a jetting action. They are the most rapid burrowers of all shellfish. Razor-shells are often gathered for food. In certain areas, such as Cuba, where they are especially popular, razor-shells are served in restaurants; they have a delicate flavour.

REINDEER *(Rangifer tarandus)* range throughout the arctic regions of Europe and western Asia, and can be domesticated. In winter, the animals eat lichens, which

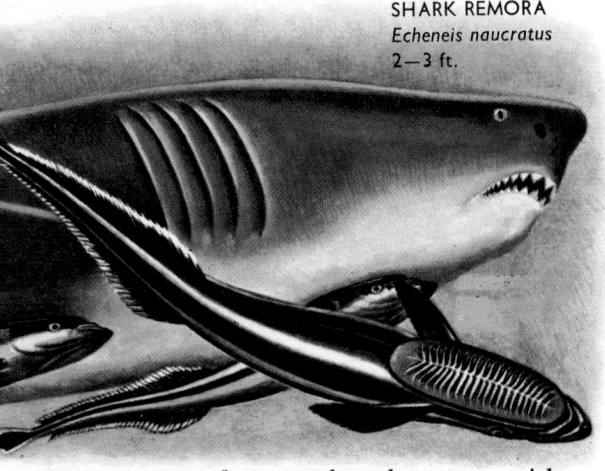

SHARK REMORA
Echeneis naucratus
2—3 ft.

swimmers, ordinarily they ride on turtles, sharks or other fishes, to which they attach themselves by means of the powerful suction disc on their head. The disc is developed from their dorsal fin, and suction is created when the muscular flaps are spread. They can release themselves, or can slide forwards or backwards along their host's body when they wish. If their host drops scraps of food, the Remora grabs them. An ancient way to fish for sea-turtles consisted of tying a line to a Remora's tail and turning it loose when a turtle was sighted. The Remora soon fastened itself to the turtle, which was then drawn in.

RHEAS are large, flightless birds of the South American pampas. They resemble the Ostrich, but are smaller and have three toes instead of two; they also swim well. Rheas breed like the Emu (see EMUS), but as many as fourdozen eggs have been found in one ground scrape. Rheas are still fairly plentiful, though natives use them for food and sell their feathers for feather-dusters. Rheas are primarily vegetarians, but also eat insects, reptiles, and even small mammals. They are said to make good pets, but have never been raised commercially.

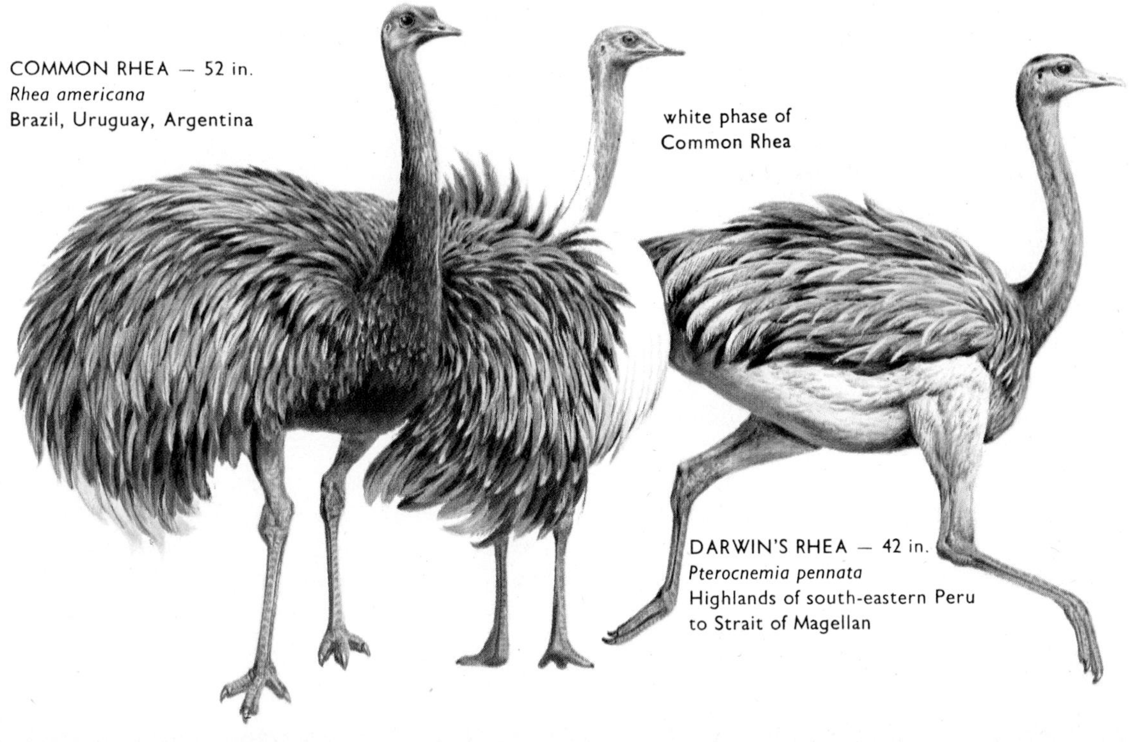

they uncover from under the snow with their hoofs. In the summer, they move into the valleys, where they eat green plants. When mosquitoes and biting flies become bothersome, they travel to the sea-coast, where they feed on kelp.

Reindeer are not well domesticated, but they can be broken in to ride, pull sleighs, or carry packs. Laplanders accompany the herds and depend on them for milk, meat, fur, leather and transport. (See CARIBOU.)

REMORAS *(Echeneis* spp.*)*, also called Shark-suckers, are noted hitch-hikers. Although these slim fishes are strong, fast

COMMON RHEA — 52 in.
Rhea americana
Brazil, Uruguay, Argentina

white phase of
Common Rhea

DARWIN'S RHEA — 42 in.
Pterocnemia pennata
Highlands of south-eastern Peru
to Strait of Magellan

WHITE RHINOCEROS
Ceratotherium simus
Length 14. 5 ft., tail 2 ft., height 5.5 ft.

GREAT ONE-HORNED RHINOCEROS
Rhinoceros unicornis
Length 12 ft., tail 26 in., height 5.7 ft.

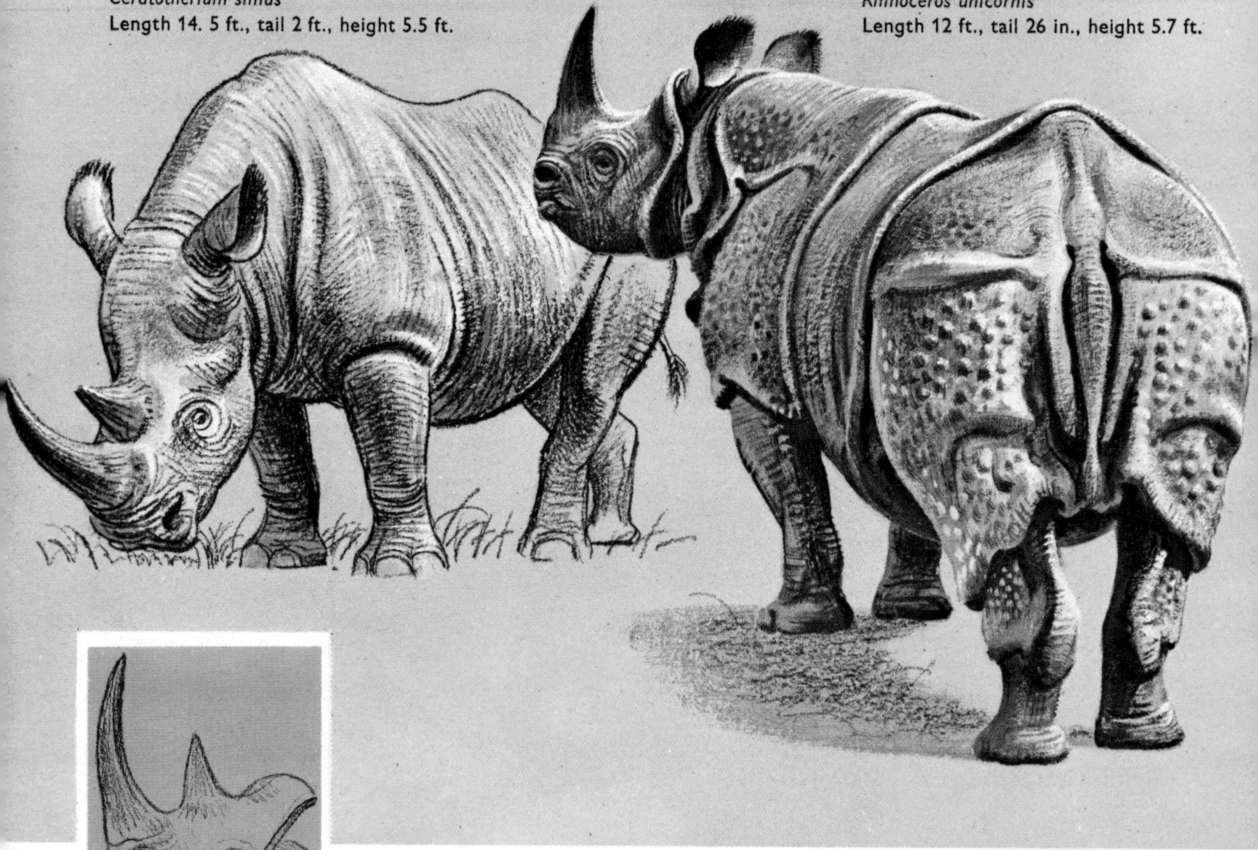

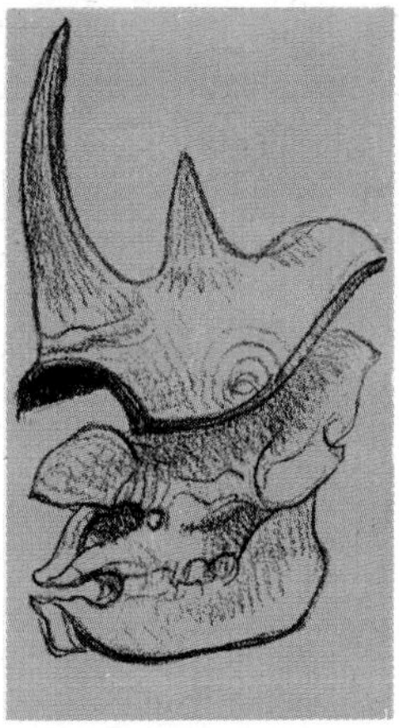

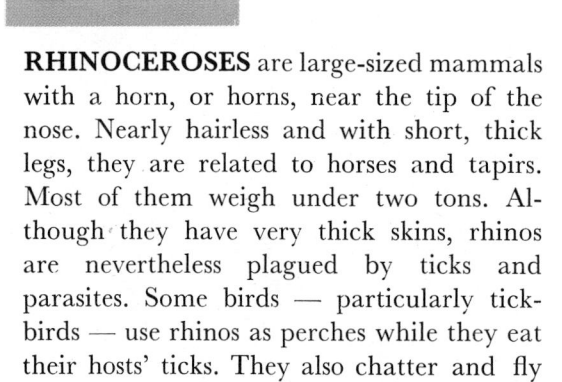

Rhinoceros horns consist of modified hair. They rest on a prominent knob of bone and are not attached to the skull.

Members of the rhinoceros family are noted for their poor vision. Their usual reaction to most disturbances is to lower their heads and charge.

RHINOCEROSES are large-sized mammals with a horn, or horns, near the tip of the nose. Nearly hairless and with short, thick legs, they are related to horses and tapirs. Most of them weigh under two tons. Although they have very thick skins, rhinos are nevertheless plagued by ticks and parasites. Some birds — particularly tick-birds — use rhinos as perches while they eat their hosts' ticks. They also chatter and fly away when an intruder is near. This warns the poor-sighted rhinos of any potential danger.

The Black Rhinoceros *(Diceros bicornis)* has two horns on its snout. The longer front horn sometimes measures 50 inches in length. Its tapered upper lip can be extended for grasping twigs and leaves, and because of this the Black Rhinoceros is frequently called the Hook-lipped Rhinoceros. The Black Rhinoceros, found in thorny country near water-holes, is the common species in Africa, south of the Sahara. Generally, a pair is seen with one young. Commonly, the offspring stays with the parents until it is about half grown.

The White Rhinoceros *(Ceratotherium simus)*, which also has two nasal horns, is actually light grey in colour. The largest of all the rhinos, it roams the open plains of Africa, eating grass, but is never very far from water-holes or thickets of thornbush.

The Great One-horned Rhinoceros *(Rhi-*

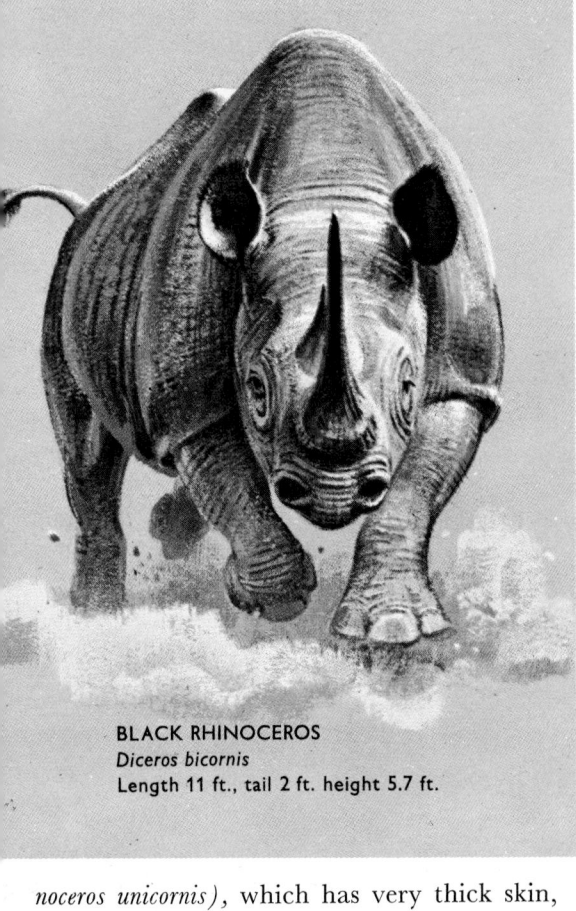

BLACK RHINOCEROS
Diceros bicornis
Length 11 ft., tail 2 ft. height 5.7 ft.

RIBBED TOADS and Tailed Toads are the only anurans, or tail-less amphibians, that, as adults, still have evidence of bony ribs. Ribbed Toads are members of the family Discoglossidae, which means "round-tongued". Their tongues are attached all round, instead of becoming free at the rear end, as are the tongues of most other frogs and toads. There are a dozen species, found only in Europe, Asia and the Philippines. Males have weak voices and no vocal sacs, and the tadpoles — unlike the tadpoles of other frogs and toads — have a spiracle opening in the middle of their bellies.

The Painted Toad *(Discoglossus)*, found in southern Europe and northern Africa, is best known for its bright colours. Also members of the group are four species of the Fire-bellied Toads, two of which occur in Europe and two in China. These toads have very poisonous skin secretions, and no animals normally prey on them. Sluggish, water-dwelling toads, they are often seen during the day and make little attempt to escape. When disturbed, fire-bellied toads

noceros unicornis), which has very thick skin, lives in the tall grasslands of northern Bengal, Assam and Nepal. Each newborn calf, weighing about 100 pounds, is able to follow its mother immediately after birth.

The Lesser, or Javan, Rhinoceros *(Rhinoceros sondiacus)* lived in the thick jungles and marshlands of southern Asia, from Burma to Java, but is now extinct over much of its former range; it weighs only about one ton and is now becoming exceedingly rare. The Two-horned Rhinoceros *(Didernoceros sumatrensis)*, smallest of all the rhinos, weighs less than a ton. It is found from Sumatra to Assam.

The greatest danger to the rhinoceros is the belief that powdered rhinoceros horn has certain medicinal properties. Western medicine dismisses this as superstition, but high prices for powdered horn in oriental pharmacies encourage poaching, even in game reserves.

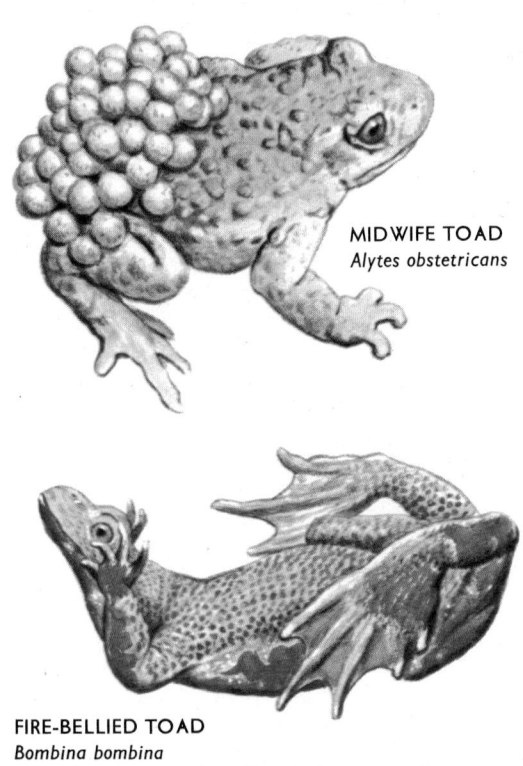

MIDWIFE TOAD
Alytes obstetricans

FIRE-BELLIED TOAD
Bombina bombina
in display position when disturbed

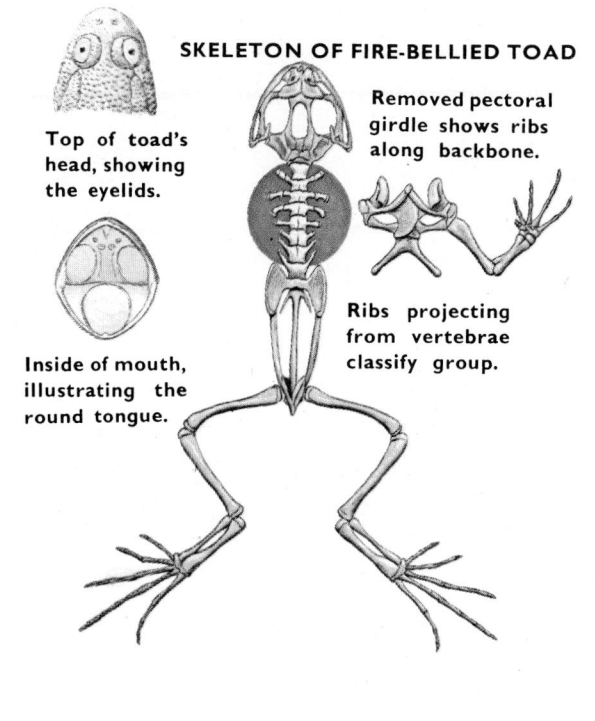

SKELETON OF FIRE-BELLIED TOAD

Top of toad's head, showing the eyelids.

Removed pectoral girdle shows ribs along backbone.

Inside of mouth, illustrating the round tongue.

Ribs projecting from vertebrae classify group.

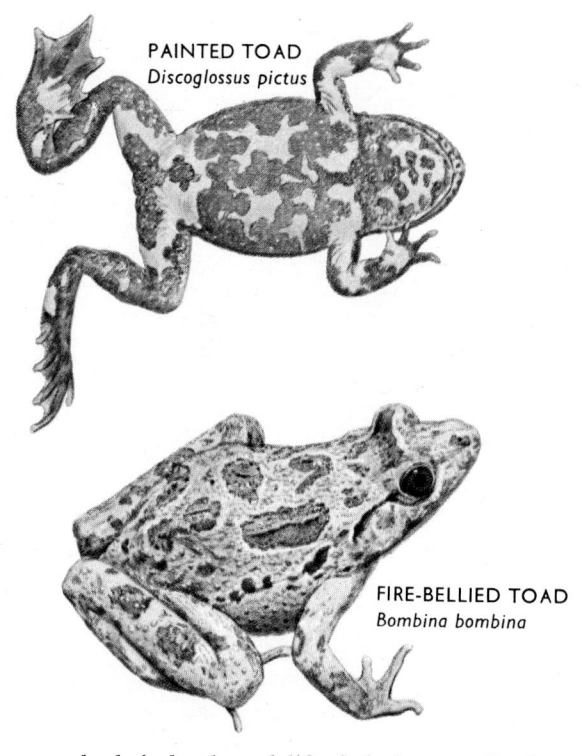

PAINTED TOAD
Discoglossus pictus

FIRE-BELLIED TOAD
Bombina bombina

arch their back and lift their legs to display their bright underparts in warning.

The male Midwife Toad *(Alytes)* of Europe thrusts his legs through the egg mass and, for about three weeks, carries it wrapped around his legs. During this time,

he hides during the day in moist, dark places. At night he hops about in dew-dampened vegetation or in water. When the larvae are fairly well developed, the male enters a pond, and the larvae escape from the eggs to complete development in the water. One other member of the family is Barbour's Toad *(Barbourula),* found only on the Island of Palawan in the Philippines.

RIBBON-WORMS, which belong to the phylum Nemertea, are mostly marine. They live both along the seashore and in the open sea, some in deep water. Ribbon-worms range in size from less than an inch to the more than 75-foot length of *Lineus longissimus.* All ribbon-worms are capable of tremendous extension and contraction. A three-inch worm, for example, may stretch to a length of three feet. Ribbon-worms are also capable of regeneration. Even a small piece can grow into an adult worm, replacing all the lost organs.

A ribbon-worm's proboscis, or tube, is normally kept inside the body, but can be extended for a great distance to catch prey. Some worms have on the proboscis one or more darts, or stylets, that pierce their prey and inject a mild poison — sometimes causing painful wounds.

RIBBON-WORM
Cerebratulus lacteus

ROBBER FLY
Asilus sp.
0.8 in.

ROBBER FLIES *(Asilidae)* are a large family of medium to large size predatory flies. Most species are slender and have long, bristly legs. Some are stout, quite hairy, and resemble bumblebees.

Robber flies feed on many kinds of insects. Some species destroy such beneficial insects as bumblebees and honeybees. It is possible that they inject a poison with their stout beaks to overcome their prey.

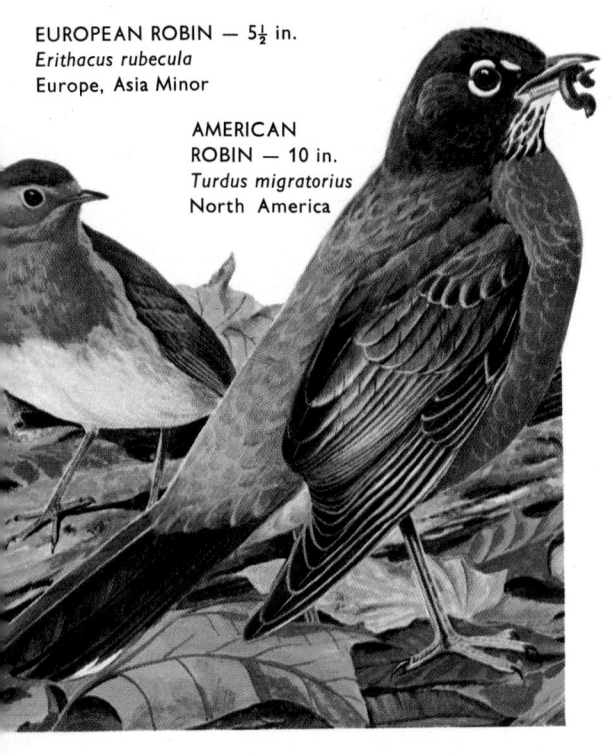

EUROPEAN ROBIN — 5½ in.
Erithacus rubecula
Europe, Asia Minor

AMERICAN ROBIN — 10 in.
Turdus migratorius
North America

ROBINS are birds of the thrush family. The small bird known to earlier scientists as the Redbreast was so tame and confiding that many people referred to it by the pet name of Robin Redbreast, and the last name has now fallen into disuse. When British people settled in any part of the world they called any familiar red-breasted bird "Robin", and

the name has been used for several species. In America, it is a migrant thrush as big as a blackbird that has the name, while in Australia it is a red-breasted, black-and-white relative of the flycatchers.

The European Robin is best-loved in those countries where it is resident all the year, on account of its habit of singing throughout the winter. Both sexes take up separate territories, and both sing. It is a very aggressive bird. In Spring, a pair will amalgamate territories and breed but adults and young become intolerant of each other after the breeding season.

ROVE BEETLES *(Staphylinidae)* are rather long beetles with short wing-covers. Their hind wings, golden beneath, are fully developed, however. After flying, the beetle uses the tip of its abdomen and its legs to fold the hind wings under its short wing-covers. More than 20,000 species are known. Most species are quite small, but a few are about an inch long. Rove beetles are rapid runners and characteristically hold the tip of the abdomen high when moving or when disturbed. Some of the larger species that are coloured black and red, or black and yellow, resemble wasps.

Many rove beetles are found around decaying plants or animals, or in dung-piles. It was once believed that they were scavengers, but apparently they feed on the maggots and other insects found also in these places. Some rove beetles live in the nests of ants and termites. They secrete a liquid used as food by the ants and termites, and the beetles are in turn fed by their hosts.

HAIRY ROVE BEETLE
Creophilus villosus
0.8 in.

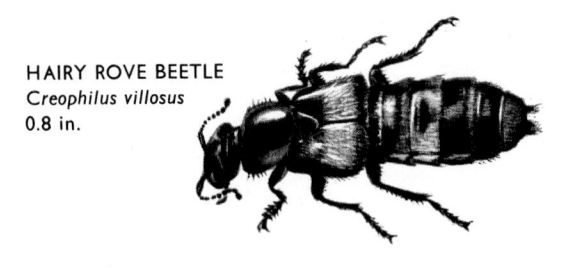

S

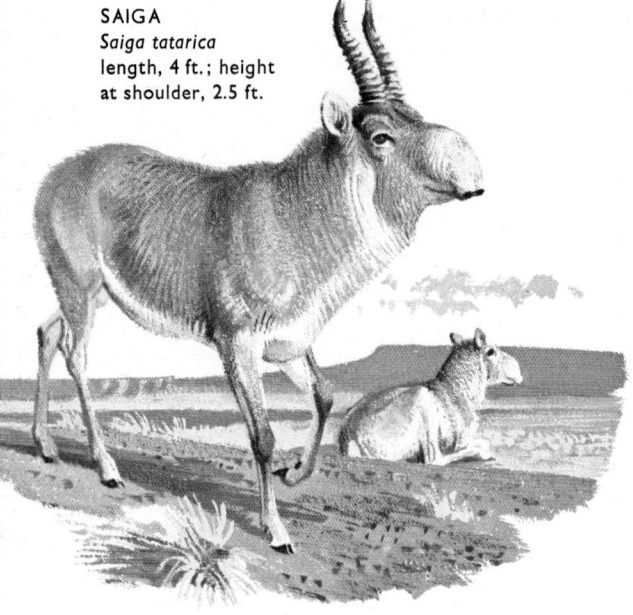

SAIGA
Saiga tatarica
length, 4 ft.; height
at shoulder, 2.5 ft.

SAIGAS *(Saiga tatarica)* are unusual antelopes. They are remarkably short-legged,
and have a greatly swollen nose that looks
like an enlarged proboscis or short trunk.
The bulbous nose may serve to filter out
dust and sand, or to warm cold air breathed
during the winter months. The muzzle is
hairy. These animals are over four feet
long, but stand only about two and a half
feet high at the shoulder. Males, about
the size of domestic sheep, have long,
curved, ringed horns which form a graceful,
lyre-shaped arch. The Saiga's coat is dirty
yellowish in summer, but longer, thicker
and whitish in winter. They live in herds
on the plains of south-eastern Russia and
were formerly found in many parts of Asia.

EUROPEAN CAVE SALAMANDER
Hydromantes fuscus

SALAMANDERS are the only group of
living amphibians with well-developed tails.
They are often mistaken for lizards, which
are reptiles. Lizards always have scales
and claws, and usually have five fingers
on their front legs. Salamanders have a
moist skin without scales. They do not
have claws and never have more than four
fingers on their front legs.

Salamanders, a small group of about
250 species, are abundant in the Northern
Hemisphere, especially in North America.
In South America there are only three
species, all rare. In Africa they occur only
along the Mediterranean, and there are
none in Asia Minor, the Indian and Malayan
peninsulas, or Australia and the islands
of the Pacific.

Like other amphibians, salamanders require an abundance of moisture. Unlike
many toads and frogs, however, they cannot
tolerate heat and are rarely found in
tropical regions. They are killed by temperatures only a little below freezing, but
many are very active, at least in the breeding
season, at temperatures only slightly above
freezing. Salamanders ordinarily move

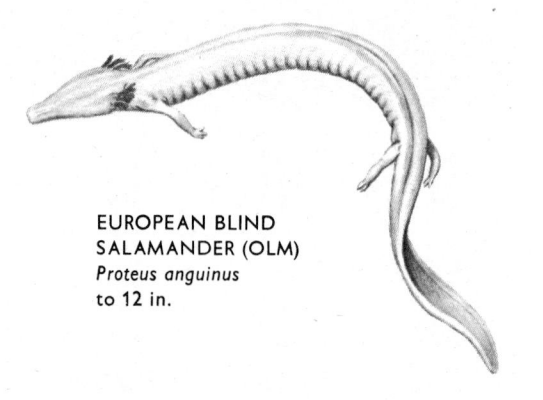

EUROPEAN BLIND
SALAMANDER (OLM)
Proteus anguinus
to 12 in.

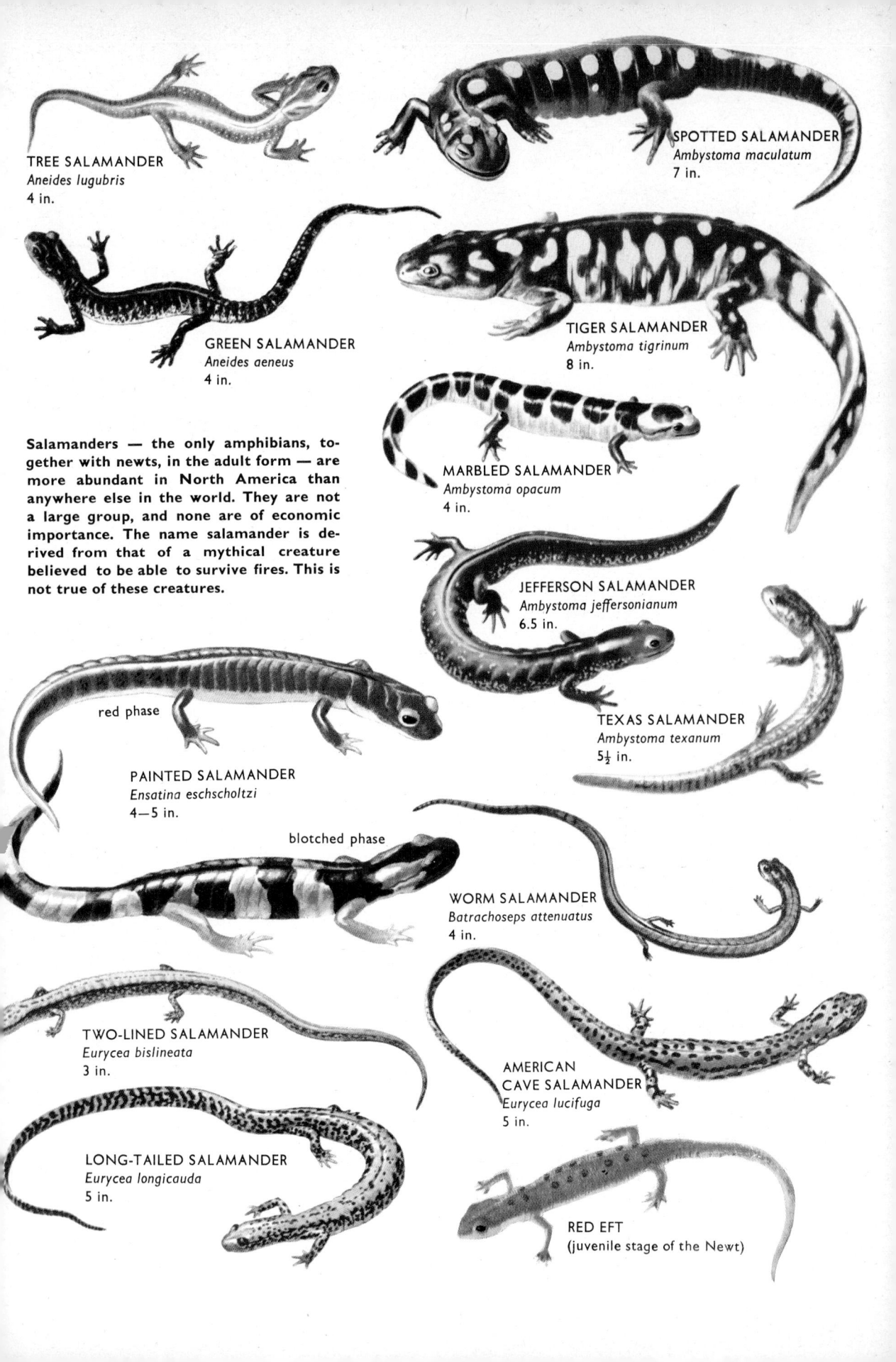

TREE SALAMANDER
Aneides lugubris
4 in.

SPOTTED SALAMANDER
Ambystoma maculatum
7 in.

GREEN SALAMANDER
Aneides aeneus
4 in.

TIGER SALAMANDER
Ambystoma tigrinum
8 in.

MARBLED SALAMANDER
Ambystoma opacum
4 in.

Salamanders — the only amphibians, together with newts, in the adult form — are more abundant in North America than anywhere else in the world. They are not a large group, and none are of economic importance. The name salamander is derived from that of a mythical creature believed to be able to survive fires. This is not true of these creatures.

JEFFERSON SALAMANDER
Ambystoma jeffersonianum
6.5 in.

TEXAS SALAMANDER
Ambystoma texanum
5½ in.

red phase

PAINTED SALAMANDER
Ensatina eschscholtzi
4—5 in.

blotched phase

WORM SALAMANDER
Batrachoseps attenuatus
4 in.

TWO-LINED SALAMANDER
Eurycea bislineata
3 in.

**AMERICAN
CAVE SALAMANDER**
Eurycea lucifuga
5 in.

LONG-TAILED SALAMANDER
Eurycea longicauda
5 in.

RED EFT
(juvenile stage of the Newt)

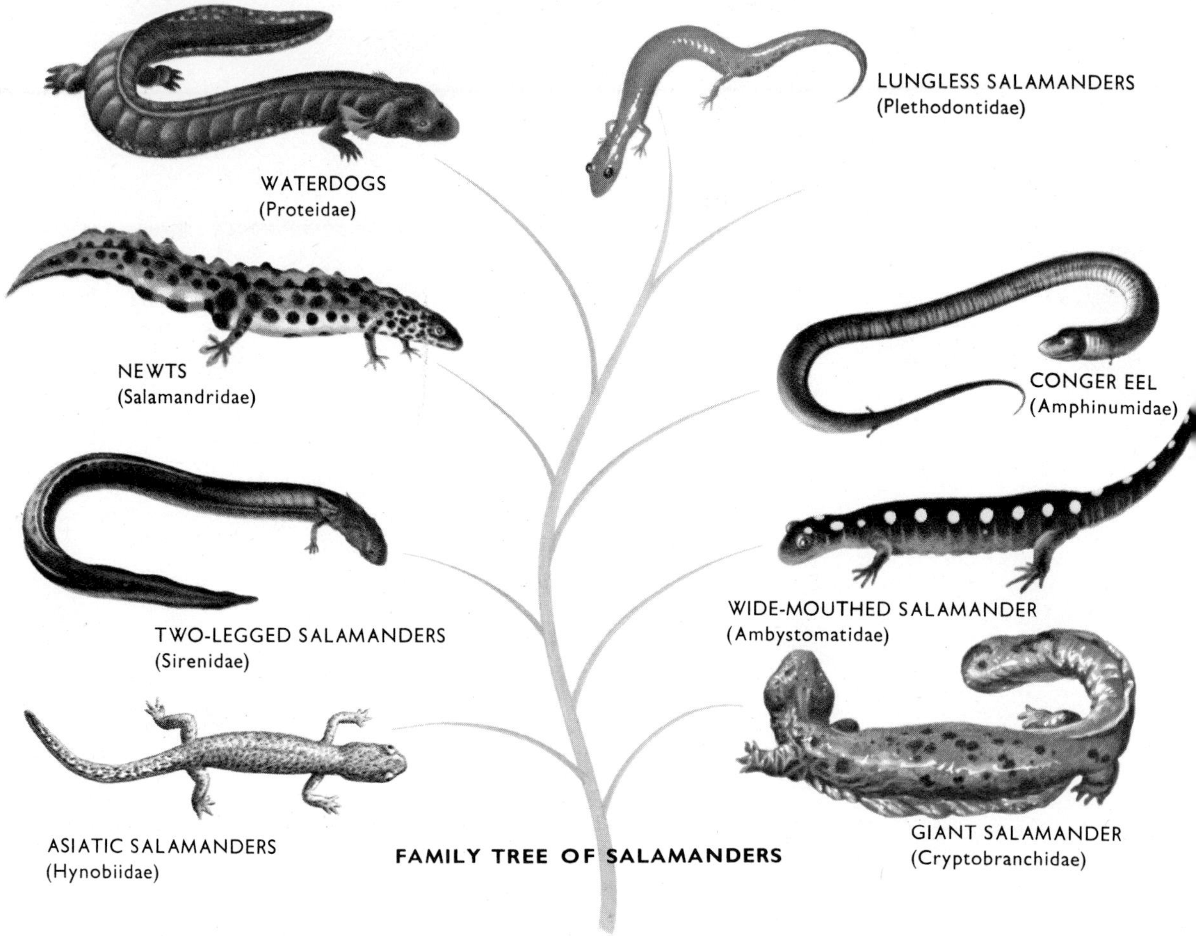

WATERDOGS
(Proteidae)

LUNGLESS SALAMANDERS
(Plethodontidae)

NEWTS
(Salamandridae)

CONGER EEL
(Amphinumidae)

TWO-LEGGED SALAMANDERS
(Sirenidae)

WIDE-MOUTHED SALAMANDER
(Ambystomatidae)

ASIATIC SALAMANDERS
(Hynobiidae)

FAMILY TREE OF SALAMANDERS

GIANT SALAMANDER
(Cryptobranchidae)

Dusky Salamanders are average in size and dull in colour. They have vertical grooves on their sides.

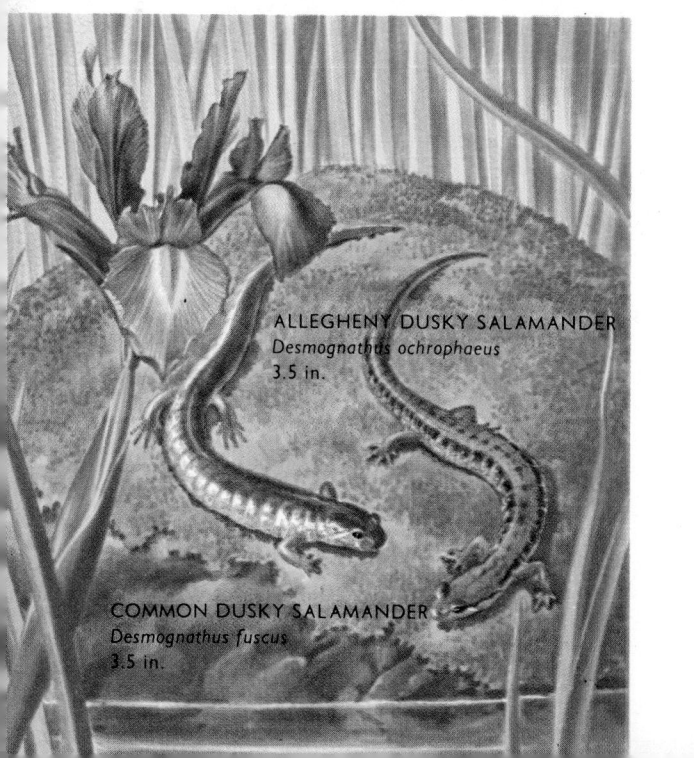

ALLEGHENY DUSKY SALAMANDER
Desmognathus ochrophaeus
3.5 in.

COMMON DUSKY SALAMANDER
Desmognathus fuscus
3.5 in.

about at night. During the day and at all times in hot, dry or cold seasons, they hide underground — in burrows made by other animals, in rotting logs, under stones and litter, or in holes in trees. In rainy periods they often crawl from one place to another, and are sometimes found in cellars.

Salamanders vary in size from tiny creatures, three-quarters of an inch long, to a heavy five-foot monster. Of those that live in water, some are slim-bodied, like eels; others are broad and flat. Some of the land-dwelling types resemble worms, although worms do not have tiny legs. Most salamanders are like lizards in body shape.

Salamanders have no eardrums or middle-ear cavities, so they are unable to hear airborne sounds; they can detect ground vibrations, however. Their well-developed sense of smell is most important to them

SALAMANDER EGGS

Some eggs are laid in jelly-coated masses, others are laid singly or in strings.

Tiger Salamander

Four-toed Salamander

Spotted Salamander   Hellbender

in the water throughout their lives. Other salamanders lay their eggs on moist soil, and imagos — miniature replicas of full-grown adults — hatch from them. Some of the newts spend several years on land in an immature stage (eft) before returning to the water.

Mature salamander larvae are easily distinguished from frog larvae (tadpoles), although the two look much alike when first hatched. A salamander larva has three gills on each side of its head; a frog larva has only two. Also, the frog larva has,

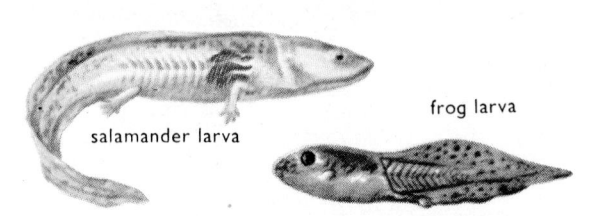

salamander larva   frog larva

The larva, or tadpole, of a salamander has three gills on each side of its head, and it keeps these external gills throughout its period of development. The frog tadpole has two gills on each side of its head when it hatches. These are soon grown over with skin.

in finding food. Some land-dwelling salamanders find their food by sight.

All salamanders are strictly carnivorous. They are not very discriminating, however, and will try to eat anything small enough for them to swallow — insects, worms, and other small creatures, alive or dead.

Eggs of some primitive kinds of salamander are fertilised in the water after they are laid. At the opposite extreme, a few kinds of salamander give birth to their young. In most kinds the male deposits clumps of sperm enclosed in gelatine; these are picked up by the female as she crawls over them, and later she deposits fertile eggs in the water. The eggs hatch as larvae with external gills, and skin over their eyes. After a time, the larvae "transform", losing their gills and gill slits, developing eyelids, and becoming capable of living on land, although some kinds remain

A salamander has four toes on its forefoot, while a lizard is equipped with five toes.

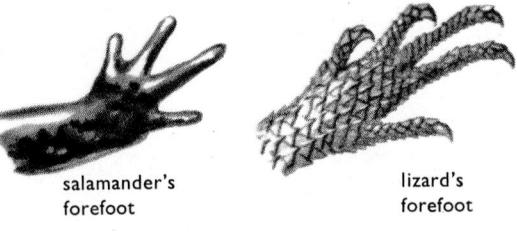

salamander's   lizard's
forefoot   forefoot

beneath its mouth, heavy adhesive organs for holding on to objects underwater. A salamander larva either has no such structures on its head, or it has much more delicate organs, called "balancers", which serve the same purpose. Salamander larvae that develop in still waters have balancers, lateral-line organs, and large gills and fins. Those found in fast-moving waters have no balancers or lateral-line organs, and have short gills and fins. (See AMPHIBIANS; LIZARDS; NEWTS.)

SALMON and trout belong to the *Salmonidae*, a small family of fishes with about five genera and some two dozen species. Salmon have small and numerous scales, and a stubby adipose (fatty) fin behind the dorsal fin. They are found in cold waters in the Northern Hemisphere, but have nowadays been introduced into many parts of the Southern Hemisphere. Salmon are important sport and commercial fishes.

Salmon spend most of their lives in the sea, but they return to fresh water to spawn. Some salmon travel thousands of miles from the ocean to the headwaters of mountain streams. In most cases, they lay their eggs in the same stream in which they themselves hatched from eggs several years before. At sea, they seldom travel far from shore and generally stay near the spawning stream. Pacific salmons exhaust themselves in spawning and die soon afterwards. The Atlantic Salmon swims back to sea after it lays its eggs, and can spawn season after season, ordinarily in autumn or early winter.

Newly-hatched salmon still carrying a pouch of yolk from the egg are called "alevins". Soon the yolk is absorbed, and the little fish get large black blotches along their sides; then they are called "parr". Some remain in fresh water only a few months, others for several years. When they start their journey to the sea, they lose the "parr" marks and become silvery; then they are known as "smolt". Occasionally, year-old salmon, particularly males, join older fish in the next season's spawning-run. These young fish, still not mature, are called "grilse"; but, typically, a salmon stays in salt water from two to as long as

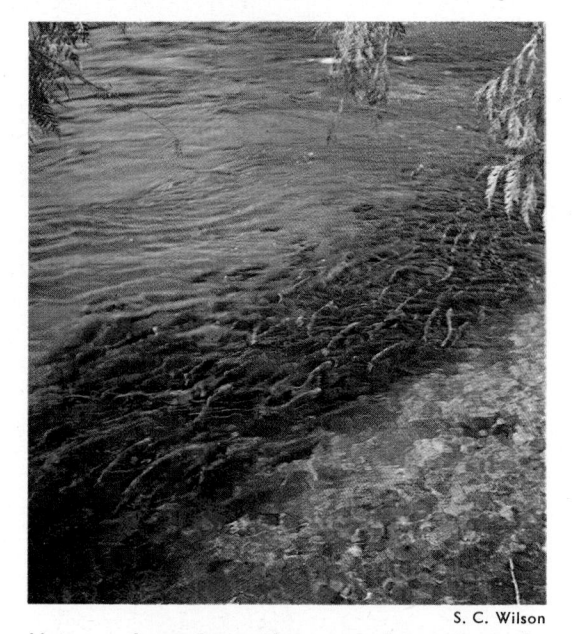

S. C. Wilson

Mature salmon leave the sea and travel to the stream in which they hatched. There they mate.

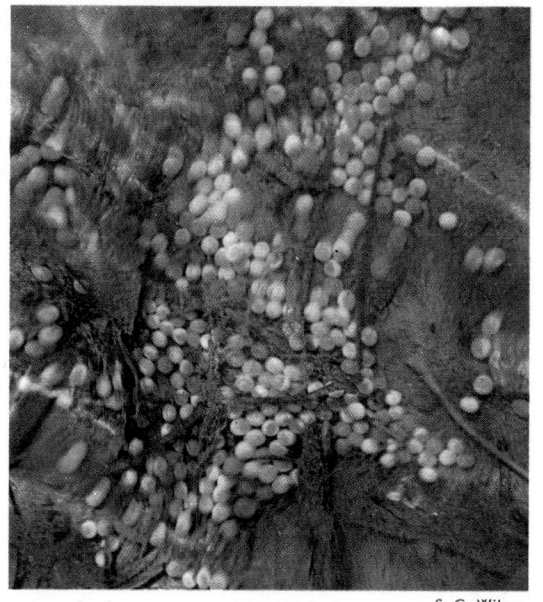

S. C. Wilson

A female salmon usually lays about 900 eggs for each pound of her own weight.

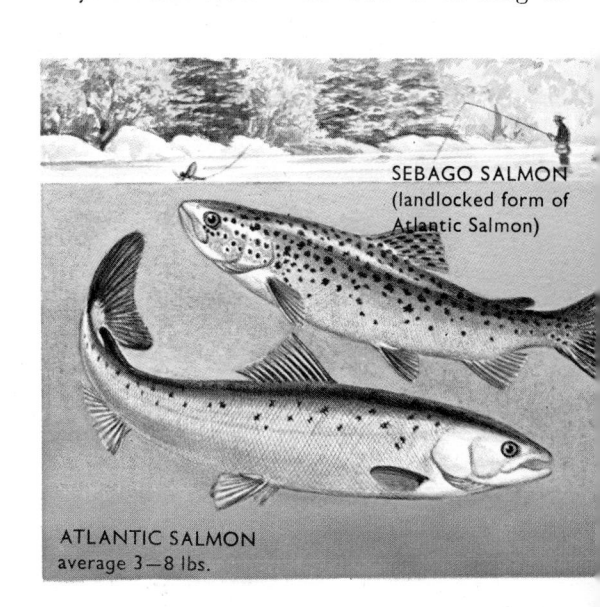

SEBAGO SALMON
(landlocked form of Atlantic Salmon)

ATLANTIC SALMON
average 3—8 lbs.

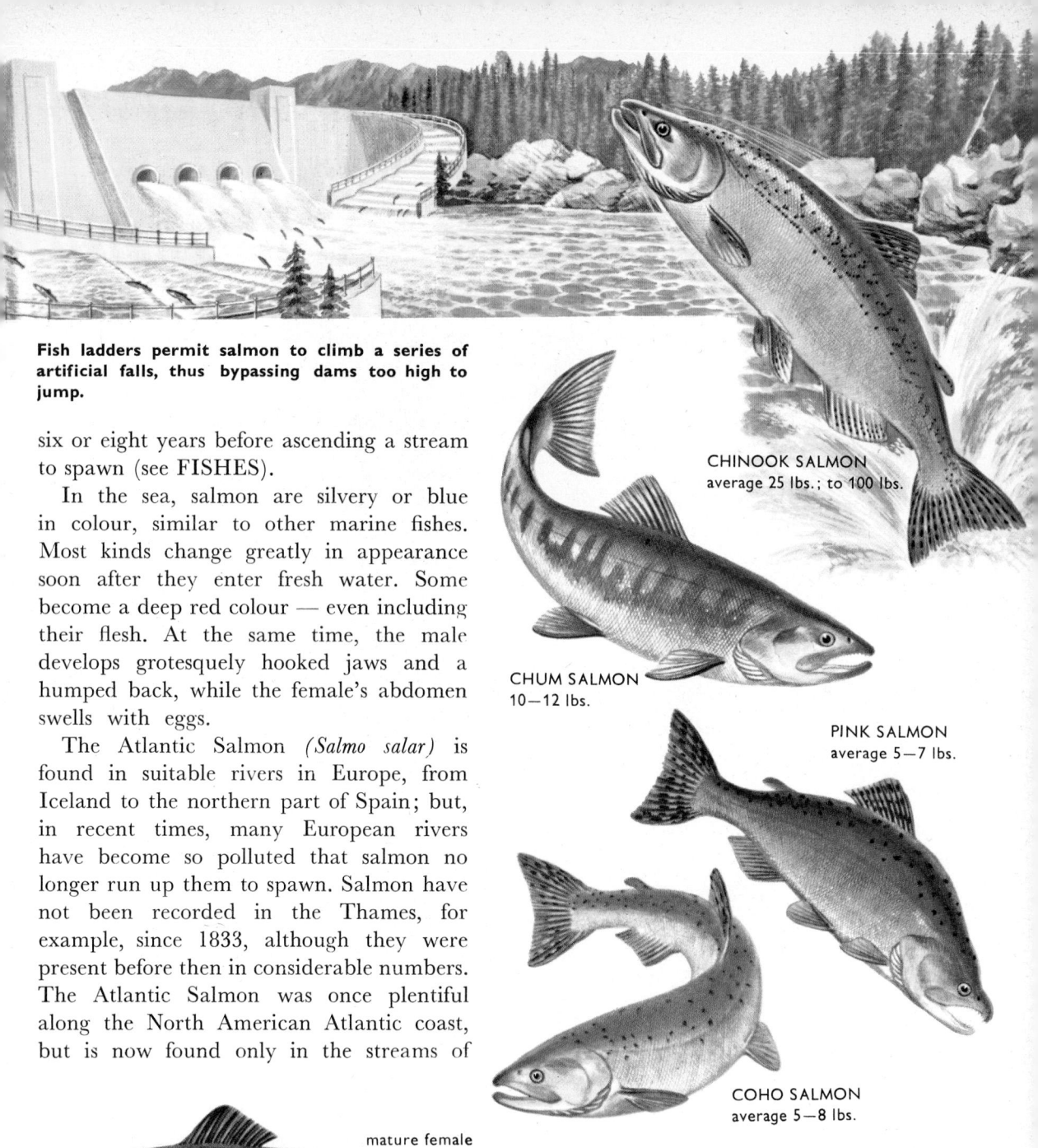

Fish ladders permit salmon to climb a series of artificial falls, thus bypassing dams too high to jump.

CHINOOK SALMON
average 25 lbs.; to 100 lbs.

CHUM SALMON
10—12 lbs.

PINK SALMON
average 5—7 lbs.

COHO SALMON
average 5—8 lbs.

mature female

spawning male

SOCKEYE (or RED) salmon

six or eight years before ascending a stream to spawn (see FISHES).

In the sea, salmon are silvery or blue in colour, similar to other marine fishes. Most kinds change greatly in appearance soon after they enter fresh water. Some become a deep red colour — even including their flesh. At the same time, the male develops grotesquely hooked jaws and a humped back, while the female's abdomen swells with eggs.

The Atlantic Salmon *(Salmo salar)* is found in suitable rivers in Europe, from Iceland to the northern part of Spain; but, in recent times, many European rivers have become so polluted that salmon no longer run up them to spawn. Salmon have not been recorded in the Thames, for example, since 1833, although they were present before then in considerable numbers. The Atlantic Salmon was once plentiful along the North American Atlantic coast, but is now found only in the streams of

Maine and northwards from there.

Nowadays great care is taken to preserve the Salmon fisheries. Fish-ladders enable the fishes to bypass hydro-electric dams, the rivers are restocked from fish hatcheries, and the rivers are watched for any signs of pollution from saw-mills or factories.

In the northern Pacific, there are six species of salmon placed in the genus *Onchorhynchus.* They are among the most valuable caught in American waters.

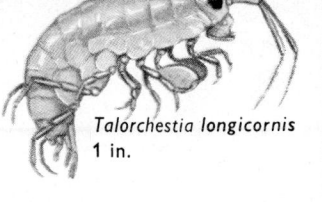

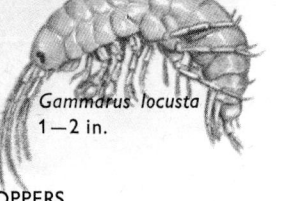

Talorchestia longicornis
1 in.

Gammarus locusta
1—2 in.

SAND-HOPPERS

SAND-HOPPERS, crustaceans of the class Amphipoda, are found both in the sea and on land. Many have highly-arched bodies that are strongly compressed from side to side. Others have enormous, curiously-shaped eyes. Sand-hoppers are small (about $\frac{1}{4}$ to 2 in. in length) and live among seaweeds washed up near the high-tide mark. When the weeds are picked up, they jump wildly about on the sand. Other marine amphipods live in shallow sands and muds, and large numbers belong to the plankton, where they are important as food for fishes.

SANDPIPERS are small, slender, wading birds, with long necks, long legs and long bills, and a nervous manner. They are always found near water and feed at the margin or on mud, the fine slender bill being designed to seize tiny insects at the surface of mud or water. They have long, narrow wings and are migrants.

The Common Sandpiper nests near fresh-water streams and rivers. It has a constant nervous habit of bobbing body and tail up and down. Its large, pear-shaped eggs are well camouflaged and laid in a mere

scrape, like those of all waders. The young can run and feed as soon as they are hatched, and are only brooded by the parents. This species is readily identified by its low flight across water, with downward-beating wing-tips and a shrill, piping "kitti-needi" call.

The Green Sandpiper nests in the Scandinavian pine-forest regions. Unlike other species, which nest on the ground, the Green Sandpiper does so in trees, in the nests of other birds or on accumulations of twigs and needles forming platforms.

SAWFLIES get their name from the saw-toothed ovipositor of the female. She uses it to drill into solid wood to lay eggs. Many species deposit their eggs in other places, however. Several families make up this group of the order Hymenoptera, which includes wasps, bees and ants (see INSECTS).

Sawfly larvae feed on plants. Many resemble caterpillars of moths and butterflies, but they have a single pair of simple eyes (ocelli), whereas caterpillars have four to six pairs. Also, they do not have hooks on their abdominal "legs", as do most caterpillars of moths and butterflies.

Some species, such as the Elm Sawfly, feed on leaves of deciduous trees and, when abundant, they may strip the trees of leaves. Female elm sawflies deposit their eggs in slits cut in leaves of elms, alders, birches, maples, or other broad-leaf trees. The larvae feed for six to eight weeks. When fully grown, they crawl to the ground and spin cocoons, in which to pass the winter.

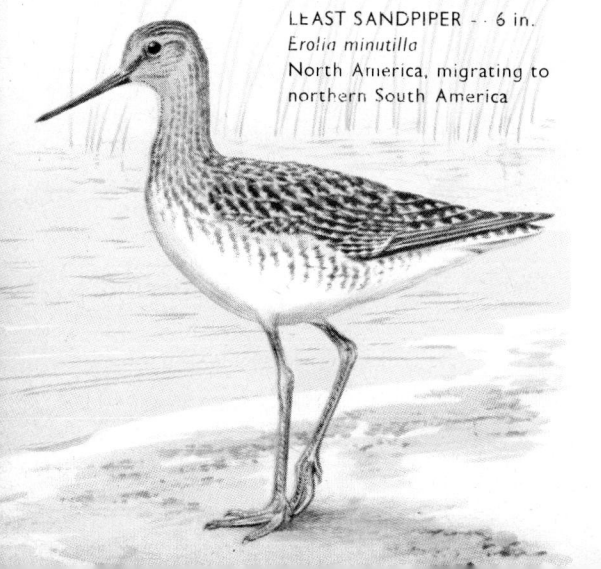

LEAST SANDPIPER -- 6 in.
Erolia minutilla
North America, migrating to
northern South America

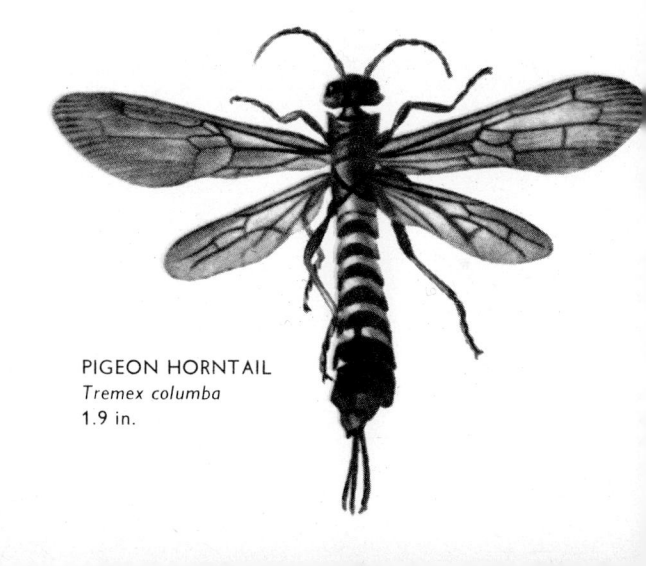

PIGEON HORNTAIL
Tremex columba
1.9 in.

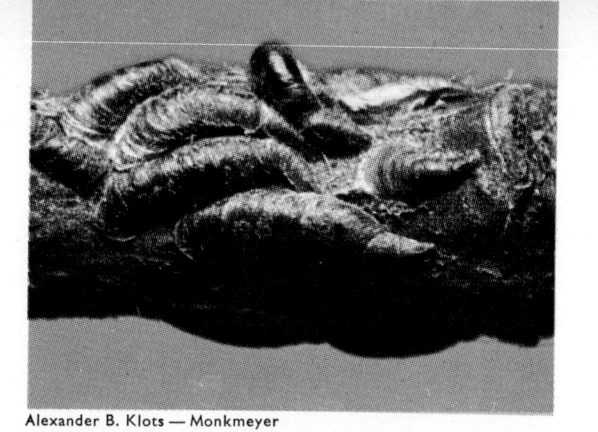
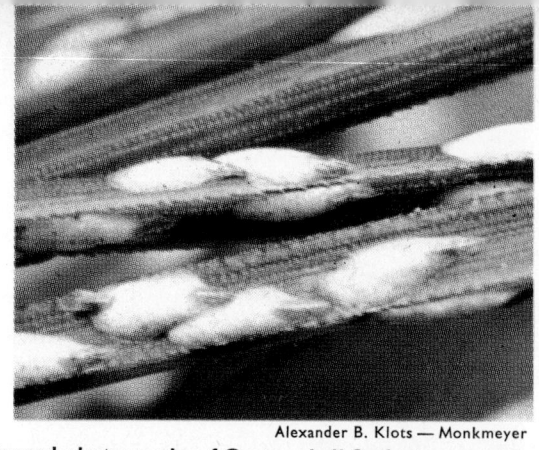

Scales are small and inconspicuous, as shown by these enlarged photographs of Oyster-shell Scales on a peach twig (left) and of Pineleaf Scales on pine needles (right). They are among the most destructive of all insect pests.

Many sawflies feed on pines or other conifers. The practice of planting conifers in several-acre blocks has undoubtedly helped to spread these sawflies. Their eggs are deposited in slits in the needles, either in the autumn or spring, depending on the species. The larvae feed on the needles and, when fully grown, spin cocoons either in litter on the ground or in foliage.

The larvae of some sawflies feed between the upper and lower surfaces of leaves. Others are stem-borers, and some are known to be gall-makers.

Horntails are closely related to sawflies, and resemble them in general appearance. Females lay their eggs in the bark or wood of trees or shrubs. Sometimes their ovipositors get stuck in the wood, and the insects are unable to free themselves. The larvae make burrows in the wood, and later spin their cocoons and pupate in these tunnels.

SCALE INSECTS, represented by several families in the order *Homoptera,* are among the most destructive pests of plants. Most scale insects are quite small and are seldom recognised as insects. They may occur in such enormous numbers on the leaves and twigs of plants that they completely cover the surface, sucking the juices off the plant through their piercing beaks. They get their name from their waxy, scale-like covering. This secretion takes various shapes — round, oval, long, star-shaped — but is always for a particular species.

Some species of scale insects give birth to their young; others lay eggs. Until their first moult, the nymphs — sometimes called "crawlers" — are quite active. They have both antennae and legs; then, after their first moult, the legs and antennae are lost or greatly reduced in size. The insects no longer move about, and begin secreting their waxy covering. Females stay in the same spot, even after becoming adults, but most adult males develop a pair of wings and resemble small flies or gnats. Like flies, their hind wings are knobs, or halteres; unlike flies, however, these structures hook on to the rear edge of the front wings. Males lack mouth-parts. hence are unable to feed. They die after mating.

Purple Scale, one of the most destructive, is found in South America, South Africa, the western Mediterranean, California, aud areas around the Gulf of Mexico. It is a serious pest of citrus trees, but also lives on several other plants. The San José Scale is common on many fruit and shade trees.

A few scale insects are beneficial. The

Scale insects look more like shellfish than insects.

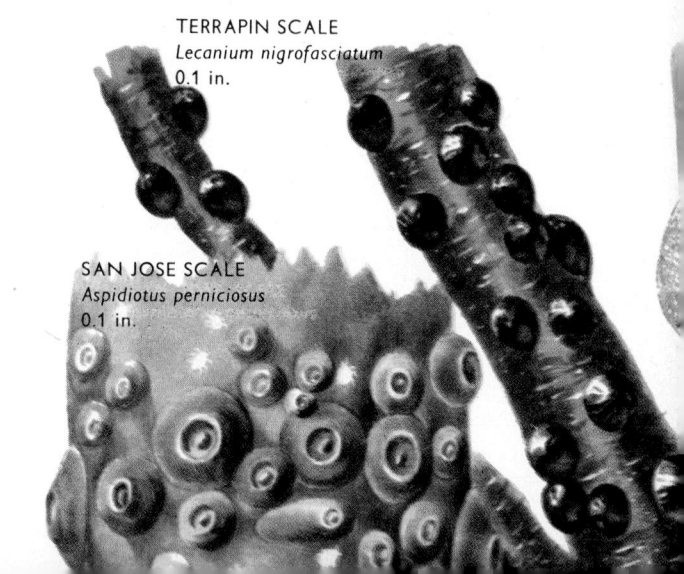

TERRAPIN SCALE
Lecanium nigrofasciatum
0.1 in.

SAN JOSE SCALE
Aspidiotus perniciosus
0.1 in.

416

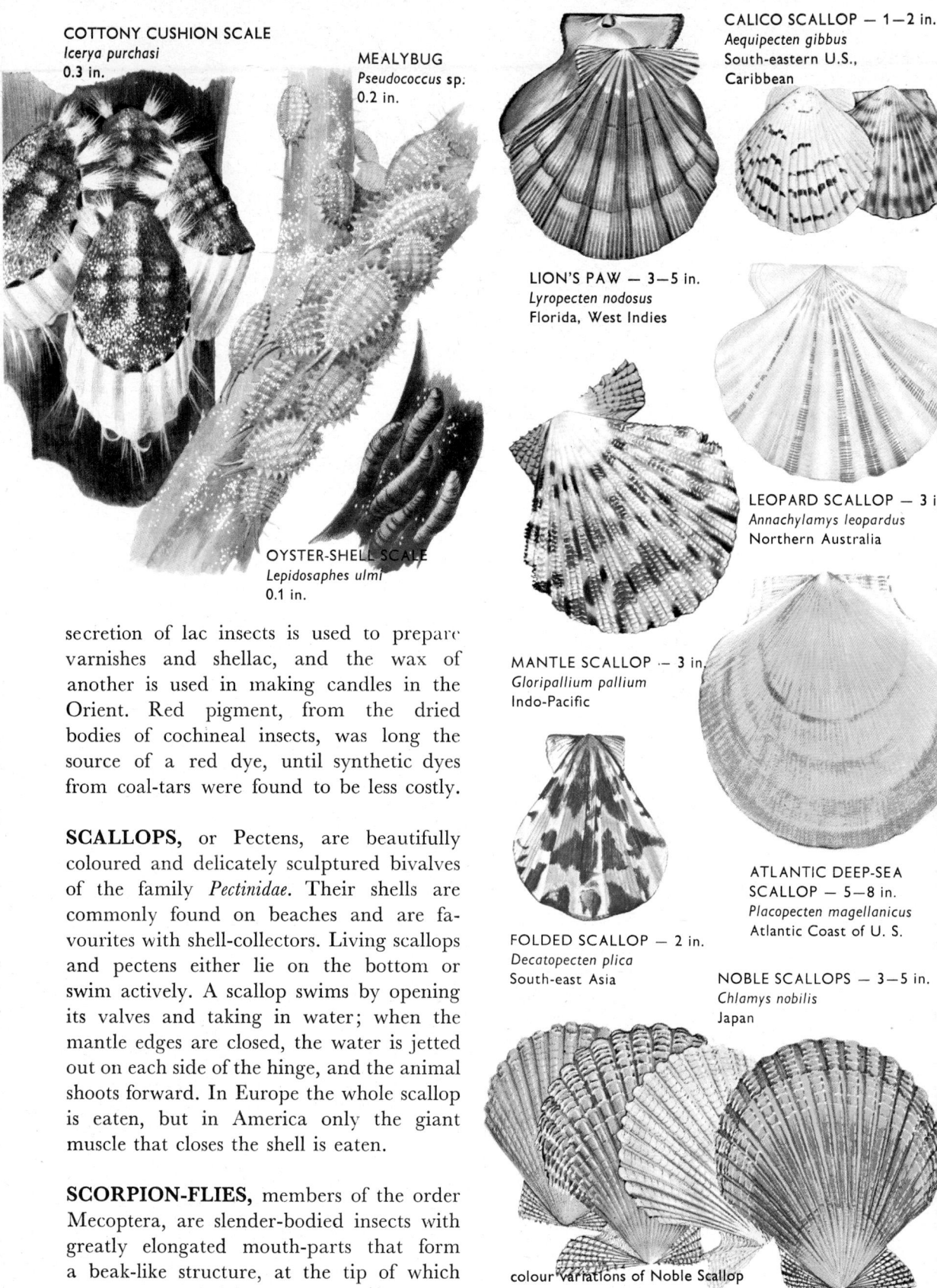

COTTONY CUSHION SCALE
Icerya purchasi
0.3 in.

MEALYBUG
Pseudococcus sp.
0.2 in.

OYSTER-SHELL SCALE
Lepidosaphes ulmi
0.1 in.

CALICO SCALLOP — 1—2 in.
Aequipecten gibbus
South-eastern U.S.,
Caribbean

LION'S PAW — 3—5 in.
Lyropecten nodosus
Florida, West Indies

LEOPARD SCALLOP — 3 i
Annachlamys leopardus
Northern Australia

MANTLE SCALLOP — 3 in.
Gloripallium pallium
Indo-Pacific

FOLDED SCALLOP — 2 in.
Decatopecten plica
South-east Asia

**ATLANTIC DEEP-SEA
SCALLOP — 5—8 in.**
Placopecten magellanicus
Atlantic Coast of U. S.

NOBLE SCALLOPS — 3—5 in.
Chlamys nobilis
Japan

colour variations of Noble Scallop

secretion of lac insects is used to prepare varnishes and shellac, and the wax of another is used in making candles in the Orient. Red pigment, from the dried bodies of cochineal insects, was long the source of a red dye, until synthetic dyes from coal-tars were found to be less costly.

SCALLOPS, or Pectens, are beautifully coloured and delicately sculptured bivalves of the family *Pectinidae*. Their shells are commonly found on beaches and are favourites with shell-collectors. Living scallops and pectens either lie on the bottom or swim actively. A scallop swims by opening its valves and taking in water; when the mantle edges are closed, the water is jetted out on each side of the hinge, and the animal shoots forward. In Europe the whole scallop is eaten, but in America only the giant muscle that closes the shell is eaten.

SCORPION-FLIES, members of the order Mecoptera, are slender-bodied insects with greatly elongated mouth-parts that form a beak-like structure, at the tip of which

are their mandibles. The reproductive organs of the males of some species resemble the scorpion's sting, hence their name. Scorpion-flies are harmless, however.

Scorpion-flies are usually found in damp, wooded areas. Females lay their eggs on the ground, and the larvae usually feed on decaying matter in humus. Some kinds eat other insects. One group of scorpion-flies looks like crane flies (see CRANE FLIES). They are very often found hanging by their front legs from leaves or twigs, ready to seize with their hind legs any small insect or spider that comes within reach. Some kinds of scorpion-fly feed on nectar and also eat the petals of flowers. Their larvae feed on the leaves of a great variety of common plants.

SCORPIONS belong to the class *Arachnida*, which includes spiders. Most abundant in the warmer regions of the world, true scorpions are rather large, some measuring nearly six inches in length. They are nocturnal, hiding by day in crevices, under boards and in holes. Although they do not ordinarily attack man, they will sting quickly if picked up or disturbed, and the sting is painful. The pain may last several

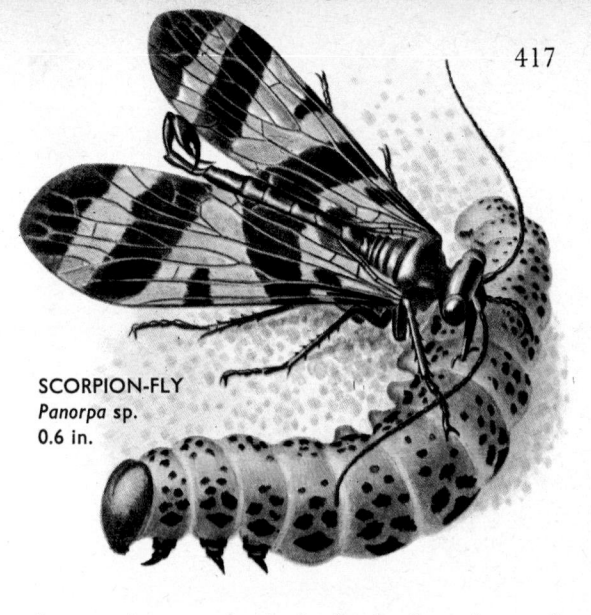

SCORPION-FLY
Panorpa sp.
0.6 in.

hours, but rarely is it fatal. Scorpions of the tropics are more dangerous than are species that live in temperate climates.

Scorpions usually feed on insects and spiders, from which they suck the body juices. They grab with their claws and then bring the abdomen up over their back to sting the prey and paralyse it.

Scorpions give birth to their young, and the female carries them on her back for some time. The young grow slowly, in some cases requiring several years to become fully adult.

Whip Scorpions are not true scorpions, but are close relatives and look like scorpions. Many have long, whip-like tails, but they do not have stingers at the tip.

Pseudoscorpions, or False Scorpions, are also near relatives. These animals are very small (less than a quarter of an inch long) and are often found under bark or leaves or in debris. They have two grasping claws, like the scorpions and Whip Scorpions, but have neither long tails nor stingers.

ANATOMY OF A SCALLOP

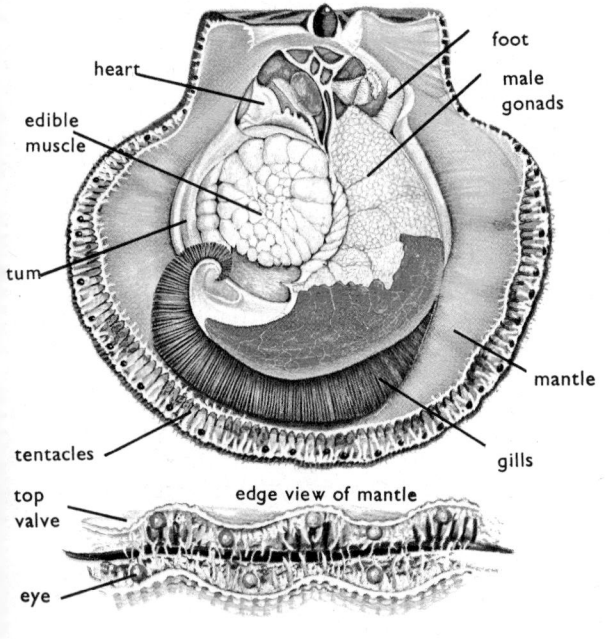

heart

edible
muscle

tum

tentacles

top
valve

eye

foot

male
gonads

mantle

gills

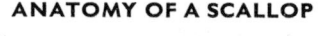

edge view of mantle

SCORPION
Centruroides sp.
Southern United States

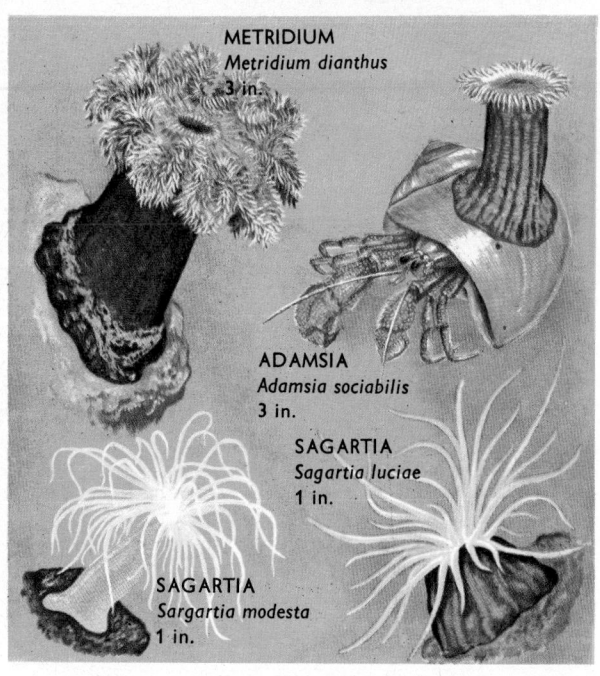

METRIDIUM
Metridium dianthus
3 in.

ADAMSIA
Adamsia sociabilis
3 in.

SAGARTIA
Sagartia luciae
1 in.

SAGARTIA
Sargartia modesta
1 in.

INTERNAL VIEW OF COMMON SEA ANEMONE

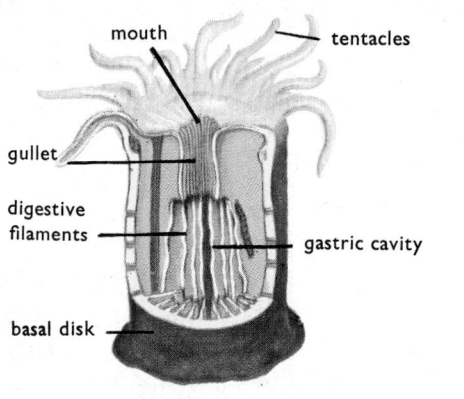

mouth — tentacles
gullet
digestive filaments
gastric cavity
basal disk

SEA ANEMONES are related to corals, but they do not have "skeletons" and do not form colonies (see COELENTERATES). Anemones have hollow body cavities, partially divided by fleshy partitions. They feed by paralysing their prey with stinging cells (nematocysts) on their long tentacles.

Sea anemones can creep slowly over the bottom, and sometimes multiply by simply pulling themselves apart, each half growing into a full animal. Sea anemones also reproduce by eggs. The small, ciliated larvae that hatch from the eggs soon settle to the bottom and grow into adults. Some anemones, such as *Adamsia*, form commensal (tenant) relationships with hermit crabs

or shrimps. Most sea anemones grow attached to rocks and timbers, but some are burrowers and others float with seaweed. The Green Anemone *(Cribrina)* occurs in Pacific tidal pools. The largest anemone in American waters is the Blue-tipped Anemone *(Condylactis)*, found in Florida and the West Indies. It may measure 18 inches in diameter and stand 12 inches high.

Sea anemones are preyed upon by sea slugs, and certain starfish. Other marine creatures apparently do not molest them.

SEA-CUCUMBERS are echinoderms of the class *Holothuroidea*. They have a long, flexible, cylindrical body. Their skeleton consists of numerous limy spicules of a great variety of shapes. One kind of sea-cucumber lives in the open sea and is

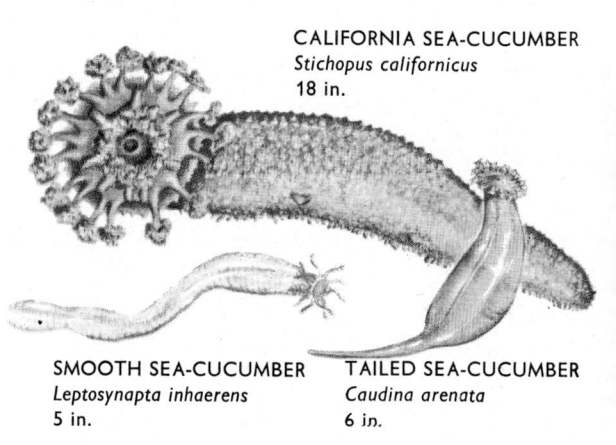

CALIFORNIA SEA-CUCUMBER
Stichopus californicus
18 in.

SMOOTH SEA-CUCUMBER
Leptosynapta inhaerens
5 in.

TAILED SEA-CUCUMBER
Caudina arenata
6 in.

seldom caught even in nets, but most sea-cucumbers crawl worm-like over the bottom, or burrow into sand or mud. They feed on dead animals or plants.

Probably due to their obnoxious taste, sea-cucumbers are seldom eaten by other marine animals. Some kinds of sea-cucumber eject all their internal organs in a mass when disturbed. Others have in their bodies a chemical that seems to paralyse the gills of small fishes, suffocating and killing them. Natives of West Indies and Pacific islands cut these sea-cucumbers into pieces and drop them into tidal pools. Any fishes in the pools soon come gasping to the surface, and are then collected. The poison does

not make the flesh of the fish inedible.

In parts of the Pacific, especially in the East Indies and along the northern coast of Australia, sea-cucumbers — there they are called trepang — are collected by divers, mainly Japanese. They are brought on deck, split open, and dried in the sun, and then are sold to the Chinese, who use them in soups. The Japanese wash the long intestines of sea-cucumbers and dry them in the sun, later eating them as *hors d'oeuvres*.

SEA-FANS and **SEA-FEATHERS** are both horny corals, and are closely related to true corals. Though found in most warm seas, they are especially abundant and conspicuous in the West Indies and Florida, where they form waving undersea forests of soft blues and yellows. Horny corals grow

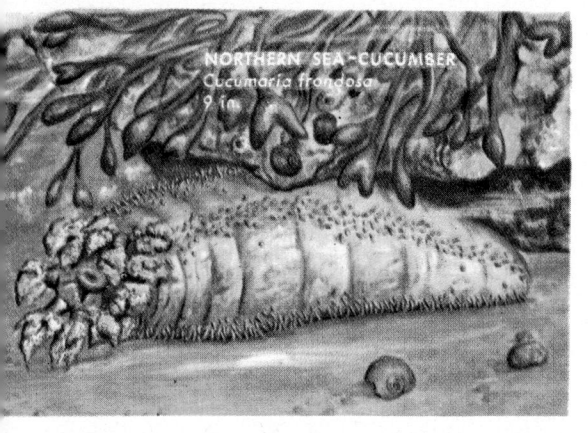

NORTHERN SEA-CUCUMBER
Cucumaria frondosa
9 in.

around a central horny, or leathery, axis. Their flesh is armed with warty spicules. Sea-feathers form slender, branching, fern-like colonies. Some, such as *Antillogorgia*, have long, graceful, purple branchlets. Others, like *Pterogorgia*, have slim, triangular blades, resembling whips. Sea-fans, like *Gorgonia*, grow flat and fan-like, with delicate traceries of blue or yellow. Each small polyp has eight finely-branched tentacles. Sea-fans and sea-feathers are often dried and sprayed with gold, silver or other colours for sale as decorations.

Precious Coral, which grows at considerable depths in the Mediterranean and eastern Atlantic, is fished for with grappling hooks and tangling devices. The hard, pink, limy core is cleaned, polished and drilled for use in bracelets and necklaces. Large pieces are carved into brooches or rings. Precious Coral was worn by the ancient Cretans, Greeks and Romans.

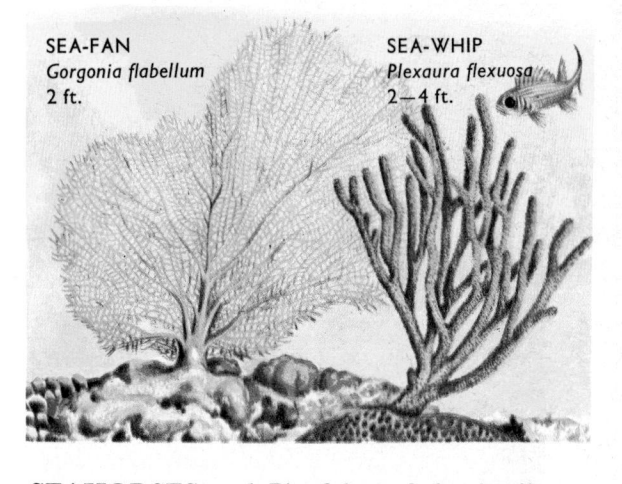

SEA-FAN
Gorgonia flabellum
2 ft.

SEA-WHIP
Plexaura flexuosa
2—4 ft.

SEAHORSES and Pipefishes of the family *Syngnathidae* live in warm seas throughout the world. Both are so unusual in appearance that they are hardly recognisable as fish. Their small mouth is at the tip of a long, tube-like snout, through which they suck tiny shellfish and other creatures on which

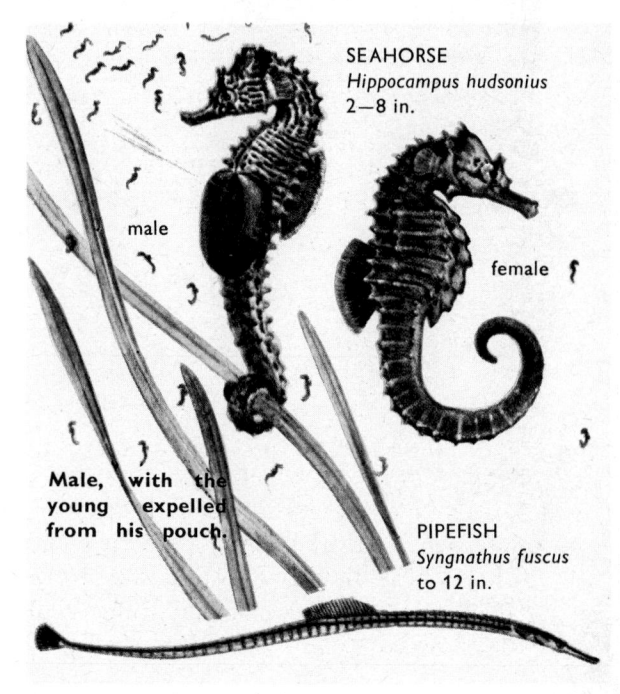

SEAHORSE
Hippocampus hudsonius
2—8 in.

male

female

Male, with the young expelled from his pouch.

PIPEFISH
Syngnathus fuscus
to 12 in.

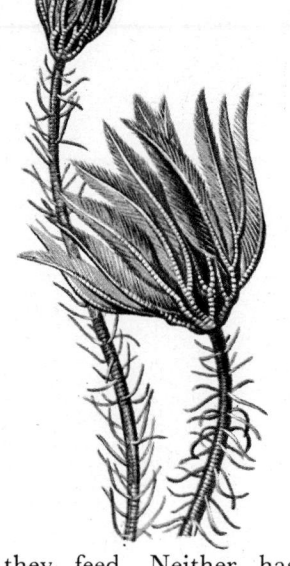

SEA-LILY
Antedon sp.
2—4 ft.

Sea-lilies grow on stems, or unbranched stalks, somewhat like plants. Some species become free-swimming as adults, but others stay fixed unless accidentally detached.

they feed. Neither has true scales, but their body is encased in horny rings.

Seahorses spend most of their time anchored to seaweeds, their slim and finless tail curled about the stems. Though not fast swimmers, they are graceful, and when they move, their dorsal fins ripple rapidly — so fast, in fact, that the vibration is hard to see with the naked eye.

Females deposit their eggs near a male, who then fertilises them and places them in a brood pouch on his belly. After the eggs hatch, the young remain in the pouch as a place of refuge for a while, until the male discharges them. They then stay in the vicinity for some time.

Seahorses make good aquarium pets. They swim stiffly, with the body held in an upright position. Their head is directed forward, at right angles to the body, and their neck is curved. Pipefishes, in contrast, swim in a horizontal position, like eels or gars. Most seahorses and pipefishes are small — less than 12 inches in length. One pipefish grows to a length of 18 inches.

SEA-LILIES are echinoderms of the class *Crinoidea*. They are feathery animals that have a number of arms fringed with delicate tentacles. Some grow on long, limy stalks and have arms measuring as much as 12 inches across. Other smaller types crawl

about among seaweeds and rocks by using the five or more slender tendrils at the base of their body disc. Most sea-lilies live in deep water, but a few American species of the tropics are found in shallow water. Many are beautifully coloured and often are striped. There are about 800 living species. In past ages, sea-lilies were more common and must have covered the floor of the warm seas of ancient times. More than 2,000 fossil species have been identified.

Sea-lilies feed on plankton which they catch on their feathery tentacles. A sea-lily's body is composed of joints of lime, and little actual flesh can be seen. Sea-lilies are commonly mistaken for plants.

Isolated plates from stems of sea-lilies, or crinoids, are common fossils in rocks of many ages. Known as "Indian beads", they were once used as ornaments and also as money. A crinoid's arms are usually branched, and often have small extensions, or pinnules. Fossil crinoids are found in rocks ranging in age from Ordovician to Recent. They developed a variety of forms (see ECHINODERMS).

SEA LIONS (*Zalophus* or *Eumetopias* spp.) are large seals. They differ from some other seals in that they have visible ears. Their hind flippers, which are modified legs, can be rotated forward. Perhaps they have been called "lions" because they bellow or roar. Sea lions may weigh as much as 1,700 pounds; the females, always smaller than the males, give birth to a single pup. They spend much time on the rocky beaches and islands of the Pacific Ocean, where they feed on fish and squid.

COMMON SEAL

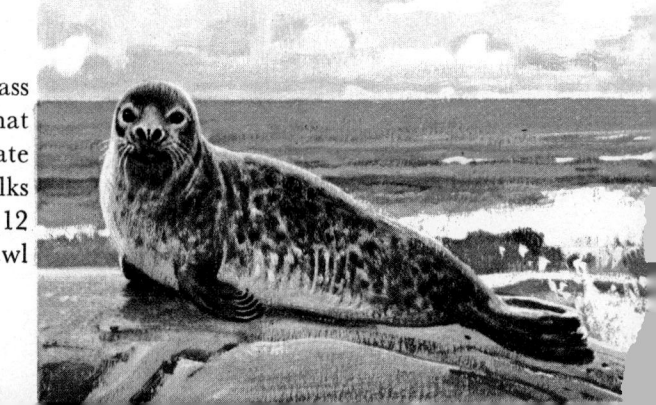

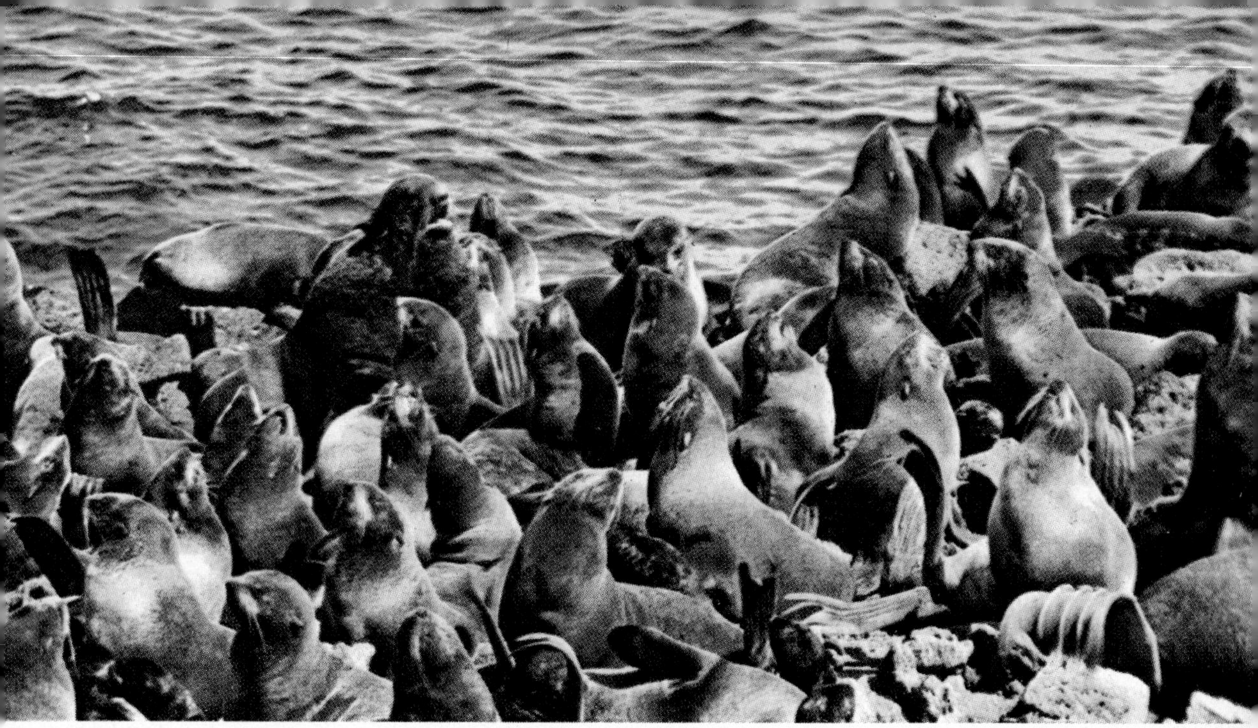

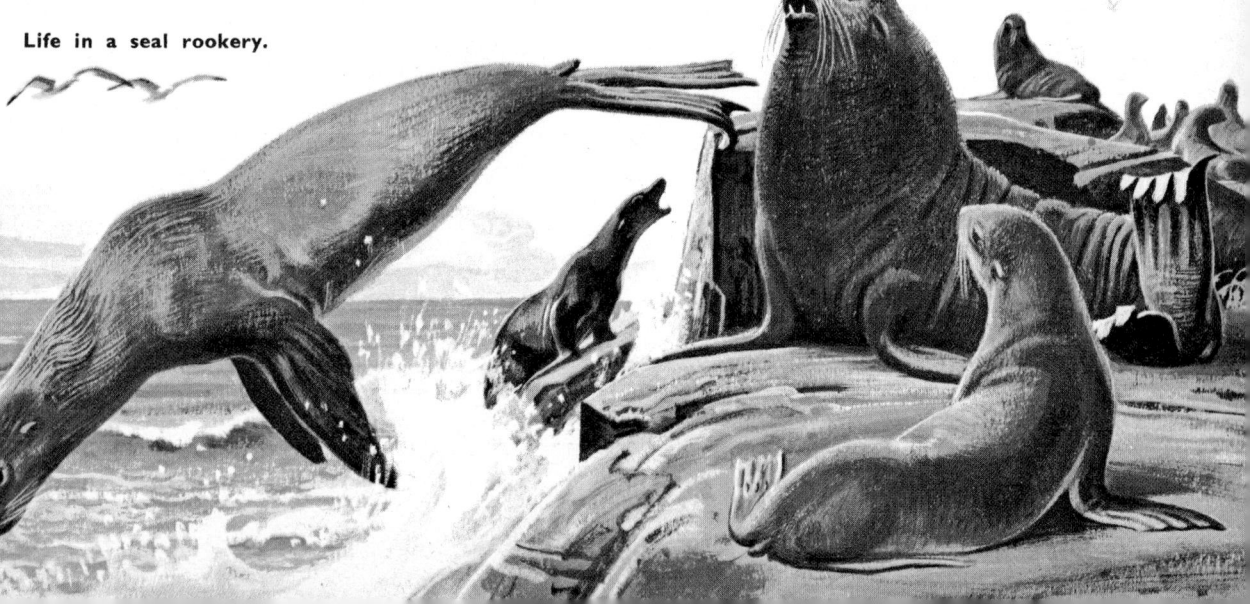

A colony of sea lions, inhabitants of Pacific Ocean coasts and islands. The Sea Lion provides an example of a mammal adapting itself to marine life, and then multiplying in its new environment.

SEALS are especially adapted for life in the water. They have a streamlined body, with arms and legs modified into powerful flippers, and a short, thick, protective coat of fur. Numerous kinds live on or near coasts of all the oceans of the world.

Common Seals *(Phoca* spp.*)* are best known around northern harbours, bays and mouths of rivers. They come on shore only to sleep, sunbathe and rest. They feed on fish and, in turn, are eaten by sharks and toothed whales, and killed by man. Leopard Seals *(Hydrurga leptonyx)*, with black spots on a greyish coat, are common in the cold seas of the Antarctic.

Elephant Seals *(Mirounga* spp.*),* found in South Pacific and Mexican waters, are large and fat, weighing as much as 5,000 pounds. Their large snouts droop about nine inches below their mouths and look somewhat like an elephant's trunk. So many Elephant Seals were killed by hunters that, at one time, they were nearly extinct.

Fur Seals *(Callorhinus ursinus* and *Arctocephalus pusillus)* are relatives of sea lions. The bulls weigh about 500 to 600 pounds;

Life in a seal rookery.

FAMILY TREE OF AQUATIC CARNIVORES

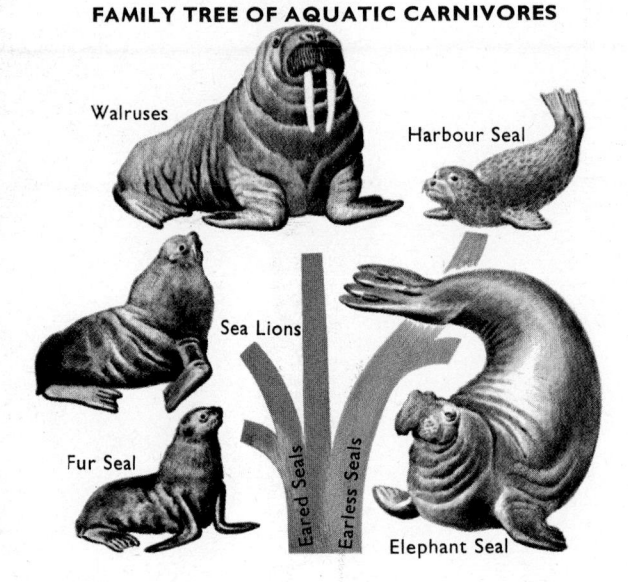

Walruses

Harbour Seal

Sea Lions

Fur Seal

Eared Seals

Earless Seals

Elephant Seal

females weigh only about 100 pounds. They have an especially fine fur, from which sealskin coats are made. So many seals were slaughtered at one time that the animal was nearly exterminated, but through wise management their numbers have been rebuilt to several millions. Most of their lifetime is spent at sea, but in late spring the Fur Seals return to the islands to breed.

SEA SLUGS are delicate, often beautifully-coloured shell-less molluscs of the order *Nudibranchia*. They swim in the open sea, or glide over rocks and seaweeds. Sea slugs breathe by means of the soft, fleshy projections on their backs. The Giant Frond Eolis, of the north-western United States, reaches a length of eight inches. The Sargussum Slug, one to two inches long, lives in the drifting Gulf Weed. The Bushy-backed Sea Slug is an Atlantic Species found along the coasts of both North America and Europe. The Plumed Sea Slug is also an Atlantic species, occurring as far north as the Arctic Ocean. Sea slugs often feed on stinging anemones; they have the peculiar ability to extract the stinging cells from their prey and transfer them into their own skin for use in defence. Sea slugs are among the most beautiful and brightly coloured of marine animals.

SEA SNAKES, members of the family *Elapidae*, are found in tropical waters of the Indian and western Pacific Oceans. One species occurs in the eastern Pacific, in the Panama region. They have never become established in the Atlantic. Sea snakes have fixed front fangs and a neurotoxic venom, similar to coral snakes, cobras and mambas. Although sea snakes have a potent venom, they rarely bite humans, and are commonly handled by fishermen who catch them in their nets.

Adaptations for a marine existence are: the flattened, oar-like tail; valves on the nostrils, preventing water from entering the lungs; and a reduction in the size of ventral plates, or even total absence. Generally the nostrils and eyes are situated on top of the head, thus enabling the snake to breathe and see with minimum exposure of the head when it surfaces. Genera that are fully aquatic are further modified to cope with marine habits by bearing young live. One genus (*Laticauda*) is known to come ashore and lay eggs; the belly plates

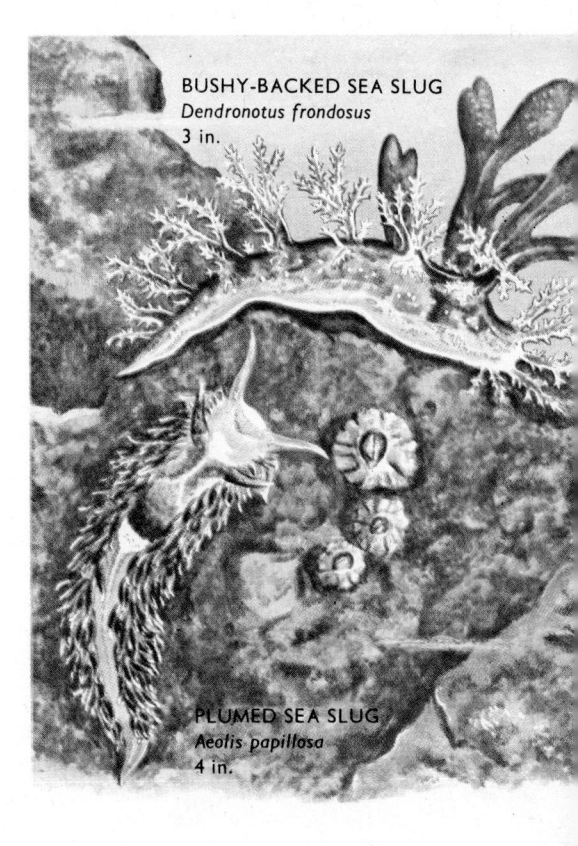

BUSHY-BACKED SEA SLUG
Dendronotus frondosus
3 in.

PLUMED SEA SLUG
Aeolis papillosa
4 in.

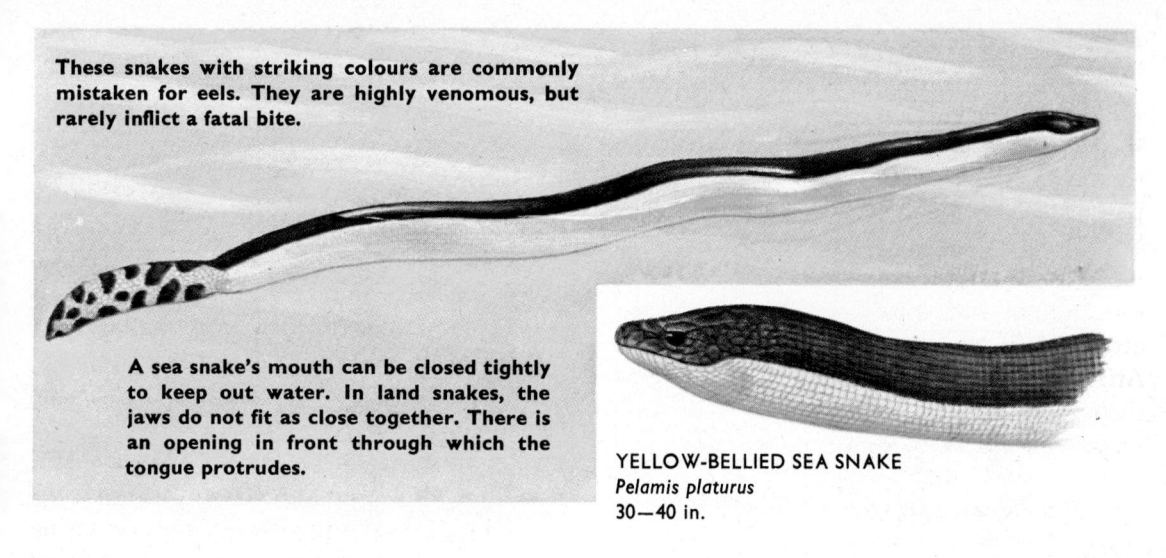

These snakes with striking colours are commonly mistaken for eels. They are highly venomous, but rarely inflict a fatal bite.

A sea snake's mouth can be closed tightly to keep out water. In land snakes, the jaws do not fit as close together. There is an opening in front through which the tongue protrudes.

YELLOW-BELLIED SEA SNAKE
Pelamis platurus
30—40 in.

of this snake are only slightly reduced in size. As many as 30,000 *Laticauda* a year have been caught in the Philippines, where they congregate before coming ashore. The snakes are used for food and skins.

Sea snakes live in relatively shallow waters near continents and islands, and never in deep seas; they feed entirely on fishes, especially eels. The bodies of many species are very thick towards the rear, and taper rapidly to a thin neck and head. The large rear part of the body offers considerable resistance to the water, and allows the slender front part to be shot forward faster and farther than would be possible otherwise.

Many sea snakes attain nine feet in length; one genus is as thick as a man's leg.

Sea snakes stretch out in the water to bask. Their stick-like form is apparently

an advantage in attracting fish, as small fish often collect near floating debris, presumably to avoid being detected by wandering predatory fish.

Congregations of millions of sea snakes — as much as 60 miles long and 10 feet wide — have been observed, the snakes swimming calmly side by side, all in the same direction. These massive "migrations" are apparently related to their breeding. (See COBRAS; CORAL SNAKES.)

SEA SPIDERS are peculiar arthropods, distantly related to crustaceans and true spiders. They occur from low tide to great depths and live under rocks or on algae, anemones or hydroids. Most sea spiders are tiny creatures found crawling about slowly, but some deep-water species have a leg-spread of about six inches. Their small bodies are equipped with seven pairs of appendages, of which four or six are long, thin, jointed walking legs. The males carry the eggs until they hatch.

The bodies and legs of these animals are so slender that they are often overlooked in the seaweeds. In some, the body is so small that the stomach extends down the legs as swollen pouches. They feed on tiny bits of food which they chew with their stalked mouths. Sea Spiders are fragile crustaceans. Among the common genera are *Pycmogonum, Nymphon,* and *Colossendeis.*

SEA SPIDER
Nymphon hirtus
body: 0.5 in.
legs: 4.5 in. spread

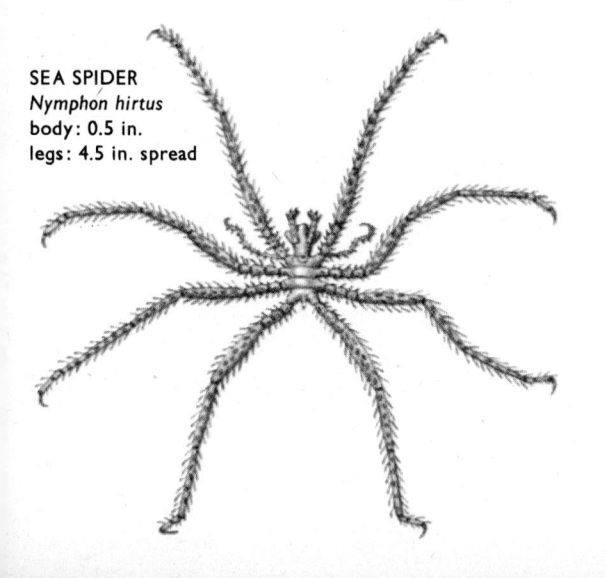

SEA-URCHINS, echinoderms of the class Echinoidea, are enclosed in limy plates fused together to form a round shell covered with sharp spines. When the spines are cleaned off, the characteristic five-rayed pattern of the tube-feet pores can be seen. Sea-urchins live in grassy or rocky areas, where they feed on algae scraped from the bottom with their jaws. Their jaws are attached internally to a structure called Aristotle's lantern. Urchins crawl by using their spines, which work on ball-and-socket joints. Their long tube feet are used to keep their bodies free of foreign material. The south-eastern Variegated Urchin, however, holds shells and bottom debris over its shell as a camouflage. Some urchins,

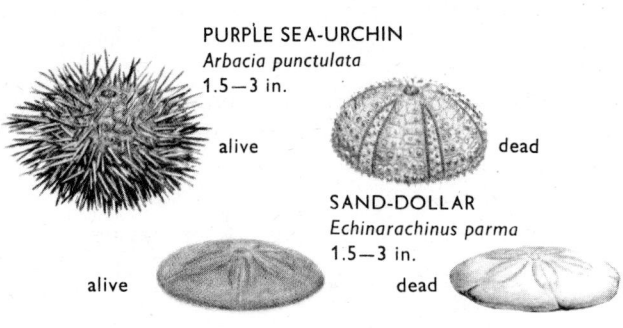

PURPLE SEA-URCHIN
Arbacia punctulata
1.5—3 in.

alive   dead

SAND-DOLLAR
Echinarachinus parma
1.5—3 in.

alive   dead

Sea-urchins are rounded echinoderms from 1½ to 10 inches in diameter, and they have long spines. Sand-dollars are flat and have short spines.

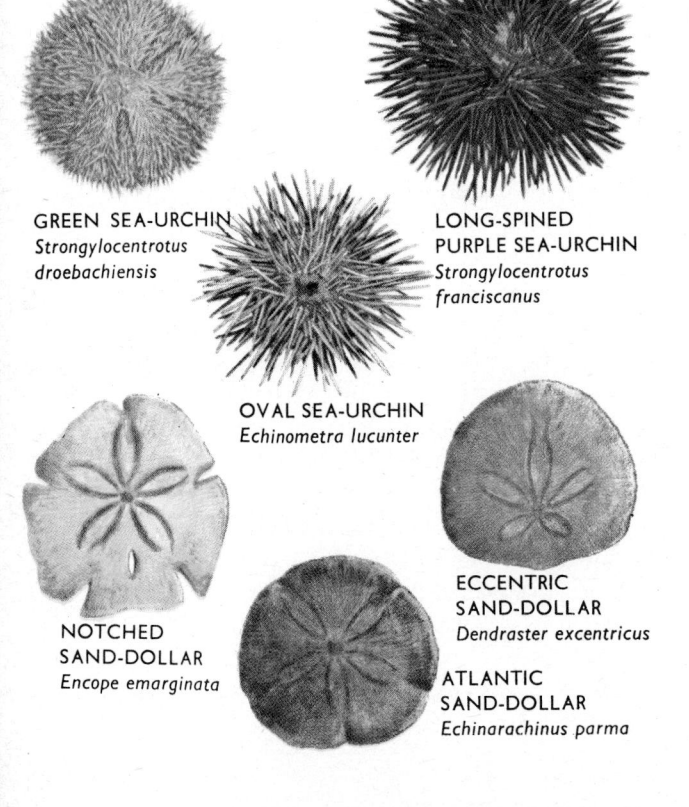

GREEN SEA-URCHIN
Strongylocentrotus droebachiensis

LONG-SPINED
PURPLE SEA-URCHIN
Strongylocentrotus franciscanus

OVAL SEA-URCHIN
Echinometra lucunter

NOTCHED
SAND-DOLLAR
Encope emarginata

ECCENTRIC
SAND-DOLLAR
Dendraster excentricus

ATLANTIC
SAND-DOLLAR
Echinarachinus parma

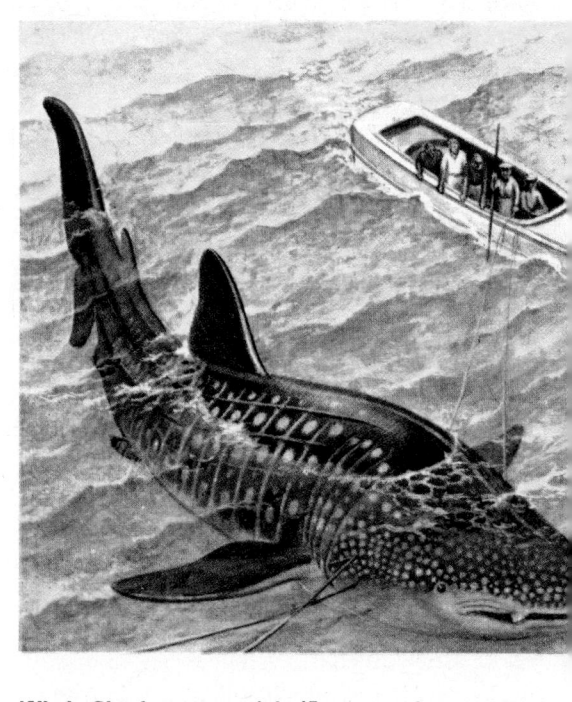

Whale Sharks may weigh 15 tons and grow to a length of 50 feet. Despite their awesome bulk, Whale Sharks subsist on plankton, microscopic plants and animals that float on the surface of the sea.

like *Diadema* of tropical waters, have long, needle-sharp spines that inflict slightly poisonous and painful stings, the poison coming from glands at the base of the spines.

Some sea-urchins can bore into rocks, or even into steel pilings. *Echinometra,* for example, lives in holes in limestone. The urchin accomplishes its boring by keeping the surface wiped so clean that the corrosive action of sea water eats away the material. Eggs of *Tripneustes,* a common sea-urchin, are eaten in the Mediterranean region and the West Indies. In Barbados, laws protect sea-urchins to conserve them for eating.

Sea-biscuits and sand-dollars are closely related to sea-urchins. Sea-biscuits are fat and oval-shaped. Spine-covered creatures,

they shovel about the bottom, feeding on organic debris. Some live below the surface, and one forms a true burrow. Sand-dollars are greatly flattened, their discs covered with very short spines. They live buried in the sand, and their bleached, cleaned shells are often found on sandy beaches. (See ECHINODERMS.)

SHARKS belong to an ancient group of fishes. They have skeletons of cartilage, or gristle, not true bone. Like their nearest relatives, the rays, they have thick skins and small, tooth-like placoid scales (see RAYS). Most sharks are swift, graceful swimmers, but they cannot stop or turn as quickly as bony fishes.

In contrast to flat-bodied, bottom-dwelling rays, typical sharks have round, streamlined bodies. Most kinds live in the open sea, but a few inhabit shallow bays and inlets or may be found far up rivers, even in fresh water. One species lives in Lake Nicaragua. Sharks are most abundant in warm seas, and many species are wanderers.

Some sharks are scavengers, living on dead animals and refuse, but the Whale Shark *(Rhincodon typus)*, which is the largest of all fishes, eats small plants and animals, as does the big Basking Shark *(Cetorhinus maximus)*. Most sharks, however, are flesh-eaters, feeding on other fishes. Large species may even eat seals, turtles, penguins, or any other large creature they can catch.

Typically, sharks locate their food by its odour, and they can track a faint trace of blood to its source. When they get close, sharks may circle several times, and even nudge the food with their snout before eating it. Even so, such odd items as wooden kegs, rubber tyres, coils of rope, and other inedibles, have been removed from sharks' stomachs. Sharks are greatly feared by man, for many kinds are truly ferocious;

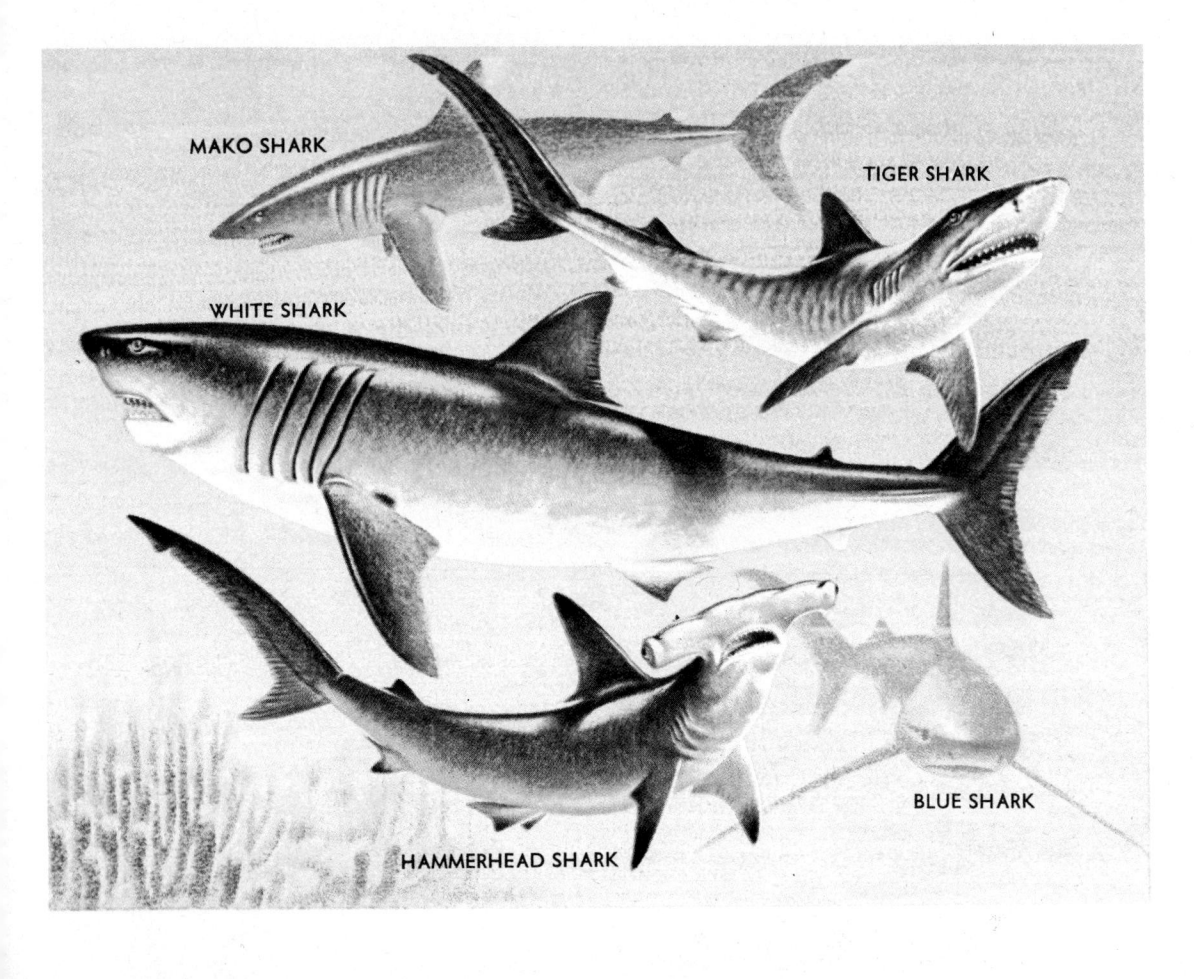

MAKO SHARK

TIGER SHARK

WHITE SHARK

HAMMERHEAD SHARK

BLUE SHARK

when excited, they bite anything nearby. Authentic reports of shark bites are numerous; death is a common result. Oddly, shark attacks seem to be increasing. In part, this is due to the growth of the sport of skin-diving in recent years. This has exposed a greater number of human beings to sharks than ever before. Divers carrying speared fish which trail blood in the water are in special danger of being attacked.

Even common Nurse Sharks *(Gingly-mostoma* spp.*)*, scavengers frequently seen close to shore and generally considered to be harmless, can be dangerous when annoyed. Faster and fiercer, however, is the Great White Shark, or Maneater *(Carcharodon carcharias)*. These giants of tropical seas will attack anything that moves. Equally voracious are the Blue Shark *(Prionace glauca)* and Tiger Shark *(Galeocerdo cuvieri)*.

Thresher Sharks *(Alopias* spp.*)* are easily recognised by their long, sickle-shaped tail-fins. They use these tails to stun smaller fishes, and several thresher sharks will team up to hold a school of fishes in a bay or inlet while they feed on them. Most unusual in appearance is the Hammerhead Shark *(Sphyrna zygaena)*. Its head is greatly flattened and its eyes are located on the tips of the hammer-like extensions, which are possibly used as a planing device. It has a reputation for ferocity and is known to have attacked swimming humans.

Sharks of many sizes and shapes are found throughout the world. Some are fished commercially for their skins, which can be made into fine leather; others are hunted for the oil from their livers. One large Basking Shark can yield several hundred gallons of oil; this is used in soaps, cosmetics and various drugs. Some shark oil is richer in vitamins than cod-liver oil. Sharks are also used as food — particularly their thick fins, which are boiled to make soup stock. Soup-fin Sharks *(Galeorhinus zyopterus)* are especially popular for this purpose. Some kinds, such as the plentiful Spiny Dogfish *(Squalus acanthias)*, are great nuisances to commercial fishermen, because they foul nets or strike at hooked fish. They can also

1. WHITE SHARK
Average 8—10 ft. Maximum 35 ft.

2. TIGER SHARK
Average 10—15 ft. Up to 30 ft.

3. THRESHER SHARK
Average 5—15 ft. Up to 20 ft.

4. NURSE SHARK
Average 5—10 ft.

5. HAMMERHEAD SHARK
Average 5—10 ft.

6. BLUE SHARK
Average 5—15 ft. Up to 20 ft.

7. BASKING SHARK
Average 30 ft. Up to 40 ft.

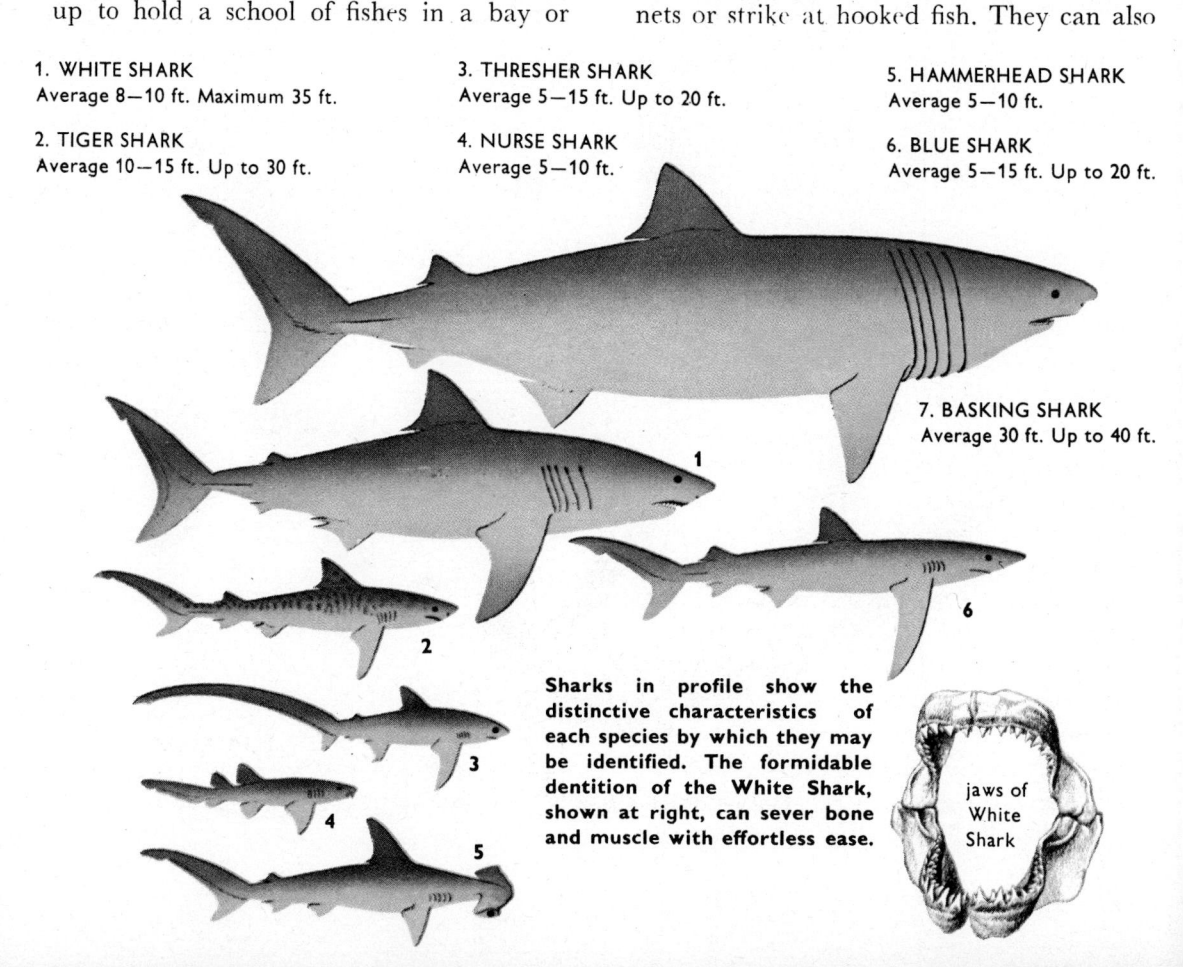

Sharks in profile show the distinctive characteristics of each species by which they may be identified. The formidable dentition of the White Shark, shown at right, can sever bone and muscle with effortless ease.

jaws of White Shark

inflict painful wounds with their spines. Dogfishes, however, are valuable laboratory specimens for college students, who study them to learn the basic anatomy of back-boned animals.

Many sharks furnish sport for fishermen; almost all kinds fight hard. Mako Sharks

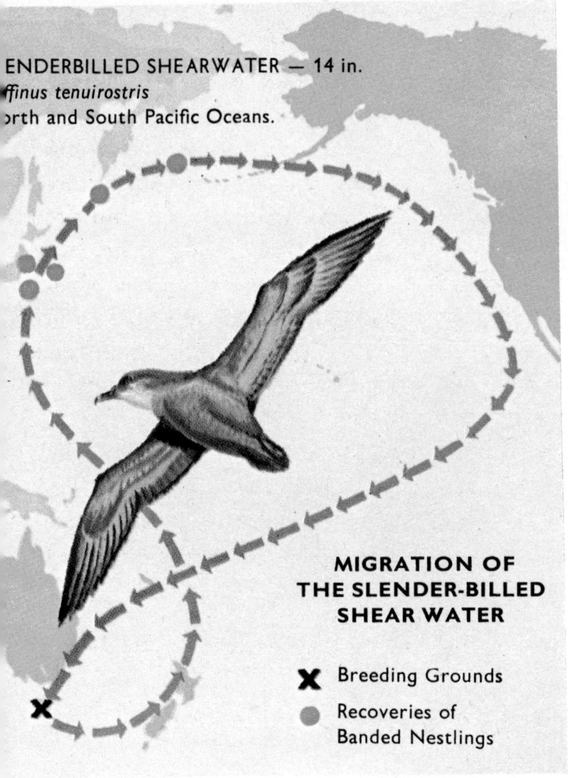

ENDERBILLED SHEARWATER — 14 in.
ffinus tenuirostris
rth and South Pacific Oceans.

MIGRATION OF
THE SLENDER-BILLED
SHEARWATER

✗ Breeding Grounds
● Recoveries of
Banded Nestlings

(Isurus oxyrinchus) leap high out of the water and are as sporting as any other game fish, though they are much more dangerous than most.

The oldest fossil sharks come from rocks of Devonian age. They increased in numbers considerably in upper Paleozoic times. Some lived in fresh water, but most types, like those living today, were marine. Early cartilaginous fish tended to be rather simple, unspecialised fish, compared with later members of the group. Most primitive forms became extinct by the close of the Paleozoic period. During Mesozoic and Cenozoic times sharks were a successful group. One giant shark of the Tertiary period reached a length of 60 feet.

SHEARWATERS are migratory sea-birds that live in all the oceans of the world and come to land only to nest. Related to albatrosses and petrels, they have tubular nostrils and long wings. While hunting for fish and squid, the birds fly so low over the water that they seem to shear foam off the waves.

Shearwaters nest in colonies on islands, and sometimes quite far inland on mountain tops. The nests are usually in burrows or in cracks between the rocks. All shearwaters lay a single egg, which both parents incubate in turn. They raise their chick together, feeding it by regurgitation, and often go hundreds of miles out to sea in search of food, leaving the chick alone in the burrow for several days.

The Greater Shearwater, one of the largest, nests on the lonely Tristan da Cunha Islands, a small British group in the South Atlantic. When not breeding, it ranges over the entire Atlantic from Cape Horn to the Arctic Circle.

The Manx Shearwater breeds on many Atlantic islands, but is no longer found on the Isle of Man, after which it was named. It nests in burrows, and the site of a breeding colony is honeycombed with nesting holes. In 1952, a Manx Shearwater was taken from its nesting burrow in Wales, banded, carried by plane across the Atlantic and released in Boston Harbour, U. S. A. In 13 days, the bird found its way back to the island burrow in Wales, crossing 3,200 miles of trackless, unfamiliar ocean waters in order to do so.

The Sooty Shearwater nests on islands in the southernmost part of the South Atlantic during our winter, and migrates to the seas around Iceland and Greenland in summer.

The chicks of the Slender-billed Shearwater, or Muttonbird, of Australia, are canned and sold as "Tasmanian Squab". Muttonbirds migrate north in the Pacific, via New Zealand, to Japan, the Bering Sea and then California, before returning to Australia (see accompanying map).

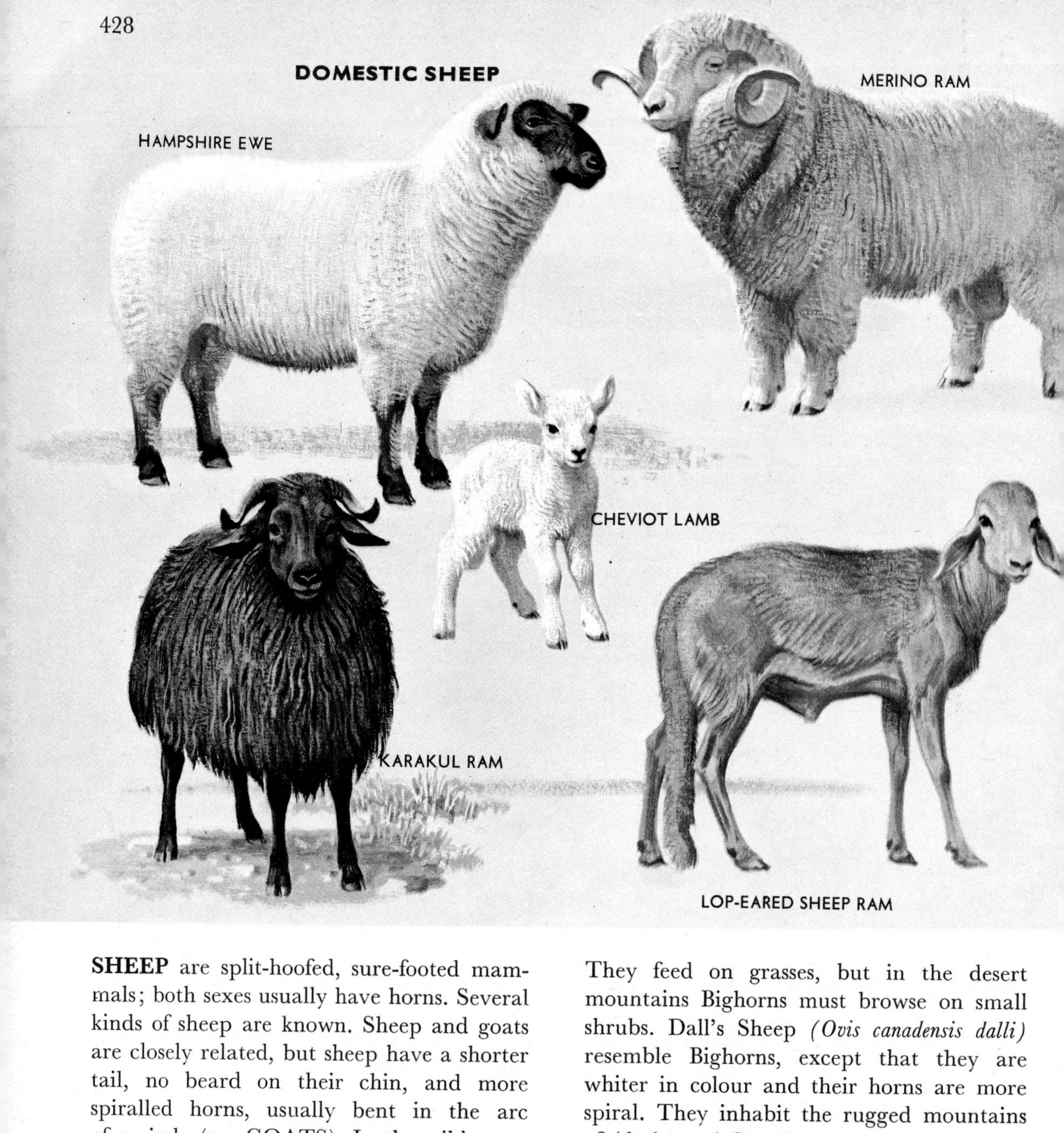

DOMESTIC SHEEP

HAMPSHIRE EWE

MERINO RAM

CHEVIOT LAMB

KARAKUL RAM

LOP-EARED SHEEP RAM

SHEEP are split-hoofed, sure-footed mammals; both sexes usually have horns. Several kinds of sheep are known. Sheep and goats are closely related, but sheep have a shorter tail, no beard on their chin, and more spiralled horns, usually bent in the arc of a circle (see GOATS). In the wild state, sheep are native to four regions: North America, the Mediterranean Basin, Central Asia, and Asia south of the Himalayas.

Big-horned Sheep, or Bighorns *(Ovis canadensis)*, of western North America and eastern Siberia, live on rocky slopes and snow-covered peaks. They are brownish-grey, shy animals, almost invisible against the rocks where they live. Bighorns usually travel in small herds, with the rams (males) separate from the ewes (females) and young.

They feed on grasses, but in the desert mountains Bighorns must browse on small shrubs. Dall's Sheep *(Ovis canadensis dalli)* resemble Bighorns, except that they are whiter in colour and their horns are more spiral. They inhabit the rugged mountains of Alaska and Canada.

The long-bearded Barbary Sheep *(Ammotragus lervia)*, frequently called Aoudads, live among the rocky crags of the mountainous regions of North Africa. These long-horned, shaggy-maned sheep are seen commonly in zoos. The horns of ewes are shorter and thinner than those of rams.

The Argali *(Ovis ammon)* is a large grey-brown sheep from the mountains of central Asia. The male has massive, wrinkled horns, which form a spiral, while the horns of

A BIGHORN

DALL'S SHEEP

the female are considerably smaller.

DOMESTIC SHEEP. Domestic sheep were probably developed from the Red Sheep (*Ovis vignei*), which is at present found wild in limited numbers in Russia and Asia Minor. Sheep have been domesticated since early times, and are often mentioned in the Bible. Cain and Abraham kept sheep, and Jesus used sheep and shepherds as subjects for many of his stories.

Sheep, like cows and goats, are ruminants, and have stomachs that are divided into four compartments. Food is swallowed whenever the sheep has a chance to graze and is stored in the first stomach. Later it passes to the honeycombed second compartment of the stomach, where it is rolled into unchewed balls, or cuds. At its leisure, the sheep returns these cuds to its mouth and chews them thoroughly. When it is swallowed again, the food goes into the third stomach, where it is digested as it filters through a series of folds in the third and fourth compartments.

Australia produces about a third of the world's wool supply. New Zealand, South Africa and Argentina also have large sheep populations. In some areas of Southern Russia, Iran, Iraq and Turkey, sheep are raised for fur, and England is noted for its mutton sheep.

Australian Merinos have been bred for long, fine wool. New Zealand mutton breeds were crossed with the Merino to produce the all-purpose Corriedale sheep.

SHIELD-TAIL SNAKES are cylindrical burrowing snakes that have a conical, pointed head no wider than their neck, and a short, blunt tail; their eyes are small and degenerate. About 45 species are known, found only on the Indian Peninsula and in Ceylon; they are members of the family *Uropeltidae*. The largest reaches a length of 29 inches; 15 inches is average. Their skin is enamel-like, and the colours are often combinations of red, yellow, orange and black. The tip of the tail often bears spines, or a sort of blunt shield believed to be helpful in burrowing. Shield-tail

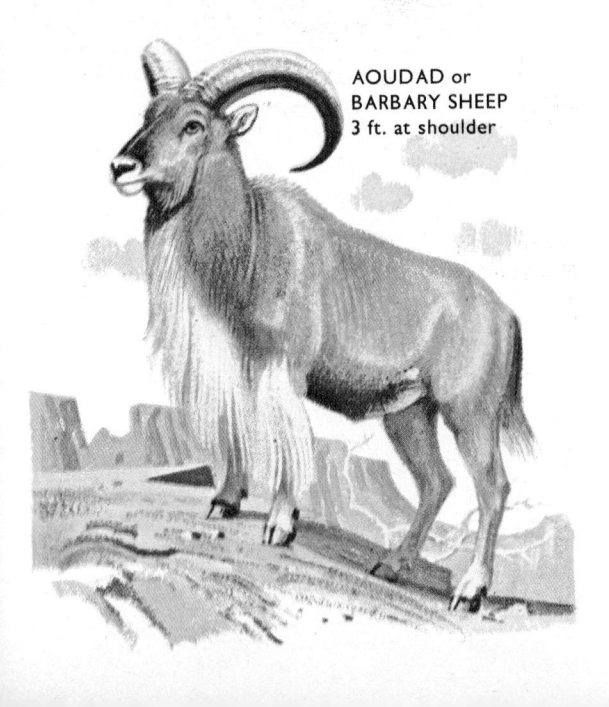

AOUDAD or
BARBARY SHEEP
3 ft. at shoulder

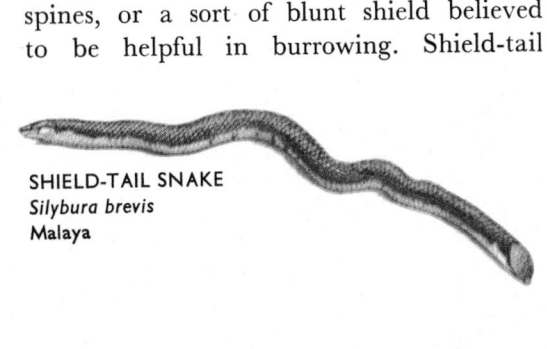

SHIELD-TAIL SNAKE
Silybura brevis
Malaya

snakes eat almost nothing but earthworms. The snakes never bite when handled. Females bear up to eight young alive.

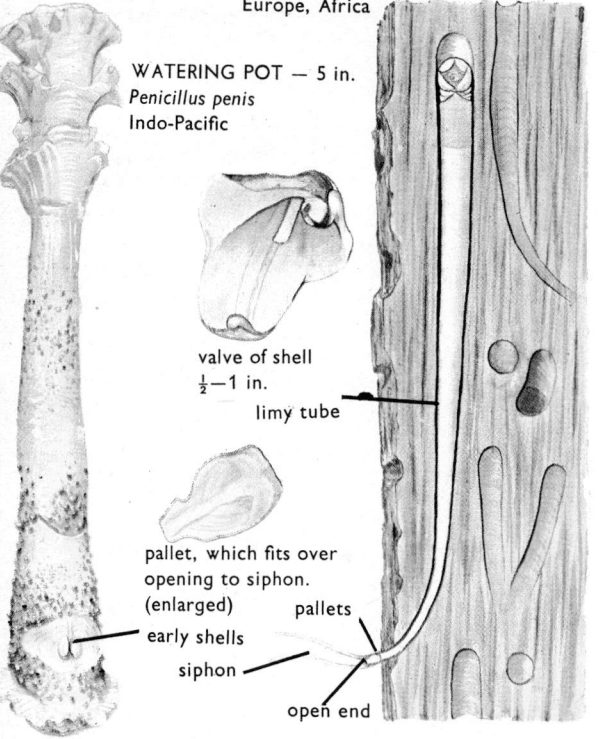

COMMON SHIPWORM—½—2 ft.
Teredo navalis
Coastal North America,
Europe, Africa

WATERING POT — 5 in.
Penicillus penis
Indo-Pacific

valve of shell
½—1 in.

limy tube

pallet, which fits over opening to siphon. (enlarged)

pallets

early shells

siphon

open end

A piling infested by shipworms may be honeycombed with burrows and reduced almost to a shell, even though the outer surface appears normal and undamaged.

actually lost on long voyages as a result of the attacks of these molluscs. Copper sheathing was one answer. Shipworms are not able to damage steel hulls, and toxic paints are used now to protect small wooden boats. In northern Australia and Africa, some people eat shipworms; they even "farm" them by placing logs in the water. (See BIVALVES; MOLLUSCS.)

SHREWS are related to moles, and much less closely to bats and rodents. Some adults weigh only one-tenth of an ounce and are the smallest of all mammals. Nearly all kinds of shrews feed on insects and earthworms and, because of their great expenditure of energy, consume as much as twice their weight in food every day. All shrews have a long, pointed nose, small

SHIPWORMS, or Teredos, are bivalve molluscs with long, tubular soft parts. A pair of limy, sharp-ridged valves (shells) at their head end are used for boring into wood. A pair of siphons at the opposite end always project from the wood to draw in water for breathing. Some biologists believe that shipworms digest wood, but there is some evidence that their digestion is aided by bacteria, as in the case of termites. Shipworms enter the wood as larvae and may grow very long. *Bankia,* for example, may attain a length of 18 inches and nearly half an inch in diameter.

Shipworms cause untold damage to water-front structures and boats each year. Most maritime governments carry out research continually to learn better and more effective ways of controlling them. In the days of wooden ships, vessels were

SHORT-TAILED SHREW
Blarina brevicauda
Length 4½ in.
Eastern U.S.A.

WATER SHREW
Neomys fodiens
Length 4 in.
Europe,
northern Asia

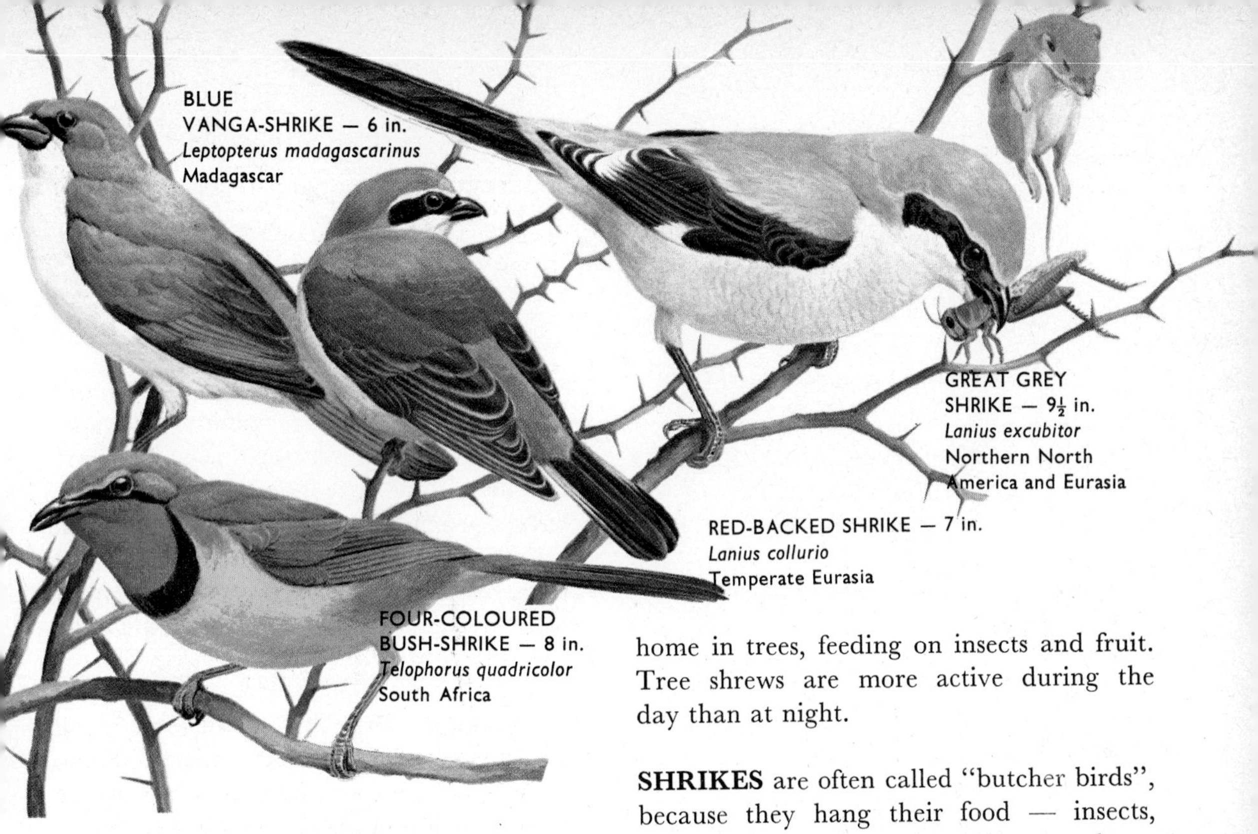

BLUE
VANGA-SHRIKE — 6 in.
Leptopterus madagascarinus
Madagascar

GREAT GREY
SHRIKE — 9½ in.
Lanius excubitor
Northern North
America and Eurasia

RED-BACKED SHRIKE — 7 in.
Lanius collurio
Temperate Eurasia

FOUR-COLOURED
BUSH-SHRIKE — 8 in.
Telophorus quadricolor
South Africa

eyes, small ears — hardly visible in their fur — and small, sharp teeth.

Common Shrews (*Sorex* spp.) are found in meadowland throughout much of Europe and northern Asia. They eat insects, snails and worms, and build a nest of grass and leaves. The young are naked and blind at birth. Short-tailed shrews (*Blarina brevicauda*) are common in the leaf-mould and soil of forested areas of central and eastern North America, and are similar in appearance and habits to the Common Shrew.

Water shrews (*Neomys fodiens*), widespread in Europe and northern Asia, are commonly found along streams and near ponds. They feed on water insects, small fish and other aquatic creatures.

White-toothed shrews (*Crocidura* spp.), found in Europe, Asia and Africa, are fairly large, grey or brown shrews. There are many kinds and they live in all kinds of habitats, from forests to dry, rocky places.

Tree shrews (*Tupaia* spp.) are about a foot long, half of which is tail. Because of their unusual features, tree shrews are sometimes classed with primates, rather than with shrews. In the Indo-Malayan region and the Philippines, they are at home in trees, feeding on insects and fruit. Tree shrews are more active during the day than at night.

SHRIKES are often called "butcher birds", because they hang their food — insects, lizards and small birds and mammals — on a thorn; then, gradually, they eat the choice parts. Shrikes do this even when kept in captivity.

These birds occur in the temperate and tropic regions of all large land masses except South America. Solitary birds, they often sit on roadside wires, watching for prey in the fields. Shrikes have weak feet and must, therefore, kill their prey entirely

The Pygmy Shrew (*Microsorex hoyi*) **weighs about 1/14 of an ounce — little more than a dram.**

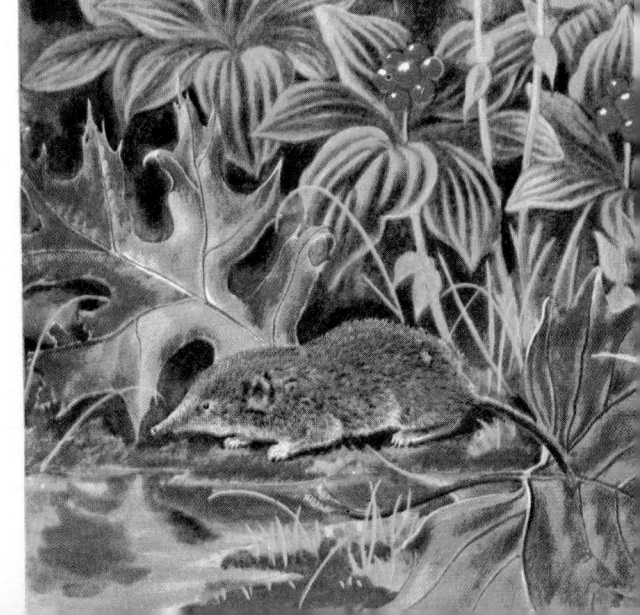

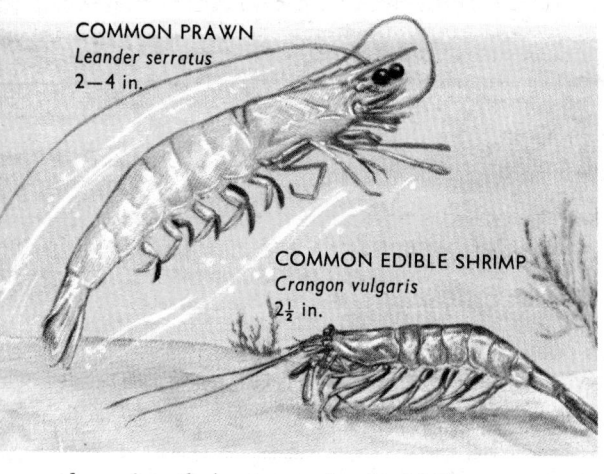

COMMON PRAWN
Leander serratus
2—4 in.

COMMON EDIBLE SHRIMP
Crangon vulgaris
2½ in.

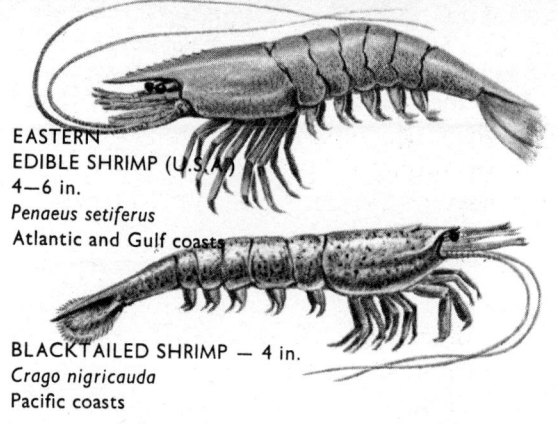

EASTERN
EDIBLE SHRIMP (U.S.)
4—6 in.
Penaeus setiferus
Atlantic and Gulf coasts

BLACKTAILED SHRIMP — 4 in.
Crago nigricauda
Pacific coasts

by using their strong, hooked bills.

The Red-backed Shrike is a summer visitor and feeds largely upon large insects. The Great Grey Shrike, a larger species nesting further north and wintering in areas of cold climates, is a much fiercer type and will not hesitate to attack small birds.

SHRIMPS and **PRAWNS** are crustaceans closely related to lobsters. Active swimmers, they can move forwards slowly by using their paddle-like legs, or dart backwards by quick strokes of their fan-like tail. In shrimps, all the plates of the tail overlap. In prawns, the plates are often sharply angled or humped, and the second plate overlaps both the one behind and the one in front. Shrimps are mainly scavengers. Some kinds are very small and are members of the plankton or live in communities; others measure as much as nine inches in length, not counting the antennae.

Most of the snapping and crackling sounds heard under water or near the sur-face are caused by snapping shrimps. They have a peculiar large claw with plunger and cylinder device. When this is discharged, it makes a noise like a cap-pistol, and it is used by the shrimp to stun small fishes and other animals.

SIDENECK TURTLES differ from all other turtles in the way they withdraw their head. The neck is drawn in sidewise, so that their head fits transversely across their body between the front legs. Sideneck turtles are found only in the Southern Hemisphere. There are two families: the hidden-neck turtles *(Pelomedusidae)*, in which the neck when withdrawn is covered by loose skin; and the snakeneck turtles *(Chelidae)*, in which the neck is not hidden.

Hidden-neck turtles of about a dozen species are found in Madagascar, Africa and South America. One group of African hidden-neck turtles *(Pelusios)* has a hinged plastron, like box turtles, and can close the shell completely. The largest hidden-neck turtle is a South American species of the genus *Podocnemis;* its carapace measures at least 30 inches. The eggs are eaten, and

The Matamata uses its long nose as a snorkel, rising to the surface to breathe with only the tip out of water.

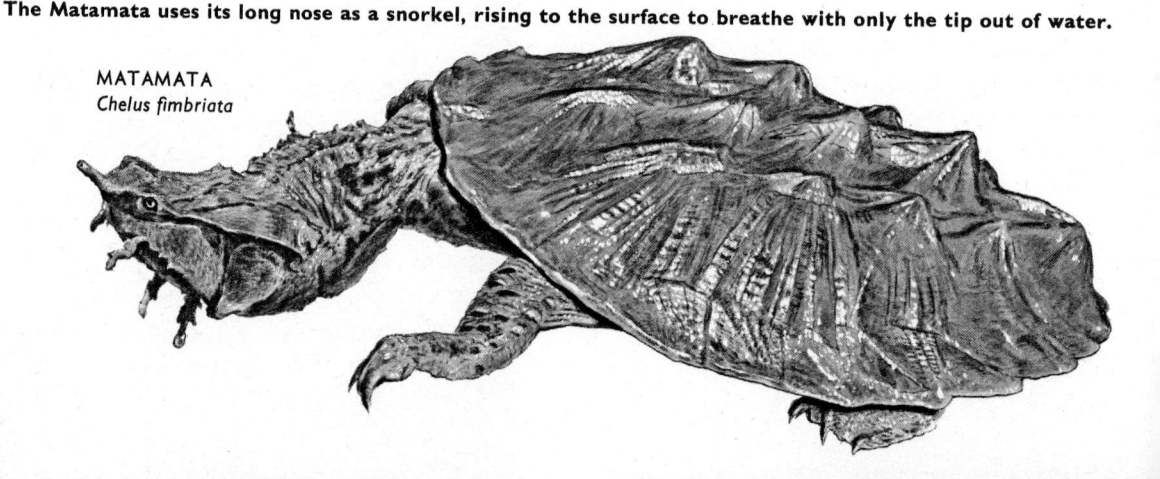

MATAMATA
Chelus fimbriata

both the young and adults are much prized as food. An estimated 50 million eggs of these species were collected every year on islands in the Amazon River.

Snakeneck turtles of about 30 species are found only in South America and Australia. All are small to medium-sized aquatic turtles that seldom come on land except to lay eggs. The most completely aquatic and largest is the bizarre Matamata (*Chelus*) of South America. This 16-inch turtle has an extremely rough, dark shell. The neck and head, as long as or longer than its shell, are very broad and flat, and have slender flaps along the sides. The snout is long and tubular, and the Matamata's tiny eyes are set in a ridge along the side of its head. This turtle feeds largely on small fish, which it captures by suddenly opening its spacious mouth when a fish is near and sucking the hapless prey inside. It then swallows the fish without chewing.

SKINKS of about 650 species form the second largest family of lizards in the world. They are as abundant in Africa and the East Indies as are the iguanids in the Americas. About 50 species occur in the Americas, seven in Europe. Largest is the Zebra Skink, about $2\frac{1}{2}$ feet in length. The Blue-tongued Skink (*Tiliqua*) and Spiny-tailed Skink (*Egernia*), both of Australia, are commonly kept in zoos.

Skinks usually have flat, rounded, tightly overlapping scales, much like fish scales. Each has a small, bony scale inside the outer horny scale. Most skinks are slick and smooth, but in some species the scales have ridges, or "keels", running lengthwise on the scales. In some species, the scales are large enough to be seen with the naked eye; in others they are microscopic. The large scales of the Spiny Skinks (*Tribolonotus*) project from the body. The Australian Shingleback is the most bizarre skink, for it has big, spiny scales, and its body looks like a pine-cone.

The Stump-tailed Skink (*Tiliqua*) has a heavy body, wide head, and short, thick

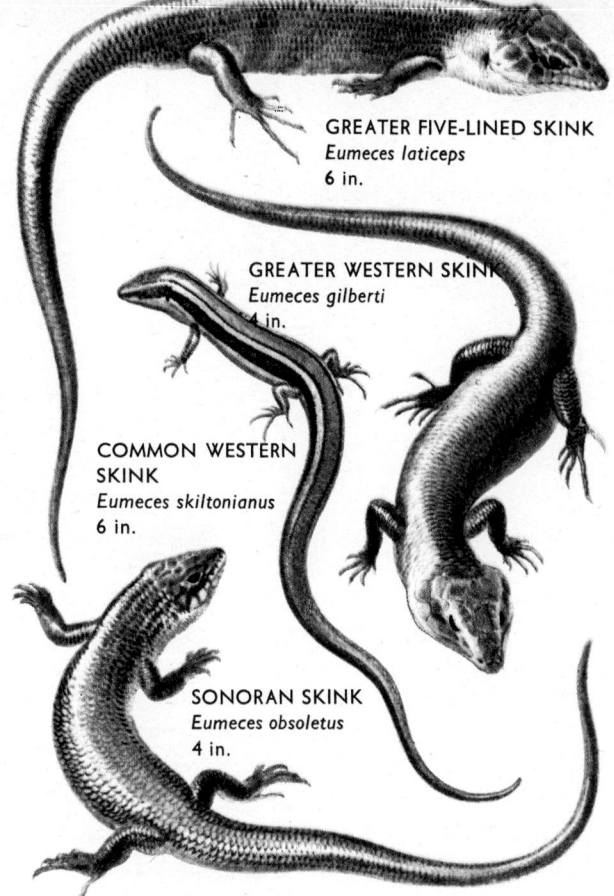

GREATER FIVE-LINED SKINK
Eumeces laticeps
6 in.

GREATER WESTERN SKINK
Eumeces gilberti
4 in.

COMMON WESTERN SKINK
Eumeces skiltonianus
6 in.

SONORAN SKINK
Eumeces obsoletus
4 in.

SOME NORTH AMERICAN SKINKS

tail. All other skinks are slender-bodied and long-tailed. In some the tail is twice as long as the head and body. Most skinks have strong legs; nevertheless, skinks move their bodies with snake-like, sinuous curves. Many kinds move entirely by serpentine movements of body and tail, and the legs, which are not needed, are held tightly against the body. Some kinds have lost their legs completely. The Florida Sand Skink (*Neoseps*) has only one toe on its front legs.

All skinks are secretive, hiding at the slightest sign of danger. Legless varieties, even shyer than the others, are considered burrowers. Legless skinks of one type (*Feylinia*) are found in Africa; another (*Anelytropsis*) in Mexico. Both are whitish, eyeless and earless. They feed on ants and termites in rotting wood on the jungle floor.

Skinks that live in deserts often have flattened snouts and countersunk jaws, adapting them for burrowing and for

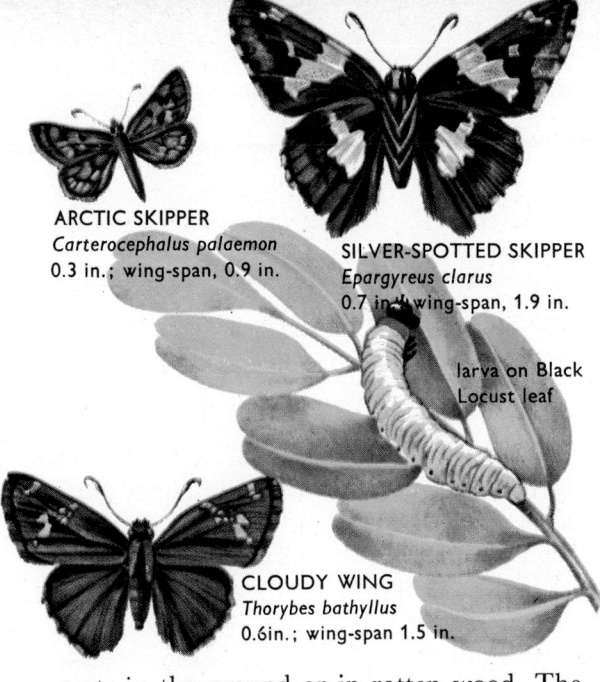

SAND SKINK
Neoseps reynoldsi
2 in.

The Sand Skink, a small lizard with degenerate legs, lives in sandy pine-woods of Florida.

ARCTIC SKIPPER
Carterocephalus palaemon
0.3 in.; wing-span, 0.9 in.

SILVER-SPOTTED SKIPPER
Epargyreus clarus
0.7 in.; wing-span, 1.9 in.

larva on Black
Locust leaf

CLOUDY WING
Thorybes bathyllus
0.6in.; wing-span 1.5 in.

"swimming" in sand. Some of these skins have no legs or only tiny ones; others have short legs and fringed toes — for instance, the Sand Fish *(Scincus)* of Africa and Arabia. Some are almost exclusively tree-dwellers: the Prehensile-tailed Zebra Skink *(Corucia zebrata)* of the Solomon Islands is an example. A few, such as the keeled skinks *(Tropidophorus)* of the East Indies, are highly aquatic.

Many skinks have a transparent scale that forms a window-pane in their lower eyelid. In many, the lower eyelid is fused to the upper one, so that the transparent scale covers the eye, as in snakes.

Most skinks are carnivorous, although the largest skinks are mainly vegetarian. Ceylon skinks *(Nessia)* feed on earthworms. They have long, slender, recurved teeth like snakes, and quite unlike the straight, heavy teeth of most other lizards.

Skinks are variously coloured, but are unable to change colour as can most iguanids, agamids and chameleons. In some species, males develop a reddish head and fight ferociously with other males in the breeding season. In many, there is a change in colour and even pattern between young and adults.

About half the species of skink are egg-layers, laying their 2 to 23 white eggs in

nests in the ground or in rotten wood. The female commonly guards the eggs until they hatch. Other skinks bear their young alive, some having a well-developed placenta, as in mammals (See LIZARDS).

SKIPPERS *(Hesperiidae)* are a distinctive group of butterflies of about 2,500 species. Their antennae are knobbed, as are those of other butterflies, but there is a curved hook beyond the knobbed portion. Also, a skipper's body is stout — more like the body of a moth, rather than slender like a butterfly's. Its wings are relatively small and pointed. Skippers fly rapidly, darting about from flower to flower, seldom in a straight line. Their name comes from this erratic flight. Their caterpillars have large heads and smooth bodies, narrowed abruptly just behind the head. These caterpillars usually live in a folded leaf or in a shelter made of leaves bound together with silk, or inside stems or fruit of plants.

The Bean Leaf Roller is a dark brown skipper with silver spots on its front wings; part of its body and wings are blue-green. With the long tails on its hind wings, this skipper resembles a swallowtail butterfly. Its caterpillars feed on the leaves of many plants, after rolling them into tight cylinders.

Most skippers are small, but members of one group — the giant skippers — may have

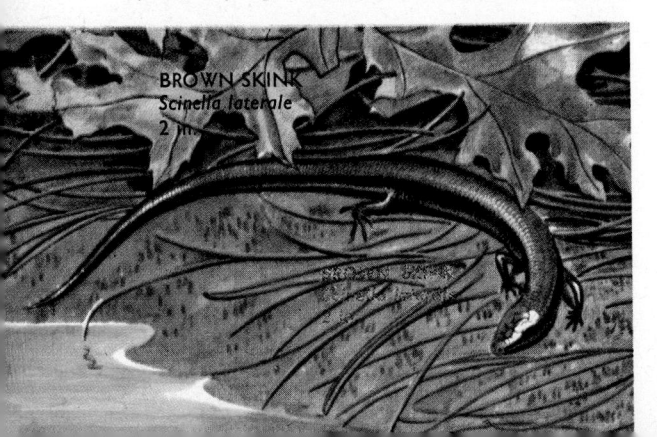

BROWN SKINK
Scincella laterale
2 in.

wing-spans of three inches. They also lack the curved hook on their antennae. Caterpillars of giant skippers bore into the stems of yucas and related plants.

SKUNKS are famed for their unique protection — a potent, foul smell — the fluid from large scent-glands under the tail. They can eject this fluid for a considerable

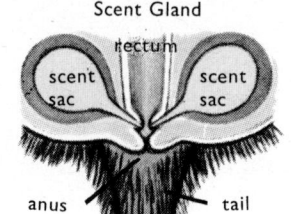

Scent Gland

Acrid scent, produced by the glands under its tail, is a skunk's best defence against enemies.

distance. These black and white carnivores will stamp their feet, hiss, and raise their tails to warn intruders. If an intruder is not frightened, the skunk squirts out the scent. Skunks are found only in the New World. Their scent-glands are better developed than those of any other members of the weasel family, to which they belong. Skunks feed on small rodents, insects, birds' eggs, and sometimes on plant material.

The Striped Skunk *(Mephitis mephitis)* measures as much as 40 inches in length. A white stripe on its head usually divides into two stripes that run along its back, all the way to its tail. Sometimes the white stripes on its back are short or absent. The Striped Skunk lives along the edge of forests, in thickets, in open meadows, or in abandoned burrows of other animals. It feeds at night. The young of Striped Skunks are blind and helpless at birth.

The Spotted Skunk, or Civet Cat *(Spilogale spp.)*, smallest of the skunks, has stripes broken into short white lines. When warning intruders, this skunk may stand on its front legs, holding its back erect and waving its white-tipped tail. This peculiar hand-stand posture sometimes frightens enemies away, and the skunks do not then emit their odour. Spotted skunks range from Central America to the central United States. Because they sometimes have rabies, once known as hydro-

phobia, they are also called phoby cats.

Hog-nosed skunks *(Conepatus spp.)* have long claws on their front feet and a long, partially bare snout, somewhat like that of a hog. With this they root in the ground for insects and worms. A broad band of white runs from the head down the back to the white tail. As large as the Striped Skunk, they are found from the southern United States to South America. The Hooded Skunk *(Mephitis macroura)* is similar in colour pattern to the Striped Skunk.

STRIPED SKUNK
to 40 in.
North America

LITTLE SPOTTED SKUNK
to 22 in.
North America, south of Canada

HOG-NOSED SKUNK
to 28 in.
Mexico and
border U. S. states

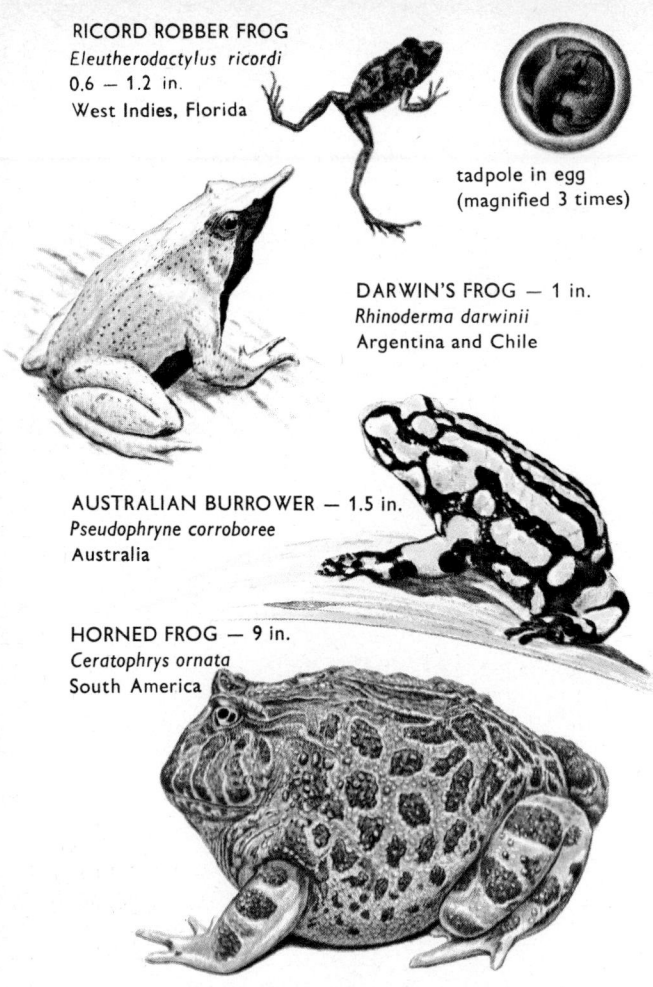

RICORD ROBBER FROG
Eleutherodactylus ricordi
0.6 — 1.2 in.
West Indies, Florida

tadpole in egg
(magnified 3 times)

DARWIN'S FROG — 1 in.
Rhinoderma darwinii
Argentina and Chile

AUSTRALIAN BURROWER — 1.5 in.
Pseudophryne corroboree
Australia

HORNED FROG — 9 in.
Ceratophrys ornata
South America

SLENDER-TOED FROGS, of the family Leptodactylidae, are a large and varied group with representatives in Australia, southern Africa, and tropical America. Many are not slender-toed, however.

Most Australian species are small land-dwelling forms without webbed feet. A few kinds live in water and have fully-webbed feet; others *(Notaden)* are bottle-bellied burrowers that spend their lives in arid or semi-arid regions.

These bulbous, desert-dwelling types fill themselves with water and remain deep under the ground during the long dry season. When in need of water, wise travellers are said to dig these frogs from their burrows and quench their thirst with the fluid stored in the frogs.

A few African species of this group live in swift mountain streams. They hang on to rocks by adhesive discs at the tips of their fingers and toes; their tadpoles anchor

themselves by sucker discs on their bellies. Most members of the family — the "true" slender-toed frogs — inhabit Central and South America, and the West Indies. One large species, living on the islands of Dominica and Montserrat, is greatly esteemed for its food value and is called the Mountain Chicken. Most of these frogs lay their eggs in small depressions near water. They beat the jelly surrounding the eggs into an airy foam. When water rises and reaches the egg mass, it floats on the surface. The tadpoles swim free as soon as they hatch.

Closely related to the "true" slender-toed frogs are the robber frogs. One *(Syrrhophus)* is found mainly in Mexico, but also ranges into New Mexico and Texas. It has a call that sounds like a weak whistle. Another *(Eleutherodactylus)* is widely distributed in the West Indies, Central and South America, and also in Florida, New Mexico and Texas.

The Horned Frog *(Ceratophrys)*, found in South America, is a giant among present-day amphibians. About nine inches long, it has a mouth a third the size of its body. The Horned Frog hides on the jungle floor, waiting for any animal small enough for it to swallow. It can easily take mice, small snakes or birds. When handled, it bites and can draw blood. In its upper jaw it has real teeth; in its lower jaw, tooth-like projections.

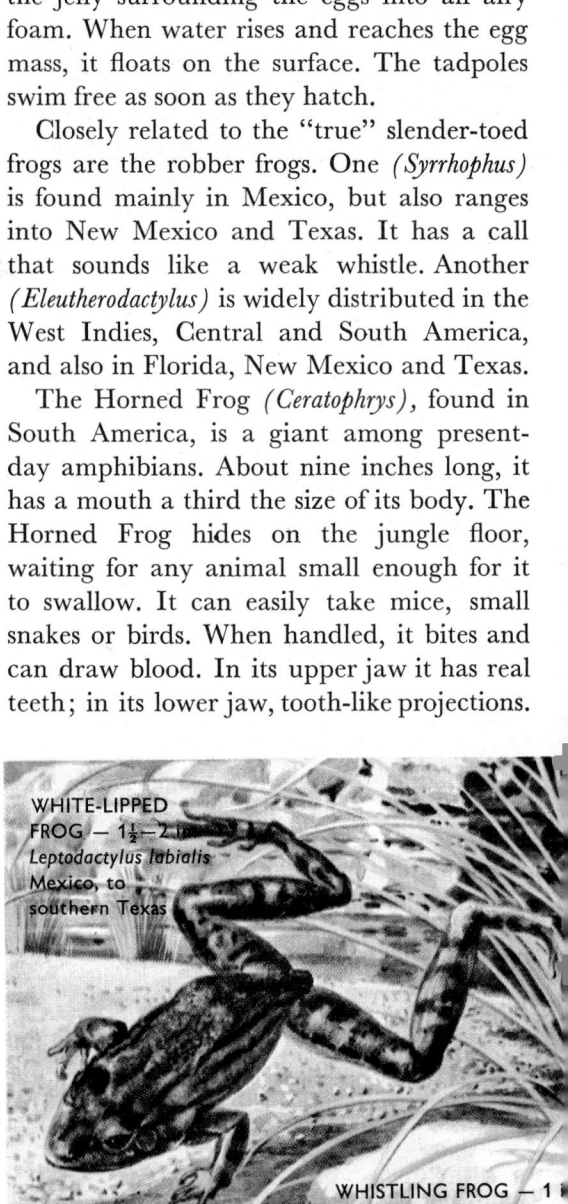

WHITE-LIPPED
FROG — 1½ — 2 in.
Leptodactylus labialis
Mexico, to
southern Texas

WHISTLING FROG — 1 in.
Syrrhophus marnocki
Mexico to southern U. S.

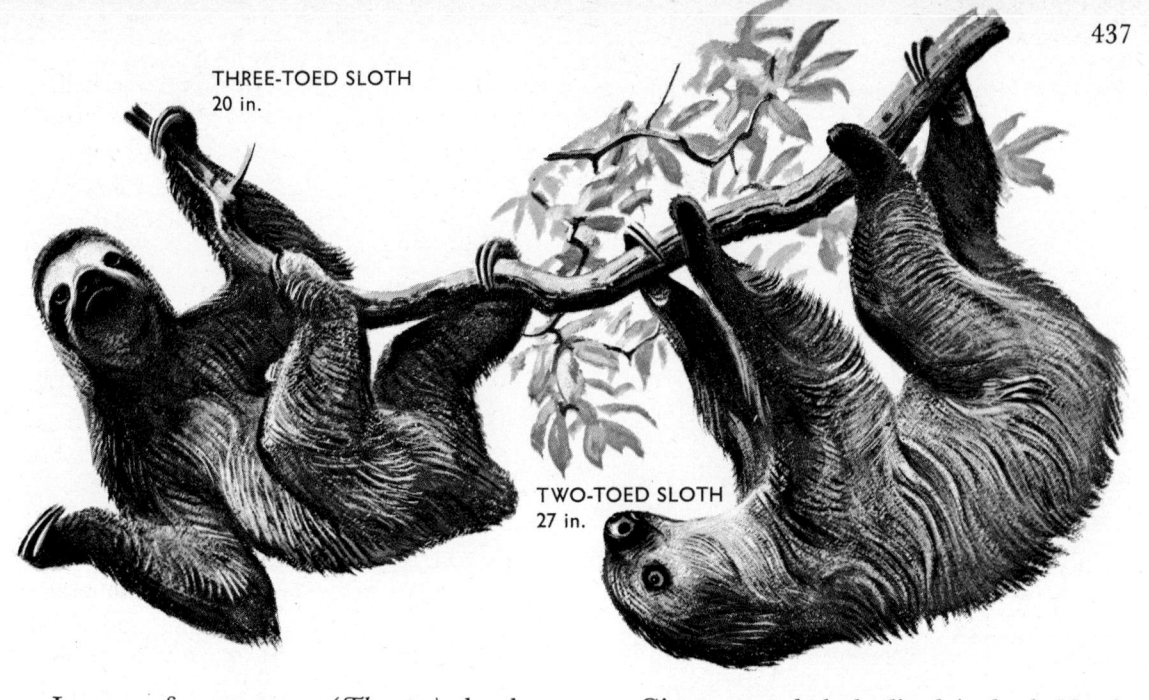

THREE-TOED SLOTH
20 in.

TWO-TOED SLOTH
27 in.

Larvae of one genus *(Thoropa)* develop entirely out of water, slithering around on mossy, wet stones with their mouth discs.

Darwin's Frog *(Rhinoderma)* is an inch-long frog that lives in South America. Males carry the eggs in their over-sized vocal pouches, which extend under the skin of their belly to the hind legs. The eggs hatch and the larvae develop in these pouches, finally emerging from the male's mouth as fully transformed froglets.

SLOTHS are sluggish, hairy mammals native to the tropical forests of Central and South America. They are tree-dwellers, feeding on leaves, and even sleeping while hanging upside down from the branch of a tree. Their coarse, straw-like fur frequently supports growths of algae, which gives sloths a greenish look — especially during the wet seasons of the year. The hair of most mammals parts along the middle of their backs and grows down their sides, but sloths have lived upside down so long that their hair parts on their stomachs and hangs down over their backs. The Two-toed Sloth *(Choloepus* spp.) has two toes on its front feet; the Three-toed Sloth *(Bradypus tridactylus)* has three. Both sloths have long, heavy, powerful claws with which they hang on to branches.

Giant ground sloths lived in both North and South America during late Cenozoic times. They were ungainly animals, some of them reaching a length of 20 feet. Both the front and hind legs were clawed, and they probably walked at times on their strong hind feet. Ground sloths probably ate plants. They became extinct fairly recently, and undoubtedly lived with early man in North America. Their remains have been found as mummies in caves of arid regions.

SLOW-WORMS *(Anguis)* are limbless, smooth, cylindrical lizards, usually chestnut brown in colour; the female differs from the male in having a smaller head and dark stripes down the body. Occasionally, blue-spotted males are found. The Slow-worm occurs in a wide variety of habitats, from woodland to gardens and heaths, throughout Europe and western Asia; it bears its young alive. It feeds mainly on white slugs and insects. A slow-worm in captivity reached an age of 54 years, a record for any lizard.

SLOW-WORM
Anguis fragilis
15—20 in.

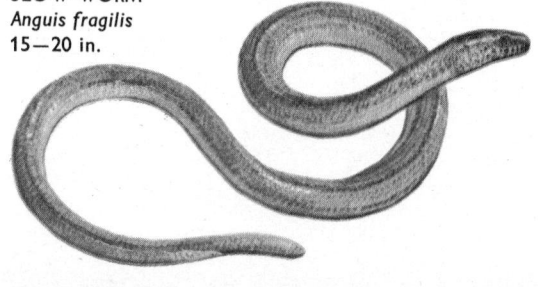

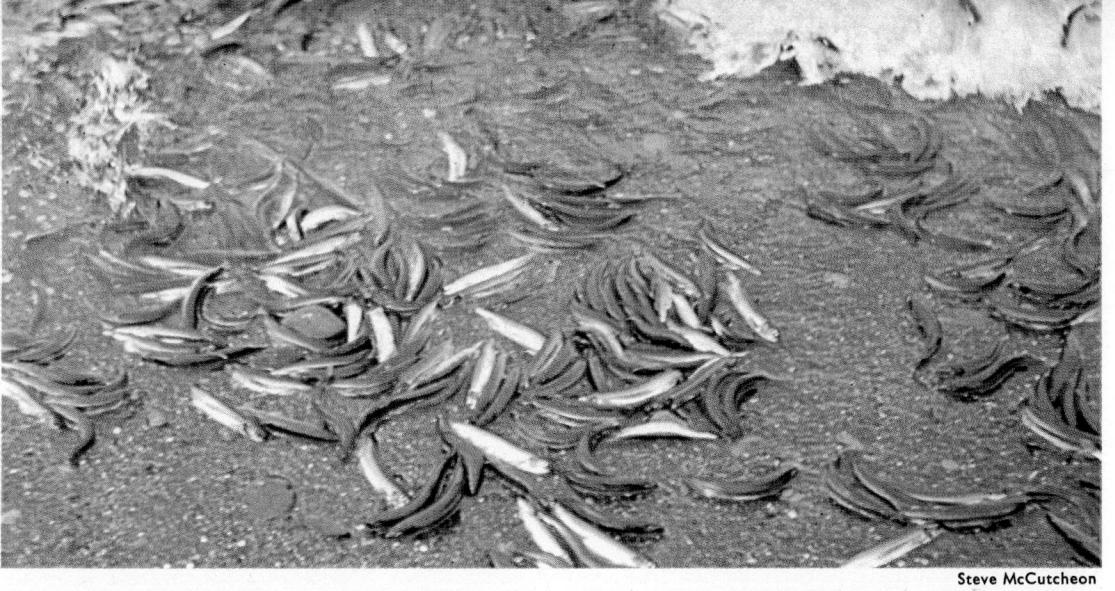

Steve McCutcheon

Eulachons *(Thaleichthys pacificus),* **slender, 12-inch smelts common in the coastal waters from northern California to Alaska, are an important food of salmon and seals. They enter the rivers in large numbers in spring to spawn.**

SMELTS are small, silvery fishes (family Osmeridae) related to trouts and salmons. About a dozen species are known, all from the colder waters of the Northern Hemisphere. They can be distinguished from the Silversides (also called smelts) by the fatty adipose fin behind the dorsal fin.

The European Smelt, or Sparling *(Osmerus eperlanus),* is an anadromous species — that is to say it migrates from the sea into fresh water to spawn. It ranges from the Seine to the Baltic and is a valuable economic species. Freshly caught, the Smelt has an odour of cucumbers.

The American Smelt *(Osmerus mordax)* is found along the American Atlantic coast, and is also an anadromous species.

One of the largest of the smelts is the Candlefish *(Thaleichthys pacificus),* which reaches a foot in length. It is found along the American Pacific coasts, and is so oily that American Indians used to tie dry candlefishes to sticks to make torches.

SNAILS, or Gastropods, are molluscs that have a long body, a broad, muscular foot, and a distinct head region that bears a pair of eyes and a pair of tentacles. Their mouth has a long, rasping "tongue" called a radula,

ANATOMY OF A SNAIL (GASTROPOD)

vent · intestine · heart · kidney · sperm duct · liv · tentacle · blo · ves · eye · test · stomac · operculu · mouth · esophagus · gill · mantle cavity · muscular foot

used to scrape food from the surfaces of plants or rocks, or for boring. Snails breathe by means of "lungs", or gills. Some live on the sea floor; others in the open ocean. Some live in fresh water; others on land. Sea slugs and garden slugs are snails that lack shells. Most snails, however, are covered by a spirally-coiled shell. A snail can withdraw inside its shell for protection, and some can close the opening by means of a small, hard plate, the operculum, attached to the foot. In some, the operculum is made of shell, in others of horn.

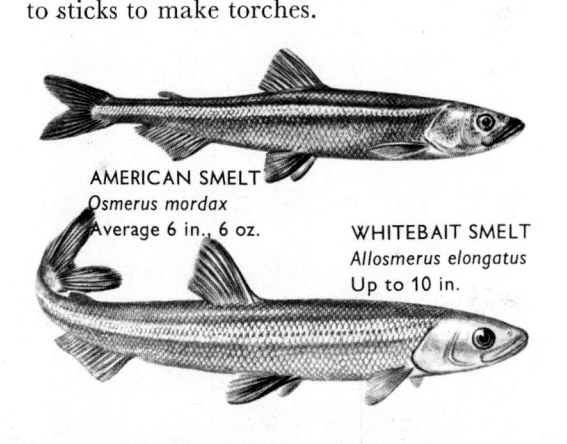

AMERICAN SMELT
Osmerus mordax
Average 6 in., 6 oz.

WHITEBAIT SMELT
Allosmerus elongatus
Up to 10 in.

Besides being much sought after by shell-collectors, who prize their rich variety of shapes and their bright colours, some gastropods are in large demand for food. The Queen Conch is a staple food in the West Indies. Nerites are often eaten, especially in the Mediterranean. Whelks are prized in England; abalones in California and the Orient; and garden snails are epicurean delights in France.

SNAKES of some 2,700 species form a group of reptiles almost as large as lizards. Each of these two groups outnumbers all other reptiles. Snakes belong to the suborder Serpentes in the order Squamata, which also contains lizards (sub-order Sauria).

Snakes are believed to have evolved from burrowing lizards. They first appeared in the fossil record in the upper Cretaceous period, some 80 million years ago (Lizards are known from the upper Jurassic period,

about 130 million years ago.). Snakes do not have legs, movable eyelids, external ear-openings, eardrums, or middle-ear cavities. The two halves of their lower jaw are joined by a ligament at the chin. No single external feature, however, is unique to either snakes or lizards. Many lizards, for example, do not have legs and also lack ears, and some snakes have stubs of hind legs or, internally, the bony girdles for their attachment.

A snake's scales are its most useful identification feature. In some groups, the scales on the head are small; in others they are large or irregular in size. Scales on the belly are called ventrals and are usually wide; the other body scales are called dorsals and are small. There are exceptions in which all the scales over the body are small (see WART SNAKES; BLIND SNAKES; SEA SNAKES.). In most snakes, the approximately diamond-shaped scales in each dorsal row alternate with those of adjacent rows. The

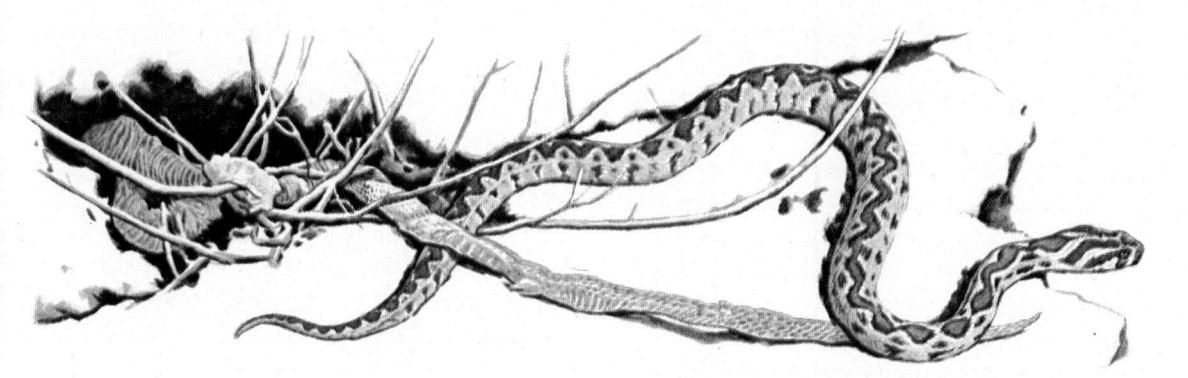

Before shedding, the outer skin of a snake is composed of dead cells. As it peels away, the bright fresh colours of the new skin beneath it are exposed.

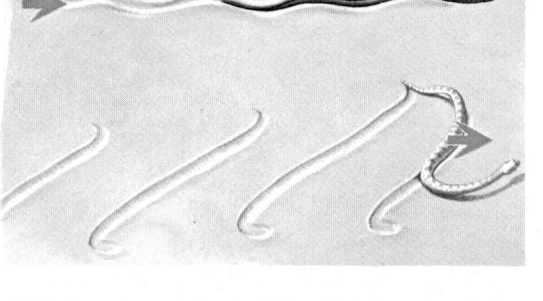

Most common movement of snakes is a serpentine wiggle of S-shaped waves that speeds the snake forwards as the waves pass backwards. A rarer movement is the sidewinder action of some rattlers, producing J-shaped tracks as only two parts of the snake's body touch the ground at any time.

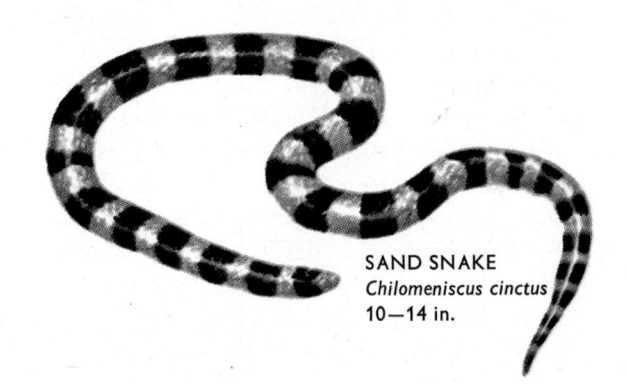

SAND SNAKE
Chilomeniscus cinctus
10—14 in.

WART SNAKE
Acrochordus javanicus

SHOVEL-NOSED SNAKE
Chionactis occipitalis
12—16 in.

number of longitudinal rows varies from 13 to about 150. Wart snakes have the most rows, since their scales are very small. In snakes with tapered bodies, the number of scale rows decreases towards both head and tail. In those with cylindrical bodies, such as coral snakes, the number is the same throughout the length of the body.

Scales under the tail are called caudals. They may be small like the dorsals, or may occur in two rows (divided), or be broad like the ventrals (undivided or entire). Their number is often important in identifying related species. In all snakes with large ventral and caudal scales, each scale corresponds exactly with one of the vertebrae. A species averaging 100 ventral scales might have a total range of from 93 to 108 ventrals. A small cone-shaped scale caps the end of the tail. This is never associated with poison, nor used as a spine or spur in combat, but is often used to assist the snake in burrowing.

Dorsal scales on both body and tail may be smooth or have a median, longitudinal ridge (keel); the free edge may be rounded or notched. In some kinds of snakes, each scale bears one or two tiny pits, usually visible only with the aid of a lens.

Male and female snakes generally look alike. In only a few species is there a difference between male and female in colour and pattern (see ADDERS). Males almost always have a longer tail and more caudal scales than females. Females usually have a longer body and more ventral scales. The total number of scales is about the same in both sexes, however. In some groups, such as water snakes, there are numerous tiny pits on the scales beneath the male's head. Some Madagascar tree snakes have a scaly projection on the snout, which is longer in the female and somewhat different in form. This, too, may be used in courtship.

Snakes feed almost exclusively on living animals or eggs. A few kinds will eat dead animals, or can be trained to do so in captivity. Snakes catch their food with the mouth and swallow it whole. Their loosely-hung jaws and flexible skin make it possible for them to swallow animals even larger in diameter than their own body. Most kinds start swallowing as soon as they catch their prey; often the prey is still struggling when it is in the snake's gullet. If the prey is an animal such as a horned lizard or a catfish, spines can puncture the snake's body wall; in most cases, this is fatal to the snake.

Some snakes use their body to hold down lengthy or struggling prey. Constrictors tighten coils of their body about the prey until it is dead. Giant boas and pythons do not "crush" their prey — they suffocate it.

Another specialised technique for killing prey is with poison, a modified saliva secreted by glands in the upper jaw. Species in five snake families have enough toxin in their saliva to be called poisonous or venomous (see COLUBRID SNAKES; CORAL SNAKES; SEA SNAKES; VIPERS). Venom is the liquid that contains the poison. The poison is always injected into the victim by hollow or grooved teeth. Some snakes hang on to their prey until their venom takes effect; this is especially true of snakes that have weak venom or short fangs, and that feed on prey, such as birds, that might escape if released. Those that have strong venom and long fangs ordinarily release their prey as soon as it is bitten, then track it down by scent as it dies.

Fangs of poisonous snakes are of three sorts. Rear fangs, as in colubrid poisonous snakes (see COLUBRID SNAKES), are not movable, and usually occur one to four on

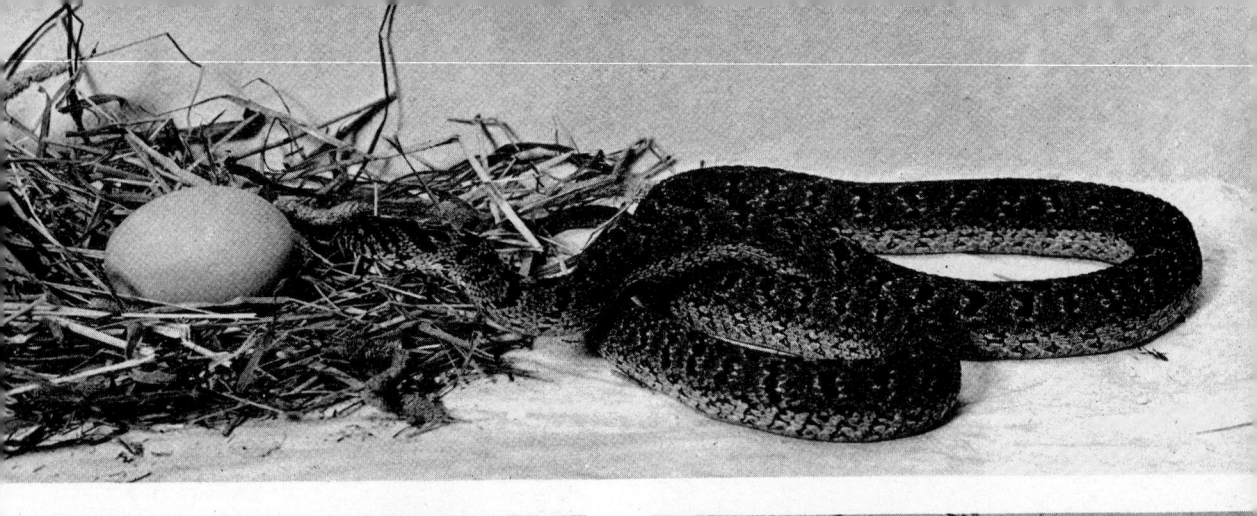

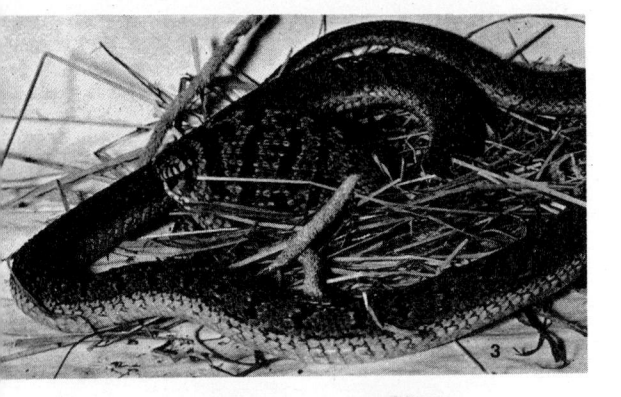

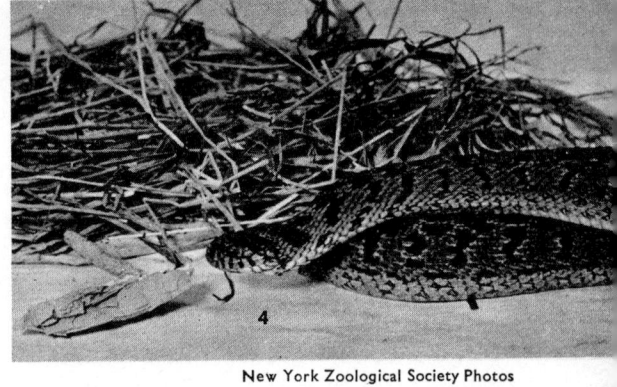

New York Zoological Society Photos

In the series of pictures above and to the left, a three-foot African Egg-eating Snake (*Dasypeltis scaber*) approaches an egg (1), which it is about to eat. The snake disjoints its jaw (2) and stretches its throat to swallow the egg. When the egg is completely contained (3), the snake constricts its powerful neck muscles; then bony projections on the neck vertebrae slice into the egg, which collapses. The contents of the egg flow into the snake's stomach, where they are digested. Meanwhile, the snake squeezes the last of the liquid from the shell, then ejects the remnants of its feast from its mouth (4). In the wild, this snake is primarily nocturnal.

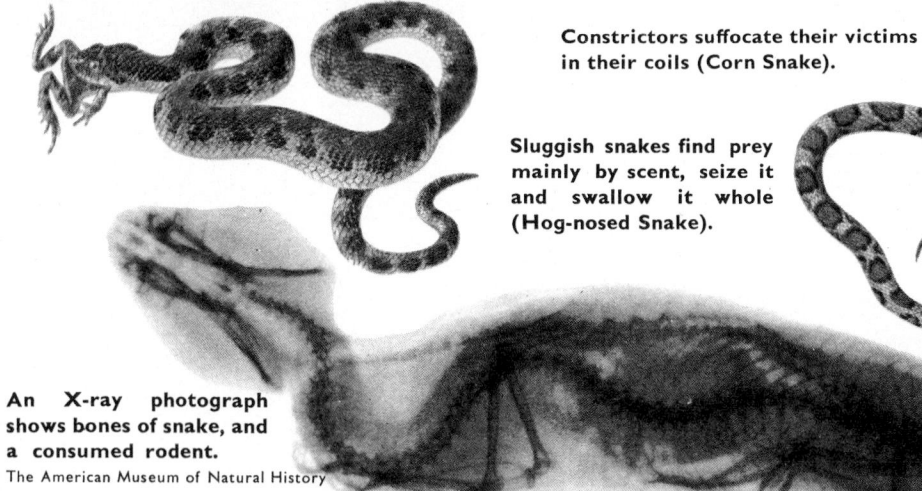

Constrictors suffocate their victims in their coils (Corn Snake).

Sluggish snakes find prey mainly by scent, seize it and swallow it whole (Hog-nosed Snake).

An X-ray photograph shows bones of snake, and a consumed rodent.

The American Museum of Natural History

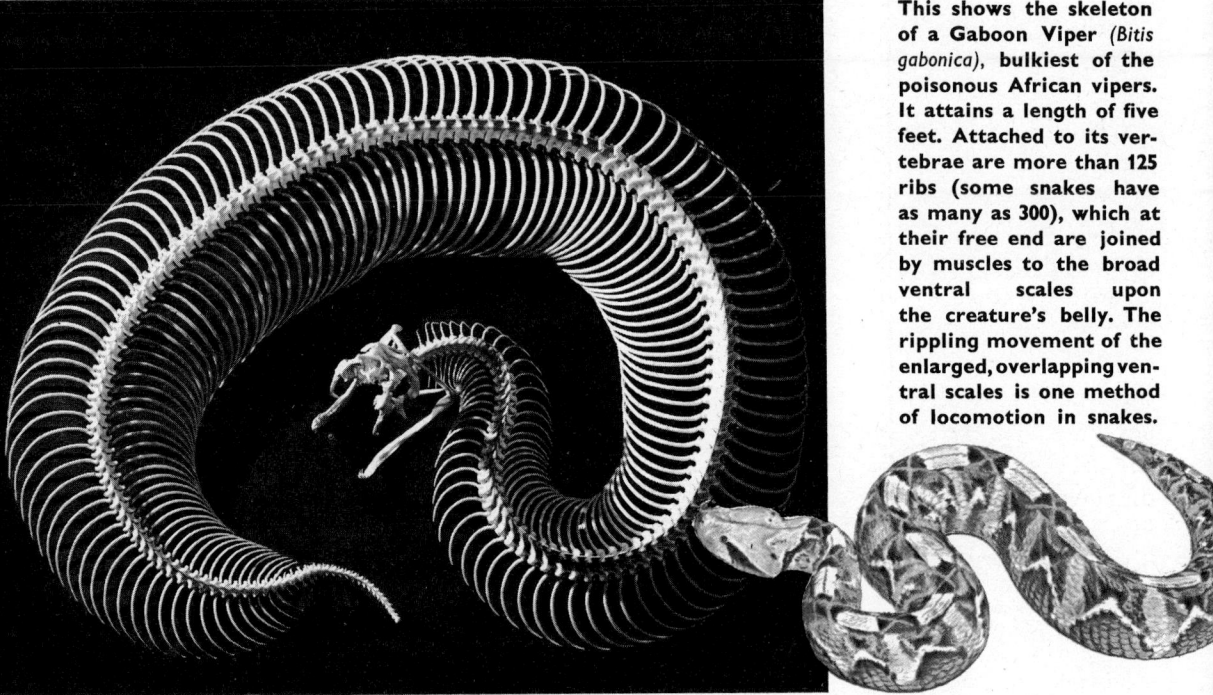

This shows the skeleton of a Gaboon Viper (*Bitis gabonica*), bulkiest of the poisonous African vipers. It attains a length of five feet. Attached to its vertebrae are more than 125 ribs (some snakes have as many as 300), which at their free end are joined by muscles to the broad ventral scales upon the creature's belly. The rippling movement of the enlarged, overlapping ventral scales is one method of locomotion in snakes.

The American Museum of Natural History

each side. These short fangs have on their front edge a deep groove, down which the venom flows into the bite. All vipers have one pair of large, movable fangs located at the front of the mouth. These fangs swing down, or even a little forward, when the mouth is opened. When the mouth closes, the fangs swing back into place (see VIPERS). Sea snakes, kraits, cobras, mambas and coral snakes have a third type: short, immovable fangs at the front of the mouth.

Snake venoms have one of two effects. Viper venoms affect the blood and the circulatory system (haematoxic). Most others affect the nervous system (neurotoxic).

Snakes find their prey in various ways, but among the most useful structures are the pit organs of pit vipers and certain boas (see BOAS; VIPERS). These pits are very sensitive heat-detectors, with which these nocturnal snakes can detect their prey at a distance.

Snakes do not have good vision, but even slight movements attract their attention. Racers rely on movement to find their prey. A motionless animal can escape detection, unless the snake comes close enough to locate it by its body heat. The snake's tongue plays an important role in detecting odours. More sluggish snakes rely almost exclusively on scent. A water snake will try to swallow anything — even itself — if smeared with the odorous secretion of a frog or a fish.

Snakes shed the outer dead layer of their skin at least once, and often three or four times, a year. The number of times they shed depends on the species and its physical condition, not on its rate of growth. An injury to the skin also stimulates more frequent shedding. The cast skin (slough) is turned back at the tip of the snout and pushed off the body, wrong side out. The snake rubs against rocks or other objects to help get the skin off.

Snakes either hatch from eggs or are born alive. Broods or clutches range from three or four to about a hundred. Snakes grow rapidly for a few seasons. Small snakes mature in one or two years; medium-sized snakes in three or four years; large snakes in five or six years. Growth continues slowly throughout life. The maximum age recorded for a snake is 28 years. Record size is about 37 feet, for the South American Giant

Anaconda, which may even exceed this length by 10 feet.

Snakes move by one of four different mechanisms, or a combination of these methods. Most commonly they wriggle their body from side to side in S-shaped waves that start at the front end of the body and move to the rear. The body is pushed forward whenever it catches on irregularities in the surface. On a smooth surface, snakes can move only very slowly by this "serpentine" movement. The "concertina" method, next most frequently used, involves hitching one part of the body forward in loops, while the remainder of the body remains anchored. "Rectilinear" locomotion is possible only in such heavy-bodied snakes as vipers, which

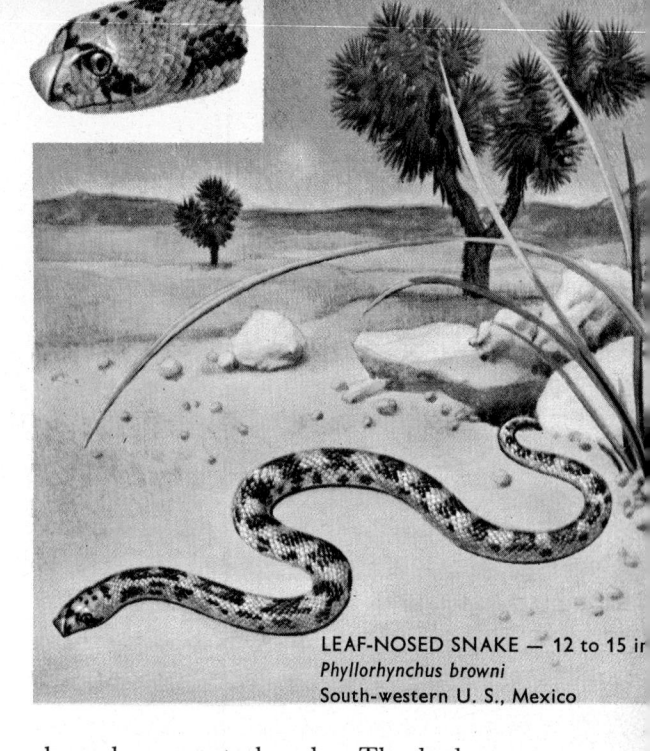

LEAF-NOSED SNAKE — 12 to 15 in
Phyllorhynchus browni
South-western U. S., Mexico

Two male Red Diamondback Rattlesnakes (*Crotalus ruber*) **engage in a combat dance, a common habit of male snakes of many species. The snakes exhaust themselves in sparring, but neither is harmed. This activity is not well understood.**

Pat Kirkpatrick from National Audubon Society

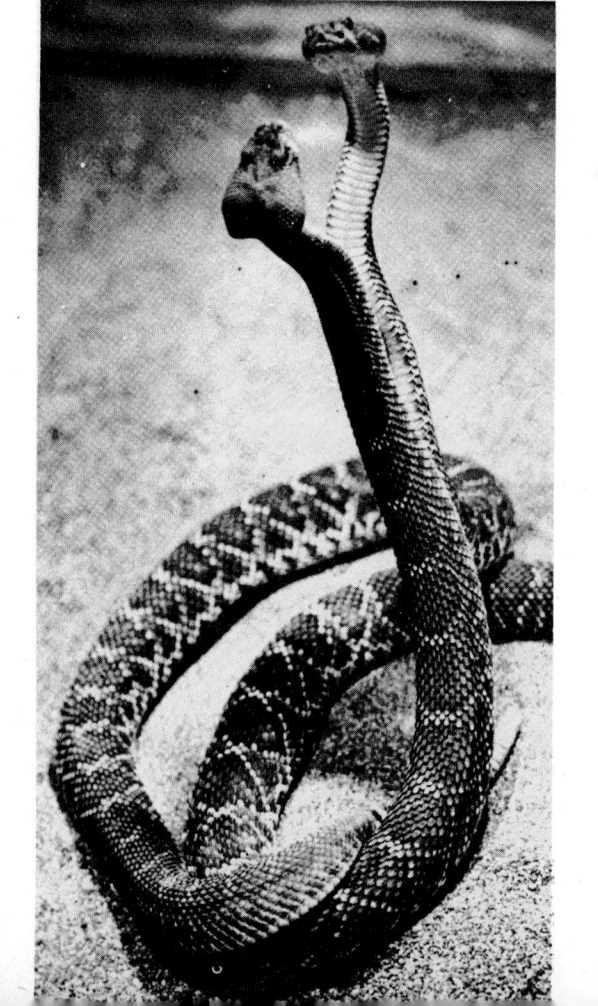

have large ventral scales. The body moves forward very slowly in a straight line, as the ventral scales move in waves over the ends of the ribs. Rarest of all is the "sidewinding" locomotion of the Horned Viper of North Africa and a Horned Rattlesnake, or Sidewinder, of south-western North America. Both live in loose sands where other types of locomotion would not be possible.

There are many mistaken beliefs about snakes — here are some of the facts. Snakes do not charm or hypnotise enemies or prey. No snake can roll like a hoop, and none can blow poisonous vapour. No snakes can "sting" with their tail, nor does any snake have a poisonous tongue. Snakes never milk cows. Mother snakes do not swallow their young to protect them. Snakes will crawl over a horsehair rope as readily as any other, and they can bite underwater. Snakes do not lick their prey before swallowing it, although the prey may be smelled with the tongue. No snake can break into pieces, as the glass-snake myth implies; and no matter how long its body or tail, a snake never uses it like a whip. Rattlesnakes do not add one button per year to their rattle. Sometimes snakes occur in pairs, but not regularly. Snakes do not wait for sundown to die.

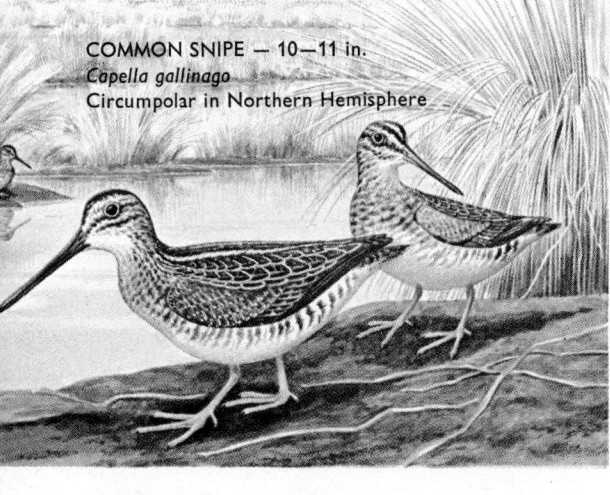

COMMON SNIPE — 10—11 in.
Capella gallinago
Circumpolar in Northern Hemisphere

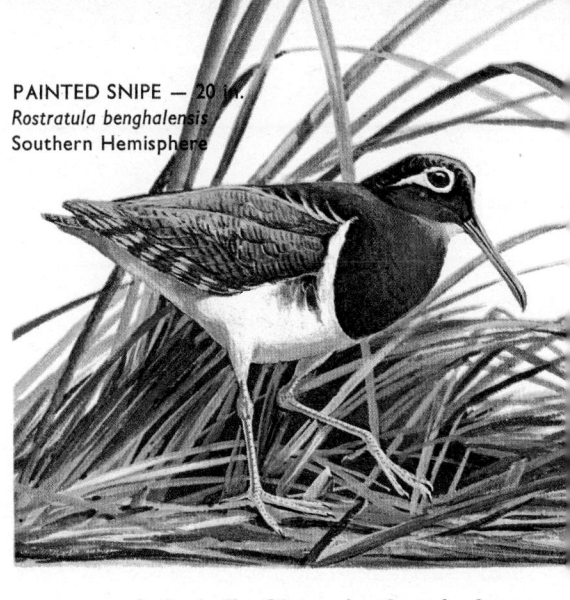

PAINTED SNIPE — 20 in.
Rostratula benghalensis
Southern Hemisphere

SNIPE Marsh birds, cousins of sandpipers, curlews, woodcocks and plovers. They sometimes nest away from water on uplands or mountain meadows, and sometimes on marshes. They feign injury, like plovers, to lead intruders from their nest. In courtship flights, they rise and then plunge down, their outer tail feathers making a bleating sound while flying. Snipe are game birds, loved by hunters because their zigzag flight is so swift and erratic that only a skilful shot can hit one. Painted Snipe are unrelated, but are similar in appearance to the Common Snipe.

SOFT-SHELL CLAMS (*Mya* spp.) are bivalved molluscs that live in shallow sand and mud-flats of the North Atlantic. The common Soft-shell Clam is found from Labrador to North Carolina, along the north-east coast of North America, and has been introduced at several locations on the Pacific Coast. The Truncate Soft-shell Clam is a more northerly species, found most commonly off Greenland and Iceland.

The Soft-shell Clam, also called Long-necked Clam or Steamer, is considered a delicacy, and commercial harvesting reached the total of 12 million clams in the peak year of 1935. The clams can be located in tidal flats at low water, when they react to approaching footsteps by squirting a jet of water into the air as they burrow deeper into the sand. They are dug from the sand or mud with clam rakes, and are eaten fried, steamed, or made into clam chowder (see MOLLUSCS).

SOFT-SHELLED TURTLES always have an elongated neck which is adapted for rapid contraction. The fore-limbs are paddle-shaped, and the snout is long and tubular, with the nostrils situated at the tip and the eyes on the top of the head, so that the minimum amount of the head is exposed when the animal surfaces or is browsing in the mud. Thoroughly aquatic in habits, soft-shelled turtles occur in rivers, canals, marshes and ponds, and come on shore only to bask in the sun and to lay their eggs. They are extremely active and quick in their movements in the water, but on land

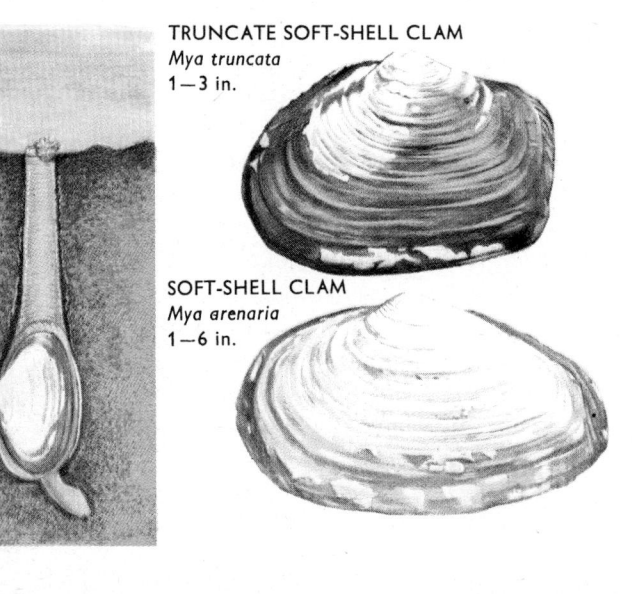

TRUNCATE SOFT-SHELL CLAM
Mya truncata
1—3 in.

SOFT-SHELL CLAM
Mya arenaria
1—6 in.

they are clumsy. Instead of hard plates over their flat, pancake-like shells, soft-shelled turtles have a soft skin which is thick and leathery around the edges of the shell.

Only one kind of soft-shelled turtle occurs in America *(Trionyx)*, the remainder belonging to Africa and Asia. Two African genera and one Asian have valve-like flaps on the plastron, under which the hind limbs can be concealed *(Cyclanorbis, Cycloderma* and *Lissemys)*.

Soft-shells often bury themselves in mud or sand. Frequently they submerge in water shallow enough for their long necks and snorkel-like snouts to reach the surface for breathing. In this position they seem to feel secure. Soft-shells can refrain from surfacing to breathe for perhaps longer than any other turtles. They definitely do obtain oxygen from water, but not with gills as fish do. They pump water into and out of their mouth and throat, the exchange of gases taking place through numerous blood vessels in the thin lining of these cavities. When hibernating, they bury in mud under water and do not breathe for weeks at a time.

The soft-shelled turtles eat insects, cray-

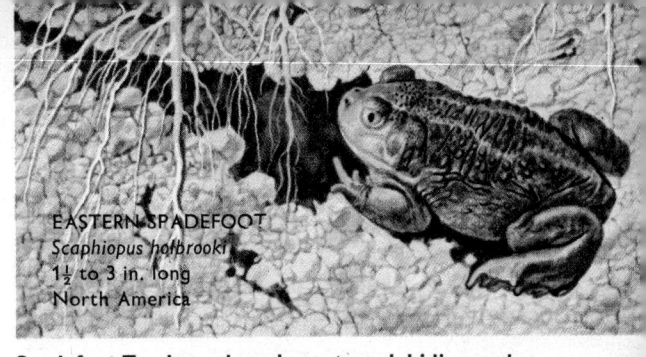

EASTERN SPADEFOOT
Scaphiopus holbrooki
1½ to 3 in. long
North America

Spadefoot Toads are largely nocturnal, hiding under rocks and fallen logs during the day.

fish, clams, fish and frogs. A small part of their diet consists of plants and carrion.

To compensate for their lack of bony armour, these turtles protect themselves by biting repeatedly and viciously, even after long periods in captivity. Their necks are so long and flexible that it is difficult to grasp them where they cannot either bite or claw. Their meat is quite tasty.

Soft-shells lay their eggs in spring and early summer, in nests dug in open sandy banks. The nests are flask-shaped hollows, narrow at the top and about six inches in diameter below. As many as about two-dozen spherical, brittle-shelled eggs, about an inch in diameter, are laid in each nest. The eggs hatch in about two months. Males have a distinctly longer and more fleshy tail than females (See TURTLES.).

SPADEFOOT TOADS of North America *(Scaphiopus* and *Spea)*, and of Asia and Europe *(Pelobates)*, have a black, sharp-edged projection on the inner side of each foot. These are used like spades for digging burrows. The toads shuffle into the ground backwards, shoving the dirt from beneath them, first with one spade, then the other.

This group apparently developed in arid or semi-arid regions, but a few species now live in areas where rainfall is plentiful. Like their ancestors, they are secretive burrowers.

Spadefoot toads breed only after hard rains, no matter what the time of year. A chorus of their loud voices can be heard for miles. Their tadpoles develop in a week, before temporary rain pools dry up.

A group that lives in tropical rain-forests of southern Asia, and nearby islands of the East Indies, do not have spades on their feet.

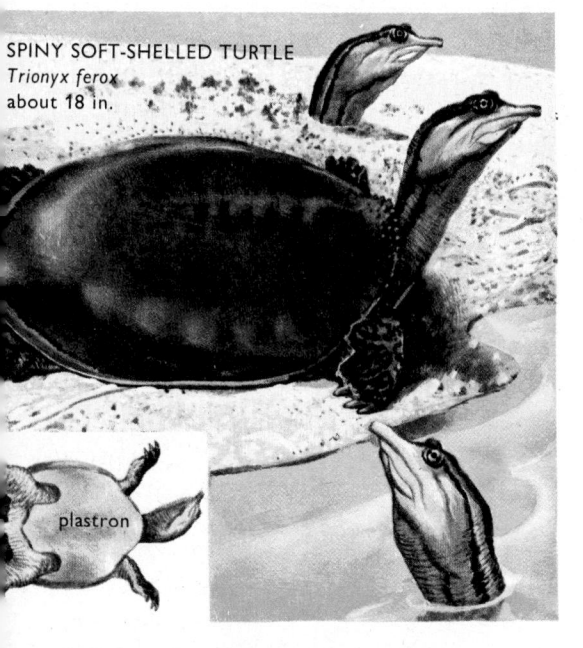

SPINY SOFT-SHELLED TURTLE
Trionyx ferox
about 18 in.

plastron

Soft-shelled Turtles are bad-tempered and can inflict deep wounds with their sharp beaks.

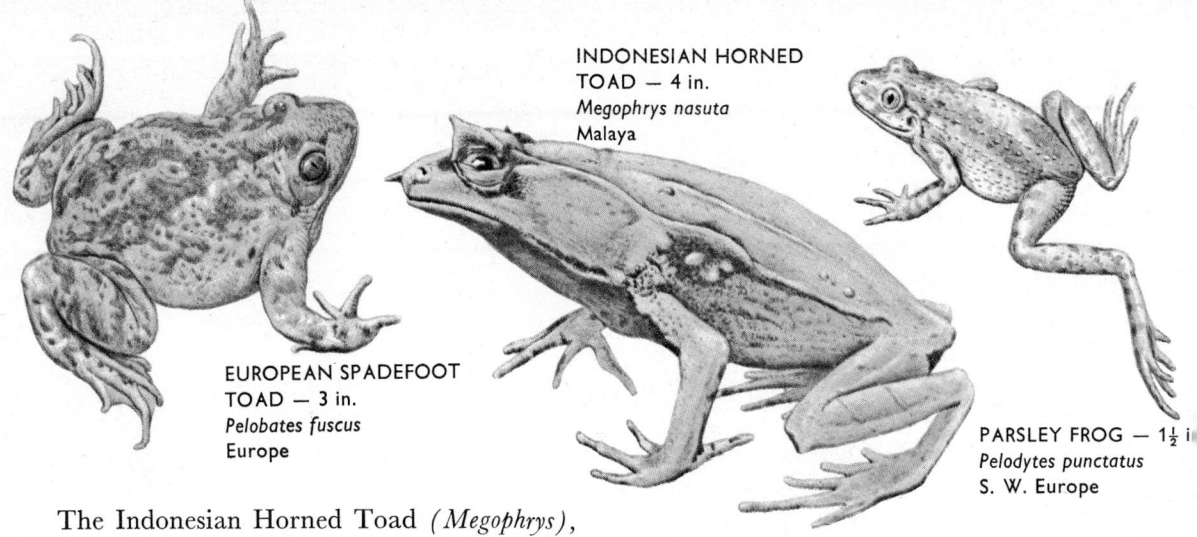

INDONESIAN HORNED
TOAD — 4 in.
Megophrys nasuta
Malaya

EUROPEAN SPADEFOOT
TOAD — 3 in.
Pelobates fuscus
Europe

PARSLEY FROG — 1½ i
Pelodytes punctatus
S. W. Europe

The Indonesian Horned Toad *(Megophrys)*, which often feeds on mice or other small mammals, is much like the South American Horned Frog in body shape and habits. It has soft, fleshy horns over its eyes and on the tip of its snout.

Toads of a genus *(Pelodytes)* found only in southern Europe and the Caucasus are called Parsley Frogs, because of the smell emitted from their glands. Though believed to be ancestors of the true spadefoots, they do not have foot spades. They do burrow into soft mud to hide when disturbed, however. (See AMPHIBIANS.)

SPARROWS are small, seed-eating birds. The true sparrows are species of the sub-family *Passerina*, of the Weaver-bird family *Ploceidae*. As with robins and flycatchers, the name has been applied to different birds in newly-settled countries and, as a result, a large group of North American buntings are known as sparrows (see BUNTINGS). The true sparrows share with the female, and young weavers, a rather nondescript, streaky-brown plumage. Most of the species are confined to the warm, dry regions of northern Africa and Asia Minor. The majority of them build domed nests with side entrances, in trees or bushes. These are not complex woven structures, like those of the weavers, but looser and bulkier masses of twigs and grasses. The House Sparrow will sometimes build a nest of this sort in a tree, but more frequently the nest is built into a crevice, while Tree Sparrows will only use natural holes for their nests.

The great success of the two latter species appears to be linked with their manner of nesting, and the fact that man has spread from the region in which the species evolved. Man has provided both a source of food and also structures (his buildings) which usually contain ideal nesting sites. The House Sparrow appears to have spread with man right across Europe, but in Asia the Tree Sparrow takes its place and becomes the species which lives on and around houses.

The warmly-lined nest hole may be used for roosting at all times of year, and enables the sparrow to survive right up into the Arctic, where other birds might freeze at night. The possession of a nest-site is as important to a sparrow as a territory is to a warbler or a robin, and once he has found one the male sits at the entrance and chirps

HOUSE SPARROW
Passer domesticus
5½ in. (including tail)

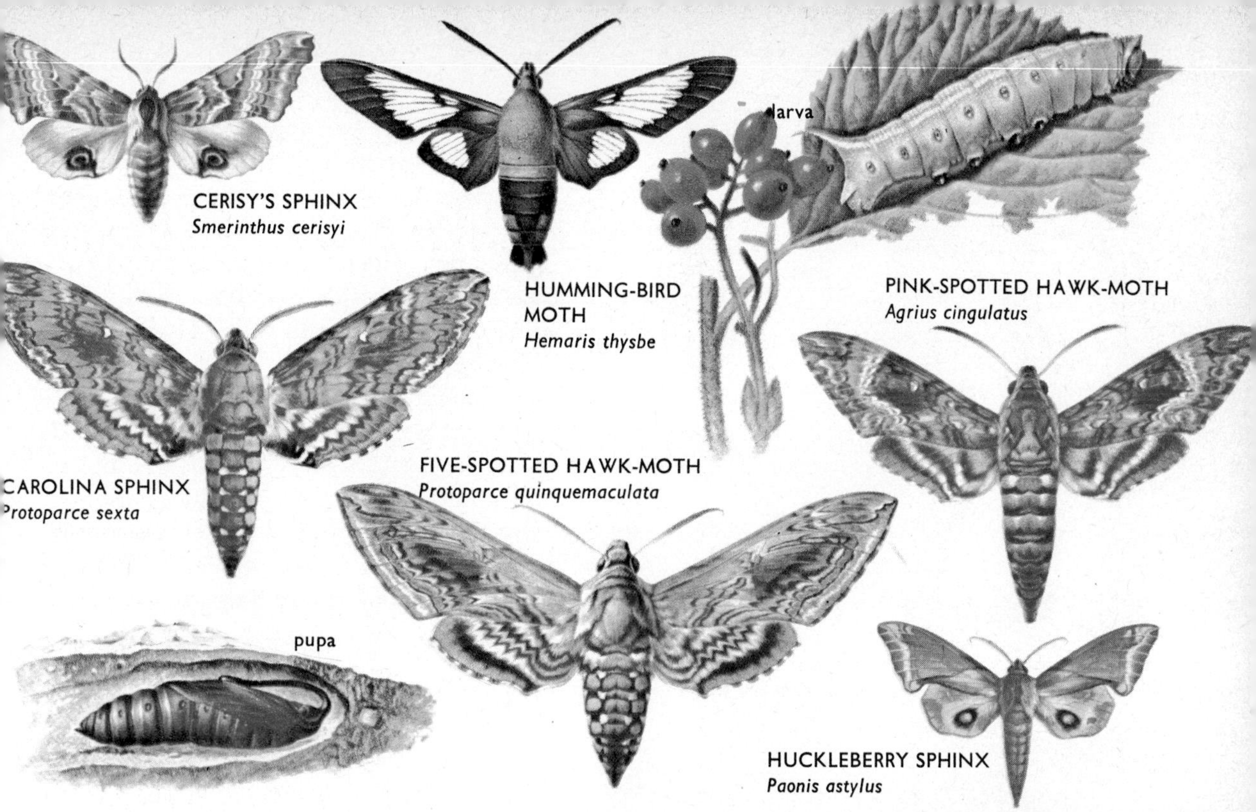

CERISY'S SPHINX
Smerinthus cerisyi

HUMMING-BIRD MOTH
Hemaris thysbe

larva

PINK-SPOTTED HAWK-MOTH
Agrius cingulatus

CAROLINA SPHINX
Protoparce sexta

FIVE-SPOTTED HAWK-MOTH
Protoparce quinquemaculata

pupa

HUCKLEBERRY SPHINX
Paonis astylus

excitedly to attract a mate to him.

Although sparrows are largely seed-eaters, the House Sparrow takes a great variety of foods and seems ready to investigate new ones. The young are at first fed entirely on insects, and the parents go to a great deal of trouble to collect these. They may be seen acrobatically searching plants, hovering in mid-air to snatch insects from the underside of leaves or the heads of grasses, or clinging to vertical walls to inspect crevices. Although young sparrows are incautious, adults are suspicious and, even if they are trapped once, they are not often trapped a second time. This makes them of little use for ringing studies. It is probably this suspicious attitude which enables them to live with man without trusting him too far, and so survive.

Although resident birds, sparrows may, especially in late summer, be found feeding in flocks and gathering in roosts at night.

Although European sparrows are rather dull in colour, some of the tropical ones — such as the Golden Sparrow — are bright yellow, while desert species are pale sandy-buff or silver-grey.

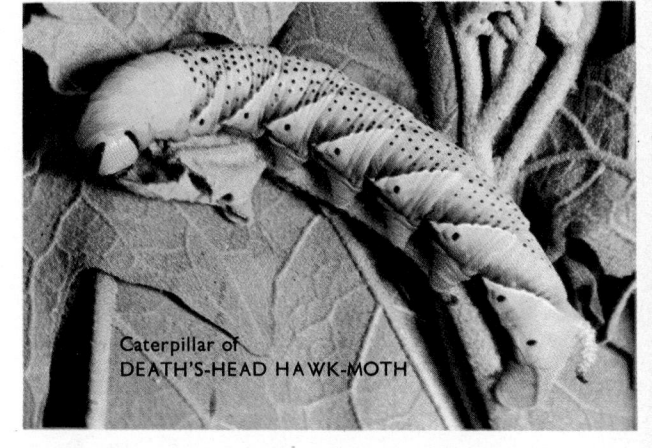

Caterpillar of
DEATH'S-HEAD HAWK-MOTH

SPHINX- (or **HAWK-**) **MOTHS** *(Sphingidae)* are easily recognised by their stout, spindle-shaped bodies and long, narrow front wings. Their hind wings are much smaller. Most sphinx-moths feed on nectar, sucking it from flowers through their tubular tongue, which in some species is several inches long. The European Death's-head Hawk, however, has a short tongue, sharp and stiff enough to penetrate bees' honeycombs and suck out the honey. The remarkable image of a human skull on the thorax of the Death's-head Hawk has given rise to many superstitions about this moth.

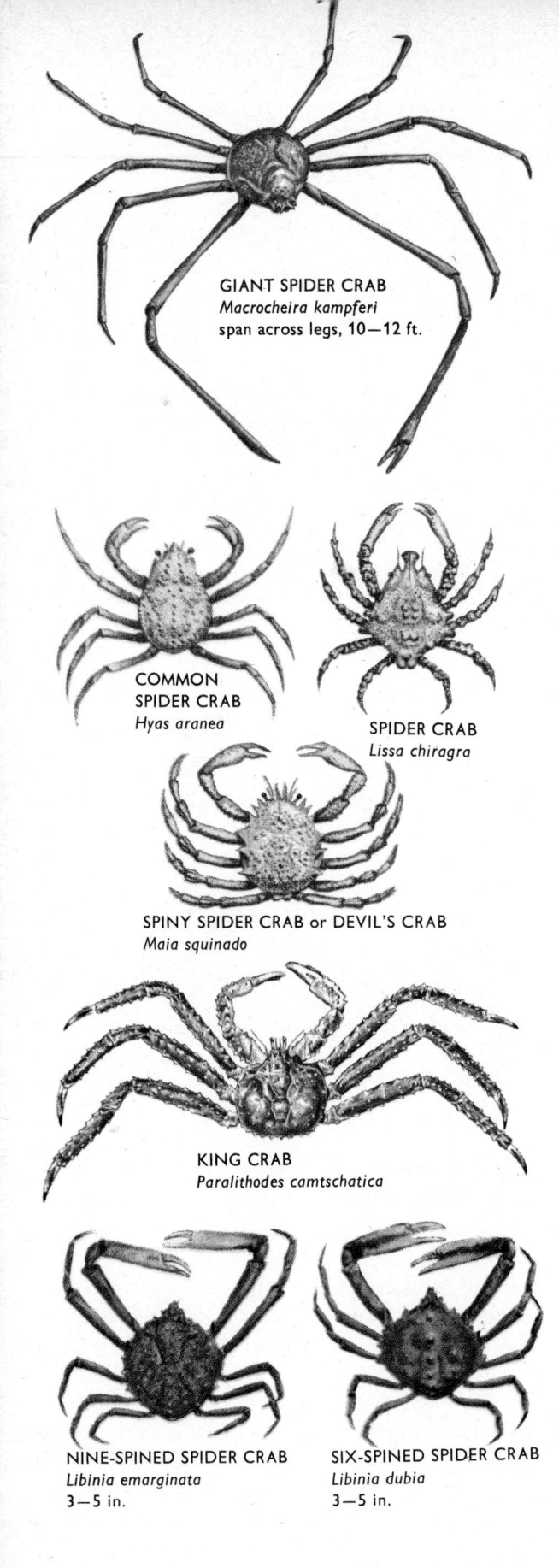

GIANT SPIDER CRAB
Macrocheira kampferi
span across legs, 10—12 ft.

COMMON
SPIDER CRAB
Hyas aranea

SPIDER CRAB
Lissa chiragra

SPINY SPIDER CRAB or DEVIL'S CRAB
Maia squinado

KING CRAB
Paralithodes camtschatica

NINE-SPINED SPIDER CRAB
Libinia emarginata
3—5 in.

SIX-SPINED SPIDER CRAB
Libinia dubia
3—5 in.

Hawk-moths are strong flyers, and are most active at twilight and in the evening. Those that fly during the day are often seen hovering in front of flowers; they are commonly called Hummingbird Hawk-moths. Other sphinx-moths with short, stubby bodies are called Bee Hawk-Moths.

Caterpillars of most sphinx-moths have a prominent horn on their eighth abdominal segment; hence they are known as Horn-worms in the U.S.A. When not feeding, the caterpillars frequently remain motionless, with the whole front part of their body elevated in a pose that suggests the Egyptian Sphinx. The caterpillars usually pupate in a cell in the ground.

SPIDER CRABS are a peculiar group of crustaceans of the family *Maiidae*. Widely spread throughout the world, they have rounded or triangular bodies, often covered with spines or warts, and long legs and claws. Despite their long legs, spider crabs are rather sluggish and are easily caught. Though their claws are not especially large, they can pinch hard. Some have the peculiar habit of picking pieces of algae and hooking them on to their oval, or sac-shaped, shell as camouflage. They change the algae to match the kind that grows where they live. The Giant Spider Crab, found in deep waters of the Pacific off Japan, may measure more than ten feet across the claws, and is the largest of the living crustaceans.

SPIDERS differ from insects in having four pairs of legs (insects have three pairs) and two body regions (insects have three). Spiders usually have eight eyes. Mites, scorpions and ticks belong to this same class (*Arachnida*) of the phylum *Arthropoda*.

Spiders, totalling some 40,000 species, live in a wide variety of habitats, from sea-shores to mountain tops. All spiders can spin silk through spinnerets at the tip of their abdomen. The silk is used to enclose their eggs, or to catch their food in webs or traps. Young spiders of many species use their silk for "ballooning" in the spring.

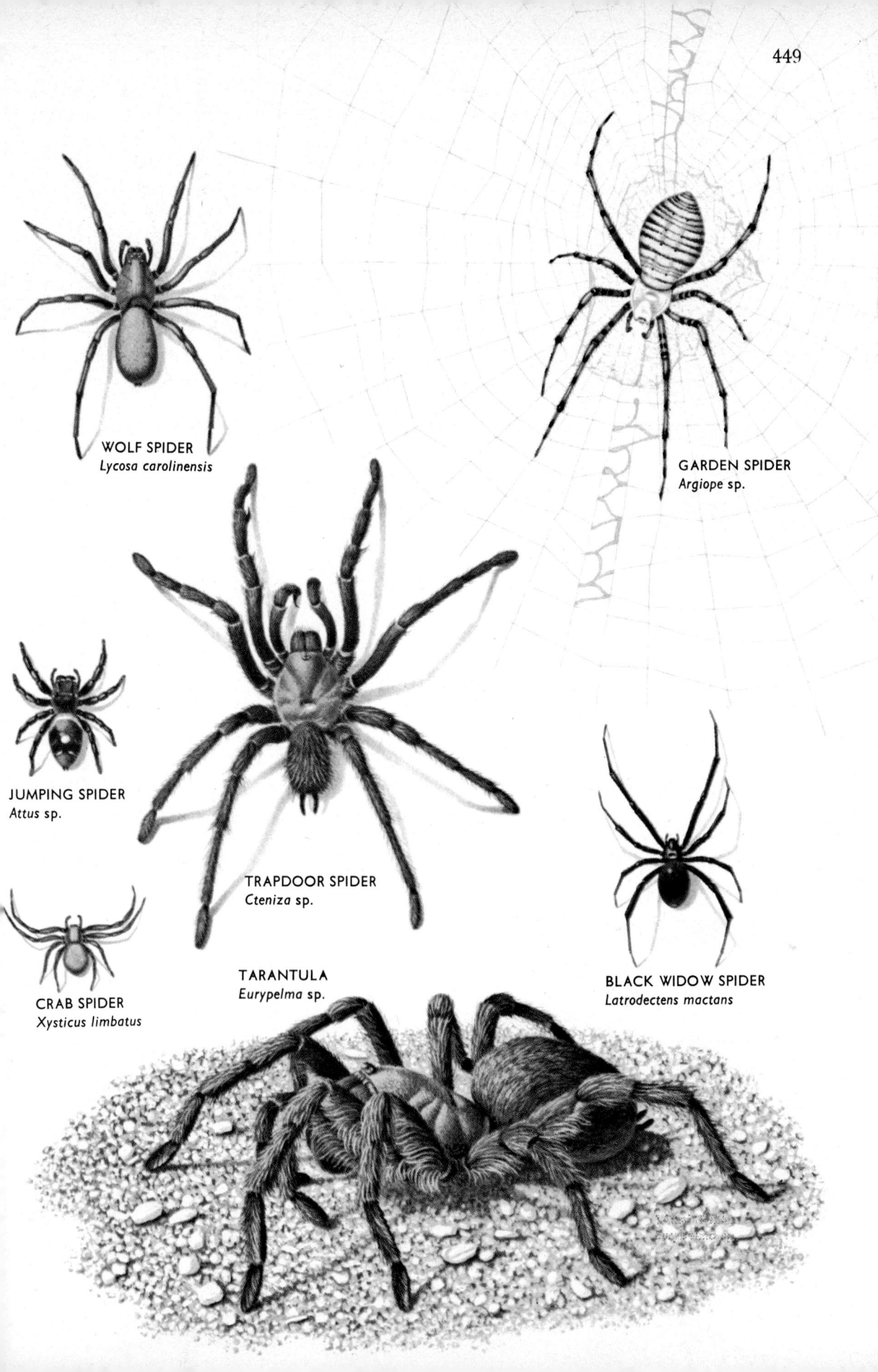

WOLF SPIDER
Lycosa carolinensis

GARDEN SPIDER
Argiope sp.

JUMPING SPIDER
Attus sp.

TRAPDOOR SPIDER
Cteniza sp.

CRAB SPIDER
Xysticus limbatus

TARANTULA
Eurypelma sp.

BLACK WIDOW SPIDER
Latrodectens mactans

450

THE CONSTRUCTION OF THE WEB OF AN ORB-WEAVING SPIDER

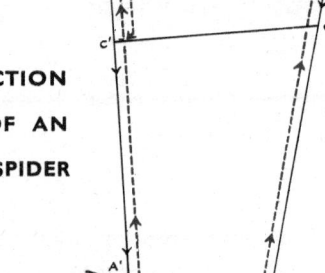
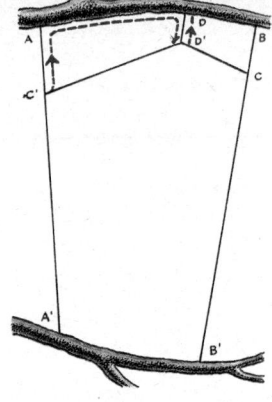
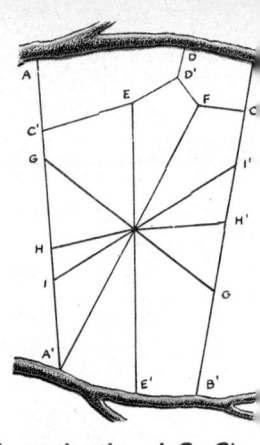

1. The spider begins the web by dropping thread from A on top branch to A¹ on bottom branch. Then it climbs back up that thread, along the branch to B, and drops down to B¹. It returns along this thread and starts a new one at C. It trails this thread as it climbs on up and across the branch and down thread A—A¹ to C¹.

2. The spider climbs back up to the branch and drops a new thread at D. This is secured around thread C—C¹ and pulled tight.

3. From the thread C—C¹, the spider drops to the lower branch for the first radial thread, then weaves the other radial lines.

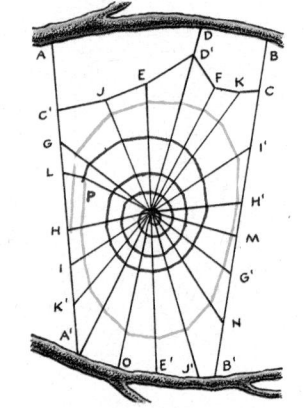
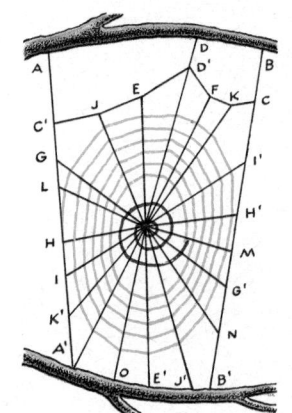
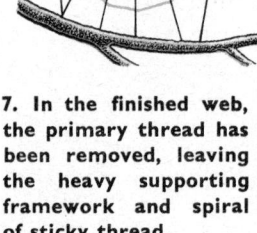

4. After completing the radial thread system, the spider begins the primary spiral (shown in red). Neither of these is sticky.

5. The viscid, or sticky, threads follow (blue), working from the outside and in towards the centre of the web.

6. As the spider nears the centre of the web, it cuts away the primary spiral, replacing it with the viscid thread.

7. In the finished web, the primary thread has been removed, leaving the heavy supporting framework and spiral of sticky thread.

They climb on to high places, spin one or more strands of silk, and then are blown by the wind — often for hundreds of miles, and lifted up a mile or more.

Most spiders lay their eggs in an egg-sac or cocoon. In some this consists only of a few strands of silk; in others it is well formed, with a tough, papery texture. The cocoons are placed under boards or stones, in crevices of bark, or may be carried about by the female. Some spiders lay only a few eggs, others several hundreds.

In a few weeks, the young spider (or spiderling) breaks out of the egg, but still remains in the cocoon. It looks much like the adult, but lacks spines and hairs and has little colour. All spiders moult, or shed, at least once before leaving the cocoon, and some moult two or three times. While still in the cocoon, the young spiders live on the remaining yolk of the egg. After leaving the cocoon, spiderlings of some species may moult a number of times before maturing.

Spiders prey chiefly on insects. They inject enzymes that dissolve the tissues of their prey, then eat the liquid mass, leaving only the dry shell.

Wolf spiders, commonly found in such damp places as under stones or leaves, are quite active feeders. They are hunters and

actually chase their prey. A few species of wolf spider build tunnels and some spin webs, but these are exceptions.

Jumping spiders are also active hunters. These brightly-coloured spiders, forming one of the largest groups, are often seen climbing along the sides of buildings, or up trees or posts, as they search for prey. Some can jump several times their body length.

Crab spiders have broad bodies and hold their legs in a crab-like position. Like crabs, they can move sideways or backwards. Most kinds are hunters and do not spin webs. Members of one group hide in flowers and wait to capture insects attracted there.

Most spiders spin webs to snare their prey, and web patterns are characteristic of various groups. The small, brownish spider, commonly found in houses, spins an irregular web in corners or beneath furniture. The Black Widow Spider also makes an irregular web. Sheet-web weavers construct a snare that forms a silken sheet, usually domed; they ordinarily wait at the lower surface of the sheet for their prey. Funnel-web spiders also spin sheet-like webs, but they wait in a tube, or funnel, at one side until an insect falls on the sheet. Orb-weavers, still another group, spin webs with distinctive designs. Black and yellow garden spiders of this group commonly build their large webs in bright, open places.

Most primitive of the spiders is a group, found largely in the tropics, to which the tarantulas and trapdoor spiders belong. Trapdoor spiders, found in the desert regions of the south-western United States, as well as in the tropics, build underground burrows which open to the surface through a hinged, tightly-fitting door. Tropical tarantulas are the largest of all spiders, some of them with a leg-span of nearly 10 inches and bodies more than 3 inches long. Tarantulas are used as food by the Tarantula Hawk, a wasp.

All spiders produce a venom, which they inject into their victims through openings at the tip of their claw-like fangs. Those that spin webs often wrap their prey in silk before eating it. Spiders cannot eat solid food, so they inject a digesting fluid into the body of the prey and then suck out the liquefied contents. Often a web, or the area around it, is littered with the empty bodies of many insects. When food is scarce, spiders can fast for long periods. (See BLACK WIDOW SPIDERS).

SPONGES are colonial animals that grow attached to the bottom. They are the simplest of the many-celled animals. Sponges feed by filtering plankton from water drawn in through in-current pores scattered over their bodies. The water is discharged through an ex-current pore (osculum) near their top. Most marine sponges reproduce sexually. Their larvae — small, free-swimming half-spheres — are discharged through the ex-current pore into the open sea, to drift about in the plankton. Eventually, they settle to the bottom, attach themselves, and develop as adults. Most kinds grow to fit the type of bottom on which they rest.

Calcareous, or limy, sponges — the simplest of the three main groups — grow in tube or vase-like colonies. Their skeletons consist of limy spicules, or needles, embedded between the two cell layers that make up the sponge's body. Most limy

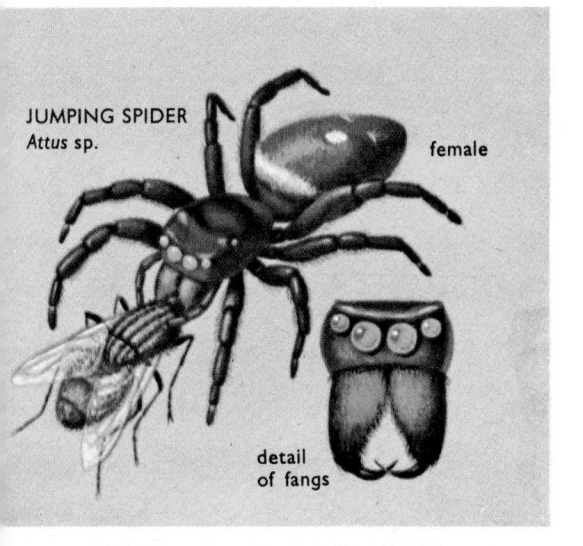

JUMPING SPIDER
Attus sp.

female

detail
of fangs

The sharp, piercing fangs of spiders are used to inject digestive juices into their victims.

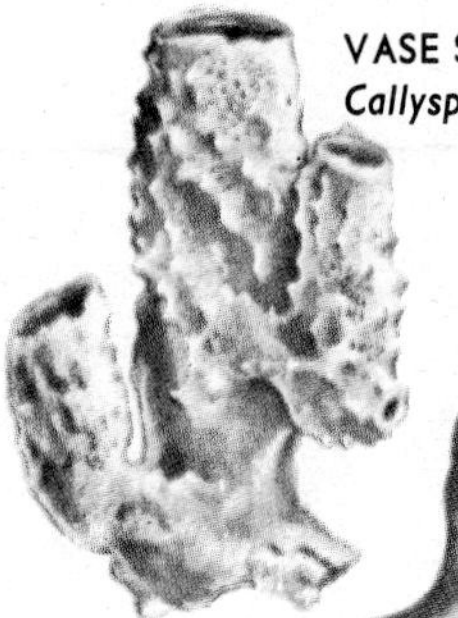

VASE SPONGE
Callyspongia vaginalis

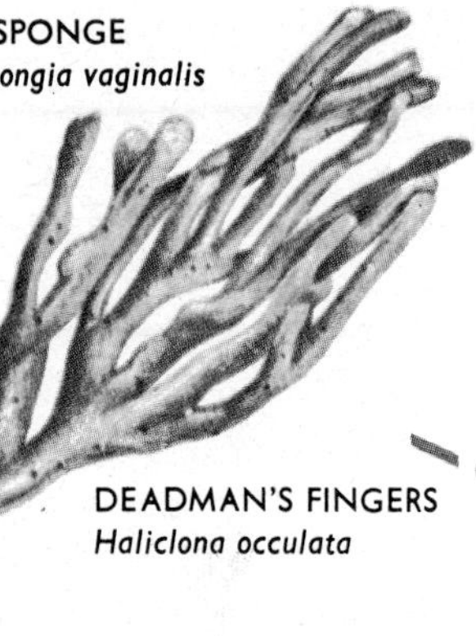

DEADMAN'S FINGERS
Haliclona occulata

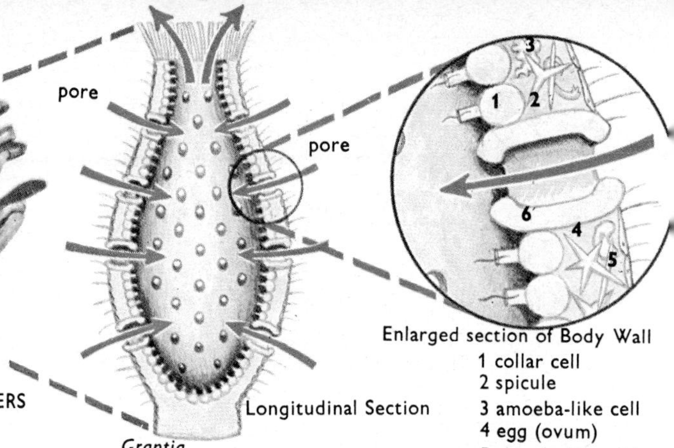

pore

pore

Enlarged section of Body Wall
1 collar cell
2 spicule
3 amoeba-like cell
4 egg (ovum)
5 skin (epidermis)
6 porecell

Longitudinal Section

Grantia
a simple sponge

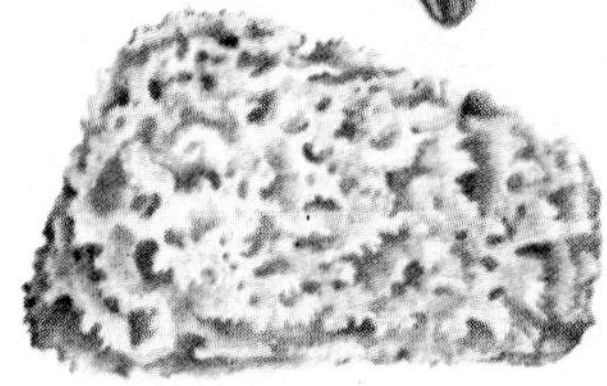

SHEEP'S WOOL SPONGE
Hippiospongia lachne

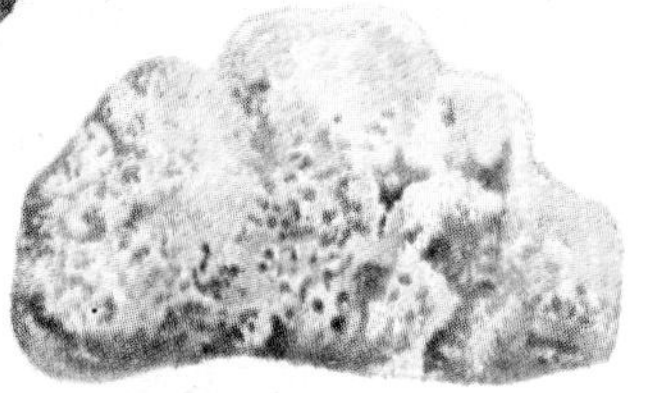

GRASS SPONGE
Hippiospongia equinoformis

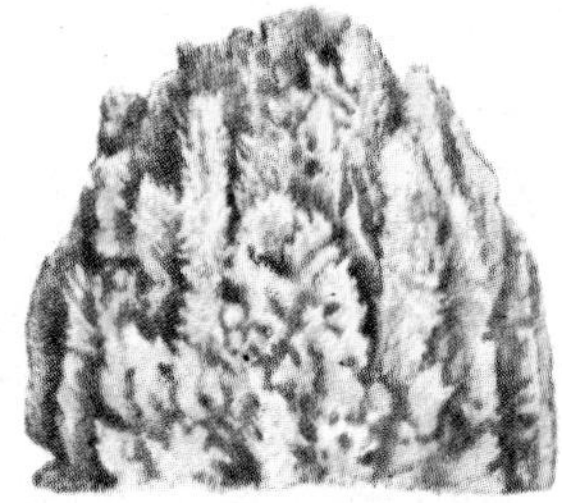

GLOVE SPONGE
Hippiospongia canaliculata

VENUS'S FLOWERBASKET
Euplectella sp.

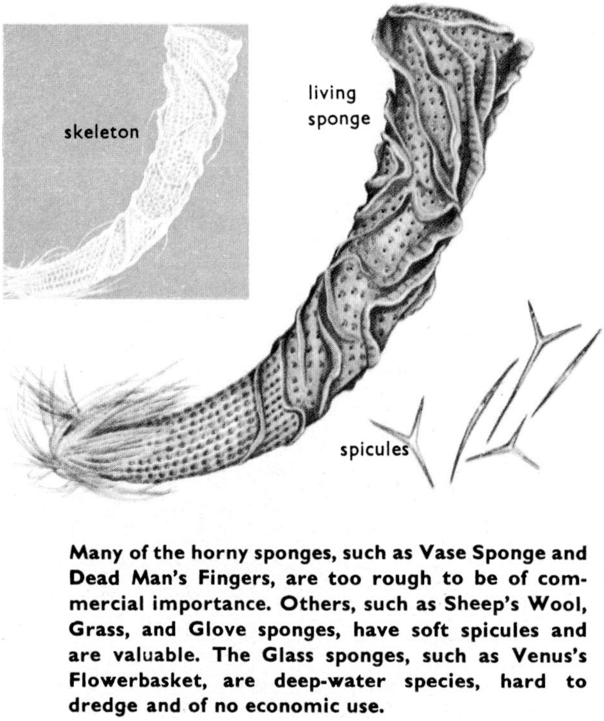

skeleton

living
sponge

spicules

sponges are less than an inch long. They grow on rocks, pilings and ship bottoms. Among the common types are *Grantia,* which forms simple, yellowish-grey tubes, and *Leucosolenia,* which grows in soft, yellowish mats or branching colonies.

Glass sponges, another of the three basic types, are found in deep water in the tropics. Some grow to over a foot in length. Their tissues are soft, but their long, glassy spicules are intricately interwoven to form beautiful, hollow tubes. A common one is Venus's Flowerbasket *(Euplectella),* found on soft bottoms off the Philippine Islands.

Horny sponges, the third type, are the most common. Many of the more than 2,000 species are commercially valuable. Their skeletons may be of horny fibres or of spicules. Some have skeletons of both horny fibres and spicules, and others have

Many of the horny sponges, such as Vase Sponge and Dead Man's Fingers, are too rough to be of commercial importance. Others, such as Sheep's Wool, Grass, and Glove sponges, have soft spicules and are valuable. The Glass sponges, such as Venus's Flowerbasket, are deep-water species, hard to dredge and of no economic use.

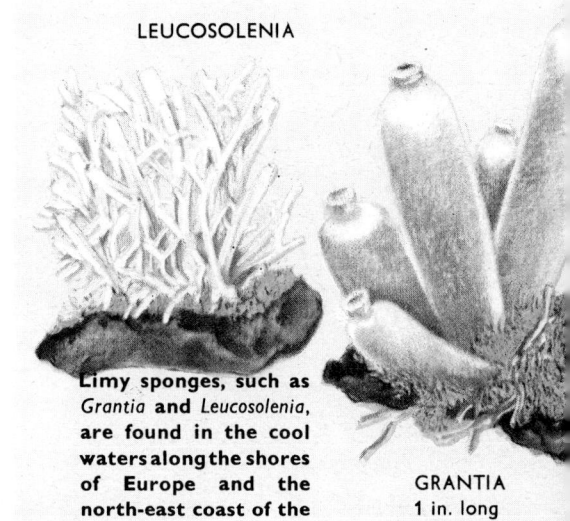

LEUCOSOLENIA

Limy sponges, such as *Grantia* **and** *Leucosolenia,* **are found in the cool waters along the shores of Europe and the north-east coast of the United States.**

GRANTIA
1 in. long

no skeletons at all. The Loggerhead Sponge, one of the largest of the horny sponges, has both spicules and fibres.

SPOONBILLS are members of the Ibis family. The Common Spoonbill more often nests in reed-beds, but the Roseate and other Spoonbills usually nest in low trees. The flattened bill is used like a duck's bill, being swept from side to side in shallow water with a dibbling movement, as the bird wades forward. Spoonbills fly well, with head and neck extended forwards, and legs stretched backwards. In general they are birds of coastal or brackish waters. Owing to the length of the bill, they cannot preen their own head-feathers, but occasionally two birds preen each other simultaneously.

SPRINGTAILS are small, wing-less insects of the order *Collembola*. More than a thousand species of these insects are distributed in nearly every part of the world.

Most live under leaves, stones, or in similar moist situations. When some occur in large numbers on the surface of swimming-pools, they become a nuisance.

Others are abundant in commercial mushroom-beds. A few kinds are pests of crops, and still others live on beaches in the tidal zones. Species found in great numbers on the surface of snow are called "snowfleas" in the United States of America.

Springtails have a unique mechanism for jumping. A forked structure, called the furcula, is held close to the under-surface of their abdomen by a clasp. When the clasp is released, the furcula snaps against the ground and propels the insect forward. Some of them can actually jump several times their own length.

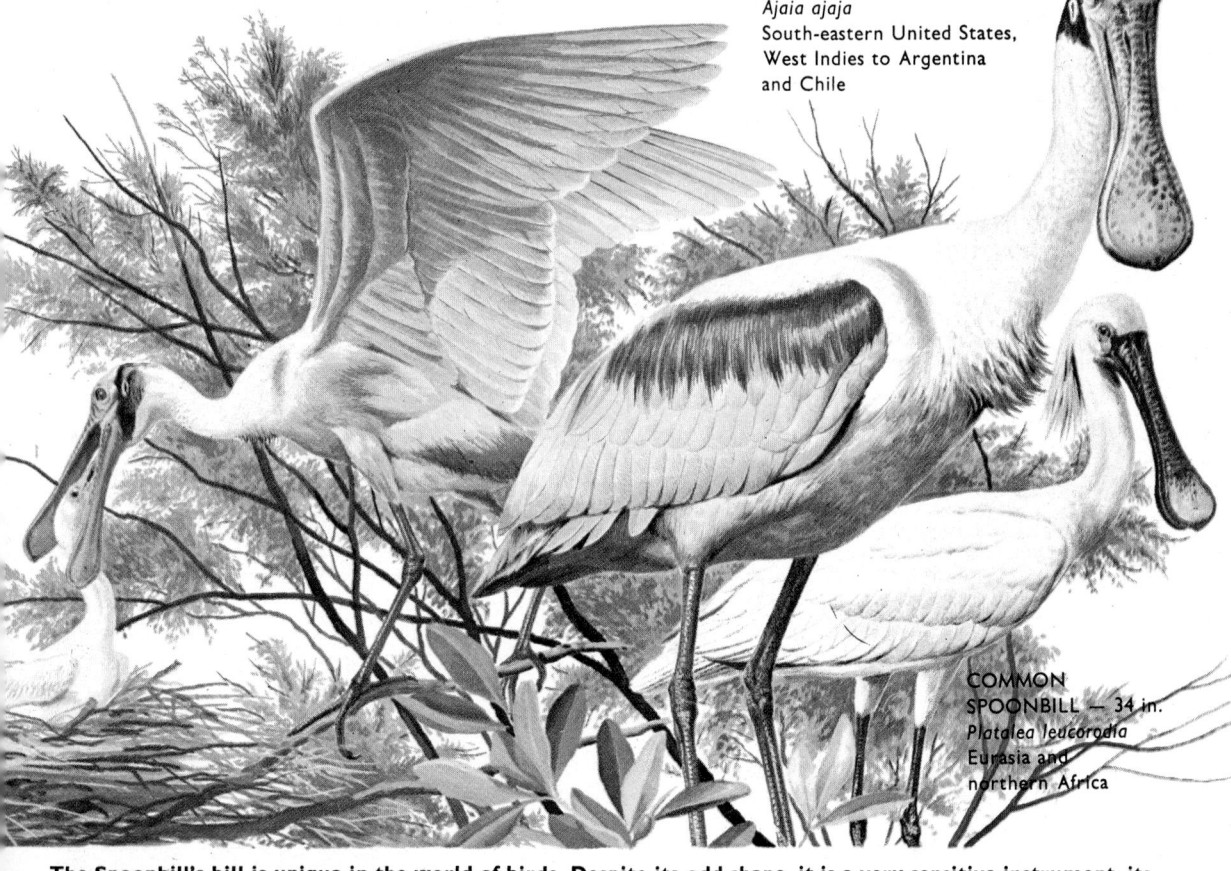

ROSEATE SPOONBILL — 34 in.
Ajaia ajaja
South-eastern United States,
West Indies to Argentina
and Chile

COMMON
SPOONBILL — 34 in.
Platalea leucorodia
Eurasia and
northern Africa

The Spoonbill's bill is unique in the world of birds. Despite its odd shape, it is a very sensitive instrument, its inner surfaces lined with membranes that detect insect larvae and small fish in the water.

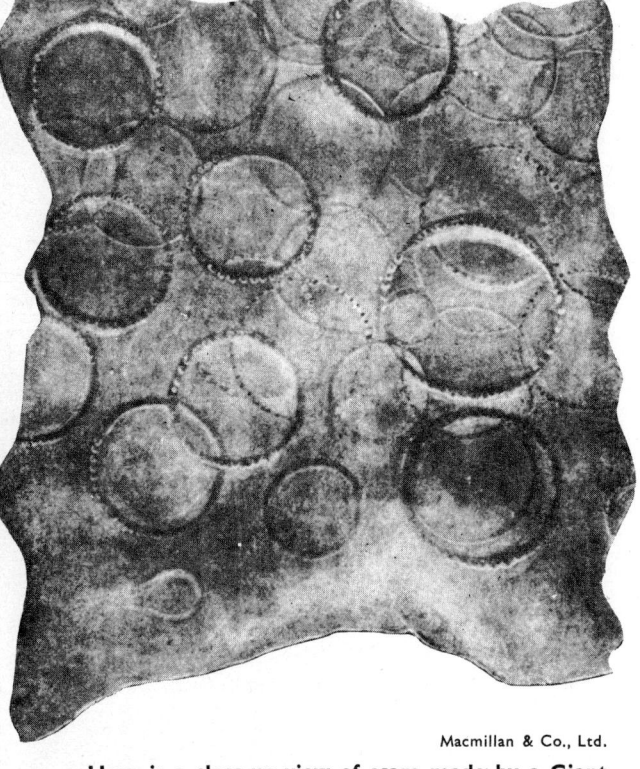

Macmillan & Co., Ltd.

Here is a close-up view of scars made by a Giant Squid on a Sperm Whale. The squid has suckers along each long tentacle. Each sucker has a ring of sharp teeth (as many as 50 in a large Giant Squid), surrounded by a membrane. Wounds from suckers may extend an inch into the flesh, leaving scars.

SQUIDS are fast-swimming, streamlined cephalopods with eight arms and two long tentacles (see CEPHALOPODS). They may swim by jet propulsion or, more slowly, by using their fins. The smallest squids are only half-an-inch long; the Giant Squid measures more than 50 feet. Squids feed on shrimps, fishes and other squids, which they capture with their long tentacles. They cut the prey to pieces with their parrot-like beaks. Some squids can swim so swiftly that they can shoot out of the water and sail for long distances, like flying-fishes. Squids are eaten by many kinds of fishes, and also by toothed whales and, in some countries, by humans. Large numbers, canned in oil, are exported by Spain and Portugal. Most squids caught in countries where they are not prized as food by people are used for fish-bait, or are processed to make fertiliser or fish meals, the latter being fed to livestock.

When alarmed, a squid shoots out ink, and this forms a cigar-shaped cloud the size of the squid. The creature then turns colourless, and swims away rapidly while its enemy tries to swallow the ink. Squids do not use the ink as a smokescreen, as is commonly believed.

Squids are among the most numerous animals in the sea, and account for about half the total volume of the Japanese fishery. Like octopuses, they can change their colours rapidly and may assume stripes, bands and dots. Many that live in the deep sea are luminescent, and some of them are arrayed with literally hundreds of tiny, jewel-like light organs that gleam in the depths. Some have light organs that look like headlights on an automobile; others have lights that shine out through their thin and transparent body wall. Presumably

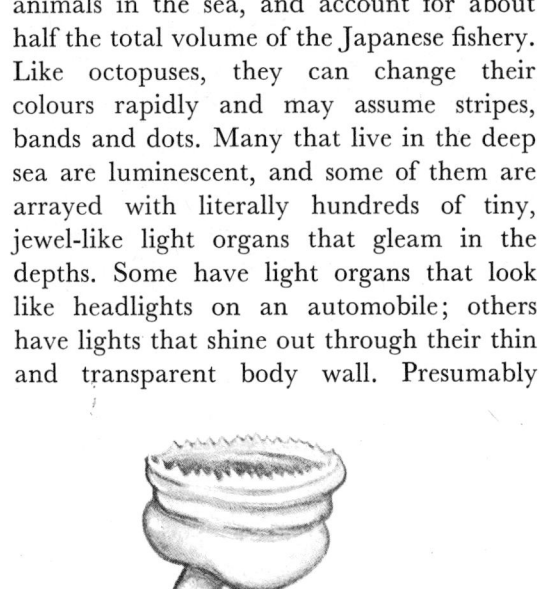

detail of sucker, showing sharp "teeth" around rim

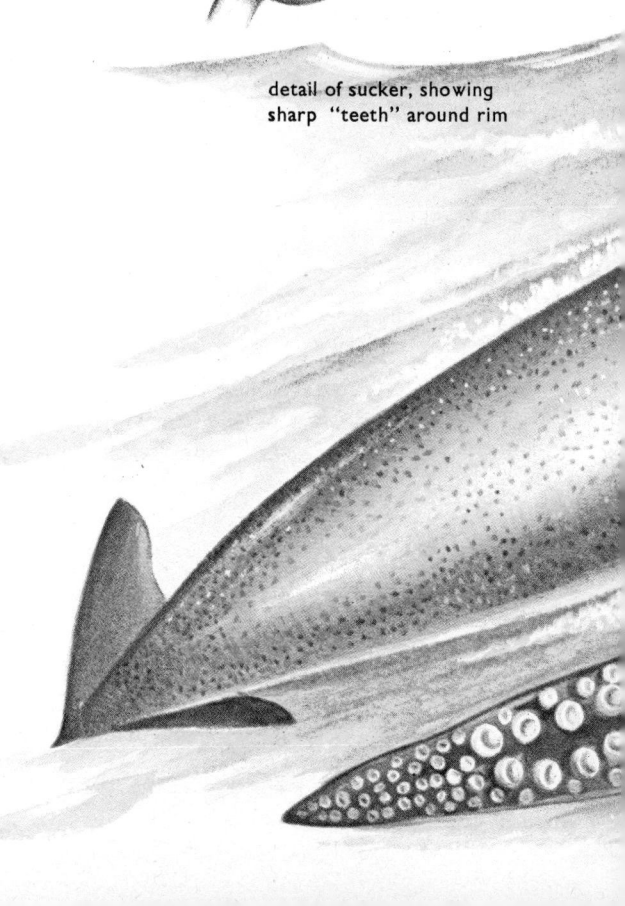

these lights attract small fish, or other food animals on which the squids feed.

One group of squids has a single big eye and a single little one, which enables them to see equally well in the dim depths of the sea or at the sunny surface. A few have their suckers modified into talons as formidable as a tiger's claws, and these are used to seize their prey.

Cuttlefish are a type of squid with a thick, limy internal shell. They are found only in deep water. Cuttlefish are used as food and their shells are sold for use in bird-cages. The shell is also used in tooth-powders, and for making castings for jewellery.

Giant Squids, the largest of all animals without backbones, live in deep waters throughout the world. They are seldom seen at the surface, and only a few specimens have ever been captured. Giant Squids are eaten mainly by Sperm Whales. In one case on record, a 47-foot Sperm Whale had swallowed a 37-foot Giant Squid. Scars on the skin of whales are evidence that such meals can be dangerous.

The Common Squid, found along the Atlantic coasts of North America, and also in the Mediterranean, is only about $1\frac{1}{2}$ feet long. As with other squids, it uses its two longest arms, or tentacles, primarily to capture prey, and the eight smaller tentacles to transfer the prey to its mouth for eating.

Illustrations of several deep-water squids accompany this entry. Though small, these squids are among the most interesting and most colourful of the group. Also illustrated is the Oceanic (or Flying) Squid of tropical seas. This squid is noted for its ability to glide above the sea, sometimes leaping high enough to land on the deck of a ship.

GIANT SQUID
Architeuthis princeps
overall length (body and tentacles): more than 50 ft.

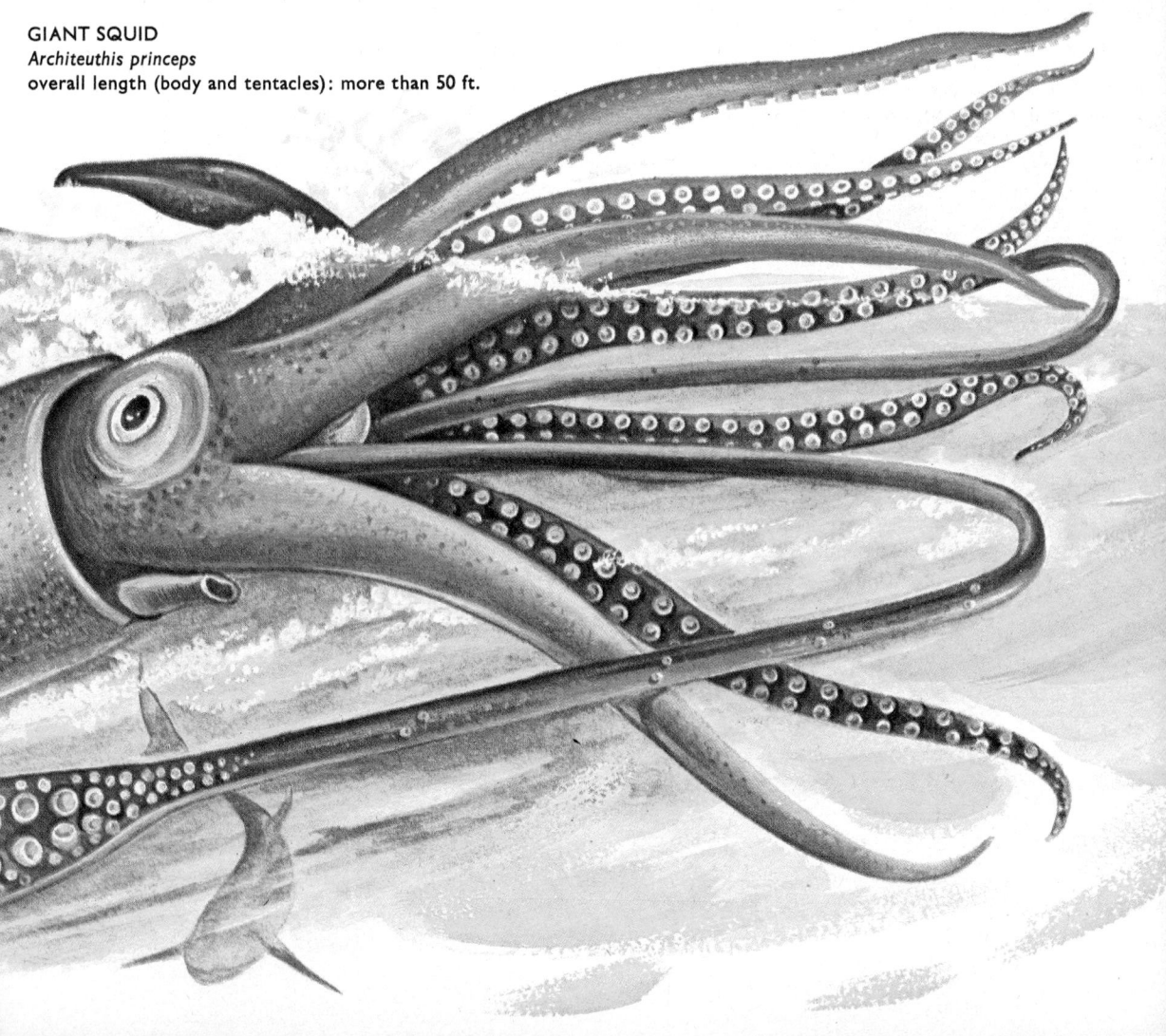

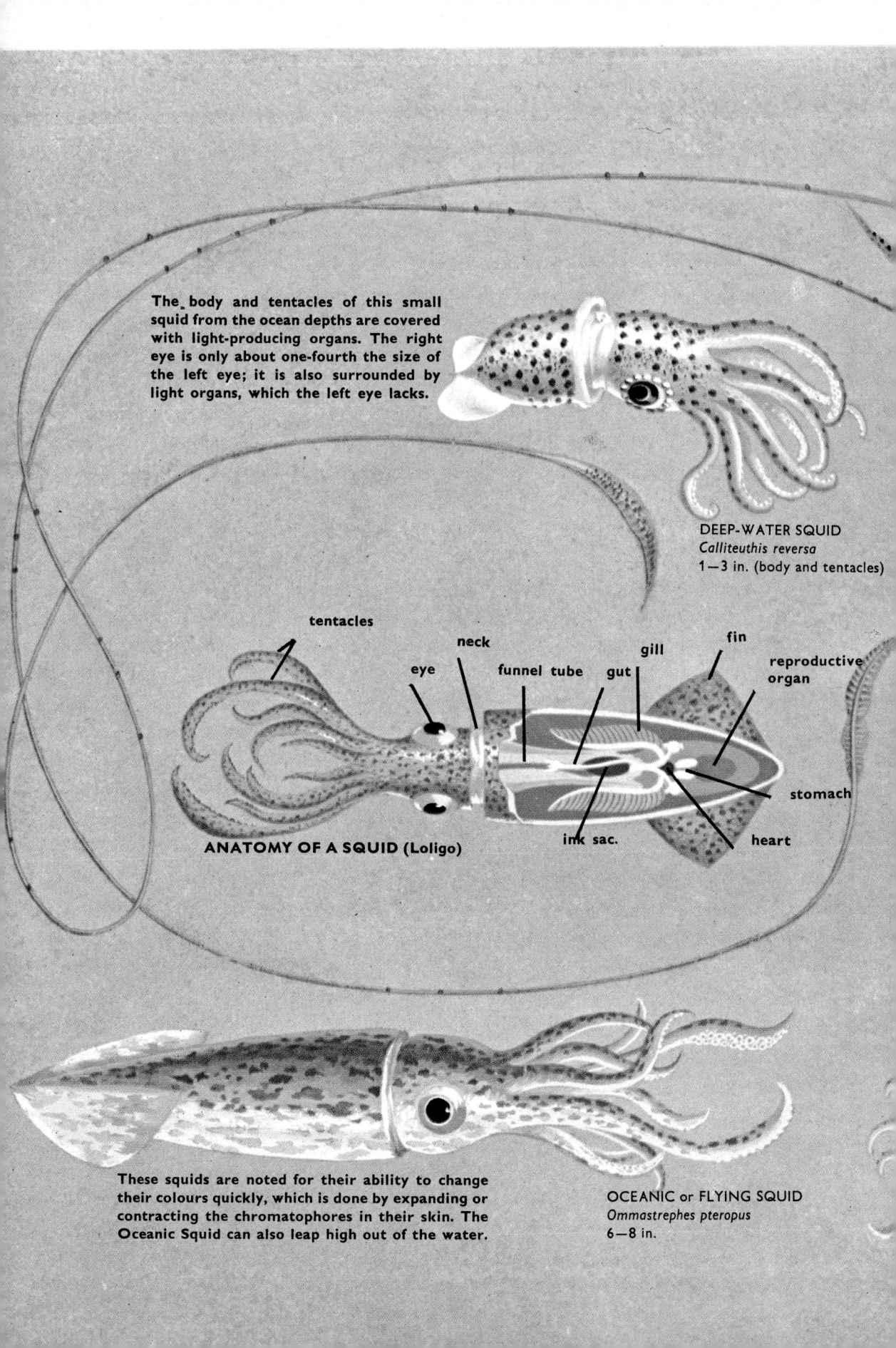

The body and tentacles of this small squid from the ocean depths are covered with light-producing organs. The right eye is only about one-fourth the size of the left eye; it is also surrounded by light organs, which the left eye lacks.

DEEP-WATER SQUID
Calliteuthis reversa
1—3 in. (body and tentacles)

tentacles

neck

fin

eye

gill

reproductive organ

funnel tube

gut

stomach

ink sac.

heart

ANATOMY OF A SQUID (Loligo)

These squids are noted for their ability to change their colours quickly, which is done by expanding or contracting the chromatophores in their skin. The Oceanic Squid can also leap high out of the water.

OCEANIC or FLYING SQUID
Ommastrephes pteropus
6—8 in.

This unusual squid of deep water can extend or retract its exceptionally long tentacles. The young, or larvae, have a pen, or interior shell, that is longer than the body of the animal.

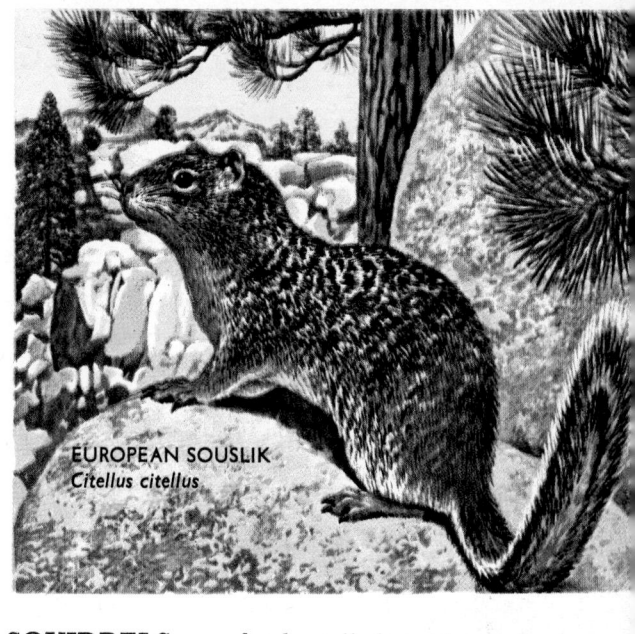

EUROPEAN SOUSLIK
Citellus citellus

DEEP-WATER SQUID
Chiroteuthis veranyi
body: 3—4 in.
tentacles: 30—36 in.

DEEP-WATER SQUID
Lycoteuthis diadema
2—3 in.

This deep-water squid, like *Calliteuthis*, has light-producing organs on its body and tentacles. There are nearly a dozen different types, varying in complexity. Some have lenses and reflecting devices.

SQUIRRELS are bushy-tailed, wide-eyed rodents found throughout the world, except in Australia. All the several kinds — tree squirrels, flying squirrels, and ground squirrels — feed on nuts, seeds, fruits and buds, and also grain. Flying squirrels are nocturnal; all the others are active during the day.

Red Squirrels are widely distributed in Europe and northern Asia. They eat pine seeds, acorns and nuts, sometimes burying nuts in the soil when there are more available than they can eat. They build round nests, or dreys, in the trees. Similar squirrels — sometimes called Pine Squirrels, or Chickarees — are found in North America.

The Fox Squirrel, common in the eastern United States, lives in or at the edge of open forests. Its usual colour is yellowish-tan specked with black, but grey and black colour phases also occur. The Fox Squirrel is the largest native North American squirrel.

The Eastern Grey Squirrel ranges from the Eastern Seaboard to the Great Plains of the United States. Like the Fox Squirrel, it builds leafy tree nests, in which it spends much of its time in warm weather. It also nests in holes or hollows in trees. An average of four young are born in each litter, and there may be two litters in one year. The young leave the nest when they are about six weeks old. The adults, which apparently mate for life, may live for fifteen years.

FAMILY TREE OF SQUIRRELS

Antelope Squirrels

Mantle Squirrels

Chipmunks

Ground Squirrels

Prairie Dogs

Tree Squirrels

Woodchucks

Flying Squirrels

GROUND-DWELLERS

TREE-DWELLERS

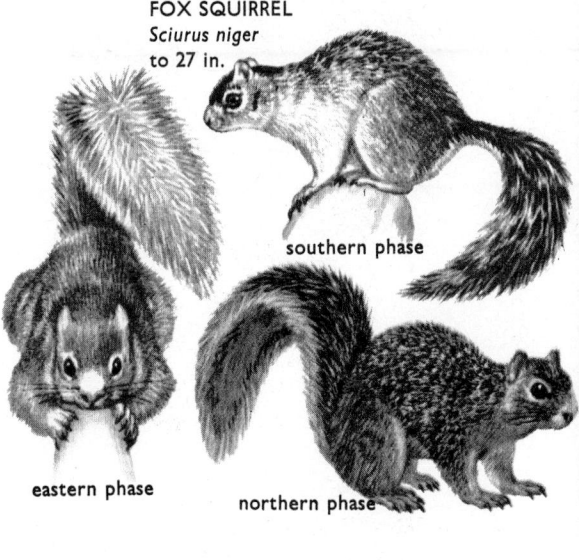

FOX SQUIRREL
Sciurus niger
to 27 in.

southern phase

eastern phase

northern phase

There are 22 species of tree squirrels (*Sciurus* spp.) **in North America. Red** (*Tamiasciurus* spp.) **and Flying squirrels** (*Glaucomys* spp.) **are also tree-dwellers.**

Black or melanistic phases of the Eastern Grey are not uncommon, and albinos also occur. This squirrel has been introduced to Britain and is now widespread. The Western Grey Squirrel, slightly larger, is found in Pacific coastal States of North America. Grey Squirrels live in forests.

A wide variety of squirrels, some of them brilliantly coloured, is found in south-eastern Asia. Others are widely distributed in Africa and in South America.

Pygmy squirrels are small-sized tree squirrels found in various parts of Central and South America, West Africa, and the islands off south-eastern Asia. One kind is about the size of a large mouse. In the Philippines, these shrew-like squirrels are active in trees during the daytime, although they are rarely seen. Those of Central and South America seek shelter in the palm forests, where they feed on fruits and nuts.

The Giant Tree Squirrel, or Ratufa, of south-eastern Asia measures about three feet in length. It runs and leaps through the tall

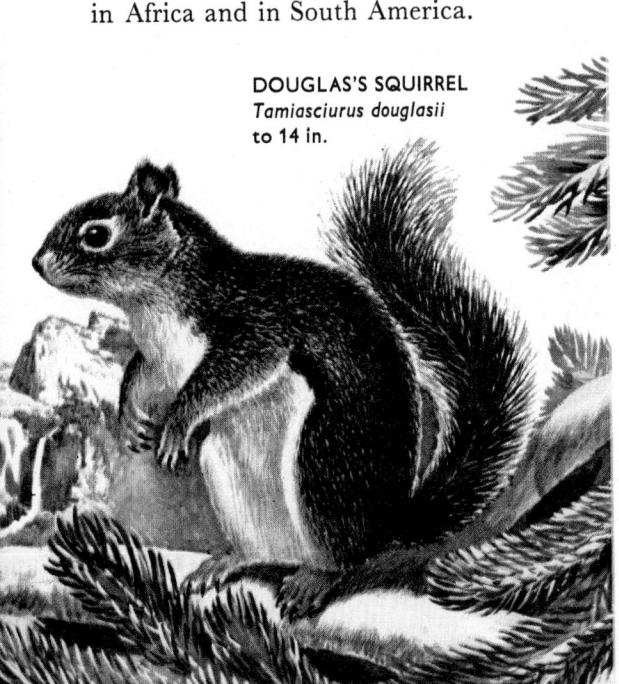

DOUGLAS'S SQUIRREL
Tamiasciurus douglasii
to 14 in.

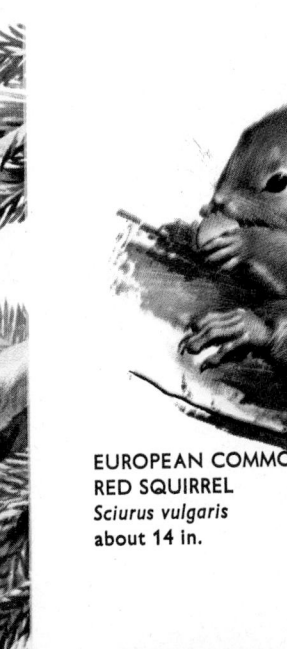

EUROPEAN COMMON
RED SQUIRREL
Sciurus vulgaris
about 14 in.

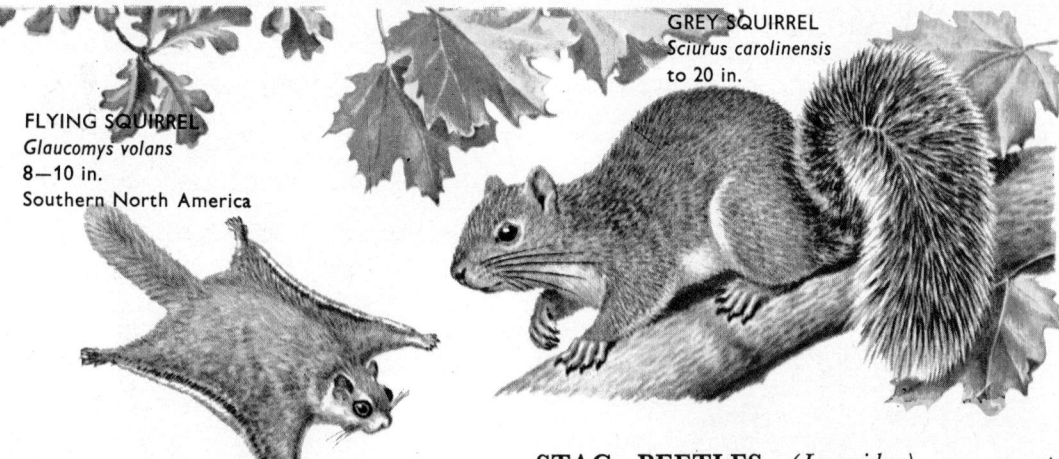

GREY SQUIRREL
Sciurus carolinensis
to 20 in.

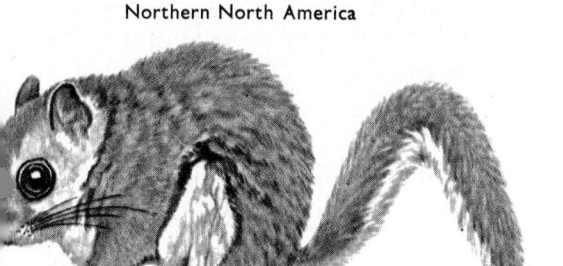

FLYING SQUIRREL
Glaucomys volans
8—10 in.
Southern North America

FLYING SQUIRREL
Glaucomys sabrinus
10—11 in.
Northern North America

trees, giving off noisy, shrill calls. It is brightly coloured — red, black or orange above and yellow to white below.

Flying squirrels have thin, hairy membranes along the sides of their body, between their fore and hind legs and, in some, between their hind legs and their tail. When they leap, they spread these "wings" and glide from one tree to another. Often they climb the next tree and repeat the process. They use their tail as a rudder for turning, and to help them to land softly and in a "head up" position on a tree-trunk. Flying squirrels of North America are about the size of large rats. They feed on nuts, fruits and seeds, and frequently live in abandoned woodpecker holes. Taguans, or Giant Flying Squirrels, of south-eastern Asia, may be three feet in length. Several types of small flying squirrel are found in south-eastern Asia.

STAG BEETLES (*Lucanidae*) are most abundant in the tropics. Males of the nearly 1,000 species have large mandibles. In some males, these may be as long as the beetle's body and branched, much like a stag's antlers. These mandibles look dangerous, but often are so long that they cannot inflict a painful pinch. The females, with shorter, stouter jaws, can bite harder.

Stag beetles are found mostly in wooded areas. Adults are often attracted to lights. The larvae live in decaying logs.

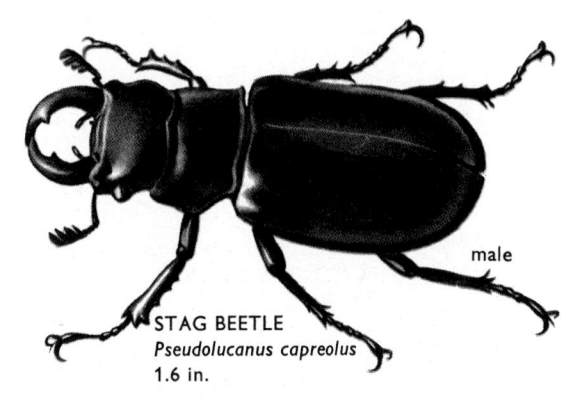

male

STAG BEETLE
Pseudolucanus capreolus
1.6 in.

STARFISH, echinoderms of the class Asteroidea, normally possess five arms (or rays) that arise from a central body. Their vital organs are concentrated in the body disc, but also extend into the tips of the arms. A star-fish's mouth is located on its under-surface. It feeds on many kinds of animals, including sponges, young crabs, clams, oysters — and even smaller starfish. The limy plates of their skeletons are not rigid, giving the arms some flexibility. They

PURPLE SUN-STAR
16—20 in.
Solaster endeca
Atlantic

MUD STAR 3—4 in.
Ctenodiscus crispatus
Atlantic

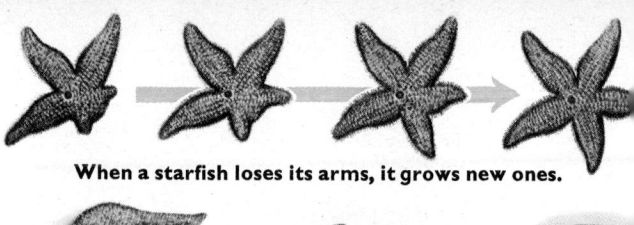

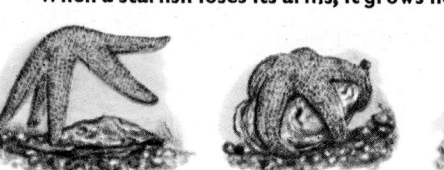

When a starfish loses its arms, it grows new ones.

SUNFLOWER
STAR — to 30 in.
Pycnopodia helianthoides
Pacific

Starfish feeding on an oyster.

SEA BAT — 7 in.
Patiria miniata
Pacific

RED STAR — 4 in.
Henricia leviuscula
Pacific

along Atlantic coasts, feeds on oysters and is often a serious pest in commercial oyster-beds. It wraps its arms around the oyster, and pulls until the oyster's muscles become so tired it can no longer hold its shell shut. As soon as the shell opens, the starfish shoves its stomach inside and digests the oyster's soft body. In years gone by, oyster-men collected starfish from the oyster-beds, chopped them to pieces, and threw them overboard. Instead of being eliminated, the starfish actually became more numerous, for most of the pieces grew into whole new animals. Now the starfish are ground into meal and fertiliser.

One of the larger starfish is the Cushion Star *(Oreaster reticulatus)*, which lives on shallow, sandy bottoms along America's east coast; its arms span over 12 inches. *Astropecten*, which is found in sandy areas on both Atlantic and Pacific coasts, has flat arms. The large Pacific *Pisaster* lives on rocky shores. The Comet Star *(Linckia)* can grow a new starfish from even a small part broken from its body. Arms with buds of new ones are often found lying on the bottom. Some starfishes have many long arms. Inca Indian carvings of the sun were copied from them.

Fossil starfish are found in rocks as old as the Ordovician, but are uncommon. Ordovician forms include brittle stars, true asteroid starfish, and somasteroids, an extinct group. (See BRITTLE or SERPENT STARS; ECHINODERMS.)

crawl by using their tube feet to pull themselves along the bottom. Long-stalked pinching organs, called pedicillariae, are scattered over the starfish's body. These pincers grab intruding organisms, such as larvae of other animals or various plants, and crush them before they become attached.

Some starfish feed by simply shoving their stomach out through the mouth and surrounding their prey, after which they digest it outside their bodies. *Asterias*, found

STARLINGS are a family of noisy, glossy-plumaged eaters of insects and fruit. The Common Starling, like the sparrow, owes

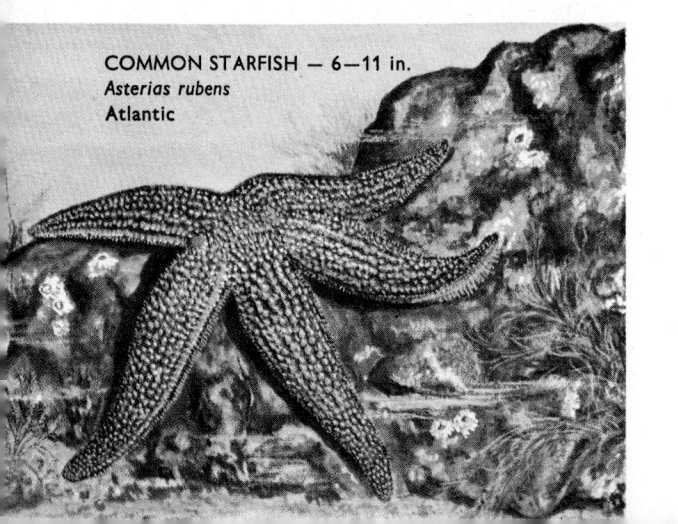

COMMON STARFISH — 6—11 in.
Asterias rubens
Atlantic

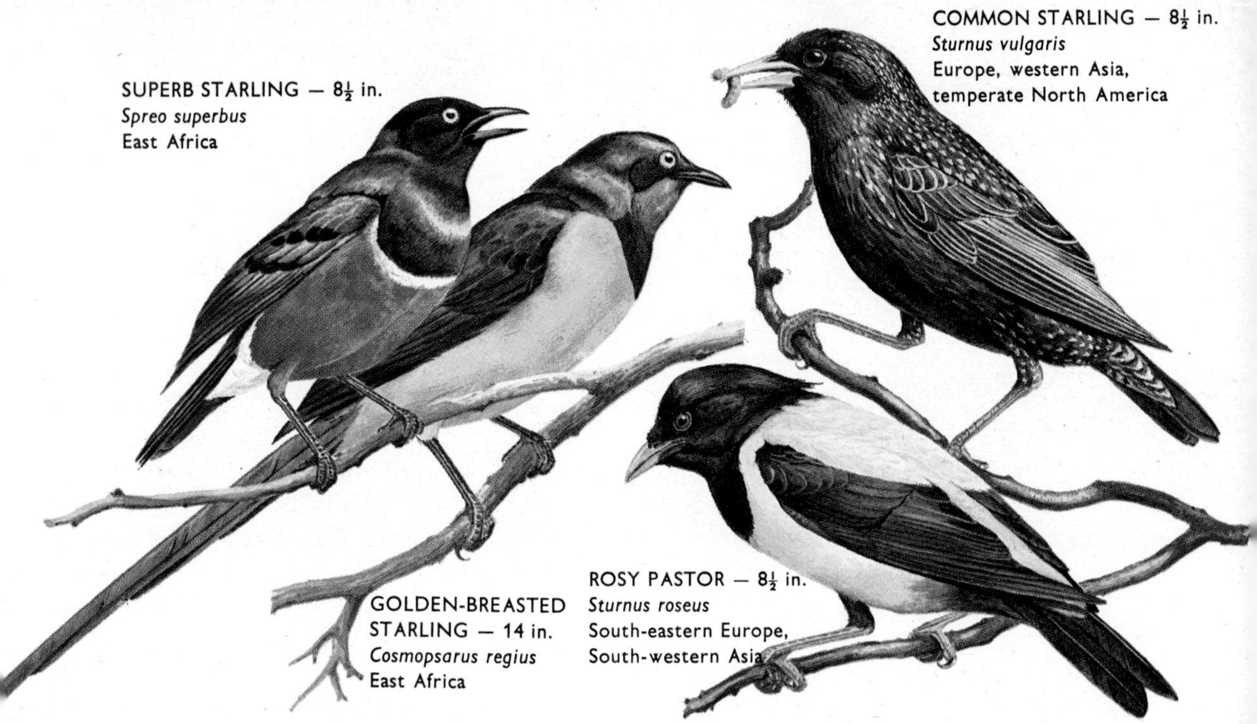

SUPERB STARLING — 8½ in.
Spreo superbus
East Africa

COMMON STARLING — 8½ in.
Sturnus vulgaris
Europe, western Asia,
temperate North America

GOLDEN-BREASTED STARLING — 14 in.
Cosmopsarus regius
East Africa

ROSY PASTOR — 8½ in.
Sturnus roseus
South-eastern Europe,
South-western Asia

All members of the starling family are medium-sized birds. Characteristically, the tail is short and squared, but in the Golden-breasted Starling, the tail is long and slim; in others round. Starlings have a sturdy bill, either straight or slightly curved. Young birds have dull, streaked plumage.

its success to its ability to utilise man's habitat. Man has provided the holes it needs for nests in his buildings, while his meadows and lawns provide the stretches of green turf on which it mainly feeds. When feeding in turf, the starling thrusts its bill in, and then opens it to force the roots apart and reveal hidden insects. It is a sociable bird and, when not breeding, forms large flocks that roost at night in woods or on the ledges of town buildings.

Among the more than 100 species comprising the Old World starling family are a number of brightly-coloured African species. Included in this group are the ox-peckers, which live in mutualism with such large animals as the Rhinoceros. Mynahs, noted for their ability to talk, are captured in the hill country of India or Indo-China, and are exported from these areas for sale as cage-birds all over the world (See BIRDS; MYNAHS.).

Oxpeckers live with rhinos, feeding on insects and other parasites that infest the big hosts' hides.

YELLOW-BILLED OXPECKER — 8½ in.
Buphagus africanus
Africa south of
the Sahara

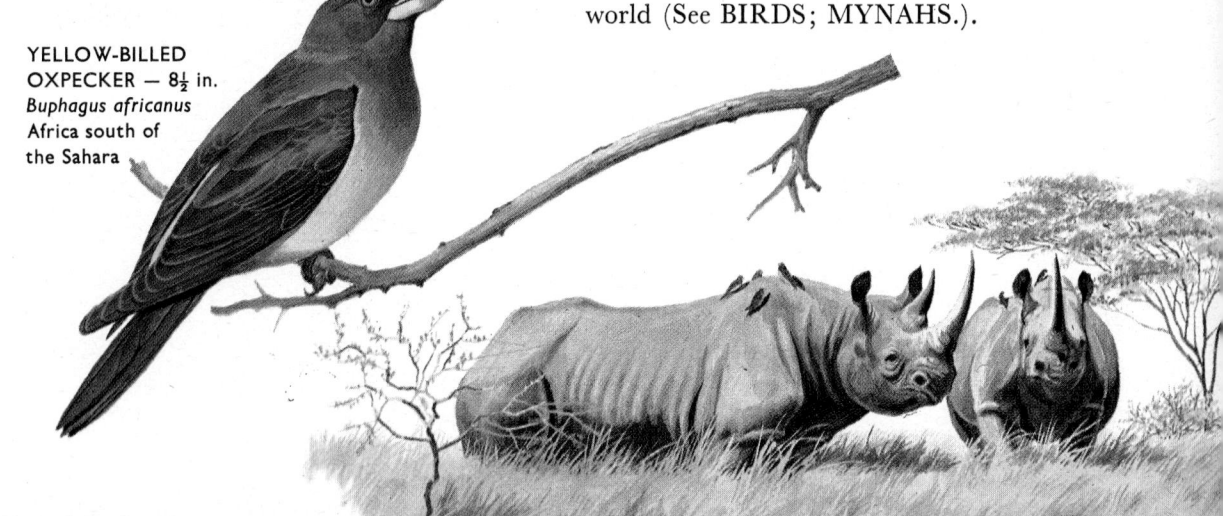

THREE-SPINED STICKLEBACK
Gasterosteus aculeatus
fresh water

TEN-SPINED STICKLEBACK
Pygosteus pungitius
fresh water

FIFTEEN-SPINED SEA-
STICKLEBACK
Spinachia spinachia

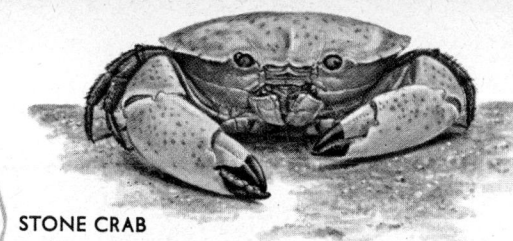

STONE CRAB
to 6 in.

STICKLEBACKS are small marine or freshwater fishes of the cold or temperate waters of the Northern Hemisphere. The name refers to the stout, thorn-like spines in the dorsal fin, and in England the number of spines can be used to distinguish the species (Three-spined, Ten-spined and Fifteen-spined Sticklebacks).

Male sticklebacks build elaborate nests out of the stems of aquatic plants, which they bind together with fine strands of mucus secreted from the kidneys. During the breeding season, the males of the Three-spined Stickleback develop a bright red under-surface. They entice the female into the nest, where she lays the eggs. The male then enters, fertilises the eggs and guards the nest until the eggs hatch, fanning the nest and eggs with its pectoral fins.

The Three-spined Stickleback (*Gasterosteus aculeatus*) occurs throughout most of the Northern Hemisphere, in both fresh and salt water (mainly in freshwater in England). The Ten-spined Stickleback (*Pyggosteus pungitius*) has a similar distribution, but does not reach so far to the south.

The Fifteen-spined Stickleback (*Spinachia spinachia*) is a purely marine species. It is found all around the coasts of Britain, and also inhabits the Baltic and North Sea. In this species, the male changes to a blue colour during the breeding season, and the seaweed nest is pear-shaped.

STONE CRABS (*Menippe mercenaria*) are relished for their delicate flavour. They live in waters off southern Florida and in the West Indies, where they are the basis for a special fishery. These heavy-shelled crabs have powerful armoured claws, one of which is much larger than the other. Their pinch is painful and may inflict a deep cut. Only the meat of the large claw is usually used for food. In Tampa Bay, where these crabs are caught commercially, the large claw is broken off, and the crab is thrown back into the bay. Within a couple of months, the small claw grows rapidly into a large claw, and a new small claw develops where the large one was broken off. This reversal may occur several times. Stone Crabs live in deep, wide burrows in shallow, sandy and rocky areas.

STONEFLIES, members of the order Plecoptera, are usually seen resting on trees or shrubs near water. They are not strong flyers. Most adult stoneflies are less than an inch long, although some exceed two inches. They are generally dull coloured, and the males are usually smaller than the females.

Females drop their eggs into the water in masses, and the immature stoneflies, or naiads, which look like the adults but lack wings, live under stones in flowing water. Most species prey on other animals, but some are vegetarians. They are not able to live in water with a low oxygen content, thus they are good indicators of water

STONEFLY
Plecoptera spp.
0.7 in.

adult

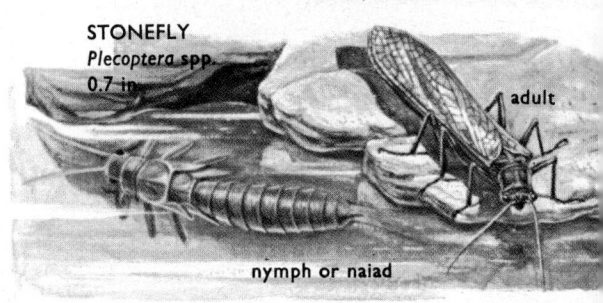

nymph or naiad

pollution. After shedding their skin a number of times and increasing in size with each moult, the nymphs (or naiads) crawl on to vegetation or rocks along the water's edge, and then shed a final time to become adults. Often the adults emerge early in the spring, when there is still ice on the water. Stonefly naiads are an important food for bass, trout, and other freshwater fishes. Most stoneflies eat very little or nothing at all as adults, but a few of the more than 1,000 species are pests of plants.

STORKS are long-legged birds related to the cranes, ibises and herons. Some species have unfeathered patches on their neck and head. Almost voiceless, storks make noises by clapping their bill. They appear very dignified and walk sedately, but when courting they hop up and down, toss their head back, clack their bill, and cavort in ungainly dances.

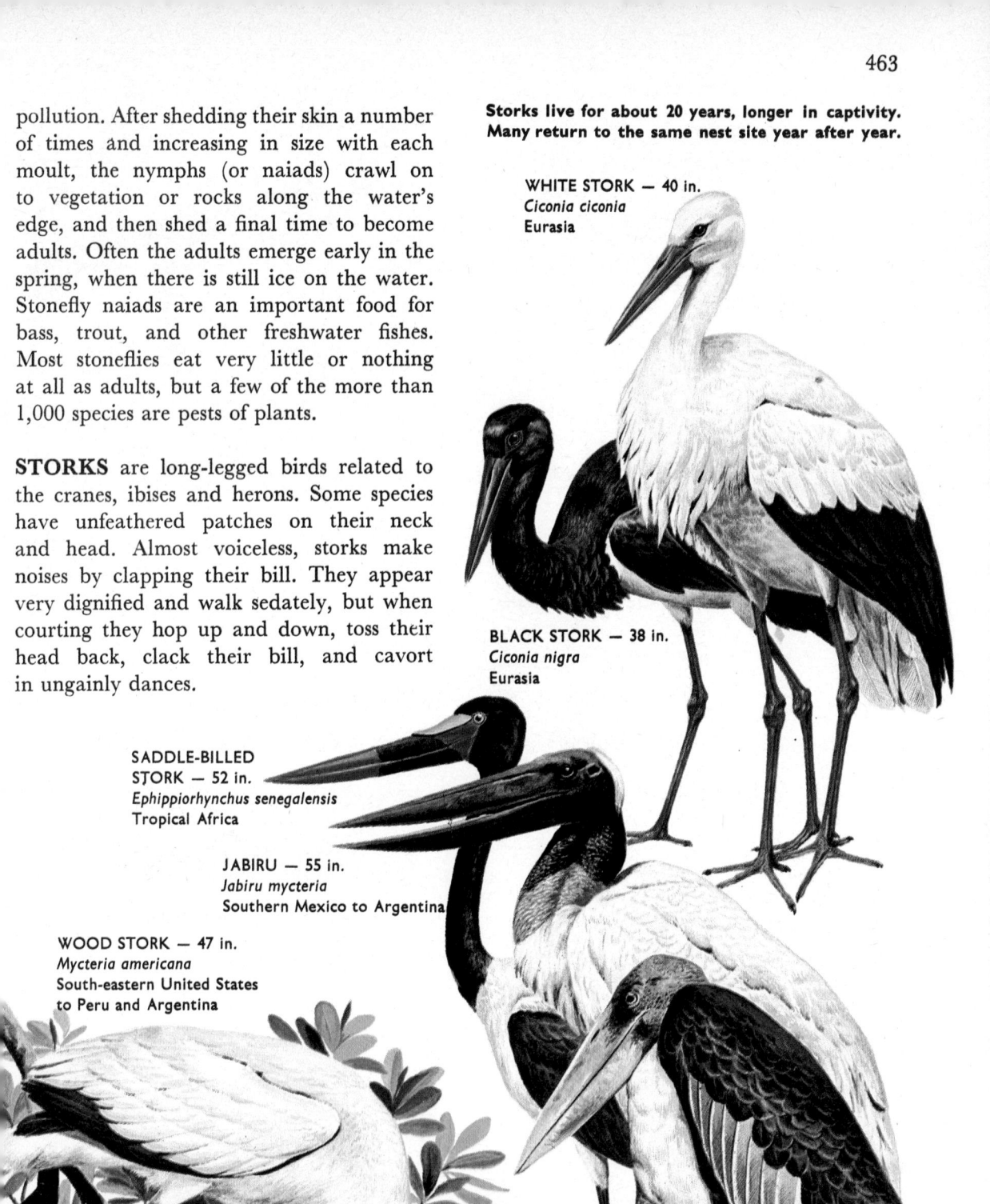

Storks live for about 20 years, longer in captivity. Many return to the same nest site year after year.

WHITE STORK — 40 in.
Ciconia ciconia
Eurasia

BLACK STORK — 38 in.
Ciconia nigra
Eurasia

SADDLE-BILLED STORK — 52 in.
Ephippiorhynchus senegalensis
Tropical Africa

JABIRU — 55 in.
Jabiru mycteria
Southern Mexico to Argentina

WOOD STORK — 47 in.
Mycteria americana
South-eastern United States to Peru and Argentina

MARABOU (ADJUTANT) STORK — 60 in.
Leptopilus crumeniferus
Tropical Africa

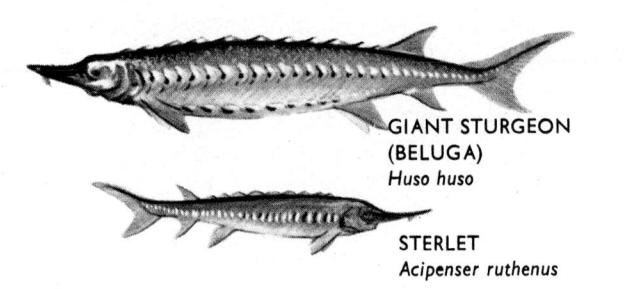

GIANT STURGEON
(BELUGA)
Huso huso

STERLET
Acipenser ruthenus

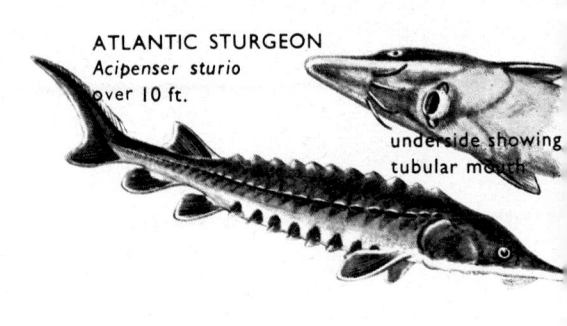

ATLANTIC STURGEON
Acipenser sturio
over 10 ft.

underside showing
tubular mouth

Storks nest in high trees, on cliffs, and on the top of buildings. Both parents take care of the naked young. The nestling birds spit out indigestible food waste in pellets.

Storks are powerful flyers that can soar and glide gracefully. Northern species are migrants. The European White Storks winter in Africa, where they may follow locust swarms and feed on them. In many parts, it is regarded as a symbol of good luck to have them nest on your house, and special platforms are therefore put up for them. They build great twig nests, which they return to year after year.

The Great-billed Marabou, with its capacious crop, is a scavenger, and feeds with vultures on a carcase.

Wood Storks feed in flocks in shallow ponds and bayous (marshy offshoots of rivers in southern North America). They trample the bottom to drive out animals that live in the mud, and eat fish, frogs, small snakes and water-beetles.

Less familiar are the now rare Black Stork of Eurasia and the tall Saddle-billed Storks of tropical Africa. The Jabiru Stork ranges from Mexico south to Argentina.

STURGEONS belong to a primitive group of fishes, once abundant but now represented by about two-dozen species. They are the largest of freshwater fishes, some specimens exceeding 2,000 lbs in weight. They are found in temperate waters of the Northern Hemisphere, some species living in fresh water and others in the sea, but returning to freshwater to breed.

The largest of all sturgeon is the Giant

Sturgeon *(Huso huso)* of the Black Sea, Caspian Sea and Volga River regions; a fish of 28 feet has been recorded. A large female may produce up to five million eggs. These are processed to make the expensive delicacy called caviar. Isinglass is another by-product of the fisheries (made from air-bladders).

The Atlantic Sturgeon *(Acipenser sturio)* was formerly caught in the Thames, but there have been no recent records of its presence. It feeds on small invertebrates, stirring the bottom with its snout.

SHOVELNOSE STURGEON (U.S.A.)
Scaphirynchus platorhynchus
Up to 32 in., 10 lbs.

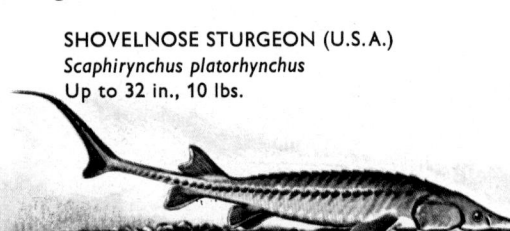

Sturgeons have a tubular mouth, which they extend to suck in food. Feelers, or barbels, on the chin help to detect small food animals.

SUNBEAM SNAKE *(Xenopeltis unicolor).* Named for its beautiful, smooth, iridescent scales, the Sunbeam Snake lives in ricefields and gardens in south-eastern Asia. About 40 inches long, this snake spends its day hidden under logs or in the earth, and emerges only at night. It eats frogs and other small ground vertebrates, including other snakes. The Sunbeam Snake is a non-venomous, docile creature whose sole method of defence is a rapid vibration of the stumpy tail. The Sunbeam Snake is related to other primitive families of snakes, including the Oriental pipesnake and shield-tail snakes (See COLUBRID SNAKES; SNAKES.).

SPOTTED SUNFISH
Lepomis punctatus
Average 6—8 in.; $\frac{1}{2}$—1 lb.

SUNFISHES are a group of North American freshwater fishes belonging to the family Centrarchidae. In appearance, most resemble the Perch, but have the spiny and the soft portions of the dorsal fin continuous. The best-known members of this family are the Black Basses (see BASSES) and the Bluegill Sunfishes *(Lepomis* spp.).

The Bluegills are known for their nest-building habit. The males construct the nest, and then entice a female to swim over it and deposit the eggs. The male then fertilises the eggs and guards them against predators. Bluegills are small fishes, mature at less than 4 inches, but under exceptional circumstances they have been known to grow to over a foot in length.

The Crappies *(Pomoxis* spp.) are slightly larger, averaging one or two pounds in weight. Large catches are made in spring, when they congregate to spawn.

Sunfishes are carnivorous, feeding on insects, worms, crustaceans, amphibians or other fishes. Some species will form hybrids.

SWALLOWS and martins, with a worldwide distribution, are specialised for catching insects on the wing. Their long, narrow wings and forked tails enable them to fly fast and manoeuvre easily. The Swallow has always been well-loved as a bird which will nest on a rafter or support of a building, using cattle-sheds in northern Europe, but, further south and east, entering the unglassed windows of houses to nest inside. The nest of mud-pellets and grass, lined with feathers, is built on a ledge. When the young have first fledged, they may be fed on the wing by the parents. The Swallow has a rambling, musical, twittering song that is uttered on a perch, or on the wing, at most times of year. Its choice of nesting place has earned it the name of "Barn Swallow" in America.

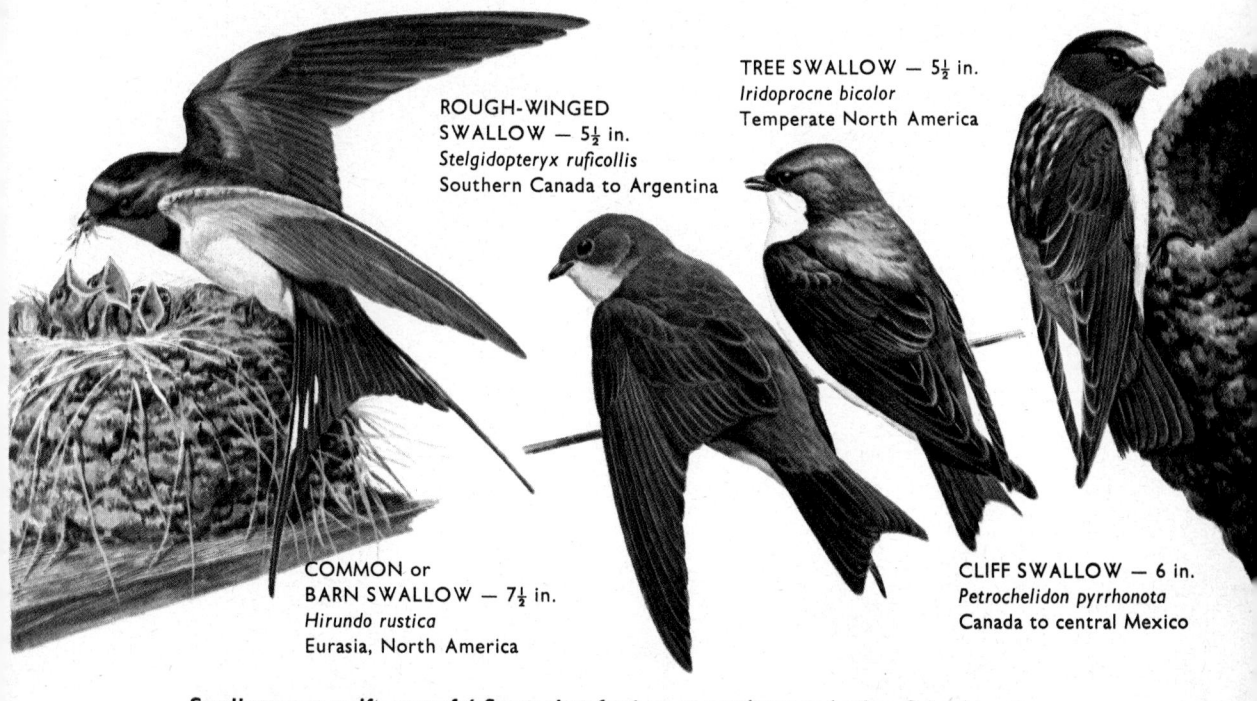

ROUGH-WINGED
SWALLOW — 5$\frac{1}{2}$ in.
Stelgidopteryx ruficollis
Southern Canada to Argentina

TREE SWALLOW — 5$\frac{1}{2}$ in.
Iridoprocne bicolor
Temperate North America

COMMON or
BARN SWALLOW — 7$\frac{1}{2}$ in.
Hirundo rustica
Eurasia, North America

CLIFF SWALLOW — 6 in.
Petrochelidon pyrrhonota
Canada to central Mexico

Swallows are swift, graceful flyers that feed on mosquitoes and other flying insects.

The Red-rumped Swallow of southern Europe is similar in appearance, but builds a mud nest with an entrance spout, stuck to the underside of a bridge or a rock.

The House Martin is another species which sticks its nest to an overhang. Originally, the mud cup must have been fixed to a rock overhang, but the usual site now is under the eaves of a house roof. It lacks the swallow's song and utters a short, harsh note. The House Martin is sociable, and nests are often placed close together.

The Sand Martin is the smallest and least colourful of the commoner species. A little brown bird with a small bill, it nevertheless burrows into a sand-quarry face to make a nest tunnel. Like the other species, it is a migrant, and in autumn great flocks are often seen feeding over stretches of water and roosting in reedbeds.

SWALLOWTAILS *(Papilionidae)* are butterflies of medium to large size, and are easily recognised by the tail-like projections at the rear margins of each hind wing. Wings of most species are black, marked

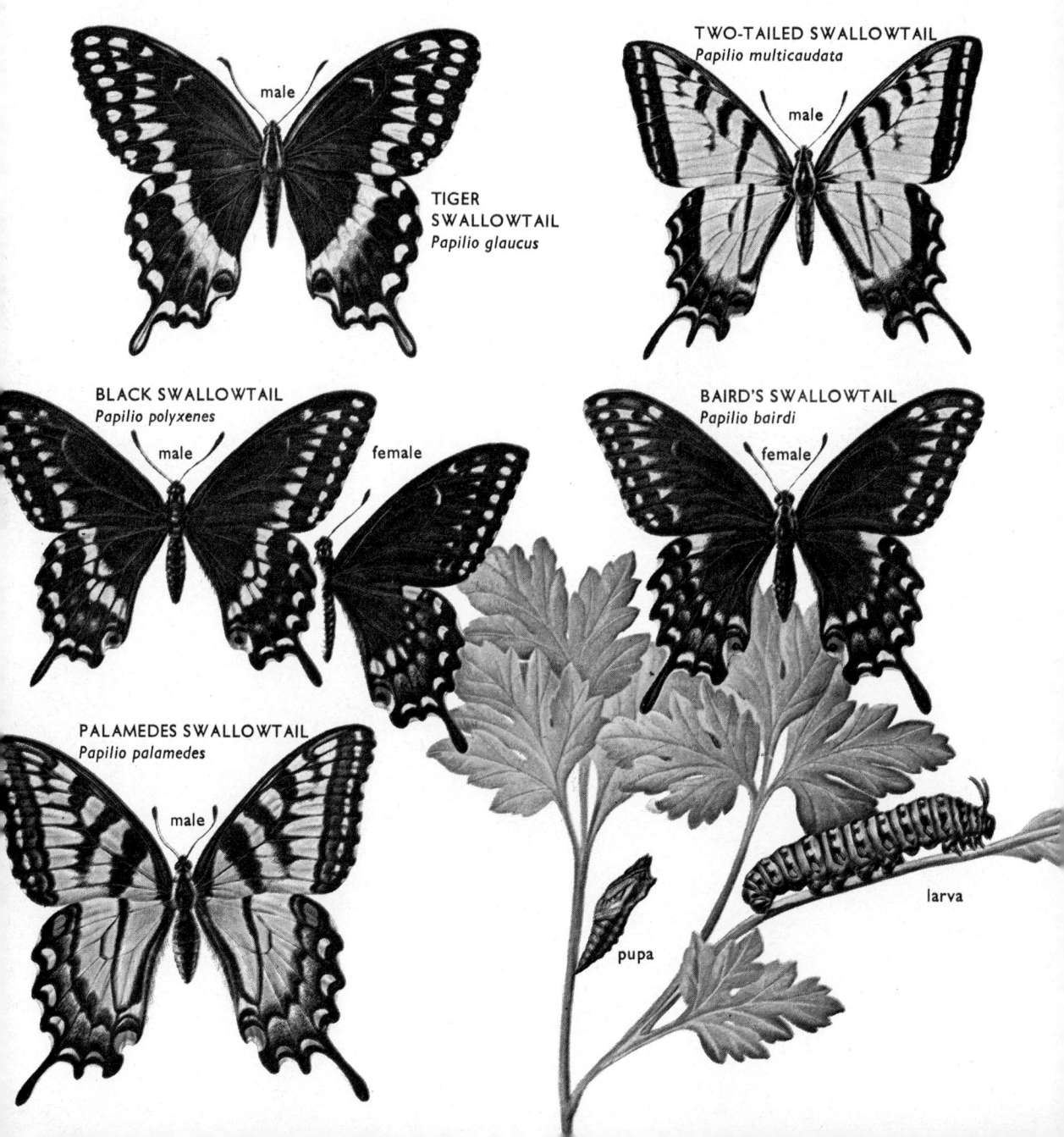

TWO-TAILED SWALLOWTAIL
Papilio multicaudata
male

TIGER SWALLOWTAIL
Papilio glaucus
male

BLACK SWALLOWTAIL
Papilio polyxenes
male female

BAIRD'S SWALLOWTAIL
Papilio bairdi
female

PALAMEDES SWALLOWTAIL
Papilio palamedes
male

pupa

larva

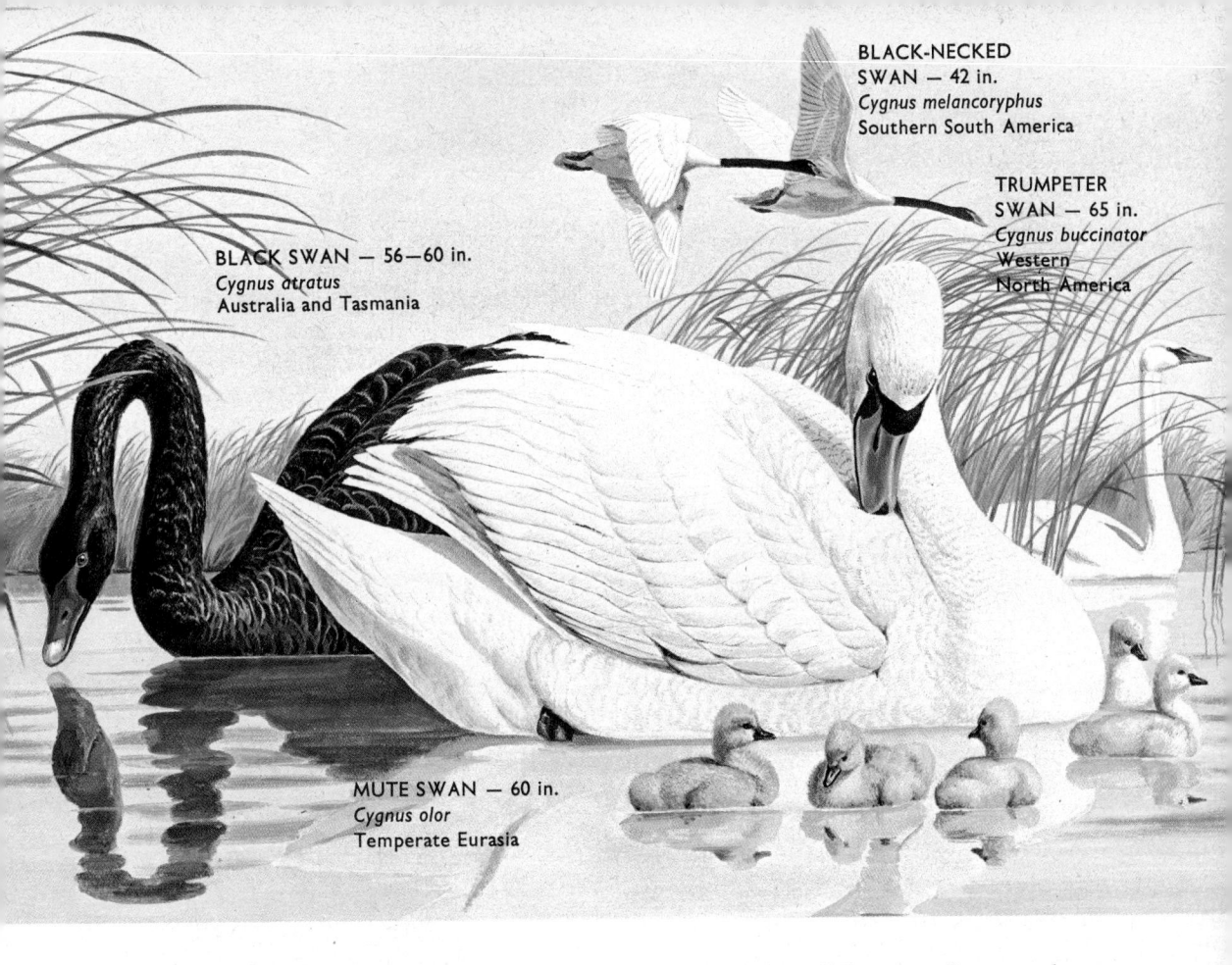

BLACK-NECKED
SWAN — 42 in.
Cygnus melancoryphus
Southern South America

TRUMPETER
SWAN — 65 in.
Cygnus buccinator
Western
North America

BLACK SWAN — 56—60 in.
Cygnus atratus
Australia and Tasmania

MUTE SWAN — 60 in.
Cygnus olor
Temperate Eurasia

with yellow, red, green or blue. Often the colour pattern of the two sexes differ.

Caterpillars of swallowtails are smooth-bodied and quite varied in colour. All have a forked, usually orange gland, located on top, near the front of the thorax. When a caterpillar is disturbed, its forked gland shoots out, and at the same time a rather strong odour is released. This defensive mechanism protects the caterpillar from enemies. Pupae of swallowtails are attached to twigs by the tail, supported in an upright position by a silken median girdle.

SWANS are the largest of the water-fowls. Their short legs are used mainly for propulsion, so they tend to waddle slowly on land, but glide majestically on the water. The long neck is used for reaching down below the surface, in order to haul up the waterweed on which they feed. Swans also graze on water-side turf to a limited extent, but sufficiently for the Icelandic farmers

to claim that Whooper Swans threaten the food of their sheep. Swans have difficulty in rising from the water, and must run along the surface before actually rising in flight. Once in flight, however, they move rapidly and strongly. The wings on Mute Swans produce a lovely musical sound as they beat, and can be heard from a distance.

The non-migratory and tame Mute Swans were once a useful source of food. They were domesticated in England well before 1186. Laws forbade the ownership of swans without a licence from the King. Swans were marked with a notch on their bills and, during the reign of Queen Elizabeth I, over 900 such ownership marks were recognised. Each spring a "swan-upping", in which young birds were marked, was held on rivers, and this custom is still maintained annually on the Thames today.

The Mute Swan is not, in fact, so silent; it grunts, hisses, growls and croaks. Other species have better voices, however, and

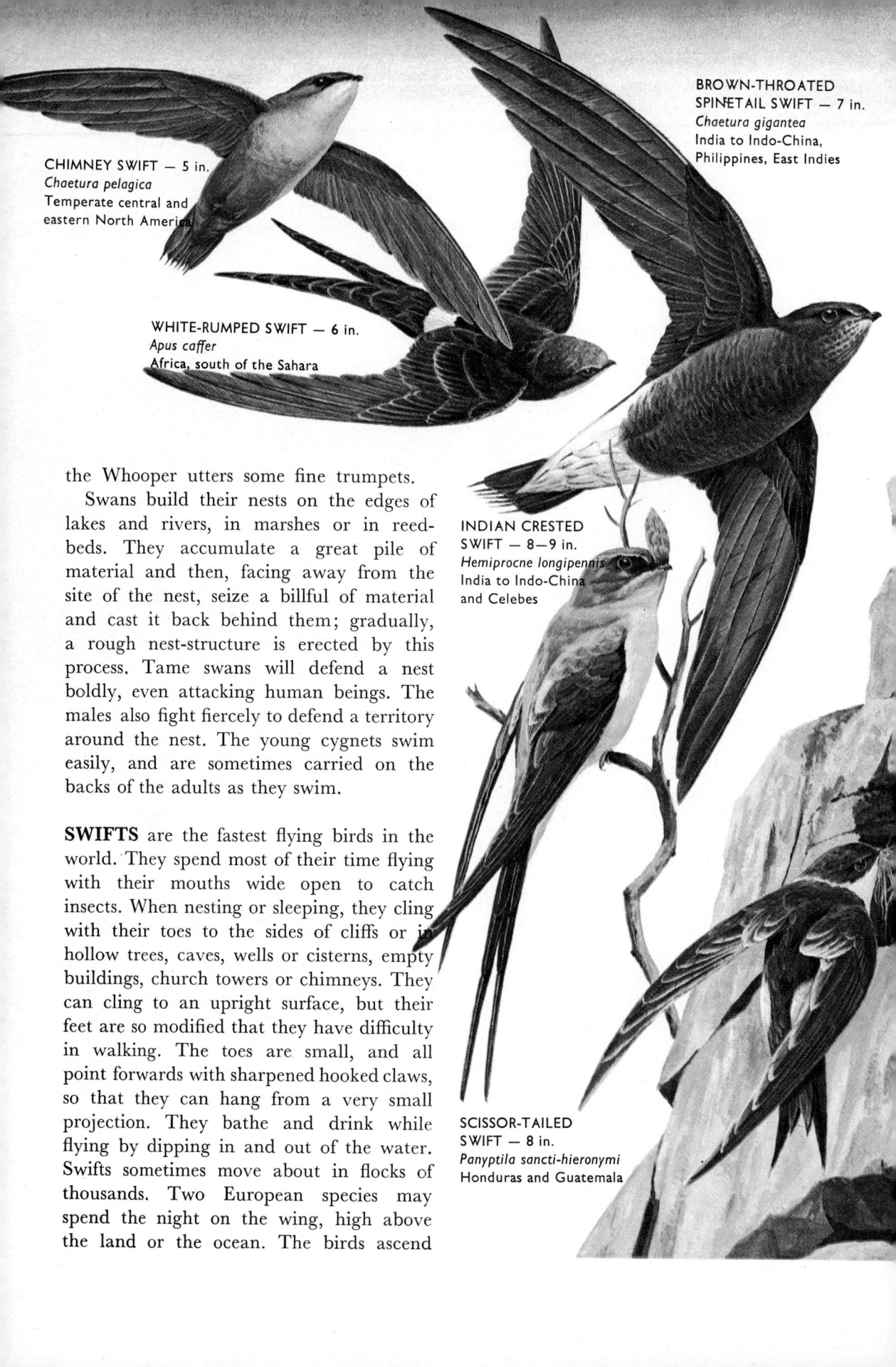

CHIMNEY SWIFT — 5 in.
Chaetura pelagica
Temperate central and
eastern North America

WHITE-RUMPED SWIFT — 6 in.
Apus caffer
Africa, south of the Sahara

**BROWN-THROATED
SPINETAIL SWIFT — 7 in.**
Chaetura gigantea
India to Indo-China,
Philippines, East Indies

**INDIAN CRESTED
SWIFT — 8—9 in.**
Hemiprocne longipennis
India to Indo-China
and Celebes

**SCISSOR-TAILED
SWIFT — 8 in.**
Panyptila sancti-hieronymi
Honduras and Guatemala

the Whooper utters some fine trumpets.

Swans build their nests on the edges of lakes and rivers, in marshes or in reed-beds. They accumulate a great pile of material and then, facing away from the site of the nest, seize a billful of material and cast it back behind them; gradually, a rough nest-structure is erected by this process. Tame swans will defend a nest boldly, even attacking human beings. The males also fight fiercely to defend a territory around the nest. The young cygnets swim easily, and are sometimes carried on the backs of the adults as they swim.

SWIFTS are the fastest flying birds in the world. They spend most of their time flying with their mouths wide open to catch insects. When nesting or sleeping, they cling with their toes to the sides of cliffs or in hollow trees, caves, wells or cisterns, empty buildings, church towers or chimneys. They can cling to an upright surface, but their feet are so modified that they have difficulty in walking. The toes are small, and all point forwards with sharpened hooked claws, so that they can hang from a very small projection. They bathe and drink while flying by dipping in and out of the water. Swifts sometimes move about in flocks of thousands. Two European species may spend the night on the wing, high above the land or the ocean. The birds ascend

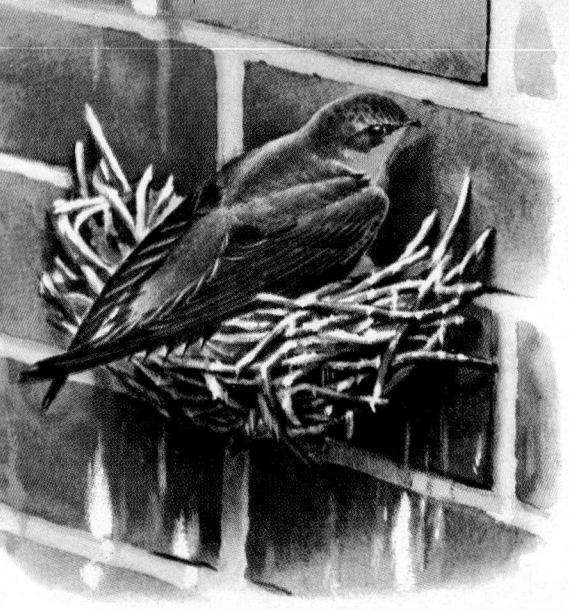

The Chimney Swift's nest is made of small twigs bonded together by the bird's saliva. It is fastened to a wall or to the inside of a chimney.

beyond sight at dusk, and are not seen again until the following day.

Swifts secrete a glue-like saliva. With this they build their nests and cement them to walls. While species like the American Chimney Swift glue cap-shaped nests of twigs to vertical walls, the Common Swift nests on a ledge in a house roof, or in a hole in a cliff, and needs little nest material. When stormy weather makes it difficult for the parents to find food, the young may go for long periods without being fed.

The Cave Swiftlets of southern Asia build nests out of their saliva, adding little or no other material. The Chinese use these nests to make bird's-nest soup; similar to gelatine, the nest is full of protein and very nourishing. Collecting, cleaning and drying Swiftlet's nests is a large industry in southeastern Asia. The birds build a second nest when the first is taken away.

SWIMMING CRABS form a large family of scavenger species that crawl about on the bottom, searching for food. Although they prefer the bottom, they can swim quite well by using their flattened and paddle-like hind legs. Thousands of people go crabbing each summer to catch the Blue, or Channel, Crab *(Callinectes sapidus)*, one of the largest of the group and a delicacy.

The Blue Crab lives during the summer in shallow, often slightly brackish water; it moves into deeper water during the cold months. When a female is carrying the orange eggs under her abdomen, she is said to be "in berry". Like most crustaceans, the Blue Crab must shed its shell in order to grow, and for a short period after moulting, the new shell is paper-thin and soft. This is the famed "soft shell" crab. In a few hours, however, the shell hardens.

Crabs have segmented bodies, as do shrimps, crayfish and lobsters. Crabs, however, have all but the first segment recurved under the first segment. These additional segments are wider in females than in males; the first segment may be wider than it is long (See CRAYFISH; LOBSTERS; SHRIMPS and PRAWNS.).

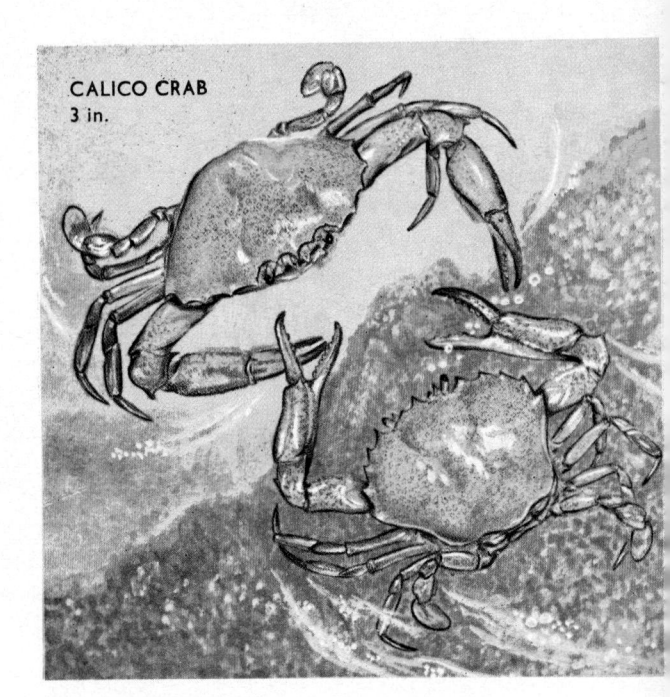

CALICO CRAB
3 in.

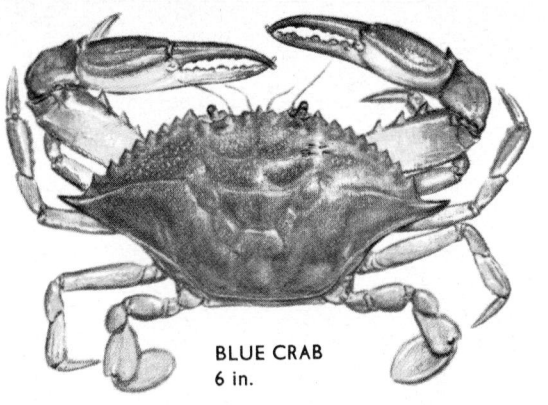

BLUE CRAB
6 in.

T

TAILED TOADS *(Ascaphus)* are the most primitive living anurans. They are found in the high mountains of the north-western United States and south-western Canada, where the cold surroundings are too severe for more "advanced" types of amphibians that have continued to evolve. By holding fast to stones with their mouth discs, the larvae live in the swift waters of mountain streams. Although referred to as tailed toads, the "tail" is actually an organ for fertilisation, and is present only in the male. It is the only frog in which fertilisation is internal. The New Zealand Leiopelma Toad is probably closely related; it lays its eggs on land, and they develop into froglets.

TANAGERS are small birds (3 to 12 in.) that live in temperate and tropic regions of the Western Hemisphere. Most tanagers are tropical birds and they are brilliantly coloured. Many are largely red; others are blue, green or yellow. These colours are

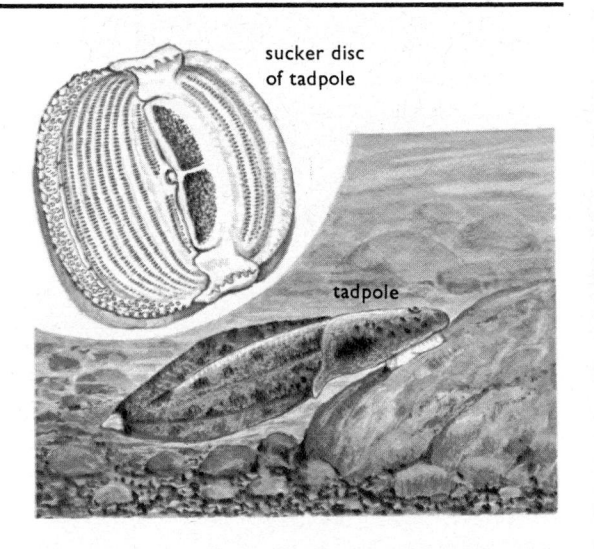

sucker disc of tadpole

tadpole

generally accented with black markings. Of the 222 known species, only 4 occur in North America. They all live in trees, many of them in the tops, 60 feet above ground.

Tanagers are closely related to finches and have similar cone-shaped bills, but usually with a notch in the cutting edge; possibly this notch is useful in eating fruit, one of the tanager's favourite foods. Tropical tanagers do not migrate, but northern tanagers do, always flying at night.

The Golden-masked Tanager ranges from southern Mexico through Central America into South America. Males and females are so much alike that often they cannot be told apart. Once mated they remain together, but only the female incubates the eggs. The male brings the female food, calls to her, and flies with her when she leaves the eggs to eat and rest. When the eggs hatch, the male joins her in feeding the young. These tanagers raise at least three broods a year, and the birds of the first brood often help to feed their younger brothers and sisters on insects, mistletoe berries, bananas and other fruits. The

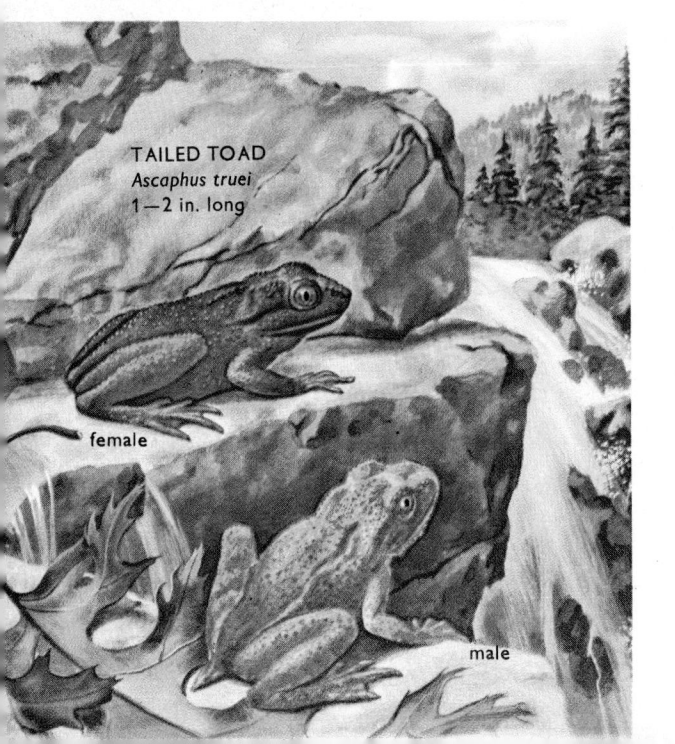

TAILED TOAD
Ascaphus truei
1 — 2 in. long

female

male

Golden-masked Tanager has no song, but mated pairs keep contact with each other by making ticking calls.

The Scarlet Tanager breeds in eastern North America, from southern Canada to northern Alabama and Georgia; it winters in north-western South America. Scarlet Tanagers are often heard when they cannot be seen in the heavy foliage overhead. Their song is much like that of the Robin, and their alarm call is a strident "chip". Their breeding habits are like those of the Golden-masked Tanager, but the Scarlet Tanager raises only one brood each year. Further south, the similar Summer Tanager occurs, but in this species the male is entirely scarlet, including the wings.

TAPIRS (*Tapirus spp.*) are mammals that resemble miniature elephants, with short, stocky legs and sawn-off trunks. Their flexible snouts, which extend only a few inches beyond the mouth, are used to pull twigs and branches from trees. Adult tapirs are dark, or with the middle part of the body white; the young are spotted or striped all over. Their tails are short, the hoofs oval. Tapirs live in swampy areas or in tropical rain-forests and often take to the water, where they swim well. Active at night, they are rarely seen in the daytime. One group of tapirs is found in Central America and northern South America, another group in southern Burma, Siam,

The South American Tapir lives in the hot, moist lowlands. It stands three feet high and is six feet long. The one illustrated is young.

Harold Schultz — Birmback

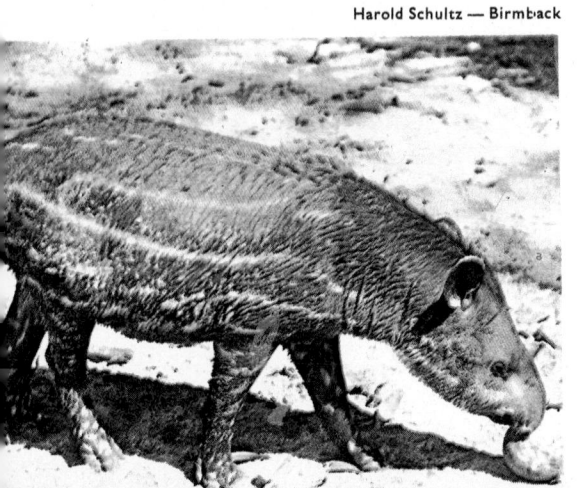

MASKED TANAGER — 5¼ in.
Tangara nigro-cincta
Mexico to Bolivia

PARADISE TANAGER — 5¾ in.
Tangara chilensis
Colombia to Brazil and Bolivia

BLACK-EARED TANAGER — 6 in.
Tangara parzudakii
Colombia to Peru

SCARLET-RUMPED TANAGER — 7 in.
Ramphocelus passerinii
Mexico to Panama

BLUE-GREY TANAGER — 7—8 in.
Thraupis virens
Mexico to Brazil

SCARLET TANAGER — 7 in.
Piranga olivacea
Eastern North America

Malaya and Sumatra. Most tapirs weigh about 500 pounds, and measure about 3½ feet high at the shoulder. One which lives high in the Andes has long hair. Those of the Malayan tropics have a band of white around their body.

TARSIERS (*Tarsius tarsier*), which weigh only a few ounces, are the smallest of the primates. Found in the East Indian islands and the Philippines, they live in bamboo

thickets and at the edges of dense forests. Tarsiers are nocturnal and use their large eyes to find their principal food, insects and lizards. During the day they hide in dark places. They can rotate their head as much as 170 degrees in each direction. The long limbs end in broad adhesive pads at the tips of their thin fingers and toes. Their very long and thinly-haired tail ends in a bushy tuft.

The importance of Tarsiers is far greater than their size would indicate. Studies of the anatomy of these creatures indicate that they are probably very close to the

A Tarsier is a primitive primate no larger than a small squirrel. It uses its padded fingers to hold on to branches and to grasp food while feeding.

Cy La Tour

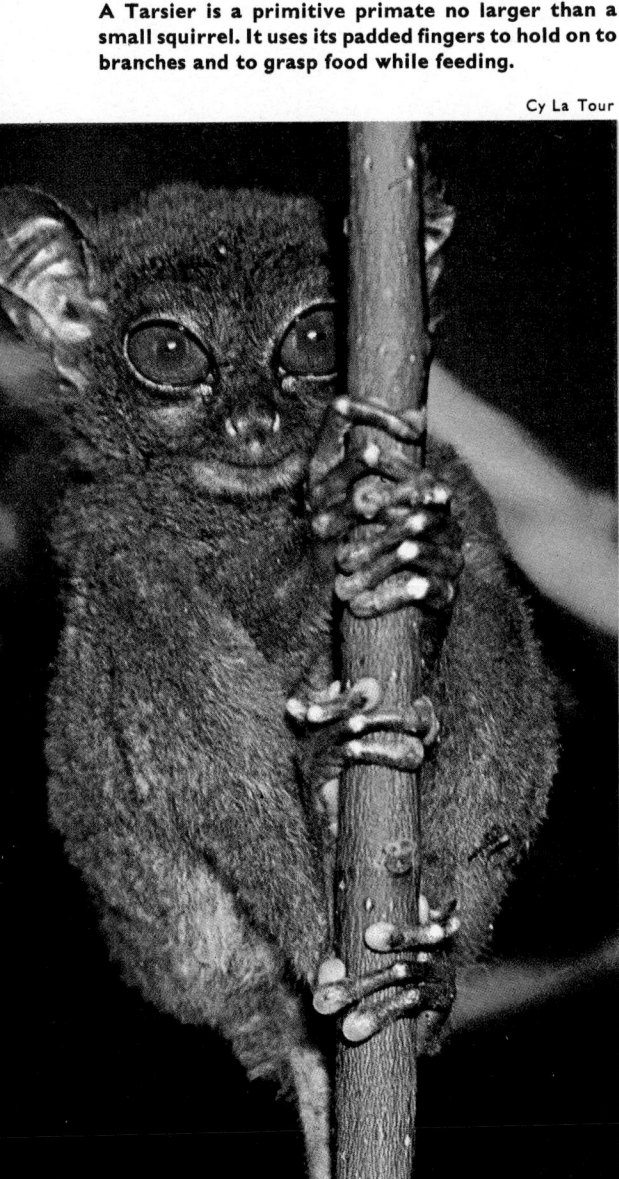

ancestral stock of all the primates. They represent a refinement of the shrew-like insectivores and include such advanced characteristics as binocular vision, opposable thumbs and upright posture. Fossil discoveries disclose that present-day Tarsiers had many quite similar relatives about 60 million years ago. (See PRIMATES.)

TEJIDS are lizards of some 225 species that are found only in the Americas. The majority of tejids occur from Mexico south into South America, where they are most numerous, but Whiptail lizards occur farther north, in the United States — the only members of this group to do so. They live in dry regions.

Largest tejids are the four-foot Caiman Lizards *(Dracaena)* living in South American swamps and rivers. Caiman Lizards feed primarily on snails and other molluscs, crushing the shells in their broad, molar-like teeth, and spitting out the broken bits.

Nearly as large is the somewhat skin-like three-foot Tegu *(Tupinambis)*, a heavy-bodied predator that eats almost all kinds of small animals, their eggs or young. This lizard is commonly kept in zoos. Equally as large is the speedy False Monitor *(Tejovaranus)* of the deserts of coastal Peru. It feeds largely on other lizards and, when chasing prey, runs on its hind legs with the forelegs outstretched.

At the opposite extreme are slender, three-inch lizards, some of them burrowers with tiny, slender, useless legs, and others with normal legs. One *(Echinosaura)* lives on the jungle floor, where it is concealed among dead leaves and twigs by its brownish colour. When touched it "freezes" in position, taking on the appearance of a dead twig.

TELLINS *(Tellina* spp.*)* are highly prized by collectors, for their array of colours, and glossy or finely-sculptured shells, make them among the most beautiful of all bivalves. They are active burrowers that live in sandy areas. Many species occur in the West Indies and in coastal waters of the south-

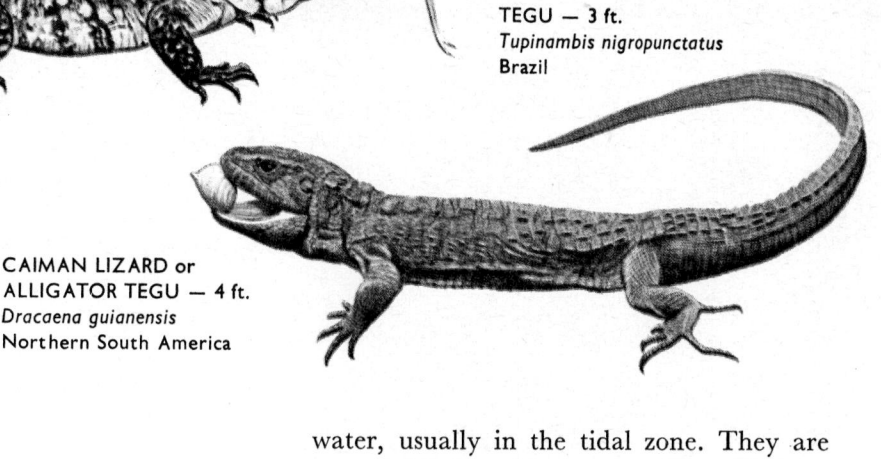

TEGU — 3 ft.
Tupinambis nigropunctatus
Brazil

CAIMAN LIZARD or
ALLIGATOR TEGU — 4 ft.
Dracaena guianensis
Northern South America

water, usually in the tidal zone. They are extremely fast burrowers. The inhalant siphon of these very narrow shells is greatly elongated, and is used in a vacuum-cleaner fashion to collect organic debris from sand.

eastern United States, and a number are also found along the beaches of the Pacific Coast. The Hatchet Tellin is found in the Mediterranean, and the Full-blooded Tellin is native to South-East Asia.

Most prized is the Sunrise Tellin, which grows to four inches and is rayed with all the colours of a tropical sunrise. Tampa, Rose Petal, Dwarf and Speckled tellins are all found along southern Atlantic beaches, while the Salmon, Carpenter's and Modest tellins are very well-known Pacific Coast species.

Most of the more than 200 species of tellins live in tropical oceans. The greatest concentration of species is along the shores of countries that surround the Indian Ocean. Tellins are edible, but are not considered to be delicacies; no substantial fishery of tellins exists in any of the regions where they are found. Tellins are found in shallow

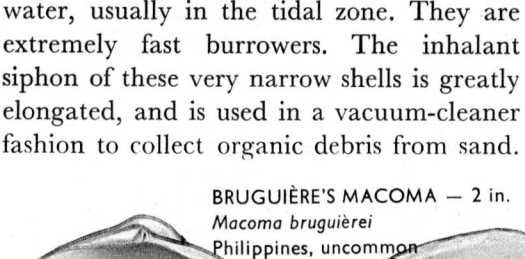

BRUGUIÈRE'S MACOMA — 2 in.
Macoma bruguièrei
Philippines, uncommon

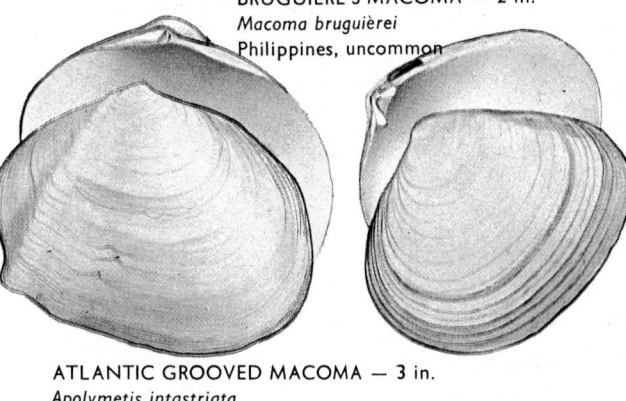

ATLANTIC GROOVED MACOMA — 3 in.
Apolymetis intastriata
Florida — Caribbean

SUNRISE TELLIN — 3 in.
Tellina radiata
Florida and West Indies
Abundant in sand

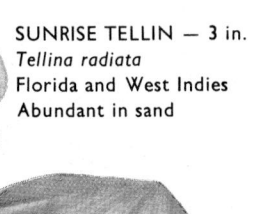

BURNETT'S TELLIDORA — 1½ in.
Tellidora burnetti
West Mexico; uncommon

LARGE STRIGILLA — 1 in.
Strigilla carnaria
S.E. U.S. — Caribbean

VIRGATE TELLIN — 2½ in.
Tellina virgata
Indo-Pacific; common

FULL-BLOODED TELLIN — 3 in.
Tellina consanguinea
S.E. Asia; rare

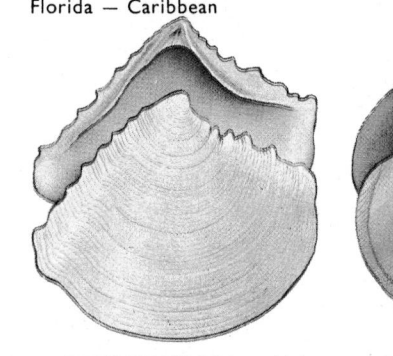
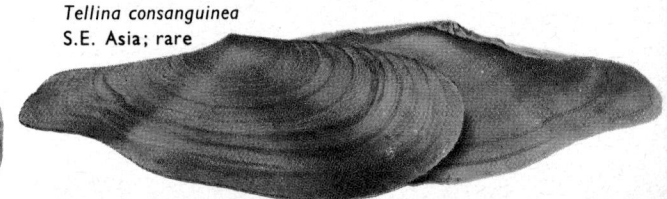

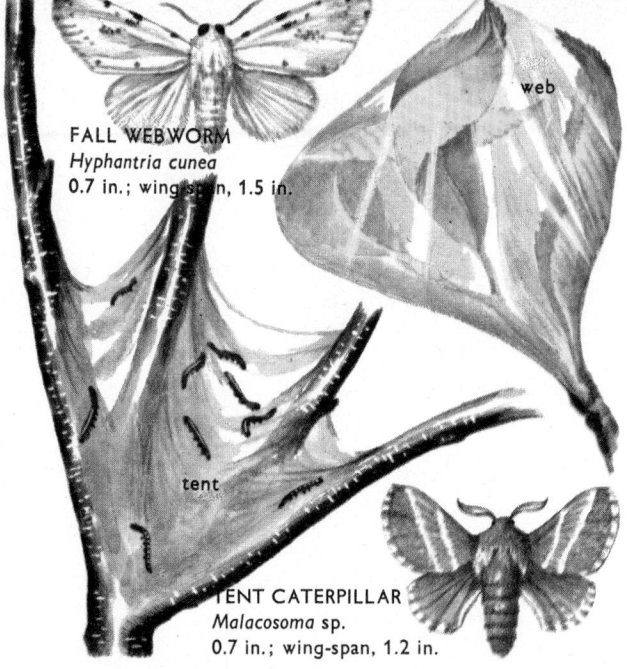

FALL WEBWORM
Hyphantria cunea
0.7 in.; wing-span, 1.5 in.

web

tent

TENT CATERPILLAR
Malacosoma sp.
0.7 in.; wing-span, 1.2 in.

Tent Caterpillars and Fall Webworms are among the most destructive insects of forest, shade and fruit trees in the United States of America.

TENT CATERPILLARS *(Lasiocampidae)* often become so numerous that they defoliate many kinds of fruit and shade trees. Female moths deposit their eggs in close-packed bands around small twigs. The several hundred eggs in each band do not hatch until the following spring. As soon as they hatch, the caterpillars begin constructing their "tents"; this nest is usually made in a fork of a branch. Each time they leave the tent to feed, the caterpillars spin a silk thread along their path. The tent is enlarged continuously as the caterpillars grow; in about six weeks, the caterpillars are ready to pupate. They usually spin their white cocoons on tree-trunks, buildings, or other objects. After pupating, they emerge as adult moths in about two weeks.

TERMITES are often called "white ants", although they are not, in fact, ants at all. Nevertheless, many termites do resemble ants in their habits and appearance. The two can be told apart easily, however, by looking at the way their abdomen joins the thorax. A termite's abdomen connects to its thorax broadly, but an ant's abdomen joins its thorax by a stem-like connection.

Termites are a primitive group, forming the order *Isoptera*; ants, with bees and wasps, are of the order *Hymenoptera*.

Most of the more than 1,500 species of termites are found in the tropics; about 60 live in North America. All termites are members of highly-organised colonies. Some live entirely underground, but others build huge, cement-like mounds above the ground, 20 or 30 feet high and as big around. A few make nests in trees or on stumps.

Inside a termite colony are individuals of several different types. Some are young termites, or nymphs; others are members of various castes, each of which performs a different function to maintain the colony.

Every year a large number of brown or black termites with fully-developed wings swarm from each colony. These are members of the first reproductive caste. When they land, they shed their wings. Then the males and females pair off and select a suitable place for a new nest. Each mated pair becomes the king and queen of the colony, and they are the only individuals in the new colony having wing-stubs. Shortly after the

A termite colony consists of a king, queen, workers, soldiers, and winged reproductives.

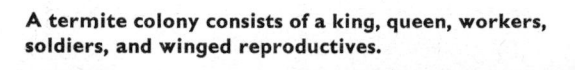

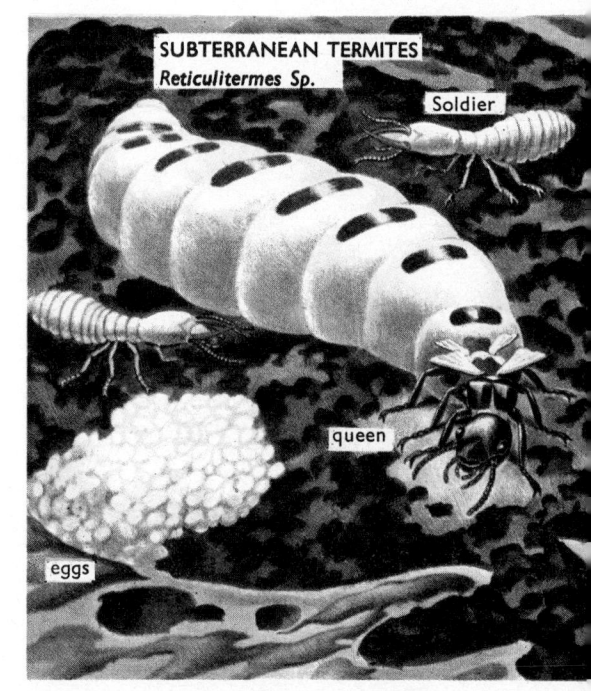

SUBTERRANEAN TERMITES
Reticulitermes Sp.

Soldier

queen

eggs

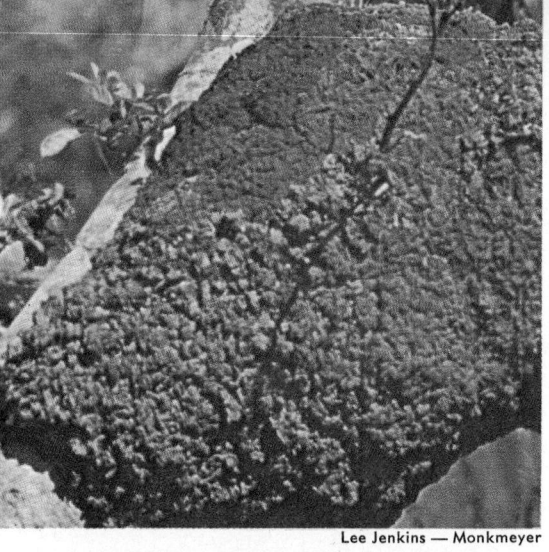

Some species of tropical termites build nests of mud in trees, connected to the ground with mud-covered paths.

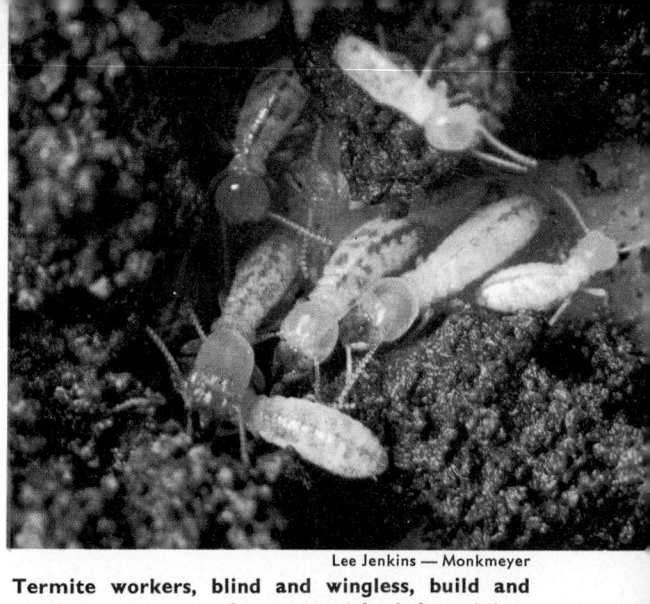

Termite workers, blind and wingless, build and repair the nest, care for eggs and feed the soldiers and the queen.

new nest has been started, the queen's abdomen becomes swollen, and she begins laying eggs; some termite queens become six to eight inches long. No longer able to move, the queens remain enclosed in the royal chamber with the king. Queens of some species lay more than a million eggs in their lifetime, and some are known to live for several years.

The second reproductive caste consists of pale termites, both males and females, with wing-buds that never develop completely.

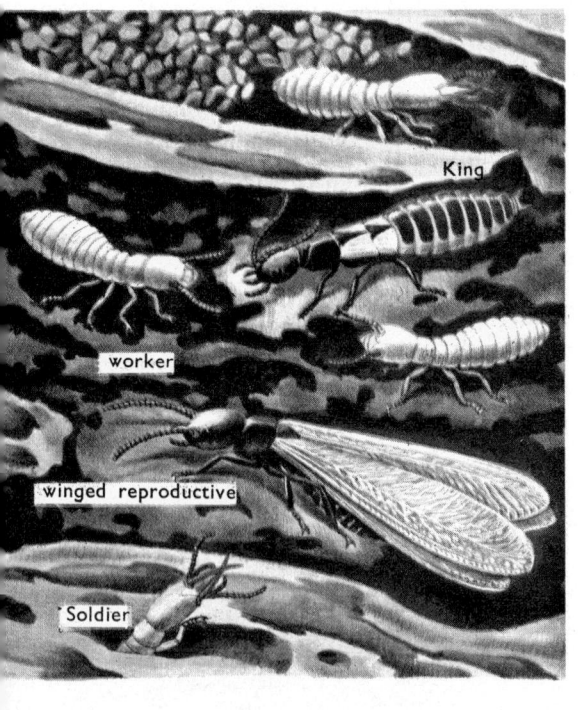

King

worker

winged reproductive

Soldier

If something happens to either the king or the queen, members of the second reproductive caste take over the task of producing eggs. Even under normal conditions, the secondary females may lay eggs to supplement those of the busily productive queen.

Members of the worker caste do the hard labour in the colony. They are either nymphs or sterile adults, and do not have wings. They collect food, feed the queen, take care of the newly-hatched young, and maintain the nest and its tunnels.

Termites in the soldier caste are also sterile adults and, like the workers, are wingless and pale. They are usually a little larger than workers, and have a large head and mandibles. In some termites, the soldiers have such large mandibles that they are unable to feed themselves. They depend on workers to put food in their mouths. Their job is to protect the colony from enemies. In some termites, a special soldier caste have heads formed into snouts, from which they squirt a sticky material at invaders.

Termites eat wood, but are unable to digest the cellulose of which wood is made. They depend on protozoa, one-celled animals in their digestive tracts, to digest the wood for them. Termites cannot live without these protozoa, nor can the protozoa live outside a termite's gut; such an association of dependency is called Symbiosis.

Destructive subterranean termites usually

live in the ground, and build tunnels up the sides of foundations to get at the wood parts of a building. The tunnels protect the termites from exposure to air, which dries out their body quickly and kills them. Termites consume all but a thin outer shell of the wood, and, if not stopped, they can cause a whole building to collapse. Dry-wood termites attack wood that does not touch the ground. They often infest furniture.

Termites are in one sense beneficial, for they convert dead and rotting trees into basic elements in the soil, to be used again by plants in the great chain of life.

TERNS, found throughout the world, are members of the gull family. They occur on all oceans, even the Arctic and Antarctic, and also on many inland lakes, rivers and marshes. Usually smaller and more graceful than gulls, they have slenderer bodies, more pointed wings, and longer, forked tails.

Terns catch their food alive. They dive from the air for fish, or snatch water insects or other small animals from the surface. Because of their slender wings and forked tails, terns are often called "sea swallows".

Terns build simple nests on or near the ground. They usually breed in colonies on uninhabited offshore islands. Terns that breed on lake shores or marshes escape

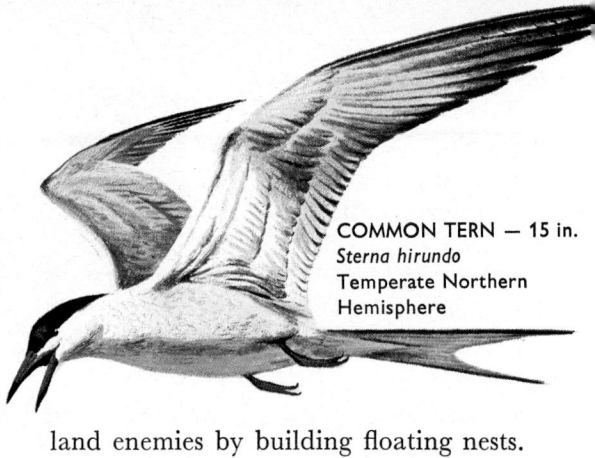

COMMON TERN — 15 in.
Sterna hirundo
Temperate Northern
Hemisphere

land enemies by building floating nests.

Best known and most familiar of the world's 39 species of terns is the Common Tern, which breeds around the world in the Northern Hemisphere, and migrates south to the equator and beyond in winter. Scientists have assembled more exact information about the Common Tern than about any other non-game bird. Since 1920, several million Common Terns have been ringed in North America and in Europe.

Of every 100 Common Tern chicks that grow up and leave the nesting grounds, about 70 die during the first winter, before they have learned to care for themselves.

After the first year, their death rate drops to 25 out of every 100 per year, and continues at this rate as long as they live. Only 7 per cent of the adults live longer than 10 years. One ringed as a chick in England lived to be 25 years of age, the oldest record so far.

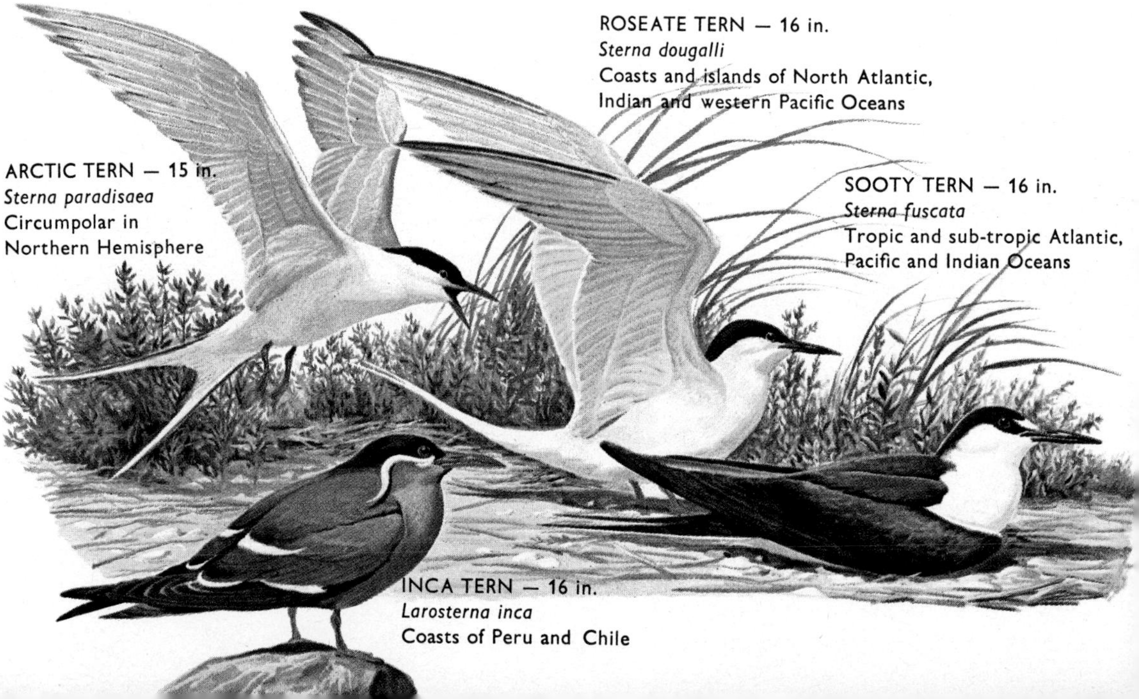

ROSEATE TERN — 16 in.
Sterna dougalli
Coasts and islands of North Atlantic,
Indian and western Pacific Oceans

ARCTIC TERN — 15 in.
Sterna paradisaea
Circumpolar in
Northern Hemisphere

SOOTY TERN — 16 in.
Sterna fuscata
Tropic and sub-tropic Atlantic,
Pacific and Indian Oceans

INCA TERN — 16 in.
Larosterna inca
Coasts of Peru and Chile

Terns do not breed until they are three years old. When young terns come from the wintering grounds to nest for the first time, they return to the island where they were hatched. They nest there, if there is room.

If there is no space, they nest nearby. When the birds return north to breed for the second time, they come first to the same spot where they nested the year before, or as close to it as they can get. Common Terns keep the same mates for life; changing mates is unknown among terns, unless one dies.

The Arctic Tern looks so much like the Common Tern that only experts can tell the two apart. It also breeds circumpolarly in the Northern Hemisphere, but farther north — on the northernmost ice-free coasts and islands. It winters farther south, going almost to the Antarctic Circle. The Arctic Tern is the world's champion migrant, for it covers at least 20,000 miles every year. As it nests in the northern summer during perpetual daylight, and winters where the nights are shortest, it probably sees more sunlight each year than any other animal in the world. The Arctic Tern also holds the tern record for longevity; one ringed in Germany in 1920 was killed in the same place by a cat 27 years later.

The Little Tern, smallest of the terns, is one of the most widely distributed. It nests on all continents and on many islands.

The Sooty Tern is commonly called the Wideawake, because of its call and the noise it makes, day and night, on its breeding grounds. One of the most famous "Wideawake Fairs", as these colonies are called, is on Ascension Island, in the eastern Atlantic near the equator. In this colony, the birds do not time their nesting by the sun, but breed every nine months. In the West Indies, and on the Dry Tortugas Islands off the Florida Keys, they nest every 12 months. They also nest on islands in the Pacific and Indian Oceans.

TERRAPINS are hard-shelled turtles inhabiting fresh or brackish water. Typical forms have a streamlined, oval shell, and webbed

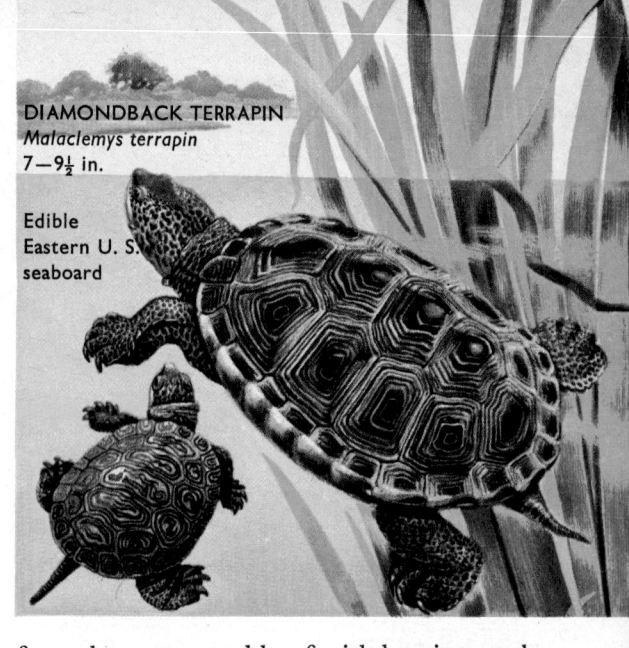

DIAMONDBACK TERRAPIN
Malaclemys terrapin
7—9½ in.

Edible
Eastern U. S.
seaboard

feet; they are capable of withdrawing neck and limbs into their shell. In America, the term terrapin is used exclusively for the edible forms, such as the Diamondback *(Malaclemys)*; but in Europe and Asia it is applied both to the aquatic, edible, gaily-coloured Dura *(Kachuga)*, and Basker *(Batagur)*, as well as to Europe's two genera — *Emys* and *Clemmys*.

The Diamondback, which is found only in the brackish water along the Atlantic coast and the Gulf of Mexico, has long been considered a delicacy and, although once abundant, numbers have dwindled through man's exploitation. Although they do make excellent eating and were the most expensive turtles ever known to man, slaves in the South once went on strike to get relief from a steady diet of terrapins. Terrapins can be

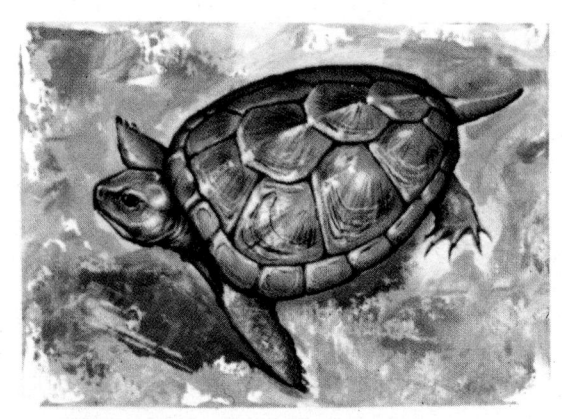

EUROPEAN POND TORTOISE (TERRAPIN)
Emys orbicularis

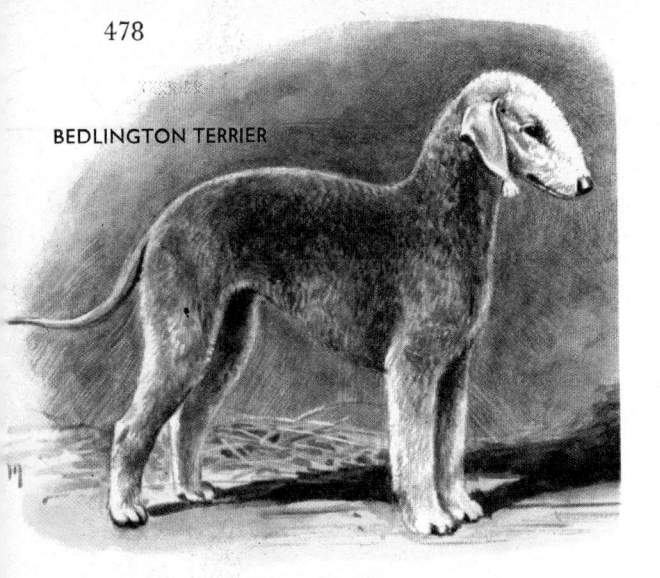

BEDLINGTON TERRIER

Schnauzer, a German breed. British terriers were developed originally as hunting dogs for such game as rabbits, weasels, foxes, otters and rats. The Bull Terrier was the product of careful cross-breeding of terrier-like mongrels and the Bulldog. The developer's purpose was to obtain a rugged, aggressive dog for use in bull pits or dog-fighting rings. Other terriers were bred for their keenness of nose, tenacity and small size.

The Airedale, with its thick muzzle and heavy, pointed chin-whiskers, appears to be only slightly different from an extinct breed known as the Black and Tan Old English Terrier. The wiry hair, tan on face and underparts, and black on the back, are significant features of the breed, which has an average weight of 40 pounds.

The Bedlington Terrier is usually white, shading into grey on the back; but it may be liver-coloured or, rarely, sandy. The soft, woolly coat of show dogs is clipped to a round-nosed, whip-tail profile. The best weights are around 22 to 24 pounds.

The Bull Terrier is an exceptionally strong

raised commercially, but the process is too expensive for the current low demand.

Terrapins are largely carnivorous, and feed on snails and small fish. Like turtles and tortoises, terrapins lay eggs on land.

TERRIERS. Most of the breeds of terrier originated in the British Isles. Exceptions are the Lhasa Apso, a long-haired, short-legged watchdog from Tibet, and the Miniature

Fox terriers were bred originally to be vermin hunters, but are now popular pets.

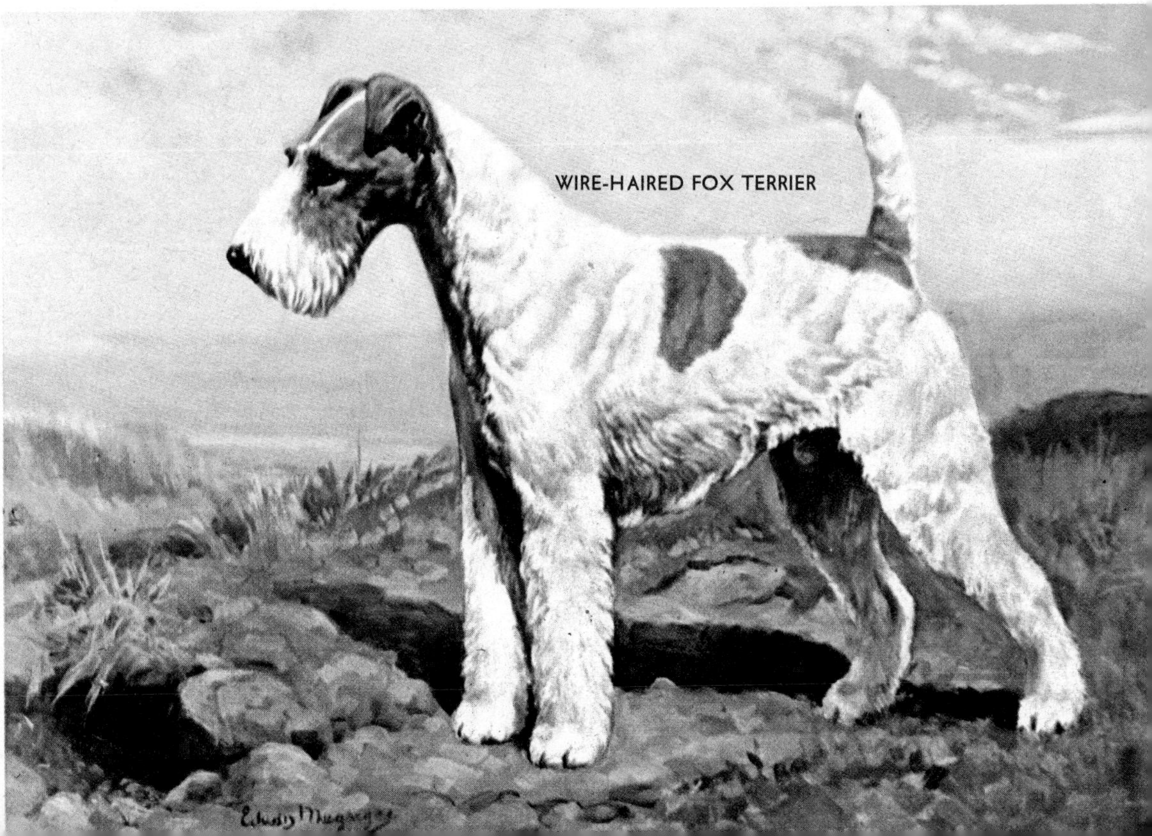

WIRE-HAIRED FOX TERRIER

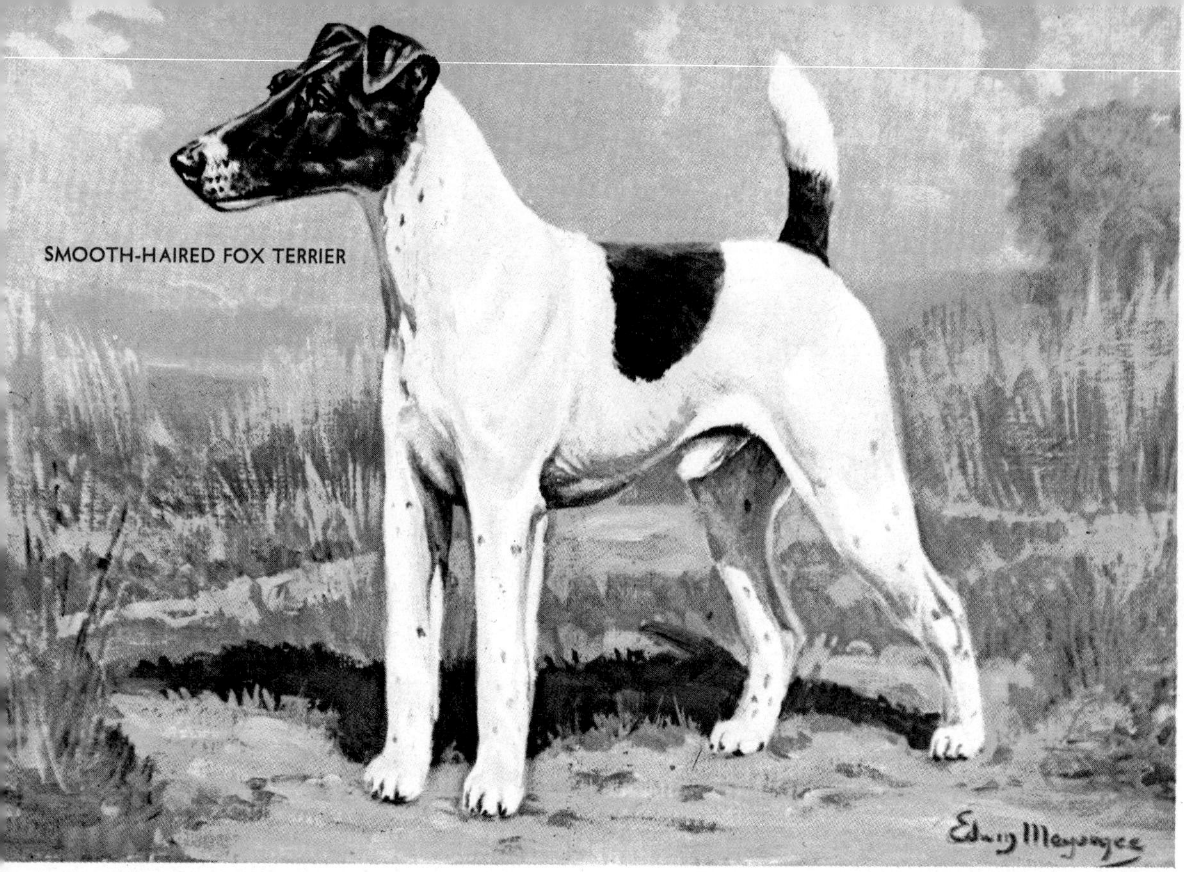

SMOOTH-HAIRED FOX TERRIER

dog that owes much of its heavy build to its Bulldog ancestry. Bred as a fighting animal, it has become a gentle and affectionate pet. There are two varieties — pure white and spotted — varying from 25 to 60 pounds.

Both the Skye Terrier and the Cairn Terrier, which claim a common ancestry, are believed to have originated on the island of Skye, off the western coast of Scotland. The Cairn has a harsh, weather-resistant winter coat with a short, soft, furry undercoat of soft hair, and is often called the Short-haired Skye.

There are two varieties of Fox Terriers — smooth-haired and wire-haired. Both are white with black or brown markings, often both, and weigh about 18 pounds.

The Irish Terrier is reddish and has no black markings. This dog is often used as a retriever of waterfowl, and has served with distinction as a war dog. About 27 pounds is an average weight.

The Miniature Schnauzer from Germany has no known connection with British terriers. It is thought to be a result of crossing the Standard Schnauzer and the toy dog,

Affenpirsher. Grey, with tufted eyebrows and pointed ears, the Miniature Schnauzer weighs about 15 pounds.

The Lhasa Apso, from Tibet, may be almost any colour, but always has a long, straight coat of rather stiff hair. It also weighs about 15 pounds.

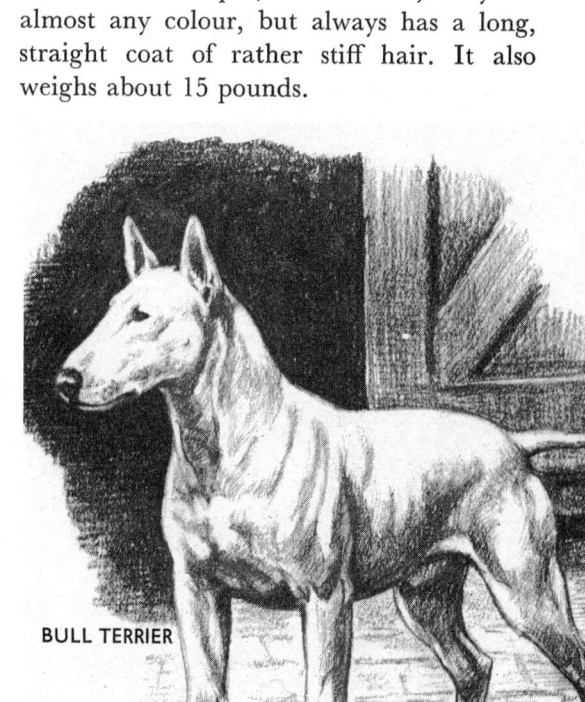

BULL TERRIER

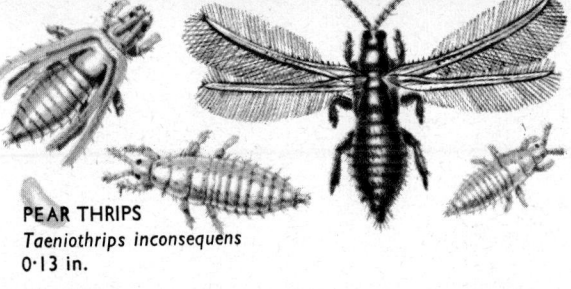

PEAR THRIPS
Taeniothrips inconsequens
0·13 in.

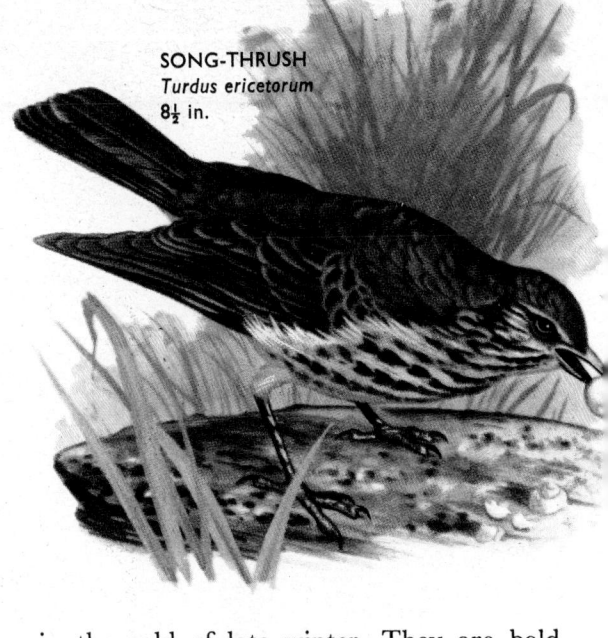

SONG-THRUSH
Turdus ericetorum
8½ in.

THRIPS, members of the order *Thysanoptera*, are slender insects, usually no more than an eighth of an inch long. Of about 3,000 species, some are wingless; others have two pairs of wings, which are narrow and fringed with hairs. A few kinds of thrip prey on other small insects and mites, but most species feed on plants by sucking out their fluids. Thrips are common in flowers and buds, but many kinds are found on leaves, fruits, and even on roots. In addition to the damage they do by feeding, thrips transmit plant diseases.

THRUSHES, fine songsters, are distributed all over the world, except on lands near the North and South poles. Most thrushes live in woodlands or at forest edges and stay hidden in foliage, nesting well up in trees or bushes. A few live and nest on the ground, among rocks, or in cavities in trees.

The Mistle Thrushes are the largest of the European species. Tree-nesting birds of more open country, they begin their harsh song

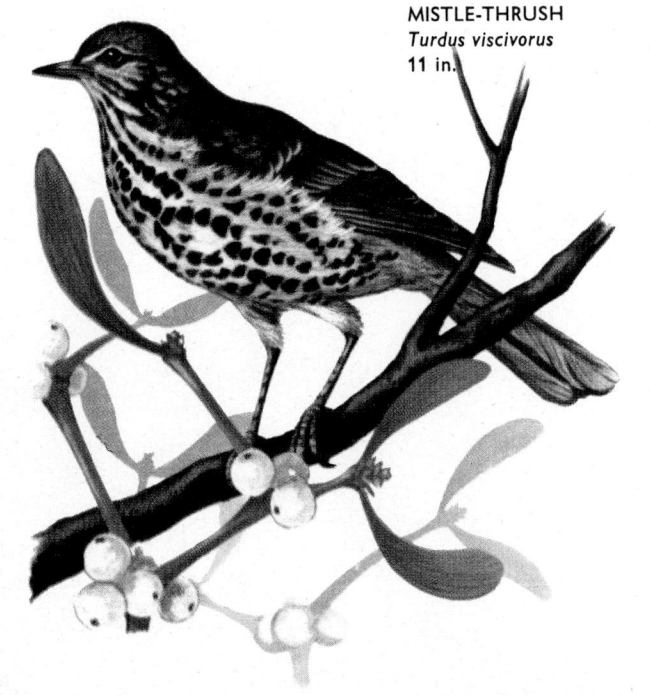

MISTLE-THRUSH
Turdus viscivorus
11 in.

in the cold of late winter. They are bold in defence of their nests, fiercely mobbing jays or cats with a loud, rattling alarm-cry. They feed mainly on open ground.

The Song Thrush is smaller and darker brown. It is a shyer bird of woodland, preferring to nest in thick cover and feeding on the woodland floor. In many places, it has become a bird of gardens, where these provide sufficient trees and shrubs. Like other thrushes, this bird uses mud in nest construction; in the case of the Song Thrush, however, it is used as a lining to produce a smoothed cup of mud in which the bright blue, black-spotted eggs are laid. In spite of its shyness, it is a bold singer with a loud, hurried song of many different phrases rapidly repeated.

There are two northern species which migrate south in winter. The large Fieldfare, with its gruff, chuckling cry, is better known for the large, strong-flying flocks that haunt open places in winter; it nests in colonies. The much smaller Redwing has chestnut colour on its flanks.

TICKS are closely related to mites, but differ from them in their larger size and leathery skin. They belong to the Arachnida, which also contains scorpions and spiders. All ticks are parasites at some stage of their development, and are second to mosquitoes

in the great number of human diseases they transmit. Most ticks complete their development in about twelve months, but may live for several years. There are records of ticks living for five years without food.

Ticks are divided into two groups: soft-bodied and hard-bodied. Soft-bodied ticks have no shield, or scutum, over their back. These ticks are mainly skin parasites of birds, but are found occasionally on small mammals. Typically they stay in the nest or burrow of the host, and move on to its body only when they feed. For this reason they are not ordinarily carried about.

Hard-bodied ticks have a shield, or scutum. It covers nearly the entire back of the male, but is considerably smaller in the female.

AMERICAN DOG TICK

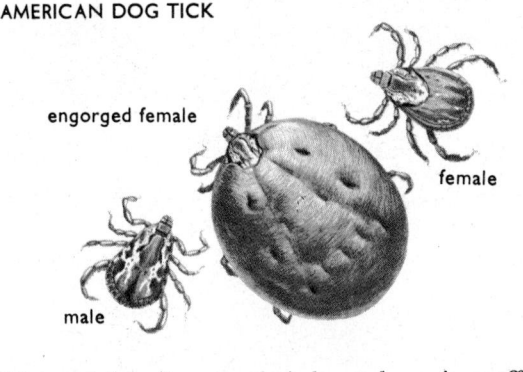

engorged female

female

male

These ticks cling to their host, dropping off only to moult, mate and lay eggs. Some species, such as the Cattle Tick, even moult while on their unwilling host.

TIGER BEETLES (*Cicindelidae*) are slender, long-legged beetles, often seen along dirt roads or paths or on sandy beaches. Some are pale cream, dull black, or brown; many are metallic blue or green. When approached they usually fly a short distance, then alight facing the pursuer. Both adults and larvae are predaceous and very active. Adults capture other insects in their strong, sharp jaws. The larvae live in burrows in the sand or mud, and wait with their jaws wide open for some hapless creature to step in. A pair of small hooks near the end of the larva's abdomen anchor the larva in its burrow, so that it is difficult to extract.

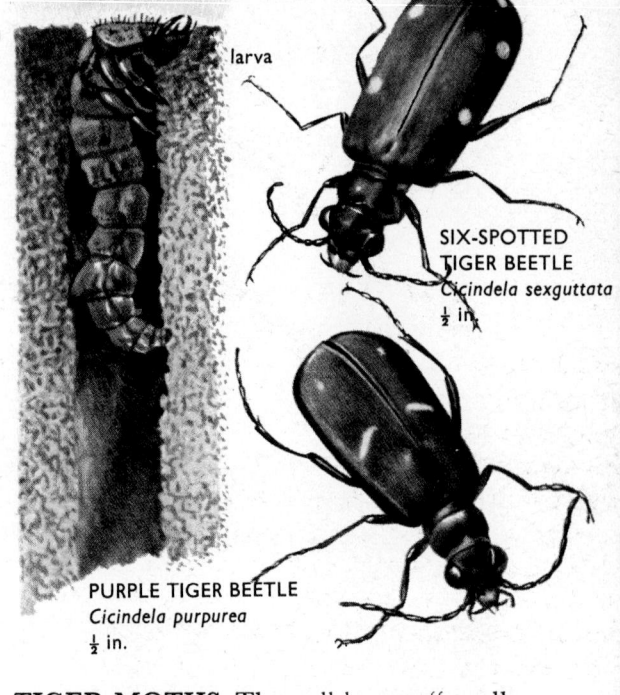

larva

SIX-SPOTTED TIGER BEETLE
Cicindela sexguttata
½ in.

PURPLE TIGER BEETLE
Cicindela purpurea
½ in.

TIGER-MOTHS. The well-known "woolly-bear" is the larva of the Common (or Garden) Tiger-moth. Woolly-bears hibernate as small larvae; then, the next spring, they change into their last skin and develop the long, hairy coat which has given them their name. Later, the hairs fall out and assist in forming part of the cocoon. The adult emerges in July. Rarer tiger-moths, occurring in certain localities in Britain, are the Jersey Tiger-moth and the Scarlet Tiger-moth.

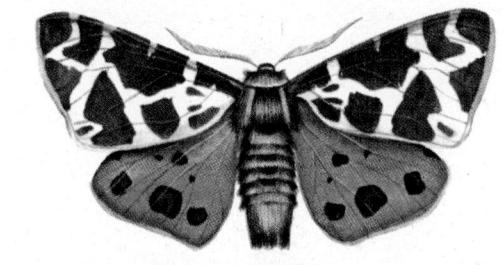

COMMON OR GARDEN TIGER-MOTH
Arctia caja
2½ in.

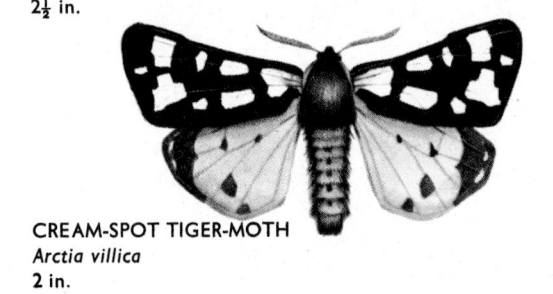

CREAM-SPOT TIGER-MOTH
Arctia villica
2 in.

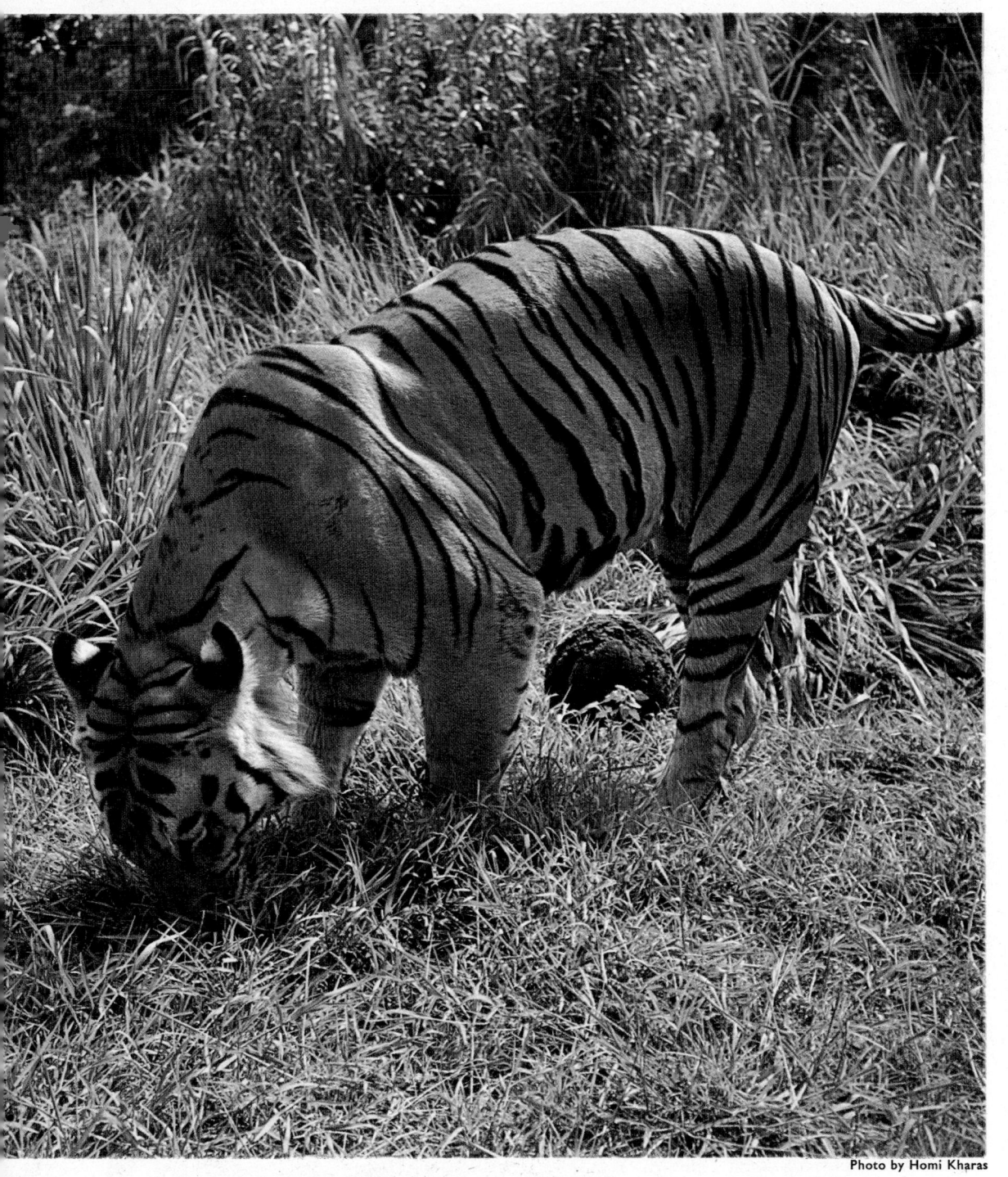

Photo by Homi Kharas

A full-grown Bengal tiger (Panthera tigris) sniffing at the paw-mark of another.

TIGERS are large, powerful, striped cats widely distributed in Asia, from India to Siberia and Java. Males weigh about 500 pounds and stand nearly three feet high at the shoulders. Tigers prey on all types of game, from full-grown elephants, bears and buffaloes to crocodiles and fish, and usually hunt their prey alone. They stalk silently and seize the unwary animal by its throat, frequently dislocating its neck with the impact

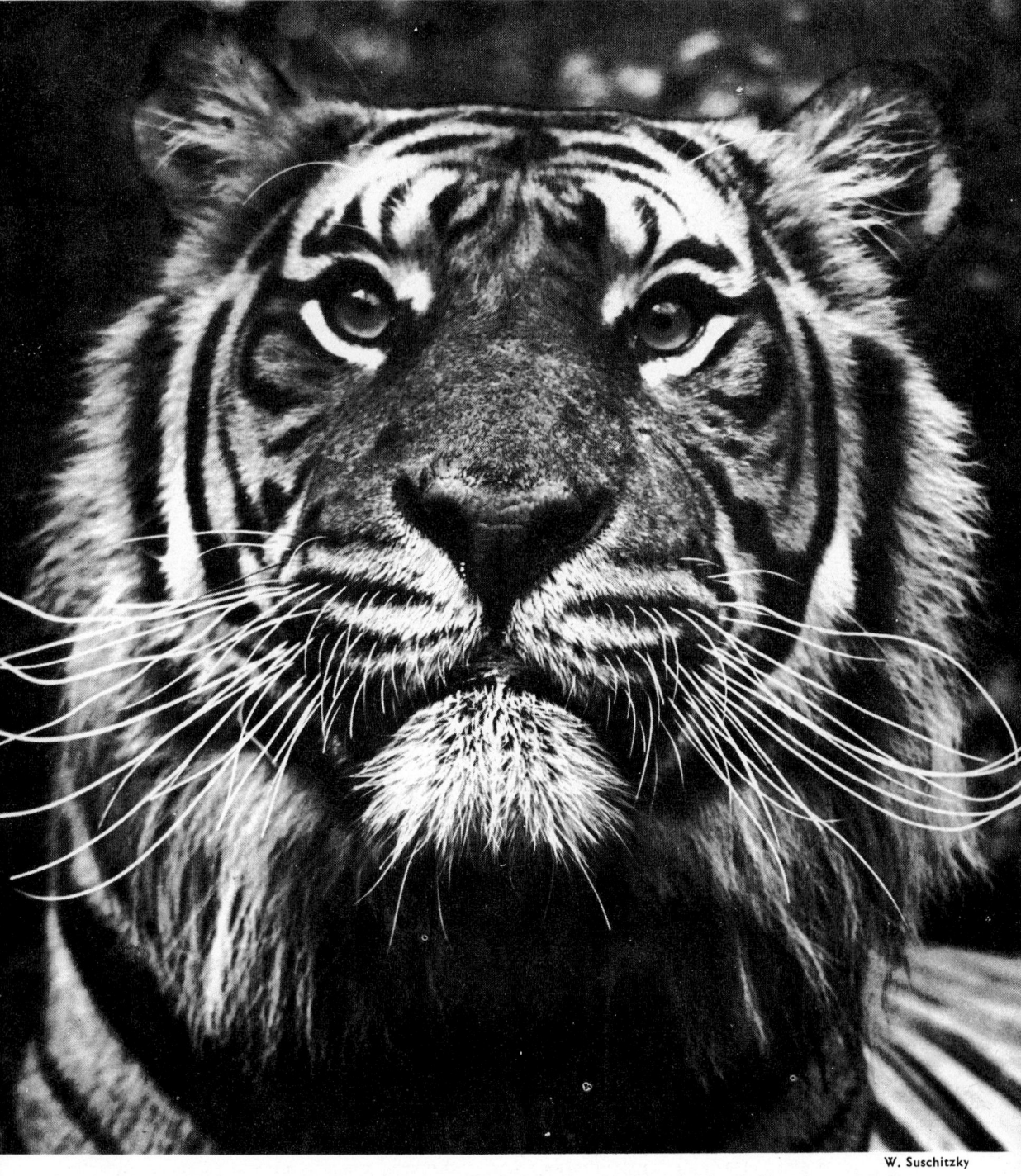

W. Suschitzky

Tigers do not have a mane, as lions do, but the white hair in the cheeks and chin of old males grows long.

of the rush. Tigers generally avoid man, but once their instinctive fear of humans has been overcome, they may become man-eaters and are, therefore, greatly feared. A tigress gives birth to as many as six cubs, or kittens, although the usual number is three. The young remain with their mother for a year or sometimes longer, learning from her the skills of survival. Tigers live in jungles and grasslands, preferring to be near water.

CRESTED TINAMOU — 14 in.
Eudromia elegans
Pampas of Argentina

VARIEGATED
TINAMOU — 9 in.
Crypturellus variegatus
Northern South America,
south to Ecuador and
the Guianas

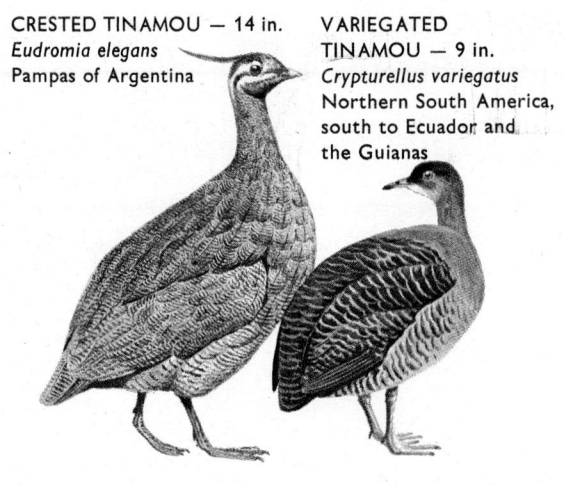

Although they resemble grouse, tinamous are more closely related to the rheas.

TINAMOUS are primitive, partridge-like birds that range from southern Mexico to Argentina. Their tails are so short and hidden by contour feathers that the birds appear to be tail-less. They are strong flyers for short distances, but do not migrate. They eat berries, seeds and insects. The females lay one to ten glossy eggs that may be green, blue, yellow or wine-purple. The male does all the incubating; the chicks are precocial.

TITMICE are found throughout the world, except in South America; they are particularly numerous in temperate regions. Titmice are usually sedentary, finding food all the year round in woods and hedgerows.

They are social birds that live — when not in the nesting period — in small groups in continual movement. They explore branches and leaves — often in acrobatic positions — in search of insects hidden in cracks in the bark. In winter they come near houses, and they may be attracted by putting out fatty substances, which they like very much.

Most titmice nest in holes in trees and often use bird-boxes. They line their nests with matted hair, fur or moss. The female incubates the four to twelve whitish eggs. Some Great Tits in England have learned to follow the milkman; they occasionally annoy housewives by picking tops off milk bottles to sip the cream. The Varied Tit of Japan is taught tricks which it enacts at shows in return for the reward of food.

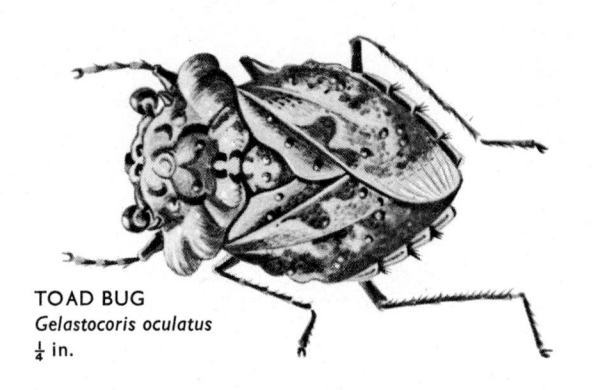

TOAD BUG
Gelastocoris oculatus
¼ in.

TOAD-BUGS (*Gelastocoridae*) are small, round-bodied bugs that resemble toads in appearance and even hop like toads. They are usually found along the banks of streams or ponds, and often bury themselves in the sand to escape detection. Because of their dull green or brown colours, toad-bugs look much like the sand or mud in which they live. They feed on other insects, which they grab with their front legs.

LONG-TAILED TIT
Aegithalos caudatus
5½ in.

TUFTED TITMOUSE
5½—6½ in.
Parus bicolor
Eastern U. S. A.

GREAT TIT — 5½ in.
Parus major
Eurasia, Java, Sumatra

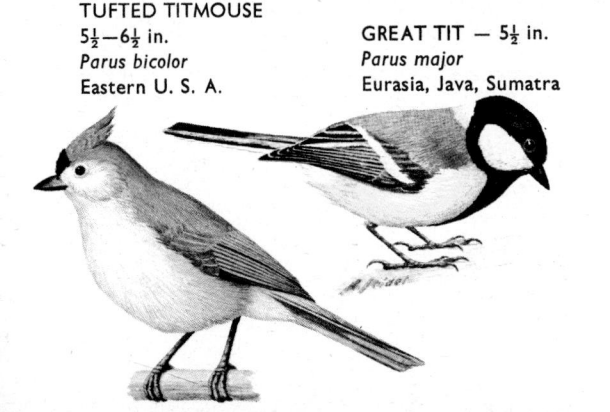

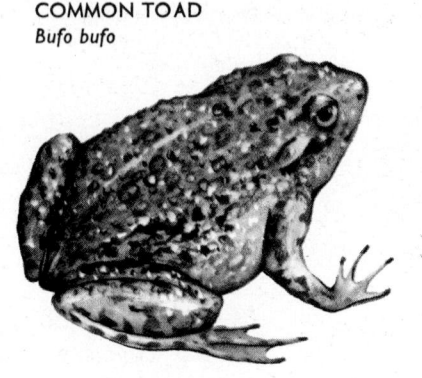

COMMON TOAD
Bufo bufo

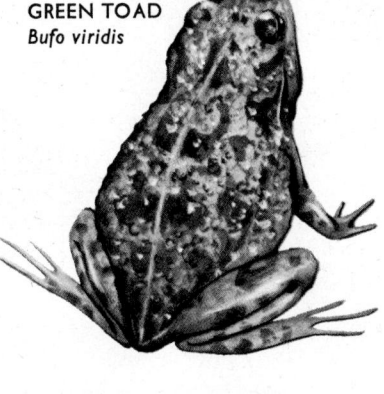

GREEN TOAD
Bufo viridis

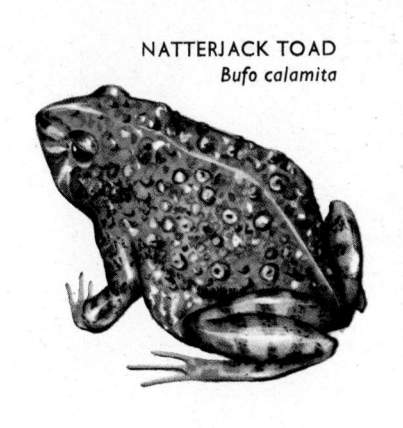

NATTERJACK TOAD
Bufo calamita

TOAD-FISHES are ugly fishes of temperate and tropical seas. They are covered with a loose, slimy, often warty-looking skin with no scales. Their head and mouth are generally so large that the body appears dwarfed.

Frequently, toad-fishes lie half-buried in sand or mud, or are hidden in vegetation among rocks. Their mottled colouration makes them almost impossible to see. Some have fleshy, iridescent lures attached to their mouth, to attract passing fish or crustaceans on which they feed. Many are caught by fishermen. They bite viciously.

TOADS are amphibians that spend most of their adult life on land, rather than in the water. This one fact, which is a popular concept rather than a scientific one, serves to differentiate them from the frogs.

Members of the family *Bufonidae* are believed to be the most "advanced" of all toads. Most of the 150 species belong to the genus *Bufo,* which is found everywhere in the world, except New Guinea, Polynesia, Australia, Madagascar, or in cold or marine regions. More than a dozen species of "true toads", or Bufos, occur in Europe. Other members occur in Africa and Asia.

Some of these toads have a rough skin, but others are smooth. All have conspicuous lumps scattered under the skin on their back and limbs. Each "wart" is the location of

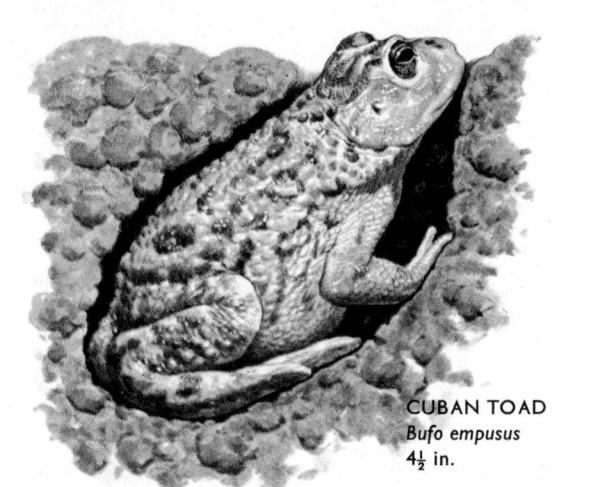

CUBAN TOAD
Bufo empusus
$4\frac{1}{2}$ in.

Cuban Toads plug burrows with their bony head.

swollen poison glands. The poison of some kinds is very powerful; any animal that bites a Marine Toad *(Bufo marinus),* for example, becomes ill at once. Dogs, snakes and other predators are frequently killed by mouthing these toads; even people have died from eating Marine Toads. Contrary to superstition, the poison produced by the skin glands of toads cannot cause warts. It has no effect on the skin, though it is toxic when taken internally through the sensitive tissues of the mouth or stomach. Their noxious skin secretions and retiring nature are the only defence toads have.

Toads of the family *Bufonidae* are toothless. Other toads, and all frogs, lack teeth in their lower jaw; most have teeth in their upper jaw. The tongue is hinged at the front of the mouth and can be flipped out quickly to catch insects, which are passed

GULF TOADFISH
Opsanus beta
to 12 in.

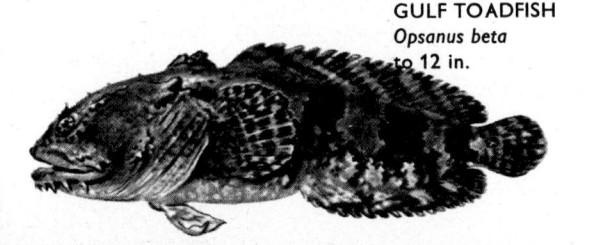

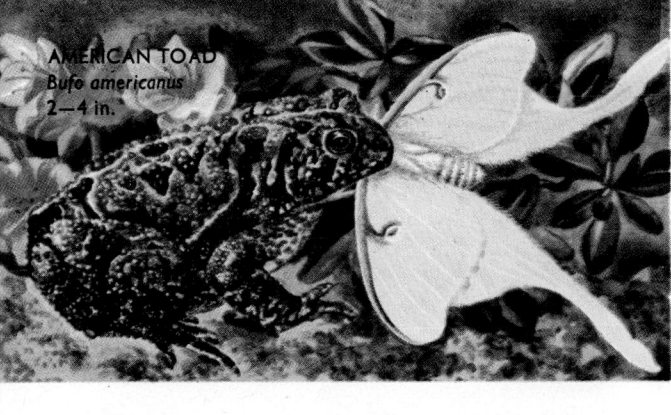

AMERICAN TOAD
Bufo americanus
2—4 in.

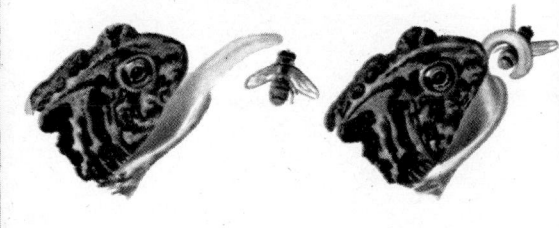

A toad's tongue is attached at the front of its mouth and can be flipped out quickly to wrap around a moving insect.

toad extends tongue   toad catches fly

directly into the throat and swallowed whole.

The largest species, the Marine Toad, measures about nine inches in length and is about six inches wide when sitting with its legs folded. A Colombian species attains a similar size. The Marine Toad is widely distributed in tropical America, and occurs as far north as Florida, Texas and the West Indies. It has been introduced to many Pacific Islands, including Hawaii, to help control insects.

The Oak Toad *(Bufo quercicus)*, of the south-eastern United States, is the smallest species of the genus *Bufo*; it measures only about an inch and a half in length. An African toad of a different genus *(Nectophryne)* is smaller.

Toads will attempt to eat almost any moving object which is small enough to swallow. Nevertheless, they never eat their young, even when they are in abundance around them, so they must be capable of some discrimination. Insects that are distasteful are spat out at once.

Marine Toads are common in American tropics.

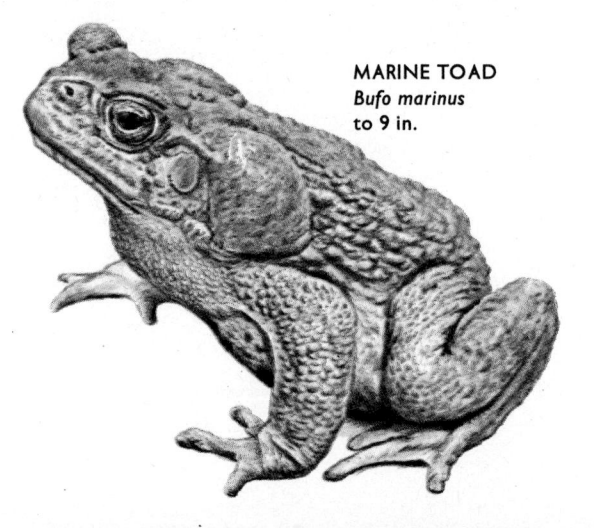

MARINE TOAD
Bufo marinus
to 9 in.

Male toads are usually smaller than females. A thick layer of horny material on the inner surface of their thumbs helps them in clasping the female when mating.

An African genus of toads *(Nectophrynoides)* are the only anurans (which means "tailless ones") that give birth to young. The female keeps the large eggs in her body while they develop. The tadpoles inside the eggs have long tails, and apparently absorb oxygen through them from the blood vessels in the wall of the uterus. Birth occurs after the eggs have been absorbed by the tadpoles, and development is completed in the water.

All other modern toads lay eggs, typically in a pair of strings in shallow, temporary pools of water. The females usually tangle the strings together over a large area, as they move about in the laying process. A female Marine Toad may lay as many as 30,000 eggs in a single clutch; the Common European Toad lays about 6,000. Some toads, however, lay as few as 30 eggs.

Tadpoles of most modern toads are small and dark. When their mouth discs are fully developed, they have horny jaws and two to four rows of "teeth" in both upper and lower halves. Their single breathing spiracle, through which water is discharged from their internal gill-chambers, is located on the left side of their body.

Toads are the longest-lived of the tail-less amphibians; the Common Toad *(Bufo bufo)* having reached 36 years in captivity.

In many parts of the world, toads are the most common of all tail-less amphibians, yet they are seldom seen in abundance.

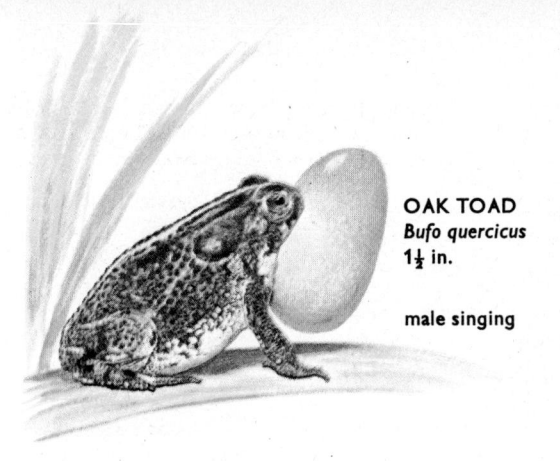

OAK TOAD
Bufo quercicus
1½ in.

male singing

During their breeding season, they congregate in huge numbers around bodies of water, and their calls can be heard for a mile or more. For the remainder of the year, they scatter and remain silent.

Of all amphibians, toads are the most resistant to drying out, and for this reason they are not confined to the immediate vicinity of water. They do not wander far from moist places, however. Often they may spend weeks or months in some protected, cool, damp spot, from which they emerge only at night to seek food. During the day, some kinds hide in crevices or under debris around houses, barns or other buildings. Others spend the day in burrows under the ground or in among moist rocks. (See AMPHIBIANS; FROGS.)

TONGUELESS TOADS are a strange family of toads found only in South America and Africa. They are completely aquatic, and therefore could not use a tongue to flick food into their mouths underwater. Their eyes, too, are small and of little use, but their feet are very large and fully webbed. When swimming, these toads stretch their slender forelegs in front of them, like feelers; their fingers are long and slim. South American species have sensory bumps in star-like clusters at the tips of their fingers. The five species of African tongueless toads are called clawed toads, because the tips of some of their toes are horny and claw-like.

Among the South American kinds of tongueless toads is the Surinam Toad *(Pipa)*. During the breeding season, the skin on the female's back thickens and, after a series of acrobatic somersaults, the female lays her eggs as she, and the male close to her, swim downwards; the male then helps to guide the eggs on to her back. Aided by the action of enzymes, the eggs sink rapidly into the thick skin. A cap of mucus forms over the pit that each egg occupies. The entire development of the eggs takes place in these chambers, and completely transformed toadlets eventually hop out and swim to the surface of the water.

The Pre-Surinam Toad *(Protopipa)*, also a South American species, has a similar life history, except that the larvae develop only a short time on the female's back. They emerge from their compartments and enter water to complete their development.

Other forms belonging to this group are the small *Hymenochirus* and *Pseudhymenochirus* of the Cameroons and West Africa.

TOOTH-SHELLS *(Cadulus* and *Dentalium spp.)* are small, bottom-dwelling molluscs that have slender, curved, shelly tubes open at both ends. They resemble the teeth of reptiles. This small group is widely distributed in seas throughout the world. Some live half-buried in sandy or muddy bottoms, feeding on microscopic organisms caught in a ring of tentacles around their head. Most are small, but a few from the Indo-

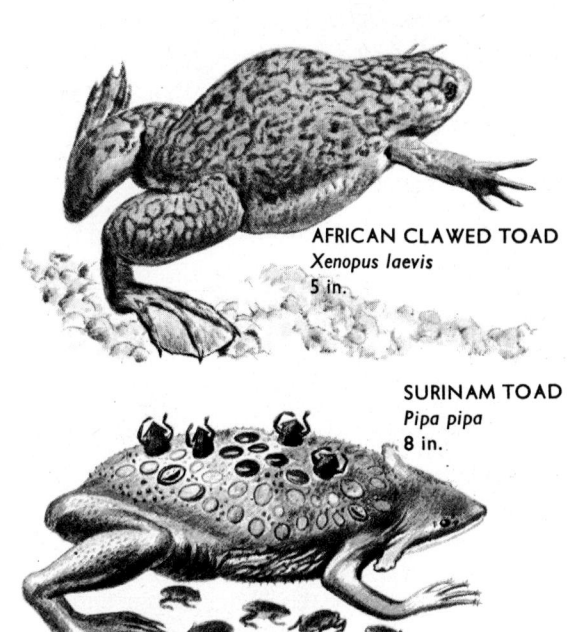

AFRICAN CLAWED TOAD
Xenopus laevis
5 in.

SURINAM TOAD
Pipa pipa
8 in.

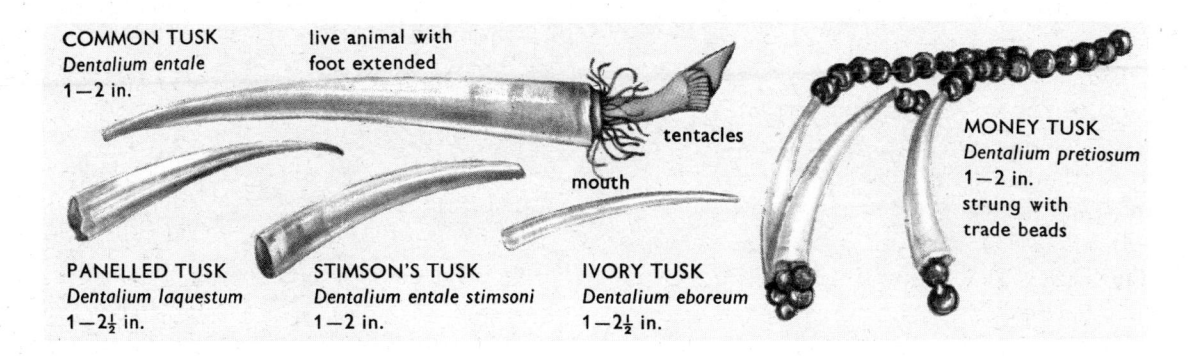

COMMON TUSK
Dentalium entale
1—2 in.

live animal with
foot extended

tentacles

mouth

MONEY TUSK
Dentalium pretiosum
1—2 in.
strung with
trade beads

PANELLED TUSK
Dentalium laquestum
1—2½ in.

STIMSON'S TUSK
Dentalium entale stimsoni
1—2 in.

IVORY TUSK
Dentalium eboreum
1—2½ in.

Pacific region attain a length of four to six inches. Primitive peoples used these shells as ornaments, and some Pacific Coast Indians used them as a kind of wampum (strung beads). Today they have no economic value, except to collectors.

TOPSHELLS and **TURBAN SHELLS** are cone-shaped shells with finely-beaded or thread-lined sculpturing. They live in shallow to deep water, from tropical to cold seas, in both the Atlantic and Pacific Oceans. Most kinds are yellowish-brown, but a few have bright colours. Largest is the West Indian Topshell, that lives in the intertidal zone and in shallow water. Natives

of the West Indies prize it highly as food. Margarites, Solariellas and pearly Gazas are closely-related types of topshells.

Most important of the topshells is the commercial Trochus, a handsome shell found in great numbers off the northern coast of Australia. The shell is used in the manufacture of buttons. The industry was a large one prior to World War II and is now being revived, largely by Melanesians licensed by the Australian Government.

Turban shells, found mainly on the Atlantic Coast, are related to topshells. The Chestnut Turban, which has a white, shelly operculum, lives on blades of turtle grass. The rare, glossy Channelled Turban

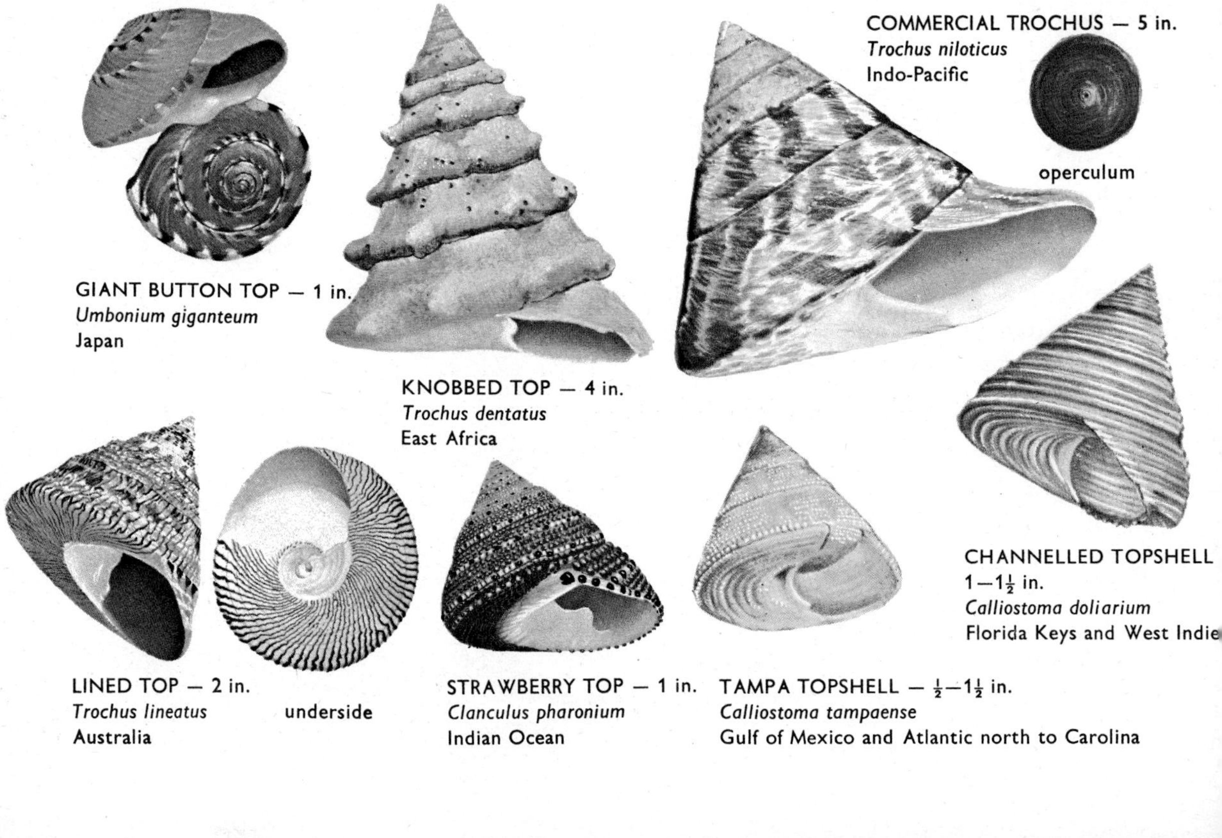

COMMERCIAL TROCHUS — 5 in.
Trochus niloticus
Indo-Pacific

operculum

GIANT BUTTON TOP — 1 in.
Umbonium giganteum
Japan

KNOBBED TOP — 4 in.
Trochus dentatus
East Africa

CHANNELLED TOPSHELL
1—1½ in.
Calliostoma doliarium
Florida Keys and West Indie

LINED TOP — 2 in.
Trochus lineatus   underside
Australia

STRAWBERRY TOP — 1 in.
Clanculus pharonium
Indian Ocean

TAMPA TOPSHELL — ½—1½ in.
Calliostoma tampaense
Gulf of Mexico and Atlantic north to Carolina

lives near coral reefs in West Indian waters.

Star shells are closely related to topshells and turbans, but are distinguished from them by their radial shells. Most star shells are Atlantic species, found in sub-tropical to tropical waters. The Long-spined Star *(Astraea phoebia)* occurs in marine grasses. The Green Star Shell *(Astraea tuber)* prefers rocky areas.

In the Pacific, star shells are common in the waters of both Australia and Japan. Pheasant shells, also closely related to the Turbans, are the largest and most common in the Indo-Pacific area.

TORTOISES are turtles that have become highly adapted to life on land and can live for long periods without water. Many species, of which there are some 41, are

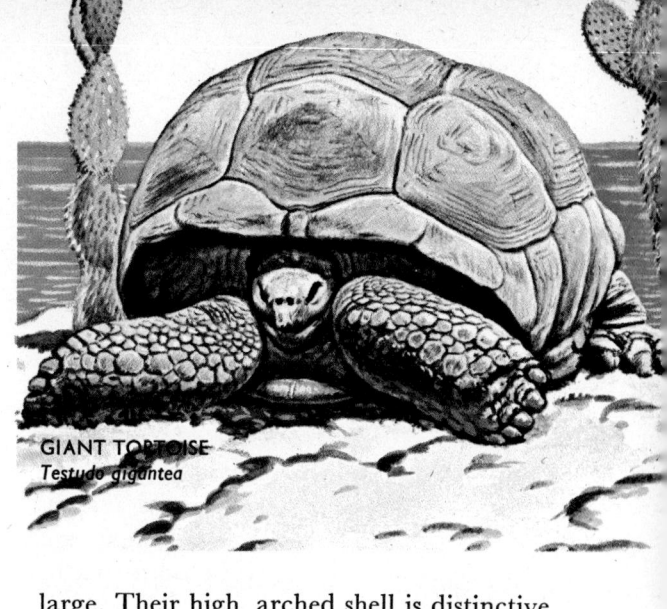

GIANT TORTOISE
Testudo gigantea

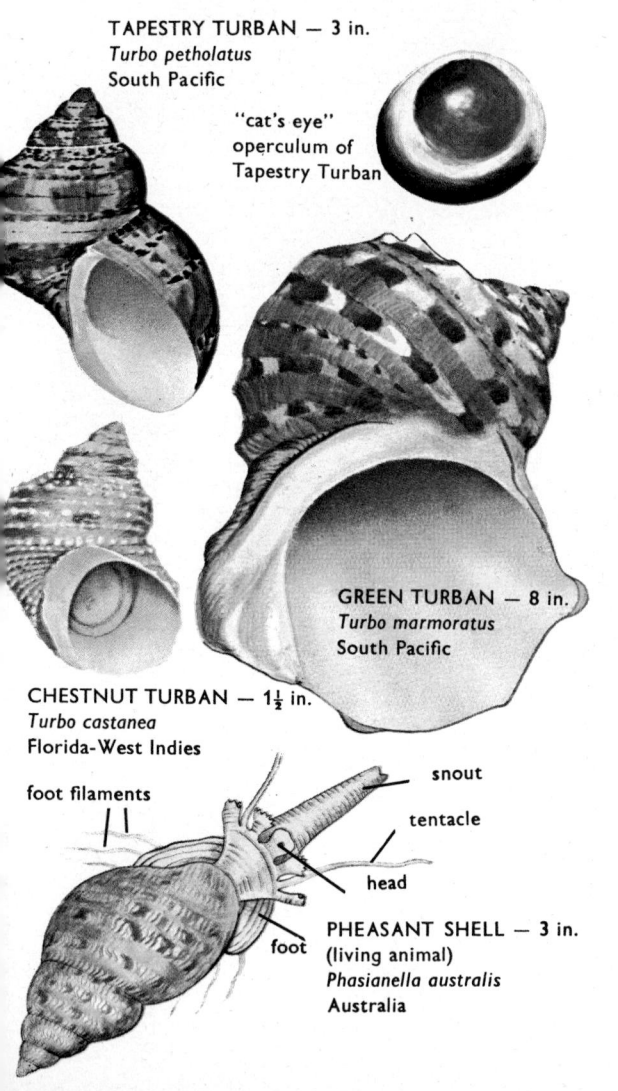

TAPESTRY TURBAN — 3 in.
Turbo petholatus
South Pacific

"cat's eye"
operculum of
Tapestry Turban

GREEN TURBAN — 8 in.
Turbo marmoratus
South Pacific

CHESTNUT TURBAN — 1½ in.
Turbo castanea
Florida-West Indies

foot filaments

snout

tentacle

head

foot

PHEASANT SHELL — 3 in.
(living animal)
Phasianella australis
Australia

large. Their high, arched shell is distinctive, but not as much so as the stump-like hind legs. Their well-scaled front legs can be pulled together to cover the front opening of the shell completely, when the head is drawn inside.

Tortoises live only in warm parts of the world, for most kinds are too large to burrow deeply enough to survive severe cold spells. They are so susceptible to predators — particularly man — that they have become extinct in many continental areas. The giants have survived in abundance only on the isolated Galapagos Islands, in the Pacific Ocean, and Mascarene Islands, in the Indian Ocean. Many kinds were exterminated during the Ice Ages.

All tortoises are vegetarians. Most have such high shells that they are unable to right themselves when turned on to their back on a nearly smooth surface. Extremely gentle, they rarely if ever bite, even in self-defence. Competing males, however, rush at each other and crash their bony shells together, seeming to be deliberately trying to turn each other over. At the same time, they grunt throatily.

Females lay their brittle-shelled eggs in moist, sandy soil. Like other turtles, they dig their nests with the hind legs. Females of species that live in semi-arid regions return at hatching time and break the hard crust of the soil, in order to help the young to escape from the nests. The adults sometimes kill young turtles by crawling over

them and crushing them with their weight; young tortoises have rather soft shells that require several weeks, or months, to harden.

Tortoises grow rapidly during their first few years, and mature in 7 to 15 years. Cool-climate species take longer to become adults than those that live in warm regions. Tortoises are presumed to reach the greatest age of any known animals; about 180 years is the oldest reliable record. It is probable that they live for as long as two centuries.

Some giant tortoises, of the genus *Testudo*, weigh as much as 500 pounds and are nearly three feet long. A century or two ago, the Galapagos and Mascarene Islands teemed with tortoises. They were highly prized as food for the crews of passing ships, particularly whaling vessels, for they could be kept alive, on their backs, for weeks or months until needed. For many years, they were the only means of providing fresh food and preventing scurvy among seamen on long voyages. This use of the tortoises was stopped about 1900, but then the people of Ecuador began killing the creatures to obtain their oil. Now only a few hundred tortoises are left on the islands, and some species, formerly abundant, are extinct. The tortoises are protected by law, but the regulation is difficult to enforce; also, dogs and pigs that have been introduced to the islands rob the nests of eggs and prey on the young.

Tortoises in other parts of the world, particularly on islands, have been exterminated similarly by man or his animals. In fact, no group of creatures has suffered more at the hands of man than tortoises.

The African Pancake Tortoise (*Malacochersus tornieri*) has a flexible shell that is not very bony. These unusual tortoises live in rocky regions, and can flatten themselves in order to crawl deep down into rocky crevices. (See GOPHER.)

TOUCANS are remarkable birds that live in the jungle treetops in Central and South America. They do not sing, but their loud

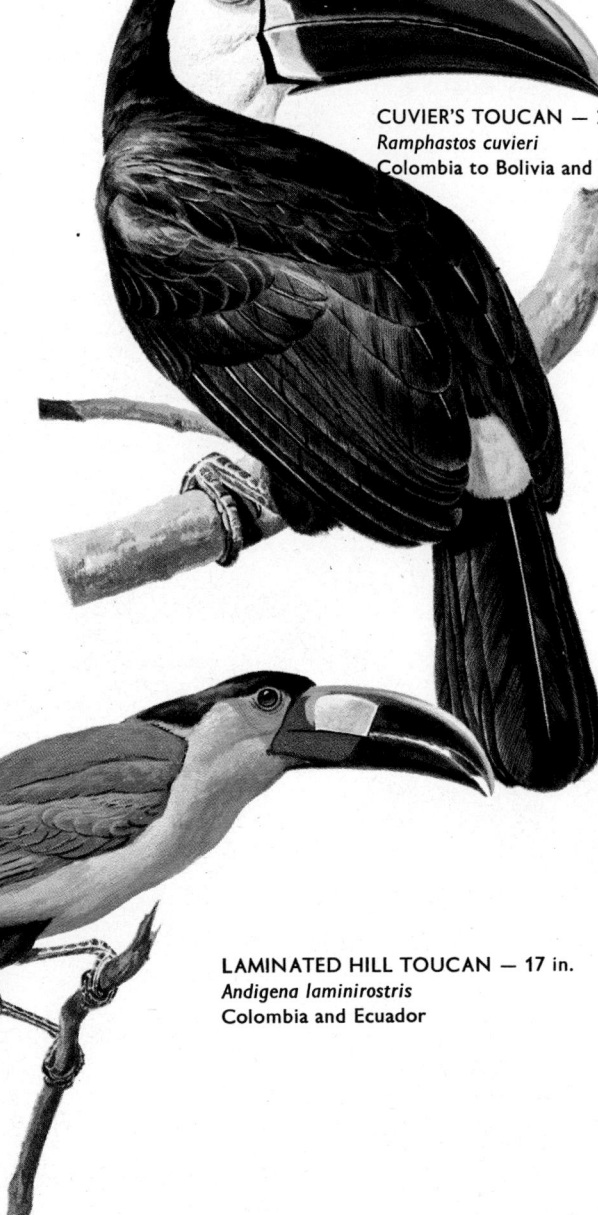

CUVIER'S TOUCAN — 2
Ramphastos cuvieri
Colombia to Bolivia and B

LAMINATED HILL TOUCAN — 17 in.
Andigena laminirostris
Colombia and Ecuador

Range of Toucans

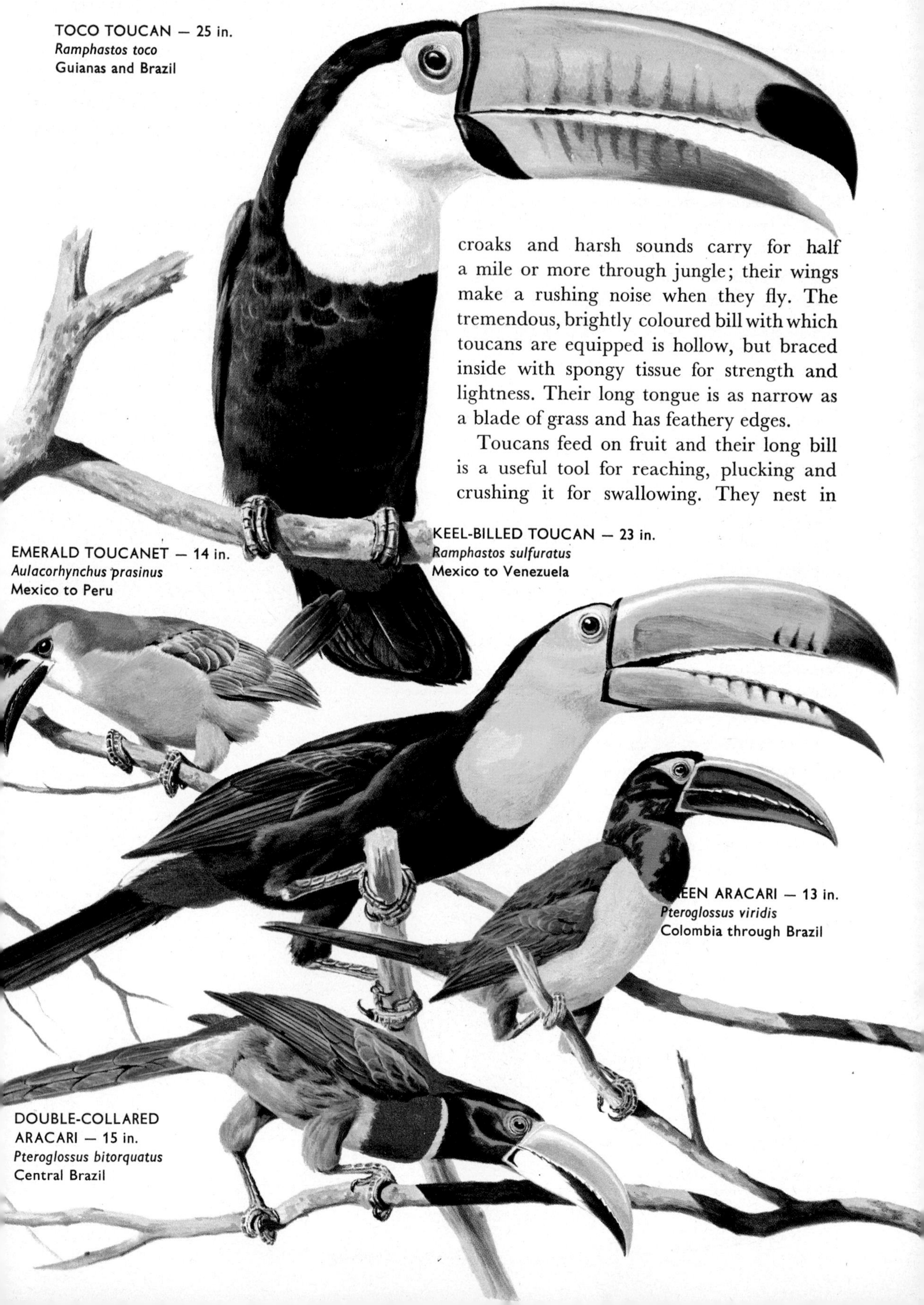

TOCO TOUCAN — 25 in.
Ramphastos toco
Guianas and Brazil

croaks and harsh sounds carry for half a mile or more through jungle; their wings make a rushing noise when they fly. The tremendous, brightly coloured bill with which toucans are equipped is hollow, but braced inside with spongy tissue for strength and lightness. Their long tongue is as narrow as a blade of grass and has feathery edges.

Toucans feed on fruit and their long bill is a useful tool for reaching, plucking and crushing it for swallowing. They nest in

EMERALD TOUCANET — 14 in.
Aulacorhynchus prasinus
Mexico to Peru

KEEL-BILLED TOUCAN — 23 in.
Ramphastos sulfuratus
Mexico to Venezuela

EEN ARACARI — 13 in.
Pteroglossus viridis
Colombia through Brazil

DOUBLE-COLLARED ARACARI — 15 in.
Pteroglossus bitorquatus
Central Brazil

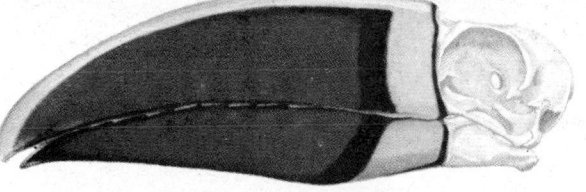

Toucan's skull, showing disproportionate size of bill.

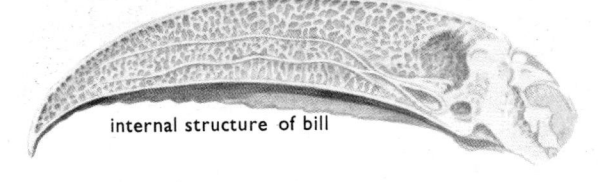

internal structure of bill

hollow trees, and lay two to four white eggs. The female Toucan pokes her bill out of the nesting-hole to drive off marauding monkeys. Toucans also sleep in tree cavities. They rest with their bill held over the centre of the back, and tail tilted forward to cover it; in consequence, a sleeping toucan looks like a ball of feathers, the colourful bill being hidden by the dull-coloured tail.

TOY DOGS, the smallest of the dog breeds, were bred primarily to provide companionship in the home. Until recently, toy dogs were usually kept by women of the nobility. The Aztecs and the Egyptians, however, used their little pets in religious ceremonies. Both in Europe and the New World, a popular belief once existed that sleeping beside a small dog would help to cure rheumatism, and certainly a dog's warm body can be as comforting as a hot-water bottle.

The Chihuahua *(Chi-WA-wa),* which weighs from one to six pounds, is the smallest of all dogs. It comes from the State of Chihuahua in Mexico, where it was valued by the Toltec Indians as long ago as the ninth century. There are two varieties — long-haired and smooth-haired.

The Mexican Hairless and its cousins in other parts of the world are surely among the most unusual of all dog breeds. They are quite bald, except for a little tuft of hair on the head and sometimes on the tail. The Mexican Hairless was established in America when the Aztecs founded their empire. There is a possibility that they came originally from Asia, and are probably related to such other hairless dogs as the Chinese Crested and the African Sand Dog.

The English Toy Spaniel was for many

The Pomeranian is a descendant of the Spitz, a watchdog, hunter and sledge-puller of northern Europe. Records show that Pomeranians once weighed 30 lbs and were used for herding sheep. Today they weigh about 5 lbs.

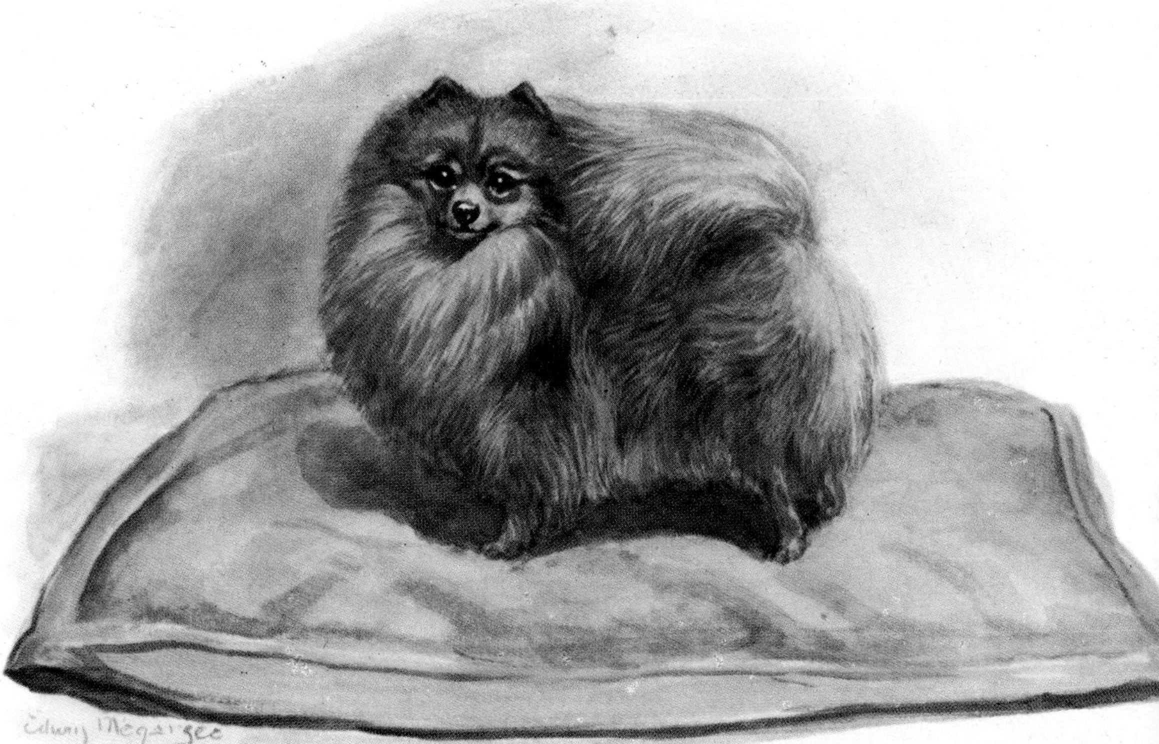

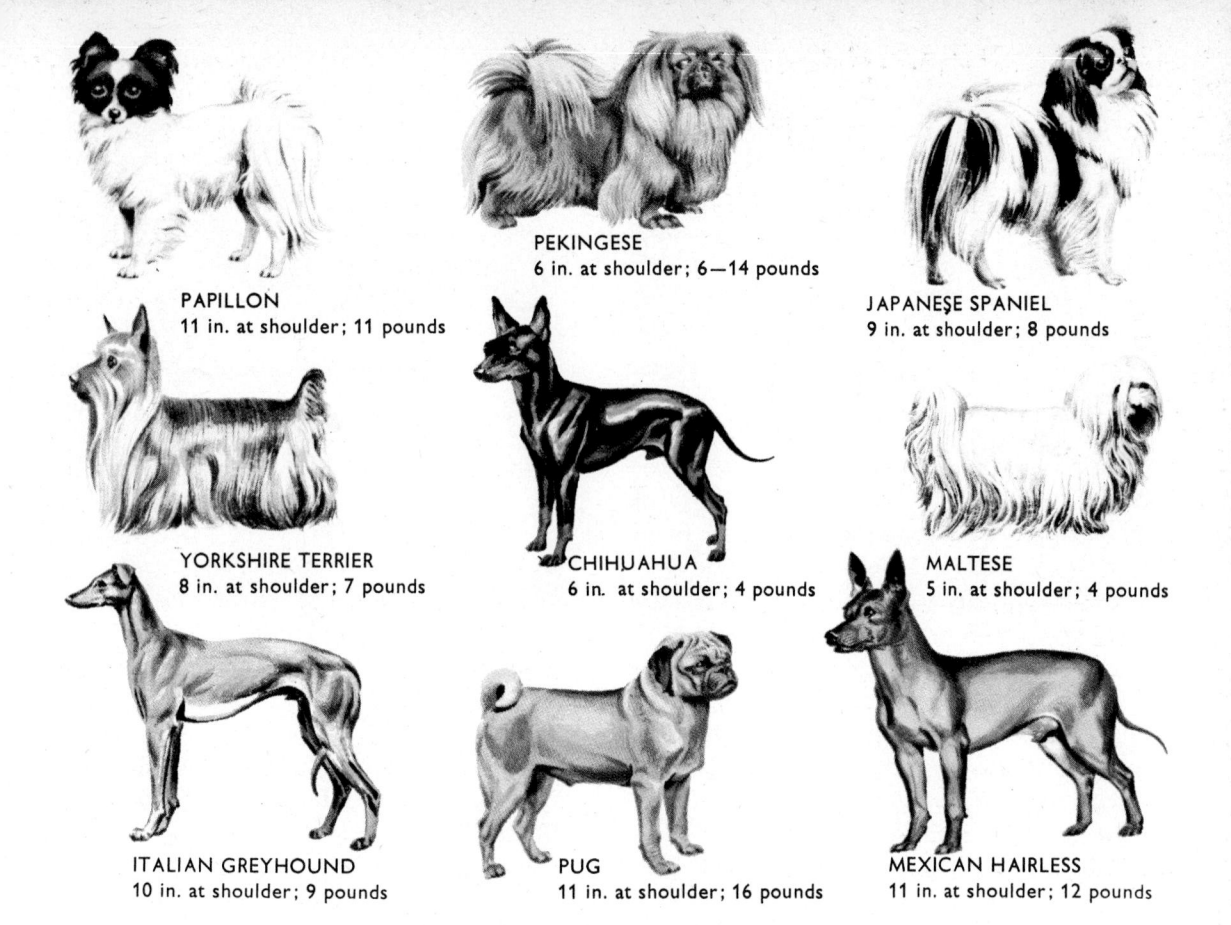

PAPILLON
11 in. at shoulder; 11 pounds

PEKINGESE
6 in. at shoulder; 6—14 pounds

JAPANESE SPANIEL
9 in. at shoulder; 8 pounds

YORKSHIRE TERRIER
8 in. at shoulder; 7 pounds

CHIHUAHUA
6 in. at shoulder; 4 pounds

MALTESE
5 in. at shoulder; 4 pounds

ITALIAN GREYHOUND
10 in. at shoulder; 9 pounds

PUG
11 in. at shoulder; 16 pounds

MEXICAN HAIRLESS
11 in. at shoulder; 12 pounds

years a favourite of English royalty. In the late sixteenth century, it was described as "the comforter", because it curled up on its mistress's bed like a furry hot-water bottle. It is said that an English Toy Spaniel accompanied Mary, Queen of Scots, to her execution. Although England adopted this toy breed, there is evidence that it originated in the Orient. It may have some Cocker Spaniel blood in its ancestry, for some strains were once used for bird-hunting.

The Italian Greyhound is a breed many centuries old, and its only purpose has been to please man with its daintiness and companionship in the home. Some say that when the Romans put up a sign reading *Cave Canem* (Beware of the Dog), they did not mean that the dog might bite — rather they were asking visitors to be careful not to step on their dog by accident! The Italian Greyhound is one of the few toy breeds that seems definitely to have been bred down from a larger breed — in this case, of course, the Greyhound. Italian Greyhounds were

very popular during the 1800s, but are now rather rare.

The Japanese Spaniel, or Japanese Chin, is not really a spaniel, and the breed's ancestors apparently came from China. The Japanese, however, were responsible for the breed as we know it today. Sometimes they kept these little Japanese Spaniels in hanging cages, like pet birds. These dogs are rather delicate. Establishing the breed has been difficult, because some of the better kennels were destroyed in World War II, and also by the earthquakes that often occur in Japan.

Papillons *(Pah-PEE-yon)* once upon a time had drooping, spaniel-like ears and were known as Dwarf Spaniels. They were very popular among the nobility; Madame de Pompadour and Marie Antoinette, for example, are said to have been fond of the earlier type. Gradually a type was developed with perky, erect ears. The French called the new breed Papillon ("butterfly").

The Pekingese, one of the most popular of the toy breeds, is an aristocrat among dogs,

for its ancestry can be traced at least as far back as the Tang Dynasty of the eighth century in China. The Chinese considered the Pekingese sacred, and stealing a Pekingese was punishable by death. There were three varieties: Lion Dogs, which had massive manes; Sun Dogs, which were a beautiful reddish gold; and Sleeve Dogs, so small that they could be carried in the sleeves of an Oriental robe. When the British looted the Imperial Palace at Peking in 1860, the defeated Chinese royalty tried to destroy their sacred dogs, to keep them from being captured. Some of the little dogs were taken alive, however, and so the Pekingese were introduced to the West.

TREE-FROGS, a cosmopolitan group, have an enlarged pad at the tip of each finger and toe. Between each pad and its toe, or finger, is a separate cartilage. This extra joint, or "intercalary cartilage", serves as a swivel, so that the pad can be placed flat against a vertical surface. It also helps to reduce the abruptness of the "take-off" when the frog jumps. Other kinds of frog have developed pads on their toes, but have no cartilages and are not as successful as climbers. They stay either on the ground or in low shrubbery. Some tree-frogs have reverted to a life on the ground.

Three families of tree-frogs are recognised:

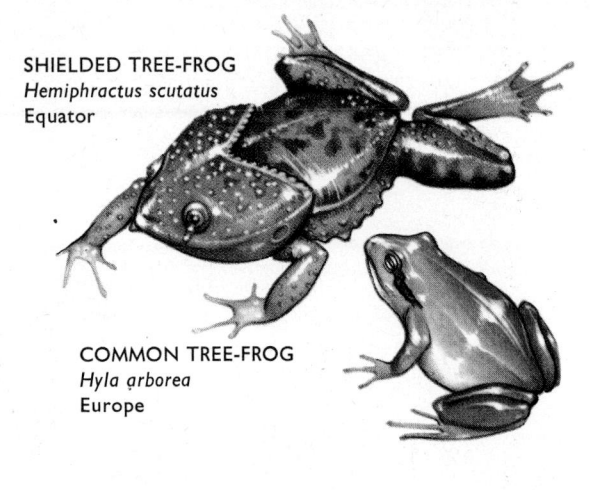

SHIELDED TREE-FROG
Hemiphractus scutatus
Equator

COMMON TREE-FROG
Hyla arborea
Europe

Rhacophoridae of Africa, Asia and Madagascar; *Hylidae,* or true hylas; and *Centrolenidae,* or glass-frogs. Members of the genus *Hyla* are found everywhere, except in Africa, Madagascar, India and the Malayan region.

Many particularly beautiful climbing forms occur in Madagascar and Africa *(Mantella* and *Hyperolius),* one being bright orange, and another jet-black with pale-blue patches. The genus *Hyperolius* is noted for its rich variety of colours and patterns. Many have "flash colours" on parts of their hind legs and on the sides of their body. When they come to rest after a leap, their folded legs hide these bright spots of colour, confusing pursuers.

Marsupial frogs *(Gastrotheca)* are unusual tropical tree-frogs: females carry their eggs

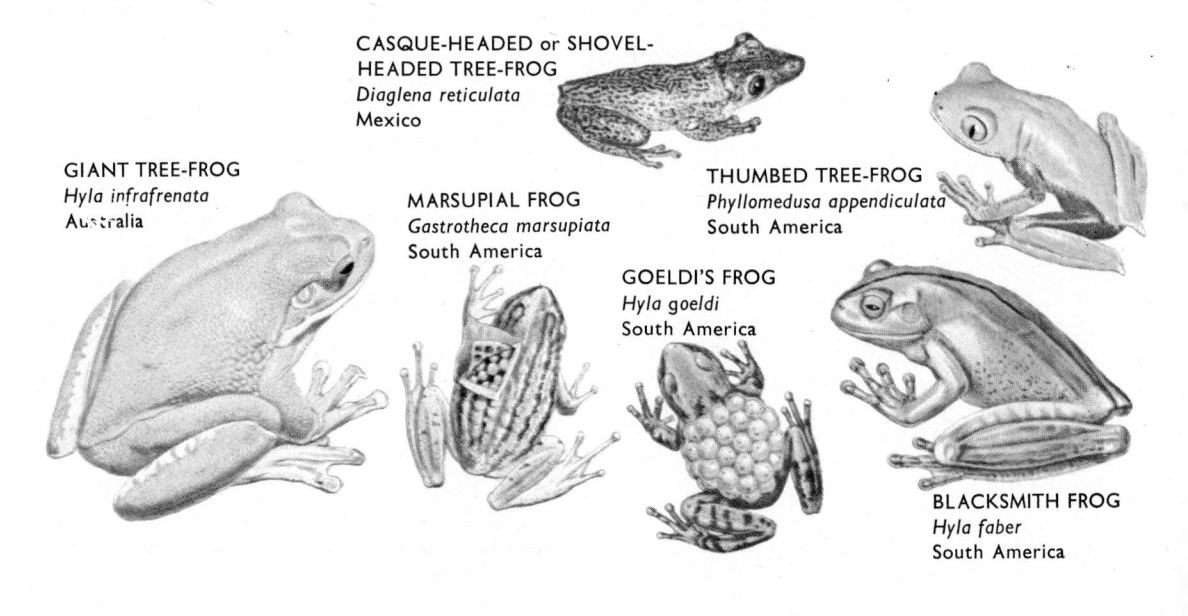

CASQUE-HEADED or SHOVEL-
HEADED TREE-FROG
Diaglena reticulata
Mexico

GIANT TREE-FROG
Hyla infrafrenata
Australia

MARSUPIAL FROG
Gastrotheca marsupiata
South America

THUMBED TREE-FROG
Phyllomedusa appendiculata
South America

GOELDI'S FROG
Hyla goeldi
South America

BLACKSMITH FROG
Hyla faber
South America

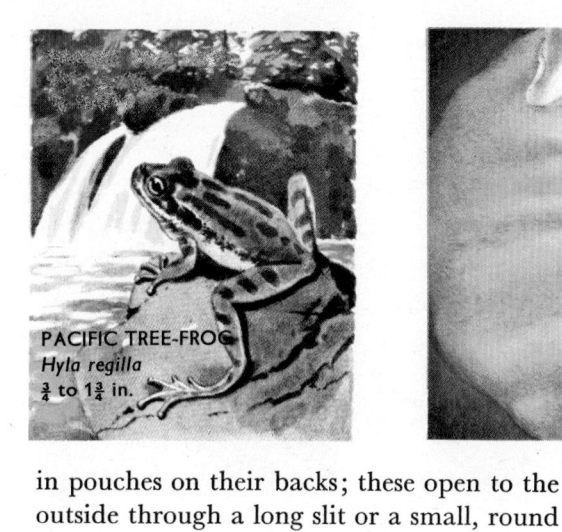

PACIFIC TREE-FROG
Hyla regilla
¾ to 1¾ in.

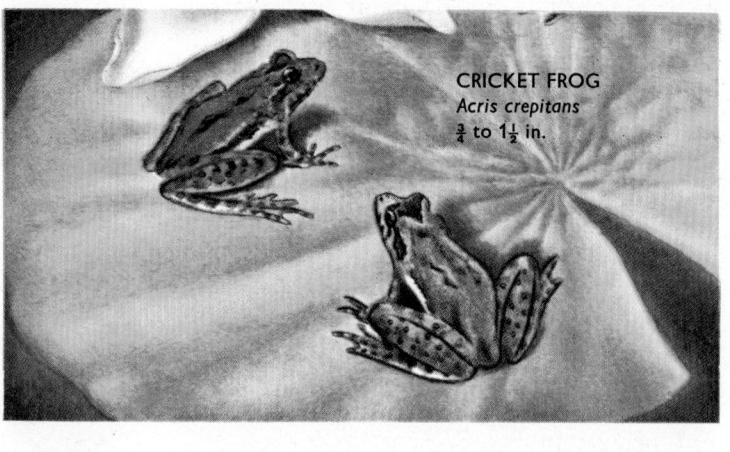

CRICKET FROG
Acris crepitans
¾ to 1½ in.

in pouches on their backs; these open to the outside through a long slit or a small, round hole. The young of some kinds emerge as tadpoles, others as transformed froglets. Eggs of the female Goeldi's Frog (*Hyla goeldi*) are held on her back in high folds of skin. The young of others exchange nutrients and waste products through wineglas-shaped gills held against the mother's skin.

Thumbed tree-frogs (*Phyllomedusa* and *Agalychnis*) wrap their eggs in tree leaves above the surface of a body of water. After the eggs have developed for a few days, and are about half an inch long, the almost completely transparent tadpoles drop into the water below. Only their large, dark eyeballs are easily visible. The Nebulous Tree-frog (*Phrynohyas nebulosa*) of Brazil lays its eggs in the large dead leaves around the trunk of a banana tree. The tadpoles die if placed in water. The Bromeliad Frog (*Hyla bromeliacea*) lays its eggs in the water that collects in air plants where the leaves join the main stem; others lay their eggs in water-filled hollows of trees. The "Smithy" Frog (*Hyla faber*) is so-called because the call of these frogs sounds like an anvil struck by a hammer. The female lays her eggs in a special mud-walled nursery built in shallow water. The young also develop in this chamber, which is about a foot in diameter. Another kind is said to line hollows of trees with beeswax, and lay its eggs in the basins, which then fill with rain-water.

Most male tree-frogs "call" during the breeding season. They have either a pair of vocal pouches or a single one, and the pouches swell when in use. In some, the sacs swell out on either side at the rear of the head; others have no vocal sacs and are seemingly voiceless. How the males of these silent frogs find females is unknown.

Most male tree-frogs have a horny pad, or spine, on the inner surface at the base of each thumb. These help them to clasp the female in mating. Some of the Dagger Tree-frogs (*Plectrohyla*) have either a single or a branched spine projecting through the skin.

Many tree-frogs also have tooth-like projections in their lower jaw. Once these were thought to be true teeth, but now they are known to be bone. Numerous kinds also have a helmet-like skull; the conspicuous, bony ridges of the "helmet" are fused with the skin. Many have powerful skin poisons. These can cause violent irritation of human skin, and also violent sneezing, a running nose and other cold symptoms.

Some of the larger tree-frogs spread their webbed fingers and toes when they jump from high perches. They can glide for considerable distances. Members of the genus *Rhacophorus*, these Asiatic species range from Japan to Malaya, and are called gliding-frogs or flying-frogs.

Suction pads on the tips of their toes permit tree-frogs to climb or cling to vertical surfaces.

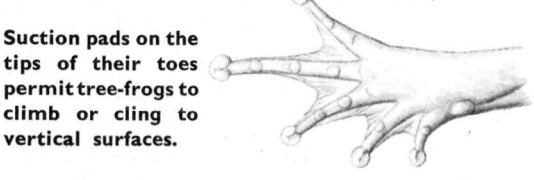

TREE-HOPPERS (*Membracidae*) are members of the order Homoptera and feed by sucking sap from plants. Most tree-hoppers live on trees and bushes, but a few feed on grasses during their nymphal stage. The front portion of a tree-hopper's thorax is greatly enlarged, and may extend back over its thorax and abdomen. In some species of the tropics, where the group is most highly developed, this structure is modified into spines, horns and other unusual shapes. Nymphs usually do not have these enlargements. Female tree-hoppers deposit their eggs in slits cut in small twigs of host trees. Often these slits cause the twigs to die, thus damaging orchard trees. Thorn Bugs are common tree-hoppers in which the enlarged thorax is sharp and thorn-like. They can be a hazard to barefooted children. The Buffalo Tree-hopper is another variety.

TROPICAL FISH. Several hundred species of jewel-coloured freshwater fish of the tropics, mostly from the Amazon Basin and south-eastern Asia, are popular aquarium pets, and many kinds are bred in captivity. Supplying tropical fish and equipment for hobbyists is a big business.

Tropical fish can be divided into two categories: the live-bearers and the egg-layers. Some of the popular live-bearers are guppies, mollies, swordtails and platyfish.

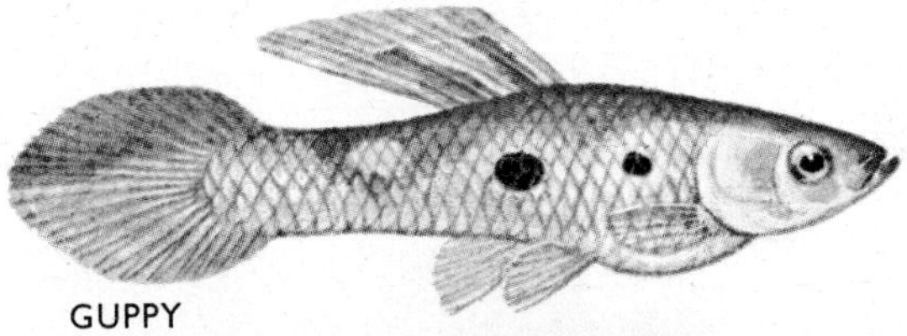

GUPPY
Lebistes reticulatus

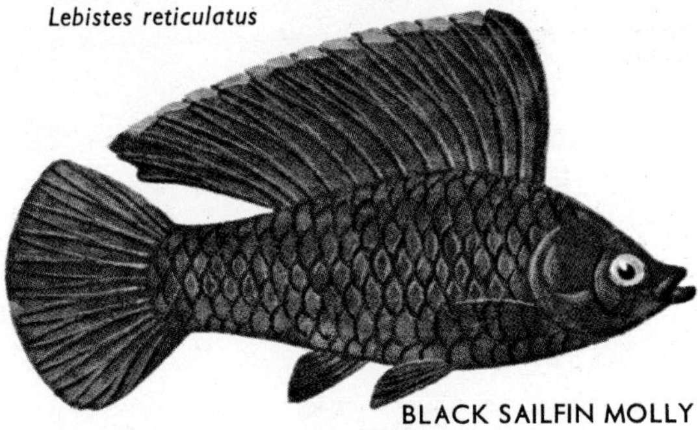

BLACK SAILFIN MOLLY
Mollienesia latipinna

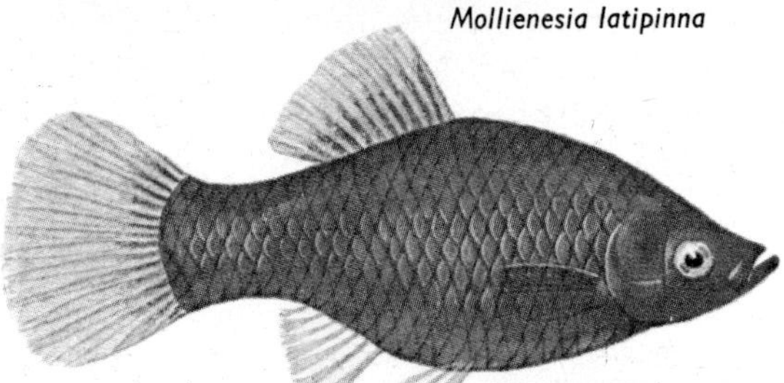

RED PLATY
Platysoecilus maculatus

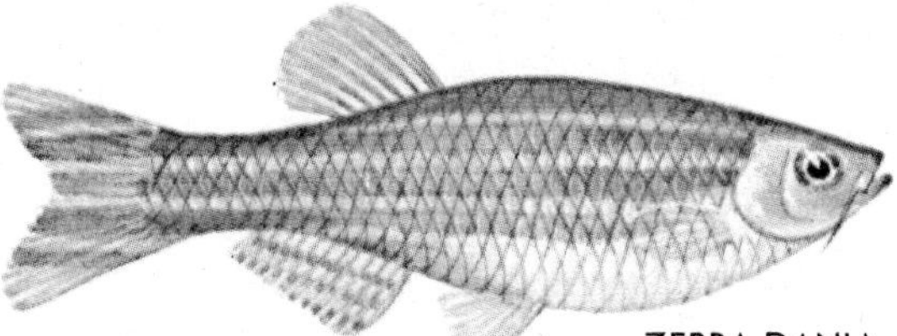

ZEBRA DANIA
Brachydanio rerio

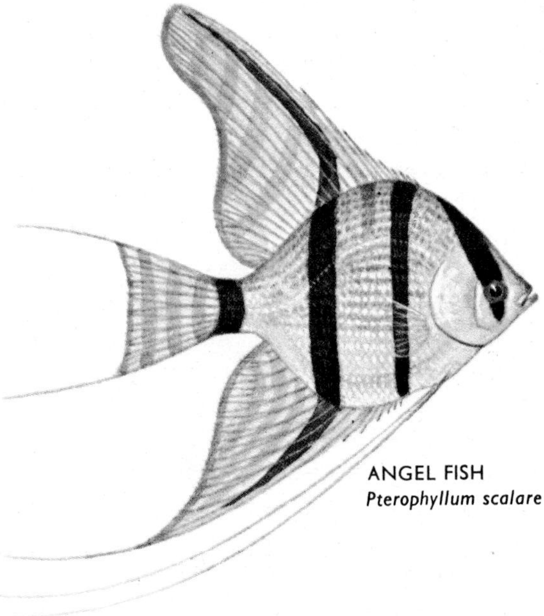

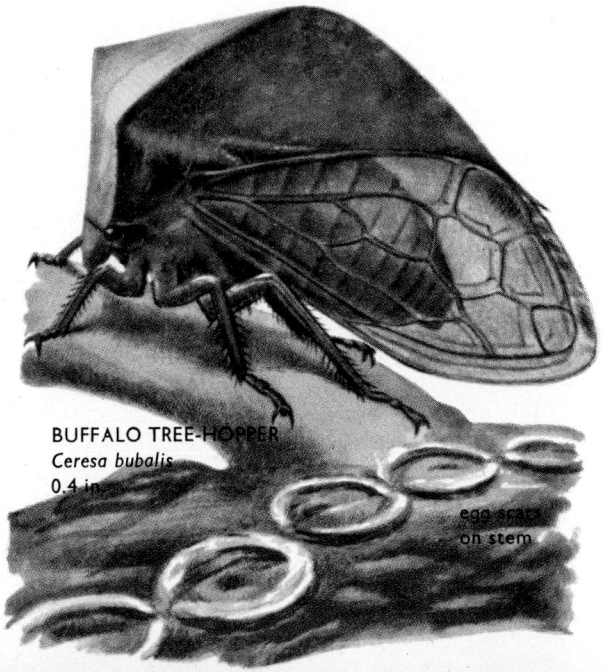

BUFFALO TREE-HOPPER
Ceresa bubalis
0.4 in.

egg scars
on stem

ANGEL FISH
Pterophyllum scalare

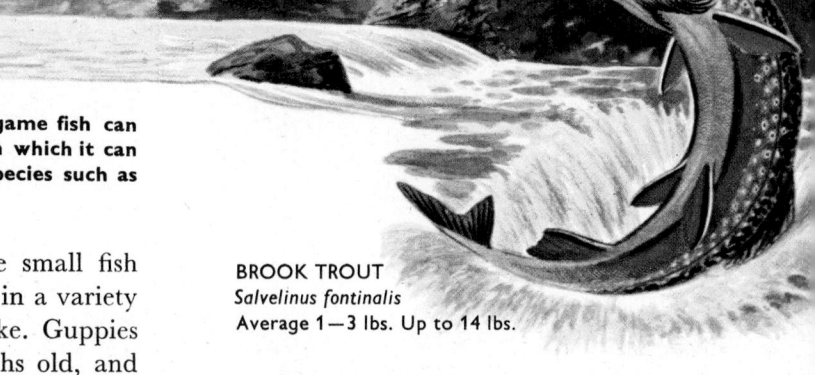

The Brook Trout's popularity as a game fish can be attributed in part to the ease with which it can be caught, compared to more wary species such as Rainbow Trout and Brown Trout.

Guppies *(Lebistes reticulatus)* are small fish (1½ in. maximum). Males occur in a variety of colours, but females look alike. Guppies mature when about eight months old, and live for about four years. Among the several species of mollies *(Mollienesia* spp.*)* kept in aquariums is the Black Sailfin Molly, so-named because of its high dorsal fin. It is native to North America, from Mexico to South Carolina. A molly from Yucatan has an even higher fin. Another group of live-bearers are the swordtails and the platys *(Xiphophorus* spp.*)*. These fish seem to like a little salt water; both come in a variety of colours — red, green, black, gold and albino. Zebra Dania *(Brachydanio rerio)* are egg-layers. They like to swim in schools and are playful, active fish, which get along well with all the other fish. Black Tetras *(Gymnocorymbus ternetzi),* however, should never be put in a tank containing fish smaller than themselves, as they will eat them. Angel Fish *(Pterophyllum* spp.*)* are large, and are considered by many to be the most beautiful of the tropical fishes.

The breeding habits of bubble-nest builders are especially interesting. Best known is the Siamese Fighting Fish, or Betta *(Betta splendens)*. The male takes a breath of air, holds it, and seems almost to chew on it; then he blows out a stream of bubbles until a floating nest (about 1½ in. by 1 in.) forms at the surface. When the female lays her eggs, the male catches them in his mouth and blows them up into the bubbles of the nest, where they incubate.

TROUT belong to the same family of cold-water fishes as salmon. Like salmon, their scales are small, and they have a fleshy adipose fin just in front of the tail.

To many fishermen, trout are the greatest

BROOK TROUT
Salvelinus fontinalis
Average 1—3 lbs. Up to 14 lbs.

TROUT FLIES

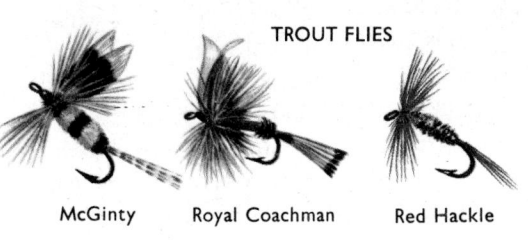

McGinty   Royal Coachman   Red Hackle

game fishes of fresh water. Most species are wary and demand skilful fishing. When hooked, they fight hard to get free; even a small trout is fun to catch.

Fly fishing for trout is an ancient sport. One fly pattern, the Red Hackle, was first described about 200 B.C. There are many different kinds of artificial flies, which are designed to imitate in appearance or in action some insect, fish, or other natural food. Some trout-anglers carry their fly-tying equipment with them when fishing, and then create flies to resemble whatever kind of insect the trout are feeding on.

The Brown Trout is found all round the British Isles and ranges from Iceland to the Mediterranean, including Corsica, Sardinia and Algeria. It has a less graceful form than the Salmon, with a deeper caudal peduncle (base of the tail-fin). The Sea Trout, once believed to be a distinct species, is now recognised as a migratory form of the Brown Trout. Sea trout are more silvery fishes; they descend rivers as smolts (see SALMON) and live a part of their lives in the sea. However, unlike the Salmon, they do not go far out to sea, and often frequent estuaries. They spawn in freshwater from September to January, the principal season being in October and November. There are many

varieties of Trout recognised from different parts of Britain, based mainly on their wide variation in colour. But the Gillaroo of Irish lakes, the Loch Leven Trout of Scotland, the Sewen and the Phinnock, all belong to the same species, *Salmo trutta*.

The natural home of the Rainbow Trout *(Salmo gairdneri)* is in the rivers of the western part of the United States. As in the case of the Brown Trout, there is a form which descends to the sea, returning to spawn in rivers. This is known as the Steelhead, and like the Sea Trout of Europe, it too is a less colourful fish than the river variety, becoming grey-blue in salt water.

The Rainbow Trout was introduced into Europe about eighty years ago. It can be distinguished from the Brown Trout by the spots on the tail and the reddish or iridescent bands on the body, although there is some variation in colour, depending on the water body in which the fish lives. In the American

Great Lakes, Rainbow Trout are referred to as Steelheads, and in the large lakes of the Pacific North-east as Kamloops Trout.

Trout lay their eggs in nests dug in the gravel of streams where the water is swift. After the male has fertilised the eggs, they are covered over with gravel to protect them from predators. The time taken to hatch depends on temperature; the larval trout, with bulbous yolk-sacs, remain in the gravel until the yolk is used up. Like salmon eggs, the eggs of trout are hardy in the "eyed" stage and can be transported. Trout are reared in hatcheries for dispatch to other parts of the world, or for restocking nearby rivers.

Related to the trouts are the various species of Char *(Salvelinus spp.)*. Char are cold-water fishes typical of mountain lakes. In the British Isles, they occur in the Lake District, North Wales, Scotland and Ireland, and may weigh up to about three pounds.

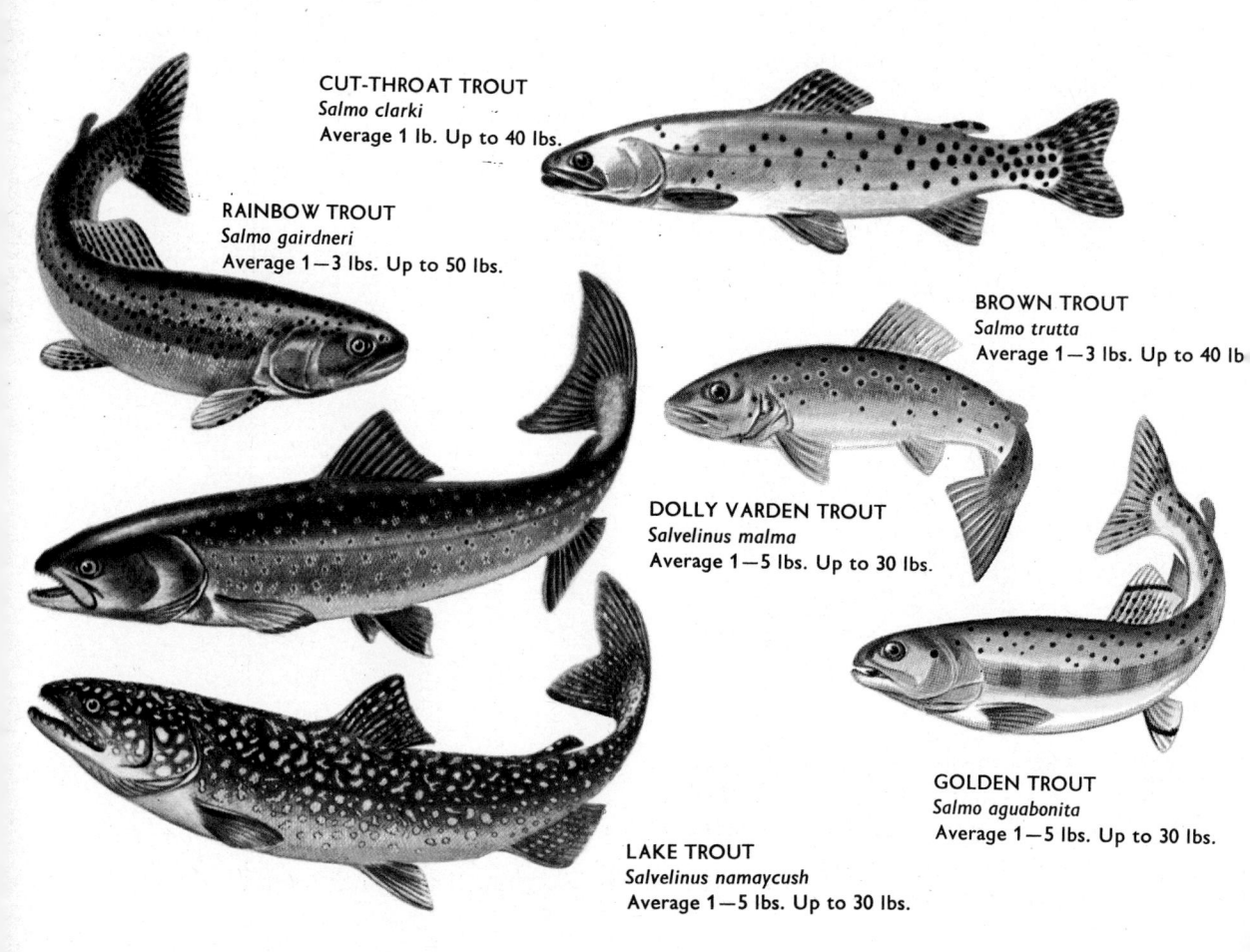

CUT-THROAT TROUT
Salmo clarki
Average 1 lb. Up to 40 lbs.

RAINBOW TROUT
Salmo gairdneri
Average 1—3 lbs. Up to 50 lbs.

BROWN TROUT
Salmo trutta
Average 1—3 lbs. Up to 40 lb

DOLLY VARDEN TROUT
Salvelinus malma
Average 1—5 lbs. Up to 30 lbs.

GOLDEN TROUT
Salmo aguabonita
Average 1—5 lbs. Up to 30 lbs.

LAKE TROUT
Salvelinus namaycush
Average 1—5 lbs. Up to 30 lbs.

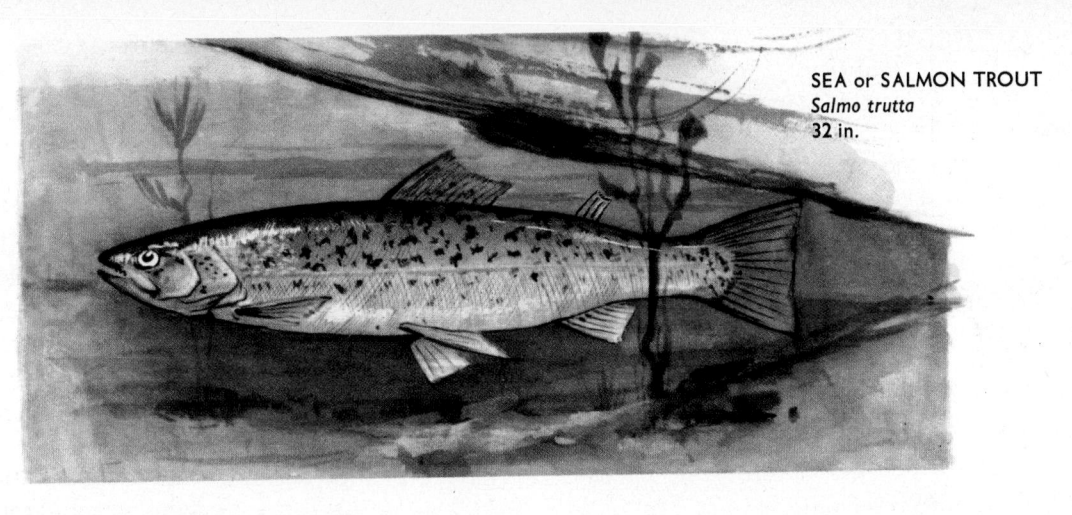

SEA or SALMON TROUT
Salmo trutta
32 in.

TRUMPET FISHES *(Aulostomus maculatus)* are common in coral reefs of the Atlantic Ocean and West Indies. These odd-looking fishes, closely related to pipe fishes, have slim, snaky bodies and long, tubular snouts. The closely related Cornet Fish *(Fistularia tabacaria)* has a whip-like filament growing from the fork of its tail. Most species measure less than a foot in length, but a few grow to a length of six feet or more. They seem to float slowly through the coral as though carried along by currents of water. They hold their body vertically, with the head sometimes up and sometimes down. Actually they propel themselves by vibrating their fins rapidly. They can also swim by rapidly lashing their slim body back and forth.

TRUMPET FISH
1—2 ft.

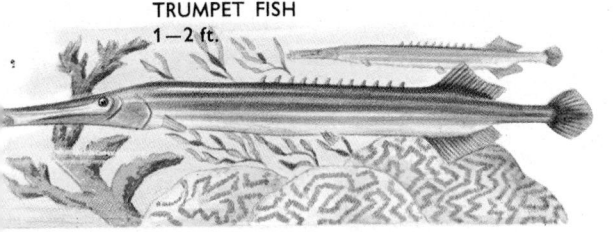

TUATARA *(Sphenodon punctatus)*. In external appearance, and in its ability to regenerate its tail, the Tuatara resembles a lizard, but internally it differs so much that it is placed in a separate order. The Tuatara, truly a "living fossil", is the sole survivor of an order of reptiles *(Rhynchocephalia)* that was common and widespread in the Triassic and Jurassic periods, 250 million years ago. More successful forms replaced

these "beakheads", except where they were safe from competition. In New Zealand, they were indeed inaccessible for millions of years, until man and his domestic animals arrived to prey on them.

Within historic times, Tuataras occurred on both the main islands of New Zealand, but are now extinct there. They survive only on some 20 small, inaccessible islands in the Bay of Plenty, off the east coast of the North Island and at the north-east tip of the South Island. Goats threatened their existence even on these islands, and the New Zealand Government has taken steps to remove the goats, and to protect the endangered and dwindling population.

Tuataras live in a bleak, cold habitat of low, bush-like trees and rocky hills. There they burrow in the deep humus under the trees, often sharing their burrows with petrels (small sea birds), but rarely if ever with another Tuatara. Despite the cold, Tuataras are active mostly at night, and have the lowest tolerance for normal activity (52 degrees Fahrenheit) of any living (and, it is suspected, of any extinct) reptile. As in many other essentially nocturnal animals, their eyes have vertical pupils. Tuataras forage on the surface for insects, snails, earthworms and other small animals. Tuataras are relatively slow-moving, never jumping or climbing, and seldom scampering. Perhaps the relatively great age attained by these reptiles — at least 77 years — is also related to the low temperature of their habitat, for all reptiles in cold regions live longer than

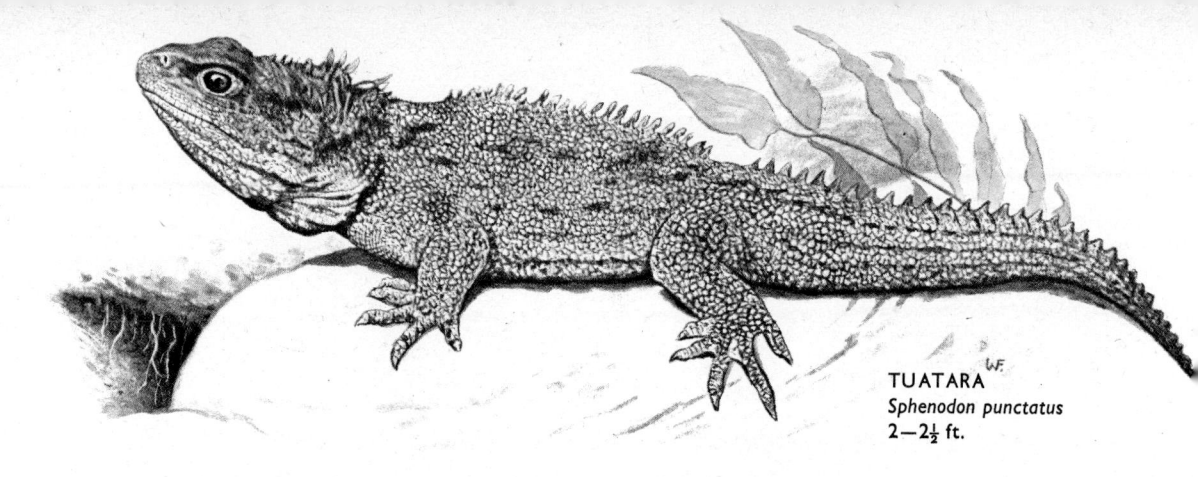

TUATARA
Sphenodon punctatus
2—2½ ft.

relatives or members of the same species found in warmer regions.

During the day, Tuataras sleep in their burrows. On sunny days the males, particularly, bask near the mouth of the burrow in the morning and evening. Petrels are "at home" during the night, Tuataras during the day. If both are present, the petrel is said most often to be found to the left and the Tuatara to the right. To a large degree, there is little conflict in the use of the burrow by both animals, although sometimes the Tuatara will eat young petrels and their eggs.

The burrow is two to three feet long and four to five inches high, not much larger than the Tuatara. The resting place at the end is about a foot and a half wide. The petrel may help to dig the burrow, and both animals dig frequently to clean the channel of debris blown in by the constant wind. The chief hazard is destruction of the deep humus in which their burrows are dug.

The Tuatara lays approximately ten flexible, parchment-like, oval eggs ($\frac{3}{4}$ in.) in shallow excavations where, because of the persistent cold, they develop for a year, or slightly longer, before hatching. This is the longest period of incubation known for reptile eggs.

TUN and **CASK SHELLS** are sea-snails found on sandy bottoms, mainly in tropical seas. Their thin shells have spiral grooving and are covered with a thin, leathery outer skin (periostracum). The Atlantic Partridge Tun, found in south-east Florida and the West Indies, grows to a length of two to five inches. The Giant Tun is fairly common in shallow, grassy sand-bottoms around the world. It has a channelled seven-inch shell. The closely-related Common Fig Shell is long and fragile, and is found commonly along beaches on the Atlantic coast of southern North America.

TUNAS are swift fishes that occur in schools in warm, temperate seas throughout the world. Called tunnies, they are closely related to mackerels. Like most other fishes that live in the open sea, their backs and sides are dark green or blue, grading into silvery-white on the belly. A tuna's body is spindle-shaped, its head is pointed, and the tail tapers towards the rear. The large tail-fin is crescent shaped, like a half-moon.

Tunas travel rapidly through the sea, their schools cruising at speeds greater than 20 miles per hour. They feed on smaller schooling fishes that cross their path. Females lay numerous small eggs which float.

This group contains some of the most famous game fishes in the world. Several are also important commercially, for tuna are delicious. Their flesh colour varies from reddish to white, depending on the species. Tunas are rich with oil, which is extracted from their livers for its vitamin content. Albacores are "white meat" tunas taken in great quantity by commercial fishermen off the Pacific coast of the United States of America (see ALBACORES).

The Bluefin Tuna *(Thunnus thynnus)* is one of the largest fishes in the sea. It reaches 14 feet and 1,800 pounds in weight. Those that weigh less than 100 pounds are called School

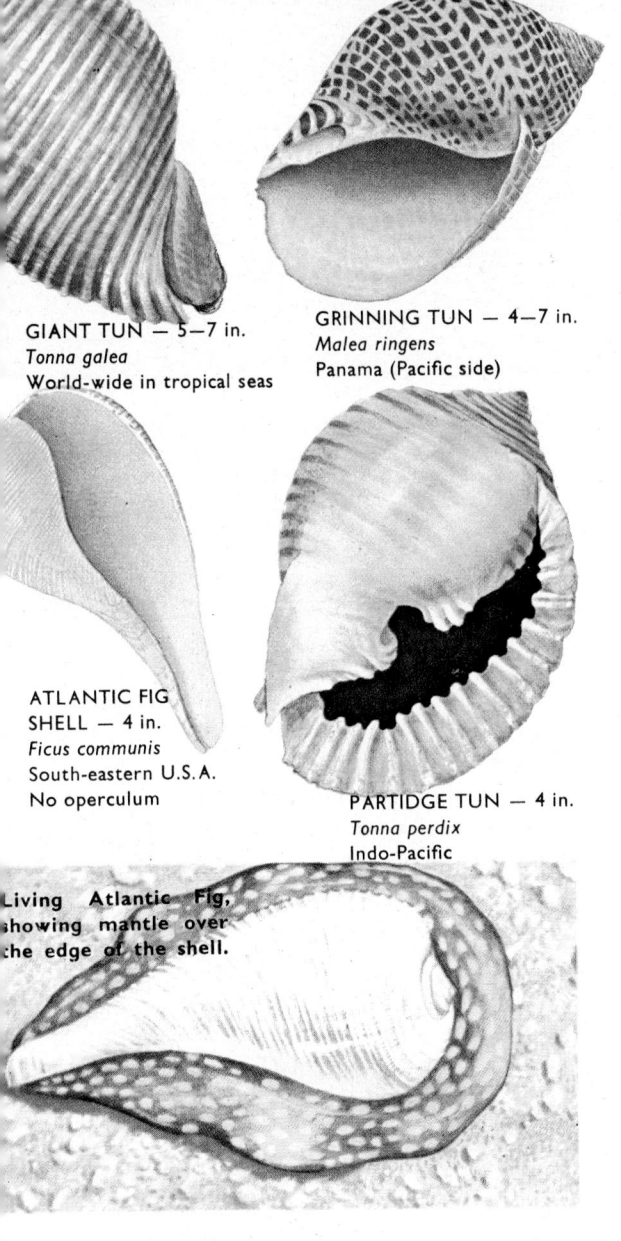

GIANT TUN — 5—7 in.
Tonna galea
World-wide in tropical seas

GRINNING TUN — 4—7 in.
Malea ringens
Panama (Pacific side)

ATLANTIC FIG
SHELL — 4 in.
Ficus communis
South-eastern U.S.A.
No operculum

PARTIDGE TUN — 4 in.
Tonna perdix
Indo-Pacific

Living Atlantic Fig,
showing mantle over
the edge of the shell.

Tuna; those that weigh more than 400 pounds are called Horse Mackerel.

Bluefin Tunas spawn early in the spring, somewhere in the southern part of their range. After spawning, they begin a northward migration, gorging as they go on herrings and other fishes. Along the east coast of the United States, the schools are sighted off the Bahamas in May. By the end of summer or early autumn, the great schools are off Nova Scotia, fattened and ready for the lean winter months. Wedgeport, Nova Scotia, is the site of a famous tuna-fishing tournament (see FISHES).

Bluefin Tunas make a similar migration along the coast of Europe from the Mediterranean to the North sea. Then, like the tunas off the coast of Nova Scotia, they turn to deeper offshore waters for the winter. Bluefin Tuna migrations also occur in the Pacific, from Chile to California, and again off Japan and Korea. Less commonly, they are seen off Africa and Australia.

Commercial fishermen catch tunas with nets and harpoons. Some are also taken on hook and line with the same type of tackle that sport fishermen use. When a tuna is hooked, it dives deep into the sea, and may battle for hours before it becomes tired enough to be brought to the boat. Commercial fishermen like to haul them in quickly.

Every year millions of pounds of tunas are caught commercially. Commercial fishing for Yellowfin Tunas (*Thunnus albacares*) in the Pacific is particularly active. Slightly

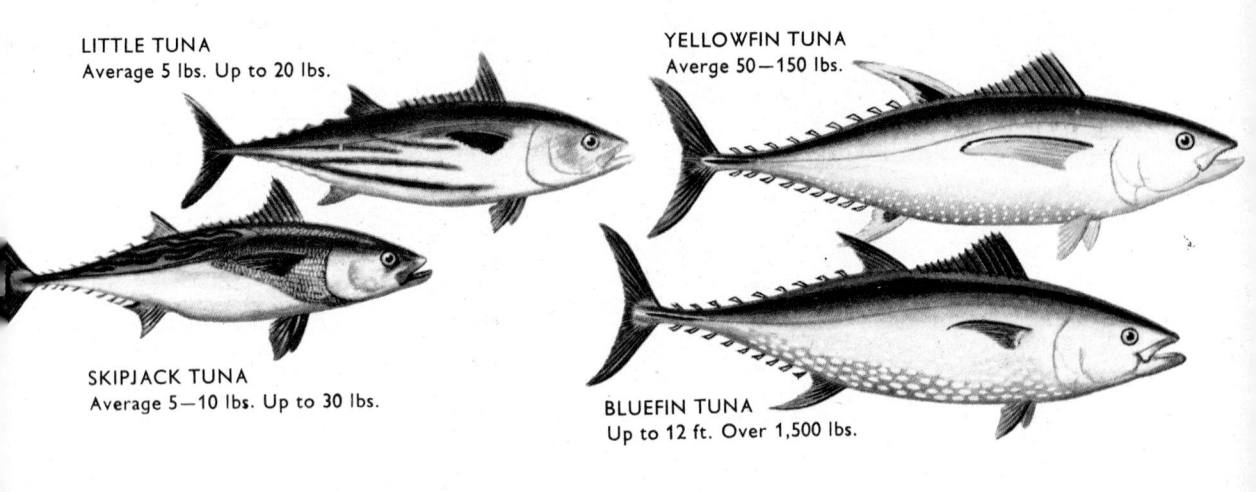

LITTLE TUNA
Average 5 lbs. Up to 20 lbs.

YELLOWFIN TUNA
Averge 50—150 lbs.

SKIPJACK TUNA
Average 5—10 lbs. Up to 30 lbs.

BLUEFIN TUNA
Up to 12 ft. Over 1,500 lbs.

smaller than the Bluefin Tuna, these fish prefer warmer water. Almost none are caught off California, but the California tuna fleet is a large one, and ranges as far south as northern South America. Yellowfin Tunas are also taken in the Atlantic and the Gulf of Mexico, though not as commonly. In these waters, Yellowfin Tuna are called Allison Tunas.

Several other fishes are commonly grouped with the tunas. Among them is the Atlantic Bonito, found in the Atlantic as far north as New York. The Skipjack Tuna, or Oceanic Bonito *(Euthynnus pelamis)*, feeds near the surface. It travels in huge schools in the Pacific, and is caught with the Yellowfin Tuna. The Little Tuna *(Euthynnus alletteratus)*, another small member of the family, is easily distinguished from the others by the spots around its pectoral fins and along its lateral line. Little Tunas, also called False Albacores, occur along western Atlantic coasts, from Massachusetts to Brazil.

TURKEYS are natives of America, and once ranged from the Canadian border as far west as the Dakotas and south to Guatemala.

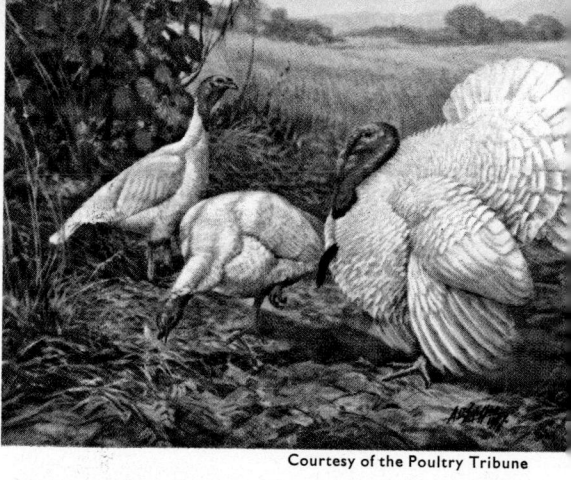

Courtesy of the Poultry Tribune

White Holland Turkeys are a domesticated breed developed for good eating. New, meatier breeds, plus improved raising and marketing methods, have made turkeys popular all-the-year-round food.

Today they are still fairly plentiful in Mexico and Guatemala, but by 1900 overhunting and destruction of their forest habitat had made them quite scarce in the United States.

The wild Mexican turkey is the ancestor of all barnyard turkeys. It differs from wild turkeys of the United States only in the whitish tips of its tail-feathers.

Turkey cocks are polygamous. During the breeding season, their red topknots swell to twice the usual size. The birds spread the great fan of their beautiful tails, scrape

The Ocellated Turkey has prominent eye-spots on its tail feathers. Except on the wattles, its head lacks the red characteristic of the common Wild Turkey.

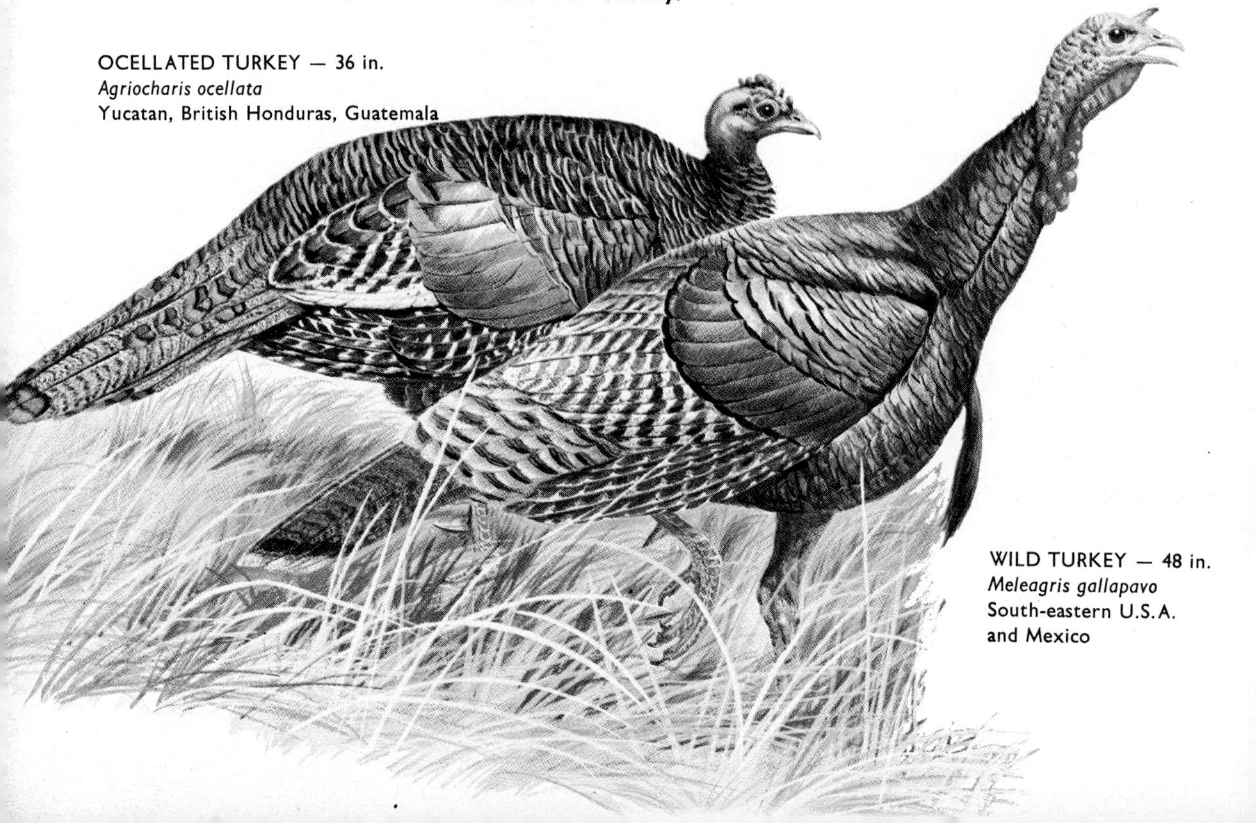

OCELLATED TURKEY — 36 in.
Agriocharis ocellata
Yucatan, British Honduras, Guatemala

WILD TURKEY — 48 in.
Meleagris gallapavo
South-eastern U.S.A.
and Mexico

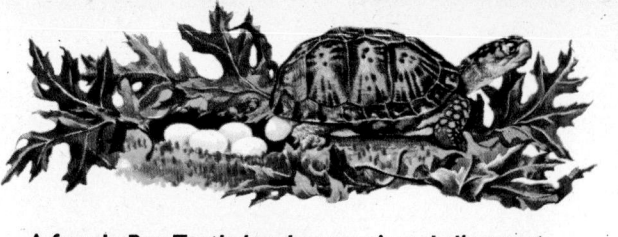

A female Box Turtle lays her eggs in a shallow nest dug in the soil in a sunny place.

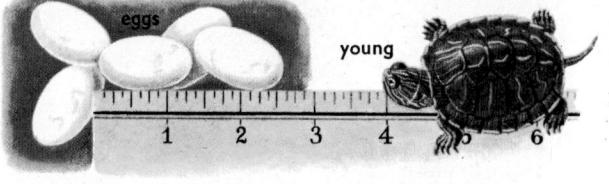

A young Elegant Slider is compared in size to a clutch of eggs. Adults are about 12 inches long.

their wide-open wings along the ground, and challenge and fight other males. The nest is a mere scrape on the ground, well-hidden in vegetation. More than one female will sometimes lay in the same nest. Each hen lays 8 to 15 eggs, which take 28 days to hatch. She does not start incubating until she has laid a complete clutch, so all the eggs hatch on the same day.

The hen leads her precocial young away from the nest soon after they hatch. When two weeks old, the young can fly to low branches to roost at night, out of reach of weasels, foxes and other enemies. Later, the sexes tend to segregate in separate flocks.

TURTLES (including terrapins and tortoises) are unique among backboned animals in having a shell that almost completely encloses the body. A number of extinct reptiles and mammals had somewhat similar protective coverings, but none was ever as successful as the turtle in coping with other problems of life, in spite of their cumbersome armour.

Different kinds of turtle are known as terrapins and tortoises, and in different regions these names have variable meanings. Commonly, all members of the order are called turtles. The mainly edible forms that live in brackish and fresh water are called terrapins, and those that live completely on land, and which have cylindrical, club-shaped limbs devoid of web, are termed tortoises (see TERRAPINS; TORTOISES).

All chelonians — the group name for turtles, tortoises and terrapins — lay eggs. Even sea turtles, the most aquatic of all, must crawl on to land to lay their eggs. Modern chelonians are toothless as adults (embryo soft-shell turtles do have teeth, as did some fossil species). Both jaws are covered with a horny sheath, much like that of the equally toothless birds; the upper jaw is not movable. The bones to which the legs are attached (the limb girdles) lie inside the rib basket, rather than outside, as in all other vertebrates. Usually there are eight neck-bones that can be moved independently.

Thirteen vertebrae of the back are fused to the upper shell. The tail is usually very short. Finally, all turtles have shells, which consist of an upper part, or carapace, and a lower part, or plastron. These are joined on each side by a bridge, either narrow or broad; the ribs are fused to the inner surface of the carapace. The bony structure of the shell is, in most turtles, covered with a series of horny plates. In a few kinds, such as the soft-shells and the marine Leatherback the bony shell is entirely covered with leathery skin.

There are some 230 species of turtle (order *Testudines),* and these are divided into two sub-orders: straight-necked turtles and side-necked turtles. Straight-necked turtles draw in their head by making

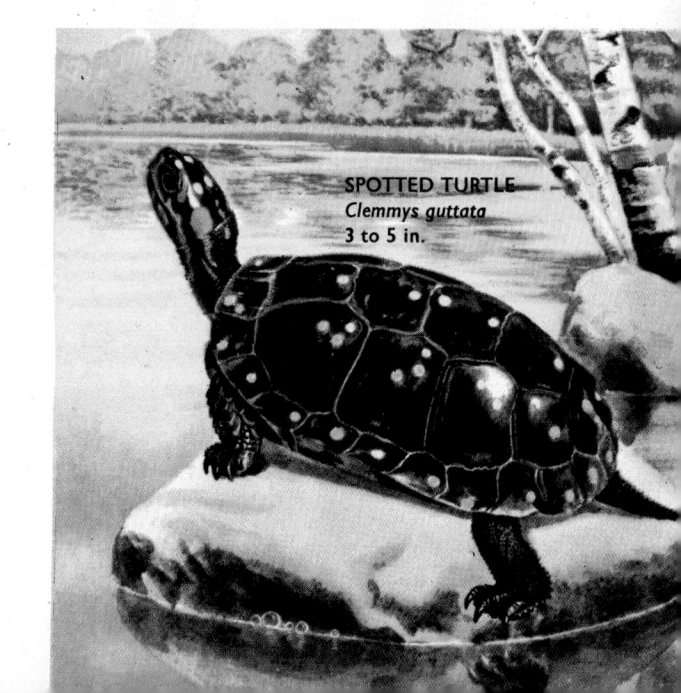

SPOTTED TURTLE
Clemmys guttata
3 to 5 in.

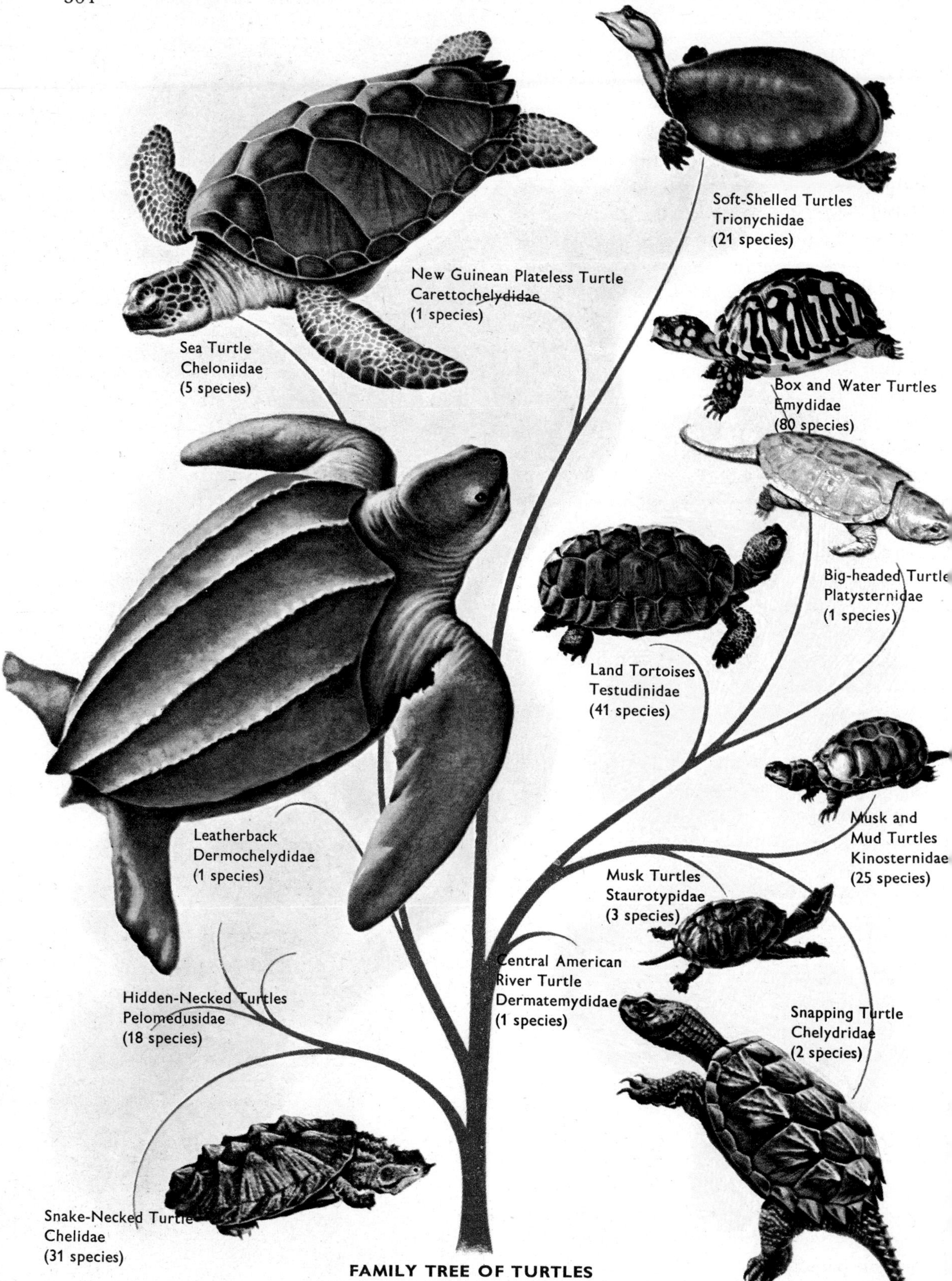

Soft-Shelled Turtles
Trionychidae
(21 species)

New Guinean Plateless Turtle
Carettochelydidae
(1 species)

Sea Turtle
Cheloniidae
(5 species)

Box and Water Turtles
Emydidae
(80 species)

Big-headed Turtle
Platysternidae
(1 species)

Land Tortoises
Testudinidae
(41 species)

Leatherback
Dermochelydidae
(1 species)

Musk and
Mud Turtles
Kinosternidae
(25 species)

Musk Turtles
Staurotypidae
(3 species)

Central American
River Turtle
Dermatemydidae
(1 species)

Hidden-Necked Turtles
Pelomedusidae
(18 species)

Snapping Turtle
Chelydridae
(2 species)

Snake-Necked Turtle
Chelidae
(31 species)

FAMILY TREE OF TURTLES
(Colours indicate related families)

a vertical S-shaped bend in the neck. Side-necked turtles make a horizontal, S-shaped bend in the neck, so that their head points to the side when withdrawn.

The age to which turtles live is amazing, but records are confusing, and in many cases considerably distorted. There are accepted records of 123 and 138 years of age for the Box Turtle, and there is a reasonable probability that a giant tortoise reached an age of about 200. The long life attained by turtles is possible only because of the slowness of their life processes.

Sea turtles live exclusively in and about the sea. Their enormous front legs are oar-like paddles with no fingers visible externally. The rudder-like hind legs are of little help in propelling them in the water. These turtles never drink fresh water, but extract salt from sea water by means of special glands located above each eye. Sea snakes and marine birds have similar glands. The huge "tears" shed by sea turtles as they move laboriously about on the shore are not really tears, but a strong salt solution secreted by these glands.

Leatherback Turtles *(Dermochelys coriacea)* do not have horny plates on their shell, but are covered instead with a nearly smooth skin. Seven heavy ridges run the full length of the carapace, and five low ones along the plastron. Leatherbacks have no claws on their long, powerful front flippers, while all other sea turtles have one or two claws on their shorter flippers.

The Leatherback, largest of all sea turtles, is said to reach a length of 10 feet and a weight of 2,500 pounds. Confirmed records are 7 feet and 1,200 pounds. Leatherbacks are found in all warm oceans, occasionally straying into cooler waters. When noosed,

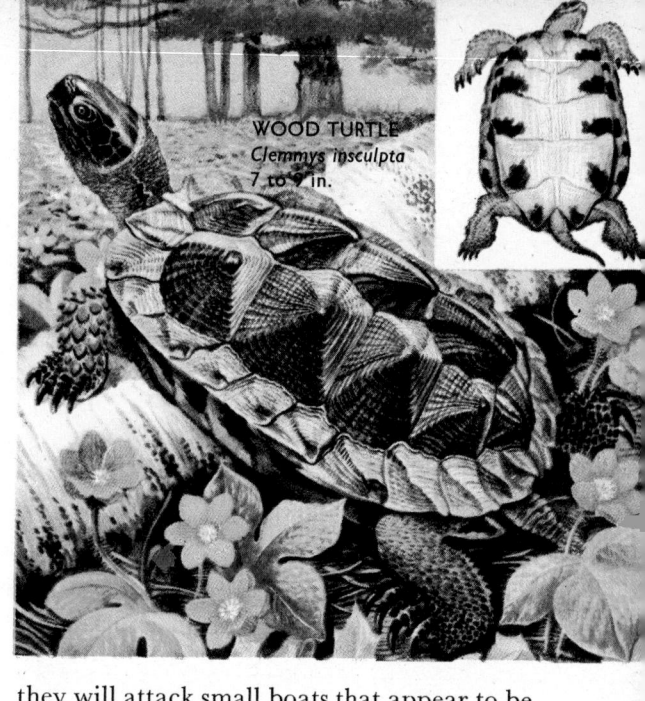

WOOD TURTLE
Clemmys insculpta
7 to 9 in.

they will attack small boats that appear to be a source of danger, and their jaws are powerful enough to bite chunks from oars.

Only the female Leatherbacks come on to land. They dig their nests on sandy shores and lay up to 175 eggs each season (May to August). They dig their nests under cover of darkness and are back in the sea by dawn. The nests are about 50 to 200 feet from water, and the eggs are laid about 3 feet below the surface, deeper than are those of any other sea turtle. When a female has begun nesting,

The bony shell of the turtle is its only defence.

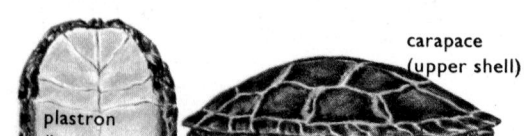

plastron
(lower shell)

carapace
(upper shell)

head and legs
retracted

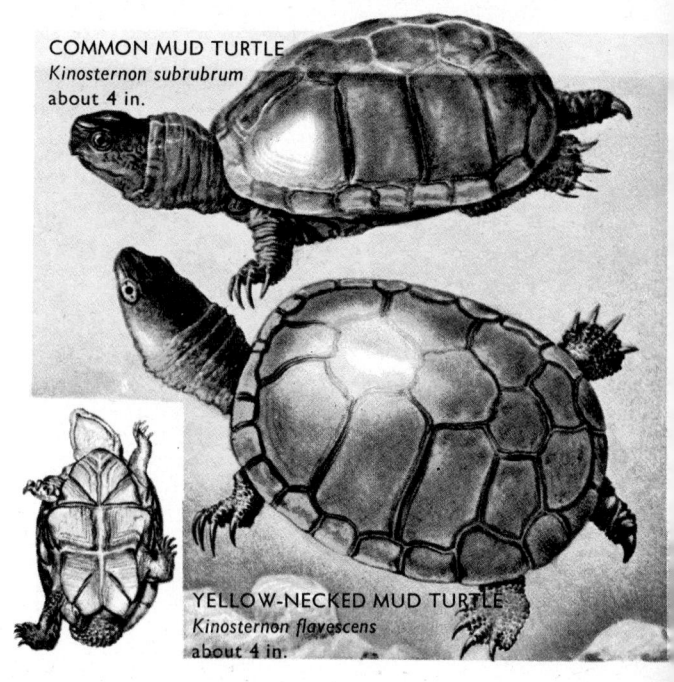

COMMON MUD TURTLE
Kinosternon subrubrum
about 4 in.

YELLOW-NECKED MUD TURTLE
Kinosternon flavescens
about 4 in.

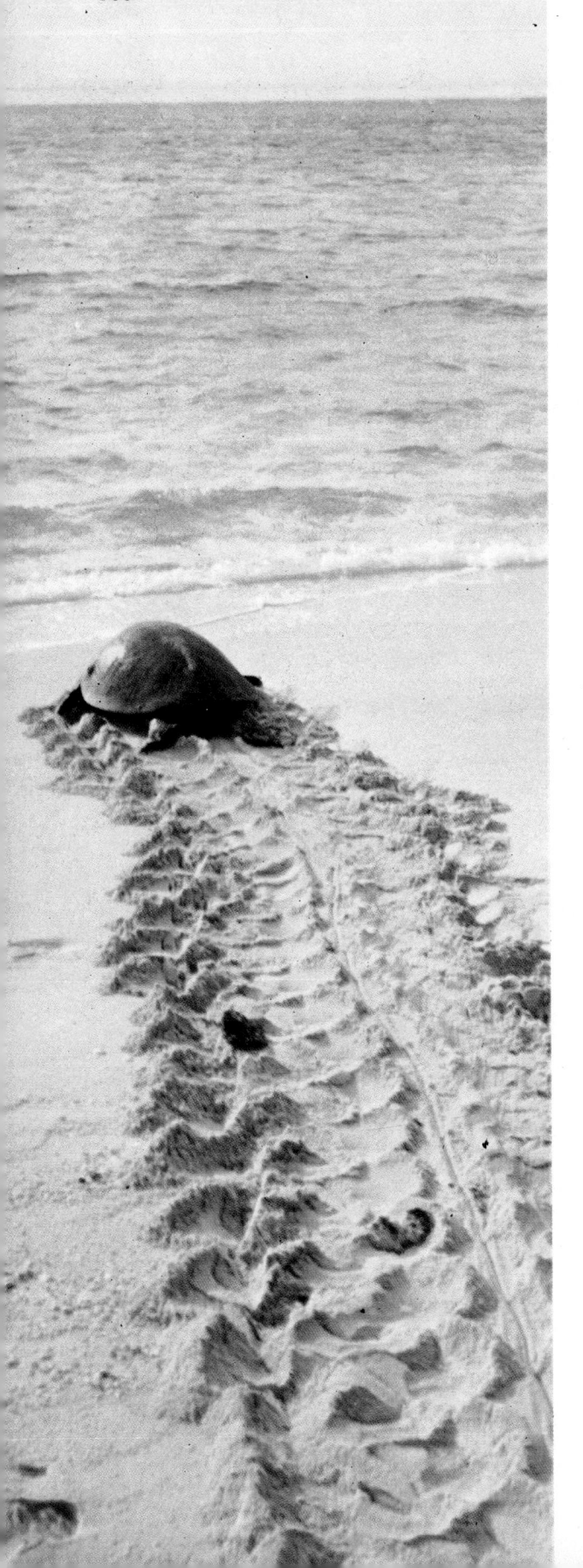

she seems unaware of any other activity around her, and may be watched from a distance of a few feet. The nearly spherical eggs are about $2\frac{1}{2}$ inches in diameter. After the eggs are laid, the nest is filled in with sand, and the location is concealed as the turtle flounders about before heading back to sea. Leatherback eggs are much prized as food, and the turtles' flesh also makes good eating. Their "shell" contains large quantities of oil.

Sea turtles are not properly adapted to crawling on shore; all movements on land require tremendous effort and frequent stops for rest. If they do not get into the water, they will die within a few hours, unless turned on to their backs; when lying on their bellies, the pressure of their weight on the heart and lungs is too great. Putting them on their backs relieves this temporarily, but they are not able to turn themselves over on to their bellies again.

Green Turtles (Chelonia mydas) have been a famous food for centuries. These turtles live in all warm oceans of the world, generally in the shallower waters over the continental shelf. At nesting time, however, they may cross oceanic deeps to reach the sandy shores which they prefer for their nests. Green Turtles are active for only part of each day. At other times they rest, or sleep on the surface of the water, or swim on the bottom of shallows and rest in favoured underwater depressions. They come to the surface every hour or so to breathe, and then go back to the same resting site. Green Turtles seldom exceed 4 feet in length and a weight of 500 pounds.

Nesting occurs chiefly in late spring and early summer, and in the Atlantic is now confined mainly to the coast of Central America and Ascension Island. In times past, Green Turtles nested on the coasts of Florida, the Bermudas, West Indies and Mexico.

Green Turtles eat mainly grasses and

A Green Turtle labours her way back to the sea after a journey above the tide-line to lay her eggs.
Fritz Goro

algae. Some small animals also are eaten, and it is thought that the young are probably mainly carnivorous. Green Turtles are mild-tempered and rarely attempt to bite.

Hawksbill Turtles *(Eretmochelys imbricata)* are small turtles that seldom weigh more than 100 pounds. The record is 280 pounds. The Hawksbill is famed primarily as a source of tortoise-shell—the unusually thick, translucent, horny plates covering their shell. These are removed by heat (the process generally kills the turtle) and can be molded to various shapes. Plastics have largely replaced tortoiseshell in North America and Europe, but elsewhere it is still cherished.

The flesh of the Hawksbill is palatable, and its eggs are much in demand. In certain parts of the world, poisonous algae may be eaten by the Hawksbill, however, and though the turtles themselves are safe from the poison, they may pass the poison on in their flesh. People are not immune to the poison, and several deaths of this origin have been reported. Other algae-eating turtles may also hold poison within their flesh.

Hawksbills eat both plants and animals, but prefer animals. They live mostly in shallow waters. Their territorial instinct is so strong that they stay in one area for years, leaving only to nest or to find food. Hawksbills grow rapidly, increasing their shell length from $1\frac{1}{2}$ inches at hatching to 14 inches or more within two years.

The Loggerhead *(Caretta)*, and the Atlantic and Pacific Ridleys *(Lepidochelys)*, are the only other sea turtles, the Ridleys being the smallest of all. Both genera have more than four pairs of shields along the sides of the carapace, and are thus distinguished from the Green and Hawksbill Turtles. Some Loggerheads attain a massive size, and weights of over 1,000 pounds have been reported, but such large specimens are rarely captured. The Loggerhead is a wanderer and, while preferring coastal bays, it is often sighted on the high seas, and has also turned up on British shores. The Ridleys have a more restricted range, and are less prone to floating on the surface than other sea turtles. Both the Loggerhead and the Ridley feed on crabs and other invertebrates, and also marine grasses. The eggs are widely appreciated, and many people also relish the flesh. Fortunately the Ridley is well protected from exploitation by the remoteness of its nesting-sites; furthermore, unlike the other sea turtles — which nest at night — the Ridley nests by day, and nesting and egg-laying times appear to be erratic.

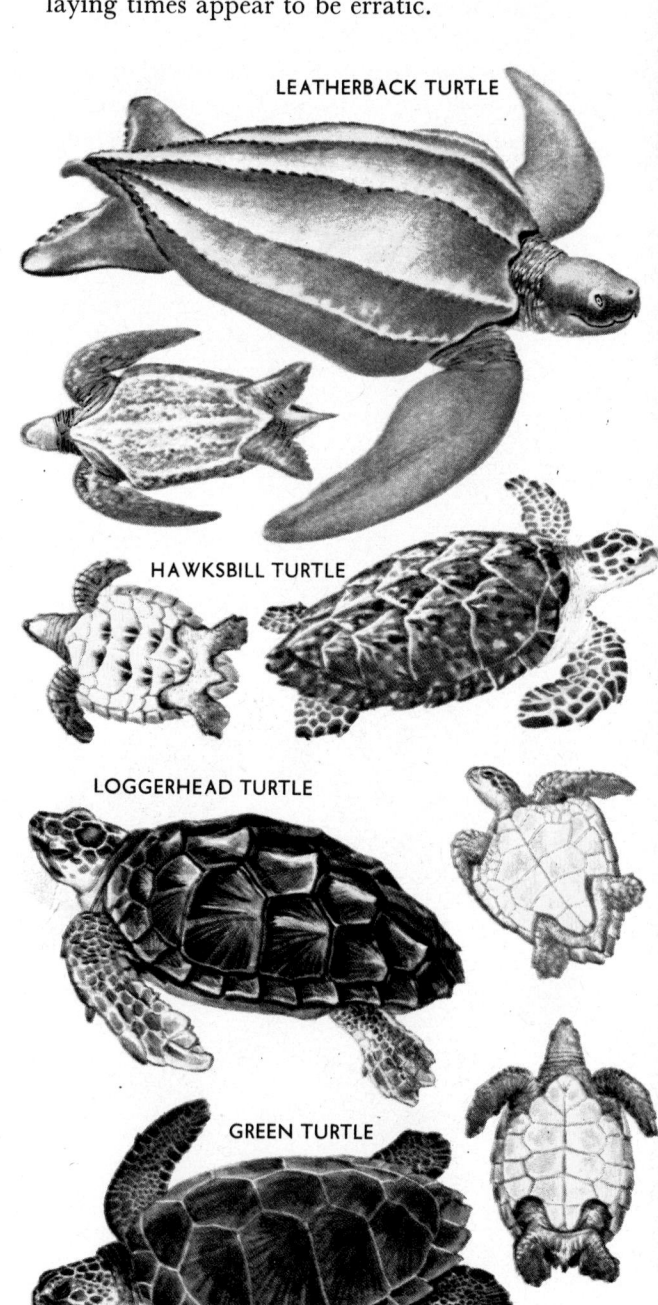

LEATHERBACK TURTLE

HAWKSBILL TURTLE

LOGGERHEAD TURTLE

GREEN TURTLE

U-V

UNDERWING MOTHS (*Noctuidae*) offer excellent examples of "flash colouration". Their brown or grey forewings are usually marked to resemble the various backgrounds on which the moths rest. Some are nearly white and marked with black, so that they blend with birch-bark. The hind wings are brightly coloured with black and red, orange or yellow bands. In flight these bright colours are much in evidence, but they disappear as soon as the moth comes to rest. Pursuers presumably continue to look for the bright colour; likewise, the sudden flash of colour as an underwing moth takes flight may startle a predator that disturbs the moth in its resting place.

VELVET ANTS (*Mutilidae*) are actually wasps, not ants. Females are wingless, and the bodies of most species are covered densely with short hairs. Females can make

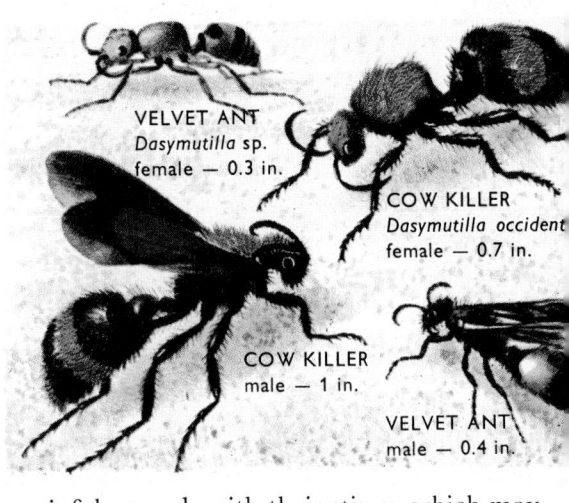

VELVET ANT
Dasymutilla sp.
female — 0.3 in.

COW KILLER
Dasymutilla occident
female — 0.7 in.

COW KILLER
male — 1 in.

VELVET ANT
male — 0.4 in.

painful wounds with their stings, which may be nearly as long as their abdomens. Some of the larger species are called Cow Killers in the U.S.A. The males lack stings, but in most species are winged.

Velvet ants deposit their eggs in nests of solitary wasps and bees. Usually a single egg is placed in each nest. When the Velvet ant larva hatches, it feeds on the provisions left for the larva of the solitary wasp or bee — which may also be eaten by the Velvet ant when it hatches.

Velvet ants are most abundant in hot, dry climates. Some are active in the heat of the day; others are nocturnal. The family contains more than 3,000 species.

VIPERS comprise two groups, the true vipers and the pit vipers, both of which have movable front fangs for injecting venom.

True vipers differ from pit vipers primarily in lacking facial pits. A few pitless vipers, such as the Ceylonese Copperhead, have venom so weak that it has no more effect on a human being than a bee-sting, but all vipers are poisonous and the majority can be fatal to man. The venom affects the

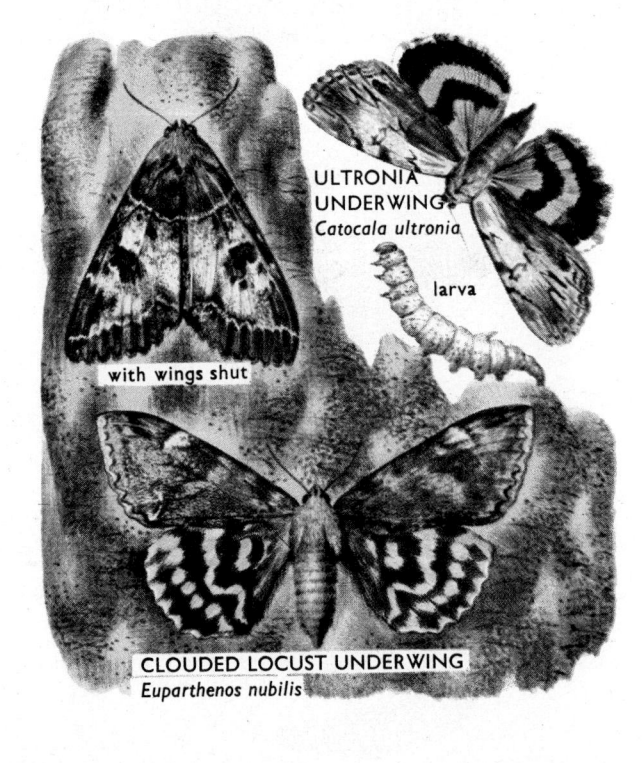

ULTRONIA
UNDERWING
Catocala ultronia

larva

with wings shut

CLOUDED LOCUST UNDERWING
Euparthenos nubilis

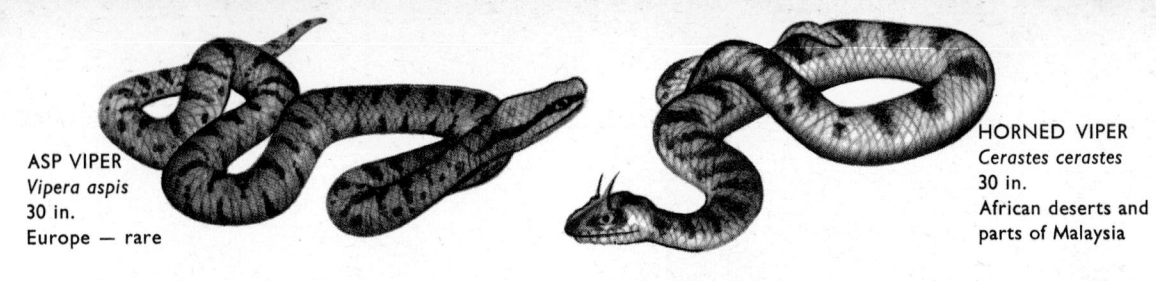

ASP VIPER
Vipera aspis
30 in.
Europe — rare

HORNED VIPER
Cerastes cerastes
30 in.
African deserts and
parts of Malaysia

blood and blood vessels. Pitless vipers of about 50 species are found only in the Old World, from England across Europe and Asia, through China southward to Java, in the East Indies, and through Africa.

Mole vipers *(Atractaspis)* are true burrowers. A dozen species are found in Africa, Asia Minor and the Arabian Peninsula. They have a slender head, tiny eyes, and only two or three teeth on each side near the middle of the lower jaw. Their fangs in the upper jaw are disproportionately enormous, scarcely clearing the lower jaws when the mouth is opened wide, so that they can be swung down along each side of the lower jaw while the mouth is closed or only partially open, and so bite a hand gripping the snake's head. Their venom is not especially powerful and is rarely fatal to man. Mole vipers prey largely on insects and small reptiles.

Four species of night adders *(Causus)* live south of the Sahara Desert, in Africa. Unlike mole vipers, these snakes have the shortest fangs of all vipers, but they resemble the Mole Vipers in having symmetrical head shields like the more primitive snakes. These snakes feed entirely on frogs and toads. Their

venom is powerful, and in two species the venom gland and sac extend back from the head for almost a fourth of the body length.

Pitless vipers of the most advanced group have a broad head with small scales, and all bear their young alive. Some burrow in sand by coiling their heavy body and sidling into the sand by movements of their ribs. Sand-dwellers live in the African deserts, and in Asia Minor eastward to the deserts of India and Ceylon. Included in the group are two species of horned vipers *(Cerastes)* and two species of false horned vipers *(Pseudocerastes)*, the Leafnose Viper *(Eristocophis mcmahoni)*, and the Sawscale, or Carpet, Viper *(Echis carinatus)*.

When disturbed, the short-tempered Sawscale Viper rubs together the very rough sawtooth-like scales on the sides of its body, and produces an awesome noise that is described as sounding like water boiling furiously. Numerous tales are told about the Sawscale Viper's jumping powers, as it flips from sandy concealment to bite hapless and unsuspecting intruders. Drop for drop, the venom of this two-foot snake is the most potent of all vipers, making it indeed

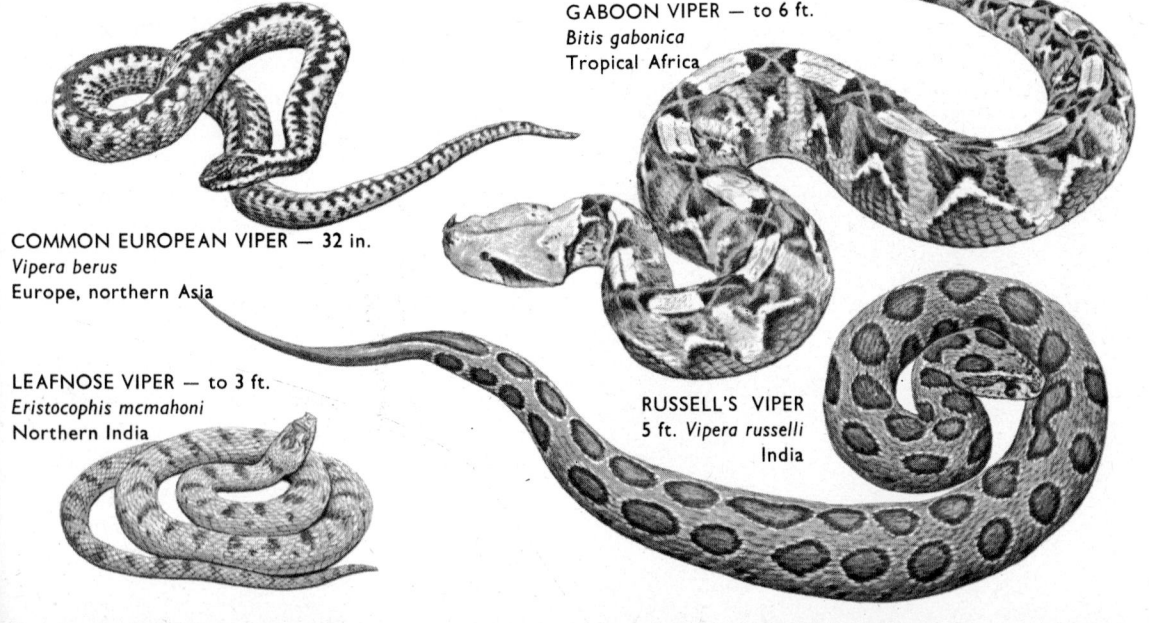

COMMON EUROPEAN VIPER — 32 in.
Vipera berus
Europe, northern Asia

GABOON VIPER — to 6 ft.
Bitis gabonica
Tropical Africa

LEAFNOSE VIPER — to 3 ft.
Eristocophis mcmahoni
Northern India

RUSSELL'S VIPER
5 ft. *Vipera russelli*
India

a justly-feared snake. At an opposite extreme of adaptation are African tree vipers *(Atheris)* that have a prehensile tail and are arboreal.

The Gaboon Viper *(Bitis gabonica)* of tropical Africa is a six-foot giant that has a head almost as large as a spread hand, and a heavy, thick body. This big snake weighs as much as 18 pounds, but is extremely docile. Its venom is powerful, and its bite is especially dangerous because of the large quantity of venom stored in its big venom sacs. Its fangs are almost two inches long. This species and the closely-related Rhinoceros Viper *(Bitis nasicornis)* are among the most beautifully coloured of all snakes. They have complex markings of brown, green, purple, black and blue, forming a "disruptive" pattern that makes them difficult to detect on the forest floor where they live. The Puff Adder *(Bitis arietans)* is a five-foot species that lives throughout most of Africa and into Asia Minor. A large proportion of the African snakebite cases, many of them fatal, are caused by the Puff Adder. These snakes wheeze and huff and puff as a warning when startled. They inhale and exhale air rapidly; all members of this genus hiss similarly, but the Puff Adder is most adept — even its nostrils are enlarged.

Russell's Viper *(Vipera russelli)* causes more human deaths than any other snake. Its habit of resting after dark on dusty trails, where the heat of the sun still lingers, makes it especially dangerous to barelegged natives. Like the Puff Adder, this viper has enlarged nostrils. Other members of this genus are smaller and have small nostrils. They are found in Europe, extreme northern Africa, Kenya, and northern Asia, the range of one species extending to Java. (See ADDERS, common European Viper.)

Pit vipers are largely American; 75 of the 115 species are found in the Western Hemisphere, the remainder in Asia. Bushmasters, lanceheads and rattlesnakes are among the kinds of pit vipers described in separate entries.

Pit vipers look essentially like true vipers, except that they have facial pits — deep depressions on each side of the head between the eye and nostril. No other snakes have these pits, which contain sense organs that can detect temperature differences as slight as a fraction of a degree. This enables pit vipers to find their prey and to strike accurately even in darkness. Rattlesnakes have been observed hunting at dusk by testing the temperature outside burrows, until one is found giving off the heat from a rat (see RATTLESNAKES).

Most vipers release their prey immediately after striking, then track the animal down by their sensitive sense of smell. Mammals that run on the ground are easily followed. Pit vipers that feed on birds have learned that their winged prey leaves no trail and so these snakes hold their victims in their mouths until the venom kills them.

Vipers have movable front fangs. These large, hollow teeth, one each side in the upper jaw, are lowered when the snake opens its mouth to strike. The fangs are shed about every two weeks, and replaced from a reserve series in the "gums" behind.

The venom sac is located next to the venom gland at the rear on each side of the head. Venom flows through a hollow fang, and thence to the exterior via an opening near the tip of the fang. Muscles around the venom sac contract to force the venom out, which then runs through the fang and is injected into the prey like the contents of a hypodermic needle. (See ADDERS.)

A viper's skull shows adaptations to its method of feeding: poison fangs and unjoined lower jawbones.

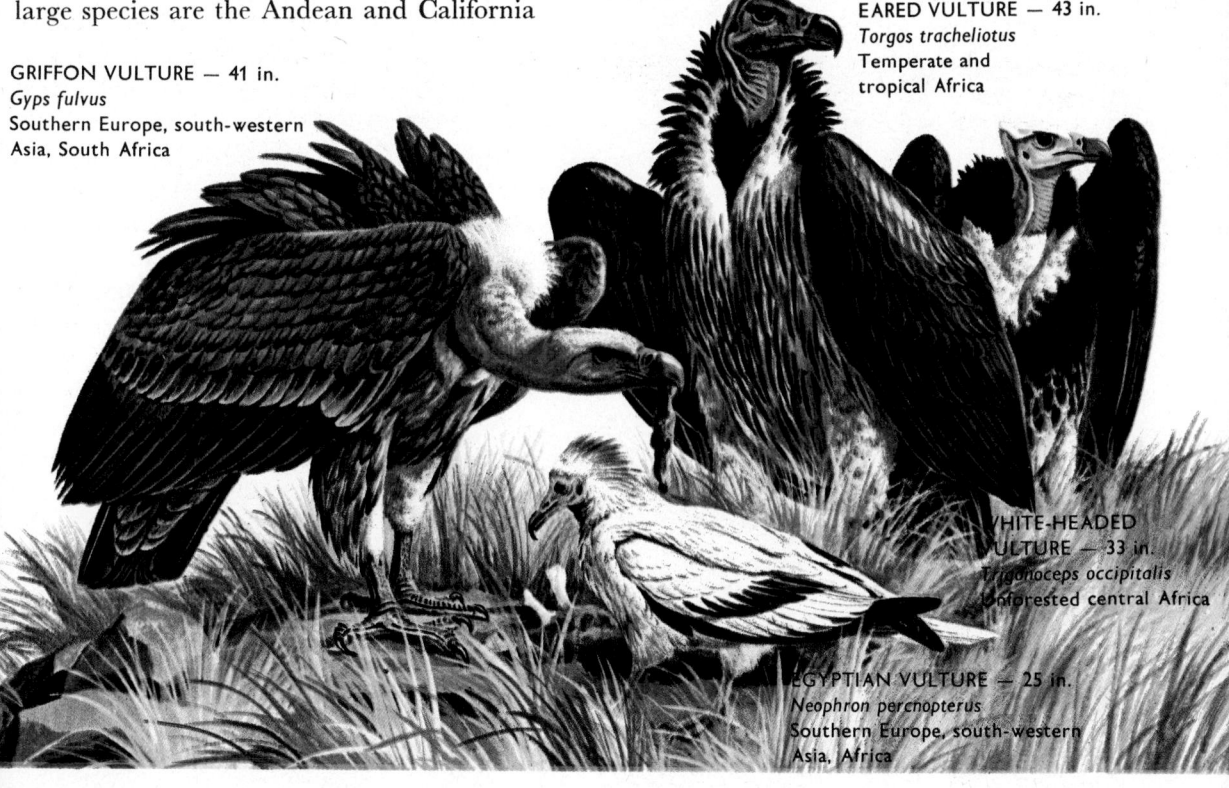

TURKEY VULTURE — 29 in.
Cathartes aura
Southern Canada to the
Strait of Magellan

BLACK VULTURE — 25 in.
Coragyps astratus
Central U.S.A., south
to Argentina and Chile

VULTURES are found in the tropical and sub-tropical regions of the world, where they play an important part in disposing rapidly of dead animals that would otherwise quickly putrify. They are characterised by weak feet, which do not allow them the crushing grip of a bird like the eagle.

There are two distinct families which have become vultures. The *Cathartidae* of the Western Hemisphere have small heads and relatively weak bills. The small species are called "Buzzards" in North America. The large species are the Andean and California

Condors. They are carrion-feeders and, like all vultures, will gorge themselves when food is plentiful until they can hardly move. They are broad-winged, with a soaring flight that uses little energy as they circle, watching the ground below for food. The sight of one descending is a signal for others to come and investigate, and where food is present a crowd soon gathers.

The American Vultures do not build nests, but nest in caves, hollow tree-stumps, or even on the ground in sheltered sites. The young develop slowly, taking three months to fledge.

The Vultures of the Eastern Hemisphere are members of the big family of hawks and eagles, the *Accipitridae*. If their heads and necks were feathered, they would, in fact, look like eagles. The lack of feathers on head and neck enables them to keep themselves clean when feeding, which they do by delving into carcases. They have heavy, tearing, eagle-like bills, build big nests of sticks on trees or rock ledges, and are relatively sociable in their behaviour.

GRIFFON VULTURE — 41 in.
Gyps fulvus
Southern Europe, south-western
Asia, South Africa

EARED VULTURE — 43 in.
Torgos tracheliotus
Temperate and
tropical Africa

WHITE-HEADED
VULTURE — 33 in.
Trigonoceps occipitalis
Unforested central Africa

EGYPTIAN VULTURE — 25 in.
Neophron percnopterus
Southern Europe, south-western
Asia, Africa

W

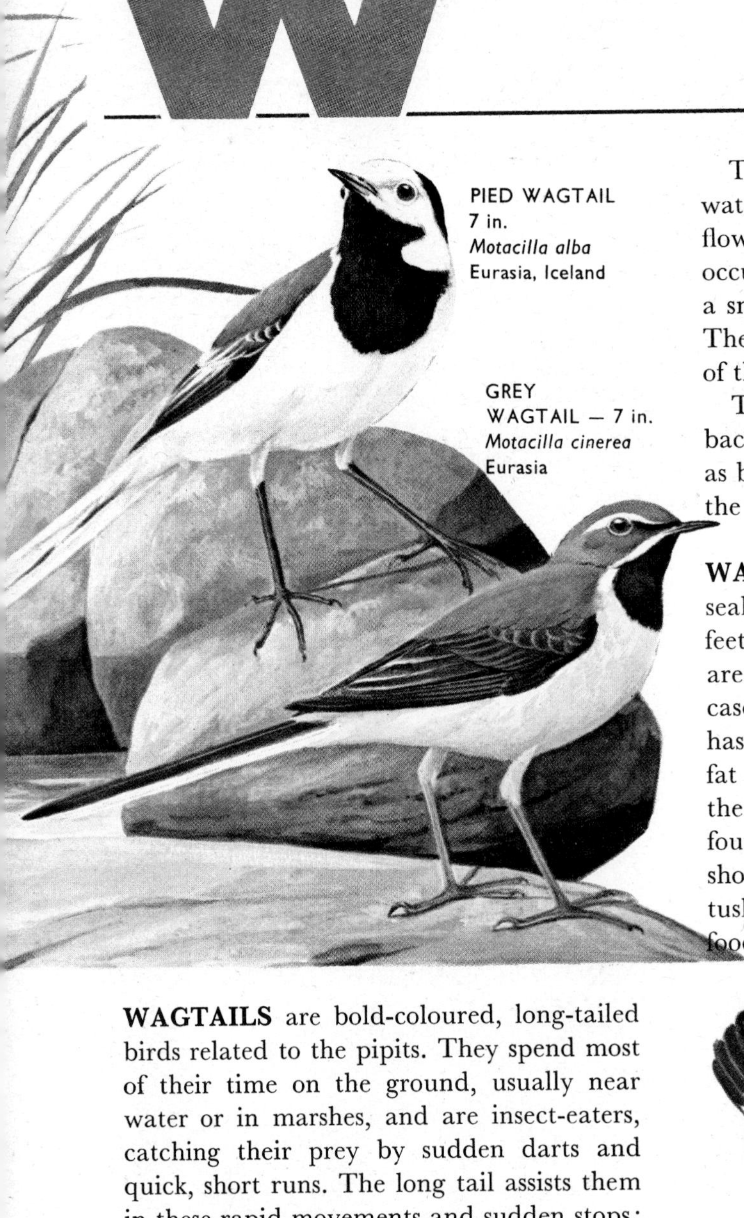

PIED WAGTAIL
7 in.
Motacilla alba
Eurasia, Iceland

**GREY
WAGTAIL — 7 in.**
Motacilla cinerea
Eurasia

The Grey Wagtail is a bird of running water. It is commonest alongside fast-flowing streams in hill country, but will occur elsewhere, usually where there is a small waterfall or some similar substitute. The black throat-patch is a spring adornment of the male.

The Yellow Wagtail male is olive on the back, but in spring the breast and head are as bright as those of a canary. It is a bird of the marshes.

WALRUSES (*Odobenus rosmarus*) are large seals. Males may measure as much as 12 feet in length and weigh $1\frac{1}{2}$ tons; females are smaller. Both have tusks, which in rare cases may be 3 feet long. The wrinkled body has relatively little hair, but a thick layer of fat insulates these animals from the cold of the arctic seas. Frequently, walruses are found basking on ice-floes, or on the rocky shores of arctic oceans. They use their long tusks in digging up clams, their principal food, and in threatening troublesome Polar

WAGTAILS are bold-coloured, long-tailed birds related to the pipits. They spend most of their time on the ground, usually near water or in marshes, and are insect-eaters, catching their prey by sudden darts and quick, short runs. The long tail assists them in these rapid movements and sudden stops; it is constantly in motion and, when not otherwise used, may be wagged up and down, thus giving the birds their name.

The Pied Wagtail is the species least tied to water. It often occurs around farms and such places, where it becomes relatively tame. In winter, Pied Wagtails flock to roost in reedbeds or trees, in some areas using warmed greenhouses.

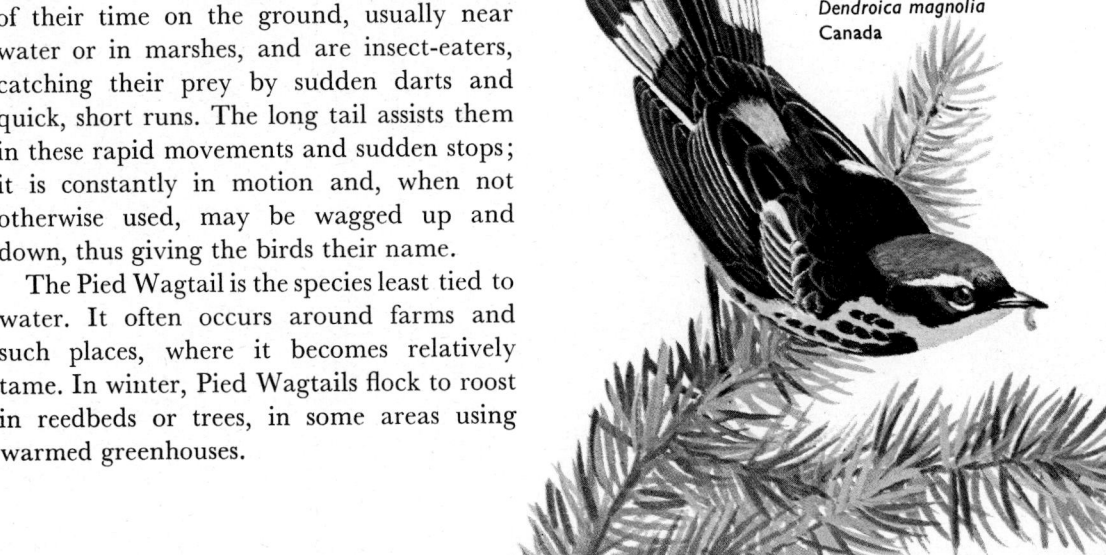

MAGNOLIA WARBLER — 5 in.
Dendroica magnolia
Canada

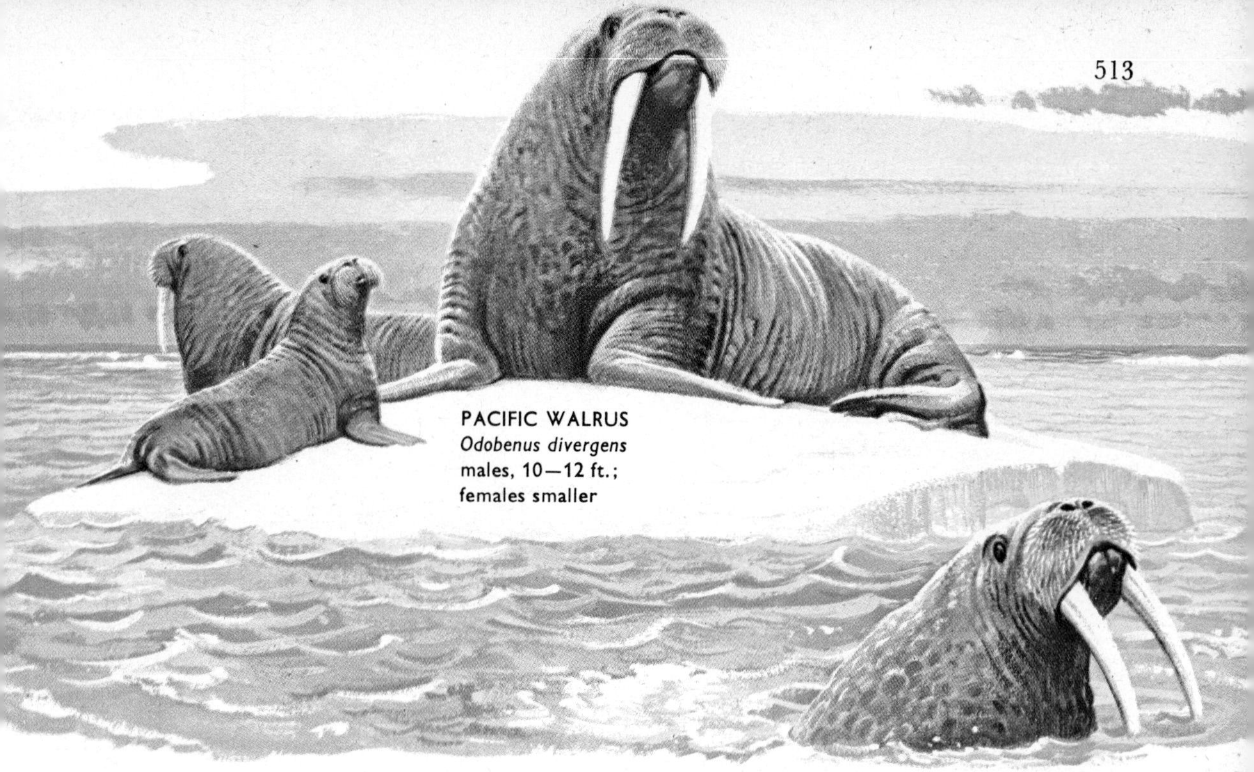

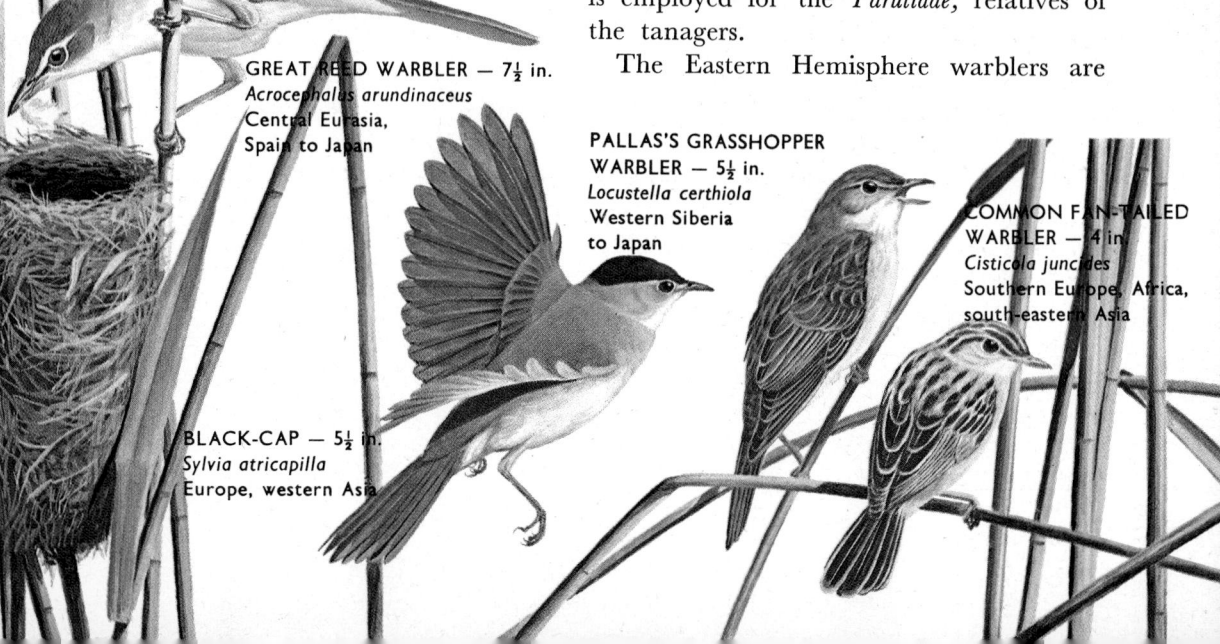

PACIFIC WALRUS
Odobenus divergens
males, 10—12 ft.;
females smaller

Walruses take turns watching for intruders. If an enemy, such as a Killer Whale or a Polar Bear, is sighted, the sentinel Walrus slides into the water to escape and the others in the herd follow.

Bears. Walruses, like many other seals, can make loud, deep bellows. Eskimos hunt walruses for food, to get their hides and oil, and also for the valuable ivory of their tusks.

Walruses are aquatic carnivores, thus sharing a common ancestor with such land-dwellers as dogs, cats and bears. The two species, the Atlantic and the Pacific, are found only in the Arctic Ocean, ranging into Hudson Bay and the Bering Sea in winter. The Pacific Walrus has stouter whiskers and longer tusks (See SEALS).

WARBLERS are small insect-eating birds. As with the flycatchers, two distinct families have been given the same popular name. In the Eastern Hemisphere the family *Sylviidae*, near relatives of the thrushes, have this name, while in the Western Hemisphere it is employed for the *Parulidae*, relatives of the tanagers.

The Eastern Hemisphere warblers are

GREAT REED WARBLER — 7½ in.
Acrocephalus arundinaceus
Central Eurasia,
Spain to Japan

PALLAS'S GRASSHOPPER WARBLER — 5½ in.
Locustella certhiola
Western Siberia
to Japan

COMMON FAN-TAILED WARBLER — 4 in.
Cisticola juncides
Southern Europe, Africa,
south-eastern Asia

BLACK-CAP — 5½ in.
Sylvia atricapilla
Europe, western Asia

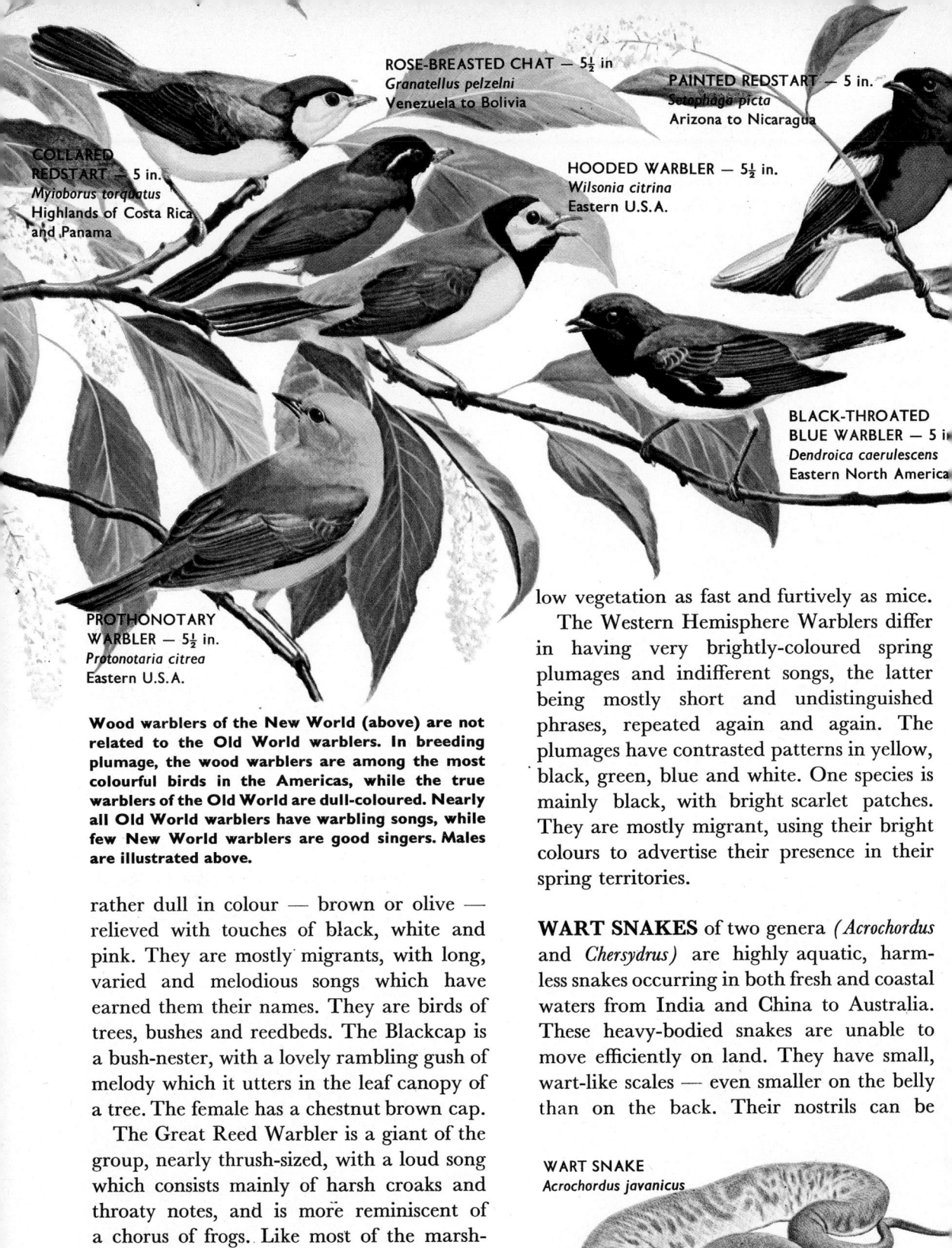

ROSE-BREASTED CHAT — 5½ in
Granatellus pelzelni
Venezuela to Bolivia

PAINTED REDSTART — 5 in.
Setophaga picta
Arizona to Nicaragua

COLLARED REDSTART — 5 in.
Myioborus torquatus
Highlands of Costa Rica
and Panama

HOODED WARBLER — 5½ in.
Wilsonia citrina
Eastern U.S.A.

BLACK-THROATED BLUE WARBLER — 5 in
Dendroica caerulescens
Eastern North America

PROTHONOTARY WARBLER — 5½ in.
Protonotaria citrea
Eastern U.S.A.

Wood warblers of the New World (above) are not related to the Old World warblers. In breeding plumage, the wood warblers are among the most colourful birds in the Americas, while the true warblers of the Old World are dull-coloured. Nearly all Old World warblers have warbling songs, while few New World warblers are good singers. Males are illustrated above.

rather dull in colour — brown or olive — relieved with touches of black, white and pink. They are mostly migrants, with long, varied and melodious songs which have earned them their names. They are birds of trees, bushes and reedbeds. The Blackcap is a bush-nester, with a lovely rambling gush of melody which it utters in the leaf canopy of a tree. The female has a chestnut brown cap.

The Great Reed Warbler is a giant of the group, nearly thrush-sized, with a loud song which consists mainly of harsh croaks and throaty notes, and is more reminiscent of a chorus of frogs. Like most of the marsh-nesting warblers, it slings its nest between upright stems.

The Grasshopper Warblers are ground nesters in marshy places, moving through low vegetation as fast and furtively as mice.

The Western Hemisphere Warblers differ in having very brightly-coloured spring plumages and indifferent songs, the latter being mostly short and undistinguished phrases, repeated again and again. The plumages have contrasted patterns in yellow, black, green, blue and white. One species is mainly black, with bright scarlet patches. They are mostly migrant, using their bright colours to advertise their presence in their spring territories.

WART SNAKES of two genera (*Acrochordus* and *Chersydrus*) are highly aquatic, harmless snakes occurring in both fresh and coastal waters from India and China to Australia. These heavy-bodied snakes are unable to move efficiently on land. They have small, wart-like scales — even smaller on the belly than on the back. Their nostrils can be

WART SNAKE
Acrochordus javanicus

closed by valves, and their flat tail helps in swimming. Wart snakes are active mostly at night and, like most other nocturnal animals, have vertical pupils in their eyes. They bear their young alive. Adults reach a length of six feet, and at this size their thick body resembles an elephant's trunk. Their skin is used for leather and is referred to as "karung".

WASPS are a large group of insects of the order *Hymenoptera*, which also contains ants and bees. There are many kinds in a number of families, differing from bees in structure and also in habits (see BEES).

Gall Wasps (*Cynipidae*) are small, usually black wasps, with abdomens flattened from side to side. They produce swellings, or galls, such as those commonly seen on leaves or twigs of oaks and other plants.

Potter, or Mason, Wasps (*Vespidae*) build vase-like nests of mud. In each nest the female deposits a single egg, suspended from the ceiling by a thread of silk. The nest is usually provisioned with a caterpillar, or some other insect, on which the larva feeds.

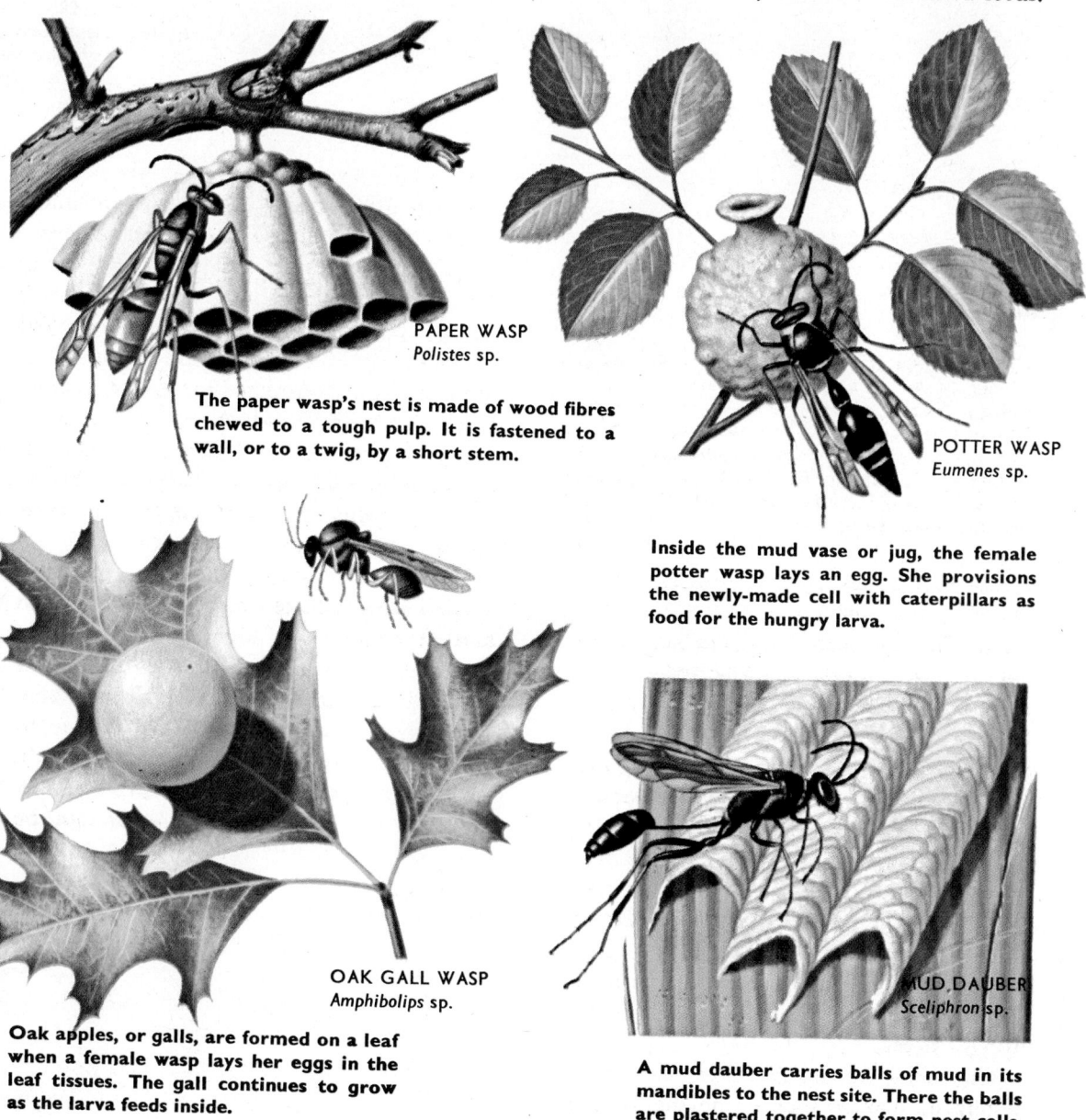

PAPER WASP
Polistes sp.

The paper wasp's nest is made of wood fibres chewed to a tough pulp. It is fastened to a wall, or to a twig, by a short stem.

POTTER WASP
Eumenes sp.

Inside the mud vase or jug, the female potter wasp lays an egg. She provisions the newly-made cell with caterpillars as food for the hungry larva.

OAK GALL WASP
Amphibolips sp.

Oak apples, or galls, are formed on a leaf when a female wasp lays her eggs in the leaf tissues. The gall continues to grow as the larva feeds inside.

MUD DAUBER
Sceliphron sp.

A mud dauber carries balls of mud in its mandibles to the nest site. There the balls are plastered together to form nest cells.

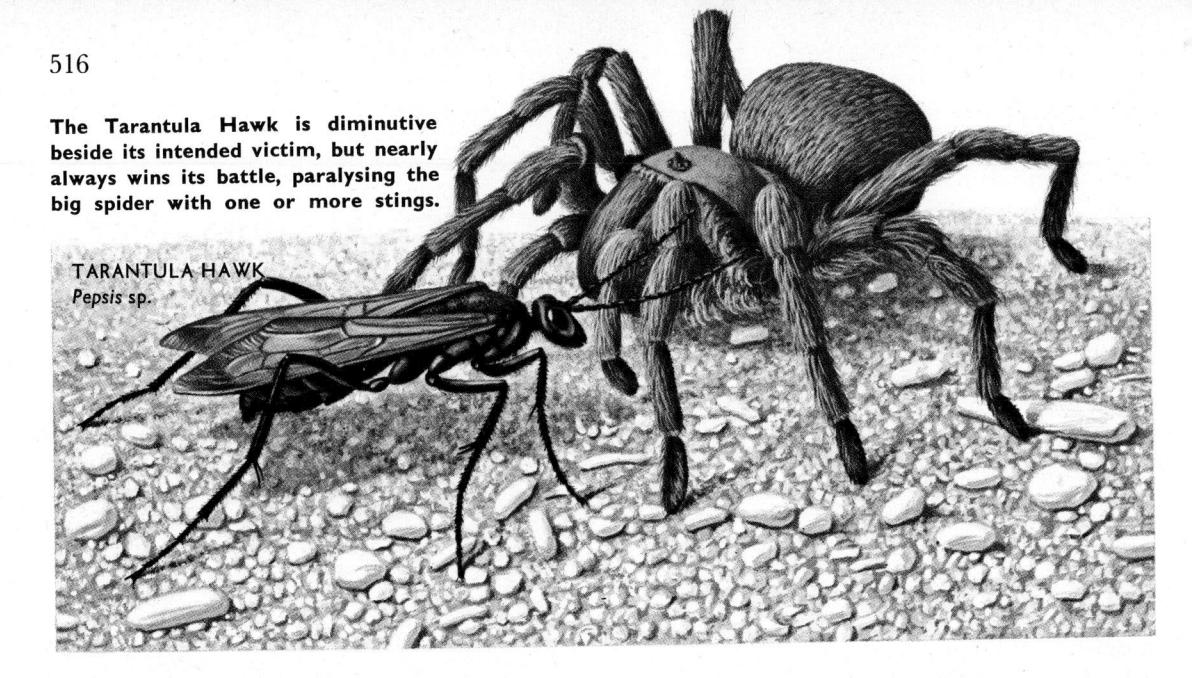

The Tarantula Hawk is diminutive beside its intended victim, but nearly always wins its battle, paralysing the big spider with one or more stings.

TARANTULA HAWK
Pepsis sp.

Paper Wasps, members of the same family, hang their nests from twigs or the eaves of buildings. These familiar, large comb-nests are made of wood fibres that the wasps convert into a paper-like material by chewing and moistening.

Spider Wasps (*Psammocharidae*) are slender, usually black or metallic blue, and have long, spiny legs. Some species are three inches long, but most are half this length or less. These wasps capture spiders and paralyse them, often after a lengthy fight. Some species place the spider in a cell in the ground or in a crevice; others use the spider's own burrow. An egg is deposited in the paralysed spider, on which the larva feeds. One of the best-known members of this family is the Tarantula Hawk of the south-western United States.

Many small wasps are parasitic on other insects. Some deposit their eggs in other insects' eggs; others attack larvae, pupae or adults. These wasps are very important in helping to maintain the balance of nature. (See HORNETS; ICHNEUMONS; INSECTS; SAWFLIES; VELVET ANTS.)

WATER-BEETLES of three separate families resemble each other in general appearance. These are the whirligig beetles (*Gyrinidae*), the water scavenger beetles (*Hydrophylidae*), and the predaceous diving beetles (*Dytiscidae*), which are carnivorous.

Whirligig beetles live in groups in pools or in quiet inlets of streams. They whirl about rapidly on the surface, going first one way and then another. If disturbed, they dive. Each eye is divided into an upper and lower section, so that the beetles appear to have two pairs of eyes — one pair for seeing above the surface, the other for seeing below. Adults feed mostly on other insects that fall into the water. Because of the row of gills on either side of their body, the slender, bottom-dwelling larvae of whirligig beetles look very much like small centipedes.

Water scavenger beetles resemble predaceous diving beetles, but have short, clubbed antennae, while those of diving beetles are long and thread-like. Many water scavenger beetles also have a spine that projects backwards between their legs. Adults feed mostly on decaying matter, but the larvae are predaceous. Females lay their eggs in silken cases which they fasten to vegetation. They breathe by means of a sheath of air carried with them over their body as they swim under the water. The film of air gives their body a silvery sheen.

Predaceous diving beetles differ in habits from other water-beetles, for both adults and larvae are carnivorous. The voracious larvae have long, sickle-shaped mandibles. When they seize another insect or fish in

their mandibles, its body fluids are sucked out through canals that open at the tip of each mandible. Adult beetles are seen hanging head down at the surface, with the tip of their abdomens sticking out of the water. By lifting their wings slightly when in this position, they can replenish the supply of air which is carried beneath their wings. These beetles fly, and are attracted to lights.

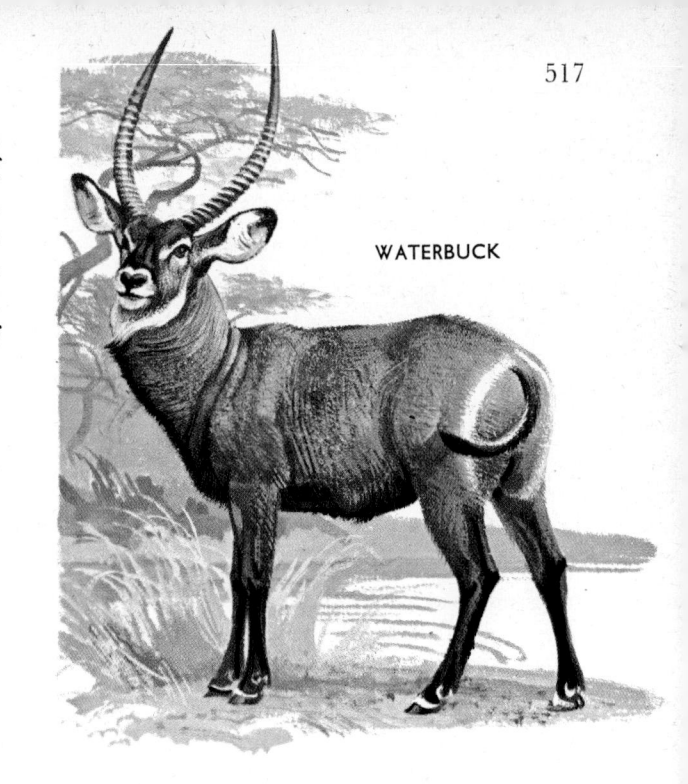

WATERBUCK

WATERBUCKS *(Kobus ellipsiprymnus)* are African antelopes that have slightly curved horns. They live near water or in swampy areas, usually in small herds. Often they swim into deep water to escape enemies. They emit a musky odour, which may be a defence mechanism against crocodiles. The odour can be detected in their flesh when fresh, but disappears when dried to make biltong (strips of sun-dried meat.) Chiefly grey, the Waterbuck has a white ring on its rump. Its coarse hair is longest on its neck. (See ANTELOPE.)

WATER-BUFFALO are large, wild cattle native to India and south-eastern Asia. Their horns may have a spread of 12 feet from tip to tip. Used as beasts of burden in most warm countries of Asia, the Arna *(Bubalus bubalis)* is so powerful that it can pull a plough through rice-fields, even through mud up to its knees. The Carabao, a smaller variety, is used in the Philippine Islands. Water-buffalo hide is strong and tough when tanned. The milk from the cows is strong and rich, and has a higher fat

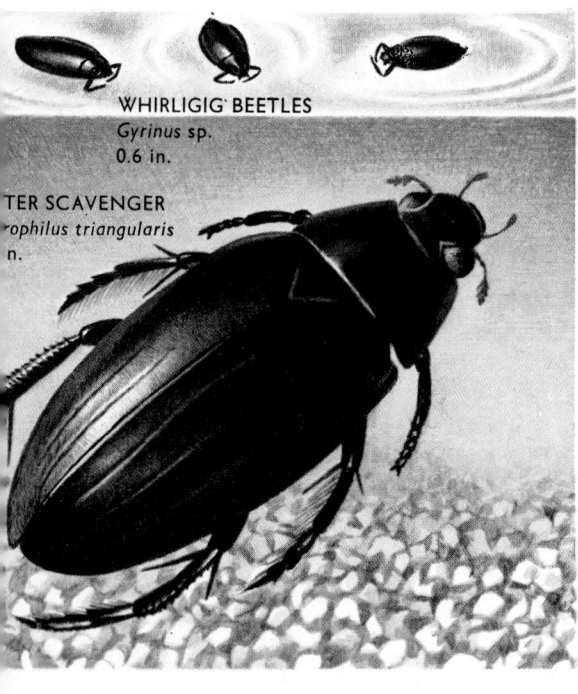

WHIRLIGIG BEETLES
Gyrinus sp.
0.6 in.

TER SCAVENGER
rophilus triangularis
n.

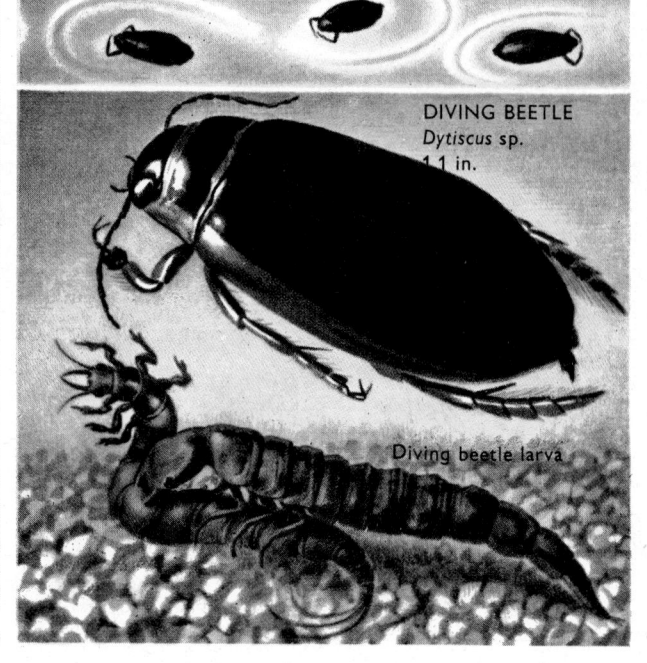

DIVING BEETLE
Dytiscus sp.
1.1 in.

Diving beetle larva

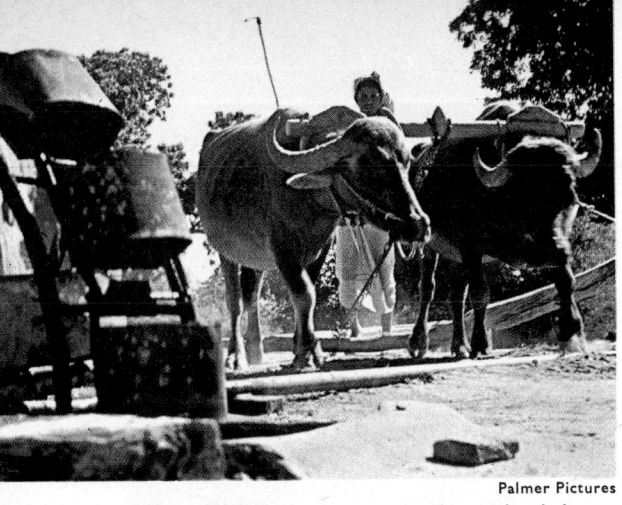

Water Buffaloes are work animals in Asia.

content than milk from domestic cattle. The semi-liquid poured from melted buffalo butter is called ghee.

The African Buffalo *(Syncerus caffer)* is also known as the Cape Buffalo. It is a fierce beast and a favourite of game-hunters. The African Buffalo has never been domesticated, although it resembles domestic cattle. It has a habit of wallowing in water-holes.

WATER-BUGS of the order *Hemiptera* can be divided roughly into two groups: those that swim at the surface of the water, and those that live below the surface.

In the surface group are water-measurers (*Hydrometridae*). These slender insects, less than an inch long, live in shallow, quiet water. They walk slowly on the surface of the water and on water-weeds, as they hunt for the small crustaceans or insect larvae on which they feed. A water-measurer's head is as long as its thorax, and it has long, elbowed antennae. Some kinds have wings.

Pond-skaters (*Gerridae*), a second group of insects found on the surface, often occur in large groups. Most kinds have long bodies, and their last two pairs of legs are very long. Their tarsi (terminal segment of limbs) are covered with fine hairs that are difficult to wet, enabling them to move on the surface without sinking. Their short front legs are used to capture other insects.

Giant water-bugs (*Belostomatidae*) are found below the surface in ponds and lakes. Because they are often attracted to lights, they are sometimes called "electric-light bugs". Some South American and Australian species attain a length of two inches. Giant water-bugs feed on other insects, small fish and tadpoles. They can inflict painful stabs with their short, sharp beaks. Females of some species lay their eggs on the backs of

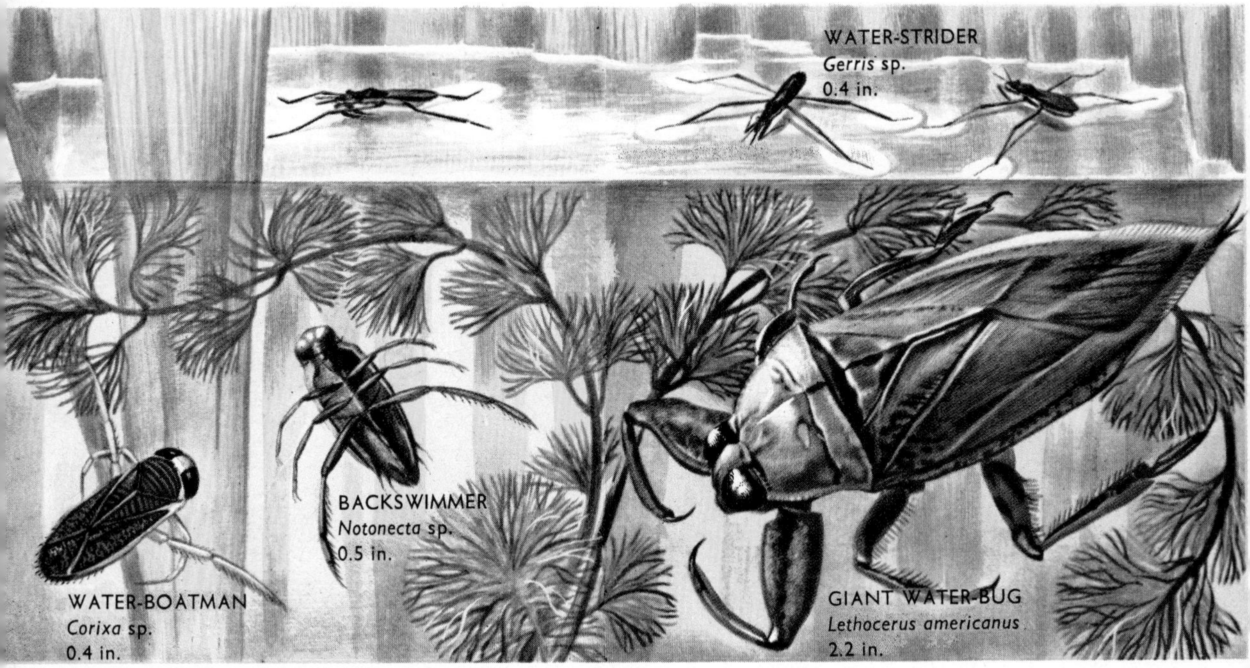

WATER-STRIDER
Gerris sp.
0.4 in.

BACKSWIMMER
Notonecta sp.
0.5 in.

WATER-BOATMAN
Corixa sp.
0.4 in.

GIANT WATER-BUG
Lethocerus americanus
2.2 in.

males, others lay their eggs on vegetation.

Water-boatmen (*Corixidae*), probably the most common of all water-bugs, use their flattened hind legs for swimming with a somewhat darting motion. Their middle legs are used to hold on to objects under water, for these insects are lighter than water and would otherwise rise quickly to the surface. They use their unusual, comb-like front legs to sweep food into their mouth from the organic ooze that collects on the bottom.

In some parts of the world, water-boatmen are used for food. Their eggs are collected and placed in ponds. Later, the bundles are removed from the water, dried, and ground into a flour. Adults are also ground into flour, or are eaten directly.

Backswimmers (*Notonectidae*) always swim upside down. The convex upper surface of their body has a ridge, or keel, down its centre, like the bottom of a boat. Their long, hair-fringed legs are used much like oars to propel them through the water, and also sweep air into a bristle-lined channel on the underside of their abdomen. This connects to the breathing spiracles.

Water-scorpions (*Nepidae*) usually live in shallow ponds, where they rest on the bottom, or among plants or debris floating on

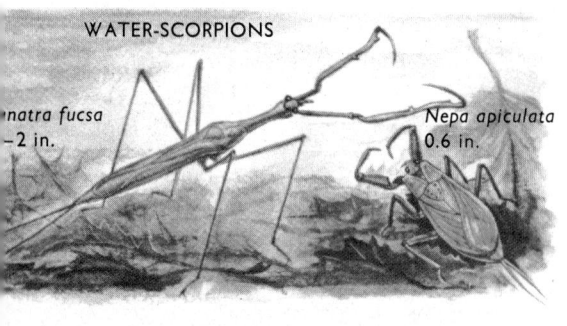

WATER-SCORPIONS

natra fucsa
–2 in.

Nepa apiculata
0.6 in.

the surface. They breathe through long respiratory tubes at the end of the abdomen. Their legs are not adapted for swimming, so they walk about slowly over the bottom or hide in the debris while waiting for prey, which they grab with their front legs. Their short, sharp beak can cause painful wounds. One kind of water-scorpion has a flat, oval body; another has a long, cylindrical body.

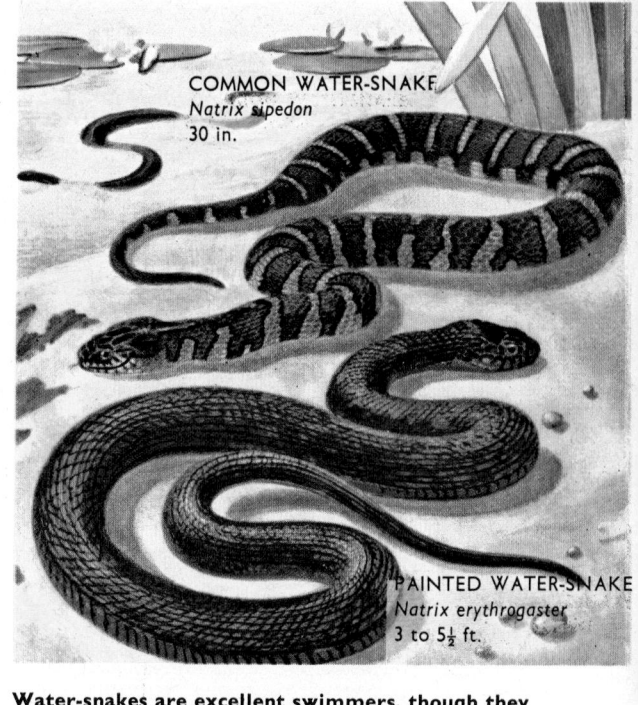

COMMON WATER-SNAKE
Natrix sipedon
30 in.

PAINTED WATER-SNAKE
Natrix erythrogaster
3 to 5½ ft.

Water-snakes are excellent swimmers, though they lack fins or other external appendages.

WATER-SNAKES *(Natrix* spp.*)* occur throughout the Northern Hemisphere. Three species — the Viperine Snake, the Tessellated Snake and the Grass Snake — occur in Europe. The Grass Snake is the only one of these to be found in Britain, where it is the larger and more widespread of the two harmless snakes occurring there. It can be recognised by a light collar behind the head which, although usually yellow, may be orange or white. The body colour is generally olive, and it attains six feet in length. Its habitat is hedgerows, open woodland and marshy places; its food is mainly frogs — although newts, fish, occasionally lizards, birds and small mammals are also eaten. The Grass Snake shows a preference for places near water, even brackish water, and there is a record of one having been found many miles out to sea.

The Viperine Snake, of Southern Europe and North-west Africa, superficially resembles the European viper, or adder, but can be distinguished from it by its round pupil. The Viperine and the Tessellated Snakes are even more aquatic than the Grass Snake.

WAXWINGS, a circumpolar family of three species of small, sleek songbirds, were named for the red, waxy tips on their wing-feathers. Waxwings' silky, soft plumage gives them unusual elegance. They erect their crests when excited and, during courtship, the male will feed his mate.

The Common Waxwing breeds as far north as the tree-line in Europe, Asia and also America.

When cedar berries, mulberries or other fruits are plentiful, waxwings often eat until they are so stuffed that they cannot fly. When they find over-ripe cherries, they become drunkards as well as gluttons. In addition to berries, waxwings eat insects.

As do most fruit- or grain-eating birds, waxwings feed their young exclusively on insects. The female does most or all of the incubating, and the male feeds her on the nest. The Cedar Waxwing, widespread in North America, migrates as far south as Central America.

Often it does not nest until mid-summer, but may raise two broods before autumn. Their nests are carelessly built in forest and orchard trees.

Waxwings are sociable, and flock at all times of year. When food becomes scarce in their normal habitat, they disperse for long distances, and flocks may then appear where they are not normally seen.

WEASELS are long, slim-bodied carnivores with exceptionally short legs. Like other members of their family, they have scent-glands. Weasels are vicious hunters, often

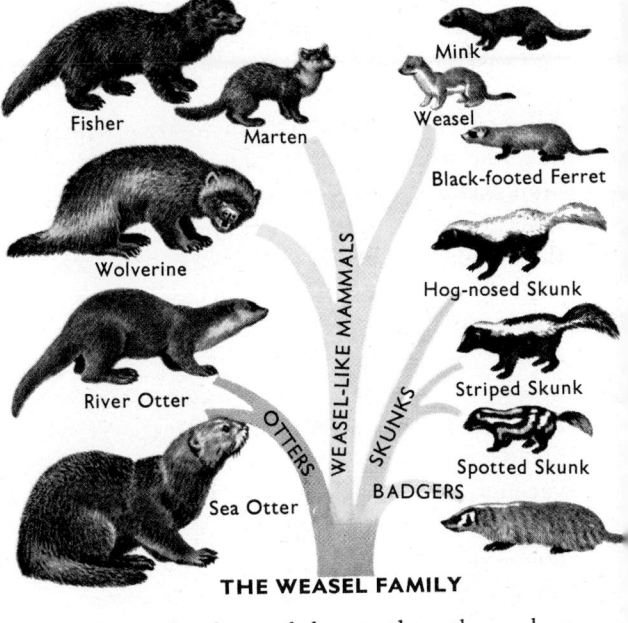

THE WEASEL FAMILY

killing animals much larger than themselves, and sometimes killing more than they can eat. They prey on rats, mice, rabbits, shrews, squirrels and some birds. Their brown fur coats turn white in winter, in some regions.

Stoats, or Ermines *(Mustela erminea)*, are about 13 inches long, the females somewhat smaller than the males. Found in Europe, Asia and northern North America, they commonly turn white in winter, but always retain the black tip on the long and slender tail. The Weasel *(Mustela nivalis)* is much smaller than the stoat, and has a shorter tail without a black tip.

The Long-tailed Weasel *(Mustela frenata),* found from southern Canada southward into South America, measures as much as 19 inches in length. It often hunts during daylight hours and kills its prey by biting at the base of the skull, severing the spinal cord.

The Least Weasel *(Mustela rixosa)*, smallest of all carnivores, measures only about 6 inches in length. It feeds principally on insects, occasionally on mice and shrews, and does not have a black tip on its tail. The Least Weasel lives in the northern areas of North America.

The Kolinsky *(Mustela sibirica)* is a large yellow weasel of cold, north-eastern Asia. Its valuable fur is used widely in coats.

WAXWING — 8 in.
Bombycilla garrulus
Eurasia, western North America

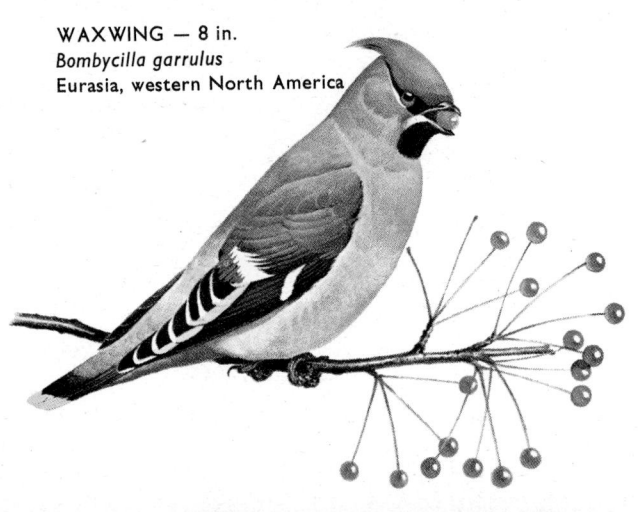

(Other members of the weasel family are treated in separate entries.)

WEEVILS, or Snout Beetles (*Circulionidae*), of more than 40,000 species, form the largest family of insects. Most kinds are less than half an inch long, but some reach a length of three inches, and the smallest measure less than one-tenth of an inch. Weevils are easily recognised by their long, cylindrical snouts, at the end of which are their mouth-parts. Some have a short, stout beak; others have a slender beak as long as their body. Weevils use these beaks to drill deep holes into various plant tissues — even into hard nuts; females usually deposit their eggs in these holes. Weevil larvae, or grubs, are pale, soft and legless, and are generally slightly curved. The grubs feed on fruits, nuts, seeds, roots or stems, depending on the species of weevil. Most species pupate in a cell near to where they feed.

Damage done by weevils has been estimated at hundreds of millions of pounds annually, for many kinds are injurious to plants or products valued by man. The Plum Curculio, for example, is a serious

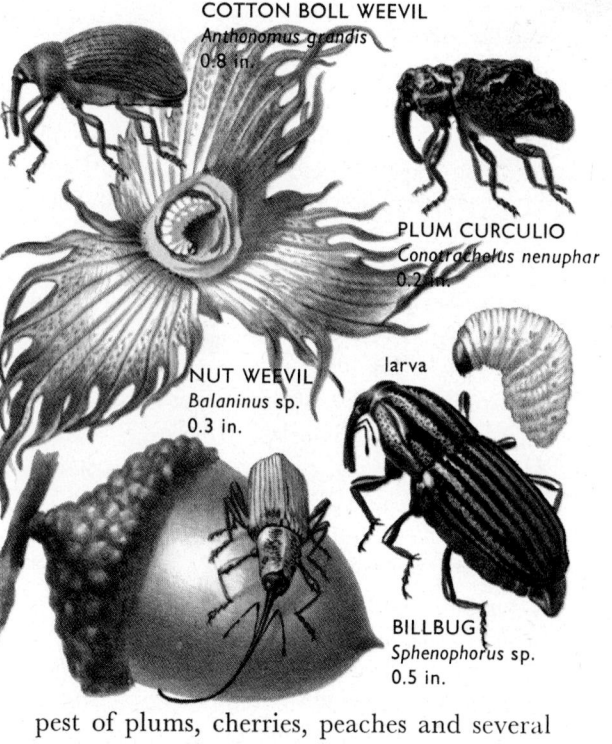

COTTON BOLL WEEVIL
Anthonomus grandis
0.8 in.

PLUM CURCULIO
Conotrachelus nenuphar
0.2 in.

NUT WEEVIL
Balaninus sp.
0.3 in.

larva

BILLBUG
Sphenophorus sp.
0.5 in.

pest of plums, cherries, peaches and several other fruits. Females lay their eggs in small holes in the young fruit, making a crescent-shaped cut around each egg-hole. The larvae feed on the fruit, and then drop to the ground to pupate. Infested fruit either falls.

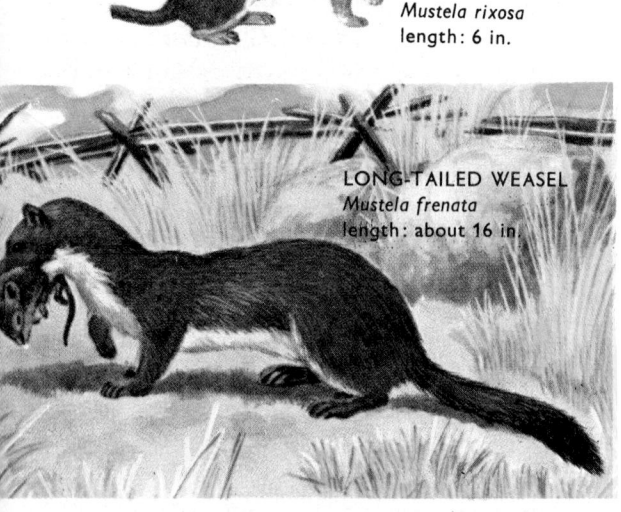

LEAST WEASEL
Mustela rixosa
length: 6 in.

LONG-TAILED WEASEL
Mustela frenata
length: about 16 in.

Weasels hunt by scent. Despite their short legs, they can move with astonishing speed.

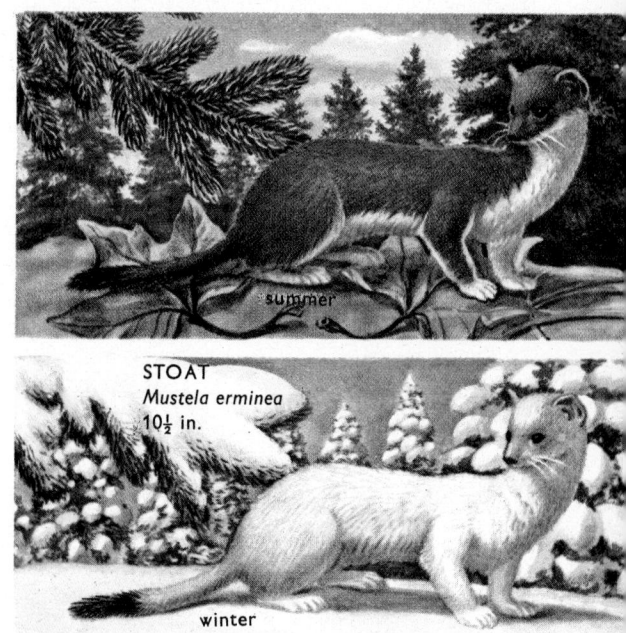

summer

STOAT
Mustela erminea
10½ in.

winter

Weasels do not burrow, but make nests for their young in abandoned dens of other species.

or is so scarred that it cannot be sold.

Nut weevils, which have a long, slender beak, bore holes in nuts where they deposit eggs. The larvae feed on the meat of the nut.

The Granary Weevil and Rice Weevil are the most destructive pests of grain in the world. Both adults and larvae feed on it.

Female leaf-rolling weevils cut slits in a leaf, and then roll the section of leaf into a tube. An egg is laid inside. The larva feeds inside the tube, and may pupate there or in the ground. (See BOLL WEEVILS.)

WENTLETRAPS, or Ladder Shells, members of the family *Epitoniidae,* are beautifully fluted shells found in shallow to deep water. They are a favourite food of some bottom-feeding fishes, and were formerly greatly prized by collectors because of the sculpture of their shells. Some shells were so valuable that the Chinese made imitations of them from a rice-paste. The many species are hard to identify.

The White Whale is also called the Beluga

Russ Kinne

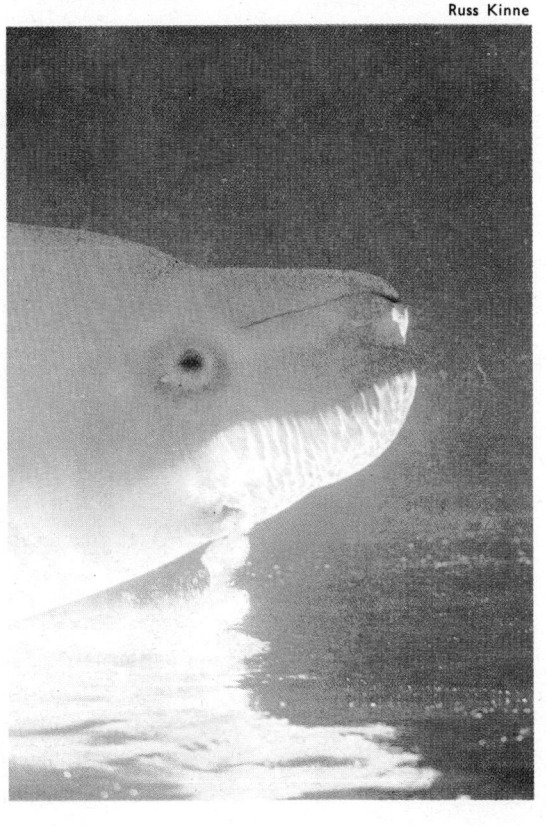

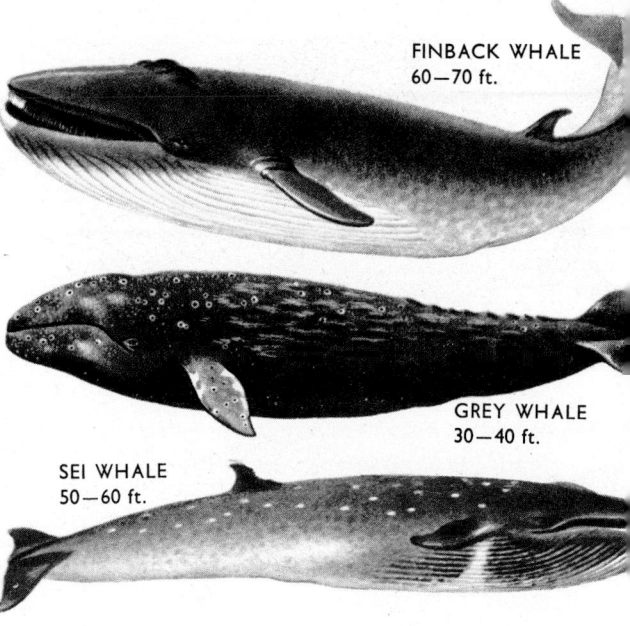

FINBACK WHALE
60—70 ft.

GREY WHALE
30—40 ft.

SEI WHALE
50—60 ft.

WHALES are mammals found in all the open seas and oceans of the world. They are members of a group, the cetaceans, that include whalebone whales, toothed whales, porpoises, dolphins and the narwhal. All have streamlined bodies and appendages modified into swimming flippers. The hind appendages are completely lost. The tails are horizontal flukes, unlike the vertical tail-fins of fishes. Whales must come to the surface to breathe, and it is their exhaled breath that causes the well-known spout. Whales are able to stay under water without inhaling for up to an hour. A female gives birth to a single young, which is nursed under water.

There are two distinct groups of whales: baleen, or whalebone, whales and toothed whales. Baleen whales have two blowholes, and instead of teeth have rows of whalebone (or baleen) hanging from the upper jaw. The whalebone traps tiny sea-animals, on which these large whales feed. Toothed whales have a single blowhole and a series of jaw teeth, sometimes as many as 30.

The Blue Whale *(Balaenoptera musculus),* largest of all whales, may be 100 feet long and weigh as much as 115 tons. The outside of its throat is deeply grooved, of furrowed. Because of its yellowish colour, it is also called the Sulphur-bottomed Whale.

The Right Whale *(Balaena mysticetus*

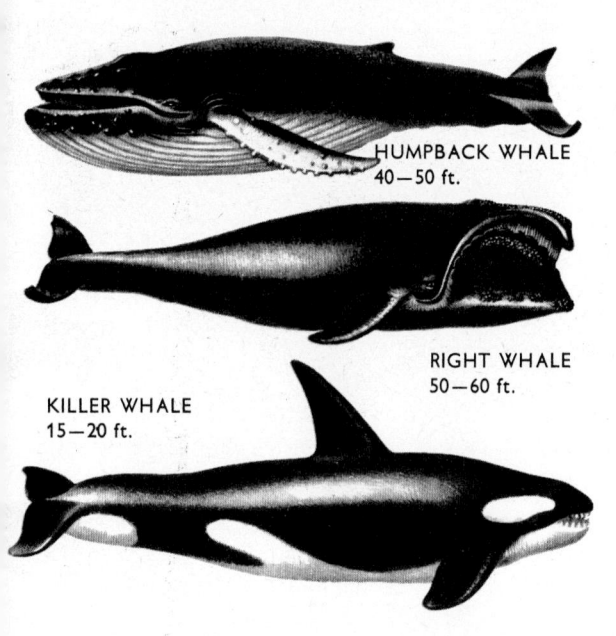

HUMPBACK WHALE
40—50 ft.

RIGHT WHALE
50—60 ft.

KILLER WHALE
15—20 ft.

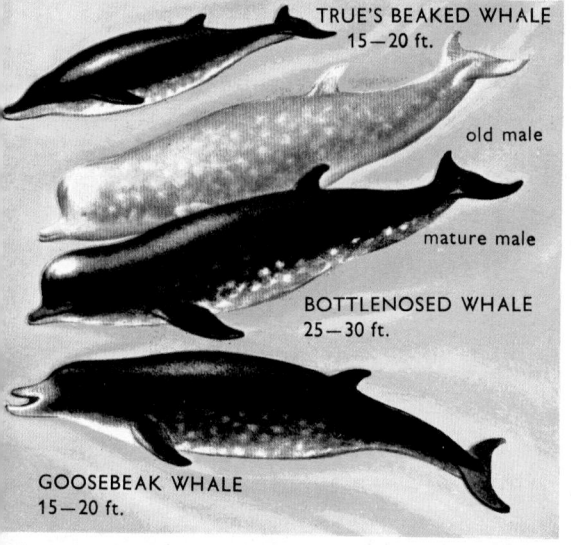

TRUE'S BEAKED WHALE
15—20 ft.

old male

mature male

BOTTLENOSED WHALE
25—30 ft.

GOOSEBEAK WHALE
15—20 ft.

to barnacles. Small Killer Whales often harass the Grey Whale, and may even kill it.

The Sperm Whale *(Physeter catodon)*, largest of the toothed whales, reaches a length of about 60 feet. Its huge, tank-like head contains a storage of oil, sperm oil, which was formerly used in lamps and for candles. Schools, or "pods", of Sperm Whales are found in all oceans. Their numerous teeth aid in grasping and holding giant squid and cuttlefish, their chief food.

Killer Whales *(Orcinus orca),* usually under 20 feet in length, are small, toothed whales closely related to dolphins. Deadly hunters, they travel in schools and attack large whales, seals, porpoises and other dolphins. Favourite targets are the tongue, lips or flippers of the animals attacked.

Beaked Whales are small to medium-sized toothed whales which are difficult to distinguish from dolphins. In this group

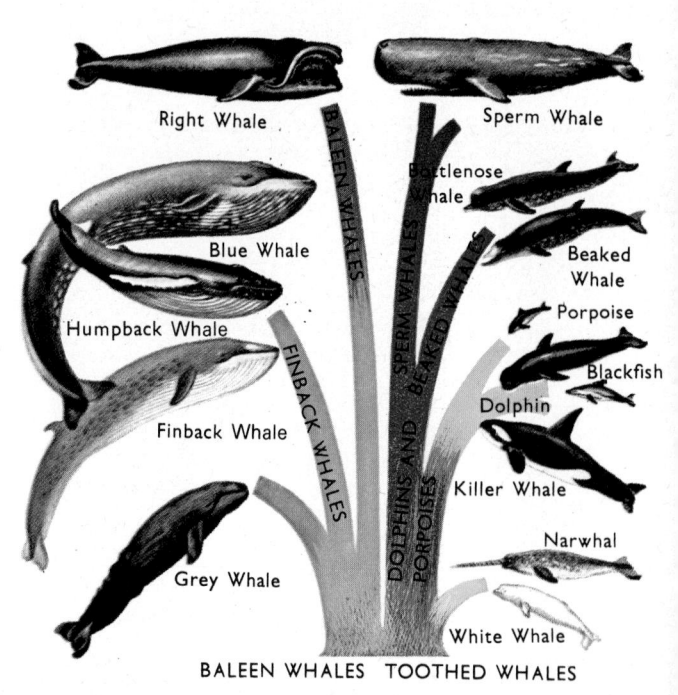

Right Whale

Sperm Whale

BALEEN WHALES

Bottlenose Whale

Beaked Whale

Blue Whale

SPERM WHALES AND BEAKED WHALES

Porpoise

Humpback Whale

Blackfish

FINBACK WHALES

Dolphin

Finback Whale

DOLPHINS AND PORPOISES

Killer Whale

Narwhal

Grey Whale

White Whale

BALEEN WHALES   TOOTHED WHALES

FAMILY TREE OF WHALES

glacialis) is much smaller and occurs mainly in northern waters. This whale usually floats when harpooned; hence it is the "right" whale for whalers, which explains its name. Another species of the same genus lives in the Pacific.

The Grey Whale *(Eschrichtius gibbosus)* of the Pacific Ocean often makes mass-migrations, near shore, from the Arctic southward to the tip of Lower California. Females give birth to their young in coastal lagoons of the more southern waters. The Grey Whale grows to a length of 30 to 40 feet and is frequently mottled with white patches, due

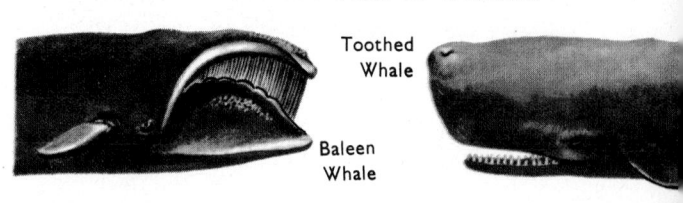

Toothed Whale

Baleen Whale

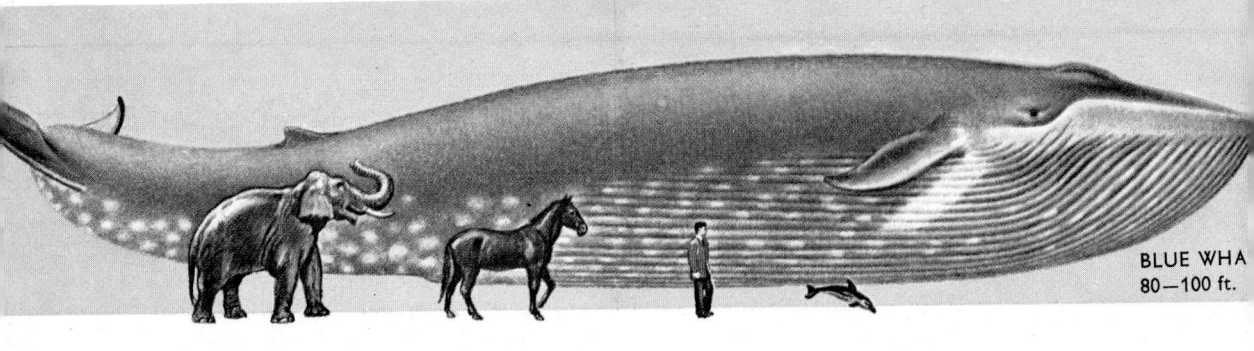

BLUE WHALE
80—100 ft.

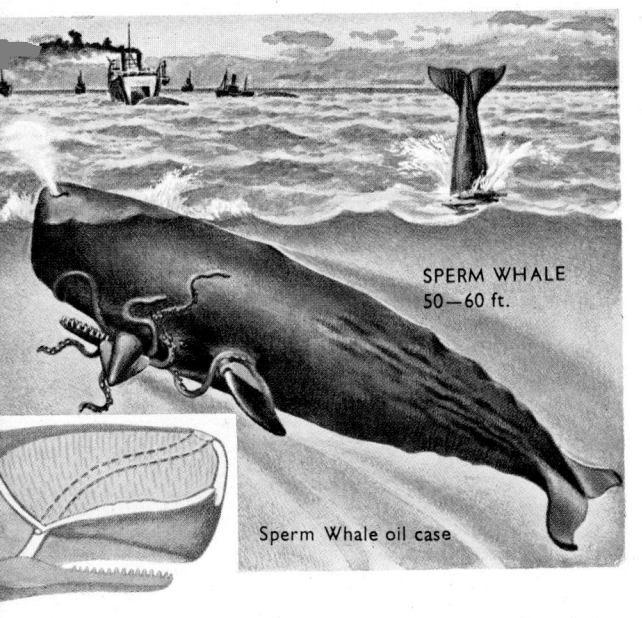

SPERM WHALE
50—60 ft.

Sperm Whale oil case

coast. They feed on bivalve shells (clams and oysters) which they kill by holding them with their foot until the valves open. Then they insert the edge of their own shell and pry the valves open. The largest is the Lightning Whelk (4 to 16 inches, and left-handed), found from South Carolina to Florida and in the Gulf of Mexico. Knobbed and Channelled whelks live from New England to Florida. The Perverse Whelk, so-called because it is often left-handed, is many times confused with the Lightning Whelk. The Pear Whelk, a smooth species, is more southern in range. Large whelks are often eaten. The name whelk is also applied to a number of other shells of a smaller size but similar form.

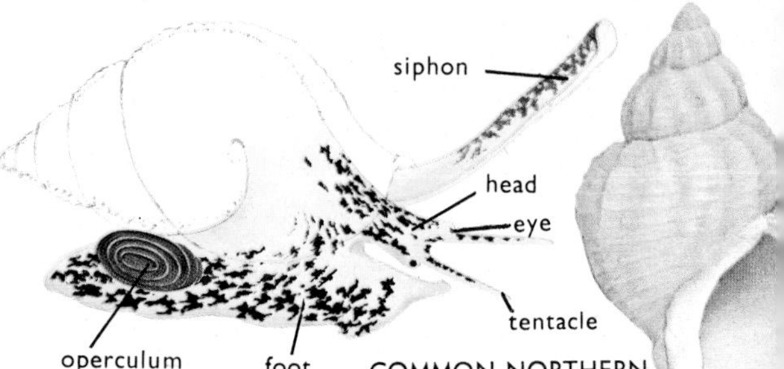

are the True's Beaked Whale (*Mesoplodon mirus*), Bottle-nosed Whale (*Hyperoodon ampullatus*), and Goose-beaked Whale (*Ziphius cavirostrus*), all of which are under 30 feet in length and live in colder waters.

The oldest fossil whales come from rocks of the Eocene period, but since they were already fully adapted to an aquatic existence, these fossils tell very little about the ancestry of whales. Whales probably arose well before Eocene times. The similarity in the body shape of dolphins, ichthyosaurs and fish is an example of a process known as "convergent evolution". These unrelated animals are modified for life in the same environment (See DOLPHINS; PORPOISES.)

WHELKS (*Busycon spp.)* are large, carnivorous, heavy-shelled gastropods that live along the sandy beaches of the Atlantic

siphon

head

eye

tentacle

operculum   foot

COMMON NORTHERN
BUCCINUM — 3 in.
Buccinum undatum
N. Atlantic: common offshore

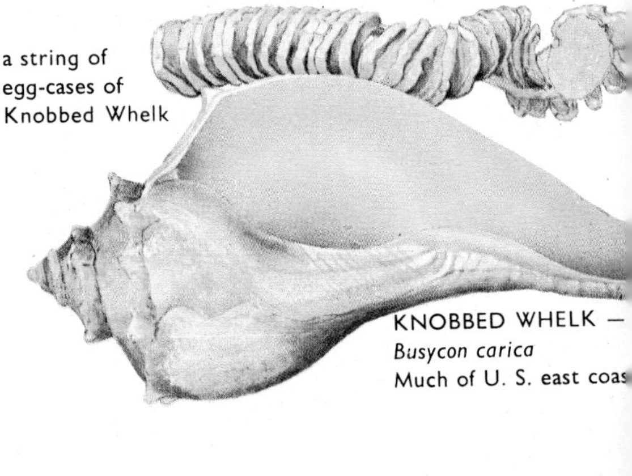

a string of
egg-cases of
Knobbed Whelk

KNOBBED WHELK —
Busycon carica
Much of U. S. east coast

NEW ENGLAND NEPTUNE — 4 in.
Neptunea decemcostrata
Canada to Massachusetts (U. S. A.)
common offshore

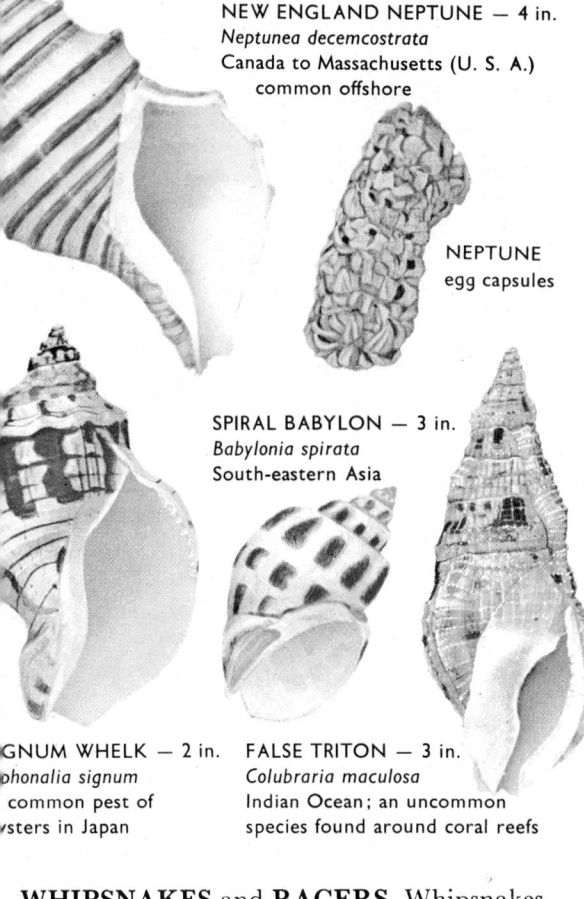

NEPTUNE
egg capsules

SPIRAL BABYLON — 3 in.
Babylonia spirata
South-eastern Asia

GNUM WHELK — 2 in.
phonalia signum
common pest of
ʏsters in Japan

FALSE TRITON — 3 in.
Colubraria maculosa
Indian Ocean; an uncommon
species found around coral reefs

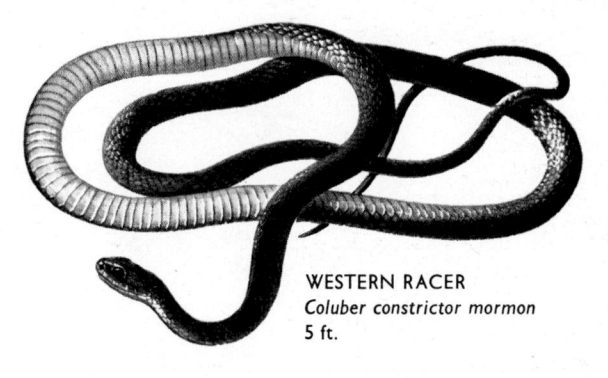

WESTERN RACER
Coluber constrictor mormon
5 ft.

tance in ridding places of rodents, and some eat other snakes. These snakes do not constrict to kill. They are not poisonous, but they bite freely and do not tame well. All lay eggs, and all are fast-moving snakes, but their speed does not exceed four miles per hour. They are deceptive, however, and are difficult to follow where there are bushes or other cover. When pursued closely, they may coil quickly in some cranny while the pursuer continues a headlong chase in the direction the snake was last seen moving. On very rare occasions, racers have become so angry, or so interested in a human being, that they have followed or even attacked.

WHIPSNAKES and **RACERS.** Whipsnakes *(Masticophis)* of some 10 species, range from the southern United States to northern South America. The closely-related Racers *(Coluber)* occur from southern Canada to Guatemala, and in Eurasia and northern Africa. Almost all have an economic impor-

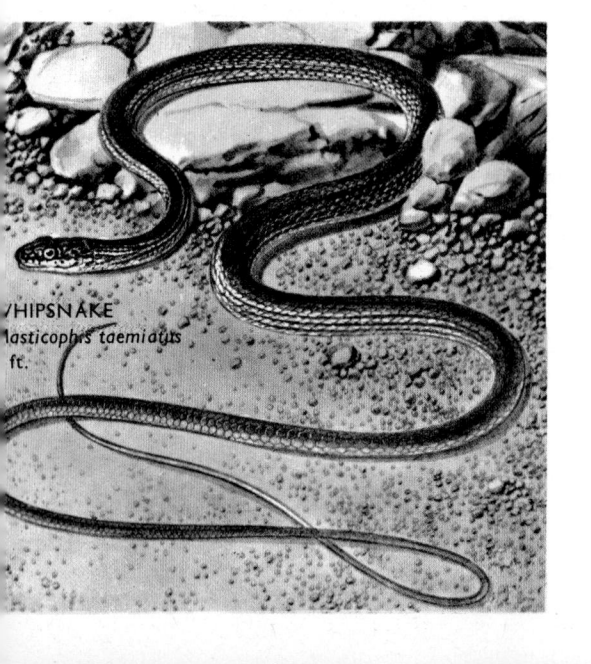

WHIPSNAKE
Masticophis taemiatus
ft.

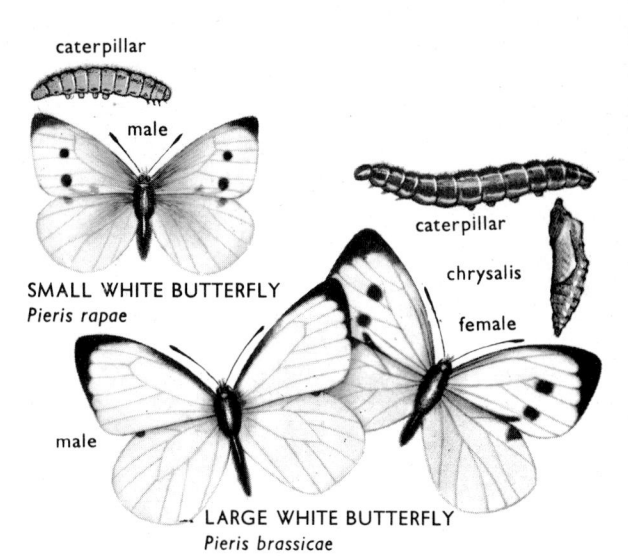

caterpillar

male

SMALL WHITE BUTTERFLY
Pieris rapae

caterpillar

chrysalis

female

male

LARGE WHITE BUTTERFLY
Pieris brassicae

WHITES *(Pieridae)* and related Butterflies. Some of the world's commonest butterflies belong to this family. They are usually predominantly white, yellow or orange in colour, sometimes marked with black and of

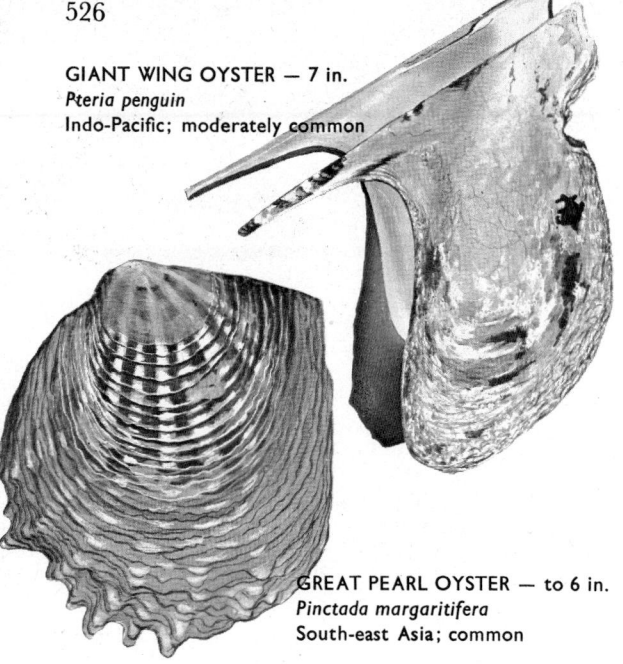

GIANT WING OYSTER — 7 in.
Pteria penguin
Indo-Pacific; moderately common

GREAT PEARL OYSTER — to 6 in.
Pinctada margaritifera
South-east Asia; common

Pearl oysters are edible but have an unpleasant flavour. Wing oysters seldom produce pearls.

This species may be only a form of the 12-inch Great Pearl Oyster *(Pinctada margaritifera)* of the Pacific Islands. Pearl shell is an important trade item that gets its iridescence from the particular arrangement of the lime crystals in the shell. Pearls are formed around natural or artificial substances that irritate the mantle and cause the animal to secrete layers of shell around it. Cultured pearls are formed by inserting small galls of pearl shell into the mantle of pearl oysters, which then secrete layers of shell about the ball until a pearl is formed.

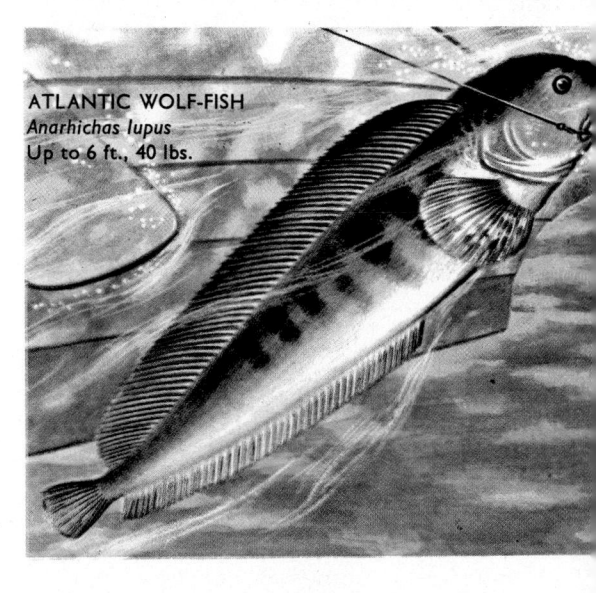

ATLANTIC WOLF-FISH
Anarhichas lupus
Up to 6 ft., 40 lbs.

Wolf-fish are found in shallow waters along shore and out to depths of 500 or 600 feet.

medium size. Many species migrate in very large numbers, a phenomenon little understood. The genus *Pieris* includes the infamous Cabbage White Butterflies, whose caterpillars are very destructive to green vegetables of the cabbage family. The chrysalids — like those of the swallow-tails, to whom they are closely related — are supported by the tail in an upright position, with a silken girdle about their middles.

WING and **PEARL SHELLS** live mostly in tropical waters. Only a few occur in waters off the coast of North America. Atlantic and Western wing shells *(Pteria* spp.*)*, found on the Atlantic and Pacific coasts respectively, are shallow-water forms that are very similar in appearance; also, only one species of pearl oyster occurs on each coast. The Atlantic Pearl Oyster *(Pinctada radiata)* grows a shell about three inches long. It is found off the coast of southern Florida and in the West Indies. In quiet waters, where it attaches to marine grasses, this creature grows beautiful scales and delicate spines. The Pacific Pearl Oyster formerly supported a large pearl-fishery in the Gulf of Lower California and Panama.

WOLF-FISH *(Anarhichas* spp.*)* are large, blenny-like fish found in the cold waters of both the Atlantic and the Pacific. Long, slim and eel-like, they have powerful jaws filled with sharp teeth. Wolf-fish feed on crustaceans and shellfish, which they can crush easily with their strong jaws. Often they are caught in nets, or on hook and line. They must be handled carefully, since their bites are dangerous. Despite their unattractive appearance, their flesh is good to eat.

WOLVERINES, or Gluttons *(Gulo luscus),* largest members of the weasel family, reach a length of 3 feet and a weight of 30 pounds.

Wolverines are found in the northern parts of Europe, Asia and North America. They ordinarily feed on birds, rabbits, squirrels or other small animals, but they are quite fearless and have been known to kill animals as large as deer. They steal food from cabins and rob trappers of their catches. Because of their cunning and viciousness, Wolverines are greatly feared and detested. Their fur, which sheds moisture, is valued for collars and parkas where moisture from breathing would form a frost. Three or four young are born during the summer in an underground den. Wolverines are seldom taken in traps.

WOLVES *(Canis lupus)* are found in cold regions throughout the Northern Hemisphere. They are the largest members of the dog family, except for certain breeds of domestic dogs. Sometimes called Timber Wolves, or Grey Wolves, they may weigh as much as 110 pounds. They usually have thick fur, round ears and slanted eyes. Their

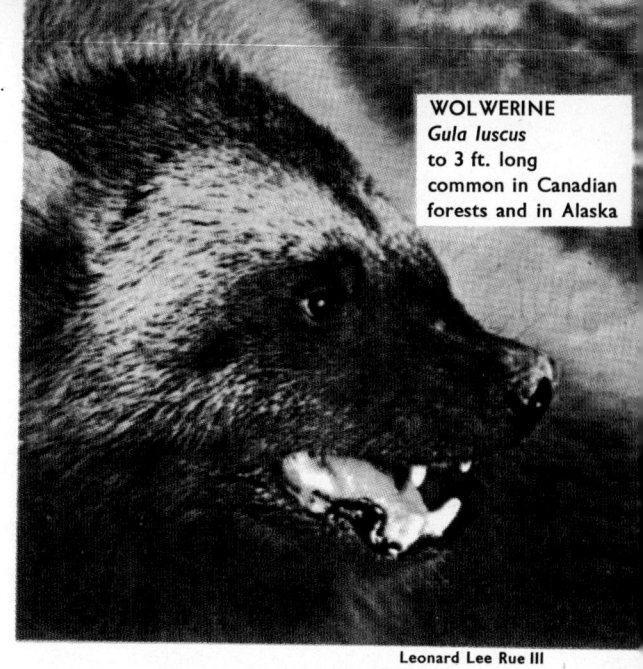

WOLWERINE
Gula luscus
to 3 ft. long
common in Canadian
forests and in Alaska

Leonard Lee Rue III

feet are large, and the tail is quite full.

Wolves prey on deer, game-birds, rabbits, and other animals, usually foraging at night on regular "runs", which may be many miles in length. In winter they frequently

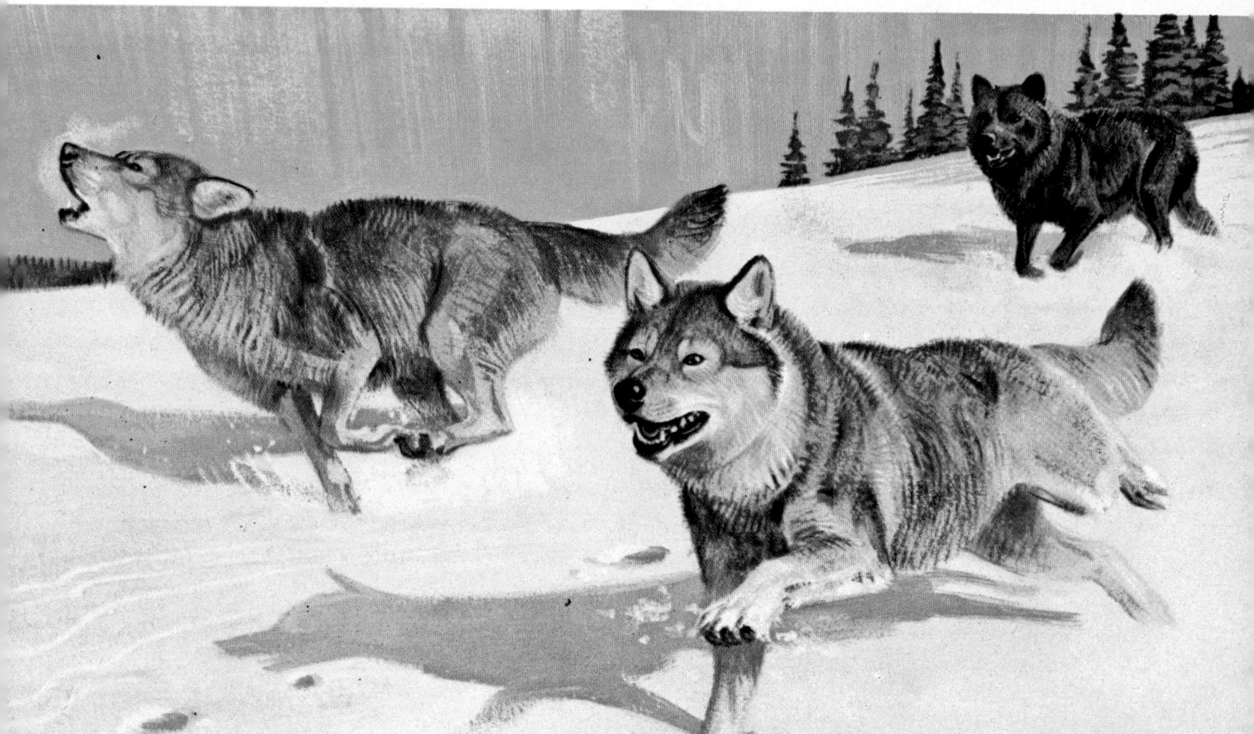

The cry of the wolf pack, as the animals pick up the trail of some luckless four-footed beast, is said to be the most awesome sound of the northlands.

hunt in packs, combining their efforts to attack and kill domestic sheep and cattle, as well as wild animals. Sometimes they feed on carrion, or even on roots, berries or other plant material, if they are very hungry. Man has continually pushed the Grey Wolf farther into the wilderness, until now it is common in North America only in Canada and Alaska. The Red Wolf, intermediate in size between the Grey Wolf and the Coyote, lives in the southern United States, mostly in Louisiana and Texas.

Except in winter, the Grey Wolf travels

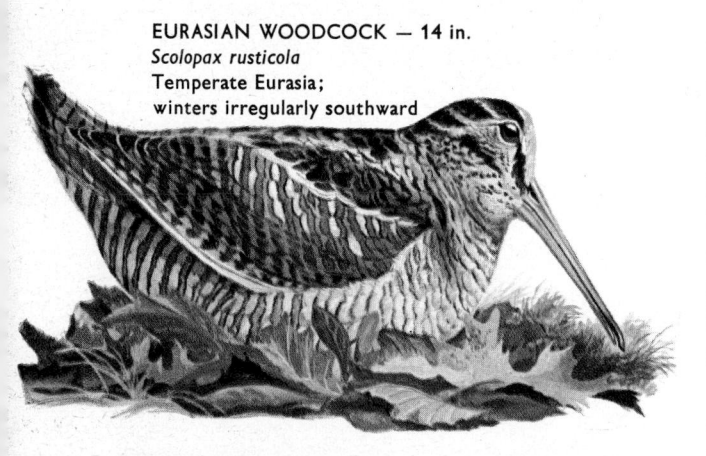

EURASIAN WOODCOCK — 14 in.
Scolopax rusticola
Temperate Eurasia;
winters irregularly southward

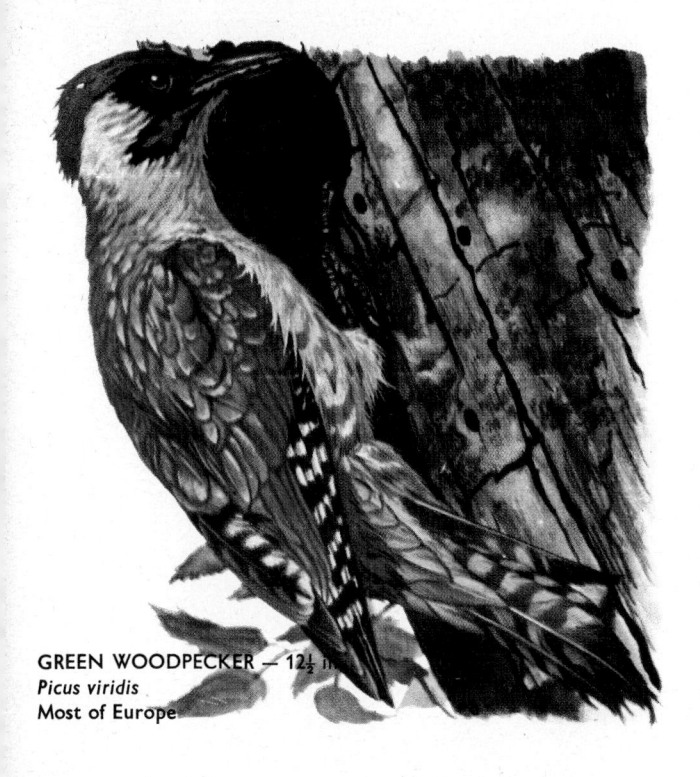

GREEN WOODPECKER — 12½ in.
Picus viridis
Most of Europe

alone or in pairs. It is believed to mate for life. The pups — usually six — are born in the spring; they stay with the parents for a year or longer, before striking out alone.

Wolves learn quickly by experience, and many tales are told about how they have outwitted trappers and hunters or their dogs. The hunting ability of wolves depends as much upon their endurance as upon their skill. They have been known to run down deer, caribou and elk in gruelling chases that have lasted for miles. Where they are common, attacks on unarmed humans are not unusual.

WOODCOCK are large waders found in woodland throughout much of the temperate Northern Hemisphere. They are a large snipe; but, unlike other waders, they have moved away from open marshland into woodland. They feed in damp woods, chiefly at night, probing deep in soft ground for worms. The long bill has a flexible, sensitive tip which can detect and seize an earthworm underground.

The Woodcock's plumage is beautifully camouflaged to match a background of dead leaves, and the bird usually sits tight until the last moment and then, if alarmed, rises suddenly and flies off, twisting through the trees in agile flight. The male displays at dawn and dusk, following a course at tree-top level with slow butterfly-like wing-beats and a croaking call.

The eggs are laid in woodland, among the leaves on the ground. Woodcocks have been seen carrying the chicks between the thighs, apparently supported by the bill.

WOOD-LICE are crustaceans, more closely related to lobsters and crayfish than to insects. Most are greyish and small — $\frac{1}{4}$ to $\frac{1}{2}$ inch long, and about half as wide. Their body is covered with a series of hard plates joined by flexible membranes. When disturbed, some are able to roll into a ball, like tiny armadillos.

Females hold their eggs in a pouch in their abdomen for eight weeks or longer

until they hatch. The young, which resemble the adults, do not emerge from the pouch to feed until all the yolk is absorbed from the egg-sac. Wood-lice feed at night and are usually found in damp places, beneath boards or stones. Closely related crustaceans live in fresh water and along seashores. (See CRUSTACEANS.)

WOODPECKERS are found in woodlands on all continents except Australia. The smallest is $3\frac{1}{2}$ inches long; the largest, 22. The South African Ground Woodpecker is the only one of the 179 species that does not peck wood; it chisels hard mud-banks to get its insect food and make a nest.

All other woodpeckers nest in holes in trees, stumps, telephone poles or fence-posts. They have a large head; slender, strong neck; and powerful, long, straight bill, which is used as a hatchet, chisel and borer. The nest cavities of woodpeckers are smooth and well-finished inside, and are not lined. They lay two to eight glossy white eggs.

Woodpeckers' feet are shaped for clinging

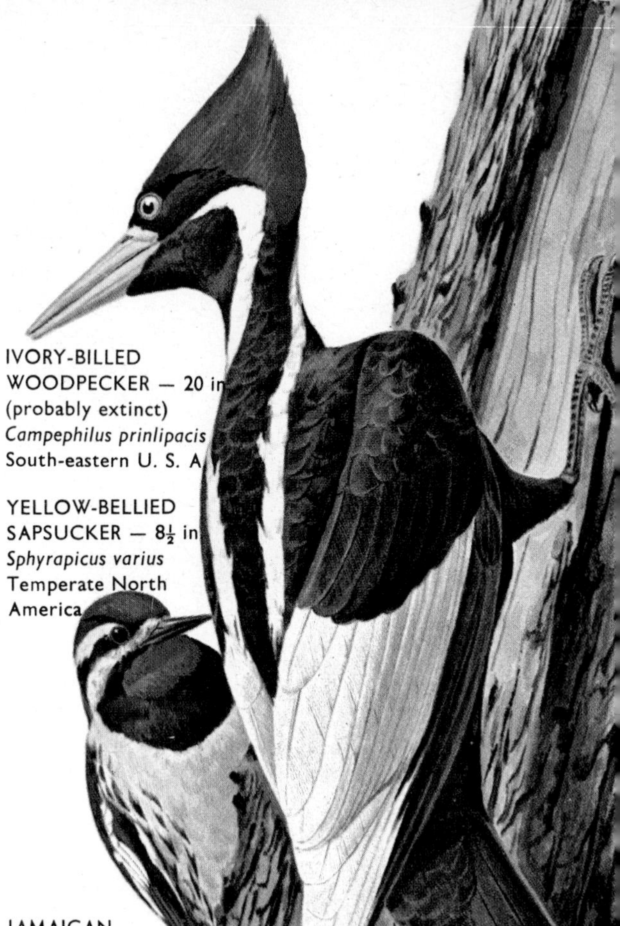

IVORY-BILLED
WOODPECKER — 20 in.
(probably extinct)
Campephilus prinlipacis
South-eastern U. S. A.

YELLOW-BELLIED
SAPSUCKER — $8\frac{1}{2}$ in.
Sphyrapicus varius
Temperate North
America

JAMAICAN
WOODPECKER
11 in.
Centurus radiolatus
Jamaica

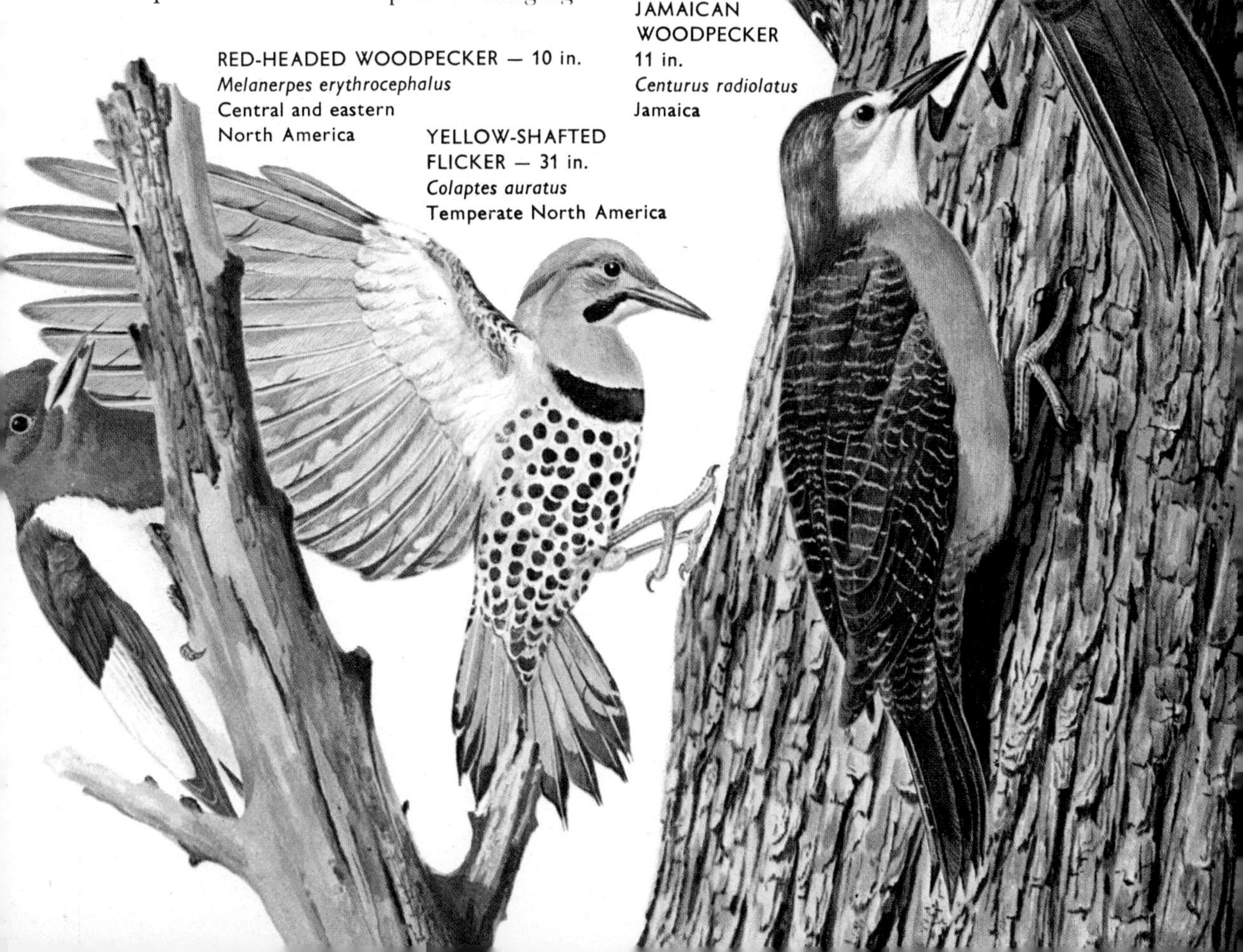

RED-HEADED WOODPECKER — 10 in.
Melanerpes erythrocephalus
Central and eastern
North America

YELLOW-SHAFTED
FLICKER — 31 in.
Colaptes auratus
Temperate North America

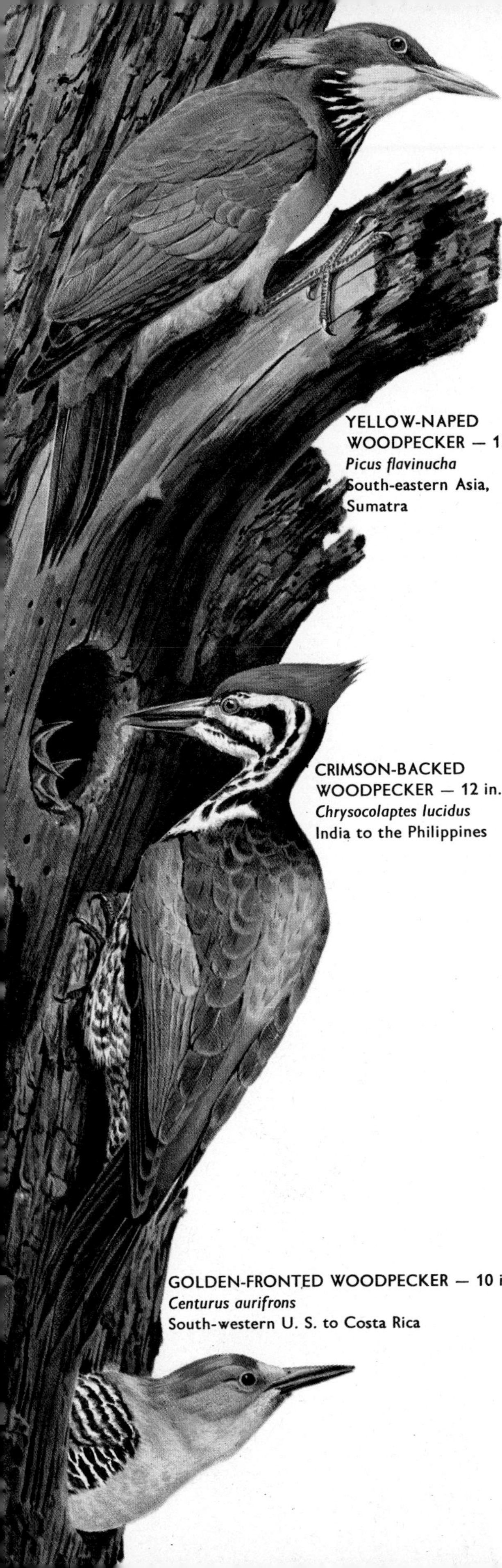

**YELLOW-NAPED
WOODPECKER — 13 in.**
Picus flavinucha
South-eastern Asia,
Sumatra

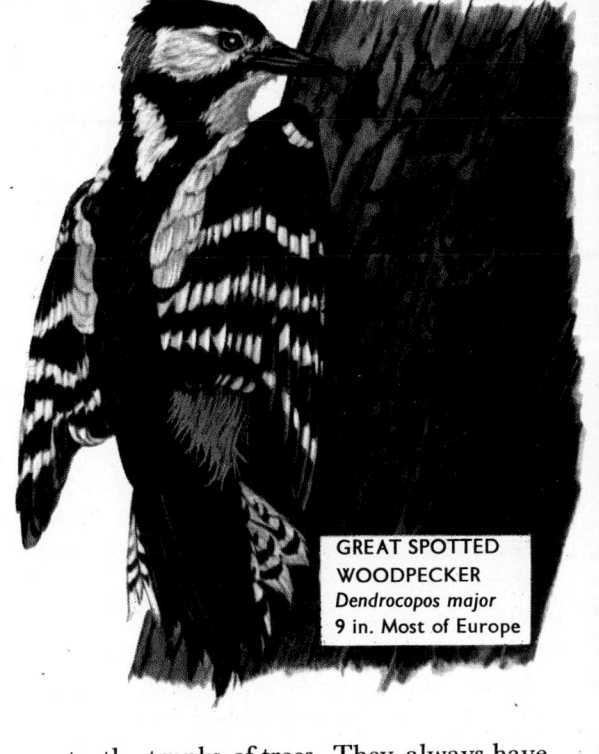

**GREAT SPOTTED
WOODPECKER**
Dendrocopos major
9 in. Most of Europe

**CRIMSON-BACKED
WOODPECKER — 12 in.**
Chrysocolaptes lucidus
India to the Philippines

GOLDEN-FRONTED WOODPECKER — 10 in.
Centurus aurifrons
South-western U. S. to Costa Rica

on to the trunks of trees. They always have
two toes in front, and most kinds also have
two toes behind, although a few have only
one. The stiff tail-feathers are used as props
to brace them as they chip away.

In addition to their chisel bills, woodpeckers have specialised tongues. These are
very long and worm-like, and can be
extended far beyond the bill. They are
barbed, and are thrust down small tunnels in
wood to harpoon and draw out the tunnelling
grubs of beetles.

Some also feed on nuts and acorns, and
the Great Spotted Woodpecker will open
pine-cones for the seeds.

The Green and Grey-headed Woodpeckers
are a little more specialised in their feeding,
being to a large extent ant-eaters. They
have the same long tongues as other woodpeckers, but these are coated with saliva and
are sticky. The Green Woodpecker, crouching on a lawn, thrusts its bill into an ant-
hole and extends the tongue; then the bird
draws in the tongue with the ants sticking to
it, without withdrawing its bill. The Wry-
neck, a very close relative of the Woodpeckers, is also an ant-eater. All these
species nest in holes in trees, like other
woodpeckers.

All woodpeckers have sharp, high-pitched call-notes, and in some species a number of these may be run together to form trilling or laughing calls, like that of the Green Woodpecker. In addition, many of them produce mechanical sounds by "drumming" on wood. This drumming is used instead of song in spring; the bird raps quickly with its bill at the end of a dead bough, in such a way that the bough vibrates and acts as a sounding-board. It produces, with a rapid series of blows, a harsh, rattling purr that can be heard for a considerable distance. The Great Spotted Woodpecker is a fine exponent of this method of advertisement. Different-sized branches produce different sounds, and some birds have used pieces of metal fixed to poles with striking results.

In addition to boring nest-holes, woodpeckers also bore holes in trees at other times of year to make roost-holes, each being used by only one bird. The numerous holes that result are used by other birds, for roosting and nesting, long after the woodpeckers have finished with them.

WORKING DOGS are trained to perform valuable services for man. Their skills range from herding sheep and cattle, or guiding the blind, to performing valiantly in time of war as carriers of messages and supplies, or acting as police and security dogs in support of the law and, often, people's safety.

The Collie, one of the oldest of the working dog breeds, weighs about 65 pounds and has a graceful body, long, narrow head, long tail, and pricked ears that droop at the tips. Some have white muzzles, ruffs and feet; markings on the rest of the body may be brown, black, and white. Collies were first bred in Scotland. Those with rough coats were developed primarily to guard sheep; those with smooth coats, also called Border Collies, to drive either sheep or cattle. The name Collie was derived from "coally", after the black coat of the early members of the breed.

The Doberman Pinscher was bred in Germany to be a guard dog and a war animal, but the Doberman also makes a good pet. The Doberman is long-legged but muscular, and weighs about 65 pounds. It has a very short tail and cropped, erect ears. Its short hair may be solid brown or black, or black marked with brown.

The Great Dane came originally from Germany, where it was bred to hunt wild boars. One of the largest of all dogs (minimum height for males is 30 inches at the shoulder), Great Danes are deep-chested and muscular but graceful, with large, lean, finely-shaped heads. Their tails are long, their ears cropped and erect. There are several colour varieties: brindle (yellow with black striping), fawn (yellow, and

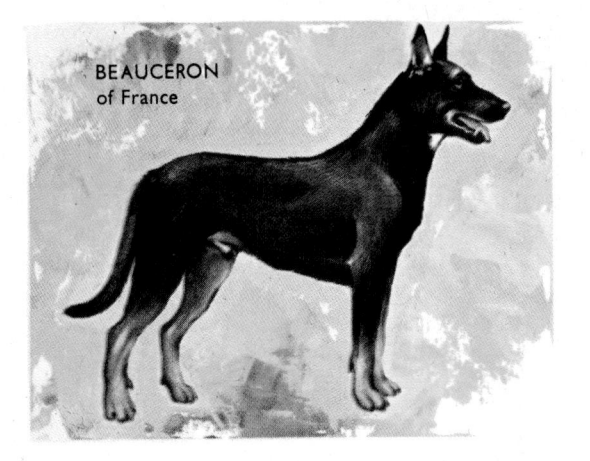

BEAUCERON
of France

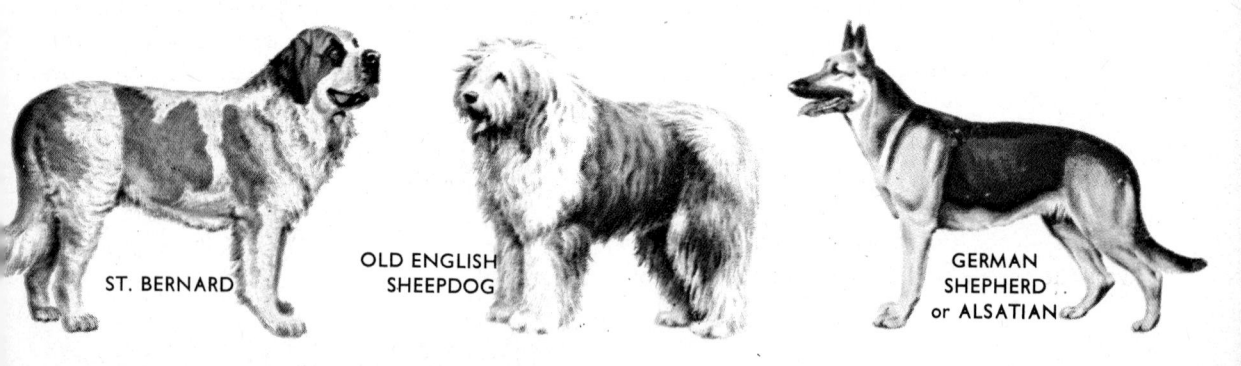

ST. BERNARD

OLD ENGLISH
SHEEPDOG

GERMAN
SHEPHERD
or ALSATIAN

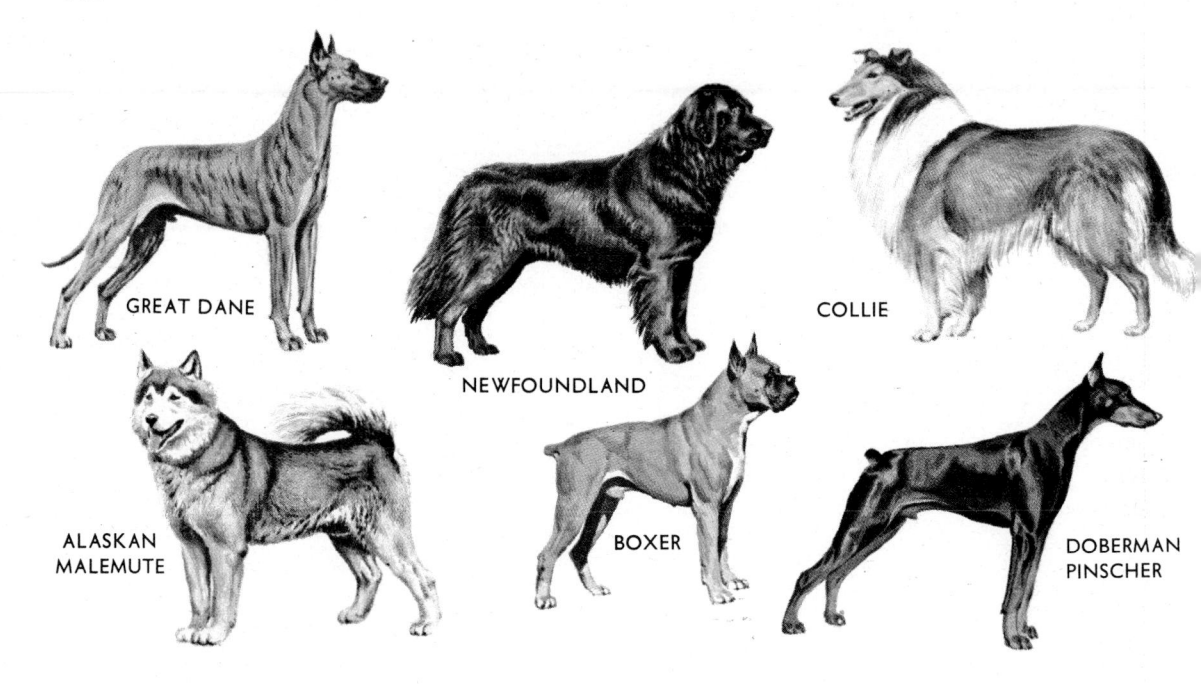

GREAT DANE

NEWFOUNDLAND

COLLIE

ALASKAN MALEMUTE

BOXER

DOBERMAN PINSCHER

usually with a black face-mask), blue (steel-grey), black (solid black, sometimes with small white marks), and harlequin (white with black spots and patches).

The Newfoundland is a hard-working American breed also prized as a pet. Because Newfoundlands are so strong and such good swimmers, they have been trained to rescue drowning people, and to swim ashore with lifelines from sinking ships. They are also sturdy enough to pull carts and to carry loads. Newfoundlands are heavily built and weigh up to 150 pounds. They have broad heads, small ears, long tails and long, dense coats, usually black.

Old English Sheepdogs make unusually fine pets because of their gentleness. Although their coats are quite thick, they require no more care than any other long-haired dog. Old English Sheepdogs are rather large and have short, or "bob", tails, drooping ears, and a rolling gait. The long coat may be grey, grizzled or bluish, with or without white.

The Alaskan Malemute, one of the oldest Arctic sledge-dogs, is a native of Alaska.

The St Bernard is a large (150 to 250 pounds) dog that has worked for years with the monks in the Swiss Alps as a rescue

Guide-dogs for the blind, often Alsatians, have exceptional intelligence and are carefully trained.

Dennis Stock from Magnum Photos

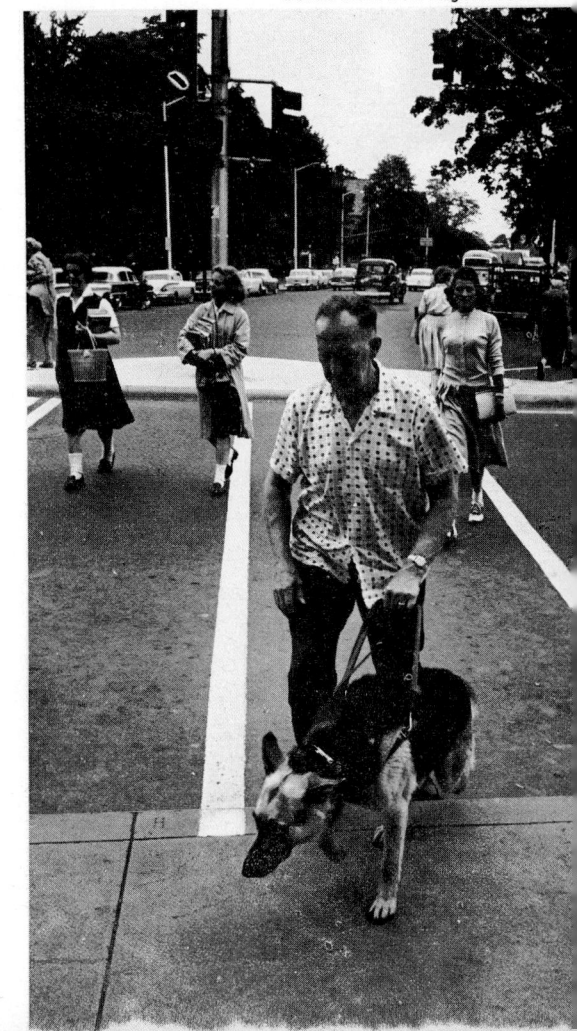

dog. St Bernards travel in packs of three or four to search for missing people, even locating those buried under avalanches of snow. The dogs carry around their necks a small flask containing brandy.

WORM LIZARDS, or *Amphisbaenids,* are a group of about 115 species of lizard found mostly in the tropics of America and Africa. Most species are blind and earth-worm-like, with a soft, pale-coloured skin. Their tail is very short — no more than a tenth the total length of the body — and usually so bluntly rounded that it is difficult at a glance to tell which is the front end. In some the tail is hard and covered with blunt spines, making it a useful stopper for their burrows.

Worm lizards use their head to tunnel through the soil, and can move in a straight line backwards as well as forwards. They do not move their body in "S" shapes as snakes do. Numerous grooves around their body make them look all the more like earth-worms. In some kinds the head is sharp-edged, rather than rounded. This spatulate shape is an aid in burrowing. Their neck muscles are especially powerful, and the skull is modified in order to cope with a burrowing existence.

Almost all worm lizards are legless. Three species of *Bipes* found in western Mexico have short front legs just behind the head. Each has distinct fingers, most of even them bearing claws. Worm lizards do not have external ears.

Worm lizards either lay eggs or give birth to their young. Egg-layers often deposit their eggs in the termite nests in which they live. These are handy incubators, since the adults feed largely on termites. Other kinds of worm lizard eat earthworms, spiders and ants. The largest are about 27 inches long.

WORMS. Often the word *worm* is used to describe almost any long, soft-bodied animal, including flat-worms and ribbon-worms. True worms (*Annelida*), however, have segmented bodies. Marine worms, earth-

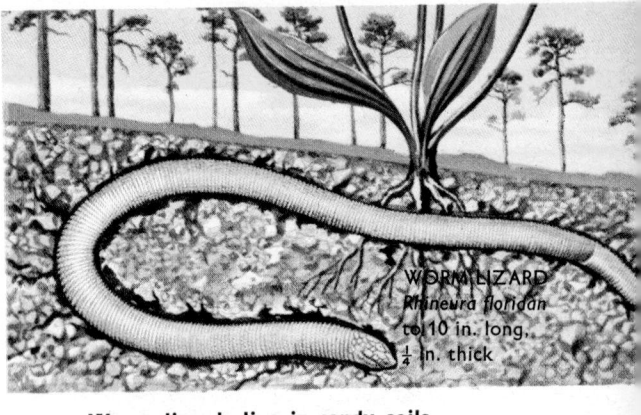

WORM LIZARD
Rhineura floridana
to 10 in. long,
¼ in. thick

Worm lizards live in sandy soils.

worms and leeches belong to this group. They have complete digestive tracts, and are the lowest animal group with a circulatory system composed of veins and arteries. Species of segmented worms are found on almost every type of beach, and also in deep water. A few exceedingly small species swim as plankton in the upper layers of the sea.

Marine worms, many of which are important as food for other animals, are divided roughly into two large groups: those that crawl or swim actively, and those that live in burrows or tubes. Crawling and swimming worms are predators. They hunt, mostly at night, for small clams, shrimps and crabs, which they catch and kill with their powerful jaws. They swim and crawl with a snake-like body motion, aided by paddle-like and often bristly projections along the sides of their body. Some possess two or

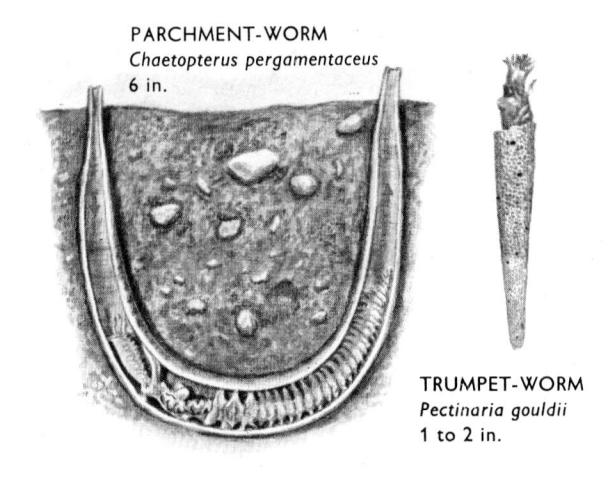

PARCHMENT-WORM
Chaetopterus pergamentaceus
6 in.

TRUMPET-WORM
Pectinaria gouldii
1 to 2 in.

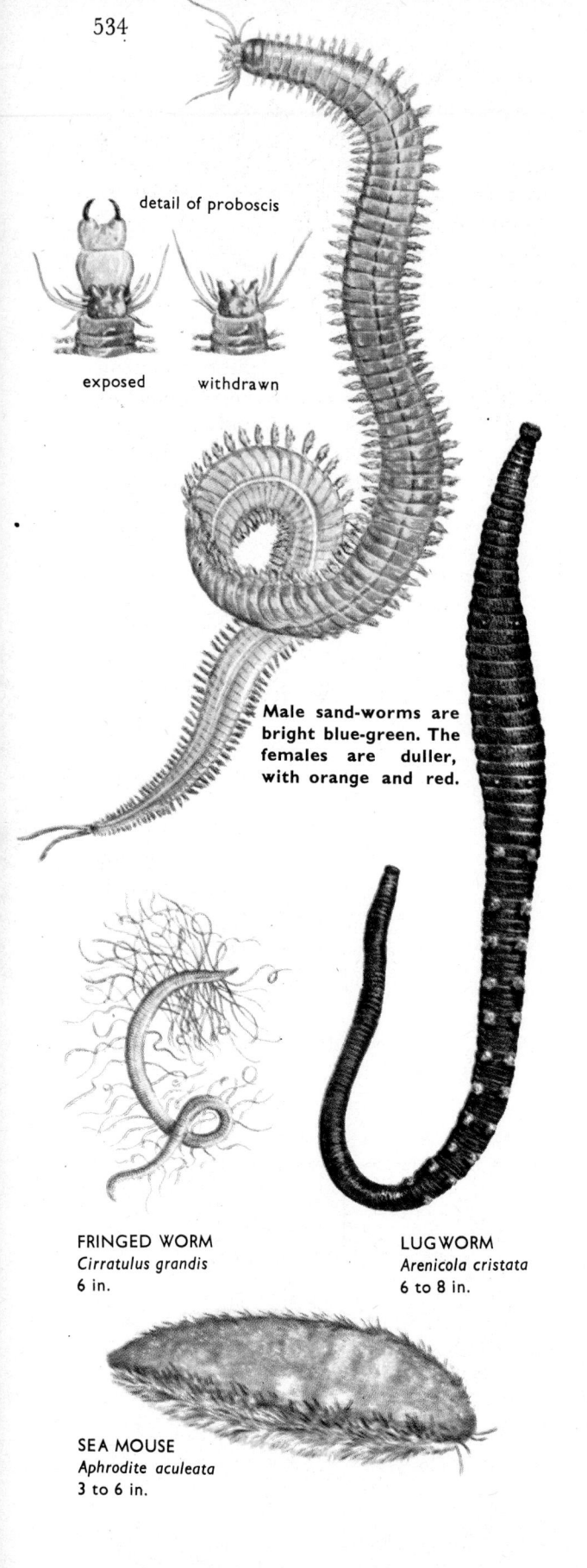

detail of proboscis

exposed

withdrawn

Male sand-worms are bright blue-green. The females are duller, with orange and red.

FRINGED WORM
Cirratulus grandis
6 in.

LUGWORM
Arenicola cristata
6 to 8 in.

SEA MOUSE
Aphrodite aculeata
3 to 6 in.

more eye-spots and several pairs of long, sensitive tentacles.

A number of kinds of sand-worm are found along both Atlantic and Pacific coasts of North America. The Clamworm, or Bloodworm *(Nereis)*, is dug from northern mudflats and used as bait by fishermen. Scale-worms, like *Holosydna* along the west coast, crawl about among weeds and rocks. Their bodies are covered by overlapping, leathery scales that give them an armour-plated appearance. In tropical waters of the West Indies, bristle-worms, such as *Chloeia viridis*, can inflict severe stings with the numerous tufts of needle-sharp bristles along the sides of their body.

The Palolo Worm *(Palolo viridis)*, of Pacific islands, normally crawls about in holes and crevices in coral reefs, but during the last quarter of the moon at low tide in October and November, it swims to the surface to spawn. The worms appear in such tremendous numbers that the water seems alive with them. Natives of Samoa and the Fiji Islands can predict to the night when the worms will appear; they harvest the worms and eat them. A similar worm spawns during early summer in Florida, and another species occurs in Bermuda.

Worms that live in tubes generally have bodies modified for their special environment. Often the paddle-like projections along the sides are lost, and the front and rear halves of these worms are generally quite different. Feather-worms form tubes, either of sand and mucus or of lime. Those that live in coral reefs may be brilliantly coloured, looking like red or orange flowers. When disturbed, they disappear in the coral.

The Lugworm *(Arenicola)*, which looks much like an overgrown earthworm, lives in a U-shaped tube in shallow, sandy or muddy areas. It swallows sand from which it digests animal and plant remains.

The Parchment-worm *(Chaetopteris)* also lives in a U-shaped tube. The parchment-like tube is constructed largely of sand grains. By beating the large paddles along the sides of its body, the Parchment-worm

pumps the water through its tube and extracts the plankton on which it feeds. One or two crustaceans, and other small species of worm, usually live in the tube, too. The Parchment-worm has the peculiar ability to give off bright flashes of luminescence; the function of these flashes is not known. In an aquarium, parchment-worms can be made to give off flashes by subjecting them to light electric shocks.

Trumpet worms (*Pectinaria*), which are small (1 to 2 in.), live in stiff, conical tubes composed of sand grains. They have plume-like tentacles for feeding.

Virtually all known fossil worms are segmented worms of the phylum Annelida. Their long, soft bodies, composed of many similar segments, are covered with bristles or appendages of various types. Many are beautifully plumed and coloured.

Because of their soft bodies, worms are rare as fossils. Only in exceptional deposits, such as the Cambrian Burgess Shale in British Columbia, are their outlines, or even the tiny bristles, preserved. Their tiny black, hook-like jaws are abundant in some Paleozoic rocks. Coiled calcareous tubes in which some worms lived are also preserved as fossils, as are their mud trails, now consolidated into rocks. (See EARTHWORMS; FLAT-WORMS; LEECHES; NEMATODES; RIBBON-WORMS.)

WRASSES are common salt-water fishes, most abundant in tropical seas, especially around coral reefs. There are more than 400 species in the family, and they range in size from tiny fish, only a few inches in length, to species that are three feet long and weigh 30 pounds or more. Almost all wrasses are good to eat, although their flesh may be poisonous if they have fed on poisonous shellfish. Many wrasses are excellent sport fish. Most of them are brightly coloured, and they can change their colours rapidly as they swim from one background to another.

Wrasses have sharp front teeth that stick out. Their lips are flexible, so that their teeth can be bared easily to scrape food from the coral. Their rear teeth are powerful grinders, used to crush molluscs and crustaceans. Many kinds also have teeth in their throat, with which they can break shells, allowing their digestive juices to work on the tender meat of the animal inside the shells.

Most wrasses make large nests. The female spreads her eggs in a single layer over the bottom of the nest, and then the male guards them until they hatch.

There are a few species of Wrasse that live in temperate waters. Around British coasts, seven species are found, although none are of economic importance. Perhaps the commonest is the Ballan Wrasse. It varies in its colour, but usually the back and

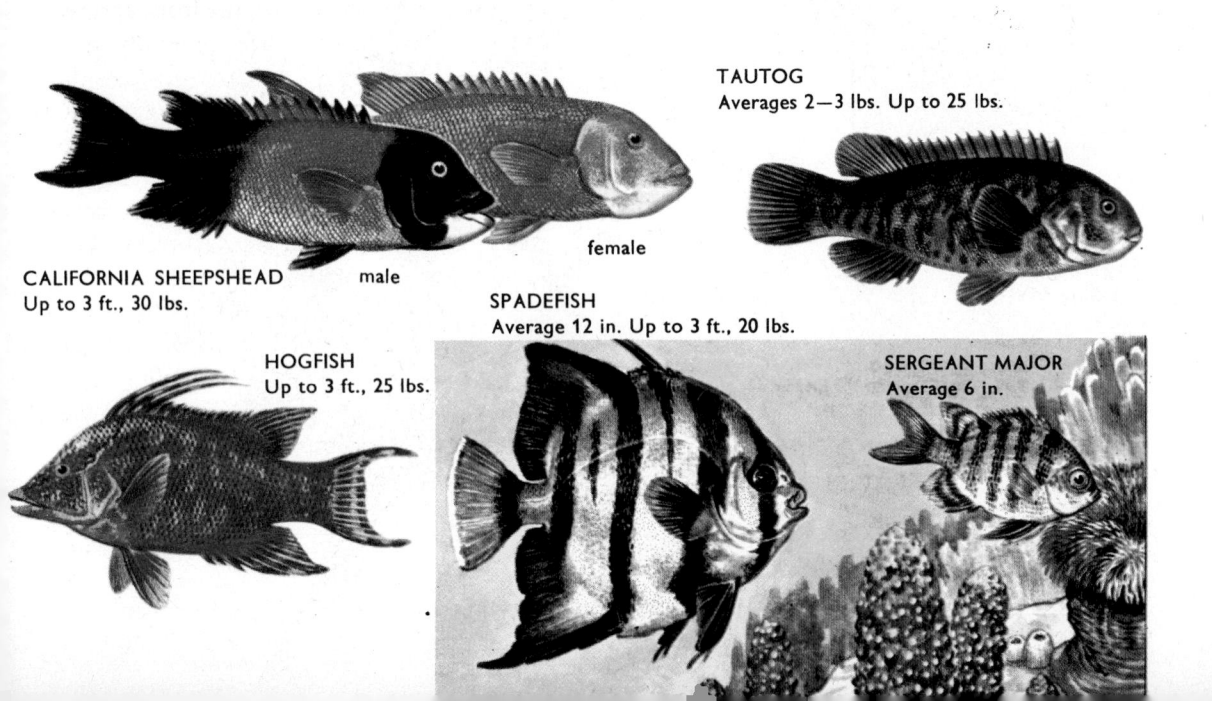

CALIFORNIA SHEEPSHEAD male female
Up to 3 ft., 30 lbs.

TAUTOG
Averages 2—3 lbs. Up to 25 lbs.

HOGFISH
Up to 3 ft., 25 lbs.

SPADEFISH
Average 12 in. Up to 3 ft., 20 lbs.

SERGEANT MAJOR
Average 6 in.

sides are blue or green, and the dorsal and anal fins have orange or yellow rings. It prefers moderately deep water, and spawns from May to July.

The Rainbow Wrasse *(Coris julis)*, well-known in the Mediterranean, is another occasional visitor to Britain.

Certain small fishes are known to remove the parasites from the head and gills of larger fishes. Some of the smaller species of Wrasse (chiefly the genus *Labroides*) perform this duty and are known as cleaner fishes. Large fishes visit the areas where the cleaners live and patiently submit to being groomed, obligingly opening their gill covers to allow the cleaners to enter the gill chamber and pick parasites off the gills. Red Shrimps *(Hippolysmata californica)* also perform cleaning duties. Obviously, both host and cleaner benefit from the service, and the large host fishes do not gobble up the cleaners.

Many other kinds of fishes abound in coral-reef waters where wrasses live. Spadefish *(Chaetodipterus* spp.*)*, members of the angel fish family, are common schooling fishes. They are caught in nets commercially, and also on hook and line for sport. Although they range from Cape Cod to Brazil, they are numerous only in tropical waters.

The black-striped Sergeant Majors *(Abudefduf saxatilis)*, also abundant in tropical waters, are found in great numbers fairly close to shore, but never in deep water. With darting movements, they satisfy their curiosity about an intruder, then disappear quickly among rocks and seaweeds.

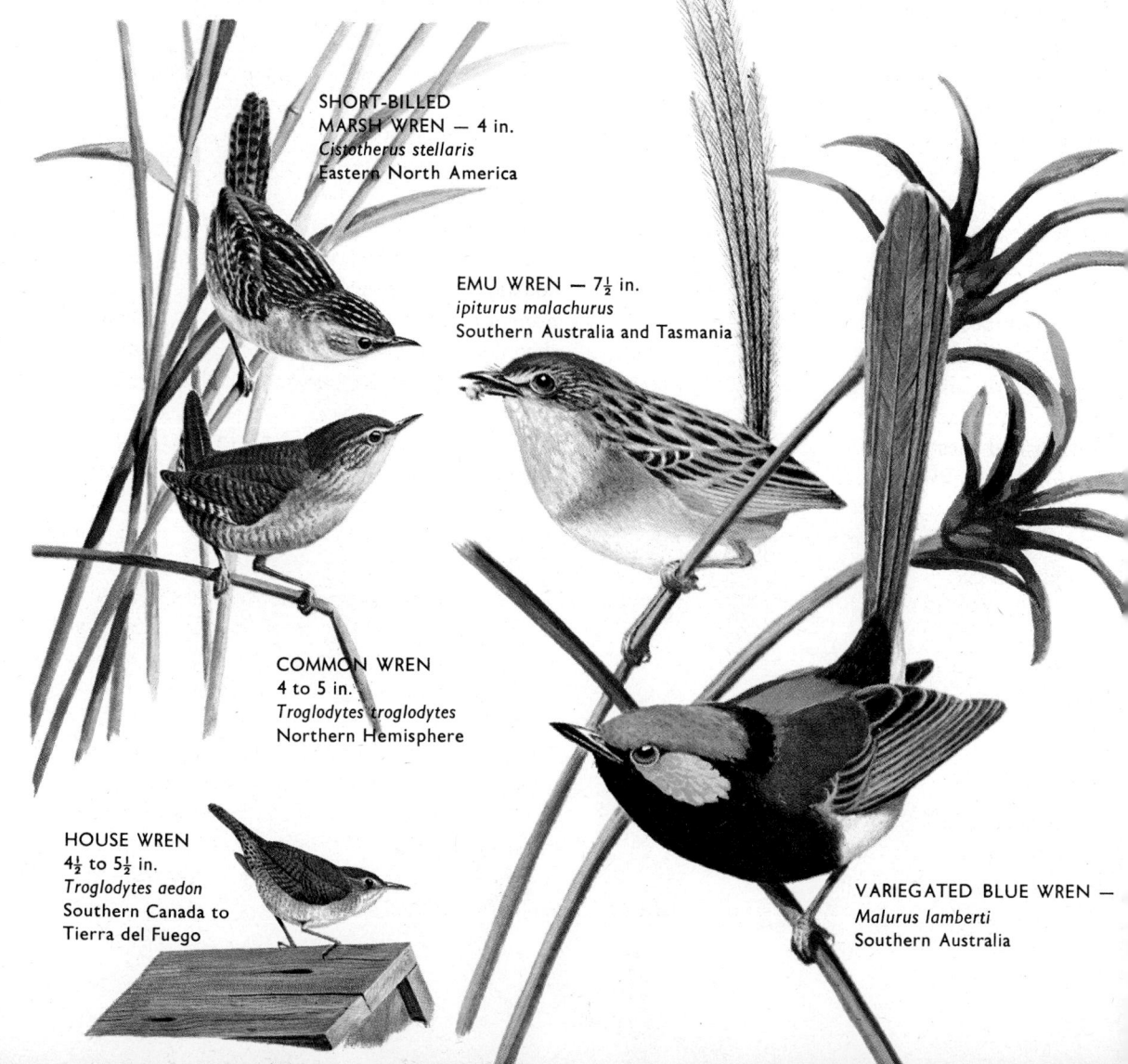

SHORT-BILLED
MARSH WREN — 4 in.
Cistotherus stellaris
Eastern North America

EMU WREN — 7½ in.
ipiturus malachurus
Southern Australia and Tasmania

COMMON WREN
4 to 5 in.
Troglodytes troglodytes
Northern Hemisphere

HOUSE WREN
4½ to 5½ in.
Troglodytes aedon
Southern Canada to
Tierra del Fuego

VARIEGATED BLUE WREN —
Malurus lamberti
Southern Australia

WRENS, the busybodies of the bird world, are plump, little, brown songsters that scurry around in the underbrush and on the ground, with the tail held erect, while they hunt and feed on insects. Wrens have rather harsh, scolding calls, but most of them — in some, both males and females — also have fine, bubbling songs. They sing all the year.

Wrens apparently originated in the New World, where they are still most abundant, both in species and in numbers. Most of the 59 species in the Western Hemisphere are found in Central and South America. They have become adapted to a wide variety of habitats, from tropical rain-forests to rocky, desert hillsides and to swamps.

The Common Wren seems able to find a place in any part of the Northern Hemisphere where there is some ground cover, from the undergrowth of forest floors to bare, rocky Atlantic islands.

It is a shy, furtive creature when feeding, creeping through the undergrowth investigating holes and crannies, but it becomes bold when it explodes into sudden loud song. The male builds a number of "cock nests" in his territory. These are the mere shells of domed nests, tucked into cavities and made of coarse dead plants. When a female joins him, she occupies one of these nests, lining it and laying her eggs. She incubates alone, and meanwhile the male will find a second mate and install her in another of his unfinished nests. While she is laying and sitting, he helps the first female to feed her brood, and then, as they fledge, returns to help the second female with hers. The families are generally large.

Although usually unsociable and aggressive in winter, the Common Wren will roost communally, huddled together in some small cavity. The birds arrive singly and enter one at a time, until ten or twenty may be present. It suffers badly in very cold winters and may become very scarce.

Although so tiny, it is fearless and will mob predators, such as owls or stoats, with a loud, rattling alarm-call.

The similar but larger House Wren of

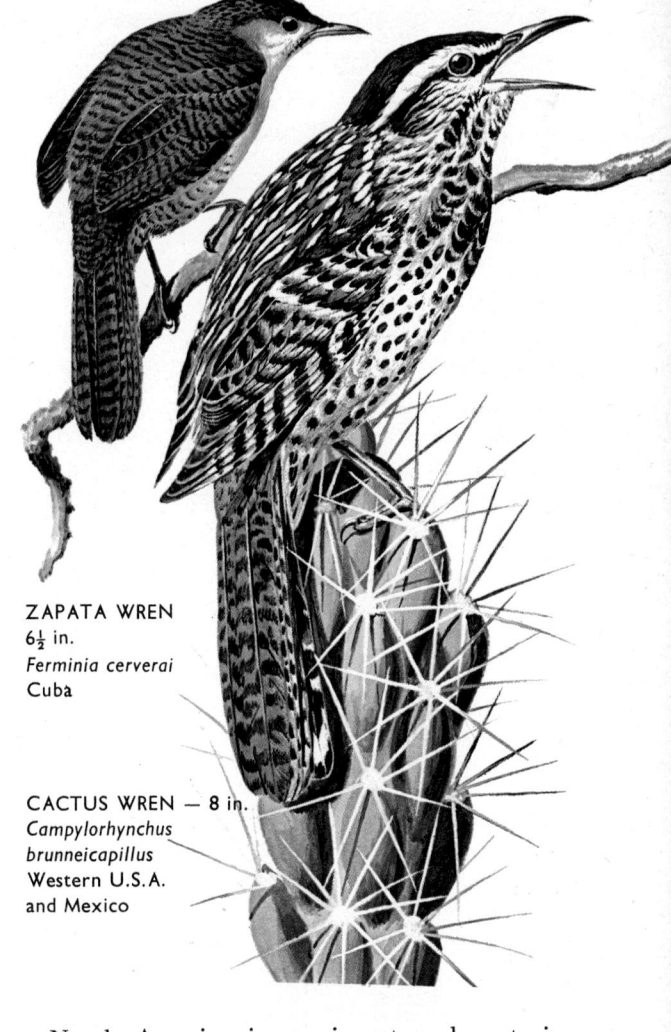

ZAPATA WREN
6½ in.
Ferminia cerverai
Cuba

CACTUS WREN — 8 in.
Campylorhynchus brunneicapillus
Western U.S.A.
and Mexico

North America is a migrant and nests in holes. It readily occupies nest-boxes.

Some tropical species tend to be large, and the boldly-marked Cactus Wren is as big as a finch. It nests in the shelter of spiky cacti, or in thorny trees or bushes. The globular nest has a long entrance-tunnel.

The Blue Wrens and Emu Wrens of Australasia are members of the *Maluridae*, a family often placed with the warblers. They have odd social habits, living in groups — not necessarily composed of one family — and the group defends a territory. When a pair nest, the other members of the group, which may include other males, help to feed the young. The Blue Wrens have an eclipse period, during which the bright colours are lost, the males being brown like the females.

Y-Z

YAK. In Tibet, the Wild Ox *(Poephagus grunniens)* is known as the Yak. The Yak's long, silky, fur is usually black and white, and hangs in a fringe along its shoulders and flanks. This fringe becomes a matted protective layer between the Yak and the snow when it lies down. Tibetans use the rich milk from the domesticated Yak, and also eat its meat. Its long hair is twisted into ropes, and the shorter silky hair is made into cloth. The animals are used for riding, and for pulling carts or carrying loads. Domestic Yaks are generally lighter in colour than the wild species. Yaks cannot live at low

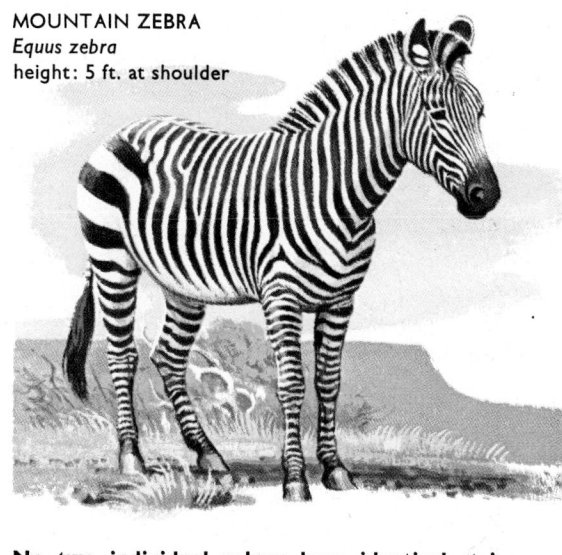

MOUNTAIN ZEBRA
Equus zebra
height: 5 ft. at shoulder

No two individual zebras have identical stripes.

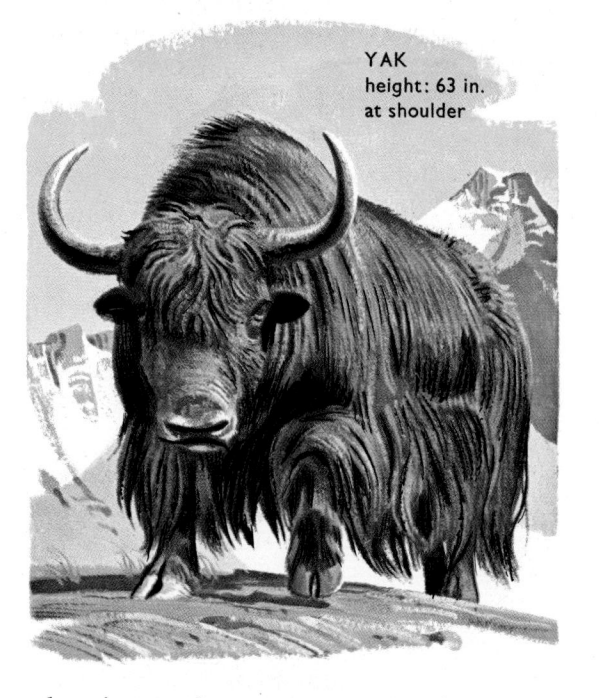

YAK
height: 63 in.
at shoulder

elevations and cannot eat corn; they must be fed on hay and grass. These animals have never been introduced successfully to other areas, although it is probable that they could live in northern Europe or North America.

ZEBRAS are small black-and-white, striped horses of Africa. Large herds, often containing a thousand or more animals, forage on grassy plains and frequent the water holes. They are a prize food of the Lion. Zebras protect themselves from enemies by slashing with their front teeth, kicking with their back feet, or biting. In many parts of Africa they are now becoming scarce, and herds are being preserved in parks and wild-life sanctuaries; once they were extremely abundant on the plains of southern and eastern Africa. Zebras do not tame easily, but a few have been trained to work in harness.

The Mountain Zebra *(Equus zebra)* lives in the mountainous areas of South Africa, usually in small herds of 20 or fewer animals. Everywhere their numbers have been greatly reduced, more by man than by lions. Unlike other zebras, this variety has a reddish nose.

Burchell's Zebra *(Equus burchelli)* of South and East Africa, and Grevy's Zebra *(Equus grevyi)* of north-eastern Africa, are larger

animals found in the open bush country in large herds. In Grevy's Zebra, the stripes are narrower than those of the Mountain Zebra. Females commonly have only one young, or foal, at a time.

ZEBUS *(Bos indicus)* are the domesticated oxen of India. They have a large hump over the shoulders, and folds of loose skin that form the dewlap beneath the throat. Zebus have abundant sweat-glands, and are adapted to live in hot climates.

Zebu bulls average 1,800 pounds; the cows are lighter, weighing about 1,200 pounds. When raised for meat and fattened for the market, the animals often weigh considerably more than these averages.

In India and the neighbouring countries of southern Asia, Zebus are used for riding, for hauling carts, and in some regions for both milk and meat. The animals are considered sacred by Hindus, and wander freely through their cities and towns; killing a Zebu is a serious offence.

Four of the 30 or more Indian breeds of Zebus have been introduced into the United States. These breeds — the Guzerat, the Nellore, the Gir and the Krishna Valley — are referred to collectively as Brahmans. Pure-bred herds exist in the United States, but most of the Zebu stock has been bred to other meat-producing breeds of cattle. The cross between the Shorthorn and the Brahman is called the Santa Gertrudis, and the Angus-Brahman cross is the Brangus.

ZONURES are lizards with large scales, each usually with a bony interior. About 50 species are found in Africa and Madagascar. Most kinds live in burrows or among rocks

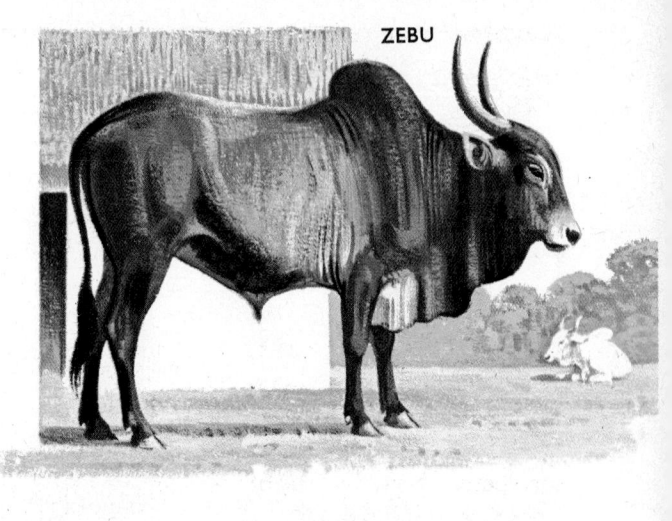

ZEBU

in mixed forests and on grassy plains. Most zonures have strong legs, but those of a small, snake-like group are reduced to a useless size, and the forelegs of some are completely lacking. Zonures have ear-openings and movable eyelids.

Zonures that live among rocks have rings of heavy spines on their tail. These aid the lizards in wedging themselves tightly into crevices so that their enemies cannot get them out; to this end, they also inflate their body slightly. The Sungazer *(Cordylus)* is not well armoured on its belly. When caught in the open, it stiffens its body, holds its limbs against its sides, and resists all efforts to turn it over; only the bone-armoured back is exposed to the enemy. The Armadillo Lizard, of the same genus, grasps its tail in its mouth and forms a circle, thus making it difficult for a predator to pick it up. All spiny-tailed types use their tail as a club, if unable to escape.

Zonures range in size from 6 to 28 inches. One group bears its young alive, others lay eggs; all eat small animals.

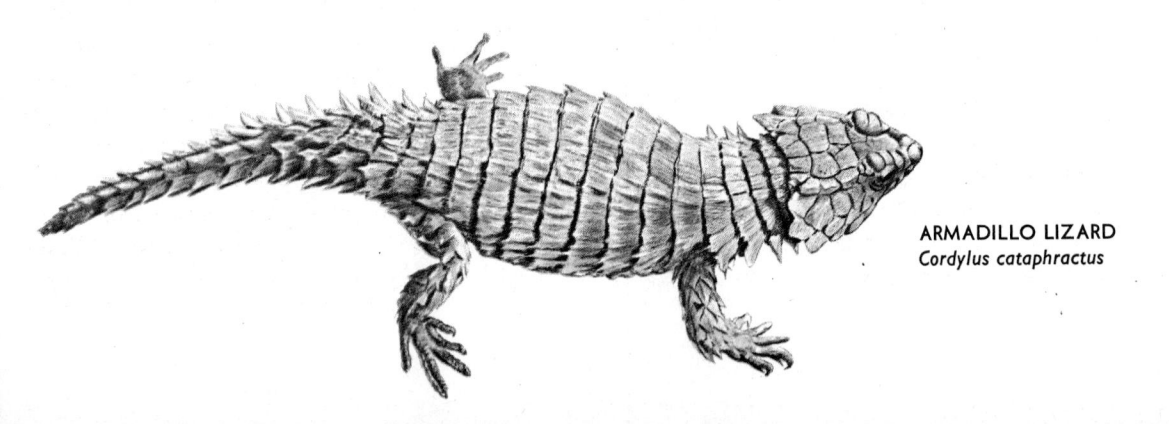

ARMADILLO LIZARD
Cordylus cataphractus

INDEX

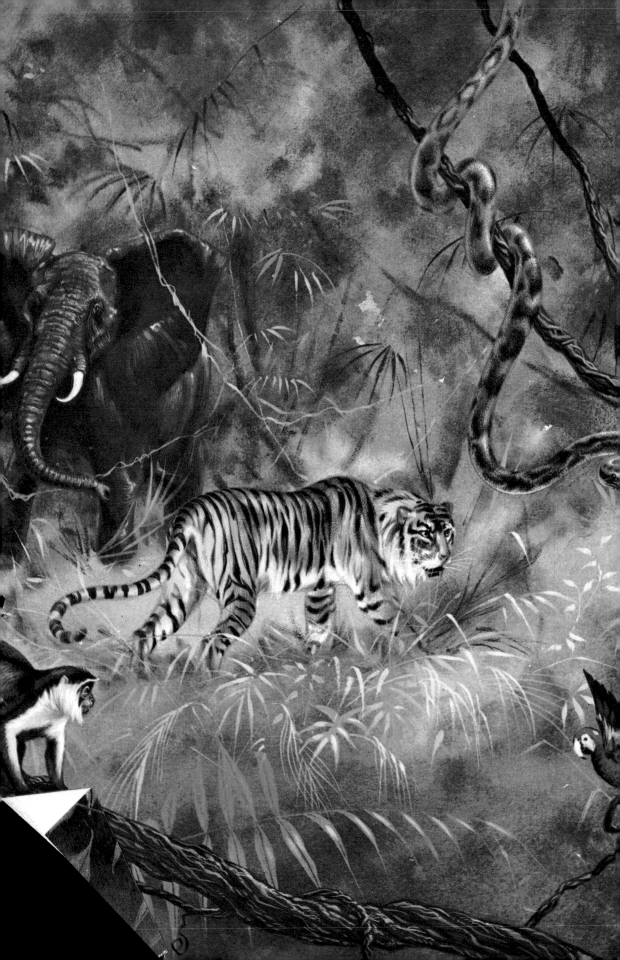

THE CHILDREN'S
ANIMAL
WORLD
ENCYCLOPEDIA
IN COLOUR

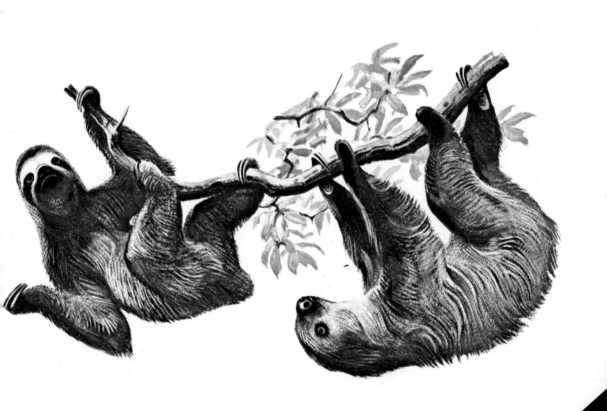